ISBN 978-1-5277-2010-7
PIBN 10884211

English
Français
Deutsche
Italiano
Español
Português

www.forgottenbooks.com

Mythology Photography **Fiction**
Fishing Christianity **Art** Cooking
Essays Buddhism Freemasonry
Medicine **Biology** Music **Ancient**
Egypt Evolution Carpentry Physics
Dance Geology **Mathematics** Fitness
Shakespeare **Folklore** Yoga Marketing
Confidence Immortality Biographies
Poetry **Psychology** Witchcraft
Electronics Chemistry History **Law**
Accounting **Philosophy** Anthropology
Alchemy Drama Quantum Mechanics
Atheism Sexual Health **Ancient History**
Entrepreneurship Languages Sport
Paleontology Needlework Islam
Metaphysics Investment Archaeology
Parenting Statistics Criminology
Motivational

THE

HISTORY

AND

ANTIQUITIES

OF THE COUNTIES OF

WESTMORLAND AND CUMBERLAND.

By JOSEPH NICOLSON, Efq; and RICHARD BURN, LL. D.

IN TWO VOLUMES.

VOL. II.

LONDON:

PRINTED FOR W. STRAHAN; AND T. CADELL, IN THE STRAND.

MDCCLXXVII.

T H E

HISTORY and ANTIQUITIES

OF THE

C O U N T I E S

OF

WESTMORLAND and CUMBERLAND.

OF CUMBERLAND IN GENERAL.

CUMBERLAND, according to Mr. *Denton*, on the fouth-weft part thereof, is divided from Furnefs, which is a part of the county of Lancafter, by the river Dudden, which falls into the Irifh fea, at Millum caftle; afcending by the banks of that river up to Ulfay or Woolfhey park at Blackhill, to the fhire ftone upon the mountain Wrynofe at the head of Dudden, where it meets with the county of Weftmorland, firft at Little Langdale in the fells; fo, leaving on the eaft Great Langdale and Grefmere, it bordereth on the fame all the way to Dunmaile Raife; and thence on the backfide of Hilvellen or Hill-Belyne hill, by the head of Glenrhodden beck, to the head of Glencune beck; and fo, down that rill or little beck Glencune, to Ulfwater; thence, by the river Aymót, which runneth forth of Ulfwater at Pooley ftank, defcending by Dacre caftle and Carleton until it receive the river Lowther under Brougham caftle, and till it be received by the great river Eden; and fo up Eden unto the foot of Kirkland and Newbiggin beck, by which it is fevered from Weftmorland until it come to the head fpring thereof. It joins again with Weftmorland in the mountains, for the fpace of five or fix miles; then meeting with a little corner of Yorkfhire, it is bounded by the fame to the head of the great river Tees, which divideth there Yorkfhire from the county of Durham; and from thence to Kellowplaw hill by the fame county of Durham. From Kelloplaw hill to Alnburne it adjoineth to the

county

county of Northumberland, which burn or little river unto Kirkhaugh (where it is received of the great river South Tyne) divideth the two counties, which in like manner on the other side of Tyne are kept asunder by another little rill falling into Tyne from the East side of the mountains in Geltsdale forest; from that little water unto the head of Hartley burn; and then along the north east side of Geltsdale forest, and on Burntippet moor (a great heath and waste), the said two counties of Cumberland and Northumberland meet again, and are not severed until a little beck called Powtrofs parts them, which falling into Irthing loseth its name. And then Irthing divides them, ascending the same river, until it receive a lesser water named Troutbeck, which in like sort falleth in between them, until they concur again at the Horsehead, the Gill cragg, and Christenbury cragg, unto Lamyford, where Cumberland makes a narrow point northwards. There the river Liddale on the north west side runs down between Scotland and Cumberland unto Canonby holme, where the water of Esk receives it, and bereaves Liddale of its name, at a place called the Mote. Then descending Esk a little way, the Scotch dyke divides the two kingdoms from Esk to Sark, which falling into Esk, and so with Esk into Eden aforesaid, are presently carried together into Solway firth, and so to the Irish sea. From the foot of Eden, Cumberland on the west side, bending all along the coast southward like a bow, is invironed by the Irish sea to the foot of the river Dudden at Millum castle aforesaid.

It extendeth in length, from the south end of Peil de Fodra on the south point of the said county, to the north point thereof near Lamyford above seventy miles; and reacheth in breadth from Allonby on the west to Newbiggin bridge on the east thirty miles; and hath in circumference upwards of two hundred miles.

Mr. Houghton tells us, from some calculations made by Dr. Halley, that it contains 1040000 acres, is a 38¼ part of the whole kingdom; that there are in it 14825 houses, and that in this respect it is about a 78¼ part of the kingdom[*]. It is supposed there may now be about 20000 houses, and near 100000 inhabitants.

Cumberland first took its name from the inhabitants, who were the true and genuine Britons, and called themselves Kimbri or Kumbri. For that the Britons in the heat of the Saxon wars posted themselves here for a long time, we have the authority of our histories and of Marianus himself[†], who calls this country *Cumbrorum terra*, that is, the land of the *Cumbri*: Not to mention the names of many places purely British; such as Caer-luel, Caer-dronoc, Penrith, Pen-rodoc, and the like.

The first inhabitants of Britain, according to Mr. Carte[‡], were a Celtic nation, who first settled here about 2000 years before the christian æra[||].

---

[*] Houghton, vol. i. p. 71.   [†] Camd. p. 1002.   [‡] Carte, vol. i. p. 21.

[||] These people generally called themselves Celts, which signified as much as a man of extraordinary worth and accomplishments, and which bishop Nicolson brings from the primitive Celt, signifying God; as they, as well as most other nations, affected to trace up their descent as high as the creation. So the word Gothic from Gott or God; and Teutch from Teut who they said was the son of God.

And

And the Britiſh government was anciently divided amongſt a great number of chieftains, much in the ſame manner as the clans in the Highlands of Scotland, and the Septs in Ireland; though they are frequently dignified by our writers with the pompous titles of kings.

And we are told, that about the year of Chriſt 448, the moſt conſiderable kingdom among the Britons was that of the *Strath Cluyd* Britons, called generally the kingdom of Cumbria, and which then comprehended all the weſtern Lowlands of Scotland as far as Dunbritton, and was further extended by the union of North Wales, upon Coil's marrying the heireſs of that principality, and by the acceſſion of the intermediate countries lying in the Iriſh channel, which upon the Romans quitting Britain had put themſelves under the protection of the Strath Cluyd princes. Theſe territories were all united under Eneon Urdd. But this union continued no longer than his life; and his dominions being divided amongſt his poſterity formed the principalities of North Wales, Cumberland, and Galloway.

Northumberland was the fifth kingdom of the Saxon heptarchy, which began under Ida, in the year 548, and was ſo called lying north of the river Humber, and extended from that river to St. Johnſton's in Scotland. Cumberland was undoubtedly included within the bounds of this kingdom, but (as is before mentioned) was always governed by its own king or rather chieftain, and lived under what was called the Danes Law till the conqueſt *.

In the year 878, Alfred king of the Weſt Saxons ſubdued the Northumbers, and indeed the whole kingdom, and reduced it again to one intire monarchy. He alſo divided the kingdom into certain parts or ſections, which from the Saxon word *ſcyran*, ſignifying to cut, he termed *ſhires* or ſhares, and appointed over every ſhire an earl or alderman, to whom he committed the rule and government of the ſame : and *comes* being latin for a count or an earl, thence came the word *county* for a ſhire; and viſcount, the ſheriff, ſhire's reeve, or county's deputy.

Theſe ſhires he broke into ſmaller parts commonly called *hundreds*, but in this county *wards*, from the watching and warding that were neceſſary againſt the neighbouring incurſions; and theſe wards are five in number, viz. Allerdale ward above Derwent, Allerdale ward below Derwent, Cumberland ward, Leeth ward, and Eſkdale ward.

In the year 945, Edmund king of England, having waſted all Galloway, and intirely ſubdued the Britons in Cumberland, gave that principality to Malcolm king of Scotland, on condition of guarding the Northumbrian territories by ſea and land from the enemy's invaſions †.

In 1032, Malcolm the ſecond and Canute quarrelling raiſed great armies againſt each other; but their difference, by the interpoſition of the prelates and nobles, was accommodated : and it was agreed, that Duncan (the Scotch king's heir apparent) and the heirs of all future kings of Scotland for the time being ſhould hold Cumberland as freely as any of their predeceſſors had done ‡.

---

* Nicolſon's Engl. Hiſt. Libr. p. 45.   † Carte, vol. i. p. 323.   ‡ Id. p. 343.

In 1068, king William the Conqueror made peace with Malcolm, who did him homage for Cumberland *.

But in the very next year Malcolm again joined the difcontented Englifh; and William having fubdued him added Cumberland to the Englifh pale: But it was miferably haraffed all along by its reftlefs neighbours out of Scotland; as were no lefs the Scotch adjoining territories by plundering parties of England.

In the 5 Ed. 2. Robert de Brus, king of Scotland, entred Cumberland by Solway with a great army on Thurfday before the day of the Affumption of the Bleffed Virgin, and burned all Gilfland, with the village of Haltwyfil in Northumberland, and great part of Tindale; and after eight days returned with much booty. In Auguft he came again to Lanercoft, ftaid there three days, and did much mifchief.

In the 8 Ed. 2. Edward de Brus, brother of Robert, entered Cumberland, and tarrying at Rofe three whole days, fent out parties to burn, deftroy, and plunder on all fides. And before Midfummer in that year the county of Cumberland alone gave 300 marks to the Scots by way of contribution.

In the 10 Ed. 2. the Scots again entred Cumberland, and proceeding as far as Richmond in Yorkfhire with all poffible devaftation, from thence turned towards Furnefs in Lancafhire, burning and deftroying all the way they went: And here they were much pleafed with finding large quantities of iron, which did not abound in Scotland, The Chronicle adds, that in this year, plague and famine raged both in England and Scotland, to a degree till then unheard of; and that the quarter of bread corn fold in the north for forty fhillings.

In the 13 Ed. 2. the Scots came again, and deftroyed all before them with fire and fword as far as Burgh under Stanemore.

In the 16 Ed. 2. Robert de Brus again entered Cumberland, burnt Rofe, plundered the abbey of Holm Cultram, and deftroyed all with fire and fword as far as Lancafhire, and returned home with much booty.

In the 5 Ed. 3. on the 22d of March the Scots again enter England by Carlifle, and there burn, kill, and deftroy as ufual. And on the Vigil of the Annunciation, Anthony lord Lucy enters Scotland, and for 12 miles kills, burns, and deftroys in the fame manner. On his return he was attacked near Dornock by Sir Humphrey de Boys, Sir Humphrey de Jardayne, William Bard, William de Douglafs, and 50 more well armed men, with the commons of the whole country. They all, with one accord rufhed upon the perfon of lord Lucy, but he was fo well defended, that the two Scotch knights, and about 24 armed men were killed, William Bard and William Douglafs taken, and the reft put to flight. Of the Englifh, only two efquires, Thomas de Plumland and John de Ormefby were flain: their bodies were carried to Carlifle, and there honourably interred. Lord Lucy himfelf was indeed wounded in the foor, hand, and eye, but foon recovered.

In the 11 Ed. 3. in the beginning of September, the earl of Warwick entred Scotland with an army, by Berwick; as did alfo Thomas Wake baron of Liddale, lord Clifford, the lord of Gilfland, and the bifhop of Carlifle, by Carlifle; and joining forces, they wafted Teviotdale, Moffetdale, and Nithef-

* Chronicon Saxonicum. 1 Dugd. Mon.

dales.

dale; and lord Lucy, with a part of the said army, ravaged Galloway. In return, the Scots entred England near Carlisle about the middle of October, and shewing themselves for three days together on the east side of the city, challenged the besieged to open battle. This they declined, but sent out archers and others to harass them in their tents. Notwithstanding which, they surrounded the town, burned the hospital of St. Nicholas, and Rose, and all the places they passed through.

In the 19th of the same king, the Scots entered England by Carlisle, burned Gilsland and Penrith with the adjacent villages. And in the next year king David in person wasted Cumberland, Derwent Fells, and Alston-moor, with fire and sword, and returned unhurt, with a great booty. But in the next year, the same king David was taken prisoner at the battle of Durham.

In the 6 Ric. 2. the Scots entred with fire and sword into Cumberland and Westmorland and the forest of Englewood, and came to Penrith fair, where they rifled booths and houses, spoiled and seized upon all the goods they found there, killing and taking many, and bringing away the rest; and so returned with great riches into Scotland: But they had small cause to joy in their booty; for with such cloth and other commodities as they took away with them, they carried into their own country such a violent pestilence, that a third part of all the people where the infection came died thereof. The English, to revenge the damage done by the earl of Douglas at the fair aforesaid, raised a power and went therewith over the water of Solway, and invaded the Scottish borders on that side with fire and sword, and took a great booty of cattle and other goods: But in the mean time the Scots hearing thereof, gathered together to the number of 500 men, and lurked privily in ambush at a strait, till such time as the Englishmen came to pass by them, and then with so large a noise and clamour they set upon them, that in their retreat there were 400 of the English slain, and a great number of the residue for haste were drowned in the water of Solway; and hereby the booty of cattle and goods, which they had taken, was recovered again by the Scots †.

In the 11 Ric. 2. Robert earl of Fife, James earl of Douglas, and Archibald lord of Galway entred into England, and came so privately over the water of Solway, that they arrived at Cockermouth, and surprized the town before the inhabitants could be prepared for any resistance. Here they continued three days, got a rich booty, and with the same returned through the counties of Westmorland and Northumberland safe, and without any encounter, again into Scotland. Amongst other things found in the rifling and ransacking of houses in this journey, there was a charter mentioned of certain lands given by king Athelstan, which shews the artless simplicity in the manner of conveyancing in those days:

> I *King* Athelstan, *gives to* Pallan,
> Odcham *and* Rodcham;
> *Als quid, and als fayre,*
> *Als ever they myne weare:*
> *And yar to witness* Maulde *my wife* ‡.

† Drake's Historia Anglo-Scotica, p 152.　　　‡ Ibid. 160.

In

In the 27 Hen. 6. the Englifh borderers of the Weft Marches fetched a great booty of cattle out of Scotland: In revenge whereof the Scots invaded England, wafted the country, burned towns and villages, flew the people, and with a great prey of prifoners, goods, and cattle returned home into Scotland. Hereupon daily followed inroads made on both fides between the Scots and Englifh, and that with fuch extreme rage and cruelty, that a great part of Cumberland was in a manner laid wafte and defolate *.

In the 16 Hen. 8. the lord Maxwell and Sir Alexander Jorden, with the number of 4000 Scots, with banners difplayed, entred by Carlifle into the Weft Marches of England, and began to harrafs the country, and to burn on every fide. The Englifh perceiving this, affembled themfelves together with all the forces they could fo fuddenly raife, and with the fame to the number of 2000 men fiercely fet upon the Scots, between whom there was a cruel fight; but at laft the Englifhmen broke the array of the Scots, difcomfited them, and took Sir Alexander Jorden and his fon, and others of meaner quality, to the number of 300 prifoners, with whom the Englifhmen that took them departed, whereby the ftrength of the refidue of the Englifhmen was much diminifhed. Which when the lord Maxwell perceived, he fuddenly rallied his men, and began a new fkirmifh, wherein he recovered almoft all the prifoners, and took and flew divers Englifhmen; fo that he returned with victory, and carried 300 prifoners home with him into Scotland †.

Such was the ftate and condition of this county in thofe days; and fuch it continued during the following reigns, even after the uniting of both kingdoms under one monarch, until the final union in the reign of queen Anne.

Befides the apportionment of the county into *Wards* as aforefaid, the Ecclesiastical ftate thereof fubjects it to another divifion, namely, of the feveral bifhops fees, and the deanries therein refpectively.

The bifhoprick of Carlifle extends into the two counties of Cumberland and Weftmorland, but not to the whole of either; for all that part of Cumberland called Allerdale Ward above Derwent, and the barony of Kendal in Weftmorland, do lie within the achdeaconry of Richmond in Chefter diocefe; fo Alfton Moor, and alfo Over Denton (as it is faid), are in the diocefe of Durham.

There are within the diocefe of Carlifle four deanries, *viz.* Carlifle, Wigton, Penrith, and Appleby.

Carlifle deanry comprehends all Efkdale and Cumberland Wards, Wigton and Kirkbride only excepted.

Wigton deanry takes in Wigton, Kirkbride, and all Allerdale Ward below Derwent.

Penrith deanry extends through the whole bounds of Leeth Ward.

The deanry of Appleby reacheth through all the bottom of Weftmorland, lying within the limits of the Eaft and Weft Wards thereof.

Within this diocefe there is but one archdeacon, who hath the rectory of Great Salkeld annexed as a corps to that dignity. He had anciently archidia-

* Drake's Hiftoria Anglo-Scotica, p. 226.   † Ibid. 336.

conal

conal jurifdiction alfo; but the fmallnefs and poverty of the diocefe rendring a concurrent jurifdiction both inconvenient and burdenfome, he gave up the fame for a penfion of *3l 19s 6d per annum*, which is ftill paid him by the bifhop, and only retained the more ancient rights of examining and prefenting perfons to be ordained, and of inducting perfons inftituted into their refpective livings; and all the reft of the archidiaconal jurifdiction is now devolved upon the chancellor of the diocefe.

This county fends two MEMBERS to parliament; of whom we have inferted a lift in our Appendix, N° XXXVI.

Alfo a catalogue of fome of the more fcarce and curious PLANTS growing in this county is inferted in the faid Appendix, N° XLI.

ALLERDALE WARD ABOVE DERWENT.

KING William the firft, having difpoffeffed the Scots of this county as aforefaid, gave it to *Ranulph de Mefchiens* one of his Norman adventurers, and left him men and munition to defend the fame from all hoftility that might difturb its peace, either by tumult of the inhabitants, or foreign invafion. Ranulph, quietly poffeffed of every part thereof, prefently furveyed the whole country; and gave all the frontiers bordering on Scotland, on Northumberland, and along the fea coaft, unto his friends and followers; retaining to himfelf the middle part between the eaft and weft mountains, a goodly great foreft, full of woods, red deer and fallow, wild fwine, and all manner of wild beafts, called the foreft of Englewood, which was fixteen miles long and ten broad, and lieth between the rivers of Shawk and Eden, extended in length from Carlifle to Penrith. The boundaries whereof, by a perambulation in the 29 Ed. 1. are fet forth to be as follows: " Beginning at the bridge of Caldew " without the city of Carlifle, and fo by the highway unto Thurfby towards " the fouth; and from Thurfby by the fame way through the middle of the " town of Thurfby to Wafpatrick wath, afcending by the water of Wampole " to the place where Shawk falls into Wampole. And from thence going up " ftraight to the head of Rowland beck; and from that place defcending to " the water of Caldbeck; and fo down by that water to the place where Cald- " beck falls into Caldew. And fo up to Gyrgwath; and fo by the highway " of Sourby unto Stanewath under the caftle of Sourby; and fo by the high- " way up to Mabil crofs; and fo to the hill of Kenwathen, going down by " the faid highway through the middle of the town of Alleynby; and fo by " the fame way through the middle of the town of Blencowe; and fo by the " fame way unto Palat; and fo going down by the fame way unto the bridge " of Amote; and fo from that bridge going down by the bank of Amote unto " Eden; and fo defcending by the water of Eden unto the place where Caldew " falls into Eden; and from that place to the bridge of Caldew aforefaid with- " out the gate of the city of Carlifle *."

* Appendix, N° IV.

The

The faid *Ranulph de Mefchiens* gave to his brother *William de Mefchiens* the great barony of Copeland, which lieth between the river Dudden; the river Derwent, and the fea; and fo much of the fame as lieth between the rivers of Cocker and Derwent, the faid William granted over to Waldieve fon of Gofpatric earl of Dunbar in Scotland, together with the five towns above Cocker, that is to fay, Brigham, Eglesfield, Dean (with Branthwaite), Craikfothen, and Clifton (with the hamlets thereof, Little Clifton and Stainburn).

The fame lord William Mefchiens feated himfelf at Egremont, where he built a caftle upon the top of an hill or mount nigh the river *Egen* (now corruptly called *End*), and thereupon he ftyled his caftle *Egermont (Ege-er mont)*; and all fuch lands as he or his fucceffors lords of Copeland granted to any perfon within the barony of Copeland, they bound the fame to be holden of the caftle of Egremont; and caufed the name of the barony to be changed from Copeland, and to be called the barony of Egremont, which name it retaineth to this day.

This William Mefchiens left no iffue at his death, fave only a daughter *Alice* married to *Robert de Romley* lord of the honour of Skipton in Craven, by whom he had iffue a daughter named *Alice*, whom the faid Robert de Romley gave in marriage to *William Fitz Duncan* earl of Murray, fon of Duncan brother of David king of Scots, which Duncan married Octhreda fifter and heir of Waldieve fon of Alan, fon of Waldieve firft lord of Allerdale, fon of Gofpatric earl of Dunbar aforefaid. By which marriage of William Fitz Duncan with Alice de Romley, the faid William Fitz Duncan became lord both of Skipton and Egremont in the right of his wife, being fole heir of Skipton by her father, and of Egremont by her mother the lord William Mefchiens's daughter.

William Fitz Duncan had iffue by the faid *Alice* his wife, a fon called *William*, who died an infant, and by her had alfo three daughters coheirs: the eldeft, named *Cicely*, was married to *William le Grofs* earl of Albemarle, and had iffue only a daughter named *Hawife*, who was married to three hufbands fucceffively; firft, to *William de Mandevill* earl of Effex, to whom fhe had no child; fecondly, to *William de Fortibus*; and thirdly, to *Baldwin Beton* earl of the ile of Wight. To her fecond hufband William de Fortibus, who in her right affumed the title of earl of Albemarle, fhe had a fon *William de Fortibus*; who had iffue the third *William de Fortibus*; whofe daughter and heir *Aveline* (wife to Edmund Crouchback king Edward the firft's brother) dying without any child, the third part of William Fitz Duncan's lands (which was Skipton in Craven) came to the king's hands, and by king Edward the fecond was granted to Robert de Clifford in exchange for the Cliffords lands in the county of Monmouth, in whofe pofterity it ftill remains.

Amabil Romley, the fecond daughter of William Fitz Duncan, had for her part of the inheritance this barony of Egremont; and was married to *Reginald Lucy*, by whom fhe had *Richard Lucy*, who had two daughters *Amabil Lucy* and *Alice Lucy*.

Dame *Alice Romley*, third daughter and coheir of William Fitz Duncan, was married to *Gilbert Pippard*, who was juftice itinerant in Wiltfhire in the

23 Hen.

23 Hen. 2. and afterwards was married to *Robert Courtney*; but had no iſſue of her body: wherefore her part of her father's inheritance (which was the liberty of Cockermouth, Aſpatric, and the barony of Allerdale beneath the river Derwent) was divided between the earl of Albemarle her elder ſiſter's huſband, and Richard de Lucy her other ſiſter's ſon, And ſo it continued divided until the eldeſt ſiſter's iſſue was extinguiſhed by the death of Aveline aforeſaid, daughter of the laſt William de Fortibus; after whoſe death, all the Romley's lands, both above and below Derwent, came wholly to the heirs of Reginald Lucy and Amabil Romley his wife, ſecond daughter to the ſaid William Fitz Duncan.

Amabil Lucy and *Alice Lucy*, daughters and coheirs of Richard de Lucy ſon of Reginald Lucy and of Amabil Romley his wife, ſucceeded in the Lucy's lands in Cumberland.

Amabil Lucy for her moiety enjoyed the barony of Egremont, all except Lowſwater; and was married to *Lambert de Multon*, who had iſſue *Thomas de Multon*, who had iſſue another *Thomas de Multon*, who had iſſue a third *Thomas de Multon*, whoſe ſon *John de Multon* left the barony of Egremont to his three ſiſters coheirs; *Elizabeth*, married to Haverington of Haverington; *John*, married to Robert Fitz-water; and *Margaret*, married to the lord Thomas Lucy. At which time that barony was broken into parts, which from the conqueſt had continued intire (except Lowſwater, and the lands between Cocker and Derwent, and the five towns, granted to Waldieve as is aforeſaid). But afterwards it became again united by the earls of Northumberland lords thereof, by gift and purchaſe, but not by deſcent from the ſaid coheirs.

This barony of Egremont or Copeland was firſt of all demeſne, but ſhortly after the conqueſt was granted away for ſervices. All between Cocker and Derwent, and the five towns, were given by William de Meſchiens to Waldieve lord of Allerdale. To Ketel ſon of Eldred ſon of Ivo de Talebois baron of Kendal, were given Kelton, Salter, Workington, and Stockhow. The manors of Beckermet, Friſington, Rotington, Weddekar, and Arlockden, to Fleming. Kirkby Begog, to the abbey of York. Mulcaſter, to the anceſtors of the Penningtons. Dregg and Carleton, to Stutevill. Milium, to Godard Boyvil. Laſtly, Sainton, Bolton, Goſforth, and Hale, to Thomas Multon of Gilſland.

MILLUM.

WITHIN this great barony and foreſt of Copeland, now called Egremont, are divers knights fees and lordſhips which are manors of themſelves, holden of the caſtle of Egremont. Amongſt which manors, the lordſhip or ſeigniory of MILLUM (in the ſouth weſt corner of the ſaid barony) is the firſt, and of greateſt liberties; containing alſo in itſelf divers manors, which are holden of Millum (as Millum is of Egremont) immediately, with ſome difference of ſervice.

Millum ſeigniory or lordſhip is bounded by the river Dudden on the eaſt, by the iſlands of Whinney and Peel de Fodra on the ſouth, the Iriſh ocean on the weſt, and the river Eſk and Hardknot and Wrynoſe mountains on the north. It is above ten miles in length, and, from the weft fea up into the mountains above the manor of Thwaites above fix miles in breadth and in form triangular. It is fo called, as it were *Meol-holme* or *Mil-holme,* being a plain ground running with a fharp point into the fea; for fo the ancient inhabitants termed every plain low ground near the fea, as Efk Meol, Kirkfantone Meole, Carl-meol (Cartmell) in Furnefs, the Mull of Galloway in Scotland, and many others.

This Millum was firft given by William de Mefchiens as aforefaid to *Godart Boyvil,* father to *Godartus Dapifer,* who being lord thereof gave to the abbot and monks of Furnefs a carucate of land with the appurtenances called Monkforce, which *Arthur* fon of Godart confirmed to that abbey, and after him *Henry* his fon and heir confirmed the fame, referving only hart and hind, wild boars, and their kinds, with all airies of hawks. But whatfoever was referved in the firft grant, whether demefne, or foreft liberties, dame Cecily Romley countefs of Albemarle, one of William Fitz Duncan's coheirs, gave and confirmed the fame to Henry fon of Arthur and his heirs,—*Henrico filio Arthuri et hæredibus fuis jus hæreditarium, videlicet, totam terram et totum feodum inter Efk et Dudden:* And dame Hawife her daughter and heir, then wife of William Mandeville, engaged her hufband to confirm it. And for a recognition of the lands made to the Boyvils by dame Cecily aforefaid, they paid to king Henry the fecond for a poft fine one hundred pounds and five couple of hounds, which the record terms *decem fugatores.*

The Boyvils took their furname from this place, and were ftyled *de Millum;* and held the fame in their iffue male, from the reign of Hen. 1. to the reign of Hen. 3. for above the fpace of one hundred years, when their name and family ended in a daughter. And their fucceffion was as follows:

1. *Godart de Boyvil,* to whom William de Mefchiens granted Millum.
2. *Godart* his fon, called Godardus Dapifer.
3. *Arthur* his fon.
4. *Henry* fon of Arthur.
5. *William* fon of Henry.
6. *Adam* brother and heir of William.
7. *Joan* daughter and heir of Adam; who by marriage transferred the inheritance into the Huddlefton family, which continued in the male line there for upwards of 500 years; and at laft, like moft of the reft, ended in a daughter.

The firft Boyvil gave his fecond fon William the manor of Kirkfanton; whofe pofterity enjoyed the fame till king Edward the fecond's time.

Godart the fecond lord gave Munkforce to the abbey of Furnefs as aforefaid, with the churches of Bootle and Whitcham: And all the parifhes between Efk and Millum, to the abbey of St. Mary's York; to which his wife gave alfo Anderfet, now called Agnes Seat.

Arthur the third lord confirmed his father's grants, and granted to Furnefs the fervice of Kirkfanton in Millum, which Robert Boyvill his coufin-german then held of him, and prefently after did mortgage the fame to the abbot of I urnefs, until he returned from the holy land.

Henry

Henry the fourth lord of Millum; confirmed his anceftors' grants, and in-feoffed Ranulph Corbet and his heirs of the manor of Brattaby with the ap-purtenances in Milium. He gave Rayfthwaite in Dunderfdale to Oime fon of Dolphin, and Leakly (now Seaton) to Henry fon of William in frank mar-riage with his daughter Gunild, with fhields for her cattle, and common of pafture in Brockbergh and in that foreft which Gunild gave afterwards to the abbey of Holm Cultram, and which after that became the poffeffion of the nuns of Seaton.

All the refidue of the fees in Millum were thus granted by the Boyvils to their children and friends, and by the Huddleftons after them; fome as ma-nors, fome as freeholds only, namely, Ulpha was granted to one Ulph fon of Everard, whofe pofterity kept it till Henry the third's time. Ulph had iffue Aylward and Ketel. Aylward paid to king Hen. 2. in the 27th year of his reign, 20 marks for a fine affeffed on him for an attaint. Ketel had divers fons, Bennet, William, and Michael. Bennet lived in king John's time; and had a fon named Alan. But the land was reduced into demefne again, and the lords of Millum inclofed there a park for deer.

The *Huddleftons* derive themfelves for feveral generations before the con-queft, but they came not to the feigniory of Millum till Henry the third's time by the marriage of Sir John Huddlefton knight with Joan daughter and fole heir of Adam de Boyvill. And with him we begin our pedigree of the Hudleftons of Milium.

1. Sir *John Hudlefton* knight, at the time of his marriage with the lady Joan, was lord of Anneys in Millum. He was fon of Adam, fon of John, fon of Richard, fon of Reginald, fon of Nigel, fon of Richard, fon of another Ri-chard, fon of John, fon of Adam, fon of Adam de Hodelfton in the county of York. Which five laft named (according to the York manufcript) were before the conqueft. In the 20 Ed. 1. before Hugh Creffingham juftice iti-nerant, it was proved that he had *jura regalia* within the feigniory of Millum, and his plea therein was allowed.

2. *John de Hudlefton*, fon of Sir John and lady Joan, died unmarried; and was fucceeded by

3. Sir *Richard Hudlefton* knight, who married Alice daughter of Richard Troughton in the 13 Ed. 2. and had iffue,

4. Sir *John Hudlefton* knight, who married Maud daughter of Sir William de Penington knight; and by her had iffue,

5. *John Hudlefton* efquire, who married Catherine daughter of Richard Tem-peft of Bowling in Yorkfhire, in the 14 Ric. 2.

6. *Richard Hudlefton,* fon of John married Anne daughter and one of the coheirs of Fenwick of a place of the fame name in Northumberland.

7. *Richard Hudlefton,* fon of Richard, married Margaret fifter of Sir Wil-liam Harrington knight of the garter. This Richard was made knight ba-neret by king Henry the fifth at the battle of Agincourt. He was fucceeded by his fon,

8. Sir *John Hudlefton* knight, who married Jane one of the coheirs of Sir Miles Stapleton of Ingham in Yorkfhire. He was made bailiff and keeper

of the king's woods and chaces in Barnoldwick in the county of York, sheriff of the county of Cumberland by the duke of Gloucester for his life, steward of Penrith, and warden of the west marches, and in the 7 Ed. 4. represented the county of Cumberland in parliament.

9. Sir *Richard Hudleston* knight, son of Sir John, married Margaret daughter of Richard Neville earl of Warwick.

10. *Richard*, his son, married Elizabeth daughter of lady Mabil Dacre, and died without issue in the reign of Hen. 7. He had two sisters; but the estate being entailed, passed to the next in the male line, namely, to his uncle John Hudleston younger brother of his father Richard Hudleston, son of the last Sir John Hudleston above mentioned. The two sisters were married, *viz.* Johan, to Hugh Fleming of Rydal esquire; and Margaret, to Lancelot Salkeld of Whitehall esquire.

11. Sir *John Hudleston* knight, uncle to the last Richard, married Joan, daughter to lord Fitz Hugh.

12. *John*, his son, married to his first wife Jane daughter of Henry lord Clifford knight of the garter, and first earl of Cumberland; by whom he had no issue. He married to his second wife Joan, sister of Sir John Seymour knight, father of the lady Jane Seymour, wife to king Henry the eighth. To his third wife he married Joyce daughter of Mr. Richley of Prickley in the county of Worcester.—By his second wife he had issue two sons, *Anthony* who continued the family at Millum, and *Andrew* who married one of the coheirs of Thomas Hutton of Hutton-John esquire, and was ancestor of the present family at Hutton-John.

13. *Anthony Hudleston* esquire, son and heir of John by his second wife Joan Seymour, married Mary daughter of Sir William Barrington of the county of Oxford knight.

14. *William*, his son, married Mary Bridges of the county of Gloucester. He served in parliament for the county of Cumberland in the 43 Eliz. and was succeeded by his son,

15. *Ferdinando Hudleston*, who married Jane daughter of Sir Ralph Grey of Chillingham in Northumberland knight, and had issue nine sons, William, John, Ferdinando, Richard, Ralph, Ingleby, Edward, Robert, and Joseph; every one of whom were officers in the service of king Charles the first. *William*, the eldest, raised a regiment of foot for the king at his own expence, and cloathed and paid them the whole war; he was made knight baneret by the king for his said services, but principally for retaking the royal standard at the battle of Edgehill. *John* was colonel of dragoons. *Ferdinando*, a major of foot. *Richard*, lieutenant colonel of foot, was slain in the minster yard at York. *Ralph*, a captain of foot. *Ingleby*, a captain of foot. *Edward*, a major of foot. *Robert*, a captain of foot. And *Joseph*, a captain of horse. *Ferdinando* the father was knight of the shire for Cumberland in the 21 Ja. 1.

16. Sir *William Hudleston* knight baneret married Bridget daughter of Joseph Pennington of Muncaster esquire.

17. *Ferdinand*

17. *Ferdinand,* their fon, married Dorothy daughter of Peter Huxley of London merchant; who had only a daughter Mary, married to Charles Weft lord Delaware, and died without iffue.

18. *Jofeph,* brother to Ferdinand, married Bridget daughter of Andrew Hudlefton of Hutton-John efquire, and had iffue Ferdinand who died without iffue, and was fucceeded by

19. *Richard,* fon of John next brother to Sir William, who married Ifabel daughter of Thomas Hudlefton of Bainton in the county of York, and had iffue,

20. *Ferdinand,* who married Elizabeth daughter of Lyon Falconer efquire, of Rutlandfhire, fon of Everard Falconer by Elizabeth daughter of Sir Maurice Trefham baronet, and had iffue,

21. *William Hudlefton* efquire, who married Gertrude daughter of Sir William Meredith of Henbury in Chefhire, and left two daughters Elizabeth and Ifabella.

22. *Elizabeth* was married to Sir Hedworth Williamfon of Monk Weremouth in the county of Durham baronet, who in the year 1774 fold the eftate to Sir James Lowther for upwards of 20,000 *l.*

The *Arms* of Hudlefton are Gules, a frette Argent.

Millum lordfhip hath feveral parifhes within it. That which lies higheft and moft fouthwardly is MILLUM PARISH; within which ftands the *caftle* of Millum, the capital meffuage and ancient feat of the lords thereof, which is placed at the foot of the river Dudden, at the eaft end of a large park well ftored with deer, and formerly with great quantities of wood, which Ferdinand Hudlefton (having no iffue but a daughter) about the year 1690 difpofed of in a great meafure in building of a large fhip, and in making charcoal for his iron forge in that park, where he confumed (as is faid) much excellent timber, to the then value of 4000 *l* and upwards, and was little or nothing profited thereby.

On the weft fide of this caftle, above the park, arifeth gradually a very high mountain, called *Blackcomb;* which, ftanding near the fea, and having the two level counties of Lancafhire and Chefhire on the fouth-eaft fide thereof, may be plainly difcovered on a clear day, from Talk on the Hill in Staffordfhire, near 100 miles diftance. And from the top of Blackcomb one may fee feveral mountains in North Wales, feven Englifh counties, and as many in Scotland, together with the Ifle of Man. This mountain, and the ridge of hills which run north-weft from thence, are efteemed the beft fheep heaths in the country.

This lordfhip was anciently exempted from the fheriff's jurifdiction, had power to licence their own alehoufes, and wreck of the fea is ftill enjoyed here, whereof much benefit is frequently made, it being almoft furrounded by the fea.

The foil is pretty fertile, being inriched by the great quantities of fea-pingle which is caft out there. Here are alfo iron mines, as is before obferved. But there is neither port nor creek within all this lordfhip. And the place is fo thinly inhabited, that the market at Millum hath been long difcontinued.

The

The *church* of Millum was given to the abbey of Furnefs in the year 1228; one moiety whereof was appropriated by the archbifhop of York to that monaftery, who were to prefent to the vicarage; the other moiety the archbifhop referved to his own difpofition, and in the year 1230 he affigned it for the maintenance of three chaplains with clerks and other charges for his chantry ordained at the altar of St. Nicolas in the cathedral church of York. It was certified to the governors of queen Anne's bounty at 26 *l* 1 *s* 8 *d*. In 1714 it received an augmentation by 200 *l* given by the reverend Mr. Poftlethwaite. The prefentation (Dr. Gaftrell fays) is in the crown, in right of the duchy of Lancafter.

There is a fchool in this parifh, to which Jofeph Hudlefton of Millum caftle gave 100 *l*, the intereft whereof is paid to the fchoolmafter, by the church jury, by whom he is chofen.

In 1722 it was certified, that they had then a poor ftock of 30 *l* 2 *s* 0 *d* given by feveral perfons not known *.

Upon the north fide of Millum, up the river of Dudden, lies ULPHA or *Ouffa*, among the rocky hills; which was granted, as is before mentioned, to *Ulfe*, who gave name to the place. In whofe pofterity it continued for feveral defcents, till at length it did revert to the lords of Millum, who have the lands and park there in demefne, of a confiderable yearly value; and having been formerly an intire manor of itfelf, when in the poffeffion of *Ulfe* and his pofterity, was again made parcel of the manor of Millum; and was fold fome few years ago by Sir Hedworth Williamfon to the prefent owner Mr. William Singleton of Drigg.

The lower part of Ulpha is very woody and good land, the upper part more rocky and barren.

The *chapel* was certified to the governors of queen Anne's bounty at 5 *l* yearly value, whereof 3 *l* 6 *s* 8 *d* was ancient chapel falary. The chapelry is reckoned a third part of the parifh of Millum. The chapel is diftant about feven miles from the parifh church, and the road from thence to the church is in fome places very rugged and almoft unpaffable.

THWAITES is another manor and townfhip within this parifh, ftanding upon the fame river, and north from Ulpha between Dudden and the mountains. Near the head whereof was heretofore the ancient feat of the Thwaitefes of Ewanrigg, who firft had their name from this place. For it being a ftony and mountainous country is not every where fo fit for tillage or meadow; but in feveral parts and parcels, as they are marked by nature, differing in form and quality of foil, or otherwife inclofed by the inhabitants from the barren wafte of the fells, fuch parts or parcels are now and were of old called *thwaits*, fometimes with the addition of their quality, as *Brackenthwaite*, of brackens or fern growing there; *Sieveythwaite*, of fieves or rufhes; *Stonethwaite*, of

---

* Many of the particulars concerning the churches, chapels, fchools and charities in this ward, we have from bifhop Gaftrell's Notitia of the diocefe of Chefter, with continuances by Mr. Commiffary Stratford. M. S.

rocks; and fuch like: and in-general, this word denotes any plain parcel of ground, from which the wood had been grubbed up, inclofed and converted into tillage.

This manor was an ancient fee holden of the lords of Millum. In the 35 Hen. 3. Eleanor wife of John Boyvil and Michael de Cornee paffed the fame by fine levied: And in the 16 Ed. 1. John Hudlefton impleaded William fon of John Thwaits for 200 acres of pafture there. The gentlemen of this family of Thwaites do bear for their arms; Or, a crofs Argent, frette Gules *.

The *chapel* of Thwaites was certified to the governors of queen Anne's bounty as having no endowment. In 1715, a new chapel was built at the expence of the inhabitants on freehold ground purchafed by them, with a chapel yard fenced in; and afterwards confecrated by bifhop Gaftrell. In 1717, John Dixon and others of the inhabitants advanced 200 *l* whereby the queen's bounty was procured, and an eftate purchafed therewith in Dent in the county of York. The place where the chapel ftands is called Hallthwaites. It is about three miles from the parifh church.

John Wennington gave 30 *l*, and Bernard Benfon 5 *l*, to the poor of this chapelry; which money is fecured upon two tenements in the neighbourhood.

PARISH OF WHITCHAM.

At the weft end of Donerfdale, near the fell of Blackcomb, and oppofite to Millum, ftands WHITCHAM or *Whittingham*; all which, or moft part of the fame, was holden of Millum, as another fee thereof. And the place took name of one *Wyche* the firft grantee thereof, who lived about the time of king Hen. 1. His two fons, William and Godfrey, were witneffes to a deed of mortgage of Kirkfanton in the reign of king Hen. 2. But the iffue general brought their lands into other families about the time of king Henry the third. For then one Radulph de Bethom had the land, and in the 6 Ed. 1. he granted eftovers to John parfon of Whitcham in his woods there. And in the 9 Ed. 1. Robert fon of Radulph (or Ralph) de Bethom did warrant lands in Silcroft and Satarton in the lordfhip of Milium. But the manors of Silcroft and Whitcham were in another family in the 9 Ed. 2. as appears by a fine thereof levied between William Corbett and Alicia his wife complainants and John de Corney deforciant.

And this manor of Whitcham is now broken into feveral parcels; part thereof, with a confiderable demefne, now belongs to Sir James Lowther, which he purchafed from the devifee of Henry Fearon of Calvey; another part belongs to Mr. John Muncafter of Cockermouth; and part thereof ftill remains to the lord of Millum.

* Sir Daniel Fleming, who was very curious in thofe matters, blazons their arms thus : *Argent,* a crofs fable, frettee Or.

The

The *church* of Whitcham is rectorial, and valued in the king's books at 8*l* 15*s* 0*d*; and was certified to the governors of queen Anne's bounty at 49*l* 13*s* 3*d*. It was granted by Reyner the fewer to the abbey of St. Mary's York. After the diffolution, Hugh Afcue efquire appears to have been patron, having prefented a rector in the year 1544. In the year 1717, Mr. Pennington is certified as patron.—The rector pays a penfion of 10*s* yearly to St Bees.

At Whitcham there is a fchool, which was built at the charge of the inhabitants, and endowed with 16*l* a year (as is faid) by one Hodgfon. The mafter is nominated by 12 truftees or governors, in purfuance of a decree in chancery in the 2 Ja. 2.

, Given to charitable ufes 33*l*, viz. 3*l* by Daniel Mafon, the intereft thereof to fix poor widows; 5*l* by Robert Crompton rector, the intereft to the poor yearly; the refidue by benefactors unknown, half of the intereft thereof applied to the repairs of the church, and half to the poor.

PARISH OF WHITBECK.

Under the mountain Blackcomb, a mile weft from Whitcham, ftandeth WHITBECK or *Whitebeck*, which William Morthing gave by fine to the prior and convent of Conifheved. Thefe Morthings and alfo the Corbets were anciently feated in Millum. Their names appear in old evidences in the reigns of Henry the third and Edward the fecond, and they were men of good worth and quality, as William de Morthing and John de Morthing, William Corbet and Ranulph Corbet. Divers of the Corbets feated themfelves in Scotland in thofe famous wars of king Ed. 1. where their pofterity remain to this day in good repute.

The church was given by Gamel de Pennington to the priory of Conifhead aforefaid, and is now only a perpetual curacy, returned at the yearly value of 9*l* 14*s* 8*d*; and Mr. Park the impropriator is alfo the patron.

In the year 1631, Henry Park of Kendal mercer left 400*l*, the intereft whereof to be given yearly to fix poor people, to be chofen upon a vacancy by the churchwardens and four of the moft fubftantial men of the parifh, who are to be nominated and appointed by the bifhop of Chefter for the time being. In 1722 it was certified that an hofpital was built for the faid poor people, and lands bought with the money, which yielded 24*l* per annum.

There was then alfo a poor ftock of 30*l*, the intereft thereof to be applied to the ufe of the poor.

PARISH OF BOOTLE.

Next to Whitbeck on the common high ftreet is BOTHILL or *Bootle*, which had its name from the beacon on the top of the *hill* above the town, which

was

was fired upon the difcovery of any *fhips* upon the Irifh feas which might threaten an invafion, by the watchmen who lay in *booths* by the beacon. And for the fupport of this fervice, the charge or payment of *Seawake* was provided [*].

At Bootle in old time ftood a manfion of the family of the *Copelands* who continued till the reign of Hen. 4. Amongft whom we find Sir *Richard Copeland* knight, father of *Alan*, father of *Richard*, who died feifed in the 26 Ed. 1. and left his eftate to John his fon, father of another Richard Copeland. They bear for their arms; Or, a bend Sable, on a canton and two bars Gules.

Bootle is a market town, and though it is at a confiderable diftance from any other market town, yet it hath but a fmall market.

The *church* is rectorial, and dedicated to St. Michael It is valued in the king's books at 19*l* 17*s* 3¼*d*; and was certified in 1717 at 70*l* 2*s* 2*d*. It pays 4*s* penfion to St. Bees. It was given to the abbey of St. Mary's York by Godard the Sewer (the fame who is above called Godardus Dapifer, fecond lord of Millum). The abbot and convent prefented to it in 1527, a little before the diffolution; in 1717, Robert Pennington efquire is certified as patron.

They have a fmall *fchool*, built at the charge of the inhabitants, and endowed with the intereft of 200*l* given by Mr. Singleton, and of 50*l* given by Mr. Hutton the rector. The fchoolmafter is nominated by the rector and four or five of the parifhioners.

They have an ancient *poor ftock* of 20*l*, the intereft whereof is diftributed every St. Thomas's day. The benefactor not known.

LEKELEY, now *Seaton*, was granted to the abbey of Holm Cultram, by Gunild daughter of Henry de Boyvill fourth lord of Millum [†]; whofe grant was confirmed by Joan daughter and heir of Adam de Millum, for the health of her foul and of the foul of John de Hodlefton her hufband deceafed [‡]. And here became eftablifhed an houfe of Benedictine nuns.

Henry duke of Lancafter (afterwards king Henry the fourth) by his charter, fetting forth that the priory of Seaton was fo poor that it could not fufficiently maintain the priorefs and nuns, grants to them in aid the hofpital of St. Leonard at Lancafter, with power to appoint the chantry prieft to officiate in the faid hofpital [||].

---

[*] In the 7 Eliz. there was a decree in the Duchy court of Lancafter, for fettling the cuftoms of the queen's tenants, late belonging to the abbey of Furnefs: *Inter alia*—It is further ordered and decreed, by the faid chancellor and council, by the full affent, confent, and agreement of the faid cuftomary tenants [in the parifh of Hawkfhead], that the faid cuftomary tenants, their heirs and affigns, being tenants of the premifes, fhall for ever, at their own proper cofts and charges, prepare, furnifh, and have in readinefs, when they fhall be thereunto required and commanded by the queen's majefty her heirs and fucceffors, or by any of her other officers fufficiently authorized for the fame, forty able men, horfed, harneffed, and weaponed according to their ability by ftatute of armory, and horfe meet to ferve in the war againft the enemies of the queen's majefty her heirs and fucceffors, for the defence of the haven and caftle called the Peel of Fodia, or otherwife upon that coaft, without allowance of wages, coat, or conduct money; or elfewhere; as need fhall require, and fhall be thereunto commanded and appointed out of the realm, having allowance of coat and conduct money and wages as inland men have.

[†] Appendix, N° V.   [‡] Regiftr. Holme.   [||] Id.

This nunnery was valued at the diffolution at 12 or 13 *l* a year; and in the 33 H. 8. was granted to Sir Hugh Afcue knight, to hold of the king *in capite* by the fervice of the 20th part of one knight's fee, and the rent of 9 *s* 2 *d* to be paid yearly into the court of augmentations. Sir Hugh fettled the fame upon his wife who was daughter of Sir John Hudlefton, and fhe after his death marrying into the Pennington family at Moncafter gave the fame to her younger fon William Pennington, in whofe pofterity it ftill continues.

In the 5 and 6 Ph. and M. Sep. 2. Thomas Reve and Nicholas Pynde of London gentlemen purchafed of the crown the faid rent of 9 *s* 2 *d*, together with divers free rents in Seaton late belonging to the faid priory.

MUNKFORCE was, as before is mentioned, given by William de Mefchien's to Furnefs abbey, and upon the diffolution was granted to the houfe of Millum, and by feveral mefne conveyances is now the inheritance of Mr. Edmund Gibfon of Whitehaven in this county.

SCOGGERBAR is another manor within the parifh of Bootle, lying weft from thence by the fea fhore; and was given by Sir William Hudlefton to his fecond fon Jofeph, who by the death of his elder brother Ferdinand, as is abovefaid, became heir of the lordfhip of Millum, and reunited Scoggerbar to the faid lordfhip.

PARISH OF CORNEY.

The parifh and manor of CORNEY lies three miles north from Bootle. Of this place Michael the falconer and his pofterity took furname, for they were thereof infeoffed in the reign of king John or king Henry the third; and by marriage of the daughter and heir of Corney the inheritance came to the Penningtons of Mulcafter where it yet remains, who are alfo patrons of the advowfon.

Middleton Place is a little hamlet within this parifh and manor, where the manor court is held, and hath been fo of old time, and the rather in regard the capital meffuage and demefne were here formerly, which gave name to an ancient family of the Middletons, and was their habitation, but hath fince been broken into tenancies.

The *church* is rectorial, dedicated to St. John Baptift; is valued in the king's books at 9 *l* 17 *s* 1 *d*, and returned to the governors of queen Anne's bounty at 22 *l* 11 *s* 10 *d*. It belonged to the abbey of St. Mary's York, who prefented to it in 1536, which was a few years before the diffolution. It is a fmall parifh, confifting only of 36 tenements.

PARISH OF WAYBERGTHWAITE.

WAYBERGTHWAIT, or the plain and valley of Waybergh, is the next parifh; which Waybergh married the daughter or fifter of Arthur Boyvil third

lord

lord of Millum fon of Godard Dapifer, with whom the faid Arthur gave this manor in frank marriage; and their pofterity took name from that place, until it was fold to the Penningtons of Mulcafter, it being only fevered from Mulcafter demefne and park by the river Efk.

Here are no demefne lands, except Efkmeals; being a bare fandy ground, wherein is a coney warren.

The cuftomary tenants pay arbitrary fines, rents, heriots, and boon fervices.

The *church* is rectorial, dedicated to St. John, valued in the king's books at $3l$ $11s$ $8d$, and returned to the governors of queen Anne's bounty at $18l$ $16s$ $6d$, clear yearly value. In the year 1421, Sir Richard de Kirkby prefented to this rectory, and again in 1425. In 1580, Henry Kirkby prefented. In 1608, the prefentation appears to have been in the Penningtons, in whom it ftill continues.

In this parifh there was an ancient *poor* ftock of 20*l*, unto which Mr. Park rector of Barton in Norfolk added 80*l*; the intereft thereof to be diftributed annually.

PARISH OF MULCASTER.

Next unto the north fide of the feignory of Millum ftands MULCASTER, upon the north-weft bank of the river Efk; an ancient feat of the Penningtons, in whofe name and family it hath continued ever fince the time of William the conqueror or near it.

1. *Gamel de Penington*, in the reign of king Henry the fecond, gave the churches of Mulcafter, Penington, Whitbeck, and of Orton in Weftmorland, to the priory of Conifhead; which grant was confirmed by king Edward the fecond in the 12th year of his reign [*].

2. *Benedict de Penington*, fon of *Gamel*, had divers children. Alan fon of Alan fon of Benedict granted lands at Orton aforefaid to his uncle Simon fon of the faid Benedict: But, according to their family pedigree, Benedict (after the death of an elder fon Robert) was fucceeded by his fon,

3. *David*, father of

4. *John*, father of

5. *Alan*, to whom Richard Lucy (as is hereafter mentioned) in the reign of king John granted the fee of Ravenglafs.

6. *Thomas*, fon of Alan.

7. *Alan*, fon of Thomas.

8. *John*, fon of Alan; of whom mention is made in the 21 Ed. 1.

9. *William*, fon of John.

10. *John*, fon of William; who being left in minority, was ward to the abbot of Furnefs; who demifed the park at Pennington to one John de Haverington in the 16 Ric. 2.

11. *William*, fon of John; who died feifed of the fixth part of a knight's fee in Mulcafter and Ravenglafs, and of the advowfons of the third part of

[*] 2 Dugd. Mon. 424.

the

the cell of St. Bees and abbey of Calder, and the advowfons of Gosforth and Diffington, as appears by inquifition taken 8 Ed. 3.

12. *John*, fon of William.

13. *William*, fon of John; who was ward to John de Multon.

14. *Alan*, fon of William; who married Margaret daughter and coheir of Sir Richard Prefton, with whom he had a moiety of the manor of Prefton Richard, which the family enjoys to this day.

15. Sir *John Pennington* knight, fon of Alan.

16. *John*, his fon; who married Mary daughter of Sir John Hudlefton, upon which marriage in the 23 Ed. 4. the eftate was fettled upon the iffue male. And he having only a daughter Ifabel married to Thomas Dykes of Warthole efquire, the eftate came to the fecond brother,

17. *William*, who had a fon,

18. *Jofeph*; father of

19. Sir *William Pennington* knight, who married Ifabel daughter of John Farrington of Warden in Lancafhire efquire, with whom he had the manor of Farrington. On an inquifition of knights fees in Cumberland in the 35 Hen. 8. it is found that this Sir William held the manor of Mulcafter of the king as of his caftle of Egremond, by the fervice of the fixth part of one knight's fee, rendering to the king yearly for Seawake 12 d, and the puture of two ferjeants; and that he held the hamlet of Ravenglafs in like manner, by homage and fealty and the fervice of the 17th part of one knight's fee, and puture of ferjeants as above.

20. *Jofeph*, fon of Sir William.

21. Sir *William*, fon of Jofeph. He married Ifabel the eldeft daughter of John Stapleton of Wartre in the county of York, with whom the manor of Wartre came to the Penningtons. He was the firft baronet of the family; being fo created 29 Cha. 2. He had iffue,

22. Sir *Jofeph Pennington* baronet, who married Margaret fifter of Henry vifcount Lonfdale. He had iffue John, Jofeph, and a daughter Katharine mother of the prefent Sir James Lowther baronet.

23. Sir *John Pennington* baronet died unmarried, and was fucceeded by his brother the prefent owner of the family eftate, viz.

24. Sir *Jofeph Pennington* baronet; who hath three fons, John now a colonel in his majefty's forces, Jofeph, and Lowther; and three daughters, the youngeft of whom is now lately married to Brooks Ofbaldifton of the county of York efquire.

The Arms of Pennington are; Or, 5 lozenges conjoined in fefs Azure.

This manor is bounded by the river Efk on the fouth eaft, the fea on the weft, and the rill or rivulet called Mite on the north. It is in the form of a long ridge of hills, running in an oblique form, from the foot of Efk unto the great and vaft mountains in Efkdale, Wafdale, and Miterdale, being in length above two miles, and about half as much in breadth. The park is large, well ftored with deer and conies, as it is faid it anciently was with wood, but there is not much appearance of it at prefent.

Ravenglafs

Ravenglass is a village within this manor, and a market town, lying a mile west from Mulcaster upon the sea shore. The word signifies a green of ferns, from *renigh*, fern, and *glass*, green, derived from the Irish. King John granted to Richard Lucy a yearly fair to be held here on St. George's day (April 23d), and a weekly market every Friday, as lord paramount. But the said Richard Lucy the same year, by fine levied to Alan Pennington, confirmed to him as mesne lord and his tenants all the land and fee of Ravenglass, to hold to him and his heirs, with estovers to make fish garths in the river Esk.

At present, the earl of Egremont holds the fair of Ravenglass on the eve, day, and morrow of St. James. On the first of these days in the morning, the lord's officer, at proclaiming the fair, is attended by the serjeants of the bow of Egremont, with the insignia belonging thereto; and all the tenants of the forest of Copeland owe a customary service to meet the lord's officer at Ravenglass to proclaim the fair, and abide with him during the continuance thereof; and for sustentation of their horses, they have two swaiths of grass in the common field of Ravenglass in a place set out for that purpose. On the third day at noon, the earl's officer discharges the fair by proclamation; immediately whereupon the Penningtons and their tenants take possession of the town, and have races and other divertisements during the remainder of that day.

The earl of Egremont hath also several fisheries upon the rivers of Esk, Mite, and Irt; where are caught great varieties of sea fish, as well as fresh water fish: Which fisheries are held in lease by the Penningtons.

And in the winter season there is so great plenty of woodcocks (which they catch in snares or springes) that the tenants are bound by the custom of the manor to sell them to the lord for pence apiece.

The *church* is dedicated to St. Michael. It was wholly appropriated to the priory of Conishead, and upon the dissolution was granted to the lord of the manor, who nominates a perpetual curate, whose stipend was returned at 10*l*. In 1723, it had an augmentation of 200*l* by lot:

Here is a school founded by Richard Brookbank, and endowed by him with the interest of 160*l*. The schoolmaster is appointed by trustees, who are some of the substantial inhabitants.

There is an ancient *poor stock* of 23*l*; and 12 loaves distributed every Sunday, given by some of the ancestors of the Penningtons.

ESKDALE CHAPELRY.

At the head of Esk river, three miles east from Mulcaster, stands *Eskdale* chapel in this ward. It is dedicated to St. Catherine. It was certified in 1717 at 9*l per annum*; 5*l* of which was interest of 100*l* given by Edward Stanley esquire, then in the hands of John Stanley esquire his son. The chapelry consists of two villages, Eskdale and Birker, which are divided by the river Esk, the latter in the parish of Millum, the other in the parish of

St.

St. Bees where the chapel ftands, being 14 miles diftant from the mother church.

About half a-mile from the chapel ftands *Awfthwaite*, now called *Dalegarth*, which gave name to the ancient family of the Awfthwaites, upon the grant thereof made by Arthur Boyvill lord of Millum. And Conftance daughter and heir of Thomas de Awfthwaite brought this manor by marriage to Nicholas Stanley efquire in king Edward the third's time. His grandfather John was a younger brother of William Stanley efquire lord of Stanleigh in the Moorlands in Staffordfhire, from whence they took their name. This manor continues in the iffue male of the faid Nicholas to this day; the prefent owner being Edward Stanley efquire. Their arms are; Argent, on a bend Azure three ftags heads cabofhed Or.

This manor lies at the foot of the mountain Hardknot, and contains a vaft tract of mountainous ground, which is reckoned an excellent fheep heath.

The aforefaid Edward Stanley efquire, who gave 100 *l* to the chapel, gave 40 *l* to the *poor*; and there was then 13 *l* more of ancient poor ftock.

WASDALE.

WASDALE (Wafte-dale) at the foot of Copeland fells lies about two miles north from Efkdale. Here are two *chapels*, holden of St. Bees, *Nether Wafdale*, and *Wafdale head* or *Upper Wafdale*.

Nether Wafdale was certified at 5 *l* a year, and is above ten miles diftant from the parifh church.

Wafdale head was certified at 3 *l* a year, and is 14 miles diftant from the parifh church. It received an augmentation by lot of 200 *l*, in the year 1719.

Thefe two chapelries, Mr. Denton fays, are parcel of the barony of Egremont, and make one intire manor; which was parcel of the third part of Egremont, which Thomas Lucy had with his wife Margaret one of the coheirs of John Multon the laft baron of Egremont of that name. But at prefent, Wafdale head is underftood to be part of the manor of Efkdale, and Nether Wafdale a diftinct manor of itfelf.

In thefe mountains is a large foreft of deer, which extends as far as Styhead in Boredale.

PARISH OF IRTON.

A mile or two below Wafdale to the fouthward, upon the fouth fide of the river Irt, lies the parifh, manor, and town of *Irt* or IRTON, fo named of the river Irt. This place gave name to the ancient family of the *Irtons*, who have enjoyed it in the male line for many ages. The firft that we meet with of certainty is,

1. *Richard de Yrton*; who had iffue,

2. *Ralph*

2. *Ralph de Yrton*; who lived in the reign of king Hen. 2. He had issue,

3. *Stephen de Yrton*; who had issue Robert, Ralph, and Thomas.

4. *Robert de Irton* died without issue; and his next brother Ralph being professed of religion, being first prior of Gisbourn, and afterwards bishop of Carlisle, the estate fell to Thomas the third brother. Ralph was made bishop in the 7 Ed. 1.

5. *Thomas Irton* had issue,

6. *Thomas*; father of

7. *Christopher*; father of

8. *Richard*; father of

9. *John*; father of

10. *Richard*; father of

11. *John*; father of

12. *Nicholas Irton*; which Nicholas appears to be one returned by the commissioners in the 12 Hen. 6. amongst the great men and gentry of the county. He had issue,

13. *John Irton*; from whom descended the family of the Irtons in Devonshire. He had issue,

14. *John*; who had issue,

15. *William Irton*; who was made receiver of the county in the 8 Hen. 7. He had issue,

16. *Richard Irton*; who was sheriff of the county in the 22 Hen. 8. This Richard in the 35 Hen. 8. is found by inquisition to hold the manor and town of Irton of our lord the king as of his castle of Egremond, by homage and fealty and one half-penny free rent and suit of court at Egremond. He held also at the same time Cleter, and a moiety of the manor of Bastinthwaite. He had issue,

17. *Roger*; who had issue,

18. *John*; who had issue,

19. Another *John*; who had issue,

20. A third *John*; who had issue,

21. *George*; who had issue,

22. *George*; who was sheriff of the county in the 24 G. 2. and dying without issue was succeeded by his brother,

23. *Samuel Irton*; who was sheriff in the 5 Geo. 3. and died in 1766, leaving three sons, George, Samuel, and Edmund; and three daughters, Frances, Elizabeth, and Martha.

Irton *hall* is said to be a good seat in a bad country; standing upon the ascent of an hill, with a large prospect over the west part of Cumberland and the Irish sea unto the Isle of Man and Galloway in Scotland. This place is well sheltered with wood; and where it is not rocky, the soil is tolerably fertile. The demesne is large. The tenants pay customary rents, arbitrary fines, and heriots, with other boons and services.

SANTON,

'SANTON, in this parish, was in Henry the third's time the inheritance of one Alan de Copeland. His capital manſion houſe was in the townſhip of Bootle. He held of Thomas de Multon of Gilſland, who held over of the lord of Egremont. Afterwards, Alan and Richard his ſons ſucceeded him, and John and Richard ſucceeded them. And in the 22 Ric. 2. Alan ſon of Richard Copeland held lands there. It is now in the families of Irton and Winder; Winder's part was purchaſed of Latus, and Latus purchaſed of one Lancaſter.

In the river Irt the inhabitants at low water gather *pearls*, and the jewellers buy them of the poor people for a trifle, but ſell them at a good price. And it is ſaid, that Mr. Thomas Patrickſon late of How in this county, having employed divers poor inhabitants to gather theſe pearls, obtained ſuch a quantity as he ſold to the jewellers in London for above 800*l*.

The *church* was appropriated to the nunnery of Seaton or Lekeley, and upon the diſſolution thereof granted to the Penningtons lords of Mulcaſter, who now enjoy the advowſon and tithes. The church is dedicated to St. Paul, and was returned to the governors of queen Anne's bounty at 4*l* 13*s* 4*d*.

Henry Calday gave 100*l*, the intereſt thereof to go to a *ſchoolmaſter* when a ſchool ſhould be built. Upon which foundation a ſmall ſchool hath been eſtabliſhed.

PARISH OF DREGG.

About two miles ſouth weſt from Irton, between Irt river and the ſea, is DREGG; which is the next pariſh, and another fee of Egremont.

The pariſh conſiſts of two hamlets, Dregg and Carleton.

Dregg had of old time great ſtore of oaks growing there, and thereof the name *Derigh* or *Dergh* ſignifying an oak in the Erſe or Iriſh language was attributed to it. It was in the poſſeſſion of the Eſtotevilles, barons of Liddall, in king Henry the ſecond's time; whoſe patrimony by a daughter came to the lord Baldwin Wake in the reign of king Henry the third. Of which Baldwin, William ſon of Thomas de Grayſtock and the lady Adingham de Furneſs in the 10 Ed. 1. held a knight's fee between them in Dregg. And in the 29 Ed. 1. the abbot of Caldre, Patrick Curwen, and the lady Margaret Multon held Dregg of John de Grayſtock and of John ſon of Robert de Harrington, and they held over of John Wake. Afterwards Harrington's part came to the Curwens by marriage of the heir general of the Harringtons, and ſo continued in the houſe of Workington, until Sir Nicholas Curwen ſold it to Sir William Pennington of Mulcaſter in king James the firſt's time, whoſe poſterity ſtill enjoy it. But the moſt conſiderable part of Dregg now belongs to the earl of Egremont, and the tenants do ſuit and ſervice at the great court at Egremont.

Dregg is bounded by the river Irt on the Eaſt and South, by the ſea on the Weſt, and by the demeſne and manor of Seaſcales on the North.

The

The church is dedicated to St. Peter. It was appropriated either to the priory of Conifhead or the abbey of Calder, but unto which of the two hath not appeared to us. Bifhop Gaftrell takes notice, that Anfelm fon of Michael de Furnefs gave the chapel of *Drog* to the priory of Conifhead, and queries whether in the manufcript it might not be miftaken for the church of Dreg. On the other hand, it hath appeared that the abbot of Caldre had part of the manor, and it feldom happened when the religious had any thing to do with the manor, but they had the advowfon alfo. However, it was fo totally appropriated, that it is now only a perpetual curacy; and was certified to the governors of queen Anne's bounty at the yearly value of *5l 6s 8d*. Upon the diffolution it was granted to the Curwens, and Sir Nicholas Curwen fold it to the Penningtons as before is mentioned, whofe pofterity now enjoy not only all the tithes, but alfo the demefne and manor. The lord hath here alfo a miln, to which the tenants are bound; and prefcribes to flotfam, jetfam, and lagan, and fo it was adjudged upon a trial at bar between Henry earl of Northumberland and Sir Nicholas Curwen in queen Elizabeth's time, and afterwards a decree in chancery for confirming the faid prefcription and fecuring that right to the claim of the fea againft the lord paramount.

CARLETON was firft *villa rufticorum*, a town of hufbandmen, and then called the *Carles town*; but it was afterwards made demefne, and fince demifed and broken into tenancies. They hold of Sir Jofeph Pennington as of his manor of Dregg. It lies on the eaft fide of Irt; and it is very obfervable, that the lands which lie on each fide of that river are of fuch different foils, as hath hardly been known elfewhere; thofe on the eaft fide being altogether a deep clay, and thofe on the weft and north nothing but beds of fand.

PARISH OF GOSFORTH.

Above Dregg two miles north lies the parifh of GOSFORTH or *Gosford*, whereof the Gosfords an ancient family in thofe parts took their furname. Robert Gosford, the laft of their houfe, left his lands to be divided among five coheirs, viz. Mariot the wife of Alan Caddy, his eldeft daughter; Ifabel wife of Henry Huftock, his fecond daughter; Johan wife of Adam Garth, the third daughter; Eleanor wife of William Kirkby, the fourth daughter; and John Multon fon of Agnes Eftholme, the fifth coheir.

In the fecond year of king Edward the third, Sarah the widow of Robert Leyburne held Caddy's part, John Pennington held Kirkby's part, and the faid John Multon the refidue.

Mr. Robert Copley, fteward to Sir William Pennington for 17 years during his minority, and chief bailiff of Copeland foreft to the then earl of Northumberland, purchafed Kirkby's part, and built a large handfome houfe, with orchards and gardens fuitable, but they are now much in decay.

Bolton in Copeland is a townſhip within this pariſh, which lies a mile eaſt from Gosford. This was the inheritance of the Waybergthwaits in Edward the firſt's time; for in the 23 Ed. 1. William de Waybergthwait held 10 *l* lands there of Thomas de Multon of Gilſland, and his land in Waybergthwaite of the lord of Millum.

In the 35 Hen. 8. William Kirkby held the manor of Bolton of the king as of his caſtle of Egremont, by knights ſervice, paying yearly 10 *s* cornage, and ſeawake, homage, ſuit of court, and witneſſman. At the ſame time he held lands and tenements in Gosforth and Cleater, by the like homage, fealty, and ſuit of court, and paying to the king a fee farm rent of 8 *s* for the lands in Gosforth, and 2 *s* for the lands in Cleater; and 2 *s* ſeawake, and alſo puture of two ſerjeants.

It was afterwards the eſtate of Lancelot Senhouſe, whoſe father was third brother of the houſe of Seaſcales, and he had it by grant from the lord thereof his brother.

Seaſcales lies a mile weſt from Gosford, and is ſo called from the *ſcales* or ſhields of cattle by the ſea ſide. It was the capital meſſuage of John Senhouſe eſquire, ſon cf William, brother of John, whoſe father alſo was John. It was puichaſed by Mr. Blaylock merchant in Whitehaven, whoſe daughter and heir was married to Auguſtine Earl eſquire, whoſe ſon dying without iſſue, it deſcended to his two ſiſters coheirs. At preſent, this, and alſo the manor of Bolton are the property of Charles Lutwidge eſquire, who has a country houſe near adjoining, where he has made great improvements in building, planting, and gardening.

The *church* of Gosforth is rectorial, dedicated to St. Mary. It is rated in the king's books at 17 *l* 14 *s* 7 *d*; and was certified to the governors of queen Anne's bounty at the clear yearly improved value of 35 *l*. In the 8 Ed. 3. William Pennington of Moncaſter eſquire died ſeiſed of the advowſon of this church. Afterwards, the patronage thereof appears to have been in the crown; and in the ſixth year of king Edward the ſixth, the ſaid king by his letters patent granted the advowſon and right of patronage to Fergus Greyme gentleman, his heirs and aſſigns. And in the 6 Eliz. March 22. there is a licence to Fergus Greyme to alienate the ſame (holden of the queen *in capite*) to Thomas Senhouſe gentleman, for the fine of 16 *s* 10 *d* paid into the hanaper. The owners of Seaſcales are now the patrons.

In 1717 it was certified that there is a *poor ſtock* in this pariſh of 24 *l*, the intereſt thereof diſtributed yearly at Eaſter.

PARISH OF PONSONBY.

PONSONBY, the habitation of *Ponſon*, was ſo denominated from a family of that name of ancient time, which family afterwards took name from the place *de Pon-*
ſonby,

sonby, of which family and name there are several yet remaining. There was one Ponson in the reign of king Stephen and Henry the first. His son John Fitz Ponson was fined in Henry the second's time because he wanted pledges. Alexander son of Richard Ponsonby lived about the time of Ed. 2. And William in the reign of Ed. 3. And Robert in Richard the second's time. It was afterwards purchased by the Stanleys, in whose name and family it still continues.

The *church* was given to the priory of Conishead by John Fitz Ponson aforesaid. It was certified to the governors of queen Anne's bounty at 9 *l* 2 *s*; viz. 6 *l* paid by the impropriator, 3 *l* given by William Cleator for monthly sermons, and 2 *s* surplice fees. In 1689, a presentation from the crown was procured to this church as a vicarage, but afterwards revoked, and there was none before that in the institution books. So that it is only a perpetual curacy, and the Stanleys impropriators nominate the curate. It is a small parish, consisting only of 24 tenements and two cottages, in which are resident about 20 families.

In 1717 it was certified that the said William Cleator abovementioned, who was doctor of physic, gave by his will 100 *l* to the minister for preaching 12 sermons every year, till the impropriation should be restored to the church, and then to go to a school in the parish. And the executors refusing to pay the money, the minister sued and recovered it in chancery, with 20 *l* arrears of interest; 9 *l* of this money was then lost, and 43 *l* thereof in the hands of the churchwardens not disposed of. The rest was laid out in lands.

PARISH OF ST. BRIDE's.

The parish of St. Bride's, or St. *Bridget's*, lies on the north side of the river Calder, upon which river stands the ABBEY within the *manor* of *Calder*; so named from the rill or beck falling down from the mountain called *Caldfell* (from its *cold* situation) into the dale where the abbey stands, and thence into the Irish sea.

This abbey (which was of the Cistertian order) was founded by Ranulph son of the first Ranulph de Meschiens, in the year 1134.[†] The revenues thereof will principally appear from a confirmation thereof by king Henry the third, which was as followeth:

By the gift of *Ranulph de Meschiens*, the ground on which the abbey stands; and Bemerton, and Holgate, with the appurtenances; one house in Egremont; two salt works of Withane; a fishing in Derwent; another in Egre; pasture for their cattle in the forest of the said Ranulph as much as they shall need; all necessaries for their salt works and fisheries and building of their houses; and liberty for their hogs without pannage:

[†] Fanner's Notitia, 75.

By the gift of *John* son of *Ada* and *Matthew* his brother, all the land of Stavenenge with the appurtenances :

By the gift of *Robert Bonekill*, one carucate of land in lesser Gilerux, and 12 acres and one perch more in the same ; and one acre of meadow between the greater and lesser Gilcrux ; and pasture for 20 oxen, 12 cows, and 6 mares, with their young of one year :

By the gift of *Roger* son of *William*, lands in Ikelinton and Brachampton, and part of the mill of Brachampton :

By the gift of *Richard de Lucy*, one moiety of the mill of Ikelinton, with all things thereunto appertaining :

By the gift of *Beatrix de Molle*, five bovates of land in lesser Gilcruce, and a fourth part of the miln of the greater Gilcruce :

By the gift of *Thomas* son of *Gospatrick*, a toft in Workington, and 20 salmon yearly at the feast of St. John Baptist, and one net in Derwent between the bridge and the sea :

By the gift of *Thomas de Multon*, a moiety of the vill of Dereham, with the advowson of the church there †.

After the dissolution, king Henry the eighth by letters patent dated the 26th of July in the 30th year of his reign, granted to Thomas Leigh doctor of laws and his heirs, the demesne and site of the late abbey or manor of Calder, and the church, steeple, and churchyard thereof, and all messuages, lands, tenements, houses, buildings, barns, dovecotes, gardens, orchards, waters, ponds, mills, ground and soil, as well within as nigh unto the site and precinct of the said monastery ; as also all lands, tenements, granges, meadows, pastures, woods, common of pasture, with divers inclosures by name, containing in the whole 217 acres, at Calder aforesaid (with divers granges elsewhere) of the clear yearly value of 13*l* 10*s* 4*d*. To hold of the king *in capite* by the tenth part of one knight's fee, and the rent of 27*l* 1*d*, in the name of tenths to be paid into the court of augmentations.

Sir Ferdinando Leigh, grandson of the said Thomas Leigh, sold the same to Sir Richard Fletcher baronet ; who gave it in marriage with his daughter Barbara to Mr. John Patrickson second brother to Joseph Patrickson of How esquire, whose son Richard Patrickson sold it to Mr. John Tiffin of Cockermouth, who gave it to his grandson John Senhouse esquire the present possessor.

There is a large demesne, but a great part of it is a barren and sandy soil, excepting what lies near the river, which is very rich and fertile, but not woody.

Above this abbey eastward stands *Caldfell* and *Wasdale* fells, mounting aloft, but yielding plenty of pasture for large flocks of sheep.

Silla park lies a mile lower upon this rill towards the sea, which was heretofore a cell belonging to this abbey, where the abbey had a park well stored

† Appendix, N°. VI. Note, This last particular, concerning the church of Dereham, was either a mistake, or a wrong claim by the abbey ; for this advowson had been given before by Alice de Romeley to the priory of Gisburn, and the said priory constantly enjoyed it.

with

with deer; and is now a very pleafant feat, by the river's fide, within a mile of the fea, the land lying in a flat, and a commodious dwelling-houfe being there built by Darcy Curwen efquire, upon whom the fame was fettled by his grandfather Sir Henry Curwen, which Sir Henry received the fame by grant from the crown upon the diffolution of chantries.

St. Bride's *church* lies half a mile more weftward between Calder beck and Beckermouth. It was dedicated to St. Bridget an Irifh faint. It was appropriated to Calder abbey; and fince the diffolution thereof was granted to the Flemings. John Fleming of Rydal efquire gave the fame in frank marriage with his daughter to Sir Jordan Crofsland knight, whofe daughters and coheirs fold the fame to Richard Patrickfon efquire; and Mr. Henry Todd is now impropriator and patron. It was certified at 7 *l* clear yearly value.

PARISH OF ST. JOHN's.

A little above St. Bride's lies the manor of (*Little*) BECKERMET, now and of old time belonging to the Flemings of Rydal in Weftmorland, who as méfne lords between the baron of Egremont and the poffeffors and land tenants of Rotington, Frifington, Arloghden, and Weddikar, did hold them as fees of Beckermet, and it felf as demefne of the baron of Egremont barony. For it is to be noted, that there are two manors of the name of *Beckermet*; one called *Great Beckermet*, in the parifh of St. Bride's, belonging to the earl of Egremont; and this other, called *Little Beckermet* in the parifh of St. John's.

The church of this parifh was given by the Fleming family to the aforefaid abbey of Calder, and in the year 1262 was totally appropriated to the faid abbey, fo as that the whole revenue thereof was applied to the ufe of that houfe. In the grant of appropriation, it is curious to obferve, upon what frivolous pretences fuch appropriations were commonly obtained. The abbot and convent in their petition to Godefride archbifhop of York fet forth, that although they had the right of patronage in the churches of St. John Baptift of Beckermet, and of St. Michael in Arlekden, yet by reafon of the importunity of great men, and provifions of the faid benefices, they had not free liberty to prefent unto the fame; and therein, where they obliged one great man they difobliged many more; they therefore requeft, that the archbifhop would take fuch order therein, as may be more beneficial to the faid abbot and convent, and alfo to the archdeacon of Richmond, to whom the fequeftration of, and inftitution to vacant benefices doth belong, and the collation thereof for various caufes may appertain: Therefore the faid archbifhop grants to the faid abbot and convent, that the church of St. John of Beckermet, which is nigh to the houfe of Calder, and contiguous to their parifh of St. Bridget, fhall, after the death or ceffion of William the then rector, be converted and perpetually remain to their own ufe, for the increafe of their alms,

and

and better fuſtentation of the convent : And that the archdeacon of Richmond may not be prejudiced thereby in his right to ſequeſtrations, inſtitutions,
and collations, he grants in recompence thereof, that the church of Arlekden,
after the death or ceſſion of Alan the then incumbent, ſhall be perpetually
annexed to the archdeaconry; and converted to the uſe of the archdeacon, ſo
that he may have a houſe in Coupland unto which he may reſort, when he or
his officials go into thoſe parts, through bogs, and floods, and various tem-
peſts, to diſcharge their eccleſiaſtical function.—And the monks in this and
other like caſes; having obtained the whole poſſeſſions, ſent out ſome of their
own body occaſionally to officiate in thoſe neighbouring churches ; and upon
the diſſolution of the religious houſes, thoſe revenues being not reſtored, the
churches were thereby left totally deſtitute, and to this day are not ſupplied
by rectors or vicars, but only by perpetual curates. And by this means,
this ſame church of St. John's, as well as that of St. Bride's, were ſo impo-
veriſhed, that they have ever ſince been ſupplied by one and the ſame curate,
nominated to both by the ſame impropriator and patron, and are looked upon
in fact as two pariſhes united. In biſhop Bridgman's time, they paid ſynodals
and procurations jointly ; but ſince that time (by reaſon of their poverty, no
doubt) they have paid nothing. In 1702, a curate was nominated by Richard
Patrickſon eſquire to the churches of St. Bridget's and St. John's. In 1690,
a curate was licenſed to the cure of the churches or chapels of Beckermond.

The church of St. John's ſtands not far from the mouth of End river. It
was certified to the governors of queen Anne's bounty at 7 l. Mr. Henry
Todd is the preſent impropriator and patron.

PARISH OF HALE.

Hale was firſt granted to the Multons of Gilſland, with Gosford ; by the
firſt lords of the barony of Egremont : And in the reign of Henry the third
was the property of *Alexander de Hale. Agnes* and *Conſtance* his daughters
held it in the 23 Ed. 1. of Thomas de Multon. But in Edward the ſecond's
time the proprietor is named *Chriſtian* in the inquiſition *poſt mortem* of John de
Multon.

The *Ponſonbys* got Agnes's part, and afterwards the whole. This family
derive their original from Picardy ; and their prime anceſtor in this county,
accompanying William duke of Normandy in his expedition into this kingdom, eſtabliſhed his reſidence here, and took their name *de Hale*. *John
Ponſonby* of Hale eſquire, was father of *Simon*, father of *Henry* ; which Henry,
by Dorothy his wife daughter of Mr. Sands of Rottenden, had two ſons
John and *Henry*, both of whom ſettled in Ireland. For in the year 1649,
when Oliver Cromwell was appointed to reduce Ireland, theſe two gentlemen
attended him, with other officers. Sir John Ponſonby, the elder brother, was
anceſtor to the earl of Beſborough ; and Henry, the younger, having lands
aſſigned him in the county of Kerry, had the ſame confirmed by patent under
the

the act of settlement June the 16th, 1666; and became seated at Stacks town and Crotto in Kerry, where his posterity still remain and flourish †.

The *church* of Hale was appropriated to the priory of Conishead in the year 1345, by the archdeacon of Richmond, reserving to himself a pension of 6 *l* 8 *s* a year. It was certified by the lord viscount Lonsdale the impropriator, who was also patron, at 7 *d* a year. It is charged 3 *s* 4 *d* synodals, and 6 *s* 8 *d* procurations, to be paid by the impropriator. The parish contains about 25 families ‡.

PARISH OF EGREMONT.

A mile north-west from Hale, stands EGREMONT town, upon the north side of the river End. It was first the seat of William de Meschines, as is before related; by whose daughter Alice the inheritance came after two descents to the family of the Lucys; the last of which family Maud or Matilda Lucy, only sister and heir of Anthony lord Lucy, was married to Henry Percy the first earl of Northumberland, in whose male line the estate continued, until the lady Elizabeth, sole daughter and heir to Jocelne the last earl of Northumberland of that line, married Charles duke of Somerset about the year 1682, and thereby transferred the same unto that family.

The Percys (who came from a place of that name in France) derive themselves in the following manner:

1. *Galfrid de Percy*, first lord of that name, was son of William de Percy, and born in Normandy.

2. *William* lord Percy, his son, born in Normandy, was for his valour created earl of Poictiers by Richard duke of Normandy in the year 956.

3. *Galfrid* lord Percy, son of William.

4. *William* lord Percy, son of Galfrid, came into England with William the conqueror. He founded the abbey of Whitby. His wife's name was Emma de Porte, by whom he had issue Alan, William, Richard, and Walter. He went with Robert duke of Normandy against the Turks, and died at the siege of Antioch; and his heart was buried in Whitby abbey.

5. *Alan* lord Percy married Emma de Gaunt, daughter of Gilfrid de Gaunt, unto whom the conqueror gave Lindsey, being the third part of Lincolnshire. This Alan had Hunmanby cum membris in frank marriage with his wife. He gave the tithes of many manors to the said abbey of Whitby; and, dying in a good old age, was buried there.

6. *William* lord Percy married Alice daughter of the lord Rosse, by whom he had issue Alan and Robert; but they both dying young, the inheritance did descend to his younger brother Richard.

7. *Richard* lord Percy, brother of William, married Jane daughter of Sir William Davise alias Bruers; and was buried at Whitby.

† Smith's History of Kerry, p. 60.   ‡ Gastrell.

7   8. *William*

8. *William* lord Percy married a daughter of Sir William Turkey, by whom he had iffue (befides feveral children who died young) William abbot of Whitby, Maud, and Agnes. He founded the monaftery of Sanly in the year 1147, and the monaftery of Hundall in 1173. He died very old, and was buried at Sanly. His fon William being profefs:d of religion, the inheritance did defcend to his daughters Maud and Agnes. Of whom, Maud was married to William Beaumont earl of Warwick, and died without iffue; whereupon Agnes fucceeded to the whole.

9. *Agnes*, lady Percy, married Joceline de Lovain, on condition he fhould take the name and arms of Percy. This Joceline was brother to Idoliza queen confort to king Hen. 2. and fon to the duke of Brabant. King Hen. 3. gave to him the honour of Petworth, where he was buried; and Agnes was buried at Whitby.

10. *Henry* lord Percy, fon of Joceline and Agnes, married Ifabel daughter of Adam de Bruce of the kingdom of Scotland, and by her had iffue William and Henry. He was buried in Sanley abbey.

11. *William* lord Percy married Helen daughter of the lord Randolf, and had iffue Richard, Gilfrid, Walter, Ormefby, Ingelram, and Alan, who all died without iffue, and the lands defcended to his brother Henry.

12. *Henry* lord Percy married Eleanor daughter of earl Warren, by whom he had iffue Henry, William, and John.

13. *Henry* lord Percy, fon of Henry, married Idonea daughter of the earl of Arundel; and by her had iffue Henry and William. He died in the 54 Hen. 3.

14. *Henry*, his fon, married Idonea daughter of the lord Clifford, and had iffue Henry, William, Thomas (bifhop of Norwich), Roger, Richard, Maud, Eleanor, Ifabella, and Margaret. He died in the 25 Ed. 3.

15. *Henry* lord Percy, fon of the laft Henry, married Mary daughter of the earl of Lancafter, by whom he had iffue Henry and Thomas.

16. *Henry* his fon, firft earl of Northumberland, fo created at the coronation of king Richard the fecond. He married to his third wife Maud or Matilda aforefaid, daughter of Thomas lord Lucy, and fifter and heir of his fon Anthony lord Lucy of this barony. And though fhe had no child to him, yet fhe made him her heir, on condition that he fhould quarter the arms of Lucy, which were, Gules, three luces or fifhes Argent; together with his own, which were, Or, a lion Azure †.

17. *Henry* his fon, furnamed Hotfpur, married Eleanor daughter of the earl of Weftmorland, and had iffue Henry, Thomas created earl of Egremont by king Henry the fixth and flain at Northampton field in his quarrel, Robert prebendary of Beverley, William bifhop of Carlifle, Ralph, Richard, John, Henry, Catherine married to the earl of Kent, Anne married to the lord Hungerford, and Joan who died young. This earl was flain in the firft battle of St. Albans on the part of king Hen. 6.

† Appendix, N°. VII.

19. *Henry*,

18. *Henry*, third earl of Northumberland, married Eleanor daughter and heir of the lord Poynings, and had issue Henry, Margaret married to Sir Walter Gascoyn, Elizabeth married to the lord Ascrook, and Eleanor married to the lord Delawar.—He was slain at Towton field on behalf of the said king Hen. 6.

19. *Henry*, fourth earl of Northumberland, married Maud daughter of the lord Herbert, and had issue Henry, Joceline, Alan, William, Anne married to the earl of Arundel, Eleanor married to the duke of Buckingham, and Elizabeth —He was slain at Thrisk by the country people in levying a tax for the king's service, and was buried at Beverley.

20. *Henry*, fifth earl of Northumberland, married Catherine daughter of Sir Robert Spencer; and had issue Henry, Thomas, Ingelram, Margaret married to Henry earl of Cumberland, and Maud who died young.

21. *Henry*, sixth earl of Northumberland, married Mary daughter of the earl of Shrewsbury, and died without issue. He wasted a considerable part of his estate, and gave the rest to king Hen. 8. which gift was confirmed by act of parliament. Thomas, his brother, had two sons Thomas and Henry: which Thomas the son succeeded to the earldom.

22. *Thomas*, seventh earl of Northumberland, married Anne daughter to the earl of Worcester, and had issue Thomas who died young, Elizabeth, Lucy, Jane, and Mary. Unto this Thomas queen Mary, in the 4 and 5 Ph. and M. gave back the estate, thus described: All that the honour, park, and forest of Cockermouth; and all those demesnes, manors, lands, tenements, and townships of the five towns, Aspatric, Newlandrawe, Allerdale, Satmurtho, Lorton, Coldale, Rogersett, Mikerkyne, Brathayte, Buttermere, Darwenfell, Wigdon, Kirkland, Rossuen alias Rossington, Aykehead, Woodside alias Woodsend, Dundraw, Waverton and Westward, Egremond, Wilton, Drege, Karleton, Ashedale, Washdale, Netherwashdale, Egremont, Boundage, Ravenglass, Kenneside, Dene, Whinfield, Byrkley, Broughton parva, Broughton magna, and Caldbeck Underfield; and the forest of Derwent fells, Westward, Ashdale, and Wasdale; and the office of bailiff and bailiwick between Eyne and Derwent, and between Eyne and Dodyne; and all messuages and tenements and other hereditaments between the said rivers, and in Carlisle and Egremont; and the fishery of salmon in the river Derwent; and the advowson of the rectories of Egremont, Deane, and Uldale, and of the vicarages of Caldebeck-Upperton, Aspatrick, Kirkbride, and Wiktoh alias Wickedon: To hold to the said Thomas earl of Northumberland and the heirs male of his body, and for default of such issue to Henry Percy esquire his brother and to the heirs male of his body, of the king and queen *in capite* by the 40th part of one knight's fee †.

23. *Henry*, brother of Thomas, succeeded; who married Catherine one of the daughters and coheirs of John Nevil lord Latimer, by which marriage

—————————

†! Other parts of the estate had been granted away by king Henry the eighth and by this queen before, and some also of the estates in this grant mentioned; as to which, this posterior grant would of course be void.

the manor of, Bolton in this county came to the Percys. He had iffue Henry,
Thomas, William, Charles, Richard, Alan, Joceline, Lucy, and Anne.

24. *Henry*, the ninth earl, married Dorothy daughter of Walter earl of
Effex; and had iffue Algernon, Henry, Catharine, and another daughter
married to Henry Sidney earl of Leicefter. He lay long in the tower in queen
Elizabeth's time for treafon; and to prevent the forfeiture of his eftate, he
killed himfelf with a dagger before he was attainted.

25. *Algernon*, the tenth earl, married a daughter of Henry Sidney earl of
Leicefter, by whom he had iffue Dorothy married to Sidney lord Lifle, afterwards earl of Leicefter; and Jane married to Arthur earl of Effex. His
fecond wife was Elizabeth daughter of James earl of Suffolk, by whom he
had iffue Joceline and Elizabeth. This Algernon in his life-time by fine and
recoveries docked, all the old intails, and made a new fettlement of his
eftate.

26. *Joceline*, the eleventh earl of Northumberland, married Jane one of
the daughters and coheirs of Thomas earl of Southampton, by whom he had
iffue a daughter Elizabeth. He died at Tholoufe in France in his return from
Rome, having in that progrefs expended at leaft 100000*l*. Of which fum he
borrowed 60000*l*, and unhinged his father's fettlement to enable him to
fecure that fum by mortgaging his lands in Yorkfhire and Northumberland.

27. *Elizabeth* lady Percy, fole daughter and heir of the laft earl Joceline,
was firft married to Thomas Thinne of Longleet in the county of Somerfet
efquire, to whom fhe had no iffue. Afterwards fhe was married to Charles
Seymour duke of Somerfet in 1682, and had iffue Algernon, and a daughter
Catharine married to Sir William Wyndham baronet.

28. *Algernon* duke of Somerfet married Frances daughter of Henry Thynne
only fon of Thomas vifcount Weymouth, and by her had iffue George who
died unmarried, and Elizabeth married to Sir Hugh Smithfon baronet. The
faid Algernon, Oct. 2. 1749, was created baron of Warkworth and earl of
Northumberland, with remainder to the faid Sir Hugh Smithfon his fon in law,
now duke of Northumberland. He was alfo on the day following created
baron of Cockermouth,and earl of Egremont, with remainder to Sir Charles
Wyndham his nephew, fon of Sir William Wyndham aforefaid by his wife
the lady Catharine Seymour, unto whom the Cumberland eftate came by
intail.

29. On the death of the faid Algernon duke of Somerfet in 1750, the faid
Sir *Charles Wyndham* fucceeded as earl of Egremont and baron of Cockermouth. He married Alicia-Maria daughter of George lord Carpenter, and
by her had iffue George, Percy-Charles, Charles-William, William-Frederic,
Elizabeth-Alicia-Maria, Frances, and Charlotte.

30. *George Wyndham*, the prefent earl of Egremont and baron of Cockermouth, born Dec. 7, 1751.

The town of Egremont was an ancient burgh and fent burgeffes to parliament; until the burghers becoming poor and unable (at leaft unwilling) to
pay their burgeffes their wages, they to free themfelves from that future burden

did petition the king and parliament that they might be exempted from that charge.

They have many privileges by ancient charters. Particularly, Richard Lucy, about the time of king John, by his charter granted to them divers privileges, and at the same time enjoined them certain duties and fervices: for inftance,—that in time of war the burghers, fhall find him and his heirs twelve men with their arms in his caftle of Egremont for the defence of the fame for 40 days at their own charges; that they fhall grant him aid to make one of his fons a knight, and to marry one of his daughters, and to ranfom his perfon if it fhall fortune that he be taken prifoner; that if any burgher fhall openly revile his neighbour, and be convicted thereof, he fhall forfeit to the lord 3 s; if he ftrike his neighbour without drawing blood 3 s, if blood be drawn with any weapon 18 s; if a burgher's wife fhall utter any contumelious language to her neighbour, fhe fhall forfeit to the lord 4 d; that every burgher who keeps a plough, fhall plough for the lord one day in the year at the fummons of the bailiff, and every burgage fhall find one man in autumn to mow and reap, who fhall have their dinner when they fo do, and for the faid fervice they fhall have common of pafture of Corkeby unto the river of Calder when the lord's corn and hay fhall be cleared away from the fame; but if their cattle fhall pafs the river Calder, they fhall pay in fummer for every ten of them one penny, in winter for every twenty of them one penny, and for fivefcore fheep one penny; that they fhall grind their corn at the lord's mill, paying a thirteenth multure of their own corn, and of corn bought by them a fixteenth; that they fhall have neceffary eftovers for their buildings without view of the forefters, faving fufficient timber for the lord; that they fhall not be obliged to expeditate their dogs within their own limits, and if any of their dogs fhall follow them out of their limits they fhall not be troubled therefore, unlefs it be within the foreft of Ennerdale *.

The *church* of Egremont was given by William Mefchiens to the cell of St. Bees belonging to the abbey of St. Mary's York. It pays ftill a penfion of 1 l 2 s 0 d to St. Bees. In 1426, the abbot of St. Mary's York prefented to it.

In 1569, queen Elizabeth prefented to it. The earl of Egremont is the prefent patron. It is valued in the king's books at 9 l 11 s 0 d. And was certified to the governors of queen Anne's bounty at 45 l 15 s 10 d.

King Ed. 6. in the fecond year of his reign granted to William Ward and Richard Venables one meffuage, one garden, and two acres of land in Brifco in the county of Cumberland, which formerly had been affigned towards the fupport of a chantry prieft in the church of Egremont.

And the fame king, in the third year of his reign, granted to Henry Tanner and Thomas Bocker meffuages and tenements in the parifh of Egremont, in the poffeffion of 18 different perfons, late belonging to a ftipendiary in St. Mary's church of Egremont.

* Appendix, N° VIII.

F 2   PARISH

PARISH OF CLEATOR.

About a mile above, north from Egremont, lies CLEATOR, being the next parish and town; severed from Egremont by a little rill or beck called *Kekell,* and so the parish was called *Kekell-terr,* and by contraction *Cleater.*

So early as the 35 Hen. 8. we find this manor in the hands of the tenants; for on an inquisition of knights fees in Cumberland in that year, it is found; that the free tenants of Cleator held jointly the manor of Cleator of the king *in capite* as of his castle of Egremont, by the ninth part of one knight's fee; rendring homage and suit of court and 12*d* seawake.

The *church* was so totally appropriated to the abbey of Calder, that it is now only a perpetual curacy. It was dedicated to St. Leonard; for the licences to the curates did anciently run in this form—to serve the cure of souls in the chapel of St. Leonard de Cleator. It was certified to the governors of queen Anne's bounty at the clear yearly value of 6*l* 13*s* 4*d, viz.* 4*l* 13*s* 4*d* from the impropriator, and 2*l* pension from the crown. In 1702, Mr. John Robertson the impropriator nominated the curate. The present impropriator and patron is John Gale esquire.

ENNERDALE.

ENNERDALE or *Enderdale* is commonly reputed a parish, although it is only a chapel under the mother church of St. Bees, as was found by verdict holden at Carlisle in the year 1690. The Irish named it *Lough Eanbeth* (lacus volucrum), from the fowls that bred there in the islands; and the river, *Eanbeth;* and the dale, *Eaner* or *Ar-ean;* and the Saxons retaining still the Irish name called the bottom and valley *Enerdale.*

In one of the charters of the priory of St. Bees (which was a cell of the great abbey of St. Mary's York) Ranulph son of William de Meschiens grants to the said abbey the lordship or manor of Enerdale, yet it was only some particular part thereof, for the manor at large continued in the Multon family, and was in the Harrington's part of the division of Egremont in the partition amongst John de Multon's coheirs, and descended to the Bonvils and Greys, and by forfeiture of Henry father of the lady Jane Grey escheated to the crown, wherein it still continues.—It is a forest, and was anciently stocked with red deer.

The *church* or *chapel* was certified to the governors of queen Anne's bounty at 4*l* 13*s* 4*d,* paid by the impropriator. It is distant about six miles from the parish church of St. Bees.

How or *Castlebow* is an ancient seat of the Patricksons, standing upon an ascent on the east side of the lough at Ennerdale aforesaid which is now the possession of John Senhouse of Caldre abbey esquire.

PARISH

PARISH OF LAMPLUGH.

THIS place was named by the Irish inhabitants *Glan-flough*, or *Glanfillough*; whereof is formed this present name LAMPLUGH: which Irish word signifies the *dale-wet* (vallis humida).

It gave name to the ancient family of the Lamplughs, a race of valorous gentlemen (saith Mr. Denton) successively for their worthiness knighted in the field, all or most part of them. The first lord of Lamplugh that we read of was *William de Lancaster* baron of Kendal, who exchanged Workington and Lamplough with *Gospatric* son of Orme lord of Seaton beneath Derwent for Middleton in Lonsdale. *Gospatric* held it all his time; but after his death, *Thomas* son of *Gospatric* gave it to *Robert de Lamplugh* and his heirs, paying yearly a pair of gilt spurs to the lords of Workington. This Robert held it in Henry the second's time; and is first in the pedigree of this family certified by John Lamplugh esquire at Dugdale's visitation in 1665; which is as follows:

· 1. Sir *Robert de Lamplugh* knight, lord of Lamplugh and of Hailkard in Lancashire.

2. Sir *Adam de Lamplugh* knight, son of Robert, lived in the time of king Richard the first and king John. To which *Adam*, Richard de Lucy lord of Egremont, as lord paramount of Lamplugh, confirmed the same and other possessions to him and his heirs, with divers privileges and immunities.

3. Sir *Robert de Lamplugh* knight, 43 Hen. 3. His wife's name was Meliora, who was an inheritrix; for on her marriage her husband paid a relief to king Henry the third.

4. *Raphe de Lamplugh*, 7 Ed. 3. Margaret his widow was impleaded by the lord of Workington for the wardship of Robert her son, whereby she lost the tuition of him.

5. Sir *Robert de Lamplugh* knight, by Constance his wife, had issue John, Raphe, William, and a daughter Christian.

6. Sir *John de Lamplugh* knight, 9 Ed. 1.

7. *Raphe de Lamplugh*, 13 Ed. 1. His wife's name was Elizabeth daughter of Preston.

8. *John de Lamplugh*.

9. Sir *Thomas de Lamplugh* knight, had issue John, Robert, Nicholas, Thomas, William, and Raphe.

10. *John de Lamplugh*, 20 Ric. 2.

11. *Hugh de Lamplugh*, 12 Hen. 4. He married Margaret daughter of Thomas Pickering.

12. Sir *John de Lamplugh* knight married Margaret daughter of John Eglesfield.

13. *Thomas de Lamplugh*, 7 Ed. 4. His wife was Eleanor daughter of Henry Fenwick.

14. *John de Lamplugh*, 19 Ed. 4.

15. *John*

15. *John de Lamplugh*, 1 Hen. 7.　He married Isabel daughter of John Pennington.

16. Sir *John Lamplugh* knight, 27 Hen. 8.　His wife was Catharine daughter and coheir of Guy Forster of Howsome in the county of York.

17. *John Lamplugh* esquire, married Isabel daughter of Stapleton.

18. *John Lamplugh* esquire, maried Isabel daughter of Sir John Pennington knight.

19. Sir *John Lamplugh* knight, married Isabel daughter of Sir Christopher Curwen knight; and by her had issue John, and two daughters Anne and Elizabeth.

20. *John Lamplugh* esquire, married to his first wife Jane daughter of Blenerhasset, and by her had issue Edward.　To his second wife he married Isabel daughter of Stapleton, and by her had issue Richard.

21. *Edward Lamplugh* esquire, died without issue.

22. *Richard Lamplugh* esquire, second son of John, married Alice daughter of Ward, and had issue John, George, Elizabeth, and Dorothy.

23. *John Lamplugh* esquire, son and heir of Richard, married Elizabeth daughter of Sir Edward Musgrave knight, and died in the 12 Cha. 1.　He had issue John, Francis, Richard, Edward, Henry, George, and a daughter Anne.

24. *John Lamplugh* of Lamplugh, esquire, was of the age of 46 at Dugdale's visitation aforesaid.　He was colonel of foot in the service of king Charles the first, and was wounded and taken prisoner in the battle of Marston Moor in 1644.　He was thrice married; first, to Jane daughter of Roger Kirkby of Kirkby in the county of Lancaster esquire, by whom he had no issue.　His second wife was Frances daughter of Christopher Lancaster of Sockbridge esquire, and widow of Sir John Lowther of Whitehaven; by whom also he had no issue.　He married to his third wife Frances daughter of Thomas Lamplugh of Ribton esquire; and by her had issue Thomas of the age of eight years at the said visitation, John, Edward, Elizabeth, and Phœbe.

The Arms of Lamplugh are; Or, a cross fleury Sable.

The demesne of Lamplugh is very large, but hilly; the soil is partly clay, and other parts are better soil, covering a limestone rock.　Here are large herdwicks and sheep heaths upon the mountains.

From hence there is a large prospect over the west part of Cumberland, the Isle of Man, a great part of the Irish sea, and of the shires of Galloway, Carrick, Clidsdale, Nithsdale, and Annandale in Scotland.

KELTON, *Ketel's town*, in this parish, was parcel of Lamplugh, and first separated from it by *Ketel* son of Eldred son of Ivo de Talebois first baron of Kendal.　Which *Ketel*, evidently, gave name to the place.　It was holden as a fee of Beckermet, as Beckermet was holden of Egremont.

Salter, the capital messuage or demesne there, was afterwards given by Gospatric son of Orme son of the said Ketel to the abbey of St. Mary's York, and the abbots made it a part of the cell of St. Bees.

But

But Kelton continued always a lay fee, and being in the Harrington division of the Multon estate, it came by an heirefs from them to the Bonvills, from them to the Greys, and by the attainder of Henry Grey marquis of Dorfet and duke of Suffolk (father of the lady Jane Grey) it was, amongst his other possessions, forfeited to the crown.

In the 3 and 4 Ph. and M. June 25, the said king and queen grant to Chriftopher Morys (called, by Mr. Denton, Moorhoufe) and Elizabeth his wife (who was laundrefs to queen Mary) and the heirs of their bodies, the manor of Kelton with the appurtenances, then efcheated to the crown by the attainder of Henry late duke of Suffolk ; together with all and fingular houfes, buildings, barns, ftables, dovecotes, gardens, orchards, lands, tenements, meadows, paftures, rents, reverfions, fervices, and hereditaments whatfoever in Kelton aforefaid, and a yearly rent of the premifes of 12 l 18 s 6 d : Excepting all bells, and all the lead of and in the premiffes (not being in the gutters and windows), and all advowfons belonging to the fame.—And the lay fee thereof was in Mr. Denton's time in the poffeffion of a grandchild of the faid Moorhoufe.

But Dr. Leigh (Mr. Denton fays) purchafed what belonged to the abbey, which was fold by Henry Leigh, fon of Thomas, fon of William, brother and heir of the faid Dr. Leigh, to Thomas Salkeld, younger fon of the Salkelds of Whitehall ; who gave the fame in marriage with Catherine his eldeft daughter and coheir to Jofeph Patrickfon of How before mentioned ; who fold the fame to Sir John Lowther baronet.

Murton, *Moor-town*, lies a mile weftward from Lamplugh, and was anciently the poffeffion of a family who received their furname from thence. Gerard, Roger, and Alan de Morton, grandfather, father, and fon, fucceffively held the fame, with ample privileges. In the reign of Ed. 2. Sir John Lamplugh held the fame, in whofe name and family it hath continued ever fince.—It is held immediately of Egremont.

The *church* of Lamplugh is rectorial. It is valued in the king's books at 10 l 4 s 7 d ; and is now worth upwards of 100 l a year. The patronage is in the Lamplugh family lords of the manor.

PARISH OF ARLECDEN.

Arlochden (*Ar-flogh-den*), in the original Erfe or Irifh, fignifies a place at the bottom of a deep valley. It is a fee of Beckermet, as Beckermet is of Egremont, and was given, together with Frifington, Rotington, Weddiker, and other places thereabouts, by William de Melchines to Michael le Fleming knight, anceftor of the prefent Sir Michael-le Fleming of Rydal baronet.

The *church* thereof was given by John le Fleming grandfon of the firft Michael to the abbey of Calder, in the 26 Hen. 3. And in the 47 Hen. 3. in confideration of the total appropriation of the church of Beckermet to the
faid

said abbey (as before is mentioned), whereby the archdeacon of Richmond would lose the benefit of inflitution thereunto, and other cafual profits, this church of Arlckden was by the archbifhop of York appropriated to the arch-deacon of Richmond; and is now only a perpetual curacy, and was certified to the governors of queen Anne's bounty at the clear yearly value of 10*l*. The bifhop of Chefter is impropriator and patron.

FRISINGTON, in this parifh, is a fee of Beckermet, holden of the Flemings as aforefaid. It lies a mile weft from Arlecden, and was anciently a gentle-man's feat of that name, whofe heir male in Henry the fourth's time left three daughters coheirs,; Johanna wife of Richard Sackfield, Agnes wife of John Lawfon, and Margaret wife of John Atkinfon: Who fold it to William Leigh, with whofe pofterity it continued, till Henry fon of Thomas fon of William fold it to Anthony Patrickfon. From the Patrickfons it paffed to a family of the name of Williamfon, who finally fold the fame to the late Sir James Low-ther of Whitehaven. The Fletchers of Hutton enjoy the parks (which are part of the demefne), by purchafe from Thomas grandfon of the aforefaid Anthony Patrickfon.

PARISH OF ST. BEES.

ST. BEES had its name from *Bega*, an holy woman from Ireland, who is faid to have founded here, about the year of our lord 650, a fmall monaftery, where afterwards a church was built in memory of her [*].
. The name *Begoth* is Britifh, derived of two words *beg og*, that is, by our Englifh interpretations *little-young*; whereupon the church was firft, and is ftill in fome ancient evidences called *Kirkby Begock*, or *Begoth*.
The aforefaid religious houfe, being deftroyed by the Danes, was reftored by William de Mefchiens fon of Ranulph and brother of Ranulph de Mefchiens firft earl of Cumberland after the conqueft; and made a cell of a prior and fix Benedictine monks to the abbey of St. Mary at York. Which William by his charter granted to God and St. Mary of York and St. Bega, and the monks ferving God there, all the woods within their boundaries, and every thing within the fame, except hart and hind, boar and hawk; and all liberties within their bounds which he himfelf had in Coupland, as well on land as on the water both falt and freth [+].
Ranulph de Mefchiens, fon of the faid William, granted and confirmed to the abbey of St Mary's York all his father's grants; and namely, the church of *St. Bee*, and feven carucates of land there; and the chapel of *Egremont*; and the tithe of his demefne in Coupland and of all his men inhabiting therein, and of all his fifheries in Coupland, and the tithe of his hogs, and of his venifon throughout his whole foreft of Coupland, and alfo of his pannage, and of his vaccaries throughout all Coupland; and alfo the manor of *Ennerdale*: And the grant which *Waltheof* made to them of the church of *Steinburn*: And *Preflun*, which they have by the gift of *Ketel*: And two bovates of land, and

[*] Tanner's Not. 73.   [+] Appendix, N° IX.

3

one

one villein, in *Rotington* ; which *Reiner* gave unto them : And the churches of *Whittington* and *Botele*, which they have by the gift of *Godard*: And *Swarthoft*, given to them by *William de Lancaſtre* ſon of *Gilbert*. And he grants to them all the woods within their boundaries, from *Cuningſhaw* to the ſike between *Preſton* and *Henſingham*, which runs down to *Whiteſhaven*, and there falls into the ſea ; and whatever they can take in thoſe woods, except hart, hind, boar, and hawk.‡.

And *William de Fortibus*, earl of Albemarle, by his charter grants and con-firms to God and the church of St. Bees in Coupland and the monks ſerving God there, all his anceſtors grants; that is to ſay, 14 ſalmons which they have by the gift of *Alan* ſon of *Waltheof*; and by the ſame gift, half a carucate of land in *Aſpatric* ; and ſix acres of land in the ſame vill, by the gift of the ſaid *Alan*: And ſix ſalmons, which they have by the gift of the lady *Alice de Rome-ley* ; and half a mark of ſilver, by the ſame donation, out of the fulling mill at Cockermouth, and one meſſuage in the ſame vill. He further grants to them one mark of ſilver out of the ſaid fulling mill yearly.*.

After the diſſolution of the monaſteries, king Edward the ſixth, in the ſe-venth year of his reign, granted to Sir Thomas Chaloner knight (amongſt other particulars) the manor, rectory, and cell of St. Bees, with all its rights, members, and appurtenances, and all the poſſeſſions belonging to the ſame in St. Bees and Enerdale and elſewhere in the county of Cumberland (not granted away by the crown before); to hold to the ſaid Thomas Chaloner, his heirs and aſſigns, in fee farm for ever, of the king, his heirs and ſucceſſors, as of his manor of ſheriff Hutton in Yorkſhire, in free and common ſocage, by fealty only, and not *in capite* ; paying to the crown yearly the fee farm rent of 143 *l* 16 *s* 2¼ *d*.

And in the 4 and 5 P. and Mar. the king and queen grant to Cuthbert bi-ſhop of Cheſter and his ſucceſſors the ſaid yearly rent, paying thereout to the crown yearly 43 *l* 8 *s* 4 *d*.

After Sir Thomas Chaloner, we find the manor and rectory in the hands of the Wyberghs, a very ancient family at St. Bees, who came to Clifton in Weſt-morland by marriage of the heireſs there. And being great ſufferers in the civil wars in the reign of king Charles the firſt, they mortgaged St. Bees to the Lowther family, and on a ſuit inſtituted by Sir John Lowther of White-haven the equity of redemption was forecloſed, and the eſtate decreed in chan-cery to him and his heirs in the year 1663, in which name and family it ſtill continues.

The *church* of St. Bees was certified by James Lowther of Whitehaven eſquire the impropriator in 1705, at 12 *l* a year.

Within the body of the church, on the ſouth ſide, is an effigy in wood of Anthony the laſt lord Lucy of Egremont; which, if a true portraiture, ſhews him to have been a large bodied man, upwards of ſix foot high, and propor-tionably corpulent.

‡ 1 Dugd. Mon. 395.   * 1 Dugd. Mon. 397.

A free *school* was founded and endowed here by archbifhop Grindall in the year 1587, for which a charter was obtained from queen Elizabeth, whereby fhe incorporates feven governors, of whom the provoft of queen's college in Oxford and the rector of Egremont for the time being are to be two. And he fettled a revenue of 50*l* a year, whereof was to be paid to the mafter of Pembroke hall in Cambridge 20*l*, to the fchoolmafter of St. Bees 20*l*, and five marks to an ufher who fhall teach the catechifm and accidence and to read and write, five marks to an exhibitioner to Pembroke hall and Queen's college alternately, and the refidue to be employed for purchafing exhibitions. The mafter to be a native of Cumberland, Weftmorland, Yorkfhire, or Lan-cafhire; and nominated by the provoft of Queen's college aforefaid: If he ne-glects for two months after notice from the governors, then the mafter of Pembroke hall to nominate. The fcholars to be taught *gratis*, paying only 4*d* entrance to the mafter, and 2*d* to the ufher, or 4*d* to the ufher if he teaches them to write. The archbifhop gave alfo 20*s* yearly to a receiver, and 13*s* for a dinner when the governors meet. He had power by the charter to make ftatutes, and afterwards the governors with confent of the bifhop of Chefter.

All which was certified by Mr. William Lickbarrow, fchoolmafter, in 1623; who alfo certified, that belonging to the fchool there were two manors, *viz.* St. Bees, the rent whereof was 18*l* 5*s*, and Sandwath, 14*l* 7*s* 3½*d* †.

Which poffeffion feem to be thofe which were granted to the fchool by king James the firft: Who by his letters patent dated June 25, in the 2d year of his reign, grants to the keepers and governors of the poffeffions and reve-nues of the free grammar fchool of Edmund Grindall late archbifhop of Can-terbury in Kirkby Begog, for the fuftentation and maintenance of the faid fchool and the fchoolmafter there, 16 meffuages or tenements in the vill of Sandwath, late parcel of the poffeffions of the cell of St. Bees, with pafture for 300 fheep in Sandwath marfh; and 48 meffuages or tenements in Kirkby Begog parcel of the manor of St. Bees, with divers quit rents, and foggage and after-paf-ture in divers fields there; and 16*s* 8*d* called walk-mill filver payable there in common amongft the tenants of the manor of St. Bees; and a rent of 24*s* iffuing out of the manor of Henfingham, and four meffuages in Henfingham and Wray: All which faid premiffes were parcel of the lands and poffeffions of Thomas Chaloner knight deceafed, of the yearly rent of 28*l* 8*s* 0¼*d*.

There is a library belonging to this fchool, moft of which was procured at the expence of Sir John Lowther of Whitehaven baronet.

ROTINGTON is the next town, north from St. Bees. It lies near the fea banks, not far from the great cliff called the Barugh, or St. Bees head; which abounds with feveral forts of fea fowl: where alfo grows moft excellent fam-phire. Bifhop Tanner fays, there was a fmall nunnery here under the cell of St. Bees *.

It belonged anciently to a family of the name *de Rotingion*; and is holden as a fee of Beckermet.

† Gaftrell.   * Tanner's Not. 72.

                                                                    It

It paſſed by an heireſs of the houſe of Rotington to the family of *Sands*, who came from Sandsfield in Burgh upon the Sands, from whence they took their ſurname. They ſold the ſame to the *Curwens* of Workington; who enjoyed the ſame until Henry Curwen eſquire, having no iſſue, deviſed his eſtate here with other lands to *Henry Belham* of Yorkſhire eſquire, who ſold the ſame in the year 1762 to Sir *James Lowther* baronet the preſent owner.

WHITEHAVEN is a creek in the ſea, at the north-eaſt end of the Bergh, or riſing hill there, about a mile north from Rotington. It is waſhed by the flood on the weſt ſide thereof; where is a great rock of hard white ſtone, which gave name to the place. It was ſo inconſiderable in Camden's time, that he doth not ſo much as mention it in his Britannia.

In the year 1566, as appears by a ſurvey of the ſhipping and trade of the county of Cumberland (taken by virtue of a commiſſion under the great ſeal) there were but ſix houſes, and no ſhipping ſave one ſmall pickard of eight or nine ton, at Whitehaven; and only one of ten ton in the whole county; no mariners, except a few fiſhermen; nothing exported, beſides a ſmall quantity of herrings and codfiſh; nor any thing imported but ſalt.

In 1582, upon a general muſter of ſhips and mariners within the county of Cumberland, taken by command of the earl of Lincoln then lord high admiral, there were only twelve ſmall ſhips under 80 tun, and mariners and fiſhermen 198, in the whole county †.

Sir Chriſtopher Lowther ſecond ſon of Sir John Lowther of Lowther purchaſed the lands here that had belonged to the priory of St. Bees, and ſettled at this place, his manſion houſe being at the weſt end of the town, at the foot of the rock. And he dying in 1644, his ſon and heir Sir John Lowther built a new houſe at the ſouth-eaſt end of the town, called the Flatt; which hath of late been greatly improved, or rather rebuilt, by the preſent owner Sir James Lowther of Lowther baronet.

About the year 1666, king Charles the ſecond granted to Sir John Lowther of Whitehaven all the derelict ground at this place; and in 1678, all the lands between the high and low water marks, for two miles northward; paying a yearly rent to the crown.

His ſon, the late Sir James Lowther baronet, by improvement of the coal works, advanced this town to ſuch a degree, that he lived to ſee about eleven thouſand inhabitants, and about two hundred and ſixty ſail of ſhips, of near thirty thouſand tun burden. About thirty of theſe ſhips are employed in foreign trade, and all the reſt in the coal trade, and export yearly above two hundred thouſand tun.

The ſaid Sir James dying in 1755, deviſed his eſtates here to Sir William Lowther of Holker baronet; who, dying in the year following, was ſucceeded in the ſaid eſtates (reckoned 14000 *l* a year) by the preſent Sir James Lowther of Lowther baronet, purſuant to the will of the ſaid Sir James Lowther deceaſed.

† Moriſon's Naval Tracts, vol. iii. p. 256.

The coal mines at this place are perhaps the moſt extraordinary of any in the known world. Sir John Lowther, father of the late Sir James, was the firſt that wrought them for foreign conſumption. It hath been computed, that the ſaid two gentlemen, in the compaſs of a century (which time they enjoyed theſe mines), expended in one of them only upwards of half a million ſterling.

The principal entrance into theſe mines for men and horſes, is by an opening at the bottom of an hill, through a long paſſage hewn in the rock; which, by a ſteep deſcent, leads down to the loweſt vein of coal. The greateſt part of this deſcent is through ſpacious galleries, which continually interſect other galleries; all the coal being cut away except large pillars, which, in deep parts of the mine, are three yards high, and about twelve yards ſquare at the baſe; ſuch great ſtrength being there required to ſupport the ponderous roof.

The mines are ſunk to the depth of one hundred and thirty fathoms, and are extended under the ſea to places where there is, above them, ſufficient depth of water for ſhips of large burden. Theſe are the deepeſt coal mines that have hitherto been wrought; and perhaps the miners have not in any other part of the globe penetrated to ſo great a depth below the ſurface of the ſea; the very deep mines in Hungary, Peru, and elſewhere, being ſituated in mountainous countries, where the ſurface of the earth is elevated to a great height above the level of the ocean.

There are here three ſtrata of coal, which lie at a conſiderable diſtance one above another, and there is a communication by pits between one of theſe parallel ſtrata and another. But the vein of coal is not always regularly continued in the ſame inclined plain, but inſtead thereof, the miners meet with hard rock, which interrupts their further progreſs. At ſuch places there ſeem to have been breaks in the earth, from the ſurface downwards; one part of the earth ſeeming to have ſunk down, while the part adjoining hath remained in its ancient ſituation. In ſome of theſe places the earth may have ſunk ten or twenty fathoms or more; in other places, leſs than one fathom. Theſe breaks, the miners call Dykes; and when they come at one of them, their firſt care is to diſcover whether the ſtrata in the part adjoining be higher or lower than in the part where they have been working; or (to uſe their own terms) whether the coal be caſt down, or caſt up. If it be caſt down, they ſink a pit to it; but if it be caſt up to any conſiderable height, they are oftentimes obliged, with great labour and expence, to carry forward a level or long gallery through the rock, until they again arrive at the ſtratum of coal.

Thoſe who have the direction of theſe deep and extenſive works, are obliged with great art and care to keep them continually ventilated with perpetual currents of freſh air; which afford the miners a conſtant ſupply of that vital fluid, and expel out of the mines damps and other noxious exhalations, together with ſuch other burnt and foul air, as is become poiſonous and unfit for reſpiration.

In the deſerted works, which are not ventilated with perpetual currents of freſh air, large quantities of theſe damps are frequently collected; and, in ſuch

works,

works, they often remain for a long time, without doing any mischief. But when, by some accident, they are set on fire, they then produce dreadful explosions, very destructive to the miners; and bursting out of the pits with great impetuosity, like the fiery eruptions from burning mountains, force along with them ponderous bodies to a great height in the air.

The coal in these mines hath several times been set on fire by the fulminating damp, and hath continued burning for many months; until large streams of water were conducted into the mines, and suffered to fill those parts where the coal was on fire. By such fires, several collieries have been entirely destroyed; of which there are instances near Newcastle, and in other parts of England, and in the shire of Fife in Scotland; in some of which places, the fire has continued burning for ages.

In order to prevent, as much as possible, the collieries from being filled with those pernicious damps, it has been found necessary carefully to search for those crevices in the coal, from whence they issue out; and at those places, to confine them within a narrow space; and from those narrow spaces in which they are confined, to conduct them through long pipes into the open air; where being set on fire, they consume in perpetual flames, as they continually arise out of the earth.

The late Mr. Spedding, who was the great engineer of these works, having observed that the fulminating damp could only be kindled by flame, and that it was not liable to be set on fire by red hot iron, nor by the sparks produced by the collision of flint and steel, invented a machine, in which while a steel wheel is turned round with a very rapid motion, and flints are applied thereto, great plenty of fiery sparks are emitted, that afford the miners such a light as enables them to carry on their work in close places, where the flame of a candle, or lamp, would occasion dreadful explosions, Without some invention of this sort, the working of these mines, so greatly annoyed with these inflammable damps, would long ago have been impracticable.

But not so many mines have been ruined by fire as by inundations. And here that noble invention the fire-engine displays its beneficial effects. It appears, from pretty exact calculations, that it would require about 550 men, or a power equal to that of 110 horses, to work the pumps of one of the largest fire-engines now in use (the diameter of whose cylinder is seventy inches), and thrice that number of men to keep an engine of this size constantly at work; And that as much water may be raised by an engine of this size kept constantly at work, as can be drawn up by 2520 men with rollers and buckets, after the manner now daily practised in many mines; or as much as can be born up on the shoulders of twice that number of men, as is said to be done in some of the mines of Peru.—So great is the power of the elastic steam of the boiling water in those engines, and of the outward atmosphere, which by their alternate actions give force and motion to the beam of this engine, and by it to the pump rods, which elevate the water through tubes, and discharge it out of the mine.

There are four fire engines belonging to this colliery; which, when all at work, discharge from it about 1228 gallons every minute, at thirteen strokes;

and

and after the same rate 1,768,320 gallons every twenty-four hours. By the four engines here employed, nearly twice the above mentioned quantity of water might be discharged from mines that are not above sixty or seventy fathoms deep, which depth is rarely exceeded in the Newcastle collieries, or in any of the English collieries, those of Whitehaven excepted*.

In 1693, there was a little old *chapel*, which was pulled down, and a large spacious chapel was erected in the place of it by Sir John Lowther and the inhabitants, which was consecrated in that year, and dedicated to St. Nicholas; and in the petition for consecration it was set forth, that formerly it had been an inconsiderable village, but by the coal trade was then become so populous, that about 268 families were to be accommodated with seats in the chapel. It was certified at about 60 *l* a year; 40 *l* of which did arise from seats by agreement with the inhabitants when the chapel was built, and the rest by contribution. When the curacy is vacant, the persons who have interest in the seats chuse two, out of whom the lord of the manor nominates one to the bishop to be licensed.

In 1715, another chapel was built by James Lowther esquire and other of the inhabitants on ground given by Mr. Lowther, and dedicated to the holy Trinity; and then it was represented that 800 families resorted to those chapels. This also was certified at about 60 *l* a year; 40 *l* whereof was to arise from the seats by agreement before the consecration, the rest by contribution. The curate is nominated alternately, by the lord of the manor one turn, and the persons interested in the seats another.

In 1753, another chapel was erected, full as large and handsome as either of the other two. It is dedicated to St. James; and has the like endowment. But the lord of the manor solely has the nomination of the curate.

At present there are in the town about 2200 families.

HENSINGHAM is the next village in this parish, lying east from Whitehaven. It is now a manor of Sir James Lowther baronet. In the 4 Ed. 1. one Robert de Branthwaite held a moiety thereof of Adam de Moresby, together with the manor of Branthwaite, by the payment of one penny yearly for all services. It descended from the Branthwaites to the lords of Little Bampton; from them to the Skeltons, who married a coheir of Thomas Whitrig lord of Little Bampton aforesaid. At the conquest one Gillesby, Gilby, or Gillsbueth, held the same; whose sons Roger and William granted to the abbot of St. Mary's York two bovates in Henfingham and the land of Snartheved. The tenants were also given to the said abbey. And Alan son of Ketel, at the instance of

---

* For these observations on the coal mines at Whitehaven, we are obliged to the very ingenious Dr. Brownrigg's Notes on a beautiful little poem of Dr. Dalton's, on the return of two young ladies from viewing those mines.

Christian

Christian his wife, gave millstones to the abbot of Holm Cultram out of his lands at Hensingham.

Besides the chapels of *Whitehaven*, there are five other chapels of ease, in distant parts of this extensive parish of St. Bees; namely, those of *Ennerdale, Eskdale, Nether Wasdale, Wasdalehead*, and *Lowswater*. The four first of which we have treated of already, together with the neighbouring places thereabouts: And *Lowswater* will fall in properly, when we come unto the parts adjoining to it. Some of these are commonly looked upon as distinct parish churches, though they are in reality no more than chapels of ease; and there is an order in bishop Bridgman's time, in the year 1622, by which the inhabitants of all these five chapelries are injoined to contribute to the repairs of the mother church of St. Bees.

PARISH OF MORESBY.

MORESBY lies about a mile north from Whitehaven, upon the coast. This, being the utmost limit of the Roman empire in this part, appears by heaps of rubbish all along to have been fortified wherever there was easy landing. For the Scots from Ireland greatly infested these parts. Mr. Camden, speaking of Moresby, says, there are many remains of antiquity about it, in the vaults and foundations of buildings; several caverns, which they call Picts holes, and several pieces of stone dug up with inscriptions. Upon one of which was LVCIVS SEVERINVS ORDINATVS; upon another COH. JVII. And in the year 1667, he saw an altar dug up there with a little horned image of Silvanus, and this inscription:

DEO SILVANO
COH. II. LINGONVM
CVI PRÆEST
G. POMPEIVS M.
SATVRNINVS.

And there was another, fragment of a Roman inscription sent to him by Mr. Fletcher then lord of the place; containing these words · · · · *ob prosperitatem culminis instituti.*

And Mr. Horseley found there two imperfect sepulchral inscriptions: And in his essay on the *Notitia*, he says; "*Arbeia* appears to me to have been the " most northerly of the stations, which were next to those *per lineam valli:* " for after mention of the stations garrisoned by horse, which were in the south-" ern part of Yorkshire, the *Notitia* sets down those which were garrisoned by " several *numeri;* and of these, *Arbeia* is the first. Camden, from affinity of " names, took this for *Ireby* in Cumberland; but as there are no remains of a " station at *Ireby*, so I could never learn upon inquiry, that there were any " other Roman antiquities ever found there; and the argument from affinity of " names is of less force, because there is another place of the same name in " Lancashire. *Harby-brow*, or *Harby-burgh*, by the name might bid as fair at
leaft,

" leaſt, as *Ireby*, from which it is diſtant about two or three miles; but I
" found the ſame objections lie againſt that. I met with the like diſappoint-
" ment at *Workington*, where ſome have ſaid, that there muſt have been a
" Roman ſtation; for I could diſcover no appearance of it, nor hear of any
" Roman coins, inſcriptions, or other antiquities found thereabout. The bo-
" rough walls, where the ſtation is ſuppoſed to have been, is about a mile
" from the town, and not much leſs from the river, but on the oppoſite ſide:
" A good part of the walls are yet ſtanding, by which it appears to have been
" only one of thoſe old towns, which we ſo frequently ſee in the north, and
" which ſometimes bear the name of *Burgh* or *Brugh*: I ſaw no appearance of
" a ditch, no remains of other buildings about it, or near it; and in ſhort, no-
" thing that looked like a Roman ſtation or town: If it has ever been a Ro-
" man fort of any kind, I think it muſt only have been one of thoſe ſmall ex-
" ploratory *caſtella*, which ſome obſerve to have been placed along the coaſt:
" It has a large proſpect into the ſea, but little towards the land. At *Moreſby*
" I met with evident proofs, though little remains, of a ſtation. In a field
" which lies between that town and *Parton*, called the Crofts, they continually
" plow up ſtones and cement, which have all the uſual appearance of being
" Roman; and, beſides the Roman inſcriptions mentioned in Camden, I ſaw
" two other monuments of that nature myſelf; yet it is not eaſy now to diſ-
" cern the limits of the ſtation. The field in which the ſtones are now plowed
" up, looked to me rather like the place of the town, than the ſtation. There
" appeared, as I thought, ſomewhat like two ſides of a fort near the church.
" Perhaps the ſtation, or part of it, has been deſtroyed, or waſhed away by
" the ſea, towards which there is a very large proſpect. The order, in which
" *Arbeia* is mentioned in the *Notitia*, ſuits very well with the ſuppoſition that
" this is the place; for *Moreſby* is nine or ten computed miles from *Elenborough*,
" which ſtation I take to be the laſt of thoſe contained under the title *per lineam*
" *valli*. The remains indeed are not ſo large and conſpicuous, as might be
" expected in a *Notitia* ſtation; but thoſe have different degrees as well as
" others. According to the *Notitia*, the *Numerus Barcariorum Tigritenſium*
" were in garriſon at *Arbeia* †."

Moreſby had its preſent name from one *Moris* a Welchman or Briton, who
was ſettled here in king William Rufus's time. For of old time men gave
names to their houſes and villages where they planted colonies; as Gumelſby
of Gamel, Ormeſby of Orme, Moriſby of Moris, and the like. So in proceſs of time this place gave name to its owners the Moreſbys; the eldeſt of
whom, called Ucknard, gave common in Moriſby to the abbot of Holm
Cultram.

This eſtate continued in the family of the Moriſbys for many generations,
till the male line ended in Sir *Chriſtopher Moriceby* knight, who had a daughter
and heir *Anne* married to Sir *James Pickering* of Killington in Weſtmorland
knight; who had a daughter *Anne*, heir both to the Moriceby and Pickering
eſtates, who was thrice married, firſt, to Sir Francis Weſtby; ſecondly, to Sir

† Horſeley, p. 483.

Henry

Henry Knevett; and thirdly, to John Vaughan esquire. Accordingly, in the 35 Hen. 8. on an inquisition of knights fees in Cumberland, it is found, that *Henry Knevett* and *Anne* his wife, in right of the said *Anne*, held the manor of Moresby with the appurtenances of the king as of his castle of Egremont, by knights service, rendring for the same yearly 52 *s* 7 *d* cornage.

In the 19 Eliz. the lady Anne being yet living, the manor of Moresby was sold by *Thomas Knevett* esquire (probably her son by the said Sir Henry Knevett) to *William Fletcher* of Cockermouth gentleman, of an elder branch of the Fletchers of Hutton. Which William had a son and heir *Henry Fletcher* of Moresby esquire; who had a son *William* who died unmarried, and was succeeded by his brother *Henry Fletcher* of Moresby esquire, who had a son *William*, who had a son *Thomas Fletcher* of Moresby esquire, who came to Hutton by the gift of Sir Henry Fletcher baronet. From him it came to the Broughams; and from the Broughams to the late Sir James Lowther of Whitehaven baronet; and from him to the present owner Sir James Lowther of Lowther baronet. The demesne is large and woody; and rich in coal mines, for the exportation of which the little harbour of Parton aforesaid is very convenient.

The *church* is rectorial, dedicated to St. Bridget. It is valued in the king's books at 6 *l* 2 *s* 3½ *d*, and was certified to the governors of queen Anne's bounty at 23 *l* clear yearly value; *viz.* tithe corn 12 *l*, glebe 2 *l*, modus for hay tithe 2 *l* 10 *s*, wool and lamb 1 *l*, prescription for the tithes of the demesne lands of Moresby hall 4 *l*, other small tithes and Easter offerings 1 *l*, surplice fees 10 *s*. The patronage is in the lord of the manor.

PARISH OF DISTINGTON.

DISTINGTON lies between Moresby and Harrington, a mile or more east from Moresby. It was the inheritance of *Gilbert* son of *Gilbert de Dundraw*, who was son of *Odard de Logis* lord of Wigton. He lived in the time of king Richard the first and king John. He was lord of Distington, Dundraw, and Crofton. He gave lands in Distington and Crofton to the abbot of Holme and priory of Carlisle.

He had issue a daughter *Isolda*, married to *Adam de Tinemouth.* They gave the fourth part of Distington, and the advowson of the rectory, to *Thomas* son of *Lambert de Multon*, in the 42 Hen. 3. He had issue also another daughter *Ada*, married to *Stephen de Crofton*; who gave their part of Distington to *Thomas de Moresby* and *Margaret* his wife in the 6 Ed. 1.

Which *Margaret* exchanged it with her brother *Thomas Lucy* for lands in Thackthwaite. And *Thomas* again exchanged Distington with the *Moresbys*, for Brackenthwait in Lowefwater. After that, we find it in the name and family of *Dykes*. In the 2 Ric. 3. 1484, *William Dykes* esquire presented a rector to be instituted to the church of Distington. In the 35 Hen. 8. *Thomas Dykes* is found by inquisition to hold then the manor of Distington of the king as of his castle of Egremont, by homage and fealty, suit of court, 10 *s* cornage, 11 *d* seawake, and puture of the serjeants. In the 4 P. and M. *Leonard Dykes* esquire presented to the vacant rectory. Finally, after several mesne conveyances, this manor was at laſt purchaſed by the late Sir James Lowther, and from him came to the preſent Sir James Lowther baronet.

Hayes caſtle is the capital meſſuage belonging to this manor, ſtanding a little below the town weſtward. It belonged to the Moreſbys, and is now the property of Mr. John Hartley, merchant in Whitehaven.

The *demeſne* is large and woody, being a fertile clay ſoil; and well ſtored with coal. And the tenants have large common right and turbary on Whilli- moor.

The church is rectorial, and valued in the king's books at 7 l 1 s 0¼ d. It was certified to the governors of queen Anne's bounty at 67 l 19 s 2 d: viz. houſe, garden, churchyard, and glebe 25 l; tithe corn of Diſtington 16 l 5 s; of Gilgarren and Stubſkills 13 l; of the outſide of Smith's gill 5 l; wool and lamb 3 l; preſcription for hay and hemp 4 l; Eaſter dues and ſurplice fees 2 l 10 s.—Deductions : tenths and acquittance 14 s 5 d; ſynodals and acquit- tance 1 s 5 d.—It is now worth upwards of 100 l a year.—The patron is the lord of the manor, Sir James Lowther baronet.

PARISH OF HARRINGTON.

HARRINGTON, Haverington, lies between Diſtington and Workington, about two miles diſtant from each of them, being north-weſt from Diſtington. It ſtands upon the river Wyre, and was at the conqueſt or ſoon after, together with Workington, granted to the Talebois family, barons of Kendal in Weſtmorland, and was holden as a fee of Workington.

This place gave name to the firſt of that ancient family of the *Harringtons*; of which houſe have ſprung divers families, as of Beaumont in this county, of Witherſlack in Weſtmorland, of Aldingham in Lancaſhire, one in Rutland- ſhire, and one in Lincolnſhire.

The firſt of this family, lords of *Harrington*, that we read of, married the heireſs of Seaton below Derwent, and therefore confirmed Flemingby to the abbey of Holm Cultram, but got not the lord of Seaton's lands, for his wife died in the life-time of her grandfather Thomas ſon of Goſpatrick, and he gave the ſaid lands to her uncle Patric de Culwen.

Afterwards, *Robert de Harrington*, in the reign of Ed. 1. married the heireſs of *Cancefield*, namely Agnes ſiſter and heir of William, ſon of Richard de Cancefield, who married Alice ſiſter and heir of Sir *Michael le Fleming*, ſon of William, ſon of the firſt Sir Michael le Fleming of Beckermet knight.

The ſaid Robert had a ſon and heir *John de Harrington* knight, who was ſummoned to parliament among the barons from the 18 Ed. 2. to the 21 Ed. 3. in which year he died.

Robert de Harrington, ſon and heir of John, married Elizabeth one of the three ſiſters and coheirs of John de Multon of Egremont, and died before his father, leaving a ſon and heir, *viz.*

John de Harrington, who died in the 37 Ed. 3. and left iſſue a ſon and heir, *viz.*

Sir

Sir *Robert de Harrington*, who received the honour of knighthood at the coronation of king Richard the fecond. He married Ifabel daughter and co-heir of Sir Nigel Loring knight of the garter; and by her had iffue,

Sir *John de Harrington* knight; who died without iffue in the 5 Hen. 4. And was fucceeded by his brother,

Sir *William Harrington* knight, who married Margaret daughter of Sir Robert Nevil of Hornby knight, and had iffue only a daughter Elizabeth married to *William* lord *Bonvil*; by which marriage fhe carried into that family the accumulated eftates of Harrington, Cancefield; Fleming, a third part of the vaft eftate of Multon, and a moiety of that of Loring.

This *William* lord *Bonvil*, who married the heirefs of *Harrington*, by her left iffue a fon and heir, *viz.*

William, commonly called from his mother's name *William lord Harrington*. He married Catherine daughter of Richard Nevil earl of Salifbury, and was flain at the battle of Wakefield in the 39 Hen. 6. fighting on the part of the houfe of York. Which party prevailing foon after, his eftate was not confifcated. He left only a daughter, *viz.*

Cecilie, married to *Thomas Grey* marquis of Dorfet, to whom fhe carried the aforefaid eftates, with the addition of that of Bonvil. To whom fhe had a fon,

Thomas Grey, marquis of Dorfet; who married Margaret daughter of Sir Robert Wotton, and died in the 22 Hen. 8. leaving iffue a fon and heir, *viz.*

Henry Grey marquis of Dorfet, who married Frances eldeft daughter of Charles Brandon duke of Suffolk by his wife Mary the French queen. And the lady Frances's two brothers dying without iffue, this Henry her hufband was created duke of Suffolk. By her he had three daughters Jane, Katherine, and Mary. The lady *Jane Grey* the eldeft was proclaimed queen after the death of king Edward the fixth, and foon after beheaded. And her father, for countenancing the faid proclamation, was alfo beheaded, in the fecond year of queen Mary; and all thefe great eftates became forfeited to the crown. And this is that Henry duke of Suffolk, on whofe attainder we find fo many grants from the crown.

Particularly, with refpect to the matter before us, king Philip and queen Mary, by letters patent bearing date the firft of July in the third and fourth years of their reign, grant to Henry Curwen efquire, all that demefne and manor of Haverington with the appurtenances in the county of Cumberland, late parcel of the poffeffions of Henry duke of Suffolk convicted and attainted of high treafon; and alfo all and every meffuages, mills, houfes, buildings, tofts, cottages, barns, ftables, dove-cotes, gardens, orchards, pools, ponds, lands, tenements, meadows, paftures, feedings, commons, ways, waftes, furze, heath, moors, moffes, rents, reverfions, and fervices referved upon any grants or leafes; and alfo fee farm rents, knights fees, wardfhips, marriage, efcheats, reliefs, heriots, fines, amerciaments courts leet, view of frankpledge, profits, waifs, eftrays, bondmen, villeins with their followers; and all rights, commodities, emoluments, and hereditaments whatfoever, with the appurtenances, fituate, lying, and being in Harrington in the faid county of Cumberland and

elfewhere

elsewhere to the said manor belonging; and all woods and underwoods of, in, and upon the premisses growing and being, and the land, ground, and soil thereof. The same being of the yearly value of 18 *l* 14 *s* 8 *d.* (Except all advowsons of livings.)—To hold to the said Henry Curwen, his heirs and assigns, of the king and queen and the heirs and successors of the queen *in capite*, by the 40th part of one knight's fee, for all rents, services, and demands.

The *demesne* is now comprehended within the wall of Workington park; and is well replenished with deer, and is a rich pasture for cattle.

Here is also a good colliery, and the present owner Henry Curwen esquire having made a new quay or wharf at the foot of the river, exports large quantities of coals to Dublin and other places.

The *church* is rectorial, and valued in the king's books at 7 *l* 7 *s* 3¼ *d.* It was certified to the governors of queen Anne's bounty at 37 *l*; viz. Glebe 8 *l*, all tithes belonging to the rectory 25 *l*; prescription for Mr. Curwen's demesne 2 *l*; Easter dues and surplice fees 2 *l*. This church, together with that of Workington, was given by Ketel son of Eldred son of Ivo de Talebois to the abbey of St. Mary's York.

After the dissolution, king Henry the eighth by letters patent bearing date Aug. 20. in the 36th year of his reign, grants to *Robert Brokelsbye* and *John Dyer* the advowson and right of patronage of both the said churches. To hold of the king in free socage by fealty only, and not *in capite*.

And on the 27 Jan. following, Robert Brokelsbye and John Dyer convey by fine the said two rectories to *Thomas Dalston* of the city of Carlisle esquire.

In the 6 Eliz. Oct. 12. there is a licence of alienation to *John Dalston* esquire, to convey the advowson and right of patronage of the churches of Haverington and Workington, parcel of the late monastery of St. Mary's York, to *Henry Curwen* esquire, in whose posterity, lords of the manor, they still continue. In 1721, the university of Cambridge presented to Harrington, the lord of the manor being then a Roman catholick.

PARISH OF WORKINGTON.

WORKINGTON, WYREKINTON, stands two miles north from Harrington, at the mouth of the river Derwent. Leland saith, that Workington had its name from the *Wyre*, a brook that runs into Derwent at Clifton. It is the seat of the ancient family of *Curwen*, who fetch their descent from Ivo de Talebois who came in with William the Conqueror; and their surname they took from Culwen a place in Galloway in Scotland; from which family Mr. Camden says he himself took his descent by the mother's side. The succession of which family is as follows:

1. *Ivo de Talebois*, brother of Fulk earl of Anjou and king of Jerusalem, married Elgiva daughter of Ethelred king of England. He was the first lord of the great barony of Kendal in Westmorland.

2. *Eldred,*

2. *Eldred*, or *Ethelred*, from the name of his grandfather by the mother's side, was the second baron of Kendal. His wife's name was Edgitha.

3. *Ketel*, son of Eldred, third baron of Kendal. His wife's name was Christiana, as appears from his grant of the church of Morland to the abbey of St. Mary's York, to which grant she was a witness. His eldest son was *Gilbert*, father of William de Lancaster the first, father of William de Lancaster the second, from whom descended in a direct line the barons of Kendal. His second son was *Orme*, from whom the Curwens are descended. He had also a third son *William*, witness to the aforesaid grant.

4. *Orme*, son of Ketel, married Gunilda sister of Waldieve first lord of Allerdale, son of Gospatric earl of Dunbar. And her brother Waldieve gave to Orme with her in frank marriage the manor of Seaton below Derwent, parcel of the barony of Allerdale, as also the towns of Camberton, Craykfothen, and Flemingby. And thereupon Orme became settled at Seaton; and the walls and ruins of this mansion house, Mr. Denton says, were to be seen there in his time.

5. The said Orme the son of Ketel had issue a son and heir by his wife Gunild (the lord Waldieve's sister) whom he named *Gospatric*, after the name of Gunild's father.

To this Gospatric son of Orme and his heirs, his cousin german by the mother's side, Alan second lord of Allerdale, son and heir of the said Waldieve, gave high Ireby, which continued the Curwens lands in a younger branch till it ended, as many of the rest have done, in daughters.

The said Gospatric son of Orme was the first of his house that was lord of Workington, by an exchange made with William de Lancaster his cousin german by the father's side; which Gospatric gave to the said William, Middleton in Westmorland, in exchange for Lamplugh and Workington in Cumberland; in which exchange, the said William reserved to himself and his heirs a yearly rent of 6*d* at Carlisle fair, or a pair of gilt spurs, and bound Gospatric and his heirs to do homage, and to discharge his foreign service for the same, to the barony or castle of Egremont.

He had issue Thomas, Gilbert, Adam, Orme, and Alexander; who took their surname (as the manor was in that age) of their father's name, and were called Thomas son of Gospatric, Gilbert son of Gospatric, Adam son of Gospatric, and so of the rest.

Gospatric their father gave two parts of the fishing in Derwent to the abbey of Holme Cultram, with the appendices; except Waytcroft, which he gave to the priory of Carlisle. Which Waytcroft John then prior of Carlisle regranted to Thomas son of Gospatric and his heirs, to be holden of the priory freely, paying yearly 7*s* rent at Pentecost and Martinmass.

6. *Thomas son of Gospatric*, succeeded his father in the inheritance, and had issue Thomas, Patric, and Alan.

To this Thomas son of Gospatric, one Roland son of Ughtred son of Fergus gave the great lordship of *Culwen* in Galloway; to which grant the brethren of the said Thomas, Alexander and Gilbert, and Thomas and William sons of the said Gilbert, are mentioned as witnesses.

The

The said Thomas confirmed his father Gospatric's grant of Flemingby to the abbot and convent of Holme Cultram, and gave them the whole fishings of Derwent; which fishings Thomas son of Thomas his eldest son confirmed unto them.

And the said Thomas son of Gospatric gave Lamplugh to Robert de Lamplugh and his heirs, to be holden of him by paying yearly a pair of gilt spurs.

And he gave to Patric his second son Culwen in Galloway.

This Thomas son of Gospatric died Dec. 7, 1152; and was buried in Shap abbey in Westmorland, to which he was a great benefactor.

7. *Thomas*, eldest son of Thomas son of Gospatric, married Joan daughter (as it seemeth) of Robert de Veteripont, by whom he had a daughter married to Harrington of Harrington. But both her father and she dying before her grandfather Thomas son of Gospatric, he gave the estate to Patric his second son, to whom he had before given Culwen in Galloway.

8. *Patric de Culwen*, second son of Thomas son of Gospatric, after the death of his elder brother, left Seaton, and came to live at Workington, and from henceforth was called Patric de Culwen of Workington, and from him all his posterity have been called *Culwens*, now corruptly *Curwens*.

He gave Camerton to his brother Alan, which before was parcel of Seaton, and bounded it out from the rest; and from that Alan the Camertons took their name.

9. *Thomas*, son and heir of Patric, died without issue; and was succeeded by

10. *Gilbert* his brother, who married Eda or Editha.

11. *Gilbert* his son, died in the 3 Ed 3.

12. Sir *Gilbert de Culwen* knight, his son, was member of parliament for the county in the 47, 48, and 50 Ed. 3.

13. Sir *Gilbert de Culwen*, his son, was knight of the shire in the 5 Ric. 2. and died about two years after.

14. Sir *Christopher de Culwen*, his son, represented the county in the 2 Hen. 5. and in 2, 3, 6, and 9 Hen. 6. He was sheriff of Cumberland in the 2d, and 6th, and again in the 12 Hen. 6. by the name of *Culwen*, and in the 6th of the said king by the name of *Curwen*, to which last name the family hath ever since adhered.

15. Sir *Thomas Curwen*, his son, represented the county in the 13, 20, 27, 38 Hen. 6. and died in the 3 Ed. 4.

16. Sir *Christopher Curwen* his son died in the 7 Hen. 7.

17. Sir *Thomas Curwen*, his son, died in the 34 Hen. 8. And in that year, on an inquisition of knights fees in Cumberland, it is found, that Thomas Curwen knight held the manor of Workington of the king by knights service, as of his castle of Egremont; viz. by the service of one knight's fee, 45s 3d cornage, 4s seawake, and puture of two serjeants. He held at the same time the manor of Thornthwaite, and one third of the manor of Bothill, and the manors of Seaton and Camerton, and divers tenements in Gilcrouse, Great Broughton, and Dereham.

18. Sir

18. Sir *Henry Curwen*, his fon, f.rved in parliament for the county in the 6 Ed. 6. and 1 Eliz —He married, firft, Mary daughter of Sir Nicholas Fairfax; and to his fecond wife he married Jane Crofby.—By his firft wife he had

19. Sir *Nicholas Curwen*, who was knight of the fhire in the 35 Eliz. which was four years before his firft father's death. He married to his firft wife Anne daughter of Sir Simon Mufgrave; and to his fecond wife Elizabeth daughter of judge Carus. He died in the 2 Ja. 1.

20. Sir *Henry Curwen*, fon of Sir Nicholas, was knight of the fhire in the 18 Ja. 1. He married, firft, Catherine daughter of Sir John Dalfton: Secondly, Margaret Wharton. He died in the 21 Ja. 1. and left iffue by his firft wife Patric and Thomas, and Eldred by his fecond wife.

21. Sir *Patric Curwen* died without iffue in the 13 Cha 2. being member of parliament for Cumberland in that year; having ferved alfo for the fame in the feveral parliaments of king Cha. 1.

22. *Thomas Curwen* efquire, his brother, died without iffue in the 25 Cha. 2. On whofe death, the eftate came to

23. *Eldred Curwen* efquire, fon of Sir Henry by Margaret Wharton his fecond wife. He died in the year next after his brother Thomas.

24. *Henry Curwen* efquire, fon of Eldred, died in the 12 Geo. 1. without iffue. With whom the direct line ended. Recourfe therefore muft be had to the children of Sir Henry Curwen at N°. 18, by Jane Crofby his fecond wife: And thefe were *George* and *Thomas*. *George* died without iffue. *Thomas* died, leaving 3 fons; *Darcy*, *Thomas*, and *Patric*.

Darcy the eldeft died and had fix fons; *Wilfrid*, *Thomas*, *Henry*, *Darcy*, *Patric*, and *Eldred*. All of whom died young, except *Henry* and *Eldred*

25. HENRY CURWEN efquire, eldeft furviving fon of Darcy, fon of Thomas, fon of Sir Henry by his fecond wife Jane Crofby, fucceeded the laft Henry, commonly called by way of diftinction 'Henry the horfe courfer; and died without iffue in the 13 Geo. 1.

26. ELDRED CURWEN efquire, brother of the laft Henry, and youngeft fon of Darcy, ferved in parliament for the borough of Cockermouth in the 7 Geo. 2. and died in the 18 Geo. 2. leaving iffue a fon,

27. HENRY CURWEN efquire, the prefent owner of the family eftate, who married Ifabella daughter of Mr. William Gale merchant in Whitehaven, and hath iffue a daughter born in 1765. He was chofen to reprefent the city of Carlifle in parliament in the 2 Geo. 3. and the county of Cumberland in the 8 Geo. 3.

The arms of Curwen are; Argent, fretty of 10 Gules, a chief Azure.

Workington *hall* ftands upon an afcent, on the fouth bank of the river Derwent, being an handfome and commodious building.

The *demefne* is large, and hath been always remarkable for fine cattle of all forts. Here are falt pans, and a good colliery, coney warren, dove cote, a large falmon fifhery, and much fea fifh.

The

The *church* is rectorial, valued in the king's books at 23 *l.* 5 *s.* and is now upwards of 100 *l* a year. It was given by Ketel son of Eldred, with two carucates of land and a mill there, to the abbey of St. Mary's York. And it still pays a pension of 2 *l* 15 *s* 4 *d* to St. Bees.

Queen Elizabeth, by letters patent, in the 15th year of her reign, granted to Parcivill Gunson gentleman, divers messuages, lands, tenements, and other hereditaments in Workington, and one messuage in Clifton, late belonging to the monastery of St. Mary's York. (Which were probably those same lands which had been given to the abbey by Ketel.)

There also appears to have been a *chapel* at Workington. For the same queen, in the 17th year of her reign, granted to the said Parcivill Gunson and John Soukey, three acres of land called *Chapel Flatt* in Workington, and also one *chapel* together with one acre of land there.

In 1534, the abbot of St. Mary's York presented to the rectory. In 1544, king Henry the eighth granted the advowson, together with that of Harrington as aforesaid, to Robert Brocklesby and John Dyer; who in the same year sold the same to Thomas Dalston esquire, and in 1556 John Dalston esquire presented to the rectory. In 1563, John Dalston esquire sold the same to Henry Curwen esquire, in whose name and family it still continues.

King Henry the eighth granted this advowson to John Bird the first bishop of Chester in exchange for divers temporalties; and it was exchanged again by queen Mary for Childwall and other places. But it having been granted before to Brockelsby and Dyer, it was found that the bishop had no title.

Here is a small *school* at Workington, which was built (as is said) by Sir Patric Curwen, and endowed by his brother Thomas with a salary of about 8 *l* a year.

STAINBURN, a *stony burn* or beck, is a township within this parish, and stands a mile or more east from Workington, upon an ascent above Derwent. Waldeve, son of Gospatric earl of Dunbar, gave this whole vill, consisting of three carucates of land, to the abbey of St. Mary's York, for the proper use of the cell of St. Bees. The prior of St. Bees built here a chapel or oratory. Afterwards, king Henry the fourth presented one Robert Hunte to this as a free chapel in the gift of the crown. The abbot of St. Mary's York remonstrated, setting forth the above particulars. And the king, upon inquiry and trial, revoked this grant.

CLIFTON Magna et Parva are the next townships in Workington parish, which make a chapelry. They lie about a mile east from Stainburn, upon a descent by the mouth of Marron water, as it falls into Derwent. These villages took name from a *cliff* or steep precipice, which hangs over Derwent at the mouth of Marron.

They were given by William de Meschines to Waldieve son of Gospatric earl of Dunbar; and by the heiress of that family came to the Lucys; from them to Benedict Eglesfield, who had a son Richard Eglesfield, whose
-daughter

daughter and heir carried the same by marriage to Adam de Berdsey, who had a son Nicholas de Berdsey, who had a son William de Berdsey, which William in the 35 Hen. 8. is found by inquisition to hold his messuage and vill of Clifton on the king as of the manor of Dean, by knights service, rendring for the same 2 *s* 11 *o d* cornage, and 17 *s* 1 *d* free rent, and suit of court, homage, and witnesman in the five towns: And he held Kirk Clifton, by the service of 3 *s* 4 *d* cornage, with suit of court, witnesman as aforesaid, and puture of the serjeants.—And by a daughter and coheir of the said William these villages came to the Salkelds of Whitehall, who sold to Sir James Lowther baronet.

The *chapel* was certified to the governors of queen Anne's bounty at 3 *l* a year. But in 1717, it was certified that there was then no maintenance for a curate, or any divine service performed; that formerly every family in the two hamlets, being about 40 in number, paid 6 *d* each to one that read prayers, and taught the children to read, and the rector gave 2 *l* a year, and officiated there every sixth-Sunday; but that these payments had then ceased for above 40 years last past.

PARISH OF DEAN.

The parish of DEAN is about four miles long from north to south, and three broad from east to west. It adjoins to the parish of Brigham and to Lowswater on the north and east, to Lamplugh and Arlecden on the south, and to Distington, Workington, and the chapelry of Clifton on the west. It consists of the villages of Dean, Dean Scales, Pardsey, Ullock, and Branthwaite, with several intermediate houses; containing in all about 136 families.

There is plenty of limestone at Dean, Dean Scales and Pardsey; quarries of white freestone at Branthwaite, and of red on the common called the Edge; on which common are also some coal pits. And at Branthwaite are pits of black stone called Cat-scalps, much used in the iron furnaces at Clifton and Seaton †.

At the same time that Ranulph de Mefchines gave the barony of Coupland or Allerdale above-Derwent to his brother William de Mefchines, who fixed his feat at Egremont, he gave the barony of Allerdale below Derwent to Waldieve fon of Gofpatric earl of Dunbar, who fixed his feat at Papcaftle, and afterwards at Cockermouth. And the said William de Mefchines gave, of his barony of Copeland, to the said Waldieve, fo much as lies between the rivers of Cocker and Derwent, and the five towns of Brigham, Eglesfield, Dean (with Branthwaite), Craikfothen, and Clifton (with the hamlets thereof, Little Clifton and Srainburn). From Waldieve the same came by Octhreda the heirefs of that family to William Fitz Duncan, from him to the Lucys, and from them to the Percys earls of Northumberland. And the manor of Dean continued in this family, till Henry Percy the sixth earl of Northum-

† Philofophical Tranf. N°. 277, in Baddam's Abr. V. 4. p 108.

berland granted it to his fteward Sir Thomas Wharton knight; in whofe
family it continued for five generations, which falling in the late duke of
Wharton's time, this manor came again by purchafe into the hands of the
lord of Egremont the then duke of Somerfet, and from him to the prefent
earl of Egremont.—The cuftomary tenants of this manor pay a ten penny
fine, by virtue of a decree in chancery.

The *church* of Dean is rectorial, dedicated to St. Ofwald; valued in the
king's books at 19 l. 3 s. 1½ d.; certified at 74 l. 9 s. viz. Parfonage houfe, garden, churchyard and glebe 50 l; prefcription for tithe corn, and fmall tithes,
let for 25 l 10 s; furplice fees 1 l. Deduct tenths and acquittance 1 l 18 s 7 d.
fynodals and acquittance 2 s 5 d. It is now worth about 150 l a year.

In 1447, the church being newly built, a commiffion was iffued to the
bifhop of Dromore to confecrate it.

In 1426, Henry Percy, earl of Northumberland, and lord of the honour
of Cockermouth, prefented to it. In 1679, Philip lord Wharton prefented a
rector to the faid church. The late Philip duke of Wharton granted the
advowfon to his fteward Matthew Smales efquire; from whom, after feveral
mefne conveyances, it came to the prefent incumbent the reverend Miles
Tarn.

Here is a *fchool*, which was founded by John Fox of London goldfmith,
and endowed by him with 10 l a year (as certified in 1723) clear value of land
purchafed with money left by him to the goldfmiths company, the mafter and
wardens of which are governors, and nominate the fchoolmafter. He is commonly recommended by the minifter and fome of the principal inhabitants.
The fchoolmafter hath alfo the intereft of 61 l; which is fecured by the
churchwardens.

It was alfo certified at the fame time, that there were legacies given to the
poor, to the amount of 49 l.

BRANTHWAITE, or Brand's plain, lies half a mile fouth from Dean, upon
the Marron; and is the next townfhip in this parifh. It was granted together
with Dean by William de Mefchines aforefaid to Waldieve fon of Golpatric
earl of Dunbar; and was given by Alan fon of the faid Waldieve in marriage with
one of his kinfwomen to a perfon who took the name *de Branthwaite*; the
heirefs of which family was married to *Skelton*; which family of *Skelton* continued here for many generations. In the 35 Hen. 8. it was found by inquifition, that *John Skelton* held the manor of Branthwaite of the king by knights
fervice, as of his manor of Dean; rendring for the fame 24 s cornage, fuit
of court at Dean, homage and fealty; and witnefman within the five towns.

And at the fame time he held a moiety of the vill of *Ulaike* of the king
as of the manor of Dean, by knights fervice, 8½ d cornage, 2 s 8 d free rent,
fervice of witnefman within the five towns, with homage and fealty.—And
John Thompfon held the other moiety by the like fervices.

The late general *Skelton*, who died in 1757, devifed Branthwaite by will to
captain Jones; whofe fon *Arnoldus Jones* efquire (who hath fince taken the
                                                          name

name of *Skelton*, the prefent owner of Branthwaite hall, is now an officer in the guards.

The cuftomary tenants of this manor purchafed their eftates to freehold of Henry Skelton efquire, having paid eighty years purchafe for their infranchifement. The demefne is worth about 200*l* a year.

PARDSEY, Bard's fhaw or wood is another hamlet in this parifh. By the aforefaid inquifition of knights fees in Cumberland in the 35 Hen. 8. it is found, that Thomas Salkeld of Corkby then held *Pardifhow* of the king as of his manor of Dean, by the fervice of the moiety of one knight's fee, 2 s 8 d cornage, puture of the ferjeants, 8 d free rent, homage and fealty.

DEAN SCALES, or *fhields* for the cattle of *Dean*, is another little village in this parifh, included in the fame townfhip with Pardfey. It lies about a mile fouth eaft from Dean, on the fide of what was formerly a common, being a place for fheltering the cattle. The common hath been fince inclofed, and granted into tenancies.

PARISH OF BRIGHAM.

BRIGHAM is the next parifh, which lies eaft and by north from Dean. Brigham is another of the five towns within the honour of Cockermouth, granted to Waldieve; who gave it to *Dolphin* fon of *Aleward*, together with Little Crofby, Applethwait, and Langrigg in frank marriage with Matilda his fifter. And after fome few defcents it fell to coheirs. For in the 40 Hen. 3. *Beatrice de Lowther* and *Thomas de Huthwaite* gave their part of the rectory of Brigham to *Ifabel* countefs of *Albemarle* widow of William de Fortibus the third, then lady paramount of Allerdale; who in the 7 Ed. 1. impleaded *Robert de Yenwith* and *Alice* his wife for the rectory. But afterwards they agreed, by fine levied, that the countefs and the heirs of *Ifabel* wife of *Walter Twinham* daughter of the faid *Alice* wife of *Robert de Yenwith* fhould prefent by turns.

In the 8 Ed. 1. *Gilbert Huthwaite* held a moiety of the manor of Brigham; and after that family, the *Swinburns* enjoyed that moiety. The other moiety defcended from *Walter Twinham* to *Adam Twinham* his fon, who died feifed thereof in the 35 Ed. 1. And *Walter* fon of that *Adam Twinham* granted the rectory by fine to *John Harcla* and his heirs in the 13 Ed. 2. And by the attainder of Andrew Harcla earl of Carlifle, the rectory was feifed for the king, though Andrew ftood feifed only in truft for Henry Harcla fon of the faid John.

But Twinham's moiety of the manor was given to a chantry in the church of Brigham; which after the diffolution of chantries came to the Fletchers of Morefby, and William Fletcher efquire infranchifed the tenants for 80 years purchafe. But the Swinburn tenants are ftill cuftomary, and pay arbitrary fines.

In the 35 Hen. 8, it is found by inquisition, that John Swynburne then held a moiety of the vill of Brigham of the king, as of the honour of Cockermouth, by knights service, 2 s cornage, puture of the serjeants, and witnesman, with suit of court at Cockermouth from three weeks to three weeks. And that he held also the land of Huthwaite by homage and witnesman in Darwent fells; and two inclosures called Dunthwait and Brunthwait by the service of one pair of gilt spurs at the feast of Easter yearly, with homage.

And that the free chantry of Brigham held the other moiety of the vill of Brigham of the king by fealty only.

The *church* of Brigham is vicarial, and dedicated to St. Bridget. It is valued in the king's books at 20l 16s ½d; and was returned to the governors of queen Anne's bounty at 44l 15s 11d; viz. Glebe lands 25l; pension out of the rectory 20l; surplice fees 2l.—To be deducted, Pension to the bishop of Chester 2l; synodals 4s 1d.

This church was appropriated to the collegiate church of Staindrop in the diocese of Durham in the year 1439. In 1544, the master or warden, chaplains, and others of the said college presented to it. In 1579, the bishop of Carlisle was patron. In 1618, Sir Richard Fletcher and Mr. Hudson were patrons. The present patron and impropriator is Sir James Lowther baronet.

Mrs. Susanna Fletcher left by will 100l to the poor to be disposed of as the minister should think fit. Accordingly the vicar in 1712 distributed 50l of it; and ordered 50l to be put out upon bonds and the interest to be disposed of by the churchwardens as the vicar shall direct.

CRAKESOTHEN is the next township within this parish. It is another of the five towns which was given by William de Meschines to Waldieve son of Gospatric earl of Dunbar.

EGLESFIELD is the next township, a mile east from Crakesothen, and one of the said five towns. This place gave name to the Eglesfields an ancient family here, and lords of the manor. Of this family was Robert Eglesfield, rector of Brough in Westmorland, confessor to Philippa queen consort of king Edward the third, and founder of Queen's college in Oxford.

[LOWES-WATER, lacus in valle vel profundo, comes next in our course of investigation, although it is not in the parish of Brigham, but a chapelry (as is abovementioned) under the mother church of St. Bees. The lake which gives name to the place is three miles south from Eglesfield, in a deep vale invironed with high mountains; it is two miles broad, and abounds with divers sorts of fish, particularly pikes, perches, and (as some say) chars.

This manor was the estate of *Randolph Lindsey*, and in Richard the first's time *William Lindsey* sued out a writ of right against Henry Clarke of Appleby, the countess of Albemarle, and Nicholas Estotevil for Loweswater and other lands.

9

It

It was an ancient demefne of Egremont, and by partition between the daughters and coheirs of Richard Lucy it fell to the fhare of *Alan Multon* and *Alice* his wife, as the 20th part of the barony of Egremont: *Thomas Multon*, calling himfelf *Lucy* after his mother's name, feated himfelf there. He purchafed Brackenthwaite of the Morefbys in exchange for a moiety of Diftington, and alfo Thackthwaite of one Agnes Drumbrough wife of Roger Lindfey, which he gave to his fifter Agnes, wife of Thomas Standley, but the fame after fome time reverted to the heirs of Lucy; and the whole defcended to Maud Lucy, who gave the fame together with the reft of her patrimony to her fecond hufband Henry Percy, the firft earl of Northumberland of that name, in whofe blood and name it continued until Henry the 6th earl gave the fame to king Henry the eighth, who fold the premiffes to *Richard Robinfon* clerk, and *John Robinfon* of London goldfmith fold the fame to *Thomas Standley* efquire; and the daughter and heir of Standley, together with her hufband Sir *Edward Herbert*, fold the fame to *Anthony Patrickfon* efquire, who fold to *Gilfred Lawfon* efquire, uncle of the prefent owner Sir *Gilfred Lawfon* baronet.

Here is no demefne, and the tenants pay only a two-penny fine; for on fome difputes arifing about the uncertainty of fines in the reign of king James the firft, who fomented thofe difputes throughout both counties, but chiefly with an eye to his own particular manors, the lord and tenants agreed, by indenture bearing date Oct. 16, 1619, that in confideration of 27 years ancient rent then paid to the lord, they fhould afterwards only pay two years rent for a fine.

Lowefwater is commonly reputed a *parifh*, fometimes it is called a *chapelry* within the parifh of Brigham; but it is in reality a chapelry within the parifh of St. Bees, though diftant eleven miles from the parifh church; and pays yearly by way of aeknowledgment 3 s 8 d to St. Bees. And it appears that the priory of St. Bees had poffeffions here, and perhaps they built the chapel. After the diffolution of the monafteries, certain of thefe poffeffions were granted to William Graye lord Graye of Wilton and John Bannifter efquire; and in the 3 Ed. 6. there is a licence to them to alienate unto Richard Robinfon clerk a cottage called Kirkftall and two little clofes called Kirkcroft and Milnehow in Lowefwater, and pafture for 300 fheep on Lowefwater moor, late parcel of the poffeffions of the cell of St. Bees, belonging to the abbey of St. Mary's York. In like manner, John Robinfon in the 3 and 4 Ph. and M. conveyed the fame by fine to Thomas Stanley efquire.

This chapel was certified at 4 l 11 s; part of it being intereft of money given by will of feveral perfons, and the reft made up by the inhabitants: which ftock was lodged in the hands of twelve individual inhabitants, who paid the curate by turns. It was augmented by lot with 200 l in 1723.

There was given to the poor of Lowefwater by William Woodvill of Carlifle the fum of 50 l, the intereft to be diftributed yearly on St. Thomas's day.]

LORTON,

Lorton, or the *lower town*, lies in a valley, which though it hath the denomination and all the semblances of a parish, yet is only a parochial chapel under Brigham. The river Cocker runs through the middle of this village, which is parcel of the manor of Derwent fells, lying on the west side thereof, and holds of the honour of Cockermouth. This is the most beautiful and pleasant, as well as the most fertile vale in the whole country, confisting of fine fields laid out in regular order, variegated with quick wood hedges, wherein alfo is a confiderable quantity of timber wood. The mountains alfo fuftain large flocks of fheep, to the no fmall profit of the inhabitants.

This manor was early broken into feveralties. In the 35 Hen. 8. *Richard Winder* held one third part of the vill of Lorton of the king as of his honour of Cockermouth, by homage and fealty, 3 s 4 d free rent, witnefman in Derwent fells, and fuit of court ; *William Sandes* held another third part ; and *William Huddlefton* the other third : Probably by marriage of, or defcent from, coheireffes.

The dean and chapter of Carlifle have alfo a manor here. And in the reign of king Richard the firft, one Radulphus de Lindefay gave to the church of Carlifle lands in Lorton, with a miln there and all its rights and appendages, and namely, the milner, his wife, and children.

Here the dean and chapter fometimes hold courts, to which their tenants in other places in that neighbourhood are amenable, and do their fuit and fervice accordingly. The cuftomary tenants pay a four-penny fine upon change of tenant by death or alienation ; but the lord never dies. And the tenants are intitled to all the wood upon their refpective cuftomary eftates.

The *chapel* is dedicated to St. Cuthbert ; and was certified at 7 l a year, paid by the impropriator. There are four townfhips within the chapelry, viz. 1. Lorton. 2. Brackenthwaite, two miles from the chapel. 3. Wythop, about three miles from the chapel. And, 4. Buttermere, 5 miles from the chapel. For which there are four chapelwardens refpectively. Two of thefe divifions have chapels of their own, namely, Wythop and Buttermere ; and hence it is, that Lorton hath been efteemed a parifh, and thefe two chapels of eafe within that parifh. But that matter amounts to no more than this ; that within the chapelry at large, two other chapels have been erected for convenience, the boundary of the original chapelry continuing ftill the fame : and this appears from the chapelwardens being appointed regularly as aforefaid from every of the four quarters.—The impropriators and patrons were for a long time the Fletchers of Hutton ; who fold their right about the year 1752 to Sir James Lowther baronet.

There is a fmall fchool at Lorton, endowed with the intereft of 100 l given by feveral perfons. The mafter to be nominated by four feoffees.

Brackenthwaite is fituate on the north fide of Lorton fell, having its name from the large quantity of brackens or fern that grows there. It was part of the poffeffions of the *Morefbys* as was before mentioned, until *Thomas Multon*, who took the name *de Lucy*, purchafed the fame ; in whofe family

3

family it continued till given by the heirefs of that family to the *Percies*, who gave the fame to king *Henry* the eighth.

From the crown it came to the lord *Grey* and *John Bannifter* efquire; for in the 3 Ed. 6. there is a licence to *William Graye* knight lord *Graye* of *Wilton* and *John Bannifter* efquire to alienate to *Richard Robinfon* clerk, all the feveral poffeffions late in the tenure of *Peter Mirehoufe*, *Thomas Wilkinfon*, *Chriftopher Stanger*, *John Robinfon*, *John Newton*, and *John Stubb*, and all thofe lands called Dalehowes and Thwaite, in Brackenthwaite; late parcel of the poffeffions of Henry late earl of Northumberland: and all lands, tenements, rents, reverfions, fervices and hereditaments whatfoever in Brackenthwaite aforefaid, and in the office or collection of the fteward of Brackenthwaite aforefaid.

There is a like licence in the 4 and 5 Ph and Mary, to *John Robinfon* to alienate the fame to *Thomas Stanley* efquire. And the Stanleys conveyed to the *Fyfhers*, in whofe family it remains difperfed into feveral branches.

WYTHOP. *Wyth-thorp*, fo called from the *wyths* or willows growing there, is one of the chapelries under Lorton. It was a wafte parcel of Allerdale above Derwent, adjoining to Embleton, only at the eaft end thereof it falls down with a fteep woody bank to the lake or meer of Baffenthwaite, and ftands between Embleton and Thornthwaite.

Alice Lucy fecond daughter and coheir of *Richard Lucy* and wife to *Alan Multon* fecond fon of Thomas Multon who married the widow of *Richard Lucy*, gave Wythorp and Whinfell near Lorton, the eighth part of Lorton, and certain corn out of Afpatric miln, and 3 meffuages and 40 acres of land in Caldbeck, unto *John Lucy* her fecond fon whom fhe had to the faid *Alan Multon*; whom fhe named *Lucy*, not *Multon*, becaufe *Lucy* was the greater family; and for that her elder fifter Amabil who was married to Lambert Multon did continue the name and arms of Thomas Multon their father in the family of Egremont, fhe caufed her children to be called Lucys, and gave the Lucy's coat to her pofterity. She did referve out of Wythorp a penny rent fervice, or a pair of gloves; and after it was inhabited, it was deemed worth 10 *l* a year, and the refidue about 8 *l* 11 *s* 2 *d*, out of which fhe alfo referved a rent fervice of 4 *d* a year. This John Lucy lived in the time of Henry the third and Edward the firft, and died in the 8 Ed. 2. or before. For Hugh Lowther fon of Hugh Lowther, after the death of the faid John Lucy, enjoyed Wythorp: and in the 8 Ed. 2. Chriftian the widow of the faid John Lucy impleaded him for her dower there.

It did defcend in the Lowthers iffue male for a long time. By the inquifition of knights fees aforefaid in the 35 Hen. 8. it is found, that John Lowther knight then held the manor of Withorppe of the king by the third part of one knight's fee as of the honour of Cockermouth, by homage, fealty, and fuit of court at Cockermouth from three weeks to three weeks, and the free rent of one penny or one red rofe.

Afterwards

Afterwards it was fold by Sir Richard Lowther knight to Thomas Fletcher father of Sir Richard Fletcher baronet, in whofe pofterity it ftill continues under the fervices before mentioned.

Here is a fmall demefne and ancient houfe called Wythop hall, and divers cuftomary tenants who pay arbitrary fines and heriots.

From this place fouthwards, there is a continued tract of prodigious high mountains as far as the Black-comb fell at Millum, and which runs fouth eaft as far as the barony of Kendal and Furnes.

The *chapel* of Wythop was certified at 2*l* 7*s*; part paid by the inhabitants out of their eftates by voluntary agreement, and part of it being intereft of money given by the will of feveral perfons.

BUTTERMERE is the other chapelry under Lorton, which was certified at 1*l*, paid by the inhabitants by voluntary affeffment upon their lands. It was alfo certified that both this and Wythop were ferved by Readers, except that the curate of Lorton officiated at each of them three or four times a year.

This village lies about a mile fouth from Lowefwater, in a low crooked deep valley, incompaffed with ftupendous mountains. Here are alfo two great lakes or meers, and in them the char is found, and excellent trout little inferior to char. In the hills above thefe lakes fprings the river Cocker.

This diftrict, with the lakes, is holden of the earl of Egremont as parcel of the manor of Derwent Fells; and was granted, as feveral others abovementioned, firft to the lord *Gray* and *Banifter*, then to *Robinfon*, and then to *Stanley*. In the feveral licences of alienation, the lands are thus defcribed: All the lands called Birknesfield or Gatefcath, with the appurtenances in Gatefcath and Buttermere Dubbs, late in the tenure of Robert Hudfon, lying and being in Buttermere in the parifh of Brigham, late parcel of the poffeffions of Henry late earl of Northumberland.

WHINFELL, another diftrict in the parifh of Brigham, lies on the weft fide of Lorton fell, and is parcel of the honour of Cockermouth. In the 35 Hen. 8. it was in the hands of coparceners, namely, Chriftopher Curwen, John Eglesfield, and Ambrofe Middleton, who held the fame (together with divers tenements in Setmorthow) of the king as of the honour of Cockermouth, by knights fervice, 6*s* 8*d* cornage, homage and fealty, feawake, and puture of the ferjeants.

It appears to have been afterwards in the Wharton family; and was fold by the truftees of the late duke of Wharton to the late duke of Somerfet, and is now the inheritance of the earl of Egremont.

MOSERGH lies a little higher weft, and is another townfhip in the parifh of Brigham. In the 35 Hen. 8. Thomas Salkeld of Corkby held the manor of Mofergh of the king as of his caftle of Egremond, by homage and fealty,
fuit

fuit of court, 13s 4d cornage, and puture of the ferjeants. It was afterwards purchafed to freehold.

Many of the inhabitants here are quakers, being fo approximate neigh-bours to Pardfey Cragg, a moft famous place formerly for quakers, being far from any church.

But before the diffolution of the religious houfes, there feems to have been a chantry or chapel here, which was pretty largely endowed; for king Ed-ward the fixth, by letters patent bearing date Dec. 13. in the fecond year of his reign, granted to Thomas Brende of London, fcrivener, the chantry of Mofer otherwife Mofargh, together with divers meffuages and tenements late in the tenure of Henry Robinfon, John Mirehoufe, John Watfon, John Williamfon, and Anthony Fletcher in the parifh of Brigham in the county of Cumberland, late belonging to the faid chantry; and alfo, late belonging to the faid chantry, one water mill, with all watercourfes, pools, and mill-dams in Brigham aforefaid.

Defcending from Lorton, by Southwaite, in a fertile country, we come to COCKERMOUTH, which is another chapelry in the parifh of Brigham. It ftands on the *mouth* of the river *Cocker*, from whence it deriveth its name. The faid river divides the town equally into two parts, fave only that the church, market place, and caftle ftand all on the eaft fide thereof, more upon an afcent; where, under the weft fide of the caftle wall, the river Derwent receives Cocker, and there they make one ftream. Camden defcribes this place to be a populous, well traded, market town, neatly built, but of a low fituation, between two hills, upon one is the church or chapel, and upon the other over againft it (which is evidently artificial) a very ftrong caftle, on the gates whereof were the arms of the Multons, Umfranvills, Lucys, and Percys.

This, together with the reft of the Lucy eftate, did Maud fifter and heir to Anthony Lucy, give to her hufband Henry firft earl of Northumberland; and although fhe had no iffue by him, yet made fhe the family of the Percys her heirs, on condition they fhould quarter the arms of Lucy.

The houfes are built of ftone, and flated moftly with blue flate. They compofe two ftreets, one above the river Cocker, in which part are the moot-hall, market houfe, corn market, and fhambles. And in the other below, is the beaft market.

This borough returned two members to parliament in the 23 Ed. 1. to wit, William Bully and Peter de Hall. From which time it was difcontinued till the year 1640, when its liberties, together with thofe of Okehampton, Hony-ton, Afhburton, Malton, and Northallerton were reftored †. The bailiff is the returning officer, and the members of parliament are elected by about 300 burghers, who hold by burgage tenure ‡.

† Brown Willis's Not. Parl.   ‡ For a lift of the burgeffes returned for this borough, fee the Appendix, No. XXXVIII.

The said bailiff is the head officer in the borough, and is chosen yearly at the Michaelmass court by the leet jury for the year ensuing. He is also clerk of the market.

The estate of the earl of Egremont in this county is managed by commissioners (whereof the steward is one), before whom all the customary tenements pass by deed, surrender, and admittance, at their audit in Cockermouth castle, as well for the barony of Wigton and Egremont, as of this honour of Cockermouth, and the several manors of the five towns, Derwent fells, Brathwaite, Coldale, Westdale, Aspatric, Bolton, and Westward. And all leases are there granted of all demesne lands, mills, mines, profits of fairs and markets; and all rents, fines, and profits are duly paid in there by the bailiffs and tenants of the respective manors. There is also an old survey book kept of the bounds of all those manors; and of all lands, tenements, farms, mills, mines, quarries, rents, customs, duties and services, arising out of or any ways belonging to any of them.

The steward keeps the courts, and at the court leet holden for this honour, all the tenants within the five towns and Derwent fells answer; and there are three juries charged, one for the borough, another for the five towns, and a third for Derwent fells.

Of the *castle*, no part is habitable but the gatehouse, and two rooms on each floor, where the old stable stood adjoining thereto; and the court house at the east angle of the castle wall, where the Christmass sessions was also held, till the new hall was built.

The castle yard hath a bowling green inclosed in it, which is all the land that did belong to it.

The *park* lies on the north east side of the castle, which ariseth with a gradual ascent eastward above a mile to the top of Hay fell, and with a like descent bends northward towards Derwent river. It was long ago disparked, and the herbage thereof sold to Sir Thomas Wharton, but is now again by purchase united to the family estate.

This castle was the seat of Waldeof lord of Allerdale and his successors, after they had removed from Papcastle; and was kept in repair till it was made a garrison in the year 1648 for the king, and being besieged by the parliament forces was by them taken and burnt.

The weekly *markets* are held here on Mondays, and a fortnight *fair* holden every other Wednesday from the beginning of May to Michaelmass for the sale of cattle, in the wide street between Cocker and Derwent bridges. There are likewise two other fairs holden in the borough yearly on Whitsun Monday and Michaelmass day.

The *chapel* was dedicated to All Saints; for in the 18 Ric. 2. it appears from a record in the tower, that Henry Percy earl of Northumberland founded a chantry in the chapel of All Saints in Cockermouth. And the said chantry was endowed probably with lands in Cockermouth; for in the 20 Eliz. there is a grant from the crown to Parcivil Gunson of two acres of land in Cockermouth late in the tenure of Alan Ribton, two acres late in the
tenure

tenure of William Thompſon, and two acres late in the tenure of Michael Bouch, parcel of the poſſeſſions of the late college of Staindrop in the county of Durham (unto which college, or collegiate church, the mother church of Brigham was appropriated).

· It was returned to the governors of queen Anne's bounty at 34*l* 13*s* 4*d*; viz. 26*l* 13*s* 4*d* paid by the impropriator, ſurplice fees about 8*l*. · The impropriator (Sir James Lowther baronet) nominates the curate.

. The preſent chapel was built in 1711, towards defraying the expence whereof a charity brief was obtained. The length of it is 100 feet, and the breadth 45; and it is galleried on both ſides.

· Here is a free *ſchool*, which in 1717 was certified at 26*l* 15*s* a year; viz. 10*l* paid by Mr. Fletcher Vane then impropriator of the church, 5*l* by Mrs. Fletcher of Tallentire, 5*l* by the duke of Somerſet, 5*l* rents of houſes in the town, 35*s* intereſt of money. The ſchool was founded by Philip lord Wharton, Sir George Fletcher, Sir Richard Grahme, Dr. Smith dean (afterwards biſhop) of Carliſle, and other contributors.

. HUGHTHWAIT lies two miles north from hence, being a ſmall hamlet in this pariſh, and a little manor of Mr. John Swinburn's; whoſe great anceſtor married the daughter and heir of Hughthwaite.

SEATMOORTHOW, called in the biſhop of Cheſter's regiſters *Secmurthy*, is another village in the pariſh of Brigham, lying upon Darwent a mile further eaſt. The chapel thereof was certified to the governors of queen Anne's bounty at 40*s* a year, being the intereſt of 40*l* raiſed by the inhabitants out of their eſtates for a Reader.

EMBLETON, villa *Amabilla*, lies ſouth from Seat Muſthow above two miles, in a pleaſant fruitful valley, pointing eaſt upon the lake of Baſſenthwaite, and weſt towards Cockermouth; being well incloſed with plenty of wood, eſpecially in the hedge rows; and girded in by two green hills on the ſouth and north ſides, whence they reap much benefit in ſummer by their great flocks of ſheep.

· In the reign of king Richard the firſt, it was parcel of the demeſne of Allerdale; then Robert Courtney and dame Alice Romley his wife (one of the daughters and coheirs of William Fitz Duncan lord of Allerdale ward from Dudden to Shalk and Wampool) gave Embleton to Orme de Ireby one of the younger ſons of Goſpatric ſon of Orme, and free common of paſture in Dockera and Wythop. This Orme de Ireby was ſeated at High Ireby which Goſpatric his father gave him, of which place his iſſue and poſterity took ſurname.

· This is another chapelry in the pariſh of Brigham. The chapel is dedicated to St. Cuthbert. It was certified at 8*l* 5*s* per annum, viz. 5*l* paid by the impropriator, 2*l* 4*s* rent of land, 1*l* 1*s* from ancient ſtock in ſeveral hands.

K 2   PARISH

PARISH OF CROSTHWAITE.

Having traverfed the large and extenfive parifh of Brigham, we come to that part of Crosthwaite parifh which lies within this ward, which is fevered from the eaft part of the faid parifh, and from Allerdale ward below Derwent, by the lake and river of Derwent, and is part of the manor of Derwent Fells, within the honour of Cockermouth.

  Thornthwaite is the firft townfhip, at the head of the broad water of Baffenthwaite, and on the eaft fide of Whinlatter a great mountain which interpofeth between it and Lorton. The tenants here are moftly cuftomary under the earl of Egremont, and pay arbitrary fines and heriots.

  Here is a chapel of eafe under Crofthwaite; the whole endowment whereof, as certified to the governors of queen Anne's bounty, was 4l 16s 0d. The vicar of Croftthwaite for the time being has the nomination.

  Portenscale is the next townfhip, a mile eaft nearer Kefwick, belonging to Coldale and Brathwaite, parcel of the manor of Derwent Fells, and lies in the middle of the valley between Brathwaite and Kefwick. Here are fome very confiderable cuftomary eftates; which, as many others in this ward, pay arbitrary fines and heriots.

  Braythwaite is the next townfhip, a mile fouth-weft from the former. The tenants here are all cuftomary except one, and pay fines arbitrary.

  Stanger and Stare make the next townfhip, a mile further fouth, upon the weft fide of Derwent lake. Here the late general Stanwicks had a fmall freehold eftate, the reft are all cuftomary and pay arbitrary fines.

  Newlands lies yet two miles higher fouth, towards the head of Derwent; where or nigh unto which, were difcovered thofe rich copper mines by Thomas Thurland and Daniel Hetchletter a German of Augfburg in queen Elizabeth's time, which occafioned a fuit between the queen and Thomas then earl of Northumberland, in whofe lordfhip of Derwent Fells thefe mines were found. But in regard of the queen's prerogative, there being in thofe mines more gold and filver than copper or lead, they were judged to be due to the queen upon the defendant's demurrer in law. In which cafe it was agreed, that where the gold and filver, extracted out of the copper or lead, was of greater value in quality than the copper or lead, it was then a royal mine *. But by the act of parliament 1 W. c. 30, no mine of copper, tin, iron, or lead fhall thence after be deemed a royal mine; provided that all gold or filver that fhall be extracted be difpofed of at his majefty's mint within the tower of London. And by another act 5 W. c. 6. the owners of mines fhall enjoy them, but the king may have the ore of any mine (other than tin ore in the counties of De-

* Plowden's Com. 3 4.   2 Inft. 578.

von and Cornwall) paying to the proprietors for the fame, within thirty days after the ore fhall be raifed and before the fame be removed, the rates following, *viz.* for copper 16 *l* a tun, tin and iron. 40 *s* a tun, and lead 9 *l* a tun.— Thefe mines, it is faid, ferved not only all England, but divers places beyond fea; until the fmelting houfes and works were deftroyed, and moft of the miners flain, in the civil wars: and the works have never fince been managed to any account.

BORROWDALE is our laft townfhip in this ward. It was anciently written *Boredale*, having its name probably fiom the wild boars which ufed in former times to haunt the woody part of Weftdale foreft; the hill above it being called *Styhead*, where the fwine were wont to feed in the fummer, and fall down in autumn into this dale, where they fed upon nuts and acorns.

Here are large flocks of fheep; and anciently were mines of lead and copper. Here alfo, in a very high and perpendicular rock, called Eagle crag, is every year an airy or neft of eagles.

This is part of the ancient manor of CASTLERIGG, the inheritance heretofore of the family of Derwentwater, and afterwards of the Radcliffs.

And here we finifh the ward of Allerdale above Derwent. The reft of the parifh of Crofthwaite lies in the ward of Allerdale below Derwent; which we proceed next to treat of.

ALLERDALE BELOW DERWENT.

AT the fame time that *Ranulph de Mefchiens* gave to his brother *William de Mefchiens* the barony of Allerdale above Derwent, afterwards called the barony of Egremont; he gave to WALDIEVE fon of Gofpatric earl of Dunbar in Scotland the barony of Allerdale below Derwent, commonly diftinguifhed by the fingle name of the barony of Allerdale, which lieth between the rivers of Derwent and Wathempool on the fouth and north parts, and upon the weft fide is incompaffed by the fea, on the eaft fide by Dalfton barony and Seburgham where it is from them divided by the brook called Shawk which falls down northward into Wathempool, and on the other fide of the hill by Rowland beck which falls fouthward into Caldbeck, then by the fame rill running eaftward until it falls into Caldew.

It is called *Allerdale* from the river *Alne*, this fyllable *er* being interpofed between *Alne* and *Dale*, which fignifies at or upon; as in other names of places in this county, as Miterdale the dale upon Mite, Eynerdale the dale upon Eyne, Anerdale the dale upon Annand, Dudden-er dale (corruptly Dunderdale) the dale upon Dudden, and others.

This Waldieve had alfo, by the gift of William de Mefchiens lord of Egremont, all the lands between the rivers of Cockar and Derwent, and the

five

five towns above mentioned. His feat was firft at Papcaftle, and afterwards at Cockermouth.

He gave divers manors within this barony to his kinfmen and followers: As, to Odard de Logis, he gave Wigton, Kirkbride, Ulton, Waverton, Dundraw, and Blencogoe. To Odard fon of Lyulph he gave Tallentire and Caftlerigg, with the foreft between Gretely and Calter. To Adam fon of the faid Lyulph he gave Ulnedale and Gilcrux. To Gamel Fitzbrun he gave Bothill. To the priory of Gifburne he gave Appleton and Bridekirk, with the patronage of the church of Bridekirk. To Milbeth his phyfician he gave Bromfield, excepting the patronage of the church there. To Waldieve fon of Gilmin, with his fifter Octhreda, he gave Broughton, Ribton, Little Brough-ton, and Bewaldeth. To Orme fon of Ketel, with Gunyld his fifter he gave Seaton, Camberton, Flemingby, and Crakefothen. And to Dolphin fon of Ailward he gave Applethwaite, Little Crofby, Langrig, and Brigham, with the patronage of the church of Brigham.

ALAN, fon of Waldieve, fecond baron of Allerdale, had iffue a fon named *Waldieve*, who died in his father's life-time; and therefore he gave to the priory of Carlifle the body of his faid fon, and Crofby now called Crofs Ca-nonby with the patronage of the church there; and the fervices of Ucthred (to which Ucthred the faid Alan had given a carucate of land in Afpatric, to be fummoner in Allerdale, which is to this day called Ucthredfeat); the patron-age of the church of Afpatric, with the fervices of Alan de Brayton; the pa-tronage of the church of Ireby, with the fervices of Waldeof de Langthwaite; and the piece of the holy crofs which his father brought from Jerufalem.

To king Henry the fecond he gave the foreft ground of Allerdale called the Weft ward, and Holm Cultram. To the priory of St. Bees he gave Stain-burn. To Ranulph de Lindfey, with his fifter Octhreda, he gave Blenerhaffet and Uckmanby. To Ucthred fon of Fergus lord of Galloway, with his fifter Gunild, he gave Torpenhow and the rectory there. To his fteward Ketel he gave Threapland. To Gofpatric fon of Orme his coufin-german he gave High Ireby. To Gamel Fitzbrun he gave Ifell and Ruthwait. To Odard he gave New-ton, with the fervices of Newton. To Gofpatric his baftard brother he gave Bol-ton, Baffenthwaite, and Eaftholme. To Symon Sheftling he gave half of Deer-ham, and to Dolphin fon of Gofpatric the other half. To Waldeof fon of Dolphin he gave Brackenthwaite. To Dolphin he gave fix oxgangs of land in High Crofby, to be the king's ferjeant or bailiff in Allerdale. And to his huntf-men Seliffe and his fellows he gave Hayton.

He died without iffue male; leaving a daughter and heir,

OCTHREDA (or, *Ethred*) married to *Duncan* earl of Murray brother to David king of Scots, and thereby fhe brought the barony of Allerdale into that fa-mily. Which *Duncan* had by his faid wife *Octhreda* a fon and heir, *viz.*

WILLIAM FITZ DUNCAN, who married the grandaughter of the aforefaid William de Mefchiens, lord of Egremont, heirefs of that family; and thereby united

united the two great baronies of Egremont and Allerdale. For the said William de Mefchiens. had only one child that furvived him, namely, *Alice* married to *Robert de Romley* lord of Skipton in Craven, who had a daughter and heir *Alice* married to this fame *William Fitz Duncan* nephew to the king of Scotland ; by which marriage fhe alfo brought her paternal inheritance, the honour of Skipton, into the fame family. . : .

This *Alice* wife of William Fitz Duncan, and daughter as aforefaid of Robert de Romley lord of Skipton, in the 1 Hen. 2. transferred the canons of Emefey, which her grandmother Cecily wife of William de Mefchiens had fettled there, unto Bolton ; and confirmed to them the poffeffions which her grandmother had given them. She gave to the monks of Fountains in the county of York a moiety of her mill at Crofthwaite, and a toft in Cockermouth. Likewife fhe gave to the monks at Pontefract one carucate of land and an houfe in Broctune, for the health of the foul of William Fitz Duncan her hufband, and of the fouls of all her progenitors ; and alfo free chafe in all her lands and woods within her fee, with liberty to hunt and take all manner of wild beafts there ; fhe alfo beftowed on them the tenth of all the deer taken within her own lands and chafes in Craven ; alfo a certain piece of ground in each of her lordfhips to make granges for their tithes ; with common of pafture for their cattle together with her own, in all her woods, moors, and fields, during the whole time of autumn. And, being lady of Skipton caftle, fhe ordained, that the perpetual chaplain, celebrating divine fervice every day in the chapel there, fhould, in augmentation of his maintenance, receive every twelve weeks one quarter of wheat, and 13 s 4 d yearly upon Chriftmafs day for his robe, out of the rents of that caftle and manor †.

The faid William Fitz Duncan, by his wife Alice de Romley, had a fon *William*, who died young ; and three daughters, *viz. Cecily*, firft married to Alexander Fitz Gerald, and afterwards to *William le Groffe* earl of Albemarle, to whom fhe brought the honour of Skipton, being her purparty of the inheritance. The fecond was *Amabil*, married to Reginald de Lucy, who had the honour of Egremont as her purparty. The third was *Alice*, firft married to Gilbert Pipard, who had with her Afpatric, with the barony of Allerdale, and liberty of Cockermouth ; and afterwards married to Robert de Courtney : but fhe died without iffue. Whereby this barony of Allerdale came to her two fifters *Cicely* and *Amabil*, or their heirs.

CICELY the elder of the two fifters, having no iffue to her former hufband Alexander Fitz Gerald, was married as aforefaid to her fecond hufband *William le Groffe* earl of Albemarle, who died in the 25 Hen. 2. leaving iffue by his faid wife a daughter and heir, *viz.*

HAWISE, who was thrice married ; firft, to William de Mandeville earl of Effex, who died in Normandy in the 35 Hen. 2. leaving no iffue by her. To her fecond hufband fhe married William de Fortibus, who in her right was earl of Albemarle and lord of Holdernefs. This William de Fortibus died in

† 1 Dugd. Mon. 586.

the 6 Ric. 1. and left issue by the said Hawise William de Fortibus the second. But Hawise surviving married again to Baldwin de Betun then earl of the Isle of Wight. He also in her right enjoyed the earldom of Albemarle. He died in the 14 Joh. leaving the same Hawise surviving, who then gave no less than the sum of 5000 marks to have the possession of her inheritance and dowries. She died not long after, and was succeeded in the sixteenth year of king John by her son,

WILLIAM DE FORTIBUS the second; who married Aveline daughter and at length coheir to Richard de Munfichet a great baron in Essex. He died upon the Mediterranean sea in the 26 Hen. 3. leaving issue his son and heir,

WILLIAM DE FORTIBUS the third; who paying 100l for his relief, had livery of his lands. This William was he who made partition with Alice wife of Alan de Multon of. the forests of Allerdale, Cockermouth, and Caldbeck. In the 41, 42, 43, and part of 44 Hen. 3. he was sheriff of Cumberland. To his first wife he married Christian daughter and coheir of Alan de Galway a great man in Scotland, but had no issue by her. To his second wife he married Isabel daughter of Baldwin earl of Denby, by whom he had issue three sons, John, Thomas, and William, and two daughters Avice and Aveline, which Avice died young and was buried in the abbey of Meaux.—This earl died in the 44 Hen. 3. and his three sons not long after; and the only remaining issue was

AVELINE, who was married to Edmund second son of king Henry the third, commonly called Crouchback, and afterwards earl of Lancaster *; and died without issue: whereby Skipton, her ancestor Cicely's purparty, came to the crown, and was granted by king Ed. 2. to Robert de Clifford, from whom it hath descended to the present owner Sackville earl of Thanet. Her remaining share of the Fitz Duncan's estates in Cumberland fell to the heirs of *Amabil* second daughter and coheir of William Fitz Duncan; and thereby the two baronies became again united.

The said AMABIL, who had Egremont for her purparty, and after the death of her sister *Alice* a moiety of Allerdale, was married to *Reginald de Lucy:*

Sir William Dugdale says, that the first mention he finds of this name is, in the render made to *Richard de Lucy* by king Hen. 1. of the lordship of Disce in Norfolk; where the record expresseth, that it was not known whether it was so yielded to him as his inheritance or for his service ‡.

In the 20 Hen. 2. this *Reginald de Lucy,* who married *Amabil* second daughter of William Fitz Duncan, upon the rebellion of the earl of Leicester and others on the behalf of young Henry the king's son, was governor of Nottingham for the king. And in the 1 Ric. 1. at the coronation of that king, he gave his attendance with the rest of the barons. By his said wife he had a son and heir, viz. RICHARD DE LUCY, who in the 1 Joh. gave to the king a fine of 300 marks for livery of all his lands in Coupland and Canteberge, and to have liberty to marry whom he pleased, as also to have his purparty of those lands

* 1 Dugd. Bar. 62.   ‡ 1 Dugd. Bar. 562.

whereunto

whereunto he had claim againſt Baldwin earl of Albemarle and Robert de Courtney and Alice his wife.

In the 5 Joh. he gave five marks and one palfrey to the king, that he might have jurors to inquire what cuſtoms and ſervices his tenants had uſed to perform and do to him and his anceſtors for their lands in Coupland; and the ſame year obtained a grant from the king to himſelf and Ada his wife daughter and coheir of Hugh de Morville of the foreſterſhip of Cumberland with its appurtenances without any partition to be made thereof with Joane her other ſiſter. And ·the king further granted to them the purparty of her the ſaid Joane in all her father's lands.—And in the 15 Joh. the ſaid *Richard de Lucy* died; leaving by his ſaid wife *Ada* two daughters coheirs, *Amabil* and *Alice*,. between whom the inheritance became again divided.

His wife *Ada* ſurvived him, and in the 15 Joh. ſhe paid a fine of 500 marks for livery of her paternal inheritance, and alſo for her dowry of her huſband's lands. After which ſhe took to huſband *Thomas de Multon*, without the king's licence; by reaſon whereof the caſtle of Egremont and other the lands whereof ſhe was poſſeſſed were ſeized into the king's hands. But afterwards, upon compoſition made, he had livery of them again. And he obtained the wardſhip of his wife's two daughters the coheirs of Lucy, and married them to his two ſons which he had by a former wife; namely, *Amabil* the elder ſiſter to *Lambert de Multon* elder of the ſaid two ſons, and *Alice* the younger ſiſter to *Alan de Multon* the younger ſon.

Ada the mother had, to this her ſecond huſband Thomas de Multon, two other children *Thomas* and *Julian*; unto which Thomas the Morvil eſtate from his mother did deſcend, and he married the heireſs of Gilſland: which two inheritances, after ſeveral deſcents from him in the male line, were carried by an heir female into the family of Dacre. The *Lucy* eſtate, by the two intermarriages aforeſaid, was transferred into the name and family of *Multon*.

The firſt of the MULTONS that Sir William Dugdale * had met with, was THOMAS DE MULTON (ſo called from his reſidence at *Multon* in Lincolnſhire); who in the reign of king Hen. 1. at the funeral of his father in the chapter-houſe at Spalding (his mother, brothers, ſiſters, and friends being preſent) gave the church of Weſton to the monks of that abbey.

After him was LAMBERT DE MULTON; who in the 11 Hen. 2. was amerced at 100 marks, reſiding then in Lincolnſhire.

After him was THOMAS DE MULTON, of whom we ſpeak; who married to his ſecond wife as aforeſaid *Ada* widow of *Richard Lucy*. In the 9 and 10 Joh. he was ſheriff of Lincolnſhire. In the 15 Joh. he attended the king in his expedition into Poictou. And having then given 1000 marks to the king for the wardſhip of Richard Lucy's two daughters, he beſtowed them as aforeſaid in marriage upon his two ſons Lambert and Alan.

In the 17 Joh. being in arms againſt the king with the rebellious barons, and taken at Rocheſter caſtle, he was committed to the cuſtody of Peter de

* 1 Dugd. Bar. 567.

Manley, to be fafely kept; who carried him prifoner to the caftle of Corff.
Whereupon he employed his fon Lambert to the king for licence of fafe conduct, on the behalf of himfelf and his friends, that he might treat of his enlargement. But at that time he did not make his peace as it feems; for it appears that the king committed his caftle of Multon in the 1 Hen. 3. together
with all his other poffeffions, to William de Albini, to hold during the king's
pleafure. However, before the end of that year, returning to obedience, he
had reftitution of them.

In the 2 Hen. 3. command was fent to the fheriff of Lincolnfhire, to feize
all his lands in that county, for the arrearages of the fine due for his own redemption then unpaid: And foon after this, Robert de Veteripont received the
like precept to take good fecurity from him, for the payment of 300*l* debt
to the king; as alfo for another fum of 164 *l* 8*s* 1*d*, due to the king by Ada
de Morvil his wife, it being a fine whereby fhe compounded with king John
for licence to marry.

In the 6 Hen. 3. he gave 100*l* fine to the king and one palfrey for the office
of forefter of Cumberland granted to him by king John, rendring 10*l* yearly
into the exchequer; it being of the inheritance of Ada his wife.

In the 17 Hen. 3. being fheriff of Cumberland, he was made governor of
the caftle of Carlifle; and was conftituted fheriff of that county for the 18th,
19th, and half of the 20th year of that king's reign. Moreover he was one of
the juftices of the king's court of common pleas, and juftice itinerant for divers
years in the reign of that king.

He gave to the monks of Calder a moiety of the town of Dereham. To
the monks of Holm Cultram, common of pafture for 500 fheep in Layfingby.
Alfo to the hofpital of St. Leonard at Skyrbec in the county of Lincoln he
gave his whole lordfhip of Skyrbec, with the chapel of Wyneftowe, and advowfon of the church of Kirketon.

In the 24 Hen. 3. he departed this life, leaving iffue as aforefaid, by his
firft wife, *Lambert* and *Alan*; and by his fecond wife, *Thomas*, and a daughter
Julian married to Robert de Vavafour.

The faid LAMBERT DE MULTON, by his wife AMABIL DE LUCY, had a fon
and heir THOMAS DE MULTON; who had another THOMAS DE MULTON; who
had a third THOMAS DE MULTON; who had a fon JOHN DE MULTON; who died
without iffue, leaving three fifters coheirs; *viz.* ELIZABETH, married to *Harrington* of Harrington; JOHAN, married to *Robert Fitzwalter*; and MARGA-
RET, married to *Thomas Lucy*, great grandfon of *Alice* fecond daughter of Richard Lucy and of *Alan de Multon* her hufband; whereby a third part of this
moiety of the Lucy inheritance remained in the Multon family. The *Harrington* fhare defcended to Thomas Grey duke of Suffolk, on whofe attainder
in the reign of queen Mary it was forfeited to the crown. What became of
the *Fitzwalter* fhare, we have not certainly found.

The Arms of Multon were; Gules, 3 bars Argent.

ALICE, the fecond daughter of *Richard de Lucy* aforefaid, had to her faid
hufband *Alan de Multon*, a fon and heir, *viz.*

THOMAS

THOMAS DE MULTON, who, by way of diftinction probably from *Thomas de Multon* his coufin-german, fon of the elder fifter Amabil, took his mother's name *de Lucy*. This Thomas married Ifabel one of the daughters and coheirs of Adam de Botteby (a great man in Northumberland), and in the 18 Ed. 1. doing his fealty, had livery of all the lands which were of the inheritance of *Alice* his mother. He died in the 33 Ed. 1. being then feifed of the manor of Langley in the county of Northumberland, which came to him by the marriage of the faid Ifabel. He died feized likewife of the manor of Afpatric and royalty of the liberty of Allerdale, as alfo of the manor of Caldbeck; leaving *Thomas* his fon and heir 24 years of age.

THOMAS DE LUCY, fon of *Thomas*, in the fame year that his father died doing his homage, had livery of his lands. In the 34 Ed. 1. he was in the wars in Scotland; and in the 2 Ed. 2. he died, without iffue.

ANTHONY DE LUCY, brother of *Thomas*, was found his next heir, being then 25 years of age; and doing his homage had livery of the lands of his inheritance. This *Anthony*, in the 34 Ed. 1. was with his brother Thomas in the Scotifh wars.

In the 4 Ed 2. he received command (with divers other noble perfons) to fit himfelf with horfe and arms, and to be at Roxborough within the month after the nativity of St. John Baptift, thence to march againft the Scots.

In the 7 Ed. 2. he was again in the wars of Scotland; and in the 10 Ed. 2. was joined in commiffion with William lord Dacre for defence of the counties of Cumberland and Weftmorland againft the incurfions of the Scots.

In the 16 Ed. 2. he was made fheriff of Cumberland; and was conftituted governor of Appleby caftle, on the attainder of Roger de Clifford for adhering to Thomas earl of Lancafter againft the king. He was likewife made governor of the caftle and barony of Egremont, and the fame year obtained from the king a grant in fee of the caftle and honour of Cockermouth, with the manor of Papcaftre pertaining thereto; to hold by the fervice of one knight's fee.

Moreover, the next enfuing year he obtained a charter for a weekly market on Tuefday at his manor of Heydon bridge in the county of Northumberland, and a fair yearly on St. Mary Magdalen's day and three days following: As alfo free warren within his liberty of Cockermouth, Papcaftre, Broughton, Bretteby, Crofby, Ulndale, Afpatric, Caldbeck, and Lowefwater.

In the fame year he received a command from the king to arreft Andrew de Harcla earl of Carlifle for high treafon, which he accomplifhed in his caftle at Carlifle; after whofe attainder, he was appointed governor of the faid caftle. He had alfo a grant of Meburn Regis in Weftmorland, which Andrew de Harcla had held after Roger de Clifford's attainder; alfo of the manor of Grendon in the county of Northumberland.

In the 1 Ed. 3. this *Anthony* was again made governor of the caftle and town of Carlifle; and there being divers hoftile invafions made by the Scots upon the marches, to retaliate thefe injuries, he entred Scotland, and by fire and plunder did much mifchief there. About this time alfo he was conftituted juftice of Ireland, and in the 8 Ed. 3. governor of the town and caftle of Berwick upon Tweed, as alfo juftice of all the king's lands in Scotland. And in the 11 and 12 Ed. 3. he was fheriff of Cumberland, and governor of the caftle of Carlifle.

He was fummoned to parliament from the 14 Ed. 2. to the 17 Ed. 3. in which laft year he died, and left iffue *Thomas* his fon and heir.

THOMAS DE LUCY, fon of *Anthony*, married *Margaret* (as aforefaid) third fifter and one of the coheirs of *John de Multon* of Egremont. In the 8 Ed. 3. he made partition with the other coheirs of the lands of their inheritance, and in the 11 Ed. 3. had livery of them accordingly.

In the 12 Ed. 3. this *Thomas*, being in the king's fervice in Flanders, had an affignation of forty facks of wool for his better fupport therein. And in the 13 Ed. 3. he had a confirmation of an annuity of 50*l*, which had been granted to his father in the 9 Ed. 3. to be received out of the exchequer, until he fhould have lands or rents of inheritance to that value.

In the 17 Ed. 3. he was one of thofe, by whofe martial conduct the fiege of Loughmaben caftle which the Scots had begun was happily raifed; being the fame year joined in commiffion with Henry lord Piercy and Maurice lord Berkeley to treat with William Douglas, and to receive him to the king's obedience. And upon the truce then made with the French, wherein the Scots were included, he was conftituted one of the commiffioners to fee the fame firmly obferved throughout all the marches of Scotland.

Thus far during his father's life. After which, in the 17 Ed. 3. having done his homage, he had livery of his lands. In the 19 Ed 3. upon the invafion of the Scots, he joined his ftrength with the bifhop of Carlifle, and fo alarmed the enemy in the night-time by frequent entering into their quarters, that at length they fled into their own country. And a truce fhortly after enfuing, he was again joined in commiffion with the fame bifhop and others to fee the fame duly obferved, and likewife conftituted fheriff of Cumberland, and governor of the caftle of Carlifle.

In the 20 Ed. 3. he went into France with the king, for raifing the fiege of Aguillon; and on his return was joined with the bifhop of Carlifle and others in the wardenfhip of the weft marches. The next year he was affociated with the lord Dacre to treat of peace with the Scots.

In the 25 Ed. 3. he was again in commiffion with the lord Piercy and others to fee the peace kept with the Scots; and the next year was conftituted one of the commiffioners for the arraying of men in the counties of Cumberland and Weftmorland for the defence of thofe parts, the French then threatning an invafion.

In the 27 Ed. 3. he was affociated with the bifhops of Durham and Carlifle and others, to treat with certain ambaffadors from Scotland, concerning the inlargement of David de Brus their king then prifoner in England: So likewife with Ralph lord Nevil and others, for guarding the marches.

In the 28 Ed. 3. he was again affociated with the fame bifhop of Durham and others to fee all things performed according to the articles concluded on for the delivery of the faid David de Brus from his imprifonment.

                                                                    In

In the 30 Ed. 3. he was again conftituted a commiffioner for the defence of the marches, and alfo governor of the caftle of Carlifle: So likewife in the 31 Ed. 3. for the cuftody of the marches, and the fame year retained to ferve the king during his life.

He was fummoned to parliament from the 15th to the 38th of Ed. 3. and died on the eve of St. Nicholas the bifhop on the 39 Ed. 3. leaving by the faid *Margaret* his wife, 1. *Anthony*, his fon and heir. 2. *Reginald*, who married Euphemia daughter of Ralph lord Nevil, and had the manors of Caldbeck, Ulnedale, and Afpatric fettled upon the iffue of that marriage, but they had no iffue. 3. *Maud*, the laft of the name of Lucy or Multon.

ANTHONY DE LUCY was 24 years of age at the death of his father, and do-ing his homage had livery of his lands. He married Joan widow of William lord Grayftoke, and died two years after his father, leaving an infant daughter and heir.

JOAN DE LUCY, daughter and heir of *Anthony*, was two years and a quarter old at her father's death, and fhe died the next year after. And her uncle *Re-ginald* being alfo dead without iffue, fhe was fucceeded by *Mavd* her aunt, fifter to Anthony de Lucy her father.

MAUD DE LUCY was firft married to Gilbert de Umfrevil earl of Angus, to whom fhe had no iffue. Afterwards fhe was married to *Henry de Percy* firft earl of Northumberland. She fettled the caftle and honour of Cockermouth, with a large portion befides of her great inheritance, upon the faid earl her hufband and herfelf and the heirs of their two bodies; and for want of fuch iffue, on the heirs of her own body; and in cafe fhe fhould die without iffue, then on Henry lord Percy fon and heir of the faid earl by his firft wife and the heirs male of his body, on condition that he the faid earl and the heirs male of his body fhould quarter the arms of Lucy. The faid Maud died without iffue; and the eftate continued in the Northumberland family, till Henry the fixth earl of Northumberland, having no iffue, gave the fame to king Henry the eighth. But the greateft part of it was reftored by queen Mary to *Thomas* earl of Northumberland, brother to the laft *Henry*; in which name and family it further continued, till in the reign of king Charles the fecond it paffed with a daughter and fole heir of Percy to *Charles Seymour* duke of Somerfet; and again by a female defcent from *Catherine* daughter of the faid Charles Seymour duke of Somerfet, to the prefent owner *George Wyndham* (grandfon of Sir William Wyndham baronet hufband of the faid Catherine) baron of Cocker-mouth and earl of Egremont.

PARISH OF CROSTHWAITE.

WE have already treated of that part of this parifh which lies within the barony of *Allerdale above Derwent*.

The greateft part of this parifh was anciently the inheritance of a family of the name *de Derwentwater*, fo called from the place; which family had alfo large poffeffions in other parts of this county and in divers other counties. In the

the 20 Ed. 1. on an inquisition concerning the furniture of a chantry in the chapel of Bolton in Westmorland, it was found (amongst other particulars) that the said chantry was founded by the ancestors of Sir *John de Derwentwater* then lord of that manor.

By several inquisitions *post mortem* it appears that the said family were owners of the said manor of Bolton for a long time. In the 20 Ed. 2. *John de Der-wentwater* held the same.

In the 48 Ed. 3. *John de Derwentwater* knight was sheriff of Cumberland: His seat at Derwentwater: And his arms, Argent, two bars Gules; on a canton of the second, a cinquefoil of the first.—He was again sheriff in the 50th of the said king; as also in the 1st and 4th of Ric 2. And likewise one of the representatives in parliament for the county in the 2d and again in the 11th Ric. 2.

This Sir *John de Derwentwater* had a daughter and heir *Margaret* married to Sir *Nicholas Radcliffe* of Dilston in the county of Northumberland knight. Accordingly in the 36 Hen. 6. we find, that *Nicholas Raacliffe* knight then held the manor of Bolton. He had issue by his said wife Margaret de Derwentwater a son and heir, *viz.*

Sir *Thomas Ratcliffe* knight, who married Margaret daughter of Sir William Parr of Kendal castle, and by her had issue; first, John who had a son also called John, who died without issue: Secondly, Sir Richard Ratcliffe knight, who had a son Richard who died without issue male: And four other sons, Edward, Nicholas, Christopher, and Rowland, the two last of whom were professed of the Romish church.

Sir *Edward Ratcliffe* knight, third son and surviving heir male of Thomas, married Anne daughter and heir of John Cartington of Cartington; and by her had issue Cuthbert and John: Which John died in the 19 Hen. 8. and was buried in Crosthwaite church, as appears from the following inscription on a brass plate in the quire:

" Of your charity pray for the soul of Sir John Radcliffe knight, and for
" the soul of dame Alice his wife; which Sir John died the 2d day of Feb.
" Ann. Dom. 1527; on whose soul Jesu have mercy."

Sir *Cuthbert Ratcliffe* knight son and heir of Edward, married Margaret daughter of Henry lord Clifford; and by her had issue George, Thomas, and Anthony.

In the 33 Hen. 8. Sir *Cuthbert Ratcliffe* knight held Bolton. And on a survey of knights fees in Cumberland in the 35 Hen. 8. it is found, that *Cuthbert Ratcliffe* knight held the manor of Talentire, and divers messuages, lands, and tenements in Castlerigg and in the island of Derwentwater, of the king as of his manor of Papcastre, by the service of two knights fees, 23 s 3 d cornage, 16 d seawake, puture of the serjeants, and suit of court at Papcastre; late in the tenure of Anne lady Ratcliffe.

Sir *George Ratcliffe* knight, son and heir of Cuthbert, married Catherine daughter of Sir John Mallory knight, and had issue only one son, *viz.*

Francis Ratcliffe of Derwentwater and Dilston esquire, who married Isabel daughter of Sir Raphe Grey of Chillingham knight; and had issue Edward,
Thomas,

Thomas, Francis, John, Cuthbert, Mary, Margaret, Catherine; Elizabeth, Dorothy, Anne, and Jane.

Edward Ratcliffe esquire son and heir of Francis, was living when this pedigree was certified at an herald's visitation of Northumberland in the 13 Cha. 1. He married Elizabeth daughter of Thomas Barton of Whenby esquire; and was afterwards advanced to the degree of baronet. He had issue a son and heir, *viz.*

Sir *Francis Ratcliffe* baronet, who married the lady Mary Tudor natural daughter of king Charles the second by Mrs. Mary Davis, and was created by king James the second baron of Dilston, viscount Langley, and earl of Derwentwater.

He was succeeded by his son *James* earl of *Derwentwater*, who married Mary-Anne daughter of Sir John Webb of Dorsetshire baronet. And being engaged in the rebellion in 1715, he was attainted and beheaded on Tower hill in 1716. His lady died in 1723, of the age of about 30 years, and was buried at Louvain in the church of the English regular canonesses of St. Austin. He had a son, who died in 1731 unmarried; and a daughter married to the lord Petre in 1732, who received with her a fortune of about 30,000 *l.*

The Arms of Radcliff are; Argent, a bend ingrailed sable.

The forfeited estates were vested in the king for the use of the public, and settled upon Greenwich hospital by act of parliament. The tenants to pay fines on the death of the king, as if he were a private person.—The estates were, the manors of Castlerigg, Derwentwater alias Kefwick, Thornthwaite, Alston moor, and Garrigill, in the county of Cumberland: And in the county of Northumberland, the barony of Langley, the manors of Whittingstall, Newlands, Dilston, Aydon, Shields, Warke, Elrington, Meldon, Spindleston, Utchester, Throckley, Coastley, Middleton hall, Thornton, Eastwestwood, and Thornborough; and other estates in about eight and thirty different places in the said county: And divers estates at Scremerston, Holy Island, Anncroft, Tweedmouth, Norham, and Lowick in the county of Durham.

Two miles east from *Borrowdale*, behind Borrowdale fells, lies WYTHBURN, being a township and chapelry within this parish. It was a manor of the Brathwaites of Warcop, until Richard Brathwaite esquire sold it to Sir George Fletcher of Hutton hall, in whose posterity it still continues.

The mountains here are very profitable to the inhabitants, for nourishing their herds of cattle and flocks of sheep, which are very numerous.

At the foot of Wythburn, there is a large and broad meer or lake called BRACKMEER, well furnished with pike, perch, and eels; being above a mile in length, and near half a mile broad: from the north end whereof issues the river Bure, which falls into Derwent below Kefwick.

A little below *Brackmeer*, at the head of Buresdale, stands an ancient seat of the Leathes's, called DALEHEAD; which gave name to a family of the *Dales*, whose daughter and heir was married to Leathes of Leathes in the parish of

Aketon.

Aketon. This townſhip bending weſtward, ſpreads itſelf wider, being leſs mountainous; hath many beautiful incloſures, rich meadows, and fertile paſture ground, till we come to Castlerigg, the ancient ſeat of the lords of the manor of Derwentwater. But after the heireſs of that family was married to the Ratcliffs, the family ſeat was removed into Northumberland, and the caſtle went to ruin; and with the ſtones thereof, the Ratcliffs built an houſe of pleaſure in one of the iſlands in Derwentwater; and the demeſne was broken into tenancies, whereof Gawen Wren's was the principal, which was alſo infranchiſed: only the ancient park, which bends towards Derwentwater ſide, continues in demeſne, and was repleniſhed with a prodigious quantity of tall ſtately large oaks; all which the truſtees of Greenwich hoſpital have cut down and ſold, but within a few years laſt paſt they have made ſome ſmall plantations.

In the neighbourhood of this place, on the right hand ſide of the road leading from Keſwick to Penrith, is a monument of great antiquity (perhaps a Britiſh place of worſhip), of about 30 yards in diameter, and conſiſting of 39 ſtones irregularly placed, and of unequal place and ſize; and on the eaſt ſide thereof, and within the circle or area, are two more rows of like ſtones, including a ſpace of about eight yards in length and four in breadth.

On the north ſide of *Caſtlerigg*, upon the river Bure, may yet be ſeen the foundations and ruins of the forges, milns, and workhouſes, made uſe of by the miners of the lead and copper mines here, which were many in number, and were kept going and in good repair till the years 1641 and 1642, when they were burned by the rebels in the civil wars.

In this pariſh in Seatallor fell is that famous mine of *black lead* or *wad*, a mineral very ſcarce elſewhere to be met with. Mr. Camden calls it that mineral earth or hard ſhining ſtone, which painters uſe in drawing their lines and ſhading their pieces in black and white; which whether it be Dioſcorides's *Pnigitis*, or *Melanteria*, or *Ochre* (a ſort of earth burnt black), he leaves to others to determine.

Mr. *Robinſon*, in his natural hiſtory of Weſtmorland and Cumberland, ſays, " Its compoſition is a black, pinguid, and ſhining earth, impregnated with lead and antimony. Its natural uſes are both medicinal and mechanical. It is a preſent remedy for the cholic; it eaſeth the pain of gravel, ſtone, and ſtrangury: and for theſe and the like uſes it is much bought up by apothecaries and phyſicians, who underſtand more of its medicinal uſes, than I am able to give account of. The manner of the country people's uſing it, is thus: Firſt, they beat it ſmail into meal, and then take as much of it in white wine or ale, as will lie upon a ſixpence; or more, if the diſtemper require it. It operates by urine, ſweat, and vomiting. This account I had from thoſe who had frequently uſed it in theſe diſtempers with good ſucceſs. Beſides thoſe uſes that are medicinal, it hath many other uſes which increaſe the value of it. At the firſt diſcovering it, the neighbourhood made no other uſe of it, but for marking their ſheep; but it is now made uſe of to glaze and harden crucibles and other veſſels made of earth or clay, that are to endure the hotteſt fire; and to

3   that

that end it is wonderfully effectual, which much inhaunceth the price of such vessels. By rubbing it upon iron arms, as guns, pistols, and the like, and tinging of them with its colour, it preserves them from rusting. It is made use of by dyers of cloth, making their blues to stand unalterable. For these and other uses, it is bought up at great prices by the Hollanders and others. This mundic ore, having little of sulphur in its composition, will not flow without a violent heat. It produceth a white regulus, shining like silver. It cannot be made malleable."

Bishop *Nicolson*, in a letter to Dr. Woodward, Aug. 5, 1710, speaks of this mine as follows :—" Having lately had notice of the opening of our wad mines above Keswick, I hasted (with some others) to see a curiosity which I never hitherto had an opportunity of viewing, and if this were omitted, I was never likely to have another. From Keswick we travelled up the valley of Borrowdale along the banks of Derwentwater six or seven miles or more, till we came to Seewhaite moor, where ascending an high mountain we at length reached the mine, and were courteously received by Mr. Shepherd one of the proprietors of the work, who was here waiting for his copartner Mr. Banks. On the first opening of the old level in the latter end of June last, great discouragements appeared ; for no search having been made in 32 years, they found that some pilfering interlopers had carried on the old work, till they had lost it in the rock. Upon the 3d of July (the day before we got thither) a new belly was happily discovered, above the fore head of the old man, which proved so rich that in less than 24 hours they had filled several sacks with fine and clean washed mineral. It lies intermixed with an hard greenish rock, but appeared in the midst of that of a full round vein or body of above three foot in diameter. Dr. *Merret*, in his *Pinax*, p. 218, would persuade one to believe, that this mineral is so very scarce, that it is no where in the universe to be met with, save only in Old and New England, and that this is the only place within the four seas where it can be had with us : Whereas Sir *Robert Sibbald* † assures us that it may be had in the shire of Aberdeen, the description and natural history whereof is now under his consideration; and Mr. *Dale*'s ‡ *inventur in fodinis* would induce one to believe it to be a very common mineral. Nay the author last mentioned particularly reckons up three several sorts of it, brought from as many distant countries, whereof he allows that of our English growth to be the best, that of Spain the next, and condemns what is brought from the East Indies as the worst of all. 'Tis strange that it should be the natural produce of so many parts of the globe, and yet that father *Kircher*, in his *Mundus Subterraneus*, should have no account of it ; and stranger yet, that none of the ancient naturalists should so much as touch upon the name or thing. Neither the *Melanteria* nor *Pnigitis* of *Dioscorides* seems to me the least related to this mineral; the former being described as a sort of liquid ink distilling from the veins of metals, and the latter appears to be of the same kind with that black chalk which Dr.

---

† Prod. Scot. b. 4 p. 42.   ‡ Pharmatelog. p, 650.

Plot † found in Oxfordshire. That learned gentleman indeed elsewhere falls in, with Mr. *Camden*'s opinion §, that this black lead (improperly so called, for that is the right name of our common lead as distinguished from tin) is a stony fort of black ochre, because it is neither subject to fusion or ductility in the fire, nor to a dissolution in the water. Yet a fusion it must have, if Dr. *Leigh* is to be credited ‡, who asserts that the Dutch use it in glazing their earthen pots; which he seems to confirm by an experiment tried in his own sight. My sagacious neighbour Mr. *Robinson* * will have it to be a mundic; which he afterwards more fully explains by a black, pinguid, and shining earth, impregnated with lead and antimony. It will, he says, flow with a great heat, but cannot be made malleable. What he reports of its easing the pains of gravel, stone, and strangury, is more than is confirmed to me; but the neighbours generally subscribe to his affertion of its being a present remedy for the cholick. That the dyers use it for the strengthening of their blues, is more than I have learned from any other hand. The chief use that Mr. *Camden* or Sir *Robert Sibbald* knew of it, was for drawing the lines and shading the pieces of the painters; but Mr. *Dale* †† hath added sundry more— *refrigerat, ficcat, repellit, usus præcipuus adversus strumas, tumoresque frigidos et phlegmaticos.* Dr. *Merret* || speaks of a certain blue stone in Lancashire which the inhabitants there call *killow*; and its use he observes to be the same as of our black lead, for drawing lines. I am very confident, that not only the uses but the matter of both are the same; and that this *nigrica fabrilis* and his *killow* differ no otherwise, than that the former name was happily coined by himself, and well expresses the true meaning of the latter. Sir *Robert Sibbald* tells us, that his countrymen give the name of *keel* to the *rubrica fabrilis* or common ruddle stone, and that the *nigrica* is called by them *killoyne*. Now, the Irish (from whom the Highland Scots may be presumed to have borrowed these two words) express all sorts of minerals or fossils by *knilen mineigh*, and *vinne* in their language is the same as *caothy*, blind or dark. We are likewise told, that the men of Kefwick** (where are also many remains of the Irish or Manks tongue) call their black lead indifferently either *kellow* or *wadf*; the latter of which is doubtless from the Saxon name of *woad* or *glaftum*, which (says Mr. *Ray* ‡‡) affords a better dye than Indico."

In the act of parliament 25 Geo. 2. c. 10. making it felony to break into any mine or wad hole of wad or black cawke, commonly called black lead, or to steal any from thence, there is a recital that the same hath been discovered in one mountain or ridge of hills only, in this realm, and that it hath been found by experience to be neceffary for divers useful purpofes, and more particularly in the casting of bomb shells, round-shot, and cannon balls.

It is hoped the very ingenious Dr. *Brownrigg* will oblige the world with a differtation on this mineral, in which he had made confiderable progrefs fome years ago.

† Natural Hift. of Oxfordfh. c. 3. s. 16, 17.   § Philof. Tranf. Nº 240.   ‡ Nat. Hift. Lanc. b. 1. p 91.   * Nat. Hift. Cumb. p. 74.   †† Pharmacol. p. 650. || Pinax, p. 218.   ** Philofoph. Tranfact. Nº 240.   ‡‡ Hift. Plant. p. 284.

The

The principal place in this large parish is the market town of KESWICK; of which, and of the lake adjoining, we find the following account in Camden's Britannia: "Derwent, after it has passed through the hills, spreadeth abroad "into a large lake: Bede termeth it *prægrande stagnum*."

The late Dr. Brown, in a letter to a friend, describes it in an elegant and very picturesque manner: "In my way to the north, I passed through *Dove-* "*dale*; and, to say the truth, was disappointed in it. When I came to "*Buxton*, I visited another or two of their romantic scenes; but these are " inferior to *Dovedale*. They are but poor miniatures of KESWICK; which " exceeds them more in grandeur, than I can give you to imagine; and more, " if possible, in beauty than in grandeur.

" Instead of the narrow slip of valley which is seen at *Dovedale*, you have " at Keswick a vast amphitheatre, in circumference about twenty miles. In- " stead of a meagre rivulet, a noble living lake, ten miles round, of an " oblong form, adorned with a variety of wooded islands. The rocks indeed " of *Dovedale* are finely wild, pointed, and irregular; but the hills are both " little and unanimated; and the margin of the brook is poorly edged with " weeds, morass, and brushwood. But at *Keswick*, you will, on one side of " the lake, see a rich and beautiful landskip of cultivated fields, rising to the " eye, in fine inequalities, with noble groves of oak, happily dispersed; " and climbing the adjacent hills, shade above shade, in the most various and " picturesque forms. On the opposite shore, you will find rocks and cliffs of " stupendous height, hanging broken over the lake in horrible grandeur, " some of them a thousand feet high; the woods climbing up their steep and " shaggy sides, where mortal foot never yet approached. On these dreadful " heights the eagles build their nests. A variety of waterfalls are seen pour- " ing from their summits, and tumbling in vast sheets from rock to rock in " rude and terrible magnificence. While on all sides of this immense am- " phitheatre, the lofty mountains rise round, piercing the clouds in shapes as " airy and fantastic, as the very rocks of *Dovedale*. To this I must add the " frequent and bold projection of the cliffs into the lake, forming noble " bays and promontories. In other parts they finally retire from it; and often " open in abrupt chasms or clefts, through which at hand you see rich and " cultivated vales, and beyond these at various distance, mountain rising over " mountain; among which, new prospects present themselves in mist, till the " eye is lost in an agreeable perplexity,

" *Where active fancy travels beyond sense,*
" *And pictures things unseen.———*

. " Were I to analyse the two places into their constituent principles, I " should tell you, that the full perfection of *Keswick* consists of three circum- " stances, beauty, horror, and *magnificence* united; the second of which is " alone found in *Dovedale*: Of *beauty* it hath little, nature having left it almost " a desert: Neither its small extent, nor the diminutive and lifeless form of the " hills admit *magnificence*. But to give you a compleat idea of these three " perfections, as they are joined in Keswick, would require the united powers " of *Claude*, *Salvator*, and *Poussin*. The first should throw his delicate sun-

M 2   " shine

" shine over the cultivated vales, the scattered cots, the groves, the lake,
" and wooded islands. The second should dash out the horror of the rugged
" cliffs, the steeps, the hanging woods, and foaming waterfalls; while the
" grand pencil of *Poussin* should crown the whole, with the majesty of the
" impending mountains.

" So much for what I would call the *permanent* beauties of this astonishing
" scene. Were I not afraid of being tiresome, I could now dwell as long on
" its *varying* or *accidental* beauties. I would sail round the lake, anchor in
" every bay, and land you on every promontory and island. I would point
" out the perpetual change of prospect: The woods, rocks, cliffs, and
" mountains, by turns vanishing or rising into view: Now gaining on the
" sight, hanging over our heads in their full dimensions, beautifully dreadful;
" and now, by a change of situation, assuming new romantic shapes, retiring
" and lessening on the eye, and insensibly losing themselves in an azure mist.
" I would remark the contrast of light and shade, produced by the morning
" and evening sun; the one gilding the western and the other the eastern side
" of this immense amphitheatre; while the vast shadow projected by the
" mountains buries the opposite part in a deep and purple gloom, which the
" eye can hardly penetrate: The natural variety of colouring, which the
" several objects produce, is no less wonderful and pleasing: The ruling tints
" in the valley being those of azure, green, and gold, yet ever various,
" arising from an intermixture of the lake, the woods, the grass, and corn
" fields: These are nobly contrasted by the grey rocks and cliffs; and the
" whole heightned by the yellow streams of light, the purple hues, and misty
" azure of the mountains. Sometimes a serene air and clear sky disclose the
" tops of the highest hills: At others, you see the clouds involving their
" summits, resting on their sides, or descending to their base, and rolling
" among the vallies, as in a vast furnace. When the winds are high, they
" roar among the cliffs and caverns like peals of thunder; then, too, the clouds
" are seen in vast bodies sweeping along the hills in gloomy greatness, while
" the lake joins the tumult, and tosses like a sea: But in calm weather, the
" whole scene becomes new: The lake is a perfect mirror; and the landskip
" in all its beauty, islands, fields, woods, rocks, and mountains are seen
" inverted, and floating on its surface. I will now carry you to the top of a
" cliff, where, if you dare approach the edge, a new scene of astonishment
" presents itself, where the valley, lake, and islands seem lying at your feet;
" where this expanse of water appears diminished to a little pool, amidst the
" vast immeasurable objects that surround it; for here the summits of more
" distant hills appear beyond those you had already seen; and rising behind
" each other in successive ranges and azure groups of craggy and broken
" steeps, form an immense and awful picture, which can only be expressed by
" the image of a tempestuous sea of mountains.—Let me now conduct you
" down again to the valley, and conclude with one circumstance more;
" which is, that a walk by still moon-light (at which time the distant water-
" falls are heard in all their variety of sound) among these inchanting dales,
                                                            " opens

" opens a scene of such delicate beauty, repose, and solemnity, as exceeds all
" description."

Dr. Dalton, in his elegant poem addressed to the two young ladies at
Whitehaven, speaking of the rocks of Lodore from whence there is a very
high cascade into this lake, has the following reflections :

" Horrors like these at first alarm,
But soon with savage grandeur charm,
And raise to noblest thought the mind :
Thus, nigh thy fall, Lódore, reclin'd,
The craggy cliff, impending wood,
Whose shadows mix o'er half the flood,
The gloomy clouds, which solemn sail,
Scarce lifted by the languid gale
O'er the cap'd hill, and darken'd vale ;
The ravening kite, and bird of Jove,
Which round th' aerial ocean rove,
And, floating on the billowy sky,
With full expanded pennons fly,
Their flutt'ring or their bleating prey
Thence with death-dooming eye survey ;
Channels by rocky torrents torn,
Rocks to the lake in thunder born,
Or such as o'er our heads appear
Suspended in their mid career,
To start again at his command,
Who rules fire, water, a'r, and land,
I view with wonder and delight,
A pleasing, tho' an awful sight :
For, seen with them, the verdant isles
Soften with more delicious smiles,
More tempting twine their opening bowers,
More lively glow the purple flowers,
More smoothly slopes the border gay,
In fairer circle bends the bay,
And last, to fix our wand'ring eyes,
Thy roofs, O Keswick, brighter rise
The lake and lofty hills between,
Where giant Skiddaw shuts the scene.'"

Amongst other particulars, he takes occasion to caution the traveller not to
be shocked with some late violations of those sacred woods and groves, by the
commissioners of Greenwich hospital ordering the woods to be cut down,
which had for ages shaded the shores and promontories of that lovely
lake : For,

" Where the rude axe with heaved stroke
" Was never heard the nymphs to daunt,
" Or fright them from their hallow'd haunt,"

there-

there is, alas, now,

" The lonely mountains o'er,
" And the refounding fhore,
     " A voice of weeping heard and loud lament;
" From haunted fpring and dale,
" Edg'd with poplar pale,
     " The parting genius is with fighing fent :
" With flower-inwoven treffes torn,
" The nymphs in twilight fhade of tangled thickets mourn."

However (he adds) the vifitant, for his confolation may ftill, notwithftanding all thofe profanations, expect to find there an affemblage of fuch
exquifite, though different, beauties, as will well deferve to be admired by
him, as much perhaps as any one part of the inanimate creation.

The lake is of an orbicular form; abounding with large pikes, eels,
trouts, and perch, a great ftore of water fowl, as ducks, mallards, teals, and
widgeons.

There are in it three iflands :

The firft ifland is about the middle of the lake, being in a manner round,
and above half a mile in compafs. It was heretofore full of wood, which
grew about a little houfe which was called St. Herbert's hermitage. In
the regifter of bifhop Appleby in the year 1374, there is an indulgence
of forty days to every of the inhabitants of the parifh of Crofthwaite that
fhould attend the vicar to St. Herbert's ifland on the 13th of April yearly, and
there celebrate mafs in memory of St. Herbert †. This ifland now belongs
to the houfe of Brayton ; and the late Sir Wilfrid Lawfon, about the year
1761, cut down all the old wood and planted the ifland anew.

The fecond ifland lies nearer to the fhore, of an oval figure, being a quarter
of a mile long, and half as much broad. This, it is faid, was inhabited by
the miners, until their works were deftroyed by the civil wars ; though now
there is fcarce fo much as the foundation of any houfe to be feen.

The third ifland contains about fix acres of ground, and lies north of the
fecond, and nearer to Kefwick. It goes by the name of the Vicar's ifland,
having belonged formerly to Fountain Abbey in Yorkfhire, to which the
church of Crofthwaite was appropriated ; and was granted by king Hen. 8.
(amongft many other poffeffions belonging to the faid abbey) to one John Williamfon. It is now the inheritance of the Ponfonbys of Hale.

The mountain *Skidaw* is about eleven hundred yards perpendicular from
the Broadwater. It rifes with two heads, like unto Parnaffus ; and with a
kind of emulation beholds Scruffel hill before it in Annandale in Scotland.
By thefe two mountains, according as the mifty clouds rife or fall, the people
dwelling thereabouts make their prognoftication of the change of the weather;
and have a common expreffion,

† Appendix, N°. 10.

If Skidaw hath a cap,
Scruffel wots full well of that.

Like as there goes also another faying concerning the height of this hill with two others in this kingdom,

Skidaw, Lanvellin, and Cafticand,
Are the higheft hills in all England.

Upon the top of this mountain, there is a blue flate ftone, about a man's height, which they call Skidaw man. And a little further fouth, upon the faid mountain top, was erected in the year 1689 an houfe five yards fquare, and four yards high, by Mr. John Adams the geographer, for placing his telefcopes and optic glaffes, having from thence a full profpect and view of thefe two counties, whereby he was enabled to give the better defcription thereof by dimenfions. But he being arrefted, firft by his engraver for debt, and not long after by death, his project proved abortive.

On the fouth fide of this mountain lies the manor of *Brundham* or *Brundholm*, being a large manor of cuftomary tenants. It was part of the poffeffions which Henry the fixth earl of Northumberland gave to king Henry the eighth. Which faid king by letters patent July 15, in the 35th year of his reign, granted the fame to Thomas Dalfton efquire, together with the manors of Uldale, Caldbeck Upperton, and Kirkbride. It afterwards belonged to the Tolfons of Woodhall; who fold the fame to Mr. Relph of Cockermouth, after whofe death it came to the Haffels of Dalemain, in which family it ftill continues. It comprehends the feveral villages of Brundham, Applethwaite, Milnbeck, and Syzick; being well fhaded with wood on the north banks of Bure. There are in this manor about 34 cuftbmary tenants who pay arbitrary fines, and about 38 freeholders.

The *church* is dedicated to St. Kentigern, and valued in the king's books at 50l 8s 11¼d. It was given by Alice de Romley to Fountains abbey in Yorkfhire aforefaid, and foon after appropriated to that abbey, the collation thereunto being referved to the bifhop of Carlifle.

The prefent revenue is about 140l a year; it enjoys all the tithes of the whole parifh, corn tithe only excepted. The late vicar Mr. Chriftian, after a long and expenfive fuit in the exchequer, recovered the fight of the wool in tithing, and alfo the tithe of hog wool and lamb; which increafed the revenue of the vicarage very confiderably.

In 1294, Mr. *Jeoffrey Whethamftede* was collated to the vicarage of Crofthwait, faving to the abbot and convent of Fountains a yearly penfion of ten marks.

In 1313, *Richard de Grayftoke* was collated, faving the faid penfion.

In 1335, Sir *Richard*, vicar of Crofthwaite, at the bifhop's vifitation, proves his being canonically ordained, and was difmiffed.

In 1340, the abbot and convent of Fountains, by their proctor prove their title to the impropriation of Crofthwaite, at the bifhop's vifitation.

In 1354, the bifhop appoints two commiffioners to judge a caufe depending between the abbot and convent of Fountains complainants, and *Thomas Lune* vicar

vicar of Crosthwaite respondent; wherein the said abbot and convent demanded a yearly pension of ten marks; and an oath of fealty from the said vicar.

In 1359, upon an appeal to the court of Rome, by *John Henry de Broughton* vicar of Crosthwaite, complaining of his sufferings by a dispute between his predecessor Thomas Lune and W. de.Celario (the pope's provisor), and the pope's apostolical letters thereupon; the bishop refers the inquiry to certain commissioners.

In 1360, *John de Welton* was collated, on his making oath (according to the canon) of personal residence. Soon after which, a prohibition came from the king against the bishop's admitting any new vicar, till his majesty's title to the advowson (then depending in court) were considered.

In 1361, *Peter de Morland* vicar of Torpenhow is .appointed commendatory-curate of Crosthwaite, during the vacancy of that vicarage: And presently afterwards, upon his resignation, the same is given in commendam to *John Boon.*

In 1567, on the death of *John Ratcliff* the last incumbent, *John Maybraye* was collated by bishop Best. And in the next year, on his resignation, *William Bennet* was collated.

In 1585, on William Bennet's resignation, institution was given to *Peter Mayson,* who was presented by Michael Benson of Loughrigg in the county of Westmorland, assignee of Laurence Charlies of Rose Castle gentleman, to whom the bishop had granted that avoidance.

In 1592, on Peter Mayson's resignation, *Robert Beck* was collated; who likewise resigning in 1597, *Peter Beck* was collated.

In 1602, on Peter Beck's resignation, Dr. *Giles Robinson,* the bishop's brother, was collated.

In 1623, on Dr. Robinson's death, bishop Milburne gave the vicarage to *Isaac Singleton,* M. A.

In 1661, *Henry Marshall,* M. A. was collated.

In 1667, *Richard Lowry,* M. A.

In 1710, *Thomas Tullie,* M. A.

In 1727, *Thomas Nicolson,* LL. B.

In 1728, *Thomas Christian,* B. A.

In 1770, James Stephen Lushington, M. A. was collated by bishop Law.

There are in this parish five *chapels* of ease; viz.

1. St. *John's,* about three miles distant from the mother church, which was returned to the governors of queen Anne's bounty at 4*l* 15*s*.; But in the year 1719, it was augmented by the said governors with 200*l*, in conjunction with 200*l* given by Dr. Gaskarth; the inhabitants also gave 100*l*. With all which sums lands were purchased within this parish; and the present revenue of the chapel is upwards of 45*l* a year. Dr. Thomas Tullie the then vicar, with the consent of the bishop, gave up the right of nomination to the said Dr. Gaskarth and inhabitants; the said Dr. Gaskarth or his heirs to present a

4   curate

curate whom they pleafe one turn, and the next turn to prefent on the nomination of a majority of the inhabitants and landowners.

2. *Wythburn* chapel, about fix miles diftant from the mother church, has an ancient falary of 2 *l* 10 *s* 0 *d*. In 1739, it was certified to the governors of queen Anne's bounty at 3 *l* 6 *s* 4 *d*. About the year 1742 it received from the faid governors an augmentation of 200 *l* by lot, and afterwards another augmentation by lot of 200 *l*. In 1772 it received another augmentation of 200 *l* in conjunction with 200 *l* given by the countefs dowager Gower. With all which fums lands were purchafed in the parifhes of Crofthwa'te, Great Salkeld, and Grefmere; now of the yearly value of about 37 *l*.

3. *Thornthwaite* chapel, diftant from the faid church full fix miles, hath an ancient falary of 4 *l* 4 *s* 0 *d*; was certified to the governors of queen Anne's bounty at 4 *l* 16 *s* 0 *d*; received an augmentation of 200 *l* by lot in 1746, and again in 1754. Whereof 300 *l* was laid out in lands in the parifh of Baffenthwaite, of the prefent yearly value of 11 *l*. And 100 *l* remains in the governor's hands, intereft whereof is paid yearly 40 *s*.

4. *Borrowdale* chapel is alfo diftant from the faid church fix miles or more. Its ancient falary is 3 *l* 5 *s* 0 *d*. It received an augmentation of 200 *l* by lot about the year 1744, and again in 1752, and in 1762 a further augmentation of 200 *l* in conjunction with 200 *l* given by the countefs dowager Gower. Which fums were laid out in lands in the parifh of Crofthwaite and in the parifh of Coulton in Lancafhire, of the prefent yearly value of 30 *l*.

5. *Newlands* chapel, about four miles from the mother church, hath an ancient falary of 2 *l* 12 *s* 0 *d*, and hath thrice received 200 *l* by lot, *viz*. in 1748, 1750, and 1757. With which fums lands were purchafed in the chapelry of Lowfwater and in the parifh of Crofthwaite, of the prefent yearly value of about 22 *l*.

The vicar nominates the curates to the four laft named chapels.

In this parifh they have a particular manner of chufing and fwearing *churchwardens* and *fidefmen*, as fettled by the commiffioners for ecclefiaftical caufes in the 13 Eliz. who decreed, that yearly upon Afcenfion-day, the vicar, the 18 fworn men, the churchwardens, the owner of Derwentwater eftate, the fealer and receiver of the queen's portion at the mines, one of the chiefeft of the company and fellowfhip of the partners and offices of the minerals then refiant at Kefwick, the bailiffs of Kefwick, Wythburn, Borrowdale, Thornthwaite, Brundholme, and the forefter of Derwent fells, fhall meet in the church of Crofthwaite, and fo many of them as fhall be there affembled fhali chufe the 18 men and churchwardens for the year enfuing, who fhall on the Sunday following before the vicar take their oath of office. In the fame decree they make order concerning the goods of the church; namely, that the 18 men and churchwardens fhould provide, before Chriftmafs then next following, two fair large communion cups of filver with covers, one fine diaper napkin for the communion and facramental bread, and two fair pots or flagons of tin for the wine; which they fhall buy with the money they fhall receive for the chalices, pipes, paxes, croffes, candlefticks, and other church goods that they have to

fell; and that they shall sell for the use of the church, such popish relicks and
monuments of superstition and idolatry as then remained in the parish; and
namely, two pipes of silver, one silver paxe, one crofs of cloth or gold which
was on a vestment, one copper crofs, two chalices of silver, two corporate rafts,
three hand bells, the Sion whereon the paschal stood, one pair of cenfures, one
ship, one head of a pair of cenfures, twenty-nine brazen or latyne candlesticks
of fix quarters long, one holy water tankard of brafs, the canopies which hanged
and that which was carried over the facrament, two brazen or latyne chrifma-
tories, the vail cloth, the fepulchral cloths, and the painted cloths with the
pictures of Peter and Paul and the Trinity: They further decree, that the
four vestments, three tunicles, five cheftables, and all other vestments belonging to the faid parish church, and to the chapels within the faid parish, be defaced and cut in pieces, and of them (if they will ferve thereunto) a covering
for the pulpit and cushions for the church be provided; and likewise the albes
and amylies fold, and fair linen cloths for the communion table, and a covering
of buckram fringed for the fame be provided; and that for the chapels in
the faid parish be provided decent communion cups of filver or tin: And that
a decent perclofe of wood, wherein morning and evening prayer shall be read,
be fet up without the quire door, the length whereof to be feven foot, and
breadth feven foot, and height five foot, with feats and desks within the fame:
And that they take care that the church be furnished with a bible of the largest
volume, one or two communion books, four pfalter books, the two tomes of
the homilies, the injunctions, the defence of the apology, the paraphrafes in
English, or instead thereof, Marlorat upon the Evangelists, and Beacon's
Postil, and alfo four pfalter-books in metre: And, that there be no fervice on
the forbidden holidays; viz. on the feafts or days of All Souls, St. Katherine,
St. Nicholas, Thomas Becket, St. George, Wednesday in Easter or Whitfun-
week, the Conception, Assumption, and Nativity of our Lady, St. Laurence,
Mary Magdalene, St. Anne, or fuch like: And that none shall pray on any
beads, knots, portaffes, papistical and superstitious latin primers, or other like
forbidden or ungodly books: And that there be no communion at the burial
of any dead, nor any months minds, anniverfaries, or fuch superstitions ufed.

At Kefwick there is a *fchool*, founded by the parishioners, and endowed with
two fmall tenements of about 18 l. a year. Concerning this fchool, the aforefaid commissioners decree, That whereas two pence for every fire-houfe hath
been paid to the parish clerk yearly, and alfo certain ordinary fees for night
watch, burials, weddings, and moreover certain benevolences of lamb, wool,
eggs, and fuch like, which feem to grow up to a greater fum than is competent for a parish clerk; the 18 men shall hereafter take up the faid two pence
a houfe for the ufe of a fchoolmafter, paying thereout to the parish clerk
yearly 46 s. 8 d.

And on a commission of pious ufes, Feb. 16, in the 13 Ja. before Sir William Hutton knight, John Fleming, Henry Blencowe, John Lowther, and
George Fletcher efquires, it is found by the inquest, that the 18 fworn men
had for time immemorial laid a tax for the maintenance of the fchoolmafter
                     and

and other occasions of the parish, and appointed the schoolmaster, and made orders for the government of the school, and that the inhabitants had by a voluntary contribution raised a school stock of 148 *l* 2 *s* 3 ½ *d*; nevertheless, that Dr. Henry Robinson bishop of Carlisle, Henry Woodward his chancellor, and Giles Robinson brother of the said bishop and vicar of Crofthwaite, had intermeddled; and that the said bishop, sometimes by authority of the high commission for ecclesiastical causes, sometimes as a justice of the peace for the county, and sometimes by his power as ordinary, had interrupted the orders of the 18 men, and had committed thirteen of them to prison. Therefore the commissioners restore the 18 men to their authority concerning the appointing of a schoolmaster, and the government of the school.

Within this parish, in the town of Keswick, was born Sir *John Banks*, a person who arrived to the highest honour in the profession of the law, and became a considerable benefactor to the place of his nativity. He was educated in Queen's college in Oxford, became student in Gray's Inn, was appointed attorney to prince Charles, and in the year 1640 constituted lord chief justice of the common pleas. In 1641 he attended the king to Oxford, and was there admitted of the privy council. He died at Oxford in 1644, and was buried in the north isle of the cathedral church there. In his last will and testament he devised to trustees two tenements in Keswick, 200*l* in money, and 30*l* a year issuing out of his lands and tenements within the parish of Crofthwaite for the building of a manufacture house, and raising a stock for the employment and maintenance of the poor of the said parish. Some of the trustees dying, and the rest neglecting the trust reposed in them, the manufacture was discontinued; and the charitable gift in a good measure neglected or misemployed for several years; till in the year 1672 the parishioners sued out a commission of charitable uses, by virtue whereof, upon inquisition and decree thereupon such just measures were taken as to answer the pious intention of the donor.

Thomas Grave bequeathed for the purchase of freehold lands so much money as raises an annual rent of 10*l*; which is yearly distributed to the poor of the parish on Good Friday.

Peter Udall gentleman gave a rent charge of 4*l* 11 *s* 4*d* out of his lands in Essex, to be yearly distributed in manner following: *viz.* To twelve poor people of Great Brathwaite; five of Little Brathwaite, Portinskall, and Ulleck; and three of Thornthwaite; 3 *s* 8 *d* each: To the minister of the parish for preaching a sermon to them on Candlemass day 8 *s*: For a dinner to the minister and trustees on the day of distribution 8 *s*: And to the person that brings the money out of the south 2 *s*. An addition of 30*l* 10 *s* 0*d* principal stock was made to this charity, by the care and management of Mr. Lowry then vicar, who recovered so much arrears from Mr. Udall's representatives; the interest whereof is given at the discretion of the vicar and trustees.

Thomas Williamson and *Agnes Williamson* gave each 20 *l* to the poor of St. John's and Castlerigg; the interest thereof to be laid out in flesh meat pickled, hanged, and dried, for their relief on stormy days in winter, that they may not in such weather be forced to hazard their lives in seeking of a daily support.

Hugh

Hugh Tickell gave lands of the yearly rent of 6 *l*, for the common ftock of the whole parifh; and Mr. *Hudleſton*, fome time fchoolmaſter at Keſwick, gave 15 *l*, the yearly intereſt thereof to be applied to the fame uſe.

Unto whom the *corn-tithes* were firſt granted after the diſſolution of the monaſteries, we have not found. But they are now enjoyed by the owners of the lands.

Other poſſeſſions which had belonged to Fountaine abbey were granted as follows; viz. King Henry the eighth by letters patent dated June 20, in the 32d year of his reign, grants to *John Williamſon* (amongſt other particulars) a yearly rent of 11 *s* and ſervices, which the heirs of *Nicholas Radcliff* had paid to the ſaid late monaſtery for the Bridge holme in the vill of Croſthwaite; and a yearly rent of 2½ *d*, and one pound of cumin and ſervices, which the heirs of *John Reede* paid to the ſaid monaſtery for the fiſh garths in Croſthwaite aforeſaid; and a rent of 6 *d* and ſervices from the heirs of *William Walles* for lands there called *Wanthwaite*; and divers meſſuages and tenements there in the tenure of *Richard Yowdall, Robert Yowdall, John Yowdall, William Howe*, the late wife of *Richard Atkinſon, Nicholas Williamſon, Richard Becke*, the daughter of *Edward Becke, Nicholas Radcliff*, and *James Radcliff*; and all that meſſuage called *Monkhall* in the tenure of *Gawin Radcliff*; and the wood, containing one acre, called the *Vicar ile* in the water of *Derwent*; and the lands and tenements called *Eſkneſs*, in the tenure of *John Wilſon* junior and *Thomas Wilſon*: To hold of the king *in capite* by the ſervice of the 20th part of one knight's fee.

And the fame king, Jan. 20, in the 37th year of his reign, grants to *Richard Greimes*, late belonging to the ſaid monaſtery, lands and tenements in *Wattenland* in the tenure of 18 different perſons; in *Stanthwait*, lands and tenements in the tenure of 20 different perſons, with the mill alſo in *Stanthwait*; a meſſuage and tenement called *Applegarth*; 12 acres of land in two incloſures called *Pykerigg* and *Thakerigg*; one acre called *Monk* acre; one acre in *Heland*, nigh *Derwent*; and divers other incloſures and parcels of land in *Braithwaite*, and *Cauſey*, of the yearly value of 22 *l* 6 *s* 0 *d*.

And king Edward the fixth, Dec. 13, in the 2d year of his reign, grants to *Thomas Brende* of London, ſcrivener, the late *chantry* of St. *Mary Magdalene* in the pariſh church of Croſthwaite; together with the meſſuages and tenements late in the ſeveral tenures of *Parcibal Wharton, Parcibal Radcliff, John Williamſon*, and *Miles Williamſon*, fituate, lying, and being in *Croſthwaite* and *Braythmyre*, to the ſaid late chantry belonging.

In the year 1740, it was certified, that there are in this pariſh 556 families; of which, Quakers 6, Preſbyterians 15.

PARISH

PARISH OF BASSINTHWAITE.

On the north-weft fide of *Crofthwaite* lies the parifh of BASSINTHWAITE; which is bounded by Crofthwaite on the fouth eaft fide; by the broad water or Derwent on the fouth weft, till Caldbeck falls into it below Ewes bridge; and by Caldbeck on the weft, unto a brook that falls into it, which fprings on the fouth-fide of Binfay fell, and fo to the head of that fpring; then crofs over Lanfketh common to the fouth-weft fide of Whitefield, as it ftands divided from the park of Baffenthwaite and the Vothial beck; fo up that water to White water Dafk on the north; and fo on the eaft fide of Skiddaw till it meets with Crofthwaite boundary at Glendermakin.

This parifh is divided into two conftablewicks; that where the church ftands near Crofthwaite being called the High fide; and the low fide goes by the name of the Hawes, where the chapel ftands: Which at firft was all one intire manor, and granted by Waldeof the firft lord of Allerdale to his baftard fon Gofpatric, whofe pofterity took upon them the furname *de Baffenthwaite*. And fo it defcended, until Sir Adam de Baffenthwaite in the time of Ed. 2. having iffue only two daughters, the elder of whom was married to *Irton* of Irton, and the younger unto *Martindale*, they by partition divided the patrimony betwixt them: Since which time they have been two diftinct manors.

Martindale's part continued in the name, until *Roger Martindale* did forfeit his part for treafon; whereupon it was granted to the earl of *Derby*, in which family it continued till the year 1714, when it was given in marriage with the lady Henrietta Stanley daughter of the earl of Derby to John lord Afhburnham, who in the next year after fold it to the tenants for 1825*l*, who are now all freeholders, about 46 in number, and they pay a quit rent to the earl of Egremont of 3*l* 4*s* 10*d*.

The coheir that married *Irton*, furviving him, married to her fecond hufband *Lawfon* of Little Ofwith in the county of Northumberland counfellor at law, and fettled the fame upon him; who, dying without iffue, gave the fame to his coufin Sir *Wilfred Lawfon* knight, who fettled the fame upon his fecond fon *Wilfred Lawfon* efquire, in whofe defcendents it ftill continues. There are in this manor about 17 cuftomary tenants, who pay arbitrary fines; and 28 indenture tenants, who pay a nine-penny fine only. The whole rent is 21*l* 12*s* 1¼*d*. And the lord pays a quit rent to the earl of Egremont of 3*l* 4*s* 10*d*.

The aforefaid divifion of the manor appears to have been before the 35 Hen. 8. for in that year on an inquifition of knights fees it is found, that *Richard Irton* then held a moiety of the manor of Baftynthwayte of the king as of his manor of Papcaftre, by the fervice of a third part of one knight's fee, 2*s* cornage, 8*d* feawake, and witnefman in Skedo: And that the earl of Derby held the other moiety, by knights fervice, 6*s* 8*d* cornage, 8*d* feawake, and fuit of court at Papcaftre.

This manor is well wooded, efpecially towards the lake, being full of inclofures and rich meadows; as that lake is of many varieties of fifh and fowl, being about five miles long, and in fome places near two miles broad.

In

In the year 1772, the right to this lake was tried at the affizes at Carlifle, in a caufe between the earl of Egremont and Sir Gilfrid Lawfon; when the following iffues were found for the faid earl:

That the lake and every part thereof is the freehold of the earl of Egremont:

That the earl is feifed of a feparate fifhery in the whole, except three draughts called Ewes bridge, Stone wall, and Ellers ftile, wherein John Spedding efquire hath a free fifhery in common with the faid earl; and that, as owner of the fifhery, he the faid earl and his tenants are intitled to the privilege of drawing and landing nets ufed in the fifhery on the grounds adjoining:

And that the earl is intitled to the fole navigation of the lake, and to land goods upon the grounds adjoining, out of boats and veffels ufed in the navigation.

The *church* ftands in Upper Baffenthwaite, and is dedicated to St. Bridget. Waldeof fon of Gofpatric gave this church to the abbey of Jedworth. In the tenth year of king John, Duncan de Lafcel and Chriftian his wife impleaded Hugh abbot of Jedworth for the advowfon of the church of Baftinthwait; and it was adjudged to belong to the abbot, by the gift of Waldeof fon of Gofpatric, father of the faid Chriftian.

The dean and chapter of Carlifle are now appropriators and patrons, and allow to the curate (by leafe) all the tithes great and fmall, he paying the ancient referved rent of 11 *l*.—But by an act of parliament for dividing and inclofing the common of Baffenthwaite, the curate after July 1, 1774, fhall have land fet out inftead of tithes; from which time all tithes, modufes, prefcriptions, oblations, obventions, furplice fees, and other dues fhall ceafe, and be no longer paid.

The curacy was returned to the governors of queen Anne's bounty, at 22 *l* 4 *s* 8 *d*.

About the year 1625, Matthew Caipe of the city of Carlifle merchant gave his leafe of the tithe corn and fheaves of corn and tithe hay of Levington, or Linton holme and Harper hill, to fupport a lecture in Baffenthwait church.

In the year 1471, divers of the parifhioners petitioned the then bifhop for leave to build a *chapel* in the faid parifh, which was granted to them, on their engaging to depofite 50 *l* for a falary, and to build a dwelling-houfe for the reader, and lay thereto one acre of land for a garden or orchard. Whereupon the chapel, called Hawes chapel, feems to have been then built; but there is no account of any curate, or any thing elfe belonging to it in the bifhop's archives. But in the year 1738, the fum of 45 *l* called by the name of chapel ftock, unto which the parifhioners added 5 *l* (probably to fupply what feems to have been loft from the ancient ftock), was laid out in a purchafe of lands for the ufe and benefit of the curate of Baffenthwaite for ever. So that all along the church and chapel feem to have been fupplied by one and the fame curate.

There are in this parifh about 68 families, all of the eftablifhed church.

PARISH OF ISEL.

The parish of Isel is bounded by the river Derwent from the foot of Cole-beck to the foot of Redmain hagg hedge on the south; and by the said hedge to the head thereof, and so cross the highways to Cockermouth and Bridekirk to a field called the Trinities as it is divided from Bridekirk demesnes to the top of Tallentine hill on the west; and by Moothay horse course unto Threapland gill head on the north; and so on the said course to the head of Colebeck, and so down Colebeck to the foot thereof on the east

This *Isel* was at first demesne of Allerdale, and did contain Rughthwaite, Blenkrake, Warthole, Redmain, half of Plumbland, and Sunderland, with their appurtenances.

Alan son of Waldieve gave Rughthwaite and a third part of the wastes of Isel, to Gamel de Brun lord of Bothill; and he gave the principal manor of Isel with the appurtenances, Blencrake, with the services of Newton, to *Ranulph Engain*.

Ranulph had issue *William Engain*; and he a daughter and heir *Ada Engain* married to *Simon de Morvil*, father of *Roger de Morvil*, father of *Hugh de Morvil* (one of the assassins of Thomas a Becket).

This *Hugh de Morvil* had two daughters coheirs *Ada* and *Joan*. Isel was of *Ada*'s purparty. She was first married to *Richard Lucy*, to whom she had no issue male. To her second husband she married *Thomas de Multon*, to whom she had a son and heir *Thomas de Multon*, who in the reign of Hen. 3. intailed Isell and Blencrake with the appurtenances on his two younger sons *Edward* and *Hubert*, and their heirs general successively: So the lords of Isel lost the services of Newton, because that tenure remained to the grantor Thomas Multon and his heirs, as it had descended to him.

By that intail *Hubert Multon* enjoyed Isel; and *William* his son after him, whose daughter *Margaret* brought the inheritance into the family of the *Leighs* in Edward the second's time. Which *Margaret*, in the 33 Ed. 3. being then widow of Sir *William de Lygh* knight, had a licence from bishop Welton for a chaplain in her private oratory within the manor of Isale.

In the 35 Hen. 8. *John Leigh* esquire held the manor of Isaill and Blencrake of the king, by the service of one knight's fee, and 46s 8d coinage, by the hands of William Dacre knight, lord Dacre receiver of the cornage there. He held also at the same time one third part of the manor of Orton in Cumberland

Thomas Leigh, the last of the name, gave it to his second wife *Maud Red-main* whom he married being then a widow: who afterwards gave it to her third husband Sir *Wilfrid Lawson*, who received the honour of knighthood from king James the first. And this brought the *Lawsons* to Isel, who were a Yorkshire family, deriving their descent from *John Lawson* of Fawkesgrave in the county of York esquire in the reign of king Hen. 3.

This

This Sir *Wilfrid Lawfon* knight died without iffue, and was buried in the quire of Ifel church, where is the following monumental infcription:

Hic jacet ille cinis, qui modo Lawfon erat.
Even fuch is time which takes in truft,
  Our youth, and joys, and all we have,
And pays us but with age and duft,
  Within the dark and filent grave:
When we have wandred all our ways, .
Shuts up the ftory of our days:
And from which earth, and grave, and duft,
  The Lord will raife me up, I truft.

Wilfridus Lawfon miles obiit 16 die Apr. Anno ætatis fuæ 87. Annoque falutis 1632.

He had a brother *Gilfrid Lawfon* efquire, who feems to have died before him: For in the year 1636, *William Lawfon* efquire (fon of the faid *Gilfrid*) appears to have prefented a clergyman to the vicarage of Ifel, being then vacant. This *William* married Elizabeth daughter and fole heir of William Beaulie efquire, with whom he had the manor of Hefket in the parifh of Caldbeck. And by her he had iffue,

Sir *Wilfrid Lawfon* baronet, who was advanced to that dignity by king Charles the firft. He married Jane daughter of Sir Edward Mufgrave of Hayton baronet, by whom he had iffue 5 fons and 8 daughters. In the line of his eldeft fon *William* did defcend the manor of Ifel. Upon his fecond fon *Wilfrid* he fettled the manors of Brayton, Baffenthwaite, Henfingham, Lowef-water, and Hefket, and alfo an eftate at Newlaythes near Carlifle. Of this Sir Wilfrid is the following epitaph in the chancel of Ifel church.

Here lies Sir Wilfrid Lawfon baronet and his lady Jane. He departed this life the 13th day of December 1688, aged 79. And fhe the 8th of June 1677, aged 65. Having married four fons and eight daughters.

Vivit poft funera virtus.

William Lawfon efquire, eldeft fon of the laft Sir *Wilfrid*, died before his father; having married Milcah daughter of Sir William Strickland baronet: By whom he had iffue,

Sir *Wilfrid Lawfon* baronet; who reprefented the borough of Cockermouth in the 2 W. and M. He married Elizabeth only daughter of George Prefton of Holker in Lancafhire efquire, by Mary only fifter of John vifcount Lonf-dale, by whom he had three fons and three daughters.

Wilfrid the eldeft fucceeded him, and was one of the grooms of the bed-chamber to king George the firft; and ferved in parliament for Cockermouth in the 2 G. 1. alfo in the 1ft and 2d parliaments of G. 2. He married Elizabeth-Lucy daughter of the honourable Harry Mordaunt brother to the late earl of Peterborough; by whom he left iffue Wilfrid, Mordaunt, Eliza-beth, and Charlotte. He died in 1737.

Wilfrid his fon and heir died two years after, without iffue.

I   He

He was succeeded by his brother *Mordaunt*, who also died without issue a few years after.

Whereupon, *Gilfrid Lawson* of Brayton esquire, son of *Wilfrid*, and grandson of the second Sir *Wilfrid* by his wife Jane Musgrave abovementioned, succeeded to the title and all the ancient estate; who died at Brayton in 1749.

He was succeeded by his brother Sir *Alfrid Lawson* baronet, who died in 1752; leaving issue,

Sir *Wilfrid Lawson* baronet, who was elected knight of the shire for Cumberland in 1761, and died in 1762 unmarried.

He was succeeded by his brother Sir *Gilfrid Lawson* baronet, the present owner of the family estate; who married Emelia daughter of John Lovett esquire, by whom he hath issue Wilfrid and Emelia.

The paternal arms of Lawson are; Parted per pale Argent and Sable, a cheveron counter-changed. The Crest: Two arms flexed, holding up the sun in his glory. Motto; Quod honestum, utile.

The parish of Isel is one entire manor, except *Redmain*; which was so called from the redness of the soil: for demesnes in former times were called *maines*. Redmain was granted by Waldeof the first baron of Allerdale to the monastery of Gisburn, and after the dissolution came to the Curwens of Camberton, who infranchised the tenants for 80 years purchase, mortgaged the demesne called the Trinities to Sir John Lowther, and afterwards sold it to Sir Wilfrid Lawson.

The tenants within the manor of Isel are customary, and pay arbitrary fines, and several boons and services, as plowing, mowing, shearing, harrowing, and the like.

Isel *bridge* being in decay in the years 1690 and 1691, was presented to the grand juries at the assizes for those years, and the presentments waved. Whereupon the lord chief justice Holt ordered that an information should be lodged in the king's bench against this county, which by rule of court was tried at Newcastle assizes before the lord chief baron Atkins, and a verdict given for the king against the county, whereby it was found to be a public bridge. Which suit, and the rebuilding the bridge, cost the county 500*l*. At this bridge there is an eel fishing, belonging to the house of Isel.

The *church* of Isel is dedicated to St. Michael. It was appropriated to the monastery of Hexham. The third Sir Wilfrid Lawson by his will gave to this church all the corn tithe within the hamlets of Blincrake, Sunderland, Isel Old Park, and Isell gate, in lieu of the tithes of Isell demesne. The vicarage is valued in the king's books at 8*l* 13*s* 9*d*. The present clear yearly value, including the aforesaid bequest, is about 60*l*.

In 1341, the prior and convent of Hexham presented one *William Burton* to the vacant vicarage of Isale.

In 1362, on the death of Sir *John Wanton* vicar of Isale, the forementioned prior and convent present Sir *John Baynard*, who is instituted thereupon.

In 1368, a licence is granted to *William de Ifale* chaplain, to officiate in a private oratory at Blencrayke, for the fervice of the lady Legh and William de Cofte and their family.

In 1385, on the death of Sir *John Baynard*, the vicarage of Ifale was given to Sir *John Mafon* by the bifhop of Carlifle, to whom the prior and convent of Hexham, under their common feal, had granted their power of prefentation for this turn.

In 1559, queen Elizabeth granted to *Thomas Leigh* efquire the rectory and church of Ifell, late parcel of the poffeffions of the late monaftery of Hexham, and all tithes to the faid rectory belonging, as alfo the advowfon and right of patronage of the vicarage of Ifell.

In 1575, on the deprivation of *William Adcock* vicar of Ifall, inftitution was given to Sir *Thomas Harrifon*, on the prefentation of Wilfrid Lawfon efquire and Maud (Redmain) his wife.

In 1577, on the refignation of Sir Thomas Harrifon, Sir *William Adcock* was reftored, being collated by the bifhop on lapfe.

In 1581, on the death of William Adcock, Sir *Leonard Cape* was prefented by Wilfrid Lawfon efquire.

In 1594, on the death of Leonard Cape, Sir *Anthony Wharton* was prefented by the fame patron.

In 1636, on Anthony Wharton's death, *Percival Head*, M. A. was prefented by William Lawfon of Ifall efquire.

In 1661, *Richard Fletcher* was prefented by Sir Wilfrid Lawfon knight.

In 1669, *George Starke*, by the fame patron.

In 1703, *Peter Farifh*, mafter of arts of Glafgow, prefented by Sir Wilfrid Lawfon baronet.

In 1711, *William Pool*, M. A. of Glafgow.

In 1719, *Thomas Leathes*, B. A.

In 1729, *John Kendal*, B. A. All thefe laft prefented by Sir Wilfrid Lawfon baronet.

There are in this parifh about 74 families; whereof, Quakers 2, Anabaptift 1, Prefbyterian 1.

PARISH OF BRIDEKIRK.

BRIDEKIRK, or the church of St. Bridget, is the next parifh to Ifel weftward, upon the north fide of Derwent; being bounded by the fame from the foot of Redmain Haggs to Ribton beck, where it falls into Derwent; and fo up that beck to the north fide of Broughton common, unto the field hedge of Tallentire; and along that hedge, until you come to Gilcrux field; and then pointing eaftward by the hedge that divides the Trinities from Bridekirk demefne, till you crofs Cockermouth road; and then down the hedge which divides Woodhall demefne from Redmain Haggs, till it reach to Derwent where it began.

It

It is a large parish, confisting of about 228 families, all proteftants. It confifts of feveral townfhips; the firft of which is that wherein the church ftands. It is a vicarage, valued in the king's books at 10l 13s 4d, certified to the governors of queen Anne's bounty at 33l; and· is now worth near 60l a year.

Waldieve firft lord of Allerdale gave Appleton and Bridekirk, with the patronage of the church of Bridekirk, to the prior and convent of Gifburn; which grant was confirmed to the faid priory by Alan fon of the faid Waldieve, and (by two feveral charters) by Alice de Romeley for the health of her foul, and of the fouls of her father and mother, and all her anceftors and fucceffors, and her hufbands Gilbert Pypard and Robert de Courtney †. And the fame were confirmed and appropriated to the faid priory by Ralph de Irton bifhop of Carlifle.

After the diffolution of the monafteries, king Hen. 8. by letters patent dated July 29, in the 35th year of his reign, granted to Henry Tolfon the manor of Bridekirk late belonging to the monaftery of Gifburn in the county of York, and a water mill and 12 meffuages and tenements in the faid parifh, and the wood called Bridekirk wood containing 25 acres, all late belonging to the faid monaftery; to be holden of the king in capite by the 20th part of one knight's fee, and the rent of 26s yearly.

And queen Mary, by letters patent July 24, in the 2d year of her reign, granted to George Catton and William Manne of London gentlemen (amongft other particulars) the advowfon and right of patronage of the vicarage of the parifh church of Bridekirk: To hold as of the manor of Eaft Greenwich by fealty only and not in capite, for all rents, fervices, and demands whatfoever.

And king James the firft, by letters patent June 18, in the 2d year of his reign, granted to Job Gillett and William Blake (inter alia) the tithe of corn and grain of Little Broughton, Great Broughton, and Papcaftle, in the parifh of Bridekirk, late in the tenure of Thomas lord Wharton or his affigns, and parcel of the poffeffions of the late monaftery of Gifburn: To hold to them and their heirs and affigns for ever of the king as of his manor of Eaft Greenwich in free focage and not in capite.

The firft incumbent that appears in the bifhop's regifters is Roger de Eboraco; who refigning in the year 1307, the prior and convent of Gifburn prefent Robert Urry one of their canons, who was inftituted thereupon.

In 1316, on Robert Urry's refignation, the prior and convent prefent another of their canons, Robert de Wilton, who is accordingly inftituted.

In 1320, Robert de Wilton refigns, and John de Thwenge (another canon of Gifburn) is prefented.

In 1359, it being fuggefted to the bifhop's commiffioners, at a vifitation, that the prior and convent of Gifburn held the vicarages of Bridekirk and Dereham to their own ufe againft common right; the faid prior and convent,

† Appendix, N° 11.

by

by their proctor, produced such grants from the papal see and from the bishop's predecessors, that they were discharged, and a certificate given them accordingly.

In 1361, several persons being accused of shedding blood in the church and churchyard of Bridekirk, were decreed to be excommunicated by the greater excommunication, and the several incumbents in all the churches of the deanry of Allerdale to publish the sentence against them on every Sunday and holiday at high mass, when the largest number of people should be gathered together, the bells ringing, the candles lighted and put out, and the cross erected.

In 1380, William, rector of Bowness, the bishop's vicar general, institutes *Peter de Derlyngton*, canon of Gisburn, presented upon the death of *William de Crathorn* the last vicar.

In 1553, *George Elletson* was presented to the vicarage of Bridekirk by queen Mary; and in the next year she sold the advowson (as aforesaid) to Catton and Manne. These, like many others, seem to have purchased for an advantage in parcelling out the particulars, and not long after we find this advowson in the Lamplughs, in which name and family it still continues.

In 1563, on the resignation of *Percival Wharton*, institution was given to *William Robinson*, being presented by Robert Lamplugh esquire.

In 1576, Francis Lamplugh of Dovenby esquire enters a caveat against any clerk being admitted on the death or resignation of William Robinson, alias Johnson, without his notice, he claiming the sole patronage. And in 1381, on the death of the said William Robinson, institution was given to *John Wheelwright* on the presentation of the said Francis Lamplugh.

In 1625, on the death of John Wheelwright, *Joseph Williamson* was instituted, having his presentation from Henry Baxter of Seburgham gentleman and Thomas Hutton of Hameshill yeoman, assignees of Sir Thomas Lamplugh knight.

In 1634, *Nicholas Beeby*, M. A. was instituted on the death of Joseph Williamson, presented by Anthony Lamplugh of Dovenby esquire.

In the time of Oliver Cromwell, we find *George Benson* minister of Bridekirk one of the associated ministers of the county of Cumberland.

In 1660, *Samuel Grasty* was instituted on a presentation by Peter Ward, M. D. and Elianor his wife, relict of Anthony Lamplugh.

In 1664, on Samuel Grasty's resignation, *Thomas Belman*, M. A. was presented by George Lamplugh gentleman, and Thomas Lamplugh esquire.

In 1680, on the death of Thomas Belman, *Richard Tickell* was presented by Richard Lamplugh esquire.

In 1685, on the cession of Richard Tickell, *David King*, M. A. was presented by the same patron.

In 1701, on Mr. King's death, *John Harrison* was presented by Robert Lamplugh gentleman.

In 1720, on John Harrison's death, another *John Harrison* was presented by Robert Lamplugh of Dovenby esquire.

I   In

In 1755, on the death of the last mentioned John Harrison, *John Bell,* M. A. was presented by the same patron.

The abovementioned Joseph Williamson, who was presented in 1625, was father of Sir Joseph Williamson secretary of state in the reign of king Charles the second. The young man, at his first setting out in the world, was entertained by Richard Tolson esquire representative in parliament for Cockermouth, in the time of the great rebellion, as his clerk or amanuensis. When at London with his master, rather than be idle and squander away his time amongst servants and livery boys, he begged that he would recommend him to Dr. Busby, that he might be admitted into Westminster school, and have his directions how he might proceed in grammatical and classical learning. Being a youth of a quick apprehension and unwearied diligence, he profited in the school to admiration. The reverend and learned Dr. Langbain, provost of Queen's college in Oxford, coming to the election at Westminster, the master recommends this northern youth to his favour, with desire that he would be pleased to take care of him and prefer him amongst his countrymen in that college. The provost, who was a great encourager of learning and ingenuity, after a strict examination of the boy, complies with the request, and takes him to Oxford, admits him of the foundation, and provides all necessaries for him at his own expence. As soon as he was bachelor of arts, his kind benefactor Dr. Langbain sends him into France, with a person of quality, as his companion and assistant in his studies. Upon his return to the college, he was elected fellow, and (as it is said) admitted into deacon's orders. Soon after the restoration of king Charles the second, he was recommended to the then secretary of state, who placed him in the paper office as Custos Archivorum, and made frequent use of him in interpreting and writing letters and memorials in French. Within a few years, he was advanced to the place of secretary of state, created doctor of laws at Oxford, and had the honour of knighthood conferred upon him. At the treaty of Nimeguen in 1679, he was one of the plenipotentiaries on the part of the king of Great Britain; and had the like character at the pacification concluded at Ryswick in 1696. In his life-time, and at his death, he gave to the said college in plate, books, building, and money, to the value of 8000 *l.* To the grandchildren of Dr. Langbain his patron he left by will 500 *l.* And he sent to this parish gilt bibles and prayer books, velvet covering and rich linen for the altar, with silver flagons and chalices for the administration of the holy communion.

In the church of Bridekirk there is an ancient font, which Camden says was found in the ruins of Papcastle, amongst many other monuments of antiquity; being a broad vessel of greenish stone, artificially ingraven with little images. Bishop Nicolson, in his miscellany account of the diocese of Carlisle, taken in his parochial visitation in 1703, says, " I took some pains in reviewing the " Runic inscription on the font in this church, some account whereof I " had long since given to Sir William Dugdale, published in the Philosophical " Transf-

"Transactions for the year 1685, N°. 178, and reprinted in Dr. Gibson's
"late edition of Camden's Britannia, p. 841. I found it in some little parti-
"culars different from what I had at first observed it to be."

Mr. *Smith*, in the Gentleman's Magazine for May 1749, describes the font
in this manner: "It stands in a square pedestal, about 8 inches high in the
"upright, and about 3 more in the perpendicular of the slope. This sup-
"ports another of about 20 inches, and over all this is the font, about
"20 inches more, pretty near a cube hollowed, being 22 inches on the south
"and north sides, and 20 on the other two. It faces the porch door, is lined
"with lead, and perforated at bottom to take off the baptismal water, and
"must be at least of 900 years standing. The front or south side engraving
"is between 3 fillets; the uppermost, I imagine, contains two *Ægoceri* or sea
"goats, the ancient representation of *Capricorn*, in whose sign the sun was at
"the birth of Christ, and probably alludes to that; the middle fillet has
"a festoon of grapes, and an human figure catching at a cluster, perhaps to
"intimate the mistery of the passion, or of the Eucharist, and the advantages
"accruing to the partaker. Betwixt that and the third fillet is the inscription;
"and below, a female figure, with a cup (as it seemeth) in her hand, and
"some festoons. The east side has only two fillets; the uppermost contains
"an *Amphisbæna*, or rather an hydra, with two heads, one bent down over its
"body to the ground; the other erect, with a branch proceeding from
"its mouth, which in its process divides into three. The second fillet has a
"tree, and Joseph and Mary (I suppose) with the child, as Joseph is called
"a fruitful branch. The north side confirms my conjecture on that of the
"south, where the two celestial signs of *Capricorn* and *Sagittary* are repre-
"sented. *Sagittary* is the concluding sign of the year, as *Capricorn* the initial
"one with regard to the solar return; intimating, that the religion which
"sprung from the person born when the sun was in *Capricorn*, would continue
"to the consummation of things, or till the sun had gone into *Sagittary*, their
"emblem for the last period. The fillet below on the same side, has an
"allusion to the slaughter of the babes at Bethlehem, and a devotee in
"a religious posture kneeling, and taking hold of the tree of life, notwith-
"standing the loss of her child, as the only means of her future acceptance
"and happiness. The west side is in the same taste, but the figures wasted
"by time."

Mr. Bell, the present learned and very worthy incumbent, observes, that
the figures in the second fillet on the east side, which Mr. Smith supposes
to be Joseph and Mary, seem evidently to be John baptizing our Saviour; for
there is the image of a dove whose wing is over the head of the person supposed to be baptized, who standeth in a sort of baptistery: but the head of
the dove is obliterated.

Mr. Bell hath also given us a very exact copy of the inscription, which
is thus:

ᚳᚱ ᛁᚢᚪᚱᛈ᛬ᚼᚼ᛬ᚣ᛬ᛁᚢᚱᛇᚣᛁ ᛬ ᛡᛏᚠᛈᛁ'
᛬ᚣᚪᚱᛥ᛬ᛉᚼᚱᛁᚱᚣ᛬ᛒᚱᚠᚣᛤ

Dr. Hickes, in, a letter to bifhop Nicolfon, fpeaking of this infeription, fays, it feems to be Dano-Saxonic, and by confequence neither good Danifh nor good Saxon; and after feveral attempts to explain it, he is forced to leave it in the dark. The moft probable interpretation of it is that of the faid learned prelate, who thinks it ought to be read. thus :

Er Ekard han men egroeften, and to dis men red wer Taner men brogten.

In Englifh,

Here Ekard was converted, and to this man's example were Danifh men brought.

He conjectures that Ekard was a Danifh general, who being baptized at this font, was the occafion of many of his officers and foldiers becoming Chriftians.

TALLENTIRE is the fecond townfhip in this parifh, ftanding half a mile northweft from Bridekirk, upon the ridge of a hill at leaft half a mile long at the weft end of Moothay; from whence one may fee in a clear day the whole Ifle of Man, and all Galloway, Annandale, and divers other counties in the fouth of Scotland, and all Solway Frith, with a great part of the Irifh fea.

This was firft granted by Waldeof fon of Gofpatric to Odard fon of Lyolph, whofe pofterity took the name of Tallentire. It was afterwards purchafed by George Fletcher efquire, fon of Lancelot, fon of Henry, fon of William Fletcher of Cockermouth; in which name it continued till that branch ended in daughters, and by Henry Fletcher efquire was given with his fecond daughter Anne in marriage to Matthias Partis a merchant at Newcaftle upon Tyne.

The tenants of this manor are all infranchifed.

DOVENBY, or *Dolphinby*, is the next townfhip, a mile weft and by fouth from Tallentire; and was at firft fo called from one *Dolphin* fon of Aleward, who firft feated himfelf here, and called the name of his houfe Dolphinby, corruptly Dovenby. *Richard de Dovenby* was lord thereof in Henry the fecond's time; and his fon *Benedict de Bridekirk* confirmed to the abbot of Caldre lands in Gilcrux.

The lord Waldeof gave to Dolphin fon of Aleward, with Maud his fifter, Applethwaite, Little Crofby, Langrigg, and Brigham, with the patronage of the church of Brigham. Aleward feated himfelf at Alewardby, calling it after his own name.

After the iffue male of Dolphin became extinguifhed in the reign of Hen. 3. one *Roger de Roll* was poffeffed of Dovenby. In the 3 Ed 1. *Thomas Lucy* enjoyed it. In the 23 Ed. 3. *Richard Kirkbride* had it and died feifed thereof, leaving his fon in ward; who died 22 Ri. 2. or 1 Hen. 4. leaving a fifter and

heir

heir married to a younger brother of Sir *Thomas Lamplugh* of Lamplugh; in whose issue male the right descended to Sir *Thomas Lamplugh*; who being married to Agnes daughter of Sir Thomas Brathwaite of Burnelhead, and having no issue of his body, made a settlement of this whole manor upon his said wife for life, remainder in tail male to his eight brothers succeffively, and for want of such issue to *George Lamplugh* son of *John* son of *Innocent* a bastard of that house. All the brothers happened to die without issue male; so that *George*, after the death of Agnes, entered. But a claim was made on the part of two daughters of *Anthony Lamplugh*, who (as pretended) had levied a fine and thereby cut off the intail. One of the daughters was compounded with. And *Abraham Moline* (the other daughter's representative) came to an agreement with *Thomas Lamplugh* son of *George*, whereby *Moline* had the demesne of Dovenby, and *Lamplugh* had the manor and rents of Dovenby and Papcaftle and the miln, which were by him mortgaged to Brown and Haftings two London scriveners, and by decree confirmed to them. The present owner thereof is *Ralph Cook* of Penrith esquire.

Moline sold the demesne to *Richard Lamplugh* esquire, who built Dovenby hall. He was succeeded by his son *Robert*, whose son *Richard* died in 1763, and after some specific legacies bequeathed the refidue of his real and personal estate to Henry Curwen esquire for the use of his niece Elizabeth Falconer.

There are in this townfhip an *hofpital* and *fchool*, founded by Sir Thomas Lamplugh of Dovenby in 1609.

The *hofpital* is for four widows, and is endowed with the tithes of Redmain in the parifh of Ifel.

The *fchool* is endowed with part of the tithes of Brough, and a clofe in Dovenby, and the schoolmaster hath also 4l a year out of the tithes of Redmain for reading prayers to the widows of the hofpital. His whole revenue is about 20l a year.

Both the hofpital and fchool are in the donation of the house of Dovenby.

PAPCASTLE ftands a mile fouth from Dovenby upon the banks of Derwent towards Cockermouth, where lies the carcafe (as it were) of an ancient caftle, which by a number of monuments layeth claim to be of Roman antiquity.

This caftle after the conquest was the feat of *Waldeof* first lord of Allerdale, who did afterwards demolifh it, and remove the materials to Cockermouth; of which materials he built the caftle there, wherein he and his posterity inhabited.

From him it came by his granddaughter *Octhreda* to *Duncan* brother of David king of Scotland. From that family it came by a daughter and coheir to the *Lucys*; of whom *Richard Lucy* settled the fame on his wife *Ada Morvil*, who marrying to her second husband *Thomas de Multon*, the fame defcended to *Thomas de Multon*, who had a daughter and heir *Margaret de Multon* married to *Ranulph de Dacre*, which brought the fame into the *Dacre* family, in which it continued till forfeited to the crown on the attainder of *Leonard Dacre* in the 12th year of queen Elizabeth.

Which

Which faid queen, by letters patent bearing date 17th March, in the 38th year of her reign, granted to *Lancelot Salkeld* and *Thomas Brathwaite* efquires and *Richard Tolfon* junior gentleman, all that manor of Papcafter with all its rights, members, and appurtenances; and all that tenement, and lands arable, meadow and pafture, containing by eftimation 34 acres, lying and being in Papcafter aforefaid, parcel of the faid manor, then or late in the tenure or occupation of John Williamfon or his affigns, of the yearly rent of 20s; and fo in like manner lands and tenements in the tenure or occupation of Richard Brumfield, William Thompfon, William Paitfon, John Watfon, Richard Parker, John Boranfkell, Richard Robinfon, Innocent Lamplugh, George Watfon, John Lamplugh, John Wilkinfon, Agnes Bromfield, William Towfon, Janet Rawes, Alan Ribton, Agnes Fearon, Chriftopher Wheelwright, and others, containing in the whole 36 tenements, 529 acres, and 16l 10s 5d rent.

Soon after, the faid manor appears to have been in the hands of Sir *Thomas Lamplugh* knight, who fettled it upon *Agnes* his wife for life (which *Agnes* was daughter of the faid Thomas Brathwaite, afterwards Sir Thomas Brathwaite, of Burnefhead); the faid Agnes lived to the age of 100 years, and after the death of her hufband (in refpect to his memory) remitted to the cuftomary tenants the payment of their general fines. And there being a controverfy after her death between the heirs general and the heirs in tail concerning the right to that inheritance, the tenants claimed to be exempt from the payment of a general fine, becaufe none had been paid within the memory of any one living, and the fame manor not long before had been in the crown, and as the king in law never dies, fo in that cafe no general fine can be due. But it appeared that all along in the time of the Dacres general fines had been paid; and it was determined againft the tenants.

BROUGHTON ftands a mile weft from Papcaftle, upon the fame fide of Derwent, juft oppofite to Brigham. It is a pleafant well built village, much like that of Papcaftle for fituation, facing the fouth fun from the fide of the hill which fhelters it from the north weft winds. This is another manor and townfhip within this parifh, which was granted by Waldeof firft lord of Allerdale with his fifter Octhreda to Waldeof fon of Gilmin, whofe pofterity had the furname de Broughton.

After the determination of that defcent, this place became the poffeffion of the earls of Northumberland, until Henry the fixth earl of Northumberland granted it, together with Dean, Whinfell, and Cockermouth parks, unto Sir Thomas Wharton; which were fold by the truftees of Philip late duke of Wharton to the duke of Somerfet, whofe reprefentative the earl of Egremont now enjoys the fame, together with Little Broughton, lying half a mile north weft: Which two townfhips make up one intire manor, wherein are no demefne lands, but divers fubftantial freeholders, and the cuftomary tenants pay only a ten-penny fine.

Jofeph Afhley of Ledgers Afhley in the county of Northampton efquire, in the year 1722, built a fchoolhoufe and four houfes for alms men or women in

VOL. II.   P   Great

Great Broughton ; and in 1735 he endowed the said school with one close called Schoolhouse close, and a rent charge of 16*l* a year issuing out of lands in Southwaite and other places ; the trustees to chuse a schoolmaster, who shall teach gratis the children of the inhabitants of Great and Little Broughton and of all the donor's kindred. The trustees also to nominate the four poor persons to reside in the houses out of the poor of Great and Little Broughton ; if not so many there, then out of any other vills in the parish of Bridekirk ; the kindred of the donor, however remote in degree, or wherever they dwell in the county, to have the preference : To have each 40*s* yearly, issuing out of the aforesaid lands. On the death of trustees, the survivors to chuse others ; persons of the name of Ashley to have the preference ; the rest to be chosen out of Great and Little Broughton, until they make up the number ten in the whole. Twenty shillings yearly to be paid out of the said lands for the expences of the trustees.

RIBTON is the sixth and last township in this parish of Bridekirk, which lies about a mile lower west from Broughton upon Derwent opposite to Clifton. This also, after the conquest, was part of the possession of *Waldeof* son of *Gilmin* ; who settled the same upon a younger son *Thomas* who took the surname *de Ribton*. He had three sons, *Alexander, William,* and *Dow* ; but *William* and *Dow* died without issue. *Thomas* had also two daughters *Magota* and *Ellota,* the latter of whom died unmarried. *Magota* was married to *Alan de Arcleby,* who had issue *John de Camerton,* who married Sir *Gilbert de Culwen's* daughter, who had issue Sir *Robert Clerke. Alexander* son of Thomas de Ribton had issue *John,* who married Matilda daughter to Benedict de Eglelfield lord of Clifton ; by whom he had issue *Thomas, Alexander,* and *Jane. Thomas* had issue *Johanna* and *Sibbot,* who were married into Wensleydale to *Thomas Lobley* and *Edward Cross : Alexander Ribton* the second brother had issue *Thomas,* who had issue *John,* who married the daughter of *Robert Heymore.*

In the 35 Hen. 8. *John Ribton* held the manor of Ribton with the appurtenances, and the vill of Ribton of the king as of his manor of Papcastre, by the service of 2*s* 8*d* cornage, 8*d* seawake, puture of the serjeants, and suit of court at Papcastre from three weeks to three weeks.

Afterwards it was purchased by *Thomas Lamplugh,* who being-born at Beverley in Yorkshire came into this country in the late civil wars, whose son *Richard Lamplugh* esquire sold the same to the late Sir *James Lowther* of Whitehaven, and it is now the possession of Sir *James Lowther* of Lowther baronet.

PARISH OF CAMMERTON.

NEXT unto Ribton, down the river a mile west, lies CAMMERTON, under an hill opposite to Stainburn. It is bounded by the river Derwent on the south, by the sea on the west, and by Flemby on the north and east.

This,

This, with *Seaton* another manor in this parish, was given by *Waldieve* first lord of Allerdale, to *Orme* son of *Ketel* with Gunild his sister, who dwelt at Seaton, and made it a manor, to which Cammerton is appendant. The ruins of which house, it is said, do yet appear.

Orme had issue a son and heir whom he named *Cospatric*, who had issue *Thomas*, who had issue another *Thomas*, to whose brother *Alan* he gave *Cammerton*, which was at first parcel of the manor of Seaton, and this *Alan* was first called *Alan de Cammerton*, and his posterity were afterwards called *Cammertons*, and then *Culwens*, from *Patric Culwen* son of Thomas and brother of the said *Alan*, who was lord of Culwen in Galloway, and by the death of Thomas was first called Culwen of Workington. *Alan* had issue *John*, who married *Isabel* daughter of *Gilbert de Culwen*, and by her had issue *Robert Clericus*, who was the first of the Cammerton branch that took the name of *Culwen*, corruptly *Curwen*, and from that time it hath continued in the male line of the *Curwens*.

The capital messuage here is an old ruinous tower, standing nakedly at the west end of the town, at the foot of Seaton hill. The demesne is good soil, lying warm and low by the river side, and very extensive.

The tenants pay arbitrary fines, and other usual services.

'SEATON is the other only township in this parish, standing a mile northwest, on the top of an hill; and is so called, because it stands close by the sea. This place continues in the male line of the Curwens of Workington, descendents of Orme, to this very day. The demesnes of Workington and Seaton being severed by Derwent river, were made more convenient one to the other by erecting a new stone bridge at Workington about an hundred years ago; and which failing was rebuilt some few years since at the expence to the county of 500 *l.*

The demesne is large, and that part which lies near the river very rich soil; whereas, contrariwise, that part which lies toward the sea is very sandy and barren, and so is the common which interposeth between the demesne and the sea, which yet hath its use, as containing a large coney warren.—Here was also formerly a very famous horse course, called the Sigget or Sea gate.—The customary tenants pay arbitrary fines, heriots, and other boons and services.

Gospatric son of Orme gave this CHURCH to the priory of Carlisle; but it was never appropriate, nor any vicar endowed; but the monastery enjoyed all the tithes according to the first original donation, some inferior members of the convent supplying the cure. Sir James Lowther is now the dean and chapter's lessee, under the yearly rent of 8 *l* 13 *s* 4 *d* to them, and 15 *l* to their curate, whom they nominate upon a vacancy.—It was returned to the governors of queen Anne's bounty at 15 *l* 10 *s.*

This parish contains about 100 families; whereof, Quakers 3, Presbyterians 15, Papists 4.

FLIMBY.

F L I M B Y.

FLEMBY, *Flemingby,* (fo called, no doubt, from fome of the *Flemings* inhabiting there) is the next village, lying a mile north from Seaton. It is bounded by the fea on the north weft, by Ewanrigg and Deerham common on the
north and eaft fides, and by Cammerton and Seaton on the fouth and weft.
It hath been commonly efteemed extraparochial, but it evidently appears to.
have been anciently a chapelry within the parifh of Cammerton ; and to this.
day they bury their dead at the church of Cammerton.

It was part of the poffeffions of Orme fon of Ketel, whofe fon Gofpatric
gave it to the abbey of Holm Cultram, as appears from the grant in the
original regifter of the faid abbey ; whereby Gofpatric fon of Orme, with the
confent of Thomas his fon and heir and of Alan his fon, grants to God and
St. Mary of Holm Cultram and the monks ferving God there, Flemingby
with the appurtenances, by the boundaries there fpecified ; with a claufe, that
he himfelf will do for the fame foreign fervice, as noutegeld and the like due
to the king ; and alfo fervices to the lord of Allerdale of feawake, caftleward,.
pleas, aids, and other fervices †.

And the fame was confirmed by the faid Thomas fon of Gofpatric § ; who
alfo granted to them (with the confent of Grace his wife) eight acres of land
in Seton, contiguous to 32 acres of their own there ‡.

And Adam, another fon of Gofpatric, who was alfo parfon of the church
of Cammerton, granted and quit claimed to them the chapel of Flemingby,
and all the lands and tithes thereof which belonged to the mother church
of Cammerton *.

And Gofpatric's grant was confirmed feverally by king John, king Henry
the third, and Richard the firft.

Alice de Romeley, daughter of William Fitz Duncan, granted to them
common of pafture on Brechton moor for the cattle of their grange of
Flemingby ‖.

And king Edward the firft granted to them free warren in their demefne of
Flemingby **.

In the 7 Ed. 1. Before the juftices itinerant in Cumberland, Robert de
Haverington, fon of Michael de Haverington, quitted claim to Gervafe abbot
of St. Mary of Holm Coltram of the manor of Flemingby ; except 380 acres;
and the abbot and convent took him and his heirs into their prayers ††.

After the diffolution of the monafteries, king Henry the eighth, 9 Jul. in
the 37th year of his reign, granted to Thomas Dalfton efquire and Eleanor
his wife (amongft other particulars) nine meffuages and tenements in Flemby,
and all other the lands there called Lambert Garths, Thwaite croft, and
Reygarths, a fifhery in Flemby, and the wood and lands called Flemby park,
late belonging to the monaftery of Holm Coltram.

† Appendix, Nᵒ·12.   § 3 Dugd. Mon. 36.   ‡ Regiftr. Holme.   * Regiftr.
Holme.   ‖ Regiftr. Holme.   ** Regiftr. Holme.   †† Appendix, Nᵒ. 13.

And

And in the 38 Hen. 8. June 11, there is a licence to Thomas Dalfton of Carlifle efquire and Eleanor his wife to alienate the faid nine meffuages and tenements, and the faid fifhery and park, and alfo twenty other meffuages and tenements elfewhere, to John Blenerhaffet efquire and his heirs, for the fine of 14 s. 1 d paid into the exchequer; and from that time Flimby hall became the chief refidence of the family, until it was now lately (1772) fold by William Blenerhaffet efquire to Sir James Lowther baronet.

This family feems to have fprung from Blenerhaffet in this county; but for many generations they feem to-have lived in or near Carlifle. One of the name was mayor of that city in 1382, fo likewife in 1430, and again in 1614, and 1620. One of them reprefented the faid city in parliament in the 9 Ric. 2. fo alfo in the 1 Hen. 5. 20 Hen. 6. 27 and 28 Eliz. and 1 Ja. In the 29 Cha. 2. William Blenerhaffet efquire was fheriff of the county. Their arms are, Gules, a cheveron between 3 dolphins naiant, embowed proper.

The chapel of Flimby hath an ancient falary of 4 l 10 s. And hath thrice received from the governors of queen Anne's bounty an augmention of 200 l by lot; wherewith lands were purchafed in the county of Lancafter, of the prefent yearly value of 18 l.

The chapelry contains about 65 families; whereof, Prefbyterians 11, Quaker 1, Papift 1.

PARISH OF DEERHAM.

THE firft townfhip in this parifh is ELNEBURGH, ftanding a mile eaft from *Flimby*: for now we turn eaftward from the mouth of Elne river to the head thereof, taking in the parifhes and townfhips as they lie on the fouth weft of that river. Camden, by the way, takes notice of a wall that was made in convenient places from Workington to Elneburg for four miles, by Stilico a commander in the Roman ftate, when the Scots annoyed the coafts out of Ireland, as appears in Claudian; and he further tells us, that it was at this Burgh upon Elne, where the firft band of the Dalmatians with their captain made their abode. Camden and Baxter both think this was the ancient *Volantium*; others call it *Olenacum*; but Horfley takes it to be *Virofidum*, and fays, there is no one Roman ftation in Britain, where fo great a number of infcriptions has been found as at this place; and moft of the originals are yet preferved at Elneburgh hall, the feat of Humphrey Senhoufe efquire, proprietor of the ground on which the ftation has been, being the defcendent of John Senhoufe efquire, whom Camden commends for his great civility to him and to Sir Robert Cotton, for his fkill in antiquity, and for the great care with which he preferved fuch curiofities. The foldiers that feem to have been in garrifon here, are the *Cohors prima Hifpanorum, Cohors prima Dalmatarum,* and the *Cohors prima Baetafiorum.*

The infcriptions that have been found here are as follows:

L

I.

Upon an altar:

I O M
L CAMMI
VS MAXI
PREFEC
I. HIS. EQ
V. S. L. M

i. e. Jovi optimo maximo Lucius Cammius Maximus, præfectus [cohortis] primæ Hifpanorum equitum, votum folvit libens merito. Importing, that Cammius Maximus, prefect of the firft cohort of Spanifh horfe, erected this altar to Jupiter.

II.

Upon another altar:

I. O. M
COH I HIS
CVI PRAE
M. MAENI
VS AGRIP
TRIBV
POS

Jovi optimo maximo cohors prima Hifpanorum, cui praeeft Marcus Maenius Agrippa tribunus pofuit.

III.

On another:

IOVI AVG
M CENSORIVS
M. FIL VOLTINIA
CORNELIANVS Ↄ LEG
X FRETENSI PRAE
FECTVS COH I
HISP EX PROVINCIA
NARBONE DOMO
NEMA V SOL L M

Jovi Augufto Marcus Cenforius Marci filius Voltinia [tribu] Cornelianus centurio legionis decimæ Fretenfis præfectus cohortis primæ Hifpanorum ex provincia Narbonenfi domo Nemaucenfi votum folvit libens merito.

IV.

PRO SALVTE
ANTONINI AVG PII F
PAVLVS P F PALATINA
POSTVMIVS ACILIANVS

9   PRAEF

PRAEF COH I DELMATAR

Pro falute Antonini Augufti pii felicis, Paulus Pauli filius Palatina [tribu]
Poftumius Acilianus præfectus cohortis primæ Delmatarum.

V.

DIS DEABVSQ
P POSTVMIVS
ACILIANVS
PRAEF
COH I DELM

Diis Deabufque Paulus Poftumius Acilianus præfectus cohortis primæ
Delmatarum.

VI.

MARTI MILITARI
COH I BAETASI
ORVM CVI PRAEEST IVLI
VS TVTOR PRAE
FECTVS
V S L L M

Marti militari cohors prima Baetafiorum, cui præeft Julius Tutor præfectus, votum folvit libentiffime merito.

VII.

I O M
C CABAL
PRISCVS
TRIBVNVS

Jovi optimo maximo Caius Caballus Prifcus tribunus.

VIII.

The next infcription, Mr. Horfley fays, is on the fineft and moft curious
Roman altar that ever was difcovered in Britain. It was found at this
ftation, and removed from Elneburgh hall to Sir James Lowther's feat at
Whitehaven.

GENIO LOCI
FORTVNÆ RED
ROMÆ ÆTERNÆ
ET FATO BONO
G CORNELIVS
PEREGRINVS
TRIB COHORT
EX PROVINC
MAVR CÆSA
DOMOS ET ÆD
DECVR - - - - -

Genio

Genio loci, Fortunæ reduci, Romæ æternæ, et fato bono, Gaius Cornelius Peregrinus, tribunus cohortis ex provincia Mauritaniæ Cæfarienfis, domos et ædem decurionum [reftituit].

On the back of the altar are the words

VOLANTI VIVAS.

IX.

The next is an infcription to the local goddefs *Setlocenia :*

DEAE
SETLO
CENIÆ
L ABAR
EVS C
V S L M

Deæ Setloceniæ Lucius Abareus centurio votum folvit libens merito.

X.

The next infcription is in a *Corona,* fupported by two victories :

VICTORIÆ
AVGG
D D
N N

Victoriæ Auguftorum dominorum noftrorum.

Befides thefe, there were formerly feveral fepulchral ftones here, but only one remains at prefent, whereon is this infcription,

D M
IVL MARTIM
A VIX AN
XII III D XXII

Dis Manibus. Julia Martima vixit annos duodecim, menfes tres, dies viginti-duos †.

At the diftance of 63 paces fouthweft from the agger of the outer fofs of the camp or ftation here, an artificial mount hath been raifed, the circumference whereof at the verge is about 250 feet, the height 42 feet, the perpendicular height 14 feet. There is a tradition amongft the neighbouring people that a king was buried here, and it has gone by the name of the King's burying-place. The late Humphrey Senhoufe efquire, about the year 1742, caufed a cut ten feet wide to be made into it as far as the center, but no urns, bones, or other matter appeared whereby to difcover for what purpofe it was raifed.—It feems indeed to have been ancienter than the Roman times, the Britons before the coming of the Romans having made ufe of fuch places for fepulture.

† Horfley, 279—285.

A little

A little fouth-weft from *Elneburg* ftands EWANRIGG or *Unerigg*, an old houfe built caftle-wife.   This place was fo called at firft from one *Ewan* who was a Scotch king or chieftain; and after the conqueft there was a family who took their name from thence; as Robert de Ewanrigg appears to have been witnefs to feveral deeds.   In the 42 Ed. 3. the lady Margaret de Multon feems to have been in poffeffion of this place; for in that year a licence was granted by the bifhop to John de Thwaytes to be domeftic chaplain to her in any convenient oratory within the manor of Unerigg.   The Thwaitefes afterwards became owners thereof, from whom it came to the Chriftians, and it is now the property of John Chriftian efquire, who fucceeded his brother Ewan, fon of John, fon of Ewan, whofe father and feveral other of his anceftors had been deem-fters or judges fucceffively in the Ifle of Man.

DEERHAM town and church ftand a mile or more fouth from *Ewanrigg*; one moiety of which town and manor was given by Alan fecond lord of Al-lerdale to Simon Sheftlings, and the other moiety to Dolphin fon of Gofpatric. Sheftlings's pofterity from hence took the name *de Dereham*; from whom it went with a daughter and heir to the family of *Barwis*; the laft of whom, *Richard Barwis* of Iflekirk efquire, had a fifter and heir married to *Lamplugh*, whofe fon *Richard Lamplugh* efquire fold the fame to Sir *James Lowther* of Whitehaven baronet, in which name and family it ftill continues.

The other moiety came to the *Multons*, and was given by *Thomas de Multon* in the reign of king Henry the third to the abbey of *Caldre*; and after the diffolution of the monafteries, queen Elizabeth by letters patent bearing date the twenty-third day of June in the fixth year of her reign granted to Thomas Lyfford and John Lyfford (*inter alia*) twenty-one tenements and two cottages in Dereham in the tenure of fo many different perfons, and alfo the water-mill there, late parcel of the poffeffions of the priory of Caldre; and alfo all houfes, lands, woods, rents, reverfions, fervices, court leet, view of frankpledge, fines, amerciaments, free warren, and all other jurifdictions, liberties, privileges, profits, and hereditaments whatfoever, in Dereham afore-faid: And this moiety foon after feems to have been conveyed to the tenants in feveralty.

The cuftomary tenants of the other moiety pay a four-penny fine certain, according to a compofition made with Richard Barwis efquire in 1633.

Alice de Rumely, daughter of William Fitz Duncan, in her widowhood granted the *church* of Dereham to God and the church of St. Mary of Gife-burne and the canons ferving God there, for the health of her foul and the fouls of her father and mother and all her anceftors and fucceffors and her hufbands Gilbert Pypard and Robert de Courtenay*.   Which grant was con-firmed by Hugh bifhop of Carlifle.

In the year 1354, the bifhop being informed that *John* vicar of Derham was grown fo old and infirm, that he was no longer able to fupply his cure, orders

* 3 Dugd. Mon. 46.

his official to inquire further into the truth of that report, and to give him an account what curate or affiftant would be moft acceptable to the old man. And in the fame year *John de Gilcrouce* refigns his living, and Sir *John de Derham* prieft was inftituted on a prefentation by the prior and convent of Gifeburn.

In 1360, on a fuggeftion that the prior and convent of Gyfeburn took the profits of the two churches of Derham and Bridekirk to their own ufe againft common right, a commiffion of inquiry was iffued by the bifhop; and the report made thereupon was, that the faid prior and convent had been in pof- feffion thereof time out of mind: fo that their title was confirmed by the bifhop.

In 1365, upon the refignation of John de Derham, the faid prior and con- vent prefent Sir *William de Hayton* chaplain, who is inftituted thereupon.

In 1368, licence was granted as aforefaid to Sir John de Thwaytes chap- lain, to fay private mafs to the family of the lady Margaret de Multon, in any convenient oratory within the manor of Unerigg; provided it be done *fubmiffa cum voce*, and without prejudice to the mother church, and upon none of the great holidays in the grant fpecified.

After the diffolution of the monafteries, queen Mary granted this advowfon to the bifhop of the diocefe; but before the diffolution the prior and con ent had granted the next avoidance of this church to two Yorkfhire gentlemen, who accordingly in the year 1563, on the death of Sir *Robert Udall* vicar of Derham, prefent Sir *Thomas Watfon* clerk, who was inftituted thereupon.

In 1573, on deprivation of the faid Thomas Watfon (for not fubfcribing the 39 articles, as it feemeth) Sir *Henry Symfon* clerk was collated by bifhop Barnes.

In 1577, on Thomas Watfon's removal to Holm Cultram, the fame bifhop collated Sir *William Troughere* clerk: who dying in the year following, Sir *Ed- ward Dykes* was collated.

In 1593, inftitution was given into the then vacant vicarage of Dereham to Sir *Henry Adcock* clerk, prefented by queen Elizabeth: Upon what occafion doth not appear. And after this, *Edward Dykes* appears to have been vicar. For he refigned the vicarage in 1600, and thereupon bifhop Robinfon collated Sir *John Bowman.*

In 1623, on the death of *Michael Hurd* vicar of Dereham, *William Harrifen* clerk was collated.

In 1686, on the death of *Mufgrave Sleddale* vicar of Deerham, *Richard Mur- thwaite* was collated by bifhop Smith.

In 1701, Richard Murthwaite refigns, and *Peter Murthwaite* was collated by the fame patron.

In 1736, on Peter Murthwaite's death, *Jofeph Ritfon* was collated by bifhop Fleming.

In 1737' on the ceffion of Jofeph Ritfon, *Anthony Sharp* was collated by the fame patron.

In Henry the eighth's Valor this vicarage is eftimated at 4*l* 13*s* 4*d*, and was certified to the governors of queen Anne's bounty at 15*l* 11*s* 9*d*. It hath fince received an augmentation of 200*l* from the faid governors, in conjunc-

tion

tion with 200 *l* given by the countefs dowager Gower, wherewith lands were purchafed in Furnefs Fells, of the prefent yearly value of 12 *l*.

In one of the windows of the church there is an infcription, which the learned antiquary Mr. Pegge reads thus: " Geofry Goding repair edthefe win-" dows in the year 1150 †."

The vicarage houfe is very fmall, being about eight yards in length, and low in proportion; and there is no other building belonging to it. Mr. Mur-thwaite, one of the poor vicars, erected it, and put over the parlour chimney,

Fecit quod potuit.

There are in this parifh about 126 families; of which, prefbyterians 2, quaker 1, anabaptift 1.

In the year 1715, Ewan Chriftian of Unerigg efquire gave to a *fchool* at this place a rent charge of 9 *l* 18 *s* 5 *d*, iffuing out of lands in the townfhip of Flimby.

PARISH OF GILCRUCE.

GILCRUCE, or *Gilcrux*, lies next unto Deerham, three miles eaft from the river, on the height of an hill on the north fide of Moothay. This little pa-rifh and manor was given by Waldeof firft Lord of Allerdale to Adam fon of Lyulph, from which Adam it defcended to a daughter and heir married to Bonekill, who granted the fame to a younger brother Robert Bonekill, whofe fons Thomas and Walter gave it to the abbey of Caldre, which Sir Ranulph Bonekill knight confirmed: But upon the appropriation, the patronage of the vicarage was referved to the bifhop.

After the diffolution, king Philip and queen Mary by letters patent dated March 18, in the 4th and 5th years of their reign granted to Alexander Armftrong gentleman, all thofe 24 meffuages and tenements and water miln with the appurtenances, lying and being in the town of Gilcrux in the county of Cumberland, in the feveral tenure of divers tenants there at the will of the lord, late parcel of the poffeffions of the late monaftery or priory of Caldre; with a free rent there of 22d, and other rents and profits of the yearly value of 14 *l* 15 *s* 10 *d*: To hold to the faid Alexander, and the heirs male of his body lawfully begotten, on condition of finding and maintaining five horfe-men ready and well furnifhed, whenfoever the king and queen and the fucceffors of the faid queen fhall fummon them within the faid county.

In the 7 Eliz. Alexander Armftrong and Herbert Armftrong conveyed by fine to William Armftrong fon of the faid Herbert and Katherine Dalfton and the heirs of the faid William, the manor of Gilcroufe with the appurtenances, and all the meffuages, lands, tenements, woods, underwoods, profits, emo-luments and hereditaments whatfoever, in the town and fields of Gilcroufe, holden of the king *in capite*.

† Gent. Mag. vol. xxi. p. 254.

In

In the 17 Eliz. 22 June, there is a grant by the said queen to John Soukey and Parcival Gunson gentlemen, their heirs and assigns, amongst other particulars, of the grange and vill of Gilcroufe, and all the messuages, lands, tenements, water mill, rents, reversions, and services, with the appurtenances, in Gilcroufe aforefaid, late in the tenure of William Armstrong, parcel of the possessions of the late monastery or priory of Caldre: To hold as of the manor of East Greenwich, by fealty only, in free and common socage, and not *in capite* nor by knight's service.

The custom of this manor gave rise to a case in queen Elizabeth's time, in a cause in chancery, wherein Dawson and other tenants of the said manor were plaintiffs, and Armstrong (lord of the said manor) and Dykes were defendants. Which was as follows : Whereas upon hearing of counsel for the plaintiffs and defendants in the said court, 18 May, 38 Eliz. touching the custom pretended by the said Armstrong, that upon every change of a lord (although the change grew by his own act, and that daily) the plaintiffs should pay arbitrable fines at the lord's will, the lord keeper conceived in his own opinion, that the said pretended custom was unreasonable and against law. And therefore it was ordered that a case should be made, and the judges opinions had for the law touching that pretended custom. And whereas by another order of the 2d of June, 39 Eliz. it appeared that her majesty's attorney general had drawn a case upon the said pretended custom, which the lord keeper having subscribed, the said case was by his lordship referred to the consideration of the lord chief justice Popham, who on conference with Anderson, Periam, Walmesley, and all the judges of Serjeant's Inn, made his report, that he himself and the rest of the said judges were of opinion, that the custom upon alienation or death of the tenant, or upon death of the lord, might stand with reason ; but the custom to take fines upon every alienation of the lord they thought unreasonable and unlawful.—Note, This is the same case with that quoted in the margin of Coke's 1 Inst. p. 59. b. though the names of the manor and county are there mistaken or misprinted.

The said family of Dykes are still lords of the manor : only the vicar has about six tenants, who pay 12 s rent, and a two-penny fine upon death or alienation.

In 1334, Sir *John Lestofon* of Penreth, priest, was collated to this vicarage by bishop Kirkby.

In 1368, bishop Strickland set out and appointed an endowment for the vicar as followeth : That the vicar shall have the mansion house opposite to the church, with the lands arable, meadow, and pasture in the fields of Gilcrux, half of the tithe hay, and all the tithes of wool, lamb, milk, mills, fishings, and oblations, with the whole altarage and other profits, except only the corn tithes ; and that the abbot and convent of Caldre shall pay moreover to the vicar four marks yearly. The vicar to bear all charges ordinary and extraordinary, except the repair of the chancel *.

* Registr. Strickland.

                                                                    In

In 1371, Sir *William de Kirkeby*, vicar of Gilcrouce, exchanged his vicarage with Sir *Richard de Irland*, for the chantry of Hoton in the Foreſt.

In 1377, the biſhop cquaints the dean (rural) of Allerdale, with a complaint from the pariſhioners of Gilcrouce, that their vicar Sir *Richard de Irland*, notwithſtanding his oath of reſidence, did not reſide on his cure; and requires the dean to admoniſh him to take better care of his duty.

In 1385, Sir *Adam Fonward*, vicar of Gilcrouce, exchanges his living with Sir *Robert de Pomfret* vicar of Aſpatryke,

In 1565, on the death of Sir *William Milner* vicar of Gilcrouce, Sir *Thomas Trowghere* clerk was collated by biſhop Beſt.

In 1589, on the death of Thomas Trowghere, Sir *Thomas Dover* clerk was collated by biſhop Meye.

In 1611, on the reſignation of *Nicholas Banks* the late incumbent, *Edward Cooke*, M. A. was collated by biſhop Robinſon.

In 1612, on the removal of Mr. Cooke to Brigham, *Richard Wilkinſon* was collated, who continued vicar there till after the reſtoration of king Charles the ſecond.

In 1664, Richard Wilkinſon was ſucceeded by *Peter Murthwaite*.

In 1675, *Richard Murthwaite* was collated on the death of his father Peter.

In 1704, *Peter Murthwaite*, ſon of Richard, ſucceeded his father; who had formerly reſigned the vicarage of Deerham in his favour.

In 1736, on the death of Peter Murthwaite, *Thomas Hobſon* was collated by biſhop Fleming.

In 1762, on the death of *William Walker* vicar of Gilcrux, *Anthony Sharp* vicar of Deerham was collated by biſhop Lyttelton.

This vicarage is valued in the king's books at 5 *l* 14 *s* 2 *d*, and was certified to the governors of queen Anne's bounty at 22 *l* 16 *s* 4 *d*.

There are only about 31 families in the whole pariſh; all of the eſtabliſhed church.

PARISH OF PLUMLAND.

THE pariſh of PLUMLAND lies eaſt from *Gilcrux*, and is bounded by Gilcrux beck on the weſt, by the river Elne on the north, by Threapland gill on the eaſt, and from the head of Threapland gill along the horſe courſe to the top of Moothay on the ſouth.

The firſt townſhip or manor in this pariſh is WARDHOLE, corruptly *Wardale* or *Warthole*, being the place where *watch* and *ward* uſed to be kept in former times when the Scots made their inroads into Cumberland, from whence the watchmen gave warning to them who attended at the beacon on Moothay to fire the ſame. It is a ſmall manor, but hath a large demeſne, and belonged formerly to the abbey of Caldre, and is now the property of the family of Dykes, who came at firſt from Dykesfield in Burgh barony, from whence they took their name.

ARCLEBY

ARCLEBY is another place in this parish, which gave name to an ancient family, as appears in many old deeds, in several of which Hugh de Arcleby and John de Arcleby are named as witnesses. But the Martindales of Newton marrying the inheritrix, it continued in that family until Roger Martindale forfeited the same by treason as is aforesaid. Whereupon queen Elizabeth granted it to Sir John Penruddock, father of Robert, whose son Sir John Penruddock was beheaded at Salisbury by the commonwealth party together with Colonel Grove in 1652. It was afterwards sold to Gustavus Thompson, M. A. then rector of the said parish, whose son Gustavus Thompson esquire built a good house there, and settled the same upon his wife who now enjoys it.

There is another little manor within this parish called PARSONBY, or the Parson's town ; which is holden of the rector for the time being : and consists of about ten tenants, who pay 3 *l* yearly rent at Whitsuntide and Martinmas by equal portions, a twenty penny fine upon change of tenant by death or aliena-tion, and each one boon day reaping.

PLUMLAND town was heretofore a manor of the Orfeurs, an ancient family in this county, who held the same for several generations ; the first of whom that we meet with was,

1. *Thomas Orfeur* esquire who lived in the reign of king Ed. 2.

2. *John Orfeur*, his son and heir, had issue,

3. *William Orfeur* ; who had issue,

4. *Robert* ; who had issue,

5. *Richard* ; who married Margery daughter and heir of Robert Birkby esquire.

6. *Richard Orfeur* his son married Margaret daughter of Sir John Lam-plugh of Lamplugh knight.

7. *Richard* his son married Elizabeth daughter of Richard Lowther of Crookdake esquire.

8. *Richard* his son married Alice daughter and heir of Thomas Colvil of Hayton Castle.

9. *Richard* his son married Jane daughter of Thomas Dykes of War-thole esquire ; and to his second wife he married Margaret daughter of John Swinburne of Hughthwaite, by whom he had issue,

10. *William*, who married Anne daughter of Robert Lamplough of Do-venby esquire. He was sheriff of Cumberland in the 44 Eliz. His arms were ; Sable, a cross argent, on a canton Argent a mullet Gules.

11. *William* his son married Mabel daughter of William Asmonderly esquire.

12. *William* his son married Bridget daughter of John Musgrave of Plumpton esquire.

13. *William* his son married Elizabeth daughter of Sir Charles Howard knight, and by her had issue,

14. *Charles*

14. *Charles Orfeur* efquire; who had iffue,

15. *William Orfeur* efquire, who married Jane daughter of Richard Lamplugh efquire and widow of John Senhoufe of Netherhall efquire, and by her had iffue Anne, Bridget, Catherine, Margaret, and Eleanor. He fold this manor to Sir Wilfrid Lawfon of Ifel baronet, whofe granddaughter and heir general now (1773) enjoys it.

The tenants of this manor are all cuftomary, and pay arbitrary fines, heriots, and ufual boons and fervices to the capital meffuage at High Clofe. The ancient demefne belonging to this manor is called the Mains, and lies lower eaftward towards Elne.

The *church* ftands near the middle of the parifh, upon an afcent. It is rectorial, and valued in the king's books at 20*l* 14*s* 9¼*d*. It hath glebe-land to the amount of about 72 acres, and the whole revenue is now of the value of 140 or 150*l per annum*.

It is dedicated to St. Cuthbert, and now in the patronage of the duke of Portland, who purchafed the fame of Adam Afkew efquire phyfician at Newcaftle upon Tyne, who purchafed from the heirs general of the late Sir Wilfrid Lawfon of Ifel, who had it from the Thompfons, and they from the Porters.

In the year 1310, on the death of Sir *Walter de Aencourt* rector of Plumland, Mr. *Peter de Aencourt* was prefented by Robert de Gofeford, who claimed the right of patronage for that turn as next of kindred to Ralph de Aencourt (fon of Ralph) the infant proprietor of the lands of Appilthwait to which the advowfon of this rectory was appendant. Thefe fuggeftions, by commiffioners and an inqueft *de jure patronatus*, are found to be true, and Peter de Aencourt was thereupon inftituted and inducted. Soon after, Robert de Waddlehoufe brought another prefentation from the king. But on a fecond commiffion it appeared that the faid Peter was lawful incumbent, and that the late Ralph de Aencourt deceafed never held any lands of the king *in capite*.

In 1358, *Adam de Baffenthwait* was rector, who gave by his will half a mark towards repairing the church, and delineating the picture of St. Cuthbert.

In 1562, on the death of Sir *William Potter* clerk, rector of Plumland, Mr. *Lancelot Walles* was inftituted, upon the prefentation of Thomas Porter of Alwarby gentleman.

In 1568, by permiffion of Mr. Henry Dethick chancellor of the diocefe, a caveat was entered for Richard Porter of Long Sleddale in the county of Weftmorland gentleman, who claimed the right of prefentation upon the death of Mr. Walles the late rector. But afterwards Sir *William Richarbie* clerk was inftituted, being prefented by George Porter fon of George Porter late of Bolton gentleman deceafed.

In 1628, inftitution was given to Mr. *Lancelot Fletcher*, prefented by Jofeph Porter of Bridekirk efquire, notwithftanding a caveat entered by Richard Skelton gentleman : This Mr. Fletcher was living in 1643, being in that year a contributor (amongft many others) towards procuring provifions for the garrifon of Carlifle.

The

The next incumbent was *Joseph Nicolson*, who was ejected by Cromwell's commissioners, and during the usurpation lived retired at his maternal inheritance at Park Brow in the parish of Stanwix, and on the coming in of king Charles the second was restored. He was father of Dr. William Nicolson bishop of Carlisle, who on a blue marble stone within the rails of the communion table in the chancel of Plumland church caused the following monumental inscription to be ingraved:

" *H. P. S.*
" *Deposita Josephi Nicolson Rectoris hujus Ecclesiæ; et Mariæ Uxoris ejus, Filiæ*
" *Johannis Brisco de Crofton armigeri. Obiit ille A. D. 1686. illa 1689. Paren-*
" *tibus religiosissimis P. Guil. Carliol. Episc.*"

In 1686, *Michael Robinson* was presented by Richard Thompson esquire.
In 1702, *Gustavus Thompson* was presented by the same patron.
In 1711, *Peter Farish* by the same patron.
In 1728, *Thomas Leathes* was presented by Sir Wilfrid Lawson baronet.
In 1760, *Adam Askew*, presented by his father Adam Askew esquire.

This whole parish, consisting of the several manors abovementioned, contains only about 39 families in the whole; of which, presbyterians 3, quaker 1.

PARISH OF TORPENHOW.

THE next parish is that of TORPENHOW; which is bounded by Threapland gill on the west from the head thereof till it cometh to the river Elne, and so up Elne until Snittlegarth beck falls into it below Torpenhow park, then up that beck to the head thereof near High Ireby, then up to the top of Binfel fell, and so down by a spring that falls into Colebeck near Burthwait, then up Colebeck to the head thereof at Stone Cowen, then across Stone Cowen westward unto Threapland gill at the north corner of Sunderland Outpasture wall.

The first hamlet in this parish is THREAPLAND *(contentionis terra)* which adjoins unto Plumland eastward. It was given by Alan second lord of Allerdale to his steward Ketel; from whose descendents it came in Edward the first's time to Michael de Harclay father of Andrew earl of Carlisle. This Michael de Harcla granted it to William de Mulcaster in the reign of Edward the second; whose brothers Thomas and John de Mulcaster held it successively; and the latter granted it by fine to Sir Henry Malton knight and Margaret his wife in Edward the third's time, whose daughter and coheir being married to Thomas Skelton a younger brother of the Skeltons of Armathwaite, it was sold by Lancelot Skelton esquire unto Lancelor Salkeld of Whitehall esquire, who gave it to his brother John, whose great grandson Roger Salkeld sold the same to Roger Gregg of Mirehouse gentleman, whose son Joseph left two sons, but they both dying young it descended to Roger Gregg's two daughters,
the

the elder of whom was married to Mr. John Story the prefent vicar of Dalfton who hath iffue one fon, the other was married to Mr. Roger Williamfon of Snittlegarth and died with iffue.—The cuftomary tenants pay arbitrary fines, and other boons and fervices.

BLENERHASSET is the next townfhip within this parifh, a mile eaft from Threapland, and ftands upon the river Elne. This was parcel of Allerdale, which Alan the fecond lord thereof gave to Ranulph de Lindfey with his fifter Octhreda. From them the inheritance came to the Mulcaftres. In the reign of king Henry the third Robert de Mulcaftre held the fame. After him, William his fon; who had iffue Walter; who had iffue William; whofe fon Robert transferred this part of the Mulcaftre's patrimony, by a daughter and coheir to the Tilliols, viz. Hayton, Torpenhow, and Blenerhaffet.

This family of Tilliol was very ancient in this county, and ended at laft, as many of the reft have done, in female heirs. The firft that we meet with was,

1. *Richard* the rider, who lived in the reign of king Henry the firft. He had a fon and heir,

2. *Simon Tilliol*, father of,

3. *Piers* (or *Peter*) *Tilliol*, who married a daughter of Jeffrey Lucy his guardian; and by her had,

4. *Jeffrey* (fometimes called *Piers-Jeffrey*) *Tilliol*; who married Mulcaftre's daughter and coheir; and by her had,

5. *Robert Tilliol*, whofe wife's name was Maud. He died in the 14 Ed. 3.

6. Sir *Peter* (or *Piers*) *de Tilliol*, fon of Robert. He was appointed a commiffioner, together with the lord Wake of Lyddal and Sir Anthony Lucy to array all men at arms, for the expedition into Gafcony. He was fheriff of the county in the 1, 2, and 3 Ed. 3. and died in the 21 Ed. 3.

7. Sir *Robert de Tilliol*, fon of Peter, by Ifabella his wife, was fheriff of the county in the 31, 32, 35, and 36 Ed. 3. and died in the 41 Ed. 3.

8. Sir *Peter de Tilliol*, fon of Robert, was fheriff in the 11 and 18 Ric. 2. and 5 and 6 Hen. 4. He was one of the commiffioners appointed to receive the oaths of allegiance in the 12 Hen. 6. and died in the year following.

9. *Robert de Tilliol*, fon of Peter, was an idiot, and died a year after his father, without iffue; and was fucceeded by his two fifters coheirs, viz. *Ifabel*, married to John Colvil; and *Margaret*, the younger, who had this part of the inheritance for her purparty, and was married to *James Merefby* efquire, who died in the 37 Hen. 6. leaving iffue,

Sir *Chriftopher Morefby* knight; who died in the 1 Ed. 4. leaving iffue a fon

Sir *Chriftopher Morefby*, who died in the 16 Hen. 7. and left a daughter and heir

Anne, married to Sir *James Pickering* of Killington in Weftmorland knight; who had iffue,

Sir *Chriftopher Pickering* knight; who had a daughter and only child; viz.

Anne Pickering, who was thrice married; 1. To Sir *Francis Wefton*. 2. To Sir *Henry Knevet*. And, 3. To John *Vaughan* efquire.

VOL. II.   R   Accordingly,

Accordingly, in the 35 Hen. 8. it is found by an inquifition of knights fees in Cumberland, that Henry Knevet and Anne his wife then held the manor of Torpenhow; but fhe had before fold the manor of Blenerhaffet, for at the fame time we find that *Thomas Salkeld* of Whitehall held the manor of Blenerhaffet of the king *in capite*, by the fervice of a third part of one knight's fee, 12 s cornage, $6\frac{1}{4}d$ feawake, and puture of the ferjeants.

This *Thomas Salkeld* was defcended from a younger brother of the houfe of Corby, and married Mary daughter of William Vaux of Caterlen : By whom he had iffue,

Lancelot Salkeld efquire ; who married Elizabeth daughter and coheir of Nicholas Berdefey of Berdefey in the county of Lancafter efquire ; and by her had iffue,

Thomas Salkeld efquire ; who by his wife Mary Copeland had a fon and heir, viz.

Lancelot Salkeld efquire ; who married Dorothy daughter of Alan Afkeugh of Skeughfby in Yorkfhire efquire by whom he had iffue, Francis, Lancelot, Mary, Margaret married to Green, Elizabeth married to Richardfon, and Agnes married to Mr. Thomas Patrickfon.

Sir *Francis Salkeld* knight, fon and heir of Lancelot, married Anne the eldeft daughter of Walter Strickland efquire, by whom he had iffue,

Thomas Salkeld efquire, who had three fons and eight daughters, viz. Thomas, Lancelot killed in Ireland, Roger, Margaret married to Edward Charleton of Haffelfide in the county of Northumberland efquire, Anne and Catherine nuns, Frances married to John Thirlwall efquire, Dorothy, Mary, Elizabeth, and Barbara.

Of thefe, *Thomas Salkeld* efquire, eldeft fon of the laft Thomas, had iffue Thomas and Henry. *Thomas* died unmarried, and was fucceeded by his brother Henry. Which Henry was bred a phyfician, and practifed fome years at York with great reputation ; but on the death of his elder brother, he left York, and married a daughter of the aforefaid Edward Charleton of Haffelfide ; and, dying without iffue, left his eftate (much incumbered) to his faid wife, who died at Whitehall in 1769.

The tenants of this manor, though it is very fmall in compafs, and although they are only about 20 in number, yet pay an annual ancient rent of 23 *l*, and arbitrary fines, and alfo heriots as well upon the widows death as death of the tenant, and feveral boons and fervices, namely, one day mowing, fhearing, ploughing, meadows dreffing, and two days leading coals.

KIRKLAND, fo called from having belonged to the church, was, in fetting out the refpective proportions of the revenues between the rector and vicar, affigned to the priorefs and convent of Roffdale as rectors, and after the diffolution of the monafteries was granted to the Salkelds of Whitehall. The tenants here have an extraordinary kind of tenure, namely, by leafe granted to them generally by Mr. Lancelot Salkeld father of Sir Francis for 999 years, paying a certain yearly rent for every tenement amounting in the whole

whole to 6*l* 15*s* 1*d* yearly, and every twenty-one years they are to pay a fine to the lord, viz. a twenty-penny fine, which they call a running greffom, and then take new leafes, but pay no general fine upon the lord's death nor upon change of tenant, but they pay an heriot upon the death of every tenant.

BOTHIL is the next townſhip in this pariſh, ſtanding half a mile higher weſt than Kirkland. This was demeſne of Allerdale until Waldeof lord of Allerdale gàve it to Gamel ſon of Brun in king Henry the firſt's time, whoſe poſterity long enjoyed the ſame in the iſſue male. His father's chief manſion was at Brunſkeugh in the manor of Linſtock near the waſtes, whereupon Radulph ſon of Gamel was called Radulph de Feritate, Ralph of the Waſtes, and ſo his ſon Robert de Feritate. They were lords of Beaùmont, Glaſſon, Drumbugh, and Bowneſs; which they held of the lord of Burgh in the reign of Hen. 3. Richard Brun was lord of Bothil and of the ſixth part of Torpenhow in Edward the fiiſt's time, and Robert Brun in the reign of Edward the third.

Afterwards Bothil and the Bruns' lands fell to three coheirs, married to Nicholas Hariington brother to the lord of Harrington, to William Culwen of Workington, and to Thomas Bowet.

To Nicholas Harrington ſucceeded Jąmes Harrington, who died in the 5 Hen. 5. After him, Sir Richard Harrington, who died in the 7 Ed. 4. Nicholas his ſon ſold it to Thomas lord Dacre, who exchanged it and Warnel with John Denton eſquire for Denton hall and the manor of Denton in Gilſland in the 12 Hen. 7. whoſe ſon Thomas ſucceeded to this inheritance, and ſo did three more of the name of Thomas ſucceſſively, the laſt of whom in the 22 C. 2. ſold Bothil park to Sir Francis Salkeld, and the remainder of that demeſne to other inhabitants of Bothil; and the old rent of 4*l* 19*s*, with the ſeigniory, to captain Anthony Wilkes.

To Culwen's part the heirs of Workington ſucceeded, until Sir Henry Curwen father of Sir Nicholas ſold it to Anthony Barwife of Iſtekirk eſquire, who ſettled it upon a daughter married to a ſecond ſon of the Egleſfields; which Egleſfield dying without iſſue, Richard Denton a third brother of the ſecond named Thomas married her, to whom ſhe had iſſue Edward Denton, who ſold the reverſion thereof (after his and his wife's death) to the Salkelds of Threapland, and it is now poſſeſſed by the owners of that eſtate.

Bowet's part was by fine levied 8 Ed. 4. ſold by Sir Nicholas Bowet knight, grandſon of the aforeſaid Thomas, to William Ellis; whoſe grandſon Bernard Ellis eſquire recorder of York ſold the ſame to ſeveral of the inhabitants.

The town ſtands on the ſide of an hill, where in old time the watch was kept day and night for ſeawake, which ſervice was performed by the country beneath Derwent at this place; and above Derwent, in Copeland, at Bothil in Millum. It is called *ſervicium de bcdis* in old evidences, whereupon this hill was named the *bode-hill*, and the village at the foot of it *Bode-hill-ton* (Bolton), or *Bodorum Collis*. The common people uſed to call a lantern a *bowet*, which name and word was then in uſe for a light on the ſhore to direct ſailors in

the

the night, properly fignifying a token, and not a light or lantern, as they call a meffage warranted by a token a *bodeword*, and the watchmen were called *bodefmen*, becaufe they had a *bode* or watchword given them, to prevent the enemy's fraud in the night feafon.

TÒRPENHOW ſtands about a mile eaſt from Bothil, upon the fame level, and was an ancient demefne of the barony of Allerdale, until Alan fon of Waldeof gave the fame with Gunild his fiſter to Ugthred fon of Fergus lord of Galloway, to be holden by him and his heirs by homage, cornage, and other fervices. In king Henry the fecond's time, Philip de Valoniis held the fame in right of his wife, who held the fame of Reginald Lucy and Amabil his wife lord of the moiety of Allerdale. In king John's time, Robert Eftotevil brother to the lord Nicholas Eftotevil lord of Liddale held it. And in the 31 Hen. 3. William fon of William de Ulfby gave three carucates of land there to Robert de Mulcaftre, and held five parts of the fame of Richard Brun : the other fixth part, which he joined to the manor of Bothil, he held of the lord of Liddale heir to Eftotevil. The faid five parts defcended to the Mulcaftres, and from them to the Tilliolls ; one of whofe coheirs transferred the fame to the Morefbys. The heir general of Morefby was married to Wefton, Knevet, and Vaughan. Accordingly, in the 35 Hen. 8. it is found, that Henry Knevet and Anne his wife, in right of the faid Anne, held the manor and town of Torpenhow of the king *in capite*, by the fervice of 24 s cornage, 6¼ d feawake, and puture of the ferjeants. Afterwards her third hufband Vaughan joined with her in levying a fine and thereby conveyed the manor of Torpenhow unto Thomas Salkeld and John Appleby. Which John Appleby, being employed by the faid Mr. Salkeld to go into the county of Durham to make the contract with the lady Knevet and her hufband Vaughan, Appleby very unworthily made himfelf joint purchafer. So they came to a divifion, and Appleby got the part which lies without the park wall, which Anthony Appleby fon of Thomas fon of the faid joint purchafer fold to Sir George Fletcher, and the tenants of the cuftomary lands he fold to Lancelot Salkeld fon of Thomas in the 12 Eliz. Thomas Salkeld had the feigniory and all the other cuftomary tenants, the park, and miln ; which defcended in the family of Salkeld, in like manner as did Blenerhaffet, according as in the pedigree is above fet forth.

It is called *Tor-pen-how*; every fyllable of which word, in the feveral languages of the people which fucceffively did inhabit the place, doth fignify after a manner one thing. The Britons firſt called a little rifing hill there *Pen*. The Saxons, next fucceeding, not well underftanding the fignification of *pen*, called it *Tor-pen*, the pinacle *pen*. The laſt, as we do yet, called it *Tor-pen-how*, the *how* or hill *Torpen*.—Others have thought it fo named upon this occafion : The Saxons call a village *Dorp*, and finding the hill there to be named of the Britons *pen*, a head or hill top, they called it *Thorp pen*, or the town hill.

The cuftomary tenants of this manor pay arbitrary fines.

WHITERIGG

WHITERIGG is the next village, which stands half a mile south from Tor-penhow, upon the height of that hill. This is a little manor belonging to Sir Gilfrid Lawson, part of the Isel estate; which they purchased about the year 1712 of the Skeltons of Armathwaite, whose ancestors had it by a marriage with the Colvills, who married one of the coheirs of Tillioll. The demesne is pretty large, and there are about eight freehold tenants, and one customary who pays 13 s rent and a twenty-penny fine.

BOWALDETH lies a mile south on the back of Binsel fell, which is the highest mountain in this tract. It is a little manor, which was granted by Waldieve first lord of Allerdale to *Gilmin*; whose posterity, residing at Bothill, took the name of Bowet.

Afterwards, Alice de Romeley daughter of William Fitz Duncan had it; who by deed without date granted to *John de Utterfield* the whole vill of Bualdeth, by the boundaries in the grant particularly specified; together with common of pasture for him and all his tenants of Bualdeth for all their cattle to feed from the water Elne to the east, to Threapland beck on the west.

After him, the *Mulcastres* had it for several descents. In the 2 Ed. 1. *Robert de Mulcastre* granted by fine to his son *Walter de Mulcastre* the manors of Bowaldeth, Bolton, Torpenhow, and Blenerhasset. And in the 2 Hen. 4. *Robert de Mulcastre* granted to *Robert de Highmore* the vill of Bowaldeth, with the water mill, and a moiety of the profits of the foldage of divers cattle upon the moor adjoining. Witnesses of which grant were, William de Legh knight, William de Lowther then sheriff of Cumberland, John de Skelton, William de Ofmotherley, William de Dykes, and others.

And in this family it continued for the greatest part of 400 years, until Mr. *Benson Highmore* son of *Charles Highmore* esquire late of Armathwaite sold the same to *James Spedding* esquire the present owner.

Here is a small demesne called BURTHWAITE, lying round a copt hill adjoining to Isel old park. The tenants are about thirteen, and their tenements all freehold.

The CHURCH of Torpenhow is dedicated to St. Michael; and was granted by Sibilla de Valoniis in her widowhood and by Eustachius de Stutevil son of Robert, to the prioress and nuns of Rossdale in the county of York; which grants were confirmed to them by king Edward the third†.

And the said prioress and nuns having the right of advowson, bishop Irton in the year 1290, in an ordinance for the endowment of the vicarage, first awards to himself the said right of advowson, and then ordains, that the vicar shall keep in his house and maintain at his own charge three priests and one subdeacon, one of the said priests to assist the vicar in all parochial offices,

---

† — Donationem insuper et confirmationem quas Sibilla de Valoniis, in libera viduitate sua, per chartam suam fecit præfatis monialibus de ecclesia de Thorppenhow, in liberam, puram, et perpe-tuam eleemosynam.—Concessionem etiam et confirmationem quas Eustachius de Stutevilla, filius Roberti de Stutevilla, per chartam suam fecit prædictis monialibus de prædicta ecclesia de Thorp-penhow, in liberam, puram, et perpetuam eleemosynam.—1 Dugd. Mon. 508.

another

another to celebrate daily the mafs of the bleffed virgin Mary, and another to fay mafs for the dead and for the profperity of the bifhop and his fucceffors; the vicar alfo to bear all ordinary charges, and to be anfwerable for the defects of the books and ornaments, and the repairs of the chancel, fo as fuch repairs do not exceed 10 s, otherwife there fhall be a contribution according to the rate of each perfon's fhare of the profits: And in confideration of the premiffes, the vicar to have the whole altarage, and all the houfes, lands, and rents in Torpenhow belonging to the church (one only excepted), and alfo the corn tithes of Torpenhow, Threapland, Alderfceugh, Appelwray, Snitelgarth, Bellafife, and Bowaldeth; and liberty to dig turf fufficient for his own ufe in the turbary of Kirkland. The priorefs and convent to have the manor of Kirkland, with the demefne and rents of the tenants, and the corn-tithes thereof and alfo of Bothil and Blenerhaffet; and the aforefaid houfe excepted out of the vicar's fhare: Paying out of the whole to the vicar yearly two marks, and difcharging all burdens extraordinary.

In 1303, Sir *Roger Peytenin* was collated to the vicarage of Thorppenhow by bifhop Kirkby. And fome years after, the faid Roger being convened before the bifhop and his official (with other affeffors) for fubtraction of the chantry by him made in his church aforefaid; on hearing the whole matter, the vicar bound himfelf by oath to maintain three priefts and a fubdeacon or fome other clerk, fo long as he fhould continue vicar there.

In 1316, on the death of Roger Peytenin, the bifhop collates Sir *Robert de Halogton* to the vicarage of Thorpenhowe.

In 1323, the faid Robert having accepted a moiety of the rectory of Aketon, Sir *Alan de Horncaftle* is collated to Torpenhow.

In 1352, a citation iffued againft Alan de Ribton (a layman), to appear in the church of Dalfton, to fhew caufe why the canonical cenfures fhall not be paffed on him, for his farming the church of Torpenhow, contrary to the conftitutions of the lords Otho and Othobon the pope's legates.

In 1359, Sir *Peter de Morland*, vicar of Torpenhowe, changes his living with Sir *Thomas de Salkeld* rector of Clifton. Which Sir Peter was collated to the vicarage of Torpenhow in 1355, upon an exchange he made with Sir *Thomas Roland* of the church of Dittenfel (or Dittinfdale, in Northumberland) in the diocefe of Durham.

In 1371, Sir *Thomas de Enghale*, vicar of Torpenhow, changes with Sir *Robert de Byx*, rector of Wardley in the diocefe of Lincoln.

In 1380, on the death of Sir *Robert de Byx*, the bifhop collates Sir *John Mafon* chaplain to the faid vicarage, with the charge of perfonal refidence, according to the form of the conftitution of the legate in that cafe made and provided.

In 1393, *John de Carlel* appears to have been vicar of Torpenhow, having brought an action in that year for an houfe in Carlifle.

After the diffolution of the religious houfes and chantries, queen Elizabeth in the 5th year of her reign, 1562, by letters patent, grants to Ciceley Pickerell of the city of Norwich widow, late wife of John Pickerell gentleman, (amongft other particulars) all the tithes of corn and grain yearly, iffuing out of of certain lands and tenements in the vills of Thorpenhow, Threapland, Bewaldeth, Whitrigge, Snittilgarth, and Alderſkewgh, heretofore aſſigned for the ſuſtentation of a prieſt and others celebrating divine offices within the pariſh church of Torpenhow.—This ſeems to have been a grant of a ſmall part only. For in the 17 El. there is a larger grant to John Soukey and Parcivall Gunſon of all the tithes of corn and hay renewing and iſſuing out of the towns, lands, fields, or other hereditaments, in Threapland, Alderſkewe, Applewraye, Snitlegarth, Bellaſis, Bowaldeth, and Whitrigge, late in the tenure of the vicar of Torpenhow, and parcel of the poſſeſſions and lands late aſſigned to the ſuſtentation and maintenance of certain prieſts in the church of Torpenhow: All which premiſſes (with others) had hitherto been unjuſtly concealed, withdrawn, and detained from the queen and her progenitors, of the yearly value of 9l 9s 7¼d.

The ſame queen, in the 15th year of her reign, granted to the ſaid Parcival Gunſon (amongſt other particulars) three roods and an half of land in Blener-haſſet, late in the tenure of Richard Whitehead, parcel of the late chapel of St. Patric in the pariſh of Torpenhow; and three acres of land in Torpenhow late in the tenure of the vicar of Torpenhow, given to the vicar there by the lord of Bowaldeth for alms to pray for the ſaid lord and his heirs.

The firſt vicar that we meet with after the diſſolution was Sir *William Dobſon*, who was deprived in the year 1568, and thereupon Mr. *Thomas Tookie* was collated by biſhop Beſt; and in the ſame year to a prebend in the cathedral church of Carliſle, on the reſignation of John Maybraye.

In 1576, on the reſignation of Thomas Tookie, Mr. *Anthony Walkwood* was collated by biſhop Barnes.

In 1612, on Mr. Walkwood's death, *Bernard Robinſon*, S. T. B. was collated by (his brother) biſhop Robinſon.

In 1632, *Bernard Robinſon*, B. A. was collated on the reſignation of his father Bernard Robinſon.

After him, we find *William Sill*, M. A. upon whoſe reſignation in 1681, *William Nicolſon*, M. A. was collated by biſhop Rainbow.

In 1698, on Mr. Nicolſon's reſignation, *Thomas Nevinſon* was collated by biſhop Smith.

In 1728, on Mr. Nevinſon's death, *Thomas Nicolſon*, LL. B. was collated by biſhop Waugh.

In 1735, on the death of Mr. Nicolſon, *William Fleming*, M. A. archdeacon of Carliſle, was collated by his father biſhop Fleming.

In 1743, on Mr. Fleming's death, *Thomas Wilſon*, M. A. (the preſent dean) was collated by the ſame biſhop Fleming.

In pope Nicholas's Valor, the rectory of this church is rated at 30l, and the vicarage at 16l. In Hen. 8th's valuation the vicarage is rated at 33l 6s 8d. The preſent yearly value is about 110l.

There are in this pariſh about 174 families; of which, preſbyterians 8, quaker 1.

There

There is a SCHOOL at Bothil in this parish, which had a small parcel of land belonging to it time out of mind. The first benefactor within memory was Mr. Salkeld of Threapland, who by will charged his estate there with the payment of 50 s yearly to the said school. Richard Smithson of Bothill by will devised four acres of land at Bothill to the same use. The parishioners of Torpenhow, encouraged by these bequests, made in the year 1686 a voluntary subscription which amounted to about 42 l, for augmenting the salary of the master; and in the year following it was resolved by the vicar and sixteen men (or select vestry) that the said school should be a free school for the whole parish; that the masters successively should be presented to the said school by the vicar for the time being, Mr. Salkeld of Threapland and his heirs, and a majority of the said 16 men. The subscription money was laid out in land. And one Watson of Whitehaven (but born at Bothil) about the year 1737 left 10 l to this school, which is lent out at interest. The whole revenue is about 11 l a year.

PARISH OF IREBY.

NEXT unto the parish of Torpenhow is the parish of IREBY; which is bounded on the north-east side of the river Elne, from the foot of Newbiggin demesne up to the head of the standing lake called Orr water, and thence to the top of Binfell fell on the south, and so to the head of the spring which falls down by Snittlegarth called West Scawbeck to the foot thereof where it falls into Elne on the north-west. There are in this parish about 70 families; whereof quakers 2, papist 1. This is the place which from the affinity of names Mr. Camden supposes to be the *Arbeia* of the Romans, but Mr. Horsley says that there are no footsteps of any Roman station having been at this place, nor any Roman antiquities have ever been found there that he could hear of, and (with more probability) supposes that station to have been at Moresby.

Ireby hath been divided into two parts more early than we have any account; viz. *High Ireby*, called in old evidences *Ireby alta*, because it stands higher; and *Ireby bassa*, or the lower Ireby, which is now also called Market Ireby.

HIGH IREBY was granted by Alan second lord of Allerdale to *Gospatric* son of Orme, lord of Seaton and Workington; which Gospatric gave it to a younger son *Orme*, who was thereupon called *Orme de Ireby*, and from him the Irebys took their surname. Robert de Courtney and Alice his wife, one of the daughters and coheirs of William Fitz Duncan lord of Allerdale gave to this Orme de Ireby his manor of Embleton in Richard the first's time; and he had also lands in Waverton.

He had issue *Adam* his heir, and *William* a priest who gave lands in Gilcrux to the abbot of Holme.

Adam had *Thomas* his heir, and *William* lord of Gamelsby and Glassonby, and *Alan* father of Isaac who gave his dwelling-house in Ireby called Isaacby to the priory of Carlisle.

Thomas

Thomas had issue *John*; and he, *Thomas* father of *William*, who by Christian his wife had issue two daughters coheirs, *Christian* and *Eva*. *Eva* had a rent charge out of the lands, and was married to Robert d'Estotevill, and after to Alan de Charters. She released her purparty to her sister *Christian* wife of Thomas Lascells of Bolton, who had issue *Armina* Lascells married to John Seaton, whose son *Christopher Seaton* was attainted in Edward the first's time, for taking part with Robert Bruce and the Scots.

After this we find at Ireby one *John de Ireby* who was sheriff of the county in the 12 Ric. 2. And also in the 15th and 19th of the same king's reign; and knight of the shire in parliament in 8, 11, and 20 Ric. 2. And this is the last of the name that hath occurred at Ireby.

In after times, this manor belonged to the *Barwifes*, who sold to one of the *Fletchers*, whose descendent *Walter Fletcher* now enjoys the same, together with Ruthwait.

The tenants in High Ireby and Ruthwait are about 20 in number; pay to the said Mr. Fletcher 14 *l* 11 *s* 6 *d* customary rent, arbitrary fines, and each tenant one boon day or 3 *d*.

Low IREBY, called also Market Ireby, lies a mile lower, north east from High Ireby. It came to the *Ballentines* (in a female heir of which family it now continues) by marriage of *Anne* eldest daughter of *William Musgrave* of Crookdake, whose ancestor *William Musgrave* married a daughter and coheir of *William Colvil*, whose father *John Colvil* married a sister and coheir of *Robert* son of *Peter de Tilliol*, which Peter de Tilliol had this manor from *Thomas Middleton*, son of *Peter*, son of *Adam*, who married *Christian* daughter of *William de Ireby*. She held it of *William Boyvil* of Thursby knight, who was son of *Guido Boyvil*, who married *Clerota* the heir general of the Thursbys, whose ancestor *Herbert de Thursby* held it as an assart in the forest of Westward, and rented it of the king. *William de Ireby*, father of *Christian*, was but a younger brother, but advanced by king John to far better estate than his elder brother, and made knight, and preferred to the marriage of Odard's daughter and heir of Glassonby and Gamelsby then the king's ward.

In the account of knights fees in Cumberland, 35 Hen. 8. it appears, that *Cuthbert Musgrave* son of *Mungo* held a moiety of the manor and vill of Low Ireby of the king as of his manor of Papcastre, by the service of 2 *s* 3 *d* cornage, 6 *d* seawake, puture of the serjeants, and witnesman in Allerdale. And *William Musgrave* son of *Thomas* held in like manner the other moiety.

The customary tenants of this manor purchased their tenements to freehold of the two last owners of the name of Ballentine.

Here is a weekly market on Thursday, and two fairs yearly on the feasts of St. Matthias and St. Matthew.

The *church* of Ireby was given by Alan second lord of Allerdale to the prior and convent of Carlisle; which grant was confirmed by king Hen 2. and king Ed. 3 *.

* Ex dono Alani filii Waldevi ecclesiam de Yreby, in terris et decimis et omnibus rebus eidem ecclesiæ pertinentibus, et sextam partem villæ de Yreby, sc. Langethweit, et Scalethweit, et alios Thweites qui pertinent ad Langethweit.

It ftill continues in the hands of the dean and chapter, who appoint the cu-rate, and require their leffee of the rectory to pay him 25 *l* a year, which is his whole falary; all forts of tithes and dues belonging to the faid leffee.

On a tomb ftone on the fouth fide of the chancel is this infcription,

> *George Crage of Prior-hall gent.*
> *Who faithfully ferved queen Elizabeth,*
> *king James, prince Henry, and Charles*
> *king of England.* 1626.

A *fchool* was founded here in 1726, for teaching the poor children of the parifh to read and write, by one Matthew Caldbeck of Ruthwait, who gave 100 *l*, the intereft whereof is paid to the mafter.

PARISH OF ULDALE.

ULDALE (Ulndale) lies oppofite to Ruthwait on the eaft fide of Elne river, and is fo named from that river, which runs through the upper end of the parifh, its chief fountains fpringing from the top of Coppeak and Caldfell, which are parted from Skiddaw mountain by Whitewater Dafh.

It is diverfely named in old evidences Elne, Alne, and Olne. And the parifh is bounded by the fame from Ireby bridge to the head of Orr water, and from thence by the ring dyke of Whitefield to the north end of Baffenthwaite park, and fo down the park hedge to White Water, and then up that water to the head thereof above White Water Dafh, and fo pointing northward along the back of Coppeak and Caldfell, and then from the top of Caldfell down by a rill that falls by Bleaberrythwait, and the weft end of Greenrigg to the head of Awhatree beck, and fo down that beck to Ireby bridge.

The parifh is long and narrow, being ftrait laced by the mountains on the eaft and Elne on the weft, and extending itfelf from fouth to north above four miles in length, though it be not a mile in breadth any where. There are in it about 50 families, one only diffenter being a quaker.

It is remarkable, that this parifh in two years time rebuilt their church, built a fchool and endowed it with 200 *l*, and purchafed their eftates to free-hold, and yet were left in good circumftances, and are now moft of them fub-ftantial freeholders.

This parifh and manor (parcel of the barony of Allerdale) Waldeof gave to Adam fon of Lyolf, brother of Phorn, fon of Lyolf baron of Grayftock, together with the manor of Gilcrux, from which Adam they defcended by a daughter to the Bonekills, who granted Gilcrux to a younger brother Robert Bonekill; and the fons of the faid Robert, Thomas Bonekill and Walter gave away their inheritance in Gilcrux to the abbey of Galdre, which Sir Ranulph Bonekill knight (then lord paramount both of Uldale and Gilcrux) confirmed. Sir Ranulph had iffue Alexander, who had iffue Adam, which Adam gave Awerthwaite, (now Awhatree) parcel of his manor of Uldale to the priory of Carlifle. The faid Adam had iffue another Alexander Bonekill; whofe daugh-

3   ter

ter and heir, firft married to John Stewart kinfman to the king of Scots, and afterwards to David Brigham a Scotifh knight of great valour, transferred the inheritance to the family of Brigham.　This David Brigham was a companion of William Wallace that was executed at London for treafon committed againft Edward the firft, by refifting that king's attempt for the fuperiority of Scotland and the Baliol's right to the crown of Scotland, taking part with Robert Bruce.　Wallace was a man of extraordinary ftrength, and David Brigham an exceeding good horfeman, whereupon the Scots made this rythme,

> The man was ne'er fo wight nor geud,
> But worthy Wallace durft him bide;
> Nor ever horfe fo wild or weud,
> But David Brigham durft him ride.

David Brigham thereby forfeited his eftate to Anthony lord Lucy then lord of Allerdale.　So Uldale efcheated, and became again parcel of that ancient barony, and the manor extinguifhed of right; yet was it continued as a manor by the Lucys pofterity and the Percys earls of Northumberland until Henry the fixth earl of Northumberland gave the inheritance of this manor to king Henry the eighth.

Which king, by letters patent bearing date July 15, in the 35th year of his reign, granted to Thomas Dalfton efquire (together with divers other poffeffions) the manor of Uldale, late parcel of the poffeffions of Henry Percy deceafed late earl of Northumberland; paying to the king for Uldale yearly 47s 3¼d.

Which Thomas Dalfton, by fine levied in the 37 Hen. 8. fettled the fame upon himfelf and his (fecond) wife Eleanor for life, remainder to his fon *Chriftopher Dalfton* (by his faid fecond wife) and the heirs of his body, remainder to his own right heirs.　Which Chriftopher Dalfton was anceftor of the Dalftons of Acorn Bank in Weftmorland, in which family this manor of Uldale ftill continues.

AWHATREE lies half a mile north beyond the common field of Uldale, upon the edge of Sandall.　And though this townfhip was granted to the prior of Carlifle by Adam Bonekill as beforementioned, yet the priory being diffolved at the time of the grant to Thomas Dalfton, and the whole manor of Uldale being granted to him, Awhatree paffed by that grant.

The CHURCH of Uldale is fituate at the weft end of the parifh near to Ireby. It is rectorial; and the patronage thereof is appendant to the manor.　It is valued in the king's books at 17l 18s 1¼d, and the prefent yearly value is about 70l.

In the year 1305, on the death of Sir *Robert de Depyng* rector of Ulnedale, Sir David de Bryghyn (Brigham) knight prefented Hugh de Rouceftre clerk, and Thomas de Lucy prefented one Sir David de Cringledike chaplain, whereby the church became litigious.　And an inquifition thereupon was taken by the clergy of the deanry of Allerdale at Wigton in the chapter held there July 20th in that year; and the return thereon was thus:

S 2　　　　　　　　　　　　　　　　　　　　　　　　" The

" The jurors fay, that the faid church is void, and hath been void from the
" feaſt of St. Dunſtan laſt paſt, by the death of Sir Robert de Depyng late
" rector of the faid church: And they fay, that Sir Alexander de Bonkill laſt
" prefented the faid Sir Robert to the faid church: That it is worth *communi-*
" *bus annis* 18*l* a year.   Alſo they fay, that the faid Sir Alexander had a
" daughter Margaret, who is now lately dead, and that in her father's life-
" time ſhe was married to Sir John brother of the Steward of Scotland, to
" whom ſhe had children (as is faid); and fo it feemeth to them, that the
" eldeſt fon of the faid John and Margaret ought of right to be the true pa-
" tron thereof: But that the church is litigious, for that Thomas de Lucy
" hath prefented Sir David a chaplain, a man fufficiently known, honeſt, and
" of good behaviour, to the faid church; which prefentee afferts the right of
" prefentation for that turn to belong to the faid Thomas, becauſe the manor
" of Ulnedale is in his hand by reafon of the death of the faid Margaret
" daughter and heir of the faid Alexander, who held the faid manor with the
" appurtenances of the faid Thomas de Lucy by the fervice of cornage, which
" yields wardſhip and relief; and that Sir David de Breghyn, who now pre-
" fents the faid Hugh to the faid church was never married to the faid Mar-
" garet in the face of the church.   The faid Hugh in like manner propounds,
" that the faid Sir David de Breghyn is patron and ought to prefent to the
" fame by the law and cuſtom of England, for that he did marry the faid
" Margaret, and during the marriage had children by her: In evidence where-
" of he produced certain letters and tranfcripts of the biſhops of St. Andrews,
" Dunkeld, and Brekyn, and the tranfcript of a bull of the late pope Bene-
" dict of bleffed memory, under the feals of the archdeacon of St. Andrews,
" and the official of Brekyn, by which it appears, that notwithſtanding the
" affinity and confanguinity between the faid Sir David and Margaret, the
" faid pope Benedict difpenfed that they might marry.   Of the condition of
" the faid Hugh, as to his birth, they know nothing: And that he is an
" Acolyte, and otherwife of good behaviour, as they believe.   Other things
" touching the faid inquifition they leave to your fatherly goodnefs."——About
Michaelmafs following, the faid Thomas de Lucy prefented another clerk, one
Sir *Adam de Eglesfield*, whereupon a fecond inquifition was taken, and a return
made thereon to the fame purpofe as the foregoing.   It is probable this *Adam*
was inſtituted, though in this particular the regiſter book is defective.

In 1336, Sir *Hugh* rector of Ulnedale had a difpenfation granted him for
one year's abfence from his cure; the reafon thereof being thus affigned in
the preamble—Quum in curia domini noſtri regis diverfis negotiis implicatus
exiſtis, circa quorum expeditionem oportet te perfonaliter intendere et vacare.

In 1354, Sir *Richard de Aſkeby*, rector of Uldale, in confideration of the
diſtance of the pariſhioners from their pariſh church, had a licence from biſhop
Welton, for one year, to perform divine fervice in the chapel in the village of
Ulnedale; which licence doth not appear to have been afterwards renewed.   In
1361, the fame Sir Richard had a difpenfation of abfence, by reafon of his
attendance on Thomas de Lucy.

Iа

In 1366, on the death of Mr. *William Aykheved* rector of Ulnedale, Sir *Thomas de Etton* chaplain is presented by the king, by reason of the lands and tenements of Thomas de Lucy knight deceased (who held of him *in capite*) being then in the king's hands.

In 1375, Sir Thomas de Etton exchanges his living with Mr. *Robert Marrays*, for the rectory of Hugate in the diocese of York.

In 1385, Sir *John Fryfell*, rector of Ulnedale, had a dispensation of absence for three years.

In 1399, Maud, relict of Henry Percy earl of Northumberland died possessed of the patronage of the church of Ulnedale.

In 1576, on the death of *John Shayres* rector of Ulnedale, Sir *Thomas Harrifon* clerk was presented by Christopher Dalston of Ulnedale gentleman.

In 1583, on Thomas Harrifon's death, *James Carlile*, M. A. was instituted on a presentation by Christopher Dalston of Ulnedale esquire.

In 1624, on the death of Mr. Carlile, *George Hudfon* clerk was presented by Sir Christopher Dalston knight.

In 1665, on the death of *Henry Fallowfield* rector of Ulndale, *William Walker*, M. A. was presented by John Dalston of Acornbank esquire.

In 1677, on Mr. Walker's death, *Henry Guy* was presented by John Dalston of Millrigg esquire.

In 1684, on Mr. Guy's resignation, *Thomas Nevinfon*, B. A. was presented by the same patron.

In 1697, on the cession of Mr. Nevinfon, *Peter Gregory* was presented by Christopher and Henry Dalston.

In 1719, on Mr. Gregory's death, *Edward Backhoufe*, B. A. was presented by John Dalston esquire.

In 1752, on Mr. Backhoufe's death, *Richard Machel*, M. A. was presented by John Dalston esquire.

In 1770, on the cession of Mr. Machel to Brougham, *Andrew Holiday* was presented by Sir William Dalston knight.

In the year 1716, a SCHOOL was founded at Uldale, and endowed with 200*l* as is before mentioned; of which, 51*l* 10*s* 0*d* is laid out in land, and the remainder is in the hands of the seven truftees.

PARISH OF CALDBECK.

CALDBECK lies east from Uldale four miles, and was long after the conquest waste forest ground parcel of Allerdale, and is bounded by the river of Caldew where Caldbeck falls into it at the foot of Hefket demefne unto the head thereof on the east side of Coppake as the water falls each way, from thence to the top of Caldfell, and so by a rill which falls down from Burblethwaite and the west end of Greenrigg to the head of Awhatree beck, then turning northwards to Thorny stone, and along a path-way till it come to Thistle bottom, and from thence up to the Rayes head, and so down to Shawk head,

head, and then turning downwards to the Brandreth ftone, then by the height to the head of Brackley beck, and down the fame till it fall into Caldbeck above the bridge.

This is the laft parifh in this ward that lies under the fkirts of the mountains. It runs from weft to eaft in length above feven miles, from the Thorny ftone to the head of Moffdale, being hemmed in on the fouth fide by a ridge of mountains called Caldfell, Caldbeck fells, Noon fell, and Carrock; and on the north, by a lower tract of hills running to Warnel fell.

This parifh was firft fo named from the beck which runs through the middle of it, and fprings from Caldfell; which, meeting with the river Caldew (Coldwater) coming down from the north fide of Skiddaw, lofeth its name of Caldbeck, and keeps the name of Caldew till it falls into Eden below Carlifle. And it juftly receives this name, being fed with at leaft an hundred cold fprings which flow into it from thefe mountains, which are often covered with fnow in the winter and fpring feafons. Yet cold as thefe mountains are, they fuftain large flocks of fheep, which are very profitable to the inhabitants. Alfo thefe mountains are replenifhed with the ore of lead and copper; infomuch that in fome parts thereof the teeth of the fheep are remarkably tinged with a gold colour, fuppofed to be by the water iffuing from the veins of copper.

Out of Weftmorland and the eaft parts of Cumberland there lying an highway through Caldbeck into the weft of Cumberland, it was anciently very dangerous for paffengers to travel through it, who were often robbed by thieves that haunted thofe woody parts and mountains, thereupon Ranulph Engain, the chief forefter of Englewood, granted licence to the prior of Carlifle to build an hofpital for the relief of diftreffed travellers who might happen to be troubled by thofe thieves, or prejudiced by the fnows or ftorms in winter. Then began the prior to inclofe part of the fame, near to the place where the church now ftands, which was ufed as part of the foreft, but the right of the foil was in the lord of Allerdale.

After this hofpital was built, they founded the church here in honour of St. Mungo or Kentigern, and the place became fully inhabited; that part which lay near the church being higher than the reft was called Caldbeck-Uppeton or Uppertown, and that part near the fell was called Caldbeck-Underfell; unto which they have fince added a third divifion, which they call the Eaft end, though they have but two conftablewicks in that extenfive parifh,

The priors had the patronage of the rectory granted to them by Gofpatric fon of Orme, which was confirmed by William de Vefcy and Burga his wife, and dame Alice de Romeley lady of Allerdale, and alfo by the kings Henry the fecond and Edward the third *. They then diffolved the hofpital, and endowed the church with the lands thereof about king John's time; which lands, as belonging to the church, have fince been called the manor of Kirkland.

In the fame king's reign, one John Franceys (Francigena) was parfon of Caldbeck, and got a great inclofure in Warnel Bank within the foreft of Engle-

* Ex dono Gofpatricii filii Orme ecclefiam de Caldbeck cum omnibus fibi adjacentibus, et hofpitalem domum de Caldbeck cum omnibus pertinentiis fuis, fecundum quod chartæ ejufdem Gofpatricii teftantur.

wood,

wood, which he joined to the glebe, and is now called the parson's park. Yet the monks of Holme so quarrelled him, that he was glad to compound with them by granting them a share, which was between the bounds of the two sikes of Gresgardgill on the west and Brottholehill on the east; which grant was confirmed not only by the bishop and his chapter, but by king Henry the third in the 16th year of his reign. Yet the parson's share was still subject to an annual crown rent of one mark, payable into the king's exchequer at Michaelmas. Parkhead is now held in tenancy under the rector, and seems to have been part of the said inclosure, though it is now held as part of the manor of Kirkland aforesaid.

The prior's successor Bartholomew granted the advowson to the bishop (Walter Malclerk) and his successors, who have ever since enjoyed it. In the 52 Hen. 3. Cicely countess of Albemarle, eldest daughter of William Fitz Duncan, claimed the right of advowson against bishop Chause; but upon a *Quare Impedit* the bishop recovered the right of collation to the church of Caldbeck.

But the lords of Allerdale continued to enjoy the seigniory through. the several descents of the Lucys, till Maud the female heir of that family carried the same to the Percys earls of Northumberland, in whom it remained until Henry the sixth earl of Northumberland granted Caldbeck to king Henry the eighth; who sold Caldbeck Uppertown to Thomas Dalston esquire, and Caldbeck Underfell to Thomas lord Wharton, who being warden of the west marches did so treat Mr. Dalston, that he was glad to sell Upperton to him: And they continued in that family till Philip duke of Wharton, the last of that family, vested the same, together with other estates, in Mr. Justice Denton, Thomas Gibson, John Jacob, and Robert Jacomb esquires, for the payment of his debts; and Charles late duke of Somerset becoming purchaser, the present earl of Egremont as his representative enjoys the same.

Both the Caldbecks were one intire manor in the time of Alice third daughter of William Fitz Duncan, to whom the same was assigned, together with the rest of the barony of Allerdale, as her purparty. But after her dying without issue, Caldbeck was divided between her sisters children, the house of Albemarl and the Lucys; and that brought the division of the manor into two graveships or collections, and the rents and profits were accounted for as of two different manors; but the wastes were not known to be divided. After the line of Albemarle was ended, all fell to the Lucys.

In this parish there are many villages and townships; as, first, *Greenrigg*, which lies next to Uldale under Caldfell, and did formerly belong to the Musgraves of Crookdake; who heretofore being officers and commanders under the earls of Northumberland, had several parcels of waste ground granted to them for their good services, which they converted into tenancies. But Sir John Ballentine, who married Anne the eldest daughter and coheir of William Musgrave esquire, sold these tenants to the lord Wharton; which tenants pay 1 l 5 s 2 d yearly rent and arbitrary fines: All the other customary tenants pay a ten-penny fine certain by decree.

Caldfell

Caldfell arifeth high above Greenrigg, from the top whereof is Caldfell fountain, which running down by *Park end* (where formerly was a red deer park)
glideth under the *Faulds,* and fo by *Whelphay* and *Pategill* or *Paddegill,* and by
Brownrigg.

And further down the north fide of this beck lies *Ratten Row,* where there
is a coal mine and flate quarry. This hamlet ftretches down to Caldbeck
bridge, where another ftream meets with Caldbeck, which hath its rife from
the weft fide of Noon fell, falls down by a little village called *Fellfide,* and fo
by *Hudfcales;* and falling from that high hill almoft in a direct courfe, runs
with a very precipitate current through *Uppeton* to the *Low-town* or *Church
town,* where the rector hath a little manor of about 24 tenants, who pay 7 *l*
17 *s* 4 *d* cuftomary rent, arbitrary fines upon an alienation, but a Gods-penny
only upon change of tenant by death, and nothing on the death of the lord.

A little weft of this town, above the meeting of the two becks, there is a
great cave or grotto in Caldbeck (near to the earl of Egremont's mill) called
the *Hawk,* which was a receptacle in former times for thieves, where many
people may have fhelter together.

The earl of Egremont hath no demefne lands here, but feveral free rents,
and about 120 cuftomary tenants who pay 49 *l* 16 *s* 3 *d* yearly rent, a ten penny
fine certain, with heriots, fuit of court, and the thirteenth moulter.

Half a mile higher fouthward within this parifh ftands *Hefket,* being a mefne
manor within the earl of Egremont's, and a market town, hav.ng a market on
Friday weekly; whereof Sir Gilfrid Lawfon of Brayton baronet is lord, who
fucceeded his brother Sir Wilfrid, fon of Sir Alfrid, brother of S.r Gilfrid,
fon of Wilfrid, who was fecond fon of Sir Wilfrid Lawfon of Ifel baronet,
which laft named Sir Wilfrid had it as heir to his mother Elizabeth, who was
daughter and fole heir of William Beauly efquire, it having continued in the
male line of the Beaulies for feveral hundred years before.

Moffdale ftands a mile higher upon Caldew, under Carrock mountain; which,
with *Swinefide* lying oppofite thereto, makes another mefne manor, held of the
faid earl of Egremont by Edward Haffel of Dalemain efquire, who purchafed
the fame of Sir Chriftopher Mufgrave of Edenhall baronet, who purchafed of
the ladies Barbara and Anne daughters and coheirs of Thomas earl of Suffex.
For George Fiennes lord Dacre dying without iffue in 1549, his only fifter and
heir Margaret was married to Sampfon Lennard efquire, whofe defcendents in
right of the faid Margaret were lords Dacre, and intitled to this little manor,
and were in 1674 advanced to the further dignity of earls of Suffex. This in
former times was a place where the Dacres barons of Grayftock kept their red
deer and wild fwine, but being afterwards divided into tenancies, there are
now fix tenements in Moffdale and two in Swinefide, each of which pays 14 *s*
yearly free rent to the faid Mr. Haffel.

This rectory is valued in the king's books at 45 *l* 13 *s* 6¼ *d*. And is now
worth about 180 *l per annum.*

The firft rector that we meet with was the aforefaid *John Franceys,* who was
a kinfman of Gilbert Franceys lord of Rowcliff; which John Franceys inclofed
the lands called Parfon's park in the reign of king John.

                                                              In

In the reign of King Henry the third, *Alan* parson of Caldbeck is witness to a grant of William de Forz earl of Albemarl to the priory of St. Bees.

In the year 1312, *Robert de Halghton* was rector of Caldbeck, and removed to Ousby on an exchange with *Adam de Appelby*. And in 1332, a commission was issued to inquire what dilapidations were in the chancel or manse at Caldbeck, and to sequester the goods and chattels of Adam de Appelby the late rector deceased towards the repairs thereof.

Robert de Bramley, professor of civil law, succeeded Adam de Appelby, and in 1334 made an exchange with *Peter de Galiciano* rector of Horncastle, which was confirmed by the bishops of Carlisle and Lincoln respectively. And in the next year after, Peter resigning, *Nicholas de Whitrigg* was collated; with leave to be absent from his cure in pursuit of his studies for three years. By his last will he bequeathed his body to be buried in the chancel of the church of Caldbeck, and to Henry de Malton and Thomas de Whitrigg knights 140 oxen.

In 1362, on the death of Nicholas de Whitrigg, Mr. *William de Ragenhill* was collated; who in the year 1369 having obtained the church of North Colingham in the diocese of York, resigned the rectory of Caldbeck.

In the same year *Thomas de Salkeld* was inducted by authority of the pope. And he dying in 1379, *Thomas del Hall*, official of Carlisle, was collated by bishop Appleby.

In 1583, on the death of Dr. *Hugh Sewell* rector of Caldbeck, *Thomas Fairfax*, S. T. B. was instituted on a presentation by Mr. Thomas Hammond chancellor of the diocese, who had a grant from the bishop of the advowson for 20 years.

In 1640, on the death of Thomas Fairfax, *Frederic Tunstall*, M. A. was collated by bishop Potter. He was ejected by Cromwell's commissioners, and died before the restoration.

In 1657, *Richard Hutton* was rector, who probably was deprived in his turn by the Bartholomew act, for in 1663 *Arthur Savage*, M. A. who had been ejected from Brougham in 1644, was collated by bishop Sterne.

In 1700, *Jeffery Wybergh*, LL. B. was collated by bishop Smith.

In 1727, *John Waugh*, M. A. was collated by bishop Waugh his father.

In 1765, Pynson Wilmot, LL. B. was collated by bishop *Lyttelton*.

There are in this parish 243 *families*; 29 of which are quakers, and all the rest of the established church.

There is an ancient *church stock* in this parish, but no account how it was first raised. It is now about 54 *l*, the yearly interest whereof is expended in repairs of the church; and if any overplus remains, it is added to the principal.

Philip lord Wharton by deed bearing date July 12, 1692, appropriated certain lands in the county of York, as a perpetual fund for the purchasing yearly 1050 bibles, 16 of which are appointed to be sent yearly to this parish.

There is a *poor stock* of 30 *l*, left by Cuthbert Brown in 1665; which is let out to interest by the overseers, and the produce divided among poor house-holders.

Arthur Savage the rector, by his will bearing date Nov. 1, 1698, gave to this parish 50 *l*; the interest thereof to be applied for the binding out poor children apprentices.

There is also a *school stock* of 103 *l*, which was raised by voluntary contri-butions in the year 1647, which is lodged in the hands of some of the most substantial inhabitants, and they pay the interest thereof to a schoolmaster. By one of the articles then made and agreed upon, every person who then con-tributed to the stock should be free to the school, and likewise his lineal de-scendents enjoying the estate of the first contributor; but in case any of their estates should be sold, it was agreed, for the encouragement of the school, that the seller should lose this freedom to the school, and the buyer should not acquire any, but be as a foreigner.

PARISH OF WESTWARD.

The parish of WESTWARD lies north from Caldbeck, and is made up of a number of houses lying scattered up and down, every one of which hath a ready forth-gate to the common.

It is bounded by Shalkbeck from the foot thereof to the head, and so as-cends over the west end of Brocklebank fell as far as Thornthwaite; so down the water by Thackthwaite, Islekirk, Parson's bridge, and Shaking bridge, till it fall into Waver, and down Waver till it come to Rook's of the bridge, then bending eastward to a place called Messengers of the Moss, and from thence on the north side of Granger houses and Brigbank to Wysa beck, then cross Tiffinthwaite to Forster folds, and then down by the foot of Manybanks on the south side of Moorthwaite to Millbeck, until it falls into Wampool river, and then up that river till Shalk falls into it.

This place at the time of the conquest was forest ground of Allerdale; and was granted by Alan second lord of Allerdale to king Henry the second; who annexed it to, and incorporated it with his forest of Englewood, and from thence it received the name of the West Ward *.

* Juratores dicunt, quod Alanus filius Waldevi quondam dominus de Alle-dale dedit domino Henrico regi proavo domini regis nunc, cervum et cervam, aprum et capreolum, inter Shauk et Alne, sicut Alne cadit in mare: Et idem Alanus dedit dicto domino Henrico regi solum cum her-bagio in libera chasea de Allerdale, viz. per has divisas; de Waspatrick wath ascendendo ad locum ubi Shauk cadit in Wathempole, et de illo loco usque ad caput de Shauk, et de illo loco usque ad Bowland bek heved' et de illo loco usque ad Randolphsete, et de illo loco usque ad caput de Thorne-thwaite bek, et de illo loco usque ad locum ubi Thornethwayte bek cadit in Waver, et de illo loco ascendendo usque ad magnum iter inter solum domini regis et solum de Waverton, et sic inter solum domini regis et solum de Wyggeton, et sic de solo de Wyggeton usque ad Troutbek, et de Trout-bek in Watkenpole, et de Watkenpole ascendendo usque Waspatrick wath: Et idem dominus rex, proavus domini regis nunc, posuit baroniam in regardo propria voluntate sua per quendam Alanum' de Nevill tunc forestarium domini regis.——From the Perambulation of Englewood forest 29 Ed. 1.

3

Afterwards,

Afterwards, king John having granted the hermitage of St. Hilda within the boundaries of this Weſtward to the monaſtery of Holm Cultram, the monks erected not far from thence a chapel or oratory, which·in proceſs of time obtained parochial rites, but was then (as, properly ſpeaking, all foreſts are) extraparochial.

And in the 18 Ed. 1. there was a memorable cauſe concerning the tithes of Linthwait and Curthwait both within the above mentioned bounds of this pariſh. Firſt, the king claimed them as of common right, he being intitled to the tithes of all places extraparochial. Next, the biſhop claimed them as within·the pariſh of Aſpatrick. Then the prior and convent of Carliſle claimed them by grant from king Henry the ſecond as of an aſſart within the foreſt of Englewood. Finally, the parſon of Thurſby claimed them as within his pa-riſh. And it was found for the king.

And the ſaid king, in the 22d year of his reign, by his charter ſetting forth his recovery of the tithes aforeſaid, grants unto the ſaid prior and convent and their ſucceſſors not only the tithes of the places above mentioned, but alſo all tithes accruing in all lands and places in the foreſt of Englewood that ſhall be hereafter aſſarted, not being within the limits of any pariſh, without the im-pediment or interruption of the king or his heirs, his juſtices, foreſters, ver-derers, or other officers of the foreſt †.

And ſince that time the church of Carliſle hath enjoyed theſe tithes of this Weſtward, ſtyling it parcel of the pariſh of St. Mary's Carliſle. The preſent leſſee is Sir Philip Muſgrave of Edenhall baronet, and the grant is in the fol-lowing words: All the tithe corn, grain, and ſheaves, and the tithe hay, hemp,, and line, within certain limits and bounds of the foreſt of Weſtward, parcel of the pariſh of St. Mary's Carliſle; that is, of Roſley, Reathwait, Brockle-bank, Haſſellſpring, Cleathow, and alſo within the limits and bounds between Cleathow aforeſaid and the bounds called St. Ellen the Old, being parcel there-of, and within Ravenſhead and Bladderſlack, and within all other the limits and bounds and places titheable within the ſaid foreſt of Weſtward. Rent to the dean and chapter 6 *l*; and to the curate 16 *l* free of all taxes.

---

† Rex omnibus ad quos, &c. ſalutem. Sciatis, quod cum in curia noſtra coram dilectis et fide-libus noſtris Hugone de Creſſingham et ſociis ſuis juſticiariis noſtris ultimo itinerantibus in comitatu Cumbriæ, verſus venerabilem patrem Johannem epiſcopum Carliolenſem, ... priorem beatæ Mariæ Carl', et Alanum tunc perſonam eccleſiæ de Thurſby, advocationem decimarum de quibuſdam aſſartis factis in foreſta noſtra de Englewood, et aliis minutis parcellis vaſti, tanquam de illis quæ fuerunt extra quarumcunque parochiarum limites, recuperavimus ut jus noſtrum ; Nos, pro ſalute animæ noſtræ et animæ claræ memoriæ Alianore quondam reginæ Angliæ conſortis noſtræ, et animarum anteceſſorum et hæredum noſtrorum, dedimus et conceſſimus, pro nobis et hæredibus noſtris, deo et eccleſiæ beatæ Mariæ Carl', et priori et canonicis ibidem Deo ſervientibus, omnimo-das decimas provenientes tam de aſſartis et parcellis prædictis quam omnes decimas proventuras de omnibus aliis landis et placeis in foreſta prædicta, extra limites parochiarum exiſtentibus, futuris temporibus aſſartandis: Percipiendas et habendas eiſdem priori et canonicis et eorum ſucceſſoribus in perpetuum, ſine occaſione vel impedimento noſtro vel hæredum noſtrorum, juſticiariorum, foreſta-riorum, viridariorum, aut aliorum miniſtrorum noſtrorum foreſtæ. In cujus rei teſtimonium has literas noſtras fieri fecimus patentes. Teſte rege apud Weſtminſter 5to die Decembris anno regni noſtri 22°.

This

This foreft having been granted, as is aforefaid, to king Henry the fecond, it continued in the crown till the reign of king Edward the third, who in the 17th year of his reign, granted the fame to Thomas Lucie on his marriage with Agnes de Beaumont a kinfwoman of the faid king ‡, whofe daughter and laft furviving heir Maud conveyed it to her hufband Henry Percy the firft earl of Northumberland, in which family it continued till Henry the fixth earl of Northumberland gave it to king Henry the eighth. Queen Mary reftored the fame to Thomas earl of Northumberland brother to the laft Henry. Which Thomas being attainted in the reign of queen Elizabeth on account of the northern rebellion forfeited the fame during his life; after which forfeiture, in the 14 Eliz. a commiffion iffued to Richard bifhop of Carlifle, Henry lord Scrope, Thomas lord Wharton, Simon Mufgrave knight, Henry Curwen knight, Francis Slingfby, Cuthbert Mufgrave, John Penruddock, Anthony Barwife, Thomas Leigh, and Robert Highmoore, efquires, to inquire upon certain articles to the faid commiffion annexed; and accordingly an inquifition was taken at Weftward Jan. 9 and 10, in the fame year, upon the oaths of Richard Salkeld, Francis Lamplugh, Roland Vaux, John Richmond, Anthony Curwen, efquires, Alexander Highmoor, John Southake, John Ellis, Thomas Bewley, Robert Vaux, Robert Dalfton, Richard Kirkbride, John Skelton, Richard Stanwix, John Pattinfon, and Robert Mulcafter, gentlemen, as follows; viz.

" Articles and interrogatories to be miniftred and inquired upon, for and " in the behalf of the tenants and inhabitants that claim common and pafture " within the foreft of Weftward:

" Firft, how the faid common and pafture hath been ufed before the late " attainted earl of Northumberland's reftitution to the fame by the late fove- " reign lady queen Mary?"

To this it is anfwered, that the tenants of the bifhop of Carlifle and of the dean and chapter of the cathedral church of Carlifle, inhabitants at Great

---

‡ Rex omnibus ad quos, &c. Sciatis, quod cum dilectus et fidelis nofter Thomas de Lucie ad requifitionem noftram confenferit dilectam confanguineam noftram Agnetem filiam Henrici de Bellomont ducere in uxorem, et nobis fupplicaverit, ut velimus ei et præfatæ Agneti in auxilium maritagii fui folum et herbagium de Allerdale (quæ valorem annuum viginti librarum non excedunt) dare et concedere gratiofe; Nos pro eo quod per inquifitionem per dilectum et fidelem noftrum Hugonem de Moriceby efchaetorem in comitatibus Cumbriæ, Weftmorlandiæ, et Lancaftriæ, de mandato noftro factam et in cancellaria noftra returnatam, eft compertum, quod folum et herbagium prædicta coronæ Angliæ annexa non exiftunt, et quod hujufmodi donatio et conceffio de folo et herbagio prædictis præfato Thomæ fic faciendæ foreftæ noftræ de Inglewood non funt prejudiciales, et quod herbagium et folum valent per annum decem et octo librarum, volentes fupplicationi ipfius Thomæ annuere in hac parte, dedimus et conceffimus pro nobis et hæredibus noftris præfatis Thomæ et Agneti dictum folum et herbagium de Allerdale: Habendum et tenendum eifdem Thomæ et Agneti et hæredibus de corporibus fuis exeuntibus, de nobis et hæredibus noftris, per fervicia inde debita et confueta, in perpetuum. Ita quod fi idem Thomas et Agnes fine hæredibus de corporibus fuis exeuntibus obierint, tunc folum et herbagium prædicta ad nos et hæredes noftros integre revertantur. Tefte rege apud Clarendon 28 die Julii anno Edwardi 17°.——The title of this Grant is, Charta domini regis Edwardi tertii facta Thomæ de Lucie et Agneti uxori fuæ filiæ Henrici de Bellomont, de le Weftward, alias dicta, herbagio de Allerdale, prius conceffa domino Henrico fecundo quondam regi Angliæ, per Alanum filium Waldevi filii Gofpatricii comitis Dunbar quondam domini baroniæ de Allerdale. 3 Dugd. Mon. 46.

Dalfton,

Dalston, Little Dalston, Hawkfdale, Cumdivock, Cardew and Cardewlees, Buckabank, Unthank, Caldew gate and Caldew ftones, Caldcotes, Newby, Great Cummerfdale, Little Cummerfdale, Brownelfton, New Lathes, and Harrington houfes; the tenants and inhabitants of the lordfhip and manor of Thurfby; the tenants and inhabitants of the manor of Crofton and Parton, Mickelthwaite and Whyney; the queen's majefty's tenants and the tenants of her majefty's freeholders of the barony of Wigton; the manor and town-fhips of Waverton and Xyket, Woodfide, Kirkland, Roofhewen, Moor-thwait, Dockwrey, Murrhoufe, Ulton, Laffenhow, Kirkbride, Caldbeck and Kirkthwait, have always ufed time without memory (before the reftitution of the late attainted earl of Northumberland by the late queen Mary) to have common and pafture within the foreft of the Weftward.

" The fecond article : What inclofures the faid late earl of Northumber-" land hath made within the faid Weftward ; what quantity of ground or " number of acres the fame inclofure doth contain ; and how the fame hath " been ufed ; and what yearly rent hath been paid and anfwered fince the " fame inclofure ?"—Anfwer : Since the reftitution of the faid late attainted earl, there have been made and improved fix fcore and feven inclofures, con-taining twenty-feven fcore, five acres, half acre, one rood, one half rood ; of which fixfcore and feven inclofures there be newly inhabited and houfes builded upon thirty-two, which thirty-two contain ten fcore five acres half acre one rood and half rood of ground ; the refidue of the faid fix fcore and feven inclofures, which be fourfcore and fifteen in number, and contain feven-teenfcore acres, are rejoined and annexed to the tenants that have ancient farmholds befides : And they find, that the rents inhanfed or referved upon the faid inclofures (as they learn and underftand by a copy of a rental fhewed by the late receiver of the faid late attainted earl of Northumberland, other than which copy of rental they can have no certain intelligence) do amount to the fum of 9*l* 19*s* 5*d*.

" The third article : How many of the inclofures may remain in what " ftate they be, without annoyance and hurt to the tenants and inhabitants " that claim common and pafture there within the fame ?"—To this they find and prefent, that none of the faid improvements and inclofures may remain in the fame ftate they be, without annoyance to the faid tenants and inhabitants fpecified in the firft article, and that claim common and pafture within the fame.

To the feveral following articles they give one general anfwer, as follows, viz. "*Art*. 4. What number of tenants and inhabitants there be, that claim " or ought to have common there, and in what lordfhips, baronies, parifhes, " towns, and villages the tenants and inhabitants that claim to have the faid " common and pafture do dwell and be ?—*Art*. 5. Whether any of them that " claim the faid common and pafture be the queen's majefty's tenants ; if " they be, then what number is there of them, and in what lordfhip, barony, " town, or parifh they do inhabit ?—*Art*. 6. What annoyance, hurt, or " hindrance would the faid inclofures be to fuch as claim the faid common " and pafture, if the fame fhould ftill remain ; and whether may any thereof

" remain

" remain inclofed without their hurt ?—*Art.* 7. To what yearly rent do
" the fame inclofures amount; and if the fame inclofures fhould be laid open
" and unclofed, how fhould the queen's majefty be anfwered of the fame rent,
" or what yearly rent or money fhould or ought fhe have yearly of or by the faid
" tenants and inhabitants that claim the faid common, if they fhould enjoy
" the fame, or what other fervice or confiderations fhould they do, or have
" they heretofore done, in refpect of or for the fame ?—*Art.* 8. Whether
" have the faid tenants and inhabitants that claim the faid common and
" pafture had the fame time out of mind of man before the faid inclofure, or
" how long or what time have they had the fame ?"——Anfwer. To thefe
articles they find and prefent, as before they have found and prefented : And
further, that they the faid tenants and inhabitants aforefaid, claiming common
for the faid grounds inclofed to be laid open and proftrate, will fubmit themfelves and ftand to her grace's order for the rent thereof.

The firft divifion within this parifh is Brocklebank, towards Caldbeck,
lying on the north eaft fide of Brocklebank fell, which is divided from Reeth-
wait or Reedthwaite by a little rill called Silverbeck, which meeting with
Wifa beck at the northweft end of Weftward park, makes one ftream till it
falls into Wampool below Wigton. This is the moft hilly and the fulleft of
wood of any part of the parifh, and hath plenty of coal about Shawk head,
Lowpgill, and Weftward park, which are moftly a cannel coal. This divifion doth alfo comprehend Haflethorp, Tonguethwait, and Clea. At which
laft place, William Mufgrave a younger fon of Sir William Mufgrave of
Crookdake was feated, and whofe daughter Anne carried the inheritance
to the Fletchers of Deerham, in whofe name and family it ftill continues.

Rosley divifion lies northeaft of the former, being divided from it by
Wyfa beck, which arifes at one end of the town of Rofley, at the other end
whereof is held yearly a great fair on Whitfun Monday, and alfo every
fortnight day after till All Saints day, for horfes, cattle, fheep, cloth, and
many other kinds of goods. Breconthwaite, Height, and Woodcock hill are
parcel of this quarter of the parifh.

Woodside is another divifion, which lies towards Wampool. The firft
hamlet is Howrigg and Eaft Kirkthwait by Shawkfoot and Weft Kirkthwait.
Sir Gilfrid Lawfon and Mr. Brifco of Crofton have here an undivided lordfhip, the tenants whereof pay yearly rents and arbitrary fines.

Stoneraise divifion lies more weft upon Wyfa, beginning at Highmoor
and Fofter's fold, then to Kirkhill and Ilekirk, then to Crofshill, fo round
Harthwait common, by Silly Wrey, Grainger houfes, and Brigbank to Red
Dial, where the ruins of Old Carlifle appear.

Ilekirk (Hildkirk) had its name from the hermitage of St. Hilda abovementioned, which king John gave to the abbey of Holm Cultram, whofe
                                                                    grant

grant bears date the firft of March in the fixteenth year of his reign ; whereby he grants to the abbey of Holme and the monks there ferving God, the hermitage of St. Hilda in his foreft of Inglewood, with the land which Roger the hermit had held there ; with liberty of a vaccary for 40 cows in the faid foreft, and their young till the age of two years ; and pafture for as many horfes and oxen as will till the faid land ; and that they fhall be free from efcape, and from puture of the forefters †. Which grant was confirmed by king Henry the third ‡. ·

After the diffolution of the monafteries, king Henry the eighth by letters patent bearing date July 15, in the 35th year of his reign, granted to Thomas Dalfton efquire (amongft many other particulars) all thofe meffuages, lands, tenements, meadows, paftures, rents, reverfions, fervices, and hereditaments whatfoever, in Hildkirke in the county of Cumberland, viz. the meffuages and tenements in the feveral tenures of Richard Barwife, John Brown, Adam Afkew, Richard Milner, and John Plumber, and all that park called Hildkirk park, late belonging to the monaftery of Holme ; rendering for the fame yearly at the feaft of St. Michael the archangel 15s 8¼d.

And in the next year, viz. May 20, 36 Hen. 8. there is a licence to Thomas Dalfton efquire to convey the capital meffuage of Hildkirke called Hildkirk grange, with four meffuages and tenements in the tenure of John Barwys gentleman, John Plumber, and Richard Milner, to Anthony Barwys gentleman, for the fine of 43s 5d paid into the exchequer.

After three or four generations, the fame defcended to Richard Barwife efquire (called the Great Barwife from his gigantic ftature) who died in the year 1648 without iffue, as appears from the following monumental infcription in the church of Weftward :

A memorative epitaph for that excellently accomplifhed gentleman Richard Barwife late of Ilekirk efquire . He died the 13 Feb. 1648, in the 47th year of his age.

Below, good Barwife clos'd in body lies, ·
Whofe faintly foul joys crown'd above the fkies.

---

† Johannes Dei gratiâ, rex Angliæ, &c. Archiepifcopis, epifcopis, abbatibus, comitibus, baronibus, jufticarns, vicecomitibus, præpofitis, et omnibus ballivis et fidelibus fuis, falutem. Sciatis nos, intuitu Dei, et pro falute animæ noftræ et anteceflorum et fucceflorum noftrorum, dedifle, conceffifle, et hâc chartâ noftrâ confirmafle abbatiæ de Holme et monachis ibidem Deo fervientibus, heremitorium fanctæ Hildæ in forefta noftra de Inglewood, cum landa quam Rogerus Croky quondam heremita illius loci tenuit integre, cum omnibus pertinentiis fuis, ficut idem Rogerus eam unquam melius et plenius tenuit ; ita quod landam illam excolant, vel ad pafturam teneant, fi voluerint, Conceffimus etiam eis, quod habeant ibidem vaccariam quadraginta vaccarum, cum paftura eorum in forefta illa, et cum fecta earundem ad duos annos ; ita tamen quod in fine fingulorum duorum annorum amoveatur de forefta noftra fecta earundem quadraginta vaccarum de duobus annis. Conceffimus etiam eifdem, quod habeant in paftura illa tot equos et boves, quot fufficiant eis ad landam illam excolendam, fi illam excolere voluerint. Et quod quieti fint de efcapio, et de receptione forestariorum nifi ad voluntatem ipforum monachorum. Hæc autem omnia prædicta eis conceffimus habenda et tenenda de nobis et hæredibus noftris in liberam, puram, et perpetuam eleemofynam, &c. Teftibus Domino P. Winton Epifcopo, &c. Data per manum magiftri Ricardi de Marifco cancellarii noftri, apud Windefore, primo die Martii anno regni noftri 16°.   · Regiftr. Holme.

‡ Ibid.

City's

City's wife guide, country's chief ornament ;
In grace, and nature's gifts, most eminent.
Grave, prudent, pious, stor'd with virtues best,
Exchanging life for death, by death lives blest.
Of whom it's said none here liv'd more approv'd,
None died more miss'd, none miss'd was more belov'd.
Whose virtuous wife in sable thoughts doth mourn
Her turtle's loss, till laid near to his urn.
Oh pity great so choice a couple should
Without grand issue be reduc'd to mould.
Nor can they well, while here they leave a name,
Shall them survive, till they revive again.

This Richard was succeeded by another Richard Barwise (probably a distant relation) called Little Richard ; who left two daughters, the elder married to major Fetherstonhaugh who died in 1708 without issue ; the younger was married to Kirkby in Lancashire, and sold the estate to Lancelot Emerson ; from whom, or from his daughter, it came to Postlethwait and Steel ; and from them by purchase to Joshua Lucock of Cockermouth esquire the present proprietor.

Old CARLISLE aforesaid stands upon the river Wisa, where (as Mr. Camden observes) the melancholy ruins of an ancient city teach us, that nothing in this world is out of the reach of fate. But what the ancient name was, he did not know, unless it was the *Castra Exploratorum* †. But Mr. Horsley takes it to be *Olenacum*. He says, " The ruins here are very grand and con-
" spicuous. It stands upon a military way, very large and visible, leading
" directly to Carlisle and the Roman wall. And there is no other station
" upon this way, between it and Carlisle or the wall. Old Carlisle is about a
" mile south from Wigton, about eight miles southwest from Carlisle, and
" about twelve or fourteen west from Old Penrith and ten or more east from
" Elenborough. The ramparts of the station lie two of them directly east
" and west, and the other north and south. There seems to have been a
" double agger quite round it. The river Wiza runs on the south and west
" sides of the station, about half a mile from it, and the descent to the
" river is steep ; yet the outbuildings have been on all sides here as well as at
" Old Penrith. From this station there is a very large prospect, especially
" westward, reaching to the sea. The *Wiza*, on which Old Carlisle stands,
" may be imagined to have some affinity with *Virosidum*, as well as the *Elne*
" with *Olenacum*, if the order of the Notitia did not disagree. According to
" the Notitia, Olenacum was garrisoned by a body of horse, called Ala
" Herculea, and it appears from inscriptions that the Ala Augusta (afterwards
" from the emperor Maximianus Herculius called Ala Herculea) was long at
" Old Carlisle. It was there, when Fusiranus and Silanus were consuls in
" the year of our Lord 188 ; as also when Apronianus and Bradua were

† Camd. 1016.

                                        " consuls

" confuls in 191. It ftill continued at Old Carlifle, when Atticus and Præ-
" textatus were confuls in 242, under the reign of Gordian."

The infcriptions found at this place, though the altars and monuments on
which they were infcribed have been fince removed to other places or loft, Mr.
Horfley exhibits as follows :

On an altar, now at Conington, and much effaced ;

```
            I O M
PRO SALVTE IMPERATORIS
M. ANTONI GORDIANI P. F.
INVICTI AVG ET SABINIAE FVR
IAE TRANQVILE CONIVGI EIVS TO
TAQVE DOMV DIVIN EORVM A
LA AVG GORDIA OB VIRTVTEM
APPELLATA POSVIT CVI PRAEEST
AEMILIVS CRISPINVS PRAEF
EQQ NATVS IN PRO AFRICA DE
TVSDRO SVB CVR NONNII PHI
LIPPI LEG AVG PROPRETO ....
ATTICO ET PRAETEXTATO
COSS
```

Jovi optimo maximo :

Pro falute imperatoris Marci Antonii Gordiani, pii, felicis, invicti, Augufti,
et Sabiniæ Furiæ Tranquillæ conjugis ejus, totaque domu divina eorum, àla
Augufta Gordiana ob virtutem appellata pofuit : Cui præeft; Æmiliius Crif-
pinus præfectus equitum, natus in provincia Africa de Tufdro, fub cura
Nonnii Philippi legati Auguftalis proprætoris ; Attico et Prætextato confulibus.

Upon an altar in the weft wall of the Garden at Drumbrugh caftle :

```
        I O M
ALA AVG OB
VIRTVT APPEL CVI
PRÆEST TIB CL TIB FI
INGM IVSTINV
PRAEF FVSCIAN
ET SILANO ∏C
```

Jovi optimo maximo ;

Ala, Augufta ob virtutem appellata, cui præeft Tiberius Claudius Tiberii
filius . . . . . Juftinus præfectus : Fufciano et Silano iterum confulibus.

In the end wall of a ftable at the fame place :

```
        I O M
        ALA
AVG OB VIRTVTEM
APPELLATA CVI PRAEEST
```

```
PVB ÆL PVB F SER
GIA MAGNVS DE
MVRSA EX PANNON
INFERIOR PR . : . . .
APRONNIANO ET BR . . . :
```

Jovi optimo maximo, ala Augusta ob virtutem appellata, cui præest Publius Ælius Publii filius, Sergia [tribu], Magnus de Mursa ex Pannonia inferiore prefectus : Aproniano et Bradua [consulibus].

On a pillar, which seems to have been one of the miliary stones that were erected at every mile's end upon the military ways; in the garden at Naworth castle :

```
IMP CAES
M. IVL
PHILIPPO
PIO FELI
CI
AVG
ET M. IVL. PHI
LIPPO NOBILIS
SIMO CAESA
TR. P. COS.
```

Imperatori Cæsari Marco Julio Philippo, pio, felici, Augusto ; et Marco Julio Philippo, nobilissimo, Cæsari; tribunitia potestate consuli.

On a pillar at Conington :

```
D N FL IVL
CRISPO
NOB CÆS
V CONS
TANTINI
MAXIMI
FILIO
DIVI
CONST
ANT PII
NEPOTI
```

Domino nostro Flavio Julio Crispo, nobilissimo, Cæsari ; Valerii Constantini Maximi filio ; Divi Constantii, pii, nepoti.

Besides these, there are three other inscriptions given by Camden, none of which are now to be found ; viz.

Deo sancto Belatucadro, Aurelius Diatova aram ex voto posuit, libentissime, meritissime.   2

Deo

, Deo Ceaiio Aurelius . . . . . . Eruracio pro fe et fuis votum folvit libentiffime merito.
Dils Manibus Mablinius Secundus eques ɔlæ Auguſtæ ſtipendiorum.

Mr. Camden fays, an infinite number of little images, ſtatues on horſeback,
eagles, lions, Ganymedes, with many other evidences of antiquity, have
been dug up at this place, which are all now periſhed and loſt.

The *church* of Weſtward was returned to the governors of queen Anne's
bounty at 23 *l*, and is now worth about 30 *l* per annum;
In the church yard is the following epitaph : " Under this ſtone lies the
" body of major Philip Fletcher of Clea ; who ſerved their majeſtys king
" William and queen Mary ſeveral years, and alſo queen Anne. He was in
" all the conſiderable actions and ſieges of her reign under the great and
" victorious duke of Marlborough. He died Mar. 10. 1744. Aged 93."

Frances Barwiſe, widow of Richard Barwiſe eſquire abovementioned, gave a
parcel of ground in Wigton then worth 40 *s* a year, three fourths of the rent
whereof to be given to the poor of Weſtward, and the other fourth to the
poor of Wigton town ; as appears from an inſcription on a plate of braſs in
the church of Weſtward.

In 1747 it was certified, that there were 155 families in this pariſh ; of
which five were quakers;

PARISH OF BOLTON.

BOLTON *(Bothilton)* is the next pariſh to Weſtward, and is bounded by
Thornthwaite cloſe beck from the head thereof to the foot where it falls into
Waver below Rookſbridge, and ſo up Waver to Little gill above Blathwait on
the weſt ſide of Waver, and ſo up that gill to the head thereof, and then
directly north weſt to Crumbock, then up Crumbock ſouthwards to above
Prieſt croft, and then in a direct line ſouthweſt to Meals Gate, and thence
following down Dowbeck to Whitehall park wall, ſo up by that wall to Cockermouth road, and then along that road to Cockbridge, from thence up Elne
river to Ireby bridge end, then up Birkby beck by Awhatree to the head
of that beck, thence turning eaſt to Thorny ſtone, and ſo to the top of
Sandale hill, then pointing north on the tops of the hills unto the head of
Thornthwait.
This is one intire manor as well as pariſh, and was anciently demeſne
of Allerdale, until Waldieve firſt lord of Allerdale gave the ſame with Baſſenthwait and the Iſle of Eaſt Holm to his baſtard ſon Goſpatric, whoſe poſte-
rity took their ſurname from Baſſenthwait.
Bolton came, with a daughter of this family, to Duncan Laſcells, in
Richard the firſt's time. In the reign of Hen. 3. Thomas de Laſcells lord of
U 2   Bolton

Bolton (who married Chriftian daughter of William de Ireby) confirmed to the abbot and monks of Holme Cultram the hermitage of St. Hilda, and granted them common in Bolton †.

His widow Chriftian de Ireby afterwards married Robert Bruce, and died in the 33 Ed. 1. feifed of Hafelfpring in Weftward, Gamelfby and Unthank beyond Eden, and of Market Ireby, which Ireby fhe held of John Boyvil lord of Thurfby.

In Edward the fecond's time, *Roger Mowbray* was lord of Bolton, and forfeited his eftate there by taking part with Robert Bruce. Afterwards it came to his fon *Robert Mowbray* in Edward the third's time; and to *Alexander Mowbray*; and after to the *Nevils*. In the 12 Ric. 2. *John Nevil* of Raby died feifed of Bolton and of the Mowbrays lands in Gamelfby and Unthank. In the 22d of that king's reign *Ralph Nevil* held Bolton and Baffinthwait of Maud de Lucy. And thenceforth the *Nevils* lords *Latimer* held the fame, until it fell to *Henry* earl of *Northumberland* by the death of his mother one of the daughters and coheirs of the laft lord *Latimer* of that name of the *Nevils*. And it hath been ever fince a manor of the houfe of *Northumberland*, and the earl of *Egremont* now enjoys it as one of the *Percy*'s heirs as is aforefaid.

There are four divifions or conftablewicks within this parifh. 1. *Bolton wood*, which beginning at Thornthwaite clofe, runneth along the weft fide of that beck to Thackthwait, and fo down to Rookfbridge below Bolton wood foot. This part of it was heretofore moft of it woodland; but the wood being much cleared away, the lands have been broken into tenancies and tillage, except part of Hildkirk demefne which lies on Bolton fide of the water. 2. *Bolton row*, which begins at Meal's Gate, and fo afcending up Newlands row by Weary Hall (heretofore the feat of the Porters) where is

† After reciting king John's grant of St. Hilda to the abbot and monks of Holm Cultram, with pafture for forty cows and as many oxen and horfes as would till the ground belonging to the faid hermitage, he proceeds ——— Concedo etiam eifdem abbati et monachis communiam herbagii ad equicium fuum et ad prædictas vaccas cum earum fequela, et ad prædictos equos et boves de quibus prædictam landam excolere debent ut prænominatum eft, per totum bofcum meum et planum de Bothilton, et quod prædicta averia poffint libere ingredi et egredi fine impedimento mei vel hæredum meorum imperpetuum. Et quod idem abbas et monachi libere et fine impedimento poffint cum carris, plauftris, et carectis et omnimodis fummagiis tranfire per bofcum prædictum et planum, ita quod non accipiant de viridi bofco vel ficco fine licentia. Concedo etiam eifdem abbati et monachis pafturam ad porcos fuos in eifdem bofco meo et plano, fine warda facta per totum nifi tempore pafnagii; et fi ita fit quod eo tempore bofcum illum ingrediantur per efcapium vel alio modo, ego Thomas vel hæredes mei prædictos porcos abfque imparcatione faciam rechaciare, et fine damno aliquo eis inferendo, nifi prædicti abbas et monachi voluerint de pafnagio refpondere. Pro hac autem conceffione et confirmatione, prædicti abbas et monachi conceff̃erunt pro fe et fucceff̃oribus fuis, quod ego Thomas vel hæredes mei, fi licentiam habere poterimus de domino rege ad aff̃artandam vel apparcandam aliquam partem prædicti bofci vel plani, poffimus aff̃artare vel apparcare, et illud aff̃artum haia includere, fine contradictione aut impedimento prædictorum abbatis et monachorum, ita quod animalia ipforum abbatis et monachorum nullâ occafione fentiant detrimentum; ita quod fi prædicta animalia per defectum claufuræ prædicta aff̃arta ingrediantur, fine damno aut jactura rechaciabuntur. Et ut ifta conceffio mea et confirmatio robur firmitatis imperpetuum obtineat, tam ego quam prædictus abbas huic fcripto cirographato figilla noftra alternatim appofuimus. His teftibus, johanne de Danill tunc jufticiario foreftarum citra Trentam, Thóma de Multon, Willielmo de Dacre, Willielmo de Vall, Ricardo de Laton, Radulpho de Glaff̃on, Ricardo de Newton, Roberto de Mulcaftre, Thoma de Bello Campo, Yfaaco de Ireby, et aliis. *(Regiftr. Holme.)*

3   **now**

now a good colliery, and paffing by the Clofe and Quarry hill as high as Cat-
lands, makes up the fecond divifion of this parifh. 3. *Newlands.* 4. *Bolton*,
which lies on the fide of Elne river, and is the church town. The earl
of Egremont hath a demefne here; and alfo the houfe of Whitehall, a little
lower, hath a demefne called Whitehall parks. The tenants are moftly
cuftomary, pay cuftomary rents, and heriots, and a ten-penny fine certain by
decree in the time of the laft lord Latimer.

In this parifh, there are about 155 families; whereof, quakers 13, prefbyterians 7, anabaptift 1.

The *church* is rectorial, dedicated to All Saints: It is rated in the king's
books at 19*l* 18*s* 4*d*; and is now worth about 80*l* a year. The patronage
was long in the lords of the manor; afterwards, being feparated from the
manor, it hath paffed through feveral hands.

In the year 1293, *Simon de Jefemwy* was prefented to this rectory by Sir
Robert de Brus and Chriftiana his wife, and inftituted thereupon, with a
provifo, that according to the tenor of a papal difpenfation of illegitimacy
granted to him, he refide upon his benefice.

In 1310, Sir Roger Moubray knight (being then at Berwick upon Tweed)
prefents *Robert de Appelby*, who is inftituted accordingly.

After him, *Henry de Appelby*; who exchanged with *Robert Bovill* vicar of
Morland.

In 1341, on Robert Bovill's death, *John de Whitrigg* was prefented by Sir
Alexander Moubray knight then refiding at Bolton.

In 1353, Sir Alexander Moubray prefented *William de Ebor'*; who in the
next year after, at the requeft of Sir Ralph de Nevil, had a difpenfation
granted to him of abfence from his rectory for one year.

In 1361, on the refignation of William de Ebor', *Adam de Crofby* was inftituted on a prefentation by Sir Alexander Moubray.

In 1567, George Porter of Bolton enters a caveat for the right of himfelf
and his affigns on the death of *George Nevill* the prefent rector of Bolton.
And in the fame year *William Turner* was inftituted on the prefentation
of the faid George Porter, as patron for that turn, by grant from Thomas
Hutton of Hutton John efquire, who claimed (in chief) from John Nevil
lord Latimer.

In 1629, on a purchafed turn from Jofeph Porter the original patron, *William Fairfax* was prefented by Richard Tolfon efquire.

In 1665, *Daniel Hickfletter* was prefented by Jofeph Porter of Weary hall
efquire.

In 1686, *Michael Robinfon* was inftituted on a prefentation by Richard
Thomfon of Kellam in the county of York efquire.

In 1702, *Guftavus Thompfon* was prefented by the fame patron.

In 1710, *Obadiah Yates* by the fame patron.

In 1752, *Adam Afkew* was prefented by his father Adam Afkew of Newcaftle upon Tyne efquire.

In

In 1761, *Daniel Fisher* was presented by Charles Christian gentleman. The present patron is Sir James Lowther baronet.

There is a small *charity* stock in this parish, of 12 *s* yearly, issuing out of a close called the Great Paddock, and distributed by the minister and church-wardens to the poor in Easter week.

PARISH OF ALL-HALLOWS.

This which is now commonly reputed a distinct parish, was anciently no more than a chapelry within the parish of Aspatria. And so late as the 4 Hen. 6. there is an award or order made by bishop Barrow (in the archives at Rose) in a controversy between the inhabitants of the chapelry of All Saints of Ukmanby annexed to and dependent upon the parish church of Aspatrick of the one part, and William Sandes vicar of Aspatrick of the other part, whereby the bishop ordains, that the said vicar and his successors shall by themselves or by a sufficient chaplain at their expence perform divine service in the said chapel at the times in the said order specified; and that the inhabitants of the chapelry shall yearly keep and observe the day of the dedication of the parish church of Aspatrick, and resort to the church on that day to perform their devotions as other inhabitants of the parish †. And in the
5 Hen.

† Universis Christi fidelibus hoc præsens scriptum visuris vel audituris, Willielmus Dei gratia Carliolensis episcopus salutem in domino sempiternam. Ad universitatis vestræ notitiam deducimus per præsentes, quod cum nuper inter parochianos incolas seu habitatores capellæ omnium Sanctorum de Ukmanby ecclesiæ parochiali de Aspatrick annexæ et dependentis ab eadem nostræ dioceseos, ex parte una; et dilectum filium dominum Willielmum Sandes perpetuum vicarium dictæ ecclesiæ parochialis de Aspatrick, ex parte altera; de et super inventione et exhibitione unius capellani apud dictam capellam omnium Sanctorum de Ukmanby celebraturi, omniaque alia et singula sacramenta et sacramentalia ibidem ministraturi, mota coram nobis fuisset materia dissentionis et discordiæ : Nos tum advertentes quod discordi in tempore non bene colitur pacis auctor, cupientesque paternis affectibus omnium et singulorum subditorum nostrorum pacem, concordiam, et quietem, in quibus ministri quam plurimum prosperantur, effectualiter procurare, et ipsos in pace fraterna conservare, potestate nostra nedum ordinaria verum etiam virtute cujusdam submissionis dictorum parochianorum de Ukmanby, nec non dicti domini Willielmi Sandes vicarii prædictæ ecclesiæ parochialis de Aspatrick, unanimi consensu et assensu in nos factæ, de stando et consentiendo totaliter in alto et in basso nostris ordinationibus et statutis in hac parte, ad honorem summæ trinitatis omniumque sanctorum, et ad tranquillum statum, pacem, concordiam, et quietem partium prædictarum ac omnium et singulorum successorum suorum in perpetuum irrefragabiliter habenda, tenenda, et conservanda, ad hujus dissentionis et discordiæ materiam finaliter terminandam, ex parte præfatorum incolarum seu habitatorum capellæ omnium sanctorum de Ukmanby prædicta, nec non et domini Willielmi Sandes vicarii antedicti, cum instantia non modica requisiti, Christi nomine invocato, statuimus et ordinamus in hunc modum : Imprimis, statuimus et ordinamus et in perpetuum teneri et observari volumus, quod dominus Willielmus Sandes vicarius antedictus, et omnes sui successores dictam vicariam de Aspatrick in posterum canonice obtinentes, per se vel per alium capellanum idoneum eorundem vicariorum sumptibus et expensis exhibendum, in omnibus et singulis festis subsequentibus, viz. Natalis domini, Epiphaniæ, Purificationis, Annunciationis beatæ Mariæ, Paschæ, Pentecostæ, Trinitatis, Corporis Christi, Johannis Baptistæ, Apostolorum Petri et Pauli, Assumptionis beatæ Mariæ, Nativitatis et Conceptionis ejusdem, Michaelis archangeli, Omnium Sanctorum, et singulis diebus Dominicis, nec non omni quarta feria et sexta cujuslibet ebdomadæ, perpetuis futuris temporibus celebrabit seu celebrari faciet, celebrabunt seu celebrari facient, in capella omnium sanctorum de Ukmanby prædicta

5 Hen. 8. we find one Robert Ynglifh, chaplain of the chapel of All Saints in the parifh of Afpatryk, witnefs in a caufe of the abbot and convent of Shap before the chancellor of the diocefe of Carlifle.

This parifh or chapelry is bounded by Dowbeck from Meals Gate to the park wall at Whitehall below the church of Allhallows, fo along that wall fouthward to the highway leading to Cockermouth, then along that road to Cockbridge, then down Elne to Afpatria miln, then by the north fide of Elnebridge clofe to the foot of Brayton demefne, fo along the ring hedge which parts that demefne from Baggray to the common, and along the fkirts of the common by King Yeat, Ucmanby, and Leefrigg to Prieft Croft, and from thence to Meal's Gate where the boundary began.

UCMANBY was anciently one intire manor, which (with Blenerhaffet) was granted by Alan fecond lord of Allerdale to Ranulph de Lindfey with his fifter Oethreda. It afterward came by marriage to the Tilliols, which family ending in daughters coheirs, this manor became divided; one part thereof was fold by the lady Knevett (the defcendent of one branch) and her hufband John Vaughan, to the Salkelds of Whitehall, together with Torpenhow; and the other part came to Robert Highmoor father of Alexander, together with Bowaldeth.

WHITEHALL ftands at the eaft end of this parifh, where the Salkelds built a large houfe, who were defcended from a younger branch of the houfe of Corby; the firft of whom that came from Corby was,

1. *Thomas Salkeld* of Whitehall, who married Mary daughter of William Vaux of Caterlen, and had iffue,

2. *Lancelot Salkeld*; who married Elizabeth daughter and coheir of Nicholas Berdefey of Berdefey in Lancafhire, and had iffue three fons (1) *Francis*, who married Dorothy daughter of Thomas Brathwaite of Burnefhead efquire, and died without iffue. (2) *Nicholas*, who alfo died without iffue. (3) *Thomas*.

prædicta, omniaque alia facramenta et facramentalia ibidem miniftrabit feu miniftrari faciet, miniftrabunt feu miniftrari facient, per fe vel per alium capellanum idoneum, congrue et debite re-quifitus et requifiti. Quod fi dictus dominus Willielmus Sandes vicarius qui nunc eft vel fui fucceffo-res nec per fe nec per alium capellanum idoneum ad celebrandum in dicta capella nec quarta feria nec fexta, caufa fubfiftente rationabili, fint parati nec difpofiti, tunc aliqua alia feria ebdomadæ quas volnerint ad voluntatem ipforum celebrari volentium celebrabit feu celebrari faciet, celebrabunt feu celebrari facient, de cætero perpetuis futuris temporibus in eodem. Volumus infuper, ftatuimus et ordinamus, quod præfati parochiani, incolæ, feu habitatores capellæ omnium fanctorum de Ukmanby celebrent et obfervent annis fingulis de cætero diem dedicationis ecclefiæ parochialis de Afpatrick prædicta, accedentes ad eandem illo die, et facientes prout cæteri parochiani ejufdem ecclefiæ paro-chialis hactenus facere confueverint. Et ut hæc noftra præfens ordinatio de cætero robur obtineat perpetuæ firmitatis, in fidem et teftimonium ordinationis hujus, cuilibet parti hujus fcripti triplici-ter indentati, figillum noftrum duximus apponendum; et figilla partium prædictarum, viz incolarum feu habitatorum de Ukmanby prædicta, ac domini Willielmi Sandes perpetui vicarii ecclefiæ paro-chialis de Afpatrick, cuilibet etiam parti præfentis fcripti ordinavimus apponi; et unam partem penes parochianos, incolas, feu habitatores de Ukmanby prædicta, aliam penes vicarios ecclefiæ parochialis de Afpatrick, et tertiam [apud Rofam] refidere. Datum apud Rofam decimo fex-to die Februarii, anno domini millefimo quadringentefimo vicefimo quarto, et noftræ tranflationis fecundo.

3. *Thomas*

3. *Thomas Salkeld*, third fon and heir of Lancelot, married Mary Copeland; and by her had iffue,·

4. *Lancelot Salkeld*, who married Dorothy daughter of Alan Afkeugh of Skeughfby in the county of York ; and by her had iffue,.

5. *Francis Salkeld*, who married Anne daughter of Walter Strickland third fon of Sir Thomas Strickland of Sizergh in the county of Weftmoreland ; and had iffue,

6. *Thomas Salkeld*, who lived in the reign of king Charles the fecond ; and had iffue *Thomas, Lancelot, Roger*, and eight daughters.

7. *Thomas Salkeld* of Whitehall, fon and heir of the laft Thomas, had iffue *Thomas* and *Henry*.

8. *Thomas* the elder brother died without iffue, and the inheritance defcended to his brother, viz.

6. *Henry Salkeld*, who alfo dying without iffue, he devifed the eftate to his widow during life, and afterwards to truftees for payment of debts.

HARBY BROW adjoins to Whitehall demefne, from which it is only fevered by the park wall, and is a diftinct manor called Leefgill fince it came to the Highmores, as appears by an old infcription on a ftone in the kitching wall at Harby brow in the ninth year of Ed. 4. This manor continued in the Highmores, until Nicholas Highmore fold the fame to Blencow, with whom it continued for feveral defcents, and they at laft fold the fame about 30 years ago to the·prefent owner Mr. Steel. The capital meffuage or manor houfe ftood upon a little afcent upon the bank of Elne river, where there are fome remains of it ftill. The principal part of the demefne lands next to the houfe is hemmed in by Elne and Dowbeck, which meet at the foot of the demefne.

BAGGREY lies half a mile lower, where there are 8 or 9 rich tenants. It is oppofite to Blenerhaffet, being feparated from it by the river Elne.

This church was certified to the governors of queen Anne's bounty at 9 *l*, and having received two allotments from the faid bounty wherewith lands were purchafed within the parifh, is now worth about 24 *l* a year.

The bifhop of Carlifle is appropriator and patron ; and Sir Gilfrid Lawfon the leffee. The grant mentions all thofe the tithes of fheaves of corn and grain and hay, yearly growing and renewing within the fields and territories of Allhallows and Ukmanby within the parifh of Allhallows or Afpatrick, with the appurtenances. Rent referved to the bifhop 8 *l*, and to the curate 5 *l*. The leffee to repair the chancel.

In 1755, the number of *families* in this parifh was certified to be 32 ; whereof two quakers, and one papift (viz. Whitehall).

They have a fmall *poor ftock* of 10 *l* given by Jofeph Ritfon ; the intereft whereof is diftributed to poor perfons that have no allowance out of the parifh.

PARISH

PARISH OF ASPATRIA.

ASPATRIA, or *Afpatrick*, was fo firft named from Gofpatric earl of Dunbar
father of Waldieve firft lord of Allerdale. This parifh is bounded by Elne
river from the foot of Elne bridge clofe to the ring dike that parts Allerby
and Crofby fields, and fo along that ring hedge northwards to the divifion
between Hayton and Canonby fields, then turning eaftward between Hayton
and Alanby meadows, and fo as the divifion parts between Newton demefne
and Afpatria's north Riving, fo directly eaftward along the common to
the middle of Broadhead, and fo into Crumbock, and then up that beck to
Prieft croft, fo turning weftward by the ring hedge of Leefrigg to King gate,
and then to Baggray lane end, and fo along the hedge which fevers Brayton
demefne from Baggray field to Elnbrig clofe, and fo to the foot thereof.

The firft townfhip in this parifh is BRAYTON. It was the habitation of
Alan de Brayton; for Alan fecond lord of Allerdale gave the fervices of
Brayton to Ughtred after he had given him Ughtredby; and his pofterity
afterwards took the name de Brayton, until the male line failed. It is now the
inheritance of Sir Gilfrid Lawfon baronet, whofe great grandfather Sir Wilfrid
Lawfon of Ifell baronet did purchafe it of the three daughters and coheirs
of Thomas Salkeld a younger brother of the houfe of Whitehall. The
manor is of a fquare form, being bounded by Afpatria common on the north
and eaft fides, by Baggrey fields on the fouth, and Afpatria field on the weft.
The capital meffuage or manor houfe ftands exactly in the middle of it, and
was much improved by the late Sir Wilfrid Lawfon, who alfo built a very
fine park wall, and purchafed the tenants lands, and made them part of
the demefne.

ASPATRIA townfhip and manor lies next, being half a mile or more weft
from Brayton; it is bounded by the common on the north, by the demefne of
Brayton on the eaft, by Elne on the fouth, and by the demefnes of Outerfide
and Hayton on the weft. It ftands upon the ridge of an hill, pointing eaft
and weft, in length above half a mile, upon a dry fand. This was demefne
of Allerdale for a long time. On the divifion of the inheritance of William
Fitz Duncan and Alice de Romley his wife among their three daughters and
coheirs, this was allotted for the purparty of Alice the youngeft fifter; who
dying without iffue, her fhare became divided between her two elder fifters or
their reprefentatives; and the line of the eldeft fifter failing, the whole
defcended to the Lucys who inherited from the fecond fifter; whofe heir
female Maud de Lucy granted the fame to her fecond hufband Henry the
firft earl of Northumberland, as we have before obferved. This is one of the
principal manors in this barony, and ftill in the poffeffion of the reprefentative
of that family the prefent earl of Egremont; and many of the inferior lords
of manors do fuit and feryice to this court.

Outerby, or *Ughthredby*, lies a mile north-weſt from Aſpatria, upon lower ground near Elne; and is bounded by the grounds of Aſpatria on the north and eaſt, by Elne on the ſouth, and by Alwardby paſture on the weſt. This is a little manor of Sir Gilfrid Lawſon's, whoſe anceſtor Sir Wilfrid Lawſon of Iſell purchaſed it from Charles Orfeur of High-cloſe, in whoſe family it had been for many generations. There is a good colliery at this place. There are about ten freehold tenants, and twenty cuſtomary, one half whereof under Brayton pay arbitrary fines, and the other half under one Mrs. Walker pay fine certain.

Alwardby lies a mile north-weſt from Outerby. It was at firſt ſo named from Ayleward father of Dolphin who was firſt planted here, and called the place after his own name. And this place afterwards did give name to a family of the Allerbys, whoſe daughter and heir was married to Porter a younger brother of the houſe of Weary-hall. Amongſt the knights fees in Cumberland in the 35 Hen. 8. it is ſet forth, that William Porter then held the capital meſſuage and town of Alwardby of the king *in capite*, rendring for the ſame yearly 3 *d* cornage, and 8 *d* ſeawake, with other ſervices due and accuſtomed. The laſt of this name having no child made his wife joint tenant with him, and ſhe ſurviving afterwards married a younger brother of the Eglesfields, in whoſe family it continued for ſeveral generations, until Richard Eglesfield, ſon of Richard, ſon of Thomas, ſon of Richard, ſold it about 90 years ago to Richard Lamplugh of Dovenby eſquire, in whoſe heir it ſtill continues. Here are about 16 freehold tenants, and two cuſtomary who pay fine certain.

Hayton ſtands a mile north from Alwardby, within a mile of the ſea, and is bounded by Alwardby fields and Mealhay on the weſt, by Alanby and Newton fields on the north, and by Aſpatria and Outerby common on the eaſt and ſouth.

The word *hay* in the foreſt language ſignified a hunting ground incloſed, and this place ſeems to have received its name upon the like account; for Alan ſecond lord of Allerdale granted this place to his huntſman Seliff and his fellows, whoſe poſterity took the name *de Hayton.*

The laſt of the name John de Hayton had a daughter and heir married to Robert de Mulcaſter, a younger ſon of the Penningtons of Mulcaſter; which family alſo ending in daughters, Hayton was by one of the coheirs of Robert de Mulcaſter transferred to Piers-Jeffrey Tilliol; in whoſe male line it continued for eight deſcents, and then came to two ſiſters coheirs, *viz. Iſabel*, married to *John Colvil* who had Hayton for her purparty, and *Margaret* married to *James Moreſby.*

Iſabel wife of *John Colvil* had two ſons in the life of her father, *William* and *Robert. William Colvil* the elder ſucceeded his mother in her part of the Tilliol's lands, and died in the 20 Ed. 4. without iſſue male, leaving two daughters coheirs, whereby the Tilliols lands became further divided. *Phyllis* the elder was married to *William Muſgrave*, from whom deſcended the Muſgraves of Crookdaik. *Margaret* the younger, who had Hayton for her purparty,

2   was

was married to *Nicholas Musgrave* brother of the said *William*, and both of them younger sons of *Thomas de Musgrave* of Edenhall who married one of the coheirs of Stapleton *.

The said *Nicholas Musgrave* died in 1500; and, by his wife Margaret Colvil, had issue,

Thomas Musgrave of Hayton, who married Elizabeth daughter of the lord Dacre of Gilsland, and died in 1532, leaving issue *William*, and a daughter *Isabel* married to John fourth son of Sir Simon Musgrave of Edenhall.

William Musgrave of Hayton esquire, son of Thomas, married Isabel daughter and coheir of James Martindale of Newton esquire, whereby the manor of Newton came to this family; and died in 1597.

Sir *Edward Musgrave* knight, son and heir of William, married Catharine daughter of Sir Thomas Penruddock of Exeter. This Sir Edward purchased of Sir Henry Weston (who was the sixth in descent from the aforesaid James Moresby who married Margaret coheir of Tilliol) all their moiety of those lands which were the Tilliols below Eden; whereby the whole became reunited in that family, but it was afterwards sold again by the second Sir Edward Musgrave.

William Musgrave esquire son and heir of Sir Edward, married Katharine a coheiress of the family of Sir Nicholas Sherburne of the county of Lancaster knight, by whom he had a son Edward, and a daughter Eleanor married to Sir Christopher Lowther of Lowther knight.

Sir *Edward Musgrave* his son was made a baronet of Nova Scotia, 20 Oct. 1638. He married Mary daughter of Sir Richard Graham of Netherby baronet, by whom he had four sons, Richard, Edward, William, and Humphrey; and four daughters, of whom Jane was married to Sir Wilfrid Lawson of Isell. He greatly distinguished himself in the civil wars, and was thereby forced to alienate above 2000 *l per annum* of his paternal estate, *viz.* Solport to Sir George Graham, Kirklinton to Mr. Appleby, Houghton to Mr. Forster, Richardby to Mr. Studholme, and Scaleby to Dr. Gilpin.

Sir *Richard Musgrave* his son married Dorothy daughter and coheir of William James of Washington in the county of Durham esquire. He died in 1710, leaving five sons and four daughters; *viz. Richard* his son and heir, *William* a Hamburgh merchant at Newcastle, *James* rector of Gransden in the county of Cambridge, *Wastel* in the six clerks office, *Ralph* bred to the law, *Dorothy* married to John Hylton of Hylton castle esquire, *Catharine* married to John Brisco of Crofton esquire, *Anne* married to Sir William Grierson of Rockhall in Scotland baronet, and *Mary* married to William Horton of Howroyde in the county of York esquire.

Sir *Richard Musgrave* baronet, son of the last Sir Richard, married Elizabeth daughter of Mr. Joseph Finch and widow of Thomas Ramsden of Crowstone in the county of York esquire. He accompanied Sir Joseph Williamson plenipotentiary at the treaty of Ryswick; and served in parliament many years

---

* The ancient pedigree of this family is further traced and illustrated in this work under the manors of Musgrave in Westmorland and Scaleby in Eskdale ward in Cumberland.

as knight of the shire for Cumberland. He died in 1711, and left two sons, Richard and William.

Sir *Richard Musgrave* of Hayton baronet, the third of the name, married (his cousin german) Anne daughter of the above named John Hylton esquire, and died in 1739, leaving four sons, Richard, Edward, William, and Thomas, and one daughter Anne : of whom Edward and Anne are dead unmarried, William is the present baronet as hereafter mentioned, and Thomas is a major in his majesty's 64th regiment of foot.

Sir *Richard Musgrave* baronet, son of the last Sir Richard, having Hylton castle left to him by his uncle John Hylton esquire in 1746, changed his name to Hylton, and married one of the daughters and coheirs of John Hedworth esquire many years member of parliament for the county of Durham : And had issue two daughters coheirs; the elder of whom died in 1768 unmarried; the younger, now sole owner of the manor of Hayton, was married in 1769 to William Joliffe esquire member for Petersfield in the county of Southampton.

Upon the death of Sir Richard Hilton (formerly Musgrave) his brother Sir *William Musgrave* succeeded to the title of baronet, and is now one of the commissioners of the customs.

The church of Aspatria is dedicated to St. Kentigern, and is valued in the king's books at 10*l* 4*s* 2*d*, and is now worth about 100*l per annum*. It was granted by Waldieve first lord of Allerdale to the priory of Carlisle, which grant was confirmed by king Henry the second and king Edward the third[*]. The advowson, so far back as the bishop's register extends, hath been all along in the bishop.

In the year 1309, Sir *Alan de Horncastle* was collated by bishop Halton to the vicarage of Aspatrick, saving to the bishop the lands and tithes great and small within the parish as had been before accustomed.

In 1318, *Richard de Melburn* was collated on the same conditions.

In 1333, *Nicholas de Stroveton* vicar of Aspatrick dying, *Robert Bully* was thereupon collated.

In 1357, on the death of Sir *Adam Deincourt* vicar of Aspatric, the bishop collates Sir *Roger de Ledes*. This collation was made by delivery of a pair of gloves (per cirothecarum traditionem) according to the form of the constitution of the legate in that case made and provided.

In the next year, on Roger de Ledes's resignation, *Adam de Alenburgh* was collated, taking the oath of personal residence.

In 1380, *William de Arthureth* was vicar of Aspatria, as appears from his will made in that year.

In 1385, *Robert de Pontefract* vicar of Aspatryke exchanges his living with *Adam Fouward* vicar of Gilcrouce.

In 1424, *William Sandes* vicar of Aspatrick was ordered by bishop Barrow to officiate or find a sufficient chaplain to officiate, in the chapel of All Saints at Ukmanby.

---

[*] Ex dono Waldevi filii Gospatricii ecclesiam de Espatric, cum carucata terræ et omnibus pertinentiis suis.

In

In 1565, on the death of *Edward Mitchell* vicar of Afpatrick, *Anthony Thwaits*, S. T. P. was collated.

In 1578, on Dr. Thwaits's death, *Lancelot Dawson* was collated.

In 1610, Lancelot Dawfon dying, *William Orbell*, M. A. was collated by bifhop Robinfon.

In 1617, *Matthew Braddel* (on Orbell's acceptance of Bownefs) was collated by bifhop Snowden.

In 1639, *Thomas Warwick* was collated by bifhop Potter on the death of Matthew Braddel.

In 1661, *Francis Palmer* was collated by bifhop Stern.

In 1686, on the death of Mr. Palmer, *Richard Holme*, M. A. was collated.

In 1695, on the ceffion of Richard Holme to the rectory of Lowther, *George Fleming*, M. A. was collated by bifhop Smith.

In 1703, on the refignation of George Fleming (who removed to Stanwix), *Robert Hume*, M. A. was collated by bifhop Nicolfon.

In 1706, *David Bell* mafter of arts of Edinburgh was collated by the fame bifhop, on the death of his brother in law Robert Hume.

In 1729, *John Brifco*, M. A. was collated by bifhop Waugh.

In 1771, on Dr. Brifco's death, *William Gilpin* was collated by bifhop Law.

The bifhop repairs the chancel of this church; on the fouth fide of which chancel is the dormitory of the houfe of Hayton, where is a large monument, under which feveral of that family lie interred, as appears by the following infcriptions.:

1. At the head, towards the eaft;
John Covil married Ifabel Tilliol: 1438.

2. On the north fide ;
Nicholas Mufgrave married Margaret Covil daughter to William the fon of Ifabel Tilliol: Died A D. 1500.
Thomas Mufgrave married Elizabeth Dacre: Died A. D. 1532.
William Mufgrave married Ifabel one of the five heirs of James Martindale of Newton: Died A. D. 1597.

3. At the weft end ;
Edwardus Mufgrave miles duxit Catharinam Penruddock, et fecit. hunc tumulum pro fuo nobili patre. A. D. 1608.

4. On the top;

Cum legis hæc videas quam infignis gloria vixi,.
Defunctique legas quam dolor acer erat.
Lapideo corpus tumulo jacet, at fua nullo
Includi tumulo gloria digna poteft.

Nigh unto this place, on the outfide in the church yard, the late Sir Richard Mufgrave was interred at his own defire. The place is railed in with iron rails, and hath an handfome monument with this infcription :.

Here

*Here lies interred the body of Sir Richard Mufgrave baronet, who departed this
life Oct. 25. 1739. Ætat 38. He was defcended from Richard Mufgrave and
Elizabeth his wife; married to Anne fecond daughter of John Hylton of Hylton
caftle in the county of Durham efquire, by whom he had iffue Richard, Anne, Edward, John, William, William, and Thomas. And of thefe, John and the elder
William he buried here.*——Arms of the Mufgraves and Hyltons—Supporters
an unicorn and Woodman, as by his patent of baron of Nova Scotia—The
creft is that of the Mufgraves, not the creft given by the patent, *viz.* a thiftle
and laurel, to which the motto relates—*manet hæc et altera vincit,* which can
have no relation to the Mufgrave annulet.

PARISH OF CROSS-CANONBY.

THE parifh of CROSBY or CROSS-CANONBY lies fouth-weft from Hayton,
being the approximate neighbour to the fea near the mouth of Elne, whereby
it is bounded on the fouth, by the fea on the weft, by Hayton fields on the
north, and by Allerby Crooks and pastures on the eaft. This was demefne of,
Allerdale, and continued in the defcendents of the lords of Allerdale till Maud
de Lucy transferred it to the earls of Northumberland, of whom Henry the
fixth earl transferred it to king Hen. 8. Which faid king, Feb. 4, in the 37th
year of his reign, granted to Richard Bridges efquire and John Knight gentleman *(inter alia)* the manor of Crofbie with the appurtenances late parcel of
the poffeffions of Henry late earl of Northumberland, and all meffuages,
granges, mills, profits, emoluments, and hereditaments whatfoever in Crofs-Canonby to the faid manor belonging, and all other meffuages, lands, tenements,
and other hereditaments whatfoever in the parifh of Crofs-Canonby, which late
belonged to the faid earl of Northumberland, of the yearly value of 4*l* 3*s* 10¼*d.*

And on the 30th of January in the fame year, there is a licence to them
(for the fine of 28*s* paid into the exchequer) to alienate the manor of Crofby
in the parifh of Crofs Canonby, and 10 meffuages, 4 cottages, 2 acres of
arable land, 60 acres of meadow, 108 acres of pafture, 140 acres of moor,
and 12*d* rent, with the appurtenances, in Crofbie, *alias* Crofs-Canonby, late
parcel of the poffeffions of Henry late earl of Northumberland, to Gabriel
Highmore gentleman. And in the 11 Eliz. Gabriel Highmore conveyed to
Anthony Highmore.

Soon after, it was purchafed by the Porters of Weary hall; which family
poffeffed it, until George Porter efquire, fon of Jofeph, fon of George, fon
of John, fon of Jofeph, whofe father was the purchafer, fold the fame to the
tenants who are now all freeholders.

BIRKBY is another fmall manor within this parifh, belonging to Humphrey.
Senhoufe efquire of Nether-hall, anciently called Alneburgh hall, within this
parifh; at which place his anceftors became fettled about the time of the reign
of king Henry the eighth. They fprang from Seafcale in this county; the
firft of whom that we meet with, lived about the reign of king Edward the
third, and their pedigree proceeds as follows:

                                                    I. WALTER

I. Walter de Sevenhouse of Seafcale.

II. Nicholas de Slvenhouse. 1 Ric. 2.

III. William Senhouse of Seafcale married a daughter and coheir of Lucy. 1 Hen. 6.

IV. Thomas Senhouse of Seafcale. 1 Hen. 7.

V. Another Thomas Senhouse. 1 Hen. 8.

VI. John Senhouse of Seafcale married *Elizabeth* elder fifter and coheir of *Richard Eglesfield* fon of *Gawen Eglesfield* of *Alneburgh hall*; and by her had iffue, 1. *Thomas Senhouse* of Seafcale, whofe pofterity enjoyed the paternal eftate of Seafcale for feveral generations, but are now extinct. 2. *Peter Senhouse* of Alneburgh hall, otherwife Nether-hall; who died without iffue. 3. John Senhoufe of Alneburgh hall. 4. *Richard Senhoufe* of London.—The faid John, the father, died in the 11 Eliz.

VII. John Senhouse of Alneburgh hall, third fon of John by his wife Elizabeth Eglesfield, married Anne fixth daughter of John Ponfonby of Hayle. This is that John Senhoufe of whom Camden makes mention in his Britannia, to be of an ancient family, and who with great induftry collected many Roman ftones, altars, lavers, ftatues, with infcriptions, which he placed very orderly in his houfes and buildings, moft of which are to be feen there at this day. He died in the 3 Ja. 1. and had iffue nine fons and five daughters. 1. *John*, who died young. 2. *John*, who alfo died young. 3. *Peter*, who fucceeded to the inheritance. 4. *Simon*, killed near Dovenby by Skelton of Armathwaite. 5. *Richard Senhoufe*, D. D. fellow of St. John's in Cambridge, afterwards made dean of Gloucefter, and in the year 1624 bifhop of Carlifle *. 6. *William*. 7. *Thomas*. 8. *John*. 9. *James*. 10. *Ellen*, married to Fletcher of Morefby. 11. *Jane*, married to Blenerhaffet of Flimby. 12, 13, 14. *Mary*, *Elizabeth*, and *Anne*, all of whom died unmarried.

VIII. Peter Senhouse of Alneburgh hall married Frances daughter of Lancelot Skelton of Armathwaite caftle; and died in 1654. By his faid wife he had iffue, 1. *John*. 2. *Peter*, drowned in the Mill-dam when a child. 3. *Lancelot*. 4. *Thomas Senhoufe* of Long Newton, who married a daughter of Whelpdale. 5. *William*. 6. *Richard*. And three daughters, *Anne*, *Catherine*, and *Mabel*.

IX. John Senhouse of Alneburgh hall, otherwife Netherhall, married Elizabeth 3d daughter of Humphrey Wharton of Gillingwood in Yorkfhire, and

* Of this Richard there is an anecdote in Mr. Sandford's manufcript account of Cumberland (of which, by the way, we do not vouch the authenticity) : He fays, he was of a younger branch of Squire Senhoufe of Netherhall. And many good jefts paffed upon him. They were a conftant family of gamefters. And the country people were wont to fay, The Senhoufes learn to play at cards in their mother's belly. And this doctor and another perfon who was a ftranger to him being engaged one day at tables, the doctor tripped the die fo pat, that the other exclaims, furely (quoth he) it is either the Devil or Dick Senhoufe. [It is certain, the common people have a faying to this day (from whencefoever it might arife) in cafe of any extraordinary difficulty, " I will do it in fpite of the " Devil and Dick Senhoufe."] When he was a fcholar at Cambridge, coming into the country to fee his friends, his horfe happened to caft a fhoe, and having no money to pay the fmith withal, Well, well, fays the fmith, go your ways, when you are bifhop of Carlifle you will pay me. Which he did in abundance of gratuity; and was a religious and honeft paftor.

died

died in 1667. He had issue, 1. *Humphrey*, who died before his father, unmarried. 2. *John*. 3. *Richard*. 4. *Patricius*, who married Elizabeth daughter of John Bromfield of Hameshill, and relict of Henry Dalton of Brigham. 5: *Frances*, who died unmarried. 6. *Isabel*, who also died unmarried. 7. *Agnes*, who likewise died unmarried. 8: *Margaret*, married to Henry Eglesfield of Cross Canonby: She died in 1691. 9. *Elizabeth*, married to William Nicholson.

X. JOHN SENHOUSE of Netherhall married first Elizabeth daughter of Jerom Tolhurst lieutenant governor of Carlisle, by whom he had no issue. Secondly, Mary daughter of Andrew Huddleston of Hutton John. He died in 1677; and by his said second wife had issue, 1. *John*. 2. *Andrew*, killed at sea, fighting against the French. 3. *Dudley*, drowned in the river Lune. 4. *Peter*, who married Catharine daughter of Skelton of Branthwaite. 5. *Humphrey*. 6. *Richard*, drowned in Virginia. 7. *Dorothy*, married to her cousin Patricius Senhouse of Hameshill. 8. *Elizabeth*. 9. *Mary*, married to Richard Richmond of Crosby.

XI. JOHN SENHOUSE of Netherhall married Jane daughter of Richard Lamplugh of Ribton, and died in 1694. He had issue *John* and *Richard*, both of whom died infants; and six daughters, *viz.* 1. *Mary*, married first to Skelton of Branthwaite; secondly, to Richard Butler of Rocliffe in Lancashire. 2. *Jane*, married to John Stephenson of Baladool in the Isle of Man. 3 *Frances*, who died unmarried. 4. *Grace*, married to Richard viscount Shannon. 5. *Isabel*, married to John Fletcher of Clea. 6. *Elizabeth*, who died unmarried. These six sisters coheirs sold the demesne of Netherhall and manor of Alneburgh (now called Ellenborough) to their uncle Humphrey Senhouse fifth son of John at N° 10.

XII. HUMPHREY SENHOUSE of Netherhall, married Eleanor daughter of William Kirkby of Ashlack in the county of Lancaster; and died in 1738. He had issue, 1. *Joseph-Richard*, who died unmarried in 1718. 2. *Humphrey*. 3. *William-John*, who died unmarried in 1727. 4. *Bridget*, married to John Christian of Unerigg. 5. *Johanna*, married to Gustavus Thomson of Arcleby: She died in 1771.

XIII. HUMPHREY SENHOUSE of Netherhall, married Mary eldest daughter of Sir George Fleming baronet lord bishop of Carlisle; and died in 1770. He had issue, 1. *Humphrey*. 2. *George*, who died an infant. 3. *George*. 4. *William*, who married Elizabeth daughter of Sampson Wood of Barbadoes in 1772. 5. *Joseph*. 6. *Fleming*, who died an infant. 7. *Mary*, married to Robert Gale of Whitehaven. 8. *Catherine*, who died unmarried. 9. *Eleanor*, who died an infant. 10. *Johanna*, who died unmarried.

XIV. HUMPHREY SENHOUSE, the present owner of Netherhall, married in 1768 Catharine daughter of Thomas Wood of Beadnell in Northumberland; and hath issue, 1. *Mary-Anne*. 2. *Joanna*. 3. *Catharine*.

The CHURCH of Cross-Canonby was dedicated to St. John, and is a perpetual curacy in the patronage of the dean and chapter. For Alan second lord of Allerdale having issue a son Waldieve who died in his father's life-time,

gave

gave the body of his faid fon, together with the church of Crofby and one carucate of land there, to the prior and convent of Carlifle; whofe grant was confirmed by the kings Hen. 2. and Ed. 3 †.

Which carucate of land makes a fmall demefne, with about eight tenants, who pay to the dean and chapter 4 l 10 s 5¼ d cuftomary rent, and a four-penny fine upon change of tenant by death or alienation.

The demefne is now in leafe to Mr. John Brougham attorney at law in Cockermouth for 21 years, under the annual rent of 2 l.

The rectory (except the herbage of the church yard, and the tithes of Ellenburgh demefne) in 1760 was demifed to Henry Harrifon, Patricius Thompfon, and John Yoward, for 21 years, under the rent of 10 l to the dean and chapter, and 25 l to the curate, free of all taxes, and the leffees to repair the chancel.

The family of Netherhall have a vault in this church, where is the following monumental infcription :

H. S. E.
Humphridus Senhoufe
de Netherhall armiger :
Qui obiit quarto die Aprilis,
Anno Domini 1738. Ætatis fuæ 69.
Uxorem duxit Eleanoram Fil. Guil. Kirkby
De Afhlack in Com. Lanc. Armig.
Erat in Com. Cumb. Pacis Jufticiarius,
Et Vice-comes Anno primo R. Georgii I.
Quando occafione infigni oblata,
fuæ erga Ecclefiam Rempublicamq; Anglicanam
felici fub aufpicio familiæ Brunfvicenfis
egregium affectionis indicium
fortiter et alacriter exhibuit.
Conjux erat amans et fidelis,
Parens indulgens et tener,
Amicus conftans et fincerus,
Civis pacificus et utilis.
In cujus memoriam monumentum hoc, qualecunq; fit,
Gratitudinis ergô,
Filius unice fuperftes,
Humphridus Senhoufe
P.

In 1747, the number of families in this parifh was certified at 64, four of which were quakers. But an harbour having been fince made at Elnefoot, and a town there built named MARY-PORT, this number of families is greatly increafed, infomuch that it is computed there are about 340 families in that

---

† Ex dono Waldevi filii Gofpatricii ecclefiam de Crofby, cum carucata terræ et omnibus decimis et omnibus quæ ad illam ecclefiam pertinent ufque ad aquam Elne.

town only. They pay for their houses and 20 yards backward a front rent yearly, some of 6*d* and some 9*d* a yard. There are at present belonging to the said port between 70 and 80 sail of shipping, from 30 to 250 tons burden   The principal branch of their trade is coal, shipped for Ireland. But several of their vessels also sail yearly up the Baltic, for timber, flax, iron, and other merchandize. They have not much of the American trade; only a few ships yearly sail to North America. They have a *furnace* for casting *iron ware*, which carries on a considerable trade. They have also a *glafshoufe*, but at present not much use is made of it.

In the year 1760, a *chapel* was erected at Mary-port, and confecrated by bishop Lyttelton in 1763 by the name of St. Mary's chapel. The late Humphrey Senhoufe efquire gave 200 *l*, whereby to procure a benefaction from the governors of queen Anne's bounty; from which, and from certain sums charged upon the pews, the curate's falary amounts to about 35 *l per annum*. The nomination was referved in the act of. confecration to the faid Humphrey Senhoufe efquire and his heirs.

PARISH OF BROMFIELD.

BROMFIELD, or *Brun's-field*, is the next parish to Canonby, north-east from thence, and is of great extent, reaching from west to east feven miles or more. It is bounded by the sea on the west, by the boundary of Holm Cultram on the north, by the boundary of Wigton barony on the east, and by the meeting of Crumbock and Waver, and up Waver to Warthole miln, and then turning westward to Crumbock, and then up Crumbock to Aketon head above Crookdake miln, thence along Crookdake moor crofs Broadhead to the ftone quarry in Newton gill, and then along the fouth fide of Newton demefne and fields to the north fide of Hayton fields, and fo to the fea.

ALANBY is the firft township, ftanding upon the sea shore, and therewith is washed every spring tide. It ftands level and flat, as doth the whole parish, there being no femblance of an hill throughout the fame, except a little rifing ground about Crookdake and Blencogo, which ftand oppofite like two butts. This place was firft fo named from Alan the fecond lord of Allerdale, who being a melancholic man was pleafed with the lonely fituation of the place, and the rather in regard it was near to the abbey of Holme, which he had undertaken to rebuild. He gave it to fome .of his kindred who took name therefrom and were called de Alanby, until the male line failed, and one of the daughters and coheirs was married to William Flemby, from whom it came by a daughter to Blenerhaffet, in whofe family the manor continued till between 60 and 70 years ago, when it was fold to the Thomlinfons with whom it ftill remaineth. The tenants are about 40 in number, all freehold, paying a fmall quit rent to the lord.

In 1743, the reverend Dr. Thomlinfon propofed to affift the inhabitants of this village to build a chapel on a piece of wafte ground affigned by him for that purpofe as lord of the manor, but was fo ftrongly oppofed by the quakers

I   that

that it did not fucceed. But the next year he, at his own coft, built a chapel and furnished it with books and ornaments, on a piece of ground at the end of the town which he purchafed for that ufe. It is in length 18 yards, and in breadth feven yards and one foot; containing 31 pews, befides a large one for the lord of the manor, another for the curate, and another for the clerk. It was confecrated by bifhop Fleming in 1745, dedicated (at Dr. Thomlinfon's requeft) to Chrift, and the faid Dr. Thomlinfon his heirs and affigns decreed patrons. Over the door is this infcription, " This chapel was built by the " reverend Dr. Thomlinfon rector of Wickham and prebendary of St. Paul's " London, 1744." The faid bifhop Fleming foon after the confecration certified the chapel to the governors of queen Anne's bounty at 7 l per annum, viz. 5 l from the feats; and the houfe, ftable, garden, and chapel yard, 2 l. In confequence whereof, it was augmented with 200 l, in conjunction with the like fum given by the faid Dr. Thomlinfon.

There is likewife a neat fchoolhoufe built adjoining to the chapel by contributions in part, but chiefly by the curate who is obliged to teach fchool there.

In the year 1755, 100 l was laid out in the name of Dr. Waugh chancellor of the diocefe in lands in Blencogo for the ufe of this fchool.

In Alanby there was a meffuage and tenement belonging to the abbey of Holm Cultram, which at the time of the diffolution was in the tenure of Michael Fawcon, and in the 37 Hen. 8. July 9, was granted to Thomas Dalfton efquire.

WEST NEWTON is the next townfhip in this parifh, two miles eaft from Alanby, and a mile north from Hayton; and is now the manor of the furviving coheir of the Mufgraves of Hayton. It was at firft one intire manor (whereof Alanby was parcel) and was granted by Alan the fecond lord of Allerdale to Odard de Wigton, who gave it to Ketel his fourth fon, father of Adam de Newton who firft took that name. Which Adam was fucceeded by his brother Richard, who gave lands at Newton to the abbey of Holme Cultram; whofe grant was confirmed by Adam de Newton his fon. Which Adam had a fon Richard, who alfo confirmed his grandfather's grant. The faid Richard had a fon Thomas, who had another fon Thomas, who had a daughter and heir married to Roger Martindale; in whofe family it continued for three or four generations, until that family ended in daughters.

Thus amongft the knights fees in Cumberland in the 35 Hen. 8. it appears, that Cuthbert Ratcliffe, John Blenerhaffet, Anthony Barker, Richard Dacre, and Humphrey Dacre, in the right of their wives, daughters and heirs of James Martindale coparceners, held jointly and undivided the manor of Newton upon the fea, with the appurtenances, and the vill of Newton, of the king in capite by knights fervice, cornage 13 s 4 d, feawake, and fuit of court. They alfo held the manor of Ormefby; fo alfo lands and tenements in Langrigg, Bromfield, Meildrigg, Crookdake, Keldfike, and Lounthwaite by like fervices.

After the partition of the eftate, Newton came to the Mufgraves, by marriage (as it fhould feem) of one of the coheirs of Martindale after the death

of

of her firſt huſband.   For Mr. Denton, who was cotemporary, ſays, " Newton
" in Allerdale is now the inheritance of Edward Muſgrave ſecond ſon to Wil-
" liam and his wife one of the coheirs of Martindale laſt of that name lord
" of Newton."   And in that family of Muſgrave it hath continued ever
ſince.

The arms of Newton were ; Argent, a cheveron Azure, charged with three
garbes Or.

The arms of Martindale ; Barry of ſix, Argent and Gules, a bend Azure.

The town of Newton is pretty long, and hath a rill running through the
middle of it from eaſt to weſt.   The capital meſſuage ſtood at the weſt end of
the town, but being uninhabited ſince that eſtate came to the family of Hayton, there is nothing left of it but the ſhell of an old tower and a dove
coat.

The demeſne lies above the town ſouth-weſt towards Aſpatria and Hayton,
which is very large and fertil.   But there is little or no wood about all the
townſhip, and few incloſures.

At the eaſt end of the town is an excellent quarry of free ſtone, for flags,
troughs, poſts, chimney pieces, and ſuch like.

LANGRIGG is the next townſhip, being a long ridge of land, pointing eaſt-
ward towards Bromfield.   This was demeſne of Allerdale, and was granted
by Waldieve lord thereof to Dolphin ſon of Aylward, with Applethwaite and
Brigham.   The family of Dolphin became extinct in Henry the third's time.
After which, we find it in the name *de Langrigg.*   In the 9 Ed. 1. Agnes
wife of Gilbert de Langrigg demanded againſt John Crookdake 25 acres of
land, 15 acres of meadow, and 2s 5d rent there ; and againſt Thomas de
Langrigg 30 acres of land, and 14 acres of meadow.

In the regiſter of the abbey of Holme Cultram we find Agnes wife of Ralph
de Oſmunderley and Alice wife of Thomas de Laithes daughters and heirs of
Thomas de Langrigg.

In the 39 Ed. 3. John de Bromfield and Thomas de Lowther held lands in
Langrigg, rendring for the ſame 6s 8d cornage, and 7d ſeawake, being of
the yearly value of 5 l.

Afterwards, we find Langrigg in the Porters and Oſmunderleys.   The
Porters held the manor and old rent, and the Oſmunderleys had the demeſne
and ſix tenements there, as appears by an inquiſition *poſt mortem* of Cuthbert
Oſmunderley 4 Oct. 41 Eliz. who alſo died ſeiſed of ſix tenements in Whay-
rigg, one in Moor raw, one in Blencogoe, two in Bowaldeth, one in Arma-
mathwait, ſix in Oughterſide, four in Meldrigg, ſeven in Waverton, and four
in Louthwaite.

This family of Oſmunderley (Oſmotherly, Oſmunderlaw) came from a
place of that name in Lancaſhire, and was of great repute in the county of
Cumberland.   In the 21 Ric. 2. William Oſmunderlaw repreſented the county
of Cumberland in parliament.   In the 4 Hen. 4. and 6 Hen. 5. he was ſheriff
of

of the county. The laft of the family, the reverend Salkeld Ofmotherly, fold Langrigg (for they had alfo purchafed Porter's part) to Thomas Barwife father of the prefent owner, in the year 1735.—The arms of Ofmunderley are; Argent, a fefs ingrailed, between 3 martlets Sable.

The Berwifes alfo are a very ancient and refpectable family in this county. Richard Barwife efquire was fheriff of the county feveral times in the reign of Cha. 1. his feat being then at Waverton. They were anciently poffeffed of Ireby, Ilekirk, Blencogoe, and Deerham.—Their arms are; Argent, a cheveron between three boars heads couped and muzzled Sable.

The abbey of Holme Cultram had divers poffeffions in Langrigg, which after the diffolution were granted (amongft others) to Thomas Dalfton; viz. a meffuage and tenement and 12 acres of arable land and a free rent of 3s 4d in the tenure of Paul Dovingby, a dove coat with the appurtenances in the tenure of John Scurre, and a yearly rent of 5d and other fervices iffuing of the lands late of Thomas Thurnebrand, and a parcel of land with the appurtenances in the tenure of William Wright.

GREENHOW adjoins to Langrigg, and is part of that townfhip, where Mr. Brifco hath a good demefne and fome tenants. He is of a younger branch of the Brifcoes of Crofton, whofe anceftor married the heirefs of the Greenhows of Greenhow.

CROOKDAKE is alfo included in this townfhip. It was for a long time the feat of a younger branch of the Mufgraves of Mufgrave and Edenhall. Amongft the knights fees in the 35 Hen. 8. it is found, that Cuthbert Mufgrave fon of Mungo held the manor and hamlet of Crookdake with the appurtenances of the king by knights fervice, and rendring for the fame yearly 2s cornage by the hands of the fheriff of Cumberland. He held alfo at the fame time lands in many other places.

This family, like moft others, ended in daughters; and Crookdake came with Anne eldeft daughter of William Mufgrave to Sir John Balantine who was born at Carros in Clydefdale and bred a phyfician, in which name and family it continued for three or four generations, and then this family alfo ended in a daughter and heir, the prefent owner, married to Lawfon Dykes efquire a younger fon of the family of Dykes of Warthole, who in the year 1773 had a licence from the crown to affume the furname and bear the arms of Ballantine.

BROMFIELD and SCALES make the next townfhip, and are fituate about the middle of the parifh. This was granted by Waldieve firft lord of Allerdale to Melbeth his phyfician, whofe pofterity took the name de Bromfield. But the patronage of the church he referved out of that grant, and gave the fame to the abbey of St. Mary's York. The faid abbey had alfo lands at Bromfield, as likewife had the abbey of Holm Cultram; and by the general term manor being applied to them both, it is difficult to afcertain their feparate poffeffions.

Soon,

Soon after the foundation of the abbey of Holme Cultram, *Adam* son of *Thomas de Brunfeld* granted to the same abbey the *manor* of Brunfield, by the boundaries in the grant specified [*].

After this grant, *Thomas de Brunfeld* (the said Adam's father) grants to the monks of Holme the cultivated lands in Brunfield called Northrig, with the marsh on the east part thereof [†].

And *Henry* son of the said Thomas confirmed his father's grant, and further granted to the said monks two acres of land lying within one of their inclosures, for one mark of silver which they gave unto him for the same.

And Walter son of Benedict the priest quit-claimed to the monks all his right and claim of common of pasture in the marsh which Adam and Thomas de Brunfeld gave to the said monks.

Agnes daughter of Adam White of Brunfeld, carpenter, gave to the said monks five acres of arable land and one acre of meadow in the territory of Brunfeld; which grant *Thomas* son of *Thomas de Brunfeld* confirmed. And *Alan* son of *Henry de Brunfeld* quitted claim of all his right therein.

---

[*] Univerfis fanctæ matris ecclefiæ filiis has literas vifuris vel audituris, Adam filius Thomæ de Brunfeld falutem. Sciatis me, affenfu et voluntate hæredis mei, pro Dei amore et falute animæ meæ, et pro animabus patris mei at Agnetis matris meæ, et pro animabus omnium anteceſſorum et fucceſſorum meorum, conceſſiſſe, dediſſe, et hac præfenti charta mea confirmaſſe, Deo et beatæ Mariæ et monachis de Holme, in liberam, puram, et perpetuam eleemofynam, manerium meum de Brunfeld per has divifas, fcilicet, ficut Langerig bec defcendit in ipfum marifcum juxta Litil-holm interius, et fic in tranfverfom ipfius marifci verfus aquilonem, ficut recta divifa inter Brunfeld et Langerig ducit in Aldelath dub, et fic defcendendo per Aldelath dub ufque ad locum ubi Cromboc cadit in Aldelath dub, et fic afcendendo per ipfum Cromboc ufque ad locum ubi foſſatum monachorum defcendit in Cromboc, et fic afcendendo per ipfum foſſatum verfus occidentem ufque ad duram terram quæ eft ad caput de Endehou, et fic extendendo verfus occidentem femper ficut dura terra et marifcus fibi obviant ufque ad locum ubi prædictus Langerig bec defcendit in ipfum marifcum. Tenendum et habendum de me et hæredibus meis, cum omnibus libertatibus et pertinentiis fuis, fine ullo retenemento, libere, quiete, et folute ab omni feculari fervicio, confuetudine, et exactione, et ita libere et quiete ficut aliqua eleemofyna poteft teneri liberius, quietius, et melius. Et ego et hæredes mei warrant zabimus prædictis monachis prædictam eleemofynam, et acquietabimus eam de omni fervicio contra omnes homines imperpetuum. *(Regiftr. Holme.)*

[†] Sciant tam præfentes quam futuri, quod ego Thomas de Brunfeld dedi, conceſſi, et hac mea præfenti charta confirmavi, Deo et beatæ Mariæ et monachis de Holme, in liberam, puram, et perpetuam eleemofynam, pro falue animæ meæ et omnium anteceſſorum, &c. quandam culturam in territorio de Brunfeld quæ vocatur Northrig, cum marifco ex orientali parte adjacente, per has divifas, fcilicet, a foſſato monachorum ex occidentali parte ipfius Northrig afcendendo per mediam vallem ficut foſſatum monachorum ducit ufque in Pettpots, et inde circuendo ipfum Northrig ex auftrali parte verfus orientem per idem foſſatum monachorum ufque in marifcum, et fic in directum verfus orientem ufque in Cromboc, quæ eft divifa inter Brunfeld et Blencoggoe, et fic defcendendo per ipfum Cromboc ufque in foſſatum monachorum quod circuit marifcum quem Adam filius meus eifdem monachis contulit in perpetuam eleemofynam; et, de incremento, unam acram terræ arabilis propinquiorem terræ ecclefiæ ex occidentali parte, cum omnibus communibus aifiamentis et libertatibus ejufdem villæ ad tantam terram pertinentibus, fine ullo retenemento : Tenenda et habenda de me et hæredibus meis hæc omnia fupradicta, ita libere et quiete et folute ab omni fervicio, confuetudine, et demanda, ficut aliqua eleemofyna poteft teneri et haberi liberius, quietius, et melius. Et ego Thomas et hæredes mei warrantizabimus et acquietabimus hanc eleemofynam prædictis monachis de omni fervicio terreno, contra omnes homines in perpetuum. *(Regiftr. Holme.)*

In

In the 20 Ed. 1. *Hugh* fon of *Alan de Brunfield* having a controverfy with the faid monks concerning common of pafture upon the aforefaid marfh, an agreement was made and a limitation prefcribed within what places and at what times each of them refpectively might depafture their cattle without the interruption of the other †. And there was a like agreement in the fame year, between the faid monks and Ralph de Ofmunderlawe and Agnes his wife, and Thomas de Laithes and Alice his wife, concerning the faid marfh.

After the diffolution of the monafteries, we find amongft the knights fees in Cumberland in the 35 Hen. 8. that William Hutton held the manor of Bromfield of the king *in capite* as of his manor of Papcaftle, rendring for the fame 18s 4d cornage, 10d feawake, 6d free rent, puture of the ferjeants, and witnefman.

In the fame year, July 15, the faid king grants to Thomas Dalfton efquire (amongft other particulars) one tenement in Bromfield with the appurtenances in the tenure of John Scurre, and one other tenement with the appurtenances in the tenure of William Scurre, late parcel of the poffeffions of the monaftery of Holme in the county of Cumberland; paying for the fame to the king yearly at the feaft of St. Michael the archangel 3s 3½d.

And king Edward the fixth by letters patent dated the 25th day of Auguft in the firft year of his reign, in confideration that Henry Thompfon had furrendered into the hands of the late king Henry the eighth, all the right, title, and intereft which he had in the late hofpital, commonly called Maifon Dieu of Dover in the county of Kent, grants to the faid Henry Thompfon *(inter alia)* the whole manor of Brumfield, and the rectory and church of Brumfield,

---

† Sciant præfentes et futuri, quod cum mota effet contentio inter Hugonem filium Alani de-Brunfield querentem, et dominum Robertum abbatem de Holme et ejufdem loci conventum defendentes, fuper communia pafturæ quam idem Hugo in marifco prædictorum abbatis et conventus de Brunfeld exigebat, quem quidem marifcum prædicti abbas et monachi conventus ex dono et conceffione Adæ filii Thomæ de Brunfeld antecefforis prædicti Hugonis in liberam, puram, et perpetuam eleemofynam habuerunt et tenuerunt; tandem die Martis proxima poft feftum fancti Michaelis anno domini 1292°, et anno regni regis Edwardi vicefimo, dicta contentio in hunc modum convenit, videlicet, quod dictus Hugo, pro bono pacis remifit et quietum clamavit, pro fe et hæredibus fuis in perpetuum, totum jus et clameum quod habuit vel habere poterit communicandi five communiam exigendi quoquo modo in marifco prædicto, ita quod nec ipfe Hugo nec hæredes fui in marifco prædicto aliquam communiam pafturæ de cætero ultra formam quæ fequitur exigere poterunt vel vindicare; quæ quidem forma talis eft, quod prædicti abbas et conventus pro prædictis remiffione et quieta clamatione concefferunt prædicto Hugoni, quod ipfe Hugo et hæredes fui et eorum tenentes de Brunfeld communicare poffint omni tempore propriis animalibus fuis in parte-occidentali dicti marifci infra divifas fubfcriptas, videlicet, ab illo foffato quod jacet propinquius verfus occidentem in medio ejufdem marifci ufque Langerig bec, et in longo et lato quamdiu illa pars marifci verfus auftrum et aquilonem infra dictum foffatum et Langerig bec fe extendit. Et prædicti abbas et conventus pafturam illam malciofe per animalia fua non fuperonerabunt, ob quod dictus Hugo et hæredes fui et eorum tenentes conceffione fibi facta minime gaudere poterunt in forma fupradicta. Concefferunt infuper prædicti religiofi prædicto Hugoni et hæredibus fuis, quod habere poffint fingulis annis imperpetuum, a die inventionis fanctæ crucis ufque ad feftum beati Petri ad vincula unum jumentum infra feparalem claufuram marifci prædicti, quoties dicti religiofi infra eandem claufuram feparalem cum Emiffario infra fefta prædicta habuerint. Et pro hac conceffione, conceffit prædictus Hugo pro fe et hæredibus fuis, quod prædicti abbas et conventus de toto refiduo ejufdem marifci quocunque modo voluerint omni tempore valeant approvare. In cujus rei teftimonium utraque pars alterius fcripto alternatim figillum fuum appofuit. Teftibus, &c. (*Regiftr. Holme.*)

with

with the appurtenances in the county of Cumberland, late belonging to
the monaftery of the bleffed Mary nigh the walls of York; and all and
fingular granges, mills, meffuages, houfes, buildings, tofts, cottages, lands,
tenements, meadows, paftures, feedings, commons, waftes, moors, moffes,
turbary, woods, underwoods, waters, fifheries, penfions, procurations, tithes,
oblations and obventions, rents, reverfions, fervices, knights fees, wardfhips,
marriages, efcheats, reliefs, fines, amerciaments, heriots, courts leet, view of
frank pledge, waifs, eftrays, goods of felons and fugitives, free warrens, and
all other rights, jurifdictions, liberties, franchifes, privileges, profits, commodities, emoluments, poffeffions, and hereditaments whatfoever, with the
appurtenances, fituate, lying and being in Brumfield aforefaid, to the faid
manor of Brumfield and to the faid rectory of Brumfield, or to either of them
in any wife belonging or appertaining; and all other meffuages, lands, tenements, rents, reverfions, fervices, and other poffeffions and hereditaments
whatfoever in Brumfield aforefaid, to the faid late monaftery belonging: Which
premiffes are extended at the clear yearly value of 34 l. To hold of the king
in capite by the 40th part of one knight's fee; and rendring for the fame yearly
to the king, his heirs and fucceffors, 3 l 8 s.

The above poffeffions afterwards became feparated into many hands. The
Porters of Weary-hall feem firft to have had the largeft fhare. Sir John Ballantine purchafed the demefne at Scales of Mr. Jofeph Porter; which Mr.
Porter fold alfo the tenements of moft of the tenants to freehold; the remainder, with the demefne lands at Langrigg hall, he fold to Ofmotherly;
and Ofmotherly infranchifed the reft of the tenants and fold the demefne
to Mr. Barwife, in whofe family it ftill continues. The demefne and tithes of
Bromfield are now held by Sir Gilfrid Lawfon baronet; the demefne of Scales,
and the tithes of Crookdake and Langrigg, by the heirefs of Ballantine:
Weft Newton by the inhabitants, who purchafed the fame of Thomas Simpfon efquire of Carleton hall and Elizabeth his wife one of the fifters and
coheirs of Chriftopher Pattinfon efquire; Alanby and Mealrigg by Mr. Raincock of Penrith in right of his wife, another of the fifters and coheirs of the
faid Mr. Pattinfon.

The church of Bromfield is dedicated to St. Kentigern or Mungo; and
is valued in the king's books at 22 l. The prefent yearly value is about
100 l.

It was granted by Waldieve fon of Gofpatric as aforefaid to the abbey of
St. Mary's York. And they had the patronage and advowfon until the year
1302, when the abbot and convent, complaining of great loffes they had
lately fuftained, and particularly of 300 marks yearly rent and 10,000 marks
of mefne profits and cofts recovered againft them by the earl of Lincoln, prevail with the bifhop of Carlifle to appropriate the rectory of Bromfield to their
monaftery; which he grants on condition of their fecuring 40 marks of
yearly revenue to a vicar there, referving at the fame time to his fee the collation of the vicar, in recompence of the injury by fuch appropriation accruing to the rights of his church of Carlifle. From which time the bifhops
have

have conftantly collated to the vicarage. And in the next year, the abbot and convent gave a proxy to Adam de Twenge one of their monks and Simon de Leyceftre clerk, to tranfact on their part with the bifhop of Carlifle, and to take poffeffion of the profits of the church of Brumfield for their ufe. And the fame year the bifhop collated *Ralph de Aile* to the vicarage of Bromfield.

In 1330, on the refignation of *William de Suthwerk* vicar of Bromfield, bifhop Rofs collates *William de Otrington*. This refignation being made in favour of the bifhop's chaplain, Suthwerk had a penfion of ten marks out of the faid vicarage.

In 1339, on a fuggeftion that the churches of Bromfield and Kirkby Stephen, after their being appropriated to St. Mary's York, were exempt from their former fubjection to the bifhops of Carlifle, the bifhop protefts (by an inftrument figned in the prefence of a notary apoftolic) that it never was the intention of himfelf or his predeceffors in any act of theirs, to countenance any fuch pretenfion.

In 1344, *Roger de Kirk Ofwald* rector of Morefby in Lincolnfhire, born in the diocefe of Carlifle, and hoping to enjoy his health and friends better than he doth in Lincolnfhire, defires a change with *Hugh de Whitelawe* vicar of Bromfield; who is alfo defirous of the change, becaufe he is inclinable to ftudy the laws in the univerfity, and cannot fo readily obtain leave of abfence from a vicarage as a rectory. The reafons are approved by their refpective diocefans; and the bifhop of Carlifle, patron of both livings, collates the one and prefents the other accordingly. This Hugh de Whitelawe had been collated to the vicarage of Bromfield this very year, on the death of William de Otrington.

In 1377, the faid Roger de Kirk Ofwald exchanged his vicarage for the rectory of Newbiggin; to which being prefented by William de Crakanthorp he is inftituted, and *John de Culwen* late rector of Newbiggin was collated to the vicarage of Bromfield.

In 1392, the chancel of the church of Bromfield being very ruinous, and it being alledged that the abbot and convent of St. Mary's York ought to repair the fame; the faid abbot and convent appear by their proctors Thomas Pygot prior of their cell at Wetherhall and Alan de Newark advocate in the court of York, and fay, that John de Culwen the vicar ought to repair the fame, and that it is well known that all his predeceffors have been known to do fo time out of mind. Which plea feems to have been allowed, the repairs of the chancel ftill lying upon the vicar.

In 1562, on the refignation of Sir *John King* vicar of Bromfield, Sir *John Corry* clerk was collated by bifhop Beft.

And two years after, on Corry's refignation, *Thomas Laythes* was collated.

In 1589, on Thomas Laythes's refignation, *Nicholas Dean*, M. A. was collated by bifhop Meye.

In 1602, Nicholas Dean refigns, on being collated to the archdeaconry with the rectory of Salkeld by bifhop Robinfon, who thereupon collates Peter Beck, B. A.

During the ufurpation of Oliver Cromwell, *William Grainger* vicar of Brom-field was ejected, and his fucceffor feems to have been deprived after the Reftoration by the Bartholomew act; for in 1663 *Richard Garth*, M. A. was collated to this vicarage, of whom there is this epitaph on the north fide of the communion table:

> Bromfield's paftor's here intomb'd,
> Richard Garth, fo was he nam'd,
> God's word to 's flock he did declare,
> Twice a day, and would not fpare.
> T' inftruct the youth, help the needy,
> Vifit the fick, always ready.
> To end debate amongft his neighbours,
> Now he refts from all his labours.
> Rebellious fpirits he always did hate,
> Obedient to the church, true to the ftate.
> Now with heaven's quire he fings
> An anthem to the king of kings.   1673.

On the faid Mr. Garth's death, *William Sill*, M. A. was collated by bifhop Rainbow.

In 1681, *John Child*, B. D. was collated by the fame bifhop; of whom there is the following epitaph in the chancel:

Depofitum Johannis Child, vicarii hujus ecclefiæ, S. T. B. Cultus primitivi contra papiftas et fectarios affertoris feduli: Qui neglectus vixit, ac lætus obiit, in πληροφορια *beatæ refurrectionis. Tu vero, viator, mortem meditari et ultimum judicium expectare cures.*

In 1692, *John Proctor*, M. A. was collated by bifhop Smith. This Mr. Proctor greatly repaired the vicarage houfe, and built a very good tithe barn of brick at Blencogoe, where that part of the corn tithe arifes with which the vicarage is endowed.

In 1714, *Jofeph Rothery*, M. A. was collated by bifhop Nicolfon.

In 1717, *Jeremiah Nicolfon*, M. A. by the fame bifhop.

In 1733, *William Wikinfon*, M. A. was collated by bifhop Waugh.

In 1752, *Obadiah Yates*, M. A. by bifhop Ofbaldifton.

And in 1765, *William Raincock*, M. A. by bifhop Lyttelton.

In the church are two large ifles; whereof that on the north belongs to the houfe of Crookdake: the other, fronting it, belongs to the eftate at Newton; but the Martindales, from whom it came, have referved a burying-place here, and in confideration thereof are obliged to keep the windows in good order. In one of thefe is painted *William Martindale* 1701. The other repairs are charged on the houfe of Newton.

In the north wall of the church is an old arched tomb, over which is infcribed,

> Here lies intomb'd, I dare undertake,
> The noble warrior Adam of Crookdake, knight, 1514.

In

In Bromfield, before the diffolution of the religious houfes, was a CHANTRY pretty largely endowed, as appears from the grant thereof by king Edward the fixth, who by letters patent bearing date Jan. 30, in the 3d year of his reign, granted to Thomas Dalfton efquire and William Denton gentleman (amongft other particulars) the chantry of St. George the martyr lying in Bromfield in the county of Cumberland, and the yearly rent of 12s and fervices iffuing out of lands and tenements in Bromfield late the inheritance of Richard Coldall, and the yearly rent of 2s and fervices iffuing out of lands and tenements in Bromfield late John Wilkinfon's, and the rent of 14d and fervices iffuing out of lands and tenements late John Harrifon's in Bromfield aforefaid, alfo the rent of 7d and fervices iffuing out of the lands and tenements late of John Lyon in Bromfield aforefaid, and the rent of 2s and fervices iffuing of the lands and tenements late of William Goldall in Bromfield aforefaid; and alfo four meffuages and tenements in the tenure of Thomas Lowes, Thomas Plafkett, and Richard Plafkett lying in Dundraw, to the faid chantry belonging; alfo one meffuage and tenement with the appurtenances in Crokedake in the tenure of William Bewley, one meffuage and tenement in Langrigg in the tenure of Robert Martindale, and all thofe lands, tenements and hereditaments in the tenure of David Matthewman, Ifabel Sym, and Miles Chamber in Meldrigg; one meffuage and tenement in Grenefdale in the tenure of Thomas Walby, and the hereditaments called Garths in Dowbeck, all in the county of Cumberland, to the faid chantry in Bromfield belonging.

The school at Bromfield was founded and endowed by Richard Ofmotherly of London, merchant taylor, in 1612; who was a native of this parifh. He left 10l per annum to be paid to the fchoolmafter by the merchant taylors company. There was alfo a long time ago 80l raifed in the parifh for the fame ufe, but by fome means or other 16l of it is loft, fo that the yearly intereft thereof is only 3l 4s. The parifhioners add 12s to it by way of affeffment. The fchoolmafter is generally the parifh clerk, which place is worth about 3l a year. So that the whole united falary is about 16l 16s.

BLENCOGOE and DUNDRAW are in this parifh; but being in Cumberland Ward, we refer them to be treated of there.

In 1747, it was certified that there were in the parifh about 307 families; 17 of which were quakers, 4 prefbyterians, and one anabaptift.

PARISH OF HOLM CULTRAM.

THE next and laft parifh within this ward is the HOLM, which was demefne of Allerdale; but king Stephen having given Cumberland and the earldom of Huntington to prince Henry eldeft fon and heir apparent of David king of Scots (for which Henry did homage, his father refufing them upon thofe

terms,

terms,' becaufe he had fworn to acknowledge no other fovereign of England but the emprefs Matildà) the faid Henry in the year 1150 gave two parts in three of the Holme to the abbey, and the remaining third to Alan fon of Waldieve for his hunting there, but Alan inftantly gave the faid third part to the abbey, as that which the faid Henry had given him at the foundation of the abbey; and Waldieve fon of the faid Alan confented to the grant which his father had made : Which grant the faid Henry confirmed†. And David king of Scots father of the faid Henry‡, and Malcolm king of Scots fon of the faid Henry, confirmed the grant which the faid Henry had made ‡.

At the death of king Stephen, Henry fon of the emprefs Matilda, being the fecond of that name king of England, entered to Cumberland, which Stephen had before given to prince Henry of Scotland, and therefore the monk's acknowledged him their founder; and he granted them by his charter the whole ifland of Holme and Raby by their right bounds, with timber and pafture in the foreft of Inglewood*; which grant his fons and fucceffors Richard* and John confirmed. The boundaries by Richard's charter are thus afcertained : By a little fyke that falls into Wampole at Kirkbride, af-cending that fyke unto Cokelayk as the mofs and hard ground meet, thence through the middle of the mofs between Waytheholm and Laurence holm, and fo crofs the mofs and wood to Anterpot, thence down Waver to the place where Waver and Crombok meet, thence up Crombok till it receives Wythe-fkeld, fo up that fyke unto the head; then turning weft unto a fyke that compaffeth Middlerigg on the north and weft till it fall into Polnewton, fo as Polnewton falls into the fea, thence along the coaft unto the foot of Wathe-pol, and fo up Wathepol unto Kirkbride aforefaid.

All this was foreft at the firft foundation of the kings: But the monks prefently erected five granges for hufbandry, at Raby, at Mawbergh, at Skinburne, at Culfhaw, and at Newton Arlofh; and turned all into tillage, meadow, and pafture. And they foon after were endowed with many other lands, tene-ments, and hereditaments. Particularly,

Anthony de Lucy gave them dead wood in his woods of ALLERDALE, for fuel for the abbey, and coal wood for their forges within Holm Cultram, but not to have coal wood for their iron mines without fpecial licence of him or his heirs‖.

Richard de Alneburgh and *William* fon of *Simon Sheftling*, lords of Alneburgh and Deerham, gave them a *fifhing* at the mouth of the river ALNE §. And *William de Holdernefs* gave a toft and croft in ALNEBURGH §.

Alice de Romeley gave three acres of land and a quarry at ASPATRICK, with common of pafture for 10 oxen, 10 cows, 1 bull, and their produce for two years; alfo for two horfes, and 40 fheep §.

Galiene, daughter of *Richard de Hervi*, gave three acres of arable land at BLENCOGON, and pafture for 100 fheep, 28 cows, and their produce for two

. † Appendix, Nº 14.   ‡ Appendix, Nº 15.   ‡ 3 Dugd. Mon. 34.   * 1 Dugd. Mon. 885.   ‖ 3 Dugd. Mon. 34.   § Regiftr. Holm.

years,

years, 1 bull, and 2 horſes, for maintenance of the infirm poor. And *Marjory* daughter of *Galiene* gave two bovates of land there. And *Adam* ſon of *Dolphin de Langrigg* half an acre§.

Thomas de Laſſels gave paſture for their ſwine in the woods of BOLTON, except in the time of pannage†.

Adam de Harrais gave them lands in BRANSTIBET‡.

· *Thomas de Brunfeld* gave lands at BROMFIELD, by metes and bounds in the grant ſpecified ╪. *Adam* ſon of *Thomas de Brunfeld* gave the manor of *Bromfield* ╪. *Henry* ſon of *Thomas de Brunfeld* gave two acres of land there *. And *Agnes* daughter of *Adam White* gave five acres of arable and one of meadow*.

At BURGH, *Hugh de Morvil* gave the church, out of the profits thereof to find lights, wine, and all neceſſaries for the ornament of their church of Holm Cultram, and for the ſervice of the altar there *. · He gave to them alſo a net at *Solleburgh* and in all other places upon Eden in common with the inhabitants of *Burgh*, with room to dry their nets*.—*Richard de Lucy* (huſband of *Ada* elder daughter of *Hugh de Morvil*) confirmed the ſaid grant of the church of *Burgh*: As did alſo his younger daughter *Joan* wife of *Richard Gernun*; which *Joan* granted to them alſo common of paſture at *Burgh* *.—After them, *Thomas de Multon* confirmed the ſaid grant, and granted to them two nets in the fiſhery of Eden for every carucate of land which they had at *Burgh* *. He granted to them alſo a toft and croft at *Burgh**.—And pope Innocent the fifth by his bull confirms to them the church of *Burgh*, and further grants, that they may retain the whole profits thereof to their own uſe for the purpoſes of hoſpitality and maintenance of the poor; ſaving thereout a ſufficiency to maintain a chaplain*.

John Franceys parſon of *Caldbeck*, with conſent of the biſhop as ordinary and alſo as patron, and of the prior and convent of Carliſle, granted to them a moiety of an incloſure called Warnel bank in CALDBECK. Which grant was confirmed by king Hen. 3*.—And *William* ſon of *Patric de Caldebeck* granted ten acres and an half in Eſkbend in *Caldbeck* *.

Guido a merchant and burgher in CARLISLE granted to them an houſe in Ricardgate; the monks to pay the houſegavil thereof as of a free burgage. And *Henry* ſon of *William* gave them his meſſuage nigh St. Mary's churchyard towards the caſtle, whereon he had built two houſes; to find a light at the altar for private maſſes*.

Lambert de Multon gave them liberty to dig for, get, and carry away iron ore in COUPLAND; they paying for the ſame half a mark of ſilver yearly ‖.

Richard de Herez gave them the meadow grounds between CROMBOC and WAVER, juſt before the meeting of thoſe two rivers**.

Gilbert ſon of *Gilbert de Dundraw* gave 24 acres of land at DISTINGTON, and paſture there for 600 ſheep, 7 cows, 1 bull, 2 horſes, and 8 oxen. And *Hugh de Moreſby* gave 6 acres of arable land there, and 4 of meadow**.

---

§ Regiſtr. Holm.   † Vid. Bolton.   ‡ Regiſtr. Holm.   ╪ Vid. Bromfield.
* Regiſtr. Holm.   ‖ 3 Dugd. Mon. 51.   ** Regiſtr Holm.

Roger

Roger de Lyndeby gave, with his body, 7 acres of land at Dundrake, under a yearly rent of 2 *s* 4 *d* payable to the lord of *Dundrake* *.

Robert Turp gave 14 acres of land at Edenhall, part of his demesne there; with pasture for 700 sheep. And *Alan Turp* gave a meadow there, by metes and bounds *.

William earl of *Albemarle* gave an iron mine at Egremont †.

Thomas son of *Gospatric* son of *Orme*, with the assent of *Alan* his brother, gave the grange of Flimby and common of pasture at *Seton, Camberton*, and *Kernepot*. And *Alice de Romeley* gave common of pasture on *Brechton* moor for the cattle of their grange of *Flimby* **. And king *Edward* the first granted to them free warren at *Flimby* ‡.

William son of *Orme de Ireby* gave his dwelling house at Gilcrux, with the garden, orchard, and other appurtenances; and the grange thereunto belonging, and 21 acres of land ††. And the abbot of *Caldre* paid to them yearly half a mark for certain lands in Gilcrux ⊥.

Agnes daughter of *Adam de Harrais* gave one acre and half a perch in Harrais §§.

Robert de Brus gave a capital messuage at Herterpol; and *Peter le Graunt* gave lands and houses there, for which *Robert le Graunt* bound himself and his heirs by oath to pay 20 *s* yearly §§.

King *John* granted to them the hermitage of St. Hilda, with liberty for 40 cows in the forest of Inglewood and their young till two years old, and for as many horses and oxen as will be sufficient to cultivate their lands there §.

Richard earl *Strongbow, John de Curcy*, and others, gave divers possessions in Ireland ⊥⊥.

Gospatric son of *Orme* gave a moiety of the vill of Kelton ⊥⊥.

William de la Ferte released to them all his right in certain waste ground nigh Kirkbride ⊥⊥.

Waldeve son of *Gamel* son of *Whelp* gave the land called Tofts and Hale at Kirkby Thore; also a marsh there, with two acres of land at the head thereof.—*Laurence* son of *Robert*, steward of Newbiggin, gave all the lands called *Sperstamrig*, and all his part of the marsh between *Newbiggin* and them, and common of pasture in *Newbiggin* field for 360 sheep, 20 cows, 1 bull, and 30 oxen.—*John de Veteripont* gave a farm called *Castlerig*, containing 25¼ acres; also pasture for 400 sheep, 20 wethers, and as many oxen, cows, and horses as they shall need to till their ground at *Hale*, 6 sows, and 1 boar; with furze, peats, and turbary.—*Arnald de Kirkby Thore* gave two acres in *Sand-flath*.—*Adam* son of *Liulph* gave all the land which was his father's in the fields called *Morlands* at Kirkby Thore towards *Sourby*; with 3 acres of arable land of his own, with the meadows adjoining thereto in the territory of *Kirkby Thore*—*Fulk* and *Amafia* his wife gave two acres of land toward *War-thebirth*.—*Robert de Broy* and *Amabil* his wife gave 16 acres in the territory of

---

* Regiftr. Holm.   † 3 Dugd. Mon. 58.   ** Regiftr. Holm.   ‡ Appendix, N° 13.
†† Regiftr. Holm.   ⊥ Stevens's Monafticon, Appendix, 208.   §§ Regiftr. Holm.
§ Vid. Ilekirk.   ⊥⊥ Regiftr. Holm.

Kirkby Thore, with a marsh at the head thereof.—*Adam* son of *Waldeve de Kirkby Thore* gave 5 acres of arable lands in the territory of *Kirkby Thore*.—*Alan* son of *Waldeve* gave one toft and one croft in the vill of *Kirkby Thore*, and 8 acres in the territory thereof.—*Gilbert* son of *Adam de Kirkby Thore* gave ten acres upon *Wartbebergh*.—*Amabil* daughter of *Robert de Bereford*, and widow of *Robert de Broy*, gave all her land in *Maidengate*, and two acres at the head of that land ††.

Hugh de Morvil gave pasture at LAYSINGBY for 500 sheep, 10 oxen, 10 cows and their young for one year, 1 bull, 2 horses, 4 acres of arable land, and 9 acres of meadow, with common of pasture in all his demesne lands there ‡. He also afterwards, with his body, gave other lands there ‡.

Renald de Carlisle gave NEWBY near Carlisle, with a reservation of 10*s* yearly rent to him and his heirs ††.

Adam son of *Ketel de Newton* gave common of pasture for all the cattle of their grange of Maiburgh, over all his land at NEWTON, except corn and meadow ground ; and liberty to make a watercourse over his land from Polnewton to Maiburgh.—*Richard* son of *Ketel de Newton* gave 8 acres of land at *Newton*.—And *Adam* son of *Edward de Newton* gave two oxgangs of land there ††.

Henry de Derham, with consent of his wife Maud, gave half an acre in ORMESBY. And *Christian de Derham*, widow of Michael de Clifton, gave all her lands there ††.

Alice daughter of *Roger* son of *Gerard* gave divers parcels of land in the territory of SACMIRDAGH, with common of pasture for 8 oxen, 2 horses, 60 ewes, and as many goats with their young for three years ††.

Walter de Berkele, chamberlain of SCOTLAND, granted to them lands in *Galloway* ; which grant was confirmed by William king of Scotland §.—*Christian* bishop of Glasgow, becoming professed of the Cistertian order, and of the house of Holm Cultram, gives his body to be buried there, and therewith the grange of *Kirkwinny* ; and charges all men to protect and defend the same grange, as they tender the blessing of God and of himself ; and threatens, if they do otherwise, that they shall incur the papal excommunication, the curses of almighty God and of himself, and the pains of eternal fire ∥.—And *Jocelin* bishop of *Glasgow* granted to them the chapel of *Kirkwinny* ; which grant was confirmed by pope Innocent the fifth †*.—And *Robert* king of *Scots*, for the health of his soul, and the souls of his ancestors and successors, and especially of his father whose body was interred in the church of St. Mary of Holm Cultram, quits claim to them of an annual rent of 10*l* which they paid out of their lands in Galloway †*.—And they had several other possessions in *Scotland*, given by private persons. And king Edward the first of England gave them 300 marks yearly out of forfeited estates in Scotland, by his charter dated at Cordoyl in Scotland, Sept. 25. in the 30th year of his reign ┼. Witnesses, Walter bishop of Coventry and Litchfield, John bishop of Cordoyl,

†† Regiſtr. Holm.   ‡ v. Lazonby.   †† Regiſtr Holm   § 3 Dugd. Mon. 38.
∥ Appendix, Nº. 16.   †* Regiſtr. Holm.   ┼ Appendix, Nº 17.

John

John earl of Warrene, Thomas de Lafci earl of Nicole, Thomas earl of Lancafter, Guy earl of Warwyk, Henry de Percy, Robert Fitzwalter, Robert de Clifford, and others †.

Gunild daughter of *Henry* fon of *Arthur* lord of Millom, in her widowhood, granted to them all the lands in *Lekeley* or SEATON, which her father had given her in marriage, and that they may have fhields for their cattle in *Crocherk*, and common of pafture within the foreft, fo far as the cattle may go and return home at night‡.—*Thomas* fon of *Gofpatric* gave 8 acres of land in *Seton*, adjoining to 32 acres of their own there ; and one net in Derwent, and one toft nigh the bank, where they may abide and manage the fifhery ††.
—And *John* fon of *Alan de Camberton* releafed to them a pool which they had made or fhould make to turn the water of Derwent, or fo much thereof as fhould be prejudicial to their fifhery of *Seton*††.

Brice de Penrith gave St. SWITHIN's holme, adjoining to the river Eamont nigh *Penrith* §.

The lands on the weft fide of WAVERTON *Magna* were given by *Adam* fon of *Gamel* ; and other lands there by *Roger* fon of *Gillefiephen* **.

John Gernon and *Margaret* his wife gave the church of WIGTON, with fome lands on condition that the abbot and monks fhould eftablifh a chantry there ; which being done, the church was foon after appropriated ‖. *Adam* fon of *Lambert*, gave another parcel of land at *Wigton* §§. And *Udard* fon of *Adam* another parcel, and pafture for 10 cows with their young for two years, 2 horfes, and 10 fheep with their young for one year §§.

William earl of *Albemarl* gave a forge at WYNEFEL, with wood for charcoal §§.

Befides thefe feveral poffeffions, they had feveral privileges and exemptions granted to them by the kings of this realm, together with a confirmation of all former grants ; as particularly, freedom from fhires, and hundreds, and wapentakes, and toll, and theam, and infangthief, and affart, and wafte (except in the king's forefts), and from regard of the foreft, and efcape, and amerciaments, and geld, and danegeld, and affizes, and feaward, and caftle-work, and tallage, and cornage, and paffage, and ftallage, and fcutage, and aids of fheriffs, and in general all fecular exaction §§.

Alfo they had many privileges and exemptions, with confirmations of charters, by the bulls of many of the popes. As a fpecimen whereof, we have inferted in the Appendix, as being one of the ampleft and moft fpecific, the bull of pope Clement the third in the year 1190+.

This monaftery was not one of the mitred or parliamentary kind, yet the abbot was fometimes fummoned to that great affembly, as particularly in the 23, 24, 28, 32, and 34 of Ed. 1. and in the beginning of the reign of Ed. 2.

---

† Regiftr Holm.   ‡ Appendix, Nº 5.   †† Regiftr. Holm.   § Appendix, Nº 18.
** Regiftr. Holm.   ‖ 1 Dugd. Mon. 886.   §§ Regiftr. Holm.   + Appendix, Nº 19

In the year 1301, bishop Halton being informed, that the inhabitants of the village or town near the port in Skinburnese were at a great distance from all manner of divine service, grants a power to the abbot and convent of Holm Cultram to erect a church there, which should be endowed with all manner of tithes, and enjoy all parochial rights. The abbot and convent to have the advowson, and the bishop of Carlisle and his successors all ordinary jurisdiction. The town of Skinburnese was at this time not only privileged with a market, but seems also to have been the chief place for the king's magazines in these parts for supplying the armies then employed against the Scots. But the case was most miserably altered very soon after. For in 1305, we find it thus mentioned in the parliament records; " At the petition of the abbot " requesting that whereas he had paid a fine of 100 marks to the king for a " fair and market to be had in Skinburnese, and now that town together with " the way leading to it is carried away by the sea, the king would grant that " he may have such fair and market at his town of Kirkeby Johan instead of " the other place aforesaid, and that his charter upon this may be renewed; " It is answered, Let the first charter be annulled, and then let him have a " like charter in the place as he desireth †." And for the same reason, as it seemeth, the church also was removed to Kirkby Johan or Newton Arlosh: For the same bishop, by his charter bearing date at Linstock the 11th of April 1303, setting forth that the lands and possessions of the abbot and convent at Holm Cultram are far distant from and not within the limits of any parish, and considering their impoverished condition by the hostile invasions and depredations of the Scots, grants to them licence to build a chapel or church within their territory of Arlosh, with all parochial rights, and all the tithes within their territories to the use of their monastery, with power to them to present a priest for institution upon a vacancy, allowing him 4l a year, and room for an house and curtilage. And in token of subjection, he to pay out of the said 4l half a mark yearly to the bishop in the name of a cathedraticum, and 40d to the archdeacon for procurations ‡.

The abbey was surrendered to the crown by the abbot *Borrowdale*, March 6, in the 29 Hen. 8. being then valued at 427l 19s 3d, which in present value would amount to upwards of 2090l. The said abbot was appointed parson of the supposed rectory of Holm Cultram for life, and had a book returned him containing an account of all the tithe big, meal, oats, and money, which had been paid by the parishioners to the abbot and convent *.

Queen

† Ryley, 245, 246.   ‡ 3 Dugd. Mon. 35.
* Viz. Sowterfield; 7 skeps and 3 bushels of big meal, and 8s.
Adlath; 2 skeps and a peck of big.
New Cowper; 6 bushels of big meal.
Edderside; 6 skeps of the same.
Plasket lands; 12 bushels of the same.
Tarnès; 3 skeps, 3 bushels and an half.
Pollahow; 5 skeps and 11 bushels.
Fowlesyke; 3 skeps and 4 bushels.

Queen Mary by her charter dated the 2d of May in the firſt year of her reign, granted this rectory (together with thoſe of Southpetheryne in the county of Cornwall, and Seiſton in the county of Leiceſter) to the chancellor, maſters, and ſcholars of the univerſity of Oxford; with the advowſon of the vicarage, and all tithes and other profits and emoluments whatſoever to the ſaid rectory and church of Holm Cultram and to the chapel of Newton Arloſh belonging or in any wiſe appertaining. And this rectory hath ever ſince been granted out upon leaſe by the univerſity; as firſt, to John Eſwicke for 25 years, next to Roger Marbeck and Richard Hawſon for 21 years, then to Sir Arthur Aty for 30 years, then to Sir George Dalſton for 31 years, and is now and for many years hath been upon leaſe in the Crofton family.

The vicarage in king Henry the eighth's valuation is rated at 6*l* 13*s* 4*d*, and was certified to the governors of queen Anne's bounty at 45*l*, and is now nearly the ſame, *viz.* 40*l* paid by the leſſee of the great tithes, a ſmall piece of ground worth about 12*s per annum*, and the ſurplice fees.

Hielaws; 6 ſkeps.
Abby Cowbier; 5 ſkeps and an half.
Dubmill; 13 buſhels and an half.
Mawbrugh Senior; 6 ſkeps, and 8 buſhels and 3 pecks.
Mawbrugh Junior; 5 ſkeps and 9 buſhels.
Mawbrugh Beck; 15 buſhels and an half.
Wolflye; 4 ſkeps, 4 buſhels and a peck.
Blatterleſs; 7 buſhels and an half.
Silleth; 14*s* in money.
Coats; two tenements uncharged.
Skinburneſe; 7 ſkeps, 11 buſhels and an half of barley.
Hayrigg; 20 buſhels of meal.
Mireſide; 7 ſkeps and 2 buſhels of meal, and half a ſkep of barley.
Calvoe; 3 ſkeps and 2 buſhels of barley, 1 buſhel and an half of meal, and 3 ſkeps and 2 pecks of oats.
Brownrigg; 3 ſkeps and 3 buſhels and an half of barley, and 5 buſhels and 3 pecks of meal.
Sivill; 2 ſkeps and 2 buſhels of meal, 6 ſkeps and an half of barley, and 8 buſhels of oats.
Sandenhouſe; 4 ſkeps of meal.
Sandenhouſe grange; 14 buſhels of barley.
Newton Arloſh; 19 ſkeps, 1 buſhel, and 1 peck of barley.
Salt Coates; 22 buſhels of meal.
Moſs Side; 3 buſhels of meal, and 6 buſhels of oats.
Rabie; 2 ſkeps and 9 buſhels of meal.
Robert Chambre payeth yearly at Eaſter for all manner of tithe at Raby Coat, 6*s* 8*d.*
Raby Grange; one ſkep and 2 buſhels of barley.
Acredale, &*c.*

To this are to be added the following ſums, ſeveral whereof are not reckoned in the abbot's book otherwiſe than at the will and pleaſure of the rector; that is, as it ſeemeth, as he and the pariſhioners could agree:

	l	*s*	*d*	
Bletterley (beſide the meal as above) - - -	5	3	5	
New Cowper - - - - - -	1	8	4	
The tenants of Silleth - - - - -	0	14	0	
Robert Barwis - - - - - -	0	8	0	
The Acredale tithe - - - - - -	0	7	0	or 12 buſhels of big.
Thomas Chambre - - - - -	0	6	8	

There

There is no charge upon this vicarage of firft fruits, tenths, fynodals, or procurations.

The firft vicar that we meet with after the diffolution of the abbey, was Sir *William Robinfon ;.* who refigning in 1564, Sir *George Stubb* clerk was inftituted on a prefentation by Humphrey Mitchel gentleman who had a grant of this avoidance from the chancellor, mafters, and fcholars of the univerfity of Oxford.

In 1576, bifhop Barnes (upon lapfe) collates Sir *William Adcock* to the vicarage of Holme Cultram, *alias* Newton Arlofh.

And in the next year, on the ceffion of William Adcock, the fame bifhop collates Sir *Henry Symfon* clerk, to the faid vicarage, as belonging to his gift and collation in full right.

In 1578, on the death of the faid Henry Symfon, bifhop Meye collates in like manner Sir *Chriftopher Symfon* clerk as of his own right.

In 1581, on the refignation of Chriftopher Symfon, the fame bifhop collates Sir *Edward Mandevil* clerk. In whofe time there is the following entry in the parifh regifter: Memorandum ; The fteeple of the church, being of the height of 19 fathoms, fuddenly fell down to the ground, upon the firft day of January in the year 1600, about three o'clock in the afternoon, and by the fall thereof brought down a great part of the chancel, both timber, lead, and walls; and after the faid fall, the fame continued in a very ruinous condition for the fpace of two years; during which time, there was much lead, wood, and ftone carried away. There was prefent at the fall Robert Chamber and myfelf (Edward Mandevile, then vicar there) both of us being within the church at the very time of the fall, and yet by the good pleafure of God we efcaped all perils.—

In 1602, by means of the bifhop of Carlifle a commiffion was granted by the chancellor, mafters, and fcholars of the univerfity of Oxford under their common feal, to George Curwen gentleman and me Edward Mandevile, for re-edifying a comely and fufficient chancel, taking and having towards the work the old materials of the chancel which was fallen and fhrunk, with the price of the lead fo fallen to rebuild a new one; which commiffion was executed by me Edward Mandevile accordingly in 1602 and 1603. This work came to 180*l* and odds.—This work being finifhed, it fo happened, that upon Wednefday the 18th of April 1604, one Chriftopher Hardon, carrying a live coal and a candle into the roof of the church, to fearch for an iron chifel which his brother had left there, and the wind being exceeding ftrong and boifterous, it chanced that the coal blew out of his hand into a daw's neft which was within the roof of the church, and forthwith kindled the fame, which fet the roof on fire, and within lefs than three hours it confumed and burned both the body of the chancel, and the whole church; except the fouth fide of the low church, which was faved by means of a ftone vault. Upon which great mifhap, Thomas Chamber and William Chamber did moft untruly and malicioufly put a bill into the exchequer, therein alledging that the faid Hardon did burn the church wilfully, by the procurement of Thomas Hardon coufin of the faid Chriftopher Hardon and me Edward Mandevile, to whom the faid Chriftopher was fervant. This falfe accufation they went about to prove by divers wit-

neffes,

neffes, but they failed in the proof; and fo the matter, when it came before the court, was difmiffed.—In the fame year 1604, I the faid Edward Mandevile did re-edify the chancel of the faid church of my own voluntary will, which coft me 88 *l* and fome odd money. And in the year 1606, the parifhioners were commanded by the bifhop to repair the body of the church, who were taxed fo to do by the churchwardens and the fixteen men, who were appointed for that purpofe.

The faid Edward Mandevile died foon after, and in the year 1607 *Robert Mandevile*, M. A. was inftituted on a prefentation by the univerfity.

In 1632, on the death of *Thomas Jefferfon* late vicar, *Charles Robfon*, S. T. B. was inftituted on a like prefentation; concerning whom we find a cafe ftated in the year 1636, and an advocate's opinion thereupon. Mr. Robfon, being bachelor of divinity, demanded of the parifh an hood proper to his degree. The queftion was, Whether the ordinary of the place hath power to command the churchwardens and parifhioners at their charges to provide an hood for the vicar, he being a graduate; becaufe, 1. The faid parifh was never before charged in this kind. 2. The vicars there have refpectively either bought themfelves hoods, or brought the fame with them. 3. The prefent vicar there hath at all times fince his firft coming to his vicarage, which is five years and more, worn a hood of his own, at fuch times as by the canons he is injoined to wear the fame, till within this half year laft paft.——Anfwer. In this cafe I am of opinion, that the ordinary cannot compel the churchwardens to provide their parifh prieft an hood at the parifh charge, becaufe an hood is *habitus fcholafticus*, and doth not belong to a prieft *quatenus* a prieft, but to a fcholar *quatenus* a graduate in the univerfity, where (at leaft in Oxford) every graduate is bound *habere intra quindenam habitum de proprio gradui competentem*. And in this cafe, as it is propounded, if the three reafons be proved, it will make the matter ftill more clear that the churchwardens are not to provide the hood; though the ordinary may compel a prieft who is a graduate, to wear his hood, according to the 58th canon.

In 1638, on the death of Charles Robfon, *William Head*, M. A. was inftituted on a prefentation by the univerfity.

In like manner, *John Hewitt*, M. A. in 1684.

John Holmes, M. A. in 1687.

John Ogle, B. A. in 1694.

Thomas Jefferfon, M. A. in 1715.

Thomas Boak, B. A. in 1730.

Matthew Kay, M. A. in 1766: now D. D.

Bifhop Nicolfon gives the following account of the CHURCH of Holm Cultram from his perfonal furvey in the year 1703. " The porch on the weft fide feems to have been built by Robert Chamber abbot*; there being his rebus or device on the infide of the roof, *viz.* a *bear chained* to a paftoral ftaff ftruck

---

* He was abbot here about 26 years in the reigns of king Hen. 7. and king Hen. 8. His three brothers Thomas, Richard, and Laurence, it is faid, were all abbots at different places at the fame time.

through

through a mitre, as alfo this infcription round the top of the door,—*Robertus Chamber fecit fieri hoc opus, A. D.* M.D.VII.

Under which, on the north fide of the entrance,

> *Exultemus Domino Regi fummo, qui*
> *hunc fanctificavit tabernaculum.*

On the fouth,

> *Non eft aliud nifi domus Dei et porta cæli.*

Below thefe are the king's arms, France and England quartered; and, I fuppofe, thofe of the abbey, a crofs floree and lion rampant.

On the weft fide of the church, and under where there hath been a ftatue on the north fide of the porch,

> Lady deyr fave Robert Chamber.

On the fide of a window in the fame wall,

> Orate pro anima Roberti Chamber ℋ

(This laft Gothic capital ftanding for the word Abbatis.)

The crofs ile and quire are both gone; but in the latter lies a great blue marble ftone, whereon there have been anciently feveral infcriptions in brafs, faid to be the grave ftone of this abbot Robert.

Under the weft end of this, on a free ftone, is this legend,

> Nov. 8, 1619.
> Thomas Chamber of Raby Coat
> buried.   Married Ann Mufgrave
> daughter of Jack.

About which are the following epitaphs upon other perfons of the fame family:

> October 21, 1586.
> Here lyeth Ann Mufgrave being
> murdered the 19 of the faid month,
> with the fhot of a piftol in her own
> houfe at Raby Coat, by one Robert
> Beckworth.   She was daughter of Jack
> Mufgrave, cap.t of Beawcaftle, kn.t.
> She was married to Thomas Chamber
> of Raby Coat, and had iffue fix fons,
> videl. Robert, Thomas, John, Row. Arth.
> Will. and a daughter Florence.

> Aprill 5, 1620.
> Here lyeth Jane Barbara firft wife
> to Fergus Grahm of Nunnery,
> and fecond wife of Thomas Chamber
> of Raby Coat.

> Feb. vii, 1655.
> John Chamber, till death brought him here,
> Maintained ftill the cuftome clear:

The

The church, the wood *, and parifh right,
He did defend with all his might :
Kept conftant holy fabbath daies,
And did frequent the church alwaies :
Gave alms truely to the poor,
Who dayly fought it at his door :
And purchas'd land as much and more
Than all his elders did before.
He had four children with two wives,
They died young, the one wife furvives.
None better of his rank could be
For liberal hofpitallitie.

" The infide of the church (the bifhop proceeds) was full of water, the rain falling in plentifully every where. The parifhioners about 15 or 16 years before took off the lead from the fouth ile (the arches of which are dropping down) to cover that on the north. The fabric is large, though only the body of the church is ftanding, of nine arches on each ile, and very high."

Dr. Waugh, the late chancellor, gives the following account : " When I firft came into the jurifdiction, I found both church and chancel in a moft ruinous condition. After having often applied to the univerfity by the vice-chancellor in vain, I fent out procefs to their farmer, to fhew caufe why the tithes fhould not be fequeftred ; which made them in earneft fet about the repair of the chancel, and their example was foon followed (after my viewing and threatning a little) by the parifhioners. They now roofed with lead the large middle ile, took away the fide iles and part of the chancel, and made the whole one good building. It is neatly and conveniently feated with handfome galleries, and is altogether a beautiful church ; but, though it ftands high, ftrangely damp. The body of the church, exclufive of the chancel, contains 93 pews, the galleries 48, in all 141 ; and hold, one with another, fix people each, in all 846."

In 1730, it was certified, that there were in this parifh 479 families ; of which, quakers 30, prefbyterians 4, anabaptifts 4.

In the year 1607, there being fome controverfy concerning the payment of the wages of the _parifh clerk_ or _fexton_, the fame having been paid in an uncertain manner, and the clerk claiming the fame to be paid in meal, and no certain meafure thereof afcertained ; it was agreed and ordered by the 16 men, with the confent of the other parifhioners, that for the future there fhall be one perfon who fhall be both parifh clerk and fchoolmafter, and that he fhall have for his wages for every copyhold tenement and leafe within the faid parifh which

___

* The wood here mentioned was the wood of Wedholme, which queen Elizabeth granted to the tenants for repairing the fea banks. This wood, after many mifapplications (as it is faid), was finally fold by the 16 men in 1761 for 2200 _l_ ; and the herbage not being theirs, it is not likely that there will be any further fpring : This herbage belongs to Sir James Lowther baronet, having been purchafed heretofore of Mr. Lamplugh of Ribton.

pays yearly above 18 *d* rent, 4 *d*; and for every cottager and undertenant 2 *d*; to be collected yearly at Easter by such person; who shall be chosen by the 16 men, and approved by the ordinary: And that he shall have further such sum quarterly for every scholar as the 16 men shall from time to time direct.—— Which order is still observed.

Unto whom the manor and demesne of Holm Cultram were first granted after the dissolution of the monasteries we have not found. They are at present the property of the heir of the late John Stephenson esquire, commonly called Governor Stephenson. Whilst they continued in the hands of the crown, there was a survey made in the 12th year of queen Elizabeth as follows:

ARTICLES to be done and executed by Henry lord Scroope lord warden of the West Marches towards Scotland, John Swift esquire one of the auditors of the exchequer, Richard Ashton esquire receiver general of our county of Cumberland, Anthony Barwise esquire, John Dalston esquire, and George Lamplugh esquire, appointed by William lord marquess of Winchester lord high treasurer of England, and Sir Walter Mildmay knight chancellor of the queen's majesty's court of exchequer and under-treasurer of the same court, by virtue of the queen's majesty's commission under the great seal of England bearing date at Westminster the 12th day of June in the 12th year of her majesty's reign (among other things) for the survey of the lordship or manor of Holm Cultram in the county of Cumberland, and other articles hereafter ensuing:

First, That you survey our lordship or manor of Holm Cultram in our said county of Cumberland, if the latter survey taken and certified by commission be in any things imperfect, or else to follow the same without further travel.

Item, Upon good consideration by you had of the premisses, that you by copy of court roll of the said manor in open court demise and let so much of the said lands and tenements of the said manor or lordship, as heretofore at any time have been used within the said manor; and that you do so demise and let the same severally to every of the tenants or occupiers thereof as will take the same, according to such usages and customs as heretofore have been used within the said lordship; reserving to us, our heirs and successors upon every such demise so much yearly rent as at any time heretofore hath been accustomed or used to be paid for the same.

Item, That you, upon every such demise or copy, tax and reserve for us our heirs and successors such fines and gressoms for the same as shall appear to you to be agreeable with the ancient custom of the lordship.

Item, That you upon every such demise or copy do reserve, to us, our heirs and successors, all timber trees (and except all the said trees to us, as before mentioned) growing and being upon any of the said lands or any part thereof so to be letten: And do bind every tenant and copyholder to whom you shall make any such demise or copy, to keep his and their houses and buildings in good and sufficient reparations; and to fence and inclose his grounds with quicksets: And also to be ready with horse and armour to attend upon the lord warden of the West Marches for the time being for the service of the prince, according to ancient tenure and custom of the borders there.

Item,

Item, That you do alfo make and appoint fuch convenient cuftoms, rules, and orders for the good ordering and government of the tenants of the faid lordfhip, that fo they fhall take by copy; and for the good and quiet ufage and enjoying of the fame lands and tenements, and for the demifing, granting, furrendering, and letting thereof hereafter, as by you fhall be thought meet and convenient: And among other things, to limit and appoint what intereft or eftate the wife of every fuch tenant fhall have in the fame or any part thereof after the death of her hufband, and how long, and upon what condition: And that you give order, that the fame lands and tenements fhall not be delivered by alienation or affignment of any of the tenants thereof, in any fuch fmall quillets or parcels, as thereby the occupier thereof fhall not therewith be able to make and do the fervice and cuftoms due for the fame.

Item, That you do alfo hear and determine all matters of controverfy between the tenants and occupiers of the faid lands and tenements now being, touching their pretended title of tenantright; to the intent, that when the fame lands and tenements fhall be fo by you demifed by copy of court roll as aforefaid, the fame may fo continue without any further vexation or trouble.

Item, Our further will and pleafure is, that you do caufe all fuch cuftoms, refervations, conditions, fines, greffoms, orders, and rules, as you fhall make, limit and prefcribe or appoint, in or about the demifing and letting of the premiffes by copy of court roll as aforefaid, and in and about the furrendering and granting of any eftate of copyhold, to be entered and recorded in the court roll of the faid manor or lordfhip of Holm Cultram; to the intent the fame may there remain to be witneffed at all times when occafion fhall ferve: And that among other things you do give order, that the fteward of the faid lordfhip for the time being, or his fufficient deputies, at the end of every third or fourth year, do caufe all the fame orders, rules, and cuftoms to be renewed, by prefentment of the tenants of the manor or lordfhip of Holm Cultram aforefaid, and to be newly recorded and entered in the court rolls, to the intent the fame orders, rules, and cuftoms may continually be kept in the memory of the faid tenants thereof for the time being, whereby they may better obferve and keep the fame.

Item, Our further will and pleafure is, that the fame lands and tenements by you to be letten and demifed as aforefaid fhall at all times hereafter by the fteward of the faid manor for the time being be fo demifed and letten, by copy of court roll of the faid manor, according to fuch orders, rules, and cuftoms, and under fuch refervations, fines, greffoms, and conditions, as by you according to the tenor and effect hereof fhall be limited, fet forth, and appointed, and not otherwife; and that the fame demifes and grants by copies by you now to be made, and hereafter by the fteward for the time being to be made as aforefaid, fhall ftand, remain, and be good againft us our heirs and fucceffors: And therefore we will and command you to caufe this our commiffion, with thefe articles thereunto annexed, to be inrolled and entered of record in our court rolls of the faid manor and lordfhip, to the intent this our will and pleafure may be known and obferved accordingly.

Item,

Item, Our further will and pleafure is, that you by authority or colour of this commiffion do not in any wife demife or let, by copy of court roll or otherwife, any of our lands and tenements which be known, ufed, or taken, as part or parcel of demain lands of our faid manor or lordfhip of Holme Cultram.

Item, Our further will and pleafure is, that you by virtue of our faid commiffion conclude with the faid tenants, from henceforth to maintain and bear all manner of reparations of the fea dykes within the faid lordfhip at their own proper cofts and charges; fo that we, our heirs and fucceffors may be thereof quite difcharged, having of us all the wood in Wedholm wood within the faid lordfhip towards the repairing of the fame.

The Certificate of Henry lord Scroope lord warden of the Weft Marches againft Scotland, Richard Afhton efquire receiver general, Anthony Barwife efquire, John Dalfton efquire, and George Lamplugh efquire, commiffioners appointed by virtue of the queen's majefty's commiffion out of the right honourable court of exchequer, concerning the furvey of the lordfhip or figniory of Holme Cultram in the faid county, and other articles annexed to the faid commiffion in manner and form following:

Firft, We the faid commiffioners, by virtue of our commiffion, the 13th day of October in the year aforefaid, did affemble ourfelves at Holme Cultram in the faid county, and examined the furvey of the faid lordfhip, as by the firft article annexed to the faid commiffion we were appointed; and for that the fame did agree with a furvey taken of late by a commiffion remaining of record in the court of exchequer, we did not fpend any long time therein, but do refer the fame to the laft certificate remaining as is aforefaid.

We, by virtue of the faid commiffion, did then and there appoint and fwear 24 of the ancient and fage tenants of the faid lordfhip of Holme Cultram, for to make due prefentments of the cuftoms and ufages of the lands and tenements within the faid lordfhip, and of all other articles contained in the faid commiffion, who upon their oaths do prefent, That they and their anceftors time out of mind of man had and yet have an ancient cuftom called tenant-right, as hereafter enfuing; that is to fay, that all lands and tenements within the faid lordfhip (demefnes only excepted) which are accuftomed to be let by leafe for a term of years, after the death of every tenant within the faid lordfhip, ought to defcend to the next heirs of the faid tenant fo dying, that is to fay, to the fon and heir of fuch tenant; and for default of fuch fon, to the eldeft daughter or daughters being unmarried; and in their default, to any other the next whole blood: And that every heir, after the death of their anceftors, ought to pay to the lord of the faid manor, for his or their admiffion to be tenants, in the name of a fine, for the lands and tenements to him fo letten, according to the cuftom of the faid lordfhip, the value of one year's rent for the fame cuftomary lands, over and befides the ufual rents for that year, and no more: And that like fine ought to be paid to the lord of the faid manor upon every alienation of the title of the faid tenants of the faid lordfhip or manor: And that every tenant ought to pay to the lord of the faid manor, holding cuftomary lands, at the change of the prince one penny: And

, to pay the running greffom at the end of every five years, according to the ancient custom of the said lordship.

Item, That every tenant within the said lordship ought to have horse and armour, for to attend upon the lord warden of the West Marches against Scotland or his deputy, to serve according to the use of the said Marches, upon command.

And that every customary tenant, from time to time, ought to repair, maintain, and uphold his houses and buildings upon the said customary lands.

And further, all the said tenants are to inclose their grounds with quicksets, upon their own costs and charges.

And further, all the said tenants do agree, that they owe their suit at every court and courts, view of frankpledge, and leets to be holden and from time to time to be appointed by the lord of the said manor or his officers, within the said lordship; and to pay to the lord of the said manor all fines and amerciaments affessed or hereafter to be affessed in any of the said courts, view of frankpledge, or leets; and also to fulfil and obey all such lawful commandments and ordinances as are made in any of the courts, view of frankpledge, or leets.

Item, Their custom is, that no tenant alien, let, or sell tenement, nor no part nor parcel thereof, without licence of the steward of the said lordship: And that every tenant, upon reasonable cause, by licence of the said steward for the time being, may make surrender of his farmhold to others' uses in open court; or if necessity require, afore the grave and four of the ancient tenants of the said lordship, and the same to be presented to the steward of the said manor at the next court there to be holden;—but not by his last will and testament: And further, that no tenant may divide his tenement by grant or surrender.

And further, the said tenants do present, that the wives of every such tenant within the said lordship, after the death of their husband being tenant or occupier of any lands or tenements within the said lordship, ought to have the third part of the said customary lands and tenements which their husbands had, according to the custom of the said lordship, during their widowhood, if they live honestly, and do not commit any fornication, without any fine or greffom to the lord to be paid, but only the rents and services due and accustomed.

Item, Their custom is, that for all matters of controversy presented for title of tenantright or touching custom and usage of the premisses, to be tried by jury within the said lordship.

Item, That every tenant appointed by the jury, or collector for his turn for the year, be the lord's grave; and shall yearly collect and gather the rents, revenues, and issues within his charge within the said lordship of Holm Cultram, and pay the same over at the mansion place of the late monastery within the said lordship of Holm Cultram, at days and terms accustomed.

And further, that if a tenant die, his son and heir not claiming his title and become the lord's tenant within one year and a day, after being within the realm; then

then it fhall be lawful for the lord by his fteward to admit the next of the whole blood tenant of the fame.

☞ *Item*, That all their cuftoms, conditions, refervations, common fines and greffoms fhall be ingroffed in the court rolls, to remain there to witnefs for the continual memory of their cuftom and ufages; and every third or fourth year to be renewed by the fteward, for the continual memory of the fame orders, rules, and cuftoms to be obferved.

And that their ancient cuftom is, that if any tenant commit felony or petty michery, and thereof be found guilty, to forfeit his title into the lord's hands.

Item, We the faid commiffioners, the day of the fitting of this commiffion, for the good order and government of the tenants, and to the intent that the queen's majefty, her heirs and fucceffors, may from time to time hereafter be well ferved upon the borders, the rents, iffues, fines, and greffoms of the faid lordfhip be duly and certainly anfwered,—by force of the faid commiffion hereunto annexed have concluded and agreed, to and with the tenants and every of them, that they and every of them fhall take and accept their faid cuftomary tenements by copy of court roll to them and their heirs, according to the cuftom of the faid lordfhip; yielding and paying therefore yearly to the queen's majefty that now is, her heirs and fucceffors, being the lords of the faid manor, the yearly rents, duties, fines, greffoms, and fervices, as before time hath been accuftomed, and as before they have confeffed to be their ufage and cuftom; and to ufe the fame cuftomary lands hereafter as copyhold lands for ever.

In confideration whereof, the faid tenants have likewife concluded and agreed to and with us the faid commiffioners, to have their agreements and ours ratified, confirmed, and allowed to be good under the queen's majefty's great feal of England, to give to her highnefs one whole year's rent of all the cuftomary lands, which is paid to the hands of her grace's receiver before the return of this commiffion; and alfo to uphold, maintain, and keep, from time to time hereafter, the reparations of the fea dykes within the faid lordfhip at their own coft and charges, which hitherto hath been very chargeable to her highnefs; and fhall pay all after duties and fervices as before they have agreed to.

And we the faid commiffioners have concluded and agreed to and with the faid tenants, that they fhall have the wood growing in Wedholm wood for and towards the reparation of the fea dykes within the faid lordfhip of Holm Cultram; and that they fhall appoint four of the ancient tenants to overfee and deliver the faid woods from time to time as need fhall require; and they to continue in the fame room or place one year, except there be a caufe to remove them. And at the end of every year to elect and appoint anew for the fame place for the better prefervation of the woods. And the jury faith, that the charge of the fea dykes are to be repaired from the now dwelling houfe of Robert Taylor at Skinburnees unto a place called John Afkew hole †.

And we the faid commiffioners have agreed with the jury and the tenants, that the cuftom is, that if any tenant within the faid lordfhip do die, his next

† This is the wood which we mentioned before, to have been lately fold as the private property of the parifh.

heir

heir within the age of fixteen years; the next of the kin fhall have the cuftody of the body and lands after the ufage of the focage tenure, putting fureties for the fervice and reparations, and to make account to the heir at full age.

And we the faid commiffioners have agreed to and with the faid tenants, that every tenant within the faid lordfhip at every change fhall be entered in the court rolls after the cuftom, and to have and enjoy all fuch lands and tenements, commons, paftures, moffes, and other eafments and rights, as aforetime have been accuftomed to their tenements.

And further, we the faid commiffioners have alfo agreed, that the fteward or his deputy fhall and may, with the agreement of the faid tenants, devife and make new orders for the good ufage and well ordering of the faid cuftomary lands and tenements, and the tenants and occupiers thereof; the fame orders to be recorded in feveral court rolls thereof, to be openly publifhed in the faid courts, that all tenants may underftand the fame: fo that they be not prejudicial to the queen's majefty's right, nor the ancient cuftom of the faid lordfhip.

The particular names of the jury now fworn and examined upon the cuftom to try and prefent the fame,

Robert Chambers, &c.

In witnefs whereof to thefe articles and agreements above fpecified, we the faid commiffioners have put to our feals and fubfcribed our names the day and year above written.

WITHIN this parifh and lordfhip ftood *Wulfty caftle*, formerly (as is faid) a very ftrong building, encompaffed with a large and deep ditch; and, according to tradition, erected by the religious here, for the fafe keeping of their charters, books, and records.

CUMBERLAND WARD.

BLENCOGO.

ALthough the manor of *Bromfield*, and the greateft part of the parifh of *Bromfield*, are within the ward of Allerdale below Derwent; yet a part of the faid parifh is within Cumberland Ward, as having been parcel of the eftate of the lords of Wigton. Of which part, the firft place is BLENCOGO, which was granted by Waldieve firft lord of Allerdale to Odard de Logis, together with Wigton, Kirkbride, Ulton, Waverton, and Dundraw. It continued in the pofterity of *Odard* for feveral generations.

The firft account that we meet with of it afterwards was in the reign of king Henry the feventh, who by letters patent dated May the firft in the 24th year of his reign, granted to *Richard Cholmeley* knight, the manor of

7

Blencogo

Blencogo with the appurtenances, and all lands and tenements called Blencogo within the parish of Bromfield, with all and all manner of commons, courts leet and view of frankpledge, free warren, and other liberties whatsoever to the said manor and other the premisses belonging or in any wise appertaining ; to hold to him and his heirs by fealty only without other account to be made thereof.

In the account of knights fees in Cumberland in the 35 Hen. 8. it is found, that *Richard Cholmeley* knight then held the manor and town of Blencogo, with the appurtenances, of the king as of his manor of Wigdon, by the service of one knight's fee, 13*s* cornage, 7*s* 6*d* for puture of the bailiff, 2*s* seawake, and witnesman, and suit of court at Wigdon from 3 weeks to 3 weeks, and 50*s* relief when it shall happen.

Afterwards, queen Elizabeth by letters patent, March 22, in the 31st year of her reign, grants to *Walter Copinger* and *Thomas Butler* of London gentlemen *(inter alia)* the manor of Blencogo with the appurtenances, and all lands, tenements, and hereditaments, called or known by the name of Blencogo, heretofore in the tenure of Richard Cholmeley knight ; to hold to them and their heirs as of the manor of East Greenwich, by fealty only and not *in capite.*

In the 10 Cha. 1. June 26. *Richard Barwise* of Ilekirk esquire, lord of the manor of Blencogo, grants to the tenants (18 in number), for 40 years ancient rent, that they shall hold to them their heirs and assigns, customary estates of inheritance of their several tenements, paying the ancient yearly rent, and two years ancient rent (and no other fine) after change of lord by death, and change of tenant by death or alienation, doing suit of court as before. Every alienation to be entred at the next court, paying for the entry 12*d* and no more. He grants to them also all trees, woods, and underwoods, on their respective tenements ; with power to get freestone and limestone in their several grounds, or in any waste ground within the townfields or commons, for their own use, but not to give or sell the same to any other.

The present lord of the manor is Mr. *Thomlinson*, now (1770) an infant.

The vicar of Bromfield is endowed of the great tithes of this township, and when the commons came to be inclosed and improved, Mr. Child the vicar supposing that the great tithes of the said commons improved were included also in his endowment, brought his action, which was tried at Carlisle assizes, wherein he was nonsuited, those tithes appearing to belong to the impropriators.

Galiene daughter of Richard de Hervi gave to the abbey of Holm Cultram 3 acres of arable land in the territory of Blencoggon, and pasture for 100 sheep, 28 cows, one bull, and two horses, for the maintenance of the infirm poor†.

And Marjoria daughter of Galiene gave to the said abbey of Holm Cultram two bovates of land in Blengoggon : Unto which her son Robert quitted claim†.

† Regiftr. Holm.

And

And Adam fon of Dolphin de Langrigg gave half an acre of arable land to the faid abbey in the territory of Blengoggon†.

And king Henry the eighth, by letters patent bearing date July the ninth in the 37th year of his reign, granted to Thomas Dalſton eſquire and Eleanor his wife *(inter alia)* the meſſuages and tenements, and all the lands, meadows, paſtures, and other hereditaments whatſoever, with the appurtenances, in the ſeveral tenures of Chriſtopher Martindale, Richard Howe, and John Meſ-ſenger, in Blencogo, late parcel of the poſſeſſions of the abbot and convent of Holm Cultram.

DUNDRAW.

DUNDRAW *(Dundragh,* an Iriſh name, ſignifying an hill of oaks) was given as aforeſaid by Waldieve to *Odard de Logis,* who gave the ſame to Gilbert his ſon, who thence took the name of *Gilbert de Dundraw.* After *Gilbert* ſucceeded *Gilbert* his ſon. And after him, Mr. Denton ſays he had read of one Symon de Dundragh in the 17 Hen. 3. But it doth not ſeem that he held the manor. For the four daughters and coheirs of the ſecond Gilbert de Dundraw did inherit his lands in Dundraw, Crofton, Thackthwait, and Diſtington; viz. *Cicely* the wife of Jordon Clapell, who gave her part by fine to William Cundall, in whoſe right ſucceeded Ralph Cundall : *Matilda* the wife of William Multon, who gave her part of Diſtington to Thomas ſon of Lambert de Multon lord of Egremont, and her part of Thackthwait to Thomas Lucy the ſon of Alice and of Alan Multon : *Iſold* the wife of Adam de Tinmouth, who ſold her part of Thackthwaite to Thomas Lucy, and of Diſtington to Thomas ſon of Lambert de Multon : And *Ada* the wife of Stephen de Crofton, whoſe part deſcended by the Croftons till the time of king Hen. 4. thenceforth to the Briſcoes who yet enjoy the ſame in Dundraw and Crofton, and ſhe gave her part in Diſtington to Thomas Moreſby and Margaret his wife and to the heirs of Thomas, and her part of Thackthwait to Margaret ſiſter of Thomas Lucy and wife of Thomas Stanley‡.

In the 35 Hen. 8. *Robert Lamplugh* held a moiety of the town of Dundraw, of the king as of his manor of Wigdon, by knights ſervice, rendring for the ſame 6*s* 8*d* cornage, 10*d* ſeawake, puture of the ſerjeants, witneſman, and ſuit of court from 3 weeks to 3 weeks : And *Robert Briſco* held the other moiety by the like ſervices.

Roger de Lyndeby gave with his body ſeven acres of arable land in the territory of Dundrake to the abbey of Holm Cultram, under the yearly rent of 2*s* 4*d* to the lord of Dundrake for all ſervices *.

PARISH OF WIGTON.

WIGTON was ancient demeſne of Allerdale, until Waldieve ſon of Goſpatric earl of Dunbar gave that barony unto *Odard de Logis.* It contained Wigton,

† Regiſtr. Holm.   ‡ Denton.   * Regiſtr. Holm.

Waverton,

Waverton, Blencogo, Dundraw, and Kirkbride (with Ulton). Which five townships are feveral manors within themfelves, known by metes and bounds, and lie within the barony of Wigton. King Hen. 1. confirmed Waldieve's grant unto him, and he lived until the reign of king John ; fo that he muft have died in a good old age.

This *Odard* had iffue *Adam*, and *Adam* had iffue *Odard* the fecond, whofe fon and heir *Adam* the fecond died without iffue ; therefore the inheritance came to his brother *Walter*, who had iffue *Odard* the third, who died without iffue, and another *Odard*, who alfo died without iffue ; wherefore their brother *John de Wigton*, fon of *Walter*, entered ; which *John* had an only daughter and heir *Margaret*, who was married to John Gernoun. In king Edward the third's time, fhe was impleaded for her birthright, and her mother Idyonife Lovetot the wife of Sir John de Wigton was for a time hindred of her dower, but her adverfary did not prevail. Wigton barony fhortly after her death came to Thomas Lucy lord of Allerdale, and thereby in right the feigniory of Wigton was extinguifhed, and became again part of the ancient barony of Allerdale, though it is ftill taken and reputed as a diftinct barony. From the Lucys it came to the earls of Northumberland, together with the reft of the Lucy eftate, and is now the property of the prefent earl of Egremont.

In the *Chronicon Cumbriæ* it is faid that the CHURCH of Wigton was built by the firft *Odard de Logis* ; and it was given by the lady Margaret de Wigton to the abbey of Holm Cultram for their better fupport after the devaftations made by the Scots.

It is dedicated to St. Mary ; rated in the king's books at 17*l* 19*s* 9¼*d* ; certified to the governors of queen Anne's bounty at 32*l* 13*s* 4*d* ; and in 1718 it was augmented by the faid governors with 200*l*, in conjunction with 250*l*, given by Mr. John Thomlinfon rector of Rothbury, wherewith lands were purchafed near Carlifle, of the prefent yearly value of about 20*l*. He alfo by his will gave a further augmentation of 13*l* a year.

The faid lady Margaret gave alfo the advowfon of this church to the faid abbey, that they might find four chaplains monks of their own houfe to perform divine fervice in the church of the abbey, and two fecular chaplains to officiate in a chantry of the church of St. Mary at Wigton, for the foul of the faid Margaret and of her hufband John Gernoun, and of her anceftors, and all faithful people†.

Not

† Inquifitio capta apud Wiggeton, coram Johanne de Louthre efcaetore domini regis ultra Trentam, quinto die Februarii anno regni regis Edwardi tertii poft conqueftum fexto, per facramentum Thomæ de Redman, Gilberti de Halteclo, Ranulphi de Ofmunderlawe, Hugonis de Bromfeld, Johannis de Ireby, Adæ de Langriggs, Thomæ de Langriggs, Thomæ de la Ferte, Ranulphi de Daneby, Roberti de Vaus, Alani de Arcleby fenioris, et Wilhelmi de Leathes, fecundum tenorum brevis huic inquifitioni confuti ; qui dicunt fuper facramentum fuum : Quod non eft ad dampnum feu prejudicium domini regis, nec aliorum, fi idem dominus rex concedat Johanni Gernoun et Margaretæ uxori ejus, quod ipfi unam acram terræ cum pertinentiis in Wyggeton, et advocationem ecclefiæ ejufdem villæ, dare poffint et concedere abbati et conventui de Holm Cultram ; habendam et tenendam fibi et fuccefforibus fuis in perpetuum, ad inveniendum quatuor capellanos monachos ordinis prædicti divina in ecclefia abbathiæ prædicti, et duos capellanos
feculares

Not long after the grant of the faid church to the abbey, upon the petition of Thomas de Talcane (then abbot) and the convent of Holm Cultram to bifhop Kirkby, the faid bifhop and his commiffaries Robert de Southayke and John de Burdon confirm the appropriation; ordaining, that there fhall be a perpetual vicar, who fhall have for his ftipend 26 marks of filver yearly to be paid by the faid abbot and convent, and one meffuage and ten acres of arable land in the vill of Kirkland, and one acre of land in the vill Wyggeton nigh to the manfion houfe: But referving to the bifhop the collation to the vicarage, in recompence of the diminution of the epifcopal right accruing by fuch appropriation †.

Queen Elizabeth, by letters patent dated Feb. 9. in the 30th year of her reign, granted the corn tithes of the villages of Wigton, Waverton, and Oulton, to Edward Downinge and Miles Dodding gentlemen; who affigned the fame to Robert Petrie; whofe heir Sir John Petrie affigned to Richard Fletcher of Cockermouth chapman for 650 l.

feculares divina in ecclefia beatæ Mariæ de Wyggeton, pro falubri ftatu ejufdem domini regis dum vitam duxerit in humanis, et pro anima ipfius domini regis cum ab hoc feculo migraverit, et pro animabus præd ctorum Johannis et Margaretæ, et antecefforum ipfius Margaretæ, et pro omnibus animabus omnium fidelium defunctorum imperpetuum celebraturos ; et eifdem abbati et conventui quod ipfi terram et advocationem prædictas a præfatis Johanne et Margareta recipere, et ecclefiam illam appropriare, et eam appropriatam tenere poffint fibi et fucceffibus fuis prædictis imperpetuum. Item dicunt, quod prædicta terra et advocatio ecclefiæ prædictæ tenentur de domino Antonio de Lucy, per fervitium reddendi eidem Antonio per annum unum obolum. Et dicunt quod prædicta ecclefia per fe valet per annum in omnibus exitibus, juxta verum valorem ejufdem, triginta fex libras. Item dicunt, quod dominus Antonius de Lucy eft dominus medius inter dominum regem et præfatos Johannem et Margaretam de terra et advocatione prædictis, et nullus alius. Et dicunt, quod remanent eifdem Johanni et Margaretæ ultra donationem et affignationem prædictas, duæ partes manerii de Wyggeton cum pertinentiis, quæ tenentur de domino Antonio de Lucy per cornagium, reddendo eidem Antonio quinque marcas per annum, et faciendo fectam curiæ ejufdem Antonii apud Cockermouth de tribus feptimanis in tres feptimanas ; et valent dictæ duæ partes dicti manerii in omnibus exitibus, juxta verum valorem per annum quadraginta libras. Item dicunt, quod terræ et tenementa ejufdem Johannis et Margaretæ, remanentia ultra donationem et affignationem prædictas, fufficiunt ad confuetudines et fervitia, tam de prædictis terra et advocatione fic datis, quam de aliis terris et tenementis fibi retentis, debita facienda. Dicunt etiam, quod dicta terra et tenementa fibi retenta fufficiunt ad omnia alia onera quæ fuftinuerunt, et antea fuftinere confueverunt ; ut in fectis, vifibus franci plegii, auxiliis, tallagiis, vigiliis, finibus, redemptionibus, amerciamentis, contributionibus, et aliis oneribus quibufcunque emergentibus fuftinendis. Et dicunt, quod idem Johannes, et hæredes ipfius Margaretæ, in affifis, juratis, et aliis recognitionibus quibufcunque, poni poffint prout ante donationem et affignationem prædictas poni confueverunt. In cujus, &c. 1 *Dugd Mon.* 886.

† Et ne dicta ecclefia in ullum eventum debitis defraudetur obfequiis, ordinamus quod fit ibi perpetuus vicarius, qui curam animarum habeat, et dicto domino epifcopo, ejufque fucceffibus et miniftris de fpiritualibus et aliis occafionibus omnibus, ordinariis et extraordinariis, pro portionis fuæ rata, refpondeat ut tenetur. Ad cujus portionem viginti fex marcas argenti, ad duos anni terminos, videlicet ad fefta Pafchæ et Sancti Michaelis, per equales portiones, per abbatem et conventum antedictos in fingulis annis perfolvendas, fine omni augmento ulteriori affignamus: Item, unum meffuagium et decem acras terræ arabilis in villa de Kirkland ; ac etiam unam acram terræ in villa de Wyggeton prope manfo ejufdem vicarii, una cum communa et aliis proficuis omnibus ad eam pertinentibus. Collationem vero vicariæ prædictæ, de confenfu dictorum abbatis et conventus, dicto domino epifcopo et fucceffibus fuis imperpetuum, in recompenfationem lefionis feu diminutionis juris fui epifcopalis in præmiffis, fpecialiter refervamus.

King

King James the first by letters patent granted all the rest of the said rectory (tithes of eggs, geese, and apples only excepted) to Francis Morice esquire and Francis Phelips gentleman; who in the 13th year of the said king assigned the same to Richard Fletcher of Cockermouth esquire.

The said king in the 5th year of his reign granted the tithes of eggs, geese, and apples, to Lewis Owen esquire and William Blake scrivener; which the house of Crofton now enjoys: as do the Fletchers of Hutton all the other tithes.

King Ed. 6. by letters patent dated the 30th day of January in the 3d year of his reign, granted to Thomas Dalston esquire and William Denton gentleman, their heirs and assigns, the *free chapel* called *St. Leonard's hospital*, in the parish of Wigton; and all the lands, meadows, pastures, feedings, and hereditaments whatsoever, in the tenure of the relict of Leonard Thompson in Wigton, and of William Robinson in the forest of Westward, to the said free chapel belonging.

The church is a very old building, which seems never to have been rebuilt since Odard's time. In the chancel are three seats, so large as to fill up most of the space below the rails of the communion table. One whereof belongs to the impropriator, and is commonly used by the officers of the court at visitations. Another was built by Mr. Dalton of Oulton, and is enjoyed by the present owners of his estate. The third was erected in 1667 by Gawen Chambers, who (having been sometime a zealous fanatic) was purchased hereby into the church by good bishop Rainbow, and is now enjoyed by Sir Gilfrid Lawson whose ancestor purchased his estate.

On the north entrance into the quire, there is a plate of brass on the wall with this inscription:

    " A memorative epitaph for the worthy and loving Colonel Thomas Barwise, who died the 15 day of December 1648. Ætatis suæ 27.

    Stay, passenger, for there bold Barwise lies,
    Whose sanced spirit soars above the skies.
    Stout, wise, yet humble, fitted in each part
    For more command, of comely body, pious heart.
    Dear to his people, country, kindred dear,
    Dear to his known associates every where.
    Who, living, was life's lively portraiture;
    And dying Colonel, lives crowned sure."

This Thomas was father to the last Mr. Barwise of Ilekirk, elder brother to captain William Barwise of Huddlesceugh and sometime of Warton.

Under the eves of the north side both of the church and chancel are several antique sculptures; which have occasioned a tradition that these stones were brought from the ruins of Old Carlisle.

Incumbents of this parish that have occurred are as follows:

Before the grant of this church to the monastery by Margaret de Wigton, *James de Daltlegh*, in the year 1308, on a presentation by Sir John de Wyggeton (father of the said Margaret) was instituted to the vacant rectory of Wyggeton.

In 1317, *William de Hilton* prieſt was preſented to the vacant rectory of Wiggeton by king Edward the ſecond (probably during the minority of Margaret); and thereupon the biſhop gives him a Commendam of the ſaid church for ſix months from the date thereof, according to a Novel Conſtitution.

In 1332, Sir *Adam de Staynegrave* rector of Wyggeton exchanges his living with Sir *Gilbert de Wyggeton* rector of the church of Botelsford in the dioceſe of Lincoln; and the ſaid Gilbert being preſented accordingly by the abbot and convent of Holm Cultram was thereupon inſtituted.

In 1336, the ſaid Gilbert reſigns his rectory, and the biſhop collates *Henry de Appelby* into the vicarage *jam de novo ordinatam* (as the record expreſſeth it) *et rite creatam, concurrentibus omnibus et ſingulis quæ de jure requiruntur in hac parte.*—This Henry was a monk of Holm Cultram, and had a licence from the abbot and convent there, to take the oaths of canonical obedience to the biſhop at his inſtitution, and was bound (together with the ſaid abbot and convent) to pay yearly to the ſaid Gilbert during his life 100 *l.*

In 1359, Sir *Thomas de Cullerdane* vicar of Wyggeton exchanges his vicarage with Sir *Richard de Aſlacby* for that of Staynwigges.

In 1367, Sir *William de Creſſop* exchanges the vicarage of Wyggeton with Sir *Richard Damyſell* for the rectory of Bampton. And in the next year, the ſaid Richard exchanges with Sir *William de Hayton* of the dioceſe of Durham; and he again in the year following with *John de Welton* of the dioceſe of York.

In 1572, on the reſignation of *John King* vicar of Wigton, biſhop Beſt collates Sir *William Lowden.*

In 1592, on the death of William Lowden, Sir *William Lowſon* was collated by biſhop Mey.

In 1612, William Lowſon being removed to Hutton, the vicarage was given by biſhop Robinſon to Sir *Thomas Warcoppe* clerk. Which Thomas, long before his death, cauſed his monument to be erected in the churchyard, with the following epitaph (all, except the date of his death, of his own compoſing):

> Thomas Warcup prepar'd this ſtone,
> To mind him oft of his beſt home.
> Little but ſin and miſery here,
> Till we be carried on our beere.
> Out of the grave, and earth's duſt,
> The lord will raiſe me up I truſt;
> To live with Chriſt eternallie,
> Who me to ſave, himſelf did die.

Mihi eſt Chriſtus et in vita et in morte lucrum: *Phil.* 1. 21. Obiit Anno 1653.

In 1661, *John Chambers* was collated by biſhop Sterne.

In 1674, *Henry Geddis* by biſhop Rainbow.

In 1715, *John Brown,* father of Dr. John Brown author of the Eſſay on the Characteriſtics of the earl of Shafteſbury, and other ingenious writings, was collated by biſhop Nicolſon.

In 1763, on John Brown's death, *Wilfrid Clarke,* M. A. was collated by biſhop Lyttelton.

Belonging

. Belonging to this church is a pretty large parochial *library*.

In 1730, there were in this parish 479 families; of which, diſſenters (chiefly quakers) 63.

There are in this pariſh and town of Wigton two public charitable foundations, to wit, The college of matrons or hoſpital of Chriſt, and the Grammar School.

The HOSPITAL ſtands near the north ſide of the churchyard, and was founded in 1725 by Robert Thomlinſon, D. D rector of Whickham in the county of Durham, and John Thomlinſon rector of Glenfield in the county of Leiceſter, executors of the laſt will and teſtament of John Thomlinſon, M. A. rector of, Rothbury in the county of Northumberland, for ſix indigent widows of proteſtant beneficed clergymen epiſcopally ordained, and incorporated by the name of governeſs and ſiſters of the college of matrons or hoſpital of Chriſt in Wigton in the county of Cumberland; and endowed by them with a yearly rent of 48 *l* iſſuing out of lands in Eaſter Haughton in the pariſh of Simondburn in the county of Northumberland, and a yearly rent of 6 *l* iſſuing out of two cloſes in the pariſh of Gateſhead in the county of Durham.

. No widow 'to be admitted' under 46 years of age, and to be the widow of a proteſtant prieſt epiſcopally ordained and beneficed either in the dioceſe of Carliſle, or in that part of Cumberland which is in the dioceſe of Cheſter, or, who had ſerved as a curate therein for two years at leaſt at the time of his death, 'or elſe was rector of Rothbury or of Whickham or had ſerved two years as curate there at the time of his death. The widows of beneficed prieſts to be preferred to the widows of curates. The widows of clergymen related to the founders, or of their ſirname, to be preferred before all others. Next to them, the widows of the rectors of Rothbury and Whickham: And the widows of curates of theſe two livings, before all other widows of curates. The widow of the vicar of Wigton (if he died treaſurer), before the widows of other beneficed clergymen within the dioceſe of Carliſle. The widows of beneficed prieſts and curates within the dioceſe of Carliſle, before the widows of all clergymen within that part of Cumberland which is in the dioceſe of Cheſter.—By beneficed prieſts are to be underſtood lecturers, perpetual curates, or chaplains of chapels, as well as rectors and vicars: and by curates are to be underſtood ſtipendiary curates.—And not to be at any time above one widow of any one living. And none to be admitted who hath an income of 10 *l* a year or 200 *l* in goods.

The chancellor of the dioceſe of Carliſle, the rectors of Aikton and Caldbeck, and the vicars of Bromfield and Wigton to be governors: If the chancellor live out of the dioceſe, or become unable or unwilling to act, then his official or ſubſtitute to act as governor: And if any of the incumbents of the ſaid four livings ſhall refuſe, or be non-reſident for two years together; the remaining governors to chuſe others for that turn, out of the incumbents of Torpenhow, Aſpatric, Bolton, and Plumland.

The founders to be viſitors during their lives; after that, Mr. William Thomlinſon of Blencogo and his heirs, till the end of 60 years from the date

of

of thefe ftatutes (viz. Mar. 25, 1725); after that the bifhop of Carlifle for the time being for ever.

On a vacancy of the governefs or any of the fifters, the place to be kept void for 30 days; and the governors, within 21 days after that, fhall fill up the vacancy: If the votes are equal, the vifitor to chufe for that time.

The governors fhall alfo have power to correct, and punifh by mulct or (after three admonitions) by expulfion; with a faving, in cafe of expulfion, of an appeal to the vifitor.

The governors to have power from time to time to make new ftatutes, provided they be not contrary to thofe of the founders.

· In cafe of precedency, next after the governefs, widows of graduates to be preferred to thofe of undergraduates, but otherwife the widows of each to take place according to the feniority of their admiffion, unlefs there was a great inequality in the preferments and univerfity degrees conferred on their hufbands, in which cafe the graduates of Oxford and Cambridge fhall always be preferred to the Irifh, and the Irifh to the Scotch.

A matron having children, fhall not keep any of them in her apartment after the age of 16 or 17, unlefs a daughter that is fickly or fhe herfelf be fickly or infirm, in which cafe fhe (with leave) may have a daughter or fervant.

The outward doors of the college to be locked at half an hour after nine every night from Michaelmafs to Lady-day, and at ten from Lady-day to Michaelmafs.

The vicar of Wigton to be treafurer, for which he fhall have 20 s yearly. And he fhall pay yearly to the governefs 8 l 10 s 0 d, and to each of the five fifters 8 l.

And there fhall be a general meeting once a year, on a day to be appointed by the chancellor of Carlifle in May, June, or July; but if he do not appoint a day before Midfummer, then on the firft Thurfday in July; for auditing the accounts, viewing the hofpital, and making orders concerning the fame: the treafurer to lay out 10 or 14 s for a dinner for the truftees, and 6 s for a dinner to the matrons.

Mrs. Reed of Newcaftle upon Tyne, fifter of Dr. Thomlinfon, gave 100 l to this hofpital, for which a rent charge of 3 l 10 s was procured on fome lands at Blencogo; and there is a further addition to the revenues of this hofpital by another rent charge of 6 l from the fame lands.

[A capital error in moft of thefe charitable foundations is, in charging a pecuniary fum iffuing out of lands, which fum almoft every year diminifhes in value: If lands had been given, the value of the lands would have increafed in proportion as the value of money decreafeth.]

Upon the front of this hofpital is the following infcription:

Collegium Matronarum
Proventu annuo
Inftruxit
Joh. Thomlinfon, A. M.
Erexit
Rob. ejus Frater, S. T. P.
A. D. 1723.

The

The other charitable foundation at Wigton is the SCHOOL. The firſt eſſay towards it was made by the ſaid Mr. Thomlinſon of Rothbury about the year 1714; which was an offer to the pariſhioners, that if they would contribute thereto according to their abilities, he would give 100*l* towards erecting a free grammar ſchool, and procure another 100*l* from his relations. Accordingly, they ſet about it; and, by a method agreed to among themſelves, they raiſed 200*l*. That money of theirs Mr. Thomlinſon took into his own hands; and for that, and the 200*l* given by himſelf and his relations, he made over to the ſchool an annuity of 20 *l* for ever, payable out of the eſtate at Haughton aforeſaid. Since that time, an additional ſtock of 80*l* was raiſed, which is let out at intereſt for the benefit of the maſter. At firſt there was no ſchoolhouſe, and they were forced to hire one, which leſſened the maſter's ſalary conſiderably. Whereupon Dr. Thomlinſon of Wickham did generouſly propoſe to the pariſhioners, that if they would find him a proper piece of ground to build on, and lead the materials, he would erect not only an houſe to teach in, but alſo a dwelling for the maſter. This propoſal was readily agreed to, and the doctor built the houſes accordingly at the expence of 125*l*. And over the door of the ſchoolhouſe is the following inſcription:

Deo et E. A. S.
·Scholam hanc vir reverendus·
R. Thomlinſon, S. T. P.
Poſuit L. M.
A. D. 1730.

It is ſaid, that Mr. Thomlinſon of Rothbury intended to have the nomination of the maſter veſted in the vicar and a certain number of truſtees, but he died before any thing of that kind was effected. And every one who was a contributor claims an equal right in the choice of a maſter; and the claimants being very numerous, there is likely to be much confuſion, until they can agree to intruſt the nomination in a ſelect number.

In 1756, Mr. Barnes of Dockray left 5*l* to this ſchool.

Under the monument of the aforeſaid Mr. John Thomlinſon, in the chancel of the pariſh church of Rothbury, upon a ſquare piece of marble, are the following benefactions recorded:

To the pariſh of Rothbury for ever, the eſtates of Shaperton, Harbottle, and Todhills, of the yearly value of 33*l* 10*s* 0*d*.

To the ſchool at Rothbury, a rent charge out of an eſtate in Bickerton in that pariſh 20*l*.

Building the ſchool-houſe there 100*l*.

To procure the bounty of queen Anne towards augmenting the vicarage of Wigton, in the year 1718, 250*l*.

Further augmentation by will to the ſaid vicarage 13*l* yearly.

To the ſchool at Wigton, 100*l*.

Building a college of matrons at Wigton, 200*l*.

Towards the endowment thereof a rent charge of 35 *l per annum*.

At Wigton is a pretty large market on Tueſday weekly.

PARISH

PARISH OF AIKTON.

AIKTON (a town of oaks) is the next parish north east from Wigton. It is a manor within the barony of Burgh upon the sands, and was the principal seat of *Johan de Morville* second daughter and one of the two coheirs of Sir *Hugh Morville* lord of Burgh. A little hamlet here, now called Downhall (and ever so named after the Scots burnt it) was the capital messuage of Aikton, where the said *Johan* and her husband Sir *Richard Gernon* lived. The said *Johan* died in the 31 Hen. 3, and had two daughters *Helwise* and *Ada*. *Ada* the younger was married to Randolph Boyvill of Levington, and afterwards to William Furniville : She died in the 55 Hen. 3. and her daughter and heir *Hawise*, did succeed in the inheritance of Ada and of Randolph de Levington her husband. *Hawise* died soon after her mother without issue ; therefore the lands of Randolph Boyvill of Levington fell to his six sisters coheirs, and her fourth part, to wit, the moiety of her grandmother's moiety of the Morvill's : lands came to *Roger* son of *Walter Colvill* and of *Margaret* his wife, in right of the said *Margaret*, who was daughter and heir of *Helwise* elder daughter of Johan de Morvill and wife of Eustace Baliol. The said *Helwise* died in the 34 Hen. 3. and her daughter *Margaret* in the 9 Ed. 1. *Roger Colvill*, son of the said *Margaret*, and in her right lord of Aikton, was succeeded by his son *Edward Colvill*; and after him, *Robert Colvill* was found heir. In the 23 Ed. 1. *Thomas Daniel* died lord of the same, in right of *Isabel* his wife the heir of *Colvill*; and left his daughter *Margaret* a child of three years of age his heir; who in the 4 Ed. 3. intailed the land to her husband *John Radcliffe* and herself for life; remainder to *Richard* their son for life; then to *Robert, Thomas, Richard,* and *John,* sons of the said *Richard*, and their heirs successively in tail male; then to the heirs male of *Henry* son of *Catharine Chiftley*; then to the heirs male of *John* son of *William Radcliffe* of Longfield; after to the heirs male of *Robert* son of *William* son of *Richard Radcliffe*; after to the right heirs of *Margaret Daniel* (the grandmother) for ever. She died in the 44 Ed. 3. Afterwards this manor was sold, in the reign of Hen. 6. to the lord *Thomas Dacre*, and thereby became united to the ancient seigniory of Burgh (as it still continues), from which it had been separated by the partition between the two daughters and coheirs of Hugh de Morvill aforesaid.

GAMELSBY within this parish stands on the north side of the river Wampool, between it and the fields of Aikton. It is called in ancient evidences Gamelsby nigh Aikton, to distinguish it from another place of the same name on the north side of the river Eden. It contains the two hamlets of *Gamelsby* and *Biglands*, which latter is so called from that kind of grain called *big* (a species of barley) growing plentifully there. These two hamlets were anciently a manor, and the chief or capital messuage stood at Gamelsby, and was so called of one Gamel who built it and inhabited there; before whose time, it was a woody waste frequented with deer. It was anciently part of Burgh, and granted

granted forth to one *William Brewer* by the Barons of Burgh to be holden as a part of the faid barony, as the baron held the fame of the king. The next lord that we meet with was *Adam de Crookdake*, who had it by fine of William Brewer. Afterwards it defcended by two daughters to the family of the *Raughtons* and *Beyvills* lords of Weftlinton. *Raughton*'s part defcended to a daughter named *Catharine* wife of *John Afpilon* a Buckinghamfhire man, who fold the fame to the *Warcops*, and they to the *Crackenthorps* or *Southaiks*, who exchanged the fame with the *Dentons* of Cardew for their land in Skelton: One of the pofterity of the Dentons fold the fame to the feveral inhabitants and tenants of that part. The other moiety (the *Levington*'s part) defcended long in the heir male, till by a daughter it was transferred to *Alexander Highmore* of Harbybrow, whofe heir fold the fame to the lord *Dacre*, and it has ever fince been enjoyed along with the barony of Burgh.

WATHINPOOL, or *Wampool,* lies next unto Biglands and Gamelfby, and is fo called of the river Wampool becaufe it ftands upon the banks of the fame. The eldeft that we read of that was lord thereof was one *Robert Brune* fon of *Radulph,* who was called *Robert de Wathinpole*. He married Margaret daughter and heir of Richard de Trute lord of Newby beneath Carlifle. This family took their name from the place, and were called *Wathinpoles*. Afterwards the *Warwicks* of Warwick were lords thereof, whofe heir *Richard Warwick* fold the fame to the inhabitants, who are now freeholders of the barony of Burgh.

LEATHES is a hamlet next unto Wampool, and was fo called from a grange or farm which the lord of Whitrigg had there. Of this place the family of *Leathes* took their furname, which anciently well nigh the conqueft enjoyed the fame; and it defcended in the iffue male until *Adam de Leathes,* in the reign of queen Elizabeth, fold the fame to the inhabitants. We call a barn for corn a *leath,* whereupon the place was fo called, being a very good corn foil, and fo kept conftantly in tillage. It was part of the demefne of *Whitrigg,* fo called being a long *white ridge* upon the banks of Wathempool, which belonged to an ancient family of the name of *Brun,* who afterwards from the place of their refidence in Scotland took the name of *Dunbritton,* and their pofterity at this place took the name of *Whitrigg*.

The CHURCH of Aikton is rectorial, and dedicated to St. Andrew. It is valued in the king's books at 14*l* 3*s* 1½*d*. And the improved yearly value is now 200*l* or upwards. In 1730 there were in this parifh 128 families; of which, Quakers 4, and no other diffenter.

This church of ancient time was prefented unto by moieties, which perhaps might be firft occafioned by the divifion of the Morvil eftate between the two daughters of Sir Hugh Morvil, Ada married into the Multon family, and Johan married (as aforefaid) to Gernon.

In the year 1304, on the death of *William de Aldewerk,* Thomas de Multon of Gillefland prefents *William de Somerfet* to a moiety of the church of Ayketon;

ton ; whereupon an inquifition was had *de jure patronatus* ; and one *Richard de Ayketon* protefted that there was no fuch vacancy as was pretended, for that he himfelf was rector of the whole. And towards consolidating the faid rectory, Richard de Ayketon refigns his title. Neverthelefs, in the regifter, there prefently follows an inftitution and mandate for induction to the faid moiety, of the aforementioned William de Somerfet.

Two years after, William de Somerfet refigns his moiety ; and *Richard de Afkelly* was inftituted into it, on the prefentation of the faid Thomas de Multon lord of Gillefland.

In 1339, on the death of *Robert de Halghton*, *William de Salkeld* is prefented to a moiety of the rectory of Ayketon by Margaret de Dacre, who dates her prefentation from Kirkofwald. And upon an inquifition of the right of patronage the jurors find the aforefaid lady Margaret (heirefs of the Multon family, and relict of Ralph lord Dacre) the true patronefs ; and accordingly the faid William has inftitution, and a mandate to *Thomas le Spencer* (rector of the other moiety) to induct him.

In 1362, *William Beauchamp* was admitted to a moiety, on the prefentation of Ralph lord Dacre.

And two years after, on the refignation of the faid William Beauchamp, inftitution was given to Sir William Chamberlayne by the fame title.

In 1371, *Robert de Kirkby* was rector of a moiety of Aketon, as appears by his will dated in that year.

In 1373, on the refignation of Sir *Thomas de Hutton*, Sir *Thomas Roke* was prefented by Ralph lord Dacre to a moiety, and inftituted thereupon.

In 1378, Hugh de Dacre lord of Gillefland, knight, prefents Sir *John de Kerby* to a moiety of Aketon, vacant by the death of Sir *John de Midylton* ; and William rector of Bownefs, vicar general in the bifhop's abfence, gives him inftitution.

In 1465, a writ of Quare impedit was brought by Sir John Savage knight, claiming the right of prefentation againft the bifhop and *Richard Morland* ; but Richard Morland continued rector (of the whole, as it feemeth, for after this we find nothing more of the moieties).

In the reign of king Hen. 7. we find *Chriftopher Caunefield*, rector of Aketon, witnefs to divers inftruments.

In 1509, the laft year of that king's reign, *Robert Lowthe* rector of Aketon was witnefs to a releafe of the manor of Glaffon to Thomas lord Dacre.

In 1542, *Nicholas Crawhall* was rector.

In 1563, on the death of *John Blyth* rector of Aketon, *William Lowden* was inftituted on the prefentation of William Dacre knight, lord Dacre.

In 1572, on William Lowden's death, *Robert Allanby* was inftituted on a prefentation by queen Elizabeth. Which Robert refigned in 1583, and feems to have been fucceeded by *Rowland Hauxbie* ; for in 1591 Rowland Hauxbie refigns, and *William Lowfon* was inftituted on a prefentation by queen Elizabeth. And in the next year *Edmund Hewitt* was prefented by the faid queen (not faid on what kind of vacancy).

6   In

In 1598, Sir *Thomas Blayne* clerk was inftituted (during the vacancy of the fee) by the archbifhop of York, who wrote the fame day to the archdeacon of Carlifle to give him induction (the patron not mentioned).

In 1642, Feb. 7. on the death of Thomas Blayne, a caveat was entred by William Head vicar of Holm Cultram, on the behalf of his brother Thomas Head; who on the 7th of March following was inftituted by archbifhop Williams then refiding in Wales, on the prefentation of Thomas Dennis a mercer in Oxford. And a monition was fent by the faid archbifhop to the archdeacon of Carlifle to give induction thereupon. [Dr. Ufher was then and had been about a year bifhop of Carlifle; but archbifhop Williams was then begun to incline to the parliament party.]

In 1650, Sir Arthur Hafferig and other commiffioners for propagating the gofpel in the four northern counties ejected Mr. *Lampit* out of the rectory of Aketon, upon account of his not having been legally prefented thereto; and fettled there Mr. *Rowland Nichols* an able and painful preacher†. This Mr. Nichols conformed after the Reftoration, and in 1667 was made chancellor of the diocefe. He refigned the chancellorfhip in 1683, and died in 1694; and was fucceeded in the rectory of Aketon by *R. Threlkeld*, B. A. on the prefentation of Sir John Lowther of Lowther baronet.

In 1707, on *R. Threlkeld*'s death, *Richard Holme*, M. A. was prefented by Richard lord vifcount Lonfdale, a minor.

In 1739, on Mr. Holme's death, *William Lindfey*, M. A. was prefented by Henry vifcount Lonfdale.

In 1753, on William Lindfey's death, *Henry Lowther*, M. A. was prefented by Sir James Lowther of Lowther baronet, with the confent of his mother and guardian Mrs. Katherine Lowther.

PARISH OF THURSBY.

THURSBY *(Thor's* town) fo called from the Saxon deity from whom we derive our word Thurfday, is the next parifh towards the fouth eaft. Alan fecond lord of Allerdale gave Thurfby to *Herbert le Brun* who was firft lord thereof, and he took the furname *de Thurfby*. His female heir carried the inheritance to *Guido Boyvill* a younger fon of the houfe of Levington. He had iffue *William*, who had a brother *John* who were both knights and forefters in Allerdale from Shawk to Elne, which was the Weft Ward of the foreft of Inglewood; which office defcended to them from the faid Herbert. In the 27 Ed. 1. Sir *William de Boyvill* knight held the fame. And in the 34 Ed. 1. *John de Boyvill* knight. Soon after, we find *Robert de Ogle* lord thereof; whofe fon *Thomas de Ogle*, in the 38 Ed. 3. being then under age, prefented a rector to the church of Thurfby. In the 9 Ed. 4. it is found by inquifition, that Sir *Robert Ogle* knight then held the manor of Thorefby, with the advowfon of the church there, of the lord Dacre as of his barony of

† From a pamphlet called Mufgrave Muzzled, p. 33.

Burgh, by knights fervice. Afterwards it came to the Dacres, who held the fame united to and as parcel of the faid barony of Burgh. And amongft the knights fees in the 35 Hen. 8. *William* lord *Dacre* held the fame of the king by knights fervice, and 25s 8¼d cornage. And from that time it hath continued to be enjoyed by the owners of the faid barony, as part and parcel thereof.

Next to *Thurfby* lies CROFTON in this parifh, being fituate between Thurfby and Parton towards the eaft and weft, and between the rivers of Wampole and the Pow on the fouth and north. It is called Crofton from the word *croft*, as the town ftanding upon or having many crofts. Mr. Denton fays, the firft lord of Crofton that he had met with was a knight Sir *Gilbert* fon of *Gilbert de Dundraw*, who lived in king John's time. He gave a parcel of Crofton to the hofpital of St. Nicholas at Carlifle, and bound that land to grind at his mill at Crofton. He had daughters coheirs; one of whom, *Ada*, was married to *Stephen de Crofton*; after whom there was *John de Crofton*, *Robert de Crofton*, *John de Crofton*, and *Clement de Crofton* who died in the 43 Ed. 3. and was fucceeded by his fon Sir *John de Crofton*, whofe daughter and heir *Margaret de Crofton* was married about the 14 Ric. 2. to *Ifold Brifco* of Brifco in this county, whereby the *Brifcoes* became poffeffed of the manor of Crofton, in which name and family it continues till this day.

Brifco is a corruption of *Birkfkeugh*, or *Birch-wood*. It is a place nigh Newbiggin in a lordfhip belonging to the priory of Carlifle, which place the Brifcoes enjoyed at that time. And when Gualo cardinal of St. Martin in king John's time, and after him Randolph in king Henry the third's time, made diftribution of the lands belonging to the church of Carlifle between the bifhop and the prior (which till then were holden undivided till the faid cardinal as legate from the pope divided them) the faid firft named *John de Crofton* held the fame land in Brifkoe as a freeholder. The word is varioufly written in ancient evidences *fkewgh*, *fceugh*, *fchowgh*, *fkaw*, *fhaw*, yet always importing a woody ground on the flope of an hill.

This family of Brifco derive their pedigree as follows:

1. *Robert Brifko* of Brifko in the county of Cumberland.
2. *Alan Brifko* of Brifko fon and heir of Robert.
3. *Jordan Brifko* of Brifko fon and heir of Alan.
4. *Robert Brifko* of Brifko fon and heir of Jordan. This Robert, by the name of *Robert de Byrcfcaye*, was witnefs to a deed in the 20 Ed. 1. His wife's name was Matilda.
5. *John Brifko* of Brifko fon and heir of Robert; unto whom, after his father's death, his mother Matilda releafed her right of dower. He died without iffue, and was fucceeded by his brother and heir, viz.

ISOLD BRISKO of Brifko, who married *Margaret* daughter and heir of Sir *John Crofton* of Crofton knight; by which marriage he had the manors of Crofton, Whinhow, and Dundraw; and Crofton became henceforth the principal refidence of the family.

6. *Chriftopher*

6. *Chriſtopher Briſko* of Crofton, ſon and heir of Iſold. It appears by an arbitrement between the prior of Carliſle and this Chriſtopher concerning the manor and demeſne of Briſko, that the manor ſhould remain to the prior and his ſucceſſors, paying to the ſaid Chriſtopher 100 marks ; and that the capital meſſuage with the woods for building ſhould remain to the ſaid Chriſtopher and his heirs. This Chriſtopher kept 14 ſoldiers at Briſko Thorn upon Eſk. He was taken priſoner at the burning of Wigton. And upon theſe and the like occaſions he was forced to mortgage a conſiderable part of his eſtate.

7. *Robert Briſko* of Crofton, ſon and heir of Chriſtopher, married Iſabel daughter of Wilham Dykes of Warthole. He had iſſue, (1) *Thomas*, a prieſt. (2) *Robert*, who ſucceeded in the inheritance. (3) *Iſold*, who ſerved againſt the Saracens, and died a hermit. (4) *Edward Briſco* of Weſtward, from whom deſcended the families of Weſtward and of Aldenham in the county of Hertford. (5) *Alexander Briſco*, from whom deſcended the Briſcoes of Yarwell in the county of Northampton. And two daughters, *Syth* married to Richard Brown, and *Suſan* married to Robert Ellis of Bothill.

8. *Robert Briſco* of Crofton, ſon and heir of Robert, married Catharine daughter and ſole heir of Clement Skelton of Pettril-Wray.

9 *John Briſco* of Crofton, ſon of the laſt Robert, married Janet daughter of Thomas Salkeld of Corby eſquire.

10. *Richard Briſco*, ſon of John, married a daughter of Leigh of Friſington. He had iſſue *Robert* and *Leonard*; which *Leonard* had a ſon Robert who married the heireſs of Coldhall, in whoſe poſterity that inheritance continued for four generations when that branch became extinct.

11. *Robert Briſco*, ſon and heir of Richard, was ſlain at the battle of Sollom-moſs ; in reward of whoſe ſervices, king Henry the eighth remitted the wardſhip of his infant ſon for the benefit of the widow and the ſaid infant.

12. *John Briſco*, ſon and heir of Robert, married Anne daughter of William Muſgrave of Hayton eſquire. He purchaſed Leigh's part of the manor of Orton in Cumberland of Sir Wilfrid Lawſon and Maud his wife late wife of Thomas Leigh of Iſell : and another third part of Thomas Blenerhaſſet of Carliſle.

13. *William Briſco*, ſon and heir of John, married Jane daughter of William Orfeur of Highcloſe eſquire. He purchaſed the remaining part of the manor of Orton, except what had been ſold before to the tenants by Nicholas Ridley.

14. *John Briſco*, ſon and heir of William, married Mary daughter of Sir Thomas Brathwaite of Burneſhead ; and by her had 16 children, viz. 10 ſons and 6 daughters. (1) *Thomas*, who died in his infancy. (2) *Thomas*, who alſo died in his infancy. (3) *William*. (4) *John Briſco* of Wampool, who married Judith daughter of Bewley. (5) *Edward*, a merchant in London, who married a daughter of Tolſon of Bridekirk eſquire, and died without iſſue. (6) *Richard*, who died young. (7) *Thomas*, who died in his infancy. (8) *Chriſtopher*, who died in Ireland unmarried. (9) *Francis*, a captain of horſe in the civil wars : he died unmarried. (10) *Nazareth*, who died in his

travels beyond the feas unmarried. (11) *Jane*, who died at the age of 18 unmarried. (12) *Dorothy*, married to Sir John Ponfonby of Hale, colonel of a regiment in the civil wars, who went over into Ireland with Oliver Cromwell and fettled there, and was ancestor of the earl of Befborough. (13) *Grace*, married to Clement Skelton of Petrel-wrey gentleman. (14) *Mary*, who died young. (15) *Mary*, married to Jofeph Nicolfon clerk, father (by her) of William Nicolfon lord bifhop of Carlifle, Jofeph Nicolfon apothecary and citizen of London, and John Nicolfon father of the prefent Jofeph Nicolfon of Hawkfdale efquire. (16) *Agnes*, married to William Rayfon of Dalfton.

15. *William Brifco*, third fon and heir of John, married to his firft wife Sufanna daughter of Sir Randal Cranfield, by whom he had iffue only one fon, who died young. He married to his fecond wife Sufanna daughter of Francis Brown merchant and alderman of London; by whom he had iffue, (1) *John*. (2) *William*, a merchant in London, who died without iffue. (3) *Thomas*, who married Jane daughter of Lancelot Fletcher of Talentyre efquire and widow of major Crifp, and by her had feveral children.

16. *John Brifco*, eldeft fon and heir of William, married Mercy daughter of William Johnfon of Kibblefworth in the county of Durham, alderman of Newcaftle upon Tyne; and by her had iffue, (1) *William*, who died unmarried. (2) *John*. (3) *Thomas*, who died unmarried. (4) *Nathanael*, who alfo died unmarried. (5) *Richard*. (6) *Henry*. (7) *Margaret*, who married George Langftaff gentleman. (8) *Sufanna*, who married David Bell clerk, rector of Orton and Afpatria. (9) *Abigail*, married to Henry Brifco of Backborough in Ireland. (10) *Mary*.

17. *John Brifco* of Crofton, fecond fon of John, married Catherine daughter of Sir Richard Mufgrave of Hayton, and by her had iffue, (1) *Richard*, who married a daughter of Lamplugh of Lamplugh, and died before his father, without iffue. (2) *John*. (3) *William*, rector of Diffington. (4) *Mufgrave*, a captain in the army. (5) *James*, collector of the cuftoms at Beaumaris. (6) *Waftel*, in Jamaica; who married the widow Campbell. (7) *Ralph*, who married Dorothy daughter of Jonathan Rowland clerk. (8) *Dorothy*, married to *Richard Lamplugh* of Ribton efquire. (9) *Catharine*, married to John Holme of Carlifle, attorney at law.

18. *John Brifco* of Crofton, D. D. fon and heir of John, was rector of Orton and vicar of Afpatria. He married Catharine daughter of John Hylton of Hylton caftle efquire, and by her had iffue, (1) *John*. (2) *Richard*, a lieutenant in the army, killed in Germany. (3) *Horton*, a colonel in the Eaft India fervice. (4) *William Mufgrave*, an officer in the army. (5) *James*, rector of Orton. (6) *Dorothy*, married to Jacob Morland of Capplethwaite efquire. (7) *Margaret*, who died unmarried.

19. *John Brifco* efquire fon and heir of John, the prefent owner of the family eftate, as yet unmarried.

The Arms of Brifco are; Argent, three greyhounds courant fable.

The

The manor of PARTON adjoins to the weſt ſide of *Crofton*, and is divided from the ſame by a rill called Cattbeck. It lies between the river of Wampool on the ſouth and Powbeck on the north, extended from Cattbeck unto the Karrs mouth where Powbeck falls into Wampool. The firſt lords thereof after the conqueſt took their ſurname of the place and were called *de Parton*. The oldeſt line of which, together with the inheritance, was by a daughter transferred to one *Richard Manſel*; whoſe ſon and heir *John Manſel* ſold it to *Robert de Mulcaſter*, who granted the ſame to *Robert de Grinſdale* in Henry the third's time. *Robert de Grinſdale* had iſſue *Gilbert*; who had iſſue *Alan* and *Robert*. *Alan* had *Thomas* and *Henry*, who both died without iſſue; and Parton fell to *Margaret* their ſiſter, who gave it to *Robert de Rooſe* her ſecond huſband, whoſe nephew and heir *Richard Rooſe* ſold the ſame to *John Carliel* parſon of Kirkland; and his brother's ſon *Robert*, ſon of *Robert Carliel*, ſold it to *William Denton* ſon and heir of *John Denton* of Cardew, whoſe iſſue male enjoyed the ſame, till *George Denton* of Cardew ſold the premiſſes to Sir *John Lowther* in 1686.

This manor contains the hamlets of Parton, Michelewaite, Nealhouſe, and Cardew leaſe (which laſt is within the pariſh of Dalſton). In the year 1672, the aforeſaid George Denton, for the conſideration of 61 years ancient rent (amounting in the whole to 336*l* 2*s* 4*d*), ſold off to the tenants all rents, fines, heriots, carriages, boon days, duties, ſervices, and demands whatſoever; reſerving only one-penny rent to be paid at Martinmaſs yearly, and ſuit of court, royalties, eſcheats, and all other matters belonging to the ſeigniory: he grants to them alſo liberty to cut wood for their own uſe, and to get ſtones within their own grounds or the waſtes for their houſes and fences.

The CHURCH of Thurſby is dedicated to St. Andrew, valued in the king's books at 11*l* 10*s* 5*d*; and is of the preſent yearly value of about 60*l*. It is vicarial, in the patronage of the dean and chapter of Carliſle, having been granted to the priory there by Sir Robert Ogle about the year 1469.

About the year 1175, one *William* parſon of Thoreſby was witneſs to a grant of *William* ſon of Udard lord of Corkeby.

In 1290, *Henry de Burton* was parſon of Thoreſby.

In 1298, *Richard de Abindon* was preſented to the rectory of Thoreſby by Sir William de Boyvill knight; which Richard in 1305, having obtained from the ſaid Sir William a grant of the advowſon, reſigns the rectory, and preſents *William de Swyndon*; whereupon a *jus patronatus* was awarded, and the jurors found the ſaid Richard the true patron, and his preſentee accordingly was admitted.

In 1316, *Robert de Boyvill* rector of the church of Thoreſby had a licence of three years abſence from his cure, in the purſuit of his ſtudies. And ſome years after he was joined in commiſſion with the dean rural of Carliſle to proceed againſt divers clerks who had neglected to appear at the epiſcopal ſynod of Carliſle. And he was conſtituted one of the biſhop's delegates, together with Sir Robert Parvyng rector of Hoton, for the hearing and determining a cauſe depending between the prior and convent of Lanercoſt
and

8

and Sir Richard de Caldecotes. In 1336, he was proceeded againft by the bifhop *ex officio* upon a report of his incontinency with Alice Grete; but after the caufe had depended for fome time, the bifhop gave him a certificate of his difcharge†. In 1355 he had a licence of abfence for two years, and again a like abfence in 1361; and he died in 1364, having been rector nigh 50 years.

After him, Sir *Robert Bix* chaplain was inftituted on a prefentation by Thomas de Ogle. And in 1366, the king claimed the right of donation, by reafon of the cuftody of the land and heir of Robert de Ogle deceafed; and upon an inquifition, his nominee, viz. *Robert Paye* was inftituted and inducted.—In 1369, Clement de Crofton gave by his will to the rector a legacy of 3 s. 4 d, fpecially to pray for his foul; and to the two affiftant chaplains of the church he gives 2 s on the fame account; and bequeaths his body to be buried in the churchyard of St. Andrew of Thorefby.—In 1376, Sir Robert Paye rector of Thorefby had a licence from the bifhop of two years abfence.—In 1380, he makes his will; and, after a few fmall legacies, conftitutes John de Crofton joint executor with Sir Thomas de Lowther and Sir John de Kirkandrews chaplains.

In 1465, a licence of non-refidence was granted by bifhop Scroop to Sir *John Thoryfby* rector of Thoryfby, and this is the laft rector of this church that we have met with. It was foon after given by Sir Robert Ogle, and prefently after appropriated to the prior and convent of Carlifle. He gave them alfo a meffuage and tenement there.

In 1563, a caveat was entred by Edward Monk of the city of Carlifle yeoman and others who claimed the next avoidance by virtue of the affignment of a grant made by the dean and chapter of Carlifle to Richard Blenerhaffet gentleman: and in 1570, the vicarage becoming vacant by the death of *Richard Walles* alias *Brandling*, *Thomas Monk* was inftituted on the fame title, being prefented by Edward Monk.

In 1600, on the death of Thomas Monk, inftitution was given to *William Walles* (upon his refignation of Penrith), being prefented by Thomas Tallentire gentleman, on a grant from the dean and chapter; although another claim was entred, in a caveat, by John Denton efquire, but what his title was doth not appear.

In 1622, *Chriftopher Peale*, M. A. was inftituted on the death of William Walles, on a prefentation by the dean and chapter.

---

† Johannes, &c. Dilecto filio Roberto de Boyvill rectori ecclefiæ de Thorefby, falutem, gratiam, et benedictionem. Cum effes impetitus coram nobis ex officio, fuper eo quod Aliciam Grete in concubinam tuam per menfem et amplius publice tenuifti, et ex eo in pœnam conftitutionis legati fuper hoc editi incidifti; quibus tibi judicialiter objectis et per te negatis, juramento fuper hoc a te præftito, et factis tibi interrogationibus judicialibus, et auditis refponfionibus tuis ad eafdem, examinatoque negotio, deliberatione habita cum patrono dictæ ecclefiæ et aliis, obfervato juris ordine in omnibus in hac parte, quia invenimus te immunem, et innocentiam tuam in præmiffis fufficienter purgaffe et oftendifle, te ab impetitione præfata abfolvimus per decretum, omnem maculam et notam infamiæ (fi quam ex hoc incurreris) penitus abolentes, teque famæ tuæ bonæ priftinæ reftituentes. In cujus rei teftimonium, figilum noftrum præfentibus eft appenfum. Datum Ebor' 15° Kal. Dec. Anno Domini 1336, et noftræ confecrationis quinto.

In

In 1662, June 17, *John Hamilton* was inftituted on the like prefentation.

In 1673, on John Hamilton's death, *Richard Savage*, B. A. was inftituted.

In 1680, *Thomas Stalker* was inftituted; and refigning in the next year, *George Theobaldes*, B. A. was prefented by the dean and chapter, and inftituted thereupon.

In 1685, on the death of George Theobalds, *Matthew Prefton*, B. A. was inftituted.

In 1699, *Jofeph White*, clerk.

In 1726, on his death, *John Story*, M. A. was inftituted.

In 1731, on the ceffion of John Story, *Robert Wardale*, B. A. was, inftituted.

In 1763, *Andrew Holliday* clerk, on the ceffion of Robert Wardale.

In 1771, *Thomas Nicolfon* clerk was inftituted on the ceffion of Andrew Holliday.

In 1774, *Nicholas Robinfon*, on the death of Thomas Nicolfon.

The vicar by prefcription is intitled to all the fmall tithes within the parifh, and to the great tithes of Michaelthwaite, Parton, Whinhow, and Nealhoufe; but the year that the two firft pay the great tithes in kind, the other two pay a prefcription, and fo alternately (though there are fome exceptions). The grounds in this parifh that belong to Drumleanny pay tithe in kind every year. The tithe hay of Thurfby is held by leafe from the dean and chapter to the vicar under the yearly rent of 30 s. There are two tenants belonging to the church; John How for a meffuage and tenement at Nealhoufe, who pays 6 s yearly rent: and Efther Twentyman, for a cottage houfe and garth at Thurfby, 2 s 4 d: And at the change of tenant a two-penny fine.

Number of families in this parifh certified in 1747, eighty-one: And no diffenters of any kind.

PARISH OF ORTON.

THIS name of ORTON, or *Overton*, is common to the parifh, manor, and town: It is fo named of the fituation and higher ftanding of the place, in refpect of the lower parts towards Carlifle and the river Eden. It is parcel of the manor of Levington, and holden of the fame. It gave furname to a family of gentlemen of note called *de Orton*; who gave for arms, Vert, a lion rampant Argent, crowned and armed Gules. The firft of the name that we meet was *Simon*, who had iffue *Alan de Orton*, to whom king Henry the third granted free warren in Orton. After him fucceeded *John* his fon (they were all knights) and after him *Gyles*, whofe daughter and heir *Joan* was married to Sir *Clement de Skelton*, to whom fhe had four daughters her coheirs; one named *Agnes* married to *Leighe* of Ifall, another married to *Bellafes*, another to *Ridley*, and the fourth to *Blenerhaffet*. They divided the manor into three parts, which *Leighe*, *Ridley*, and *Blenerhaffet* enjoyed refpectively, and charged the land with a rent of 8 l to *Bellafes*, who fold the fame to one Coldall a merchant in Carlifle, which afterwards came by marriage to a younger branch of the

the *Brifcoes*. Afterwards *John Brifco* purchafed *Leigh*'s part of Wilfrid Lawfon and Maud his wife, and of Thomas Blenerhaffet another third part. Accordingly in the 30 Eliz. it is found by inquifition that *William Brifco* of Crofton (fon of the faid *John*) died feifed of the manor of Orton, with 20 meffuages, 400 acres of land, 40 acres of meadow, 200 acres of common, 100 acres of wood, in Orton aforefaid, together with the donation and right of patronage of two parts in three to be divided of the parifh church of the aforefaid manor of Orton, holden of Edward Mufgrave gentleman as of his manor of Levington, by two parts of one knight's fee: And that the third part of the faid manor of Orton, late the inheritance of *Nicholas Ridley* efquire deceafed, and all and every the meffuages, lands, tenements, and hereditaments, to the faid third part belonging, were holden of the queen *in capite* by the fervice of the third part of one knight's fee: And that the faid two parts were worth by the year above reprizes 5 *l* 6 *s* 8 *d*, and the faid third part 2 *l* 13 *s* 4 *d*.

And *Ridley*'s part not long after came into the family by purchafe. For in the 23 Jac. *John Brifco*, fon of the faid *William*, claimed the intire patronage; which, being appendant to the manor, was when it was fevered and divided into three parts enjoyed alternately by all the three; but ever fince that time he and his defcendents have enjoyed the whole.

The church is rectorial, valued in the king's books at 9 *l*. The prefent yearly value about 100 *l*.

The firft incumbent that we meet with was in the year 1303, when one *John* rector of Orreton gave a bond of ten marks to bifhop Halton, to be forfeited whenever it fhould thereafter appear that he was guilty of incontinency.

In 1337, Sir *John de Orton* knight prefents *John de Whytrigg* to the vacant rectory of Orreton; and in the fame year, upon Whitrigg's refignation, the faid Sir John prefents *William de Arthuret*.

In 1376, the faid William de Arthuret's will was proved at Rofe; and foon after, Sir *Richard de Langwathby* was prefented to the rectory by Clement de Skelton and Joan his wife.

In 1407, *Thomas de Raughton* appears to have been rector.

In 1578, on the death of Sir *Richard Place* late rector of Orton, one caveat was entered, in claim of the patronage, by Thomas Blenerhaffet gentleman; and another by Marian relict of John Twentyman late of Little Orton, to whom this avoidance had been granted by Richard Blenerhaffet of the city of Carlifle efquire, who had married one of the coheirs of Sir Giles Orton knight; and inftitution was given on this latter claim to Mr. *Leonard Lowther*.

In 1585, Mr. Lowther refigned: And the next day *William Mey*, B. A. was ordained deacon, and immediately prefented to the vacant rectory by John Lowther of Crton patron for that turn, and inftituted thereupon.

In 1625, *John Brifco* of Crofton efquire enters a caveat, claiming the prefentation; and two years after, on bifhop White's coming to the fee, he renews the caveat.

In 1643, one Mr. *Burton* was rector, being in that year a contributor towards procuring provifions for the garrifon of Carlifle.

In 1665, *John Pearfon* was prefented by John Brifco efquire.

In

In 1693, on the death of *Gawen Noble* rector of Orton, *Rowland Noble* was inftituted on a prefentation by William Brifco efquire.

In 1709, on Rowland Noble's death, *David Bell*, M. A. was prefented by John Brifco efquire.

In 1730, on the death of David Bell, *John Brifco*, M. A. was prefented by (his father) John Brifco efquire.

In 1771, on John Brifco's death, *William Taylor* clerk was prefented by Jofeph Nicolfon efquire, devifee for this purpofe by the will of the late patron and incumbent Dr. Brifco. And in 1772, on William Taylor's refignation, *James Brifco* fon of the faid Dr. Brifco was inftituted on the like prefentation.

The number of families in this parifh in 1732 was certified to be 81. Of whom Quakers 8. Prefbyterians 3.

PARISH OF KIRKBAMPTON.

BAMPTON (villata *Bembæ*, vel *Bombæ*) was anciently divided into *Bampton Magna* and *Parva*; that where the church ftands was called *Great Bampton*, the other is ftill called *Little Bampton*. The whole parifh is within the barony of Burgh, and feems anciently to have been all one manor. It was the principal feat of *Hildred de Carliell* (a knight) in the time of king Henry the fecond. After whofe death his grandchildren *Richard* and *Robert*, the fons of *Odard* fon of *Hildred*, parted this manor. And *Eudo de Carliell* tenant of the fame gave in the 11 Hen. 3. four carucates in Uchtredby and Little Bampton to *Walter de Bampton* by fine, which by inquifition taken 23 Ed. 1. was valued to 20 *l* land, and to be holden of the manor of Burgh. Another part dame *Elizabeth Mountacute* countefs of *Salifbury* held in the 36 Hen. 3. as of the inheritance of *William Mountacute* earl of *Salifbury*: And in the fame year Sir *Brian Stapleton* of Bedal in Yorkfhire held it (by purchafe, as it feemeth); whofe pofterity in king Henry the eighth's time fold it to *Thomas Dacre* of Lanercoft, whofe fon *Chriftopher* fold it into many parts to the inhabitants.

In the 24 Eliz. *Thomas Brifby* gentleman, in confideration of 240 *l*, conveyed to *John Southaick* efquire and *Richard Tolfon* gentleman, their heirs and affigns, all that the manor or lordfhip of Little Bampton, with all thofe meffuages, tenements, or farmholds within the faid manor, which were then in the feveral tenures of John Twentyman and 20 other tenants: And their cuftomary rents amounted to 8 *l* 7 *s* 10 *d*, and alfo 3 *s* 4 *d* quit rent iffuing out of the lands of Thomas Smallwood; with all houfes, commons, moors, moffes, and franchifes. Four years after, *Southaick* and *Tolfon* conveyed the faid premiffes in fee to *John Dalfton* efquire; who fold the fame in the year following to the faid feveral refpective tenants.

The CHURCH is rectorial, and dedicated to St. Peters valued in the king's books at 14 *l* 17 *s* 11 *d*: the clear yearly value about 60 *l*. It pays a penfion of 3 *s* 4 *d* to the bifhop of Carlifle.

About the 27 Hen. 2. a moiety of the rectory was given by the patron Adam son of Robert to the hospital of St. Nicholas near Carlisle, upon condition of having always two almsmen from this parish. This is now held by Mr. John Liddale of Moorhouse of the dean and chapter of Carlisle by lease of 21 years, under the annual rent of 40's: which said dean and chapter enjoy all the possessions of the said hospital.

In the year 1293, Walter de Bampton, in right of Robert son and heir of Robert de Castlecayroke, presented *John de Culgayth* to a moiety of the rectory of Bampton, vacant by resignation of *Walter de Batyler*; and after inquisition; institution was given thereupon. (The other moiety, as aforesaid, belonged to the hospital.)

In 1341, upon the death of John de Culgayth, R. de Bampton presents John son of Thomas de Bampton: And at the same time, John Grainger was presented to the said moiety by John de Moresby and others. Hereupon a commission *de jure patronatus* was granted, and upon the return *John Grainger* had institution.

In 1343, on resignation of *John de Appleby* rector of a moiety of the church of Bampton, a presentation was given by William de Eglesfield and others to *William de Appleby*: And upon inquisition, the said William de Appleby was instituted.

In 1359, *Thomas de Bampton* was rector of a moiety of this church, having in that year a dispensation of absence granted him by the bishop. This Thomas came in by the presentation of Elizabeth Montacute.

In 1361, Sir Brian de Stapilton knight presents Sir *Robert de Gaytton* to a moiety of the church of Bampton, vacant by the resignation of *John de Thornton.*

In 1367, the said Sir Brian de Stapilton presents Sir *William de Cressopp* vicar of Wigton to a moiety of this church, on an exchange with *Richard Damysell* then rector of the said moiety.

In 1561, Sir *John Aketon* clerk was instituted into the rectory of Kirkbampton, on the resignation of *Edward Michell.* (The patron not mentioned.)

In 1586, on the death of John Aketon, three several claims are made to the advowson of this rectory, and caveats thereupon entred, by Cuthbert Musgrave of Crookdayke esquire, William Briscoe of Crofton esquire, and Christopher Dacre of Lanercost esquire; who seem by consent to have lapsed it into bishop Mey's hands: for he, after the expiration of six months collated Sir *Roland Hauxbie* clerk. (One Thomas Brisby of Penrith gentleman had some years before made the like claim.)

In 1598, Feb. 1. on Roland Hauxbie's death, a caveat was entred on the behalf of Mrs. Jane Briscoe widow and John her son: but on the 12th of November following, bishop Robinson (as his predecessor had done before) collated by lapse *Joseph Lowden*, M. A.

In 1610, on Mr. Lowden's resignation, *Cuthbert Roper* was instituted, being unanimously and jointly presented by Henry Dacre, Cuthbert Musgrave, and John Brisco esquires.

In

In 1639, on the death of *Robert Brown* rector of Kirkbampton, institution was given to *Otho Polewheele*, who was presented by William Brisco esquire, notwithstanding that Sir Thomas Dacre had entred his claim by a caveat.

In 1679, on the death of *John Bell* rector of Kirkbampton, *Thomas Story* clerk was presented by Henry Dacre of Lanercost esquire, patron (as he asserts) for that turn.

In 1740, on the death of Thomas Story (who had been incumbent 61 years, and had buried every one of the parishioners that was living at his induction) *Michael Burn* was instituted on the presentation of Henry viscount Lonsdale, notwithstanding that caveats had been entred by John Brisco of Crofton esquire, John Ballentine of Crookdake esquire, and William Robinson of Bothel gentleman, as well as by the said viscount Lonsdale.

There are in this parish about 97 families; of which, Quakers 3, Presbyterians 2.

PARISH OF KIRKBRIDE.

THE church at this place was founded before the conquest, and dedicated to the honour of a religious Irish woman of great sanctity called Brydoch, and corruptly St. Bride, which gave name to the town. It is parcel of the barony of Wigton, and was first granted forth from the same by *Adam* son of *Odard* second baron of Wigton in king John's time, to *Adam* his second son a knight, and brother to *Odard* the second of that name, who was the third baron of Wigton. His posterity, as was usual in those days, took their name from the place, and were styled de Kirkbride. *Adam* son of *Adam* had issue *Richard de Kirkbride*, and *Richard* had issue *Robert*, who dying without issue was succeeded by his brother *Richard* in the 23 Ed. 1. *Richard* had issue *Walter*, who was knight of the shire in the 9 Ed. 2. whose issue male for several descents, all of the name of *Richard*, enjoyed the manor of Kirkbride, until a coheir of *George Kirkbride*, the last of that house, transferred a moiety thereof to the *Dalstons* of Dalstonhall. The other moiety went off with the other coheir, whose posterity sold the same to the lord paramount of Wigton, where it continued till Henry the sixth earl of Northumberland gave it with the rest of his patrimony to king Henry the eighth, who by letters patent in the 35th year of his reign granted the same to *Thomas Dalston* esquire, whereby the *Dalstons* became entire lords of the whole manor. Accordingly it is found by inquisition in that year, that *Thomas Dalston* esquire held of the king *in capite* by knights service the town and manor of Kirkbride with the appurtenances, as of his manor of Wigdon, rendring for the same yearly 13 s 4 d cornage, for puture of the serjeants 22 d, seawake 16 d, and suit of court at Wigdon from 3 weeks to 3 weeks. It continued in the *Dalston* family till about the year 1764, when Sir George Dalston baronet, the last of the name at Dalston hall, sold the same to *Joseph Wilson* of Pomfret esquire the present owner.

The tenants of the manor are about 40 in number; 13 of whom purchased their estates to freehold (heriots included) for five fines and an half at the rate of a twenty penny fine, of the said Sir George Dalston about the year

E e 2   1763.

1763. The ancient cuftomary rent of the whole manor was 14*l* 14*s* 0*d*; the remaining rent is 7*l* 10*s* 0*d* upon the tenements not infranchifed, for which they pay a twenty penny fine, and a heriot upon the death of the tenant, and no other duties or fervices but fuit of court.

The church is rectorial, and valued in the king's books at 5*l*. It was cer-tified to the governors of queen Anne's bounty at 44*l*; and is now worth about 60*l*. There are only about 55 families in the whole parifh; of which, Quakers 4, and one Prefbyterian.

In the year 1341, on an inquifition *de jure patronatus* it appeared, that Sir John de Wefton knight was the true patron of the vacant rectory of Kirkbride. And thereupon a commiffion was granted to Nicholas de Whytrigg rector of Caldbeck to give inftitution to the faid Sir John's prefentee *Robert de Bromfield*; who refigning in the next year, the faid Sir John de Wefton prefents *John de Mifterton*, who upon his inftitution contracts to pay 60 fhillings to the bifhop, whereof 30 at Martinmafs and 30 at Candlemafs next following.—On this prefentation it was found, that Sir John de Wefton was patron in right of the lady Joan de Wigton his wife.

In 1580, on the death of *Cuthbert Fifher* rector of Kirkbride, inftitution was given to *Robert Allanby* M. A. prefented by John Dalfton of Dalfton gentleman.

In 1586, on Robert Allanby's death, *Gyles Hemmerford* was inftituted on a prefentation by John Dalfton efquire. And the faid *Gyles* dying within a year, Sir *Nicholas Dean* clerk was inftituted upon the faid patron's prefentation.

In 1643, one Mr. Hudfon was rector.

Sep. 20, 1660, *Thomas Lumley* was inftituted on the prefentation of Sir Wil-liam Dalfton baronet.

In 1678, Thomas Lumley dying, *Henry Hall* was prefented by Sir William Dalfton of Heath hall in the county of York baronet.

In 1717, on Henry Hall's death, *John Walker*, B. A. was prefented by Sir Charles Dalfton baronet.

In 1743, on the death of John Walker, *John Cowper*, B. A. was prefented by Sir George Dalfton baronet.

In 1750, on John Cowper's refignation, *George Gilbanks* clerk was prefented by the fame patron:

PARISH OF BOWNESS.

Bowness, *Bulnefs*, is the common name of the manor, town, and parifh; and is parcel of the barony of Burgh: one of the firft barons whereof after the conqueft gave it to *Gamel le Brun*, whofe pofterity enjoyed the fame for many generations. Their capital meffuage was at Drumbugh, which being near the wild waftes, they were promifcuoufly called *de la Feritate*. *Richard le Brun*, and after him *Robert le Brun*, enjoyed it in king Edward the firft's time; *Richard le Brun*, in the reign of Edward the fecond; *Robert le Brun* in the reign of Edward the third; and *John Brun* in the reign of Richard the fecond.

I   The

The laſt of this name and family at Bowneſs was *Richard le Brun,* who had three daughters coheirs; one, called Hellen, married to the houſe of Workington; another, to the Harringtons of Harrington; and the third to one Bowet. After whom, this manor in proceſs of time became again united to and conſolidated with the barony of Burgh.

The village of Bowneſs is ſituate on the ſouth ſide of the Solway frith, at the weſtern extremity of that memorable Roman work commonly called the *Piƈts wall*; extending from hence quite acroſs the iſland, through this county and Northumberland, unto the German ocean, being of the length of 63 Engliſh miles and 3 furlongs.

Mr. Denton as alſo Mr. Camden think this was the *Blatum Bulgium* of the Romans; but Mr. Horſley ſeems to prove from the diſtances, that this *Bulneſs* was not the *Blatum Bulgium* (which Mr. Camden only conjeƈtured to be ſo from the ſimilarity of the names), but that this was the ſtation called by the Romans *Tunnocelum*; and that *Blatum Bulgium* was at *Middleby* on the Roman way, on the oppoſite ſide of Solway frith.

This work was firſt a line of forts or *ſtations* built by Agricola. Theſe ſtations were generally oblong, comprehending three or four acres of ground, with houſes therein or barracks for ſoldiers, and buildings all about near to the ſame, in nature of a town: ſo that a *ſtation* was in effeƈt a ſmall town fortified. Theſe ſtations at a medium were about four miles diſtant from each other; but they were cloſer or nearer together where there was moſt danger, and where there was leſs danger they were further off.

Communicating with, and as it were conneƈting theſe ſtations, the emperor Hadrian built a vaſt wall of turf, ſometimes mixed with ſtone, with a ditch on the north ſide thereof three yards deep, and near four yards over; a large military way accompanying the wall all along. And behind this wall, on the ſouth ſide, another wall or rampart with a ditch, about five paces diſtant from the former.

Within this, on the north ſide towards the enemy, by way of further and ſtronger fortification, the emperor Severus built a wall of freeſtone; and in ſome places where the foundation was not good, they made uſe of oaken piles: It was faced with hewn ſtone, and the inner part (as appears from what remains of it) filled after a remarkable manner; the filling ſtones are generally pretty large, and moſtly broad and thin; theſe are always ſet edgeways, and uſually not ereƈt, but ſomewhat obliquely; upon theſe the running mortar or cement has been poured, and by this contrivance (together with the great ſtrength of their cement in moſt places) the whole wall hath been bound as firm as a rock *. This wall of Severus was about four yards high, and from ſeven feet four inches to nine feet thick; and his ditch (on the north ſide) wider and deeper than that of Hadrian; with a paved military way on the ſouth ſide thereof about ſeventeen foot broad. Between the *ſtations*, there were *caſtles (caſtella)* ereƈted along this wall, generally about 66 foot ſquare, and between ſix and ſeven furlongs diſtant from each other. And between theſe

* Horſley's Brit. Rom. 123.

again,

again, there were *turrets*, about four yards fquare at the bottom, at the diftance one from another of about 308 yards, wherein were centinels placed within call of each other, without having recourfe to the fiction of a founding trumpet or pipes under ground †.

At this ftation of *Bulnefs* or *Tunnocelum* the *Cobors Ælia Claffica* were in garrifon; which, from the fignification of the word *claffica* and the vicinity of that place to the fea, feem to have been marines. Bifhop Gibfon fays, there have frequently been found here Roman coins and infcriptions, and that there was lately dug up a fmall brazen figure of a Mercury, or a victory, which came into the poffeffion of John Aglionby efquire ‡. Mr. Horfley fays, that he could not fee nor hear of any infcriptions remaining there. That which is at Appleby fchool in Weftmorland feems (he fays) to have come from Bulnefs, but is no original: However, it is an argument that fome Roman infcriptions, as well as other antiquities, have formerly been found there; for Mr. Bainbrigg (the fchoolmafter) had an humour of cutting out or copying upon ftones any Roman infcriptions which came in his way; of which fort this manifeftly appears to be, becaufe in his ufual manner he hath annexed what he took to be the Roman name of Bulnefs, namely, Blatum Bulgium. The whole is as follows:

IMP. M. AVRE
TRIVMPHAI
PERSAR
MARC. AVREL:
PHILO
BLATI BULGII.

The three firft lines, *Imperatori Marco Aurelio triumphatori Perfarum*, have been evidently a copy of fome Roman infcription found at Bulnefs; the laft three, *Marco Aurelio Philofopho Blati Bulgii*, feem to be Mr. Bainrigg's own comment upon it, with a defign to fhew, that this monument was found at Bulnefs (which he believed to be Blatum Bulgium), and that the emperor Marcus Aurelius, called the philofopher, was intended in the infcription *.

At *Drumbugh* (the *Gabrofentum* of the Romans) is a fort about five chains fquare, whofe ramparts are large, and the ditch very deep. Out of this fort abundance of ftones have been taken. It is very probable, that the houfe and garden walls have been built with the ftones of the wall and ftation, and that it has the name of *caftle* from the old Roman fort; for the feat is not built in the form of a caftle ‖.

The name *Drumbugh* (Drumbogh) is derived from that fenny mire or bog frequented with bitterns, which are here called mire-drums; fo that the word Drumbug fignifies the bittern's fen.

The church alfo hath probably been built out of the ruins of the ftation. It is dedicated to St. Michael, and the advowfon is and hath been all along appendent to the manor. It is rectorial, and valued in the king's books at

† Horfley's Brit. Rom. 120.   ‡ Camd. 1017.   * Horfley 267.   ‖ Ibid, 157.

21 *l* 3*s* 11¼*d*; and is now worth about '130*l*. There are in the parifh about 155 families; of whom, 2 Prefbyterians, and 2 Quakers.

In the year 1300, *Roald de Richmond* an infant' was prefented to the rectory of Bownefs by the lady Ada de Feritate; whereupon the bifhop commits the care and cuftody of the faid rector and his church to Mr. John de Bowet till the infant fhould come of age.

In 1307, Sir Richard le Brun knight prefented *Reginald de Northburgh* to the faid rectory.

In 1322, the claim of the advowfon was afcertained to Robert le Brun.

In 1342, Richard Brun lord of Drumbugh prefented *William* fon of *Walter de Kirkbythore*; and upon an inquifition it was found, that one *Walter* was predeceffor to this William, and that Sir Robert Brun father of Richard the prefent pation had prefented laft.

In 1354, on the refignation of William rector of Bownefs, Robert Brun lord of Drumbugh prefents *William del Hall*.

In 1369, Robert Broyne (as they now writ their name) makes his will dated at Bothill, and bequeaths his body to be buried at the parifh church of Bonnes, with a mortuary according to the cuftom of the country; and as his anceftors had done, and conftitutes the faid William del Hall one of his executors

In 1381, William del Hall having agreed to exchange his rectory with *Thomas de Barton* rector of Caldbeck, the faid Thomas was prefented to the rectory of Bownefs by John Broyne lord of Drumbugh, and William is collated to Caldbeck by the bifhop.

In 1399, *William de Bownefs* was rector; being in that year one of the commiffioners appointed by bifhop Appleby to hear and determine a caufe concerning the repair of the chancel of Bromfield.

In 1565, on the death of Sir *John Robinfon* alias *Kendal*, rector of Bownefs, Mr. *William Talentyre* was prefented by Sir Thomas Dacre knight lord Dacre of Grayftock and Gilfland.

In 1572, on Mr. Talentyre's refigning, Mr. *Arthur Caye* was inftituted on a prefentation from queen Elizabeth.

In 1580, on the refignation of *James Taylor* rector of Bownefs, bifhop Mey collates Mr. *Leonard Lowther*, by virtue of a grant to him from Philip earl of Arundel and the lord William Howard.

In 1597, Mr. Lowther refigning, *Richard Sibfon*, S. T. B. was inftituted, but upon whofe prefentation is not mentioned in the regifter.

In 1617, on the death of Mr. Sibfon, a caveat was entered by Henry Hudfon vicar of Brigham, who claimed the right of prefentation, and although he lived in the diocefe of Chefter, he allowed himfelf on any occafion of controverfy hereupon to be cited in the parifh church of Plumbland. But in the fame year *William Orbell* was inftituted, on a prefentation by Henry Spiller of Latham in the county of Middlefex, purchafer from Anne countefs of Arundel.

In 1629, on William Orbell's death, *Thomas Warwick*, A. M. was prefented by Mr. Thomas Weft of Stoake in the county of Surrey, a like purchafer, and inftituted by Lancelot Daws, D. D. the bifhop's commiffioner.

In 1643, one Mr. Watwick was rector.

In

In 1660, *George Troutbeck* was rector; who dying in 1691, *Henry Aglionby*, M. A. was presented by John Aglionby esquire.

In 1697, on the death of Mr. Aglionby, *Gerard Lowther*, M. A. was presented by John viscount Lonsdale.

In 1731, Gerard Lowther resigning, *Henry Lowther*, A. M. was presented by Henry viscount Lonsdale.

In 1753, on the resignation of the said Henry Lowther, *Hugh Robinson*, A. M. was presented by Sir James Lowther of Lowther baronet, by the consent and advice of his mother and guardian Mrs. Katherine Lowther.

In 1763, on the death of the said Hugh Robinson, *James Watson*, M. A. was instituted on the presentation of the said Sir James Lowther baronet.

PARISH OF BURGH UPON SANDS.

THE large barony of BURGH lies upon the north side of the river Wathimpool, which towards the north-west is washed by the sea flowing up into the foot of the river Eden, and by the said river towards the north-east to a place called Boonby gill; from thence it adjoins upon the manor of Dalston to Neelhouse bars; then to Jack dyke, and down Jack dyke to the river of Wampool aforesaid. In this barony are divers manors holden of Burgh; and some within this boundary, yet no part of the barony (as Orton and Crofton) nor holden of the same.

This barony was given by the earl *Ranulph de Meschiens* to *Robert de Estrivers* or *Trevers* who married a sister of the said *Ranulph*. He gave also to the said *Robert* the chief forester's office in the forest of Englewood; which office, with great and many liberties belonging to the same, all the lords of Burgh enjoyed successively, until Thomas de Multon of Gilsland forfeited the same by treason against king Henry the third in the insurrection made by Simon de Montfort earl of Leicester.

This *Robert de Trevers* had a daughter and heir *Ibria Trevers* married to *Ranulph Engayn* lord of Isell. Which Ibria and Ranulph her husband gave Henrickby, otherwise Hernsby, near Carlisle to the priory there, which gift Hugh Morvil confirmed.

The said *Ranulph Engayn* had issue *William Engayn*; who had issue a daughter and heir *Ada Engayn*; who by marriage transferred this barony of Burgh to the *Morvils*. She was married to *Simon de Morvill*, son of *Hugh de Morvill* who in the third year of king Stephen was one of the witnesses to the charter of the protection then made by David king of Scots to the monks of Tinemouth.

This *Simon de Morvill* in the 3 Hen. 2. gave fifty marks for livery of the Engayn's lands. He had issue by his said wife two sons, *Roger* and *Richard*. Which *Richard* in the 16 Hen. 2. gave two hundred marks to the king for livery of those lands which he claimed with the daughter of William de Lancaster, and left issue Helene his daughter and heir married to Rowland de Galweie.

Roger

Roger de Morvill, elder fon of *Simon*, had iffue a fon and heir *Hugh de Mor-vill*, who was one of thofe four knights who in the 17 Hen. 2. murdered Thomas a Becket archbifhop of Canterbury : which done, they entred the archbifhop's ftables, and taking away his horfes rode to Knarefburgh in York-fhire (a town belonging to this Hugh) where they ftaid till all the inhabitants were weary of them. Mr. Denton fays, the fword that killed Becket was in his father's time at Ifell, which place belonged to the Morvils as heirs of En-gain ; after that, the faid fword remained with the houfe of Arundel.—The faid *Hugh* took to wife Helewife de Stutevill, with whom he had the manors of Kirkofwald and Lafingby ; and in the fecond year of king John he obtained licence to inclofe his woods in Kirkofwald, as likewife to fortify his manor houfe and to have a fair there once every year with a market every week. Moreover he gave unto the king 15 marks and 3 good palfreys to enjoy his court, with the liberties of toll, theam, infangthief, fire and water ordeal, and all other fuch privileges as belonged to the crown, during the continuance of Helewife his wife in a regular habit.—He had alfo confiderable poffeffions in Weftmorland.

He had iffue only two daughters, *Ada* and *Joan*. *Ada* was married in his life-time to *Richard* fon of *Reginald de Lucy* of Egremont, and afterwards was married to *Thomas de Multon*. *Joan* the younger daughter was married, after her father's death, to *Richard Gernun*. Whereupon in the 6 Joh. upon parti-tion of the lands of this *Hugh* betwixt thefe his daughters and coheirs, *Ri-chard de Lucy* gave a fine to the king of 900 marks and five palfreys for the purparty of *Ada* his wife and forefterfhip of Cumberland, as fully as he the faid Hugh enjoyed the fame : And *Richard Gernun* gave 600 marks for liberty to marry *Joan*, with the purparty belonging to her of thofe lands whereof her father died feifed.

Ada to her firft hufband *Richard de Lucy* had only two daughters Amabil and Alice. To her fecond hufband *Thomas de Multon* fhe had a fon *Thomas de Mul-ton*, heir to her purparty of the Morvil's lands. Which *Thomas* thefon, in the 25 Hen. 3. paying 40 *l* for a fine, had livery of his lands ; and being forefter of Cumberland by defcent from *Ada* his mother, paid a fine of 400 marks the next year to the king for trefpaffing in that foreft, and to enjoy all thofe liber-ties which his anceftors had ufed in that office, excepting the pleas of vert.— And in the next enfuing year he obtained to himfelf and Maud his wife daugh-ter and heir to Hubert de Vaux baron of Gilfland a charter of free warren in all his demefne lands, in Cumberland, Yorkfhire, Norfolk, and Suffolk, and that they and their heirs after the deceafe of Maud de Vaux her mother (then the wife of William Everard) fhould have free warren in all the demefne lands they held in the counties of Somerfet and Devon, being of the dowry of her the faid Maud the mother, and of the inheritance of Maud the daughter.— In the 42 Hen. 3. he received fummons to prepare himfelf with horfe and arms, and to march with the reft of the northern barons into Scotland for refcuing the king of Scots then in minority and in reftraint by his own fubjects : So likewife to be at Chefter on Monday next before the feaft of St. John Baptift to reftrain the incurfions of the Welfh.—He died in the 53 Hen. 3. leaving

Thomas de Multon his fon and heir; who, doing his homage had livery of his lands.

Which *Thomas de Multon*, upon the death of Helwife de Levington (56 Hen. 3.) widow of Euftace de Baliol, was found her heir as to the whole manor of Aketon and the other moiety of Burgh upon Sands, Kirkofwald and Layfingby; all which Euftace de Baliol (having had iffue by her which lived for fome time) held of her inheritance as tenant by the curtefy of England till his death, which happened in the 2 Ed. 1. at which time this *Thomas* had livery, and died in the 21 Ed. 1.

Thomas de Multon, fon and heir of the laft *Thomas*, was 26 years of age at his father's death, and doing his homage in the fame year had livery, and died in the 23 Ed. 1. being then feifed of the manor of Denham in the county of Norfolk, as alfo of the manor of Burgh upon Sands and Kirkofwald, alfo of the barony of Gilfland, and divers lands in Santon, Irton, Bolton, and Gofford; leaving *Thomas* his fon and heir 13 years of age, and Ifabel his wife furviving, who had for her dowry an affignation of the manor of Denham.

Which faid laft *Thomas de Multon*, paying 100l for his relief, was in the 31 Ed. 1. in the Scots wars; fo likewife in the 34 Ed. 1.—And in the 1 Ed. 2. he received command to fit himfelf with horfe and arms (together with John de Lancafter and Ingelram de Gyfnes) for refifting the incurfions of Robert de Brus of Scotland and his accomplices. In the 3 Ed. 2. he was again in thofe wars of Scotland; fo likewife in the 4 Ed. 2. And in the 10 Ed. 2. he obtained for himfelf and Margaret his wife a fpecial charter from the king for a market on the Wednefday every week, and two fairs yearly, one on the eve, day, and morrow after the feftival of our lady, the other on the eve, day, and morrow after the feaft of Simon and Jude at Ayfhall in the county of Somerfet; as alfo free warren in all his demefne lands at Seven Hampton in the faid county of Somerfet, and Pynho in the county of Devon. Moreover he was fummoned to parliament amongft the barons of this realm from the 25 Ed. 1. till the 7 Ed. 2. inclufive; and died foon after, leaving iffue *Margaret* married to *Ranulph de Dacre*, which *Ranulph* performing his fealty to king Edward the fecond, fhe the faid *Margaret* then making proof of her age had livery of her lands. But this *Thomas de Multon* had a brother called *William*, who being his heir male held the manor of Layfingby in the county of Cumberland during his life; which *William* died in the 15 Ed. 3. leaving the faid *Margaret* then wife of *Ranulph de Dacre* his next heir 36 years of age.

And thus this great inheritance was transferred by a female heir to the *Dacres* of Dacre-caftle in Cumberland; which family received further a large addition of fortune by marriage of the heirefs of Grayftock. The eldeft branch of Dacre ended in a daughter, to whom the original eftate at Dacre (with fome others) did defcend: The reft, viz. Grayftock, Gilfland, Burgh, and others, were fettled upon a younger branch of the Dacres of the male line, which continued in that name for four defcents further, and then that branch ended in coheirs; for *George* lord *Dacre*, in the 11th year of queen Elizabeth, dying without iffue, was fucceeded by his three fifters; one of whom dying unmarried,

ried, the eftate came to the other two fifters, *Anne* the elder married to *Philip* earl of *Arundel,* and *Elizabeth* the younger married to the lord *William Howard,* both of them fons of *Thomas* duke of *Norfolk.* The barony of Burgh, in the partition, was allotted to the lady *Anne,* whofe defcendent in the fourth gene-ration, *Henry Howard* duke of *Norfolk,* fold the fame about the year 1689 to Sir *John Lowther* of Lowther, anceftor of the prefent owner Sir *James Lowther* baronet.

The *cuftoms* of the *manor* of Burgh were afcertained by agreement between the lord and tenants, and confirmed by a decree in chancery about the year 1674; whereby the tenants fubjected themfelves to pay a twenty-penny fine or two years improved value, at the option of the lord, upon every general fine or change of tenant by death; and a thirty-penny fine or three years im-proved value, upon every change of tenant by fale or alienation, at the like option.

In the year 1685, Henry Howard duke of Norfolk erected a *monument* on Burgh marfh, in memory of king Edward the firft, who died there, with this infcription;

Memoriæ æternæ
Edwardi I. regis Angliæ longe
clariffimi: Qui in belli apparatu
contra Scotos occupatus, hic
in caftris obiit, 7 Julii
A. D. 1307.

The church of Burgh is dedicated to St. Michael. It was given by Sir Hugh de Morvil to the abbey of Holm Cultram, for the finding of lights, wine, and other neceffaries for the ornament of the church of Holm Cultram, and the fervice of the altar there *. Whofe grant was confirmed by Richard de Lucy former hufband of his daughter Ada †; and afterwards by Thomas de Multon her fecond hufband, who granted further to the abbot and convent common of pafture in the vill of Burgh after the hay and corn fhould be car-ried off, and two acres of arable land in Burgh marfh, lying next unto the lands of Joan de Morvil there, and a fifhery in Eden with two nets for every carucate of land which they had in Burgh ‡. Alfo Joan de Morvil, fecond daughter of Sir Hugh, confirmed the faid grant, for the health of her foul and of the foul of her hufband Richard de Gernon, of her father Hugh de Morville, and all her anceftors and fucceffors ||. The fame was likewife con-firmed by pope Innocent the third, who granted to them liberty to apply the

---

* Univerfis fanctæ matris ecclefiæ filiis Hugo de Morevilla falutem. Noverit univerfitas veftra me conceffiffe, dediffe, et hac præfenti charta mea confirmaffe Deo et ecclefiæ fanctæ Mariæ de Holm Coltram, et monachis ibidem Deo fervientibus, pro falute animæ meæ et uxoris meæ, et pro ani-mabus patris mei et matris meæ, et animabus omnium antecefforum et fuccefforum meorum, in liberam, puram et perpetuam eleemofynam, ecclefiam de Burgo ad primam vacationem, cum om-nibus pertinentiis fuis et libertatibus, ad invenienda luminaria, vinum, et omnia quæ neceffaria funt ad ornatum ecclefiæ de Holm Coltram et minifterium altaris et facramentorum Chrifti. His tefti-bus, Thoma filio Cofpatricii, Thoma de Brunfeld, &c. *Regiftr. Holm.* (

† Regiftr. Holm.   ‡ Ibid. || Ibid.

F f 2

revenues

revenues of the faid church to the ufe of their own houfe, for hofpitality
and maintenance of the poor: referving a competent portion for a chaplain to
officiate there *.

In the year 1234, one *Peter* a chaplain was inftituted to the vicarage by
Walter Mauclerk bifhop of Carlifle, who made a taxation for the vicar's maintenance, to wit, the obventions, the whole altarage, with the tithes of hay and
all other vicarial tithes except of wool and lamb and falt: the vicar to bear all
ordinary charges †. And the abbot and convent grant fpecially to the faid
Peter three marks yearly out of the altarage with divers obventions particularly
by name ‡.

In 1337, the abbot and convent of Holm Cultram prefent *Hugh de Hayton*
to the vicarage; and the bifhop recommends the inquiry, as in like cafes, to
Mr. Robert de Suthayke his official.

In 1368, *John de Kerby* vicar of Burgh and *Eudo de Ravenftandale* vicar of
Edenhall procure the confents and prefentations of their refpective patrons
(the abbot and convent of Holm and the prior and convent of Carlifle) in order
to an exchange of their livings. And in the next enfuing year *Eudo de Ravenftandale* dying, the abbot and convent prefent *John Lakeffon* who is inftituted
accordingly.

In 1381, upon the refignation of *John de Kane* vicar of Burgh, *Richard
Garth* is prefented and inftituted.

In 1473, *William Nicholfon* occurs as vicar.

In 1535, *Thomas Langton* was vicar; in whofe time the valuation was made
of all ecclefiaftical benefices and promotions throughout the kingdom, and the
values recorded in what are called the king's books: the particulars in relation
to this vicarage are as follows;

The vicarage of Burghe.

	l	s	d
Thomas Langton clerk, vicar of the church of Burgh nigh the Sands, whofe rectory is appropriated to the religious men the abbot and convent of the monaftery of Holme Cultrayme in the diocefe of Carlifle, hath a manfe and glebe appertaining to the faid vicarage, worth *per annum*	0	12	0
The fame Thomas hath the tithe of hay, flax, and hemp of the faid parifh, worth *communibus annis*	2	13	4
Carried forward	3	5	4

---

* Regiftr. Holm.   † Ibid.

‡ Univerfis fanctæ matris ecclefiæ filiis, ad quos præfens fcriptum pervenerit, Fr. W. abbas et
conventus de Holm Coltram falutem. Ad univerfitatis veftræ notitiam volumus pervenire, nos divini
amoris intuitu conceffiffe Petro capellano, nomine perpetuæ vicariæ in ecclefia noftra de Burg, tres
marcas argenti fingulis annis per manum cellerarii noftri, de obventionibus altaragii prædictæ ecclefiæ noftræ percipiendas. Ad hoc etiam ei charitative concedimus fecundam divifam morientium, et
manuportum altaris, exceptis quibuflibet decimis et oblationibus; et de fingulis miffis, fi evenerint,
fingulos denarios, præter dominicales denarios cum pane benedicto provenientes, cum omnibus aliis
rationabilibus acquifitionibus fuis, juxta canonum ftatuta recipiendis. Huis teftibus, Johanne priore
de Lannercoft, magiftro A' decano de Salopefb', magiftro Ada de Kirkeby, Alexandro de Daker
tunc officiali, Adamo decano de Allerdale, et multis aliis.

The

	l	*s*	*d*
Brought forward	3	5	4
The fame Thomas hath the white tithe, worth *communibus annis*	1	0	0
The fame Thomas hath the oblations, altarage, with the other profits of the Eafter book, worth *communibus annis* - -	1	0	0

| Sum total of the value | 5 | 5 | 4 |

Paid to the bifhop of Carlifle for Synodals yearly 2 *s* 8 *d*. And procurations of vifitations from three years to three years 2 *s* 8 *d*; and fo yearly 10¼ *d*——The fum deducted - - -

| | 0 | 3 | 6¾ |

| There remaineth | 5 | 1 | 11¾ |

The faid vicarage was certified to the commiffioners of queen Anne's bounty at 13 *l* 8 *s* 0 *d*. It was augmented in 1756 by the governors of the faid bounty jointly with Mr. Jofeph Liddel merchant in Newcaftle upon Tyne, with the fum of 400 *l*, which was laid out in lands in the parifh of Kirklinton, of the prefent yearly value of about 16 *l*.

In 1581, after the diffolution of the monafteries, inftitution was given by bifhop Meye to Sir *William Blane* clerk, on a prefentation by two yeomen of the neighbourhood, proving their title from the grantees of the abbot and convent before the diffolution.

In 1681, *Thomas Story* was prefented by king Charles the fecond.

And on Thomas Story's death in 1739, *Thomas Ifmay* was inftituted on a prefentation under the great feal.

In 1747, there were in this parifh 191 families; of which, 28 diffenters, all Quakers.

The *rectory* of this church, belonging to the monaftery of Holm Cultram as aforefaid, was after the diffolution of that religious houfe granted by king James the firft in the 6th year of his reign unto Henry Fanfhaw knight; John Ofburn, and Francis Gofton, to be holden of the king as of the manor of Eaft Greenwich, by fealty only, in free and common focage and not *in capite*; under the yearly rent of 17 *l* 12 *s* 0 *d*: Saving only to the king, his heirs and fucceffors, the donation and advowfon of the vicarage. Thefe grantees, in the year following fold the premiffes unto John Dyx *alias* Ramfay and Owen Shepherd efquires. And they again in the year 1612, for the fum of 660 *l*, fold the fame to Henry Curwen and Michael Hodgfon in truft for themfelves and their fellow partners (then leffees and farmers of the faid rectory), whofe heirs and affigns are ftill the impropriators.

Mr. Richard Hodgfon late of Weftend left 100 *l*; the intereft thereof to be applied yearly for the relief of poor houfholders, and teaching poor children, in equal portions.

There is alfo a fum of 11 *s* 2 *d* paid yearly out of fome lands, which with the intereft of 12 *l* in ftock, is applied to repairs and other public ufes.

The

The very name of *Burgh* (which was the *Axelodunum* of the Romans) leads one to look for a ftation here. And this appears to have been a little eaftward from the church, near what is called the Old Caftle, where there are manifeft remains of its ramparts. On the weft fide of the ftation thefe remains are moft diftinct, being about fix chains in length. And Severus's wall feems to have formed the north rampart of the ftation. Stones have been often plowed up here, and lime with the ftones. Urns have alfo frequently been dug up here. Mr. Horfley fays, he faw, befides an imperfect infcription, two Roman altars lying at a door in the town, but neither fculptures nor infcriptions vifible upon them†. But the late Dr. Lyttelton bifhop of Carlifle found upon an altar dug up in the vicar's garden here, the following infcription,

DEO
BELA
TVCA

The latter word certainly ftands for *Belatucadro*, and he fays it is the fifth infcription which has been difcovered in Britain, addreffed to this local deity*. About a quarter of a mile weft from the town there feems to have been a *caftellum*, for at this place there hath been dug up a larger quantity of ftones, than the bare thicknefs of the wall could well have afforded. They call the field the Watch-hill, and a remarkable tree in it is called the Watch-tree, and the tradition runs that upon this fpot there was anciently a watch-tower‡.

PARISH OF ROCLIFFE.

ROCLIFFE, the next parifh in this ward, lies on the north fide of the river Eden, abuts on Cargoe on the eaft, on Levington on the north, and is bounded by the river Eden on the fouth and weft.

This manor was anciently the inheritance of *Radulph de Bray*, who gave the fame to *William* fon of *John de Rocliffe* in the fixth year of king John. And in the fifth year of king John, one *Adam de Bray* gave the rectory to John prior of St. Mary's in Carlifle, who did appropriate the fame to their church of Carlifle. In the 33 Hen. 3. *William de Hardrigill* and *Maud* his wife (who feems to have been a daughter of the *Brays*) granted the manor to *John Ladbrook* and *Joan* his wife, to be holden of the faid *William* and *Maud* and their heirs under the yearly rent of 5l. In the fame year *John Francis* redeemed it of the faid John Ladbrook and Joan. The land was then holden as a fee of Burgh, under the yearly payment of 2s or one fparhawk. In the 54 Hen. 3. *Gilbert Francis* held the fame by the fame. fervices, and died in the 6 Ed. 1. and his fon *Richard Francis* being then under age, *Michael de Harcla* took him and married him to his daughter; wherefore the king feized Michael's lands, and fined him. The faid king, in the 22d year of his reign, gave the manor

† Horfley, 156.   * Tranfactions of the Antiquarian Society, v. i. p. 308.   ‡ Horfley, ibid.

of Rocliffe to *Richard Gernon* for life, and to remain after him to *Richard* his fon and to his wife *Eleanor* daughter of *Gyles Fyennes*, and the heirs of their two bodies, which manor the king had of *Richard Gernon* the father's gift. In the 23 Ed. 3. *Thomas Daniel* died feifed of Rocliffe, whofe daughter and heir *Margaret* was married to *John Radcliffe* and intailed all her inheritance upon the Radcliffs and their heirs male, whofe pofterity finally fold the fame to the *Dacres*, whereby this manor of Rocliffe became united to the barony of Burgh. But the demefne lands and the caftle were fold by *Henry Howard* duke of *Norfolk* in the year 1682 to *Charles Ufher* clerk, for the fum of 15,000*l*; whofe grandfon lawyer Ufher left the fame to *Hannah* his fifter, who devifed the fame to Mr. *Strong* a kinfman of the family, who now (1770) en- joys the fame and lives at Peterborough.

The *rectory* being given to the church of Carlifle as aforefaid, and totally appropriated thereto, was granted by king Hen. 8. to the dean and chapter there, who nominate a perpetual curate, and oblige their leffee of the rectory to pay him 20*l* a year. There is neither houfe nor glebe belonging to the curate. In the year 1753 an allotment of 200*l* of Queen Anne's bounty fell to this church, which ftill remains in the hands of the governors undifpofed of.

About the year 1234, an award was made by Walter bifhop of Carlifle, between the prior and convent of Carlifle, and the abbot and convent of Holm Cultram, concerning their refpective tithes of fifh caught in Eden; whereby the prior and convent were to have the tithes of fuch as were landed within the parifh of Rocliffe as rectors of the faid parifh, paying to the abbot and convent 2*s* yearly for ever†.

In 1745, John Grearfon leffee of the corn tithes of Ricardby bequeathed 26*s* yearly to be paid out of the fame, to the churchwardens and overfeers of the poor of this parifh, to purchafe fix penny loaves to be given to fix poor perfons weekly on Sunday after divine fervice in the forenoon.

In 1730, there were in this parifh 122 families; of which, Quakers 4, Prefbyterians, 4.

PARISH OF BEAUMONT.

BEAUMONT is the next parifh in this ward, but on the fouth fide of the river Eden. The town ftands upon a fair hill, from whence lieth every way a good profpect, which gave occafion to the name. It was anciently a manor belonging to the *Bruns* lords of Bownefs, who were alfo patrons of the church; but before the year 1380 it was come into the hands of the *Dacres* lords of

† Regiftr. Holm.

the

the barony of Burgh, and from thence forward went along with the said
barony, and therefore nothing further need to be said concerning it in
this place.

The CHURCH is dedicated to St. Mary, valued in the king's books at 8 *l* 1 *s*
8 *d*., The clear yearly value, as certified to the governors of queen Anne's
bounty, 18 *l* 1 *s* 6 *d*. In 1772, it received an augmentation of 200 *l* from the
governors of queen Anne's bounty, in conjunction with 200 *l* given by the
countess dowager Gower; wherewith lands were purchased in the parish of
Sedbergh, of the present yearly value of 14 *l*. About the year 1692, this
small rectory was presented to jointly with Kirk Andrews upon Eden, and
hath ever since been so held. And Kirk Andrews having had an augmentation by lot, the income of the two together may be about 60 *l per annum*.

In 1747, it was certified that in this parish there were 34 families; of
which, one quaker, and one presbyterian. [Note, the presbyterian families
in this and all other like places in the borders, are chiefly farmers that come
out of Scotland; who resort, as to their place of worship, to a presbyterian
meeting-house at Carlisle, or else go over on Sundays into their native country
of Scotland.]

Here is a small church at Beaumont, which serves both this parish and
Kirk Andrews; for there is no church at Kirk Andrews. But the rector
lives at Kirk Andrews, where there is an house and a small glebe, and none at
Beaumont; which house was built by the present rector the reverend George
Bownes, for which use the bishop permitted him to take the stones that were
the ruins of the old church there.

About the year 1680, when the commons in Burgh barony were allotted,
divided, and inclosed by agreement with the lord of the manor, a portion of
land called Priest-hill, containing about 30 acres, was assigned to Mr. Wilson
then rector, and to his heirs for ten years after his death, in consideration
of the present charge it was like to bring upon him. The said Mr. Wilson,
when he died, was indebted 20 *l* to Mr. Reed, who entered upon the premisses for his security. Afterwards Mr. George Hume, Mr. Wilson's immediate successor, gave bond for the said 20 *l*, and had thereupon possession of
the said Priest-hill. And Mr. Hume's widow keeping possession of the land as
her husband's inheritance, it hath never yet been recovered back to the
church.

In the year 1296, Robert de la Feritate [the same that at Bownes is called
Robert le Brun] presented Sir *Elias de Thirkwall*, chaplain, to the vacant
rectory of Beaumont; and dates his presentation *apud Bellum Montem*.

In 1306, *Walter de Arthuret* was presented by Sir Richard le Brun knight,
who is also in the register said to have presented *Adam* the last incumbent
lately dead.

In 1339, on the death of *William Broune* late rector of Beaumont, Matilda
Brune lady of Beaumont, presents *Richard Broune* to the rectory.

In 1365, *Thomas de Sourby* was rector of Beaumont; who in that year
made

made his will, and bequeathed 20*s* to find lights in the church of St. Mary of Beaumont.

In 1366, on the death of *Adam de Caldberk* rector of Beaumont, *Walter de Ormesheved* was presented by William Beauchamp rector of Kirk Ofwald, Thomas de Tughale vicar of Torpenhow, and Robert Paye chaplain [truftees, as it feemeth, upon a fettlement].

In 1380, on the death of Walter de Ormesheved, Sir Hugh de Dacre lord of Gillfland prefents *Robert Croft,* who was inftituted by William rector of Bownefs the bifhop's vicar general.

In 1490, *Robert Chapman* rector of Beaumont was witnefs to an indenture of Thomas lord Dacre.

In 1562, on the deprivation of *John Thompfon* for obftinately refufing the oath of fupremacy, *Henry Hafelhead* was inftituted on the prefentation of Sir William Dacre knight, lord Dacre of Grayftock and Gillfland.

In 1581, on the death of the faid Henry Hafelhead, inftitution was given to Sir *Lancelot Wilfon* clerk, prefented by Philip earl of Arundel.

In 1611, on the refignation of *Edward Johnfton, Thomas Thompfon* was inftituted on the prefentation of Anne countefs dowager of Arundel.

In 1615, Sir *John Wilfon* was prefented by the faid countefs dowager.

And in 1616, *Thomas Robinfon* was inftituted on the fame title.

In 1625, on the death of Thomas Robinfon, a citizen of London (patron for that turn) prefents *Thomas Warwick,* who was inftituted thereupon.

In 1634, *Andrew Smith* was prefented by Thomas earl of Arundel and Surry, earl marfhal of England.

In 1663, on Andrew Smith's death, *Patricius Hume* was prefented by the countefs of Arundel and Surry.

In 1692, on the death of *Richard Wilfon* rector of Beaumont, *George Hume* was prefented by Sir John Lowther baronet.

In 1703, *Gabriel Trant* was inftituted both to this rectory and to that of Kirk Andrews upon Eden, vacant by the death of George Hume, on the prefentation of Richard vifcount Lonfdale.

In 1705, on Mr. Trant's death, *Thomas Lewthwaite* was prefented by the fame patron.

In 1762, on the death of Thomas Lewthwaite, *George Bownefs* clerk was inftituted to this rectory and that of Kirk Andrews upon Eden jointly, upon the prefentation of Sir James Lowther baronet.

PARISH OF KIRK ANDREWS UPON EDEN.

THE parifh of KIRK ANDREWS UPON EDEN is parcel of the barony of Burgh, and there is nothing in the civil ftate thereof to diftinguifh it from the reft of that barony.

The CHURCH of this place, as the name imports, was dedicated to St. Andrew, though there is now no church remaining. The parifhioners have long

VOL. II. G g attended

attended divine service at Beaumont, but they still continue to bury in the churchyard here. There are only about 26 families in this whole parish.

In pope Nicholas's Valor in the year 1291 this church is not rated, because it did not exceed four marks, and the rector had no other benefice. Also in Edward the second's Valor it is not rated. In Henry the eighth's taxation it is rated at 3 l 11 s 5¼ d †. It was certified to the governors of queen Anne's bounty at 9 l 9 s 8 d, and having since had an augmentation by lot, it may now be worth (together with Beaumont, as is aforesaid) about 60 l a year.

In the year 1361, on the resignation of Sir *John Palmer* rector of this church, the prioress and convent of Marrig or Maryke in the county of York present Sir *John de Bempton*, who was thereupon instituted by bishop Welton. And the former of these rectors had a certificate from the bishop of his voluntary resignation and fair demeanor in the diocese of Carlisle, and the latter a dispensation for one year's absence.—And this is all that occurs in the bishops registers concerning this church before the reformation.

In 1576, on the death of *Thomas Watson* rector of Kirkanders, *Christopher Lowther* was instituted on a presentation by queen Elizabeth.

In 1587, on Christopher Lowther's death, bishop Meye collates *William Witton* by lapse.

In 1611, on William Witton's death, *George Millikin* was presented by one George Rumney.

In 1692, on the death of *Richard Wilson* rector of Kirk Andrews and of Beaumont, *George Hume* was instituted to the said rectories on a presentation by Sir John Lowther baronet.

And since that time both the said rectories jointly have been presented to by the house of Lowther.

PARISH OF GRINSDALE.

GRINSDALE, *Greensdale*, lies next, being a parish, town, and manor, within Burgh barony, and holden of the same. It gave surname to a family of gentlemen, the eldest of whom that Mr. Denton had met with was *Odard de Grinsdale*, and after him *Asketill* son of *Robert de Grinsdale*. They lived in the time of Henry the first, Stephen, and Henry the second. The eldest line failed about king John's time, when the inheritance fell to two daughters, whereof one was married to the lord Newton in Allerdale, and *Thomas de Newton* held by that right a moiety of Grinsdale of Thomas Multon lord of Burgh in Henry the third's time. And the other moiety was then so holden by one *William de la Sore*, whose ancestor had married the other coparcener.

A second brother of *Asketill*, named *Robert*, was a citizen of Carlisle, and became an inheritor of lands at Grinsdale and in Parton, which descended to *Gilbert* son of Robert, which Gilbert had a son *Robert de Grinsdale* who in the 23 Ed. 1. and again in the 33 Ed. 1. represented the city of Carlisle in parlia-

† For an account of these different Valors, see the Appendix, N° 42.

ment.

ment. The said *Robert* had a son *Alan de Grinsdale*, who was burgess for the said city in the 33 and 34 Ed. 1. and one of the representatives for the county in the 6 Ed. 2. After him was *Robert de Grinsdale*, who represented the said city several times in the reigns of Ed. 2. and Ed. 3. The last of the name was *Henry de Grinsdale*, who had two daughters coheirs, *Marriott* and *Margaret*, whose heirs sold their inheritance to the *Dentons* of Cardew in Henry the fourth's time, the last of which name was *George Denton* esquire, who sold his estate to Sir *John Lowther* about the year 1686.

Newton's moiety of Grinsdale fell by marriage to *Martindale*; the last of which name, *James Martindale*, had 5 daughters coheirs: two of which daughters were married to *Richard Dacre* and *Humphrey Dacre*, who joining with their kinsman Leonard Dacre in his rebellion in the reign of queen Elizabeth, were attainted, and their estate here seized by the crown; which was afterwards granted to *Whitmore* esquire, and by him or his representative to *Joseph Dacre* of Kirklinton esquire, in whose name and family it still continues.

The *Studholmes* also had a portion here, which they purchased of the lord of Kirk Andrews; for and heir of John de Parton and Kirk Andrews about the year 1336, and continued in that family for 10 or 12 descents, and after that was sold out into several freeholds.

The CHURCH of Grinsdale is dedicated to St. Mungo or Kentigern. It was given by Hugh de Morvil the first of that name lord of Burgh, and Eustachia his wife, to the prior and convent of Lanercost, who shortly after got it totally appropriated to that house, and supplied the same with one of their own members, without any endowment of a vicarage. It is not mentioned in king Henry the eighth's valuation, nor is there any presentation or other account of it in the bishops registers.

After the dissolution of the monasteries, king Edward the sixth by letters patent bearing date June 6, in the sixth year of his reign, granted to Sir Thomas Dacre senior knight (amongst other possessions of the priory of Lanercost) the whole rectory of Greensdale, with the advowson of the church there. And his descendents have ever since enjoyed the same, and nominated a curate, with a stipend of 40 s a year. At which sum it was certified to the governors of queen Anne's bounty; and having been augmented by lot with 200 l in 1737, and again in 1757; and again in 1771, the whole revenue now amounts to about 30 l a year.

The church for many years laid totally in ruins, until Joseph Dacre esquire the impropriator about the year 1743 rebuilt it at his own expence.

In 1747 it was certified, that there were in this parish 22 families; of which, 1 Quaker, and 1 Presbyterian.

CARLISLE.

WE come next to the ancient and famous city of CARLISLE, called by the Romans *Luguvallium*, standing in the north west corner of the forest of Engle., wood, environed with the rivers of Eden on the north east side, Petterel on, the south east, and Caldew on the south west. It is situate along Severus's wall, and from the colony there placed received its denomination. For *Llu gyda gwal*, in the ancient British, signifies an *army by the wall*; from whence the Romans framed their *Luguvallium*. The Saxons afterwards, by contraction, called it *Luell* and *Lu wall*; and the last British inhabitants there, prefixing to it the word *caer*, which is the general appellation of a *city*, called it *Caer Luell*, or *Caer Leyll*; and the common people pronounce it according to the said orthography to this day.

Upon the recess of the Romans, this place was utterly ruinated by the incursions of the Caledonians, and other barbarous northern nations; until Egfrid king of Northumberland, in the 7th century, rebuilt it and encompassed it with a wall of stone; and placing here a college of secular priests, gave it to the famous St. Cuthbert, bishop of Lindisfarne (from whence the see was afterwards transferred to Durham), in these words: " I have likewise " bestowed upon him the city called Luguballia, with the lands fifteen miles " about it." The citizens (says Bede) carried Cuthbert to see the walls of the city, and a well of admirable workmanship built in it by the Romans.

On the coming in of William the conqueror, in the year 1066, he issued out his writ to the inhabitants of Carlisle and Cumberland, commanding them to be subject to the bishop of Durham as their diocesan, from whose predecessors they had received Christianity†. And in the year 1082, in a charter of William de Karilepho bishop of Durham reckoning up the contents of his diocess, and in several other following instruments to that purpose, Carlisle with all the circumjacent country is mentioned as part of the diocess of Durham ‡.

But the city at that time having been most grievously shattered by the Danes, had lain buried in its ruins for near 200 years, until it began to flourish again by the favour and assistance of William Rufus, who built it and added a new wall with a castle, and placed a garrison in it, first of Flemings, whom upon better consideration he quickly removed into North Wales and the Isle of Anglesey; and then of southern English, who, as the Saxon Chronicle intimates, were to cultivate those parts. To this colony it is that all the records ascribe the first tillage that was known thereabouts. It is certain the whole forest of Englewood lay uncultivated for many years after. At that time (as Malmesbury has it) was to be seen a Roman *triclinium* or dining room of stone, arched over, which neither the violence of weather, nor fire could destroy. On the front of it was this inscription *Marti Victoriæ*; some will have this Marius to

† Leland, Vol. 3. p. 200.   ‡ 1 Dugd. Mon. 43.

be

be Arviragus the Briton; others, the Marius who was saluted emperor in oppofition to Gallienus. Yet it is faid that fome copies have it, not *Marii Victoriæ*, but *Marti Victori*; which latter may probably be favoured by fome, as feeming to come nearer the truth.

Leland fays, that the wall is near a mile in compafs; that it is right fair and ftrong, and built of redifh fquare ftones: That in it there are three gates, Bocher, Caldew, and Richard gate; otherwife known by the name of South, Weft, and North gates; and likewife called Englifh, Irifh, and Scotch gates †.

After the death of William Rufus, king Henry the firft, in the fecond year of his reign, founded here a college or priory of fecular priefts, and made Athelwold his confeffor or chaplain (prior of St. Ofwald's at Noftell in York-fhire) the firft prior of Carlifle, dedicating the church to the honour of the bleffed virgin Mary; but being hindred by the tumults and troubles of his time, he could not perfect all things before the 33d year of his reign, and then by the counfel of the prior Athelwald he erected a bifhop's fee at Car-lifle, and made the faid Athelwald firft bifhop there, whom the archbifhop of York (named Thurftan) did confecrate in that year. And in his ftead another chaplain of the faid king Henry, named Walter, was made the fecond prior of that houfe; who a little before his election had taken upon him by the king's licence the habit of a regular canon there, which order of canons the king and bifhop Athelwold had placed in that houfe, banifhing the fecular priefts immediately upon his confecration. The faid Walter gave to the church of Carlifle in pure alms for ever his lands in Lynftock, Richardby, Crofby, Little Crofby, Walby, Brunfkewgh, Carleton, and the wood, and the churches and rectories of St. Cuthbert in Carlifle, and Stainwiggs, which the king had given him. And the fame gift was confirmed both by the king and bifhop Athelwald ‡.

This city, from its fituation as a frontier againft Scotland, hath been fubject to various viciffitudes. In the reign of king Henry the fecond a great part of it was burned by the Scots, in which fire their charters and other records perifhed. And king Henry the third having renewed their charter of privi-leges, his charter alfo perifhed by fire, as king Ed. 1. recites in his charter of renewal granted to them in the 21ft year of his reign: But this latter fire was not occafioned by the enemy, but accidental; in which a great part of the city was laid in afhes; which happened on Sunday within the octaves of Afcenfion day in that year.

In the 32 Ed. 1. it appears from an entry in the regifter book of the abbey of St. Mary's York, that on the 4th of the Calends of June in the fame year, one half of this city was burned down, as far as the gate of Rickardby *.

The 35th year of the faid king will be ever memorable in the annals of this city, for the parliament then held at Carlifle. The king having refided here and in the neighbouring parts for feveral years, being intent upon his ex-pedition into Scotland, fummoned a parliament to meet at Carlifle on the 20th

† Leland, v. 7. p. 48.   ‡ Denton.   * Leland's Collectanea, vol. 1. p. 24.

of January in this year; which met accordingly, and continued till Palm Sunday following. And what great things they did in that time, in opposing the papal extortions, furthering the expedition against Scotland, concluding prince Edward's marriage with a daughter of France, and other public transactions, our histories abundantly inform us. The king continued at Carlisle till the 28th of June; and then setting forward towards Scotland, he was seized with a flux, and died at Burgh upon Sands on the 7th of July following.

In the 9 Ed. 2. Robert de Brus, king of Scotland, came with his whole force, and besieged Carlisle for ten days, laying waste the whole country as far as Allerdale, Coupland, and Westmorland. They made many attacks and erected several warlike engines, but at last raised the siege in so great an hurry, that they left all the said engines behind them, and were followed by the English, who took John de Moravia and Sir Robert Bardolf prisoners, and brought them to the castle at Carlisle, for whom a large ransom was paid.

In the 15 Ed. 2. Andrew de Harcla, having vanquished the earl of Lancaster, with his adherents the lords John de Moubray and Roger de Clifford, at Burrough-bridge in Yorkshire, was for this his great service made earl of Carlisle. In the next year, king Edward prepared a large army against Scotland, which king Robert de Brus being informed of, he entered England near Carlisle, and burnt Rose and the country of Allerdale, and plundered the abbey of Holm Cultram (though his father was buried there), and proceeded through Copeland as far as Preston, burning and destroying all the way he went: And returning with great spoil, he lay in the neigbourhood of Carlisle for five days, still continuing the devastation. Whereupon Andrew de Harcla, concluding that king Edward neither knew how to govern nor defend his kingdom, and fearing that he would in the end lose it, did on the third of January privately repair to king Robert at Lochmaben, and there they mutually agreed to assist and succour each other with all their might. And it was further agreed, that if the king of England should within one year approve thereof, that then king Robert should cause one monastery to be built in Scotland and endowed with 500 marks of yearly revenue for ever, to pray for the souls of all those that had perished in the wars between England and Scotland; and should pay 4000 marks of silver to the king of England within ten years: and that the king of England should have the prince of Scotland and marry him to a relation. The earl returning to Carlisle summoned all the chief of the county, as well clergy as laity; and there, more out of fear than love, they all swore that they would keep and defend the said convention with their whole power. And all the common people were much pleased therewith, hoping they might now live peaceably at home. But an account of all these proceedings being carried to king Edward, he was greatly surprised and troubled at it; and publickly proclaiming the earl a traytor, sent to Anthony lord Lucy to apprehend him, promising that he and his assistants should be well rewarded. Whereupon the lord Lucy, having his squires and other men properly dispersed here and there upon various pretended causes, on the morrow of St. Matthias the apostle, he and they entered the castle of Carlisle where the earl was, as upon common business. With

lord

lord Lucy were three stout and daring knights, Sir Hugh de Louther, Sir Richard de Denton, and Sir Hugh de Moriceby, with four squires, all well armed. And as they entered the castle, they carefully left a guard at every gate. Then lord Lucy with his three knights went through the great hall to the place where the earl was sitting, and thus accosted him; Sir, you must either surrender or defend yourself instantly. Upon which, he submitted. Then some of his servants calling out treason, the keeper of the inner gate would have shut it upon the knights that had entered, but Sir Richard Denton killed him with his own hand, and this was the only person that was slain in the whole affair. But all that were in the castle surrendred themselves and it to the lord Lucy. But some of the family repaired with all speed to High-head castle, to acquaint his brother John therewith, who immediately fled into Scotland, and with him Sir William Blount and many others. A special messenger being dispatched to king Edward at York to acquaint him with all that was done and to know his pleasure, the earl in the mean time, appre-hending what would be the consequence, confessed himself to several monks, who gave him absolution, and assured him of eternal happiness. On the feast of St. Cedde, six days after the seizing of the said earl, an armed force with Sir Jeffrey de Scroop chief justiciar arrived at Carlisle; who the next day tried and sentenced the said earl to be degraded, hanged, and quartered. After the pronouncing of which sentence, the earl said, You have disposed of my body at your pleasure, but my soul I give to God. And then with an un-changeable countenance, and uplifed hands and eyes he was carried to the gallows and executed, having first fully explained the intention of the treaty.

In the 11 Ed. 3. the Scots besieged the city of Carlisle, but being not able to take it, they burned the hospital of St. Nicholas, and all the places adjacent.

In the 6 Ric. 2. the Scots made an inroad into the forest of Englewood, whence they drove home 40,000 head of cattle†, sacked Penrith in the fair time, but attempted nothing against Carlisle, being at that time too strongly guarded.

In the civil wars between the two houses of York and Lancaster, in the reigns of Hen. 4, 5 and 6, this city was miserably harassed, the suburbs burned, and all the adjacent parts destroyed even to the gates of the city. In consideration whereof, and of their impoverishment thereby, king Edward the fourth remitted to them one half of their ancient fee farm rent of 80l.

In the 29 Hen. 8. in the insurrection during Aske's rebellion, Nicholas Musgrave, Thomas Tilby, and others, favourers of that cause, besieged Car-lisle with 8000 men, but were repulsed by the city, and in their return encountered by the duke of Norfolk, who caused all the captains (save Mus-grave who escaped) and about 70 other persons by law martial to be hanged on Carlisle walls‡.

It is said that king Henry the eighth built the citadel of Carlisle. How-ever, be that as it may, it is certain both that and the rest of the fortifications

† Hollingsh. 428.   ‡ Herbert's life of Hen. 8. p. 490.

were

were greatly gone to decay in the reign of queen Elizabeth, as appears by the following return to a commiffion of inquiry for that purpofe, viz.

"*Certificate of the decays of the caftle, town, and citadel of Carlifle, by Walter Strykland, Richard Lowther, John Lamplugh, Anthony Barwick, Alan Bellingham, and Thomas Denton efquires, appointed commiffioners for the fame,* 12 *June,* 1563."

Decays within Carlifle caftle:

Firft the dungeon tower of the caftle, which fhould be principal part and defence thereof and of the town alfo, on three fides is in decay, that is to fay, on the eaft and weft fides in length 66 foot, and on the fouth fide 66 foot, in decay; and every of the fame places fo in decay, do contain in thicknefs 12 foot, and in height 50 foot: So as the fame dungeon tower is not only unferviceable, but alfo in daily danger to fall, and to overthrow the reft of the faid tower.

Item, there is a breach in the wall in the outer ward, which fell the 12th of March 1557, containing in length 69 foot and an half, in thicknefs 9 foot, and in height with the battlement 18 foot; through which breach men may eafily pafs and repafs.

Item, the captain's tower and other principal defence wanteth a platform and the vawmer, about 44 foot, in breadth 40 foor, and in thicknefs 8 foor.

Item, three parts of the walls of the inner ward is not vawmer, containing in length 344 foot, and in thicknefs 12 foot, and in height 3 foot, with one half round.

Item, the caftle gates are in decay, and needful to be made new.

Item, there is not in the faid caftle any ftorehoufe meet for the ordnance and munition; fo as the fame lieth in the town very dangeroufly for any fudden enterprize.

Item, there is decayed the glafs of two great windows; the one in the great chamber, and the other in the hall of the faid caftle.

Decays within Carlifle town:

Firft, there is a breach in the town wall, betwixt the caftle and Rickardgate, containing in length 40 foot, and in height with the battlement 18 foot, fallen down in fuch decay, that men may eafily pafs and repafs through the fame; and at either end of the faid breach, 40 foot of the fame wall is in danger of falling, and very needful to be repaired from the foundation.

Item, on the eaft part of the city is 120 foot of the vawmer in decay.

Item, there is a part of the vawmer of the new wall unfinifhed, containing in length 400 foor, and in height 6 foot.

Item, there is in the fame wall, near unto Caldergate, 36 foot in decay, and very needful to be repaired.

Item, one half round tower, called Springold tower, being chief and principal piece and defence of two parts of the city, and helping to the caftle, unferviceable and very needful to be repaired.

Item, the vawmering of Calder tower is in decay; and it is very needful to have a platform thereon.

8   Item,

'Item, It is needful that Ricardgate have a new roof, and be covered with lead, and thereupon a platform, being a meet place for service.

Item, The gates of the city, being of wood, are in decay, and one broken; which are to be repaired with celerity.

Decays within the citadel:

First, The great round tower, at the east end of the fort of the citadel, being paved with stone and sand upon the lead roof, was thereby so overcharged, as that a great part thereof is fallen to the ground, and is very needful to be repaired, for that it is the principal of that fort, and standeth upon the most danger of the town.

Item, There be two houses within the said fort, called the buttery and boulting house, standing within the rampire wall, the roofs and timber whereof are fallen to the ground, by means of the like being overcharged with earth, so as the same are both unserviceable.

Item, It is needful to have a platform upon the old gatehouse tower, being a requisite place of service.

Item, Another platform were needful upon the half round tower towards the town.

Item, There is the glass of a great window in the hall of the said fort utterly decayed, by means of a great thunder and hailstones.

Ordnance, artillery, and munition:

‹ In the castle: Sagars 2, fawcons 4; all dismounted. Fawconets 2, whereof one not good. One little potgun of brass. Demibomberders 2. Basses double and single 12, lacking furniture. Half staggs 39, not serviceable. Bows of ewe, none. Arrows, sixscore sheafs; in decay. Morispikes 30, not good. Sagar shot of iron 58. Sagar shot of lead 70.

In the City: Fawcons of brass 5, all dismounted. One small potgun of brass. Fawconets of brass 4, dismounted; fawcons of iron 2, dismounted also; to serve the warden in the field. Fowlers 2, small serpentines 2, basses 2; all lacking their furniture. Hagbuts 13, whereof 12 unserviceable. Harquebusses 30, decayed and past service. Bows of ewe 1?, Bows of elm 70, not serviceable. Sheafs of arrows 18, in decay. Serpentine powder one last and an half, both for the city and the castle; being all placed in the city, because there is no ordnance house in the castle. Corned powder one demibarrel and an half. Hacks and picks 52, worn and decayed with work. Shovels and spades 10 dozen. Quarrel picks 12. Cart furniture for 30 horse draught. Hemp rope, two coil; small. Sagar shot of iron 50. Fawcon shot of iron 50. One quarrel mall. Wallers hammers 40. Setting chissels 9. Hand baskets 10 dozen. Gavelocks 5. Iron 12 stone. Lantirons 20, in decay.

In the Citadel: Sagars 2, fawcons 4, of brass; dismounted. Double basses 3. Single basses 8. Small serpentines 2, fowlers 2, murderers 2; all unfurnished. Harquebuses 9, not serviceable. Half haggs 14, decayed and past service. Morispicks 40, not good. Corned powder two demi-barrels; whereof four

of the grained fort. Bows of ewe 20, not good. Arrows, 26 ſheafs; in decay. Sagar ſhot of iron 50 †."

In purſuance of this report, the queen cauſed many and conſiderable repairs
to be made, and ſupplies to be furniſhed of artillery and ammunition.

In the 40 and 41 Eliz. the plague raged exceedingly at Carliſle and other
parts of the country, infomuch that there died of it at Carliſle alone 1196 perſons,
which was about one third part of the whole number. During which time collections were made as ſet forth in the following report:

"A brief note to poſterity of all ſuch ſums as did accrue for the relief of
the diſeaſed of the plague, which began in this city at Michaelmafs in the year
of God 1597, and continued until Michaelmafs 1598; with a remembrance
of the benevolence of the country there, and the particular gifts of certain
well affected gentlemen, with the affeffments of the citizens themſelves, and
the charge taken forth of the common cheſt;

	£	s	d
Imprimis, From the juſtices of the peace of this county, re-ceived and brought in by Mr. Richard Bell then mayor — —	20	0	0
Item, More ſent by Mr. Lawſon then high ſheriff of the county about the 10th of June — — — —	10	0	0
Item, From the dean and chapter at ſeveral times, which came to the ſum of — — — — —	5	7	0
Item, From the biſhop of Carliſle, then being (Dr. Meye) —	6	13	4
Item, From the biſhop of Carliſle that now is, upon his entry (Dr. Robinſon) — — — — —	2	0	0
Item, From John Dalſton eſquire of Dalſton — —	1	10	0
Item, From Mr. Dethick chancellor — — —	1	0	0
Item, From Mr. Francis Highmore of Harby-brow — —	0	18	0
Item, From Mr. Warwick of Warwick hall — —	0	10	0
Item, From Mr. Pearſon Warwick of Marpitt — —	0	10	0
Item, Taken out of our common cheſt at ſeveral times, for relief of the ſaid ſick perſons — — — — —	85	2	0
Item, The whole remainder of the revenue upon chamberlain Pattinſon's account the year before, being the ſum of —	61	14	8
Item, The ſeveral collections of the citizens themſelves	14	4	10
The total ſum	209	9	10

In October, 20 Cha. 1. (1644) ſiege was laid to the city of Carliſle by the
parliament forces commanded by lieutenant general David Leſley, and continued till June following; during which time, notwithſtanding the proviſions

† From the Cotton MSS. in the Britiſh Muſeum.

that

that had been voluntarily fent in by the country *, and otherwife provided by the governor, upon the apprehenfion of a fiege, the city was fo reduced that horfe
fleſh

* Proviſions fent unto the garriſon at Carliſle in the years 1643 and 1644, to the amount as follows :

	l	s	d
Sir Philip-Muſgrave baronet	20	0	0
Sir Patricius Curwan baronet	20	0	0
Sir Richard Graham knight and baronet	20	0	0
Sir William Dalſton baronet and Sir George Dalſton	15	0	0
Sir Henry Fletcher baronet	20	0	0
Sir John Lowther baronet	20	0	0
Sir Edward Muſgrave baronet	10	0	0
Sir Edward Radcliffe baronet	10	0	0
Sir Francis Howard knight	10	0	0
Sir Charles Howard knight	5	0	0
Sir Richard Sandford knight	10	0	0
Sir Chriſtopher Lowther baronet, his fon and heir	5	0	0
Sir William Muſgrave knight	5	0	0
Sir Timothy Fetherſton knight	5	0	0
Sir Thomas Dacre knight	5	0	0
William Pennington eſquire	10	0	0
Symon Muſgrave eſquire	2	0	0
William Carleton eſquire	4	0	0
Leonard Dykes eſquire	4	0	0
The earl of Anandale's eſtate	10	0	0
The lord Wharton's eſtate	10	0	0
Mr. Howard of Naward	20	0	0
John Dalſton of Uldale eſquire	5	0	0
William Lawfon of Iſell eſquire	10	0	0
Mr. Salkeld of Whitehall	5	0	0
Mr. Lamplugh of Fells	4	0	0
Mr. Senhoufe of Netherhall	2	0	0
Mr. Senhoufe of Seafcales	2	0	0
Mr. Barwife of Hildkirk	2	0	0
Mr. Salkeld of Brayton	2	0	0
Mr. Skelton of Armathwaite	5	0	0
Mr. Lamplugh of Dovenby	2	0	0
Mr. Blencoe of B'encoe	2	0	0
Mr. Fletcher of Morefby	5	0	0
Mr. Whelpdale of Penrith	5	0	0
Mr. Pennington of Seaton	4	0	0
Mr. Laton of Dailmain	2	0	0
Mr. Kirkbride of Ellerton	2	0	0
Mr. Fleming of Skerwith	2	0	0
Mr. Standley of Delegarth	2	0	0
Mrs. Hutton of Penrith	2	0	0
Mr. Patrickfon of Paifwellhow	3	0	0
Mr. Richmond of Highet	2	0	0
Mr. Brifcoe of Crofton	2	0	0
Mr. Denton of Cardew	2	0	0
Mr. Graham of Nunnery	2	0	0
Mr. Curwen of Camerton	2	0	0
Lady Curwen of Rottington	4	0	0
Mr. Warwick of Warwick brig	2	0	0

     Mr,

flesh without bread or salt, hempseed, dogs, and rats were eaten; and in the end was surrendered upon honourable terms; *viz.*

" ARTICLES:

	l	*s*	*d*
Mr. Tolson of Bridekirk	2	0	0
Mr. Fletcher of Tallentyre	2	0	0
Mr. Skelton of Branthwaite	2	0	0
Mr. Highmore of Armathwaite	2	0	0
Mr. Huddleston and his son of Hutton John	2	0	0
Mr. Irton of Irton	2	0	0
Mr. Latus of Millum	2	0	0
Mr. Harrington of Woolakes	4	0	0
Mrs. Fletcher of Calder Abbey	4	0	0
Mr. Dalston of Thwaites	2	0	0
Mr. Irton of Threlkeld	2	0	0
Mr. Swinburn of Lewthwaite and mother	2	0	0
Mr. Dalton of Brigham	3	0	0
Mr. Blennerhasset of Flemby	2	0	0
Mr. Joseph Porter	2	0	0
Mr. John Aglionby	2	0	0
Mr. Orfeur of Highclose	4	0	0
Mr. Brougham	2	0	0
Mr. Denton of Warnell	2	0	0
Mr. Dudley	2	0	0
Peter Winden of Lorton	1	0	0
Mr. Robert Fisher	1	0	0
Mr. Thomas Benson	1	0	0
Mr. Osmotherly of Langrigg	1	0	0
Mr. Chambers of Raby Coat	1	0	0
Mr. Salkeld of Threapland	1	0	0
Mr. Richard Eglesfield	1	0	0
Mr. Denton of Bothel	1	0	0
Mr. Dalston of Murkeholme	1	0	0
Mr. Anthony Bouch	2	0	0
Mr. Lathes	1	0	0
Mr. Ewan Christian of Unerigg	1	0	0
Mr. Wivell of Johnby	1	0	0
Mrs. Buckle of Lamonby	1	0	0
Mr. Henry Baxter	1	0	0
Mr. Miles Halton	1	0	0
Mr. Fielding	2	0	0
Mr. Threlkeld of Melmerby junior	1	0	0
Mr. John Pildrem	1	0	0
Mr. Lamplugh of Ribton	1	0	0
Edward Walker of Lasonby	1	0	0
Dr. Sybson for temporalities	1	0	0
Mr. William James	1	0	0
Mr. Barrow of Skelton	1	0	0
Mr. Clement Skelton	1	0	0

Clergymen:

	l	*s*	*d*
The dean and chapter of Carlisle, viz. the dean 4*l*, and every prebend 30*s*	10	0	0
Mr. Usher of Kirk Andrews	3	0	0
Mr. Constable of Arthuret	3	0	0
Mr. Welchman of Stanwix	1	0	0

Mr.

" ARTICLES agreed upon between the right honourable David Lefley lieutenant general of the Scotifh cavalry, on the one part; and the right honourable Sir Thomas Glenham knight, commiffioner in chief in the four northern counties of Weftmorland, Cumberland, Bifhoprick, and Northumberland, and Sir Henry Stradling knight, governor of the caftle, city, and citadel of Carlifle for his majefty on, the other part; touching the delivery of the faid city, caftle, and citadel of Carlifle, with the forts, towers, cannons, ammunition, and furniture belonging thereto, to the faid lieutenant general, for the ufe of the king and parliament, on Saturday next enfuing at ten of the clock in the forenoon or thereabouts.

1. That Sir Thomas Glenham knight, commander of thofe four northern counties of Weftmorland, Cumberland, Bifhoprick, and Northumberland, and Sir Henry Stradling governor of the city, caftle, and citadel of Carlifle, with fuch as do unto them belong, and likewife all officers and foldiers belonging to the train, fhall march out of the caftle, city, and citadel, with their arms, flying colours, drums beating, matches lighted at both ends, bullets in their mouths, with all their bag and baggage, and twelve charges of powder a piece; and that all fuch as are willing to march fhall have the liberty of this article.

2. That to every member of the foundation of this cathedral now refident, fhall be allowed a livelihood out of the churches revenues, until the parliament determine it.

	l	s	d
Mr. Head of Aikton	3	0	0
Mr. Warwick for Bownefs and Brampton	2	0	0
Mr. Burton of Orton	2	0	0
Mr. Prieftman for Kirklinton	1	0	0
Dr. Sibfon for Bewcaftle or the fequeftrators	2	0	0
Mr. Gibfon for Caftle Carrick	1	0	0
Mr. Morland for Grayftock	5	0	0
Mr. Weft for Addingham	1	0	0
The fequeftrators of Great Salkeld parfonage	1	0	0
Mr. Goodwin of Lafonby	1	0	0
Mr. Sharplefs of Croglin	1	0	0
Mr. Milburne for Skelton and Oufeby	2	0	0
Mr. Langbaine for Kefwick	2	0	0
Mr. Tunftell for Caldbeck	2	0	0
Mr. Hudfon for Uldale and Kirkbride	2	0	0
Mr. Robinfon for Torpenhow	2	0	0
Mr. Fairfax for Bolton	2	0	0
Mr. Fletcher of Plumland	2	0	0
Mr. Wilkinfon of Gilcrux	1	0	0
Mr. Beck of Brumfield	1	10	0
Mr. Cookfon of Brigham	1	0	0
Mr. Fletcher of Dean	2	0	0
Mr. Lowther of Workington	2	0	0
Mr. Antrobus of Egremond	1	10	0
Mr. Fletcher of Diftington	1	10	0
Mr. Hudfon of Harrington	2	0	0
Mr. Tubman of Whitcham	1	0	0
Mr. Braithwaite of Lamplugh	1	0	0

The fum total 463 .10 0

3. That

3. That no church be defaced.

4. That no oath fhall by any officer belonging to the Scotifh army, be impofed upon any perfon now refident within the garrifon; and in cafe fuch an oath be impofed by authority from the parliament or the army, that then every perfon to whom the benefit of this capitulation belongeth, who fhall refufe to take the faid oath, fhall have free liberty at any time within a month after his refufal, to depart with his goods and family, if he pleafeth, with a pafs of conduct, unto what place he or they fhall think fitting; and fhall enjoy the full profit of their eftates as formerly, during the time of their abfence, and according to the laws of this land.

5. That no officer or foldier be required or inforced to march further than with convenience they may; and that they fhall accommodate themfelves with free quarters during their march, and a fufficient convoy, to what place the king or either of the king's armies fhall happen to be, or to any of the king's garrifons, or which Sir Thomas Glenham fhall pleafe to nominate, to maintain them in their quarters and upon their march free from all injuries and uncivilities that fhall any ways be offered unto them; and likewife that the privileges of this article be offered unto all perfons which fhall march along with the garrifon; and that there be horfes to the number of 150, and carriages to the number of 20, provided for the accommodation of the officers, themfelves, and their bag and baggage.

6. That all troopers as have not by accident loft their horfes, may march out with their horfes and arms.

7. That no officer, foldier, or any other perfon, fhall in their march, rendefvous, or quarters, be ftopped or plundered upon any pretence whatfoever.

8. That two officers fhall be appointed by the lieutenant general Lefley, the one for accommodating free quarter for officers and foldiers, and the other for providing of horfes and carriages for officers and baggage.

9. That no man whatfoever fhall entice away any officer or foldier upon their march, on any promife or other ground of preferment.

10. That all fuch officers, foldiers, and others, who are fick and hurt and cannot now march out of the town, fhall have liberty to ftay until they be recovered; and they may have liberty to go whither they pleafe, either to any of the king's armies, or to any of his majefty's garrifons wherefoever they be, or to their own houfes or eftates where they may reft quietly; and that in the interim, they being fick or hurt, the general lieutenant would receive them and take care of them.

11. That officers and foldiers wives, children, and families, and fervants, and all other now in town, may have liberty to go along with their hufbands, or to them, if they pleafe to return into their own country, houfes, or eftates, to enjoy them under fuch contribution as the reft of the country pays: That they have liberty to carry their goods with them, or any time within a month, and have carriages allowed them for that purpofe, paying reafonable rates.

12. That the earl of Nidfdale, the lord Harris, with their families and followers, fhall have free liberty to march out to any of the king's armies, or

otherwife

otherwife to their own houfes, or places of abode, at their pleafures; and to take with them, at any time within a month, all fuch goods as are belonging to them in the caftle, citadel, or city of Carlifle.

13. That gentlemen, clergymen, citizens, and foldiers, and every other perfon within the city, fhall at any time when they pleafe have free liberty to remove themfelves, their goods and families, and difpofe thereof at their plea-fure, according to the ancient laws of the land, either to live at their own houfes or elfewhere, and to enjoy their goods and eftates without moleftation, and to have protection for that purpofe, fo that they may reft quietly at their abodes, and may travel freely and fafely about their occafions, having letters of fafe-conduct, and be furnifhed with horfes and carriages at reafonable rates.

14. That the citizens and inhabitants may enjoy all their privileges as for-merly before the beginning of thefe troubles; and that they may have free-dom of trade both by fea and land, paying fuch duties and cuftoms as all other towns under the obedience of king and parliament. And no free quarter fhall be put upon any within this city, without his free confent. Likewife, that there fhall no oath be impofed upon any of them, or any other now within this garrifon, but they fhall freely and voluntarily take it according to the 4th article.

15. That in all charges, the citizens, refidents, and inhabitants fhall bear only fuch part with the country at large, as hath been formerly ufed in all affeffments.

16. That all perfons whofe dwellings are within this city (although they be now abfent) may have the benefit of thefe articles as if they were prefent.

17. That all gentlemen and others that have goods within this city, and are abfent themfelves, may have free liberty within a month to carry away and dif-pofe of thofe goods.

18. That there be no plundering or taking away any man's perfon, or any part of his eftate; and that juftice according to the law fhall be adminiftred within this city in all caufes by the magiftrates, and that they be affifted therein (if need require) by the garrifon."

During this liege, 3s pieces were coined out of the citizens plate; which are now become a great curiofity, and fome of them have been lately fold for above twenty times the original currency.

In 1745, this city was furrendred to the rebels in their march fouthwards, being garrifoned only by an undifciplined new-raifed militia, who were not in number fufficient to defend fo large an extent of wall; and the caftle likewife furrendred, being guarded only by the governor and about 70 or 80 invalids, and of thefe one half at leaft not fit for fervice. In their retreat into Scotland, the rebels left a fmall garrifon here, who after a few days fiege furrendered, on the 30th of December in that year, to William duke of Cumberland, on the fole condition of not being prefently put to the fword, but referved to his majefty's pleafure : Prifoners taken therein were; of the Manchefter regiment, colonel Townley; 5 captains, 6 lieutenants, 7 enfigns, 1 adjutant, and 93 non-commiffion

commiffion officers and private men.   Of the Scotch, John Hamilton governor,
6 captains, 7 lieutenants, 3 enfigns, 1 furgeon, and 256 non-commiffion officers and private men.   Of French, 3 commiffion officers, 1 ferjeant, and 4
private men.

THIS city hath had great and ample privileges granted to it, by the CHAR-
TERS of feveral princes of this realm.   The firft charter whereof we have any
account was in the reign of king Hen. 2. which was burned by the Scots;
which charter king Hen. 3. by his charter bearing date Oct. 26, in the 35th
year of his reign, recites and confirms; whereby was granted to the citizens
freedom from toll, paffage, pontage, and all cuftoms belonging to the king,
with privilege of dead wood for fuel, and timber for their houfes in divers
places within the foreft of Carlifle, by the affignment of the king's ferjeants
and forefters, with a free guild for trade and merchandize *.

King Ed. 1. by his charter dated 23 June in the 21ft year of his reign, fetting forth that Hen. 3d's charter was alfo burned, recites the tenor thereof from
the inrollment in chancery, and confirms the fame verbatim.

King Edward the third, by his charter bearing date 7 Feb. in the 26th year
of his reign of England and 13th of France, fetting forth, that it having been
found upon inquifition taken by his trufty and well beloved Richard de Denton
and John de Harrington, and returned into the chancery, that the citizens of
the city of Carlifle had for time immemorial enjoyed the following privileges,
grants and confirms the fame to them accordingly; viz. return of writs; a
market on the Wednefday and Saturday every week; and a fair yearly on
the feaft of the Affumption of the bleffed virgin Mary and 15 days after; a
free guild, and election of mayor, bailiffs, and two coroners; affize of bread,
beer, and wine; trial of felonies, infangthief, and all pleas of the crown which
belong to the office of fheriff and coroner; goods of felons and fugitives; freedom from all fines, amerciaments, and fuits to the county court and wapentake; common of pafture for all their beafts at all times of the year upon the
king's moor, and liberty to get turf there; with freedom throughout the whole
realm of England from toll, pontage, paffage, laftage, wharfage, carriage,
murage, and ftallage; and that they fhall have the place called Battail-holme,
for their markets and fairs; and fhall have power to divide, and devife their
tenements; and fhall have the city mill, and the king's fifhery in the water of
Eden †.

King Richard the fecond, May 6, in the 5th year of his reign, by his charter
recites and confirms all the fame.

King Ed. 4. Dec. 19. in the firft year of his reign, on the petition and re-
prefentation of the citizens, that the city had fuffered greatly in the late civil
wars, when befieged by the faid king's enemies Margaret late queen of England, Edward late prince of Wales, and Henry duke of Exeter, by burning
the fuburbs, and even the very gates of the city, and the mill, and other devaftations, remits unto them 40 l yearly of their fee farm rent of 80 l, and fur-

* Appendix, No 20.   † Appendix, No 21.

6   ther

ther grants unto them the keeping of the king's fisheries of Carlisle, otherwise called the sheriffs net, otherwise called the fishery of frithnet in the water of Eden ‡.

King *Henry* the seventh, 11 Feb. in the third year of his reign, recites and confirms their former charters.

The like by king *Hen.* 8. Feb. 27. in the first year of his reign.

The like by king *Edward* the sixth, Feb. 11, in the 5th year of his reign.

The like by queen *Elizabeth.*

The like by king James the first, in the second year of his reign of England and thirty-seventh of Scotland.

Finally, king *Charles* the first, July 21, in the 13th year of his reign, by Infpeximus recites and confirms all the aforesaid grants, except the free election of mayor, bailiffs, and coroners; and further grants, that in all time coming the mayor and citizens shall be one body corporate and politic, by the name of *mayor, aldermen, bailiffs, and citizens of the city of Carlisle,* and shall have a common seal: That one of the aldermen shall be *mayor:* That there shall be besides the mayor eleven other *aldermen,* two *bailiffs* and two *coroners:* That there shall be within the said city 24 other men who shall be *capital citizens,* to be of the common council and assistance to the mayor, aldermen, and bailiffs.

The mayor, aldermen, bailiffs, and 24 capital citizens, or the major part of them in Guildhall assembled, on the Monday next after Michaelmas day, shall have power to chuse annually one of the aldermen to be *mayor;* and in case of an equality the mayor to have the casting vote: and the mayor so chosen shall be sworn into his office by the last mayor (if he be living), otherwise by the aldermen or major part of them, and shall continue therein until another shall be chosen and sworn.

In like manner the two *bailiffs* and two *coroners* annually shall be chosen and sworn.

On the *death* of an *alderman,* the mayor and surviving aldermen, or the major part of them, in Guildhall assembled, shall chuse another; who shall be sworn by the mayor, and to continue during life.

Capital citizen dying, or for just cause removed, the mayor and aldermen or the major part of them shall chuse and swear another; who shall continue during life, unless by the mayor and aldermen or the greater part of them for just cause amoved.

Mayor chosen and refusing to act shall be fined not exceeding 20*l*; any of the 24 capital citizens chosen for alderman and refusing to act shall be fined not exceeding 10*l*; bailiff, 5*l*; capital citizen, 5*l*.

The *recorder* shall be chosen by the mayor, aldermen, bailiffs, and capital citizens; to continue during their pleasure.

Town clerk to be chosen by the mayor, aldermen, bailiffs, and capital citizens.

And there shall be one *swordbearer,* and three *serjeants at mace* for the execution of process: the swordbearer and one of the serjeants to be chosen yearly on

‡ Custod' piscar' nostrarum Karl·ol', alias dict' rethis vicecom', alias dict' piscar' de frithnet in aqua de Eden.

the Monday after Michaelmaſs day by the newly elected mayor; the other two ſerjeants, by the major, aldermen, bailiffs, and 24 capital citizens; to continue during pleaſure.

And the mayor, aldermen, bailiffs, and capital citizens, or the major part of them, of whom the mayor ſhall be one, upon public ſummons by the mayor, ſhall have power in the guildhall to aſſemble and make by-laws (not contrariant to the laws of the land), and inforce them by penalties corporal or pecuniary, or both.

And the mayor, recorder, and two ſenior aldermen ſhall be juſtices of the peace; the mayor to take the juſtice's oath of office before the aldermen and recorder, and the two ſenior aldermen and recorder before the mayor and the reſt of the aldermen.

And the mayor ſhall be clerk of the market, and ſhall exerciſe that office by himſelf or his ſufficient deputy.

And, finally, the mayor, aldermen, bailiffs, and citizens ſhall have ſuch and the like courtleet and view of frankpledge, and other courts, iſſues, fines, ranſoms, penalties, forfeitures, amerciaments, waifs, eſtrays, deodands, goods of felons and fugitives, felons de ſe, and perſons put in exigent and outlawed, and other emoluments, as former mayors, aldermen, bailiffs, and citizens have enjoyed, by whatever name of incorporation they were called or known.

This charter, comprehending all the reſt, was ſurrendered Aug. 7, 1684, to the lord chief juſtice Jeffreys, judge of aſſize, for the uſe of his Majeſty *. Which ſurrender being not inrolled, was therefore a void ſurrender; and this charter, like as many others, was reſtored and declared valid and effectual by proclamation of king James the ſecond a little before his abdication, viz. Oct. 17, 1688 †.

This city ſends two members to PARLIAMENT, who are choſen by the freemen of the city, reſident or non-reſident; who are now about 700.

On a diſpute in the houſe of commons, Feb. 11, 1711, it was declared, that the ſons of burgeſſes born after their father's freedom, and perſons ſerving ſeven years apprenticeſhip within the city, have a right to be made free ‡.

The ASSIZES for the county are held at this city by a ſpecial act of Parliament, 14 Hen. 6. c. 3. which enacts as follows: " Whereas by a ſtatute made in the time of king Richard the ſecond, it was ordained, that the juſtices aſſigned or to be aſſigned to take aſſizes and deliver gaols ſhall hold their ſeſſions in the principal and chief town of every county, that is to ſay, where the ſhire courts of the counties heretofore were and hereafter ſhall be holden; our lord the king, willing the ſame ſtatute to be obſerved and kept in the county of Cumberland, conſidering that the city of Carliſle is the principal and chief city and town of the ſaid county, and in which the ſhire court of the ſame county hath been holden before this time, hath granted and ordained by the

* Flem.   † Appendix, Nº 29.
‡ For a liſt of the burgeſſes, ſee the Appendix, Nº 36.

authority

authority of the same parliament, that the session of the justices to take assizes and to deliver gaols in the county of Cumberland, be holden in time of peace and truce in the said city of Carlisle, and in none other place within the same county, as it hath been used and accustomed of old time."

THE BISHOPRICK of Carlisle was founded by king Henry the first (as is aforesaid) in the 33d year of his reign; as the PRIORY had been before by the said king soon after his accession to the throne. And many grants have been made by the said king and his successors and others, to both the episcopal see and to the priory.

The said king *Henry* the first, before the foundation of the bishoprick, granted to the priory the churches of Newcastle upon Tyne and Newburne *, and the churches which Richard de Auriville his chaplain then held, after they should become vacant by the death of the said Richard de Auriville, which churches were those of Wertheord, Colebruge, Witingham, and Rodebery †.

The same king *Henry* the first granted to them also a fishery in Eden, and a mill upon the bridge there; as appears by a charter of confirmation by king Henry the second ‡.

The same king *Henry* the second confirms to them likewise the several grants following:

By the gift of the king of *Scotland*, a carucate of land with the appurtenances in *Hathetwisel.*

By the gift of *Waldieve* son of *Gospatric*, the church of *Espatric*, with a carucate of land there; a *mansion house* nigh the church of St. *Cuthbert* in Carlisle; also the church of *Crosseby* with a carucate of land there, and all the tithes and other things to the said church belonging as far as the water of *Alne*; and the chapel of St. *Nicholas* upon the sea, with the land adjoining thereunto.

By the gift of *Alan* son of *Waldieve*, *Little Crosseby* nigh *Scaddebothes*; and the church of *Yreby*, with a sixth part of the town of *Yreby.*

By the gift of *Waldeve* son of *Alan*, *Great Crosseby* with the appurtenances.

By the gift of *Radulph de Lindesey*, all the said *Radulph*'s lands in *Arthureth* and *Lerton*, with the mill, and all appurtenances to the said lands.

By the gift of *Gospatric* son of *Orme*, the church of *Caldebeck*, with the hospital there; and the lands which *Anulph* held of him nigh *Flemingby.*

By the gift of *Radulph Engaine* and his heirs, all *Henrickby*, with the mill, and other things pertaining to the said village.

By the gift of *William Engaine*, four *saltworks* between *Burgh* and *Drumbogh*, a moiety of his land in *Scadbothes*, and an house in *Carlisle.*

By the gift of *Hugh de Morvil*, two bovates of land in *Mebrune*, *viz.* 32 acres in the field there, with the meadow at the head of his corn land, and common of pasture for the goods of their tenants there, with the crofts which they had in the time of *Waldeve.*

* Appendix, N° 22.　　† Appendix, N° 23.

‡ Henricus, &c. Sciatis me concessisse et præsenti charta mea confirmasse Deo et ecclesiæ sanctæ Mariæ Karleol' et canonicis ibidem Deo servientibus, donationem quam Henricus avus meus eis fecit de piscaria una et molendino uno faciendo super ponte Hedene ubi voluerint in competente loco super terram suam, ita ut exclusa ab alia parte sit super terram meam.

I i 2　　　　　　　　　By

By the gift of *John Morvil* and his heirs, half a carucate of land in *Crekeſtot*, and four acres at *Tympaurin*.

By the gift of *Uchtred* and *Adam* his heir, *Fithvenni*, that is, the land which was in debate between *Boolton* and *Colleby*.

By the gift of *Ranulph* ſon of *Walter*, a carucate of land in *Stainton*; and two dwelling houſes given by *Ivo* ſon of *Forn* and *Agnes* his wife and *Walter* her father.

By the gift of *Theobald de Dacre*, lands in *Tympaurin*.

By the gift of *Gilbert Aclugh* and his heir, lands in *Tympaurin* and *Carliſle*.

By the gift of *Halth le Malchael* and *Eva* his wife, lands in *Crakenthorp*.

By the gift of *Humphrey Malchael*, one third part of the church of *Lowther*.

By the gift of *Adam Aculph*, the lands in *Tympaurin* which the canons poſſeſs by the donation of *Theobald* his grandfather and *Gilbert* his father and his mother *Gunild*.

By the gift of *Robert de Vaulx*, a carucate of land of his demeſne in *Hottone*, and common of paſture for the ſame, and alſo the church of *Hottone*.

By the gift of *William Dean* of *Carliſle*, three acres of land without the walls of *Carliſle*, and an houſe within the walls.

By the gift of *Adam* ſon of *Uchtred*, two bovates of land in *Tallentyre*.

Afterwards, king *Henry* the third granted to God and the church of St. Mary of Carliſle, and the reverend father Walter biſhop of Carliſle, the manor of *Dalſton*, with the advowſon of the church there, and that the ſaid manor of Dalſton ſhall be diſafforeſted, and held ſeparate from the king's foreſt of Englewood [*].

And by his charter bearing date 15 July, in the 15th year of his reign, the ſame king *Henry* the third grants to God and the church of St. Mary of Carliſle, and to the reverend father Walter biſhop of Carliſle and his ſucceſſors, and the prior and canons of the church of Carliſle ſerving God there, that they ſhall have, throughout all their lands and tenements, thol and theam, and infangtheif and outfangthief, and that they and all their men ſhall be free againſt the king and his officers from paſſage, pontage, leſtage, ſtallage, cariage, works of caſtles, houſes, walls, ditches, bridges, pavements, ponds, incloſures of parks, and all other works; and from ſuits of ſhires, wapentacks, hundreds, trithings, aids of ſheriffs, view of frankpledge, fines, amerciaments, juries, and aſſizes: And that they ſhall have the goods of felons and fugitives, amerciaments and forfeitures within their fees [†].

And by another charter bearing date Oct. 18, in the ſame year, the ſaid king grants to them, that their woods adjoining to their manors of Carleton and Briſcaihe, ſhall be free from waſtes, and regards, and aſſarts; and that they ſhall be free from eſcapes of beaſts in the foreſt, and from chiminage, and particularly that chiminage which is called foreſtage, and that they ſhall have liberty to chaſe the deer or game out of the foreſt of Dalſton into the king's foreſt, and take them there, and return without the hindrance of the foreſters [‡].

* Appendix, N° 24.   † Appendix, N° 25.   ‡ Appendix, N° 26.

King

King *Edward* the firft, by his charter bearing date 5 Dec. in the 22d year of his reign, reciting his having recovered before the juftices itinerant, againft the bifhop and prior and the parfon of Thurfby, the tithes of certain affart lands within the foreft of Englewood, as not being within the limits of any parifh, grants for the good of his foul and of the foul of his wife Eleanor of famous memory fometime queen confort, and the fouls of all his anceftors and fuc-ceffors, to God and the church of St. Mary of Carlifle and the prior and canons ferving God there, as well all tithes iffuing out of the affart lands aforefaid, as all other tithes of all lands and places within the faid foreft being without the limits of any parifh in time coming to be affarted *.

The fame king Edward the firft, in the 32d year of his reign, in confideration of the manifold grievances and oppreffions which the prior and convent had fuftained by the burning of their houfes and churches and divers depredations by the Scots, grants unto them the church of Adingham with the chapel of Salkeld to the fame annexed †, and alfo the church of Sourby ‡, to be appropriated to their own ufe.

This priory was furrendered to the crown in the 31 Hen. 8. which king, by his charter on the 8th of May in that year, in the place thereof, erected and incorporated the dean and chapter, by the name of The Dean and Chapter of the holy and undivided Trinity of Carlifle. And by his charter bearing date the fixth day of May, in the 33d year of his reign, the faid king grants unto them all thofe the manors of Newbiggin, New-laithes, Ellerton, Catcottys, Botchergate, Hofpital of St. Nicholas, Hen-derbye, Sebergham, Lorton, Ifakeby alias Prior hall, Newbiggin in Aller-dale, Crofby in Allerdale alias Crofby Canonby, Allerthwait, and Little Salkeld, in the county of Cumberland; and the manor of Corbridge in the county of Northumberland; together with poffeffions in 126 other different places by name: All late belonging to the priory of Carlifle. Alfo he grants to them (late belonging to the faid priory) the rectories and advowfons of the churches of St. Mary's and St. Cuthbert's in Carlifle, Sowreby, Adyngham, Kirkland, Thurefby, Beghokirke, Sebergham, Ireby, Canaby, Camerton, Hutton, Caftle Carrock, Cumwhitton, Cunrew, Edenhall, Rocliffe, a moiety of the rectory of Stanwix, and the rectories and churches of Whyttingham and Corbridge, and a moiety of the rectory of Newcaftle upon Tyne: Alfo penfions out of the following churches; Hakemonby 2s 6d. Hutton in the Foreft 2s. Ullerby 6s 8d. Caftlecarrock 2s. Aketon 40s. Thurfby 13s 4d. Bewcaftle 6s 8d. Whittingham 8l. Lowther 26s 8d. Alfo the advowfons and donations of all the chantries of St. Catherine, St. Crofs, and St. Roch in the cathedral church of Carlifle, and St. Alban in the city of Carlifle, and of St. Mary of Skelton. He grants to them alfo all the revenues of the priory of Wetheral. Paying to the crown for the whole 82l 11s 9¼d yearly by way of tenths; and referving to be paid by them, 3s per annum to the chantry of the hofpital of St. Catherine in Caftlegate, 46s 8d to the chaplain of the hofpital of St. Nicholas, and 5l 17s to three poor bedefmen there, 2s 4d a fubfidy to the bifhop, 6l to the curate of St. Mary's Carlifle, 6s 8d to two priefts to hear

* Appendix, N° 27.   † Vid. Addingham.   ‡ Vid. Sourby.

confeffions

confeſſions in the ſame church, 4 *l* to the chaplain of the chapel of St. Mary of Haſcott, 20 *s* for a compoſition to the vicar of Layzonby, 5 *l* 6 *s* 8 *d* to the curate of St. Cuthbert's Carliſle, 2 *s* 10¼ *d* to the biſhop for a ſubſidy of the churches of Sowreby and Adyngham, 4 *s* to the biſhop for ſynodals, 13 *s* 4 *d* to the vicar of Adyngham, 6 *s* 8 *d* to the vicar of Kirkland by compoſition, 53 *s* 4 *d* to the vicar of Edenhall, 8 *l* to the biſhop of Durham out of the moiety of the rectory of Newcaſtle, 8 *l* out of the rectory of Whittingham, and 12 *l* to the biſhop of Durham out of the rectory of Corbridge, and except the fee of 3 *l* to the collector of the rents of the late priory or cell of Wetheral.

King Philip and queen Mary, by their charter bearing date 7th March in the 4th and 5th years of their reign, granted to the biſhop the advowſon and collation of all the four prebends.

The ſame queen, by the advice of cardinal Pole, intended to give the advowſons that then remained in the crown which had belonged to the religious houſes, to the ſeveral biſhops within their reſpective dioceſes ; and accordingly there is a grant by Philip and Mary to the biſhop of Carliſle of the ſeveral advowſons of Bampton, Croſby, and Overton in the county of Weſtmorland, and Burgh, Kirkoſwald, and Dacre in Cumberland (together with divers others in Cumberland, which, by miſtake, are ſet forth to be in the dioceſe of Carliſle, but are in reality in the dioceſe of Cheſter). But the queen ſeems to have died before this grant was carried into full execution. It bears date 14 Nov. 5 and 6 P. and M. and ſhe died three days after, *viz.* on the 17th of the ſame month.

In this city there are two *pariſh churches*. The firſt and more ancient is that of St. CUTHBERT, founded in honour of that holy man, who was made biſhop of Durham in 685 ; in whoſe dioceſe Carliſle then was. When the ſteeple of this church was rebuilt in the time of queen Elizabeth, there was found a large parcel of ſmall ſilver coins to the quantity of near a Wincheſter buſhel, called St. Cuthbert's pence ; ſuch as that biſhop and ſome of his ſucceſſors biſhops of Durham had a privilege to coin ; and which were ſuppoſed to have been oblations at the building.

This pariſh conſiſts of Botchardgate within the city ; and without the city, of the ſeveral diviſions of Botchardgate, Carleton, Briſco, Uprightby, Harraby, and Bleckhill. It conſiſts of 364 families : And hath received divers augmentations from queen Anne's bounty both by lot and in conjunction with the ſubſcriptions of the pariſhioners and others, wherewith lands have been purchaſed in the neighbourhood, to the value of about 40 *l* a year.

All the ſaid diviſions without the city (except Bleckhill) are parts and parcels of the manor of Botchardgate or Prior lordſhip (as it is called) belonging to the dean and chapter ; only the houſe of Crofton have ſeveral tenants at Briſco and thereabouts, and during the time of the uſurpation they were lords of the whole, and the cuſtoms were ſettled during that period.

Blackhill, at the time of the Norman conqueſt, was barren ground, and ſo received the name of *Blackhill*. King Hen. 1. gave it to Odard de Logis, baron of Wigton and citizen of Carliſle ; who held part of it in demeſne, and

granted

granted the reft in fervices. It defcended in his iffue male until the time of Ed. 3. when Margaret de Wigton fole daughter and heir of John de Wigton knight (laft iffue male of that houfe) fo defend her birthright was glad to give away this manor, together with Melmerby and Stainton, to Robert Parving then the king's ferjeant at law, againft Sir Richard Kirkbride the heir male. It continued in the Parvings for fome few defcents, and then came to heirs female; by whom it was fold to William Stapleton and Matilda his wife, of whom the lord Dacre purchafed.

Sir Richard Flenes, chamberlain to king Ed. 4. having married Joan daughter and fole heir of Thomas lord Dacre of the north, and being accepted and declared lord Dacre of the fouth and baron of the realm in the 37 Hen. 6. became proprietor not only of this manor, but likewife of Kirk Ofwald, Baron-wood, Dacre, Martindale foreft, and other places; all which were fold in the year 1716, for the fum of 15,000*l*, to Sir Chriftopher Mufgrave baronet father of Sir Philip Mufgrave the prefent owner, by the ladies Barbara and Anne daughters and coheirs of Thomas earl of Suffex fon of Francis lord Dacre.

In the year 1698, Thomas earl of Suffex, in confideration of 36 years ancient finable rent, granted to the tenants (48 in number) a difcharge from fines and dry multure, with the wood upon their tenements, but referving the ancient rent, fuit of court, moor farm and greenhue; with liberty to alienate their tenements without licence of the lord, giving notice thereof within 40 days; paying only a penny fine on death or alienation, and to the fteward for an alienation 4 *d*, and for furrender and copy thereof 6 *d*, and inrollment 4 *d*, and 2 *d* to the bailiff upon every defcent or alienation.—And about the fame time the common was divided and granted in fee to the tenants without any rent referved, the lord having 150 acres for his fhare in land, which is now called Blackhill park, and is the inheritance of Mrs. Wardale of Carlifle.

The parifh of St. MARY's confifts of the feveral divifions within the city of Scotchgate, Fifhergate, Caftlegate, and Abbey gate; and without the city, of the feveral divifions of Caldewgate, Cumberfdale, Richardgate, and Wreay; and contains in the whole about 193 familes.

Scotchgate divifion is within that which is called the manor of the focage of Carlifle; which manor, by virtue of a commiffion under the feal of the exchequer, bearing date Nov. 21, 1610, and directed to the commiffioners Sir William Hutton and Sir Chriftopher Pickering knights, Aaron Rathborne and Lancelot Skelton efquires, Andrew Oglethorpe and Henry Baines gentlemen, was defcribed and certified as follows : " Beginning on the fouth fide of the river Eden over againft Etterby, and there leaving the fame river it extendeth fouthwards by Wearnholme unto Dowbeck fike, the lands on the right hand being the inheritance of Mr. Brifcowe; from thence it extendeth eaftward againft Bifhops lands to the river of Caldew at Caldew bridge; where croffing over the fame bridge againft Caldewgate, it extendeth up the river againft the abbey lands and Denton Holme, until it cometh to a parcel of Denton Holme lying on the weft fide of Caldew containing about nine

4 acres

acres of land, where it leaveth the river and inclofeth the fame parcel of land
on the weft fide thereof on the river-fide againft the fouth weft corner of
Walk miln clofes; and fo croffing over the river, and leaving the fame, it
extendeth fouthwards towards Curreck by the weft fide of the fields of
Blacall, Curreck, and Uprightby; and fo about the fame fields to a crofs
way at the weft end of Uprightby town; and fo fouthwards by the highway,
to Cruny beck which falleth into the river of Pettrell; and there leaving the
fame way, it extendeth down the fame beck to Pettrell; and from it turneth
northwards down the fame river to the fouth eaft corner of Paradife, where
croffing the river and leaving it, it goeth down a fmall miln water on the
fouth fide of Paradife, and inclofeth the fame at Gallows bridge; from whence
croffing over the highway, it inclofeth part of the Spittle Crook lying on the
fouth-eaft fide of Pettrell; and fo extendeth ftill down Pettrell to the foot
thereof, where the fame falleth into Eden; from thence up, over the faid
river of Eden, to the foot of a beck falling thereinto againft Kinnyholme,
and fo up the fame beck on the weft fide of Richardby to the-north-eaft corner
of Stanwix grounds; then leaving the fame beck, it extendeth northweft-
wards to the highway leading from Carlifle to Tirraby; and fo croffing over
the.fame way, it paffeth on the north fide of Horfemanfield to the north-weft
corner thereof, and from thence extendeth fouthwards to a highway dividing
Horfemanfield and the weft part of Stanwix; and fo croffing the fame way, it
extendeth on the weft fide of Stanwix to the river of Eden, and from thence
down the fame river to Etterby where it firft began."

The body of St. Mary's church, which is the cathedral, was before the
civil wars in 1641 a fpacious building, comprehending all the weftern part of
the church from the great tower, and extending in length 135 feet. But this
being deemed fuperfluous by the fanatical reformers, was in a great meafure
demolifhed, as the cloifters and chapter houfe were afterwards, and the materials applied to build a guard houfe at every gate, erecting two batteries in
the caftle, and a main guard-houfe in the market place.

.   The eaftern part of the cathedral or quire is faid to have been built by contributions in the reign of king Edward the third. And there are about that
time in the bifhop's regifters many letters patent or orders granted by the
bifhops, recommending to the clergy of the feveral parifhes fuch proctors as
the chapter thought fit to appoint from time to time, with a command to
publifh an indulgence of forty days penance to fuch of the laity as fhould
generoufly contribute towards the charge of the faid building. The door with
the work about it near the bifhop's throne was the work of prior Haythwaite
about the year 1480, his name having been on the backfide of it. And the
oppofite door with the workmanfhip about it feems to have been erected by
prior Senhoufe about the year 1500, his known adage having been upon it of
Vulnera qu nque Dei, fint medicina mei. The whole dimenfions of this fabrick,
before part of it was deftroyed as aforefaid, were as follows: The quire, on
the eaft of the crofs ifle, in length 137 feet; the crofs ifle 28 feet; on the
weft of the crofs ifle 43 feet; which when the intire weftern part was ftanding,
before the civil wars when 92 feet were deftroyed, made the whole fabrick 300

feet

feet in length. The breadth of the choir and ifles is 71 feet, and of the great north ifle from-north to fouth 124 feet. The height of the choir to the center of the ceiling is 75 feet, and of the tower 127 feet, which had a fpiré of lead upon it of 13 or 14 feet, before the fame was taken down to the fquare tower foon after the reftoration, it having for want of care in the preceding times of confufion become ruinous. The weftern part is a Normanic Saxon ftructure. But the choir is a noble and exact piece of Gothic architecture. It has a ftately eaft window of 48 feet in height, and 30 in breadth, and is adorned with pillars of moft curious workmanfhip. The roof was elegantly vaulted with wood, and embellifhed with the coats of arms of all the founders and contributors. But this failing by length of time, together with the lead roof, the dean and chapter fome few years ago new laid the roof; and the ceiling being totally ruined and deftroyed, they in the year 1764 contracted for a ftucco groined ceiling, and for cleaning and whitening the whole church. And finding the new lead much torn and broken by wind, for want of a ceiling underneath, the upper tire of that was done again, and a coping added to the rigging. And thus proceeding from one repair to another, the whole expence hath amounted to upwards of 1300*l*; towards which, dean Bolton contributed 50*l*, bifhop Lyttelton 100*l*, and the countefs dowager Gower 200*l*. The reft was made up by the dean and chapter from fales of wood and from their own revenues.

Within this church of St. Mary's, was a *chapel* dedicated to St. *Catherine*, founded by John de Capella citizen of Carlifle, and endowed by him with certain rents, lands, and burgage houfes; fome of which being detained and concealed, bifhop Appleby in the year 1366 required the chaplains of St. Mary's and St. Cuthbert's to give public notice that reftitution be made within ten days, and at the end of the faid ten days to excommunicate with bell, book, and candle all fuch unjuft detainers.—In this chapel bifhop Barrow was buried, which was at the fouth fide of the cathedral.

Bifhop *Whelpdale*, who died in 1423, gave by his will 200*l*, for founding and endowing a *chantry* in this cathedral for praying for the fouls of Sir Thomas Skelton knight and Mr. John Glafton both of this diocefe.—This perhaps might be what was called the chantry of *St. Roch*, endowed with feveral burgage houfes in the city of Carlifle.

Within this city of Carlifle was alfo a *free chapel* dedicated to *St. Alban*; concerning which there is an entry in bifhop Welton's regifter in the year 1356, that the bifhop being informed that divine fervice was frequently had in the chapel of St. Alban's, and the dead buried in the yard of the faid chapel, he therefore iffues a commiffion to the prior of St. Mary's and others, to inquire by men of credit as well clerks as laymen, whether both or either of thefe had ever been confecrated. And it appearing that they were not, the chaplains of St. Mary's and St. Cuthbert's are commanded to give public notice that none hereafter prefume to read or hear divine fervice in the faid chapel, on pain of suspension in the reader, and excommunication in the hearers.—After the dissolution of the chantries and free chapels, king Ed. 6. by letters patent bearing date the 30th of January in the 3d year of his reign, grants to Thomas Dalston esquire and William Denton gentleman, the chantry of St. Alban in the city of Carlisle, and all those messuages, tenements, burgage houses, buildings, shops, curtilages, and hereditaments whatsoever, with the appurtenances, in the tenure of John Thompson, Robert Monke, Robert Patten, Robert Pattenson, Anthony Rumpnay, Henry Mawson, John Slayter, John Dunken, Cuthbert Pattenson, Elizabeth Young, John Cardall, Elizabeth Barnefadere, Alice Stephenson, and Nicholas Studdard, in the city of Carlisle, to the said chantry of St. Alban belonging,

There was also a chantry of *St. Cross*; as appears by a grant of king Ed. 6. bearing date March 28, in the third year of his reign, whereby (amongst other particulars) he grants to Henry Tanner and Thomas Bucher, their heirs and assigns, the chantry of *St. Cross* in the cathedral church of Carlisle, with all messuages, lands, tenements, profits, and hereditaments whatsoever, in the city of Carlisle and in Kirklinton to the said chantry belonging.

Without the gates of the city, was the hospital of *St. Nicholas:* which was of royal foundation (but by which of the kings we have not found) for thirteen lepers, men and women.

In the time of bishop Bernard, about the year 1180, a moiety of the tithes of Little Bampton was given to this hospital by Adam son of Robert, on condition to have always two almsmen from the parish of Bampton.

In the year 1336, Thomas de Goldyngton, then master of the hospital, brought a prohibition against the bishop who was about to visit this house, on a suggestion that it was a royal foundation, and therefore only visitable by the king's chancellor or commissioners: And in 1341, the said bishop, with Robert Eglesfeld rector of Burgh and others, was commissioned by the king to visit this hospital.

In 1371, on complaint made by the master, brethren, and sisters of the hospital of St. Nicholas, that the house was defrauded of a great part of their necessary sustenance, the bishop issues out a monition to all rectors and vicars in the neighbouring parts, requiring them to give notice to their parishioners, that all such detainers of threaves of corn or other goods belonging to the said hospital, shall make full payment or restitution within the space of ten days, on pain of the greater excommunication.

In the year 1477, 17 Ed. 4. this hospital and the revenues thereof were given to the prior and convent of St. Mary's Carlisle, which priory was afterwards given to the dean and chapter. The site of the hospital is now holden of the dean and chapter by Mr. John Stordy on a lease for 21 years; and Mr. John Lyddel, on a like lease, holds the moiety of the tithes of Little Bampton.

The chapel of *Wrea*, in the parish of St. Cuthbert, is as ancient, at least, as the reign of king Edward the second; for in the year 1319. bishop Halton
allowed

allowed a chaplain to it, to attend divine offices, on condition that he conftantly refided upon the place. The chapelry confifts of the villages of *Wrea* of 20 families, and *Newbiggin* (a grange belonging to the dean and chapter) of 6 or 7 families, with fome other fcattered houfes. The late Dr. Bolton dean of Carlifle, having procured fome money for augmentations, gave 200*l* to this chapel, and the governors of queen Anne's bounty gave other 200*l*, wherewith an eftate was purchafed; and bifhop Fleming confecrated the chapel, in the year 1739. The revenue or falary is now about 20*l per annum*, and the curate hath a good houfe at Petrel Crooks, being part of the purchafed eftate. In the act of confecration, the nomination of the curate is referved to the dean and chapter; neverthelefs the curates, as appears from the bifhop's archives, have been appointed by the 12 men or felect veftry; as,

1728. Philip Robinfon.
1731. David Graham.
1733. John Parker.
1738. Jofeph Parker, the prefent curate.

Hiftory of the Bifhops of Carlifle.

THAT which is now the diocefe of Carlifle, was heretofore part of the diocefe of *Lindisfarne*, from whence the fee was removed to *Chefter on the Street*, and afterwards to *Durham*; and by reafon of the diftance of Carlifle from the epifcopal fee, king Henry the firft, in the year 1133, founded this bifhoprick of *Carlifle*, and beftowed it upon *Athelwald* (or *Adelulph*) then prior of Carlifle, who was alfo prior of St. Ofwald's in Yorkfhire, the king's confeffor.

1. ADELULPH, firft bifhop of Carlifle, appears as a witnefs to a charter of king Stephen, in 1136. He was one of the electors of Henry Murdac abbot of Fountains to the archbifhoprick of York, and notwithftanding king Stephen's denunciation of wrath againft all that primate's adherents, received him as his metropolitan when he came to vifit David king of Scots then refiding at Carlifle†.

Though fome learned perfons have affirmed, that before the ftatute of mortmain 7 Ed. 1. impropriations were very rare in England; yet this bifhop *Adelulph*, or *Athelwald* (as he is now called), who died above 100 years before the enacting of that law, confirmed the churches of Wetheral and Warwick, St. Michael and St. Laurence Appleby, Kirkby Stephen, Ormefhead, Morland, Clibburn, Bromfield, Croglyn, and the hermitage of St. Andrew in the parifh of Kirkland, to the abbot and convent of St. Mary's York, with this fingle provifo, that the faid abbot and convent fhould allow fuch a portion to the officiating minifter, as thereby he may be decently maintained, and be able to pay his fynodals ‡.

This bifhop died in 1155.

† Pryn. v. 1. p. 521.　　　　‡ Regiftr. Wetheral.

2. BER-

2. BERNARD.—The church of St. Mary Magdalen of Lanercoft, was dedicated by bifhop Bernard in the year 1169, being the 12th of his pontificate † ; and he died in 1186. After whofe death, it was a long time before the fee was regularly fupplied. King Hen. 2. being then at Carlifle, offered the vacant bifhoprick to one Paulinus de Leedes, who refufed it, notwith-ftanding that the king promifed, upon his acceptance of it, to augment the revenues by an acceffion of 300 marks rent out of the churches of Bambrough and Scarborough, with the chapel of Tickhill, together with two of his own manors which lay near that city ‡.

In 1188, the temporalties continuing in the king's hand, the following particulars amongft others were brought into account at the treafury : For oil for the facrament at Eafter two terms and carrying the fame from London to Carlifle 14 l. In work of the greater altar and pavement in the church of St. Mary Carlifle 27 s 9 d. In work of the dormitory of the canons 22 l 19 s 2 d.

In 1200, king John granted this bifhoprick to the archbifhop of Sclavonia, to fupport him for the prefent.

In 1203, the fame king confirms a grant from the pope of the vacant bifhoprick of Carlifle to the archbifhop of Ragufa, who was forced to abandon his own fee, and had not wherewithal to fupport himfelf.

In the firft year of king Henry the third, the canons of Carlifle (fays Prynne) contemning both the pope's and his legate's authority and cenfures, contumacioufly celebrating divine fervice and facraments, notwithftanding their interdicts ; adhering, fubmitting, and fwearing fealty to the king of Scots, king Henry's and the pope's declared enemy ; yea electing an interdicted and excommunicated clerk for their bifhop againft the king's and the legate's will ; and dividing the ancient revenues of the bifhoprick amongft themfelves : the young king's council, thereupon fent this epiftle to the pope Honorius the third in the king's name, totally to remove thefe fchifmatical canons, and place prebends in their rooms, to augment the bifhop's revenues, (being fo fmall, that no able and loyal perfon would accept thereof), and to difplace the obtruded bifhop : " Reverendo domino ac patri in Chrifto chariffimo Honorio Dei gratia fummo pontifici, Henricus eadem gratia rex Angliæ, &c. falutem et debitam cum omni honore et fubjectione reverentiam. Noverit fancta paternitas veftra, quod canonici Carleolenfis ecclefiæ, faventes et adhærentes regi Scotiæ et aliis adverfariis et inimicis veftris et noftris ; procurantes quantum in ipfis eft exhæredationem noftram, fpreta penitus authoritate veftra et fedis apoftolicæ legati ; in locis interdictis et excommunicatis, irreverenter et impudenter et contumaciter divina celebrare non verentes ; prædicto etiam regi Scotiæ, inimico Romanæ ecclefiæ et noftro, interdicto et excommunicato, urbem Carliolenfem hoftiliter occupanti, feipfos fubdiderunt, et ipfum in patronum et dominum receperunt, et fidelitatem ei fecerunt. Ita etiam quod in præjudicium juris noftri ac ecclefiæ Eboracenfis, ad inftantiam dicti regis Scotiæ inimici noftri, quendam clericum fuum interdictum et

† 2 Dugd. Mon. 130.   ‡ Regiftr. Wetheral.

excom-

excommunicatum elegerunt fibi in epifcopum et paftorem. Cum etiam præ-dicta ecclefia Carliolenfis fita fit in confinio regni Scotiæ, maxime expediret tranquilitati et paci noftræ et regni noftri, quod tale ibi conftitueretur caput, et talia membra, per quos nobis et regno noftro utiliter et efficaciter provideri, et adverfariis noftris facultas nocendi poffit recludi; paternitati veftræ devote fupplicamus, quatenus confulentes nobis et regno noftro ftatum ecclefiæ præ-dictæ in melius commutare. velitis, amoveatis (fi placet) funditus ab eadem prædictos febifinaticos et excommunicatos. Cum enim ipfi in multis abun-dent, epifcopus ita hactenus egeftate afflictus eft et inopia, quod vix habet ubi caput fuum reclinet, et non invenitur aliquis qui in aliquo nobis utilis effe poterit aut neceffarius, qui epifcopatum illum recipere voluerit. Scientes pro certo, quod non poterit nobis melius provideri in partibus illis, prout de confilio fidelium et magnatum noftrorum evidenter intelleximus, quam fi prædicti fchifmatici et excommunicati penitus amoveantur, et loco eorum qui dicuntur regulares (cum fint prorfus irregulares et ecclefiæ Romanæ inimici et inobedientes) conftituantur præbendarii, qui Romanæ ecclefiæ obedientes, et nobis et concilio fint prudentes et in auxilio efficaces; ut eorum pœna a confi-mili delicto alios deterreat : Et fuper. his voluntatem veftram chariffimo amico noftro domino legato fignificare velitis. Et quia nondum habuimus figillum, has literas figillo comitis Willielmi Marefcalli rectoris noftri et regni noftri figillavimus. Tefte eodem comite apud Wynton 26 die Aprilis."—Upon which letter, the pope ordered Gualo his legate, by the king's royal affent, to conftitute Hugh abbot of Belieu bifhop of Carlifle†.

The chapter in the mean time were but in a forry fituation, which the Chro-nicle of Lanercoft thus defcribes :—The canons of Carlifle were banifhed by Gualo the legate, becaufe through fear of death they had performed divine-fervice to the excommunicated king of Scotland.

3. Hugh. By two records in 1218, tranfcribed by Mr. Prynne, it appears that this bifhop Hugh was abbot of Belieu, and promoted to this fee by car-dinal Gualo the pope's legate; yet king Hen. 3. acknowledges him to be *fidelis nofter, cui multo tenemur debito*; *ac fanctæ Romanæ ecclefiæ devotiffimus*: and hereupon begs the pope's affiftance in getting the rectories of Penrith, Newcaftle, Rothbury, Corbridge, and Whittingham reftored to him. The former of thefe is a letter to the pope dated Feb. 17; and the other a letter to the cardinal dated the 24th of January following ‡.

In fome of this bifhop's grants made to the abbot and convent of St. Mary's York, in or about the year 1220, he ftyles himfelf Hugo Dei gratia Karleo-lenfis ecclefiæ vocatus facerdos ‡.

In the fame year, he granted the impropriations of the churches of Kirkby Stephen and Morland; the former to the ufes of the abbot and convent of St. Mary's York, and the latter to the monks of Wetheral‡. And about the fame time he ordered the prior and convent of Lanercoft to quit a referved

† 1 Rymer, 219.　　‡ Pryn. v. 2. p. 375.　　‡ Regiftr. Wetheral.

7

rent

rent out of the church of Burgh by Sands, as not having been canonically obtained [†].

This bishop was one of the sureties of king Hen. 3. for the performance of that memorable accord now made with Alexander the second, king of Scotland, who was to marry one or other of the king's sisters [‡].

The author of the Chronicle of Lanercost seems to have been no friend to this bishop. He says, Hugh bishop of Carlisle, who alienated the possessions of the see, and made a fraudulent division thereof, returning from the Roman court, by the just judgment of God perished miserably, at the abbey of *la Ferte* in the parts of Burgundy.

4. WALTER MALCLERK, (so called from his deficiency in learning,) was about Ascension day in 1223 consecrated bishop of Carlisle, by Walter Grey archbishop of York and lord chancellor; and on the 26th of October following the king confirmed the election, and restored to him the temporalties [‡].

A year or two before this, the order of Dominicans (or Friers predicants) came first into England; and this bishop was one of their most early and most generous benefactors, giving them a considerable plot of ground in the Old Jewry, and two mills without the south gate at Oxford [*].

Before his promotion to the see of Carlisle, king John (whose great favourite he was) had employed him as his ambassador at Rome, on the contest with his barons [§].

In 1230, king Hen. 3. granted to this bishop and his successors the manor of Dalston, in a more full and ample form than was usual in that age [‖].

In 1232, king Hen. 3. in the 6th year of his reign, by his charter granted the treasury of his exchequer of England to Walter Mauclerk bishop of Carlisle, to hold during his life; with all the liberties and appurtenances to the said treasury belonging: so that he should have and keep the said treasury at the king's exchequer in his own person, or by a discreet and sufficient deputy, which deputy should be sworn to serve faithfully in his office; and if such deputy should die, or become professed of religion, or for reasonable cause should be removed by the king or the treasurer, or should himself be unwilling to serve any longer, then the said treasurer should substitute some other discreet and fit person to serve in the room of such deputy; and the person so substituted was to be likewise sworn to serve faithfully. The next year the king, at the instigation of Peter bishop of Winchester his chief justiciar, and to make way for strangers of Poictiers, removed most of his court officers, and among the rest turned this bishop out of his office of high treasurer in a disgraceful manner, fining him 100*l*, and cancelling several grants which he had made to him for life, and by patent committed the treasury of his exchequer with the appurtenances to Peter de Rivall, to hold during the king's pleasure. And Walter was commanded to deliver by view and testimony of

---

† Regiſtr. Holm.   ‡ 1 Rymer, 240.   ‡ Matt. Paris, 317.   * Hiſt. and Antiq. Oxon. b. 1. p. 63.   § Pryn. v. 3. p. 29.   ‖ Appendix, N°. 24.

true men the keys of the treafury and all things belonging to it by inventory to Peter de Rivall or to Robert Paffelowe his attorney nominated by him for that purpofe before the king. Afterwards the king commanded S. de Segrave his jufticiar to give poffeffion of the treafury to the faid Peter or Robert his attorney, in cafe the bifhop of Carlifle refufed to deliver it †.

The late treafurer feems to have intended to go to Rome for redrefs, and got as far as Dover, where he put himfelf on board a fhip ; but prefently fome of the king's officers brought both him and his effects on fhore again, requiring him not to depart the kingdom, without the king's fpecial licence in that behalf firft obtained. The bifhop of London happening to arrive there from Rome at that inftant, and being an eye-witnefs to the outrages done to his brother prelate, immediately excommunicated all the affailants ; and pofting thence to the king at Hereford, renewed his fentence, and was there feconded by all the bifhops then prefent at court ‡.

In 1234, the king again received bifhop Walter into favour ‡.

And in the next year, at the inftance of the faid bifhop, king Henry was affianced to the earl of Winchefter's fair daughter ; but the match was broken off for certain reafons of ftate. She was afterwards married to Alphonfus king of Caftile ‖.

In 1236, he was one of the witneffes to the king's ratification of the great charter, the king being then arrived to the age of 21 years* ; and to the duke of Brabant's engagement to conduct the princefs Ifabella (the king's fifter) to her hufband the emperor §.

In 1239, he was appointed catechift to prince Edward.

In 1243, king Henry being beyond the feas, conftituted the archbifhop of York, the bifhop of Carlifle, and William de Cantilupe, lords juftices of the realm in his abfence, to whom he gave feveral authentic inftructions for the preventing of innovations and incroachments upon the ancient laws of the land. In one of thefe they are particularly directed to reftrain the prior and convent of Canterbury from the exercife of archiepifcopal authority (*fede vacante*) over the fuffragan bifhops of that province, and this upon folemn complaint of the faid bifhops themfelves, alledging that fuch an ufurpation was not only a great injury to themfelves, but in manifeft prejudice of the royal dignity †*.

In 1244, he had the wardfhip of Walter fon of Odard de Wigton (a child of two months) granted to him by the king ; and with him the manors of Wigton, Melmerby, Stainton on Eden, Blackhill, and Warwick.

In 1245, that this bifhop might make his will, and therein difpofe of his goods and chattels, he procured the following royal difpenfation, according to the cuftom of thofe times : " Rex omnibus, &c. falutem. Sciatis quod tefta-mientum, quod W. Karliolenfis epifcopus condidit, vel conditurus eft, quo-cunque tempore et quocunque loco, tam de bladis in terra, quam de wardis et firmis, et omnibus fuis mobilibus, pro nobis et hæredibus noftris gratum

---

† Madox Exch. 563. ‡ Matt. Paris. 384. 387. ‡ Chron. Lanerc.
‖ Matt Paris. 417. *3 Prynne, 94. § 1 Rymer, 361. †* 1 Rymer,
400.

habemus.

habemus et acceptum, et illud concedimus et confirmamus; prohibentes ne aliquis balli vus noster vel hæredum noftrorum quæ idem epifcopus reliquerit ad executionem teftamenti fui faciendam manum mittat, vel in aliquo fe inde intromittat, vel aliquo modo teftamentum illud impediat; quia tam teftamentum fuum, quam executores teftamenti fui cepimus in protectionem et defenfionem noftram et hæredum noftrorum. In cujus rei, &c. Tefte rege apud Wind' 5 Julii **.

In this fame year, the pope granted to the bifhops of Scotland (jealous of falling under the archbifhop of York's jurifdiction) that none of his delegates fhould call any of their caufes farther than the cities and diocefes of Durham or Carlifle ‡‡.

The annals of Waverley give this farther account of him: In the year of our lord 1246, Walter bifhop of Carlifle, divinely infpired (as it is believed), refigning his bifhoprick, betook himfelf to the order of friers predicant at Oxford; and having done many memorable things in buildings and other matters, he died at Oxford on the 28th of October 1248.

'5. SYLVESTER DE EVERDON; archdeacon of Chefter, was confirmed bifhop of Carlifle on the ninth of November 1246, and had reftitution of the temporalties on the 8th of December following.

In 1247, this bifhop, by an inftrument fealed at London, confirms the grants of his predeceffors of the churches of St Michael and St. Laurence in Appleby, Kirkby Stephen, and Morland, to the abbot and convent of St. Mary's York *. And in the next year, the faid abbot and convent made a grant to the bifhop and h's fucceffors of the perpetual advowfon of the vicarage of St. Michael's, taxed at 20 marks †.

In the fine rolls, 32 H. 3 are the following pleas: Between Silvefter bifhop of Carlifle and William Huntecomb for 20 l land and rent in Tynton, Maringes, and Horncaftle; and between the fame bifhop and John de Leweby‖ for 20 l land and rent in Enderby, Wilhiby, and Caningeby, and the advowfon of the church of Morefby; as the right of his fee and church of Carlifle. And he granted to the faid William and John the homage and fervices of Ivo fon of Odo in Tymleby for the eighth part of one knight's fee: and their freemen were to do fuit of court to the bifhop and his fucceffors at Horncaftle at two law days after the feaft of St. Michael and Eafter, and at other times upon reafonable fummons when judgment is to be given on a plea moved by the king's writ, or a felon is to be tried in the fame court.

In 1253, this bifhop, with the archbifhop of Canterbury and others, oppofed the king's incroachments upon the liberties of the church; particularly in the freedom of electing bifhops. The fharp return which the king made to this bifhop is very remarkable, " Et te, Silvefter Carleolenfis, qui diu lam" bens cancellariam clericorum meorum clericulus extitifti, qualiter poftpofitis " multis theologis et perfonis reverendis te in epifcopatum fublegavi ‡."

_____

** Pryn. v. 2. p. 636.   †† 1 Rymer, 438.   * Regiftr. Wetheral.   † Ibid.
‡ Pryn. v. 2. p. 795.

Bifhop

Bifhop Silvefter's fuit with one of the great barons (Michael de Harcla, as it feemeth) and his procurement thereupon of the king's protection, is advantageoufly reported by Matthew Paris ‖.

About this time the bifhop of Rochefter petitioned the pope.for an enlargement of his revenues, fetting forth that his bifhoprick was of all the bifhopricks in England the pooreft, and was exceeded even by that of Carlifle §.

Silvefter Karleolenfis is one of the bifhops that, at the requeft and in the prefence of king Henry the third, folemnly excommunicated and curfed with bell, book, and candle, the infringers of the liberties of England +.

In 1255 this bifhop died by a fall from his horfe. It is faid, that the feal which he made ufe of in all publick inftruments had on one fide a bifhop cloathed in his pontificals, and on the reverfe the figure of the bleffed virgin with our Saviour in her arms, with this motto around, according to the barbarous latin of thofe times, " Te rogo, virgo Dei, Sis vigil erga mei."

. 6. THOMAS VIPONT, or *de Veteriponte,* of the illuftrious family of the then lords of Weftmorland. On the 5th of November 1255 the king confirms the election of the bifhop, and on the 24th of December following, reftores the temporalties, requiring Robert de Dacre (cuftos of the vacant fee) to refign up his charge. This bifhop died in October following. When the bifhop of Durham fequeftring all the benefices of the faid deceafed prelate within his diocefe, and the guardian of the vacant bifhoprick of Carlifle (Walter de Rudham) endeavouring to fue out an inhibition for the removal of the faid fequeftration, the king iffued his royal writ to the guardian, commanding him to let all things continue in the ftate they then were, till the day he had appointed to hear and determine the matter. Afterwards the bifhop of Durham had a day affigned him.in the king's court, to fhew what right he had or pretended to have to the fequeftration of the benefices belonging to the bifhoprick of Carlifle during the vacancy in the king's hand. At length it feems the king was fatisfied of the juftnefs of the faid bifhop's claim ; and therefore he commanded not only the prefent profits, but thofe alfo of a former vacancy to be delivered to him. This writ was in the following form : " Rex abbati de Novo Monafterio [Newminfter near Morpeth], falutem. Quia de confilio magnatum qui funt de concilio noftro recognovimus et redidimus pro nobis et hæredibus noftris Deo et beato Cuthberto et venerabili patri Waltero Dunelmenfi epifcopo et fucceforibus fuis et ecclefiæ fuæ Dunelmenfi, ut jus dictorum epifcopi et ecclefiæ fuæ, fequeftrum ecclefiarum quas epifcopus Karliolenfis et ecclefia fua habent ufibus fuis propriis in epifcopatu Dunelmenfi affignatum. De quo quidem fequeftro toram pecuniam provenientem de duabus vacationibus epifcopatus Karleolenfis proxime præteritis, de confilio prædictorum magnatum per manus vicecomitis Northumbriæ et Johannis de Eftlington ex parte noftri et per alios duos ex parte prædicti epifcopi colligi præcepimus, et in abbatia veftra fub figillis prædictorum quatuor refervari, donec inter nos et ipfum difcuteretur

‖ M. Paris, 784.　　§ Pryn. v 2. p. 766.　　+ Ann. Burt. p. 223.

ad quem noftrum pertinere deberet fequeftrum prædictum ; vobis mandamus, quatenus totam prædictam pecuniam de fequeftro prædicto provenientem et in abbatia veftra depofitam prædicto epifcopo vel ejus certo nuncio fine dilatione deliberari faciatis. In cujus, &c. Tefte rege apud Weftm' *."

Another fort of claim was alfo fet up by the bifhop of Glafgow. For we are told by the author of the Chronicle of Lanercoft, that in the year 1258, John de Glenham fucceeded in the church of Glafgow, being collated thereto by the pope, and confecrated at Rome; an Englifhman born, but no friend to the Englifh. For in the latter part of his days, his covetoufnefs increafing with his years, he pretended an ancient right in the parts of Cumberland and Weftmorland, faying that his diocefe extended as far as Rerecrofs upon Stanemore. And haftening upon that occafion to the court of Rome, he died in his journey.

7. ROBERT CHAUSE. This bifhop's furname is varioufly written, occafioned probably from the difficulty of reading it in old records, and the furname of a bifhop being feldom mentioned. Bifhop Nicolfon fays, his name in the record is *Robert de Chaury.* Bifhop Goodwin, as alfo Ifaacfon in his chronological account of the bifhops, call him *Robert Chaufe.* In the lift of fheriffs for the county of Cumberland (of which county this bifhop was fheriff in the 56 Hen. 3. and 1 Ed. 1.) his name is written *Chauncey.* He was archdeacon of Bath; his election to this fee was confirmed on the 12th of February 1258, and his temporalties reftored on the 19th of September following.

In 1266, at Bewley, this bifhop releafed the guardianfhip of the cell of Wetherhall (being then vacant of a prior) in confideration of the remiffion of two marks annual penfion out of the rectory of Denton.

In the firft year of Ed. 1. the then lord chancellor was informed by Richard de Crepping fheriff of the county of Cumberland, that the bifhop of Carlifle had forbidden his tenants to take the oath of fealty to the king; whereupon that prelate certified the lord chancellor that the information was falfe and groundlefs; for that he had by meffage requefted the faid fheriff (then refiding at Appleby in Weftmorland) that he would either by himfelf or his deputy adminifter to them the faid oath. He therefore humbly requefts, that the chancellor would either command the fheriff to receive that fealty which they were thus ready to pay, or to appoint fome other perfon to do it; profeffing (for himfelf and his dependents) that they were ever ready to give all imaginable affurances of their juft duty and fidelity to his majefty.

This complaint feems to have occafioned the bifhop's excommunicating the faid fheriff, upon application of the abbot of Holm Cultram, on whom the fheriff had made fome diftreffes for debts owing to the crown. And this occafioned a writ of prohibition, requiring the bifhop to revoke his ecclefiaftical cenfure.

Mr. Prynne takes notice of a record after the death of this bifhop, to the following purport: The prior and convent of Carlifle were attached to an-

* Pryn. v. 2. p. 912. 942. 970.

fwer

fwer our lord the king, why after the death of Robert bifhop of Carlifle, when they had requefted and obtained (according to cuftom) leave to chufe another bifhop, and they had chofen William dean of York, whofe election was folemnly notified and publifhed; yet they, on the faid William's refufal to accept the office, had proceeded to chufe another bifhop, without any leave requefted or obtained; to the prejudice of the king and his crown, and his damage of fixty thoufand pounds;—and why, after they had received an inhibition from the king's jufticiars John de Vallibus and Thomas de Satrington, they yet proceeded to chufe another bifhop, in contempt of the king and to his damage of forty thoufand pounds. The prior returneth anfwer and faith, that he and his convent did not underftand that they had done any contempt or prejudice to the king; for that having obtained leave to elect, and the perfon elected difagreeing to the election, they thought it was *res integra*, and they might proceed to chufe again; but if it was a contempt, they fubmit themfelves to the king's pleafure †.

. Which matter is fet in a fuller light by a bull of pope Nicholas the third, dated 5 Id. Apr. A. D. 1280, and directed to the aforefaid king Edward the firft. His holinefs therein informs his dear fon, that the prior and convent of Carlifle, upon the death of their late bifhop Robert, had proceeded to the election of a new bifhop by way of compromife among themfelves, according to the accuftomed rule which then generally obtained in chufing of bifhops; and that in fuch their election they had chofen one mafter William dean of York, who refufed to accept of the charge, and fent back an authentic difclaimer of all the right which could accrue to him by virtue of the faid choice. Hereupon they proceeded to a new election, but according to their old form. No new application upon this was made to the king, though there had been upon the other vacancy. But a certain day was appointed, and notice given to the chapter to convene. Being met, their firft work (in obfervance of the methods of a capitular compromife on fuch occafions) was to devolve the whole power of their body upon five of their members, who were, the prior Robert de Everdon, the precentor, the fuccentor, the cellararius, and the fubfacrift. Thefe five elect Ralph prior of Gifburne, and the whole chapter prefent him to Walter archbifhop of York, who happened to die before he could confirm the election. Upon this the chapter of York is prefently applied to for the faid confirmation.—But fuch delays were made by them, that the electors were neceffitated to appeal to Rome. The pope, to make a fhort end of a vexatious caufe, forthwith appoints three commiffioners, who find (and make their report accordingly) that the election is null; forafmuch as it was not, according to the ufage and canons of the Roman fee, pronounced by one of the electors fingly, notwithftanding it did not appear but that they had all unanimoufly concurred in it. However, the pope refolves, through the plenitude of his own power, to remedy this irregularity; and therefore, being well fatisfied of the good learning and other extraordinary qualifications of the man, confers the vacant bifhoprick upon Ralph by way of provifion, declaring all

† Pryn. v. 3. p. 1230.

his

his title to be once more void and null, if claimed upon any other foundation ‡.

Mr. Prynne takes notice, that the parliament to which the prior and convent were fummoned to fhew caufe as aforefaid, was held foon after Eafter, whilft the bifhop elect was foliciting his caufe at Rome in perfon ; the chapter, uncertain what would be the iffue, thought fit (in cafe judgment fhould be given againft them here at home) to throw themfelves into the king's mercy. And the pope, cautioufly declining the giving countenance (barefaced) to an election thus independent on the king's authority, difcovers another fort of nullity in the proceedings, which makes way for the exercife of his provifionary power, in making this prelate a creature of his own. And we quickly fee king Edward as tamely fubmits to the Roman pontiff, as the prior and convent had done before to their liege fovereign.

8. RALPH IRTON, being of the family of Irton in Cumberland, and then prior of Gifburne, was elected by the prior and convent of Carlifle as aforefaid, and appointed thereto by the pope by way of provifion ; which king Ed. 1. fubmitting to, reftored him the temporalties on the 10th of July 1280.

This bifhop held a convocation of his clergy at Carlifle in October in the fame year ; when they granted the tenth of all their ecclefiaftical livings according to their real value for two years.

In 1281, he recovered the manor and church of Dalfton againft Sir Michael de Harcla.

In 1290, he was one of the plenipotentiaries of king Edward the firft in the treaty with the commiffioners of Scotland, for a marriage to be had and folemnized between prince Edward and Margaret daughter of Eric king of Norway, hereditary princefs and queen of Scotland. Which treaty, with conceffions of privileges to the Scottifh nation, was fully concluded, and was alfo immediately ratified by the king himfelf*.

The fame year commenced a remarkable fuit between the king, the bifhop, the prior and convent, and the parfon of Thurfby, feverally claiming right of tithes in fome new improved lands within the foreft of Englewood. " Radul-
" phus epifcopus Karleolenfis petit verfus priorem ecclefiæ Karleolenfis decimas
" duarum placearum terræ de novo affartarum in forefta de Inglewood, quarum
" una vocatur Lynthwait et alia Kyrthewayte, quæ funt infra limites parochiæ
" fuæ de Afpatric. Et fuper hoc fimiliter venit magifter Henricus de Burton
" perfona de Thorefby, et eafdem decimas clamat ut pertinentes ad ecclefiam
" fuam. Et prior venit et dicit, quod Henricus rex vetus conceffit Deo et
" ecclefiæ fuæ beatæ Mariæ Karliolenfi omnes decimas de omnibus terris quas
" in culturam redigerent infra foreftam, et inde eos feoffavit per quoddam cornu
" eburneum quod dedit ecclefiæ fuæ prædictæ. Et Willielmus Inge qui fequi-
" tur pro rege dicit, quod decimæ prædictæ pertinent ad regem et non ad
" alium, quia funt infra bundas foreftæ de Inglewood ; et quod in forefta fua
" prædicta poteft villas ædificare, ecclefias conftruere, terras affartare, et ec-

‡ Rymer, v. 2 p. 147. * Pryn. v. 3. p. 395. Rymer, v. 2. p. 483.

" clefias

" clefias illas cum decimis terrarum illarum pro voluntate fua cuicunque vo-
" luèrit conferre. Et quia dominus rex fuper præmiffis vult certiorari, ut
" unicuiquique tribuatur quod fuum, affignetur, &c. Et certificent regem
" ad proximum parliamentum †:"—The right was finally adjudged to the
king; and he granted the fame afterwards to the prior and convent ‡.

The *cornu eburneum* they have yet in the cathedral of Carlifle, a fymbol (very
probably) of fome of king Henry the firft's grants to the priory; but in none
of thofe grants, of which any copy is now extant, do thofe tithes appear. The
ceremony of inveftiture with a horn or other like fymbol is very ancient, and
was in ufe before there were any written charters. We read of Ulf, a Danifh
prince, who gave all his lands to the church of York: And the form of the
endowment was this; he brought the horn, out of which he ufually drank, filled
with wine, and before the high altar kneeling devoutly, drank the wine, and
by that ceremony enfeoffed the church with all his lands and revenues.

King Canute, another Dane, gave lands at Pufey in Berkfhire to the family
of that name there, with a horn folemnly delivered as a confirmation of the
grant; which horn, it is faid, is ftill there to be feen.

So king Edward the confeffor granted to Nigel the huntfman an hide of
land called Dere Hide, and a wood called Hulewood, with the cuftody of the
foreft of Bernwood, to hold of the king to him and his heirs by one horn,
which is the charter of the faid foreft.

So that not the Danes only, but the Englifh Saxons alfo, were acquainted
with this ancient cuftom. Thus Ingulphus abbot of Crowland, who lived in
the time of William the Conqueror, acquaints us that it continued down to
his time. He tells us, that many eftates were granted by word only, without
writing; as by delivery of a fword, an helmet, a horn, or cup, and fuch like:
but this mode, he fays, in after times was changed.

Ulf's horn at York, when the reformation began in king Edward the fixth's
time, was fwept away amongft many other coftly ornaments, and fold to a
goldfmith, who took away from it the tippings of gold wherewith it was
adorned, and the gold chain which was affixed to it. After which time, the
horn itfelf, cut in ivory, of an octagon form, came into the hands of general
Fairfax; who being a lover of antiquities, preferved it during the confufions
of the civil wars; whofe memory is defervedly honoured for other generous
actions of this nature, fuch as allowing Mr. Dodfworth the antiquarian a yearly
falary to preferve the infcriptions in churches, the giving his valuable manufcripts to the univerfity of Oxford, and his preferving the public library there,
as he did the cathedral at York from being fpoiled and defaced after the furrender of the city. And he dying in 1671, this horn came into the poffeffion
of his next kinfman Henry lord Fairfax, who ornamented it anew, and reftored
it to its ancient repofitory, where it now remains a noble monument of modern as well as ancient piety *.

† Coke's 4 Inft. 307. ‡ Appendix, N° 27.
*. Tracts of the Antiquarian Society, p. 168.

In

In the same year 1290, the king granted to this bishop the advowson of the church of Rothbury, which he had recovered from his predecessor Robert Chause: as also free warren in his manors of Dalston and Linstock.

In 1291, a protection was granted under the king's great seal of Scotland, bearing date Aug. 14, to Ralph bishop of Carlisle and A. bishop of Cathness, for their joint collection of the tenths of that kingdom †.

In this same year, June 5, the said bishop was one of king Edward's commissioners for adjusting the right claim to the crown of Scotland; and was there present at the debates on the 13th of the same month, as likewise on the 14th of August following ‡.

He is also one of the witnesses to king Edward's claim of right to the kingdom of Scotland, upon the death of the forementioned queen Margaret, dated at Norham 12 May 1291 ||

On the first of March following he died at Linstock. For being fatigued (says the Chronicle of Lanercost) with a tedious journey in deep snow in returning from the parliament at London, and refreshing himself very plentifully, he had a mind to go to rest; and a vein bursting in his sleep he was found suffocated with blood.

9. JOHN HALTON. He was some time canon regular at Carlisle; and was on the 9th of May 1292 elected bishop. Which the king approving, he sent his mandate to John de Crancumb the archbishop of York's vicar general (the archbishop himself being then in foreign parts) to do his duty herein; who confirming the election, the king restored the temporalties by a writ to his escheator. Dated at Berwick upon Tweed, July 18 §.

It seems that this bishop was presently admitted into his predecessor's place in king Edward's commission for hearing the plea of the several pretenders to the crown and realm of Scotland; since we find him present in November 1292, when sentence was given against Robert Bruce, and when John Baliol did homage for the whole kingdom of Scotland with the appurtenances to his sovereign lord the king of England ⊥.

About this time, this bishop entertained the archbishop of York John Romanus at his castle of Linstock, going to view his manor of Extildes, with three hundred attendants *.

In 1294, being commanded by Edward the first to go on some special errand to (his vassal) John Baliol king of Scots, he had letters of safe conduct for himself and family from that feudatory prince, dated at Edinburgh *.

And at this time, as well as a good while before and after, he was authorised by the pope for the collecting of the tenths in the several dioceses of Scotland, which gave him a great deal of trouble in sending minatory letters and sometimes bulls of excommunication, against the bishops, abbots, and others *.

† Pryn. v. 3. p. 450.   ‡ Pryn. v. 3 p. 504. 508. 512. || Rymer, v. 2. p. 543.
§ Pryn. v. 3 p. 473.   ⊥ Rymer, v. 2. p. 588. 593.   * Regist. Halton.

The

The king about this time lodged at the bishop's house at Rose; for from thence (on the 25th and 26th of September) are some of his letters dated *.

In 1302, this bishop was governor of the king's castle at Carlisle, and had therein the keeping and care of all the Scotch hostages and prisoners of note that lay there; many of whom, as appears from his accounts, died in durance. He also took care of all repairs there in timber, stone, and other materials. The whole of one year's receipt from the crown amounts to 270*l* 2*s* 0*d*, and his disbursements to 275*l* 14*s* 7*d* †.

In 1305, pope Clement the fifth, in the first year of his pontificate, at the request of king Edward, gave a commission to the archbishop of York and bishop of Carlisle, to excommunicate by bell, book, and candle, Robert de Brus earl of Carrick and all his adherents, for the murder of John Comyn in the church of Dumfries; which was executed accordingly ‡.

In the year following, the said bishop of Carlisle (together with the abbots of York, St. Albans, and Waltham) had another commission from the same pope, to absolve all such prelates, clergy, and other English subjects, as had or might think themselves to have incurred the sentence of irregularity or excommunication, by slaying any of king Edward's enemies, wounding the clergy, or defacing churches, in his late wars in Scotland ‖.

On the 8th of September 1305, he petitioned the pope to canonize St. Thomas de Cantelupe late bishop of Hereford §.

In 1307, in the parliament holden at Carlisle this year, he petitioned the king for a piece of ground within the precincts of the castle towards Caldew, but within the city walls, for building an house for himself and successors; whereupon an inquisition *ad quod damnum* was directed, but the return is not mentioned ⊥.

In 1308, bishop Halton was summoned *(pro forma)* to attend the coronation of king Edward the second ‡‡.

In 1314, this bishop was with the neighbouring gentlemen in Carlisle, when the town was blocked up by Edward Bruce. And from thence he dates a proxy to two clergymen of his own diocese, the rectors of Levington and Burgh under Stanemore, to appear for him in the parliament at Westminster, excusing his personal attendance on account of these Scotch troubles **.

In 1318, in recompence of the many and great services and sufferings of the (now aged) bishop of Carlisle, king Edward the second addressed the pope for the appropriation of the church of Horncastle in the diocese of Lincoln (being in the patronage of the said bishop) to his own use, and to annex the same for ever to the bishoprick of Carlisle; that he and his successors, during the ravages of the neighbouring enemy, may have a place of refuge, and out of the profits of the church may be able to support themselves ††. Some years before this, the king had granted his own royal licence, insignificant (as it seems) without a confirmation from Rome, for the said appropriation. And

---

* Rymer, v. 2. p. 865, 867.   † Regiftr. Halton.   ‡ Pryn. v. 3. p. 1122.   ‖ Ibid. 1186.
§ Reg. Halton.   ⊥ Ryley, 328.   ‡‡ Rymer, v. 3. p. 52.   ** Reg. Halton.
†† Rymer, v. 3. p. 741.

in this fame year, the bifhop himfelf defires one of the cardinals to make the like interceffion to the pope; as alfo for a remiffion of a penfion paid to the papal fee out of the rectory *.

In 1320, William archbifhop of York, John bifhop of Carlifle, Robert de Baldock archdeacon of Middlefex, and Jeoffrey le Scrop, were appointed the king's plenipotentiaries in a treaty of peace with Robert de Brus and his ac-complices; to whom afterwards fome other commiffioners were added †.

About the beginning of November in the year 1324 bifhop Halton died; and in January following the chapter elected William de Ermyn canon of York, who was confirmed by the king on the 17th of the fame January. But the pope thought fit to take the difpofal of the bifhopric into his own hand, and accordingly gave it to John de Rofs.

10. JOHN ROSS, fome time before Midfummer 1325, brought his credentials from Rome; and had thereupon reftitution of the temporalties.

In 1330, he petitions the pope for fome preferment for his two kinfmen John and Henry de Rofs (brothers, born in the diocefe of Hereford) bachelors of the civil law.

The fame year he was cited to appear before the prior of Durham delegate of the court of Rome, on a complaint made againft him by the prior and con-vent of Carlifle, for debarring them of the peaceable enjoyment of their ap-propriated churches of St. Mary and St. Cuthbert within the walls of Carlifle, Routhecliffe, Hayton, Ireby, Crofby, Camberton, and Beghokirk; as like-wife for the arbitrary feizing and difpofal of their rents and other goods.—Af-terwards, the prior neglecting to pay fome tenths that were in his hands, the bifhop excommunicated him.

In 1331, this bifhop refided at Horncaftle, and there confirmed a grant made by fome of his tenants to the abbot and convent of Kyrkftede.

In 1332, he died at Rofe; and was carried into the South to be buried ‡.

11. JOHN KIRKBY, prior of this cathedral, was elected bifhop, and con-firmed by the king, May 8, 1332, and had the temporalties reftored to him on the 9th of July following. Soon after, follows this demand of a provifion for one of the king's clerks:—Edwardus Dei gratia, &c. Venerabili in Chrifto patro Johanni eadem gratia epifcopo Karliolenfi, falutem. Cum vos ratione novæ creationis veftræ teneamini, unum de clericis noftris, quem vobis nominaverimus, in quadam annua penfione fuftinere, donec eidem clerico noftro de beneficio ecclefiaftico per vos fuerit provifum; ac nos, promotionem dilecti clerici noftri Philippi de la Mare de Wefton; fuis meritis exigentibus, affectantes, ipfum ad hoc vobis duximus nominandum: Vobis mandamus ro-gando, quatenus eidem clerico noftro talem penfionem a vobis annuatim reci-piendam quæ dantem deceat et recipientem fortius obligari debeat, concedere velitis; literas veftras patentes, figillo veftro fignatas, eidem Philippo inde ha-bere facientes. Et quod inde ad hunc rogatum noftrum duxeritis faciendum,

* Peg. Halton.　　　† Rymer, v. 3. p. 851. 851. 866.　　　‡ Chron. Lanercoft.

nobis

nobis per latorem præfentium refcribatis. Tefte meipfo apud Weftminſter 12 die Sept. anno regni noſtri fexto *.

It doth not appear what return was made to this writ nor any other of the like nature either before or after in this diocefe. Yet fuch claim feems to be well founded. For notwithſtanding the ſtatute of the 1 Ed. 3. ſt. 2. c. 10. whereby " the king granteth that from henceforth he will no more fuch things " defire, but where he ought ;" yet by the common law, the king as founder of archbiſhopricks, biſhopricks, and many religious houfes, had a corody or penſion in the feveral foundations ; a corody for his vadelets who attended him, and a penſion for a chaplain, fuch as he ſhould fpecially recommend, till the re- fpeßive poffeffor ſhould promote him to a competent benefice †.

In October 1337, the Scots burned Rofe, and wafted the country all around ‡.

In the foregoing fpring, the biſhop was fet upon in his paffage through Pen-rith, and feveral of his retinue wounded by a band of unknown ruffians ; who were denounced excommunicate, by bell, book, and candle ‖.

In the fame year, he certifies the barons of the exchequer, that it is im-poffible to levy the tenths, moſt of the clergy being fled from the Scots ‖.

In 1341, a privy feal is directed to the king's receiver of the funds for the carrying on the war againſt the Scots, requiring him to pay 200l to the biſhop of Carliſle, in part of an arrear of 529l 4s 0d for the wages of him and the men abiding with him for the fafe keeping of the marches againſt Scotland. And with this advance, the biſhop promifes immediately to engage again in the fame fervice +.

In 1342, the chapter of York (the fee being vacant, and the dean living in remote parts) fell hard upon the biſhop upon an appeal from the pariſhioners of St. Mary's in Carliſle, to whom the chapter there (too much countenanced by the biſhop) had refufed an eſtabliſhed vicar §.

The fame biſhop alfo, after fufpenfion, was excommunicated, for non-pay-ment of 60l 5s 8¼d tenths in Lincolnſhire to the pope §.

In 1343, Richard biſhop of Durham, and John biſhop of Carliſle, with fome great men of the laiety, were appointed commiffioners to treat with others from Scotland, touching the fettling and preferving of peace and commerce, in all places except in caſtles and walled towns upon the borders **.

But in the next year, both thefe biſhops, as likewife the archbiſhop of York, are required to be aiding and affiſting to Edward Baliol king of Scots, whom our king Edward conſtitutes his captain general of all his northern forces, and to pay the fame regard to his orders and commands, as they would do to thofe of their fovereign himfelf.††.

In 1348, the biſhop of Carliſle being appointed to convey the princefs Joan (affianced to Alphonfus king of Caſtile, and bearing the title of queen of Spain) to her hufband, notwithſtanding the unfortunate iffue of that journey, had on his return a warrant to the lord treafurer, barons, and chamberlains of the

---

* Regiſtr. Kirkby.   † Gibfon's Codex, p. 16.   ‡ Chron. Lanercoſt.   ‖ Reg. Kirkby.
+ Rymer, v. 5. p. 281.   § Regiſtr. Kirkby.   ** Rymer, v. 5. p. 379.   †† Ibid. 425.

king's exchequer of fuch daily allowance of board wages (*viz.* 5 marks) as he had prudently contracted for before his fetting out *.

This bifhop feems to have had a very uneafy time; being conftantly alarmed and inveterately perfecuted by the Scots in his own diocefe. And for that reafon he was frequently abroad, holding many of his ordinations at or near Horncaftle and Melborn, and fometimes at London, Durham, and Corbridge. He was alfo engaged in abundance of fuits with his chapter, archdeacon, and others, in the courts of Rome, Weftminfter, and York.

He died in 1352; and thereupon the chapter of Carlifle, with the king's leave, once more made choice of their own prior John de Horncaftle to be their bifhop; who was confirmed, and had reftitution of the temporalties: But the pope thought proper to appoint another, *viz.*

12. GILBERT WELTON, who being confecrated by the pope or his order, the king in humble obedience to the pope's plenitude of power revoked the writ for reftitution of the temporalties to John de Horncaftle, and granted the fame to Gilbert de Welton.

One of the firft things in this bifhop's regifter is, a commiffion to convene the clergy of the diocefe of Carlifle for granting a fubfidy to the bifhop. How much was given is not faid. But that the fynod had done gracioufly, was acknowledged in another commiffion for the collecting of the bounty in March following. And in his fourth year they gave him 200 marks.

Edward the third being in a manner oppreffed with the multitude of his Scotch prifoners taken at the battle of Durham, and being inclinable to fet at liberty on reafonable terms the king of Scotland David de Brus his captive brother-in-law, conftituted the bifhops of Durham and Carlifle his commiffioners in a treaty of peace, and granted to them and others the ample powers following:—Rex univerfis ad quos, &c. falutem. Sciatis quod nos, de circumfpectione et fidelitate dilectorum et fidelium noftrorum venerabilium patrum Thomæ Dunelménfis et Gilberti Karleolenfis episcoporum, nec non Willielmi de Bohun comitis Northamptoniæ confanguinei noftri chariffimi, Henrici de Percy, Radulphi de Nevil, Thomæ de Lucy, Willielmi baronis de Grayftock, et Henrici le Scrop, plenius confidentes, ad tractandum, concordandum, et conveniendum cum David de Brus, et cum prælatis, comitibus, et aliis nobilibus, cæterifque hominibus de Scotia apud villam Novi Caftri fuper Tinam, fuper deliberatione ejufdem David, ac finali pace et concordia, ac treugis vel fufferentia belli inter nos et homines de Scotia ineundis, et ad falvum et fecurum conductum prædictis prælatis, nobilibus, et aliis de Scotia et cuilibet eorundem (cujufcunque ftatus feu conditionis fuerit) ad veniendum ad dictam villam Novi Caftri fuper Tinam, ibidem morando ex exinde in Scotiam redeundo, ad certum tempus (ad hoc limitandum) concedendum, Et ad ea quæ fic tractata, concordata, conventa, et conceffa fuerint, quacunque fecuritate nomine noftro vallandum, Et ad fecuritatem quæ nobis in hac parte fieri debeat, a parte adverfa

* Rymer, v. 5. p. 648.

ftipulandum

ftipulandum et·recipiendum; Et ad omnia alia et fingula quæ circa præmiffa neceffaria fuerint vel opportuna, et quæ nos ipfi faceremus fi præfentes effemus, nomine noftro faciendum, eifdem epifcopis, comiti, Henrico, Radulpho, Thomæ, Willielmo, et Henrico, vel tribus eorum (quorum præfatum epifcopum Dunelmenfem, vel comitem Northamptoniæ, aut Radulphum de Nevil, unum effe volumus) plenam tenore præfentium concedimus poteftatem; ratum habituri et gratum quicquid per eos nomine noftro factum fuerit in premiffis et quolibet præmifforum. In cujus, &c. Tefte rege apud Weftmonafterium 15 die Octobris. Per ipfum regem *. The fame powers were granted to the fame perfons, and in the fame words, on the 18th of June following. And thereupon it was agreed with the commiffioners of Scotland, that the faid David fhould be releafed, paying a ranfom of 90,000 marks fterling in nine years. But the bifhop of Carlifle is not mentioned as prefent at this treaty, though all the reft (as likewife Gilbert de Umfrevill earl of Angus, who was added to the fecond commiffion) are faid to have been there; but his name is inferted in all the king's inftruments of ratification thereupon.—Another commiffion was again granted in 1356, to the bifhops of Durham and Carlifle, with their forementioned fellows; in purfuance whereof it was agreed, that David fhould be delivered up to his friends at Berwick the year following: And to this purpofe other powers were given to the commiffioners; unto whom were now added the archbifhop of York and Thomas de Mufgrave †.

In 1359, July 8, the king conftitutes the bifhop of Carlifle and Thomas de Lucy, jointly and feverally, wardens of the weftern marches ‡.

In 1360, king Edward the third having accepted the furrender of the kingdom of Scotland (in exchange for a penfion of 2000l fterling) from Edward Baliol, and fent back Edward de Brus to his friends in that country, began now to think of perfecting a defign which he had long been forming; which was, the entering into a firm bond of peace and amity with his aforefaid brother-in-law David, and formally acknowledging him king of Scots; and for that end grants a commiffion to the archbifhop of York, the bifhops of Durham and Carlifle, and others ‖. And in 1362, the bifhop of Carlifle was again joined with the fame commiffioners, with new powers to the like effect §.

Bifhop Welton dying in the latter end of this year, the king (Jan. 18.) granted his Conge d'Eflire to the chapter, upon their humble petition to elect a new bifhop.

In this bifhop's regifter are many letters and commiffions for the raifing of charitable contributions towards the repair of the public bridges at Carlifle, Salkeld, Kirkby Thore, as likewife for the fupport of his own and other cathedrals.

13. THOMAS APPLEBY. The prior and convent of Carlifle, by virtue of the king's Conge d'Eflire aforefaid, made choice of him (being one of their

* Rymer, v. 5. p. 761.   † Ibid. v. 5. p. 763—847.   v. 6. p. 31—68.   ‡ Regiftr. Welton.
‖ Rymer, v. 6. p. 207.   § Ibid. p 375.

own

own canons) to succeed in the paftoral charge. But the pope thought fit to vacate the election, but appointed the fame perfon by provifion to be their bifhop. He was confecrated at Avignon on the 18th of June 1363, and had reftitution of the temporalties on the 10th of Auguft following.

In 1364, the bifhop of Carlifle is enumerated amongft thofe prelates, who took an oath in the king's prefence, in his palace at Weftminfter, to obferve inviolably all the articles of peace lately concluded and agreed upon by his majefty and the French king †.

In 1366, a commiffion for wardens of the weftern marches was granted to Thomas bifhop of Carlifle, Roger de Clifford, Anthony de Lucy, and Ralph de Dacre.

In 1369, the dean rural of Cumberland is required by the bifhop, in obedience to the king's writ, to fummon all abbots, priors, and other religious and ecclefiaftical perfons, to array all the fencible men between the ages of 16 and fixty, upon apprehenfion of a defcent from France. And in the fame year, a commiffion for wardens of the weft marches is granted to the bifhop of Carlifle, Roger de Clifford, Thomas de Mufgrave, and divers others ‡.

In 1372, the king being alarmed with the new league, offenfive and defenfive, made between the French king and Robert king of Scots, and the great provifions made thereupon by the French king for the invafion of England, iffues out his proclamation for the fpeedy arming of all his liege people, clergy and laity, between the ages of 16 and 60, throughout the whole realm of England. And becaufe he was moft efpecially apprehenfive of the Scottifh king's breaking in at the fame time upon the borders, his firft care was to write a circular letter to the bifhops of Durham and Carlifle, Gilbert de Umfranvil earl of Angus, Henry Percy, Roger Clifford, and Ralph lord Dacre, requiring them forthwith to repair to their eftates and interefts in the north, there to keep their conftant refidence, and to put themfelves into the beft condition they can, with the whole power of their refpective retinues and followers, to oppofe any fudden incurfion or attempt that fhould happen from their neighbouring enemies. And to encourage them the better herein, he affures them that the county troops and others, under the power of general array within all the northern counties, together with the hobelarii (or light horfemen) and archers in thofe parts fhould join them and be under their command, as intirely as their own domeftics ‡.

In 1373, a commiffion was iffued to Thomas bifhop of Durham, Thomas bifhop of Carlifle, Edward Mortimer earl of March, Roger de Clifford, Ralph de Dacre, Richard de Stafford, Henry le Scrop, Thomas de Mufgrave, and mafter John de Appleby (probably the bifhop's brother) dean of St. Paul's, or any fix of them, to hear and determine all complaints and caufes of action upon the borders, on occafion of the breach of the articles of truce agreed on in any late convention there; requiring them to fee fatisfaction made for injuries done by any of the king's fubjects §.

---

† Rymer, v. 6. p. 436.   ‡ Regiftr. Appleby.   § Rymer, v. 7. p. 9.

In 1374, great differences having arisen between Henry lord Percy and William earl of Douglas, touching the forest of Jedburgh; the bishop of Carlisle and others are made arbitrators ‡.

In 1384, king Richard the second appoints John bishop of Durham, Thomas bishop of Carlisle, Henry de Percy earl of Northumberland, John de Nevil baron of Raby, and master John de Waltham subdean of York, special commissioners and ambassadors, impowering them or any two of them to treat with his adversary of Scotland, for the renewal of a truce and cessation of arms between the two kingdoms, and adjusting all differences amongst the borderers ‡.

In 1392, the bishops of Durham and Carlisle, together with the earl of Northumberland and others, are appointed commissioners to put in due execution that part of a late treaty of peace, concluded with the French king, which relates to the kingdom of Scotland *.

On the 3d of May in the same year, bishop Appleby confirms a grant at his manor of Rose, of certain lands given by some tenants of his at Horncastle to the priorefs and convent of Greenfeld.

In 1393, John bishop of St. David's lord treasurer, and Thomas bishop of Carlisle, together with the earl of Northumberland, the lord Nevil, and others, are commissioned to treat with the commissioners of the king's adversary of Scotland, either for a perpetual or temporary peace †.

And the same commissioners for England are the next year commanded to proclaim on the borders the articles of a truce concluded with France and Scotland §.

In 1395, on the death of bishop Appleby, the chapter obtained a Conge d'Eslire for a new election, which was signed by the king at Chiltern Langley on the 13th of December; whereupon they chose William Stirkland: But the pope refused to confecrate him, and sent them the bishop of Lismore, Robert Reed.

14. ROBERT REED was made bishop by the papal authority in 1396; and on the 26th of March following obtained the king's warrant for all the mesne profits of the fee from the time of the death of Thomas the late bishop. He was translated to Chichester before the end of the year, and nothing further memorable is recorded of him at Carlisle.

Mr. Bowchier archdeacon of Lewes, in a letter to bishop Nicolson dated Aug. 9. 1704, says that he could find but little of this bishop at Chichester, whither he was quickly removed from Carlisle; and nothing as to his country, education, monastery, benefactions, or place of burial. His register is one of the few preserved in that church, but there is nothing in it worth taking notice of, save that he was forced by the archbishop to wear the habit of his order, which he had some years thrown off after he was made bishop. Godwin says little of him, and one thing very false, that he built the cross in the

‡ Rymer, v. 7. p. 45.   ‡ Ibid. p. 432.   * Ibid. p. 725.   † Ibid. p. 754.
§ Ibid. p. 781.

market

market place at Chichester, which was the work of good bishop Story. Reed gave Yapton and Binsted to the church of Chichester. And his register there begins Feb. 10, 1396, and ends Apr. 13, 1414.

15. THOMAS MERKS, one of the monks of Westminster, and master of divinity, had restitution of the temporalties of this see from king Richard the second, on a provision made to him by the pope, in the year 1397.

In 1399, in the will of king Richard the second, which bears date the 16th of April in this year, Thomas bishop of Carlisle is one of the five prelates whom that unhappy prince thought fit to join with his nephew the duke of Surry and others of his royal relations in the executorship, to each of whom he bequeathed a gold ring of 20*l* value †. And he is the only bishop, who took letters of protection, about the 20th of the same month, from that prince; obliging himself thereby to a personal attendance on his majesty towards the coast of Ireland ‡.

Henry the fourth came to the crown Sept. 30, in that year: and in his first parliament in the very next month, where it may well be thought that Richard had not many friends in the house, and if any disapproved of the proceedings against him they were too much awed to venture to speak in his behalf, there was one however bold enough to say publickly what others only thought, namely, Thomas Merks bishop of Carlisle; who without regarding the motives which might induce him as well as the rest of Richard's friends to keep silence, made a long speech, wherein he alledged every thing that could with any plausibleness be said for the king deposed and against the king on the throne ‡. On the tenth of January following he was committed for high treason, and the king gave particular directions to his judges how to proceed against bishops on such trials §. And he was soon after deprived of his bishoprick. And having for some time continued a prisoner in the Tower, the king consented that he should be removed June 23, 1400, to the abbey of Westminster. And on the 21st of March following the king was yet more compassionate to him, and by his letters patent granted to him licence to obtain from the pope in the court of Rome benefices (episcopal excepted) to the yearly amount of 100 marks *.

And in the year following, it appearing that the said Thomas Merks, instead of the king's abovementioned allowance of 100 marks, had procured bulls from the pope for preferments of the yearly value of 300 marks, king Henry not only pardons the misprision in accepting such bulls, but allows him to put them in execution ||.

In 1404, Aug. 13. He was instituted to the rectory of Todenham in Gloucestershire; and on the 13 Jan. 1409, Robert Ely was admitted to the said rectory, upon the death of Thomas Merks.

16. WILLIAM STIRKLAND, the same that we saw four years ago duly elected, but rejected by the pope, was now at the petition of the king ap-

---

† Rymer, v. 8. p. 77.   ‡ Ibid. p. 79.   + Tindal's Rapin, v. 1. p. 486.   § Rymer, v. 8. p. 123.   * Pat. 2 H. 4. p. 2. m. 11. || Pat. 3 H. 4. p. 1.

pointed

pointed by his holiness; consecrated by the archbishop of York at Cawood Aug. 24, 1400; and had restitution of the temporalties the 15th of November following.

The inhabitants of the diocese of Carlisle seem to have long retained somewhat of the spirit of their late bishop in adhering to the interests of king Richard the second, in opposition to those of his successor Henry the fourth; which occasioned a commission from the reigning king to bishop Stirkland and others, setting forth that the king was informed that divers persons as well ecclesiastical as secular within the diocese of Carlisle had given out, that Richard the second was living and abiding in the parts of Scotland; he therefore requires them to arrest all such persons and carry them to the next gaol, there to remain till the king's pleasure therein be further known †.

In November following, the king, in consideration of the great losses lately sustained by his good subjects in the counties of Northumberland and Cumberland, remits all arrears of fines and amerciaments, tenths, and fifteenths; which was done upon the petition of their representatives in parliament, setting forth the misery of those parts, occasioned by the late incursions and devastations of the Scots ‡.

. In the same year the bishop passes a fine, in confirmation of the appropriated tithes of Horncastle.

· In 1404, amongst the records in the Tower there is an extraordinary grant (confirmed first by the prior and convent, and afterwards by the king) of the office of constable of Rose Castle for the salary of ten marks yearly, and maintenance for himself, one valet, and two horses :—Hæc indentura facta inter venerabilem in Christo patrem dominum Willielmum Dei gratia Karliolensem episcopum ex una parte, et Johannem de Dockwra armigerum ex altera parte, testatur, Quod dictus venerabilis vir, ex consensu et assensu prioris et capituli ecclesiæ suæ cathedralis beatæ Mariæ Karliolensis, dedit et concessit eidem Johanni officium constabularii castri sui de Rosa; Habendum et tenendum ad totam vitam suam, percipiendo inde annuatim de dicto venerabili patre et successoribus episcopis Karliolensibus unum annuum redditum decem marcarum bonæ monetæ, ad festa Natalis domini, Annunciationis beatæ Mariæ, Nativitatis sancti Johannis Baptistæ, et sancti Michaelis archangeli, per equales portiones, et talem sustentationem pro se et uno valetto et duobus equis, qualem Johannes de Dalston quondam constabularius dicti castri in vita sua percepit de bonæ memoriæ domino Thoma Appleby quondam episcopo loci prædicti. Et si contingat dictum redditum decem marcarum a retro esse in parte vel in toto post aliquem terminum supradictum, vel dictam sustentationem ab eodem subtrahi, bene liceat dicto Johanni et attornatis suis in maneriis venerabilis patris de Dalston et Horncastre distringere et districtionem captam retinere, quousque de dicto annuo redditu et ejus arrearagiis ac de sustentatione prædicta plenarie fuerit satisfactum. Et liceat dicto Johanni per sufficientem deputatum suum dictum officium constabularii in sua absentia gubernare. In cujus rei testimonium partes prædictæ partibus hujus

† Rymer, v. 8. p. 255.   ‡ Ibid. p. 283.

indenturæ

indenturæ figilla fua alternatim appofuerunt. , Datum Karl' primo die Decembris anno regni regis Henrici quarti fexto †.

In 1406, the bifhop of Carlifle was one of the prelates that figned and
fealed the act of fucceffion, which intailed the crowns of England and France
upon the king's four fons ‡.

It is faid that he built the tower and belfrey in the cathedral church, and
furnifhed it with four large bells, covering the pyramid on the tower with
lead ; and that he furnifhed the tabernacle work in the quire. He built the
tower at Rofe, which ftill goes by the name of Stirkland tower. And he
was at the expence of drawing a watercourfe from the river Petterel through
the town of Penrith, to the great benefit of the inhabitants. He likewife
founded a chantry in the church of St. Andrew in Penrith.

After he had prefided here 20 years, he died Aug. 30, 1419; and lies
buried in the north ifle of the cathedral, under his portraiture elegantly cut
in plain ftone.

17. ROGER WHELPDALE, born in Cumberland at or near Grayftock, was
firft fent to Baliol college in Oxford, where he was fometime fellow; from
thence he was tranfplanted into a fellowfhip of Queen's college in the fame
univerfity, where he was chofen provoft. Having firft obtained the pope's
provifion in his favour, he had the king's licence to the chapter of Carlifle to
elect him, dated at Maule in Normandy Oct. 12, 1419, in the fame form as
at this day ‡. After his election, he was confecrated at London by the
bifhop of Winchefter and others, and had reftitution of the temporalties
the 12th day of March following.

He died on the 4th of February 1422, at Carlifle place in London. And
having made his will Jan. 22. preceding, he therein ordered his body to be
buried in the church of St. Paul London in the porch or fome other private
place. He gave books, veftments, and 10 l in money to the faid Queen's
college; alfo books to Baliol college; and to the fcholars of the univerfity
20 l. He alfo bequeathed 200 l for the founding and endowing a chantry
within the cathedral of Carlifle (as is aforefaid) for Sir Thomas Skelton knight
and Mr. John Glafton both of this diocefe, and (as may be fuppofed) his particular friends. He placed a cheft in Queen's college (as Anthony a-Wood
fays) wherein he depofited the fum of 36 l 13 s 4 d as a ftock to be increafed
by the liberality of other benefactors.

Pits and Bale (who feldom agree in the characters they give of any perfon)
do both allow that this bifhop was a learned man. He writ a book De
invocato Deo, and another of Mathematical Tracts, befides feveral Logical
performances.

18. WILLIAM BARROW. He was doctor of canon law, and three years
together (1413, 14, 15) chancellor of the univerfity of Oxford ; and upon
bifhop Whelpdale's death, the pope by his authority apoftolic tranflated him

† Pat. 10 H. 4. p. 1. m. 22.   ‡ Rymer, v. 8. p. 463.   ‡ Ibid. v. 9. p. 804.

from

from Bangor to Carlifle; and the king's-writ for the reftitution of the temporalties is dated at Weftminfter, Jan. 16. 1423.

In 1429, bifhop Barrow was one of thofe Englifh prelates who protefted
againft the great cardinal Beaufort's appearing at Windfor on St. George's
day; as prelate of the garter in right of his bifhoprick of Winchefter†.

In July following, the faid bifhop was one of the king's commiffioners
(together with the earls of Northumberland and Salifbury) for the truce concluded with Scotland at Hawden Stank †.

This bifhop died at Rofe Caftle, 4 Sept. 1429; and was buried in St. Catharine's chapel on the fouth fide of his own cathedral.

19. MARMADUKE LUMLEY, of the noble family of the barons Lumley in
the palatinate of Durham, was upon bifhop Barrow's death elected by the
chapter and confirmed by the king, and yet was not to have reftitution of the
temporalties till the pope's confent was obtained, as appears by the writ itfelf
dated at Canterbury the 15th day of April 1431.

In the fame year, upon allegation by the king's ferjeants and attorney general, that fuch archbifhops and bifhops of England as had heretofore accepted
of the cardinals hat were thereupon deprived of their prelacies here, and praying
that the like judgment might be given for the king in the prefent cafe of
Henry Beaufort bifhop of Winchefter; the bifhops and other lords of parliament unanimoufly agreed, that the ancient rights of the crown in this cafe
ought to be maintained and preferved: but forafmuch as the faid cardinal was
nearly related to his majefty, that the cardinal fhould be fairly heard; and
that till this could be done, fearch fhould be made in the records of the kingdom. The diffent of the bifhop of Carlifle is entered on the foot of the
record thus: The bifhop of Carlifle differed in his anfwer from the reft, and
held, that until the coming of the cardinal nothing at all ought to be done
in the affair.

In 1433, upon his being licenfed, with many other Englifh bifhops to the
general council at Bafil, he is thus varioufly defcribed in the record, " Mar-
" maduke bifhop of Carlifle, otherwife called Marmaduke Lumley bifhop of
" Carlifle, otherwife called Marmaduke bifhop of Carlifle late parfon of the
" church of Stephenhithe in the county of Middlefex, otherwife called
" Marmaduke bifhop of Carlifle executor of the teftament of John Lum-
" ley knight ‡."

In 1435, the bifhops of Durham and Carlifle, with other lords temporal,
are commiffioned to treat with the commiffioners of the king of Scots *.

This bifhop, great and noble as he was, found fome difficulties, through
the great loffes he fuftained by the daily incurfions of the Scots, in raifing
funds fufficient for the fupport of his epifcopal dignity; and therefore upon
application to the throne he had a royal grant of the churches of Caldbeck
and Rothbury to be annexed to his fee for ever, bearing date June 21, 1441 ‖.

---

† Rymer, v. 13. p. 144.   ‡ Ibid. v. 10. p. 549.   * Ibid. p. 620.   ‖ Pat.
21 H. 6. p 2. m. 22.

But neither of thefe appropriations took place, and the two churches ftill continue rectorial.

In the year 1449, he was tranflated to Lincoln.

20. NICHOLAS CLOSE, archdeacon of Colchefter, and one of the king's chaplains, was called by the pope's provifion to this fee in 1449, and had reftitution of the temporalties in the ufual form on the 14th of March following.

The occafion of his being advanced to this bifhoprick was probably the good fervices he had done the year before in a treaty of peace concluded with the king of Scots, he being one of the commiffioners (together with the lord privy feal, lord treafurer, and lord comptroller of the houfehold, and others) in the faid treaty, by the name and defignation of Nicholas Cloos chancellor of the univerfity of Cambridge, and doctor of divinity‡.

In 1451, Nicholas bifhop of Carlifle, with Robert bifhop of Durham, and others, were commiffioned to infpect the confervators of the truce and wardens of the marches, and to punifh their negligence and irregularities†.

In 1452, the bifhop of Carlifle, with the earls of Salifbury and Northumberland, and others, were commiffioned to take the homage of James earl of Douglas and all other Scottifh noblemen who fhould apply for that purpofe§.

On the 30th of Auguft in the fame year, he was tranflated by the pope to Litchfield, made his profeffion at Lambeth on the 15th of October, and died before the firft of November following‡.

21. WILLIAM PERCY, fon to the earl of Northumberland, and fometime chancellor of the univerfity of Cambridge, bringing the now ufual provifionary bulls from Rome, had the temporalties of the vacant fee given him by king Henry the fixth, on the 24th of October 1452.

[It is here obfervable, to what an exorbitant height the papal power was at this time advanced. Acts of parliament were made, and then in full force, that if any refervation, collation, or provifion fhall be made by the court of Rome, of any archbifhoprick, bifhoprick, dignity, or other benefice, the king fhall prefent for that time; and if the king's prefentee be difturbed by fuch provifors, the difturber fhall be imprifoned till he make fatisfaction.—— And if any fhall go or fend out of the realm to provide for himfelf a bene-fice; he fhall be out of the king's protection, and the benefice fhall be void.—— And if any fhall accept fuch benefice; he fhall be banifhed out of the realm for ever, and his lands and goods forfeited to the king. And notwithftanding all this, the contrary was in conftant practice: So weak was the executive power, and fo prevalent the hierarchy at that time]

In 1462, this bifhop Percy died. Upon whofe death king Edward the fourth granted the profits of the bifhoprick during the vacancy to Dr. John

‡ Rymer, v. 11. p. 231.   † Ibid. p. 283.   § Ibid. p. 310.   ‡ Anglia Sacra, v. 1. p. 453.

Kingfcott,

Kingfcott, in confideration of his faithful fervices, and of 600*l* owing to the faid John Kingfcott by the king's father, which the king acknowledged as his own debt: And foon after, he was promoted to the bifhoprick.

22. John Kingscott. Whatever influence his being a creditor of the king might have upon the election, it is certain he was chofen by the chapter, and approved by the pope; and had thereon reftitution (or rather continuance) of the temporalties from the king on the 20th of October 1462, before it was poffible for him to have reimburfed himfelf of the 600*l* debt. And he died in little more than a year after. For on the 16th of Dec. 1463, the faid king Edward the fourth, then refiding at Pontefract, granted the temporalties of the bifhoprick of Carlifle, vacant by the death of mafter John Kingfcott late bifhop there, to Richard Nevil earl of Warwick aad Salifbury †.

23. Richard Scroop. The pope upon the death of bifhop Kingfcott, who hardly enjoyed the bifhoprick fo long as to have all his fcores paid off, provided mafter Richard Scrope (elect of the fame church, fays the record) to fucceed, and he had the temporalties reftored on the 5th of June 1464. The provifion, if it may be fo called, was from the famous Æneas Sylvius, pope Pius the fecond, in the latter end of the year 1463; and he fent a recommendation of him to the clergy and others of the diocefe of Carlifle, as followeth : " Pius epifcopus, fervus fervorum Dei, dilectis filiis in populo civitatis et dioces' ecclefiæ Karliol', falutem et apoftolicam benedictionem. Hodie ecclefiæ Karliolenfi, per obitum bonæ memoriæ Johannis epifcopi Karliolenfis extra Romanam curiam defuncti, paftoris regimine deftitutæ, de perfona dilectiffimi Ricardi electi Karliolenfis nobis et fratribus noftris ob fuorum exigentiam meritorum accepta, de eorundem fratrum confilio auctoritate apoftolica duximus providendum, præferendo ipfum eidem ecclefiæ in epifcopum et paftorem : Quocirca univerfitatem veftram rogamus, monemus, et hortamur attente, per apoftolica vobis fcripta, quatenus eundem electum, tanquam patrem et paftorem animarum veftrarum devote fufcipientes, ac debita honorificentia profequentes, ejus falubribus monitis et mandatis humiliter intendatis; ita quod ipfe in vobis devotionis filios, et vos in illo patrem inveniffe benevolum gaudeatis. Datum Romæ apud fanctum Petrum anno incarnationis Domini 1463, Kal. Feb. Pontificatus anno fexto."
Bifhop Scroop died May 16, 1468.

24. Edward Story, being elected by the chapter, and approved by the pope, had reftitution of the temporalties Sept. 1, 1468.
In 1471, there is a confirmation of the vicarages of Bampton, Shap and Warcop, granted by him to the abbey of Shap.
In the fame year, Edward bifhop of Carlifle was one of the lords fpiritual who, with many of the chief nobility and other great men of the kingdom,

† Rymer, v. 11. p. 512.

took

took an oath of fealty to Edward the fifth then prince of-Wales. And in the following month, he with the bishop of Durham and the earl of Northumberland and others was a commissioner appointed to treat with those of Scotland at Alnwick; and the year following at Newcastle; and in 1473 at either of the former, or indefinitely at any other place: And in 1474, in the treaty for marriage betwixt the prince of Scotland and the princess Cecily king Edward the fourth's second daughter †.

In 1477, he was translated to Chichester. Archdeacon Bowchier, in his aforesaid letter to bishop Nicolson, says, As for bishop Story, I persuade myself, that he left some remembrance and considerable benefaction either to the fee, church, or city of Carlisle: Otherwise it is the only place to which he had any relation, whereunto he was not a benefactor. He gave to Pembroke hall a good estate; was benefactor to the church of Ely; founded the free school at Chichester, and built the new cross in the market place there, leaving a good estate to the corporation for its constant repair; bestowed lands on his see, and also on the dean and chapter. I find by bishop Wren's account or history of the fellows of Pembroke hall, that Edward Story was a north-country man, but the place is not set down. Where and when he took his several orders, what preferments he had in the church before he was bishop, I have no where found. He lies buried at Chichester, under a tomb which he built in his life time. He died Jan. 29, 1502.

Probably this bishop might be descended of some of the many families, on the borders, in Cumberland, that still bear this name.

25. RICHARD BELL, prior of Durham, was by the pope's command made bishop, consecrated by his predecessor, and had the temporalties restored to him 24 Apr. 1478.

Before he was bishop, he had been several times one of king Edward the fourth's commissioners in treaties with those of the king of Scots.

He built the tower at Rose, which still bears the name of Bell's tower.

He died in 1496, and was buried in his own cathedral, under the Litany desk, where is his portraiture in his pontificals, drawn at full length. On a brass plate are some rude latin verses; and on a brass margin about the stone,

> Hic jacet reverendus pater Ricardus Bell, quondam episcopus Karliolensis; qui ab hac luce migravit vicesimo quarto die . . . . Anno Domini . . . . . omnium defunctorum.

26. WILLIAM SEVER, born at Shinkley in the county of Durham, educated at Oxford, probably at either Gloucester or Durham college, nurseries for the Benedictines, of which order he was ‡. He was abbot of St. Mary's York, and created bishop of Carlisle in 1496. His temporalties were given him on the 11th of December in the same year, and at the same time a royal licence granted for the holding his abbotship in commendam ╪.

---

† Rymer, v. 11. p. 714. 717. 733. 776. 814.   ‡ Ath. Oxon. v. 1. p. 553.   ╪ Ibid.

In

'In 1496, king Henry the feventh grants a commiffion to Richard bifhop of Durham, William bifhop of Carlifle, and others, to treat about the intended marriage of his daughter Margaret with James king of Scots ‡.

In 1497, William bifhop of Carlifle, Sir Thomas Dacre of Dacre, and William Warham mafter of the Rolls (afterwards archbifhop of Canterbury) were the king's plenipotentiaries in a general treaty with the faid James king of Scots ‡.

In 1499, this bifhop was one of the confervators of the truce, figned and fworn to by Henry king of England and James king of Scotland, which was to continue during the joint lives of the contractors, the life of the longer liver of them, and one whole year after the death of the fame *.

In 1502, this bifhop was tranflated to Durham by the pope's bull ‡‡.

27. ROGER LEYBURN was defcended from an ancient family of that name in Weftmorland, was educated at Cambridge, mafter of Pembroke hall there, and archdeacon and chancellor of Durham. He was confecrated Sepr. 1. 1503, and the temporalties were reftored to him Oct. 15 following †.

His will bears date July 17, 1507; wherein he defires to be buried in St. James's hofpital near unto Charing Crofs by London; but whether he died in that or in the year following is not certain. Walter Redman, doctor in divinity, and mafter of the college at Grayftock, was one of his executors §.

28. JOHN PENNY, LL. D. educated in Lincoln college in Oxford, abbot of Leicefter, and afterwards bifhop of Bangor. The pope's bull for the tranflation of bifhop Penny from Bangor to Carlifle is dated at Rome on the 21ft of September 1508; and on the 23d of January following he paid his obedience to the archbifhop of York §.

He died in 1520, and was buried (as Dr. Todd fays) in St. Margaret's church in Leicefter, where is his effigies in alabafter curiously wrought, though without any infcription.

29. JOHN KYTE. He was born, as it is faid, within the city of London, and was educated for a time in the univerfity: But in what houfe, or what degrees he took, appears not. Afterwards he had feveral dignities conferred on him, being fubdean of the king's chapel, and by Hen. 7. fent ambaffador into Spain. In the latter end of 1513 he was made archbifhop of Armagh by provifion from pope Leo the 10th, and had the temporalties thereof on the 29th of May in the year following ‖.

On the third of Auguft 1521, being newly made bifhop of Carlifle, he refigned the archbifhoprick of Armagh, and was made archbifhop of Thebes in Greece. Thefe things were done through endeavours made to the pope by cardinal Wolfey, whofe creature Kyte was. The fees of the tranflation, with the commendams for Carlifle and his other benefices amounted to 1790 ducats;

‡ Rymer, v. 12. p. 635.   ‡ Ibid. p. 638.   * Ibid. p. 721. 726.   ‡‡ Rymer, v. 13. p. 28.   † Ibid. v. 13. p. 91.   § Ath. Oxon. v. 1. p. 562.   ‖ Ibid. p. 575.

8

but

but out of respect to the cardinal 270 of these were remitted, though the world went then very hard at Rome ‖.

In 1524, bishop Kyte was one of king Henry the eighth's commissioners (jointly with Thomas duke of Norfolk and Thomas lord Dacre) to treat with the commissioners of the king of Scots for abstinence from war †.

In 1526, he was a plenipotentiary, with Ralph earl of Westmorland and others, in a treaty of perpetual peace and amity with James the fifth, king of Scots ‡.

In 1529, he was one of the bishops who signed an instrument approving the reasonableness of the king's scruples concerning his marriage, and advising recourse to the pope for a speedy decision of the cause ‡.

This bishop Kyte, after he came to the see of Carlisle, was an intimate acquaintance of cardinal Wolsey, who conversed freely with him in his prosperity, and applied to him for necessaries (as a faithful friend) in his adversity *.

In 1530, he was one of the four bishops, who with cardinal Wolsey, archbishop Warham, and the whole peerage of England, signed the bold letter to pope Clement the seventh in the case of the king's divorce ††.

In 1533, by the title of archbishop of Thebes and perpetual commendatory of the see of Carlisle, he purchased several messuages and tenements in London of Sir Thomas Kyrfon knight §.

In 1536, he was one of those bishops who adhered to Lee archbishop of York, in opposing the progress of the reformation, which was favoured by archbishop Cranmer and his party in convocation †*.

He built not only the tower on the west side of the castle at Rose which retains his name; but, as it is thought, the whole pile of building from the south end of what is now the servants hall to the present staircase (which was built by bishop Rainbow), and which at that time composed the whole habitable house; the letters J K and his arms being also on the east side of that building not far from the chapel.

He died at London June 19, 1537; and was buried near the middle of the chancel of the church of Stepney. Over his grave is a marble stone, with the following inscription (in metre, such as it is):

> Under this stone closyde and marmorate
> Lyeth John Kytte Londoner natyffe;
> Encreasyng in virtues, rose to high estate;
> In the fourth Edward's chapel by his yong lyffe:
> Sith which, the seventh Henry's service primatiffe,
> Proceeding still in vertuous efficace,
> To be in favour with this our king's grase.
> With witt endowy'd, chosen to be legate,
> Sent into Spayne, where he right joyfully
> Combyned princes in peace most amate.

‖ Ath. Oxon. v. 1. p. 575. † Rymer, v. 14. p. 21. 29. ‡ Ibid. p. 119.
‡ Ibid. p. 301, 465, 6. * Sir W. Cavendish's memoirs of the Cardinal, 119, 146.
†† Herbert, 334. § Rymer, v. 14. p. 465. †* Fuller's Ch. Hist. B. 5. p. 212.

In

In Greece archbifhop elected worthely;
  And laft of Carlyel rulyng paftorally,
   Kepyng nobyl houfhold with grete hofpitality.
One thoufand fyve hundryd thirty and fevyn,
  Invyterate wyth paftoral carys, confumyd wyth age,
The ninetenth of Jun reckonyd full evyn,
  Paffed to Heavn from worldly pylgrimage.
Of whofe foul good pepul of cherite
Pray as ye wold be prayd for, for thus muft ye lie.
  Jefu merfy, Lady help ! *

30. ROBERT ALDRIDGE, was born at Burnham in Buckinghamfhire, and educated at Eaton, whence in 1507 he was chofen fcholar of king's college in Cambridge. Here he proceeded in arts; about which time, Erafmus in one of his epiftles gives him the title of *blandæ eloquentiæ juvens*. Afterwards he was proctor of the univerfity of Cambridge; and then fchoolmafter, fellow, and provoft of Eaton. In 1529, he was incorporated bachelor in divinity at Oxford, and the year following commenced doctor there in the fame faculty. About this time he was made archdeacon of Colchefter, and in 1537 was inftalled canon of Windfor, and the fame year conftituted regiftrary of the moft noble order of the garter. He was an eminent orator and poet, having left fome epigrams and other pieces in proof of his abilities that way. His friend John Leland (the antiquarian poet) has recommended him and his performances to pofterity in his Encomia, &c. +.

In Henry the eighth's mandate for his confecration, Aug. 7, 1537, he is called chaplain and almoner of our beloved confort Jane queen of England. He had reftitution of his temporalties Aug. 24 §.

He was one of thofe bifhops, who (with archbifhop Cranmer) fet out the godly and pious inftitution of a Chriftian man, commonly called The bifhops book +.

About this time, the houfe at Lambeth Marfh, called Carlifle-houfe, formerly the bifhop of Rochefter's, was given by king Hen. 8. to bifhop Aldridge and his fucceffors in exchange for his houfes near Ivie bridge, now Beaufort's buildings, for which the duke of Beaufort pays a yearly quit rent of 16*l* to the bifhop of Carlifle.

In 1540, bifhop Aldridge was one of thofe eight bifhops whom king Henry the eighth confulted (with other learned divines) about the doctrine of the feven facraments; and the anfwers which he gives to all the feventeen feveral quæries thereupon feem to be as learned and as well confidered as any of the reft. In the main he adheres to the Roman profeffion of faith in thefe particulars, and difagrees with archbifhop Cranmer and fome other favourers of the reformation ‡.

---

* Weaver's monum. p. 539.   + Ath. Oxon. v. 1. p. 79, 583, 679, 680.   § Rymer, v. 14. p. 583.
+ Strype's life of Cranmer, p. 54.   ‡ Burnet's Hift. Reform. v. 1. b. 3. p. 289.

He

5

He alfo, with the archbifhop of York and the bifhops of Durham and Win-chefter, vigoroufly promoted the act of the fix articles (31 H. 8. c. 14.) in parliament, againft the contrary endeavours of archbifhop Cranmer and moft of his fuffragans ‖.

In 1547, this diocefe, with the whole province of York, was vifited by Edward the fixth's commiffioners; who firft adminiftred the oath of fupremacy to each bifhop, and then gave him the king's injunctions.

In 1555, this bifhop died at Horncaftle, and (as is fuppofed) was buried there. Anthony a-Wood obferves of him, that he lived during the time that many and great changes were made both in church and ftate; that he held his preferments during all thofe changes, and confequently complied with all.

31. OWEN OGLETHORP. He was born at Newton Kyme, a little village near Tadcafter in the county of York; was educated at Magdalen college in Oxford; and was proctor of the univerfity in 1531. Soon after this, viz. in 1535, being then bachelor of divinity, he was chofen prefident of his college; and vicechancellor in 1551. The year following he quitted his headfhip for a canonry in king Henry the eighth's new erected college, and forthwith from a canon he was inftalled dean of the royal chapel of Windfor. And in the firft year of queen Mary he was chofen fecretary of the order of the garter. In the fame year he was re-elected prefident of Magdalen college, being at the fame time rector of Newington and Hafely both in the county of Oxford, as well as dean of Windfor. In 1554 he was one of the Oxford doctors, appointed to difpute with Cranmer, Ridley, and Latimer; and on the 7th of April 1555 he finally refigned his prefidentfhip, being then within view of the bifhoprick of Carlifle §.

On the 27th of October 1556, the cuftody of the temporalties of the bi-fhoprick of Carlifle was granted to the faid Owen Oglethorp being then bifhop elect; and on the 28th of January following as foon as the pope's confirmatory bull was arrived, the faid temporalties were fully reftored to him in the ufual form ‡.

In 1558, when Heath archbifhop of York, and all the reft of the bifhops, refufed to crown queen Elizabeth (the fee of Canterbury being then void), bifhop Oglethorp was with much ado prevailed upon to fet the crown on her head. For which fact, when he faw the iffue of the matter; and both himfelf (faith Anthony a-Wood) and all the reft of his facred order deprived, and the church's holy laws and faith againft the conditions of her confecration and acception into that royal office violated, he fore repented him all the days of his life, which were for that fpecial caufe both fhort and wearifome *. When he was appointed to execute the folemnity of the queen's coronation, the lords of the council fent to Bonner bifhop of London for all the pontifical ornaments ufed in fuch like magnificent inaugurations of the moft illuftrious princes †. We are alfo told, that bifhop Oglethorp ftanding ready to fay mafs before the

‖ Strype's life of Crann.er. p. 73.   § Ath. Oxon. v. 1 p. 688.   ‡ Rymer, v. 15. p. 415, 485.
* Ath. Oxon. v. 1. p. 553.   † Strype's Annals, p. 28.

queen, fhe commanded him not to elevate the confecrated hoft, to prevent the idolatry that the people were wont to commit at that ceremony, but to omit it becaufe fhe liked it not ; which the fa.d bifhop neverthelefs conftantly refufed to obey ‡.

In the queen's firft parliament this year, he was prefent and gave his diffent to the bills for reftitution of firft fruits, for reftoring the fupremacy, for exchange of bifhops lands, and for the uniformity of common prayer ||.

In 1559, May 11, he was fined by the queen's council 250l, for his contempt amongft others of her majefty's command to appear at a public difputation on the challenge of Jewell. And he was not long after deprived of his bifhoprick ; the reputed value whereof at that time was 268l §.

He died of an apoplexy, and was buried privately, with fix efcutcheons of arms, at St. Dunftan's in the Weft ‡.

His will bears date Nov. 10. in the firft year of Elizabeth by the grace of God of England, France, and Ireland, queen. (So that thereby it appeareth that he owned her title.) In purfuance of a royal licence in the 4 and 5 Ph. and M. referred to in his faid will, he injoins his executors, viz. Andrew Oglethorp his brother, Clement Oglethorp his nephew, Richard Shipley his brother, his coufin Robert Oglethorp, and Robert Thurlby his fervant, that for the endowment of the grammar fchool at Tadcafter, and for the erecting and endowing of an hofpital or an almfhoufe there for twelve poor people, with fo many diftinct lodgings, a common kitchen, and an hall to dine in, to be built in the form of a quadrangle, with a fair door into the church yard, and a fair image of Chrift ftanding on the top of the door, and to be called Chrift's hofpital, they fhould within a convenient time after his deceafe purchafe lands of the clear yearly value of 40l over and befides all charges, of which the manor of Cobcroft purchafed by the teftator and given to the fchoolmafter fhould be part, for the ufe of the faid fchool and hofpital for ever : And that of this 40l per annum fo much as fhould make the manor of Cobcroft 40 marks per annum fhould be affigned to the fchoolmafter as his falary, and the refidue to the faid twelve poor people and their fucceffors, who were to have 12d each weekly for their lives, if the rents fhould be able to anfwer the charge ; if not, then power is given to his executors or fupervifors to diminifh the number of the poor people as they fall vacant, 6, 8, or 10. And for the making this purchafe, and building the hofpital, he gives in plate and money the fum of 600l, and the rent of Snedal in the county of York, or fo much yearly rent as that of Snedal amounts to, to be affigned and affured to this ufe by his brother Andrew Oglethorp, which the teftator had purchafed with his own money of Sir Arthur Darcy.

This is the fubftance of the will fo far as it relates to the fchool and hofpital. And archdeacon Pearfon, in his letter of May 9, 1709, to b.fhop Nicolfon, fays, " The fchoolmafter's falary is ftill about 40 marks ; but as to the hofpital, it was not built according to the direction of the charitable founder, and is now only the ruins of a poor forry houfe. And for the poor people, they have been

‡ Strype's Annals, p 51. || Ibid, p. 57, &c. § Strype's Eliz. p. 95, 154. ‡ Ibid, p. 145.

many years ago reduced to four. And what allowance thofe have, I cannot yet learn. The foundation or ftatutes of the fchool I have not feen. But the archbifhop nominates the mafter, and the dean and chapter during the vacancy of the fee."

After the death of bifhop Oglethorp, Mr. Bernard Gilpin, rector of Hougton in the Spring, in the county of Durham, and commonly known by the name of the northern apoftle, had upon the requeft of his kinfman Edwin Sandys then bifhop of Worcefter a Conge d'Eflire fent to him to be elected into the vacant bifhoprick, but he abfolutely refufed it.

32, John Best. He was a Yorkfhireman born; bred in the univerfity of Oxford; and afterwards dignified in the church of Wells and elfewhere; but leaving all in the beginning of queen Mary's reign for religion's fake, he lived obfcurely and as occafion ferved *.

He was confecrated bifhop on the 2d of March 1560, aged 48 years; and had his temporalties from the queen on the 18th of April following †.

In 1564, he had the queen's commiffion procured by fecretary Cecil, at the interceffion of Edmund Grindal bifhop of London, to arm him againft the ill dealings of papifts and other difaffected perfons in his diocefe ‡.

In 1566, he was one of the five bifhops created doctors in divinity at London by Dr. Humphrey the queen's profeffor at Oxford, by virtue of a fpecial commiffion from the univerfity for that purpofe ‖.

The fame year he was one of the 13 bifhops, who together with the two archbifhops, fubfcribed the Saxon homilies, then publifhed by archbifhop Parker in confutation of the errors of the church of Rome §.

In 1567, Ap. 9. he wrote to archbifhop Parker the following letter:——— " I have a commendam of a parifh called Rumald Church. It will expire within a year or lefs. The advowfon of the fame is offered to be fold to gentlemen of this country at unreafonable fums of money. So that it is apparent the revenues thereof are like to come into the temporal mens hands, and the cure into fome unlearned afs's, as many others are like to do in thefe parts, unlefs your grace be a good ftay therein. For this caufe, and for that my charge here in the queen's fervice doth daily increafe, and alfo that in time of wars I have no refuge left to fly unto but only this, I am compelled to be a fuitor to your grace, for the renewing of my commendam for the time of my life. In doing whereof, your grace fhall both ftay the covetous gripe that hath the advowfon from his prey, the unlearned afs from the cure, where I have now a learned preacher, and bind me as I am otherwife moft bound to ferve and pray for your grace's long continuance in honour and godlinefs; your grace's poor brother to command, Joannes Carliolenfis ┼"

On the 22d of May 1570, he ended his days, and was buried in his cathedral church of Carlifle **.

---

* Ath. Oxon. v. 1. p. 593.   † Ibid. p. 599.   ‡ Strype's Grindal, p. 85.
‖ Strype's Eliz. p. 431. § Strype's Parker, p. 240. ┼ Ibid. p. 256.
** Ath. Oxon. v. 1. p. 599.

33, Richard

25. RICHARD BARNES. He was bred in Brazen-Nose college in Oxford, whereof in 1553 he proceeded bachelor of arts, and in 1556 was admitted master. He afterwards took his bachelor of divinity's degree in Cambridge. He was born at Bould near Warrington in Lancashire, and was admitted fellow of Brazen-Nose by authority of the king's council in 1552. About the time that he took the degree of master of arts, he also took holy orders, and was made minister of Stonegrave in Yorkshire. In 1561 he was admitted chancellor of the cathedral church of York, and about the same time was made canon residentiary and prebendary of Laughton in the said church, as a so public reader of Divinity therein. About 1567, he was consecrated suffragan bishop of Nottingham in the church of St. Peter at York †.

On the 25th of June 1570, he was elected bishop of Carlisle, had his election confirmed on the 13th of July following, and had the temporalties restored on the 26th of the same month ‡.

He was allowed to hold his chancellor's stall and dignity in the metropolitical church of York in commendam with the bishoprick of Carlisle for one year after his consecration, and the rectories of Stockeslay and Stonegrave during his life, provided that as soon as he should be possessed of the church of Rumbold kirk, the rectory of Stockeslay should become vacant ‖.

In 1577, he was elected to the see of Durham, and confirmed the 9th of May in that year: and in 1579 was created doctor of divinity at Oxford. He died in 1587, and was buried in the choir, sometimes called the Presbytaries, of the cathedral church of Durham. Over his grave was a monument soon after put, with this inscription thereon:

" Reverendo in Christo patri ac Domino, Domino Ricardo Barnes Dunel-
" mensi episcopo, præsuli præcocto, liberali, et munifico. Obiit 24 Aug.
" Anno domini 1587. Ætatis suæ 55."

34. JOHN MEYE. He was in 1560 chosen master of Catherine hall, and Mr. Strype supposes was brother to William Meye dean of St. Paul's. In 1570, he was vice-chancellor of Cambridge, and procured for the university a new body of statutes. In 1575, he was made archdeacon of the East Riding in Yorkshire.

In 1577, June 12, he was chosen bishop of Carlisle; was consecrated at London on the 29th of September following, and had restitution of the temporalties on the 8th of October.

Mr. Strype tells us, that this Dr. Meye was made bishop by the intercession of his friend the earl of Shrewsbury, which favour he acknowledged by a letter dated from Huntingdon, where (inter alia) he requests the said earl to obtain a commendam for him where he might reside, Rose castle being then taken up by a temporal lord, the lord Scrope; therefore he besought him to move the earl of Leicester for his commendam, viz. the benefice of Darfield.—Lord Scrope was at that time warden of the west marches, and might upon that account borrow Rose castle to reside in for a time, but had certainly no other claim to it. And what the bishop says of him was a mere pretext to obtain a

† Ath. Oxon. v. 1. p. 606—708.   ‡ Rymer, v. 15. p. 684.   ‖ Ibid. p. 685.

O o 2   commendam

commendam for Darfield. And Dr. Todd fays, he attempted to have had fome concurrent leafes of good value given in reverfion to fome of his near relations, but the dean and chapter refufed to confirm them.

This bifhop died at Rofe caftle on the 15th of February 1597 at eight in the morning, and was buried at Carlifle at eight in the evening of the fame day; the plague raging at that time, of which diftemper probably he died.

35. HENRY ROBINSON. He was born within the city of Carlifle, and was entred upon the foundation of Queen's college in Oxford about the year 1568, where he became fellow, and was efteemed an excellent difputant and preacher. In 1576, being then only mafter of arts, he was chofen principal of Edmund hall; nor had he taken any other degree, when in 1581 he was unanimoufly elected provoft of the faid Queen's college; which office he enjoyed about 18 years, and in that time reftored the college and made it flourifh, after it had been long in a declining condition through the negligence of former governors.

In 1583, archbifhop Grindall by his laft will and teftament bequeathed to his chaplain Henry Robinfon (then provoft of Queen's) the advowfon of a dignity and prebend in the church of Litchfield, or of another in that of St. David's.

In 1590, he commenced doctor in divinity.

In 1598, May 27, he was elected bifhop of Carlifle; confecrated July 23; and had his temporalties reftored Aug. 5.

In 1599, he was appointed one of the queen's commiffioners for ecclefiaftical caufes.

In 1613, George Denton of Cardew-hall within the manor of Dalfton efquire, refufing all fuit to his lordfhip's mills and courts, the bifhop filed a bill againft him in the exchequer and obtained a decree againft him, and thereby fecured the juft rights of his fee againft that mefne lordfhip.

From an entry in the Regifter of the parifh of Dalfton it appears, that this bifhop died at Rofe the 19th day of June 1616, about three of the clock in the afternoon, and was buried in the cathedral church of Carlifle about eleven of the clock of the night of the fame day.

On a plate of brafs, behind the hangings on the north corner of the high altar in the cathedral, was a draught of a bifhop in his pontificals, kneeling before one church in ruins, and another fair built. Upon the former whereof, was infcribed,

Invenit deftructum, reliquit extructum et inftructum.

On the latter,

Intravit per oftium, manfit fidelis, receffit beatus.

And after many other conceits and fhort mottoes, there is under all;

Henrico Robinfono Carleolenfi, S S. Theologiæ Doctori, collegii Reginæ Oxonii præpofito providiffimo, tandemque hujus ecclefiæ per annos XVIII epifcopo vigilantiffimo, 13 Calend. Julii, Anno a partu Virginis 1616, Ætatis fuæ 64, pie in domino obdormienti.

Bernardus Robinfon, frater ac hæres hoc qualecunque MNHMEION, amoris teftimonium, collocavit.

7

Non

Non fibi, fed patriæ, præluxit lampadis inftar,.
Deperdens oleam, non operam, ille fuam ::
In minimis fido fervo, majoribus apto,.
· Maxima nunc domini gaudia adire datur.

This is, in the main, only a copy of what the college aforefaid had put up for him in their chapel, in a grateful commemoration of his great benefactions to that fociety *..

36. ROBERT SNOWDEN. He was third fon of Ralph Snowden of Mansfield Woodhoufe in the county of Nottingham, and was fome time prebendary of Southwell. He was confecrated bifhop of Carlifle in St. Peter's church at York, Nov. 24, 1616, by archbifhop Matthews; and the temporalties were given to him on the 20th of December following †.

He died at London in the latter end of May 1621, whilft the parliament was fitting; and left a fon Rutland Snowden of Horncaftle in the county of Lincoln efquire, by his wife Abigail daughter of Robert Orme of Elfton in Nottinghamfhire †.

37. RICHARD MILBURNE. He was born at Utterbank in Gilfland in this county; was firft vicar of Sevenoake in Kent, afterwards dean of Rochefter, then bifhop of St. David's, and from thence tranflated to Carlifle. He married Frances daughter of Francis Traps and widow of one Pett of Sevenoake aforefaid, and by her had iffue one fon and two daughters. Chryfogon the elder of which daughters was married to Ifaac Singleton chancellor of the diocefe.

The royal affent for his tranflation to the fee of Carlifle paffed the privy feal Sep. 11, 1621; as did the reftitution of the temporalties the third of October following ‡.

He died in the year 1624, and left money (as it is faid) for the endowing of a fchool and building of an hofpital, which bifhop Godwin fays was 300 l. to each. He had a fermon in print concerning the impofition of hands, preached at a metropolitical vifitation Sept. 7, 1607, when he was minifter at Sevenoake ‖.

38. RICHARD SENHOUSE was of the ancient family of Senhoufe of Netherhall in this county; was firft admitted a ftudent in Trinity college in Cambridge, and afterwards removed to that of St. John's in the fame univerfity, of which he was made fellow; and continuing there many years, took the degree of doctor of divinity in 1622. He was firft chaplain, as it is faid, in the earl of Bedford's family; afterwards to prince Charles, and at length to king James the firft, who advanced him firft to the deanry of Gloucefter, and afterwards to the fee of Carlifle ‖.

His Conge d'Eflire is dated 13th June 1624, the royal affent July 20, and the reftitution of the temporalties the 14th of October following,.

* Hift. and Antiq. Oxon. l. 2, p. 124.   † Ath. Oxon. v. 1. p. 620.   ‡ Rymer,
v. 17, p. 324.   ‖ Ath. Ox. v. 1. p. 620.

He:

He was killed by a fall from his horse on the 6th of May 1626, and was buried in his own cathedral.

39. FRANCIS WHITE, D. D. was consecrated at London, Dec. 3, 1626. Dr. Heylin says of him, that he was a man who having spent the greatest part of his life on his own private cures, grew suddenly into esteem by his zealous preaching against the papists, and his book against the jesuit Fisher.

He was appointed by king James the first to have a special eye to the countess of Denbigh, whom the priests much laboured to pervert. He was encouraged thereto by the deanry of Carlisle, and advanced on the same account to the bishoprick thereof in the year 1626.

On the 9th of February 1628, he was translated to Norwich. In the heads and articles to be infisted on in an intended declaration of the house of commons, and agreed upon in a subcommittee for religion the 25th of Feb. 1628, complaint was made of the growth of Arminianism, and that those persons who maintained and published that sort of doctrine were favoured and preferred. One instance (amongst others) of this was in the late bishop of Carlisle, who since his last Arminian sermon on Christmass-day foregoing preached at court, was advanced to the bishoprick of Norwich.

On the 8th of December 1631 he was translated to Ely, and died in his palace at Holborn in February 1637, and was buried at St. Paul's with much funeral solemnity.

40. BARNABY POTTER. He was born within the barony of Kendal in Westmorland, and was educated in Queen's college in Oxford, whereof he was made fellow, and afterwards entring into orders he became a puritanical preacher at Totnes in Devonshire, where he was much followed by that party. In 1615 he proceeded in Divinity, and in the year following was elected provost of his college. Which place he resigned, after he had held it about ten years, and was now the king's chaplain, and procured his nephew Christopher Potter an interest to be his successor in the college §.

He was consecrated in the chapel of Ely-house in Holborn on the 15th of March 1628, and had the temporalties restored to him on the 23d of the same month. His consecration sermon was preached by his nephew Dr. Christopher Potter, and printed. Upon a second edition of it, a notable passage in Theodoret, concerning laymen reading the scriptures, was expunged. Which Mr. Prynne supposes to have been done by the direction of the then bishop of London Dr. Laud.

He died in his lodgings within the parish of St. Paul in Covent Garden London in the beginning of January in 1641, and was buried in the church belonging to that parish on the sixth day of the same month.

41. JAMES USHER. He was eldest son of Mr. Arnold Usher, one of the six clerks in chancery in Ireland, by Margaret daughter of James Stanihurft

§ Ath. Oxon. v. 2. p. 6.

recorder

recorder of the city of Dublin. He was born in that city Jan. 4, 1580, and educated in the college at Dublin. In 1620 he was promoted to the bishoprick of Meath, and upon Dr. Christopher Hampton's death in 1624 he was advanced to the archbishoprick of Armagh. The troubles coming on afterwards in that kingdom, he suffered great losses thereby; in consideration whereof king Charles the first, in the year 1641, granted him the bishoprick of Carlisle in commendam; upon the revenues of which bishoprick, though much diminished by the quartering of the English and Scotch armies, he made shift to support himself, till the parliament seized on all bishops lands; and then, in consideration of his great merits they allowed him a pension of 400*l*, but he never received it above once, or twice at most ┼.

The grant of the Commendam runs in the following words:

" Carolus Dei gratia, Angliæ, Scotiæ, Franciæ, et Hiberniæ rex, fidei defensor, &c. Omnibus ad quos præsentes literæ pervenerint, salutem. Sciatis,, quod datum est nobis intelligere, ex parte reverendissimi in Christo patris Jacobi Usher archiepiscopi Armachani et totius Hiberniæ primatis, quod propter tumultus in dicto regno nostro Hiberniæ nuper ortos, fructus, proficua et commoditates dicti archiepiscopatus percipere non poterit; cujus causa, et propter multas alias rationes humiliter nobis supplicatum est, quatenus de opportuno aliquo subventionis et auxilii remedio in præmissis providere et clementia nostra regia dignaremur: Nos igitur ex parte sua supplicationi favorabiliter inclinati, ac volentes ut ei in præmissis commode provideatur, de gratia nostra speciali, certa scientia, et mero motu nostris, et ex nostræ regiæ potestatis plenitudine pariter et prerogativa nostris, concessimus et licentiam dedimus, ac pro nobis, hæredibus, et successoribus nostris per præsentes concedimus et licentiam damus, præfato Jacobo Usher archiepiscopo Armachano prædicto, quod ipse episcopatum Carliolensem et sedem episcopi et pastoris sive dignitatis episcopatus ejusdem in regno nostro Angliæ post mortem naturalem ultimi episcopi ibidem jam vacantem et ad nostram donationem liberamque dispositionem spectantem, una cum archiepiscopatu Armachano prædicto in commendam accipere, retinere, possidere, frui, et gaudere possit et valeat; nec non episcopatus prædicti fructus, redditus, proventiones, pre eminentias, privilegia, proficua, commoditates, et alia emolumenta prædicta, etiamsi in divinis, in ecclesia cathedrali omnino non interfuerit, aut officiis ejusdem ecclesiæ non deserviet, perinde ac si eundem episcopatum in titulo episcopatus obtinuisset, ac divinis officiis in eadem ecclesia cathedrali pariter interesset, ac aliis officiis ejusdem episcopatus deserviret, in usus suos et utilitates, donec prædicti archiepiscopatus plenos proventus et redditus rursus recuperaverit, convertere et applicare libere et licite valeat ac possit; aliquo jure, constitutione, lege, ordinatione, actu, consuetudine, statuto (generali, speciali, locali), aut aliqua alia re vel causa quacunque in contrarium faciendis in aliquo non obstantibus. Quibus omnibus et singulis præmissis, seu eorum aliquod quovis modo tangentibus,, quatenus huic nostræ dispensationi seu concessioni obveniant, tenore præsentium derogamus; volentes et mandantes, quod hæc præsens nostra concessio et dispensatio exponatur et adjudicetur in omnibus curiis nostris et alibi, in benignissimo

┼ Ath. Oxon, v. 2. p. 653.

fimo fenfu et pro maximo commodo et beneficio dicti Jacobi fecundum veram
intentionem noftram in hac parte. In cujus rei teftimonium, has literas noftras
fieri fecimus patentes. Tefte meipfo apud Weftminfter decimo fexto die Februarii, anno regni noftri decimo feptimo.":

He died on Friday the 21ft of March 1655 at the countefs of Peterborough's houfe at Rygate in Surry, aged 75 years. Sir Timothy Tyrrel, his
fon-in-law, and the countefs of Peterborough, had refolved to bury him in a
decent manner, but without pomp, at Rygate, in the vault of the Howards,
of which family the countefs was. But Oliver Cromwell ordered him to be
interred with great magnificence in Weftminfter abbey, and figned a warrant
to the lords of the treafury to pay to Dr. Bernard 200 *l* to defray the expence
thereof. And this Cromwell did out of an honourable refpect to the memory
of fo pious and learned a champion of the proteftant caufe as the archbifhop
was. On Thurfday the 17th of April following, his body was conveyed from
Rygate to St. George's church in Southwark; at which place, about 12 of the
clock, his friends and many of the clergy met the corps, and accompanied
it from thence to Somerfet houfe, where lying for fome time, it was from
thence carried to Weftminfter abbey: Where, after the faid Dr. Bernard had
preached to a numerous auditory, it was interred.

Cromwell injoined the archbifhop's executors not to fell his library without
Cromwell's confent. Part of it was purchafed by the officers and foldiers of
the then army in Ireland; and many of the books and more of the beft manufcripts had been ftolen or imbezzled during the times of confufion. What
remained was by king Charles the fecond given to the college at Dublin, and
is ftill a confiderable part of the library there.

42. RICHARD STERNE, upon the reftoration of king Charles the fecond, was
nominated to this fee. He was fon of Simon Sterne of Mansfield in the
county of Nottingham, defcended from thofe of his name in Suffolk, and was
educated in the univerfity of Cambridge, where he became doctor of Divinity,
and was mafter of Jefus college. He was alfo chaplain to archbifhop Laud,
whom he attended on the fcaffold whereon that primate was beheaded. He
himfelf was alfo a prifoner in the Tower with fome other heads of houfes,
upon a complaint from Oliver Cromwell then burgefs for Cambridge, for con-
veying their college plate to the king at York. Hereupon he was ejected
out of his mafterfhip, and lofing all he had, lived obfcurely till the reftoration *.

This bifhop built a chapel at Rofe, and arching it underneath, the walls
were infufficient to fuftain the weight, and thereby it became fo ruinous, that
his next fucceffor was obliged to take it down and rebuild it.

In 1664 he was tranflated to York, and died there on the 18th of June
1683. Bifhop Burnet, in the Hiftory of his own Times, fays of him, that he
was a four, ill-tempered man, and minded chiefly the inriching his family:
That he was fufpected of popery, becaufe he was more than ordinarily com-

* Ath. Oxon. v. 1. p. 856.

pliant

pliant in all things to the court, and was very zealous for the duke of York. On the contrary, in a letter from York to his fucceffor at Carlifle, bifhop Rainbow, it is faid, " He was greatly refpected and generally lamented. All the " clergy commemorate his fweet condefcenfions, his free communications, " faithful counfels, exemplary temperance, chearful hofpitality, and bounti- " ful charity. He contributed largely to St. Paul's. Nor did he forget St. " Peter's; for by his will he bequeathed to our cathedral at York all his chapel " plate, to repair the lofs of our own, by facrilegious hands not long fince " ftolen out of our veftry. He carefully provided for all his family, even to " the meaneft fervant. He was very exact in every thing he meddled with " and had time to difpatch, and I wifh that his Hebrew criticifms upon the " facred text do not want his laft hand. In his Logic (which is ready for the " prefs) I defired him not to omit the inftances which. (for illuftration) he " had made out of the bible : He told me, that it was like to come into the " hands of boys, that might not ufe it with that reverence which was meet. " But I hope that what I replied prevailed with him to retain them."

His will was, to 'go quietly to the grave, without exenteration, lying in ftate, or funeral fermon. He regarded not pomp whilft he lived, and he provided againft all indications of it when he was dead. He was buried under a noble monument in St. Stephen's chapel at the eaft end of the cathedral, on which is the following infcription :

Hic fpe futuræ gloriæ fitus eft
Richardus Sterne, Mansfeldiæ honeftis parentibus ortus.
Tria apud Cantabrigienfes collegia certatim,
Ipfum cum fuperbia arripiunt et jactant fuum.
Sanctæ et individuæ Trinitatis fcholarem,
Corporis Chrifti focium, Jefu tandem præfectum meritiffimum ;
Gulielmo Cantuarienfi martyri a facris in fatali pegmate reftitit,
Aufus et ipfe inter peffimos effe bonus, et vel cum illo commori.
Poftea honefto confilio nobili formandæ juventuti operam dedit,
Ne deeffent qui Deo et regi, cum licuerit, rite fervirent.
Quo tandem reduce (etiam cum apologia et prece) rogatur,
Ut Carleolenfis effe epifcopus non dedignaretur.
Et non illi, magis quam Soli, diu latere licuit.
In humili illa provincia fat's conftitit fummam meruiffe ;
Ad primatum igitur Ebor', ut plena, fplenderet gloria, electus eft.
In utroque ita fe geffit, ut Deo prius quam fibi profpiceret.
Ecclefias fpoliatas olim de fuo vel dotavit vel ditavit amplius.
Non antiquis ecclefiæ patribus impar fuiffet, fi coævus.
Omnis in illo enituit quæ antiftitem deceat, et ornet virtus ;
Gravitas, fanctitas, charitas, rerum omnium fcientia :
In utraque fortuna par animi firmitas et conftantia :
Æquiffimus ubique vitæ tenor, regiminis juftitia, et moderatio :
In fexto fupra octogefimum anno corpus erectum,
Oris dignitas, oculorum vigor auriumque, animi præfentia.

Nec ulla in feneĉtute fæx, fed adhuc flos prudentiæ,
.Satis probarunt quid menfa poffit et vita fobria.

Obiit Jan. 18. { Salutis 1683.
{ Ætatis fuæ 87.

43. EDWARD RAINBOW was born at Bliton near Gainfborough in the county of Lincoln, on the 20th of April 1608, his father Mr. Thomas Rainbow being then minifter there. After he had been educated in the fchools of Gainf-borough, Peterborough, and Weftminfter, he was admitted in Corpus Chrifti college in Oxford in July 1623, his elder brother John being then fellow of that houfe. But within lefs than two years, he removed thence to Magdalen college in Cambridge, where he was fcholar, fellow, and an eminent tutor, and as fuch the two fons of the right honourable Theophilus earl of Suffolk were committed to his care, as were alfo two fons of the lord Daincourt. In Oĉtober 1642, he was admitted to the mafterfhip of the faid laft named college. In 1646, he commenced doĉtor in divinity. He loft his faid mafterfhip in 1650, for refufing to fign a proteftation againft the king. In 1652, he had the living of Chefterford near Audley Inn in Effex, and in the fame year married Mrs. Elizabeth Smith his predeceffor's daughter. In 1659, the rich rec-tory of Benefield in Northamptonfhire was given him by the earl of Warwick; and by the favour of lord Broghill he was excufed from going to the triers, a thing he never would fubmit to for any preferment whatever. Soon after the reftoration of king Charles the fecond he was reftored to his mafterfhip of Magdalen college, and made dean of Peterborough. In 1662 he was made vicechancellor of the univerfity of Cambridge, and in 1664 bifhop of Carlifle, to which he was confecrated by archbifhop Sheldon in the chapel at Lambeth on the 10th of July in that year, and in September following he fettled at Rofe caftle, the only remaining habitable houfe then belonging to the fee; and finding even this in a moft miferable condition, a great part of it having been burnt by the Scots in the late rebellion, and the chapel (which was the only repair bifhop Sterne pretended to, notwithftanding what is faid in the flattering epitaph above mentioned, although he had received the immenfe advantages of coming to the fee when all the leafes were either totally or near expired) yet being fo ill done that it was neceffary to take it entirely down, the bifhop thought it expedient to proceed againft his metropolitan and immediate predeceffor for dilapidations. Whereupon the archbifhop made a tender of 400l for repairing the chapel, and pleaded the aĉt of indemnity and oblivion (12 Car. 2. c. 12.) in bar of all other dilapidations. The court of delegates adjudged the faid tender fufficient for repairing the faid chapel, and that all the other dilapidations were covered by the faid aĉt, and fo difmiffed the caufe without cofts on either fide. The bifhop being thus totally defeated of all aid from his rich predeceffor (the expences of the law-fuit having coft him more than 400l) fet about the repairs himfelf with all poffible care and expedition; built the chapel; with the two good parlours below, entirely anew, as alfo the ftair-cafe, and paffage or entry wherein it ftands, with feveral other additions

I   and

and conveniencies, which all together coft him upwards of 1100*l* (over and above the 400*l* recovered for dilapidations).

In 1667 he gave 130*l* for augmenting the vicarage of Melborn in Derby-fhire; which was to advance it 10*l per annum* at the prefent, and 20*l per annum* after the life of lady Hartop.

He died at Rofe caftle on Wednefday the 26th day of March 1684, at the age of near 76 years, and was interred on Tuefday following in Dalfton church-yard, under the fouthern wall of the chancel; where, according to his own direction, a plain common freeftone is laid over his grave with this in-fcription:

Depofitum Edwardi Rainbow
Epifc. Carliol. Obiit vicefimo
Sexto Die Martii. MDCLXXXIV.

He left no works in print, but three occafional fermons:

The firft of which was preached at St. Paul's Crofs, Sept. 28, 1634, in-titled, Labour forbidden and commanded.

The fecond was preached at the funeral of Sufannah countefs of Suffolk, 13th May, 1649, on Eccl. vii. 1.

The third was preached at the interment of Anne countefs dowager of Pem-broke, Dorfet, and Montgomery, at Appleby in Weftmorland, 14th Apr. 1676. on Prov. xiv. 1.

44. THOMAS SMITH was born at Whitewall in the parifh of Afby in the county of Weftmorland. He was educated in the neighbouring free fchool of Appleby, and in the 16th year of his age was admitted in Queen's college in Oxford.

After he had taken the degree of mafter of arts, and was preferred to a fel-lowfhip, he became a very eminent tutor, moft of the gentlemen of the col-lege being committed to his care.

When king Charles the firft refided at Oxford, Mr. Smith was one of thofe who were appointed to preach before him at Chriftchurch, and before the par-liament at St. Mary's.

When afterwards faction, and the fanatical and furious zeal of a new fet of vifitors, had rendred Oxford as uneafy to perfons of loyalty and generofity, as before it had been acceptable, he withdrew into the north; living there in great privacy, till upon the reftoration of king Charles the fecond, the king's pleafure was intimated to the univerfity, that there fhould be a creation in all faculties of fuch as had fuffered for the royal caufe. Whereupon, on the 2d of Auguft 1660, he was with many more of his fellow-fufferers created ba-chelor of divinity, and on the 11th of December following was diplomated doctor in the fame faculty.

The king was alfo pleafed to make him a fharer with others of his royal bounty, in the difpofal of vacant benefices and dignities in the church, and to honour him with being one of the king's chaplains in ordinary. A prebend in the church at Carlifle was what he had firft given him, into which he was inftalled Nov. 14, 1660. At the fame time he had the offer of a good rectory in the king's difpofal; the diftance whereof not fuiting his other circumftances, he declined it himfelf, and procured it for his friend.

Within a few months after this, he was collated by bifhop Cofins to a prebend in the church of Durham; where, looking upon himfelf as invefted with a preferment as agreeable as his modefty would give him leave to wifh for, he began immediately to repair his prebendal houfe, fparing no coft to make it a dwelling fuitable to the honour and endowments of that cathedral.

Upon the promotion of Dr. Carleton to the bifhoprick of Briftol in 1671, Dr. Smith had the deanry of Carlifle conferred upon him. The dean's houfe was left by his predeceffor in the fame ruinous condition the rebellious times had brought it into: But was now, moftly from the ground, rebuilt at his own great expence. The altar of the cathedral had his offering of a large fet of double gilt communion plate; and his praifes were addreffed to God on an handfome new organ given by him to the quire.

Upon the death of bifhop Rainbow, he was to his own great furprize, and no lefs fatisfaction of the whole diocefe, recommended by king Charles to the chapter for their bifhop, and by them elected May 3, 1684. On the 29th of June following he was confecrated in St. Peter's church at York, and about the middle of July did his homage at Windfor and had reftitution of the temporalties of his fee.

In 1698, his wife died at Rofe, and was buried in the cathedral at Carlifle a little below the rails of the communion table, and over her grave is a fair marble ftone, upon which is very well cut,

D. S.
Hic intus jacet Anna Smith,
R. P. D. D. Thomæ Carliolenfis Epifcopi
Conjux chariffima: Quæ fincera erga Deum
Pietate, indefeffa erga pauperes liberalitate,
Et fingulari erga omnes morum candore
et benevolentia, pofteris præluxit magnum
Chriftianis virtutis exemplar. Vixit annos
LXVII. Obiit fexto die Octobris Anno Chrifti
1698. Et hic requiefcit in Domino.

The faid bifhop Smith died at Rofe caftle Apr. 12, 1702; and lies buried in the cathedral before the altar, under a plain blue marble ftone, with this modeft infcription by his own direction:

D. S.
Thomas Smith, S. T. P.
Hujus ecclefiæ primum canonicus,
Dein decanus, tandemque epifcopus,
Placide in Domino requiefcit.
Vixit annos LXXVIII.
Obiit duodecimo die Aprilis
MDCCII.

The

The fums expended by this good bifhop in publick buildings and charities, as far as hath come to our knowledge, are as follows:

			l
The fchool and mafter's houfe at Appleby and cloifters there	—		626
The poor and fchool at Afby	— — — — —		100
Towards building St. Paul's	— — — — —		150
New library at Queen's college	— — — —		100
More to the faid college	— — — — —		500
Other colleges and chapels	— — — — —		50
Prebendal houfe at Durham and organ	— — —		300
Building deanry houfe at Carlifle	— — — —		600
Organ at Carlifle 220*l*, communion plate 100*l*	— —		320
Prebendal houfe at Carlifle	— — — —		50
Altering houfe and building ftables at Rofe	— —		300
New tower there and court walls	— — — —		167
School at Dalfton 30*l*, tenement there 80*l*	— — —		110
Court houfe at Dalfton	— — — —		50
Library and Regifter's office at Carlifle	— — —		120
To the dean and chapter	— — — — —		100
Pigeon coat at Rofe	— — — —		53
To the feveral parifhes in the diocefe by his will	— —		230
School at Carlifle	— — — — —		500
Vicarage of Penrith	— — — — —		500
Vicarage of Dalfton	— — — —		300
		Total	5226

45. WILLIAM NICOLSON. He was born at Orton near Carlifle, where his father Mr. Jofeph Nicolfon formerly of Queen's college in Oxford was then rector. In 1670, being then 15 years of age, he was admitted member of the faid college.

In 1678, he was fent by Sir Jofeph Williamfon (fecretary of ftate) to Leipfick, in order to get acquaintance with the high Dutch and other feptentrional languages. Here he tranflated an effay of Mr. Hook's towards a proof of the motion of the earth from the fun's parallax, out of Englifh into Latin, which was there printed by the profeffor who put him upon it.

In 1679, he was elected and admitted fellow of the faid Queen's college, after a fhort tour into France in the fummer, having firft compleated his degree of mafter of arts.

In 1680, he publifhed an account of the ftate of the kingdoms of Poland, Denmark, and Norway, as alfo of Iceland, in the firft volume of the Englifh Atlas; whereof he afterwards compofed the fecond and third volumes (treating of the empire of Germany) without any affiftance. The fame year he was fent by the vicechancellor to wait on George Lewis prince of Brunfwick-
Hanover

Hanover at Tetſworth in his way to the univerſity, where the next day his highneſs was complimented with the degree of a doctor in the civil law.

In 1681, he was collated by biſhop Rainbow to a vacant prebend in the cathedral church of Carliſle, and alſo into the vicarage of Torpenhow, and in the year following to the archdeaconry of Carliſle, vacant by the reſignation of Mr. Thomas Muſgrave.

In 1685, he wrote a letter to Mr. Obadiah Walker maſter of Univerſity college, concerning a Runic inſcription at Bewcaſtle in Cumberland, printed in the Philoſophical Tranſactions, Numb. 178. And likewiſe a letter to Sir William Dugdale, concerning a Runic inſcription on the font in the church of Bridekirk, dated at Carliſle Nov. 23, 1685, and printed in the ſame Tranſaction.

In 1696, he publiſhed the firſt part of his Engliſh Hiſtorical Library: The next year he publiſhed the ſecond part: And in 1699, the third and laſt part. In 1702, he publiſhed one for Scotland; as he did likewiſe one for Ireland in 1724.—Dr. Atterbury having reflected on ſome parts of the Engliſh Hiſtorical Library, particularly relating to convocations, in his rights, powers, and privileges of an Engliſh convocation; the biſhop vindicated himſelf in a letter to Dr. White Kennet publiſhed in the third edition of the ſaid Hiſtorical Library.

In 1702, on the eve of Aſcenſion day, he was elected biſhop of Carliſle, confirmed June 3, and conſecrated June 14 at Lambeth; which promotion was obtained by the intereſt of the houſe of Edenhall.

In 1704, Sept. 15. Dr. Francis Atterbury waited upon the biſhop at Roſe for inſtitution to the deanry of Carliſle. But the letters patent being directed to the chapter and not to the biſhop, and the date thereof being July 15, though the late dean Doctor Grahme did not reſign till the 5th of Auguſt, and moreover ſome diſputes ariſing about the regal ſupremacy, inſtitution was then refuſed, but the biſhop declared at the ſame time that the affair ſhould be laid forthwith before the queen; and that if her majeſty ſhould, notwithſtanding theſe objections, be pleaſed to repeat her commands for giving Dr. Atterbury poſſeſſion of the deanry, inſtitution ſhould be given. The queen was pleaſed, by her principal ſecretary of ſtate, to intimate her pleaſure to the biſhop to inſtitute the dean, which was inſtantly obeyed.

In 1705, the biſhop publiſhed his Leges Marchiarum, or Border Laws, with a preface, and an Appendix of charters and records relating thereto.

In 1707, Dr. Atterbury the dean, never at reſt, and continually raiſing freſh diſputes with his chapter, the biſhop endeavoured to appeaſe them by viſiting the chapter, in purſuance of the power given by the ſtatutes of king Hen. 8. at the foundation of the corporation of dean and chapter. But Dr. Todd, one of the prebendaries, was inſtigated by the dean, to proteſt againſt ſuch viſitation, inſiſting upon the invalidity of king Henry the eighth's ſtatutes, and that the queen, and not the biſhop, was the local viſitor. During the courſe of the viſitation, the biſhop ſuſpended, and afterwards excommunicated Dr. Todd. Whereupon the doctor moved the court of common pleas for a prohibition, and obtained it unleſs cauſe ſhewn.

In

In the mean time thefe proceedings alarmed the archbifhops and bifhops, as the aforefaid objeċtions ftruck at the root of all the new foundations of deans and chapters by king Henry the eighth; and the archbifhop of Canterbury writ the following circular letter to all his fuffragans:

Right reverend Brother,

Lambeth, 2 Feb 1707.

I doubt not but all my fuffragans are apprifed of what is doing in the cafe of the bifhop of Carlifle. Though he is not of our province, I take it to be a common caufe, and of great concern to this church; which will never be quiet, fo long as that evil generation of men, who make it their bufinefs to fearch into little flaws in ancient charters and ftatutes, and to unfix what laudable cuftom hath well fixed, meet with any fuccefs. I write not this as if I fufpeċted your zeal in fuch a cafe, but to affure you of my ready concurrence with you in any proper and legal means, whether by bill or otherwife, to make this excellent church fafe in this point, both now, and to late pofterity. Such provifions are to be endeavoured in a good reign, left in an evil one we feel the want of them.—I am,

Your affeċtionate brother,

Tho. Cantuar.

Very foon after this a bill was carried into parliament, and paffed into a law (6 An. c. 21.), which took away thofe doubts, by eftablifhing the validity of the local ftatutes given by king Hen. 8. to his new foundations as aforefaid.

In 1713, he wrote an effay or difcourfe, to be affixed to Mr. Chamberlain's book, containing the Lord's prayer in one hundred different languages. Of which, Dr. Hickes gives the following charaċter, in a letter to Mr. Chamberlain:—" I give you many thanks for communicating to me the bifhop of Carlifle's moft excellent letter, which fhews him to be a very great man, and to have a moft exaċt judgment, and which will be a great ornament to your book. I know not which is to be moft admired in it, the vaft variety of reading, or the putting all his obfervations together in fo fhort, clear, and eafy a difcourfe, which mightily confirms the hiftory of Mofes, and refutes the vain cavils which atheifts and deifts and latitudinarians are wont to make againft the truth of it. But, from the date of the letter, I wonder you would defire me in laft February to write a differtation of the fame nature, to be prefixed to your book. What could I have written of the fame nature, though never fo juftly or elaborately, but what he had written before, undoubtedly with great pains and ftudy, though he has reduced all his reading of that kind into the compafs of a fhort letter; which fhews him to be a great mafter builder, as well as a great colleċtor of proper materials, upon that curious fubjeċt. You may fee from his citations, how truly I told you that I had not the proper books for fuch a difcourfe; or, if I had them (and I will now add, his ftrength), that I would not undertake to write fuch a difcourfe in lefs time than half a year. I wonder much more, that when you had imparted

his

his lordfhip's admirable letter to me, you would again defire me to write a difcourfe of that nature. In doing of which, had I all his abilities of body and mind, I fhould expofe myfelf as an impertinent, though I could write as well as he hath done upon that fubject ; and as a man of great vanity, if my difcourfe came fhort of his. Therefore, befides my utter prefent inability, I muft plead how arrogant it would be in me to write any thing of that nature, after fo excellent a difcourfe, to which nothing can be added (I think) by a club of the beft antiquaries, if they fhould attempt to write on the fame fubject, which he has exhaufted in fhort."

In 1715, he was by the king made lord almoner, which office was refigned in his favour by the lord archbifhop of Canterbury.

In 1717, a collection of papers fcattered about the town in the Daily Courant and other periodical papers, with fome remarks addreffed to the bifhop of Bangor, was publifhed in Octavo.

In 1718, letters patent paffed the great feal of Ireland for his tranflation to the fee of Londonderry, to which he was nominated on the 17th of March, but was allowed to continue bifhop of Carlifle and almoner till after Eafter.

In 1719, he wrote a preface to the third edition of Dr. Wilkins's Leges Anglo-Saxonicæ.

He alfo publifhed feveral fermons, and left three manufcript volumes in folio to the dean and chapter of Carlifle, confifting of copies and extracts from various books, manufcripts, regifters, records, and charters, relating to the diocefe of Carlifle, and from whence many things in thefe collections are tranfcribed. There is alfo a large octavo manufcript of his, containing mifcellaneous accounts of the ftate of the churches, parfonage and vicarage houfes, glebe lands, and other poffeffions, in the feveral parifhes within the diocefe, collected in his parochial vifitation of the feveral churches in the years 1703, 1701, and 1707, now in the poffeffion of his nephew Jofeph Nicolfon of Hawkfdale efquire.

In the year 17 6, Feb. 9. he was tranflated to the archbifhoprick of Cafhell in the fame kingdom of Ireland ; but died fuddenly on the 14th of the fame month, and was buried in the cathedral church of Londonderry, without any monumental infcription.

He married Elizabeth youngeft daughter of John Archer of Oxenholme near Kendal efquire, and by her had iffue eight children 1. Thomas, who lived only a few days. 2 Jofeph, chancellor of Lincoln, who married and had two daughters. 3. John, a clergyman, who alfo married but had no child. 4. Mary, married to the reverend Dr. Thomas Benfon, and died without iffue. 5. Catherine, yet living, and unmarried. 6. Elizabeth, married to Bellingham Mauleverer clerk, and to him had 13 children, moft of whom are now (1772) living. 7. Anne, married to Bolton efquire, to whom fhe had two fons. 8. Sufanna, who died unmarried.

This bifhop was of Cumberland extraction both by his father and mother's fide. His father, the reverend Jofeph Nicolfon aforefaid, was fon and heir of Jofeph Nicolfon of Averas Holme in the faid county gentleman, by his wife Radigunda Scott, heirefs to an eftate at Park Broom in the parifh

of

of Stanwix, which eftate yet continues in Catharine eldeft furviving daughter of the faid bifhop Nicolfon. His mother was Mary daughter of John Brifco of Crofton efquire.

46. SAMUEL BRADFORD. He was prebendary of Weftminfter, rector of Marybourn in Middlefex, and mafter of Bennet college in Cambridge. His Conge d'Eflire for the bifhoprick of Carlifle was dated Ap. 30. 1718, and he was confecrated on the firft of June following.

In 1723, he was tranflated to Rochefter after bifhop Atterbury's expulfion; and died in 1731. He was interred in the north crofs ifle of Weftminfter abbey, with the following epitaph:

Ex adverfo fepultus eft Samuel Bradford, S. T. P.
Sanctæ Mariæ de Arcubus Londini diu rector.
Collegii corporis Chrifti apud Cantabrigienfes aliquando cuftos.
Epifcopus primo Carleolenfis, deinde Roffenfis, hujufque
Ecclefiæ et honoratiffimi ordinis de Balneo
Decanus.
Concionator fuit dum per valetudinem licuit affiduus;
Tam moribus, quam præceptis
Gravis, venerabilis, fanctus;
Cumque in cæteris vitæ officiis,
Tum in munere præcipue paftorali,
Prudens, fimplex, integer.
Animi conftantia tam æquabili tam fæliciter temperata,
Ut vix iratus, perturbatus haud unquam fuerit.
Chriftianam charitatem et libertatem civilem
Ubique paratus afferere et promovere.
Quæ pie, quæ benevolé, quæ mifericorditer,
In occulto fecerit (et fecit multa)
Præful humillimus, humaniffimus,
Et vere evangelicus,
Ille fuo revelabit tempore,
Qui in occulto vifa palam remunerabit.
Obiit 17 Die Maii, Anno Dom. 1731.
Suæque Ætatis 79.

47. JOHN WAUGH. He was born at Appleby in Weftmorland, educated at Appleby fchool, from thence was removed to Queen's college in Oxford, where he became fellow. He was afterwards dean of Gloucefter, prebendary of Lincoln, and rector of St. Peter's Cornhill London.

He was elected to the fee of Carlifle, Aug. 23, 1723; and died in Queen's Square, Weftminfter, Oct. 29, 1734, in the 79th year of his age, and was buried under the communion table in St. Peter's Cornhill aforefaid.

48. GEORGE FLEMING. He was born in 1667 at the family feat at Rydall hall in the county of Weftmorland; being in order of birth the fifth of ele-

ven fons, and the ninth of fifteen children of Sir Daniel Fleming knight (afterwards baronet) by Barbara eldeft daughter of Sir Henry Fletcher of Hutton baronet. He was entered in Edmund hall in Oxford in 1688, and: having paffed through his degrees in arts, he became domeftic chaplain to Dr. Thomas Smith bifhop of Carlifle, was by him collated to the vicarage of Af. patrick in 1695, and foon after to a prebend in the cathedral church of Car. lifle. In 1705, he was collated by bifhop Nicolfon to the archdeaconry. In 1727, he was promoted to the deanry; and in 1734 was advanced to the bifhoprick of Carlifle. He died at Rofe caftle in 1747, in the 81ft year of his age; and was buried at the eaft end of the fouth ile in the cathedral at Carlifle, where is a marble monument with the following infcription :.

Here is depofited till a general refurrection.
whatever was mortal of
the right reverend father in God:
Sir George Fleming baronet late lord bifhop of Carlifle ;:
whofe regretted diffolution was July 2, 1747,
In the 81ft year of his age, and the 13th of his confecration.
A prelate,.
who by gradual and well merited advancements,
having paffed through every dignity to the epifcopal,
fupported that,
with an amiable affemblage of graces and virtues :
which eminently formed, in his character,
the courteous gentleman, and the pious chriftian ;
and rendred him a fhining ornament.
to his fpecies, his nation, his order;
His deportment
in all human relations and pofitions,
was fquared by the rules of morality and religion,
under the conftant direction of a confummate prudence ;
whilft his equanimity
amidft all events and occurrences,
in an inviolable adherence to the golden medium,
made him eafy to himfelf and agreeable to others,
and had its reward
in a chearful life, a ferene old age, a compofed death.
His excellent pattern
was a continual leffon of goodnefs and wifdom,
and remains in his ever revereable memory
an illuftrious object of praife and imitation.

This bifhop, having cut down and fold fome wood belonging to the bifhop-rick, ordered an exact account thereof, and how the money raifed thereby was difpofed of, to be entred in his regiftry.

49. RICHARD

49. RICHARD OSBALDISTON. He was of the rich family of Hunmanby in the county of York; was bred at Cambridge; made dean of York; and in 1747 bishop of Carlisle. He was translated to London in 1762, and died in 1764.

50. CHARLES LYTTELTON, was born in 1714 at Hagley hall in Worcestershire, being the third son of Sir Thomas Lyttelton of Hagley and Frankley baronet, by Christian daughter of Sir Richard Temple of Stowe in Buckinghamshire baronet, sister to the late lord viscount Cobham. He was bred at Eaton school, and afterwards at University college in Oxford; from whence he removed to the Middle Temple London, and was called to the bar; but want of health not permitting him to follow that laborious profession, he took orders, and returned to Oxford. In 1742, he became rector of Alve church in Worcestershire, on the collation of old bishop Hough. In 1747, he was appointed one of the chaplains in ordinary to king George the second; and in the following year was promoted to the deanry of Exeter. In 1762, he was advanced to the bishoprick of Carlisle, on the translation of bishop Osbaldiston; and died at his house in Clifford Street London, Dec. 22, 1768; and was buried in the family vault at Hagley.

He was a gentleman of extensive learning, and particularly in matters of antiquity, upon which account he was made president of the Antiquarian Society. He was of a noble, generous, and humane disposition; a friend to all mankind, and never had an enemy.

He was succeeded in the presidentship of the said society, by the reverend Dr. Milles dean of Exeter; who in his speech to the society upon that occasion, pays a due and just tribute to his memory —" I cannot repeat the
" name of our late most respected and much lamented president, without
" paying that grateful tribute to his memory, which his services to the
" society whilst he lived, and his generosity perpetuated to them at his death,
" do most justly demand of us; and I am persuaded, that every absent as
" well as present member will join in this acknowledgment with a most will
" ing and grateful voice. It is not in my power to draw such a portrait
" of his lordship, as can in any respect do justice to the original. His merits
" and good qualities are so universally acknowledged, and so deeply impressed
" on the minds of those who hear me, that their own ideas will paint them
" in more just and lively colours than any words of mine can express: I may
" be indulged however in recalling to your minds such parts of his character
" as particularly endeared him to the society, and therefore make his loss
" more sensibly felt by us. The study of antiquity, especially that part of it
" which relates to the history and constitution of these kingdoms, was one of
" his earliest and most favourite pursuits; and he acquired great knowledge
" in it by constant study and application, to which he was led, not only by
" his natural disposition, but also by his state and situation in life. He took
" frequent opportunities of improving and inriching this knowledge, by judi
" cious observations, in the course of several journies which he made through
" every county in England, and through many parts of Scotland and Wales.

Q q 2 " The

" The fociety has reaped the fruits of thefe obfervations, in the many valua-
" ble papers which his lordfhip from time to time has communicated to us ;
" which are more in number, and not inferior either in merit or importance, to
" thofe conveyed to us by other hands. Bleffed with a retentive memory,
" and happy both in the difpofition and facility of communicating his know-
" ledge, he was enabled alfo to act the part of a judicious commentator and
" candid critic; explaining, illuftrating, and correcting, from his own obfer-
" vations, many of the papers which have been read at this fociety. His
" ftation and connections in the world, which neceffarily engaged a very con-
" fiderable part of his time, did not leffen his attention to the bufinefs and
" interefts of the fociety. His doors were always open to his friends,
" amongft whom none were more welcome to him than the friends of litera-
" ture, which he endeavoured to promote in all its various branches, efpe-
" cially in thofe which are the more immediate objects of our attention.
" Even this circumftance proved beneficial to the fociety; for, if I may be
" allowed the expreffion, he was the center in which the various informations
" on points of antiquity from the different parts of the kingdom united, and
" the medium through which they were conveyed to us. His literary merit
" with the fociety received an additional luftre, from the affability of his
" temper, the gentlenefs of his manners, and the benevolence of his heart;
" which united every member of the fociety in efteem to their head, and in
" harmony and friendfhip with each other †."

51. EDMUND LAW. He was born in the parifh of Cartmel in Lancafhire
in 1703, whofe father was a clergyman of Weftmorland extraction from Afkham. He was educated at the fchools of Cartmel and Kendal. From the
latter he removed to St. John's college in Cambridge; and after to Chrift's
college in the fame univerfity, where he was chofen fellow. He was prefented
by the faid univerfity to the valuable rectory of Grayftock in the county of
Cumberland; and afterwards was elected mafter of Peter-Houfe, vice-chancellor of the faid univerfity, principal librarian, and profeffor of cafuiftical
divinity. He enjoyed alfo feveral dignities fucceffively in divers of the cathedral churches; having been made archdeacon of Carlifle, afterwards archdeacon of Staffordfhire and prebendary of Sandiacre in the church of Litchfield, prebendary of Impingham in the church of Lincoln, and prebendary
of the twelfth ftall in the cathedral church of Durham.

He firft became eminent by *A tranflation of archbifhop King's Origin of Evil,*
with notes.

He alfo publifhed *An Inquiry into the ideas of fpace, time, immenfity, and
eternity.*

Confiderations on the theory of religion; and fubjoined thereto, *Reflections on
the life and character of Chrift* : Which laft were publifhed in 1776.

The nature and neceffity of Catechifing ; reprinted at Dublin.

† Tracts of the Antiquarian Society, p. xli.

Single

Single Sermons: viz. *On Litigiousness*; an assize sermon, preached at Carlisle in 1743.

The true nature and intent of religion, at Durham.

The grounds of a particular providence; before the lords, Jan. 30. 1770.

He published also several pieces in the controversy concerning an intermediate state.

And divers other anonymous tracts.

LIST OF THE PRIORS OF CARLISLE.

1. It is before observed, that king William Rufus, about the year 1092, ordered the city of Carlisle to be rebuilt, and appointed one Walter a Norman, overseer or director of the work. This Walter, being extremely rich, began a monastery to the honour of the blessed virgin Mary; but he dying before the work was finished, king Henry the first, in the year 1101, compleated it, and placed regular canons therein, appointing *Athelwald* his confessor and chaplain the first prior.

2. Afterwards, the same Athelwald being made bishop of Carlisle, he was succeeded by prior *Walter*; whose name often occurs in confirmations of grants.

3. *John* prior, in bishop Bernard's time. He gave Waitcroft and Flimby to the lords of Workington.

4. *Bartholomew*, prior, is a witness to several old charters. He and the convent confirmed the appropriation of the church of Orton in Westmorland to the priory of Coningsheved.

5. *Ralph*. He and the convent confirmed the appropriation of the church of Burgh upon Sands to the abbey of Holm Cultram.

6. *Robert de Morville.*

7. *Adam de Felton.*

8. *Alan.*

9. *John de Halton*, afterwards made bishop, viz. in 1292.

10. *John de Kendall.*

11. *Robert.*

12. *Adam de Warthwic.* About the year 1300, the bishop in his visitation objected a long schedule of articles, against *Adam* prior of Carlisle. (Registr. Halton.)

In the year 1304, this same prior *Adam de Wartbwyke*, being old and infirm, resigns the priorship into the hands of the subprior and convent. The subprior notifies the resignation to the bishop, who grants licence to elect another in his place, and grants a pension to the late prior of 20 marks out of the tithes of Langwathby, for the support of himself, one servant, and a boy.

13. *William de Hautwyssel*; who held the priorship four years, and then resigned.

14. *Robert de Helperton*, in 1308; who continued prior about 17 years.

15. *Simon*

15. *Simom de Hautwyffel.*

16. *William de Haftworth,* 1325. In this prior's time, in 1331, the office of Cellerarius (or fteward of the houfehold) being vacant, the prior and chapter prefent two of their brethren to bifhop Rofs ; who refiding then at Melburne in Derbyfhire, commiffions the prior of Lanercoft, and his own official Adam de Appleby to elect one of the two and admit him to the faid office.—Again, in 1338, two are prefented to the bifhop for the office of fubprior ; and the official is impowered to make choice of one of them.

17. *John de Kirkby.*

18. *Galfrid* prior.

19. *John de Horncaftle,* in 1352.—Bifhop Welton, in his vifitation of the prior and convent in 1355, makes inquiry, by what right and title the churches of St. Mary's and St. Cuthbert's in Carlifle, with the chapel of Seburgham, the church of Hayton with its chapels of Cumrew and Cumquinton, the churches of Crofby in Allerdale, Camberton, Ireby, and Beghokirk, Soureby, Routhcliff, Edenhall with the chapel of Langwathby, and Adingham with the chapel of Salkeld, were held by the faid prior and convent appropriate, and how it comes to pafs that there are no inftituted vicars in the faid churches of St. Mary's, St. Cuthbert's, Hayton, Routhecliff, Ireby, Crosfby, Camberton, and Beghokirk ; as alfo how they come to demand a penfion of 26*s* 8*d* out of the rectory of Louthre, of 26*s* from Kirkland, of 6*s* 8*d* from Ulnefby, of 2*s* from Hayton, and the like from each of the churches of Caftlecayrock and Cambok, of 6*s* 8*d* from Buthecaftre, of 2*s* 6*d* from Ukmanby, and 6*l* from the abbot and convent of Holm Cultram : And being fatisfied, by the teftimony of authentic records and living witneffes, in each of thefe particulars, he gave them a certificate thereof accordingly under his epifcopal feal.

In 1357, bifhop Welton received a command and powers from the fee of Rome (upon fome efpecial occafion) to vifit the prior and chapter.

In 1360 the fame bifhop again vifits them ; and in 1365 they are vifited by bifhop Appleby, and again in 1373.

In 1376, John de Horncaftle the prior complaining to the bifhop by petition, that by reafon of age and infirmities he is not able to govern the convent any longer, and therefore requefting permiffion to refign ; the bifhop accordingly commiffions his archdeacon John de Appleby to take his refignation, and foon after grants licence to the fubprior and convent (on their requeft) to proceed to the election of a new prior.

20. *Richard de Rydale* ; who having the bifhop's leave of abfence, one Martin de Brampton was appointed by the bifhop to take care of the affairs of the convent.

21. *John de Penrith.* In the year 1378, there were great differences between him and one Roger de Clifton a member of the convent, which the bifhop at laft compofed.

In 1381, John de Penrith refigns ; and two canons being prefented to the bifhop, he approves and confirms William de Dalfton.

22. *William*

22. *William de Dalfton*, being appointed prior, refufed to fwear canonical obedience to the bifhop. Whereupon the bifhop excommunicates him. He appeals to the temporal court, the priory being of royal foundation. And the king's writ iffues to ftop proceedings. At laft the difference was agreed; and to make all things quiet, the prior was preferred, and refigned his priory.

23. *Robert de Edenhall*, one of the canons, was chofen in the place of William de Dalfton, and approved and inftituted by the bifhop, and thereupon inftalled by the archdeacon, in the year 1386.

24. *Thomas de Hoton:* of an ancient family in Cumberland.

25. *Thomas Elye*; who built the grange of New Lathes near the city, on the walls of which his name is legible.

26. *Thomas Barnaby* prior, 1433.

27. *Thomas de Haythwaite*. He erected the bifhop's throne in the quire, on the back part whereof his name was infcribed.

28. *Thomas Gondibour* prior, about 1484. He was a great benefactor to the priory. He enlarged and improved the buildings within the abbey. The initial letters of his name are to be feen, cut in ftone, in fome places yet ftanding. And in the veftry on an old aumery (or cheft) is legible this verfe,

En domus hæc floruit Godibour fub tegmine Thomæ.

29. *Simon Senhoufe* of the houfe of Seafcales in Cumberland was chofen prior in 1507. He repaired or beautified the fquare tower within the precincts of the priory, and caufed feveral Englifh verfes to be infcribed on the beams over the middle room, with this moral rule often repeated *Loth to offend*. The fhort ejaculation which he often writ and figned with his name, was,

Vulnera quinque Dei, fint medicina mei.

30. *Chriftopher Slee*. He built the weft gatehoufe from the foundation, which is yet ftanding. On the infide whereof, this infcription is graved round the arch, "Orate pro anima Chriftophori Slee prioris, qui primus hoc opus fieri incepit A. D. 1528;"

Growing old and infirm, he refigned about the year 1532, and had an allowance of 25 *l per annum* granted him for life.

31. *Lancelot Salkeld* the laft prior. He was of the houfe of Corby nigh Carlifle. On the 9th of January 1538, he refigned the priory into the king's hands, with all its lands, revenues, and poffeffions, to be difpofed of at his majefty's pleafure.

DEANS OF CARLISLE.

OUT of the diffolved priory, king Henry the eighth, by letters patent bearing date May 8, 1542, founded and eftablifhed the body corporate of a

dean

dean and four prebendaries of the holy and undivided Trinity of Carlisle, and appointed the last prior to be the first dean, viz.

1. *Lancelot Salkeld*, who continued dean all king Henry the eighth's time, but was ejected in the reign of king Edward the sixth, restored by queen Mary, and again ejected by queen Elizabeth in 1559, and died the year after, and was buried in the cathedral.

2. On Lancelot Salkeld's first deprivation by king Edward the sixth, Sir *Thomas Smith* knight, secretary of state, was made dean, but on queen Mary's accession Sir Thomas Smith was deprived, and afterwards by queen Elizabeth restored. He was doctor of laws of Queen's college in Cambridge, and public professor of civil law for some time in that university. He was in deacon's orders; and presided as dean 20 years, but seldom or never visited his deanry. He writ a book intitled " The commonwealth of England ;" which was tranflated into latin by two different hands : Another, styled " De recta et emendata linguæ Græcæ pronunciatione :" And another, intitled " Dialogus de recta et emendata linguæ Anglicanæ scriptione." He was much employed in the affairs of the reformation, and was one of those employed in compiling the book of common prayer. In his time we meet with many grants of the advowsons of livings for 2, 3, or 4 turns succeffively, and leases for long terms, and concurrent leases to take place after the expiration of the former. But this was not the fault of his time only; for the practice continued more or less, till the restraining statutes were made in the reign of queen Elizabeth. He died in 1577, and was buried at Mount Theydon in Effex, on the north side of the chancel, where is his effigies and a monumental inscription.

3. *John Wooley*, M. A. was constituted dean Oct. 11, 1577. In the prefentation he is styled esquire, and secretary of the latin tongue; and therein is a Non obstante of his not being in holy orders, and of his having married a widow (which by the ancient canons it was not lawful for clerks to do). He died at Pyrford in Surry about the begining of March 1595, and was buried in St. Paul's cathedral London, under a stately monument.

4. *Christopher Perkins*, LL. D. afterwards knighted as his predecessor had been, succeeded to this deanry in 1596, and died in August 1622.

5. *Francis White*, S. T. P. presented Sept. 14. and installed Oct. 15, 1622. He was made bishop of this see in 1626, and was succeeded by

6. *William Peterson*, S. T. P. being presented Dec. 4. 1626. He was in 1629 promoted to the deanry of Exeter; and succeeded in this by

7. *Thomas Comber*, S. T. P. presented Aug. 28, 1630. He was born in Suffex, being the 12th child of his father. He was educated at Trinity college in Cambridge, of which he became master. In 1642, being concerned (amongst the rest) in sending the plate of that university to the king, he was deprived of all his preferments, and died in 1653, and was buried in St. Botolph's church in Cambridge. His successor, at the restoration of the church and monarchy, was,

8. *Guy Carleton*, D. D. presented June 29, 1660. He was born in this diocese at Brampton Foot, of a gentleman's family; and educated at Queen's

college

college in Oxford. In November 1660 he was made prebendary of Durham. In 1671, he was made bishop of Bristol, and was succeeded by,

9. *Thomas Smith*, D. D. who in 1684 was made bishop of this see, and was succeeded by,

. 10. *Thomas Musgrave*, D. D. who was prebendary of Durham, and died there in 1686, over whom in Durham cathedral was put the following monumental inscription :

" Here lies interred Thomas Musgrave, D. D. dean of Carlisle, and late prebendary of this cathedral. He was the fifth son of Sir Philip Musgrave of Hartley Castle in the county of Westmorland baronet, who died the 28th of March 1686 in the 47th year of his age. He first married Mary the daughter of Sir Thomas Harrison of Allerthorp in the county of York knight, by whom he had issue Margaret. His second wife was Anne the daughter of Sir John Cradock of Richmond in the said county knight."

11. *William Grahme*, D. D. succeeded, being installed June 23, 1686. He resigned in 1704, being promoted to the deanry of Wells. He died in 1712, and was buried at Kensington nigh London. He was succeeded by,

. 12. *Francis Atterbury*, D. D. who was installed Oct. 2. 1704; and in 1711, was removed to the deanry of Christ-church in Oxford; and was afterwards made bishop of Rochester. ·

13. *George Smallridge*, D. D. succeeded; who also was removed to the deanry of Christ-church in 1713 : And was succeeded by,

. 14. *Thomas Gibbon*, M. A. (afterwards D. D) rector of Graystock. He died in 1716, and was interred in the cathedral, within the rails of the communion table, on the north side of bishop Smith.

1𝑐. *Thomas Tullie*, M. A. (afterwards made Doctor of Laws) succeeded Dr. Gibbon, and died Jan. 16, 1726.

16. *George Fleming*, M. A. was presented on Dr. Tullie's death, and thereupon obtained a doctor of laws degree at Lambeth, and was instituted on the 13th of April 1727. In 1734, he was promoted to the bishoprick ; and was succeeded by,

17. *Robert Bolton*, LL. D. (of Lambeth) who died in 1764. He was succeeded by,

. 18. *Charles Tarrant*, D. D. who in the same year was promoted to the deanry of Peterborough ; and was succeeded by,

. 19 *Thomas Wilson*, D. D. who was instituted July 23, 1764; and installed the 2d of August following.

CHANCELLORS, VICARS GENERAL, AND OFFICIALS.

1. In 1220, *Adam de Kirkby Thore* appears as vicar general.

2. In 1311, *Adam de Appleby* was constituted official by bishop Halton, when he retired out of the diocese for fear of the Scots. Which Adam in 1312, was collated to the rectory of Caldbeck.

3. In the same year 1311, the bishop being called to the General Council of Vienna, appointed the prior of Carlisle and *William de Gosford* rector of

Ormefhead his vicars general. And in 1314, the aforefaid Adam de Appleby the official was conftituted vicar general.

4. In 1335, *Thomas de Halton* (nephew of the bifhop of that name) was vicar general, and *Robert de Scuthayke* official ; to whom bifhop Kirkby granted a commiffion of inquiry of the right of patronage on a vacancy of the church of Croglyn. This Robert de Southayke was rector of Bewcaftle.¹

5. *John de Stoketon*, rector of Mufgrave, was in the year 1342 confirmed official by patent ; having been formerly invefted with that jurifdiction by delivery of the feal of the faid officialty.

6. In 1353, bifhop Welton conftituted the abbot of Holm Cultram vicar general of the diocefe.

7. In 1354, Mr. *Nicholas de Whitby* official publifhed a fentence of divorce, which was ratified under the feal of the bifhop.

8. In 1355, *Adam de Caldbeck* was appointed official by bifhop Welton, and employed by him to collect a fubfidy granted by the fpiritualty, and alfo ftrictly charged not to fuffer any friers mendicant to go about from church to church to expofe their exceffive indulgences to the people.

9. In 1363, a patent is granted by bifhop Appleby, to the prior of Carlifle, *John de Appleby* rector of Kirk Ofwald, and the late bifhop's official *Adam de Caldbeck*, jointly and feverally, to execute the office of vicar general.

10. *William de Bownefs* official, about the year 1373, at the inftance of Ralph baron of Grayftock, was ordered by bifhop Appleby to inquire into the value of the living of Grayftock, in order to found a collegiate church there.

11. *William del' Hall*, official, in the year 1379, was collated to the rectory of Caldbeck.

12. In 1397, *Richard Pyttes* was vicar general, againft whom the abbot of Shap appealed to the pope, for having fequeftered the revenues of the church of Shap, which he alledged belonged to the faid abbey, for the debts or offence incurred by the vicar.

[Here is a vacancy of 150 years, occafioned by the deficiency of the bifhops regifters.]

13. In 1543, *Nicolas Williamfon*, official, was an arbitrator (with three others) in a caufe between Hugh Machel and the widow of Thomas Roos, concerning the executorfhip of her late hufband.

14. In 1552, *Henry Dethick,* LL. B. being then in deacon's orders, was made chancellor by bifhop Aldrich.

15. In 1569, *Gregory Scott*, chancellor of the diocefe, was collated to the vicarage of St. Michael's Appleby. And in the next year, bifhop Barnes, on his coming to the fee, granted him by patent the conjoined powers of vicar general and official principal, which mode hath continued ever fince.

16. In 1576, *Thomas Burton,* LL. B. fucceeded him, as chancellor, vicar general, and official principal ; and alfo as vicar of St. Michael's.

17. In 1577, bifhop Meye, in his firft year, conftitutes *Thomas Hammond*, LL. B. his chancellor during pleafure, as other of the patents had run before.

And

And in 1583, he had a grant from the same bishop of the rectory of Cald-beck for 20 years.

18. In 1586, the same bishop grants the said office to *Henry Dethick*, M. A. and LL. B. for term of life; which grant was confirmed (as the rest were afterwards) by the dean and chapter.

19. In 1597, the same bishop Meye grants the like patent to *Henry Dethick*, LL. B. then in deacon's orders.

20. In 1615, *Henry Woodward*, in a dispute concerning the schoolmaster of Kefwick, is mentioned as chancellor.

21. In 1622, *Isaac Singleton*, M. A. was collated to the archdeaconry by his father-in-law bishop Milburn, and probably to the chancellorship about the same time. In both of which offices he continued, till they and episcopacy were laid aside.

22. In 1661, Apr. 21. bishop Sterne directs his mandate for calling the clergy together to elect proctors for the convocation, to *Robert Lowther* his vicar general and official principal. Which Robert Lowther in 1663 was instituted to the rectory of Bewcastle.

23. In 1666, on Mr. Lowther's resignation, *Henry Marshall*, M. A. was made chancellor by bishop Rainbow; and in the same year was collated to the vicarage of Stanwix: And in the year next following was barbarously murdered at his own door.

24. In 1667, on Mr. Marshall's death, *Rowland Nichols*, M. A. rector of Aikton was made chancellor. In 1682, he was suspended (for what cause we have not found), and in the next year he resigned his patent and office.

25. In 1683, *Thomas Tullie*, M. A. was made chancellor by bishop Rainbow.

26. In 1727, *John Waugh*, M. A. was made chancellor by his father bishop Waugh.

27. In 1765, *Richard Burn*, LL. D. vicar of Orton in Westmorland, was made chancellor by bishop Lyttelton.

ARCHDEACONS.

1. *Gervase de Lowther*, was archdeacon in the reigns of Hen. 2. Richard the first, John, and part of Hen. 3.

2. *Robert*, archdeacon in 1230.

3. *Peter de Rofs*, in 1233.

4. *Richard*, 1293.

5. *Peter de Insula* was instituted to the archdeaconry of Carlisle, with all its rights, members, and appurtenances, in 1302.

6. In 1311, on the death of Peter de Insula, *Gilbert de Haloghton* (or *Halton*) was collated to the archdeaconry by bishop Halton.

7. *Henry de Karliol*, in 1320, by the same bishop.

8. *William de Kendale*, by the same bishop, in 1323. This William in 1337 was cited to shew cause, why he held both the archdeaconry and the parish

church

church of Salkeld without a dispensation (which had been complained of to the archbishop of York).—And this is first mention of the living of Salkeld being held with the archdeaconry; unto which it hath been ever since annexed.

9. *Richard de Arthureth*, in 1354.

10. *William de Rothbury*, in 1363.

11. *John de Appleby*, in 1364; who resigned in 1377.—After whom, there is a great vacuity, for want of the registers during that time.

12. *George Nevill*, in 1548.

13. *Edward Threlkeld*, LL. D. in 1567.

14. *Henry Dethick*, in 1588; who resigned in 1597.

15. *Richard Pickinton* succeeded Dethick; and resigned in 1599.

16. Dr. *Giles Robinson* (the bishop's brother) was instituted in 1599, and resigned in 1602.

17. On Dr. Robinson's resignation, *Nicholas Dean*, A. M. was collated by the said bishop Robinson.

18. *Isaac Singleton*, M. A. in 1622.

19. *Lewis West*, in 1660.

20. *John Peachill*, B. D. on the death of Lewis West, in 1667.

21. On the resignation of John Peachill in 1668, *Thomas Musgrave*, M. A. was instituted to the archdeaconry, and collated to the rectory of Salkeld.

22. In 1682, on the resignation of Thomas Musgrave, *William Nicolson*, M. A. succeeded.

23. In 1702, Mr. Nicolson being promoted to the bishoprick, the crown presented Mr. *Joseph Fisher*.

24. On Mr. Fisher's death in 1705, *George Fleming*, M. A. was collated by bishop Nicolson.

25. On George Fleming's promotion to the bishoprick, *William Fleming*, M. A. was presented by the king in 1734.

26. On William Fleming's death in 1743, *Edmund Law*, M. A. was collated.

27. On Dr. Law's resignation in 1756, *Venn Eyre*, M. A. was collated.

PREBENDARIES.

FIRST STALL.

1. *William Florens*, monk of Carlisle, by the foundation charter 1542.

2. *Hugh Sewell*, D. D. rector of Caldbeck and vicar of St. Laurence Appleby, 1549.

3. *Edmund Bunnie*, B. D. 1585.

4. *Richard Snowden*, 1617.

5. *Lancelot Dawes*, M. A. vicar of Barton, Westmorland; 1619.

6. *Thomas Smith*, D. D. (afterwards bishop), 1660.

7. *Thomas Canon*, B. D. 1661.

8. *William Sill*, M. A. vicar of Adingham, 1668.

5

9. *William*

9. *William Nicolfon*, M. A. (afterwards bifhop), 1681.
10. *John Atkinfon*, M. A. vicar of Kirkby Stephen, 1702.
11. *Edward Birket*, M. A. vicar of Kirkland, 1733.
12. *John Waugh*, M. A. vicar of Bromfgrove in Worcefterfhire, 1768.

SECOND STALL.

1. *Edward Lofh*, by the charter of foundation, 1542.
2. *William Parrye*, D. D. 1546.
3. *John Emanuel Tremelius*, profeffor of Hebrew in Cambridge, 1552.
4. *Edwin Sands*, 1552.
5. *Edward Mitchell*, LL. B. 1554, rector of Rothbury.
6. *John Maybray*, vicar of Crofthwaite, 1566.
7. *Thomas Tookie*, LL. B. vicar of Torpenhow, 1568.
8. *John Barnes*, 1574.
9. *Thomas Fairfax*, rector of Caldbeck, 1577.
10. *John Meye*, LL. B. 1595.
11. *William Meye*, M. A. (brother of the former) 1596.
12. *Thomas Fairfax*, vicar of St. Michael's Appleby, about 1600.
13. *Frederick Tunftall*, M. A. 1640.
14. *Arthur Savage*, M. A. rector of Caldbeck, 1660.
15. *George Fleming*, M. A. (afterwards bifhop) 1700.
16. *John Waugh*, M. A. (fon of bifhop Waugh) 1727.
17. *Robert Wardale*, M. A. 1765.
18. *John Law*, M. A. (fon of bifhop Law) 1773.

THIRD STALL.

1. *Bernard Kirkbride*, 1542.
2. *Gregory Scott*, M. A. 1564.
3. *Thomas Burton*, LL. B. rector of Brougham, 1576.
4. *Anthony Walkwood*, rector of Hutton, 1577.
5. *Bernard Robinfon*, vicar of Torpenhow and rector of Mufgrave, 1612.
6. *Lewis Weft*, M. A. 1637.
7. *John Peachell*, B. D. 1667.
8. *Thomas Mufgrave*, 1669.
9. *John Ardrey*, M. A. rector of Clibburn and Mufgrave, 1676.
10. *Thomas Tullie*, M. A. vicar of Crofthwaite, 1684.
11. *Thomas Benfon*, M. A. vicar of Stanwix and Dalfton, 1716.
12. *Richard Holme*, M. A. 1727; rector of Lowther.
13. *William Fleming*, M. A. (fon of bifhop Fleming) 1738.
14. *Thomas Wilfon*, M. A. vicar of Torpenhow, 1743.
15. *Roger Baldwin*, M. A. 1764.

FOURTH

FOURTH STALL.

1. *Richard Brandling*, monk of Carlisle, 1542.
2. *Arthur Key*, rector of Bownefs, 1570.
3. *Thomas Burton*, LL. D. 1575.
4. *George Flower*, 1576.
5. *Edward Haufby*, rector of Grayftock, 1582.
6. *Edward Mayplate*, rector of Clifton, 1584.
7. *John Fletcher*, B. D. rector. alfo of Clifton, 1624.
8. *William Dodding*, M. A. rector of Mufgrave, 1632.
9. *Richard Smith*, B. D. rector of Rothbury, 1637.
10. *Henry Hutton*, M. A. rector of Marton, 1643.
11. *George Buchanan*, M. A. vicar of Stanwix, 1660.
12. *Henry Marfhall*, M. A. vicar of Crofthwaite, 1666.
13. *Jeremy Nelfon*, M. A. vicar of Stanwix and Corbridge, 1667.
14. *Hugh Todd*, M. A. vicar of Penrith and rector of. Arthuret, 1685.
15. *Thomas Tullie*, LL. B. 1728.
16. *Erafmus Head*, M. A. vicar of Newburn, 1742.
17. *Jofeph Amphlett*, LL. D. 1763.

PARISH OF DALSTON.

DALSTON is the next parifh fouthward. In the regifter of bifhop Kirkby, about the year 1333, the boundary of it is thus defcribed : " Limites et bundæ ecclefiæ parochialis de Dalfton ex una parte incipiunt ab aqua de Caldew fubtus Parva Dalfton, et fic afcendendo per Potkoke ufque le Brend-thwayt, et fic per le Merfike ufque Thornholm, et deinde ufque ad le Redgate, et deinde per ficetum inter Winflowe et foreftam domini regis ufque le Bifhopfkale, et tunc afcendendo per Peterel ufque ad le Roanciwath, ufque ad Appletrethwayt, et fic ad novum parcum quem dominus Thomas de Nor-manvil quondam erexit, et deinde ufque ad Crokellerbeke, et deinde ufque ad Lefakihat, et fic ufque ad Ivetonfeld, et deinde ufque ad Skarnpoofyke, et deinde ufque ad aquam de Ive, et deinde ufque ad aquam de Raugh, et deinde ficut parochia de Dalfton et Sowerby inter fe dividunt ufque in aquam de Caldew."

Mr. Denton fays, that earl Ranulph de Mefchiens gave the barony of Dal-fton to *Robert de Vallibus*, brother of Hubert de Vallibus firft baron of Gilf-land, who thereupon took the name of *Robert de Dalfton*; and that the de-fcendents of the faid Robert poffeffed that barony in a lineal defcent, till king Stephen gave Cumberland to David king of Scots. However, not long after, we find it in the hands of the crown. For by the record of an affife in the 6 Ed. 1. the jurors find, that the barony of Dalfton, wih the advowfon of the church there, efcheated to the king, by reafon of the owner thereof Henry

fon

fon of Maurinus (Morifon) being attainted of felony. *Morifon* is a Scotch name; and perhaps king David granted this barony to him, and upon Henry the fecond's recovering the fame from the Scots, the felony might eafily accrue. It continued in the crown till the reign of king Henry the third, who by his charter in the 14th year of his reign, grants to Walter (Malclerk) bifhop of Carlifle and his fucceffors the manor of Dalfton, with the advowfon of the church there, with fac, and foke, and woods, and mills, and all other appurtenances: To hold the fame difafforefted, with power to affart and make inclofures, and difpofe of the wood at their will and pleafure, without the view or interruption of his forefters, verderers, regarders, or other officers; and that they fhall be free from fuits, and fummonfes, and pleas of the foreft; and have liberty to hunt and take deer and other game within the faid manor, and no other fhall have fuch liberty without their permiffion; and fhall hold the faid manor as a foreft, as the king held the fame before the faid grant. The faid bifhop and his fucceffors to find one canon regular to fay mafs every day in the church of St. Mary Carlifle, for the fouls of the king and of his father and all his anceftors and fucceffors *.

. And by another charter the fame king further grants, that if they or any perfon with their permiffion fhall chafe any game within their foreft of Dalfton, and the faid game fhall fly into the king's foreft, they may purfue and take the fame within the king's foreft, and return without the moleftation of any of the king's forefters or other officers †.

Neverthelefs, in the laft year of Hen. 3. Michael de Harcla brought an action againft bifhop Coucy for this manor; and although the record fays, that the bifhop recovered, yet in the 7 Ed. 1. it feems to have been again ftirred, for in that year bifhop Irton paid to the faid Michael 320 marks of filver, which feems to have been for an abfolute difcharge. How Harcla's title accrued doth not appear: he only fets forth that he was fon of *William*, fon of *Michael*, fon of *Walter*, fon of *Michael*, fon of *Walter*, brother of *Robert*, brother of *Hervicius*, who was duly feifed in the reign of king Henry the firft, and whofe clerk and prefentee (Americk Talbot) was admitted and inftituted into the rectory of Dalfton aforefaid.

There are in this manor about 20 freeholders, 114 copyholders, and 40 cuftomary tenants, befides about 40 leafeholders for lives.

A *copyholder*, at the death of tenant or upon alienation, pays to the lord one year's rent for a fine, and no more; may leafe out his lands for any term he pleafes; and hath power to fell or difpofe of all the wood growing upon his copyhold land. The widow is intitled to thirds of all the lands her hufband at any time poffeffed during the coverture, if fhe does not join in the furrender and be privately examined by the fteward. The hufband, if he furvives, enjoys her lands for life. Female heirs inherit in coparcenary. In mortgages, there muft be a furrender, and one year's rent for a fine paid: And as long as the mortgagor continues in poffeffion, his heir, and not the heir of the mortgagee is admitted, though it has been a forfeited mortgage never fo long.

---

* Appendix, N° 24.   † Appendix, N° 26.

The

The *customary* tenants pay two years rent as a fine to the lord, upon every change of tenant by death or alienation; and before such time as he hath paid the said fine or made tender thereof, he cannot sell nor make a lease of his customary lands. But nothing is paid upon the death or translation of the bishop. The eldest female heir inherits, and the wife is only intitled to the thirds of such lands as her husband died possessed of. Nor is the husband intitled to a life's estate in his wife's lands after her death. In mortgages, as well as absolute sales, no title is had but by deed, surrender, and admittance. A full fine is paid upon a mortgage, and the heir of the mortgagor (so long as he continues in possession) is always admitted.

The customary tenant, as well as the copyholder and freeholder, is intitled to all the wood upon his estate, and to open quarries of stone for lime, either upon his own estate or the common, as also to dig clay for bricks to be used upon their own estates within the manor respectively, but not otherwise.

All the tenants of whatever denomination are to do suit and service at the lord's courts, and to grind all their corn at his miln, and to pay the 13th moulter for all such as they grow, and the 20th for the corn that they buy.

About the year 1698 a suit in chancery was commenced between the corporation of Carlisle on the one part, and the bishop of Carlisle and his tenants of Dalston, Crosby, and Linstock on the other part, concerning their paying toll to the corporation. Which after several issues at law, and an expence of above 1000*l* on the part of the bishop's tenants only, was July 7, 1707, decreed upon the equity reserved, that the tenants of Crosby and Linstock shall pay toll, but that those of Dalston, as such, are exempted from the payment of any toll. Which decree was further explained Dec. 15, 1708, *viz.* that the tenants or farmers of the said manor of Dalston ought to have the privilege of exemption as well for corn as other goods and things bought for the use of them and their families, as for any goods or commodities wrought up or manufactured by them, or cattle bought, fed, or grazed on their lands; but that such exemption ought not to extend to badgers, or those who carry on a trade of buying of corn or grain, selling it again without manufacturing, or of other goods unmanufactured to sell the same again, or to drovers of cattle or others who by fraud come in to buy or rent lands or tenements, or take a cottage without land barely to get or gain an exemption from toll.

Rose has been the principal mansion-house of the bishops of Carlisle, since the first grant of this manor to the see. It seems to have had its name from the British word *Rôôs*, which signifies a moist dale or valley. King Edward the third in the 10th year of his reign granted leave to embattle it, from which time it hath had the title of *Rose-Castle* (though the Scots burnt it the very next year).

It suffered many outrages and violence from the Scots from time to time; nevertheless, being repaired again as fast as the Scots demolished it, it continued a comfortable habitation until its total demolition in the civil wars in the reign of king Charles the first. Before that time, it consisted of a compleat quadrangle, with a fountain in the middle; with five towers, and other

lesser

leffer turrets; and incompaffed with a mantle-wall, which had little turrets in feveral parts of it. The *north* fide of the quadrangle contained the conftable's tower, with three rooms in it; the chapel, with three chambers under it; Bell-tower at the back of the chapel, with two rooms in it, befides the clock houfe. Next to the chapel, the bifhop's chamber, and another chamber under it; a large chamber called the council chamber, and one chamber under it called Great Paradife; Strickland's tower, which had three chambers in it, befides the vault. In all 17 rooms.

The *eaft* fide contained the great dining-room, with a cellar underneath; a large hall and a buttery, with a cellar under each; a turret, and one chamber near it; a large kitchen, with two chimneys, and a place for a cauldron or boiler; a lodging below for the cook; and alfo an arched cellar or vault. In all fix rooms.

The *fouth* fide contained a long gallery leading to the hall; a ftorehoufe and larder, and a little turret or two near the fame; over the fame a granary for corn, and underneath a vault or woodhoufe; alfo a brewhoufe, bakehoufe, and offices, and over thefe another granary. In all ten rooms.

The *weft* fide contained Pettinger's * tower, in which were three lodging rooms and a vault; a wafh-houfe and dairy; one chamber below, and three above: Adjoining to thefe, Kite's tower, with two chambers. In all twelve rooms.

There were within thefe, feveral clofets, woodhoufes, and other conveniences.

In the midft of the court, a fountain, which conveyed water to all the offices in the houfe.

Rooms without, in the turrets upon the mantle wall; one turret called the porter's lodge, containing one room below and one above. Between the porter's lodge and the ftables, a chamber for the grooms. One turret over againft Kite's tower, in the wall, containing one lodging room. The other turret containing one chamber below, and one above.

What ftate this place was reduced to by the civil wars, will appear from the furvey made in order for the fale thereof in the time of Oliver Cromwell, as follows:

Imprimis: A decayed caftle, with a large mantle wall, built with hewn ftone; the caftle by eftimation containing about half an acre, with a void quadrangle in the middle of it about one rood, the houfe incompaffing it, *viz.* the chapel on the north fide; the great chamber and hall on the eaft fide; the granary, brewhoufe, and bakehoufe on the fouth; and feveral decayed chambers on the weft: with one tower, called Conftable Tower, on the north quarter; one tower on the eaft quarter, called Strickland Tower; the kitchen and two little-turrets on the fouth; and one tower, called Pettinger's, on the weft. The whole caftle being full four fquare. There is a mantle wall diftant from the caftle on the weft fide about eighteen paces, on the fouth about four,

---

* There is a tradition that one Pettinger hanged himfelf in this tower, whence it had its name.

on the eaſt about ſix paces, with courts on the north ſide about one rood and an half.

About the wall are little watch-houſes, in great decay. The caſtle is a great part of it covered with lead, *viz.* all excepting the hall, kitchen, two little turrets, Pettinger's tower, the watch-houſes, and the ſtables in the weſt ſide of the north court; which are all covered with ſlate.

One dove-cote built with hewn ſtone; one ſlaughter-houſe; a little barn in great decay, the wood being burned by the ſoldiers belonging to the garriſon at Roſe, and by the Scots. A malt-houſe, in great decay. A kiln for drying malt, burned to the ground. An orchard on the ſouth and eaſt quarters of the caſtle, containing about three roods of ground.

One orchard belonging and adjoining to the ſaid caſtle, worth *per annum* — — — — — — 2 10 0

The caſtle, as it ſtands, with lead, iron, ſtone, glaſs, timber, wainſcot, and the outhouſes belonging to the ſame, worth — 2000 0 0

Utenſils belonging to the caſtle, now remaining there, *viz.* one copper bottom of a large furnace for brewing, one great braſs beef pot ſet in a furnace in the kitchen, a little brewing lead, one lead ciſtern in the kitchen, one maſh vat lined with lead in the bottom, a large cooler lined with lead in the bottom, two old tables and frames in the hall; all worth — — 16 13 0

All which are now in the poſſeſſion of Philip Ellis gentleman farmer of the ſame.

The woods growing upon the demeſne, and the parks belonging to the ſame, *viz.* oak, aſh, elm, and elder worth — 1500 0 0 Out of which ought to be repaired the chancel of the church of Dalſton, the vicarage there, the miln, the mill-dam and wears belonging to the ſame; two wood bridges, *viz.* Dalſton bridge, and Hawkſdale bridge.

Decays of the caſtle and other houſes belonging to the ſame:

Impriimis, In lead — — — — 80 0 0
In timber, iron, glaſs, wainſcot, ſlate — — 120 0 0
Decays on the outhouſes — — — 40 . 0 0

One cloſe barn, one high barn with a workhouſe at its end, one cow bier or ſtall, one ox ſtall; in great decay.

Mem. There is in the midſt of the ſquare of the aforeſaid caſtle, a very uſeful fountain which runneth continually, and ſerveth the offices in the ſaid houſe with water. There are very many fine ſprings about the ſaid houſe, and large fiſh ponds, but grown up with weeds. There are fine walks of oak and aſh about the ſaid houſe; and there are coal pits within five miles of it, and the market (*viz.* Carliſle) within five miles of the ſaid houſe; but the ſea not near it by many miles, nor any great roads.

The hewn ſtones of the walls in and about the ſaid caſtle, containing 5170 yards, at 8 *d per* yard, are worth to be ſold — 172 0 0

The timber in and about the ſaid caſtle, ſtables, barns, and other outhouſes ſtanding and fallen, worth to be ſold — 120 0 0

The

The lead lying upon the feveral rooms, gutters, and walls,
by computation twelve hundred weight, worth to be fold   —   120   0   0
The flate upon the feveral houfes is worth to be fold   —   6   0   0
The brewing lead, mafh fat, cooler, and guile fat, all bot-
tomed with lead ; worth   —   —   —   —   7   0   0

Total value of all the materials in and about the caftle and
buildings about the fame ; worth to be fold   —   —   425   0   0

The trees growing near and about the caftle, being in number 120, are worth to be fold   —   —   —   —   80   0   0
The trees and ftumps of trees ftanding and growing in and
upon the ground called the High hagg, confifting of 934 trees
and ftumps ; worth to be fold   —   —   —   155   0   0
The trees and ftumps ftanding and growing upon the Middle
hagg, in number 845, worth to be fold   —   —   —   128   0   0
The trees and ftumps ftanding and growing in and upon the
ground called the middle ground, in number 620 ; worth to be
fold   —   —   —   —   —   —   90   0   0
The trees and ftumps of trees, the moft part being old decayed trees, of little ufe but for firing, ftanding in the hedge
rows and other grounds of Dalfton belonging to the manor of
Dalfton, in number 680 trees ; worth to be fold   —   —   68   0   0
The value of all the woods above expreffed are worth to be
fold for ready money   —   —   —   —   521   0   0

Mem. The furveyors had the caftle viewed by very able artifts, which they
carried with them for that purpofe ; and they valued the fame (all charges dif-
burfed) at 1000 *l.* Yet we are of opinion, that the fame to be fold to a
gentleman who will purchafe the whole demefnes, and make it his habitation,
to be worth 1500 *l.*
  When bifhop *Rainbow* came to the fee, no part of the houfe was habitable,
fave only from the chapel fouthward to the end of the old kitchen. He built
the two parlours, chapel, entrance or paffage, and the great ftair-cafe. Bifhop
Smith built the tower adjoining, ftables, dairy, brewhoufe, fitted up the two
parlours, and altered the whole houfe. Bifhop *Fleming* wainfcotted the firft
parlour, and three rooms above ftrairs, with the ftair-cafe, and laid the floors
of the faid three rooms all anew ; for which he fold wood belonging to the fee,
according to an account entred in his regifter. When bifhop *Ofbaldifton* came
to the fee, he bullied bifhop Fleming's executors out of 200 *l* which the faid
bifhop Fleming had allowed to his leffee of Buley caftle in Weftmorland for
his intereft in the wood fold there, and for damages and fpringing it again.
The faid bifhop Ofbaldifton cut and fold all the alder wood upon the demefne
at Rofe, with large quantities of oak and afh, to the value of many hundred
pounds. Indeed he new floored and wainfcotted the inner parlour, new flagged
the halls and kitchen, and put a new coping upon the old walls on the fide
of

of the garden. He also built a new farm house, and a poor sorry small barn in the lingy park; all which together might perhaps cost about 350*l.* Being thus several hundred pounds into pocket, he was glad to compound with his successor bishop *Lyttelton* for 250*l* dilapidations, which his said successor chose to accept, rather than be at the trouble and expence of a long litigation. The said bishop Lyttelton built a very fine new kitchen, laundry, and brewhouse, repaired Strickland tower, and altered and improved the whole house so much, that it is now a convenient and comfortable habitation; of all which additions, and improvements he caused a particular account to be entered in his register.

Anciently, every bishop of Carlisle, at his death, was obliged to leave to his successor a certain number of books of divinity and canon law; and likewise 104 oxen, 16 heifers, and other quick goods in proportion *.

Notwithstanding the poverty of this see, the bishops here lived formerly in great splendor. For at the end of bishop White's rental in 1627, a very large family establishment is mentioned; and after reciting the name and office of every servant, concludes thus: " The constant houshold, besides workfolk, and strangers, about 35 or 36; amongst whom are, a gentleman usher, a steward, a chamberlain, and the bishop's solicitor."

The first mesne lordship within this barony is Little Dalston ; of which, Dalston hall is the capital or mansion-house. It was granted (as is aforesaid) to,

1. *Robert* brother to Hubert de Vallibus first baron of Gilsland, who thereupon assumed the name *de Dalston.* He had a son,

2. *Reginald de Dalston*; who had issue,

3. *Henry de Dalston*; who gave Brownelston to the priory of Carlisle. He had issue,

4. *Adam* ; who had issue,

5. *Henry* ; father of

6. *Simon*; father of

7. *Henry*; father of

8. *John*; father of

9. *John*; who, having no issue, was succeeded by his brother, *viz.*

10. *Henry de Dalston*; who had a son and heir,

11. *Robert*; who married a daughter of Southaic.

12. *John*, son of Robert, married a daughter and coheir of Kirkbride.

13. *Thomas*, son of *John*, married Mabel Denton of Cardew. Unto this Thomas, king Henry the eighth by letters patent bearing date July 15, in the 35th year of his reign, granted the manors of Brundholme, Uldale, Caldbeck, Upperton, and Kirkbride, parcel of the possessions of the late Henry earl of Northumberland, and the manor of Temple Sowerby, parcel of the possessions of the late priory of St. John of Jerusalem.—From this Thomas descended by a son of a second marriage the Dalstons of Acorn Bank in the county of Westmorland.

14. Sir *John Dalston* knight, son and heir of Thomas, married Catharine Tolson.

* Rot. Cart. 20 Ed. 1. N° 66.

15. Sir

15. Sir *John Dalston* knight, son of the last Sir John, was sheriff of Cumberland in the 10 Ja. 1. He had issue,

16. Sir *George Dalston* knight, who was sheriff of the county in the 16 Ja. 1. and its representative in parliament in the 16 Cha. 1.

17. Sir *William Dalston* son of George, was created baronet in the 16 Cha. 1. He and his father were both great sufferers in the royal cause. He resided mostly at Heath hall in Yorkshire, and died there Jan. 13, 1683.

18. Sir *George*, his son, was knighted in his father's life-time, and married the eldest daughter of Sir William Ramsden of Byrom, and died in his father's life-time, leaving only one daughter.

19. Sir *John Dalston* baronet, his brother, married Margaret the second daughter of the said Sir William Ramsden, and had issue two sons, Charles and John.

20. Sir *Charles Dalston* baronet, the elder of the two sons, married a daughter and coheir of Sir Francis Blake; by whom he had issue one son George and four daughters.

21. Sir *George Dalston* baronet, the last of the name at Dalston, having no issue male, sold this estate in 1761 to Mr. Monkhouse Davison grocer in London for 5060*l*, and died at York March. 9th 1765, leaving an infant daughter.

This little lordship consists of a few tenants dispersed in several places within the manor and barony of Dalston, who pay a yearly customary rent of 2*l* 15*s* 9*d*, with arbitrary fines; but seem intitled, like as the rest, to the wood growing upon their customary tenements.

CARDEW is another mesne-lordship within this barony, and consists of about 14 tenancies at Cardewlees. It was anciently called *Carthieu*, having taken the name from that great fenny ground at the head of the river Wathempole, now called Cardew-mire, and by the ancient inhabitants *Car-thieu,* which is by interpretation *God's fen,* or *God's meadow*; and so denominated by them, for that it adjoined unto *Thursby,* where the Saxons had a house of sacrifice or temple of worship, where those pagans offered up the blood of the captives to a god whom in that sort they honoured called *Thor.*

It was anciently forest ground, and parcel of that great forest of Englewood, and became first inhabited, according to Mr. Denton, in the reign of king William Rufus or Henry the first. The said Mr. Denton, whose manuscript account of Cumberland we have often had occasion to quote, was owner of this manor, and resided at Cardew hall. In one of the copies of the said manuscript which bishop Nicolson says was lent to him by Mr. Bird of Brougham in 1708, is the following pedigree:

Manor of Cardew in the county of Cumberland, and lords thereof:

1. *Thor,* lord of the manor.
2. *Thorpin de Cardew.*
3. *Stephen de Cardew;* in the time of Hen. 2.
4. *Hugh de Cardew,* in the time of king John.

5. *Adam*

5. *Adam de Cardew*, t. Hen. 3.

6. *Henry*, fon of Adam, t. Hen. 3.

7. *Walter*, fon of Henry, t. Ed. 1.

8. *William* fon of Walter, t. Ed. 1. This William fold his patrimony to one *Barrington* a prieft; which *Barrington* conveyed the fame to the bifhop of Carlifle in truft for the ufe of *John Burdon*.

The faid *John Burdon* had alfo a fon *John Burdon*, upon whom his father intailed the manor of Cardew and the heirs of his body; and on default of fuch iffue, to *John de Denton* and *Joan* his wife, kinfwoman and heir of Bur. don, if John Burdon the fon fhould die without iffue, which event accordingly happened. And here begins the pedigree of the *Dentons* of Cardew.

1. *John de Denton*, by his wife Joan de Kirkbride (daughter of Walter de Kirkbride by his wife Alice daughter and heir of William de Burdon knight, brother of John de Burdon the father aforefaid) had iffue a fon,

2. *William de Denton*, t. Hen. 6.

3. *William*, t. Ed. 4.

4. *John*, t. Ed. 4.

5. *Henry*, t. Hen. 7.

6. *William*, t. Hen. 8.

7. *John*, t. Hen. 8.

8. *Henry*, t. Eliz.

9. *John Denton*, author of the aforefaid manufcript account of Cumber-land. He married a daughter of Sir John Dalfton of Dalfton knight, and by her had iffue,

10. *Henry*, who married Julian daughter of Sir Richard Mufgrave of Norton in the county of York, and by her had iffue,

11. *George*, who married Catharine daughter of George Graham of Nunnery, and by her had iffue 4 fons and 4 daughters. He was colonel of a regiment of foot in the fervice of king Charles the firft; and fuffered greatly in that king's caufe.

12. *George Denton* of Cardew efquire, fon of George, was of the age of 15 at Dugdale's vifitation in 1665.

In 1672, for 61 years ancient rent, he fold to the tenants their meffuages and tenements free from all rents, fines, heriots, carriages, boons, and other fervices; referving only one penny yearly rent, fuit of court, and royalties. And in 1686 he fold the whole remainder to Sir John Lowther of Lowther baronet, anceftor of Sir James Lowther baronet the prefent owner.

In 1690, the faid Sir John Lowther fold to the tenants a parcel of common called Cardew leafe ftint, containing 35 acres, for the yearly rent of .17s; referving to himfelf the royalties, and fuit of court for the manor of Parton (of which this lordfhip or manor of Cardew now is parcel).

The paternal arms of the Dentons of Cardew were, Argent, two bars and three martlets in chief Gules. The Creft; On a tower Sable breathing out flames at the windows Gules, a demi-lion Or, holding a fword in his paw Argent. (Which creft, the faid Mr. Denton fays they took, on one of their
anceftors

anceſtors (John Denton) holding a caſtle in Annandale in Scotland for Baliol againſt Bruce till it was fired under him.)

GATESKALE and RAUGHTON were at the conqueſt all foreſt and waſte ground, and were firſt incloſed by way of purpreſture by one Ugthred, to be holden of the king in fee farm by ſerjeanty for keeping the eyries of hawks for the king, which bred in the foreſt of Englewood.

Gateſkale being a whinny place, where the inhabitants of Raughton made *ſcales* or ſhields for their *gates* (or goats), from thence took its name; as *Raughton* did from the beck or river, called *Raugh* (or Raghe), which ſignifies a *rough*, rapid water.

The poſterity of Ughtred took their ſurname of the place, and gave the ſparhawk for their cognizance. It continued in this name and family for ſeveral generations; till the laſt of the name ſettling it upon his wife Margaret (Stapleton), and ſhe dying without iſſue, her brother William Stapleton of Edenhall ſucceeded to the inheritance. In like manner the Muſgraves ſucceeded the Stapletons by a female heir, and towards the end of the fourteenth century ſettled it upon a younger ſon, whoſe chief ſeat was at Hayton, in which houſe it ſtill continues.

Here are in this manor 22 freehold tenants, who pay 1 *l* 8 *s* 8¼ *d* yearly free rent, do ſuit and ſervice at the lord's court when called upon, and alſo pay yearly to the duke of Portland as chief lord of the foreſt of Englewood the ſum of 2 *l* 13 *s* 2 *d* or thereabout, and likewiſe ſend a man to appear for them at the foreſt court at Heſket every St. Barnabas's day, who is to be upon the inqueſt.

ABOUT four miles from the church, and within the ſaid pariſh of Dalſton, ſtands. HIGH-HEAD caſtle within the manor thereunto adjoining and belonging.

By an inquiſition in the 16 Ed. 2. it is found, that John de Harcla held the caſtle of High-head *(pelam de Higheved)* with 60 acres of land there newly aſſarted; and that the ſaid John enfeoffed his brother Andrew thereof after the death of the ſaid John.—When this Andrew de Harcla was ſeized at Carliſle for treaſon by the lord Lucy, word thereof was immediately ſent to his brother at High-head who forthwith fled into Scotland, and with him Sir William Blount and many others. Upon Andrew's conviction, and his brother's flight as aforeſaid, this inquiſition ſeemeth to have been taken, and the premiſſes ſeized by the king: who ſoon after (as it ſeemeth) granted the ſame to Ranulph de Dacre; for in the 2 Ed. 3. it is found by inquiſition, that Ranulph de Dacre *tenuit pelam de Higheved*, by the ſervice of five marks.

In the 18 Ed. 3. *William Engliſh* (Lengleys) held the manor of Higheved of the king by the ſervice of one roſe yearly: *William Engliſh* being his ſon and heir. Which William the ſon in 1358 obtained a licence from biſhop Appleby to build a chapel here, and to have a chaplain to attend in it.

In the 35 Hen. 8. *William Reſtwold* held of the king the manor of High-head as an approvement of the foreſt of Englewood *in capite* by fealty and the

4   ſervice

fervice of rendring at his exchequer of Carlifle one red rofe at the feaft of St. John Baptift yearly.

It was purchafed of *Reftwold* by *John Richmond* efquire; who had a fon *John Richmond*, who in the 2 Eliz. was impleaded for a purprefture of 60 acres, which he feems to have fully juftified. In the pleadings the following boundary is infifted on : " Incipiendo ad Siplingill hedge, et fic defcendendo verfus occidentem ad Boreftayn gill, et ab inde ut regia via ducit ad manerium de Rofe vocata Bifhopfgate, et fic in occidentem ex auftrali parte de Hemfkin howe ad Brokelfyke, et deinde ad aquam de Ive."

This *John Richmond* (according to a pedigree certified at Dugdale's vifitation in 1665) married to his firft wife a daughter of Dacre a younger brother of the lord Dacre, by whom he had no iffue. To his fecond wife he married Margaret daughter of Thomas Dalfton of Uldale efquire; and by her had iffue, 1. Chriftopher. 2. John, who died young. 3. Francis, who married a daughter of Lancelot Fletcher of Tallentire, and died without iffue. 4. Margaret, married to Sir Richard Fletcher of Hutton knight. 5. Mabel, married to John Simpfon of Sowreby.

Chriftopher Richmond efquire, eldeft fon of John, was thrice married. He married, firft, Anne daughter of Thomas Mayplate of Little Salkeld, and by her had iffue a fon John Richmond, who died unmarried. His fecond wife was Elizabeth daughter of Anthony Chaytor of Croft-hall in the county of York efquire, and by her he had iffue, 1. Francis, who died an infant. 2. Chriftopher. 3. Margery, married to John Aglionby of Carlifle. 4. Elizabeth, married to Richard Baxter of Sebergham, gentleman. 5. Mary, married to John Vaux of Little Mufgrave in the county of Weftmorland. To his third wife he married Eleanor daughter of Richard Beauley of Hefketh hall in Cumberland, and by her had iffue William, Jane, and Mabel. He died in 1642.

Chriftopher Richmond of High-head efquire, fon and heir of Chriftopher, married Mabel daughter and heir of John Vaux of Catterlen efquire, and by her had iffue, Chriftopher aged 17 at the faid vifitation, John aged 16, Magdalen aged 12. To his fecond wife he married Magdalen daughter of Andrew Huddlefton of Hutton John efquire, and by her had iffue Dorothy at the faid vifitation aged one year, and Margery aged 7 weeks.

Chriftopher Richmond efquire, fon and heir of the laft Chriftopher, married Ifabella Towerfon about the year 1678, and had iffue Henry, and 6 daughters, 5 of which daughters married, and are dead; one of the faid daughters, Sufanna, is now (1773) living and unmarried.

Henry Richmond of High-head efquire died unmarried about the year 1716, and devifed all his eftate to his mother the faid Ifabella.

Ifabella, widow of Chriftopher Richmond, and devifee of her fon Henry Richmond, married to her fecond hufband Mr. Matthias Miller, and by her laft will and teftament in the year 1730 devifed High-head to her faid daughter Sufanna Richmond the prefent proprietor.

The manor confifts of about 39 tenements, the owners whereof pay 19 *l* 4 *s* 7 *d* yearly cuftomary rents, and arbitrary fines.

Nigh

Nigh unto the caftle ftands the chapel, the foundation whereof feems as ancient as the days of William Englifh aforefaid. It hath never yet been made parochial, for they chriften and bury at the mother church, but the holy communion is adminiftred at the chapel by the vicar every Maundy Thurfday.

The ftock or endowment is 300*l*, now fecured in the hands of John Gale of Whitehaven efquire, as executor of Henry Richmond Brougham efquire who pays 5 *per cent.* The truftees nominate the curate, who feem to manage the revenue as public charities or benefactions are too often managed. Their account for the year 1748 (which is the only one we have feen) ftands thus:

	£	s	d
To the curate at four quarterly payments	6	10	0
To the fame by way of prefent	4	11	6
Mr. Blain for 8 fermons	2	0	0
Mr. Relph for 2 fermons	0	10	0
Jon. Mandeville for ringing the bell	0	3	0
Wafhing furplice	0	2	0
Houfe-room when fettling accounts	0	2	0
Glazing windows	0	2	6
Ale, &c.	0	7	0
Balance in the truftees hands	0	12	0
	15	0	0

The CHURCH of Dalfton is dedicated to St. Michael; and valued in the king's books at 8*l* 18*s* 1¼*d*. Having been given to the fee of Carlifle, along with the manor as aforefaid, it was foon after appropriated thereto. And the vicars, in the year 1307, were endowed as follows:—" Affignamus vicariis perpetuis ecclefiæ noftræ de Dalfton, aream principalem ex parte orientali ipfius ecclefiæ, quam rectores ejufdem inhabitare confueverunt, cum edificiis fuis (Salva nobis et fuccefforibus noftris una placea competenti pro quadam grangia conftruenda ibidem, ac libero et fufficienti exitu et ingreffu) ac omnes obventiones, altaragia, et minores decimas ad ipfam ecclefiam fpectantes. Exceptis decimis lanæ, agnorum, vitulorum, molendinorum, ac vivis mortuariis, terris, tenementis, et redditibus ad ipfam ecclefiam pertinentibus, præter aream antedictam; quæ omnia, cum decimis garbarum cujufcunque bladi crefcentis infra dictam parochiam ubicunque, nobis et fuccefforibus noftris fpecialiter refervamus. Vicarius vero qui pro tempore fuerit, fuis fumptibus ipfi ecclefiæ deferviet in divinis, facramenta canonica miniftrabit, fynodalia perfolvet, et archidiaconum ficut convenit procurabit, ac libros et alia ornamenta dictæ ecclefiæ bene cuftodiet et honefte: Onera etiam extraordinaria qualitercunque emergentia, pro rata fuæ portionis quam ad centum folidos taxamus, de cætero fuftinebit. Et quia Levitæ et miniftri ecclefiaftici defervientes altari præ cæteris quibufdam immunitatibus gaudere debent, fin-

gulis vicariis ipfius ecclefiæ qui pró tempore fuerint a præftatione decimarum
de animalibus fuis quibufcunque, nobis et fucceffóribus noftris auctoritate
prædicta quietos effe decernimus et immunes."

After the Reftoration, the following augmentations were given to this
vicarage:

				£ s d.
Out of the tithes of Raughton and Gatefkill.	—		—	7 0 0
—— Unthank 1 10 0 Skiprig 1 10 0.	—		—	3 0 0
—— Cummerfdale and Brownelfton.	—		—	5 0 0
—— Cumdivock 2 l. Highead and Ivegill 4 l.	—	..1 —		7 0 0
—— Cardew and Cardewlees.	—	—	—	3 0 0
—— Caldew-ftones 2 l. Little Dalfton 1 0 8.	—	. —		3 0 8
—— Little Raughton.	—	—	—	: 3 0 0
				...31 0 8

And bifhop Smith left 300 l to this vicarage. So that it may now be worth
80 l a year or better.

Incumbents, fo far as we have any account, have been as followeth.

In 1203, whilft this church was rectorial and in the patronage of the crown,
king John gave it to *Americ Theobald* archdeacon of Carlifle; and in the year
following, Alexander Lucy had the archdeaconry, and *Robert Pickering* this
rectory.

In 1292, in the vacancy of the fee, king Edward the firft prefented *John de
Drockenford* to the rectory of Dalfton; concerning which a difpute arofe with
the archbifhop of York's official.

In 1303, *Gilbert de Derington* was collated to the vicarage by bifhop
Halton.

In 1310, *John de Carlifle* was collated by the fame bifhop.

In 1356, on the death of Sir *Henry Hand* vicar of Dalfton, Sir *Richard
Aflakby* was collated, with a charge of perfonal refidence according to the
form of the Legatine conftitution in that behalf provided.

In 1358, Sir *Roger de Ledes* was collated in like form.

In 1369, Sir *John Middleton* chaplain was collated.

In 1371, *John del Marfh*, rector of Kirk Andrews, makes an exchange for
the vicarage of Dalfton.

In 1378, on the death of vicar Marfh, Sir *John de Alanby* was collated by
William rector of Bownefs, who had the bifhop's commiffion, and admini-
ftered the oath of refidence. And in the fame year this Alanby exchanged with *John Mayfon* rector of Croglin, who was collated by the bifhop
himfelf.

In 1570, on the death of Sir *George Bewly* vicar of Dalfton, *Mark Edgar*
was collated.

In 1586, Sir *Thomas Nicolfon* fucceeded the faid Edgar.

In

In 1596, on the death of Thomas Nicolson, *Robert Collier*, B. A. was collated. He died in 1630, as appears from the parifh regifter. His fucceffor feems to have been *William Griffith*; for in the fame regifter it appears, that William Griffith vicar was buried in December 1642.

Edward Baker, B. A. fucceeded, on the collation of archbifhop Ufher. He was buried, as appears by the faid parifh regifter, Nov. 18, 1659.

In 1661, Oct. 14. *Richard Garth*, M. A. was collated by bifhop Sterne.

In 1663, on the ceffion of Richard Garth, *John Walker*, B. A. was collated by the fame bifhop.

In 1714, on John Walker's death, *Thomas Benfon*, M. A. was collated by bifhop Nicolfon.

In 1727, *William Nicolfon*, M. A. was collated on the death of Thomas Benfon.

In 1731, *John Story*, M. A. was collated upon the death of William Nicolfon.

The school at Dalfton is endowed with a ftock of 138*l*, and a tenement in Hawkfdale called New Hall, of about 7*l* yearly value, given (upon the attainder of John Lowther of the Cawfey at Rofe Caftle for murder) by bifhop Smith, who alfo rebuilt the fchool-houfe.

About the year 1343, forty days indulgence was granted by bifhop Kirkby, to all fuch as fhould give any money, books, veftments, or other things, towards the repairs of the *chapel* of St. Wynemius the bifhop, or to the fupport of Hugh de Lilford an *hermit* there, made overfeer of the repairs of the faid chapel in the parifh of Dalfton: No tradition now remains, what this chapel was, or where fituate, nor of the hermit or his hermitage. Indeed, there is a field, about a mile from the parifh church, called Chapel Flat, in a part of which freeftones have frequently been dug up, which feems to indicate fome fort of building there. And the fituation, amongft rocks, water, and wood, is not unlikely for the folitary retirement of an hermit.

And that there was anciently here a Britifh temple or fomething of that fort, is evident, for that a good many years ago a circle of rude ftones about three foot in diameter was difcovered, the whole circle being about 30 yards in circumference. And within the circle, towards the eaft point, were found four ftones, much of the fame form as the reft, lying one upon another, fuppofed to be fomething of the Keft-vaen kind.

Not far from hence is a very regular tumulus or barrow, about eight yards in diameter at the bottom and two at the top, and about three yards in height. When opened, there were found near the top two freeftones about three foot long, one broad, and about fix inches thick, wh ch had a fort of circle very rudely cut out or marked near the top, but nothing was found underneath, though the ground was opened above 4 foot below the level.

About half a mile S. S. W. from hence was a fmall Roman camp of about fifty yards diameter; and much about the fame diftance N. N. E another Roman camp of the like dimenfions. Alfo a third, about a mile S. E. much

larger

larger than the other. None of thefe three camps are above a mile from Rofe Caftle, and the firft not one fourth of that diftance, where Mr. Camden places the Congavata of the Romans, but Mr. Horfley upon much better grounds fixes that ftation at Stanwix. The two fmaller of thefe camps are now arable land, and have been frequently plowed, but no coins or infcriptions have been difcovered. The other is upon an uncultivated moor, and hath never been any way fearched or tried. But fmall hand mill-ftones and other things have been found in them all, fufficient to evince them to be Roman.

About a mile or fomewhat more from Rofe Caftle weftward, is *Shalk* beck, where are large and fine quarries of freeftone, from whence it is fuppofed a great part of the ftone which built the Roman wall from Carlifle to Bownefs was taken. From the appearance of the place, it is certain that immenfe quantities have been carried away from thence ; and lately, on removing a vaft heap of rubbifh from before the rock in one part, in order to carry the works further back, was found upon the face of the rock the following infcription ;

LEG II AVG.
MILITES PEIU
COH III COH IIII

(Legionis Secundæ Auguftæ milites pofuerunt, Cohors tertia, Cohors quarta †.)

Dalfton is no market town, yet there is a very large *crofs*, which feems to have been built at the expence of the neighbouring gentlemen, as the feveral coats of arms thereupon do indicate. The three kites heads, on one of the coats, which were the arms of bifhop Kite, refer the erecting of it to his time. Croffes, foon after the eftablifhment of chriftianity in this ifland, were put up in moft places of public concourfe, to remind the people of the benefit vouchfafed to us by the crofs of Chrift. The poor folicited alms at thofe croffes (as the faying is to this day) *for Chrift's fake*; and when a perfon is urgent and vehement, we fay, he begged like a cripple at a crofs. At thofe croffes, the corps in carrying to church was fet down, that all the people attending might pray for the foul of the departed. In perambulating the boundaries of parifhes, croffes were erected at certain diftances, where the people prayed, and at the fame time regaled themfelves. We fign children in baptifm with the fign of the crofs. And in many ancient charters, where a man could not write his name, he put the fymbol of the crofs ; which kind of fignature is even yet not out of ufe ‡.

It was certified in 1747, that there were in this parifh 220 families, all of the church of England.

---

† Tracts of the Antiquarian Society, p. 227.

‡ In the original *Solemn League and Covenant*, which hath been lately difcovered, and is now in the Britifh Mufeum, there are abundance of markfmen, all of whom, from their abhorrence of popery at that time, leave the crofs unfinifhed, and fign in the fhape of the letter T.

PARISH OF SEBERGHAM.

Sebergham, or *Sebraham*, is the next parifh to Dalfton, and the laft in this ward towards the fouth. It was fo called from the place where it ftands, which is a hill or rifing ground in the foreft of Englewood, whereof the eaft and fouth eaft parts were woodland and dry ground ; but the fouth, weft, and north weft parts were wet fpringy ground covered with rufhes, which the country people call *fieves*; and thereupon the place was called *Sievy-burgh*, or fievy hill. At the time of the conqueft, it was a great wafte and wildernefs. Afterwards, in the latter end of king Henry the fecond's time, one William Waftall, or *de Wafte-dale*, began to inclofe fome part of it. He was an hermit, and lived there to an extreme old age, by the labour of his hands, and the fruits of trees. He came hither in Henry the firft's time, and died about the end of king John's reign, or in the beginning of Henry the third's. King John granted him the hill Sebergham, and he left it to the priory of Carlifle.

The parifh in general is the manor of the duke of Portland, who hath here about 80 tenants, who pay an ancient free rent of 4*l* 7*s* 4*d*, copyhold rent 5*l* 11*s* 6*d*, and pannage 1*s* 11*d*. But they are now all made freeholders by the improvement of the commons, for which they pay an additional free rent of 58*l* 2*s* 4*d*.

The dean and chapter of Carlifle have alfo an independent manor here (perhaps from the hermit aforefaid) which is likewife called the manor of Sebergham; which confifts of about 16 cuftomary tenants, five leafeholders, and one freeholder. The cuftomary tenants are now all made freeholders, by their fhares of the faid commons; for which they pay a quit rent of 4*l* 7*s* 3¼*d* to the faid dean and chapter. And to prevent for the future all interference of manerial rights or jurifdictions, it is agreed and declared by the act of parliament for dividing and inclofing the faid commons, that the manor of the faid dean and chapter fhall extend only to the leafehold and cuftomary eftates held under them, and to the feveral parcels of the faid common or wafte ground allotted to the faid leafehold and cuftomary eftates, by virtue of the faid act.

Mr. *Denton* of Warnel hall holds alfo a mefne manor of Warnel hall within this parifh; who is of an ancient family fprung from Denton in Gilfland in this county, whofe pedigree was certified at Dugdale's vifitation in 1665, as follows:

1. *Thomas de Denton* of Denton lived in the reigns of Ed. 3. and Ric. 2.

2. *Adam de Denton* died 10 Hen. 4.

3. *Thomas Denton*, efquire, married Alice daughter of Thomas Moore.

4. *Richard Denton* of Gilfland, efquire, married Jane natural daughter of Sir Humphrey Dacre knight lord Dacre of Gilfland, and died in the 2 Ric. 3.

5. *John Denton* of Denton hall, efquire, married Agnes Sithe, and died in the 27 Hen. 7.

6. *Thomas Denton* of Warnel, efquire, died in the 6 Eliz.

7. *Thomas*

7. *Thomas Denton* of Warnel, efquire, died in the 6 Ja. without iffue ; and was fucceeded by his brother's fon, viz.

8. *Thomas Denton* fon of George, by his wife a daughter of Lafcells in the county of York. Which Thomas died unmarried, and was fucceeded by his brother,

9. *Henry Denton*, who married Elizabeth Oglethorp of the county of York; and died about the 12 Cha 1.

10. *Thomas Denton.* He was a captain of foot under the earl of Newcaftle, in the fervice of king Charles the firft, and died of the wounds he received at Hull in 1643. His wife was Lettice daughter of John Lowgher of Perton in the county of Stafford efquire.

11. *Thomas Denton* of Warnel, barrifter at law, and recorder of Carlifle and Appleby, married Lettice daughter of Thomas Vachell of Cowley in the county of Berks efquire. He was of the age of 27 at the faid vifitation.

12. *Thomas Denton* his fon married Margery daughter of Crackenthorp of Newbiggin in Weftmorland efquire.

13. *Thomas* his fon married a daughter of Pattinfon of Penrith, and died in 1736.

14. *John Denton* of Warnel hall efquire, his fon, married Mary daughter of Mr. Thomas Wilkin of Brough Sowerby in Weftmorland ; and by her hath iffue Thomas and Barbara : but in the year 1774 he fold the eftate to Sir James Lowther baronet.

The Arms of Denton of Warnel are ; Argent, two bars Gules, in chief three cinquefoils Sable.

The CHURCH is dedicated to St. Mary, and is a perpetual curacy, in the patronage of the dean and chapter of Carlifle, who are the appropriators. It doth not occur in any of the ancient valuations ; but was certified in 1739 to the governors of queen Anne's bounty at 19 *l*, and having received an augmentation by lot, and another in conjunction with 200 *l* given by John Simpfon efquire, and being greatly advantaged by the late inclofure and divifion of the common, it is now worth upwards of 100 *l per annum.*

The parifh contains about 111 families ; all of the church of England, except only 1 Quaker.

PARISH OF WARWICK.

WE muft now turn to the eaft fide of Carlifle, and the firft parifh that there prefents itfelf is WARWICK, which feems to have been anciently a chapelry in the parifh of Wetheral. It begins at the foot of Sawbeck, where the faid beck falls into Eden below Warwick bridge, fo along the river Eden to the Dead water (or ancient courfe of the faid river) to Pow Maugham beck, then up that beck to the Carr fyke, and along the Carr fyke through

Holm

Holm mire to the foot of Sawbeck aforefaid.—It is divided into *Aglionby* quarter, and *Warwick* quarter.

The firft is the manor of the family of *Aglionby*, who finally fettled at Nunnery in this county, and was fo called of *Agullon* their firft anceftor, who came into England with William the Conqueror and feated himfelf here.

This *Agullon* had iffue *Everard, Laurence,* and *Werrye.* The two firft feem to have died without iffue, for *Elias* fon of *Werrye* fucceeded to the inheritance. *Elias* had iffue *Alan,* who had iffue *William,* who had iffue *Adam,* who had iffue *John,* who had iffue *Adam* that lived in the reign of Edw. 1. and married Julian Whitfield.

·*Thomas* fon of the laft *Adam* lived in the reign of Ed. 2. and had iffue *John,* father of *William,* who married Maria daughter of Alan Blenerhaffet efquire, and reprefented the city of Carlifle in parliament in the reign of Ric. 2. as did many of his pofterity in feveral fucceeding reigns.

This William had a fon *Thomas,* who married Katherine daughter of Skelton efquire, 3 Hen. 5.

John fon of *Thomas,* 14 Ed. 4.

Thomas his fon, 3 Hen. 7.

Edward Eglionby of Eglionby, fon of *Thomas,* was fheriff of Cumberland in the 36 Hen. 8. His arms were; Barry of four, Sable and Argent, On a chief of the laft, 3 fheldrakes of the firft.

- *John,* fon of *Edward,* married a daughter of Salkeld of Corby.

Thomas, fon of *John,* married a daughter of Cuthbert Mufgrave of Crookdake.

About this time lived *John Aglionby,* a younger brother (as it feemeth) of this family, who was a ftudent in and fellow of Queen's college in Oxford, became a moft polite and learned preacher, was principal of Edmund Hall in 1600, and the year after rector of Iflip in Oxfordfhire. He had a confiderable hand in the tranflation of the New Teftament in the year 1604, and died at Iflip in 1609.

Edward Aglionby, brother of *Thomas,* fucceeded to the inheritance, and married a daughter of *Henry Brougham* efquire; and by her had iffue *John,* who was recorder of Carlifle many years.

The faid *John* married Barbara daughter of John Patrickfon of Caldre abbey efquire, and had iffue *John,* who was difinherited; and *Henry* fon of this laft *John* fucceeded, and married Elizabeth daughter of Wilfrid Lawfon of Brayton efquire, and by her had iffue *Henry Aglionby* of Nunnery efquire, who married Anne daughter of Sir Chriftopher Mufgrave of Edenhall baronet, by whom he had iffue Henry, John, and Chriftopher, and four daughters, Elizabeth, Anne, Julia, and Mary married to John Yates of Skirwith efquire.

Henry the father died in 1770, and his fons Henry and John died before him unmarried, and *Chriftopher Aglionby* efquire the third fon (yet a minor, 1773) now enjoys the family eftate.

This manor confifts of about 26 tenements and 17 cuftomary tenants who pay a yearly rent of 7 l 6 s 9 d, arbitrary fines, and heriots. Here are alfo nine fmall free rents, which amount to one fhilling only.

The

The manor of *Warwick* was given by Hubert de Vallibus and Robert his fon to Odard firft lord of Corkeby, to be holden of his barony of Gilfland. This Odard, in the pedigree certified by Thomas Warwick efquire at Sir William Dugdale's vifitation in 1665, is faid to be Odard de Logis firft baron of Wigton. But the fubfequent account doth not at all agree with the family of the lords of Wigton; therefore this muft have been another Odard, concerning whom the pedigree proceeds as follows:

1. *Odard*, firft lord of Corby and of Warwick, had iffue *Ofbert* and *William*. To *Ofbert* the elder he gave Corby, and to *William* his younger fon he gave Warwick. *Ofbert* died without iffue, fo *William* became lord of them both.

2. *William* had iffue *John* and *Robert*, with divers other children. *John* the eldeft had Warwick, and *Robert* had Corby.

3. *John de Warthwyke*, lived in the reign of Ric. 1.

4. *William de Warthwyke*, 17 Hen. 3. He was knighted in the 44 Hen. 3.

5. *Robert de Warthwyke*, 31 Ed. 1.

6. *William de Warthwyke*, in the time of Ed. 2.

7. *John de Warthwyke* knight, fon of William, died without iffue: And was fucceeded by,

8. *John de Warthwyke*, nephew and heir of John, and fon of Edmund de Warthwyke deceafed. He lived in the reign of Ed. 3.

9. *George de Warthwyke*, in the reign of Ric. 2.

10. *John de Warthwyke*, in the fame reign of Ric. 2.

11. *John Warthwyke*, in the time of Ed. 4.

12. *Lancelot Warwike*, in the time of Hen. 7.

13. *Richard Warwike*. In the 35 Hen. 8. it is found, that Richard Warwick then held the manor and vill of Warwike of the king *in capite* by knight's fervice and cornage.

14. *Chriftopher Warwike*, fon of Richard, married Frances daughter of Salkeld of Corby.

15. *Richard Warwike*, married to his firft wife Frances daughter of Salkeld of Whitehall, and by her had iffue *Thomas*, and a younger fon *George* who died without iffue. To his fecond wife he had a fon *John Warwike* of Lockwayt nigh Hartley caftle in the county of Weftmorland. This Richard died about the 10 Cha. 1.

16. *Thomas Warwick*, married a daughter of Gawin Brathwaite of Amblefide, and died in his father's life-time.

17. *Thomas Warwick* of Warwick, married Frances daughter of John Skelton of Armathwaite efquire; and had iffue *John* who died unmarried; *Thomas*; *Mary* married to Rowland Nichols rector of Aikton; and *Catherine*. He died in 1654.

18. *Thomas Warwick*, aged 22 at the faid vifitation, married Frances daughter of John Dalfton of Acorn Bank in Weftmorland efquire; and had iffue,

19. *John Warwick*, who married Mary daughter of Francis Howard of Corby efquire; and by her had iffue,

20. *Francis Warwick* efquire, who married Jane daughter of Thomas Howard of Corby efquire, by Barbara daughter of John vifcount Lonfdale; who

who died without iffue in 1772, and was fucceeded by his only furviving fifter and heir Mrs. Anne Warwick, after whofe deceafe the eftate is devifed to Ralph Maddifon of Gatefhead near Newcaftle upon Tyne efquire, grandfon of Mary, fifter of John Warwick efquire, father of Francis Warwick efquire the devifor. , .The Arms of Warwick, certified at the aforefaid vifitation, are ; Azure, 3 lions rampant Argent. The Creft ; an armed arm and hand, with a gantlet, holding a poleax.

The *church* of Warwick is dedicated to St. Leonard (who was an holy man of France, that lived in the fifth century, whofe commemoration-day in the Romifh Kalendar is the fixth of November) ; and was given by Ranulph de Mefchiens, by the name of the Chapel .of Warthewick, together with the church of Wetheral and the cell of St. Conftantine there, to the abbey of St. Mary's York. After the diffolution of the monafteries, king Henry the eighth gave the fame to the dean and chapter of Carlifle, who ftill enjoy the rectory, and nominate a curate from time to time to the two parifhes of Warwick and Wetheral jointly, and allow him a falary of 52 *l per annum.* This parifh contains about 47 families ; of which Quakers 4, Papifts 3.

PARISH OF WETHERAL.

THE next parifh is WETHERAL, in which are contained feveral manors. The firft of which is that of *Wetheral,* where Ranulph de Mefchiens in the year 1088 founded a cell of a prior and eight Benedictine monks, and gave the fame, together with the church, mill, fifhery, wood, and the chapel of Warthewick, and two bovates of land at Corkeby, to the abbey of St. Mary's York. The boundary of which manor, Dr. Todd defcribes from an old manufcript as follows :

" Hæ funt metæ & bundæ circumfcribentes territorium et villam de Weder-
" hâl. Prima meta ejufdem territorii incipit ad mediam partem aquæ de
" Edene fubtus pontem vulgariter vocatum Werwykbrigge, ficut eadem præ-
" dicta aqua de Edene ab inde decurrit verfus occidentem, et ab inde afcendit
" ufque ad unum torrentem vocatum Sawbeke, ufque ad quandâm crucem quæ
" vocatur Wederhal-girth croffe verfus occidentem, et ftantem fuper prædic-
" tum torrentem prius nominatum, et ab hinc percurrit ad Holmfmyr verfus
" Carfyke, ficut Girthcrofs de Wederhal extendit, et ab hinc afcendit ufque ad
" Scotby beke, et ab eadem foffa ufque ad Cumwhynting beke, et ab inde
" afcendit ufque ad marifcum qui vocatur Wragmire, et ab eodem percurrit
" ufque ad Merefike, et hoc ex parte auftrali ; et ab inde ufque ad Sandwak,
" et ab eodem ufque ad Taykingate, et ab inde pertranfit per ftratam regiam
" quæ vocatur Highftreet quæ ducit de Carliolo ufque ad Appilby way, et ab
" inde ufque ad Drybeke, et a Drybeke, defcendit ufque ad mediám aquæ de
" Edene, et hoc ex parte orientali ; et fic defcendit per mediam aquæ de Edene,
" ufque ad prædictum pontem vocatum Werwickbrigg verfus boream."

The said Ranulph de Mefchiens granted to them alfo the water of Eden towards Corby, and the river bank on the fide of the water next to Corby wherein their fifh pool was ftrengthened and fecured, *(in qua ftagnum firmatum eft)*: And for this fifhery all along they feem to have been peculiarly folicitous.

King William Rufus by his charter confirms to the abbey of St. Mary's York the cell of St. Conftantine of Wetherhal and the manor there, with the chapel of Warthwyke, and the pond and fifhery and mill, which they had by the gift of Ranulph de Mefchiens. And he confirms to them, of his own proper gift, the whole pafture between Eden and the king's highway which leads from Carlifle to Appleby, and from Wetheral to Drybeck +.

They had a like confirmation from king Henry the firft, with a grant to feed their fwine in the king's foreft without pannage ‡.

William fon of Odard lord of Corkeby, with the affent of his lord Robert de Vallibus and Ofanna his wife and John his fon, by his charter quits claim to God and the churches of St. Mary's York and St. Conftantine of Wederhale, all the land between Wederhale and Warwic called the Cell *(cameram)* of Conftantine, and two bovates of land in Corkeby ; and grants that neither he nor his heirs fhall hinder the monks to fortify their fifh pool, ftank, or wear, *(ftagnum fuum)* upon the river bank of Corkeby.

And finally, Richard de Salkeld lord of Corkby by his charter grants and confirms to the monks of Wetheral their fifhgarth or wear, with liberty to conftruct, fortify, and repair the fame, upon the bank as far as a place called Monkwath towards the Brigend, and to make fluices and trunks in the fame, and freely to difpofe of the falmon and other fifh therein taken, and alfo to take ftone and branches of trees for making the faid wears ; and grants to them the whole water of Eden, and the whole fifhery, from the upper part of the faid wear towards Corkeby unto the faid place called Monkwath.

King Richard the firft granted them an ample charter of privileges ; that all their lands then in poffeffion or which they fhould afterwards acquire, and their manors, cells, and other poffeffions, fhould be quit of pleas, and plaints,

---

+ This, and all other charters here referred to, are to be found in the original regifter of the faid priory, in the poffeffion of the dean and chapter.

‡ Henricus rex Angliæ, archiepifcopo Eboraci, et jufticiariis et vice-comitibus et omnibus baronibus et fidelibus fuis Francis et Anglis Eboracifcire et de Karliolo falutem. Sciatis, me conceffiffe et confirmaffe Deo et ecclefiæ Sanctæ Mariæ Eboraci et abbati Gaufrido et Monachis ibidem Deo fervientibus Cellam Sancti Conftantini cum manerio de Wederhale, et cum capella de Warthewic, et cum exclufagio et ftagno de pifcaria et de molendino de Wederhale, quod eft fitum et firmatum in terra de Chorkeby, ficut habuerunt quando Randulphus comes Ceftriæ habuit Karliolum. Et confirmo eis ex dono meo totam pafturam inter Edene et regiam viam quæ ducit de Karliolo ad Appelby, et a Wederhale ufque ad Drybec. Et concedo eis foreftam meam ad porcos fuos de Wederhale fine pannagio Et concedo eis et confirmo ecclefia*, res, poffeffiones, terras, et omnia quæ eis data funt et confirmata, per chartas meorum proborum virorum ; et prohibeo ne aliquis eis inde contumeliam faciat. Et præcipio, ut ita habeant confuetudines fuas, et terras fuas, et res, quietas ab auxiliis et tallagiis, et ab omnibus rebus, ficut habet ecclefia fancti Petri in Eboraco, vel ecclefia fancti Johannis in Beverlaco, et omnes eafdem libertates habeant quas habent iftæ duæ ecclefiæ. Teftibus, Roberto de Sigillo, et Pagano filio Johannis, et Euftachio fratre ejus, et Pagano Peverell. Apud Windefhores.

and

and murder, and robbery, and fcutage, and gelds, and danegelds, and hidage, and affizes, and works of caftles bridges and parks, and from ferdwite, and hengwite, and flemenefrenith, and averpeni, and blodwite, and flitwite, and hundredpeni, and tethingpeni, and legerwite, and toll, and paffage, and pontage, and leftage, and ftallage, and gridelbreke, and hamfoken; and he grants to them alfo fridftal, and foke, and fack, and theam, and infangthiefe, and out-fangthiefe.

They had, befides thefe, many fpecial grants of poffeffions in particular places; which reduced into alphabetical order, and collected from the faid Regifter of the priory, are as follows:

Aghonby. Laurence de Agullonby gave four acres of land there.

St. *Andrew*'s hermitage. Adam fon Suane gave the hermitage of St. Andrew; confirmed by David king of Scots.

Appelby. Ranulph de Mefchiens gave the churches of St. Michael and St. Laurence of his caftle of Appleby: Witneffes, his wife Lucia, and William his brother, and Gilbert Tyfun, and Godard.—Alfo Walter fon of Robert gave a fmall parcel of land there.

Aynftable. Michael de Ainftapelit gave nine acres and a half there; John Muflie, 7 acres; and Henry de Terriby, 7 acres.

Bewcaftle. Robert fon of Buet gave 4 acres, with pafture for 300 fheep. Mabel daughter of Adam fon of Richer of Buthcaftre gave 14 acres, with two tofts.

Bochardby. Richard fon of Richard fon of Trute gave a toft without Botchardgate.—Walter de Botchardby gave the lands called Elwrick Flat, between Scotby dike and the rivulet running from St. Helen's well.—And Adam brother of the faid Walter gave a parcel of ground at the head of his croft, adjoining to the faid rivulet.

Brumfield. Waldeve fon of Gofpatric gave the church of Brumfield, and the corps of the manor there.

Burdofwald. Walter Bavin, for the health of his foul and of the fouls of his lords Ranulph de Vallibus and Robert his fon, gave 20 acres in the fields called Haithwaite, bounded by the highway leading from Trewerman thro' the old wall.

Burgh. Ranulph Engaine and William his fon gave two falt pits there; whofe grant was afterwards confirmed by Joan de Morvil, Richard de Lucy, Thomas de Multon, and others.

Carlifle. King Hen. 1. gave them dead wood in his foreft of Carlifle, for their houfes and fuel.

Coleby. Enfiant fon of Walter gave a carucate of land there.

Corkby. Ofbert fon of Odard gave the tithe of the mill of Corkby, and of all the hogs depaftured in the woods there. Robert fon of William fon of Odard gave four acres of land. And William fon of Roger and Ofanna his wife gave for their buildings and fuel dead wood ftanding and dry, throughout the whole wood of Corkeby; alfo green oaks ftanding and deficient in cropping, and any other oaks except only thofe whofe leaves are green throughout from top to bottom, and are profitable for bearing acorns, and eafy to cleave for timber.

Cringledyke. Alice and Mabel fisters and heirs of R. de Beauchamp gave the lands there called Gildefhill or Gildhoufe Hill, with one inclofure called Ox Clofe: Whofe grant their faid brother confirmed, with his body to be buried in the church of Wederhale.

Croglin. The lady Ibria (d'Eftrivers) gave half a ploughland ; whofe grant was confirmed by Symon de Morvil.—William de Croglin *(i. e.* of Little Croglin) gave two oxgangs and two acres of land there, and alfo his bondmen Ralph and his fon, and alfo Alan and his wife Alice, with all their families and chattels ; confirmed by Robert de Vallibus.

Culgaith. Alexander de Creuquer gave part of Kirkandrew's wood, with half the mill, and pafturage throughout the fields and wood of Culgaith : Alexander fon of Swain gave the other half of the mill. And both the grants were confirmed by David King of Scotland.

Cumquinton. Uchtred fon of Liolf gave half a carucate of land ; confirmed by William de Heris, with common of pafture.—Eudo de Karliel gave the dead wood and liberty of cutting oaks which were dry in the cropping ; confirmed by Robert de Leverfdale.—Adam fon of Roger de Karliel gave 8s yearly rent out of certain lands there, and alfo the heath where his fhields ftood under a rent of 6d to him and his heirs ; which rent Eudo his grandfon (fon of William) changed to a rofe on Midfummer-day.—John fon of Gamel verderer of Cumquinton, gave four roods of land and a toft there.

Cumrew. Adam de Cumreu, fon of William de Ravenwick, gave two oxgangs of land, with pafture for 60 fheep, and 8 cows, and 4 oxen ; and alfo gave Roger fon of Hughtred with all his goods and chattels.

Denton. Robert de Buet gave the church of Denton with the glebe land thereunto belonging, and 8 acres more of his own. (This grant was equally between the priories of Wederhale and Lanercoft.)

Eafton. Uctred fon of Liolf gave two bovates of land there.

Farlam. Solomon de Farlam gave 16 acres of land in feveral places within the territories of Farlam. Two acres more, in the field called Ruthwait, were given by Richard fon of Bernard de Farlam.

Gilfland Robert de Vaux confirmed to them all the lands that had been given to them in Gilfland.

Hedresford. Gervas de Lafcells gave 21 acres and one rood of land, with pafture for 300 wethers, 300 ewes, 9 oxen, and 4 horfes, and the ufe of his mill at Levington moulter free.

Kaberth. John de Hermine fon of William gave two oxgangs of land there : To which Henry de Ulvefthwayt added the meadow of Smallwaths lying between Kaberth and Croglin.

Kirk Ofwald. Ralph de Hoff, for the health of the foul of his lord Hugh Morville, gave certain lands in Huddlefceugh in the parifh of Kirk Ofwald.

Kirkby Thore. A toft here, formerly in the occupation of Roger Abbot, and lying below Borrains, was given by William fon of Gilbert.

Man ifland. Maurice de Man gave licence to erect a falt pan there, with the like conveniences as had been formerly given to the monks of St. Begh's.

Meaburn.

Meaburn. Ranulph de Mefchiens gave two parts of the tithes of his demefne at Meaburn. And John fon of Walter de Ravenfby gave a fmall parcel of ground in King's Meaburn, 112 yards long and 50 broad (for a tithe barn, as it feemeth) in confideration of their having taken him into their prayers.

Melmerby. Gervafe de Melmerby gave one oxgang in the town fields, and one acre and a half in another part of the territories. And Adam de Mora gave two oxgangs there.

Morland. Ketel fon of Eldred gave the church of Morland and three carucates of land there. Henry de Legat (in the time of Walter bifhop of Carlifle) gave all his lands at Morland, referving a yearly rent of half a pound of cummin, payable to the bifhop at Carlifle fair. And Peter de Legat (brother of the faid Henry) gave other lands.

Newby. Walter, porter of the priory, gave with his body two oxgangs of land, with a toft and croft. And Anfelm de Newby gave fifteen acres and a half (being two oxgangs) in the fame vill; confirmed by others of his name and family.

Ormfby. Adam fon of Alan gave half a ploughland in Ormefby field. And Adam fon of Robert gave another half, called Mirland. To which were added other lands by Eudo de Karliel.

Oufby. Robert de Robertby gave three acres and a half in the town fields, with right of common and other appurtenances: Saving the multure of the 20th difh due to the mill there.

Salkeld. Ranulph de Mefchiens gave two parts of the tithes of the demefne lands there. And Waldeve fon of Gofpatric afterwards gave the whole.

Scotby. David king of Scots gave one mark of filver yearly out of the rent of his mill of Scotteby, and alfo the tithes of the vill of Scotteby. And Uchtred fon of Liolf gave afterwards the mill.

Scotland. David earl of Dunbar gave the town and church of Karkarevil.

Slegill. One meffuage, with the appurtenances, given by Gilbert de Sleygilk.

Sourby. The whole tithe of the demefne lands there, and half a carucate of land, given by Uchtred fon of Liolf.

Staffole. Alice and Mabel, fifters and heirs of R. de Beauchamp, gave right of common and other privileges.

Strickland. Walter de Stirkland knight gave four acres in Stirkland fields; whofe grant was confirmed by Sir William de Stirkland.

Thrymby. John fon of William de Thrymby gave four perches and an half at Thrymby.

Warwick. William fon of Odard gave 3 oxgangs of land, and the tithe of his mill there.—John fon of the faid William gave a toft and croft.—Alan de Langwayt gave all his land there, and fireboot in his woods at Langwayt, with pafture for their horfes or other cattle in carrying wood, lime, or ftone.—Henry Birkenheved and Beatrice his wife gave three acres in the Holme near the bridge.

Wetheral. Befides the grants at Wederhale above fpecified, Robert fon of William fon of Udard remitted the eighth fifh, which he and his anceftors had out of the coffin or coup of the monks.—And John Spendlowe and Margaret his wife gave an houfe and four acres of land; and granted a leafe for 60 years to the

prior

prior and convent of an oxgang more, in confideration of 3 marks of filver given them in their great need : Which faid Margaret and her children foon after quitted claim for ever to the faid oxgang.

Workington. Ketel fon of Eldred gave the church of Workington.

Wynfell. John de Veteripont, for the good of his foul and of the foul of Sibil his wife, gave twenty carts load of firewood yearly out of his foreft of Wynfell.

And they had many confirmations of all thefe grants by the kings, bifhops, and popes.

It was for fome time contefted between the bifhop of the diocefe and the abbot of St. Mary's York, which of them fhould have the appointment of the prior, and the guardianfhip of the priory during the vacancy. But at laft, in the time of bifhop Chaufe, it ended in a compromife, that the abbot fhould prefent and the bifhop fhould inftitute, and that the abbot fhould have the guardianfhip during the vacancy; in confideration whereof, the abbot and convent make over to the bifhop and his fucceffors two marks and an half yearly payable unto them out of the church of Denton.

In a difpute concerning the cuftoms of the manor, between John fon of Elmin and Robert abbot of St. Mary's York, it was fettled, that the faid John, like as the reft of the tenants of Wederhale, fhall carry the abbot's corn one day in autumn yearly, and fhall find for the abbot one reaper, and fhall plow one day in the year, and carry wood for the fifh garth and mill of Wetheral, and (together with the reft of the tenants) fhall repair the wear and mill, and grind his corn at the faid mill, paying the thirteenth moulter.

In the year 1539, Oct. 20, Ralph Hartley prior and the convent furrendered the priory into the king's hands; and the faid king by his charter bearing date 6th May, 33 Hen. 8. grants the revenues thereof to the dean and chapter of Carlifle, fpecifying; All that the fite of the priory or cell of Wetherell, with the church, fteeple, churchyard, and all other lands and poffeffions in and about the fame; and alfo the manor of Wetherell; and fundry parcels of land there, defcribing the fame by their feveral names, quantities, and abuttals; and one chapel there called St. Anthony's chapel, with two inclofures adjoining thereto; with the water mill, and fifhery at the bay of Wetherell; and alfo all thofe manors, meffuages, lands, and tenements, in the feveral parifhes or hamlets of Corkby, Cumwhynton, Botcherby, Morehoufe, Holmehoufe, Frodelcrooke, Penreithcottys, Bridgend, Cryngledyke, Anaftable, Armathwayte, Brodwall in Gilfland, Newby, Ferlame, Kaybridge, Gallowfeld, Ruke, Skallmelock, St. Mary's and St. Cuthbert's Carlifle: Alfo the rectories and advowfons of the churches of Morland, St. Michael's and St. Laurence's in Appleby: Alfo the tithes of corn and hay in the vills of Bolton, Mykelftry, Reland, Thurneby, Thurneby Grange, Morland, Sleagill, Newby in the Stones, King's Meburn, Little Strickland, Skyteigate, Langton, Crackenthorp, Hilton, Bondgate, Moreton, Drybeck, Fallowfield, Barwis, Rutter, and Coleby; and a penfion of 15 s out of the rectory of Great Salkeld. All belonging to the late priory of Wetherell. (Saving to the king the rectory of Wetherell, and other profits to the faid rectory belonging.)

8   And

And by another charter, 15 Jan. 38 Hen. 8. the faid king grants to the dean and chapter the reverfion of the rectory of the parifh churches of Wetherell and Warwick, and the chapels of St. Anthony and St. Severin to the fame annexed ; and alfo the advowfon of the fame two churches.

In the year 1650, Oliver Cromwell's commiffioners for the fale of dean and ehapter's lands, fold the manor of Wetheral and all the late dean and chapter's poffeffions within the faid manor, to Richard Bancks of Cockermouth gentleman, for the fum of 1044*l* 5*s* 1¼*d*. On the reftoration of king Charles the fecond, the dean and chapter came again into poffeffion, in which they have ever fince continued.

Near the fite of the late monaftery are three remarkable cells, communicating with each other by means of a gallery in front. They are cut out of the folid rock, about 40 feet above the level of the river, which wafhes the bottom of the rock ; and are difficult of accefs, the only way to come at them being by a narrow and difficult pafs, and from thence a perpendicular afcent of about 7 feet, which could only be furmounted by means of a ladder, which the perfon afcending might draw up after him. The wall in front that makes the gallery is founded on a ledge of a rock about 8 feet below the floor of the cells, and is raifed a little above the top of the cells, and heretofore was joined to them by a roof covered with lead or flate. In the middle of the wall is a chimney, and there are three windows in it, one oppofite to every cell, to give light to them. They are from 22 feet and upwards to 20 feet long ; from 12 foot 4 inches, to 9 foot 7 inches broad; and in height near 9 foot. They feem to have been intended for a place of concealment or refuge in cafe of danger ; and perhaps might be made ufe of by way of religious retirement †.

Within this parifh is the manor of CORBY, which lies on the eaft fide of Eden, and is part of Gilfland. King Hen. 2. gave it *(inter alia)* to *Hubert de Vallibus,* who gave it to one *Odard,* who was fucceeded by his fon *Ofbert.* Ofbert dying without iffue was fucceeded by his brother *William.* Which *William,* by his wife Ofwinx, had iffue *John* and *Robert.* *John* was the elder, yet he feated himfelf at Warwick, and *Robert* poffeffed Corby After *Robert* fon of William, fon of Odard, there was one *Adam de Chorkbye* knight. And *William* fon of Roger and Ofanna his wife *de Corkeby* granted to the priory aforefaid the dead wood in their wood of Corkeby, in the reign of Ed. 1.

Next, it feems to have come into the name of *Richmond.* For in the 31 Ed. 1. there was a grant to *Thomas de Richemont* of free warren in all his demefne lands in Korkbie.—In the 6 Ed. 2. *Richard de Richemound* releafes the manor of Corkby to Sir *Thomas de Richmound* knight.—In the 16 Ed. 2. *Rowland de Richmound* releafed the fame to Sir *Andrew de Harcla* earl of Carlifle ; and foon after, *Richard de Richmound* and *Margery Lafcells* releafed the fame to the faid earl.

On the attainder of *Andrew de Harcla,* it efcheated to the crown ; and king Ed. 3. in the 10th year of his reign, granted the fame to *Richard de Salkeld* knight. This is that *Richard* who made that ample and explicit grant above-mentioned to the monks of Wetheral of the fifhery within his liberties as far as Monk-

† Tracts of the Antiquarian Society, vol. 1. p. 84.

wath.

wath.—The faid *Richard* had a fon *Hugh de Salkeld*, who married the heirefs of Rofgill in Weftmorland, whereby the houfe of Corby came to that inheritance, in whom it continued for many generations: The faid *Hugh* reprefented the county of Weftmorland in parliament during the reign of king Ric. 2. and part of the reign of Hen. 4. *John de Salkeld*, brother of *Hugh*, continued at Corby, and had iffue, *Richard Salkeld*, who died in the 17 Hen. 7. In the church of Wetheral, betwixt the north ile and the chancel, are the effigies of a man and woman in alabafter, which feem to reprefent this Richard and his wife; with this legend in old characters almoft obliterated:

> Here lies Sir Richard Salkeld that knight,
> Who in this land was mickle of might.
> The captain and keeper of Carlifle was he,
> And alfo the lord of Corkbye.
> And now he lies under this ftane,
> He and his lady dame Jane.
> The eighteenth day of Februere,
> This gentle knight was buried here.
> I pray you all that this do fee,
> Pray for their fouls for charitie,
> For as they are now, fo muft we all be.

This Sir *Richard* left five daughters coheirs; the two eldeft whereof, viz. *Catherine* and *Mary*, had the eftate at Corby. *Catherine* the elder was married to *Thomas Salkeld* of Whitehall efquire, and *Mary* was married to *Thomas Blenkinfop* of Helbeck efquire. Each of thofe families enjoyed their feveral moieties for five generations; and then *Henry Blenkinfop* fold his moiety to the lord *William Howard* in the year 1606, and *Thomas Salkeld* fold his moiety to the faid lord *William* in 1624.

The Salkelds of Whitehall were a younger branch of this fame family.

The arms of Salkeld are; Vert, a frette Argent.

The faid lord *William Howard* married Elizabeth one of the fifters and co-heirs of George lord Dacre, and with her had Naworth caftle. By his faid wife Elizabeth Dacre, he had fix fons and two daughters. The fons were, 1. Sir *Philip Howard* knight, from whom the prefent earl of Carlifle is defcended. 2. Sir *Francis Howard* knight, to whom he gave Corby. 3. Sir *Charles Howard* of Croglin hall knight. 4. Colonel *Thomas Howard*, who was flain at Pierfebridge in the county of York in the year 1643, on the part of king Charles the firft. 5. Sir *William Howard* knight, who died without iffue. 6. *Robert Howard*. The daughters were, *Anne* married to Sir John Winter of Lydney in the county of Gloucefter knight. And another daughter married to Sir Thomas Cotton of Connington in the county of Huntingdon baronet.

The faid Sir *Francis Howard* of Corby, the fecond fon, was twice married: firft, to Anne daughter of John Prefton of the manor in Furnefs in the county of Lancafter efquire, and by her had iffue *Thomas* who died unmarried, being

flain

flain in the year 1643 at Atherton moor in Yorkfhire, being colonel of horfe for the king: And a daughter *Elizabeth*, married to Edward Standifh of Standifh in the county of Lancafter efquire. To his fecond wife he married Mary daughter of Sir Henry Widderington of Widderington in the county of Northumberland knight, and by her had iffue, *Francis*, *Henry*, *Thomas*, and *William*; and four daughters, *Margaret* married to Thomas Haggerfton of Haggerfton in the county of Northumberland efquire, *Alathea*, *Catherine*, and *Anne*.

Francis, the eldeft furviving fon, was of the age of 29 at Dugdale's vifitation in 1665. He married Anne daughter of Sir William Gerard of Brynne in the county of Lancafter baronet, and had iffue by her a fon, who died an infant, and three daughters, 1. *Mary*, married to John Warwick of Warwick hall efquire. 2. *Frances*, who died unmarried. 3. *Anne*, married to Langdale of High-Cliffe in the county of York efquire.—To his fecond wife he married Mary-Anne-Dorothy Townley of Townley in the county of Lancafter; by whom he had a fon and two daughters who died in their infancy, and a daughter who furvived him and died unmarried.—He died in 1702, without iffue male; and devifed the eftate to his fourth brother *William*.

Of this *Francis*, Mr. Sandford in his manufcript account of Cumberland fpeaks with great glee, being (as one would conjecture) of a congenial fpirit: " The " laft Thomas Salkeld fold Corby to the lord William Howard third fon of " Thomas the great duke of Norfolk, great grandfather to the now earl of " Carlifle, and grandfather of the now brave monfieur Francis Howard a great " houfekeeper and horfe-courfer, and in all jovial gallantries expert, and be- " loved of all men, and lord of Corby caftle his manfion houfe, and has many " towns adjacent, and eftate of 2000*l per annum*, and his mother fifter to the " late lord Widderington, and his wife daughter to one of the famous families " of the Gerards in Lancafhire.". Of him there is the following epitaph in the north ile of Wetheral church:

" Here lies Francis Howard efquire, eldeft fon of Sir Francis Howard,
" who was the fecond fon of the lord William Howard of Naworth.
" On his right hand lies his father; on his left hand lies his fifter Anne; at his
" feet, his four children, viz. a fon by Anne Gerard his firft wife, and a fon and
" two daughters by Mary-Anne-Dorothy Townley his fecond wife, who fur-
" vived him. He died Dec. 17, 1702, much lamented by all that knew him,
" but moft of all by his widow and relict,
                " M. A. D. Howard.
        " Eternal reft give unto them, O lord!
                " Amen. Amen."

William Howard efquire, fourth brother of Francis aforefaid, married Jane daughter of John Dalfton of Acorn Bank efquire; and by her had iffue four fons, *Francis* who died unmarried, *Thomas*, *William* and *John* both profeffed of the Romifh church; and five daughters, *Dorothy* who died unmarried, *Elizabeth* married to William Sanderfon of Armathwaite caftle efquire and *Lucy*, *Mary*, and *Bridget*, all nuns.. The said William Howard the father died in 1708, and was succeeded by his eldest surviving son *Thomas*.

Thomas Howard of Corby, esquire, married to his first wife Barbara daughter of John viscount Lonsdale, and by her had issue three sons, who all died in their infancy ; and three daughters, *Mary* who died an infant, *Elizabeth* now living (1772) and unmarried, and *Jane* married to Francis Warwick of Warwick hall esquire.—To his second wife he married Barbara sister of Sir Christopher Musgrave of Edenhall baronet ; and by her had issue *Charles* who died in the 12th year of his age, and another son *Philip*; and three daughters, viz. *Anne* who died an infant, and *Catherine* and *Mary* both nuns.—To his third wife he married Mary sister of Francis Carthington of Wooton esquire; by whom he had no issue.—He died in the year 1740.

Philip Howard of Corby esquire, son and heir of *Thomas* married Anne daughter of Henry Witham of Cliff in the county of York esquire; and by her hath issue, *Henry, Philip, Catherine*, and *Maria*.

. In the division of *Combquinton* and *Coathill* in this parish, the owner of ·Armathwaite castle hath a manor, having at Coathill 7 customary tenants, who pay 18 s 6 d customary rent, arbitrary fines, and heriots ; and at Combquinton 12 tenants pay 1 l 11 s 4 d customary rent, with like fines and heriots. Also the Aglionbys of Nunnery have here a manor, having 34 tenants, who pay yearly 7 l 3 s 9 d, with like arbitrary fines and heriots. They also pay boondays shearing and leading coals, with a certain quantity of oats called *Foster oats* (perhaps heretofore for the use of the *foresters*, this part being within the forest of Englewood). Six pecks of which oats are equal to four of Carlisle measure.

The church of Wetheral is dedicated to the holy and undivided Trinity, and is in the patronage of the dean and chapter of Carlisle ;. unto which, jointly with Warwick, they present a perpetual curate, and allow him a salary of 52 l a year: There is also a little neat house belonging to it, with a small field adjoining.

In 1747, it was certified, that there were in this parish 229 families ; of which,, quakers and presbyterians 4, and papists 10.

L E E T H   W A R D.

PARISH OF HESKET.

ADVANCING from Carlisle towards the South and South-East, we come to LEETH WARD ; in which the first parish is that of HESKET, which is generally supposed to have been a chapelry only within the parish of St. Mary's Carlisle. But so early as the reign of king Edward the third, by an inquest then taken, the parishes of St. Mary Hesket and of Wetheral are severally and distinctly ascertained. But being appropriated to the priory of Carlisle, it was supplied (as was usual in churches belonging to the religious houses, that lay near to such house) by one of their own body. And perhaps the prior, in ease of his

2 ·

canons, might require them to bring their dead to be buried at Carlisle, or possibly they might defire it as a particular favour; for the people in thofe days were ambitious, and fometimes gave large donations, to be interred amongst thofe holy brethren.   Dr. Todd relates a tradition, that the firft erection of a chapel here was about the year 1530, when an infectious diftemper raging in the country, and the people bringing their dead as ufual to be buried within the city of Carlisle, the mayor and citizens shut the gates upon them, and from the walls advifed them to carry back the corps and bury the fame at a place then called Walling Stone; and that if they did fo, and complied with their advice, they and others would endeavour to prevail with the bifhop of the diocefe, to have a chapel built and confecrated there, which would be of perpetual ufe to them and their pofterity.   And they complying with this propofal, as foon as the plague was ceafed, a chapel was built, and the then bifhop (John Kite) attended by Sir Chriftopher Dacre knight, Sir John Lowther knight, and a great number of gentlemen and others of the country and neighbourhood, did in a folemn manner confecrate it and the church or chapel yard, and by proclamation fet out and fixed the bounds thereof.—All which perhaps may amount to this, that the church or chapel was then rebuilt, and had then firft the right of fepulture granted to it.

. The dean and chapter of Carlisle, as fucceffors of the prior and convent, are the impropriators, and nominate a perpetual curate, and oblige their leffees of the tithes to pay him yearly 18 l 5 s o d; befides which, Mr. John Brown of this parifh gave 200l, whereby an augmentation of 200l was procured from the governors of queen Anne's bounty: with which fum of 400l lands were purchafed at Hefket and Mill Yate, now of the yearly value of 14l.

Of this Mr. Brown, his nephew and heir Mr. Lofh caufed the following memorial to be infcribed in the church of Hefket:

Mr. John Brown

of Mellguards in the parifh of Hefket,

By an almoft conftant refidence in that parifh

from the time of his birth,

Became not only a true patron to it in his life-time,

But willing to extend his regard to its welfare

Even after death,

Gave by his will

To the church of Hefket	— —	200l
To the fchool of Hefket	— —	200l
To the fchool of Wreay	— —	200l
To the chapel of Armathwaite	—	100l.

He died on the 15th day of July 1763,

Aged 69 years,

And had this juftice done to his memory

By John Lofh efquire his nephew and heir,

A. D. 1765.

This parifh is all within the foreft of Englewood, and the tenants are moftly copyholders under the duke of Portland (tho' there are fome mefne lordfhips

X x 2

within

within the fame). The duke's tenants are faid to be near 200, who pay a yearly copyhold rent, and a fingle year's rent upon change of tenant, and nothing upon the death of the lord. And the tenant has all the wood that grows upon his eftate.

One of the principal mefne manors is that belonging to ARMATHWAITE CASTLE; unto which there are feveral appendages, the tenants of all which places do fuit and fervice to the court at Armathwaite. In *Armathwaite*, are 4 freeholders, who pay 10½d yearly free rent; and 12 cuftomary tenants, who pay yearly 3l 18s 4d cuftomary rent, 16 days boon fhearing, and fuit of mill. At *Nether Southwaite*, one freeholder, who pays yearly 2l 3s 4d free rent. At *Coathill* 7 cuftomary tenants, who pay yearly 18s 6d cuftomary rent, 8 days boon fhearing, and 7 heriots. At *Cumwhinton*, 12 cuftomary tenants, who pay yearly 1l 11s 4d cuftomary rent, 13 days and one third of a day boon fhearing, and 15 heriots. At *Caftlecarrock*, 12 cuftomary tenants, who pay yearly 2l 12s 6d cuftomary rent. And the cuftomary tenants throughout pay arbitrary fines.

Armathwaite caftle anciently belonged to the *Skeltons*, which family is of great antiquity in this county, and whofe chief place of refidence was for many ages here: But they were likewife poffeffed of feveral lands in the weftern parts of this county, as at Whitrigg, Threapland, Bellafis, Thornbank, Kirkthwaite, Lynthwaite, Arkleby, Langlands, and Branthwaite. From the name, there feems to be no doubt but that they came from Skelton in this county, but of that we have not met with any account. There is not any regular pedigree of the family that hath fallen under our notice, except one of 5 generations only, certified by John Skelton efquire at Dugdale's vifitation in 1665. Therefore the following account is not to be looked upon as a regular fucceffion from father to fon, but only a lift of names that have occafionally occurred, including (very probably) many collaterals.

1. The firft that we meet with was *John de Skelton*, who was knight of the fhire for Cumberland, in the parliament holden at Lincoln in the 10 Ed. 2.

2. *Adam de Skelton* reprefented the faid county in parliament in the 12 Ed. 2.

3. *John de Skelton* was member for the county in the parliament holden at London in the 18 Ed. 2. and in that holden at York 2 Ed. 3.

4. *Richard de Skelton* was burgefs for the city of Carlifle in the parliament holden at Winchefter in the 4 Ed. 3.

5. *Thomas de Skelton* was knight of the fhire in the 11 Ed. 3:

6. *Clement de Skelton* was knight of the fhire in the 2, 6, 17, and 20 Ric. 2.— In the 16th year of the fame king, Sir Robert de Mulcaftre lord of Hayton granted to Sir Clement de Skelton knight and Thomas de Skelton feveral lands in Threapland, Alderfcogh, and Blenerhaffet. He married Johanna daughter of Sir Giles de Orton.

7. *John de Skelton* was member of parliament for the county in the 3d and 8th of Hen. 4. and in the 1 Hen. 6.—In the 7 Hen. 6. Sir William Clifford grants to Sir John Skelton knight feveral lands in Whitrigg and Torpenhow; to which grant Richard Skelton then fheriff of Cumberland was a witnefs. This
                                                                              Richard

Richard then lived at Branthwaite. He was prefent with king Hen 5. in France at the famous battle of Agincourt: And probably was a younger brother of the family.

8. *John Skelton* efquire was fheriff of the county in the 10th, 19th, 24th, and 29th of Hen. 6. and reprefented the faid county in parliament in the 28 Hen. 6. —He was retained by Humphrey duke of Gloucefter to ferve him in the wars. For by a deed in the 2d year of Hen. 6. the duke grants to him an annuity of 20 *l*, on condition to ferve him in the wars during life. The duke's ftyle in this grant is fomewhat particular; it begins " Humfridus regum filius, frater, " et patruus; dux Gloceftriæ; comes Hannoniæ, Hollandiæ, Zeelandiæ, and " Pembrochiæ; dominus Frifiæ; et magnus camerarius Angliæ."

9. *Robert Skelton* efquire was reprefentative of this city of Carlifle in parliament in the 12 Ed. 4.

10. *John Skelton* efquire was fheriff of Cumberland in the 3 Hen. 8.—In the 35 Hen. 8. it was found by inquifition, that John Skelton of Armethwaite held the capital meffuage of Armethwaite in the foreft of Inglewood, as a purprefture, with the appurtenances, of the king *in capite*, by the fervice of rendring to the king yearly by the hands of the fheriff of Cumberland a free rent of 30 *s*: And that he held one clofe called Southwaite in the faid foreft, of the faid lord the king, by the fervice of paying 22 *s* 2 *d* 2*q* yearly to the faid lord the king, by the hands of the receiver of the foreft: And one hundred acres in Armenayle bank of the faid lord the king in focage, paying yearly to the faid lord the king 5 *s* 4 *d* by the hands of the faid receiver of the foreft: Alfo that he held of the faid lord the king the manor of Threpland, as of the manor of Papcaftre, by knights fervice, rendring yearly to the faid lord the king 4 *s* 6 *d* cornage, 8 *d* feawake, and puture of the ferjeants.

11. *William Skelton* efquire, fon of John, married Anne daughter of John Leigh of Ifall efquire, and died Aug. 29, in the 27 Eliz. And was fucceeded by,

12. *Lancelot Skelton*, his fon: And with him begins the pedigree certified at Sir William Dugdale's vifitation aforefaid. He married Catherine daughter of Thomas Dalfton of Dalfton efquire, and died Dec. 28. in the 20 Ja. 1. in the 63d year of his age.

13. *John Skelton* efquire, fon of Lancelot, married to his firft wife Julian daughter of Sir Philip Mufgrave of Edenhall baronet, and by her had iffue *Richard* his fon and heir. To his fecond wife he married Barbara daughter of Fletcher of Cockermouth, and by her had iffue *Lancelot, John, William*, and *Marmaduke*; and two daughters, *Frances* married to Thomas Warwick of Warwick hall efquire, and *Mary* married to John Simpfon of Grinfdale. This John Skelton died about the year 1652.

14. *Richard Skelton* efquire, fon of John, married Lettice daughter of Burdet of Biamcoat in the county of Warwick efquire, and fifter of Sir Thomas Burdet baronet; and by her had iffue *John* his fon and heir, and *Philip* who died young: And two daughters, *Catherine* married to William Harrington of Wooloaks in Cumberland, and *Julian* married to George Fothergill of

4. Tarnhoufe

Tarnhouse in Ravenſtonedale in Weſtmorland. This Richard was of the age of 65 at the time of the ſaid viſitation.

15. *John Skelton* eſquire, ſon and heir of Richard, married Elizabeth daughter of Gerard Salvin of Croxdale in the county of Durham eſquire, and was of the age of 40 at the ſaid viſitation; and then had iſſue, *Richard* aged 13 years, *Gerard, John, Philip, Mary,* and *Lettice.*

16. *Richard Skelton* eſquire, ſon and heir of' John, married Mary daughter of George Meynell of Dalton Ryal in the county of York eſquire, and was the laſt of this family who enjoyed the eſtate at Armathwaite; for he ſold it in 1712 to *William Sanderſon* eſquire then of Conſtable Burton in the county of York, who died in 1727; and was ſucceeded by *Robert Sanderſon* his brother, who died in 1741, and left this eſtate to his widow for life, and afterwards to his nephew *William Milbourne* eſquire, who dying without iſſue deviſed the ſame to his ſiſter Mrs. *Margaret Milbourne* for life, and after her deceaſe to his couſin german Mr. *Robert Milbourne* of Newcaſtle upon Tyne merchant, and his iſſue male.

The Arms of Skelton are; Azure, a feſs between 3 flower de luces Or.

Richard Skelton, grandfather of the laſt Richard, by his will dated in 1668 gave 100*l* for the endowment of a chapel here at Armathwaite, after he had firſt built the ſaid chapel. But it is ſuppoſed it had been an ancient cha‑ pel long before his time, and that he only rebuilt it. And one Chriſtopher Rickerby, who was curate at this chapel ſoon after the ſaid endowment, in a kind of poem intitled " An elegy upon the death of that virtuous old gentle‑ " man Richard Skelton eſquire late of the caſtle of Armathwaite in the " county of Cumberland," ſays,

> He did rebuild a chapel which will be
> A monument of his fidelity.
> I heard this worthy perſon often ſay
> He walk'd unto his chapel on a day,
> And beaſts were lying in't (ere he begun)
> To ſhade them from the ſcorching of the ſun.
> This prick'd his tender heart, that when, oh! when
> He ſaw the temple of the Lord a den,
> Then he in haſte conſidered where to find
> Workmen to build according to his mind.
> His purſe cried plenty, when he thought upon
> The building up again of mount Sion, &c.

It is a very neat fabrick, the quire part eſpecially, being handſomely wain‑ ſcotted about.

Beſides the intereſt of the ſaid 100*l*, it hath been augmented with 200*l* by the governors of queen Anne's bounty in conjunction with 100*l* given by Mr. Brown aforeſaid, and 100*l* by the counteſs dowager Gower; which
ſums

sums were laid out in a purchase of lands in the parishes of Lazonby and Ainstable, of the present yearly value of 26l.

Nunclose also lies within this parish of Hesket, which king William Rufus in the second year of his reign granted to the prioress and nuns of Ermithwaite in the following words: " Ducentas et sexdecim acras terræ, exiftentes " infra foreftam noftram de Ingelwode, jacentes ex parte boreali cujufdam " aquæ vocatæ Tarnwadelyn, cum omnibus proficuis et commoditatibus." And king Edward the fourth in the 13th year of his reign, regranted and confirmed the same to the said houfe—" Et fpecialiter, cujufdam antiqui " claufi vocati Le Nonne clofe."

After the diffolution of the religious houfes, Nunclofe was granted by Ed. 6. in the 6th year of his reign to William Greyme *alias* Carlyfle gentleman, in whofe family it continued for feveral defcents; and was afterwards conveyed to John Pattenfon gentleman, who fold it to Sir John Lowther of Lowther baronet, who in 1695 granted the same in exchange for other lands to Chriftopher Dalfton of Acorn Bank efquire, in whofe family it remained till 1762, when it was fold by Sir William Dalfton knight to William Milbourne of Armathwaite caftle efquire, who devifed the same to his fifter Mrs. Margaret Milbourne for life, and after her deceafe to his kinfman (as aforefaid) Robert Milbourne of Newcaftle upon Tyne merchant.

It is now deemed a manor of itfelf, and is ftyled the manor of Armathwaite otherwife Nunclofe; and confifts of one freeholder who pays yearly 1s free rent, and 17 cuftomary tenants who pay yearly 4l 10s cuftomary rent, and 9s yearly in lieu of boon days. The fines upon the death of lord or tenant are twenty penny, upon alienations arbitrary.

At Armathwaite caftle, in Mr. Machel's time, was a broad fword, with a bafket hilt: On one fide of the blade was this infcription, ƐDWARDVS; on the other fide, PRINS ANGLIƐ. It was probably left there in king Edward the firft's time, at which place the prince might lodge, when his father's head quarters were at Lanercoft.

In the church of Hefket, on the north wall, over a feat belonging to Ellerton and Hayclofe is the following monumental infcription:

M. P. Q. S.

Bernardus Kirkbride de Howes et Ellerton, armiger; unus, dum vixit, jufticiariorum pacis pro comitatu Cumbriæ; et bis vice-comes ejufdem comitatus: Stirpe gentilitia et antiqua natus, et illuftrioribus in comitatibus Cumbriæ et Weftmerlandiæ familiis cognatione et agnatione conjunctus: Pietate, fortitudine, hofpitalitate, et aliis animi et corporis dotibus ornatiffimus: Decimo die Martii Anno Dom. 1677, fine prole, extinctus, et gentis fuæ poftremus, hic fælicem in Chrifto refurrectionem expectans, Pofitus.

Of

Of this Bernard Kirkbride (the laſt of his name and family) the following pedigree was ceitified by himſelf at Sir William Dugdale's viſitation in 1665:

1. *Richard Kirkbride* of Ellerton eſquire, married Eleanor daughter of Edmund Cliburne of Cliburne in Weſtmorland, and by her had iſſue *Bernard* and *Randal*, the latter of whom lived at Newbiggin in Cumberland.

2. *Bernard Kirkbride* eſquire, ſon and heir of Richard, married Dorothy daughter of Edmund Dudley of Yanewith in the county of Weſtmorland; and had iſſue (1) *Richard.* (2) *Chriſtopher*, who died unmarried. (3) *Cliburne Kirkbride*, a merchant at Newcaſtle upon Tyne, who died without iſſue. (4) *Iſabel*, married to John Saunderſon of Newcaſtle upon Tyne. This Bernard died about the year 1622.

3. *Richard Kirkbride* of Ellerton eſquire, ſon and heir of Bernard, was colonel of a regiment of foot in the ſervice of king Charles the firſt, under the command of William marquis of Newcaſtle. He married Bridget daughter of Edward Mayplate prebendary in the cathedral church of Carliſle; and by her had iſſue (1) *Bernard.* (2) *Mary*, married to William Graham of Nunnery. (3) *Barbara*, married to Leonard Barow of Ainſtable. He died in 1659.

4. *Bernard Kirkbride* of Ellerton eſquire, ſon and heir of Richard, was lieutenant colonel to Sir Henry Fetherſtonhaugh knight in the ſervice of the ſaid king Charles the firſt. He married Jane eldeſt daughter of Sir Timothy Fetherſtonhaugh of Kirk Oſwald knight (and ſiſter of Sir Henry); was of the age of 36 at the ſaid viſitation; and died (as his epitaph above expreſſeth) in 1677 without iſſue.

Adjoining to the churchyard a little *ſchool* hath been erected; which had an ancient endowment by the annual intereſt of 40*l*; and was augmented as aforeſaid by Mr. Brown with the ſum of 200*l*.

At Heſket yearly on St. Barnabas's day, by the highway ſide under a thorn tree (according to the very ancient manner of holding aſſemblies in the open air), is kept the court for the whole foreſt of Englewood; to which court the ſeveral manors within that vaſt circumference (above twenty in number) owe ſuit and ſervice; and a jury is there impannelled and ſworn for the whole foreſt. It is a ſhadow or relick of the ancient foreſt courts; and here they pay their compoſitions for approvements, purpreſtures, agiſtments, and *puture* of the foreſters; and the jurors being obliged to attend from the ſeveral manors, ſeems to be part of that ſervice which was called *witneſman*.

In 1730 there were in this pariſh 269 families; of which preſbyterians 6, and papiſts 2.

The hamlets of Brathwait and Middlesceugh are deemed part of the pariſh of St. Mary's Carliſle; but they lie in Leeth Ward. They conſiſt of about 25 tenements, and pay a yearly quit rent of 16*l* 3*s* 4¼*d* to Henry Brougham eſquire of Scales hall. They adjoin to the pariſhes of Dalſton northwards, Heſket eaſt, Hutton and Skelton ſouth, and Caſtle Sowerby weſt.

PARISH

PARISH OF SOWERBY.

, The parish of Sowerby, or *Caſtle Sowerby*, lies wholly within the foreſt of Englewood, and adjoins upon the pariſhes of Dalſton on the north weſt; Sebergham and part of Caldbeck on the weſt and ſouth weſt; Grayſtock on the ſouth; Skelton, Hutton, and the hamlets of Brathwait and Middleſceugh. on the eaſt. The tenants hold immediately of the duke of Portland lord of the ſaid foreſt, and pay a copyhold yearly rent, and a fine of one penny only upon change of tenant by death or alienation, 'and nothing upon the death of the lord. The tenants alſo have the wood. The land deſcends to coheir-eſſes; and the wife muſt be privately examined and conſenting, otherwiſe ſhe will have her thirds, notwithſtanding any ſale made by her huſband.

. In the 7 G. 3. an act of parliament was paſſed for dividing and incloſing the common and ſeveral waſte grounds within this manor and pariſh; which being now effected, the ſaid ſeveral copyholders are thereby become free-holders. By the ſaid act, 557 acres are allotted to the dean and chapter of Car-liſle as appropriators, and 203 acres to the vicar, in lieu and perpetual dif-charge of all tithes rectorial and vicarial, a modus of 20 s out of Thiſtlewood only excepted. And ſo much of the ſaid common is ordered to be ſold as will raiſe 700l, for incloſing and erecting proper houſes upon the ſaid two al-lotments. And one eighth part of the remainder (viz. 470 acres) is aſſigned to the lord, with a reſervation of the royalties and ſeigniory.

The church is dedicated to St. Mungo or Kentigern. It is ſituate at the very extremity of the pariſh; the reaſon of which probably might be, as in many other like inſtances, that the founder (who was moſt commonly the lord of the manor) did inhabit nigh thereunto. And to this day we ſee in abundance of pariſhes the church and manor-houſe to be nearly contiguous.

In 1294 (which was the 22d year of king Edward the firſt of England) John Baliol king of Scots preſented a clerk to the rectory of Sowerby, being vacant by the removal of the late rector *Richard de Wytton* to the church of Hawyk in the dioceſe of Glaſgow. The form of whoſe preſentation is ſome-what remarkable:—" Johannes Dei gratia rex Scotorum, venerabili in Chriſto patri ac amico ſuo quamplurimum confidenti domino Johanni eadem gratia Carliolenſi epiſcopo, ſalutem et ſinceram in domino charitatem et dilectio-nem. Ad eccleſiam de Soureby veſtræ dioceſeôs curam animarum habentem, per acceptationem et admiſſionem magiſtri *Ricardi de Wytton* quondam rectoris ejuſdem de eccleſia de Hawyk Glaſguenſis dioceſeôs conſimilem curam habente vacantem, cujus eccleſiæ de Soureby jus patronatus ad nos ſpectare dignoſ-citur, magiſtrum *Willielmum de Londors* clericum noſtrum dilectum et fidelem vobis charitatis intuitu preſentamus per præſentes, paternitatem veſtram atten-tius rogantes, quatenus dictum magiſtrum Willielmum ad prædictam eccle-ſiam de Soureby benigne ac ſine difficultate admittentes, in eadem inſtitui, et in corporalem poſſeſſionem ejuſdem cum pertinentiis induci, et inductum defendi faciatis. Per quod, a Deo meritum, et a nobis grates ſpeciales, recipere valeatis. In cujus rei teſtimonium, præſentibus literis ſigillum noſ-

trum apponi fecimus. Teftibus, Johanne Comyn, Alexandro de Ballo came-
rario Scotiæ, Galfrido de Moubray jufticiario noftro, Laoden' et Thoma Rau.
militibus. Apud Jedd' 20 Apr. anno regni noftri fecundo."

In June following, the famous Anthony Beck, bifhop of Durham, prefents
a clerk, by virtue of a grant from the faid king of Scotland ; whofe prefen.
tation is no lefs remarkable than the former :—" Venerabili in Chrifto patri
domino Johanni Dei gratia Karliolenfi epifcopo, Antonius eadem permiffione
Dunelmenfis epifcopus falutem et fraternæ charitatis continuum incrementum.
Ad. ecclefiam de Soureby veftræ diocefeôs vacantem, et ad noftram advocationem fpeclantem ratione donationis et conceffionis domini J. Dei gratia regis
Scotorum quondam patroni ejufdem, dilectum nobis in Chrifto dominum
Johannem de Langeton cancellarium Angliæ vobis præfentamus ; fupplicantes
quatenus ipfum ad eandem ecclefiam per hanc noftram præfentationem admit-
tere et rectorem inftituere velitis in eadem. In cujus rei teftimonium has
literas noftras vobis tranfmittimus patentes. Dat' London' 14 die menfis
Junii annô Domini 1294, et confecrationis noftræ undecimo.".—One would
think this church, whilft it continued a rectory, was very confiderable ; fince
no lefs confiderable a man than the lord chancellor of England was prefented.
to it, the fame that was afterwards made bifhop of Ely.

In 1295, Sir *Henry de Rye*, fubdeacon, was prefented by the faid Anthony.
Beck bifhop of Durham, and inftituted thereupon.

In 1300, *Henry de Rither*, fubdeacon, was prefented to the rectory of Soureby by the bifhop of Durham, and difpenfed with for 3 years abfence.

In 1307, king Edward the firft (by what right is not declared) granted the
advowfon of this church to the prior and convent of Carlifle, and the appropriation of the revenues thereof to their own ufe † ; which grant was in the
fame year confirmed by bifhop Halton, and a certain portion of the revenues
affigned to the vicar ; which endowment is now fuperfeded by the aforefaid:
act of parliament, giving a portion of land in lieu thereof.

Notwithftanding the faid appropriation, on the death of the rector Henry
de Rither in the year 1309, the faid Anthony bifhop of Durham (and now
being alfo patriarch of Jerufalem) prefents one Sir *John de Jargole* to the
rectory, but the bifhop would not admit him, but inftituted *Alan de Frifington* prefented to the vicarage of Souerby by the prior and convent of
Carlifle.

---

† Edwardus Dei gratia, rex Angliæ, dominus Hiberniæ, et dux Aquitaniæ, omnibus ad quos
præfentes literæ pervenerint falutem. Sciatis, quod ob devotionem quam erga gloriofum cognomen
Mariam et reliquias beati Thomæ Martyris et aliorum fanctorum in ecclefia beatæ Mariæ Karleoli
exiftentes gerimus et habemus, necnon in relevationem oppreffionum et damnorum quæ dilecti
nobis in Chrifto prior et conventus ejufdem loci per invafiones et combuftiones Scotorum, inimicorum et rebellium noftrorum, hactenus fuftinuerunt; dedimus eis et conceffimus pro nobis et hæredi.
bus noftris, quantum in nobis eft, advocationem ecclefiæ de Soureby, Karliolenfis diocefeôs in co.
mitatu Cumbriæ; ita quod iidem pr.or et conventus ecclefiam illam, cum eam vacare contigerit,
fibi in proprios ufus poffidendam appropriare, et eam appropriatam tenere poffint fibi et fucceffori.
bus fuis imperpetuum. Tefte meipfo apud Karleolum quarto die Aprilis anno regni noftri 35°.

In

In 1312, Alan de Frifington refigns; and *John de Schilton* (a canon of St. Mary's) was prefented by the prior and convent, and inftituted thereupon.

In 1334, Sir *John de Carlifle* vicar of Sourby refigns his living; and the prior and convent prefent Sir *Richard de Wylford* (one of their canons), who was inftituted with a charge of perfonal refidence.

In 1338, on the death of the faid Sir Richard, the prior and convent prefent (another of their canons) *Patricius Culwen*.

In 1360, on the death of Patricius Culwen, the prior and convent prefent *John de Penrith* another of their canons, who is thereupon inftituted.

In 1385, Sir *John de Carlifle* was inftituted.

In 1571, bifhop Barnes collates (by lapfe) *Thomas Scott* clerk to the vicarage of Sourby, vacant by the death of Sir *John Brifco* clerk, and thereon fends his mandate for induction directed to all and every rectors and vicars, and particularly to Robert Pearfon dean of Cumberland.

In 1584, *Thomas Scott* refigns, and inftitution is given to *Leonard Scott* prefented by the dean and chapter.

In 1623, on Leonard Scott's death, *William Fairfax*, B. A. was inftituted on the prefentation of Francis White D. D. (dean) and the chapter of Carlifle.

In 1664, William Fairfax refigns, whereupon the dean and chapter prefent *Edward Waterboufe.*

On his death in 1705, *Chriftopher Whittingdale* was collated by lapfe.

In 1718, *James Clerke*, B. A. was prefented on the ceffion of Chriftopher Whittingdale.

In 1739, on the death of James Clerke, *Jofeph Sevithwaite* was prefented by the fame patrons.

In 1762, Jofeph Sevithwaite dying, *John Twentyman* clerk was inftituted on a like prefentation.

This church is valued in the king's books at 17*l* 10*s* 5*d*. It was certified to the governors of queen Anne's bounty at 40*l* 2*s* 2*d*. Before the late alteration by affignment of common, it was worth about 90*l* a year; and now by the faid improvement may be worth 130*l* a year or upwards.

In the year 1750, May 3, John Sowerby furrendred to the lord of the manor by the hands of his fteward by the rod a meffuage and tenement at Sowerby Row within Row Bound in the manor of Caftle Sowerby, and two clofes adjoining to the faid tenement called Topping Garth and Croft, to the ufe and behoof of Jofeph Robinfon and his affigns according to the cuftom of the manor; conditioned to pay yearly to three truftees 5*l* for the ufe of a *fchoolmafter* within the liberty of the faid Row Bound to be chofen by the faid truftees: of which truftees, the vicar of Caftle Sowerby fhall be always one, Jofeph Robinfon during his life fhall be another, and Ifaac Monkhoufe another, and after the death of either of them, the two furvivors to chufe another within 20 days after fuch death, and in default of fuch choice the heir at law of the deceafed (being a tenant of the manor) fhall be a truftee. The fchool

to

to be free for all boys and girls, those within the parish paying quarterly 2 *s*
each, out of the parish 2 *s* 6 *d*; except that the master shall teach two of the
poorest persons children in Row Bound, one in How Bound, and one in
Southernby Bound, for 6 *d* a quarter each. And to be taught English, Latin, writing, and accounts.

RAUGHTON HEAD *chapel* in this parish, having long laid in ruins, was rebuilt in 1678, and consecrated by bishop Rainbow. It was again rebuilt by
the inhabitants about the year 1760 at the expence of above 300*l*. The ancient salary was about 3*l* a year. It was augmented by lot with 200*l* in 1737,
and since with 200 *l* in conjunction with 200*l* given by the countess dowager
Gower. All which being laid out in lands, the whole revenue is now worth
about 30*l per annum*. The present curate Mr. Bewley was appointed by bishop
Osbaldiston on suggestion of a lapse; but the nomination is by custom in the
trustees or twelve men.

Adjoining to the chapelyard, a neat little *schoolhouse* was erected in 1744 by
Mr. John Head of Foxleyhenning at his own expence.

The vicar Mr. Sevithwaite (who died in 1762) left by his will 20*l* to the
said school; and other 20*l*, the interest whereof (after his widow's death) to
be laid out yearly in purchasing bishop Beveridge's Thoughts upon Religion,
and the bishop of Man's Essay for the instruction of the Indians, to be
given to the poor housekeepers of the said parish.

This parish contains about 170 families; of which, quakers 4, presbyterians 2, papists 2.

PARISH OF GRAYSTOCK.

GRAYSTOCK, *Grayftoke*, (a place of badgers, brocks, or grays,) consists of
the following townships, or constablewicks; Grayftock, Penruddock and
Hutton Soil, Hutton John, Watermillock, Matterdale and Warkthwaite,
Threlkeld, Grisedale, Hutton Roof, Berrier and Murrey, Johnby, Little
Blencow, Motherby and Gill. It is a large barony, comprehending all that
part of the county of Cumberland above or on the south side of the forest
of Englewood, between the seigniory of Penrith and the manor of Castlerig
towards Keswick.

This barony the earl Ranulph de Meschines gave to one Lyolf or Lyulphe,
and king Henry the first confirmed the same unto Phorne son of the said
Lyulphe, whose posterity took their surname of the place, and were called
de Grayftock. Whose succession was as follows:

1. *Lyolf* or *Lyulphe* was the first baron of Grayftock.
2. *Phorne* his son, in the reign of Henry the first.
3. *Ivo* his son.
4. *Walter* son of Ivo.
5. *Ranulph* son of Walter. He died in the twelfth year of king John.
6. *William* son of *Ranulph*.

7. *Thomas*

7. *Thomas* his fon had livery of his lands in the 1 Hen. 3.—He obtained the king's charter for a weekly market on Saturday at his manor of Grayftock, and alfo for a fair for three days yearly, to begin on the eve of St. Edward's tranflation.—He married Chriftian daughter of Robert de Veteripont, the firft of that name of Appleby caftle ; and by her had iffue,

8. *Robert* lord Grayftock, who had livery of his lands in the 31 Hen. 3.— He was fucceeded by his brother,

9. *William* lord Grayftock, who had livery of his lands in the 38 Hen. 3. He married Mary the elder of the two daughters and coheirs of Roger de Merlay, who held the barony of Morpeth and other large poffeffions in Northumberland, a moiety whereof by this match came into the Grayftock family †. By his faid wife he had iffue John, William, and Margaret. He died in the 17 Ed. 1.

10. *John* de Grayftock, fon of William, was 25 years of age at the death of his father. He died without iffue in the 34 Ed. 1. and was fucceeded by Ralph fon of his brother William.

11. *Ralph* lord Grayftock, nephew of John married Margery widow of Nicholas Corbet, one of the two daughters and coheirs of Hugh de Bolebeck ; by which marriage he obtained a moiety of the barony of Bolebeck. He died in the 9 Ed. 2.

12. *Robert* his fon fucceeded, and died in the year following, viz: 10 Ed. 2. By an inquifition taken at Carlifle on Monday next before the feaft of St. Barnabas in that year, the jurors find, that Robert fon of Ralph de Grayftock died feized of the manor of Grayftock with the appurtenances, holden of the king *in capite* by homage and the fervice of 4 *l per annum* for cornage : That the faid manor is worth by the year in all iffues at this time 62 *l* 13 *s* 9 *d* ob. q. and no more, becaufe it is deftroyed by the Scots : But before thefe times, in time of peace, it was ufually worth in all iffues 200 marks. He married Elizabeth daughter of Neville of Stainton in the county of Lincoln ; and had iffue,

13. *Ralph* lord Grayftock, who was 18 years of age at the death of his father, and had livery of his lands in the 14 Ed. 2. He married Alice daughter of Hugh lord Audley, and was poifoned in the 17 Ed. 2. by the accomplices of Sir Gilbert de Middleton whom he had been the principal inftrument of feizing in the caftle of Mitford for treafon.

14. *William* his fon was very young at his father's death, for he had not livery of his lands till the 16 Ed. 3.—He obtained the king's licence to make a caftle of his manor houfe at Grayftock. He built alfo the caftle of Morpeth. He married firft Lucy daughter of the lord Lucy, from whom he was divorced ; and afterwards he married Joan daughter of Henry lord Fitzhugh of Ravenfwath, by whom he had iffue Ralph, William, Robert, and Alice married to Robert de Harrington.—He was one of the commiffioners to treat about the ranfom of David king of Scotland, who was taken prifoner at the battle of Durham. He died at Brancepeth in the county of Durham, and was buried

† Our account of the family from this time is chiefly taken from an ancient manufcript quoted by Mr. Wallis in his Hiftory of Northumberland, v. 2. p. 291.

at

at Grayſtock; for whom there was a moſt pompous funeral, whereat the biſhop of Carliſle ſaid maſs. There were preſent Ralph lord Nevil, Thomas de Lucy lord of Cockermouth, Roger lord Clifford of Appleby caſtle; Henry le Scrope, and Thomas Muſgrave ſenior, knights.; the prior of Carliſle, and the abbots of Holm Cultram and Shap.' This was in the 32 Ed. 3 †. And in the chancel of Grayſtock church is this monumental inſcription : " Icy gſt " William le bone Baron de Grayſtok plys veillieant, noble et courteyous chvia- " ler de ſa paiis en ſon temps; Quy. mufult le x jour de Jully l'an de grace " Mill. CCCLIX. Alme de guy Dieu eyt pete and mercy. Amen."

15. *Ralph* lord Grayſtock, ſon of William, was but young when his father died, for he had not livery of his lands till the 48 Ed. 3. He married Catherine daughter of Roger lord Clifford ‡. He had the direction of the military expe- dition againſt the Scots in the 4 Ric. 2. when he was taken priſoner at Horſridge in Glendale by George earl of Dunbar. His brother William went as an hoſ- tage for him to Dunbar, where he died of a fever. His ranſom coſt 3000 marks, which ſeems to have been raiſed by way of aſſeſſment on his tenants, for thereunto the burgeſſes of Morpeth paid for their proportion 7*l* 13*s* 10*d*,— He died in the 6 Hen. 5.

16. *John* lord Grayſtock, ſon of Ralph, was of the age of 28 at the death of his father. He married Elizabeth one of the daughters and coheirs of Robert Ferrers and Elizabeth his wife ſole daughter and heir of William Boteler lord of Wemme.; and died in the 14 Hen. 6.

17. *Ralph* lord Grayſtock was of the age of 22 at his father's death. He married Elizabeth daughter of William Fitzhugh lord Ravenſwath, and died in the 2 Hen. 7. He had only one child *Robert Grayſtock* knight, who married Elizabeth daughter of Edmund Gray duke of Kent, and died before his father, in the 3 Ric. 3. leaving only an infant daughter *Elizabeth*.—And thus ended the male line of the lords of Grayſtock; and the inheritance was transferred by marriage of the heireſs into another family.

There was at that time a very conſiderable and ancient family at Dacre in Cumberland of the name of DACRE ; who, to their paternal inheritance had received a large addition by marriage of the heireſs of *Multon*, whoſe anceſtor had married the heireſs of *Vaux (de Vallibus,* of Gilſland,) and was deſcended from a daughter and coheir of *Morvil*, whoſe anceſtor had married the heireſs of *Engain*, who married the heireſs of *Trivers*, who married a ſiſter of *Ranulph de Meſchiens* ſo often mentioned, to whom William the Conqueror gave Cumber- land. Of this family, THOMAS lord DACRE of GILSLAND married the ſaid *Elizabeth* baroneſs of Grayſtock and Wemm, in the 22 Hen. 7. in which year ſhe had ſpecial livery of her lands. He was ſon of *Humphrey de Dacre*, who ſuc- ceeded to the Gilſland and Grayſtock eſtates as heir male of the family by intail; whilſt the paternal eſtate of Dacre deſcended by a female heir to the lords Dacre
                                                                                       u l

‡ So ſays the manuſcript above mentioned ; which ſeems to be ſufficiently authentic. Altho' this daughter hath eſcaped the notice of the compiler of the counteſs of Pembroke's memoirs.

of

of the fouth. The faid lady Elizabeth died in the 8th year of king Henry the eighth, and her hufband Thomas lord Dacre (by way of diftinction ftyled lord Dacre of the north) died in the 18th year of the fame king.

They had iffue WILLIAM lord Dacre of Gilfland, Grayftock, and Wemm; who married Elizabeth daughter of George Talbot fourth earl of Shrewfbury, and died in the 6 Eliz. leaving iffue *Thomas, Leonard, Edward*, and *Francis*.

THOMAS, the eldeft, fucceeded in the title and eftate. He married Elizabeth daughter of Sir James Leiburne of Cunfwick in Weftmorland, and died in the 8th year of queen Elizabeth, not three years after the death of his father, leaving four infant children, *George, Anne, Mary* and *Elizabeth*. Their mother married again to *Thomas Howard*, duke of Norfolk, being his third wife.

The faid GEORGE lord Dacre, in the 11th Eliz. was killed by the fall of a wooden horfe whereon he practifed to leap, leaving his three fifters coheirs. *Leonard Dacre* their uncle claimed as heir in tail male; but in the 12 Eliz. he was attainted of high-treafon and banifhed for being concerned in the affair of Mary queen of Scots, and died in the 23 Eliz. without iffue. His brother *Edward* was attainted at the fame time, and died before him, in the 21 Eliz. The furviving brother *Francis* was alfo attainted at the fame time and for the fame caufe, but lived a long time after; for he died not until the 8 Cha. 1. He had a fon *Ranulph*, who died without iffue two years after his father†; and a daughter *Mary*, who lived to a very great age, and died alfo without iffue. A confiderable part of the eftate feems to have gone by the intail, which was forfeited during the lives of the faid three brothers and the iffue male of the laft of them; for there is a grant in 44 Eliz. to Edward Carrill, John Holland, John Cornwallis, and Robert Cansfield of divers lands and poffeffions in Cumberland and elfewhere, until, and fo long as there fhould be an heir male of the body of Francis Dacre efquire late attainted of treafon in full life: The particulars, in Cumberland, were; the lordfhip of Burgh, alfo the demefnes and manors of Burgh upon Sands, Beamonde, Kirk-Andrews, Weftlington, Bowes, Drombrugh, Whitrigg, Whitrigleas, Langcroft, Aynethorne, Cardronock, Glaffon, Eafton, Fingland, Roughcliffe, Etterby, Ayketon, and Thurfby: Alfo the lordfhip of Gilfland, with the demefnes and manor of Lyverfdale, Brampton, Denton, Walton, Farlam, Talkin, Caftle-carrock, Cumrew; Hayton, Fenton, Corby, Tradermayne, Afkerton, and Cumwhitton; the forefts of Brierthwait, and Ternehoufe; and the fifhery in Talkin terne; and all thofe rents called land ferjeant fees in Linfdale, Newby, Crogling, Newbiggin, Ormefby, Fenton, Corby, Over Denton, Nether Denton, Eaft Farleham, Weft Farleham, Hayton, Cumwhitton, Irthington, Cummackhill, and Tradermain: Alfo the lordfhip of Grayftock, with the feveral manors of Grayftock, Motherby, Stainton, Skelton, Matterdale, Grayfdale, Wethermelock, Sparkhead, Berrier, Murrey, and Newbiggin: With divers rents iffuing out of feveral tenements in the city of Carlifle,

---

† In the parifh regifter of Grayftock in the year 1634 is the following entry: (Buried)
" Randal Dacre efquire, fonne and hyre to Francis Dacre efquire deceafed, being the youngeft
" fonne of the late lord William Dacre deceafed, being the laft hyre male of that lyne; which faid
" Randal dyed at London, and was brought downe at the charges of the right honourable Thomas
" earle of Arundell and Surreye and earle marfhal of England."

Fulkholme, Standwick, Caldcote, and Thiftlethwaite : And the rents of divers cuftomary tenants in Melmerbye ; free rents of feven different tenants in Penrith, one in Carleton, with feveral meffuages and tenements in Ullefby, Kirkland, Staffoll, Kirk-Ofwald, Glaffonby, Ravenwick, Scalehoufe, and Ainftable †.

The

† There is a letter from the faid Francis Dacre to queen Elizabeth complaining of his hard ufage ; of which letter he fent copies to feveral of his acquaintance before his departure out of England in the 42 Eliz.

"Moft dread fovereign,

"The caufe of this my prefumptuous boldnefs in writing to your majefty is, my fudden, unwil-
"ling, and forced departure from your majefty and realm, for the which I moft humbly crave par-
"don, being the firft thing that ever was committed by me, wherein I might hazard your highnefs's
"difpleafure, and yet betwixt God and my confcience am free from all difloyalty or evil practices in
"thought, word, and deed againft yonr majefty and realm, whatfoever hath been or may be inform-
"ed to the contrary by my unfriends, whereof I have gained many by my lord and father's poffef-
"fions, efpecially fuch as have been brought up by him from mean eftate to be gentlemen, and now
"live in all wealth and pleafure upon the lands that were my anceftors, who have laboured to incenfe
"your majefty and council many untruths againft me, which often hath taken effect with the lords
"of your council, whereby I have endured many and great diftreffes, but never with your majefty
"before this time ; upon whom, as upon a fure pillar, next under God, I have always trufted, hop-
"ing ftill for happy performance of your majefty's moft gracious promifes : In regard whereof, with
"the great and dutiful love and obedience that I have always born to your majefty, hath caufed me
"not only to many hard fhifts for maintenance, after all that I had was fpent, with the benevolence
"of all my friends, but alfo to fuffer fo many and open injuries at my adverfaries hands, as the
"world may wonder that flefh and blood was able to fuffer the fame. It were too long to trouble
"your majefty with the recital thereof, but leave them untouched and proceed in my purpofe, to
"fignify to your majefty the true caufe that hath driven me to take this courfe. Now continuing
"ftill inthis good hope, I have made my laft and moft hard fhift for providing a little money in felling
"my houfe, wherein I have received great lofs, to bring me up to attend your majefty's good plea-
"fure, ftill expecting an happy end ; but in the mean-time, being within a week of taking my
"journey, your majefty's commiffioners in the furvey of the faid lands have not only difpoffeffed
"me, by virtue of a letter from my lord treafurer and written by your majefty's command, of all
"thofe tenements which were returned to me both of the Grayftocks lands, and alfo of the Dacres
"which were purchafed and out of the concealment, but alfo have called me and very earneftly de-
"manded the rents again at my hands that I have received thereof, (under favour be it fpoken)
"a hard cafe, that my lord of Arundel's attainder fhould forfeit my lawful poffeffion, I being a true
"fubject. All thefe things confidered, with the want of friends to further your majefty's good
"meaning towards me, the many and mighty adverfaries that I have fo near about you, which I
"fear me hath withdrawn your gracious favour from me, the many delays for anfwer of my laft
"petition put unto your majefty at Eafter laft, wherein I made it known to your highnefs that I
"was not able to endure any longer without fome fpeedy relief, whereof I never had anfwer ; the
"rents of the Dacres lands, which was the moft part of my maintenance, being received to the ufe
"of your highnefs, without any confideration of my poor eftate ; and now my lawful poffeffion of
"all the reft taken from me by another man's fault. The favour and commodity of the Lowthers
"and Carletons, which never deferved well at your majefty's hands, is like to receive and be pre-
"ferred unto before me, of thofe lands which were my anceftors, and gone from me not by any
"offence committed by me or my means, and by my only life and my fon's your majefty doth keep
"them. Under correction be it fpoken, my heart cannot endure that fuch evil men as they be,
"being the only maintainers of theft, befides their other bad behaviours, which is well known to all
"men that have had dealings with them, who have concealed your majefty's title thefe 20 years,
"and would have done for ever, if my adverfaries right had proved better than mine. They did
"make means to me, to have compounded with them to have defrauded your majefty thereof; which
"if I had done, I had made a better match for myfelf than I have done as the cafe ftandeth. And
"now in the end they be fo liberally dealt with, and myfelf (who I proteft may compare with the
"beft

The faid three fifters, coheirs of George lord Dacre, Sir William Dugdale fays, were married by their father-in-law the duke of Norfolk to his three fons by his former wives. It is probable enough the duke intended fo to do ; but the fecond fifter died. The eldeft fifter *Anne* was married to the faid duke's eldeft fon *Philip* earl of Arundel, and the third fifter *Elizabeth* was married to the faid duke's third fon the lord *William Howard*, and divided the inheritance between them. (The fecond fon of the faid duke of Norfolk, the lord *Thomas Howard*, married a daughter of Sir Henry Knevett, and was anceftor of the prefent earl of Suffolk.)

The lord *William Howard*, with his wife the lady *Elizabeth*, fettled at the Dacre eftate at Naworth, and was anceftor of the prefent earl of Carlifle. *Philip Howard* earl of Arundel, with his wife the lady *Anne*, fettled at the Dacre eftate at Grayftock, in whofe name and family it ftill continues †. And this renders it neceffary to deduce the hiftory of this illuftrious family.

I. The firft was an eminent and learned lawyer (as many of the great families both in ancient and modern times were raifed by the law) *viz*. WILLIAM HOWARD, a judge of the court of common pleas in the latter part of the reign of king Ed. 1. and beginning of the reign of king Ed. 2.

" beft for my loyalty and true heart) to be fo little efteemed of, and without any reward at all ; thefe " things have not only driven me out of all good hope at your majefty's hands, but of all other " refuge, in fuch fort, as knowing my title to be clear to Strangwaie's lands; yet confidering the " intereft that my lord chamberlain and Sir Thomas Scifell's fon hath in thefe lands from your " majefty, no hope there is at all for me to attain unto them, but muft let them reft in their hands " that have no right, arming myfelf with patience to abide what poverty may enfue. Now con- " fidering all thefe aforefaid hard dealings, as alfo all that was towards my lord of Arundel and the " lord William doth receive credit and commodity of thofe lands, and thofe that were towards me " difplaced of their offices with moft hard fpeeches; feeing the cafe to ftand fo hard againft me, " and that I have the laft penny of maintenance that ever I can make, befides the great debt I am " in, having no fhift now left me whereby to live, To beg I am afhamed, To work I cannot, To " want I will not, Therefore I am forced to feek for maintenance where I may with credit gain the " fame, and have determined to employ that little that fhould have brought me to attend upon your " majefty, to carry me elfewhere. I have taken my fon with me, for that I have left him nothing " to tarry behind me withal ; and if God hath provided a living for us we will live together ; if not, " we will ftarve together. And for my daughters, I commit them to God and fuch friends as it " fhall pleafe him to provide for them. Thus trufting in your majefty's moft princely clemency in " tolerating this my forced and moft unwilling departure, which I moft humbly crave at your " majefty's hands, I will daily pray to the Almighty for the prefervation of your majefty's reign in " all happinefs to continue. From Crogling the 17th of September 1589.

. Francis Dacres.

† The particulars upon the divifion that were affigned to the faid lady Anne in Cumberland were, the caftle, barony, and lordfhip of Grayftock, the parks there ; the manors, lordfhips, towns, hamlets and villages of Stainton, Wethermelock, Sparkhead, Papcaftre, Thurfby, Burgh by Sands, Aikton, Rowecliffe, and Bownefs. The advowfons of the churches of Grayftock, Skelton, Aikton, Beaumond, and Bownefs. Meffuages, lands, and tenements in Skelton, Newbiggin, Blencowe, Motherby, Matterdale, Berrier, Murray, Grifedale, Caftle Sowerby, Tallentire, High Ireby, Cleter, Langrigg, Lafenby, Glaffonby, Kirk Ofwald, Staffoll, Parkhead, Skarrowmannock, Marwhenby, Robertby, Ulfby, Robertby-fields, Hunfenby, Melmerby, Crewgarth, Kirkland, Great Salkeld, Penrith, Carleton, Ainftable, Etterby, Thiftlethwaite, Beaumond, Carlifle, Stanwicks, Kirkanders, Weft Linton, Fingland, Dromebough, Glaffon, Wetherigg, Wetherigg Leas, Langcroft, Aynethorn, Eafton, Cardroneck, Pavy fields, Wearyholme, and Takeholme.

II. To him fucceeded JOHN his fon; who was of the bedchamber to king Ed. 2. fheriff of the counties of Norfolk and Suffolk from the 11th to the 16th or that king's reign; governor of the caftle of Norwich; and who ferved that king in his wars both againft Scotland and France. He died in the 5th of Ed. 3.

III. To him fucceeded Sir JOHN HOWARD his fon; who in the 10 Ed. 3. was conftituted admiral of all the king's fleet, from the mouth of the Thames northward.

IV. Sir ROBERT HOWARD knight, fon of John, married Margaret daughter of Robert lord Scales, and dying in the 12 Ric. left iffue by her,

V. Sir JOHN HOWARD knight, who was retained (according to the cuftom of thofe times) to ferve king Ric. 2. for life. He married to his firft wife Margaret daughter and heir of Sir John Plaiz of Tofts in the county of Norfolk knight, and by her had a fon *John* who died in his father's life-time, leaving only a daughter. To his fecond wife he married Alice daughter and heir of Sir William Tendering of Tendering hall in the county of Suffolk knight, and, by her had iffue,

VI. Sir ROBERT HOWARD knight; who married Margaret one of the two daughters and coheirs of Thomas de Mowbray *duke of Norfolk*, and died in his father's life-time, leaving a fon John.

VII. Sir JOHN HOWARD knight fucceeded his grandfather, and began early to diftinguifh himfelf in the wars with France under king Hen. 6.

In the 1 Ed. 4. he was fheriff of the counties of Norfolk and Suffolk, as likewife conftable of the caftle of Norwich, and one of the king's carvers.

In the 2 Ed. 4. he had a grant of feveral manors in the county of Norfolk, Suffolk, Effex, and Dorfet, efcheated to the crown by the attainder of John earl of Wiltfhire and John earl of Oxford; and in the fame year he had the joint command, with the lords Falconberg and Clinton, of the king's fleet, and did confiderable fervice againft the French.

He was alfo at that time treafurer of the king's houfhold, and in the 10th of that reign made captain general of the king's forces at fea, for baffling the attempts of the Lancaftrians, then making powerful head under Richard Nevil the ftout earl of Warwick.

In the 12 Ed. 4. he (with the lord Haftings) was conftituted deputy governor of Calais and the Marches, and in the year following was fummoned to parliament among the barons.

In the 18 Ed. 4. he was made conftable of the Tower of London, and the next year captain general of the king's fleet againft the Scots, as alfo in that reign made knight of the garter.

In the 1 Ric. 3. he was made *earl marfhal* of England, and created *duke of Norfolk*; Thomas his fon being at that time alfo created earl of Surry.

He was then likewife made lord high-admiral of England, Ireland, and Aquitain, for life; and at the fame time had a grant of 86 manors and lordfhips

from

from that prince. But he did not long enjoy thofe great honours and vaft pof-feffions, for in the very next year he was flain (together with the king) in the battle of Bofworth-field, and in the firft parliament of king Hen. 7. was attainted.

He married to his firft wife Catherine daughter of William lord Molines, and by her had *Thomas* his fon and heir; and four daughters, *Anne* maried to Sir Edmund George knight, *Ifabel* to Sir Robert Mortimer knight, *Jane* to John Timperly efquire, and *Margaret* to Sir John Windham knight. To his fecond wife he married Margaret daughter of Sir John Chetworth knight, and by her had a daughter *Catherine* married to John Bourchier lord Berners.

VIII. THOMAS HOWARD, fon and heir to John late duke of Norfolk, was efquire of the body to king Edward the fourth, and retained to ferve in his wars; and in the 1 Ric. 3. was created (as is aforefaid) earl of Surry; and tho' he took part with that king, and was taken prifoner at the battle of Bofworth-field, yet did king Hen. 7. in the 3d year of his reign receive him into favour and make him one of his privy council, and in the 4th of that reign he was re-ftored to his title of earl of Surry.

In the 15 Hen. 7. he attended the king and queen to Calais, and in the next year was made lord high treafurer of England, and afterwards knight of the garter.

In the 1 Hen. 8. he was made earl marfhal of England for life. And in the 4 Hen. 8. he was with that king at the taking of Therouenne and Tournay; and afterwards being fent general againft the Scots, routed their army at Flod-den field, where king James the fourth was flain; in which battle his fon Tho-mas lord admiral attended him, and another of his fons Edmund led the van. For which fignal fervice, he had a fpecial grant from the king, to himfelf and the heirs male of his body, of an honourable augmentation of his arms, viz. to bear on a bend in an efcutcheon, the upper half of a red lion (depicted as the arms of Scotland) pierced thro' the mouth with an arrow, together with a grant of 29 manors †.

He

† It is thought proper here to fubjoin a beautiful piece of elegiac poetry upon the fubject of this battle; which, though it is only in the form of an old Scotch ballad, yet it is fuch as ancient Greece or Rome might not be afhamed of.

The moans of the foreft after the battle of Flodden field.

I have heard a lilting, at the ewes milking,
A' the laffes lilting before break of day;
But now there's a moaning, in ilka green loning,
Since the flowers of the Foreft are weeded away:

I have heard] That is, formerly, whilft the young men were living.

Lilting] Singing chearfully, with a brifk lively air, in a ftyle peculiar to the Scots; whofe mufic, being compofed for the bagpipe, jumps over the difcordant notes of the 2d and 7th, in order to prevent the jarring which it would otherwife produce with the drone or bafs, which conftantly founds an octave to the key note. Hence this kind of compofition is commonly ftyled a Scotch lilt.

A'] All.

Ilka] Each.

Loning] Lane; a word ftill in ufe in the nor-thern parts. The word *green* is peculiarly empha-tical; the lane being grown over with grafs, by not being frequented as formerly.

At

He was also advanced to the dignity of duke of Norfolk, which title John his father (deriving his descent thro' the heirs female of Mowbray and Segrave from Thomas of Brotherton son of king Edward the first) did enjoy.

He married to his first wife Elizabeth daughter and sole heir of Sir Frederic Tilney baronet and widow of Humphrey Bourchier lord Berners; and by her had issue eight sons and three daughters, 1. *Thomas*, his eldest son and heir. 2. *Edward*, who was a person of the greatest account in his time, and was knight of the garter. In the 1 Hen. 8. he was made the king's standard bearer; and in the 4th of the same king was made high-admiral, at which time he convoyed the marquis of Dorset from Spain in aid of the emperor Ferdinand against the French; and having with his fleet cleared the seas from enemies, he landed in Britany, did great execution in the country, and brought away rich spoils. He likewise fought and took Sir Andrew Barton the famous Scotch pirate. But afterwards resolving to attempt the French in their harbours, he entered a galley and boarded the admiral of the French gallies; but

> At Bughts in the morning, nae blythe lads are scorning,
> Our lasses are lonely, and dowie, and wae;
> Nae daffing, nae gabbing, but sighing and sobbing,
> Ilka lass lifts her leglin and hies her away.
>
> In Har'st at the shearing, nae swankies are jeering,
> Our Bansters are wrinkled and lyard and grey;
> At a fair or a preaching, nae wooing nae fleetching,
> Since the flowers of the Forest are weeded away.
>
> At e'en in the gloming, nae youngsters are roaming
> 'Bout stacks with the lasses at Boggles to play;
> But ilka lass sits dreary, lamenting her deary,
> Since the flowers of the Forest are weeded away.
>
> Dool and wae fa' the order—sent our lads to the Border!
> The English for once by a guile won the day:
> The flowers of the Forest, that shone aye the foremost,
> The pride of our land now ligs cauld in the clay!
>
> We'll ha' nae mair lilting, at the ewes milking,
> Our women and bairns now sit dowie and wae:
> There's nought heard but moaning in ilka green loning,
> Since the flowers of the Forest are weeded away.

Bughts] Circular folds, where the ewes are milked.
Scorning] Bantering, jeering.
Dowie] Dowly, solitary.
Wae] Full of woe or sorrow.
Daffing] Waggish sporting.
Gabbing] Jestingly, prating, talking gibble gabble.
Leglin] Can, or milking pail.
Swankies] Swains.

Bansters] Bandsters, binders up of the sheaves.
Lyard] Hoary; being all old men.
A preaching] A preaching in Scotland is not unlike a country fair.
Fleetching] Fawning, flattering.
Gloming] Glimmering, twilight.
Dool] Dolour, sorrow.
Wae fa'] Woe befal, evil betide.
Aye] Always.
Ligs] Lies.

the grapplings giving way, the gallies fheered afunder, and left 'him in the
hands of his enemies; when, in the heat of the action, he was thrown over
board and perifhed.   3. *Edmund*, who with his brother Thomas led the van-
guard (as is aforefaid) at Flodden field, at which time he was a knight and
marfhal of the hoft.   And in the 12 Hen. 8. at the famous interview between
the faid king and Francis king of France, where all feats of arms were performed for 30 days, he was one of the chief challengers there on the part of the
Englifh.   By his wife Joyce, daughter of Sir Richard Colepepper of Holling-
bourne in Kent knight, he had eight children, one of whom was the lady
Catherine Howard fifth wife of king Hen. 8.—4. *Henry*, 5. *John*, 6. *Charles*,
7. *Henry*, 8. *Richard*.   Thefe five laft all died young.—The daughters were,
Elizabeth married to Thomas vifcount Rochford, *Muriel* married firft to John
Grey vifcount Lifle and after to Sir Thomas Knevit knight, and *Mary* married
to Henry Fitz-Roy duke of Richmond natural fon of king Hen. 8.

To his fecond wife he married Agnes daughter of Sir Philip Tilney knight,
and by her had iffue, 1. *William*, created baron Howard of Effingham.
2. *Thomas*, who having married the lady Margaret Douglafs daughter of Margaret queen of Scots and niece to king Henry the eighth, was attained of treafon upon fome fufpicion of his afpiring to the crown, and died in the Tower of
London in the 29 Eliz.   3. *Richard*.   And 4 daughters; *Anne* married to
John Vere earl of Oxford, *Dorothy*, to Edward Stanley earl of Derby, *Elizabeth*
to Henry earl of Suffex, and *Catherine* married firft to Sir Rhefe ap Thomas and
after to Henry Daubeny earl of Bridgewater.

IX. Thomas Howard duke of Norfolk fucceeded his father in the
16 Hen. 8.   He was in his father's life-time created earl of Surry; and upon
the death of his younger brother the lord Edward, was conftituted lord admiral
in his ftead.   In the 12 of Hen. 8. he was made lord deputy of Ireland; and
upon his father's death he was made general of the army at that time raifed to
advance into Scotland to fet the young king free whom the duke of Albany
kept at Stirling; and afterwards attended king Henry into France.   In the
15 Hen. 8. he was appointed earl marfhal of England.   In the 18 Hen. 8. he
was fent to the affiftance of the earl of Shrewfbury towards fuppreffing that
memorable infurrection in Yorkfhire called the Pilgrimage of Grace.

Afterwards, upon fome infinuations againft him, the king committed him
prifoner to the Tower, ordered his goods to be feized, and gave notice to his
ambaffadors abroad, that the duke and his fon the earl of Surry had confpired to
take upon them the government during the king's life, and after his death to
get the prince into their hands; for which he was attainted in parliament,
and nothing but the king's death prevented his execution.   He continued prifoner during all the reign of king Ed. 6. but was difcharged, and his attainder
reverfed in the firft year of queen Mary.

He married to his firft wife Anne daughter of king Edward the fourth, by
whom he had a fon named *Thomas*, who died young.   To his fecond wife he
married Elizabeth daughter of Edward duke of Buckingham, and by her had
                                                                          iffue,

· iffue, 1. *Henry*, earl of Surry. 2. *Thomas*, who in the 1 Eliz. was advanced to
the title of vifcount Howard of Bindon in the county of Dorfet.

X. Henry Howard, earl of Surry, was atainted in parliament at the fame
time with his father, and was beheaded. He married Frances daughter of John
Vere earl of Oxford; and by her had iffue, 1. *Thomas*. 2. *Henry*, who being
reftored in blood, was by king James the firft created lord Howard of Marnhill
and earl of Northampton, and made lord privy feal. 3. *Jane*, married to Charles
earl of Weftmorland. 4. *Margaret*, married to Henry lord Scroop of Bolton.
5. *Catherine*, married to Henry lord Berkeley.

XI. Thomas Howard, elder fon of the faid Henry earl of Surry, fucceeded
his grandfather Thomas duke of Norfolk in his honour and eftate; his faid
grandfather's attainder being reverfed (as is aforefaid) in the firft year of queen
Mary. And in the 2d year of that queen, this Thomas was fent againft the
infurrection headed by Sir Thomas Wiat. In the 1 Eliz. he was made knight
of the garter, and two years after lieutenant-general for the northern parts:
But in the 11th of that reign, the queen began to fufpect him as too much inclined to the queen of Scots, whom it was reported he defigned to marry; to
which marriage the queen being averfe, the duke retired into Norfolk, with a
refolution (notwithftanding) to purfue his former courtfhip; which being difcovered, he was imprifoned in the 14th of that reign, and the next year brought
to his trial for high treafon, in having confpired the dethroning of the queen,
and bringing in foreign forces, and applying to the Pope and Spaniards for that
purpofe, and having endeavoured the enlargement of the queen of Scots; of
which he was found guilty and beheaded in the 15 Eliz.
He married to his firft wife Mary daughter of Henry Fitz-Alan earl of Arundel (with whom he had the manor and caftle of Arundel in the county of Suffex),
and by her had *Philip* his fon and heir. To his fecond wife he married *Margaret* daughter and fole heir of Thomas lord Audley of Walden; by whom he
had *Thomas* the firft earl of Suffolk of this family, and the lord *William Howard*
who married Elizabeth one of the coheirs of Dacre as aforefaid, and a daughter
Margaret married to Robert Sackville earl of Dorfet. To his third wife he
married Elizabeth widow of Thomas lord Dacre mother of the faid coheirs,
who feems to have died not long after; for her former hufband died in the
8 Eliz. and we find this her fecond hufband in the 11th year of the fame queen
afpiring after the marriage of Mary queen of Scots.

XII. Philip Howard, his eldeft fon, was ftyled earl of Arundel, as owner
of Arundel caftle by defcent from his mother (for whoever is poffeffed of that
caftle becomes thereby an earl without any other creation); and was fummoned
to parliament by that title in the 23 Eliz. and in the fame parliament by a fpecial
act was reftored in blood; but not long after, by the contrivance of the earl of
Leicefter and fecretary Walfingham (for queen Elizabeth's minifters feem to
have been peculiarly fufpicious and jealous of this noble family, being Roman

                                              Catholics)

Catholics) confined to his houfe; and endeavouring to go beyond fea was difcovered and fent prifoner to the Tower; and foon after a charge was brought
againft him in the Star-chamber, for fupporting Romifh priefts and holding
correfpondence with Jefuits and other traytors, for which he was fined 10,000*l*,
and to fuffer imprifonment during the queen's pleafure. But this did not fuf-
fice; for in the 32 Eliz. he was tried for high treafon by his peers: the
particulars of the charge were, his contracting a ftrict friendfhip with cardinal
Allen and Parfons the Jefuit for reftoring the Romifh religion; that he was
privy to the excommunicating bull of pope Sixtus the fifth, and that he caufed
mafs to be faid for the fuccefs of the Spanifh Armada. And being found guilty, he had fentence of death pronounced againft him; but being remanded
to the Tower, his execution was refpited, and he died a prifoner in the 38 Eliz.

He married (as is aforefaid) *Anne* eldeft daughter of Thomas and fifter and
coheir of George lord Dacre, and with her had Grayftock. He had iffue by her
Thomas his only child.

XIII. Thomas Howard, fon of Philip earl of Arundel, was reftored in
blood by the parliament in the firft year of James the firft, and to all the titles
of honour and precedence loft by his father's attainder; was inftalled knight
of the garter in the 9th of the fame king, and in the 19th was conftituted earl
marfhal for life.

In the 9 Cha. 1. he was conftituted chief juftice of all the king's forefts north
of Trent; being alfo in the 16th of the fame king made general of the army
raifed to march againft the Scots; and in the 20th of the fame king's reign advanced to the title of earl of Norfolk; and going over fea, with many others,
in the decline of that king's affairs, he died at Venice in 1646.

He married Alathea one of the daughters and coheirs of Gilbert Talbot earl
of Shrewfbury, and by her had two fons, 1. *Henry*, lord Mowbray and Maltra-
vers. 2. *William*, knight of the Bath, was alfo created baron of Stafford on his
marrying the lady Mary fifter and fole heir to Henry lord Stafford.

XIV. Henry Howard, lord Mowbray, fucceeded his father in his honours;
and was alfo earl marfhal, and knight of the garter. He married Elizabeth
daughter of Efme Stewart lord Aubigny and earl of March, and afterwards
duke of Lenox; and by her had iffue nine fons, *Thomas, Henry, Philip, Charles*
(from whom the prefent family at Grayftock are defcended), *Talbot, Edward,
Francis, Bernard*, and *Efme*; and two daughters, *Catherine* married to John
Digby of Gothurft in Northumberland efquire, and *Elizabeth* married to Alexander Macdonnel grandfon to the earl of Antrim.

XV. Thomas Howard, eldeft fon of Henry, fucceeded his father in his
honours and titles of earl of Arundel, Surry, and Norfolk, in the year 1652.
And in 1661 he was reftored to the title of duke of Norfolk. He died at Pa-
dua in Italy unmarried, in the year 1678.

XVI. Henry

XVI. HENRY HOWARD, duke of Norfolk, succeeded his brother Thomas. He was in the life-time of his elder brother created lord Howard of Castle Rising in the county of Norfolk; and in 1672 was created earl of Norwich to him and the heirs male of his body; and also by the same patent had granted to him the office and dignity of earl marshal of England and to the heirs male of his body; and for default of such issue, to the heirs male of the body of Thomas earl of Arundel, Surry, and Norfolk, grandfather of the said Henry earl of Norwich; and for default of such issue, to the heirs male of the body of Thomas late earl of Suffolk; and for default of such issue, to the heirs male of the body of the lord William Howard of Naworth.

He married to his first wife Anne daughter of Edward Somerset marquis of Worcester, and by her had issue, 1. *Henry*. 2. *Thomas*. 3. *Anne-Alathea*, who died young. 4. *Elizabeth*, married to Alexander duke of Gordon. 5. *Frances*, married to the marquis Valparesa, a Spanish nobleman.

To his second wife he married Jane daughter of Robert Bickerton esquire, and by her had issue, 1. *George*, who married Arabella daughter of Sir Edmund Allen, and widow of Francis Thompson esquire. 2. *James*, who died unmarried, being drowned in attempting to ride over Sutton Wash in Lincolnshire. 3. *Frederic Henry*, who married Catherine daughter of Sir Francis B'ake. And three daughters, *Catherine* and *Anne* both nuns in Flanders, and *Philippa* married to William Standish of Standish hall in Lancashire esquire.

XVII. HENRY HOWARD, duke of Norfolk, succeeded his father in 1685., In his father's life-time, he was summoned to parliament by the title of lord Mowbray; and in 1652, upon the death of Prince Rupert, he was made constable of Windsor castle, and lord lieutenant and custos rotulorum for the counties of Norfolk, Surry, and Berks. On the landing of the prince of Orange in 1688, he immediately declared for him, and brought over several parts into his interest.

He married Mary daughter and sole heir of Henry Mordaunt earl of Peterborough, but died without issue in 1701.

His brother Thomas died before him; being of the Romish religion, this Thomas withdrew with king James the second into France, and attended him from thence into Ireland, and in his return to Brest he was cast away and perished at sea in the year 1689; leaving by his wife Mary Elizabeth daughter and heir of Sir John Savile of Copley in the county of York baronet, five sons and one daughter, *Mary*, married to Walter Aston baron Aston of Forfar in Scotland. The sons were, 1. *Thomas*, who succeeded his uncle Henry. 2. *Henry*, who died unmarried. 3. *Edward*, the present duke, who succeeded his brother Thomas. 4. *Richard*, who died unmarried. 5. *Philip*, who married to his first wife Winifred daughter of Thomas Stonor of Watlington Park in the county of Oxford esquire, by whom he had issue *Thomas* who died 1763, without issue, and *Winifred* married to William lord Stourton and died in 1753. To his second wife he married Henrietta daughter of Edward Blount of Blagdon in the county of Devon esquire widow of Peter Proli of Antwerp esquire and sister to the late duchess of Norfolk, and had one son *Edward* who died

in

in 1767 unmarried, and a daughter *Anne* married to Robert Edward lord Petre.

XVII. THOMAS HOWARD duke of Norfolk was born in 1683, and succeeded his uncle, Henry in 1701. He married Mary daughter and sole heir of Sir Nicholas Shirburne of Stonihurst in Lancashire baronet; but died without issue in 1732.

XVIII. EDWARD HOWARD, the present duke, succeeded his brother Thomas, and married Mary daughter of Edward Blount of Blagdon in the county of Devon esquire, and hath no issue. And there being no male issue remaining of any of his brothers or uncles, the honours of this family will devolve upon the descendents of *Charles Howard* brother to the present duke's grandfather, and fourth son of Henry Howard lord Mowbray and earl of Norfolk abovementioned.

The said CHARLES HOWARD, after a long and expensive suit in chancery and an appeal to the house of lords, obtained a decree for the whole barony of Graystock *. He married Mary daughter and heir of George Tattershall of Finchamstead in the county of Berks esquire; and by her had issue *Charles* who died young, and another son *Henry-Charles*.

HENRY-CHARLES HOWARD esquire succeeded his father, and at great expence repaired Graystock castle, and made it a very convenient and delightful habitation. He married Mary daughter of John Aylward esquire, descended of the family of Aylward in the kingdom of Ireland; and by her had issue, *Henry, Charles, Thomas, Mary, Catharine,* and *Francis.* Of these, *Henry* died before his father unmarried: and of the rest, *Charles* only now surviveth.

Which said CHARLES HOWARD esquire married Catharine daughter of John Brockholes of Claughton in Lancashire esquire, and had issue *Charles,* and six other children who died young.

Which last CHARLES HOWARD esquire, son of Charles, married to his first wife Marian daughter of Coppinger of Ballamalow in the county of Cork esquire, who died in 1768 without leaving issue. To his second wife in 1771 he married Frances daughter and sole heir of the late lord Scudamore of Home-Lacy in the county of Hereford.

This barony is held of the king *in capite* by the service of one intire barony, rendering 4l yearly at the fairs of Carlisle, suit at the county court monthly, and serving the king in person against Scotland. Here are 257 customary tenants and 106 freeholders within the barony, and about 120l *per annum* customary rent. The customary tenants pay a twenty penny fine upon the death of lord or tenant, and a thirty penny fine upon alienation. They also pay foller rents, foster corn, miln rents, greenhue, peat silver, and boon mowing and leading peats.

* Appendix to Chancery Cases. (Duke of Norfolk's case.)

The CHURCH of Grayſtock is dedicated to St. Andrew, and is rectorial, valued in the king's books at 40*l* 7*s* 8 ¼ *d*, and now worth upwards of 300 *l per annum.*

In the year 1302, Mr. *Richard de Morpeth* was inſtituted to this church, upon the preſentation of Sir John de Grayſtock knight.

In 1314, *Ralph de Erghome*, an acolite, was preſented by *Ralph* ſon of William lord of Grayſtock, and inſtituted thereupon, with a diſpenſation for four years abſence at his ſtudies. He had afterwards no fewer than five diſpenſations of abſence, and ſeems indeed never to have reſided there at all. And after he had been rector here above 40 years, he reſigned the rectory, on his being inſtituted into the living of Foulſtowe in the diroceſe of Lincoln, in the year 1357, and thereupon *Richard de Hoton Roof* was preſented by Sir William de Grayſtock knight; who immediately, upon his inſtitution, took out a commiſſion of inquiry into the dilapidations in the parſonage houſe and chancel, occaſioned by the long non-reſidence of his predeceſſor.

In 1359, there is a confirmation by biſhop Welton of a grant made by the ſaid William lord of Grayſtock, to one maſter and 6 chaplains, viz. Sir Richard de Hoton (then rector) maſter or cuſtos, Andrew de Briſcoe, Richard de Brampton, William de Wanthwaite, Robert de Threlkeld, and William de Hill, chaplains.

In 1365, on the death of Richard de Hoton, inſtitution was given to *John de Herinthorp* prieſt, who was preſented by king Ed. 3. in right of his ward Ralph baron of Grayſtock then a minor.

In 1377, on the petition of the ſaid Ralph de Grayſtock, ſetting forth that the income of that rectory is very conſiderable, and the cure ill ſupplied, the biſhop iſſues out a commiſſion of inquiry: and the commiſſioners return (amongſt other particulars) that the yearly revenues of the rectory of Grayſtock amount to about 100*l*, out of which deductions being made for procurations and other eccleſiaſtical duties, the parſon may clear about 80 *l*. That there are ſeveral chapels in the pariſh; one at Wethermelock, 3 miles from the pariſh church; and another, 4 miles diſtant, at Threlkeld; that each of theſe hath a chaplain and a chapel clerk (clericum aquæ bajulum); that the pariſh is 7 miles long, and 4 broad.

In 1379, another commiſſion of inquiry, to the ſame purpoſe, is ſent by the biſhop to his official, who makes return (upon the oaths of the jury, conſiſting of an equal number of eccleſiaſtics and laymen thereupon ſummoned) that it would be for the honour of God and the good of the pariſhioners, to have more clergymen to officiate in that large pariſh.

In the ſame year, Sir *John de Claſton* the rector had a diſpenſation for two years abſence, with allowance to let his rectory to farm for that term.

In 1382, the mother church of Grayſtock being much out of repair, the walls crazy, the bellfry fallen, and the wooden ſhingles on the roof moſtly ſcattered, and the inhabitants of Threlkeld and Wethermelock refuſing to contribute their proportion of the charge; the biſhop, at his ordinary viſitation, iſſues out his injunction to all and every of them under pain of the greater excommunication.

In

In the fame year, Alexander (Nevil) archbifhop of York, the pope's legate, converts the rectory of Grayftock into a college; whereof he conftitutes *Gilbert Bewett* prieft the firft mafter; and gives the chantry of St. Andrew in the faid church to John Lake of the diocefe of Litchfield, the chantry of St. Mary to Thomas Chamberlayne of the diocefe of Norwich, the chantry of the altar of St. John Baptift to John Alve of the diocefe of York, the chantry of the altar of St. Katherine to Richard Carwell of the diocefe of Lincoln, the chantry of St. Thomas the martyr (meaning Becket) to Robert Newton of the diocefe of Litchfield, and (laftly) the chantry of the altar of St. Peter to John de Hare of the diocefe of York: and all thefe were obliged at their inftalment to fwear canonical obedience to the bifhops of Carlifle, in like manner as the rectors of Grayftock had been before accuftomed to do.

In 1386, upon the death of Thomas Chamberlayne, Adam de Aglionby was inftituted into the chantry of the altar of St. Mary in the collegiate church of Grayftock, being thereunto prefented by the noble lord Ralph baron of Grayftock.

In 1420, *Adam de Aglionby* appears to be then mafter of the college of Grayftock; being fued in that year by William Rebanks and his wife for fome lands in Raughton.

In 1526, died *John Whelpdale*, LL. D. mafter of the college of Grayftock and rector of Caldbeck; as appears from his epitaph in the church of Grayftock.

Not long after, the monafteries, collegiate churches, and chantries were diffolved. At which time, the revenues of the feveral chantries aforefaid in this church were twenty nobles a year to each. Afterwards it was difputed whether the church did continue rectorial, or the rectory and profits thereof became vefted in the crown by the faid diffolution. For the incumbent it was alledged, that he was poffeffed by prefentation, admiffion, inftitution, and induction: That the church was indeed made collegiate, but it was by the pope's authority only: That they had no common feal, and therefore were not a legal corporation. And judgment was given againft the king; and the church continued rectorial and parochial.—Judge Dyer, who reports this cafe, feems to lay the ftrefs upon the want of a common feal [*]. Lord Coke lays the ftrefs upon its being made collegiate by the pope's authority only, without the king's affent [†]. (Either of them fufficient arguments of the invalidity of the eftablifhment.)

In 1567, on the death of Mr. *John Dacre* rector of Grayftock, inftitution was given to Sir *Simon Moffe* clerk prefented by Thomas duke of Norfolk earl marfhal of England and knight of the garter and Elizabeth his wife (widow of Thomas late lord Dacre).

In the next year, on the death of Simon Moffe, Mr, *Edward Hanfby* was inftituted, on a prefentation by queen Elizabeth in right of her ward George lord Dacre fon and heir of Thomas lord Dacre, Grayftock, and Gilfland.

In 1584, Mar. 6. on the death of Mr. Hanfby, one caveat was entred by Francis Dacre of Croglin efquire, claiming the patronage of the rectory of

[*] Dyer, 81.   [†] 4 Co. 107.

Grayftock; and on the 13th of the fame month, another caveat was entred by Philip earl of Arundel and the lady Anne his wife. Hereupon a commiffion of Jus Patronatus was iffued, and the jury brought in the following verdict :

" To the reverend father in God John by God's divine providence bifhop of Carliel, Thomas Fairfax bachelor of divinity, Anthony Walkwood, William Bennet, Robert Corney, maflers of arts, John Whelewright, John Symfon, clerks, Symon Mufgrave, Henry Curwen, Wilfrid Lawfon, Henry Crackenthorp, Lancelot Salkeld, and Thomas Layton, efquires, being named, elected, and fworn jurors for the trial of the Jus Patronatus or right of patronage of the parifh church of Grayftock in the county of Cumberland and within the diocefs of Carliel, fend greeting in our lord God everlafting. Whereas we the faid jurors had certain articles miniftred unto us in writing by your lordfhip, and were charged with a corporal oath well and truly to inquire of all and every the faid articles according to our evidence, do give our verdict and anfwer unto the faid articles in manner and form following: To the 1ft, viz. Whether the parifh church of Grayftock be now void, how long that hath been void, and by what means? We anfwer, that the parfonage of Grayftock is void by the death of Mr. Edward Hanfbye late incumbent there, who died the fecond day of March laft paft. To the 2d, viz. Whether there be many patrons which pretend title unto the paronage and prefentation of the parfonage of the faid parifh church, how many they be, and who they be? We anfwer, That there be two which pretend title to prefent to the faid parfonage, viz. Philip earl of Arundel and Anne (Dacre) his wife, and Mr. Francis Dacre. To the 3d, viz. Whether any of the patrons pretending fuch title have given and granted any advowfon or advowfons of the faid rectory or parfonage, by whom were fuch advowfon or advowfons given or granted, to whom, and in what manner? We anfwer, That Philip earl of Arundel and the lady Anne his wife, pretending title to the patronage of the faid parfonage, have granted an advowfon of the faid parfonage unto William Cantrell, as by the faid advowfon under their hands and feals appeareth. To the 4th, viz. Whether the faid parfonage of the parifh church of Grayftock be appendent to any manor, and to what manor it is appendent, or is it a rectory or parfonage in grofs? We anfwer, That for any evidence we have feen, we find the faid parfonage of Grayftock appendent to the manor of Grayftock. To the 5th, viz. Who prefented to the faid church, and by what right and title he did fo prefent? We anfwer, That the queen's majefty that now is prefented the laft time to the faid parfonage of Grayftock in the right of George lord Dacre fon of the lord Thomas Dacre, the faid George then being in minority. To the 6th, viz. Who at this prefent is in poffeffion of the patronage of the faid parifh church? We find, That William Cantrell is for this prefent vacation in poffeffion of the patronage of the faid parfonage, by virtue of the faid advowfon granted by the earl of Arundel and lady Anne his wife. To the 7th, viz. Who hath the right and title of lawful intereft to prefent to the faid parifh church of Grayftock, this prefent time of the vacation thereof? We Symon Mufgrave knight, Wilfrid Lawfon, Henry Crackenthorp, Anthony Walkwood, William Bennet, Robert Corney, and John Symfon,

feven

seven of the said jurors, answer, That whereas Mr. Francis Dacre made his title to the patronage of the parsonage of Graystock by an intail supposed to be made by his father William late lord Dacre, which intail was impugned for divers imperfections therein alledged by the counsel learned of William Cantrell; yet we by reason of other matter of record given us in evidence, not entering into the consideration of the validity or invalidity of the same intail, do find, that William Cantrell hath right to present to the church of Graystock for this time, as by grant thereof made from the earl of Arundel and lady Anne the countess his wife: And we Henry Curwen knight, Lancelot Salkeld, Thomas Fairfax, Thomas Layton, and John Whelewright, five of the said jurors, answer, That according to such evidence as we have had, we find the right of the patronage of Graystock in William Cantrell, as in the right and by the grant of Philip earl of Arundel and lady Anne his wife: So we all twelve agree, conclude, and find, that William Cantrell hath right to present to the church of Graystock for this time, as by grant thereof made from the earl of Arundel and lady Anne the countess his wife. To the 8th, viz. How many be presented at this time to the said church, and by whom they be presented? We answer, That there be two presented at this vacation, the one (viz. Mr. Hugh Thornly) by William Cantrell in the right of the earl of Arundel and lady Anne his wife; the other (viz. Mr. Henry Evans) by Mr. Francis Dacre. To the 9th, viz. Whether be the clerks now presented, and every of them, of such qualities as be required by the laws and statutes of this realm to be in such persons as are to be admitted by the ordinary to the said parish church of Graystock? We answer, That for any thing we know, they are qualified as the law requires. In witness whereof, we the said jurors to this our verdict have put our seals and subscribed our names. Given at Rose castle the 16th day of August, in the year of our lord God a thousand five hundred eighty and five, and in the 27th year of the reign of our sovereign lady Elizabeth."

In pursuance of which verdict, *Hugh Thornly*, M. A. was instituted into the said rectory on the 30th of January following, on the presentation of William Cantrell esquire. And nine years after, the said Hugh Thornly was again instituted on a presentation from the queen, to prevent any hazard, by lapse or otherwise, in the former title.

In 1597, Mr. *Leonard Lowther* had institution on the death of Hugh Thornly, being presented by Richard Lowther of Lowther esquire, by virtue of a grant of the present avoidance from the queen (the earl of Arundel the patron being then under attainder).

In 1616, a cause was determined (as appears from lord Hobart's Reports, p. 107.) between the bishop of Carlisle as rector of Graystock (having that living in Commendam), and one of his parishioners; wherein the bishop recovered a sight of the wool in tithing. This bishop (according to the course of chronology) was Dr. *Henry Robinson*.

In 1633, on the death of *Jerome Waterhouse* rector of Graystock, *William Pettie* B. D. was presented by Thomas earl of Arundel and Surry, earl marshal.

In

In 1639, *William Morland*, M. A. was prefented by the fame patron. In 1650, he was ejected for ignorance and infufficiency by Sir Arthur Hazlerig and other commiffioners for propagating the gofpel in the four northern counties; which fentence, upon Mr. Morland's appeal, was confirmed by the committee for plundered minifters. He was firft fucceeded by one *Weft*, who died in about two years time. After him came Dr, *Gilpin*, who delivered up the rectory to Mr. Morland on king Charles the fecond's reftoration *.

In 1663, on Mr. Morland's death, *Alan Smallwood*, D. D. was prefented by Jofhua Colfton of London, M. D. by virtue of a grant from Elizabeth countefs dowager of Arundel and Surry.

In 1686, on Dr. Smallwood's death, *Richard Fowke*, M. A. was prefented by the honourable Charles Howard efquire.

In 1692, a caveat was entered on behalf of the univerfity of Cambridge, claiming by their right of prefenting as to a popifh living; and on Mr. Fowke's death, *Thomas Gibbon*, M. A. was inftituted on their prefentation. In 1711, he refigned, and was reinftituted upon the prefentation of Gilfrid Lawfon efquire grantee of Charles Howard efquire the lord of the manor.

In 1717, on Mr. Gibbon's death, *Thomas Bolton*, M. A. was inftituted on the prefentation of the faid Gilfrid Lawfon efquire.

In 1737, on Mr. Bolton's death, caveats were feverally entered for Williams Gibbon clerk, for the univerfity of Cambridge, and for Mr. Crosfield King, executor of John King deceafed. The firft withdrew his caveat; and *Edmund Law*, M. A. the univerfity's prefentee, and the faid Mr. King, having proceeded to try their right in Weftminfter hall, the faid Mr. Law (now bifhop of Carlifle) obtained a fuperfedeas to the writ of Ne Admittas, and in 1739 was inftituted. In 1746, Sep. 9. he refigned the faid rectory, and on the 19th of the fame month was readmitted on the prefentation of Adam Afkew of Newcaftle upon Tyne efquire, purchafer of the advowfon from Charles Howard efquire lord of Grayftock.

HUTTON JOHN, within this parifh, for a long time was the property of a family of the name of Hutton; defcended from a younger brother, very probably, of the Huttons of Hutton in this county. From what *John* in particular it received this appellation, we have not found. In the 36 Edw. 3. it is found by inquifition, that *William de Hoton John* held the manor of *Hoton John* of the barony of Grayftock, by homage and 20s cornage, with fuit of court at Grayftock from three weeks to three weeks, and by the fervice called witnefman and puture of the forefters of Flafcowe.

In the 2d year of queen Mary, *Cuthbert Hutton* died feifed thereof, and *Thomas* his fon inherited the fame, with the appurtenances, and alfo a certain pafture called Hutton Moor †. and Mellfell, and certain amerciaments called

Muremaile,

* Walker's fufferings of the clergy, 306.

† Which moor is thus defcribed: Incipiendo apud quendam locum vocatum Akerbeck, et deinde afcendendo antiquam fepem campi de Motherby ufque lapidem immobilem ex parte occidentali de Motherby, et deinde ex parte occidentali ufque lapidem immobilem fubtus Pilowe, et deinde ultra Merefyke ufque de Bromehowe, et deinde ex parte occidentali ufque lapidem immobilem juxta

Muremaile, and lands and tenements in Penruddocke, Whitebarrow, and Stodehow.

This *Thomas* died without iffue, and was fucceeded by fifters coheirs; one of whom, *Mary*, was married to Andrew Hudleston of Farington in the county of Lancaster efquire, fecond fon of Sir *John Hudlefton* of Millum; and this brought the Hudleftons to Hutton John. The faid Mary was daughter of Cuthbert Hutton aforefaid, by his wife Elizabeth one of the four daughters and coheirs of Sir Robert Bellingham of Burnefhead in the county of Weftmorland; which Elizabeth was educated with the lady Katherine Par of Kendal caftle, who when fhe was married to king Hen. 8. fent for the faid Elizabeth up to court, and made her one of the ladies of the bed chamber, where her faid daughter Mary was born, and the princefs Mary (afterwards queen) was her godmother: Mr. Sandford fays, he had feen a piece of gilt plate which was her godchild's gift.

The paternal eftate of the faid *Andrew* confifted of the feveral manors of Abbington in Oxfordfhire, Prefton Richard in Weftmorland, and Farrington hall in Lancafhire, with feveral other poffeffions both in Weftmorland and Cumberland. He was an officer in the body guards to king Hen. 8. Ed. 6. queen Mary, and queen Elizabeth.

He had iffue by this marriage 7 fons, viz. *Jofeph, John, Edmund, Byham, William, Andrew,* and *Richard*; and 3 daughters, *Dorothy, Joyce,* and *Bridget.*

Joseph Hudleston of Hutton John efquire, eldeft of the faid feven fons of Andrew, married Eleanor daughter of Cuthbert Siffon of Dacre, and by her had iffue 6 fons, viz. *Andrew, John, Richard, Cuthbert, William,* and *Ferdinando*; and 8 daughters, viz. *Mary, Dorothy, Jane, Margaret, Joyce, Bridget, Helen,* and *Elizabeth.*

John the fecond fon was brought up to the church; and had his education in the Englifh college at Doway in Flanders, and was ordained prieft in the Romifh church. He was happily inftrumental in preferving king Charles the fecond after the battle of Worcefter. For which, and other his fervices, he was after the reftoration appointed firft chaplain and father confeffor to Catherine queen confort of Charles the fecond, and private confeffor to the king himfelf; and was in fo great confidence both with king and parliament, as to be excepted by name out of all the fevere acts made againft popifh priefts.

---

juxta Skytwatche, et deinde afcendens le Sykett ufque Troutker ex parte boreali, et deinde afcen dens le Sykett ufque lapidem immobilem juxta Beryerfield, et deinde ufque parvum lapidem fuper Calfrigge, et deinde ufque le Carfaile juxta Beryer, et deinde defcendendo le Sykett fubtus Grenecragge, et fic inde defcendendo aquam de Berryerbecke ufque Lanftowhowe ex parte occidentali, et defcendendo ufque caput Nirmerfyke ex parte auftrali, et deinde afcendendo ufque pedem de Fermerfyke, et deinde afcendendo ex parte auftrali ufque lapidem immobilem in Troutbeck gill juxta Lickaclofe, et deinde a dicto lapide in Troutbeck gill afcendendo Troutbeck gill ficut Kittofyke, cadit in le Troutbeck, et deinde afcendendo Kittofyke ufque caput ejufdem, et deinde afcendendo recte et ex parte auftrali ufque lapidem immobilem juxta Materdale Mofs, et deinde defcendendo ufque Rayfet Dubbs, et inde defcendendo le Stanftobeck ufque Grenedubbs, et fic defcendendo aquam de Dakerbecke ufque Bowcrofte, et deinde ex parte boreali ufque Dudfethowe, et fic defcendendo le Ellerfyke ufque le Gillbecke, et fic afcendendo le Gillbecke ufque le Akerkelde.

3   When

When king Charles the second lay upon his death-bed, he adminiftred to him the facraments according to the rites of the church of Rome ; which when he had finifhed, and pronounced the abfolution, the king feemed at great eafe, and turning to the reverend father, exprefled his thanks in thefe remarkable words : " You have faved me twice ; Firft, my body after the fight at Worcefter, And now my foul." And afked if he would have him declare himfelf of that church ?   To which the father anfwered, that he would take upon himfelf to fatisfy the world in that particular.   After king James the fecond came to the crown, he caufed father Hudlefton to atteft and publifh to the world, that the late king Charles the fecond died a catholic, and that he gave him the Eucharift and Extreme Unction.   And therewith he publifhed two papers found in the late king's ftrong box, all of his own handwriting, tending to prove the neceffity of a vifible church and guide in matters of faith ; together with a little treatife called " A fhort and plain way to the faith and church," which father Hudlefton fays was written by his uncle Richard Hudlefton [7th fon of Andrew abovementioned] of the Englifh congregation of the order of St. Benedict ; which treatife, the father affirms, made great impreffion upon the mind of Charles the fecond, whilft he fecreted him from the fearch of the rebels at Bofcobel after the battle of Worcefter.—— For thefe and other faithful fervices, this reverend father had an appointment in the queen dowager's palace at Somerfet houfe, where he had the fuperintendency of the chapel, and alfo had a handfome penfion fettled upon him for life.   Both which he enjoyed quite through the reigns of king James the fecond and king William, and till the 3d year of queen Anne, 1704, when he died, being of the age of 96 years, and was buried in the body of that chapel.   He expended the greateft part of his income and effects in rebuilding the chapel of the Englifh college at Doway aforefaid, and endowing feveral new fcholarfhips there, and in the abbey or convent of Lambfpring in Weftphalia ; and at his death, by will, left the refiduum of his effects to the (popifh) lord Feverfham, in truft to fee thofe undertakings finifhed.

ANDREW HUDLESTON of Hutton John efquire, eldeft fon of Jofeph, married Dorothy fecond daughter of Daniel Fleming of Skirwith efquire, and by her had iffue 4 fons, *Andrew*, *Jofeph*, *John*, and *Richard* ; and five daughters, *Mary*, *Jane*, *Dorothy*, *Magdalene*, and *Bridget*.

This family fuffered greatly for their loyalty and fervices to king Charles the firft and fecond, from Oliver Cromwell, who caufed all their manors and poffeffions in the counties of Oxford, Lancafter, and Weftmorland to be feized and fold, or otherwife difpofed of amongft his partizans.   So that the family had little or nothing left except the eftate at Hutton John (being under fettlement on the marriage of the faid Andrew and Dorothy), which was for many years under fequeftration, and not reftored until the return of king Charles the fecond, when they got this eftate again, but no recompence for their lofs and fufferings.   *

ANDREW HUDLESTON of Hutton John efquire, eldeft fon of Andrew and Dorothy, was the firft proteftant of the family: He was a man of great learning and parts, much refpected in the county, and a zealous promoter of the Revolution. In October 1688, being informed of a fhip put into Workington, loaded with arms and ammunition intended for king James the fecond's garrifon of Carlifle, he immediately went over to confult Sir John Lowther of Lowther, who was alfo extremely affected to the Revolution, how they might feize and fecure the fhip and loading for the ufe of the prince of Orange, who was then daily expected to land. It was agreed to make the attempt, by immediately arming their fervants and tenants, and mounting them on horfeback to march privately in the night, fo as to be ready for the attack by break of day the next morning. This was fo happily effected, that after very little refiftance, the crew furrendered, and the fhip, arms, and ammunition were all taken and fecured for the prince of Orange. This was one of the firft open acts of hoftility againft king James the fecond in favour of the Revolution, but had like to have coft the parties dear. For they had fcarce got home, when news arrived of the prince of Orange's fleet being difperfed in a ftorm and obliged to put back, and of having received fo much damage, that the prince could not purfue his enterprize till next fpring. This advice gave the parties fome uneafinefs for a few days. But the damage to the fleet was fo foon repaired, that on the firft of November it put to fea again, and on the 5th arrived at Torbay, and the prince's landing happily effected before night.

This Andrew married Katharine daughter of Sir Wilfrid Lawfon of Ifell baronet, and by her had iffue fix fons, viz. *Andrew* (who died before his father without iffue), *Wilfrid, William, Richard, Lawfon,* and *John*; and 9 daughters, *Dorothy, Jane, Katharine, Elizabeth, Mary, Anne, Judith,* and *Bridget*.

WILFRID HUDLESTON of Hutton John efquire, fecond fon and heir of Andrew, about the year 1703 married Joyce daughter and heir of Thomas Curwen of Workington efquire, and by her had iffue, 1. *Andrew.* 2. *Curwen*, minifter of the old church in Whitehaven, and rector of Clifton in Weftmorland; who married to his firft wife Elizabeth fifter of Richard Cooke of Workington efquire, and by her had iffue a daughter Joyce married to William Shammon efquire a lieutenant in the royal navy: He married to his fecond wife Elianor one of the daughters and coheirs of John Dove of Cullercotts in the county of Northumberland, and by her had two fons Wilfrid and John; which Wilfrid fucceeded his father in both his churches of Whitehaven and Clifton. 3. *Ifabella*, married to Edmund Gibfon of Barfield in the county of Cumberland gentleman, and to him had one fon and 3 daughters.

ANDREW HUDLESTON, of Hutton John efquire, fon and heir of Wilfrid, fucceeded his father in 1728, and is the prefent owner of the family eftate. In his younger days he fpent much of his time in the ftudy of the laws in Gray's

Inn, and was called to the bar from that house in Hilary term 1728. He
hath been one of the deputy lieutenants and justices of the peace, and chair-
man at the quarter sessions, for the county of Cumberland·for near 40 years.
He married Mary daughter and sole heir of Richmond Fenton of Plumpton hall clerk, and by her hath had issue two sons, *Andrew* and *William*;
and 5 daughters, *Joyce, Mary, Julia, Isabella,* and *Katherine.* William, John,
and Katherine are all dead without issue, and lie interred in the family burying-
place in the south ile of the parish church of Graystock. Andrew, Joyce,
Mary, and Isabella are now living (1772) and unmarried. This last named
Andrew was likewise brought up to the bar at Gray's Inn, where he now
resides.

WATERMILLOCK in this parish, the seat of John Robinson esquire, sheriff
of this county in the year 1769, is (like the rest) part of the barony of Gray-.
stock; and is commonly called Newkirk parish, probably from a chapel
having been erected there, which was consecrated by bishop Oglethorp in the
year 1558 : It hath the parochial rights of baptism and burial ; and is endowed with a dwelling house and outhouses, with about ten acres of land; worth
about 7 *l* a year; a prescriptive payment out of 66 tenements amounting to
6 *l* 11 *s* 4 *d*, out of which is paid yearly to the rector of Graystock 2 *l*; surplice fees about 1 *l*; and lands purchased with two allotments of queen Anne's
bounty at Glenridding in Patterdale worth about 14 *l* *per annum :* The whole
amounting to about 26 *l* a year.

There was a chapel here before, so early as the reign of Ed. 3. but not
made parochial (as it seemeth) till the time abovementioned.

MATTERDALE and *Warthwaite* is another division within this parish ; all
holden of the barony of Graystock. Here also is a *chapel* of ease, unto
which bishop Meye in the year 1580 granted parochial rights in the following
form : " To all christian people to whom these presents shall come, John by
the providence of God bishop of Carlisle sendeth greeting in our Lord God
everlasting. Know ye, that at the reasonable suit of the whole inhabitants
of the chapelry of Matterdale, complaining, that by reason their parish
church of Graystock is so far distant from them, and from the great annoy-
ances of snow or other foul weather in the winter season in that fellish part,
they be often very sore troubled with carrying the dead corpses dying within
the said chapelry and the infants there born unto burial and christening to
their said parish church of Graystock, sometimes the weather being so foul
and stormy that they be driven to let their dead bodies remain unburied
longer time than is convenient, or else to abide that annoyance and danger in
carrying them to burial as is not reasonable, and therefore have divers times
made humble suit for remedy of their said inconveniences and griefs : We the
said bishop, with the consent of Mr. Edward Hansbie bachelor in divinity and
parson of the said parish church of Graystock, have given and granted unto
all the inhabitants which now be, or which from henceforth shall be of the
chapelry aforesaid, full authority to cause to be baptized and christened in the
                                                              chapel

chapel of Matterdale all and fingular the infants which fhall at any time hereafter be born within the faid chapelry ; and all women which within the fame fhall bring forth any child, to go to the faid chapel, and to have the prayers faid for her deliverance fet forth by public authority, which commonly hath been called the purification of women ; and that it may alfo be lawful unto the faid inhabitants from time to time hereafter to caufe their marriages to be celebrated within the fame chapel ; both the faid perfons which fhall be married or the one of them being an inhabitant and dweller within the fame chapelry ; and fuch perfons as fhall from time to time happen to die or depart this world within the faid chapelry, to bury them within the fame chapel or churchyard of the fame : Giving and granting unto the faid chapel the right to receive infants to baptifm, women to be purified, perfons to be mar-ried in the faid chapel, and all manner of perfons dying within the faid cha-pelry, to whom the laws of this realm do not deny chriftian burial, to be buried in the faid chapel or churchyard : Befeeching the Almighty, that as we do not doubt but that he hath already fanctified and hallowed the faid chapel and churchyard through the prayers of the faithful made therein and the preaching of his moft bleffed word ; fo it may pleafe him to grant unto all thofe which fhall be baptifed within the faid chapel, that they may receive remiffion of fins, perfect regeneration, and be made heirs of the kingdom of heaven ; and to fanctify the marriage of all fuch as fhall be married in the fame chapel ; and to fuch as fhall be buried in the faid chapel or churchyard to grant refurrection unto life everlafting. Thefe in no wife to prejudice or hinder the right of the parifh church of Grayftock aforefaid, nor the eftate of the faid Mr. Edward Hanfbie now parfon of the fame, or his fucceffors parfons there, in any the tithes, rights, oblations, duties, commodities, or emoluments, due unto the faid parifh church or to the faid Edward Hanfbie and his fucceffors parfons of the fame out of the faid chapelry, or the inhabi-tants of the fame or any of them from time to time there dwelling ; the righ', intereft, and eftate of which church and the faid Edward Hanfbie and his fucceffors parfons there, we do referve and fave by thefe prefents. Provided always, that the inhabitants of the faid chapelry fhall at their own proper cofts and charges (as hath been before ufed) find and maintain a good and able prieft to be refident within the faid chapelry, to minifter divine fervice and holy facraments, as fhall be allowed by us the faid bifhop and our fucceffors ; and fhall provide unto him fuch convenient dwelling and habitation within the fame chapelry; and give him fuch wages for his relief and maintenance, to the wor-thynefs of his eftate and calling, as fhall be thought meet and convenient unto us the faid bifhop and our fucceffors bifhops of Carlifle ; and fhall alfo elect, with the confent of the minifter there from time to time, an honeft perfon to be the parifh clerk of the fame chapel, and fhall give to him convenient wages for keeping the faid church and things belonging to the fame in good order, and doing other duties which appertain to the office of a clerk ; and fhall yearly elect and chufe, by the content of the faid minifter, two church-wardens and fome fidemen, to do the duties which unto their office doth be-long ; and fhall repair, maintain, and uphold the faid chapel and walls of the 'yard thereof, with all needful and convenient reparations whatfoever, and shall from time to time fee and provide that the faid chapel and churchyard be ufed with that feemly and reverend manner as becometh the houfe and place dedicated to the fervice of God; and finally fhall, from time to time, and at all-times hereafter, receive and obey all fuch injunctions, general and particular, which fhall from henceforth be given by us the faid bifhop and our fucceffors, for the fervice of God and good order to be maintained within the faid chapel and chapelry: Under which conditions, we do dedicate, the faid chapel and churchyard to the ufe aforefaid, and none otherwife. In witnefs whereof, we have to thefe prefents put the feal of our bifhoprick. Given the 30th day of October, in the year of our Lord God a thoufand five hundred and eighty, and in the 22d year of the reign of our moft gracious fovereign lady Elizabeth by the grace of God queen of England, France, and Ireland, defender of the faith, &c. and of our confecration the fourth.

To the curate of this chapel there are 34 tenements that pay yearly 2 s 6 d each. There is land anciently belonging to it of about 3 l 10 s per annum; and it hath had two allotments of 200 l each of queen Anne's bounty, and 200 l more in conjunction with 200 l given by the countefs dowager Gower; with 600 l whereof lands have been purchafed in the parifhes of Thornton and Sedbergh, of the prefent yearly value of about 23 l, and 200 l remains in the hands of the governors of the faid bounty after the rate of two per cent. intereft.

In 1716, a fmall parcel of common on the weft fide of the chapel, commonly called Butt Hills, containing about 6 roods, with confent of Henry-Charles Howard efquire lord of the manor, and of the tenants refpectively, was inclofed; whereon the reverend Robert Grifdale of St. Martin's in the Fields Weftminfter built a very handfome *fchool*, and by indenture bearing date Aug. 6, 1722, fettled upon the fame the fum of 200 l, in the hands of 13 truftees, for the benefit of a fchoolmafter or fchoolmiftrefs to be chofen by them; but rather a fchoolmiftrefs, if it can be agreed upon, for the improvement of the girls in the faid dale. On the death of truftees, or removal out of the dale (not having any eftate therein), the furvivors fhall within 3 months chufe others, whereof the perfon inheriting the eftate of the faid Mr. Grifdale's father to be one, and the perfon inheriting his brother Edward's eftate to be another. If the faid 200 l fhall fall fhort of yielding 10 l a year, or the fchoolhoufe fhall want reparation; the truftees fhall-make up the deficiency by quarteridge of the fcholars belonging to Matterdale that fhall be taught therein. If any difpute arife about the management of the fchool, upon complaint of three truftees to the chancellor of the diocefe, he fhall have power to determine the fame.

In the fchoolhoufe is a neat little ftudy, furnifhed with 189 volumes (given by Mrs. Elizabeth Grifdale of St. Martin's in the fields in 1723) for the ufe of the dale; being moft of them books in divinity.

THRELKELD

Z

THRELKELD is another chapelry and manor within the barony and parish of Grayſtock. It belonged to a family who took their name from thence, who had alſo poſſeſſions at Yanwith and Croſby Ravenſworth in Weſtmorland.

So early as the reign of king Ed. 1. *Henry de Threlkeld* obtained a grant of free warren in his eſtates in Weſtmorland (the like having probably been obtained before for the family eſtate at Threlkeld). He appears to have had the ſame grant renewed in the 14 Ed. 2.—Neverthelefs, in the 11 Ed. 2. we find that *John de Derwentwater* held this vill of the lord of Grayſtock, by homage and ſuit of court at Grayſtock; which ſeems to have been only by way of truſt in a ſettlement.

In the 30 Ed. 3. *William de Threlkeld* was owner of this manor under the Grayſtocks, and in the ſame year was ſheriff of the county of Cumberland. In the 40th of the ſame king, he paid a relief for a moiety of Yanwith, which he held of the barony of Grayſtock. In the 13 Ric. 2. *William de Threlkeld* was member of parliament for this county.

This *William* ſeems to have been ſucceeded by a collateral of the ſame name: For in the 5 Hen. 4. *William Threlkeld* then lord of Croſby Ravenſworth, couſin and heir of *William Threlkeld* knight, father of *William Threlkeld* of Ulveſby, ſon of *John*, ſon of *William*, paid his relief for two parts of the moiety of the manor of Ulveſby.

In the 10 Hen. 6. an agreement was made between Sir *Henry Threlkeld* knight lord of the manor of Threlkeld and the rector of Grayſtock, concerning the appointment of a curate of the chapel of Threlkeld (as is herein after more particularly expreſſed).

In the reign of Ed. 4. *Lancelot Threlkeld* married Margaret daughter and heir of Henry Bromflett lord Veſcy widow of John lord Clifford; and by her had iſſue,

Sir *Lancelot Threlkeld* knight, who had three daughters coheirs; one married to Thomas Dudley, with whom he had Yanwith; another married to James Pickering, with whom he had Croſby Ravenſworth; and the third *Winifred*, married to *William Pickering*, brother of the ſaid James (and both of them ſons of Sir James Pickering of Killington in Weſtmorland), with whom he had Threlkeld.

The ſaid *William Pickering* ſeems to have had a ſon *Chriſtopher Pickering* knight, who was ſheriff of Cumberland in the 33 Eliz. and the 4th and 6th of James the firſt.

It is ſaid the hall and demeſne went with a daughter to the Irtons, whoſe deſcendent James Spedding of Armathwaite eſquire now (1769) enjoys the ſame. The manor and tenants were ſold to the Lowthers of Lowther; and in the year 1635, June 16, Sir *John Lowther* of Lowther and *John Lowther* eſquire his ſon and heir apparent, in conſideration of 1360*l* agreed with the tenants for a four penny fine certain; the number of tenants ſpecified in the indenture and decree were 39, and 8 cottagers. The total of the rent is 30*l.* 16*s* 4*d*; beſides a free or quit rent of 2*s* 11*d* paid by a few of the tenants to the lord of Grayſtock. Each tenant here was obliged to find half a draught for one day ploughing; one day mowing; one day ſhearing; one day clipping.

ping, and one day falving fheep; one carriage load once in two years, but not to go above ten miles; to dig and lead two loads of peats every year: The tenants to have fufficient meat and drink when they performed thefe fervices. The cottagers to perform the fame fervices, only inftead of half a plough, they were to find one horfe with a harrow, and a footman inftead of a carriage load. The tenants are alfo bound to the lord's miln, pay the fortieth corn, and to maintain the wall and thatch of the miln to the louder. The tenants to have houfe boot, to be fet out by the lord's bailiff; peats, turves, ling, whins, limeftones, and marle, with ftones and flates for building.—But about thirteen years ago, half of the tenants bought off thefe fervices at five guineas each tenement; the miln fervice only excepted.——The widow has the whole eftate during her chafte viduity. The tenements pay 2 *d* yearly each as greenhue rent.

There has been a *chapel* here of ancient time: And in the year 1431, there was a reference to bifhop Lumley, by the rector or mafter and chaplains of the collegiate or parifh church of Grayftock on the one part, and Sir Henry Threlkeld knight lord of the manor of Threlkeld and his lay tenants on the other part, concerning the appointment of a curate in the church or chapel of Threlkeld, and the manner of tithing corn and hay, and concerning other things tithable, within the lordfhip of Threlkeld aforefaid: Whereupon, the bifhop awards, and at the requeft of both the faid parties decrees for ever to be obferved, that upon a vacancy of the curacy, the faid Sir Henry Threlkeld and his heirs, with the advice of his tenants, fhall within one month nominate a curate to the rector or mafter aforefaid, who fhall within fix days admit him if he finds him fufficient; if he finds him infufficient, he fhall then fend him to the bifhop or his official principal, for further examination; and if they find him infufficient, then the rector or mafter, with confent of his chaplains, fhall for that time nominate one to the bifhop within ten days after the rejection of the former; and if the bifhop finds this latter fufficient, he fhall admit him; otherwife, the bifhop fhall have the nomination for that turn only: —And that the rector or mafter fhall receive all the tithes, great, fmall, and mixed, within the faid lordfhip, except the tithes of corn and hay; and that he fhall pay in lieu of the tithes of corn and hay to the curate aforefaid 3*l* 17*s* 10*d*; and over and above the fame, the fum of 12*s* yearly *.

This chapel enjoys all parochial rights; and was certified in the year 1720 to the governors of queen Anne's bounty at 8*l* 16*s* 6*d*, and in the year 1747 received an augmentation of 200*l* by lot, wherewith lands were purchafed nigh Kendal of the prefent yearly value of 6*l* 10*s*.

Grisedale, or *Mungrifedale*, is another chapelry within this parifh. The hamlet is holden, like many of the reft, of the lords of Grayftock. The *chapel* is endowed with a dwelling houfe, and a fmall enclofure wherein it ftands.

---

* Entered in bifhop Smith's Regifter at Rofe, July 27, 1698, by Mr. Archdeacon Nicolfon from the original at Lowther, by permiffion of John vifcount Lonfdale.

And

And every tenement in Mungrifdale, whereof there are twenty, pays to the curate 3s 10d yearly; feven in Murray, each 1s 1d yearly; four in Boufgill, 1s 1d each; feven houfes in Mofedale, four in Gill, and four in Swinefide, 4d each; alfo there is a ftipend of 6s 8d from the caftle of Grayftock; and the intereft of 10l yearly; and 8d for every churching. It has alfo been augmented with 200l by lot in 1745, 200l given by the inhabitants in 1766, 200l given by the countefs dowager Gower in conjunction with 200l given by the governors of queen Anne's bounty in 1773; with all which fums lands have been purchafed at Blackburton and Dilliker, of the prefent yearly value of 29l.

JOHNBY, in this parifh, is a fmall demefne and manor, which formerly belonged to the *Mufgraves* of Hayton, who gave it to a younger fon, whofe heir female married one Mr. *Wyvil* of the county of York, who fold it to Mr. *Williams*, who came out of Wales and was fteward at Grayftock caftle; who had four daughters coheirs, the eldeft of whom was married to Sir *Edward Hafel* knight, who for her purparty had Johnby; the fecond married to John Winder of Lorton counfellor at law, father to the late Williams Winder of Dufton efquire; the third to Mr. Relph of Cockermouth; and the fourth to Dr. Gibbon dean of Carlifle.

Of this Mr. *Williams* there is the following epitaph in Grayftock church :

"GUILLIELMUS WILLIAMS de St. Nicolao in comitatu Glamorgan, gene-
" rofus (toga fumpta virili) fub fignis Car. I. R. A. conftanter militavit.
" Dein, lapfis aliquot annis, Cumbriam aufpicatò veniens, ingeffit fe curis
" tam diu fraterno confilio profpere euntibus, quam mox turbidis quorundam
" livore. Ducitur fibi interea uxor BARBARA, chariffima, pia. Hic, qua-
" tuor filiabus (intercifis aliquot) beatus, poftquam domi biennium morbo
" contabuit, charus amicis, Deo animam pie conceffit (cunctis fuis mœrenti-
" bus) 12 Januarii, A. D. 1679."

LITTLE BLENCOW gives name to a family which is of ancient ftanding in thefe parts. Their firft feat was at *Great Blencow* clofe by, but on the other fide of the river Petterell, where they ftill have a demefne; and where the ruins of an old tower are to be feen. The prefent manfion houfe, within this parifh of Grayftock, was purchafed from the family of Lyddal. Here is a ruinous *chapel*, with a yard belonging to it, in the midft whereof is a large receiver for pure fpring water which bubbles up plentifully in the bottom of it, and probably was ufed in former times as a baptiftery. Over the door are the arms of Blencow cut in ftone, viz. Azure, a bend Argent charged with three chaplets of Rofes Gules; with this motto, *Quorfum vivere mori, mori vita*+.

Near

+ This is according to the blazoning of their arms in the heralds office, and to the blazoning exhibited by Mr. Machel from a vifitation of Cumberland in 1580. But from the original grant of thefe arms by the lord Grayftock in the 30 Ed 3. it appears that the colours have been mif-taken. Which grant, being curious (as proving the power of the great barons to grant arms in ancient times) it is thought proper here to fubjoin, " To all to whom thefe prefents fhall come
" to.

Near the houfe, by the highway weftward, is an inclofed burying-place for the conveniency of the family, with a ftone crofs erected, whereon the arms of Blencow are alfo engraven.

1. The firft of the name that we have met with was *Adam de Blencowe* aforefaid, who ferved in the French wars in the reign of king Edward the third, under the banner of William de Grayftock his fuperior lord. He was twice married; his firft wife's name was Emma, by whom he had three fons; *William*, who died in the lifetime of his father unmarried; *Thomas*; and *John*, whofe wife's name was Johanna.

2. *Thomas de Blencowe* fucceeded his father; and married Elizabeth daughter and heir of Nicholas Vefpont, by whom he had iffue,

3. *William de Blencow*, who married Johanna Brifco in the reign of king Hen. 6. and by her had iffue,

4. *Richard*, who lived in the reign of king Edward the fourth.

5. *Chriftopher*, fon of Richard, had iffue *Richard*, and a daughter *Ifabella* married to James Halton.

6. *Richard Blencowe* efquire married Eleanor Crackenthorp, and by her had iffue *Anthony*, *Chriftopher* and *Cuthbert* who both died unmarried, *Elizabeth* married to Richard Hutton, and *Marzen* married to Matthew Bee.

7. *Anthony Blencowe* efquire, fon and heir of Richard, married Winifrid Dudley; and by her had iffue *Richard*, *Anthony* provoft of Oriel college in Oxford, who left 1300*l* to the faid college; and another fon *George*, who had iffue a fon George who died unmarried.

8. *Richard Blencowe* efquire had iffue *Henry*, and another fon *Richard* who died unmarried.

9. *Henry Blencowe*, fon and heir of Richard, was knighted by king James the firft. He married Grace fifter of the firft Sir Richard Sandford of Howgill caftle in Weftmorland; and by her had iffue, *Chriftopher*; *John*, who had two daughters, Elizabeth married to Henry Thompfon of Hollin hall near Rippon, and Anne married firft to George Barwick and then to major Farrer; and two other fons *Anthony* and *Henry*, who both died unmarried.

10. Sir *Chriftopher Blencowe* knight, fon and heir of Sir Henry, married Mary Robinfon of Rookby hall in the county of York; and by her had iffue *Henry* who died before his father unmarried, *Chriftopher*, *Thomas* who died unmarried, and four daughters, *Mary*, *Frances*, *Margaret*, and *Catharine*.

11. *Chriftopher Blencowe* efquire, fon and heir of Sir Chriftopher, married Anne eldeft daughter and coheir of William Layton of Dalemain efquire, and by her had iffue,

" to be feen or heard; William baron of Grayftock, lord of Morpeth, wifheth health in the
" Lord: Know ye that I have given and granted to Adam de Blencowe an efcutcheon Sable with a
" bend cloffelted (or barred) Argent and Azure, with three chaplets Gules; and with a Creft
" cloffelted Argent and Azure, of my arms. To have and to hold to the faid Adam and his heirs
" for ever. And I the faid William and my heirs will warrant to the faid Adam and his heirs the
" arms aforefaid. In witnefs whereof, I have to thefe letters patent fet my feal. Written at the
" caftle of Morpeth the 26th day of February in the 30th year of the reign of king Edward the
" third after the conqueft."

12. *Henry*

12. *Henry Blencowe* efquire, who married to his firft wife Dorothy daughter and heir of George Siffon of Penrith gentleman ; and by her had iffue (befides three fons that died young) *Chriftopher*, *Dorothy* married to Tobias Croft M. A. vicar of Kirkby Lonfdale, *Bridget* married to Mr. Reay of Newcaftle, and *Mary* who died unmarried. Of this Dorothy, daughter of George Siffon, there is the following epitaph on a brafs plate in Penrith church :

" Subtus inhumata jacent corpora Dorotheæ uxoris Henrici Blencowe de
" Blencowe in comitatu Cumbriæ armigeri, filiæ unicæ et hæredis Georgii
" Siffon de Penrith generofi ; et trium filiorum, Henrici, Georgii, et Georgii.
" Illa ab hac luce migravit 29 die Octobris A. D. 1707, Ætatis vero 32 :
" Poft fe relinquens filium Chriftophorum ; filias vero tres, Dorotheam, Bri-
" gettam, Mariam. Dum in vivis, omnia fœminæ Chriftianæ, confortis fidæ,
" et matris indulgentiffimæ, officia præftitit. Hoc pofteros non nefcire voluit
" Henricus Blencowe fuperftes, qui pro illibati amoris monumento laminam
" hanc poni curavit."

The faid Henry, to his fecond wife, married Elizabeth daughter of William Todd of Wath in the county of York, and by her had iffue *Henry* ; and a fecond fon *William*, who married the eldeft furviving daughter of Ferdinando Latus efquire counfellor at law, and had iffue George who died abroad, Eliza-beth, William-Ferdinand, Henry who died an infant, and John ; alfo a third fon *Peter*, who married Frances Benn of Whitehaven, and had iffue Eliza-beth and Henry.

The faid Henry Blencowe died in 1721, and was fucceeded by his fon,

13. *Chriftopher Blencowe* efquire, counfellor at law ; who died upon the circuit in 1723, aged 25, and unmarried : Whereupon the next heir male of the family fucceeded, viz. his brother in-law,

14. *Henry Blencowe* efquire, who married Mary Prefcott of Theby, and by her had iffue *Henry Prefcott*, and a daughter *Mary* now living and unmarried.

15. *Henry-Prefcott Blencowe* efquire, the prefent owner of the family eftate, as yet unmarried.

The tenants are about 60 in number ; who pay about 30*l* yearly cuftomary rent, and a twenty-penny fine.

In this whole parifh of Grayftock, in the year 1747, it was certified, that there were 347 families ; of which, quakers 15, prefbyterians 16, papift one (viz. at the caftle).

PARISH OF DACRE.

THE parifh of DACRE confifts of the hamlets or conftablewicks of Dacre, Soulby, Newbiggin, Stainton, and Great Blencow. It is noted for having given name to, or rather perhaps received its name from, the barons of *Dacre*, who continued there for many ages. It is mentioned by Bede, as having a monaftery there in his time ; as alfo by Malmefbury, for being

the place where Conftantine king of the Scots and Eugenius king of Cumberland put themfelves and their kingdoms under the protection of the Englifh
king Athelftan.

The true name of the family was *D'Acre*, from one of them who ferved at
the fiege of *Acre* (or Ptolemais) in the Holy-Land ; who from his atchievements
there having received the name of the place, imparted the fame at his return
to his habitation in Cumberland.

I. The firft of the name that hath occurred to us (who is one generation
further back than in any of the Dacre pedigrees that we have met with) was
RANULPH DE DACRE, lord of a moiety of the manor of Orton in Weftmorland;
who, with THOMAS DE MUSGRAVE owner of the other moiety, obtained a charter
in the 6 Ed. 1. for a market at Orton. The Dacres continued in the poffeffion of
the faid moiety till the reign of king James the firft, when they fold the fame
to the tenants. He had a fon and heir,

II. WILLIAM DE DACRE knight; who married Joan daughter of Sir William Buet knight. He died in the 12 Ed. 2. leaving iffue,

III. RANULPH DE DACRE; who married Margaret daughter and heir of
Thomas de Multon lord of Gilfland, and who was in right of his wife the ninth
lord of that barony who had fate in parliament. This Thomas de Multon's
anceftor came to this barony by marriage of the heirefs of Vaux (de Vallibus);
and was fon and heir of Ada one of the two daughters and coheirs of Sir Hugh
de Morvil. Morvil's anceftor married the heirefs of Engain, who married the
heirefs D'Eftrivers, whofe father Robert D'Eftrivers married a daughter of
Ranulph de Mefchiens firft lord of Cumberland.—This Ranulph de Dacre
died in the 13 Ed. 3. and Margaret his widow died in the 35th of the fame
king.

IV. WILLIAM DE DACRE, eldeft fon of Ranulph by his wife Margaret, fucceeded his father, but died in the life-time of his mother, without iffue ; and
was fucceeded in his paternal inheritance by his brother and heir,

V. THOMAS DE DACRE, who alfo died in the life-time of his mother, without iffue ; and was fucceeded by the third brother,

VI. RANULPH DE DACRE, who was in the life-time of his elder brother
rector of the church of Preftecotes. Upon his mother's death he became the
tenth parliamentary lord of Gillefland. He died in the 49 Ed. 3. without iffue ;
and was fucceeded by the fourth brother,

VII. HUGH DE DACRE, who died in the 7th of Ric. 2. leaving a fon and
heir, '

VIII. WILLIAM DE DACRE. In the 18 Ric. 2. *William de Dacre*, fon and
                                                                    heir

heir of *Hugh de Dacre*, brother and heir of *Ranulph de Dacre*, held a burgage in Appleby of the king *in capite*, rendering to the king *ad hufgabulum* (an houfe rent) of 4 *d* yearly. He died in the 23 Ric. 2. as appears by the regifter book of Lanercoft.

IX. THOMAS DE DACRE, fon of William, married Phillippa daughter of Ralph Nevil firft earl of Weftmorland, and by her had iffue, 1. *Thomas*, his eldeft fon, who died in his father's life-time, leaving only a daughter. 2. *Ranulph*, who (as his next heir male) fucceeded his father in the barony of Gillefland, as appears by the regifter book of Lanercoft, where he is ftyled the 14th parliamentary lord of Gillefland: He was flain in the battle of Towton field, and died without iffue. 3. *Humphrey*, who fucceeded his brother Ranulph, and was anceftor of the lord Dacre of the north, barons of Gilfland, and afterwards of Grayftock.

X. THOMAS DE DACRE knight, eldeft fon (as aforefaid) of the laft Thomas, married a daughter of Richard Bowes efquire ; and dying before his father, left iffue *Johan* his only child.

XI. JOHAN lady Dacre fucceeded her grandfather as heir general of the family, and inheritrix of the eftate at Dacre. She was married to Sir *Richard Fynes* knight, who in her right was declared lord Dacre of the South, and became poffeffed of the manors of Dacre, Kirk-Ofwald, Blackill, Glaffonby, Staffold, Lazonby, Brackenthwaite, and Newbiggin in the county of Cumberland ; and alfo of the barony of Barton, and manors of Patterdale and Martindale, with the foreft of Martindale and Grifedale in the county of Weftmorland : together with feveral rents, fifhings, lands, tenements, and hereditaments within the faid counties. She died in the 1ft of Hen. 7.

XII. THOMAS FYNES knight, fon of Sir Richard Fynes and Johan lady Dacre, died before his father and mother ; leaving iffue,

XIII. THOMAS FYNES lord Dacre, who died in the 25 Hen. 8.

XIV. THOMAS FYNES, knight, died in the life-time of his father ; leaving iffue,

XV. THOMAS FYNES lord Dacre ; who was attainted of felony, and died in the 34 Hen. 8. leaving iffue *Thomas*, *Gregory*, and *Margaret*.

XVI. THOMAS FYNES, eldeft fon of Thomas late lord Dacre, died in the 1 Mar. without iffue.

XVII. GREGORY FYNES, fecond fon of Thomas lord Dacre, was reftored in the 1 Eliz. to the honour of lord Dacre ; and died without iffue in the 36 Eliz.

XVIII. MAR-

XVIII. MARGARET, fifter and heir of Gregory lord Dacre, was married to
Sampfon Lennard of Chevening in Kent efquire.   This Margaret laying claim to
the title upon her brother's death, queen Elizabeth referred the matter to the
lords Burleigh and Howard, to examine and inquire if her claim was good,
which they both allowed it to be after mature confideration : but this affair not
being quite finifhed before the queen's death, it was again laid before commiffioners appointed in the fucceeding reign ; and fhe was then, in the 2 Ja. 1.
allowed and declared baronefs Dacre.   She died in the 9 Ja. 1.

XIX. HENRY LENNARD lord Dacre, fon and heir of Sampfon Lennard and
Margaret lady Dacre, married Chryfogona daughter of Richard Baker of Siffing-
hurft in Kent; by whom he had three fons, *Richard, Edward,* and *Fynes,*
whereof the two laft died without iffue ; and four daughters, *Margaret, Penelope,*
Philadelphia, and *Barbara.*   This Henry died in the 14 Ja. 1.

XX. RICHARD lord Dacre married firft Elizabeth daughter and coheir of
Sir Arthur Throgmorton, by whom he had four fons, *Francis, Richard, Tho-*
mas, and *Henry;* which three laft died without children.   His fecond wife was
Dorothy daughter of Dudley lord North, by whom he had a fon named *Richard,*
who took the furname of Barret ; and a daughter *Catharine* wife of Chaloner
Chute of the Vine in Hampfhire.   This Richard lord Dacre died in the 6 Cha. 1.
at his feat at Hurftmonceaux, and was buried in the parifh church there.

XXI. FRANCIS lord Dacre married Elizabeth fifter and fole heir of Paul
vifcount Bayning ; and had iffue *Thomas* ; *Francis* who died a bachelor ; and
Henry who left iffue Margaret, Anne, and Catharine, and three daughters,
Philadelphia married to Daniel Obrien vifcount Clare, *Elizabeth* married to John
Barbafon earl of Meath, and *Margaret* who died unmarried.   This Francis died
in the 14 Cha. 2. and was buried at Chevening in Kent.

XXII. THOMAS LENNARD lord Dacre married the lady Anne Fitz-roy, natural daughter of king Charles the fecond by Barbara duchefs of Cleveland, and
in the 26 Cha. 2. was created earl of Suffex.   He had iffue two fons, *Charles*
and *Henry,* who died in their infancy ; and two daughters *Barbara* and *Anne,*
who were his heirs.   He died in 1715, and in the year following his widow
and the faid two daughters fold Dacre and all other the premifes above-mentioned in Cumberland and Weftmorland for the fum of 15,000l to Sir Chriftopher Mufgrave of Edenhall baronet ; who foon after conveyed the caftle and
manor of Dacre (inter alia) to *Edward Hafell* efquire the prefent proprietor.
The title of lord Dacre, upon the death of the faid earl of Suffex, was held in
abeyance between the two daughters, till the lady *Barbara,* who married Charles
Skelton efquire a general officer in the fervice of the king of France, dying without iffue in the year 1740, the lady *Anne* her fifter then became fole heir to her
father and lady Dacre.   She married firft Richard Barret-Lennard efquire, to
whom fhe had a fon *Thomas Barret-Lennard* the prefent lord Dacre.   Her fecond hufband was Henry lord Teynham, to whom fhe had *Charles* who died

in

in 1755 leaving feveral children, and *Henry* a clergyman who married the daughter of William Chetwynd efquire, and a daughter *Anne*.

The prefent lord Dacre was born in 1716, married Anne daughter of Sir John Pratt knight and fifter of the prefent lord Camden, and had iffue a daughter *Anna Barbara* who died in the year 1749.

The CHURCH of Dacre is dedicated to St. Andrew, and feems to have been appropriated to the monaftery which Bede fpeaks of as exifting there in his time, tho' there are now no veftiges thereof remaining. In pope Nicholas's Valor in 1291, the rectory and vicarage of Dacre are rated feparately, viz. the rectory at 50*l*, and the vicarage at 9*l* 2*s* 8*d*. In Edward the fecond's Valor in 1318 they are eftimated as being united, viz. the church of Dacre with the vicarage 13*l* 6*s* 8*d*. As to the total annihilation of that monaftery, perhaps we need go no further than to the Scots to account for it. However, the church from the time not long after pope Nicholas's furvey appears to have been rectorial, and fo to have continued till late in the reign of king Henry the eighth, when (as tradition reports) it was given to the college of Kirk-Ofwald and totally appropriated thereto.

In 1296, on the death of *Nicholas de Appleby* the laft incumbent, Sir William de Daker prefents *Henry de Harcla* to the rectory of Dacre, to whom the bifhop firft grants the living by fequeftration, and afterwards gives him inftitution being then a fubdeacon. Tho' ftyled clerk, yet he feems only to have been an acolite when firft prefented.

In 1328, *William de Burgh* was rector of Dacre, and a truftee in a fettlement by the lord Dacre.

In 1359, *William Bowett* rector of Dacre made his will, and therein bequeathed his body to be buried in the quire of St. Andrew's church in Daker; and was fucceeded by *Walter de Loutheburgh*, on a prefentation by Sir William de Dacre. And the bifhop grants him a licence of three years abfence, making a decent allowance to a curate, and paying to the bifhop 10*l* fterling each year for the faid licence.—In 1369 he exchanged his rectory with *Peter de Stapilton* rector of Waldnewton in the diocefe of Lincoln, with confent of the refpective patrons and ordinaries. And in the next year Peter exchanges with *William de Orchards* rector of Whitburn in the diocefe of Durham, who is prefented by Ranulph de Dacre lord of Gilfland. And the faid William de Orchards again refigns, in favour of *John Ingelby*.

After the diffolution of the religious houfes, *John Brockbank* in the year 1571 was collated by the bifhop to the vicarage of Dacre, vacant by the refufal or neglect of *Roland Dawfon* the late vicar to fubfcribe the 39 articles according to act of parliament.

In 1574, the fame bifhop (Barnes) collates Sir *Richard Sutton* clerk.

In 1582, on the death of Richard Sutton, Sir *William Martin* was collated. In whofe time, viz. in 1586, a leafe of the rectory and tithes was granted by the crown to Thomas Hammond for 21 years, he paying to the vicar an annual ftipend of 8*l*.

In

In 1591, on the death of William Martin, Sir *Thomas Wrae* was collated by bishop Meye.

In 1742, *William Richardson* clerk was presented under the great seal, and instituted accordingly.

In 1768, on William Richardson's death, *William Cowper*, M. A. was instituted on a like presentation under the great seal.

The aforesaid stipend of 8 *l* a year was the whole endowment, until about the year 1669, when Mr. William Mawson of Timpaurin gave by his will a lease of the tithes of Slegill and Thrimby in Westmorland to the vicars of Penrith and Dacre equally between them. The trustees, with consent of all parties, separated the tithes, and the vicar of Penrith had the tithes of Slegill, and the vicar of Dacre the tithes of Thrimby, each in a distinct lease. This at first was a considerable augmentation to the church of Dacre. But afterwards the village of Thrimby was mostly bought up by the first lord viscount Lonsdale, and the lands taken into Lowther park. Which lease being suffered to run out, the said tithes were sold by the dean and chapter of Carlisle to the said lord Lonsdale for 200 *l*; which sum they gave in augmentation of the vicarage, unto which the governors of queen Anne's bounty gave 200 *l* more, wherewith lands were purchased at Black Burton, of the present yearly value of 21 *l*.

The church is a neat and elegant building; and the tradition goes, that it was erected by the Dacres, instead of a very mean one about half a mile distant. (Perhaps out of the ruins of the monastery above-mentioned.)

On the north-side of the communion table, is a stone pourtraiture of a knight, with his legs crossed; probably one of the old lords Dacre. The arms of that noble family are frequent in the windows; both single, and quartered with the Veteriponts and Cliffords.

At each corner of the churchyard, there stands a bear and ragged staff, cut in stone; which bishop Nicolson says looks like some of the atchievements of the honourable family that so long resided at the neighbouring castle : which has since been illustrated by a very worthy descendent of the family; who supposes they were cognizances taken by the family, on account of their claim to the hereditary foresterfhip of Englewood forest. And the more so, as one sees those jagged branches over and over introduced in the chapel at Naward castle, which is so rich with arms and cognizances, and where this jagged branch is in some places even thrown across the Dacres arms fess-wise. Ranulph de Mefchines lord of Cumberland granted this office of forefter to Robert D'Eftrivers lord of Burgh upon Sands in fee. His arms were ; Argent, 3 bears Sable. The heiress D'Eftrivers married Engain. The heiress of Engain married Morvill. The heiress of Morvill married Multon. And Dacre married the heiress of Multon, and by her had the same right as the others to the foresterfhip of Englewood : which was so honourable, and gave so great command, that there is no wonder the family should wish by every means to set forth their claim to it, and (amongst others) by cognizances taken in allusion thereunto ; especially as the crown about this time seems to have interfered with them in regard to

4

this

this right. And surely nothing could be more naturally adapted to this idea, than this bear, which was the arms of their anceſtor, the firſt grantee of the office. And the branch of a tree, which ſeems ſo very alluſive to foreſts and woods, agrees with the ſame notion. And it is not improbable, but that this might originally be a badge uſed by Robert D'Eſtrivers himſelf; and that he choſe the bears in his arms, becauſe they were inhabitants of foreſts.

Matthew Brown late of Whitehaven gave to his executor Dr. Joſeph Brown of Queen's College in Oxford 55*l*, to which the ſaid Dr. Brown added 10*l* more; the intereſt of 60*l* thereof to ſupport a petty ſchool, and the intereſt of the remaining 5*l* to go to the poor of the townſhip of Dacre. John Dawſon left 5*l* to the ſame uſes equally. Mr. Troutbeck late of Corbridge left 50*l*, the intereſt thereof to be diſtributed yearly at the diſcretion of a Troutbeck of that family, as long as there are any ſuch at Blencow; and on failure of ſuch, by the miniſter and churchwardens. They had alſo here ancient poor-ſtock of 4*l*. All which ſums together amount in the whole to 124*l*. And a convenient purchaſe offering of an eſtate at Motherby holden under the dean and chapter of Carliſle, they purchaſed the ſame for 144*l* 10*s*. Edward Haſell of Dalemain eſquire gave the ſum of 20*l* 4*s*, to make up the deficiency, and took the purchaſe in his own name, and is to direct the uſes thereof.

DALEMAIN, within this pariſh, is holden of the barony of Grayſtock by cornage and other ſervices, as a fee of the ſame. Mr. Denton ſays, the firſt that he had read of who poſſeſſed the ſame was *John de Morvil* in the reign of Hen. 2. *Nigell* his ſon in the 10th of king John; and *Walter* ſon of Nigell in the 38 Hen. 3.

In the reign of the ſame king Henry the third, Sir *Richard de Layton* knight was lord thereof, in whoſe name and family it continued for many generations. One of whom, *William Layton*, in the time of king Henry the ſixth, by his firſt wife (who was of the name of Tunſtal) had 28 children; and by his ſecond wife (who was ſiſter of Sir Lancelot Threlkeld) had two more. Of this family, *William Layton* was ſheriff of Cumberland in the 5 Cha. 1. and again in the 20 Cha. 2. At length the iſſue male failing, the eſtate came to ſix daughters coheirs, and was ſold to Sir *Edward Haſell* knight.—The arms of Layton were; Argent, a feſs between ſix croſs croſslets Sable.

The ſaid Sir *Edward Haſell* married to his firſt wife Jane eldeſt daughter of Sir Timothy Fetherſtonhaugh of Kirk Oſwald knight, by whom he had no iſſue. His ſecond wife was Dorothy eldeſt daughter of William Williams of Johnby hall, by whom he had iſſue William, Edward, and John.

Of his firſt wife, there is the following monumental inſcription on a braſs plate within the rails of the communion table in the church of Dacre:

Here lies the body of Mrs Jane Haſell, *eldeſt daughter of* Sir Timothy Fetherſtonhaugh *of* Kirk-Oſwald *knight, who was beheaded for his loyalty to king* Charles. *She was firſt married to* Bernard Kirkbride *eſquire, and after married to* Edward Haſell *eſquire. Born, May* 14, 1629. *And died July* 18, 1695.

OF

'Of himfelf, there is a marble monument on the wall on the north-fide of the chancel, with this infcription:

Near this place lies the body of Sir Edward Hafell *knight, juftice of the peace, and deputy lieutenant of the county of* Cumberland; *high fheriff in* 1682; *elected knight of the fhire for the fame* Anno 1701. *He was twice married; firft, to* Jane *eldeft daughter of Sir* Timothy Fetherftonhaugh *of* Kirk-Ofwald *in the faid county knight, but had no iffue by her. His fecond wife was* Dorothy *eldeft daughter of* William Williams *of* Johnby *hall in the faid county gentleman, by whom he had three fons* Williams, Edward, *and* John. *Having always been inclined to do juftice, to love mercy, and promote peace, and lived a virtuous and fober life, he died the twelfth day of* September 1707, *in the fixty-firft year of his age.—To whofe memory the faid* Dorothy *his widow hath caufed this monument to be erected.*

Of the faid three fons, *Williams* and *John* died unmarried. *Edward,* the prefent proprietor of Dalemain, married Julia daughter of Sir Chriftopher Mufgrave of Edenhall baronet; by whom he has iffue *Williams, Edward, Chriftopher,* and *John;* and three daughters, *Julia, Jane,* and *Mary.*

Their Arms are; Or, on a fefs Azure, three crefcents Argent, between three hazel flips proper.

At GREAT BLENCOW in this parifh a free grammar fchool was founded and endowed by Mr. Thomas Burbank in the 19 Eliz. unto which he gave a meffuage or burgage in Grayftock in the county of Cumberland; one meffuage and tenement, 3 roods of land, and one rood of meadow at Weftpurye alias Paulefpurye, one other meffuage and tenement in Brixworth, and 3 clofes of pafture ground in Geddington, all in the county of Northampton: to be 8 feoffees, who by writing indented under their hands and feals fhall nominate a fchoolmafter; and as the feoffees die away, two of the furvivors, or the heir of the furvivor, fhall make new feoffments to others being inhabitants within Great Blencow or Little Blencow. The feoffees may fell the Northamptonfhire lands, and buy others in Cumberland or any adjoining county. The lands were then worth 10 *l* a year, and are now let at 50*l* or upwards.—Befides the lands aforefaid, the founder gave 300 *l;* 50*l* whereof was laid out in building the fchool, 50 *l* more put into one Tolfon's hand and loft, 100*l* more laid out in a rent charge out of Yanwath hall of 6*l per annum,* 20*l* loft upon a mortgage of one William Lazonby's lands in Skelton, 45*l* more lent to Mr. Blencow, 26*l* to Henry Stephenfon, 5*l* to Henry Cockburn, which three laft fums with 4*l* more were all loft.

In this parifh in 1747 it was certified that there were 151 families; of which, quakers 4, prefbyterians 3, and papifts one.

PARISH OF SKELTON.

SKELTON, *Scale-town,* is a village in the foreft of Englewood, in that place where of ancient time the country people that had their fheep, fwine, and milk

beafts

beasts agisted in the forest, had certain *scales*, shields, or little cottages to rest in, whilst they gathered the summer-profits of such goods. And about the time of Hen. 1. the Boyvills then-lords of Levington first planted an habitation there for themselves, and afterwards set some tenants there. It continued in the heir male of that-family until the death of Randolph de Levington. And his daughter and heir Hawise, wife of Sir Eustace Baliol knight, dying without issue, the Boyvills lands in Levington, Kirk-Andrews, and Skelton were divided among the six sisters of Ranulph, aunts and next heirs to the said Hawise, for the seigniory thereof. Howbeit, their father Richard and his ancestors had given forth before that descent divers parts of the same in frank marriage to them and others to whom it descended.

The purpart of Euphemia, the eldest, wife of Richard Kirkbride, continued in her blood six descents; then Walter Kirkbride sold it to Robert Parving: Sir Adam Parving, sister's son to the said Robert, sold it to John Denton of Cardew; and his posterity enjoyed it four descents, until they sold it to the Southaics; who held it three or four descents, and then John Southaics sold it to the customary tenants.

The second part fell to Margery wife of Robert de Hampton; whose grand-child William Lockard son of Symon Lockard sold the same to John Seaton; whose son Christopher Seaton forfeited his right to king Edward the first; and the said king gave it to Robert de Clifford lord of Westmorland, in whose blood it remained till George earl of Cumberland sold it to the inhabitants.

The third portion was allotted to Isabel wife of Patrick Southaic, son of Gilbert, son of Gospatric de Workington; from which Patrick it descended to John Southaic, who sold it to the customary tenants there.

The fourth part one Walter Corry held in the right of Eva his wife; but their son and heir, taking part with Robert Bruce and the Scots against the king, forfeited his estate, which the king granted to one William Marmion.

The fifth coheir Julian, wife of Patric Trump, had issue another Patric Trump, who sold that part to Robert Tillioll knight.

The sixth portion fell to Agnes wife of Walter Twinham knight, who had issue Adam, father to Walter the younger; and he sold it to Walter Kirkbride. Amongst the knights fees in Cumberland, in the 35 Hen. 8. it is found, that John Southaic held 14 messuages, 80 acres of arable land, 20 acres of meadow, 200 acres of pasture, 100 acres of wood, and a miln, with the appurtenances, in Skelton, of the king *in capite* by knight's service, with homage and fealty: and that the vill of Skelton pays yearly to the king 4*s* 6*d* cornage, by the hands of the sheriff of Cumberland.

In the 7 Eliz. Sir Thomas Dacre knight lord Dacre of Gilsland and Elizabeth his wife granted by fine the manor of Skelton (amongst other particulars), and the adwowson of the rectory of Skelton, to Thomas Daws and others, during the life of the said Elizabeth.

That part of the seigniory which remained to the Cliffords, after they had sold the tenants free, descended to Elizabeth daughter and sole heir of Henry Clifford earl of Cumberland, who was married to Richard first lord Clifford of Lanesborough, afterwards earl of Burlington; from whom it descended to the late earl of Burlington, who dying in 1750 his whole English estate came to his only daughter the marchioness of Hartington, who thereby brought this part into the duke of Devonshire's family, who receive about 3*l* 12*s* 6*d* quit rents.

The other part of this lordship belongs at present to Walter Fletcher of Hutton hall esquire.

In 1767, an act of parliament passed for dividing and inclosing the common and several waste grounds within this manor and parish of Skelton. And after quarries, watering places, roads, drains, watercourses, and one thirteenth part to the rector in lieu of tithes, are set out ; one sixteenth part of the residue is assigned to the said lords equally to be divided between them, in lieu and full discharge of all seignioral right (royalties excepted).

The CHURCH of Skelton, according to bishop Nicolson, is dedicated to St. Mary ; according to Dr. Todd, to St. Michael. And there seems to be ground for the two different opinions. Upon one of the two bells belonging to this church is an inscription, *Ave* Maria *gratiæ plena* ; on the other, *Sancte* Michael *ora pro nobis*. And the difference perhaps may be thus accounted for. When the feast of the dedication of the church (which originally was on the day sacred to the Saint to whom the church was dedicated) happened to be at an inconvenient season, as in seed-time or harvest, it became usual to transfer it to the most vacant time of the year, about Michaelmas, when the harvest was got in. And king Hen. 8th's injunctions required all the feasts of dedication to be kept at that season. Hence in many churches, by length of time, St. Michael hath obtained the reputation of the tutelar saint ; more churches being supposed to be dedicated to him, than to any other saint in the calendar.

The church is rectorial, and is valued in the king's books at 43*l* 2*s* 8¼*d*. The present yearly value about 130*l*, exclusive of the benefit to arise by the allotment of common.

In the year 1291, *Adam de Levington* was rector ; who in that year assisted the archdeacon in valuing the livings in the diocese of Carlisle.

In 1305, upon the death of the said Adam de Levington, *Nicholas de Kirkbride* was presented unanimously (but by various letters of presentation) by Sir Richard de Kirkbride and Sir Robert Tyllioll knights, Christopher de Seton, Walter de Corry, Adam de Twynham, Gilbert de Sothayk, Patric Tromp, and Matilda de Carrigg. Hereupon an inquisition *de jure patronatus* reports, that the advowson descended to Helwise daughter and heir to Sir Ralph de Levington, whose heirs the present presenters are ; except Sir Robert Tyllioll, who claims by a pretended grant from the said Patric Tromp. But all agreeing in the person presented, he was instituted accordingly.

In 1317, on Nicholas de Kirkbride's death, Sir *William de Kirkeby* was presented by the several presentations of king Edward the second, Sir Richard de Kirkbride, and the rest.

In 1322, Sir *Symon de Kyrkeby* was collated by the bishop upon a lapse, and had a dispensation for 3 years following his studies abroad.

5   In

In 1333, Sir *Simon de Semcer*, rector of Skelton, had a dispensation for 3 years absence.

In 1342, Sir *David de Wallore* was presented to the vacant rectory of Skelton by Sir Robert Parving knight.

In 1358, on the resignation of Sir *John Parving* rector of Skelton, *Robert Parving* clerk was presented by Adam Parving knight.

In 1368, king Edward the third, in right of the infant heir of Richard Kirkbride, presented one Sir *John Miles* to the rectory.

In 1377, on the death of Sir *Adam de Armstrong* rector of Skelton, Ralph baron of Grayftock presents Sir *John Fox* chaplain, who is instituted accordingly.

In 1412, *Adam de Aglionby* rector of Skelton furrenders certain lands to Ralph lord Grayftock.

In 1561, the queen's commissioners for ecclesiastical affairs within the province of York, viz.' the lord archbishop of York, the earl of Rutland, and others, declared *Hugh Hodgson* rector of Skelton to be deprived, on his obstinate refusal to take the oath of fupremacy : and thereupon institution was given to *Henry Dacre*, A. B. presented by Sir William Dacre knight lord of Dacre, Grayftock, and Gilfland.

In 1566, the whole rectory of Skelton, with the glebe lands, was granted by the lady Elizabeth Dacre, to John Lamplowe for 16 years, if Sir Henry Dacre clerk parson of the said rectory shall fo long live and continue parson there.

In 1579, a caveat was entered upon a grant made of the next avoidance of this church, to *Ambrose Hetherington*, B. D. (then vicar of Kendal) by Philip earl of Surry and the lady Anne his wife, and the lord William Howard and the lady Elizabeth his wife.

In 1597, Mr. Henry Dacre resigned the rectory, into which *Leonard Scott*, M. A. was instituted on a presentation from Christopher Pickering of Threlkeld esquire, by grant of John Southwyke esquire and Francis Southwyke his son and heir apparent.

In 1607, Francis Southwyke esquire sold the advowson of this rectory to Corpus Christi college in Oxford, who have ever since presented by trustees for that purpose appointed.

In 1623, a caveat was entred by Sir E. Musgrave knight, on the death of the aforesaid Lancelot Scott; but *Leonard Milburn*, M. A. was instituted on a presentation by Daniel Fearclough, D. D. and other trustees for the college. He was son to bishop Milburn, and was ejected by Cromwell's commissioners in 1653; and was restored on the return of king Charles the second.

In 1673, on Leonard Milburn's death, *Nathanael Cole*, M. A. was presented by Richard Busher and Catharine his wife.

In 1683, on the cession of Mr. Cole, *William Ward*, M. A. was presented by Robert Newton and William Gilliflower.

In 1711, on Mr. Ward's death, *Richard Nelmes*, M. A. was presented by Thomas Porter, B. D. W. Adams, and Matthew Adams of the university of Oxford.

In 1714, Richard Nelmes, M. A. resigned; and *John Morland*, M. A. was presented by the same patrons.

In

In 1748, on the death of John Morland, *Peter Peckard*, M. A. was inftituted on the prefentation of Gilbert Jackfon of Titchfield, D. D. John Thompfon of Corpus Chrifti college in Oxford, B. D. and John Hefter of Oxford yeoman.

In 1760, on the ceffion of Peter Peckard, *Samuel Starky*, D. D. was inftituted on the prefentation of Charles Hall, D. D. H. Pinnell, John Forde, John Huifh, and John Baker, all of the fame college.

There was a *chantry* in the church of Skelton, which feems to have been pretty largely endowed. King Ed. 6. by letters patent bearing date Sep. 7. in the 2d year of his reign, granted to *William Ward* of London gentleman, and *Richard Venables* efquire ferjeant at arms, one clofe of land with the appurtenances containing by eftimation one acre late in the tenure of John Coupland, one acre late in the tenure of the wife of Robert Skelton, one rood of land late in the feveral tenures of John Wilfon and Chriftopher Wilfon, one rood late in the tenure of Edward Grayfon, one meffuage or tenement and 16 acres of land late in the tenure of Thomas Ellerton, all lying and being in Skelton in the county of Cumberland, late belonging to the chantry of St. Mary in Skelton aforefaid. And the fame king, by his letters patent, Jan. 30, in the third year of his reign, granted to Thomas Dalfton efquire and William Denton gentleman, the late chantry of St. Mary in the church of Skelton, and all thofe meffuages, lands, tenements, and hereditaments, in the feveral tenures of Thomas Allerton, John Dixon, John Lawfon, Cuthbert Milner, John Robinfon, John Lankton, Robert Wifeman, John Milner, Richard Porter, John Taylor, the relict of John Wilfon, Robert Dixon, William Harrifon, and Nicholas Stoderte, lying in Skelton and Unthanke, or elfewhere in the county of Cumberland, to the faid late chantry belonging.

In the year 1747, it was certified, that there were in this parifh 119 families; of which quakers 2, prefbyterians 2.

PARISH OF HUTTON.

THE parifh of HUTTON, called in ancient evidences by way of diftinction *Hutton in the Foreft*, hath on the eaft Lazonby parifh, on the fouth weft Skelton, on the north eaft Hefket, and on the fouth Grayftock. It is about four miles in length and one in breadth.

In an efcheat roll in the 5 Hen. 7. it is found, that the manor of Hoton is holden of the king *in capite*, by the fervice of keeping the foreft in the Hay of our lord the king of Plumpton; and further, by the fervice of holding the ftirrup of the king's faddle whilft he mounts his horfe in the caftle of Carlifle, and paying yearly into the king's exchequer of Carlifle 33 s 4 d by the hands of the fheriff †.

This place continued long in a family that took their name from thence.

† Todd.

In

In the reign of Ed. 1. *Thomas* son and heir of *John de Hoton in Foresta* gave and confirmed to Henry de Hoton chaplain, one moiety of the capital messuage of his manor of Hoton, with 20 acres of land called *le Flatt*, with a miln at Hoton and suit to the same belonging.

King Ed. 3. in the 16th year of his reign, in consideration of the good services that *Thomas de Hoton* had done him in his wars against Scotland, restored to him and his heirs the bailiwick and office of keeping the king's land at Plumpton. And in the reign of Ric. 2. *William de Hoton* enjoyed this place, under the style of *Forestarius regis de landa et custos Haiæ de Plumpton*, which that king and his successor Hen. 4. confirmed to him and his heirs. And from thence it was probably that they took for their arms a bugle horn.

In the 35 Hen. 8. amongst the knights fees in Cumberland, it appears, that *William Hutton* held the manor of Hutton in the Forest of the king *in capite* by knights service, and rendering to the king 40 s yearly by the hands of the sheriff of Cumberland.

In the reign of king James the first, *Thomas Hutton* esquire sold this estate to the *Fletchers* ; the first of whom that we meet with, was

1. *William Fletcher* of Cockermouth merchant; who had issue,

2. *Henry Fletcher* of Cockermouth merchant, who increased the family estate very considerably. He entertained Mary queen of Scots at his house at Cockermouth with great magnificence, in her journey from Workington (where she landed) to Carlisle in the year 1568, and presented her with robes of velvet. He died in the 16 Eliz. and had issue, (1) *William*, who purchased Moresby and Distington, and was ancestor to the Fletchers of Moresby. (2) *Lancelot*, from whom descended the Fletchers of Talentire. (3) *James*. (4) *John*. (5) *Henry*. (Which three last died without issue.) (6) *Thomas*. (7) *Robert*. And three daughters.

3. *Thomas Fletcher* of Cockermouth, sixth son of Henry, married Jane daughter and heir of Bullen, and by her had issue, (1) *Richard*, who purchased Hutton. (2) *Thomas*, a merchant in London. (3) *Philip*, father of John, father of Richard, who married a daughter and heir of Musgrave of Clea, and was ancestor of the Fletchers of Clea. (4) *Lancelot*. (5) *Henry*. And four daughters.

4. Sir *Richard Fletcher* knight, eldest son of Thomas, succeeded his father in the trade at Cockermouth, and acquiring great riches, purchased Hutton and other estates to a great value. He was sheriff of the county in the 14 James 1. and had the honour of knighthood conferred upon him, and fixed his seat at Hutton. He married to his first wife a daughter of Richmond, and by her had issue *Thomas*, *Frances*, and *Mary*, who all died unmarried. To his second wife he married Barbara daughter of Henry Crackenthorp of Newbiggin esquire, and had issue by her, (1) *Henry*. (2) *Bridget*, married to John Patrickson of Calder abbey esquire. (3) *Isabel*, married to Richard Lowther of Ingleton in the county of York esquire. (4) *Mary*, married to Sir John Lowther of Lowther baronet. (5) *Catherine*, married to Thomas Lister of Gisburn in the county of York esquire. (6) *Winifrede*, married first to George Brathwaite of Warcop in the county of Westmorland esquire; secondly, to Sir Richard Dacre knight; and thirdly, to Christopher Lister esquire.

5. Sir

5. Sir *Henry Fletcher* of Hutton baronet (fo created by king Charles in the year 1640), was fheriff of the county in the firft, and again in the 18 Cha. 1. He married Catherine daughter of Sir George Dalfton of Dalfton baronet, who furvived him, and afterwards married to Dr. Thomas Smith dean and afterwards bifhop of Carlifle. He raifed a regiment, chiefly at his own expence, for king Charles the firft, and was killed at the battle of Rawton heath not far from Chefter in the year 1645.—He had iffue (1) *Richard*, who died before him un_ married. (2) *George*. (3) *Henry*, who died young. (4) *Barbara*, married to Sir Daniel Fleming of Rydal knight. (5) *Frances*, married to William Fletcher of Morefby efquire. (6) *Bridget* married to Chriftopher Dalfton of Acorn-bank efquire.

6. Sir *George Fletcher* of Hutton, baronet, was a minor at the time of his fa_ ther's being killed; and he, his mother and fifters, were all fent prifoners to Carlifle. But afterwards, compofition being made for the eftate, he was fent to Queen's college in Oxford under the care of the aforefaid Dr. Smith then fellow of that houfe. He married firft Alice daughter of Hugh earl of Colerain, and by her had iffue (1) *Henry*. (2) *Lucy*, married to Francis Bowes efquire, fon of Sir Thomas Bowes. (3) *Catherine*, married to Lyonel Vane fon of Sir Lyonel Vane of Long Newton in the county of Durham. (4) *Alice*, who died unmar- ried. His fecond wife was Maria Johnfton daughter of the earl of Annandale, and widow of Sir George Graham of Netherby baronet; and by her he had iffue, (1) *George*, who ferved in the wars abroad, and was commonly called colonel Fletcher, for which he had a breviate. (2) *Thomas*, a merchant in London. (3) *Sufanna*. (4) *Mary*. All of which four died without iffue. —This Sir *George* died at Hutton, and was buried in the parifh church there, beneath a mural monument of white marble with this infcription:

To the facred memory of the honourable Sir George Fletcher baronet, who died July 23, A. D. 1700: Aged 67 years. He married firft Alice daughter of Hugh lord of Colrain, who alfo lieth here interred; and by whom he had iffue George, Lucy, Catha- rine, Alice, and Henry. Secondly, Mary daughter of the earl of Annandale; by whom he had George, Mary, Sufanna, and Thomas An affectionate hufband, and an in- dulgent father, careful of his childrens education, regular in his own life and conver- fation. Pious without affectation, and free without vanity; charitable, hofpitable, and eminently juft. So great a patriot to his country, that he was chofen knight of the fhire for Cumberland near 40 years. Much beloved in his life-time, and much lamented at his death; but by none more than by his daughter Alice, who erected this monument.

7. Sir *Henry Fletcher* of Hutton baronet, fon and heir of Sir George, was a perfon of great hopes and expectation. For feveral years, he came from Lon- don, and vifited his eftate in the country; but growing weary of rural diverfions, and thofe many troubles and diffipations of thought that necessarily attend a large revenue, he fettled all he had (being about 1500l *per annum*) upon a remote relation, *Thomas Fletcher* of Morefby efquire, referving only for himfelf a fmall competency for life, and retired to Doway in Flanders, where he fhortly after died in a convent of Englifh monks, and lies buried in a magnificent chapel which he built for them at his own expence. He reconciled himfelf to the
church

church of Rome without the knowledge of any of his friends; and when his inclinations were suspected, he refused to admit any arguments to the contrary. Dr. Todd says of him, that he was of a temper positive and resolute, and not very capable of reasoning in points of controversy.

After his death, his sisters, as heirs at law, prosecuted their title to the whole estate for several years in the court of chancery. After great expence on both sides, they came to terms of accommodation, that *Thomas Fletcher* esquire should enjoy the demesne and lordship of Hutton, with some other parts of the estate, to the value of 500 *l per annum*, for his life; and if he died without issue, then *Henry Fletcher Vane* esquire, second son to *Catharine Vane* eldest sister of Sir Henry Fletcher, and relict of Lionel Vane of Long Newton in the palatinate of Durham, should have and enjoy the whole.

The said *Thomas Fletcher* died without issue, and *Henry Fletcher Vane* aforesaid succeeded accordingly: who also dying without issue, his brother *Walter Vane* (now *Fletcher*) became possessed, and now (1772) enjoys the whole estate.

. The church of Hutton is dedicated to St. James. It was anciently called the chapel of Hutton in the Forest, but for several ages it has been reputed a rectory. The present church was built about the year 1714.

Robert de Vaux gave this church, and one carucate of land at Hutton, to the priory of Carlisle; whose grant was confirmed by king Hen. 2. and afterwards by king Ed. 2 †. And the dean and chapter, as successors of the prior and convent, continue patrons.

It is valued in the king's books at 18 *l* 10 *s* 1 *d*. viz.

		£ s d
Manse and glebe — — — — 24s		
Tithes of wool and lamb — — 20s		
Tithes of corn and hay — — — 13 *l* 0 *s* 1 *d*		18 16 1
White tithes of flax, hemp, geese, hens, colts, and other small tithes — — — — 40s		
Oblations, with profits of the Easter book — 32 *s*		

Out of which deduct,

Pension to the prior of Carlisle . — 2 *s*		
Another payment to the priory by composition 12 *d*		0 6 0
To the bishop for synodals — 12 *d*		
Triennial procurations 6 *s*, therefore yearly — 2 *s*		

And there remains   18 10 1

It was certified to the governors of queen Anne's bounty at 39 *l* 10 *s* 2 *d*. and is now worth about 52 *l per annum*.

† Ex dono Roberti de Vauls unam carugatam terræ de dominio suo in Huttone, et communiam pasturæ et alia afiamenta sua communiter cum hominibus suis in eadem villa, quanta ad unam carugatam terræ pertinent. Ex dono ejusdem Roberti ecclesiam de Huttona, cum omnibus pertinentiis suis, secundum quod carta ejus testatur.

Incumbents,

Incumbents, that have occurred, were as follows :

In 1263, Mr. *John de Boulton* was rector, being in that year witness to an accord between the abbot of Holm and Sir Richard de Newton knight.

In 1309, on the death of Sir *Richard* the late rector, the prior and convent present Sir Robert Parvyng, who has institution given him, with a reservation of an ancient annual pension of 2 *s* due to the said prior and convent.

In 1369, Sir *Robert de Lowther* was instituted on a presentation by the prior and convent. And in 1381, the said Sir Robert exchanges with Sir *John de Welton* vicar of Wigton.

In 1465, Sir *Robert Thorp*, rector of Hutton, had a licence from bishop Scroop for 5 years non-residence.

In the reign of king Hen. 8. when the aforesaid valuation in the king's books was made, *John Deyne* was rector.

In 1569, on the death of Sir *Richard Tolson* rector of Hutton, Mr. *Anthony Walkwood* was instituted on the presentation of John Middleton gentleman, to whom Sir Thomas Smith (the queen's secretary) dean, and the chapter of Carlisle, had granted the first avoidance.

In 1612, on the death of Anthony Walkwood, Sir *William Lawson* clerk was instituted on a presentation by the dean and chapter.

In the time of the usurpation, *Thomas Todd* the rector was ejected by Cromwell's sequestrators, and imprisoned at Carlisle. The crimes laid against him were, that he used the Lord's prayer, baptized children, visited the sick, and sometimes preached privately to his parishioners and others. And one *Jackson* was appointed to succeed him †.

In 1689, *Nicholas Thomlinson* was instituted on a presentation by the dean and chapter.

In 1695, *Joshua Borrow*, B. A. was presented on the cession of Nicholas Thomlinson.

In 1728, on the removal of Joshua Borrow to Asby, *William Kilner* was instituted on a like presentation.

In 1752, on William Kilner's death, *Sandford Tatham*, M. A. was presented by the dean and chapter, and instituted thereupon.

In the year 1361, upon the humble remonstrance and petition of Thomas de Hoton to the bishop, setting forth that the old CHANTRY at Bramwra in this parish, erected for the soul's good of Thomas de Capella, was now wholly lost, the lands for its support being wasted and untilled ; the said bishop confirms his erection of a new chantry in the parish church of St. James at Hoton, and his settling thereon six messuages and 44 acres of arable land and meadow, besides all the lands that were formerly settled upon the chantry of St. Mary at Bramwra aforesaid, reserving to himself and his heirs the right of presentation to the said chantry. Whereupon Sir Richard de Brampton was presented to the said new erected chantry of the altar of St. Mary in Hoton, and had institution and induction given him.

† Walker, 375.

The

The valuation of the said chantry in the king's books stands thus:

The chantry of the blessed virgin Mary in the church of Hoton—Bernard Hayfty chaplain of the said chantry hath a mansion house with 9 acres of arable land belonging to the same, worth yearly *communibus annis 9 s.* The same Bernard hath divers lands and tenements lying in divers hamlets and villages within the county of Cumberland, worth yearly *communibus annis 6 l 5 s 10 d.*

After the dissolution of chantries, king Edward the sixth by letters patent bearing date Dec. 13, in the 2d year of his reign, grants to Thomas Brende of London scrivener (amongst other particulars) all that the late chantry of the blessed virgin Mary founded in the parish church of Hoton in the county of Cumberland, with messuages, lands, and tenements in the possession of 13 different persons in Hoton, Newton, Newbigging, and Gatescales in the said county of Cumberland, late parcel of the said late chantry: To hold to the said Thomas Brende and his heirs of the king as of his castle of Windsor, by fealty only, in free socage, and not *in capite*, for all rents, services, and demands.

In 1730, it was certified, that there were in this parish 62 families; only one single person a presbyterian, and two old maiden sisters papists.

PARISH OF NEWTON.

THE parish of NEWTON lies within the forest of Englewood, and consists of two townships or constablewicks, called *Newton* and *Catterlen.*

Newton, by way of distinction, is called *Newton Regny,* of one *William de Regny* sometime owner thereof. In the 33 Hen. 2. *William de Regny* was impleaded in a writ of right, by one William de Lascells for a knight's fee of land in Newton Regny, but he did not prevail; for *John Regny* succeeded his father *William* in the 4th of king John. And in the 4 Ed. 1. *William* his son was owner, and died in that year; when it descended to his four daughters coheirs. But very soon after, it was the possession of *Robert Burnel* bishop of Bath, who in the 18 Ed. 1. granted this manor by fine unto *Hugh de Lowther,* who died in the 10 Ed. 2. and his son *Hugh* succeeded, and held the village of Newton Regny (as the inquisition finds) of the king *in capite,* by the service of finding to the said lord the king in his war against Scotland one horseman with a horse of 40's price, armed with a coat of mail, an iron helmet, a lance, and a sword, abiding in the war aforesaid for 40 days with the king's person.

In an account of knights fees in Cumberland in the 35 Hen. 8. this tenure is expressed with some little variation: viz. John Lowther knight holds the village of Newton Reny of our lord the king *in capite* by knights service, and pays to our said lord the king for cornage by the hands of the sheriff of Cumberland 2 s *per annum*; and it is holden by the serjeanty of finding to our said

VOL. II.   E e e   lord

lord the king with his army one horfeman, with habiliments, one lance, and one long fword; as appears of record in the 9 Ed. 3.

And this manor ftill continues in the houfe of Lowther, in the perfon of the prefent owner Sir James Lowther baronet.

CATTERLEN, in the reign of William the conqueror was the poffeffion of *Haldan* father of *Willifrid,* father of *Cartimer, Walter,* and *Alexander,* lords of Farlam †. *Hubert de Vallibus,* lord of Gifland, accufed *Willifrid* of high treafon, as taking part with king Stephen againft Henry the fecond; and thereupon wrefted the manor from him and got it into his poffeffion, which the faid king Hen. 2. confirmed to him ‡.

The defcendents of Hubert, by the name of Vaux of Caterlen enjoyed it for many generations. In the 35 Hen. 8. *John Vaux* held the capital meffuage and vill of Caterleyn by the fervice of paying to the king 22 *d* yearly. In the reign of queen Elizabeth *Rowland Vaux* held the fame. In Mr. Machel's time, over the old kitchen door at Caterlen hall were the arms of Vaux in a roundel, viz. Or, a fefs checky Or and Gules, between 3 garbs Gules banded Or. With this legend round in Old Characters, " LET MERCY AND FAITHFULNES NEVER GOY FROME THE." And underneath, " AT THIS TIME IS ROWLAND VAUX LORD OF THIS PLACE, AND BUILDED THIS HOUSE IN THE YEAR OF GOD 1577." With the letters RV. AV. viz. Rowland Vaux, Anne Vaux (the name of his wife, who was daughter of Salkeld).

The laft of the name at Caterlen, viz. *John Vaux,* dying without iffue male, it defcended to two daughters coheirs, who were married to *Chriftopher Richmond* efquire and *Richard Graham* of Nunnery gentleman. Mrs. *Sufanna Richmond,* by virtue of her mother's will, who held the fame in purfuance of the laft will and teftament of her fon *Henry Richmond* efquire the laft male heir of that family, now (1773) enjoys both the demefne and manor.

The *church* of Newton feems to have been very early appropriated to the fee of Carlifle. It is of ancient time moft commonly ftyled a *chapel,* but no other parifh is mentioned of which it may be fuppofed to have been part.

In the year 1338, bifhop Kirkby granted to Nicholas de Claufe prieft for the term of his life the whole altarage of the chapel of Newton, rendering to the bifhop and his fucceffors two marks of filver yearly, and taking care that divine fervice in the faid chapel by himfelf or fome other be duly performed.

In 1357, Sir Gilbert Baker, keeper of the chauntry in the chapel of Newton, refigned his charge, and Sir John de Bramwra was collated to the faid vacant chantry.

---

† Todd.

‡ Henricus, &c. Sciatis me conceffiffe, dediffe, et confirmaffe Huberto de Vallibus in feodo et hæreditate fibi et hæredibus fuis . . . . Kaderleng cum molendino, quam Uctredus filius Haldani tenuit. Quare volo, &c.

In

In 1360, bishop Welton grants licence to the prior of St. Augustine in Penrith, to supply the chapel of Newton by some of his brethren.

In 1365, bishop Appleby grants licence to frier R. sacrist of the frery at Penrith, to officiate in the chapel of Newton for four years.

In 1523, bishop Kite let to farm the chapelry of Newton with all its appurtenances for 25 years to Sir Christopher Dacre knight and others, at the annual rent of ten marks.

In 1593, bishop Meye (on the death of Edward Nicolson the late curate), styling himself the appropriator of the parish church of Newton, confers the perpetual curacy of the said church on Robert Troutbeck clerk.

In 1635, an information was filed in the name of the attorney general against bishop Potter and Sir Thomas Carleton knight his lessee of the rectory for not allowing a sufficient maintenance to the curate. Whereupon it was agreed and ordered, that the curate for the time being should from thenceforth have all the rectory, the tithe corn only excepted; and should from the said corn tithe have 6*l* 13*s* 4*d* yearly. This rent was afterwards advanced to 10*l* 13*s* 4*d*; and the stipend as certified to the governors of queen Anne's bounty is 21*l* 12*s* 7*d*. In 1765 this church received an augmentation of 200*l* from the governors of queen Anne's bounty, in conjunction with 200*l* given by Dr. Holme, wherewith lands were purchased at Kirkstone foot, of the present yearly value of 14*l*.

Mrs. Isabella Miller by her will devised to her daughter Susanna Richmond, her heirs and assigns, her messuage and garth or garden with the appurtenances, late Atkinson's at Catterlen, in trust for the use of a *schoolmaster*, to instruct the children of the tenants within the manor of Catterlen, in the principles of the christian religion as now by law established and in reading and writing.

In 1747, there were in this parish 55 families; of which, presbyterians two, and quakers two.

PARISH OF PENRITH.

PENRITH, as our best antiquaries affirm, signifies in the British *red Hill*, and hath its name from the hill of red stone adjoining: Although Dr. Todd says it hath its denomination from a Roman colony *Petriana*, where the *Ala Petriana* kept garrison about three miles north of it, out of whose ruins (he says) the town had its original.

This parish lies in the southern extremity of the forest of Englewood, and is bounded by the parishes of Barton, Dacre, Newton, Hesker, Lazonby, Edenhall, and Brougham: And in Dr. Todd's time contained 424 families.

In the reign of queen Elizabeth, a commission was issued to Henry lord Scroop, John bishop of Carlisle, John Vaughan esquire, John Swift auditor, Edward Dacre esquire, Richard Dudley esquire, Simon Slingsby esquire, and

Ambrose Lancaster gentleman, to inquire of all trespasses on the wastes within the villages and precincts of Penrith, with an injunction to the sheriff to impanel a jury. The complaint was against Rowland Vaux and his tenants of Catterlin for incroachments on that side; but on the inquiry, the ancient boundary of the cow pasture of Penrith, belonging to the queen's majesty's manor of Penrith, was found necessary to be inquired into and ascertained †.

And on the side of Edenhall, the boundaries of the said manor of Penrith were ascertained and finally settled, on a reference to William Milbourne and Joseph Nicolson esquires, in the year 1765*.

At the time of the Norman conquest, this manor of Penrith and the forest of Englewood (within which forest Penrith is situate) were in the possession of the Scots; of which they were soon after dispossessed. Nevertheless the Scots did not thereupon relinquish their claim. For in the reign of king John, William king of Scots claimed the whole three counties of Northumberland, Cumberland, and Westmorland; which three counties John seems to have consented to cede unto him, on William's having paid to John 15000 marks of silver (a commodity John had great need of), and John's covenanting that Henry or Richard sons of John should marry Margaret or Isabella daughters of William (neither of which marriages took effect).

Afterwards, the two next kings of England and Scotland, viz. Henry the third king of England son of John, and Alexander king of Scotland son of William, renewed these differences, and had a further dispute in relation to an agreement of marriage to be solemnized between the said Henry and Margery sister of the said Alexander, which agreement the said Henry on his part had failed to carry into execution.

These differences at length were compromised by the pope's mediation, and an agreement entred into by Henry and Alexander in presence of the pope's legate, by an instrument purporting to be an Agreement between Henry the third king of England and Alexander king of Scotland, concerning all plaints which Alexander had against Henry until Friday next before the feast of St. Michael in the year of our Lord 1237, concerning the counties of Northumberland, Cumberland, and Westmorland, which Alexander claimed as his inheritance, and 15000 marks of silver which king John father of Henry had received of William king of Scotland father of the said Alexander for certain agreements between John and William, which on the part of John had not been fulfilled; and also concerning certain agreements between the said Henry and Alexander, in relation to a contract of marriage between the said Henry and Margery sister of the said Alexander, which on the part of the said Henry had not been performed: By which present agreement, Alexander releases and quits claim to Henry king of England and his heirs the said three counties, and also the said sum of money, and all agreements made between the said John and William concerning marriage to be had between the said Henry or Richard his brother and Margaret or Isabella sisters of Alexander, and also all agreements between Henry and Alexander concerning a marriage between the said Henry and Margery sister of the said Alexander. In consideration whereof, the said Henry gives and grants to the said Alexander 200 librates of land in the said counties of Northumberland and Cumberland, if the said 200 librates can be found in any of the towns where no castle is situate; if not, the deficiency to be made up in places near to the said two counties: To hold to the said Alexander and his heirs kings of Scotland, of the said Henry king of England and his heirs, paying for the same yearly one soar-hawk at Carlisle by the hands of the constable of the castle of Carlisle for all services. And if any of the said lands shall be within the bounds of the forest, the king of England's foresters shall make no claim of puture there or other demand, except only for attachment of pleas of the forest, and this by view of the bailiff of the king of Scotland, if on notice he shall chuse to be present †.

In 1251 the said Alexander died, and was succeeded by his son Alexander who married Margaret daughter of the said king Henry the third, who confirmed to Alexander the said two hundred librates of land, and gave to him a bond of 5000 marks of silver, for her marriage portion. And from thence those lands received the name of the Queen's haims (or demesnes).

What these lands were, will appear from an assize in the 6 Ed. 1. *Juratores pro rege ad assizas dicunt, quod rex Scotiæ tenet villatam de Penrith, Langwaldeofby, Scotby, Salkeld Magna, et Carleton.* And more particularly, from the inquisition *post mortem* of the said Alexander the son taken at Carlisle (for the Cumberland estates) in the 21 Ed. 1. 1292; before Thomas de Normanville the king's escheator beyond Trent: viz. " An inquisition taken at Car-
" lisle on Tuesday in Easter week in the twenty-first year of the reign of king
" Edward, before Sir Thomas de Normanvil escheator beyond Trent, by Hugh
" de Muleton, Hubert de Muleton, Thomas de Newton, Robert de Joneby,
" Robert de Croglyn, Adam de Ulvesby, Adam de Hoton, Adam Turpp,
" John de Stafholl, John de Salkeld, Robert de Tympauron, and Thomas
" de Lowther. Being sworn how much land Alexander king of Scotland
" held of our lord the king of England on the day on which he died, they
" say, that the same Alexander held of our lord the king of England on the
" day of his death *in capite* the manors of Penrith, Soureby, Languetheby,
" Salkild, Carlatton, and Scotteby. How much of others: They say, that
" he held nothing. By what service: They say, by rendring one soar-hawk
" yearly at the feast of the assumption of the blessed virgin Mary at the
" castle of Carlisle, and by doing homage to our lord the king of England
" and his heirs and fealty for the said lands. How much those lands are
" worth yearly in all issues: They say, that the said manors are worth yearly
" two hundred pounds. And who is next heir, and of what age: They say,
" that John de Balliol is next heir, and is of the age of 30 years ‡."

This John Balliol was he to whom king Edward the first, upon a reference to him by the several competitors, had awarded the crown of Scotland. The said Alexander the son having died without any descendent from him (except

† Appendix, N° 30.   ‡ Ibid. ut supra.

one granddaughter who died foon after him) the three principal claimants of the
crown of Scotland, were Baliol, Bruce, and Haftings; defcended from the three
daughters of David earl of Huntingdon brother of the aforefaid William king
of Scotland. Their feveral claims were; *Baliol*, defcended from the eldeft
fifter, claimed that the kingdom of Scotland was an indivifible fief, and therefore that he folely was intitled in right of primogeniture. *Bruce* claimed, that
altho' he was defcended from the fecond fifter, yet he was in a nearer degree of
confanguinity, as being grandfon, whereas Baliol was great grandfon of the common anceftor. *Haftings*, defcended from the third fifter, claimed a third part,
which being decided in favour of Baliol, Haftings neverthelefs claimed a third
part of the Englifh eftates, as being divifible amongft coparceners. And therefore when Baliol, in purfuance of the faid office being found in his favour, fued
for livery of the lands of Tindal, Penrith, and Scotteby, with the appurtenances,
as next heir to Alexander; Haftings put in his claim for a third part. But he
not appearing further to profecute his claim, and it being found, that Penrith
and Soureby with the appurtenances were given to Alexander and his heirs
kings of Scotland, and not fimply to him or his heirs, Baliol had livery accordingly, doing his homage for the fame †.

Afterwards, king Edward, quarreling with Baliol, feized all thofe lands, and
in the 26th year of his reign granted them to Anthony Beck the military bifhop
of Durham, who had affifted the king at the battle of Falkirk with a confiderable number of foldiers, and was greatly inftrumental in obtaining the victory.
But the parliament held at Carlifle in the 33d year of that king's reign, not approving of the grant, fummoned the bifhop to fhew by what title he had them;
and he not appearing, they were adjudged to the crown.

In the 19 Ed. 3. the Scots to the number of 30,000, enter Cumberland, burn
Penrith, and carry away great numbers of the inhabitants captives into Scotland,
where they were fold as fo many cattle to the beft bidder. And in the 37th of
the fame king, the tenants of the manors of Penrith, Salkeld, and Soureby, of
the ancient demefne of the crown within the foreft of Englewood, by their petition fetting forth that their lands and tenements for which they paid a large
rent to the crown were wafted by the Scots, and their corn there growing often
deftroyed by the beafts of the foreft; the king thereupon grants them and their
heirs common of pafture for all their goods in the faid foreft, in as ample manner as the prior of Carlifle and William Englifh and other tenants within the
foreft have by grant of the faid king or any of his progenitors ‡.

In the 8 Ric. 2. the Scots made another inroad into the county, and deftroyed
Penrith, and carried off the goods of the inhabitants. In confideration of
which loffes, the fame king, by his charter bearing date Feb. 10, in the 11th
year of his reign confirms his grandfather's grant ⊬.

Which fame king Richard the fecond, in the 19th year of his reign, granted
the manors of Penrith and Soureby, with the hamlets of Langwathby, Scotby,
Carleton, and Salkeld, with their appurtenances, to John duke of Bretaign and
earl of Richmond; and fhortly after, by letters patent grants them in ample

† Appendix, N° 30. ut fupra.   ‡ Ibid.   ⊬ Ibid.

manner

manner to Ralph de Nevil earl of Weftmorland and Johanna his wife. Richárd de Nevil earl of Warwick and heir of the faid Ralph, being flain in the battle of Barnet in the 11 Ed. 4. the whole eftate for defect of heirs male reverted to the crown, and continued as part of the royal demefne, till king William the third gave the honour of Penrith and all its dependences with the appurtenances, within the foreft of Englewood, to William Bentinck whom the king afterwards created earl of Portland, for his fervices to the faid king in bringing about the révolution in this kingdom, and thereby fecuring our religion and liberties. Of which family our account is as follows :

I. WILLIAM BENTINCK efquire was page of honour to William prince of Orange, and afterwards gentleman of the bedchamber. In the year 1677 he was fent by the prince to folicit a match with the lady Mary, eldeft daughter to James then duke of York, which was foon after concluded. On the duke of Monmouth's invafion of this kingdom, he was fent over to offer his mafter's affiftance to king James, both of his troops and perfon. In 1688, when the prince of Orange had thoughts of an expedition into England, he fent Mr. Bentinck, on the elector of Brandenburgh's death, with his compliments to the new elector, and to lay before him the ftate of affairs, and to know how much he might depend upon his affiftance; and was fo fuccefsful in his negotiations, that he carried to his mafter a full promife of all that was defired. He attended the prince in the faid expedition, and it is faid was principally relied on in that enterprize. After his mafter's acceffion to the throne of thefe realms, he was made privy purfe, and groom of the ftole, a lieutenant-general of his majefty's forces, colonel and captain of a regiment of Dutch horfe, knight of the garter, baron of Cirencefter, vifcount Woodftock, and earl of Portland. He attended king William in all the dangers and fatigues of the wars both in Ireland and Flanders, and afterwards had a principal management of the peace, which was firft agreed between him and marefchal Boufflers in the field between the two armies, and afterwards finifhed at Rifwyk. And being thereupon fent ambaffador extraordinary to the court of France, he fulfilled that employment with equal honour to himfelf and the Britifh nation.

Befides this grant of Penrith and its dependencies, he had a grant of the lordfhips of Denbigh, Bromfield, and Yale, with other lands, comprehending the beft part of one of the counties of Wales; but that grant was refumed, on an addrefs of the houfe of commons for that purpofe. Alfo he had a grant of one hundred and thirty-five thoufand acres of the forfeited eftates in Ireland; but this grant alfo was refumed by the parliament in 1699.

He married to his firft wife Anne daughter of Sir Edward Villiers knight, and by her had iffue, 1. *William*, who died in his infancy. 2. *Henry*. 3. *William*, who died young in Holland. 4. *Mary*, married to Algernon earl of Effex, and after to Sir Conyers Darcy only brother to Robert earl of Holdernefs. 5. *Anna Margaretta*, married to Mr. Duyvenvorde, one of the principal nobles of Holland. 6. *Frances-Williamyna*, married to William lord Byron. 7. *Eleonora*, who died unmarried. 8. *Ifabella*, married to Evelyn Pierrepont duke of Kingfton.

4   He

He married to his second wife Jane daughter of Sir John Temple of Eaſt Sheen in the county of Surry baronet, and widow of John lord Berkeley of Stratton; and by her had iſſue, 1. *William*, one of the nobles of Holland. 2. *Charles John*, an officer in the army of the States General. 3. *Sophia*, married to Henry Grey duke of Kent. 5. *Harriot*, married to James Hamilton earl of Clanbraſſil in the kingdom of Ireland. 6. *Barbara*, married to William lord Godolphin.

After king William's death, the ſaid earl of Portland betook himſelf to a retired life, and died at his ſeat at Bulſtrode in Buckinghamſhire in the year 1709, aged 61; and was buried in the vault under the eaſt window of king Henry the ſeventh's chapel in Weſtminſter abbey.

II. HENRY, earl of Portland, ſucceeded his father; and married Elizabeth eldeſt daughter and coheir of Wriotheſley Baptiſt Noel earl of Gainſborough: with whom he had (amongſt other poſſeſſions) the lordſhip of Titchfield in the county of Southampton, and a noble manſion-houſe there, which came to the ſaid earl of Gainſborough on the deceaſe of the counteſs his mother, who was eldeſt daughter and coheir of Thomas earl of Southampton, lord high treaſurer of England in the reign of king Charles the ſecond. In his father's life-time he ſerved as knight of the ſhire for the county of Southampton in two parliaments of queen *Anne*. He was one of the lords of the bedchamber to king George the firſt, and by him made marquis of Titchfield and duke of Portland. In 1721, he was appointed captain-general and governor of Jamaica, where he died in the year 1726, in the 45th year of his age.

He had ſeveral children, of whom two ſons and three daughters ſurvived him; 1. *William*. 2. *George*, a colonel of foot. 3. *Anne*, married to lieutenant-colonel Daniel Paul. 4. *Iſabella*, married to Henry Monk eſquire, of Ireland. 5. *Amelia*, married to Jacob Arran Van Waſſener, one of the nobles of Holland.

III. WILLIAM BENTINCK, duke of Portland, ſon and heir of Henry, married Margaret Cavendiſh Harley daughter and ſole heir of Edward Harley earl of Oxford and earl Mortimer by his wife Henrietta Cavendiſh Hollis daughter and heir of John Hollis duke of Newcaſtle, who married the heireſs of Cavendiſh of Welbeck in Nottinghamſhire.

He died in 1762, and had iſſue, 1. *William-Henry Cavendiſh*. 2. *Edward-Charles*, in the 8 Geo. 3. choſen repreſentative in parliament for the city of Carliſle. 3. *Elizabeth*, married to Thomas Thynne viſcount Weymouth. 4. *Henrietta*, married to George-Harry Grey earl of Stamford. 5. *Margaret*, who died unmarried. 6. *Frances*, who alſo died unmarried.

IV. WILLIAM HENRY CAVENDISH BENTINCK, duke of Portland, marquis of Titchfield, viſcount Woodſtock, and baron of Cirenceſter, ſucceeded his father William; and married Dorothy ſiſter to William Cavendiſh the preſent duke of Devonſhire: by whom he hath a ſon *William*, born in 1768.

The

The arms of the duke of Portland are; Azure, a crofs moline Argent. The creft: out of a marquis's coronet Proper, two arms counter, embowed and vefted Gules, gloved Or, and holding each an oftrich feather Argent. Supporters: Two lions-double queve, the dexter Proper, the other Sable.

Within this parifh of Penrith there are two or three fmall mefne manors; one of which belongs to the bifhop of Carlifle, called Bishop-row, confifting of about twelve leafehold tenants within the town of Penrith, and feveral other leafehold and cuftomary tenants both in Cumberland and Weftmorland; who have always been deemed amenable here, as appendices of the manor of *Bifhop-row.*

Another belonged to the Huttons of Hutton hall in Penrith, a family that continued there for many generations, and was not extinct till within our own remembrance.

The firft, of whom we have any account, was *Adam de Hoton* of Penrith, in the reign of king Ed. 1.

His fon *Alexander de Hoton* of Penrith, in the reign of Ed. 3.

Thomas de Hoton, fon of Alexander, lived till the beginning of the reign of king Hen. 5. His wife's name was Helen. Thefe two (fays the pedigree taken by Richard St. George Norroy king at arms 1615) lay intombed under the higher fouth window of St. Andrew's quire in Penrith, where were the figures of both, with this infcription in the window, *Orate pro animabus Thomæ Hoton et Elenæ uxoris ejus.*

They had iffue *John de Hoton,* who married Ifabel daughter of Hugh Salkeld of Rofgill in the county of Weftmorland efquire, and lived in the reign of Hen. 6.

William de Hoton, fon of John, appears to have been living in the 4 Hen. 7.

John de Hoton, fon of William, married Elizabeth one of the four daughters and coheirs of Thomas Beauchamp of Crogling, efquire; whofe arms were, Argent, on a bend Gules three plates.

Anthony Hutton of Penrith, fon of John, in the reign of Hen. 8. married Elizabeth daughter of Thomas Mufgrave of Comcach by his wife Elizabeth baftard daughter of Thomas lord Dacre of Gilfland. He had iffue, 1. William. 2. Richard, who was one of the judges of the court of common pleas. This Richard married Agnes one of the four daughters and coheirs of Thomas Briggs of Caumire in the county of Weftmorland, and by her had iffue Chriftopher, Richard, Thomas, and Henry; and five daughters, Elizabeth married to John Dawney fon and heir apparent of Sir Thomas Dawney knight, Jane, Mary, Catharine, and Julian married to Sir Philip Mufgrave of Hartley caftle baronet. [The other three coheireffes of Briggs were, Anne married to John Skelton of Appletreethwayte, Frances married to John Sawrey of Plumpton, and Anne married to Edward Stanley of Dalegarth.]

Sir *William Hutton* of Penrith knight, elder fon of Anthony, married to his firft wife Jane daughter of Rowland Vaulx of Caterlen, and by her had iffue Thomas who died in his father's life-time without iffue male, and William who died unmarried. To his second wife he married Dorothy daughter of Benson, and by her had issue Anthony, upon whom his father settled the estate on failure of issue male of Thomas, another son Bernard, and two daughters, Susan married to Simon Musgrave of Musgrave hall in Penrith, and Anne married to Sir Christopher Dalston of Acorn-bank.

Anthony Hutton of Penrith esquire, eldest surviving son of Sir William, married Elizabeth daughter of Robert Burdett of Bramcourt in the county of Warwick esquire, and died without issue in the year 1637.

On a brass plate on the floor near the middle of the chancel of the old church of Penrith was the following monumental inscription :

Here lyeth Mary *daughter of* Thomas Wilson *secretary of state to Queen* Elizabeth, *who was first married to* Robert Burdett *of* Bramcourt *in the county of* Warwick *esquire, by whom she had Sir* Thomas Burdett *baronet, and several sons and daughters : And afterwards was married to Sir* Christopher Lowther *of* Lowther *in the county of* Westmorland, *knight. Her daughter* Elizabeth Burdett *married to* Anthony Hutton *of* Penrith *in the county of* Cumberland *esquire, with whom she lived, and dyed the last day of* May, *Anno Domini* 1622.

On the north side of the chancel was erected a fair monument, inclosed with iron rails ; whereon, under the portraitures of a man and woman in plaister of Paris in full proportion were the following inscriptions.—On the south :

Here lies interred Anthony Hutton *esquire, who was a grave, faithful and judicious counsellor at law, and one of the masters of the high court of chancery ; son and heir of that renowned knight Sir* William Hutton *of* Penrith, *and was matched into the noble family of Sir* Thomas Burdett *of* Bramcourt *in the county of* Warwick *baronet, by the marriage of his virtuous sister* Elizabeth Burdett *; whose pious care and religious bounty hath erected this marble tomb to perpetuate the memory of such a worthy commonwealth's man and of so dear a husband, who died the* 10th *of* July 1637.

On the north :

Here lies the portraiture of Elizabeth Hutton *the wife of the late deceased* Anthony Hutton *; who, though living, desired thus to be placed; in token of her union with him here interred, and of her own expected mortality.*

Maritus ⎰ *Multum dilecta conjux, vita et morte individua comes, non amisisti quem*
uxori ⎱ *præmisisti.*

Uxor ⎰ *Unica cura mea sic vivere, ut tecum Christo fruar, et tuo lateri in æter-*
marito ⎱ *num sim conjunctior.*

Bernard Hutton of Penrith succeeded his brother Anthony, and married Anne daughter of Hugh Stamper of Snittlegarth in the county of Cumberland, by whom he had issue William, Richard, John, Bernard, and Thomas ; and four daughters, Dorothy, Anne, Grace, and Catharine.

William Hutton of Penrith esquire, son and heir of Bernard, married Elizabeth daughter of Christopher Lancaster of Sockbridge esquire, and by her had issue, Anthony, Beehard, John, Henry, Dorothy, and Anne. This William was of the age of 39 at Dugdale's visitation in 1665, and his eldest son Anthony of the age of 17.

The

The faid Anthony had a fon Richard Hutton, who died in the year 1717. On a blue ftone in the floor on the fouth of the chancel of Penrith church, is the following infcription:

Depofitus
Richardus Hutton armiger, Qui
Obiit octavo die Maii Anno Domini
1717. Anno Ætatis fuæ 41:
Et depofita
Barbara Filia fua, nata 26
Die Octobris Anno Domini 1716.
Quæ obiit 15 Junii Anno Domini
1717.

The laft of the name and family at Penrith was *Addifon Hutton* efquire, fon of Richard, who died about thirty years ago.

The arms of thefe Huttons were; Argent, on a fefs Sable three bucks heads cabofhed Or.

Mrs. Gafgarth now enjoys Hutton hall in Penrith; and (which is fomewhat extraordinary) holds divers lands there of the bifhop of Carlifle, called Bifhop's Flat, by leafe for 21 years, which faid lands have been long held by cuftomary tenure of the bifhop's leffee.

Another mefne manor was held by the CARLETONS of Carleton hall: of which family the following pedigree was certified by Sir William Carleton at Dugdale's vifitation of Cumberland in 1665.

The firft five in the pedigree are barely named, *Baldwyn, Jeffrey de Carleton, Odard de Carleton, Henry de Carleton,* and *Gilbert de Carleton*; the firft of whom, by the courfe of chronology, afcending from thofe that are dated afterwards, muft go nearly to the time of the conqueft.

The next is *William de Carleton,* who married Helena daughter of Geoffrey Stainton.

Adam de Carleton, 15 Ed. 1. married Sarah daughter of Adam de Newton.

John de Carleton, 32 Ed. 1. married Dorothy daughter of Henry Brougham.

Thomas de Carleton, 19 Ed. 2. married Joan daughter of Roger de Lancafter.

John de Carleton, 30 Ed. 3. married Margaret daughter and heir of John de Mofton.

Thomas de Carleton, 22 Ric. 2. 8 Hen. 4. and 27 Hen. 6. He married Alice daughter and heir of George Dawbury of the county of York.

Thomas de Carleton married Ifabel daughter of Gilbert Brougham of Brougham, and died in the 11 Hen. 8.

Thomas Carleton married Agnes daughter of Thomas Wibergh of Clifton in the county of Weftmorland, and died in the 22 Hen. 8.

Thomas Carleton married Anne daughter of Thomas Layton of Dalemain, and died in the 4 Phil. and Mary.

Thomas

Thomas Carleton married Mabel daughter and coheir of Carlisle of the city of Carlisle, and died in the 29 Eliz.

Thomas Carleton married Barbara daughter of Hugh Lowther of Lowther, and died in the 40 Eliz.

Sir *Thomas Carleton* of Carleton knight, the seventh in succeffion of the name of Thomas, married Elizabeth daughter of John Shelly of Woodborough in the county of Nottingham, and widow of Marmaduke Conftable. He died in the 14 Cha. 1. without iffue. His brother Gerard Carleton died before him; which Gerard married Nichola daughter of Elliot of Redhugh in Scotland, and by her had a fon William who fucceeded to the inheritance.

Sir *William Carleton* of Carleton knight, fon of Gerard, married to his firft wife Dorothy daughter of Sir Chriftopher Dalfton of Acorn-bank, and by her had iffue Mary of the age of 18 years at the faid vifitation of Sir William Dugdale. To his fecond wife he married Barbara daughter of Robert de la Vale of Cowpan in the county of Northumberland efquire, and had iffue by her at the time of the faid vifitation Robert aged 8 years, and a daughter Alice.

This *Robert* died without iffue male in the year 1707; and John Pattinfon of Penrith attorney at law purchafed Carleton hall. He was fucceeded by his fon Chriftopher Pattinfon efquire; who dying unmarried, the eftate defcended to his three fifters coheirs, and Carleton hall was affigned to the eldeft fifter Elizabeth then wife and now widow of Thomas Simpfon efquire, an eminent attorney at law, and juftly celebrated for his learning, integrity, and extraordinary natural endowments.

The Arms of Carleton are; Ermin, a bend Sable, charged with 3 pheons Argent. The Creft: On a wreath an Arm dexter Proper, ready to difcharge a dart or arrow.

The town of Penrith hath a very large MARKET on Tuefday weekly, and a fair on Tuefday in Whitfun-week, and on every Tuefday fortnight after until Lammafs.

Bifhop *Strickland* was at the expence of drawing a *watercourfe* from the river Petterel thro' this town; which is of exceeding great benefit to the inhabitants.

On the weft fide of the town ftands the CASTLE, of fquare ftone, inclofed with a ditch; which by its largenefs and ruins feems to have been a place of fome ftrength and confideration. But it feems not to have been very ancient. For when the 200 librates of land (as is aforefaid), of which Penrith was part, were given to the king of Scots, there was a fpecial refervation, that thofe lands fhould not be where there were any caftles. King Richard the third, when he was duke of Gloucefter, that he might be more at hand to oppofe the Scots, and keep the country in obedience, which was generally of the Lancaftrian intereft, refided in this caftle for fome time, and inlarged and ftrengthened it with towers and other works. The ftones for that purpofe, it is faid, he had from an old ruin, fuppofed to have been a place of Druid worfhip, at Mayburgh, about a mile diftant, on the fouth fide of the river Eamont. In the
                                                                                        civil

civil wars in the time of king Charles the firſt, this fabrick was totally ruined, and all the lead and timber ſold for the uſe of the commonwealth.

On the eaſt part of the pariſh, upon the north bank of the river Eamont, are two *caves* or *gròttoes*, dug out of the ſolid rock, and ſufficient to contain 100 men.   The paſſage to them is very narrow and dangerous, and perhaps its *perilous* acceſs may have given it the name of *Iſis Parlis*, tho' the vulgar tell ſtrange ſtories of one Iſis a giant who lived here in former times, and like Cacus of old uſed to ſeize men and cattle, and draw them into his den to devour them. But it is highly probable, that theſe ſubterraneous chambers were made for a ſecure retreat in time of ſudden danger ; and the iron gates, which were taken away not long ago, do not a little confirm that ſuppoſition.

The CHURCH of Penrith is dedicated to St. Andrew, and is vicarial, having been given by king Hen. 1. to the biſhop of Carliſle at the firſt erection of the ſee.   It is valued in the king's books at 1 2 *l* 6 *s* 3 *d.*   And is now worth about 100 *l per annum* (including an augmentation of 32 *l* out of the great tithes, and other benefactions).

About the year 1326, king Ed. 2. iſſued a writ of Certiorari to the then guardian of the temporalties, concerning his receipts from this and Dalſton vicarages, and the return as to Penrith was, that it having been appropriated *ad menſam epiſcopi,* tithe wool and lamb had been uſed to be paid to the biſhop, and therefore was now received by him, but all oblations and obventions belonged to the vicar.   And by the leaſe of the rectory now granted to John Richardſon. eſquire, all the tithes of corn, grain, hay, lamb, wool, and milns are demiſed.

For the augmentation of this ſmall vicarage and of the vicarage of Dacre, about the year 1669, Mr. William Mawſon of Timpaurin, having then a leaſe from the dean and chapter of Carliſle of the corn tithes of Sleagill and Thrimby in the pariſh of Morland for 21 years (ſeveral years being run) gave the ſame by will to the vicars of Penrith and Dacre in truſtees who were to renew the leaſe from time to time, each of the legatees to have an undivided clear moiety. This being found inconvenient by the truſtees, a diviſion was made by mutual conſent of the parties concerned, and the vicars of Penrith had the whole tithe of Slegill aſſigned to them in a diſtinct leaſe, and the vicars of Dacre that of Thrimby.   In proceſs of time, the truſtees for Penrith neglected to renew the leaſe, and left the ſole care of that to the vicar, to whoſe cuſtody the leaſe was committed.   Mr. Child the then vicar renewed the leaſe ; but thinking that the term might laſt his time, neglected to renew it again, tho' it was more than ſeven years run.   Mr. Farrington the next vicar, upon his being inducted, thought it hard for him to renew for years of which he had received no profit ; and, living only four years after, left the leaſe unrenewed.   Dr. Todd, the next ſucceſſor, being a member of the chapter, after ſome years were run out in his time, did prevail with the dean and chapter (with conſent and at the requeſt of the ſurviving truſtees) to put upon the leaſe an additional yearly rent, which by a moderate eſtimate might amount to the ſum of a fine every ſeven years, and ſo to have the leaſe granted to him and his ſucceſſors vicars of Penrith for ever.

Dr.

Dr. Smith bishop of Carlisle, who died in 1702, by a clause in his will says, "Item, I give and bequeath for and towards the augmentation of the vicarage of Penrith and the better maintenance and encouragement of the vicars incumbent there for ever the sum of 500 *l*; and my will is, that the said sum be paid within six months next after my decease unto the dean and chapter of the cathedral church of Carlisle, whom I do hereby constitute and appoint supervisors of this my last will and testament and trustees for the said charity, requesting them to see the same duly settled and secured according to my intention and will herein, unless I shall dispose, settle, and pay the same in my life-time." Which sum was afterwards laid out in a purchase of lands at Clifton.

By indenture bearing date Dec. 19, 1740; Mary Bell of Penrith, spinster, grants to the churchwardens of the parish of Penrith and their successors 240 *l*, in trust to lend out the same upon such security as the vicar shall under his hand approve of, and pay the interest thereof to the vicar for reading morning prayers in the parish church of Penrith in every week day in the year, and also evening prayers on every week day during the time of Lent; first deducting thereout their own reasonable expences in carrying the said trust into execution.

The first incumbent of this parish that we meet with was *Walter de Cantilupe*, who in the year 1223 was presented by the king to the then bishop elect of Carlisle.

In 1318, on the death of Sir *Thomas de Kirk-Ofwald* vicar of Penrith, Sir *Alan de Horncaftle* was collated by bishop Halton. And in 1323 the said Alan resigned, and the same bishop collated Sir *Gilbert de Kirkby*.

In the year 1355, bishop Welton constitutes Sir *John* vicar of Penrith to be dean rural of Cumberland. And in the same year the bishop sends out his mandate to Sir Thomas rector of Burgham and John de Docwra chaplain, to denounce the sentence of the greater excommunication against certain unknown persons, who had broken up a paved way, and done some other outrages in the churchyard at Penrith, reserving to himself the sole power of absolution. Hereupon several of the parishioners came to the bishop at Rose, confessed themselves guilty, and prayed for a remission of the heavy sentence; which was granted, on condition of each man's offering (by way of penance) a wax candle of three pounds weight, before the image of St. Mary in the parish church of Penrith on the Sunday following.—In the same year, Sir John vicar of Penrith hath a licence granted to him, to continue from the 8th of March till Easter following, to hear the confessions of all his parishioners, and to give absolutions upon the performance of penance injoined, except in cases specially reserved to the bishop; which reserved cases were those of the violaters of the rights and liberties of the bishop and his church of Carlisle, ravishers of nuns or having carnal knowledge of them, and perjured persons in assizes, or causes of matrimony or divorce, or disherison, or loss of life or limb.

In 1428, *John Hawekin* was vicar of Penrith, being in that year made a trustee in the settlement of some lands at Yanewith.

In 1477, *Thomas Befle* was vicar.

In 1565, on the death of Sir *Thomas Ellerton* vicar of Penrith, Sir *Robert Peatfon* was collated by bishop Best; and on his resignation in 1574, bishop Barnes

                                                                 collates

collates Sir *Robert Robson*; who also resigning in the next year, the same bishop collates Sir *William Walleis* clerk.

In 1600, William Walleis resigns, and *John Hastie*, M. A. was collated by bishop Robinson. Which John Hastie continued till after the abolition of episcopacy, and his living was sequestred. During the time of his being ejected, one *Baldwin* had his place, who repaired the vicarage house with part of 100 *l* given to him for that purpose out of the sequestred livings. On the return of king Cha. 2. Mr. Hastie was restored, but died soon after. And in 1661, *Simon Webster* was collated by bishop Sterne.

In 1663, on the cession of *Simon Webster* to Dufton, *Robert Fisher*, B. A. was collated by the same bishop.

Robert Fisher dying in 1665, bishop Rainbow collates *Charles Carter*, M. A.

On the cession of Charles Carter in 1667, the same bishop collates *Marius D'Assigny*, S. T. B. a Frenchman, author of several tracts. On whose promotion to Dover in the next year, *Joshua Bunting*, B. A. was collated by the same bishop. Who also removing within less than a year, *John Child*, M. A. was collated.

On the death of John Child in 1694, *Alexander Farington*, B. A. was collated by bishop Smith.

In 1699, on Alexander Farington's death, *Hugh Todd*, S. T. P. was collated by the same patron.

In 1728, on Dr. Todd's death, *John Morland*, M. A. was collated by bishop Waugh.

In 1748, John Morland dying, *Gustavus Thompson*, M. A. was collated by bishop Osbaldiston.

In 1749, on Mr. Thompson's death, *Battie Worsop*, LL. B. was collated; who resigning in the next year, *John Cowper*, M. A. was collated by the same patron.

The present church was built in the years 1720, 1721, and 1722; and is by far the most compleat and elegant parish church in the diocese. The galleries are supported by twenty stones, brought from the quarry of Crowdundale, each ten feet four inches high, and four feet two inches in circumference. It was consecrated by bishop Nicolson then bishop of Londonderry, at the request of bishop Bradford the diocesan. The whole expence of it was 2253 *l* 16*s* 10¼ *d.* Of which, 344 *l* 1*s* 5 *d* was received by a brief (though the whole collection thereupon was 944 *l* 6*s* 9 *d*). By other voluntary contributions, 236 *l* 4*s*. By the parish, 1673 *l* 11*s* 5½ *d.*

Upon the wall of the old church, on the right hand coming in at the south door, were the following inscriptions:

Hic jacet Christophorus Moresby miles, qui obiit 26° die Mensis Julii, A° Di 1499. Jesu. Maria.

Crate

Orate pro anima Chriſtophori Moreſby militis et Elizabethæ uxoris ejus. Quorum animabus propitietur Deus.

Orate pro anima Chriſtophori Pykryng militis ; qui obiit 7° die menſis Sept: Anno Dom. Milleſ°. D°. XII°.

Which inſcriptions are preſerved in the wall on the ſouth ſide of the chancel of the new church : As alſo this following, which in the old church was on the ſouth ſide of the eaſt window :

Orate pro anima Ricardi Coldall nuper de Plumpton in Comitat. Cumbr. armigeri. Qui obiit apud Plumpton 27 die menſis Decembr. Anno Domini Milleſimo CCCCLXII. Cujus animæ propitietur Deus. Amen.

And on the floor below (in the old church) was,

> *Cum Domini Coldall ſecuerunt fila ſorores,*
> *Excipe tres dies atque December abit,*
> *Armiger ille fuit præclaro ſanguine natus.*
> *Terra tenet corpus, ivit at ille Deo.*

Dr. Todd ſays, this *Richard Coldall* was a famous warrior in thoſe times, being the ſame that the country people ſtill frighten children with by the name of *Dicky Cow.*

On the north ſide of the eaſt window of the old church (which is now on the ſouth ſide of the eaſt window) on a monument of white marble adorned with drapery and the arms of Dalſton quartered with Wharton :

Hic prope Thomæ filii cineres, jacet Jana filia e tribus lectiſſima Johannis Wharton de Kirby Thore arm. Filia parente, parens filia, quam digniſſim'. Fidelis conſors et ſolamen vitæ Thomæ Dalſton Hoſpitii Grayienſis armigeri. Cui per quinquennium marita, fælicis conjugii dedit pignora Johannem, Luciam, et Thomam. Summa pietate vel illa quoad Deum, ſingulari ſtudio erga maritum, priſca ſimplicitate inter omnes, per dotes corporis et animi, olim hominum, nunc Dei, amata. O maritæ, ex illa deſcribite maritam ! O poſteri, veſtrum deflete damnum !

> Obiit Chriſtiane et pie ⎰ Ætatis xxvii.
> 12 die Auguſti Anno ⎱ Salutis 1678.
> *Amoris ergo poſuit*
> *Triſtiſſimus*
> T. D.

There were other inſcriptions in the old church, as alſo ſome in the new, which we have inſerted with the families to which they belong elſewhere.

From

From the many trifling monumental inscriptions that one meets with every where, and the very few good ones, it should seem that this is one of the most difficult species of composition. The following epitaph by Dr. Todd on two of his children, on a brass plate in the wall on the north side of the chancel, is much above the common level, and breathes something of elegance, mixed with parental tenderness, and christian magnanimity.

Infra reconduntur duo parvuli infantes, immatura morte abrepti, breves parentum deliciæ, Edvardus *et* Johannes, *filii unici* Hugonis Todd, *S. T. P. et* Luciæ *consortis ejus. Dum in ipso vitæ limine agebant, ingenium illis scitum, forma elegans, indoles blanda, futuræ virtutis et illatæ gratiæ specimina mira. Hos ad se præpropere transire voluit, Qui dixit, Ex talibus constare regnum Dei.*

Illi in portu perierunt : Tu, lector, in alto navigas. Mors ubique in propinquo. Aude sapere ; & quum momenta, quæ legentem fugiunt, in incerto sint, æternitatem fælicem cogita.

Edvardus *natus est* 14 *Sept. A. D.* MDCCII. *mortuus Febr.* 13. MDCCV. Johannes *natus Festo S. S. Innocentium A. D.* MDCCIII. *Innocens denatus Ap.* 15. MDCCVI.

On the south wall, by the side of the second window, on white marble, is the following :

H. S. E.

Thomas Bolton, S. T. P.

Thomæ, *rectoris olim de* Graystock
Filius natu tertius.
Collegii Reginæ Oxon'
Socius dignissimus !
Et non ita pridem apud Algerenses
Sacellanus Regius.
Vir erat spectabilis
Procero corpore et venusto :
Vultu ingenuo,
Honesti pectoris indice :
Moribus insuper suavissimis,
Sale conditis ac facetiis ;
Adeo ut ubicunque gentium
Gratissimum se semper
Exhibuit hospitem.
Amicos visendi studio
Huc proficiscens
Cognatorum inter amplexus
Repentina morte
Correptus est.
Ob. 30 *Sep. A. Dom.* 1763.
Ætat. suæ 44.
Richardus *Frater P.*

On the wall in the chancel is an infcription giving an account of the plague in the year 1598.

A. D. MDXCVIII.

Ex gravi pefte, quæ regionibus hifce incubuit, obierunt apud

Penrith	—	2260
Kendal	—	2500
Richmond		2200
Carlifle	—	1196

This plague is mentioned in the regifter book of Penrith, and alfo in that of Edenhall.

William de Strickland (the fame who was afterwards bifhop) founded a *chantry* in the church of Penrith, and fettled a yearly falary of 6*l* to be paid out of his lands in Penrith to a chantry prieft who fhould teach children in church mufick and grammar.

There was alfo a houfe of *grey friers* of St. Auguftine in Penrith, founded in the reign of Ed. 2. or before; which after the diffolution was granted, in the 34 Hen. 8th, to Robert Tyrwhit efquire.—In the 30 Ed. 3. Agnes Denton widow gave to them by her will 10*s*. And it was the cuftom to maintain this poor fort of monks by fuch bequefts and voluntary charities. In the 33 Ed. 3. the bifhop grants an indulgence of 40 days, to all fuch as fhould be prefent when the Auguftine monks lighted their candles on Chriftmas day and gave them fome charity becaufe they were very poor.

In the church-yard of Penrith, on the north fide thereof, ftand two pyramidal ftones, near four yards in height, at five yards diftance from each other; and having feveral fegments of circular ftones erected between them. Thefe laft the fancy of the people will have to reprefent wild boars; and they have a tradition, that a famous knight-errant, one Sir Ewan Cæfarius, was buried here, who in his time made mighty havock amongft thofe beafts in Inglewood foreft. Mr. Sandford, in his manufcript account of Cumberland, fays, he was told by Mr. Page (who was fchoolmafter at Penrith from 1581 to 1591) that a ftranger gentleman coming to an inn there, defired to have fome of the confiderable inhabitants to fup with him, whereupon this Mr. Page and fome others attended him. The ftranger told them he came to fee the antiquities of the place; and drawing out a paper faid, that Sir Hugh Cæfario had an hermitage fome-where thereabouts called Sir Hugh's parlour: And Mr. Sandford adds, that when he was at fchool at Penrith this place was opened by William Turner, who there found the great long fhank bones of a man and a broad fword.

Within the town of Penrith there was a free grammar school of ancient time. In the year 1340, the bifhop granted a licence to John de Efkeheved clerk to teach here the art of Grammar; the fchool (as is there faid) being

the

the bishop's and under his patronage and of that of his predecessors in former times. In 1361, another licence was granted to Robert de Burgham chaplain to teach boys and youth the psalter, Priscian's grammar, and singing : With an inhibitory clause against all others. Bishop Strickland (as aforesaid) required his chantry priest to teach music and grammar for the salary of 6*l* a year. Upon the dissolution of the chantries this revenue continued in the crown until the 6th year of queen Elizabeth ; at which time she, moved thereto by the humble petition of the inhabitants of Penrith, and at the instance of Sir Thomas Smith knight then dean of Carlisle and secretary of state, did by her letters patent bearing date the 18th day of July in the same year found and erect a free grammar school, in this her seigniory and chief town within the forest of Inglewood, under the style and title of The Free Grammar School of Queen Elizabeth in Penrith ; and did endow it at the same time with 6*l* ancient salary of the chantry priest ; to have one master and usher ; and to be governed by five of the most discreet persons of the town and parish, with power to chuse both master and usher, and to elect new governors upon the death of any of their number.

In 1633, Sir John Lowther conveyed to Mr. William Whelpdale some seats under Archer's hall (the Cross) at 1*l* 6*s* 8*d* rent, which was given by the town to the school. In like manner, a large piece of ground called Ling Stubbs was given to the school by the joint consent of the town and the king's commissioners ; but the same was sold by Mr. Andrew Whelpdale to John Benson, reserving only a quit rent of 20*s* to the school, whereas the land was at the time of its first settlement valued at 40*s per annum*, and is now worth ten times that sum. There are also several leases of houses in the school register, which run for 21 years ; but the premises have long been wholly unknown, and the rents turned into free or quit rents. Dr. Todd says, Upon a law suit in chancery concerning the revenue of the school, Mr. William Whelpdale having got the writings and evidences of the school into his custody and possession, and refusing to give an account thereof, it was decreed, that neither any of the governors, nor any nearly related to them, should be farmers of the school lands, or have any thing to do with the revenue.

In the year 1661, William Robinson of London citizen and grocer, gave by his will to the grocers company all his lands, rents, and hereditaments in Grubstreet to the uses following ; viz. To pay out of the rents and profits thereof 20*l* yearly to the churchwardens, vestrymen, and overseers of the parish of Penrith, for the use of 20 *poor* people, ten men and ten women, of the said parish, on the 25th day of December ; and 20*s* for a sermon to be preached in the parish church of Penrith on that day ; with 5*s* to the clerk and sexton ; and 15*s* to the churchwardens, vestrymen, and overseers for a collation : And 10*l* yearly to the use of the free *school* of Penrith : And also 20*l* yearly to the churchwardens, for the educating and bringing up of *poor girls* in a free school to read and seamstry work or such other learning fit for that sex, to be admitted by and with the consent of the churchwardens for the time being: Also 20s yearly for a sermon to be preached in the said church on Ascension day, and 5s to the clerk and sexton, and 35s for a collation for the churchwardens, vestrymen, and overseers on the said day.

Mrs. Joan Laffells by her will in 1671, gave the residue of her personal estate, after debts and legacies paid, to the said school founded by Mr. Robinson; the interest thereof to be applied towards the employing of poor children in the working of worsted and knitting in the said school, at the discretion of her executors, with power to them to nominate two able persons to carry the said will into execution. The effects came to about 100 l; for which the surviving executor granted an annuity of 5 l out of certain lands, to four trustees and their heirs male; if any of them die without an heir male, the survivors to chuse another in the town of Penrith; and they to appoint the girls so to be taught, with the assistance of the owner of the lands out of which the rent charge issues.

Mr. Roger Sleddale by his will in 1690 gave 10 l to be lent to the master or mistress of the said school without interest, on their giving security for the same to be repaid when they die or cease to teach.

PARISH OF EDENHALL.

EDENHALL (the next parish) is bounded by the river Eden on the east, Eamot on the south, the parish of Penrith on the west, and Salkeld on the north. It was first given to *Henry Fitz-Swene*, younger brother of *Adam Fitz-Swein*. In Henry the third's time *Robert Turp* died seized thereof, his son *Adam Turp* being then an infant of seven years of age. Which *Adam* had a son *Robert Turp*, who had two daughters coheirs, of whom *Julian* in the 1 Ed. 3. was married to *William Stapilton*.

The *Stapiltons* held it for five descents; then *Joan* second daughter and coheir of Sir *William Stapilton* knight transferred it to *Thomas de Musgrave* about the 38 Hen. 6. in which name and family it still continues.

The ancestor of this family most probably came in with William the Conqueror, for very soon after the conquest we find them seated at Musgrave in Westmorland, where they had large possessions, and to which place they gave name. After their purchase of Hartley castle, and the acquisition of Edenhall by this inter-marriage, they transferred their habitation to Hartley and Edenhall alternately, and of late years chiefly to Edenhall; saving that the present owner having received Kempton Park in Middlesex by his mother, daughter of Sir John Chardin, he now frequently resides in Middlesex. This family we have deduced at large at Musgrave aforesaid, which was their first habitation in these counties, and of which they still continue proprietors.

The *church* of Edenhall is dedicated to St. Cuthbert; and is vicarial, having been given by king Edward the first to the prior and convent of Carlisle, who soon after got it appropriated to their priory. It is valued in the king's books jointly with Langwathby at 17 l 12 s 1 d; was certified to the
                                                                    governors

governors of queen Anne's bounty at 43 *l* 7 *s* 8 *d*; and is now worth about 70 *l* yearly.

In the year 1299, *John de Ludam* deacon was presented to this church by the prior and convent of Carlisle; who assigned to him for his support the whole altarage of the church, and a moiety of the land and meadow of Edenhall (that is, of the *glebe* land, as it seemeth) and four pounds of silver out of their chamber yearly.

. In 1341, the bishop being informed of the infirm state of Sir *Adam* vicar of Edenhall, directs his official to give him tender notice to pitch upon some coadjutor, who may be licensed to assist him in his cure.

In 1362, upon the death of Sir *John de Lendham* vicar of Edenhall, Sir *John de Mareshall* was presented by the prior and convent, and thereupon instituted, on his having taken the oath of personal residence according to the form of the constitution of the legate in that case provided.

· In 1368, the prior and convent having procured the profits of the church of Edenhall and chapel of Langwathby to be appropriated to themselves; refer the allowance for the supply of both the said cures to be settled by the bishop, and impower their subprior to be their proctor to consent to the same. And in the same year *John de Kirkby* was presented to the vicarage, on his exchanging Burgh by Sands with *Eudo de Ravenstandale* then vicar of Edenhall.

In 1465, *Robert Goodylow* was vicar; having in that year a legacy given him in the vicar of Stanwix's will proved by the bishop.

In 1565 *Alan Scott*, M. A. was presented: He was provost of Queen's College in Oxford, and resigned his provostship, and resided and died at Edenhall.

· In 1578, on the death of *Alan Scott*, Sir *William Smith* clerk was presented by virtue of an assigned grant long before made by Sir Thomas Smith knight dean and the chapter of Carlisle.

In 1609, on the death of William Smith, institution was given to *Thomas Maplett*, M. A. who was presented by Sir Christopher Parking knight dean and the chapter of Carlisle.

· In 1669, *Gilbert Burton* was presented upon the death of *Simon Green*.

In 1683, *John Leigh*, M. A. on the death of Gilbert Burton.

In 1690, on the deprivation of *John Leigh*, *George Moon* succeeded.

In 1743, upon Mr. Moon's death, *Christopher Musgrave*, M. A. was collated by bishop Fleming on a lapse.

In 1763, on the cession of Christopher Musgrave (then D. D.) *Joseph Rowland* clerk was instituted on a presentation by the dean and chapter.

In 1774, on the death of Joseph Rowland, *Roger Baldwin*, D. D. was in like manner presented and instituted.

The abbey of Holme Cultram had 14 acres of land at Edenhall given by Robert Turp; and other lands there given by Alan Turp: With pasture for 1700 sheep, and for other goods as much as belonged to the said lands †.

† Registr. Holme.

And.

And in the 37 Hen. 8. Mar. 20, the said king grants to Thomas lord Wharton one messuage and tenement, and all those several parcels of land lying in the fields of Edenhall, and one holme or pasture containing 8 acres, then in the tenure of Edward Musgrave knight, late belonging to the monastery of Holm Cultram.

The parish register of Edenhall takes notice of 42 persons (about a fourth part of the parish) dying there of the *plague* in 1598; who were buried near their lodges on Penrith fell, Shaddow Burgh or Edenhall fell, Flatt's close, and other places.

There are now in the parish about 35 *families*; all of the established church.

They have a small charity here of about 7*l* a year, given at different times by the Musgrave family; which is chiefly applied for the maintenance of a petty school.

PARISH OF SALKELD.

THE parish of SALKELD, or *Great Salkeld* (as it is often styled in the bishops registers), adjoins upon Edenhall on the south, Lazonby on the west and north, and the river Eden on the east. It is one of those places that was granted to the king of Scots as we have mentioned above, and afterwards resumed by the crown of England, upon which account it is sometimes called Salkeld Regis, and finally granted by king William the third to the ancestor of the duke of Portland the present proprietor.

The CHURCH here is dedicated to St. Cuthbert, and is annexed to the archdeaconry of Carlisle. When it was first appropriated to or made a corps of the archdeaconry doth not appear. There are no institutions or collations to it separately in the oldest registers at Rose: therefore it seemeth to have been annexed to the archdeaconry at the first foundation of the see.

As to the *value* thereof, in bishop Appleby's register, in the year 1366, it is certified by John de Appleby the archdeacon, that the church of Salkeld Regis annexed to his archdeaconry was taxed at 12*l* sterling according to the old valuation (namely, that of pope Nicholas), and at 40*s* according to the new valuation (of king Edward the second). In Henry the eighth's taxation it is rated at 22*l* 10*s* 10*d*; and is now worth about 90*l* per annum.

The church and steeple seem to have been built at different times. The steeple seems to be of a much later erection; and intended, upon occasion, for a secure hold or habitation for the rector himself: So the iron door below, and the good cellar, with several chimnies within, persuade us to believe. Bishop Nicolson supposes it to be the work of archdeacon Close, brother to the bishop of that name. The said archdeacon lies buried in the quire under a large blue gravestone, with an inscription in brass, whereof nothing is now legible.

legible. There were alfo anciently the like commemorations of him in the windows, with an *Orate pro Anima.*

The parfonage houfe was left in a ruinous condition by archdeacon Weft; but Mr. Thomas Mufgrave, afterwards doctor in divinity and dean of Carlifle, repaired it handfomely and at confiderable expence, and built the ftable and granary from the ground. The reft of the outhoufes (the old kitchen only excepted and a fmall part of the little barn) were all built by archdeacon Nicolfon.

There are about 60 *families* in this parifh, of which feven are prefbyterians.

There is a *parifh ftock* of 9*l* 6*s.* And a *poor ftock* of 34*l* 4*s* 4*d.*

Alfo here is a free *fchool*, which was founded about the year 1515; endowed with feveral fmall rents, charged on fundry parcels of land in the faid parifh, together with fines upon defcents and alienation. Some of which rents and fines having been withholden, the matter is and hath been long contefting in the court of chancery.

In the year 1360, the bridge at Salkeld being fallen, bifhop Welton publifhed an indulgence of 40 days to all who fhould contribute to the repair of it. We have met with accounts of many other indulgences granted on like occafions, and are enabled from that bifhop's regifter to exhibit the form of fuch indulgence, which therefore as a curiofity we fhall here infert: " Uni- " verfis fanctæ matris ecclefiæ filiis, ad quorum notitiam præfentes literæ " pervenerint, Gilbertus permiffione divina Karliolenfis epifcopus falutem in " finceris amplexibus Salvatoris. Reparationem pontium et viarum quam- " plurimum fore neceffariam attendentes, mentes fidelium ad fubveniendum " fabricis pontium et viarum per allectiva indulgentiarum munera duximus " excitandas. De Dei igitur omnipotentis mifericordia; ac gloriofæ Virginis " Mariæ matris ejus ac beatorum apoftolorum Petri et Pauli omniumque fanc- " torum meritis et interceffionibus confidentes; omnibus parochianis noftris et " aliis qui Diocefanam hanc noftram indulgentiam ratam habuerint, de pecca- " tis fuis vere contritis pænitentibus et confeffis, qui ad fabricam pontis de " Salkeld diruti et proftrati de bonis a Deo fibi collatis g,a,a contulerint fub- " fidia caritatis, vel manus porrexerint quomodolibet adjutrices, quadraginta " dies de injuncta fibi pænitentia, Deo propitio, mifericorditer relaxamus. In " cujus rei teftimonium figillum noftrum præfentibus eft appenfum. Dat' etc." —And at the fame time a monition was directed to all rectors, vicars, and cha- plains in the diocefe, to warn all that have any fums of money in their hand for the ufes aforefaid, to pay the fame forthwith to Roger de Salkeld or Richard Hunter the receivers, on pain of the greater excommunication.

5

The priory of Wetheral had two parts of the tithe in certain parcels of the demefne of Salkeld Regis, and the rector only the remaining third part †.

PARISH OF LAZONBY.

THE parifh of LAZONBY adjoins upon Salkeld on the fouth, Penrith and Hutton on the fouth weft and weft, Hefket on the north weft, and the river Eden on the eaft and north eaft: And contains in the whole about 115 families, four whereof are prefbyterians.

Lazonby lies within the foreft of Englewood, but has been long a feparate manor; heretofore in the poffeffion of the *Stutevils*, and by marriage of the heirefs of the Stutevils came to the *Morvils*, then to the *Multons*, and from them came to the *Dacres*. It was fettled upon a younger branch of the Dacres and their iffue male, and on failure thereof to go to the heirs general of the family, who were the lords Dacre of the fouth. *Leonard Dacre*, fecond brother of Thomas lord Dacre of the north, being feized thereof in tail male, was attainted in the 12 Eliz. for being concerned in the affair of Mary queen of Scots, as were alfo his two younger brothers *Edward* and *Francis*. *Edward* died in the 21 Eliz. and *Leonard* died in the 23 Eliz. after whofe death the intailed eftate continued in the crown during the life of *Francis* and any who fhould claim as heir male of his body. And this feems to be the reafon why thefe brothers were not executed, but only banifhed, as the crown held the eftate by the tenure of their lives.

On the death of *Leonard*, a commiffion iffued to Henry lord Scroop, the bifhop of Carlifle, and others, to inquire what goods and chattels, and what lands and tenements, the faid Leonard Dacre had or held at the time of his death; who return, that he had no goods and chattels, and that Philip earl of Arundel in the right of Anne his wife, and the lord William Howard in the right of Elizabeth his wife, had and received to their own ufe all the rents and profits of the Dacre eftate, except what were in the hands of the queen; and that *Francis Dacre* fon of the late William lord Dacre, and brother of the faid Leonard Dacre, hath iffue male Francis Dacre of his body lawfully begotten; which faid Francis the father and Francis the fon are in full life, to wit, at Carlifle in the county aforefaid.

The faid Francis the fon had a fon Ranulf, who died in the 10 Charles 1. without iffue, whereby the intail ended. Neverthelefs, the king continued in poffeffion, and after him the commonwealth of England, until the year 1657, when Francis lord Dacre of the fouth, heir general of the family of Dacre, fued in the court of exchequer for the recovery of Lazonby (and other pof-

---

† Terræ five culturæ de dominio in villa feu territorio de Salkeld Regis; de quibus prior de Wederhal habet percipere duas partes decimæ et rector unum: In le Croftes 6 acræ. Item, in le Fittes 36 acræ, viz. in Holme. Item, in Langiigg 18 acræ. Item, in le Taythes 6 acræ. Item, in Haperfhowe 9 acræ. Item, in Halborwan, vel in les Ronylandes, 12 acræ. Item, in Smekergill bank 18 acræ. Item, in le Wym 18 acræ. Item, in le Northfeld in er vias 6 acræ. Item, in le Kingflat 12 acræ. Item, in le Waterlands 5 acræ.—Regiftr. Wetheral.

feffions);

ſeſſions); whereupon " the barons on mature conſideration adjudge, that the " hands of the keepers of the liberty of England by authority of parliament " be amoved from the poſſeſſion of the manor of Leyſingby with the appur- " tenances, and that Francis now lord Dacre be reſtored to his poſſeſſion " thereof, together with the iſſues and profits thereof from the time of the " death of Ranulf de Dacre."

From which time Lazonby continued in the Dacres till about the year 1716, when it was ſold (amongſt other particulars) to Sir Chriſtopher Muſ- grave of Edenhall baronet, by the coheirs of Thomas earl of Suſſex, being heirs general of the eſtate of the Dacres of the ſouth.

The tenants pay yearly to the preſent lord of the manor Sir Philip Muſ- grave baronet, a free rent of $2l$ $7s$ $1\frac{1}{4}d$; indenture rent, by agreement Dec. 4, 1676, $9l$ $15s$ $7\frac{1}{4}d$; arbitrary rent $3s$ $2d$; Potter rent $1l$ $4s$; and for im- provements $3s$ $11d$.—The Potter rent is ſaid to be for liberty to get clay, of which there is a very fine white ſort, for making of earthen ware.

Within theſe precincts there is a ſmall meſne cuſtomary manor belonging to Timothy Fetherſtonhaugh eſquire, whoſe anceſtors have long reſided at the neighbouring town of Kirkoſwald.

The CHURCH of Lazonby is dedicated to St. Nicholas, and was given by Sir Hugh de Morvil to the priory of Lanercoſt, and in 1272 was appropriated to that houſe: And an endowment was made for the vicar, and the collation to the vicarage reſerved to the biſhop.

In 1300, Sir *William de Haloghton* was collated by biſhop Halton.

In 1316, upon the death of the ſaid Sir William de Haloghton, the biſhop collates Sir *Adam de Ottley* chaplain.

In 1367, the laſt will and teſtament of *William de Threlkeld* vicar of Ley- ſingby was proved at Roſe. He was ſucceeded by *Richard de Whitton*, who in the next year made an exchange with *John de Caſtro Bernardi* vicar of New- ton in Glendale in the dioceſe of Durham, who thereupon is collated to the vicarage of Leyſingby.

In 1477, *Edward Rothion* was vicar, being alſo at the ſame time vicar of Stanwix.

In 1484, an award was made by biſhop Bell, between the priory and con- vent of Lanercoſt (proprietaries of the rectory) and *John Boon* the vicar, touching the tithes of wool and lamb and other ſmall dues; which award was in favour of the vicar. And in 1513, at the inſtance of the ſaid vicar Boon, the bounds betwixt the pariſhes of Penrith and Lazonby in Plumpton Park were found by a jury to be " per cloacam putei in-pariete parcæ de Plumpton, " vulgariter, *the Watdobe*; et ſic extendendo linealiter et directe uſque ad " rivulum de Petrel, habuttando directe a cloaca prædicta ad locum vocatum " uſualiter *the Harrys* ultra ripam præfati rivuli de Petrel infra parcam de " Plumpton."

In 1588, *Edward Denton* clerk was collated by bifhop Meye.

In 1614, on the death of the 'faid Mr. Denton, bifhop Robinfon collated *Anthony Haydock.*

In 1637, Mr. Haydock being dead, a caveat was entered by Sir Thomas Dacre knight, then mayor of Carlifle, who claimed the patronage : But not. withftanding this, bifhop Potter collated *Jonathan Goodwin.*

In 1661, on the refignation of Jonathan Goodwin, *Robert Simpfon* was collated by bifhop Sterne.

In 1668, on Robert Simpfon's death, *John Symfon,* B. A. was collated by bifhop Rainbow. And after him was *Robert Hume ;* who removing in 1703, *George Parker,* M. A. of Glafgow was collated by bifhop Nicolfon.

In 1737, on the death of George Parker, *Erafmus Head,* M. A. was collated by bifhop Fleming.

In 1739, on Mr. Head's refignation, *William Wilkinfon,* M. A. was collated by the fame bifhop.

In 1752, on Mr. Wilkinfon's death, *John Brown,* M. A. was collated by' bifhop Ofbaldifton : And he refigning in 1757, his father John Brown vicar of Wigton was collated.

In 1763, on the death of John Brown the elder, *James Evans,* M. A. was collated by bifhop Lyttelton.

In 1771, on Mr. Evans's death, *Jofeph Blain* was collated by bifhop Law.

Upon the diffolution of the religious houfes, this rectory was granted by king Edward the fixth to Sir Thomas Dacre knight ; which was afterwards pur. chafed by Dr. John Barwick dean of St. Paul's, and together with the demefne of Harefkeugh nigh Kirkofwald, was given by him and his brother Dr. Peter Barwick to the chapel and poor of Witherflack in Weftmorland, paying there. out yearly to the vicar of Lazonby 40 *s.*

The abbey of Holm-Cultram had divers poffeffions at Layfingby given to them by Sir Hugh de Morvil ; who for the health of the fouls of himfelf and his wife, and his father and mother and all his anceftors and fucceffors, gave to God and the church of St. Paul's, pafture at Lafyngby for 500 fheep, 10 oxen, 10 cows and their followers of one year, one bull, and two horfes, and divers parcels of arable and meadow ground *. And he afterwards gave unto them

* Univerfis fanctæ matris ecclefiæ filiis, Hugo de Morevill falutem. Sciatis me conceffiffe et de. diffe et hac præfenti charta mea confirmaffe, Deo et ecclefiæ fanctæ Mariæ de Holmcoltram et mo. nachis ibidem Deo fervientibus, pro falute animæ meæ et uxoris meæ et pro animabus omnium an. tecefforum et fuccefforum meorum, in liberam, puram, et perpetuam eleemofynam pafturam de Layfingby quingentis ovibus, et decem bobûs, et decem vaccis et fectæ earum unius anni, et uni tauro, et duobus equis; et quatuor acras terræ arabilis, videlicet, illas fuper quas edificia fua funt inter ovile fuum et viam regiam, et novem acras prati infimul ad Keldefelde inter pratum domini' H. et meum de Salychild; et communem pafturam ipfis averiis et omnibus fuis, in omnibus locis ubi mea dominica averia et averia prænominatæ villæ pafcunt; et ayfiamenta in bofco ad omnia neceffaria

them, with his body, other parcels of land †. Which land, king Hen. 8. by his letters patent dated July 9, in the 37th year of his reign, granted (among other particulars) to Thomas Dalſton eſquire and Elizabeth his wife,

PLUMPTON PARK, in this pariſh; being a demeſne of the crown, was leaſed out for a long term to *Jack Muſgrave* captain of Bewcaſtle, who planted there (Mr. Sandford ſays) five ſons on five ſeveral tenements, with many other tenants beſides. And in the 26 Eliz. whilſt the captains of Bewcaſtle were farmers thereof, there was a decree in the exchequer aſcertaining to the tenants within the ſaid park their ſeveral tenements as they had been accuſtomed.

After the expiration of the Muſgrave leaſe, king James the firſt by letters patent bearing date July 19, in the 3d year of his reign, granted the premiſſes to John Murray eſquire (afterwards earl of Annandale) for the term of forty years, paying for the ſame to the king yearly 121 *l* 6*s* 3*d*. This John Murray, being poſſeſſed of the ſaid grant, ſued the tenants for ejecting them; ſetting forth, that they holding their lands by border ſervice, and that ſervice being now ceaſed by the union of the two kingdoms in his majeſty's perſon, their tenure was at an end. At length it was agreed (by conſent of all parties) that on their payment of 800 *l* to the ſaid John Murray, they ſhould hold their tenements as before; and the cuſtoms, on the footing of the decree in the 26 Eliz. were aſcertained and decreed as followeth: That after the death of a tenant, having a tenement within the ſaid park, manor, or lordſhip of Plumpton, the eldeſt ſon ſhall inherit and enjoy the ſame to him and his heirs for ever; and if ſuch tenant have no ſons, but hath iſſue a daughter or daughters, the eldeſt daughter only ſhall inherit. And if a man marry a wife that hath right to have a tenement within the ſaid park or manor, the huſband ſhall enjoy the ſame during the life of his wife; and afterwards, if he hath iſſue by her, until ſuch iſſue ſhall attain the age of 21 years, he finding and bringing up ſuch iſſue in convenient manner at his own coſts and charges. If ſuch tenant die without iſſue male or female, the tenement ſhall deſcend to the next heir; and if there be divers heirs female in equal degree, it ſhall deſcend to the eldeſt of them and not be divided amongſt them as coparceners. And after the death or alienation of a tenant, the heir or purchaſer ſhall pay within one year in name of a fine two years rent of the lands deſcended or aliened; the ſame to be preſented by the tenants of the manor at the next court. The widow to have a

ceſſaria ſua facienda. Quare volo, ut prænominati monachi prædictam eleemoſynam habeant et teneant de me et hæredibus meis liberam et quietam ab omni ſeculari ſervicio, conſuetudine et exactione. Et ego et hæredes mei warrantizabimus prædictis monachis prædictam eleemoſynam contra omnes homines imperpetuum. Teſtibus; Thoma filio Coſpatricii, &c. *Regiſtr. Holme.*

† Univerſis ſanctæ matris, &c. Hugo de Morevill Salutem Sciatis me dediſſe et conceſſiſſe et hac præſenti charta mea confirmaſſe, voluntate et conſenſu uxoris meæ Helewiſæ et hæredum meorum, cum corpore meo, Deo et beatæ Mariæ et Monachis de Holm Coltram, pro ſalute animæ meæ et omnium anteceſſorum et ſucceſſorum meorum, in puram et perpetuam eleemoſynam, totam terram illam in territorio de Laiſingby, quæ jacet inter quatuor acras terræ quas prius dedi eis et rivulum qui eſt diviſa inter Laiſingby et Salkild, et extendit ſe a via regia uſque ad vaſtum domini regis. Teſtibus, &c. *Regiſtr. Holme.*

H h h 2   third

third part during her widowhood, paying rents and fervices according to her rate and proportion. All the faid lands to be holden by the tenants (being about fourfcore in number) as cuftomary tenants, by copy of court roll, as in the nature of copyholds.

Afterwards, king Charles the firft, by letters patent dated April 26, in the firft year of his reign, grants in fee and perpetuity to the faid John Murray earl of Annandale, all that the park or land of Plumpton, within the foreft of Inglewood, containing by eftimation in meadow, pafture, and arable ground 2436 acres, and common of pafture in the foreft of Inglewood to the fame appertaining, of the yearly rent of 121 *l* 6 *s* 3 *d*; being parcel of the poffeffions affigned to the faid king before his acceffion to the crown, and heretofore parcel of the poffeffions of Richard duke of Gloucefter : To be holden of the king as of his manor of Eaft Greenwich, by fealty only, in free and common focage, and not *in capite* nor by knights fervice, for all fervices, exactions, and demands.

Finally, James earl of Annandale, Aug. 19, 1653, for the fum of 3000 *l*, grants to dame Ellinor Lowther of Mauls Meaburn widow, and others, (whereby the fame came into the Lowther family) all that the manor or lordfhip of Plumpton, Plumpton Park, Plumpton Park Head, and Plumpton Head, together with all meffuages, lands, tenements, woods, underwoods, waters, fifheries, warrens, chafes, commons, waftes, heaths, courts leet, courts baron, view of frankpledge, heriots, waifs, eftrays, goods and chattels of felons, felons of themfelves, and of fugitives and perfons outlawed, franchifes, liberties, privileges, and emoluments whatfoever, to the faid manor and lordfhip belonging or in any wife appertaining [except one meffuage and tenement called Wallas tenement, and 13 other tenements and parcels of ground by name, of the yearly rent in the whole of 15 *l* 7 *s* 10 *d*, and foggage rent 1 *l* 1 *s* 6 *d*.] With a covenant of warranty aganft the faid earl James, John late earl of Annandale, James late king of England, and Charles late king of England.

In the year 1767, a very handfome new chapel was erected at Plumpton Wall, at the expence of about 200 *l*, raifed by contributions in the neighbourhood. Mr. John Brown late of Plumpton aforefaid endowed it with 200 *l*, and the feats make 3 *l* 9 *s* 6 *d*. It was confecrated by bifhop Lyttelton in 1767, and dedicated to St. John the evangelift; and the nomination of the curate declared to be in Mr. John Sanderfon heir to Mr. Brown.

OLD PENRITH lies within this divifion, of which we fhall give Mr. Horfley's account, as much the moft accurate and fatisfactory of any thing hitherto publifhed :

" *Old Penrith* (he fays), which I take to be *Bremetenracum*, ftands upon the grand military way that leads directly to Carlifle or to the wall, and is vifible almoft all the way to it. And excepting Carlifle (which I believe to be *Luguvallium ad vallum*, but abandoned before the writing of the *Notitia*) there feems never to have been any ftation on this way nearer to the wall than *Old Penrith*. The remains of the outbuildings here continue very confiderable, as well

2

well as thofe of the ftation itfelf. The fort is about 6 chains (or 132 yards) in length, 5 in breadth, containing about 3 acres; which is a ftation of a middle fize. The place near the ftation is called Plumpton Wall, being a long and fcattered village. The fort itfelf is called Caftle-Steeds, and the houfe that ftands neareft it *The lough*, from a fmall lake, as it feemeth, juft before it. The faid *Plumpton Wall* takes in the whole row of houfes, of which the *Lough* is one. The ftation lies about 200 yards from the river Peterel, which runs on the weft fide of it. The ramparts are ftill very high, and the ditch round them very perfect. The four gates, or entries, are all very vifible, and juft in the middle of the ramparts. The *Prætorium* alfo appears, though by working ftones out of it they have fpoiled its figure. On the weft fide there is a defcent, as ufual, towards the river, and great ruins of a town. The ruins of buildings alfo on the other fides, particularly on the eaft and fouth, are very remarkable, and the whole like a Notitia ftation, though the ftones have been wrought away, and ufed in building the village. The eaft and weft ramparts are about 140 yards long, and the north and fouth about 120. The *prætorium* is near the north rampart. The fituation of the fort is alfo very remarkable, being one of thofe that have the profpect every way terminated by hills or rifing ground, overlooking the vale in the middle. The diftance to New Penrith is about 5 miles, and to Carlifle 13. This ftation appears to have been poffeffed by the Romans in the reign of Alexander Severus from the infcription at Great Salkeld. This ftation feems to be that which is called *Voreda* in the Itinerary, and *Bereda* by the anonymous *Ravennas*. According to the *Notitia*, the *cuneus armaturarum*, that is, horfe compleatly armed, kept garrifon at *Bremetenracum*. To this it muft be added, that there is a military way, though now much ruined, which goes out from Old Penrith towards Kefwick, but not quite fo far weft. This joined the other way that paffeth from Elenborough by Papcaftle to Amblefide, from whence it is moft probable that a branch went off to Morefby *."

Mr. Camden has given us feveral infcriptions found at this place, which (he fays) he copied himfelf; the originals of which are not now to be found. The firft is,

GADVNO	Gaduno
VLP TRAI	Ulpius Trajanus
EM. AL. PET.	emeritus alæ Petrianæ
MARTIVS	Martius
F. P. C.	faciendum procuravit.

Mr. Burton (from the authority of this infcription, as it feemeth) reckons *Gadunus* among our northern tutelar deities; but by the conclufion of the infcription, *faciendum procuravit, Gadunus* feems rather to have been the name of a perfon deceafed, for whom *Ulpius Trajanus Martius* an *emeritus* of the *ala Petriana* took care to have this funeral monument erected. Mr. Ward thinks it more likely that the *emeritus* was the deceafed perfon, and therefore

* Horfley iii.

reads.

reads this infcription, *Gaduno Ulpio Trajano emerito alæ Petrianæ Martius frater ponendum curavit.*

The next is,

D M	Diis Manibus,
FL. MARTIO SEN	Flavio Martio fenatori
IN C CARVETIOR	in cohorte Carvetiorum,
QUESTORIO	queftorio :
VIXIT AN XXXXV	Vixit annos quadraginta quinque.
MARTIOLA FILIA ET	Martiola filia et.
HERES PONEN	heres ponendum
CVRAVIT	curavit.

The reading in the third line is according to the conjecture in Camden; of which Mr. Horfley fays, though he cannot fay it is fatisfactory, yet he knows not how to mend it. Mr. Ward thinks the three firft lines after D M fhould be read *Flavio-Martio fenatori in civitate* (or, *colonia*) *Carvetiorum queftorio. Vir quæftorius* is one who hath been *quæftor* or treafurer; in the fame manner as *prætorius* and *cenforius* denote fuch perfons as have difcharged thofe offices. So that this *Martius* had been a fenator and treafurer among thefe *Carvetii*, whoever they were.

The next infcription in Camden is,

DM CROTILO GERMANVS VIX.
ANIS XXVI. GRECA VIX ANIS IIII
VINDICIANVS FRA. ET FIL. TIT. PO.

Dis Manibus. Crotilo Germanus vixit
Annis viginti fex. Græca vixit annis quatuor.
Vindicianus fratri et filiæ titulum pofuit.

The laft infcription in Camden is this:

D M	Dis Manibus.
AICETVOS MATER	Aicetus mater
VIXIT A XXXXV	vixit annos 45.
ET LATTIO FIL VIX	Et Lattio filia vixit
A XII. LIMISIVS	annos 12. Limifius
CONIV. ET FILIÆ	conjugi et filiæ
PIENTISSIMIS	pientiffimis
POSVIT	pofuit.

Next follow fuch infcriptions as Mr. Horfley himfelf met with:

" Deabus Matribus tramarinis et numini imperatoris Alexandri Augufti et
" Juliæ Mammeæ matri Augufti noftri et caftrorum totique domui divinæ
" æternaque vexillatio . . . . .

This was found at Lough, and is in the garden of the archdeacon at Salkeld. *Julia Mammea* the mother of the emperor is here called *mater caftrorum*, which title is given to the empreffes in feveral infcriptions in Gruter. It occurs likewife

wife in the later writers; for Trebellius Pollio informs us, that Victorina the mother of Victorinus was fo called. And Capitolinus fays the fame of Fauftina. But the greateft curiofity of it lies in its being confecrated to the *Deæ matres tramarinæ* (or *tranfmarinæ*). We have the *matres domefticæ* upon an altar at Scaleby caftle, which feem to be diftinguifhed from thefe *matres tranfmarinæ*, and the two characters may ferve to explain each other.

The next is upon an altar;

J O M	Jovi Optimo Maximo
C O H	Cohortis
II G A L E Q	fecundæ Gallorum Equitum
T D,O M I T I	Titus Domiti-
V S H E R O N	us Heron
D N I C O M E D I A	de Nicomedia
P R E F	Præfectus.

Another, upon an altar;

I O M	Jovi Optimo Maximo
E T G D D	et Genio Dominorum
N N P H I	noftrorum Phi-
L I P P O R V	lipporum
A V G G C O H	Auguftorum Cohors
G A L L O	Gallorum.

The laft is, upon a fmall altar;

D E O	Deo
M O G T I	Mogonti.

Mogon was a local deity, that was worfhipped by the *Gadeni.*

PARISH OF KIRKOSWALD.

KIRKOSWALD is the next parifh, but on the eaft fide of Eden. It is fo called from St. Ofwald, to whom the church is dedicated.

Mr. Denton fays, it is part of that great barony which was granted to Adam fon of Swene, from whom it came with a daughter to Trivers lord of Burgh, from a daughter of Trivers to Engain, and from a daughter of Engain to Morvil. But Sir William Dugdale fays, it came (together with Lafingby) to Sir Hugh Morvil by marriage of his wife Helwife de Stuteville. And in difparagement of the former account, it is well known, that Trivers married a daughter of Ranulph de Mefchiens firft grantee of Cumberland.—But however it came to the Morvils, it is certain Sir Hugh Morvil was in poffeffion of it, from whom it defcended to the Multons, and from them to the Dacres, and by Joan daughter of Thomas lord Dacre to Sir Richard Fynes knight, and by the heirefs of that family to Sampfon Lennard, and from him to Thomas Lennard

4   lord

lord Dacre, who married the lady Anne Fitzroy natural daughter of king Charles the second by Barbara duchess of Cleveland, and by that king made earl of Suffex; whose two daughters and coheirs Barbara and Anne sold this lordship *(inter alia)* to Sir Christopher Musgrave of Edenhall baronet, father of Sir Philip Musgrave baronet the present proprietor.

The *demesne lands* here are excellent; and let for upwards of 600*l per annum*. The customary tenants pay about 9*l* yearly customary rent, and a god's-penny only for a fine.

The *castle* of Kirkoswald is very ancient. It was much improved by Sir Hugh Morvil; who in the second year of king John had a grant of a market at this place on Thursday weekly and inclosed the park. Thomas son of Thomas de Multon and John de Castro (who married his widow) enlarged this castle and fortified it. Thomas de Dacre encompassed it with a large ditch for its better security, and beautified it at a great expence. The pictures of all the kings of England from Brute (real or imaginary) were carried from hence to Naworth castle, where many of them yet remain.—Mr. Sandford, speaking of this place, says, "Northward (from Ousby) on the river Eden standeth the " capital grand castle of Kirkoswald, and a very fine church there, and quon- " dam college; now the noble mansion-house of the late Sir Timothy Fether- " stonhaugh, colonel of the king's side, taken at Wigan, where the late lord " Witherington was slain. Sir Timothy was taken prisoner, and executed " by beheading at Chester, by the command of unworthy colonel Mitton, " after the said knight had quarter given him. This great castle of Kirk- " oswald was once the fairest fabrick that ever eyes looked upon. The " hall, I have seen, 100 yards long; and the great portraiture of king " Brute lying in the end of the roof of this hall, and of all his succeeding " successors kings of England, portraicted to the waist, their visage, hats, fea- " thers, garbs, and habits, in the roof of this hall; now translated to Naward " castle, where they are placed in the roof of the hall, and at the head thereof. " This castle was the ancient palace of the lord Multon marrying the lord Vaux's " heir, lord of Naward and Gilsland; and afterward of the late lords Dacre; " and now come by lineal descent to the noble earl of Suffex: with the lands " adjoining, and many brave parks and villages belonging thereto."

The Fetherstonhaughs were a Northumberland family, whose ancient seat was at a place of that name. Their house, it is said, was formerly upon a hill (where are two stones called Fether Stones) and was moated about for a defence against the Scots. But upon the ruin of this, the house was afterwards built in the holme or valley under the hill, which they there call *haugh*; and thence it was called Fetherstonhaugh: and the family writ their names de Fetherston, and sometimes de Fetherstonhaugh †.

1. The first of the name that came to Kirkoswald, was *Henry Fetherstonhaugh*, second son of Albany Fetherstonhaugh of Fetherstonhaugh in Northumberland esquire, by his wife Lucy daughter of Edmund Dudley of Yanwath in the county of Westmorland esquire. The elder brother was Alexander, who mar-

† Machel.

ried

ried Anne daughter of Sir Richard Lowther of Lowther knight.—The faid Henry died in the year 1626; and had iffue by his wife Dorothy daughter of Thomas Wybergh of Clifton efquire, a fon . *Timothy*, and a daughter *Dorothy* married to John Stanley of Dalegarth efquire.

2. Sir *Timothy Fetherftonhaugh* of Kirkofwald, knight, married Bridget daughter of Thomas Patrickfon of How efquire, and by her. bad 18 children. He was beheaded, as aforefaid, by the ufurping power of Cromwell in 1651. His children were (1) *Henry*, who was killed in the fame caufe at Worcefter fight, and died without iffue. (2) *Thomas*. (3) *Richard*, who married Catherine daughter of William Grahme of Nunnery, and had iffue two daughters. (4) *John*, who married Ifabel daughter of Leonard Wharton of Wharton Dykes, and had iffue two fons. (5) *Philip*, who died without iffue. (6) *William*, who alfo died without iffue. (7) *Mary*. (8) *Jane*, married firft to Bernard Kirkbride of How efquire, and afterwards to Edward Haffel of Dalemain efquire, but had no iffue by either of them. (9) *Dorothy*, married to Robert Whitfield of Randleholme efquire. (10) *Bridget*, married to Peter Bell of Lazonby. (11) *Frances*, married to Chriftopher Wyvil of Johnby afterwards of Winderwath, and to her fecond hufband fhe married Thomas Addifon of Whitehaven efquire; and to her faid two hufbands fhe had 16 children. (12) *Elizabeth*, married to Mr. Simpfon of Thackwood Nook. The other 6 children died before they arrived at their full age.—Two of the fons, viz. John and William, were of the life-guard to king Charles the fecond, which was all the recompence made to the family for their fervices and fufferings in the royal caufe.

3. *Thomas Fetherftonhaugh* of Kirkofwald efquire, fecond fon and heir of Sir Timothy, was 37 years of age at Dugdale's vifitation in 1665; whereby it appears that he was only 23 at the death of his father, and was then the eldeft of 17 children. He married to his firft wife Katherine daughter of Thomas Mufgrave 3d fon of Sir William Mufgrave of Crookdayke knight, and by her had iffue *Mary*, of the age of 12 at the faid vifitation. His fecond wife was Mary daughter of Henry Dacre of Lanercoft efquire, by whom he had iffue, (1) *Timothy*. (2) *Henry*, who died without iffue. (3) *Thomas*. (4) *Bridget*, married to Mr. James Nicholfon, to whom fhe had feveral children. (5) *Jane*, married to Mr. John Bowerbank of Culgaith.

4. *Timothy Fetherftonhaugh* efquire, fon and heir of Thomas, married Bridget daughter of James Bellingham of Levins in the county of Weftmorland efquire; by whom he had iffue *Elizabeth, Agnes, Dorothy, Mary, Bridget, Heneage, Thomas, Henry*, and *Timothy*.

5. *Heneage Fetherftonhaugh* efquire, fon and heir of Timothy, married one Lidftone a Devonfhire lady, and had iffue *Timothy*, and a daughter married to the reverend Charles Smallwood vicar of Kirkofwald.

6. *Timothy Fetherftonhaugh*, efquire, now living and unmarried.

The Arms of this family, as certified by Thomas Fetherftonhaugh efquire, and confirmed by Sir William Dugdale, are; Gules, a cheveron between three oftrich feathers Argent. The Creft: On a wreath, an antelope's head couped Gules.

STAFFOL lies between Kirkofwald and Ainftable, from the river Eden to the mountains, and is a fee of Kirkofwald, and gave name to a family of gentlemen of that place. The iffue-male ended about Henry the fifth's time; and then the inheritance fell to three daughters, who transferred it by marriage to the families of Chambers, Mulcafter, and Blenerhaffet of Carlifle. It is now the property of the Fletchers of Hutton.

LITTLE CROGLIN ftands in the fame parifh and townfhip, and is a fee of Kirkofwald. It was anciently the Beauchamps till king Henry the feventh's time, when the Dacres lords paramount purchafed it to their feigniory. Before that, towards the time of Hen. 1. one Uchtred held a part thereof, and Ibria de Trivers another part. And afterwards one Elias de Croglin, William his fon, and William fon of William; who gave fome part of the fame to the houfe of Wetheral; which Reginald Beauchamp confirmed: that is, the fifth part of the town, now called Cringledyke, which is held by leafe under the dean and chapter of Carlifle. At Sir William Dugdale's vifitation of Cumberland in 1665, a pedigree was delivered in by George Towry of Crogling hall in Kirkofwald parifh, juftice of the peace; whereby it appears that he was of a younger branch of the Towrys of Towry Hagg in the county of York; that he married Anne daughter and heir of William James of Carlifle, and had a fon William then aged 13 years.

HARESCEUGH, or *Harefcow*, was given by Ada de Engain to the priory of Lanercoft, and Sir Hugh de Morvil confirmed the fame, in king Henry the fecond's time, or in the beginning of king John's reign, and before it belonged to Kirkofwald as parcel of that feigniory; being bounded as followeth: "Sicut magna via venit de Apelbi ufque ad Ravin, et inde furfum per Ravin ufque ad caput ejufdem aquæ, et a capite Ravin ufque ad Crofcrim, et a Crofcrim ufque ad Hartifhevede et ufque ad Snartegill, et fic per aquam quæ defcendit a Snartegill ufque 'ad muffam, et deinde ufque ad ficam quæ defcendit ufque ad Kenerhen ufque ad viam prædictam." After that houfe or priory was diffolved, Henry fon of Chriftopher fon of Sir Thomas Dacre knight purchafed it from the crown, and his fon or grandfon fold it to Dr. Peter Barwick phyfician in ordinary to king Charles the fecond, who gave it to the chapel and poor of Witherflack in Weftmorland. There are alfo eleven cuftomary tenants belonging thereto, who pay 29s yearly rent and a twenty-penny fine.

The CHURCH of Kirkofwald was turned into a college of 12 fecular priefts about the year 1523, which was not many years before the diffolution of colleges and other religious houfes. And the revenues thereof by the faid diffolution being come into the hands of the crown, queen Elizabeth in the 29th year of her reign granted a leafe of the rectory to Thomas Hammond for 21 years, paying thereout to the vicar 8l yearly. And in the very next year fhe granted the reverfion thereof to Edward Downinge and Miles Doddinge gentlemen, to wit, all thofe glebe lands of the rectory of Kirkofwald, and all other lands and tenements in the parifh of Kirkofwald, late parcel of the poffeffions of the late college

college of Kirkofwald, and all the tithes of corn and grain within the faid parish belonging to the faid rectory and late parcel of the possessions of the faid college; to hold to them and their heirs as of the manor of East Greenwich in free and common focage.

All these glebe lands and tithes are now the property of the family of Fether-stonhaugh, except the tithes of Staffol and Blunderfield which belong to Mr. Edward Towry.

The aforefaid yearly fum of 8*l* to the vicar is still paid by the king's receiver in thefe parts, and feems to have been the whole endowment of the vicarage after the diffolution, until the fum of 200*l* was raifed by contribution of the parifhioners, which with 200*l* more given by the governors of queen Anne's bounty was laid out in lands in 1725, and makes about 20*l* a year to the vicar. And the vicarage having been again augmented in conjunction with 200*l* given by the countefs dowager Gower, the whole revenue is now better than 40*l per annum.*

In the year 1246, one *Martin* was rector of Kirk-Ofwald; in which year, in a fuit between him and Ranulph de Levington and Ada his wife (which Ada was daughter of Joan one of the two coheirs of Sir Hugh Morvil), it was adjudged, that they fhould permit the faid Martin to have houfboot and hayboot in their woods of Kirkofwald (except in the woods inclofed), and common of pafture in the town of Kirkofwald.

Whilft the fame Martin was rector, in the year 1263, between Simon prior of Norwiche complainant, and Thomas de Multon and Ranulph de Levington and Ada his wife deforciants, concerning the church of Kirkofwald; it was fettled, that the faid church was the right of the faid Thomas (who was fon of the other coheir of Morvil) and Ada, and their heirs; fo that the faid Ranulph and Ada his wife prefent firft after the death of Martin then incumbent, and afterwards alternately the faid Thomas de Multon and Ada and their heirs. And for this recognition, the faid Thomas de Multon and Maud (Vaux) his wife, at the inftance of the faid Ranulph and Ada his wife, have given to the faid prior and his fucceffors the church of Denham, and a meffuage and grange and five acres of arable land there, to hold to the faid prior and his fucceffors for ever.

In 1293, *Walter de Langton* refigning the rectory of Kirkofwald, Thomas fon of Thomas de Multon of Gilfland prefents Mr. *Nicholas Lovetoft*; who, before he received any profits, had a writ of fequeftration for debt brought againft him.—During the incumbency of this Nicholas, in the year 1305, bifhop Halton held a great ordination in the parifh church of Kirkofwald, whereat were ordained 17 acolites, 25 fubdeacons, 26 deacons, and 21 priefts; in all 89. Whereof a good many were monks of Furnefs, Holme, and other religious houfes.

In 1323, *Richard de Monte* fubdeacon was inftituted into the rectory of Kirkofwald, being thereto prefented by Sir John de Caftre knight (who, as is aforefaid, married the widow of Thomas de Multon). In 1371, the bifhop, being informed that this Richard was grown fo old and infirm as not to be able to attend

attend his cure, orders him to be cited to shew cause, why a coadjutor, should not be assigned him. In the next year he died, and Mr. *John de Appleby* was instituted on the presentation of Ralph de Dacre lord of Gilsland. And the said John resigning in two years after, the same patron presents Sir *William Beauchamp*; who upon his institution into Kirkoswald resigns a moiety of the rectory of Aketon.

From 1436, to 1460, *William Marshall* rector of Kirkoswald appears as a witness to several deeds of Thomas lord Dacre and others.

In 1523, Mr. *John Heryng*, provost of the collegiate church of Kirkoswald, was one of bishop Kite's lessees at Newton.

In 1561, on the death of Sir *John Scales* vicar of Kirkoswald, Sir *James Shepherd* clerk was instituted on a presentation by queen Elizabeth.

In 1668, *George Yeates*, rector of Croglin, had a licence to serve this cure, by way of sequestration in the hands of the bishop, it not being worth the expence of a presentation under the great seal. In like manner, *George Sanderson, John Rumney*, and *James Wannop* were successively licensed to serve the same. But in the end, the said James Wannop, in the year 1714, tendred a presentation under the great seal, and was thereupon instituted.

In 1719, *William Milner* was licensed to be curate. So also *John Rumney* in 1723: upon whose death in 1739, *John Mandeville* was instituted upon a presentation under the great seal.

Upon Mr. Mandeville's death in 1761, *Charles Smalwood*, B. A. was instituted on a like presentation.

And upon Mr. Smalwood's death in 1771, *John James*, M. A. was presented under the great seal and instituted thereupon.

The quire of the church seems greatly disproportioned to the adjoining body. Bishop Nicolson supposes it was rebuilt by some of the lords Dacre, whose seat was at the neighbouring castle, as the arms of that family and of the Cliffords are painted in most of the windows. And he is inclined to think that it was put into this figure when the rectory was turned into a college; being made thus capacious for the reception of the members of that society. He also supposes, that the spring which issues from under the west end of the church was the great motive for the founding of it in this place; as the well-worship of the Saxons was notorious.

The belfrey is placed without the church, on the top of an hill, towards the east, that the sound of the bells might be more easily heard by the circumjacent villages.

The priory of Armathwaite had a close called The Holme, and some other small possessions, in the parish of Kirkoswald; which, after the dissolution were granted to William Greyme of Carlisle gentleman.

In 1737, it was certified, that there were in this parish 157 families; of which, presbyterians 31.

Which

Which number of prefbyterians is owing to an eftablifhed diffenting meeting-houfe in this parifh ; to which there have been feveral benefactions.

At Highbank in this parifh there is a *fchool*, endowed with the fum of 124 *l.*

PARISH OF AINSTABLE.

AINSTABLE, *Ainftaple, Eynftable, Aynftapelith*, is a manor or lordfhip on the fouth fide of Gilfland, divided from that barony by Northfkeugh beck ; and reacheth from the river Eden on the weft up eaftwards into the mountains ; and bordereth upon Staffol lordfhip towards the fouth.

This feigniory king Henry the firft gave to Adam fon of Sweine, from whom it defcended in king Henry the fecond's time to William de Neville, whofe lands in Cumberland in the time of king John were in the holding of Roger de Monte Begon, Simon fon of Walter, and Alexander de Neville. In king Henry the third's time, Ainftable lordfhip became the inheritance of John Maffey and Henry Terriby. Michael de Vallibus fon of David held it in the 33 Hen. 3. And in the latter end of that king's time, Sir William Boyvill of Thurfby knight was lord thereof, and held the fame of Richard Neville. When he died, it fell to his fon John Boyvill, whofe brother Edmund fold it to Sir Andrew Harcla who was attainted in the 15 Ed. 2. Which king granted it to Sir Richard Denton (the fame probably that was very active in feizing Sir Andrew), and from him it came to John Denton of Cardew, whofe pofterity William and John Denton enjoyed it as lords thereof fucceffively from father to fon, until Thomas lord Dacre (Mr. Denton fays) extorted it from the faid laft John Denton in the time of king Henry the fixth, for that the faid John Denton was towards the party of king Edward the fourth. Which tyranny of the Dacres (the faid Mr. Denton, who was a defcendent of thefe Dentons of Cardew, further remarks) God feemed to take revenge for fhortly after, when the faid lord Dacre and Ranulph his fon were both flain at Towton field, or drowned in the river at Ferrybridge, when king Edward got the victory againft Henry the fixth, and thereby obtained the crown. Afterwards the lord Humphrey Dacre (Mr. Denton proceeds) by marrying of dame Mabil Parr daughter of the king's favourite Sir William Parr of Kendal caftle, recovered the Dacres lands; and, amongft thefe, Ainftable: which, in the partition of the Dacre eftate between the two fifters and coheirs of George lord Dacre, fell to the fhare of the younger fifter married to the lord William Howard anceftor of the prefent owner Frederic Howard baron Dacre of Gilfland and earl of Carlifle.

NUNNERY, in this parifh, was a fmall houfe of Benedictine nuns, founded by king William Rufus ; who by letters patent bearing date the fixth day of January in the fecond year of his reign, for the fouls of his progenitors and of all chriftian people, eftablifhes an houfe or monaftery of Black nuns of the order of St. Benedict, fituate nigh the water called Croglin ; and grants unto them two acres of land whereon the faid houfe and monaftery are fituate, and three

carucates.

carucates of land and two acres of meadow lying nigh to the said monaftery ; and alfo two hundred and fixteen acres of land within his foreft of Inglewood, lying on the north fide of the water called **Tarnwadelyn** ; with common of pafture for all the cattle of them and their tenants throughout the whole foreft of Inglewood, and fufficient timber for their houfes by delivery of the foreft- ers ; alfo a yearly rent of 40*s* out of his tenements in his town of Carlifle, to be paid by the hands of his governor of the faid town ; and that they and their tenants-fhall be toll-free throughout England : And he grants to them common of pafture for all their cattle within the town and common of Ayn- ftapylith ; and free warren in all their lands wherefoever : To have and to hold all the faid premiffes as freely AS HERT MAY IT THYNKE OR YGH MAY IT SEE †.

King Ed. 4. by his charter, 9 Apr. in the 13th year of his reign, on the lamentable complaint of the priorefs and nuns, that their houfes and lands were totally ruined and deftroyed by the Scots, and that all their books, charters, and other muniments were burnt or carried away, regrants and con- firms to them all their poffeffions whatfoever ‡.

At the time of the diffolution here were only a priorefs and three nuns. By which it fhould feem that the revenues of thefe religious women had been embezzled or mifapplied ; for very ample revenues they had,- as will appear from the grant thereof by the crown after the diffolution of the religious houfes, whereby king Edward the fixth by his letters patent bearing date March 9, in the 6th year of his reign, grants to William Greyme alias Carlifle gentleman, the houfe and fite of the late priory of Armethwaite, with one garden, three orchards, one parcel of inclofed ground called the Lyngclofe containing two acres, one clofe of arable land called the Petebank containing 4 acres, one clofe called the Studholes containing 4 acres of arable land, 10 acres of meadow and 4 acres of wafte, 3 clofes of arable land called Wheat clofes containing 20 acres, one clofe called Holme Cammock containing one acre, one clofe called Kirkholme containing one acre, one clofe called High- field containing 5 acres ; one clofe of land, wood, and wafte containing 18 acres, and one other clofe called Broadmeadow containing 9 acres ; alfo all thofe meffuages, tenements, and lands containing 216 acres (in the tenure of 17 different tenants) in the Nonneclofe ; alfo 5 meffuages and tenements, in the tenure of fo many different perfons, in Dale in the county of Cumber- land ; 6 meffuages and tenements in Rewcroft in the faid county ; 12 in Anaftaplethe in the faid county, with feveral quit rents there ; two meffuages and tenements in the parifh of Kirkofwald ; two in Coumwhitton ; one in Blen- karn ; one in the parifh of Kirkland ; one in Glaffonby ; and one in Crofton. —The rectory and church alfo of Ainftable were appropriated to the faid nunnery.

The faid William Greyme, in the 3 Eliz. levied a fine of the premiffes, and fettled the fame upon his fon Fergus Greyme alias Carlifle and the heirs male of his body, remainder to the right heirs of the faid Fergus.

† Appendix, N°. 31.   ‡ Ibid. N°. 32.

Of

Of this family of the Grahams of Nunery, the following pedigree was certified at Dugdale's vifitation of Cumberland in 1665, beginning with the faid Fergus; viz.

1. *Fergus Graham* of Nunnery, a younger brother of the Grahams of Rofe-trees.

2. *William Graham* of Nunnery, fon of Fergus, married Elizabeth Somers of the county of Kent; and by her had iffue George and Henry.

3. *George Graham* of Nunnery, fon of William, married Katherine daughter of John Mufgrave of Plumpton head; and had iffue (1) William. (2) Richard Graham of Smerdale in Weftmorland. (3) George Graham of the fame place. (4) Fergus Graham of Dublin. (5) Catherine married to George Denton of Cardew efquire. (6) Elizabeth married to Robert Tomlinfon of Cumdubbrick in Cumberland. (7) Bridget married to William Chollerton of the county of Northumberland. (8) Frances.—This George Graham of Nunnery was of the age of 72 at the faid vifitation.

4. *William Graham*, eldeft fon of George, was dead before the time of the faid vifitation. He married to his firft wife Mary daughter of John Vaux of Caterlen, and by her had iffue Catharine married to Richard Fetherfton of Langwathby, Magdalen married to John Routldge, Mary married to Thomas Lowthian of Staffol, and Mabel. His fecond wife was Mary daughter of Richard Kirkbride of Howes; by whom he had Richard aged 8 years at the faid vifitation, and Bridget.

The arms of thefe Grahams are the fame as the arms of the Grahams of Netherby.

George Graham efquire, perhaps fon of the laft named *Richard*, fold Nunnery about the year 1690 to Sir John Lowther baronet for 1436*l*. And Sir John exchanged it with John Aglionby efquire for Drumbugh caftle, whofe defcendent Chriftopher Aglionby efquire is the prefent owner.

Upon a bedhead at Nunnery, called the nun's bed, is this infcription:

Mark the end and
yow fhall never doow amis.

The church of Ainftable is dedicated to St. Michael, and is vicarial, having been appropriated to the faid Nunnery. It is valued in the king's books at 8*l* 8*s* 6¼*d*; was certified to the governors of queen Anne's bounty at 35*l*, and is now worth about 40*l per annum*.

There is no prefentation or inftitution to this vicarage in the bifhops regifters before the diffolution of the religious houfes. It feems to have been totally appro-

appropriated to the nunnery, and fupplied by the chaplain of their own houfe. In 1565, on the death of *Thomas Rumney* vicar of Ainftable, Sir *John Preeft-man* was inftituted on the prefentation of Robert Dalfton gentleman in the right of his wife.

In 1597, on the death of John Preeftman, inftitution was given to *Robert Watfon* prefented by Henry Barrow and Hugh Lowther gentlemen.

In 1661, *George Dacres* clerk was prefented by Leonard Barrow gentleman.

In 1680, *George Hodgfon* clerk, on the death of George Dacres, was prefented by Barbara Huggatt widow.

In 1737, *John Verty* was prefented, upon George Hodgfon's death, by Bridget Lowthian.

In 1749, *Charles Smallwood* was prefented by Richard Lowthian of Dumfries gentleman.

In 1771, on the death of Mr. Smallwood, *Thomas Railton* clerk was prefented by the fame patron.

The rectory and advowfon of this church were granted away from the crown in the reign of king Edward the fixth; who by his letters patent bearing date the 20th day of December in the third year of his reign, grants to Thomas Peryent knight, and Thomas Rewe gentleman *(inter alia)* the rectory and church of Anaftaplethe and the advowfon and right of patronage of the vicarage of the faid church, late belonging to the priory of Armathwaite, together with all houfes, glebe lands, tithes of corn, hay, wool, lamb, and all other tithes to the fame belonging; to hold to them and their heirs as of the manor of Eaft Greenwich, by fealty only, in free focage, and not *in capite.*

The aforefaid Mr. Richard Lowthian is the prefent impropriator, and as fuch hath a feat in the chancel : But it is faid that the eftate at Nunnery ftands obliged with the repairs of the north fide of the chancel, as the vicar is with thofe of the fouth.

Near the middle of the church is a large gravestone with a coat of arms (two bars, and three martlets in chief), which is alfo above the fouth window in the quire in freeftone; and round the gravestone is this legend : " Hic " jacet Johannes de Dentoun dominus de Aunftaple."

Here is in this parifh a fmall parochial library; a poor ftock of 50l; and a fmall fchool endowed with 2l 10s, iffuing out of land.

In 1747, there were 98 families in this parifh; of which, five were prefbyterians.

PARISH OF CROGLIN.

CROGLIN was fo called from two Britifh words *Çareg (crag)* a rock, and *Lyn* water. The parifh is coextenfive with the manor. It joins upon Gilfland towards the north eaft, upon the manor of Knarefdale at a place called Gyllian
bridge

bridge towards the eaft, Renwick on the fouth, and Kirkofwald towards the weft. It was anciently the freehold of one Philip Haftings, in whofe iffue male it defcended until Edward the firft's time, and then Croglin and his other lands fell to his two daughters, one married to Wharton, and the other to Warcop.

One of this family of Haftings was with king Richard the firft at the fiege of Jerufalem, and obtained a grant there of thefe lands.

Croglin, from and after the faid intermarriage with Wharton, continued in the Whartons of Wharton hall in Weftmorland till the late duke of Wharton's time ; and it is fomewhat remarkable, that the Whartons did not (as it is ufual on the marriage of heireffes) impale or quarter the arms of Haftings, but affumed fingly the Haftings' arms, which are the paternal arms of Wharton to this day, namely, Sable, a manch Argent.

The late duke of Wharton's truftees fold this manor of Croglin to the duke of Somerfet (together with divers other poffeffions), whofe reprefentative George Wyndham earl of Egremont is the prefent owner thereof.

The number of tenants finable is about 24, who pay a yearly cuftomary rent of 5*l* 15*s* 0*d*, and a ten-penny fine. There is alfo a free rent of 2*s*, and a mill let for about 6*l* a year, and the lime kilns about 11*l* a year.

It is faid in 1 Dugd. Mon. p. 389. that Uchtred fon of Lyolf gave to the abbey of St. Mary's York a third part of Croglin with the church there ; as is fpecified among the particulars in the charter of confirmation by king Hen. 2. —But this concerning the church feems to have been brought in by a fleight of the monks ; for it doth not appear that the faid abbey (or Wetheral, which was a cell thereof) had ever any poffeffions here, but the land which Uchtred had was at Little Croglin in the parifh of Kirkofwald, where the monks of Wetheral had fome poffeffions. And this church continued always rectorial, and in the patronage of the lord of the manor, until the late duke of Wharton fold the fame in grofs to Matthew Smales gentleman, grandfather of the prefent patron Henry Chaytor, L L. D. vicar of Kirkby Stephen.

It is valued in the king's books at 8*l*; was returned to the governors of queen Anne's bounty at 47*l*; and is now worth about 90*l* per annum.

In the year 1293, the bifhop confirms a leafe made of the rectory of Croglin by *Adam* the rector, faving all dues to the crown and ordinary. And in 1309, another like leafe was allowed to be made by the rector *Symon de Layton*, for defraying the charges of affeffments for the holy-land.

In 1317, *William de Edenhall* was inftituted at Horncaftle, on a prefentation by Henry de Qwerton. Which faid Henry, on a vacancy in 1335, prefented *John de Wetewang*.

In 1362, *Patrick de Edenham* was inftituted on a prefentation by Hugh de Qwerton. And again in 1377, the faid Hugh prefented *John Mayfon* to the rectory, being vacant by the death of *William de Willerdby.*

In 1380, on the refignation of John Mayfon inftituted to Torpenhow, *William de Hoton* was prefented by Sir William Beauchamp rector of Kirkofwald.

In 1452, *Henry Staynesforth* was rector, who in that year appears as witnefs to a deed of lands in Aynftaplyth.

In 1527 Sir *William Wharton* was rector; who in that year paid the abbot of Shap's composition to the vicar of Burgh under Stanemore.

In 1564, on the death of Sir *Percival Warthcopp*, institution was given to Sir *Philip Machell*, who was presented by Barnabas Machell and Hugh Machell gentlemen, to whom Thomas lord Wharton had granted this avoidance.

In 1568, Sir *John Hudson* was instituted on the death of the said Philip Machell, being presented by Richard Lowther of Lowther esquire and Thomas Wybergh junior of Clifton gentleman, by a like grant from Thomas lord Wharton.

In 1574, on the resignation of John Hudson, *Thomas Barnes* clerk was instituted into the church of Croglin Magna or Kirk Croglin, on the presentation of Gerard Lowther. Which Thomas dying in 1578, *Marmaduke Cholmley* was presented by Philip lord Wharton: on whose resignation in 1582, *Roger Haslehead* was presented by the same patron.

In 1611, on Roger Haslebead's death, *John Allan* was presented by Philip lord Wharton.

In 1639, on the death of John Allan, *Richard Sharples* was instituted on a presentation by Philip lord Wharton.

In 1660, *John Rogers*, M. A. was presented by the same patron.

In 1663, on the deprivation of John Rogers (probably for non-conformity), *George Yates* was collated by lapse.

In 1671, on George Yates's death, *George Sanderson* was presented by the last named Philip lord Wharton.

In 1691, on the death of George Sanderson, *Thomas Hunter* was presented by the same Philip lord Wharton,

In 1724, on *Thomas Hunter*'s death, *Henry Noble* was presented by Matthew Smales gentleman.

In this parish are 39 families, all of the church of England.

PARISH OF RENWICK.

RENWICK, *Ravenwick*, a town on the river Raven, belonged from almost the time of the conquest to a family of the name of Staveley: for king Henry the first gave it to one Adam de Staveley and his heirs. And one Thomas de Staveley and Margaret his wife held it in the 20 Ed. 1. Afterwards it came to the Eglesfields. And Robert de Eglesfield, chaplain and confessor to Philippa queen consort of king Edward the third, which Robert was also founder of Queen's college in Oxford, granted the same in the 15th year of the said king to his said college then incorporated by the name of the provost and scholars of Queen's Hall in Oxford, which style in the 22 Eliz. was altered to that of the provost and scholars of the Queen's college in the university of Oxford †.

This

---

† Sciant omnes tam præsentes quam futuri, quod ego Robertus de Eglesfeld dedi, concessi, et hac præsenti mea charta confirmavi, præposito et scholaribus aulæ Reginæ Oxon per me fundatæ,

This parish and manor are coextensive; consisting of about 9 freeholders; and 23 customary tenants, who pay yearly 6l 10s 9¼d customary rent, and a twelve-penny fine upon change of tenant, by indenture settled between the provost and scholars of the one part and the several tenants of the other part, bearing date Nov. 2. in the 16 Cha. 2. Whereby also the tenants are obliged to scour and cleanse the watercourse to the lord's mill from the bottom up to the mill trough head, and maintain the said mill with wall and thatch, and bring the millstones to the same, and grind their corn thereat, paying a 24th multure: and that they shall cut down no timber trees, except what shall be set out to them by the steward for the necessary repairs of their houses.

The college hath also a colliery upon Renwick fell, now let at 33l 5s 0d a year.

The church of Renwick is dedicated to All Saints. It was rectorial at the time of pope Nicholas's Valor, and rated at 9l 11s 4d. It was afterwards appropriated to a religious house at Hexham (as is commonly supposed); but by the grant thereof after the dissolution it should seem that it belonged to the abbey of St. Mary's York. For by letters patent bearing date the 24th day of February in the 20th year of the reign of queen Elizabeth, the said queen grants to her trusty and well beloved cousin and counsellor Edward earl of Lincoln knight of the garter and Christopher Gowffe gentleman, all that the chapel or church of Renwicke, called or known by the name of Renwick chapel, with all its rights, members, and appurtenances in the county of Cumberland, formerly belonging to the late dissolved monastery of St. Mary nigh the walls of the city of York and parcel of the possessions thereof, and late demised to Thomas Owen for the yearly rent of 13 s 4 d. Except the advowson of the church and

totum hameletum meum de Ravenwicke in comitatu Cumbriæ, cum omnibus suis pertinentiis, ut in dominicis, domibus, ædificiis, terris, pratis, pasturis, redditibus, serviciis, molendinis, boscis, vastis, et aliis rebus quibuscunque, ad dictum hameletum qualitercunque pertinentibus: Incipiendo ad pedem syket vocati Sykergill, et sic ut aqua dividit ascendendo ad caput ejusdem syket, et linealiter usque ad unum lapidem jacentem super le Scalerigg, et a prædicto lapide linealiter ad caput le Bromeryge dike super Langmore, et sic linealiter ad pedem Reydyke, quod se extendit in Briggill, sicut aqua descendit usque ad unum le reyd quarreium, et sic linealiter usque ad unum le Mosse super Medlemore, et sic linealiter usque ad pedem unius fossati ex parte boreali quarundam terrarum vocatarum le Nonnefelde, et sic ascendendo sicut prædictum fossatum dividit usque ad portum vocatam Burden ad caput Davygyll, et sic linealiter usque ad unum acervum lapidum vocatum Ceyll currock super fidem Thake mire egge sicut aqua dividit usque ad caput le Blakebury gill sicut aqua descendit in aquam de Croglyng, et sic ascendendo ut aqua dividit ad pedem syket vocati Rays syke, et sic ascendendo usque ad placeam albam terræ super le Blakefell, directe descendendo ad caput Bullgrave sicut aqua descendit ad le Great force, et ut aqua descendit vocata Ravyn usque ad unum vicum vocatum Appleby street, ff ut aqua prædicta Ravyn descendit usque ad pedem prædicti syket le Sykergill; fine ullo retenemento ceu quacunque exceptione: Habendum et tenendum prædictis præposito et scholaribus et eorum successoribus in perpetuum. Et ego prædictus Robertus et hæredes mei prædictum hameletum cum pertinentiis prædictis præposito et scholaribus et eorum successoribus sicut prædictum est contra omnes warantizabimus et defendemus in perpetuum. Salvis domino regi et aliis, serviciis inde debitis et de jure consuetis. In cujus rei testimonium huic præsenti chartæ meæ sigillum meum apposui   Hiis testibus, Andrea de Wyrminhall tunc majore villæ Oxon, Ricardo Cary, Simone Gloucester, burgensibus ejusdem villæ, Johanne de Darwentwater, Petro Telyol, militibus, Richardo Saikelde, et aliis. Datum Oxon. 17 die Junii, anno regni Edwardi illustris regis Angliæ tertii post conquestum regni sui Angliæ 15°, Franciæ vero 2°, et anno domini 1341.

chapel,

chapel; with all bells and lead of, in, and upon upon the premiffes; to hold to the faid earl of Lincoln and Chriftopher Gowffe their heirs and affigns of the faid queen and her fucceffors as of the manor of Eaft Greenwich in Kent, by fealty only, in free focage and not in capite, rendering for the fame yearly to the queen and her fucceffors the fum of 13 s 4d.

Neverthelefs this probably might be a miftake, in reciting it as belonging to the faid abbey; which might be occafioned by the fame grantees having purchafed divers other poffeffions belonging to the faid abbey of St. Mary's York. And if it had indeed belonged to that abbey, we fhould probably have met with it amongft the grants or confirmations of grants to that houfe, and more efpecially in the Regifter of Wetheral priory.

Thefe vendees conveyed to Thomas Compton and Edward Braddil. Braddil releafed to Compton, and Compton again conveyed to others, and the rectory and tithes are now in feveral hands. A very fmall portion was allowed all this while to the curate, and about the year 1749 the curacy was certified to the governors of queen Anne's bounty at 4l per annum. In 1748 it received an augmentation of 200l by lot from the governors of queen Anne's bounty, and again in 1748, wherewith lands were purchafed in the parifh of Addingham; and in 1761 it received another augmentation of 200l in conjunction with 200l given by the countefs dowager Gower, wherewith lands were purchafed in the parifh of Ainftable: the whole being of the yearly value of about 36l per annum.

The revenue being for a long time fo very fmall, it would be difficult to procure any clergyman to accept of it. And it feems that fometimes the owner of one part of the impropriation, and fometimes of another, hath appointed the curate. But unlefs a title from the crown, pofterior to the grant to the earl of Lincoln and Mr. Goff can be produced, the right of nomination feemeth ftill to remain to the crown.

The church of Renwick was rebuilt in the year 1733 in a very decent manner, at the expence of the parifhioners.

There are in this parifh about 40 families, all of the church of England.

PARISH OF OUSBY.

Ousby, *Ulnefby*, or more properly *Ulffby*, was the habitation of *Ulf* or *Olave* a Dane, who before the Norman conqueft feated himfelf here under the edge of the eaft mountains. He was one of the three fons of Haldan; which fons were Thorquell, Melmor, and Ulf. Melmor was placed at Melmerby, and Thorquell (Mr. Denton fays) was placed at Thorquelby nigh Kefwick. Near the time of the conqueft, this manor of Oufby feems to have been parted between two fifters; and fhortly after, a moiety thereof between four fifters. For in the time of Henry the third one Julian Falcard and William Armftrong held each a moiety; and foon after, Henry le Serjeant and Patrick de Ulnefby held each an eighth part. The refidue by alienations was broken into fmall parcels; whereof fome were given to Lanercoft, fome to the prior of St. John of Jerufalem, fome to the prior and convent of Carlifle, fome in frank marriage, and

many

many fmall parcels fold, and diftributed amongft the families of Crofton, Sal-keld, Beauchamp, Raughton, and Crackenthorp.

The church of Oufby is rectorial, and dedicated to St. Luke. It is valued in the king's books at 13 *l* 13 *s* 4 *d*. And is now worth about 100 *l per annum*. The bifhop of Carlifle is patron.

In the year 1245, *Roger* furnamed *Peytenin* a fubdeacon, and a baftard, was collated to the vacant rectory of Ulvefby; provided that, according to the tenor of his difpenfation from the apoftolic fee upon account of the defect of his birth, he keep perfonal refidence in the fame. And faving to the prior and convent of Carlifle their annual penfion of 6 *s* 8 *d*. And upon Roger's refignation in 1304, bifhop Halton collates Gilbert de Haloughton.

In 1312, on the refignation of *Adam de Appleby* rector of Ulvefby, Sir *Robert de Halghton* was collated by William de Gosford the bifhop's vicar general, having the bifhop's fpecial mandate for that purpofe, the bifhop then being abfent in foreign parts. The faid Robert refigning in 1316, *Thomas de Caldbeck* was collated; who alfo refigning foon after, *John Grayvill*, B. D. fucceeded.

In 1359, on the death of Sir *William de Denton* the then rector, Mr. *John de Welton* was collated; and in the next year *Robert de Welton* was collated by bifhop Welton; and on Robert's refignation in the very next year, Sir *Richard de Ulvefby* was collated.

The faid Richard de Ulvefby died in the year 1361, before he had been one year rector, and his will was proved at Rofe; wherein he bequeathed to the bifhop (if he pleafed to accept of them) a pair of oxen, to Richard Aflackby his robe, and to the nuns of Lamley in Northumberland an heifer that runs at Denton. And in the fame year Sir *Thomas de Kirkland* is collated. In lefs than three years after this, Sir *Nicholas de Stapleton*. Who in lefs than three years again exchanged with *William de Strickland* for the rectory of Stapleton; which exchange was made in April, and in December following Sir *John Watreward* was collated. Neither did this John continue long; for in 1376 we find a difpenfation for three years abfence granted to *Symon de Wharton* rector of Ulvefby, to enable him the better to follow his ftudies in fome of the public fchools in England.

In 1583, on the death of *Hugh Sewell* rector of Ulvefby, bifhop Meye inftituted Sir *Hugh Rayfon* clerk on a prefentation by Barnabas Sewell of Caldbeck yeoman, who (with others) had procured this avoidance from bifhop Barnes.

In 1611, on Hugh Rayfon's death, Mr. *Nicholas Deane* was collated by bifhop Robinfon.

In 1644, we find *Leonard Milburne* rector of Ulvefby amongft the contributors of provifions to the garrifon of Carlifle then befieged.

In 1672, the faid Leonard Milburne died, and *Thomas Robinfon*, B. A. (author of the book intituled an Effay towards a natural hiftory of Weftmorland and Cumberland) was collated by bifhop Rainbow.

In 1719, on Thomas Robinfon's death, *George Fleming*, M. A. was collated by bifhop Bradford.

In

In 1735, on the faid George Fleming's promotion to, the bifhoprick, *Lancelot Pattenfon*, M. A. was inftituted on a prefentation under the great feal.

In 1759, on the death of Lancelot Pattenfon, *John Delap*, M. A. was collated by bifhop Ofbaldifton.

In 1766, on the refignation of John Delap, *William Raincock*, M. A. was collated by bifhop Lyttelton.

In this parifh are 48 *families*, 3 of which are prefbyterian.

PARISH OF ALSTON.

A S the boundary of the parifh and manor of ALSTON, or (as it is moft commonly called) *Alfton-Moor*, is more accurately and diftinctly' fet out, by, thofe natural and unremovable bounder marks of mountain tops and rivulets, than moft others we have met with, we have thought fit here to give it a place: " Beginning at the foot of Aleburn, from thence to the head thereof; from thence to Willyfhaw rig end; from thence to the top of Willyfhaw rig; from thence in a direct line to Long clough hill; from thence in a direct line to Long-crofs pool eaft of Long-crofs; from thence to the foot of Mirefyke, fo to the head thereof; from thence in a direct line to Hardrig end; from thence as heaven water deals to Blakelawes crofs; from thence as heaven water deals to High-raife; from thence to Welhope head; from thence as heaven water deals to Dodd End; from thence as heaven water deals to Guddamgill head; from thence as heaven water deals to the foot of the ditch at Ramfgill otherwife Red Groves-head; from thence along the faid ditch to the end thereof; from thence as heaven water deals to Killhope head; from thence along Killhope head as heaven water deals to a place fifty yards eaft of Killhope crofs, where the faid crofs formerly ftood, it being fome time ago removed as a mark for the convenience of travellers; from thence as heaven water deals to a place 200 yards eaft of Short's crofs, where the faid crofs alfo formerly ftood, it being likewife removed as a direction or guide for travellers; from thence as heaven water deals to the Nag's head; from thence as the water divides to the road on Wellhope edge; from thence as the water divides to Red ftones; from thence as the water divides to Pennymea hill; from thence up Pennymea, leaving the turns a little on the right hand, to Burnhope feat, otherwife Scraith head; from thence as the water divides to a part of Sciaith head, where the bifhop of Durham's, the earl of Darlington's, and the Greenwich hofpital lordfhips join in a point. From thence in a direct line to Crookburn head; from thence down Crookburn to the foot thereof where it joins Tees water; from thence up Tees to the head thereof; from thence to the fummit of Crofs-fell; from thence as heaven water deals to the north end of Crofs-fell; from thence as the water divides to Greyhound ftone; from thence in a direct line to Cafhburn head or well; from thence down Cafhburn to the foot of Dirtpot burn, where the faid Cafhburn alters to the name of Shield water. From thence down the faid Shield water to the foot of Swarthbeck burn, where there ftands a fold called Swarthbeck
fold.

fold. From thence down the said Shield water to Snittergill burn, where the name alters to Greencastle water. From thence to Rowgill burn foot; from thence up Rowgill burn to Mereburn foot. From thence up Mereburn to Dick Lee's cabbin; from thence up the said burn to the place where the said burn divides; from thence up the westermost burn called Mereburn to the half dyke; from thence to Parkin stones on the south of, and near unto, Parkin stones fold; from thence to Benty hill currock; from thence as the water divides to Rowgill head; from thence to the height of Hartside; from thence to Colecleugh head; from thence to Little Daffinside currock; from thence to Great Daffinside currock; from thence to Black-fell currock; from thence to Thief syke head; from thence as the water divides to the head of Candlesieve syke; from thence in a direct line to Woogill tarn; from thence as the water divides to Tom Smith's stone; at which place, the boundaries of the earl of Egremont, Queen's college in Oxford, and Greenwich hospital in Cumberland, and of Knaresdale and Kirkhaugh in Northumberland, do all meet. From thence to Calfless head; from thence down Woogill burn to Gilderdale burn, and down that burn to the foot thereof; and from thence up Tyne to Aleburn, where it first began."

In the 8 Ed. 2. by an inquisition *post mortem* of *Nicholas de Vipont* it was found, that the said Nicholas on the day whereon he died held the capital messuage in Alderstone, with 14 acres of arable land, and 100 acres of meadow, had 33 tenants at Gerardsgill who held 33 shieldings and paid 5*l* 18*s* 0*d* yearly rent, 13 tenants at Amotes-halth who paid yearly 3*l* 8*s* 4*d*, 22 tenants at Nent and Corbrig-gate who held 22 shieldings and paid 5*l* 2*s* 0*d* rent, also one water corn miln and one fulling miln, and 3,000 acres of pasture in Alderstone moor; all which premisses were held of the manor of Werk: and that Robert Vipont was his son and heir.

In the 10 Hen. 5. *John de Clifford* held the manors of Alderston, Elryngton, and Gerardsgill of the king *in capite*, paying yearly into the exchequer at Carlisle 6*l*.13*s* 4*d*.

In the 21 Hen. 6. *Thomas Whytlaw* granted the said manors to *William Stapilton* and *Margaret* his wife.

This William and Margaret had two daughters coheirs; *Mary* married to Sir William Hilton of Hilton, and afterwards to Richard Musgrave second son of Sir Richard Musgrave of Hartley castle; and *Joan* married to Thomas Musgrave elder son and heir of the said Sir Richard. They were heirs of Edenhall as well as of Alston-moor. And in the 9 Ed. 4. there was a partition executed between Richard Musgrave and Mary his wife of the one part, and Johan relict of Thomas Musgrave of the other part; whereby it was agreed, that Alston moor should go to the said Richard Musgrave and Mary his wife and the heirs of the said Mary, and that Edenhall should go to the said Joan and her heirs.

Mary's heir was a son which she had to her first husband *Hilton*, in whose name and family Alston moor continued till the reign of king James the first; when, in the 15th year of that king, *Henry Hilton* of Hilton mortgaged the same to *Francis Ratcliffe* baron of Dilston, and soon after released it to him absolutely. From which time it continued in the family of the Ratcliffes till the attainder of

3   James

James earl of Derwentwater in the year 1715, upon which it became vested in the crown, and by act of parliament was settled upon Greenwich hospital.

The lands in Aldston-moor and Garrigill are mostly leasehold, granted in the years 1611 and 1616, by the said Henry Hilton, for 999 years, paying a twenty-penny fine at the end of every 21 years.

The annual rent, by virtue of these leases, payed to the receiver of the hospital is 63 *l*.

The number of inhabitants in this parish, exclusive of miners that come from various parishes and work 4 or 5 days in the week, is about 4,500.

The value of the lead mines, as taken from the Moor Master's books, for three years successively, appears to be as follows: In the year 1766, 18,600 byng of ore: In 1767, 24,500 byng: In 1768, 18,730 byng: Each byng upon an average being worth 2 *l* 15 *s* 0 *d*.

There are 103 lead mines leased under the hospital in Aldston-moor. Six leased under Mr. Emerson of Temple Sowerby, the late Mrs. Railton, and Mr. Wilkinson, in Prior's Dale. And 12, under the hospital, Mr. Hopper, and Mr. Gill of Guernesey, at Tyne-head.

Prior's Dale (as the name imports) belonged to a religious house at Hexham.

That part of Tyne-head, which belongs to Mr. Gill is freehold, and he hath also the royalties. The rest of Tyne-head is held by lease as aforesaid.

Lord Coke, in his Second Institute, page 578, reports a notable case that happened in these mines of Aldernefton, in the 18 Ed. 1. Henry de Whiteby and Joan his wife impleaded several of the miners for cutting down and carrying away their trees. The miners answer, that they farm the mine of the king, and plead that for working a vein of silver (as now they do) the miners have a right to take any wood whatsoever that shall be near to and convenient for the said work, and that they have also a right at their will and pleasure to use and dispose of that wood for burning and smelting, and for paying the workmen their wages, and also to give what they think fit thereof to their poor workmen of the mine; and they state, that they have exercised their right for time immemorial. The said Henry and Joan acknowledge the miners' right to take the wood for burning and smelting for the use of the mine, but charge, that the miners had cut down, carried away, and sold large quantities of wood, from which the king received no kind of benefit, and which never came to the use of the mine at all. And upon this they pray to have judgment —It doth not appear what was the event of the cause, nor is it now very material to inquire, for two reasons; first, for that by act of parliament no mine shall be deemed a royal mine, notwithstanding any gold or silver that may be found in it, only the king (if he pleases) may have the ore, paying for the same a stated price. Secondly, here is now, as may well be supposed, scarce a tree to be seen in the whole country.

This parish is in the diocese of Durham, and the church was appropriated to the monastery at Hexham. After the dissolution, king Edward the sixth by letters patent dated Dec. 20, in the 3d year of his reign, granted to John Peryent

7   knight,

knight, and Thomas Reve gentleman, all that the rectory and church of Alder-
ſtone in the county of Cumberland, and the advowſon and right of patronage of
the vicarage thereof, with all houſes, buildings, glebe lands, woods, tithes of
corn, hay, wool, lambs, calves, flax, hemp, and other tithes and profits whatſoever, belonging to the ſaid rectory, late parcel of the poſſeſſions of the late
monaſtery of Hexham in the county of Northumberland.—The preſent impropriators are the governors of Greenwich hoſpital, Henry Stephenſon eſquire,
and John Walton gentleman, who preſent to the vicarage by turns, and have
amongſt them about 90 *l* a year in tithes.—The vicarage is worth about 80*l* a
year.

The church was handſomely rebuilt ſome few years ago, at the expence of the
pariſhioners.

PARISH OF MELMERBY.

MELMORBY was the habitation of *Melmor* a Dane, who firſt improved and
cultivated the country, about the ninth or tenth century. It is a ſmall manor
and pariſh, bounded on the eaſt with Crofsfell and part of the biſhoprick of
Durham, and on the other ſides with the pariſhes of Ouſby and Adingham.

It was parcel of the barony of *Adam* ſon of *Swene*. In the reign of Hen. 3.
Odard then lord of *Wigton* was ſeized thereof; after whoſe death, his ſon *Walter
de Wigton, John* ſon of Walter, and *Margaret* ſole daughter and heir of the ſaid
John, were ſucceſſively owners thereof. Margaret had two huſbands Sir John
Gernon knight and Sir John Weſton knight, but had no iſſue. She granted
Melmerby to Sir *Robert Parving* knight, the king's ſerjeant at law. His ſiſt-r's
ſon *Adam* ſon of John Peacock ſucceeded, and called himſelf *Adam Parving*.

This Adam died in the 4 Ric. 2. and then *Henry de Threlkeld* entered, in
whoſe family it continued for many generations.—In the 35 Hen. 8. *Chriſtopher
Threlkeld* held Melmerby of the king *in capite* by knight's ſervice, rendering for
the ſame yearly to the ſaid lord the king 13*s* 4*d* cornage.—In the 11 Eliz. we
find *Chriſtopher Threlkeld* patron of the church of Melmerby (and conſequently
lord of the manor, unto which the advowſon is appendent). In the 15 Eliz.
John Threlkeld. In the 7 Ja. 1. *Humphrey Threlkeld.* Which Humphrey had
a ſon *Lancelot Threlkeld*, who had five daughters coheirs: 1. *Anne*, married to
William Threlkeld clerk, of a collateral branch of the family. 2. *Katherine*, married
to Richard Studholme of Wigton gentleman. 3. *Mary*, married to Thomas
Crackenthorp of Newbiggin gentleman. 4. *Dorothy*, married to Anthony
Dale of the county of Durham gentleman. 5. *Margery.*—The arms of theſe
Threlkelds (who are a branch of the Threlkelds of Threlkeld) were; Argent,
a manch Gules.

William Threlkeld, who married the eldeſt daughter, purchaſed the ſhares of
the other ſiſters, and had iſſue a daughter and heir *Elizabeth* married to *Thomas
Pattenſon* of Breeks in the county of Weſtmorland eſquire; to whom ſucceeded
Lancelot Pattinſon clerk his ſon, who married Margaret fifth daughter of Charles

Orfeur of High Clofe efquire; and had iffue an only fon *Thomas Pattinfon* efquire the prefent lord of the manor, who in the year 1769 married Barbara fourth daughter of John Grainger of Bromfield gentleman.

The church is dedicated to St. John; and is rectorial; valued in the king's books at 12*l* 11*s.* 5¼*d:* and is now worth about 80*l per annum.*

In 1332, Sir *Thomas de Berneston* was prefented to the rectory of Melmerby by Dionifia relict of Sir John de Wigton knight; and the inquifition thereupon taken finds the faid lady to be the true patronefs in right of her dower in the manors of Wigton, Kirkbride, Blackhall, and Melmerby; that her late hufband was fon and heir of Sir Walter de Wigton, who laft prefented.

In 1334, the patronage was recovered by Robert de Parving knight from Margaret wife of Sir John Gernoun.

In 1342, *Thomas de Blythe* rector of Melmerby, with confent of the patron and ordinary, exchanges with *John de Manferghe* rector of Bright Walton in the diocefe of Sarum.

In the next year after, *Roger de Cromwell* was collated by lapfe.

: In 1346, *Robert de Bromfield* was prefented by Margaret de Wigton.

· In 1354, on the death of Robert de Bromfield, Sir *Henry de Wakefeld* was prefented by Adam Parving. And in 1359, Sir *William de Pulbow* was prefented by the fame patron.

In 1526, *Roland Threlkeld* was rector; who in that year, as official to Dr. William Burbank archdeacon of Carlifle, iffued his mandate for the induction of the abbot of Shap to the rectory of Kirkby Thore.

In 1565, on the death of Roland Threlkeld, inftitution was given to Sir *Edward Stampe* clerk, prefented by Chriftopher Threlkeld gentleman. Which Edward being deprived in 1572 for not fubfcribing the articles, Sir *George Threlkeld* clerk was prefented by John Threlkeld gentleman.

In 1609, *George Warwick*, M. A. was inftituted on a prefentation by Humphrey Threlkeld gentleman.

In 1684, on the death of *Richard Singleton* rector of Melmerby, *William Threlkeld* was prefented by William Jamefon and Richard Hutton yeomen patrons for that turn (grantees, as it feemeth, of the five fifters abovementioned, the eldeft of whom was married to this William Threlkeld). Which William dying in 1701, *William Lindfey*, M. A. was prefented by Thomas Pattenfon gentleman.

In 1739, on the ceffion of William Lindfey, *Lancelot Pattenfon* M. A. was prefented by (his father) Thomas Pattenfon efquire.

In 1760, on Lancelot Pattenfon's death, *John Jamefon* was inftituted upon a prefentation by John Stephenfon efquire, Francis Blackburne, and Charles Smalwood, clerks, executors in truft of the faid Lancelot Pattenfon.

In this parifh there are about 50 families; all of the church of England, except one prefbyterian.

PARISH

PARISH OF KIRKLAND.

KIRKLAND is the next parish, and is the eastern boundary of the county of Cumberland on that side, being divided from Westmorland by the rivulet which springs on the top of Crosfell, and empties itself in the river Eden a little below Temple Sowerby bridge. It seems to have received the name of *Kirkland*, from its having belonged to the church of Carlisle. The township itself of *Kirkland* is but of small extent, consisting of about 14 tenements holden of Sir Michael le Fleming baronet, all now purchased to freehold. But there are in the parish three other considerable manors, viz. *Blencarn, Skirwith,* and *Culgaith.* And the whole number of families in the parish is about 145, all of whom are of the established church.

The *church* of this parish is dedicated to St. Laurence, and was for a long time rectorial and in the patronage of the bishop of Carlisle. In the reign of king Hen. 6. it was granted, and soon after appropriated, to the prior and convent of Carlisle; since which time the prior and convent, and after them the dean and chapter, have been patrons thereof. It is valued in the king's books at 8 *l* 10 *s* 0 *d per annum*; and may now be worth about 130 *l.*—The incumbents thereof, so far as appears from the bishop's registers at Rose, have been as follows:

In 1294, *Adam de Newcastle* was collated by bishop Halton to the rectory of Kirkland; saving to the religious men the lord prior and convent of the church of St. Mary of Carlisle 20 *s* of silver yearly due to them out of the same.

In 1306, Sir *Gilbert de Haloghton* was collated by the same bishop; with a reservation of the said pension to the prior and convent.

In 1336, *William de Denton* rector of Kirkland, with consent of his ordinary and patron, subjects his rectory to an annual rent charge of 20 marks, to be paid to John Skelton during the life of the said John; and in case of failure of such payment, he subjects himself (for want of better security) to the greater excommunication —This Skelton was a clergyman, recommended by proviso from the court of Rome.

In 1372, a demand was made of *John de Langholme* rector of Kirkland, by the collector of the apostolic chamber, of a provision out of the profits of the rectory, on behalf of one John de Kirkby; which the rector refused to pay, having never consented to any such provision.

In 1379, on the death of John de Langholme, bishop Appleby collates *John de Penreth,* and grants unto him a licence to be absent from his cure, as well out of England as in it, for seven years.

In 1581, on the death of Sir *Thomas Aglionby* vicar of Kirkland, *Anthony Gosling* deacon was collated, upon a lapse, by bishop Meye.

In 1631, on the resignation of *John Robinson* vicar of Kirkland, *Edward Slegg,* B. D. was instituted on a presentation by the dean and chapter.

In 1681, *John Ardrey,* B. D. was presented by the same patrons. In like manner, *Hugh Todd,* M. A. in 1684; who resigning in the next year, *Daniel Mayer,* M. A. was presented by the same patrons.

On

On Daniel Mayer's death in 1694, *Nathanael Spooner*, M. A. was presented. And on his death in 1703, *George Fleming*, M. A. was presented; who resigning in 1717, the dean and chapter present *John Christopherson*, B. D.

In 1720, John Christopherson resigning, *Edward Birket*, M. A. was presented.

In 1768, on the death of Edward Birket, *Henry Richardson* clerk was instituted on a presentation by the dean and chapter.

BLENKARN, in this parish, was parcel of the barony of *Adam Fitz-Swein*, and *William de Nevill's* lands at first; but afterwards it was granted forth in frank-marriage, and was holden of the heirs of Adam and William Nevill; and some part in frankalmoigne was granted to the priory of Carlisle. In the reign of king John and before, the Thursbys of Thursby held a moiety, and the Whitbys the other moiety. In the 11 Hen. 3. Evon de Vipont and Sibell Thursby (daughter of Adam) his wife gave six bovates of land in Blenkarn to Bernard Thursby, and her lands in Ainstable and Waverton; all which William Boyvill had in possession in his own right as heir to the Thursbys. In the 6 Ed. 1. he granted part thereof to the priory of Carlisle. The residue descended to Edmund Boyvil his second son, who sold it to John Harcla; upon whose flight, after his brother Sir Andrew de Harcla was apprehended for treason, king Edward the second seized the same, and granted it to William English, father of William; whose sister and heir Julian was married to William Restwold, whose heirs sold it to Lough. It is now the property of Mr. Lough Carleton, attorney at law in London, who has here 24 tenants, who pay 3 *l* 12 *s* 5 *d* yearly rent, arbitrary fines, and boon services of plowing, mowing, raking hay, and reaping.

Mrs. Adderton, one of the sisters and coheirs of Christopher Pattenson late of Carleton hall esquire deceased, hath also 11 tenants here, who pay her 1 *l* yearly rent, arbitrary fines, and boon services. Likewise lieutenant-general Honywood has 10 tenants, who hold of him as of his manor of Milburne Grange. pay yearly a customary rent of 1 *l* 1 *s* 11¼ *d*, a twenty-penny fine, and some boons. And lastly, the dean and chapter of Carlisle have 8 tenants, who pay 2 *l* 16 *s* 11 *d* yearly customary rent, and a four-penny fine at change of tenant. only.

SKIRWITH also was parcel of Adam's barony. In the time of king John, one Jordan Spiggurnel had freehold, and others rent there. In the reign of Ed. 1. and the latter part of the reign of king Hen. 3. Robert Fitz-Walter held it. After, one John Lancafter of Holgill held the same, and died seized thereof. in the 8 Ed. 3. From him it descended to his cousin Richard son of Richard Place, whose heir gave it by fine to one William de Lancafter, whose heir general married to John Crackenthorp, father of William Crackenthorp, father of John Crackenthorp, whose three daughters and heirs were married to Hutton of the Forest, Sandford of Askham, and to Middleton. Afterwards the Middletons were lords thereof: so in the 35 Hen. 8. Ambrose Middleton and Anne his wife, in right of the said Anne, held the capital messuage and town of

Skirwith

Skirwith of the king *in capite*, paying yearly for the same 4*s* 4*d* cornage. Afterwards Hutton married a daughter and one of the coheirs of Middleton; and by purchasing the share of the other coparceners, enjoyed the whole. Finally, Agnes widow of William Fleming of Rydal esquire purchased the same in the 4 Ja 1. from whom it hath descended to the present owner Sir Michael le Fleming baronet.

There are in this manor about 38 tenants, who paid customary rent, fines, and many boon services, as reaping, mowing, ploughing, harrowing, carrying coals, and spinning so many hanks of yarn. But they have all been now lately infranchised by the said Sir Michael le Fleming.

Besides the demesne belonging to the said Sir Michael, there is another demesne within these liberties called *Bankhall*, belonging to the Crackenthorps of Newbiggin, who claim the sole right of common upon the fells, exclusive of Sir Michael and his tenants. And when the late Sir William Fleming came to the estate, he and the late Mr. Crackenthorp both rode the same fell-boundary. But Mr Crackenthorp did not further prosecute his claim, and the inhabitants of Skirwith still enjoy the privilege of common.

There is likewise another freehold estate, formerly Bird's, late Adderton's, and now belonging to John Yeates esquire; under whom are held four customary tenements which pay a yearly rent of 17*s* 6*d*.

CULGAITH was part of the large barony aforesaid given, or confirmed, by king Hen. 1. to Adam Fitz-Sweine son of Alaric: which barony was holden of the king by the payment of 112*s* cornage. Adam's two daughters, named Amabil and Matilda, were married to Alexander Crevaquer and Adam de Montbegon. The said Alexander de Crevaquer granted to the monks of Wetheral his moiety of the mill of Culgaith, with the miller and his family [*cum tota sequela pertinente*]. Witnesses of which grant were, Adam de Montbegon, Robert the Sheriff, Simon de Crevaquer, and others †. Amabil was wife afterwards to William de Nevill, to whom she had issue Thomas de Burgo, or a daughter to him married. And Thomas had issue another Thomas de Burgo, who gave or confirmed to the monks of Brecton in Yorkshire his right to those lands which William Nevill his grandfather and Amabil wife of the said William had given unto them, and which Adam son of Sweine gave them before.

The said Thomas de Burgo the younger gave to Symon son of Walter and Sara his wife divers of the lands by fine in the 7th year of king John; in whose time Roger de Montbegon, Symon son of Walter, and Alexander de Nevill held the lands in Cumberland that were the inheritance of Adam Fitz Swein. The said Roger de Montebegon was son to Adam de Montebegon by Matilda his wife aforesaid. They had issue Clementia a daughter married to Longviller, who seems to have been heir to Roger her brother.

In the 16 Hen. 3. one William son of John (by fine) gave the moiety of Culgaith to one Gilbert de Nevill and Mabel his wife.

† Regiftr. Wetheral.

In

.·- In the 6 Ed. 1. Michael de Harclay father to Andrew de Harclay earl of Carlisle, held, a moiety of Culgaith; and Walter Mulcaster and Gilbert son of Robert Hawkſley held the other moiety.

Andrew Harclay's part was forfeited by treaſon in Edward the ſecond's time: which king granted the ſame to Sir Chriſtopher Moreſby knight; on whoſe death in the 22 Ed. 3, the inquiſition finds, that the ſaid Chriſtopher died ſeiſed of the manor of Culgaith, holden of Robert Nevill of Hornby, who held *in capite* by the ſervice of 16 *s* 8 *d* cornage. From Sir Chriſtopher it deſcended to the lady Knevett heir general of the Pickerings and Moreſbys, who ſold the ſame to Henry Crackenthorp of Newbiggin eſquire, and the lands to four feoffees, who aſſigned to the tenants.

The lands are now all freehold, except one tenement only, which is at preſent in four or five different hands, and is holden of lieutenant-general Honywood as parcel of his manor of Milburn Grange, under the annual rent of 10 *s* 9 *d* and a twenty-penny fine. The freeholders pay a yearly quit rent of 28 *l* 4 *s* 1 *d* to the owners of Acorn-bank, but no court hath been holden by any lord of the manor for time immemorial.

The *chapel* of Culgaith was founded of ancient time by the lords of the manor, as appears by a commiſſion from the pope (which in biſhop Nicolſon's time was in the hands of ſome of the inhabitants) directed to the biſhop of Carliſle, to inquire of certain neglects of duty by the rector of Kirkland in not ſaying maſs on the week days in the chapel of All Saints at Culgaith, and for not finding on Sundays in the ſaid chapel the ſacramental bread and holy water, to the peril of his ſoul, the damage of the inhabitants, and the diminution of the divine worſhip †.

·-+ Calixtus epiſcopus, ſervus ſervorum Dei, venerabili fratri Epiſcopo Carliolenſi ſalutem et am-pliſſimam benedictionem. Querelam dilecti filii nobilis viri Chriſtophori Moreſby domicelli tuæ diocefeos accepimus, continentem, Quod licet rector parochialis eccleſiæ loci de Kirkelland dictæ diocefeos, pro tempore exiſtens, in capella Omnium Sanctorum loci de Culgayth ejuſdem diocefeos ſita infra limitem parochiæ præfatæ eccleſiæ, quæ per predeceſſores dicti domicelli fundata fuit, cujus idem domicellus verus patronus exiſtit, certas miſſas ſingulis ebdomadis ex cauſis legitimis celebrari, nec non ſing lis diebus dominicis aquam et panem benedici facere teneatur, prout etiam rectores ejuſdem eccleſiæ qui pro tempore fuerunt facere conſueverunt; tamen modernus rector dictæ eccleſiæ id facere hactenus recuſavit et recuſat, in animæ ſuæ periculum, et detrimentum habitatorum dicti loci, et diminutionem divini cultus: Quare pro parte præfati domicelli nobis fuit humiliter ſupplica-tum, ut ſuper præmiſſis opportune providere paterna diligentia curaremus. Quocirca Fraternitati tuæ per Apoſtolica ſcripta mandamus, quatenus vocatis qui fuerint vocandi, et auditis hinc inde propoſitis, quod juſtum fuerit (appellatione remota) decernas; faciens quod decreveris per cenſuram eccleſiaſticam firmiter obſervari. Teſtes autem qui fuerint nominati, ſi ſe gratia, odio, vel amore ſubſtraxerint, cenſura ſimili (appellatione ceſſante) compellas veritati teſtimonium perhibere. Datum Romæ apud Sanctum Fetrum, anno incarnationis domini milleſimo quadringenteſimo quinquageſimo ſexto, quinto die Maii, pontificatus noſtri anno ſecundo.—[*Domicellus*, is an old word uſed to ſignify one of the houſhold or family; here it ſeems to denote an inhabitant, having (as the civilians term it) a *domicil* or habitation in that place.]

'In '1739' the revenues of this chapel were certified to the governors of queen Anne's bounty as follows:

			l	s	d
Ancient falary by the inhabitants	—	—	3	5	8
Further additional falary —	—	—	2	6	8
Chapel yard worth *per annum*	—	—	0	3	0
One graffing in the town pafture	—	—	0	5	6
Total			6	0	10

It was augmented in the fame year with 200*l* by lot. Afterwards, John Dalfton of Acorn-bank efquire bequeathed 60*l* to this chapel. The reverend Chriftopher Bowerbank rector of Weyhill in Hampfhire gave by his will 160*l*, to which his brother and executor added 40*l* more. The late Dr. Bolton dean of Carlifle gave 70*l* from an unknown hand. With which benefactions another augmentation of 200*l* was procured from the faid governors of the bounty of queen Anne. With part of the bequefts they rebuilt the chapel, one John Sewell giving 10*l* towards it; and other deficiences were made up by the inhabitants. The reft of the money was laid out in lands, which now procure a revenue to the curate of upwards of 30*l* a year. And the new chapel was confecrated by bifhop Ofbaldifton in 1758.

PARISH OF LANGWATHBY.

Langwathby, Mr. Denton fays, in the ancient records is called *Long-Wa'de-ofby*; wherein it is alfo recorded, that king Henry the firft gave it to *Henry Fitz-Swein*, together with Edenhall. Howbeit this did not long continue with him or his pofterity; for the king held it as a royal demefne. King John had it in poffeffion. Henry the third gave it to Alexander king of Scots in part of 200 librates of land granted to the Scots in the year 1237, by compofition for the releafe of Cumberland and Northumberland and other things in demand. The king of Scots enjoyed it, until John Balioll forfeited thofe lands. Thenceforth they continued until Richard the fecond's time in the crown: but he granted thofe in Cumberland to Ralph Nevil earl of Weftmorland and Johan his wife and the heirs of their bodies; whofe grandfon Richard earl of Warwick did forfeit them to Edward the 4th. And he granted them to the duke of Gloucefter his brother, afterwards king by the name of Richard the third. From which time they continued in the crown, till king William the third granted them to the earl of Portland, in whofe family they ftill continue.

Langwathby confifts of one fingle townfhip or manor. The river Eden divides it from Edenhall on the weft. It adjoins upon Kirkland on the fouth and fouth eaft, and Aldingham on the north and north eaft. The tenants are copyholders under the duke of Portland, and do fuit and fervice at the courts at Penrith, tho' they are feparated from the foreft of Englewood by the river Eden.

As

As to the ecclefiaftical ftate, this feems to have been anciently part of the parifh of Edenhall, and therefore doth not occur in the valuations of pope Nicholas or of king Edward the fecond. And the church or chapel here was probably firft erected for want of a bridge over Eden, whereby the inhabitants were often hindred from repairing to divine fervice. But by length of time it hath gained parochial rights. And in the vifitation rolls, it is called a vicarage, and churchwardens are always fworn for the parifh of Langwathby.

The church was lately rebuilt at the expence of the parifhioners; and the vicar of Edenhall officiates here and at Edenhall alternately : and enjoys the profits by virtue of his inftitution and induction to Edenhall.

The revenue confifts chiefly of about 8 acres of glebe land, 10l a year paid out of the corn tithes by Timothy Fetherftonhaugh efquire the prefent leffee, prefcription for tithe hay 1l 1s 11d, tithe wool and lamb, and other fmall dues, amounting in the whole to about 25l per annum.

The number of families is about 36, one of which is prefbyterian.

PARISH OF ADDINGHAM.

Dr. Todd fuppofes this place to have received its name from a remarkable monument of antiquity, on the top of the hill, nigh unto the place where the church now ftands, a little to the north eaft of it, where there is a circle of ftones, fomething like Stonehenge in Wiltfhire ; and *Aldingham*, (*Hald hing-ham*,) he fays, fignifies an habitation nigh the hanging ftones (*oppidum ad lapides antiquum penfiles*). The circle is about 80 yards in diameter, and confifts of about 72 ftones, from above three yards high to lefs than fo many feet. There is one ftone larger than the reft, which ftands about 40 yards from the circle towards the fouth weft, being four yards in height and near two yards fquare at the bottom ; and is hollow at the top, like a difh or Roman altar. This the country people call *Long Meg*, and the reft they call *her daughters*. Dr. Todd further obferves, that the northern people, as the Scythians, Scandians, and others, who were moft tenacious of ancient cuftoms, and from whom the Britons are more immediately defcended, did endeavour to perpetuate the memory of all their great affairs, as the inauguration of their kings, the burials of their generals and nobles, or victories over their enemies, by raifing and order-ing ftones and pyramids of prodigious magnitude. We are told that the election of a king of Denmark in ancient times was commonly had in this folemn manner : as many of the nobles as were fenators, and had power to give their votes, agreed upon fome convenient place in the fields ; where feating themfelves in a circle upon fo many great ftones, they gave their votes. This done they placed their new-elected monarch upon a ftone higher than the reft, either in the mid-dle of the circle, or at fome fmall diftance at one fide, and faluted him king. In Iceland to this day, there is fuch a company of ftones, which bear the name of *Kingstolen*, or the king's feat. Near St. Buriens in Cornwall, in a place which the Cornifh men call Bifcow-Woune, are to be feen 19 ftones fet in a circle, diftant every one about 12 feet from the other, and in the very center one
pitched

pitched far higher and bigger than the reſt. So in Ròllrich ſtones in Oxford-ſhire, the largeſt ſtone is at ſome little diſtance from the circle. From all which, Dr. Todd concludes, that ſome Daniſh or Saxon king was elected here for Cumberland.

All which may be very true, and yet theſe places not ſolely ſet apart for the inauguration of their kings, but for many other ſolemn rites and obſervances; and, generally, they ſeem to have been the places dedicated to religious uſes. It is well known, that the Druids in this kingdom performed their adorations in the open air, and within this kind of incloſure. And the hollow or baſon in the top of the largeſt ſtone here ſeemeth ſomewhat to confirm this notion, as be-ing intended for a place of ſacrifice and oblation.

LITTLE SALKELD, a manor in this pariſh, was about the year 1292 given, or rather confirmed, by king Ed. 1. to the prior and convent of Carliſle; for it is ſaid that Walter the Norman had long before purchaſed and given it to that church. The dean and chapter (who ſucceeded the prior and convent) now hold this manor, and have a large number of tenants here and in the neighbouring parts, who attend their courts here, and pay about 8 ʟ 14 s 0 d annual rent. Thoſe of the tenants that are cuſtomary pay a four-penny fine on change of tenant, but the lord never dies; and they have all the wood growing upon their eſtates.

There was anciently a chapel at Little Salkeld, which in the year 1360 being deſecrated and polluted by the ſhedding of blood, and the pariſh church at a great diſtance, the vicar was allowed to officiate in his own vicarage houſe, till the interdict ſhould be taken off from the chapel.

GLASSONBY and GAMELSBY in this pariſh were anciently both one ſeigniory, bounded on the north by the rill or little beck that falleth from the eaſt moun-tains weſtward, through Kirkoſwald parks, into Eden, which doth bound it on the weſt; from whence the lordſhip is extended of great breadth into the moun-tains, till bounded by the waſte belonging to Alſton-moor on the eaſt. They were given by king Hen. 1. unto one Hildred and his heirs, to be holden of the crown *in capite* by the payment yearly of 2 s cornage; from whom it deſcended to a daughter named Chriſtian being ward to king John, who gave the ward-ſhip to William de Ireby. She was daughter of Odard, ſon of Odard, ſon of Adeline, ſon of the ſaid Hildred.

William de Ireby had iſſue by the ſaid Chriſtian two daughters Chriſtian and Eva. Eva had a rent charge out of the land, and was married to Robert de Eſtotevil, and after to Alan de Charters. She releaſed to her ſiſter Chriſtian wife of Thomas Laſcells of Bolton, who had iſſue Arminia married to Thomas Seaton, whoſe ſon Chriſtopher Seaton forfeited the ſame and other lands to king Ed. 1. by taking part with Robert Bruce and the Scots.

The king gave his lands in Gamelſby and Unthank to William Latimer, fa-ther of William, who had iſſue William Latimer, father of Elizabeth, wife of John Nevill, father of Ralph Nevill earl of Weſtmorland; who gave his lands in Cumberland, and divers others, to George (his fecond fon) lord Latimer, whofe daughter and fole heir was married to John lord Nevill of Raby.

The male line failing in the reign of Hen. 8. thefe lands fell to four coheirs; from them to the Dacres; fo to Fienes; fo to Lennard earl of Suffex; fo to Sir Chriftopher Mufgrave baronet by purchafe from the two daughters of Thomas earl of Suffex.

The CHURCH of Addingham is dedicated to St. Michael, and is vicarial; valued in the king's books at 9 *l* 4 *s* 7 *d*, and of the prefent yearly value of about 110 *l*. It was anciently in the patronage of the lord of the manor, as appears from a fine levied in the year 1245, whereby Thomas de Lafcells and Chriftian his wife and Eva widow of Robert Avenal fettle the manor of Gamelfby and Glaffenby on William de Ireby for life, and the prefentation to the church of Glaffenby (as it is there called) to go by turns between the faid Chriftian and Eva. Afterwards, the faid Chriftian being then a widow, granted the faid church to the prior and convent of Carlifle. And having married again to the lord Robert de Brus, fhe and the faid Robert in the year 1282 petition bifhop Irton to confirm the appropriation of the faid church and rectory, with the chapel of Salkeld, to the faid prior and convent, which the faid bifhop confirms accordingly; and ordains, that after the death of the then rector *Euftachius de Trewick*, they provide fufficiently for the fupply of the cure. And the fame was afterwards confirmed by bifhop Halton; who taxed the vicarage at 20 marks. And finally, king Edward the firft, on the part of the crown, upon the grievous complaint of the prior and convent of their fufferings by the Scots, confirms the fame unto them †.

In 1292, the prior and convent prefent *Robert de Scardeburg*, whereupon a commiffion *de jure patronatus* iffued, Adam de Crokedayk having alfo prefented Richard de Longwardby; but judgment was afterwards given in the king's court for the prior and convent.

In 1316, on the refignation of *William de Beverley* vicar of Addingham,

---

† Edwardus Dei gratia, rex Angliæ, dominus Hiberniæ, et dux Aquitaniæ, omnibus ad quos præfentes literæ pervenerint, talutem. Quia accepimus per inquifitionem quam per vicecomitem noftrum Cumbriæ fieri fecimus, quod non eft ad damnum vel prejudicium alicujus, fi concedamus dilectis nobis in Chrifto priori et conventui beatæ Mariæ de Carliolo, quod ipfi ecclefiam de Adingham fui patronatus et Carliolenfis dioceleos, cum capella de Salkeld eidem ecclefiæ annexa, in proprios ufus in perpetuum poffidendam appropriare, et eam fic appropriatam retinere poffint fibi et fuccefforibus, nifi ad damnum noftrum in hoc, videlicet, quod fi epifcopatu et prioratu Karliolenfi fimul et femel vacantibus, et in manu noftra exiftentibus, dictam ecclefiam de Adingham vacare contigerit, non poffemus poft appropriationem hujusmodi, idoneam perfonam ad dictam ecclefiam præfentare, ficut antea temporibus hujufmodi vacationum facere potuimus : Nos, ob diverfa gravamina et oppreffiones quæ iidem prior et conventus, tam per combuftiones domorum et ecclefiarum fuarum, quam per deprædationes diverfas eis per Scotos inimicos et rebelles noftros factas multipliciter fuftinuerunt, conceffimus e·s pro nobis et hæredibus noftris, quantum in nobis eft, quod ipfi ad relevationem ftatus domus fuæ, prædictam ecclefiam de Adingham, cum capelli prædicta, fibi in ufus proprios perpetuo poffidendam appropriare, et eam fic appropriatam retinere poffint fibi et fuccefforibus fuis, fine occafione vel impedimento noftri vel hæredum noftrorum imperpetuum. In cujus rei teftimonium has literas noftras fieri fecimus patentes. Tefte meipfo apud Strivelyn, octavo die Julii anno regni noftri tricefimo fecundo.

Jeffrey

Jeeffrey de Generton was inftituted on the prefentation of the faid prior and convent.

In 1362, *Adam de Wigton* was vicar; who dying in that year, *Walter de Kelton* was inftituted.

In 1477, *Thomas Lowther*, brother and heir of Hugh Lowther of Afkham, appears to have been vicar.

In 1574, *George Stubb* was inftituted on the death of *John Auften*, prefented by John Blenerhaffet of Flimby efquire, who had this avoidance granted to him by Lancelot Salkeld fometime dean and chapter of Carlifle.

In 1591, *Edward Mayplet* was inftituted.

In 1636, *Lewis Weft*, M. A. was inftituted: He was alfo prebendary of Carlifle; and was ejected by Cromwell's commiffioners. On the return of king Charles the fecond he was reftored, and was the only member of the chapter who furvived the ufurpation. He died in 1668, and was fucceeded by *William Sill*, M. A. who in the year 1678 commenced a fuit in chancery againft the dean and chapter, which by the mediation of bifhop Rainbow was compromifed; and a leafe of the tithes of Little Salkeld was granted by the dean and chapter in augmentation of the vicarage.

In 1697, on the death of *Henry Aglionby* the then vicar, *Thomas Nevinfon*, B. A. was inftituted; who in the next year removing to Torpenhow, *William Nicolfon* the archdeacon was inftituted. On whofe promotion to the fee of Carlifle in 1702, *John Chriftopherfon*, M. A. was prefented by the crown.

In 1758, on John Chriftopherfon's death, *Edward Birket*, M. A. was inftituted on a prefentation by the dean and chapter.

And on *Edward Birket*'s death in 1768, *John Temple* clerk was inftituted on a like prefentation.

There is a fmall *poor ftock* in this parifh of about 52*l*, lent out upon land fecurity at Windfcales in the faid parifh.

At *Maughanby* in this parifh is a free *fchool*, founded in 1634 by Mr. Mayplet vicar here, who was alfo prebendary of Carlifle. The revenues thereof, as certified by the fchoolmafter and churchwardens at bifhop Nicolfon's primary vifitation in 1704, are as follows:

Imprimis, a large fchool-houfe, a manfion-houfe, a barn, and oowhoufe. Item, the clofes following: viz. the Low Clofe, containing by eftimation 8 acres; the School field, 12 acres; Baron Croft, 4 acres; Crook tree, 6 acres; Low Whins, 10 acres; High Whins, 20 acres; New Ruft, 8 acres; The whole is a cuftomary eftate, paying yearly 8*s* finable rent to the lord of the manor of Melmerby, and 3*s* 4*d* free rent to the dean and chapter of Carlifle, and 1*s* cornage rent.

The truftees being all dead, the bifhops of Carlifle have for fome time, as ordinary, appointed fchoolmafters. About the year 1726, Jofeph Hutchinfon devifed an eftate at Gawtree in this parifh, after the death of his mother, to the ufe of a fchool in that quarter, now let for about 20*l* a year; the fame to be

under

under the care and management of the churchwarden and overfeer of the poor, for that quarter.

The number of families in this parish is about 128; of which four are pref- byterians.

ESKDALE WARD.

PARISH OF STANWIX.

THE firſt pariſh in this Ward is that of STANWIX, *Stanewick*, which word ſignifies a town or village on the ſtony way. It conſiſts of the following townſhips or conſtablewicks, viz. Stanwix, Rickerby, Linſtock, Terraby, Houghton, Etterby, Stainton, and Cargo.

STANWIX is held as parcel of the manor of the ſocage of the caſtle of Car- liſle. And the lands are all freehold. At this place, according to Mr. Hor- ſley, was the Roman ſtation of *Congavata*, upon the courſe of the wall. The ditch which appears diſtinctly to the weſt of the village, between it and the river Eden, ſeems to have been Severus's; whoſe wall has formed the north rampart of the ſtation here, as it has generally done with reſpect to the other ſtations upon the wall. This ſituation ſuits exactly with thoſe rules which the Romans obſerved in building theſe ſtations. For here is a plain area for the ſtation, and a gentle deſcent to the ſouth, and towards the river, for the out- buildings. And by all accounts, and the uſual evidences, it is upon this deſcent, and chiefly to the ſouth eaſt, that the Roman buildings have ſtood. Abundance of ſtones have been dug up in this part; and ſome which re- ſembled the ſtones of an aqueduct. The ruins of the wall are viſible to the brink of the precipice, over which it ſeems to have paſſed in going down to the river †.

RICKERBY is a meſne manor under the barony of Croſby, or manor of Linſtock, and pays a yearly quit-rent as ſuch to the biſhop of Carliſle for the time being of 13s 4d, with ſuit of court. This little manor was anciently part of the Tilliols' eſtate, then of the Pickerings and Weſtons; of which laſt Sir Edward Muſgrave purchaſed, and ſold to Cuthbert Studholme, who con- veyed to the Gilpins, in whom it continued for three deſcents, and is now moſtly ſold off to the tenants, and what remained of the ſeigniory Mr. Ri- chardſon of that place has purchaſed.

† Horſley, 155.

At

At *Drawdykes*, a capital meſſuage within this pariſh, belonging to the Aglionbys, is a Roman inſcription :

·COH·IIII PR POS	*Cohortis quartæ prætorianæ*
ᴐ IVL VITALIS	*poſuit centuria Julii Vitalis.*

This is one of that ſort of inſcriptions which are uſually found on the face
of the wall ; but it has this peculiar curioſity in it, that the century ſeems to
have belonged to the guards, or to a prætorian cohort.

Alſo there is another inſcription, which is ſepulchral :

DIS MANIBV	*Dis Manibus*
S MARCI TROIANI	*Marci Trojani*
AVGVSTINIII TVM FA	*Auguſtiniani tumulum fa-*
CIENDVM CVRAVI	*ciendum curavit*
T AEL AMMILLVSIMA·	*Aelia Ammilla Luſima*
CONIVX KARISS	*conjux kariſſima.*

There is another at Scaleby caſtle, which Mr. Horſley thinks belongs to
Stanwix :

MATRIBVS	*Matribus*
DOMESTICIS	*domeſticis*
VIS MESSO	*Vis. Meſſorius*
SIGNIFER V SLL	*ſignifer votum ſolvit libentiſſime.·*

There is another at Carliſle, which Mr. Horſley is likewiſe of opinion belongs to this ſtation :

LEG VI	*Legio ſexta,*
VIC P F	*vctrix, pia, fidelis,*
G P R F	*Genio populi Romani fecit †.*

LINSTOCK was granted (together with Carleton) by king Hen. 1. to Walter
his chaplain, to hold in cornage by the yearly rent of 1*l* 17*s* 4*d.* This
Walter (with the king's licence) took upon him a religious habit of a regular
canon in the priory of St. Mary's Carliſle ; and with the king's conſent he
gave Linſtock and Carleton to that houſe of religion in pure alms for ever :
whereupon the king releaſed the ſaid rent. And the ſaid Walter was made
prior there.

For ſome time, the biſhop and convent held all their lands in common and
undivided. But after the firſt partition made by the pope's legate Gualo, this
barony fell to the biſhop, and Linſtock caſtle was his only ſeat for a long
time. For ſo late as the year 1293, we find the biſhop of Carliſle entertaining
the archbiſhop of York Johannes Romanus, at his caſtle of Linſtock.

† Horſley, 265.

There

There are in this manor about 10 freehold tenements, which pay a yearly rent of 2*l* 13*s* 10½*d*. There are also about 90 customary tenants who pay yearly 37*l* 6*s* 1¼*d* And about 14 leaseholders, who pay 17*l* 15*s* 10*d*. The customary tenants pay only a small piece of current silver coin at the change of tenant, and nothing at the change of the lord. Yet it appears from some old evidences at Rose, that they were anciently arbitrary. They also have all the wood that grows upon their tenements. Twenty pounds of the said customary rents are paid for the commons which were divided and inclosed about the year 1707, and are held as customary estates, and conveyed as such. The tenants seem anciently to have been bound to the lord's miln, and it was then of considerable value, but is now of very little account.

Terraby and Houghton came anciently by marriage to the Aglionbys, who were lords thereof for several generations; until John Aglionby esquire exchanged the same with Sir John Lowther baronet, who again exchanged the same with Christopher Dalston esquire for the manor of Melkinthorp in Westmorland, whose heir general Sir William Dalston knight sold the same about the year 1764 to the tenants.

Etterby in old writings is called *Arthuriburgum*, which seems to imply that it had been a considerable village. Some affirm, that it took its name from Arthur king of the Britons, who was in this country about the year 550 pursuing his victories over the Danes and Norwegians. But there are no remains of antiquity at or near this place to justify such a conjecture. It now consists of about 12 tenements, holden of Sir James Lowther as parcel of the barony of Burgh; pays 5*l* yearly customary rent, and arbitrary fines.

Stainton is the next township, and is parcel of the manor of Westlinton, and holden of Sir James Lowther; consists of about ten tenements, is very high rented, and pays a twenty-penny fine.

Cargo, *Carg-bow*, a craggy hill, is a village on the north east side of the river Eden, between Stainton and Rockliffe. It was first a manor and demesne of John de Lacy constable of Chester, who held the same of the king immediately by cornage. This John Lacy granted the same and Cringledyke (a territory thereunto belonging) to William de Vescy and his heirs, lords of Alnwick in Northumberland and of Malton in Yorkshire, to be holden of the donor and his heirs, for a mew'd hawk yearly in lieu of all services. William Vescy granted it to Ewan Carlisle knight for lands in Yorkshire, reserving to him and his heirs the same services. And afterwards, in the 2d year of Ed. 1. Robert de Ross lord of Werk in Tindale died seised thereof, having held the same of William de Carlisle the younger, tendring yearly an hawk or mark of silver in lieu of all services. From this Robert de Ross it descended for many generations in the issue male, until the 32d year of Ed. 3. and shortly after, Elizabeth Ross the heir general transferred the

inheritance

Inheritance to the family of the Parrs of Kendal with other lands, where it remained until William Parr marquis of Northampton dying without iffue, his widow dame Ellin exchanged it with queen Elizabeth, and took other lands for her jointure From the crown it was granted to the Whitmores; who fold it to the prefent poffeffor Jofeph Dacre efquire.

The CHURCH is dedicated to St. Michael, and was given by Walter aforefaid or king Henry the firft to the church of Carlifle, and foon after appropriated. The corn tithes are divided between the bifhop and the dean and chapter, and the bifhop hath always had the right of patronage. It is valued in the king's books at 9*l*, and is now worth 100*l per annum*.

In the year 1300, one *Adam* was vicar, who appeared at the county court and at the affizes, as the bifhop's ordinary, to receive fuch as had the benefit of clergy, and to fee them committed to fome of the bifhop's prifons.

In the year 1309, on the death of the faid *Adam*, bifhop Halton collates Sir *Gilbert de Derlyngton*; faving to himfelf and his fucceffors the accuftomed penfion of half a mark.

In 1316, on the death of Sir *John de Appleby* vicar of Stayneweggs, Sir *Thomas Hagg* was collated by the fame bifhop, with a like refervation of half a mark penfion.

In 1358, Sir *Richard de Caldbeck* was vicar; who dying in that year, Sir *Richard de Aflacby* was collated: Who, in the next year, exchanged with Sir *Thomas de Cullerdonne* for the vicarage of Wigton.

In 1465, the laft will and teftament of Sir *William Byx*, vicar of Stanwix, was proved at Rofe before bifhop Scroop. The next that occurs was *Thomas Beft* in 1473; in like manner *Edward Rotbion* in 1477, and *Thomas Boyet* in 1487.

In 1577, Sir *Richard Phayer* clerk was collated by bifhop Barnes, on the death of Sir *Henry Brown* the late vicar. And two years after, *Mark Edgar* was collated; on whofe death in 1585, a caveat was entred by Robert Dalton of Carlifle gentleman, on a grant of the firft, fecond, or third avoidance, made by bifhop Beft in 1569, and confirmed by Sir Thomas Smith knight (then dean) and the chapter of Carlifle; but in September following Sir *John Braythwaite* clerk was collated by bifhop Meye in his own right.

In 1602, John Braythwaite died; whereupon *Thomas Langhorn*, B. A. was collated by bifhop Robinfon. And on Thomas Langhorn's death in 1614, the fame bifhop collates *John Robinfon*, M. A.

In 1625, on the refignation of *John Jackfon* vicar of Stanwix, bifhop Senhoufe collates *Robert Brown*, M. A. On whofe death in 1639, *Richard Welfbman* was collated by bifhop Potter.

In 1661, *George Buchanan*, M. A. was collated: And on his death in 1666, *Henry Marfball*, M. A. who died in the year following, and was fucceeded by *Jeremiah Nelfon*, M. A.

In 1676, on the ceffion of Jeremiah Nelfon, *John Tomlinfon*, M. A. was collated; and on his death in 1685, *Hugh Todd*, M. A. was collated by bifhop

bifhop Smith. And Hugh Todd refigning in 1688, the fame bifhop collates *Nathanael Spooner.*

In 1703, on Mr. Spooner's death, *George Fleming,* M. A. was collated by bifhop Nicolfon. And two years after, the fame bifhop collates *Thomas Benfon,* M. A. on Mr. Fleming's refignation:

In 1727, on Dr. Benfon's death, *John Waugh,* M. A. was collated by (his father) bifhop Waugh.

In 1765, on Dr. Waugh's death, *James Farifh* clerk was collated by bifhop Lyttelton.

The number of *families* in this parifh is about 182; of which, ten are quakers, and ten prefbyterians.

In the year 1356, bifhop Welton publifhed an indulgence of 40 days, to all that fhould contribute towards the repairs of the *bridge* over Eden, between the city of Carlifle and Stanwix.

PARISH OF CROSBY.

AFTER the barony of *Linftock* came to the church of Carlifle, a grange was erected here and was called *Crofby,* as belonging to the church. The civil ftate whereof being before fet forth in *Linftock,* the ecclefiaftical ftate only re_ mains to be confidered.

It is a vicarage, valued in the king's books at 7*l* 11*s* 4*d*; was certified to the governors of queen Anne's bounty at 27*l* 10*s*; and. is now worth about 27*l per annum.* It is in the patronage of the bifhop of Carlifle. What occurs concerning it in the archives at Rofe, is as follows:

In 1303, *William de Infula,* vicar of Crofby, gives bond to the bifhop for the payment of 40*s* in three years time, for a certain favour to him done. What that favour was, feems to appear from another bond immediately following, which obliges him to the payment of 10*l* to the bifhop or his official, if here_ after he be found guilty of incontinency with Maud (a parifhioner of his) or any other woman.

In 1310, William vicar of Crofby refigns, and *John Wafchipp* was collated; faving to the bifhops of Carlifle an annual penfion of 2*s.*

In 1337, Sir *Thomas de Dalfton* appears, by the ftyle and title cf vicar of Crofby juxta Lynftoke.

In 1355, *Robert Merke* vicar of Crofby refigns; and two years after, an_ other vicar refigns, viz. *Roger de Ledes*; upon whofe refignation, *John de Grandon* was collated.

In 1362, *Thomas de Kirkland* was collated; and in lefs than 4 months after, *John Fitz Rogier* was collated.

In 1379, *Robert Caylles* was collated, and in the year following exchanged with *Elias* rector of Scaleby.

In

In 1577, Sir *Thomas Twentyman* was collated and inftituted into the vicarage of Crofby nigh Eden, on the death of Sir *Simon Gate* the laft incumbent. And after the death of feveral vicars fucceffively, *Thomas Wilfon* was collated in 1585. *Thomas Shaw* in 1612. *Thomas Milburn* in 1627. And *Richard Welfhman* in 1635.

On the ceffion of Richard Welfhman in 1639, *William Hodgfon* was collated.

In 1661, *John Theakfton* was collated; on whofe death in 1666, *Philip Fielding*, M. A. fucceeded. And he refigning four years after, *Robert Hume* was collated.

On the ceffion of Robert Hume in 1680, *Nathanael Bowey* was collated. And on his death in 1713, *Richmond Fenton*, B. A. And he dying in 1730, *William Gibfon* was collated by bifhop Waugh.

In 1758, on William Gibfon's death, *Henry Shaw* was collated by bifhop Ofbaldifton.

In this parifh are about 61 families; of which one is a quaker.

PARISH OF SCALEBY.

SCALEBY is a fmall parifh, encompaffed with thofe of Stanwix, Crofby, and Kirklinton. It hath its name from the *fcales* or booths made of branches of trees and earth, which the inhabitants erected for the fhelter and defence of themfelves and their flocks and herds, efpecially in the fummer time, when all the country round was foreft.

When king Hen. 1. had eftablifhed Carlifle, he gave that lordfhip unto one *Richard* the Rider (fo called from his expertnefs in horfemanfhip) whofe name was *Tylliolfe*, who firft placed thofe habitations. From him it defcended unto *Symon Tylliolfe*; whofe fon *Piers* (or *Peter*) *Tylliolfe*, in the latter end of Henry the fecond's time, was ward to Jeoffrey de Lucy by the king's grant, and lived through the reigns of Ric. 1. and king John, and until the 31 Hen. 3. They held the caftle and manor of Scaleby of the crown as alfo Houghton and Etarby. They were alfo lords of Solpart, which they held of Lyddal; and of Richardby in the barony of Linftock, which they held of the bifhop of Carlifle. At Richardby the faid Richard their firft anceftor feated himfelf, whereupon it was fo called after his name.

At that time the Scots haraffed all this country to an high degree, which obliged the gentlemen to dwell in Carlifle, and therefore every man provided himfelf with land whereon to produce grafs, hay, and corn, as near to the city as they might; as this Richard at Richardby, Botchard at Bothard-by, Hubert the baron of Gilfland at Hubertby, Henricus father to Ranulph Engain (or grandfather to his wife Ibria) at Henrickby, Agillon at Aglionby, Pavya widow of Robert de Grinfdale in the territory called Pavy-

VOL. II.   N n n   field,

field,, Avery fon of Robert in Haverfholme, Albert fon of Yervan (or Hervy) inHarveyholme afterwards called Dentonholme, and divers others.

The faid Piers Tylliolfe married the daughter of the faid Jeffrey Lucy (his tutor and guardian), and had iffue two fons; one named *Jeoffrey* after her father's name, who fucceeded in the inheritance, and died in the 23 Ed. 1. and another named *Adam*, that married the daughter of Henry de Cormanure, and by her he got the inheritance of the fixth part of Houghton. This Adam had Richardby for term of life, and was therefore called Adam de Richardby; and of that family the Richardbys are defcended.

Jeoffrey had iffue *Robert Tylliol*, who purchafed a third part of Levington, and died in the 14 Ed. 3. He had iffue a fon *Peter Piers* or *Tylliol*, and a daughter Elizabeth married to Anthony Lucy.

Robert fon of *Peter* and Ifabella his wife died in the 41 Ed. 3. and had iffue by his wife Alice a fon *Piers* who fucceeded him, and a fecond fon Jeoffrey lord of Emelton.

Piers Tylliol fon of *Robert* died in the 13 Hen. 6. having enjoyed the eftate 67 years. He had iffue one fon *Robert de Tylliol* who was an idiot, and died in the next year after his father without iffue; whereby the eftate came to be divided between his two fifters and coheirs, *Ifabel* and *Margaret*.

Ifabel the elder fifter was married to *John Colvil*, and died in the 17 Hen. 6. having iffue *William* and *Robert*.

William died in the 20 Ed. 4. without iffue male; leaving only two daughters *Phyllis* and *Margaret*. Whereupon *Robert* the younger brother claimed the eftate by virtue of an intail; alledging that his grandfather Sir Peter de Tilliol had made a feoffment to the ufe of his will, and that afterwards he made a will, by which he ordered that William Colvil his grandfon fhould take the name of Tilliol, and have the manors of Houghton, Richardby, Ireby, Sol. part, his moiety of Newbigging, and a third part of Kirklevington, together with the caftle of Scaleby, to him and the heirs male of his body; remainder to Robert the fecond fon of his daughter Ifabel in the like manner and upon the fame condition that he take the name of Tilliol. But Robert had not this will to produce, and fo was forced to go without the eftate, which was enjoyed by the daughters of William. Neverthelefs, to keep on foot his pretenfions, he affumed the name of Tilliol. And this accounts for what we find in 'fome ancient evidences, that thefe Colvils are called Colvil *alias* Tilliol. And the late Mr. Gilpin, faid he had in his cuftody an authentic inftrument under the feal of the commiffary general of York, dated Sept. 27, in the 22 Ed. 4. which teftifies, that one Sir William Martindale knight did in the court of York, for the difcharging of his confcience, fwear, that he faw the will, and that it purported an intail as aforefaid; and that he and others, in favour of *Margaret* fecond daughter of the faid Peter de Tilliol had deftroyed it. Be that as it may, it is certain Robert failed in his claim, and the eftate defcended to the two daughters and coheirs of William, between whom their moiety of the Tilliol's lands became further divided; *viz. Phyllis*, married to William Muf. grave, who had Crookdake for her purparty, and was anceftor of the Muf.

'graves

graves of Crookdake; and *Margaret*, married to Nicholas Mufgrave brother of the faid William, who had Hayton (and, as it feemeth, Scaleby), and was anceftor of the Mufgraves of Hayton.

This *Margaret* to her hufband Nicholas Mufgrave had a fon *Thomas*; which *Thomas* had a fon *William*; which *William* died in the 40 Eliz. leaving iffue a fon and heir Sir *Edward Mufgrave* knight, who purchafed the other moiety of Sir Peter de Tilliol's lands.

For, as was obferved before, the faid Sir Peter de Tilliol had two daughters; of whom, *Margaret* the younger was married to *James Morefby* efquire, who had iffue Sir *Chriftopher Morefby* knight, who had iffue another Sir *Chriftopher*, who had iffue a daughter and heir *Anne* married to Sir *James Pickering* knight, who had iffue a fon Sir *Chriftopher Pickering* knight, who had a daughter and heir *Anne*, married firft to Sir Francis Wefton knight, fecondly to Sir Henry Knevet knight, and thirdly to John Vaughan efquire. To her firft hufband fhe had a fon and heir Sir Henry Wefton knight, who fold to Sir Edward Mufgrave aforefaid the moiety of all the lands that were the Tilliols below Eden, whereby Sir Edward became poffeffed of the whole.

This Sir *Edward Mufgrave* rebuilt Scaleby caftle in the year 1696. *William Mufgrave* efquire his fon fucceeded; who had iffue Sir *Edward Mufgrave* baronet, who fuftained great loffes on the account of his faithful fervices to king Charles the firft and fecond, and was forced to difmember a great part of his eftate. He fold Kirklevington to Mr. Edmund Appleby, Houghton to Arthur Forfter of Stonegarth fide, Richardby to Cuthbert Studholme, and Scaleby to *Richard Gilpin*, who afterwards purchafed Richardby of Michael Studholme fon of the faid Cuthbert.

Mr. Sandford (in the true fpirit of thofe times) fpeaking of Scaleby, fays, " It was fometime the eftate of Sir Edward Mufgrave of Hayton baronet, but " now fold to Mr. *Gilpin* a quondam preacher of the fanatical parliament, " and his wife Mr. Brifco's daughter of Crofton, brethren of confufion in " their brains, knew what they would not have, but knew not what they would " have if they might chufe."

The faid *Richard Gilpin* had a fon *William Gilpin* efquire, of whom Dr. Todd gives this encomium, " that he was a learned councellor at law, recorder of " the city of Carlifle, and a lover of antiquities, in which he was well fkilled."

Richard Gilpin efquire, fon of William, fold Scaleby to *Edward Stephenfon* efquire, commonly called governor Stephenfon, who died in 1768; and was fucceeded by his brother *John Stephenfon* efquire, who alfo died, leaving a fon the prefent owner, unmarried.

There are now only three cuftomary cottages within this manor, which pay 2s yearly rent and a twenty-penny fine; and 40 freehold tenements, which pay no rent, nor other fervices, but only fuit of court.

The CHURCH of Scaleby is dedicated to All Saints, and is rectorial; valued in the king's books at 7l 12s 1d; was certified to the governors of queen Anne's bounty at 18l 3s 0d; and having received an allotment of 200l from the faid governors, is now worth about 30l per annum.

It

It is in the patronage of the bifhop of Carlifle, the advowfon whereof was confirmed to the bifhop by fine in the 21 Ed. 1. for which the bifhop gave to Jeoffrey de Tylliol the lord of the manor 25 marks of filver *.

In the year 1315, upon the death of Mr. *John de Blencou, Stephen* called *Marefcall* was collated to the rectory of Scaleby; faving to the bifhop and his fucceffors a yearly penfion of 20s of old time accuftomed.

In 1342, Sir *Stephen* called *Marefcall* refigns his rectory, and Mr. *William de Carleton* is collated. And in the fame year Sir *Robert de Howes* was collated; who foon after exchanged with *Roger de Crumwell* rector of Whytefeld in the diocefe of Durham.

In 1356, on the death of Sir *Walter Swetehop*, Sir *Henry Martin* chaplain was collated. Which Henry died in 1362, and by his will bequeathed his body to be buried in the quire of the church of *All Saints* at Scaleby; and Sir *John de Grandon* was collated in his ftead.

In 1380, Sir *Robert Cayllis* was collated, on an exchange with Sir *Elias* rector of Scaleby.

In 1578, a collation was given by bifhop Mey to Sir *George Howell* clerk (in the perfon of Leonard Lowther his proxy, who fubfcribed and fwore for him) on the death of Sir *Henry Munich* the late rector.

In 1585, on the ceffion of Sir *Rowland Vaux, Thomas Nicholfon* was collated; who removed in two years after, and *Chriftopher Witton* fucceeded. Next to him, *Thomas Kirkby*. And afterwards, *Thomas Wilfon* : On whofe death in 1641, *William Green*, M. A. was collated.

In 1680, *Nathaniel Bowey* was collated upon the death of *Robert Prieftman*.

In 1713, *James Jackfon*, B. A. was collated by bifhop Nicolfon.

In 1723, on the ceffion of James Jackfon, *Chriftopher Hewitt* was collated by bifhop Bradford.

In 1759, on Mr. Hewitt's death, *Henry Shaw*, clerk, was collated by bifhop Ofbaldifton.

The number of families in this parifh is about 45.

* Hæc eft finalis concordia facta in curia domini regis apud Karliolum in craftino Sancti Michaelis, anno regni regis Edwardi filii Henrici vicefimo primo; Coram Hugone de Creffingham, Willielmo de Ormefby, Johanne Wogan, Magiftro Johanne Lovel, et Willielmo de Mortuo mari, jufticiaris itinerantibus, et aliis domini regis fidelibus tunc ibi præfentibus, inter Galfridum de Tylliol petentem per Henricum Meatton pofitum loco fuo ad lucrandum vel perdendum, et Johannem epifcopum Karliolenfem deforcientem per Rogerum Peytenyn pofitum loco fuo ad lucrandum vel perdendum, de advocatione ecclefiæ de Scaleby : Unde recognitio magnæ affifæ fummonita fuit inter eos in eadem curia; fcilicet, Quod prædictus Galfridus recognovit prædictam advocationem ejufdem ecclefiæ effe jus ipfius epifcopi et ecclefiæ fuæ beatæ Mariæ Karliolenfis et illam remifit et quietam clamavit de fe et hæredibus fuis prædicto epifcopo et fuccefforibus fuis et ecclefiæ fuæ prædictæ in perpetuum. Et pro hac recognitione, remiffione, quieta clama.ione, fine, et concordia, idem epifcopus dedit prædicto Galfrido viginti et quinque marcas argenti. Et fciendum eft, quod prædicti jufticiarii finem iftum coram eis tranfire permiferunt, eo quod per folempnem inquifitionem coram eis inde factam convictum fuit, quod prædeceffores prædicti epifcopi fuerunt in feifina de prædicta advocatione prædictæ ecclefiæ per longum tempus ante ftatutum de tenementis ad manum mortuam ron ponendis editum. Eo quod quidam Walterus quondam epifcopus Karliolenfis prædeceffor ipfius epifcopi, ante prædictum tempus, contulit prædictam ecclefiam cuidam Ricardo de Hardres clerico, et ipfum in eadem inftituit.

PARISH

PARISH OF KIRKLINTON.

THE barony of LEVINGTON was granted in the time of the Conqueror by the earl Ranulph de Mefchiens to *Richard Boyvill*, a commander under him in the royal army; which was confirmed by king Henry the firſt. The ſaid *Richard* and his poſterity from thence took the name *de Levington*, and the chief of the family reſided at *Kirk Levington*. And a younger brother, named *Reginald*, ſettled at Weſtlinton (or Weſt Levington); which was enjoyed by his poſterity *Adam, Hugh, John*, and *John*, whoſe daughter transferred the inheritance to Alexander Highmore of Harbybrow, and his heirs of marriage in Edward the fourth's time; and in Henry the eighth's time, one of the heirs of the ſaid Alexander ſold the ſame to the Dacres: And it is now the property of Sir James Lowther baronet. Another brother of the Boyvills, named *Randolph*, ſeated himſelf at Randolph Levington (now corruptly Randilinton) in Liddal barony, ſo naming the place of his dwelling, which by his daughter in the next deſcent became the Kirkbride's lands. Another brother named *Robert*, was placed upon a carucate of land in Bothcaſtre, and thereupon was called Robert de Bothcaſtre. Another brother married the daughter and heir of Thurſby, lord of Thurſby and of Waverton; his name was *Guido Boyvill*, who had iſſue two ſons William and John, both of them knights, and foreſters in Allerdale from Skawk to Elne; which office deſcended unto them, from Herbert de Thurſby firſt lord of Thurſby, by the gift of Alan ſecond lord of Allerdale, ſon of Waldeof.

The ſaid *Richard Boyvill*, the eldeſt brother, was ſucceeded at Levington by his ſon and heir *Adam de Levington*, who died about the 12th year of king John; leaving iſſue *Richard* and *Ranulph*, and ſix daughters, *viz*. *Euphemia* married to Richard Kirkbride, *Margery* married to Robert de Hampton, *Iſabel* married to Patric Southaic, *Eva* married to Walter Corry, *Julian* married to Patric Tromp, and *Agnes* married to Walter Twinham.

The ſaid *Richard de Levington*, elder ſon of Adam, in the 12 Joh. gave 300 marks fine and three palfreys for livery of the lands of *Adam* his father; and departed this life in the 34 Hen. 3. leaving *Ranulph* his brother his next heir.

The ſaid *Ranulph de Boyvill* of *Levington* married Ada daughter and coheir of Joan de Morvill and had of her inheritance the manors of Aketon, Layfingby, and a moiety of the manor of Burgh upon Sands, which had been allotted to her upon partition between her and Helwiſe her ſiſter wife of Richard de Vernon. And in the 34 Hen. 3. giving ſecurity for the payment of 100*l* for his relief, and doing his homage, had livery of the lands of the ſaid *Richard de Levington* his brother, and died in the 38 Hen. 3. leaving iſſue an infant daughter and heir *Hawiſe*, whoſe wardſhip was given by the king to Euſtace de Baliol, to whom (or to whoſe ſon of the ſame name) ſhe was afterwards married.

The ſaid *Hawiſe* died without iſſue, and her inheritance of the barony of Levington fell to the ſix ſiſters of her father or their repreſentatives; who were, at that time, Richard Kirkbride, William Lokard, Euphemia wife of John
Seaton,

Seaton, Walter Twinham knight, Gilbert Southaic, Maud wife of Nicholas Aghenlochs, Maud Carick, Patrick Tromp, Walter fon of Walter Corry; and Margaret wife of Henry Malton.

Tromp's purparty of this barony was in the fecond defcent fold to *Robert Tilliol* knight, as was alfo another of the purparties; whereby he became pof-feffed of one third part of the faid barony; which from him came at laft, amongft other of the Tilliols lands, to the *Mufgraves*; of whom Sir *Edward Mufgrave* of Hayton caftle baronet fold the fame to *Edmund Appleby* efquire, who died in 1698; leaving iffue *Jofeph*, *James*, *William*, and *Mary*.

Jofeph Appleby efquire, fon and heir of the faid Edmund, married Dorothy daughter of Henry Dacre of Lanercoft efquire, who after the failure of the other iffue from the faid Henry, became fole heir of the Dacres of Lanercoft. By her he had iffue (befides feveral other children who died in their infancy) *Jofeph* who fucceeded his father in the inheritance, *Mary* married to Abraham Anderfon of Newcaftle upon Tyne merchant, *Dorothy* married to James Jack-fon of Whitehaven merchant, *Terefa* married to Anthony Wilton, M. A. rec-tor of Kirklinton, and *Margaret* who died unmarried.

Jofeph Applely efquire, fon and heir of Jófeph, married Sufanna-Maria daughter of William Gilpin of Scaleby efquire; and by her had iffue *William*, *Jofeph*, *James*, *Richard*, and *Henry*, all of whom, except Jofeph, died young; and three daughters, *Dorothy* married to George Carlyle, M. D. *Mary*, who died unmarried, and Sufanna married to William Bowes of Clifton in the county of Cumberland merchant.—Unto this Jofeph, fon of Jofeph by his wife Dorothy Dacre, James Dacre efquire brother of the faid Dorothy, dying without iffue, left the lordfhip of Walton, together with the demefne of Caftle Steads, and Kelwood tithes, with a requeft that he would take and ufe the name of Dacre; which he did: But believing that he could not drop his own name without an act of parliament, he ufed the name of Dacre-Appleby.

Jofeph Dacre-Appleby efquire, fon and heir of the laft Jofeph, married Ca-tharine daughter of Sir George Fleming baronet lord bifhop of Carlifle, and by her had iffue *Jofeph*, *George*, and *Richard*, who all died without iffue, and a fourth fon, *William-Richard*; and four daughters, *Catharine* married to Edward Anderfon of Newcaftle upon Tyne merchant, *Sufanna-Maria* as yet unmarried, *Dorothy* married to Richard Lacy of North Shields in the county of Northumberland efquire, and *Mary* (1769) unmarried.—This Jofeph, the prefent owner of the manor of Kirklinton, being fatisfied that he might take the name of Dacre only, without an act of parliament, about the year 1743, began to take it accordingly; and all his children that were then born, and all that were born afterwards, have gone by the name of Dacre.

In Kirklinton are 23 cuftomary tenants, who pay yearly 1*l* 17*s* 2¼*d* rent, a twenty-penny fine, and fuit of court: And 62 freeholders, who pay no rent nor fine; but for the late improved commons is paid a free or quit rent of 5*l* 18*s* 11¼*d*.—In Weftlinton are 20 freeholders.

The church of Kirklinton is dedicated to St. Cuthbert, and is rectorial, in the patronage of the lord of the manor; valued in the king's books at 1*l* 1*s*
o*d*

o*d* (which low valuation fhews what deftruction had been made by the Scots), and is now worth 70*l per annum.*

In the year 1293, on a conteft arifing concerning the prefentation to the then vacant rectory of Levington (occafioned, as it feemeth, by the great number of claimants from the fix fifters of Ranulph de Levington), the patronage for that turn lapfed to the bifhop, who collated Mr. *John de Bowes.*

In 1316, upon refignation of *William de Ayreminne,*rector of Kirklevington, the bifhop grants the rectory *in commendam* for fix months to *Richard Ayrminne.*

In 1332, upon the refignation of *Robert de Tymparon,* king Edward the third (in right of Patric de Southayke's heir then the king's ward, and of Walter de Corry's lands forfeited for rebellion) joins with Sir Peter Tilliol knight and Walter de Kirkbride, in prefenting *Thomas de Barton,* who was inftituted accordingly. On whofe death, in 1362, Sir *John Bone* was inftituted on the prefentation of Sir Robert Tilliol knight.

In 1375, Sir *Robert de Kirkby* clerk was prefented by king Edward the third, in right of his then ward the heir of Sir Robert de Tilliol knight.

In 1378, *John de Norfolk,* rector of Levington, was fummoned to refidence by William rector of Bownefs the bifhop's vicar general.

In 1567, on the death of *Cuthbert Deane,* Sir *Robert Hobfon* was prefented by William Mufgrave efquire. Which Robert Hobfon being deprived in 1576, Sir *Robert Beck* was prefented by the fame patron.

In 1584, a caveat was entered by Richard Graham of Kirklinton (commonly called Dick of Woodhead) on a grant made to him of the next avoidance by Sir Henry Wefton knight, with a provifo that in cafe this firft turn on the death of Robert Beck fhould not appear to be his due, his right fhould ftand good for the fecond, third, or fourth avoidance. But on Beck's death in 1599, the bifhop collated *George Watfon* by lapfe. Which George refigned in 1604, and *Edward Johnfon,* M. A. was inftituted on the prefentation of Sir Edward Mufgrave of Hayton knight.

On Mr. Johnfon's death in 1611, the faid Sir Edward Mufgrave prefents, *Chriftopher Parrot,* M. A. Which *Chriftopher* refigned to the commiffioners of archbifhop Ufher (commendatory bifhop of Carlifle) in 1643. And *Robert Prieftman* fucceeded, but upon whofe prefentation doth not appear. Which Robert Prieftman, as appears on a tomb-ftone in the churchyard, died in the year 1679.

In 1694, *George Story* (being nominatad to the deanry of Connor in Ireland) refigned this rectory; whereupon *David Bell* was prefented by Edmund Appleby gentleman. Which David refigned in 1706, and *John Murray,* M. A. was prefented by Jofeph Appleby efquire.

The faid John Murray died in 1722, and *Anthony Wilton,* B. A. was prefented by Jofeph Dacre Appleby efquire: And *John Stamper* in 1731, by the fame patron.

In 1761, on the death of John Stamper, *William Baty* clerk was inftituted. on the prefentation of Jofeph Dacre efquire.

Mr. David Bell built the parfonage houfe at his own expence; and for a memorial thereof put the arms of his family (three bells) over the door.

In this parifh are 316 families; whereof quakers 32, prefbyterians 6.

PARISH OF ARTHURET; including the ancient parifh of ESTON, and the modern parifh of KIRK ANDREWS UPON ESK.

WE come now into the barony of LYDDALE; which comprehends what is now the parifh of ARTHURET and the parifh of KIRK ANDREWS UPON ESK (including the ancient parifh of *Efton*): And confifts of *Efk, Arthuret, Stubhill, Carwindlaw, Speer Sykes, Randilinton, Efton, North Efton, Brackenhill, Nicol Foreft,* and the Englifh part of the *Debatable lands.*

This barony was granted by Ranulph de Mefchiens to *Turgent Brundey* a Fleming, which grant was confirmed by king Hen. 1.

In the reign of king John it was in the hands of the STUTEVILLS; of which family Sir William Dugdale gives the following account:

1. *Robert de Stutevill,* in the time of William the Conqueror.

2. *Robert de Stutevill,* who married Erneburga.

3. *Robert de Stutevill,* whofe firft wife's name was Helwife; and to his fecond wife he married Sibilla 'fifter of Philip de Valois.

4. *William de Stutevill,* who married Berta niece of the famous Ranulph de Glanvill chief juftice of England. Which William, upon king John's acceffion to the crown, ftood in fuch high efteem with him, that he had the whole rule of the counties of Northumberland and Cumberland (which he afterwards held for divers years), as alfo that of Weftmorland, together with all the caftles therein committed to his truft.

5. *Robert de Stutevill,* fon of William, died without iffue, in the 7th year of king John.

6. *Nicholas de Stutevill,* fucceeded his brother Robert; from which Nicholas, the north part of this barony, which lies towards Northumberland, received the name of Nichol Foreft, which it bears to this day. He married Gunnora daughter of Hugh de Gorne, and relict of Robert de Gant; and by her had iffue *Johan* and *Margaret,* which latter was married to William Mafter, and died without iffue, whereby *Johan* the elder daughter became the fole inheritrix.

7. *Johan,* daughter and heir of Nicholas de Stutevill, was married to HUGH DE WAKE, and thereby brought the inheritance into that family *.

Which *Hugh de Wake,* lord of Wake, Colingham, Lyddale, and Bruń, dying in the 18 Hen. 3. left iffue,

Baldwin Wake, who married Elianor daughter of Sir John Montgomery, and died in the 10 Ed. 1.

John de Wake, fon of Baldwin, died in the 33 Ed. 1.

* 1 Dugd. Baron. 456.

Sir

Sir *Thomas Wake* knight, fon of John, married Blanch daughter of Henry Plantagenet earl of Lancafter, and died in the 17 Ed. 3. leaving iffue a fon *John* lord Wake, who died without iffue; and a daughter *Margaret* married to *Edward Plantagenet* of Woodftock, earl of Kent, third fon of king Edward the firft; whofe daughter *Joan*, the fair maid of Kent, was married to *Ed-ward* the Black Prince, father of king Richard the fecond †.

And thus the barony of Lyddal having come to the crown, it feems to have continued in the fame until the reign of king James the firft; when that king by letters patent bearing date the 20th day of February in the firft year of his reign, granted to George (Clifford) earl of Cumberland, all that the foreft of Nichol commonly called Nichol foreft in the county of Cumberland in the borders of England towards Scotland; and alfo all thofe lordfhips and manors of Arthureth, Liddel, and Randilington, within the limits of the foreft aforefaid in the faid county of Cumberland, parcel of the duchy of Lan-cafter; and alfo the fifhery of the water of Efk in the county aforefaid: With all meffuages, mills, houfes, and hereditaments whatfoever within the faid foreft, or to the faid foreft or manors aforefaid belonging or in any wife ap-pertaining: All and every which faid premiffes are and of old time have been parcel of the lands and poffeffions of the honour of Dunftanburgh in the county of Northumberland, parcel of the duchy of Lancafter: To hold to him, his heirs and affigns, of the king *in capite*, by the 20th part of one knight's fee; and rendring for the fame yearly 100l, for all rents, fervices, and demands.

In like manner the faid king James, by letters patent bearing date the 31ft day of March in the eighth year of his reign, granted to Francis earl of Cum-berland, all thofe his lands called the debateable lands in the county of Cum-berland, abutting upon part of the fea called Solway Sands towards the fouth, the river of Sarke towards the weft, the Scotch Dyke towards the north, and the river of Efk towards the eaft; extending in length by eftimation five miles, and in breadth three miles; and containing in quantity 2895 acres of meadow and arable land called Known Grounds, 400 acres of marfh land, 2635 acres of pafture, and 1470 acres of moffy grounds, in all 5400 acres; and two wa-ter corn mills, within the limits and metes aforefaid; and alfo the advowfon of the church of Kirkandrews; to hold to the faid earl and his heirs, under the yearly fee farm rent of 150l.

Thefe eftates were fold by the faid Francis earl of Cumberland to *Richard Graham* efquire (afterwards baronet); and finally king Charles the firft, by let-ters patent bearing date the 11th day of July in the fourth year of his reign, reciting the grants made by king James the firft to George and Francis earls of Cumberland, and alfo that *Richard Graham* efquire by virtue of affurances and conveyances in the law to him and his heirs, was then feifed of the premiffes,— grants and releafes to the faid *Richard Graham* and his heirs the yearly rent of 50l, parcel of the 100l rent referved for Nichol foreft and all other the premiffes granted in the firft year of king James, and the yearly fum of 100l parcel of

† Stukeley's Itinerarium Curiofum, p. 9.

the rent of 150 *l* referved for the debateable lands; and further grants and confirms the faid premiffes to the faid *Richard Graham* and his heirs, referving the
yearly rent of 50 *l* for the foreft of Nichol and the manors of Arthuret, Lyddal, and Randelinton, and alfo a rent of 50 *l* for the debateable lands.

This family of *Graham* (otherwife written *Grahme*, but almoft univerfally of
former times *Grame*) is defcended from the earls of Monteith in Scotland, of
the name of *Grahme*: Whofe pedigree, approved by the Scotch heralds, and
by Sir William Dugdale at his vifitation of Cumberland in 1665, proceeds as
follows:

I. MALICE earl of *Monteith* came to that title by defcent from his mother,
who was of the name of *Stuart*, and was fole heretrix of *Monteith*. He had
iffue, 1. *Patric Grahme*, earl of Monteith; who married a daughter of the lord
Erfkine. 2. *John Grahme*, from whom the principal Grahmes in the borders
are defcended. 3. *Walter Grahme*, who married a daughter of the lord Montgomery in Scotland. 4. *Mary*, married to Archibald earl of Douglafs, and
afterwards to Sir James Hamilton. 5. Another daughter married to Archibald earl of Argyle.

II. JOHN GRAHME, fecond fon of *Malice* earl of *Monteith*, commonly furnamed *John with the bright fword*, upon fome difpleafure rifen againft him at
court, retired with many of his clan and kindred into the Englifh borders in
the reign of king Henry the fourth, where they feated themfelves, and many
of their pofterity have continued there ever fince. Mr. Sandford fpeaking of
them, fays, [which indeed was applicable to moft of the borderers on both
fides] " They were all ftark mofs-troopers and arrant thieves : Both to Eng-
" land and Scotland outlawed : Yet fometimes connived at, becaufe they gave
" intelligence forth of Scotland, and would rife 400 horfe at any time upon a
" raid of the Englifh into Scotland. A faying is recorded of a mother to her
" fon (which is now become proverbial), *Ride, Rowley, hough's ith' pot :* that
" is, the laft piece of beef was in the pot, and therefore it was high time for
" him to go and fetch more.—Late in queen Elizabeth's time, one Jock
" (Grahme) of the Peartree had his brother in Carlifle gaol ready to be
" hanged; and Mr. Salkeld fheriff of Cumberland living at Corby caftle,
" and his fon a little boy at the gate playing, Jock comes by, and gives the
" child an apple, and fays, Mafter will you ride; takes him up before him,
" carries him into Scotland, and never would part with him till he had his
" brother home fafe from the gallows."

This John with the bright fword married a daughter of the lord Grey of
Fowlis; and by her had iffue, *viz.*

III. RICHARD GRAHME, fon of John; who, according to the Scotch pedigree, had a fon,

IV. MATTHIAS GRAHME, who had a fon *Fergus*. But in Sir William Dugdale's pedigree there is a chafm between *Richard* and *Fergus* (for want of
proofs, probably, of the connexion). Then the pedigree goes on.

V. FERGUS GRAHME of Plomp. He married Sibill daughter of William Bell of Blacket-houfe in Scotland; and by her had iffue, 1. *William*, who married Anne daughter of Carlifle of Bridekirk in Scotland, and had a daughter Catharine married to John Armftrong of Sarke in the fame kingdom of Scotland. 2. *Richard.* 3. *Reginald Grahme.* 4. *Francis Grahme.*

VI. RICHARD GRAHME, fecond fon of Fergus, when a youth, in the reign of king James the firft, went to London, and by the recommendation of fome friends got entertained in the duke of Buckingham's fervice; with whom he became fo much in favour, that the duke made him his mafter of the horfe, and introduced him not only to the knowledge but to the particular favour both of the king and prince. He was one of thofe few who were intrufted with the fecret of the prince's going to Spain, and who waited on him thither. Sir Henry Wotton, in his life of the duke of Buckingham, giving an account of their travel through France upon this occafion, relates the following circumftance :—" They were now entered into the deep time of Lent, and " could get no flefh in their inns. Whereupon fell out a pleafant paffage, " if I may infert it by the way among more ferious. There was near Bay- " onne a herd of goats with their young ones; upon the fight whereof, Sir " Richard Graham tells the marquis (of Buckingham), that he would fnap " one of the kids, and make fome fhift to carry him fnug to their lodging. " Which the prince overhearing, Why, Richard, fays he, do you think you " may practice here your old tricks upon the borders ? Upon which words, " they in the firft place gave the goatherd good contentment; and then while " the marquis and Richard, being both on foot, were chafing the kid about " the ftack, the prince from horfeback killed him in the head with a Scottifh " piftol. Which circumftance, though trifling, may yet ferve to fhew, how " his royal highnefs, even in fuch flight and fportful damage, had a noble " fenfe of juft dealing."

This is that Sir Richard Grahme, who purchafed the barony (as is aforefaid) of the earl of Cumberland. After which, he was created baronet. In the rebellion which began in the year 1641, he armed in defence of his royal mafter. At the battle of Edgehill he received many wounds, and lay amongft the dead all night. He took his laft leave of the king in the ifle of Wight in 1648, and with his permiffion retired into the country, where he lived very private. He died in, 1653, and was buried in the parifh church of Wath in the county of York.

By his wife Catherine, who was daughter and coheir of Thomas Mufgrave of Cumcatch, he had iffue, 1. *George.* 2. Sir *Richard Grahme* of Norton Conyers in the county of York baronet, from whom is defcended the prefent Sir Bellingham Grahme baronet. 3. *Catharine,* who died unmarried. 4. *Mary,* married to Sir Edward Mufgrave of Hayton caftle baronet. 5. *Elizabeth,* married to Sir Cuthbert Heron of Chipchafe in Northumberland. 6. *Sufan,* married to Reginald Carnaby of Halton in the faid county of Northumberland efquire.

VII. Sir

VII. Sir GEORGE GRAHME of Netherby, baronet, married lady Mary Johnston eldest daughter of John earl of Hartfield in Scotland, who was afterwards married to Sir George Fletcher of Hutton baronet. By her he had issue five sons, and a daughter *Margaret*. The sons were, 1. *Richard*. 2. Colonel *James Grahme*, whose daughter and heir Catharine was married to Henry-Bowes Howard- earl of Berkshire, grandfather of the present earl of Suffolk and Berkshire. 3. *Fergus Grahme*, who left no issue. 4. *William Grahme*, D. D. dean of Carlisle, and afterwards of Wells, who had two sons Charles and Robert, and one daughter Anne. 5. *Raynold Grahme*, who left issue Metcalf Grahme of Pickhill in Yorkshire.—The said Sir George died at Netherby in 1657, in the 33d year of his age.

VIII. RICHARD GRAHME (eldest son of Sir George Grahme) was educated at Westminster-school and Christ-church college in Oxford. In 1670 he married the lady Anne Howard second daughter of Charles earl of Carlisle; by whom he had issue, 1. *Edward*. 2. *Catherine*, married to William lord Widdrington. 3. *Mary*, who died unmarried. 4. *Susan*, who also died unmarried.

In the year 1680 he was created by king Charles the second viscount Preston in the kingdom of Scotland, and sate in the Scotch parliament under that title. In 1685 he was knight of the shire for Cumberland. He was several years ambassador at the court of France, and on his return was made master of the wardrobe and after that secretary of state to king James the second. Upon the revolution he was sent to the Tower, but in a short time was released from his confinement; upon which, he retired to his seat at Nunnington in Yorkshire. Afterwards, intending to go to king James in France, he (with some others) was apprehended in a boat on the river Thames, and committed prisoner to Newgate. Upon his trial (which was printed) he was found guilty of high treason, and received sentence accordingly; but by the intercession of friends he was pardoned, and died at Nunnington in 1695, and was buried in the chancel of the parish church there, under a black marble stone, with this inscription, according to his own desire: " Here lies the body of Richard " viscount Preston, son of Sir George Graham of Netherby in the county of " Cumberland baronet, who died the 22d day of December, A. D. 1695."

IX. EDWARD GRAHME, viscount Preston, was 17 years of age at the death of his father. He married Mary daughter and coheir of Sir Marmaduke Dalton of Hawkswell in the county of York knight; and by her had one daughter *Anne* who died young, and one son *Charles*.—He died at Nunnington in 1709, and was succeeded by his said son, viz.

X. CHARLES viscount Preston, who was 16 years of age at his father's death. He married a wife of the name of Cox, but died without issue in the year 1739; and was succeeded by his father's two sisters, coheirs, *Catharine* and *Mary*; the other sister *Susan* being dead some time before, and unmarried.

Of

Of the faid two.coheirs, MARY died unmarried in 1753, whereby the whole came to the furviving fifter CATHARINE, who was married (as aforefaid) to William lord Widdrington, whom fhe furvived; and dying in the year 1757 without iffue, devifed the eftate to the reverend ROBERT GRAHAM, M. A. (fecond fon of her uncle *William Graham* dean of Carlifle and of Wells as aforefaid) the prefent owner (1775) of this vaft tract of country, and rector alfo of the two churches of Arthuret and Kirkandrews upon Efk.

The *Arms* of Graham are, quarterly, 1ft, Or, on a chief Sable 3 efcallops of the field; being the paternal coat of Monteith. 2d. Or, a fefs checky Azure and Argent, and in a chief a cheveron Gules; being the maternal coat of *Stuart*. 3d. As the fecond. 4th. As the firft. Over all, in the cœur point, a crefcent Gules for. difference. The *Creft:* Iffuing from a wreath Or and Sable, a demivol Or. *Motto:* "Reafon contents me."

The family feat here is called *Netherby*, which ftands on the fouth bank of the river Efk, and about five miles from the fea. Here, Mr. Camden fays, the ruins of fome ancient city are fo very wonderful and great, and the name of *Efk* running by them doth fo well accord, that it feems very probable the old *Æfica* ftood here, in which the tribune of the firft cohort of the *Aftures* was in garrifon againft the Barbarians. Mr. Horfley thinks, from the vaft monuments and remains of antiquity, that here muft certainly have been the *Caftra Exploratorum*.

Concerning the fculptures and infcriptions found here Mr. Horfley delivers himfelf as follows:—" I muft firft take notice of a curious infcription men-" tioned in Camden, and faid by him to be then in the walls of the houfe;

IMP. CÆS. TRA.
·HADRIANO
AVG.
LEG. II. AVG. F.

" This ftone is not now to be found. Mr. Gordon inquired for it, and I like-
" wife fought after it, but in vain; and as part of this houfe is pulled down
" and altered, I doubt this ftone has been deftroyed, or loft in the ruins.
" However this makes it evident, that the Romans were poffeffed of this fta-
" tion in the reign of the emperor Hadrian; and by the medals both of the
" high and low empire that have been found here, it feems probable they were
" long in poffeffion of it.

" In the additions to Camden we are alfo told of two other ftones with in-
" fcriptions upon them, together with a gold coin of Nero that was found at
" this place; but both thefe ftones are alfo loft, and the copies of the infcrip-
" tions feem not to be very accurate. One of them, as it ftands in Cam-
" den, is,

IMP. COMM. COS.

" *Imperatori Commodo confuli*, which is fuppofed by this author to have been in
" the year 184, when Commodus was faluted *Imperator Britannicus*. But if
" the

" the infcription be rightly copied, I take it to have been when he was firft
" time confful, that is, in the year 177, and fo may ferve to fhew that the Ro-
" mans were then alfo poffeffed of this fort.

" The other infcription is thus reprefented :

DEO MARTI
BELATVCADRO
RO. VR. RP. CAII
ORVSII. M.

". It is juftly remarked, that this infcription argues *Mars* and *Belatucadrus*
" to be the fame deity. But the two latter lines have certainly been ill co-
" pied; for the laft letters, I think, muft have been the ufual V S L L M
" *(votim folvit libentiffime merito)*, and fome of the preceding letters may have
" contained the name of the perfon who erected the altar. The four laft letters
" in the third line, and the two firft in the laft line, look very like G A L L O R
" for *Gallorum*.

" There is another incription, publifhed by Mr. Gordon :

DEO   Deo
MOGONT   Mogonti
VITI RES FLAV   Vitæ reftitutori Flavius
Æ SECVND   Ælius Secundus
VS L M   Votum folvit libens merito.

" It was built up in the wall in a corner of the old garden, at the end of the
" houfe. The altar feems to have been erected upon a recovery from
" ficknefs.

" There have alfo been found here three fculptures; the firft, Mr. Gordon
" takes for Commodus the Roman Hercules, but from the youthful air of
" the face, I fhould rather take it for Caracalla under the appearance of Alex-
" ander; which emperor had fo profound a veneration for the name and me-
" mory of Alexander, that for the moft part he made ufe of fuch arms and
" cups as that king had formerly ufed, filling the camp and Rome itfelf with
" his ftatues.

" The next fculpture, Mr. Gordon fuppofes to be the emperor Hadrian,
" from a 'medal of the faid emperor in the fame attitude. The figure has a
" *corona muralis* on his head, a *cornucopia* on his left arm, and a *patera* in his
" right hand, which he holds as ufual over an altar.

" The third fculpture was in a ftair-cafe without the houfe, but juft at the
" entrance. It is Hercules in an Armenian habit, with a *cornucopia* in his
" left hand, and a *patera* in his right over an altar. Befide him on the left
" are reprefented his club, with a boar under it, which I fuppofe was de-
" figned for the Erymanthian boar, or perhaps Caledonia (if the Hercules
" was intended for Commodus) *."

About the year 1737, a remarkable altar to Fortune was difcovered here in
an outer room of a large Roman bath, with the following infcription :

* Horfley, p. 271, 272.

DEAE

DEAE SANCT,	Deæ fanctæ
AE FORTVNAE	Fortunæ
CONSERVATRICI	Confervatrici
MARCVS AVREL	Marcus Aurelius
SALVIVS TRIBVN	Salvius tribunus
VS COH Ī AELIHI	Cohortis primæ Æliæ
SPANORVM	Hifpanorum
OO EQ	Milliaria equitata
V S L M	Votum folvit libens merito.

Mr. Camden fays, that where Lid joins Efk, formerly ftood a *caftle:* Of this there are now no remains, nor any tradition concerning it. There is indeed a ftrong fort, with a very deep double ditch, called Liddal Strength; where Sir Walter Selby and 200 Englifhmen were taken prifoners by David the fecond, king of Scots. Sir Walter would gladly have compounded for his life by ranfom; but the cruel tyrant ordered his head to be ftruck off, after he had firft caufed his two fons to be ftrangled before his face.

THE PARISH of ARTHURET at large, before *Kirkandrews* was feparated from it, and including alfo the ruinated parifh of *Efton*, according to a boundary thereof taken in 1624, and entered in the parifh regifter, is bounded on the north weft, north, and north eaft by Scotland; on the eaft by the parifhes of Bewcaftle, Stapleton, and part of Kirklinton; and on the fouth and fouth weft by the river Leven or Line, and part of the parifhes of Rocliffe and Kirklinton.

The name of *Arthuret*, or Arthur's head, was appropriated originally to the afcent whereon the church and parfonage-houfe are placed: nor is there any other place, village, or hamlet here that bears that name.

The CHURCH of Arthuret is dedicated to St. Michael; and is valued in the king's books at 1*l* 2*s* 1*d*. Which low valuation was owing to its fituation in the neighbourhood of Scotland. If the prefcriptions were abolifhed, it would now be worth 300*l per annum*.

It was given to the abbey of Jedburgh in Scotland, but by reafon of the almoft continual differences between the two kingdoms, the abbey feldom enjoyed it. In the year 1296, John Wake lord of Lyddal prefented his brother *Baldwyn Wake* to it, referving to the bifhop his ufual portion out of it.

In 1304, *Thomas de Leyceftre* was vicar; who exchanging in that year for Kirkby Stephen, *Thomas de Capella* was prefented by the abbot and convent of Jedburgh, according to the tenor of the compofition (as the prefentation expreffeth it) between the bifhop and the abbot and convent.

In 1312, *Richard de Wethermeleck* was prefented by the abbot and convent.

In 1332, on the death of *John Aurifaber* (Goldfmith, or Orfeur) *John de Penrith* was inftituted on the prefentation of the faid abbot and convent, by the king's nomination. And, in the next year, the king prefents *John de Pokelyngton* to the vacant church of Arthuret, belonging (as he afferts) to his prefentation by reafon of the forfeiture of the abbot of Jedworth the king's rebel and enemy. Whereupon the bifhop iffues a *jus patronatus*; who return, 1. That they

do

do not know that the vicarage is vacant further than that the king is pleased to tell them so.   2. Who is true patron they cannot otherwise find, than that the abbot and convent of Jedworth had of a long time held the said church to their own use and still hold the same.   3. They find, that his late majesty, father of the present king, did give the last presentation in the same form with this. (And so indeed it was: for although John de Penrith was instituted on the abbot and convent's presentation, upon the king's nomination of him ; yet there was likewise a distinct presentation from the king himself.)   The event was, *John de Pokelyngton* was instituted.

In 1337, the said John de Pokelyngton rector of Arthuret exchanges for the rectory of Glafton in the diocese of Lincoln, whereupon *Ralph de Lepyngton* was presented by the king to the rectory of Arthuret and instituted thereupon.

During all this time, though these several persons were rectors of Arthuret, yet *John de Penrith* aforesaid continued vicar.   And in 1353 he makes his will, wherein (amongst other considerable legacies) he gives all his vestments and consecrated clothes to the altar of St. Michael of Arthuret.

In 1354, the bishop nominates *William de Ragenhill* to the king, according to the tenor and effect of a composition made of old time between the bishop of Carlisle and the abbot and convent of Jedworth, and now being in the king's hands by reason of the temporalties of the said abbot and convent, praying that the king, as the abbot and convent had used to do, will present the said William for institution; which was done accordingly, and he thereupon instituted and inducted.   This William in the same year resigned, and *William de Arthuret* was in like manner nominated, presented, and instituted.

In 1361, *John de Bouland* was presented by the king to the rectory of Arthuret, on the death of *Richard de Tiffington* the late rector.   And in 1370, *John de Wyke* was presented by the king, on an exchange with John de Bouland.

In 1565, on the death of *John Berwife*, Sir *Michael Fryfel* clerk was instituted to the vicarage of Arthuret on the presentation of Richard Graham of Netherby gentleman.

In 1639, *Cuthbert Curwen*, D. D. resigns the rectory of Arthuret ; whereupon institution was given to *George Conftable*, presented by Sir Richard Graham baronet.

And on the death of the said George Conftable in 1673, *George Usher*, B. D. was presented by Sir Richard Graham baronet, grandson of the last Sir Richard.

On *George Usher*'s death in 1688, *Hugh Todd*, M. A. was presented by Richard viscount Prefton.

In 1728, on the death of Hugh Todd, *William Lindfey*, M. A. was presented by Charles viscount Prefton.

In 1735, William Lindfey resigning, *Robert Graham*, M. A. was instituted on a presentation by the same patron.

The church stands upon an eminence towards the western sea.   It was built in the year 1609 by the help of a charity brief ; having before been a mean, low, ruinous building, and often destroyed by the Scots.   But the persons employed in the building, going off with a considerable part of the money collected, the

tower

tower was left unfinifhed ; towards which, Dr. Todd the rector expended about
60 *l*, and procured contributions of 20 *l* or 30 *l* more. It was new roofed, flagged, and feated by the honourable Mary Graham in 1750.

Near the church is a well of excellent water, called St. Michael's well ; it being ufual upon the firft erection of churches, to place them near to fome fountain,
which fometimes had a confecration, and ferved for the dipping and baptizing
of children, and other religious purpofes.

The parfonage-houfe was built by Mr. Ufher the rector, at the expence of
about 300 *l*. And rebuilt by the prefent incumbent Mr. Graham in the year
1765.

In the churchyard is the following monumental infcription, which is fomewhat remarkable : " Here lies the body of lieutenant William Graham of Moate
" efquire, who faithfully ferved the crown of England in the reigns of queen
" Elizabeth, king James, king Charles the firft, and king Charles the fecond ;
" and died the 19th of May, A. D. 1657, in the 97th year of his age."

Archy (Armftrong) jefter to king James and king Charles the firft, often mentioned in the annals of thofe times, was born in this parifh, and lies buried here
amongft his fellow parifhioners. He was banifhed the court upon the following occafion : When news came to London that the Scots were all in an uproar
about the liturgy which archbifhop Laud was for forcing upon them, the archbifhop haftening to court, Archy, as he paffed by, fays, " Who's fool now ?".
Whereupon, prefently after, appears an order in the council book,—" Ordered,
" That Archibald Armftrong, the king's fool, be banifhed the court, for fpeak-
" ing difrefpectful words of the lord archbifhop of Canterbury."

Within this parifh lies a noted morafs, commonly called *Solom mofs*, from a
fmall village of that name on the Scotch fide. It is famous in hiftory for the
defeat of the Scots in king Henry the eight's time by Sir Thomas Wharton.

In that part called *Solway-Flow*, in the year 1771, was a memorable outburft
of water, mofs, gravel, fand, and ftones, which fpread over and deftroyed about
600 acres of fine, level, fertile ground, and totally altered the face of that part
of the country. The mofs had been obferved to have rifen imperceptibly for a
long time before. It began to move in the night of the 16th of November,
and continued in motion for three days, flowly forward, fo that the inhabitants
generally had time to get off their cattle and other moveables, before their
houfes were buried or rendered inacceffible. The mouth of the breach was
about 20 yards wide, and when it began to flow was in depth between 5 and 6
yards. By this eruption, 28 families were driven from their habitations, and
their grounds rendered totally ufelefs, and feemingly irrecoverable, by reafon of
the depth of covering of the morafs and other rubbifh : But by the means of
hufhing, upwards of an hundred acres have been cleared, and by the indefati-
gable induftry of the owner it is thought the whole will be recovered, tho' it will
be attended with great expence.

Out of the aforefaid mofs (Dr. Todd fays) have frequently been dug human
bones, filver coins of the later ages, earthen pots, iron and brafs weapons, with
oak and fir trees of unufual magnitude.

Near the place called the *Chapel Flofh*, ftood anciently a fmall oratory, the chapel of Sollom ; in which, in the year 1343, a league between the Scots and Englifh about fixing the limits of both kingdoms, was in a folemn and religious manner fworn to and confirmed by commiffioners appointed for that purpofe. At prefent nothing remains of this chapel but the name.

The number of families in this parifh is about 294 ; whereof 4 prefbyterians, 4 quakers, and 1 papift.

PARISH OF KIRKANDREWS UPON ESK.

King Charles the firft, by letters patent bearing date the firft day of May in the feventh year of his reign, reciting that the church of Kirkandrews had been demolifhed, grants power to Sir Richard Graham baronet to erect, build, and refound a church, with all materials, in the place where the church of Kirkandrews formerly ftood ; and by the faid letters patent doth unite, confolidate, and annex the faid parifh of Kirkandrews and Nichol Foreft into one intire parifh.—When Dr. Todd was rector of Arthuret, he complained of this as illegal, contending that it could not be done without an act of parliament. But by the tenor of the grant there feems to have been a church here before ; and in ancient times, in this border fituation, efpecially before the partition of the debateable lands, the boundaries and diftinctions of parifhes in thefe parts perhaps might not be clearly defined.

The boundary as fixed by the faid letters patent is to be on the north fide of the river Efke (as the current then ran) and of the two burns of Carwinley and Rayburn : and all tithes and emoluments within the faid limits were appropriated to the faid church. A great part of the lands within thefe limits were part of the ancient ruinated parifh of Efton, the other part of the faid parifh of Efton (and Efton itfelf) is within the prefent parifh of Arthuret.

Sir Richard Graham having finifhed his new parifh as aforefaid, prefented thereto in the year 1637 *Charles Ufher*, M. A. who had inftitution thereupon accordingly.

In 1682, on the death of the faid Charles Ufher, *William Graham*, M. A. was prefented by (his brother) Richard vifcount Prefton. And on the ceffion of the faid William Graham in 1685, *Edward Wiltfhire*, M. A. was prefented by the fame patron.

In 1730, on *Edward Wiltfhire*'s death, *William Torford*, M. A. was prefented by Charles vifcount Prefton : and the faid Edward Wiltfhire dying in two years after, *Richard Baty* clerk was prefented by the fame patron.

In 1759, Richard Baty dying, *Robert Graham*, M. A. was inftituted to the rectory of Kirkandrews upon Efke, with Nichol foreft annexed, on the prefentation of George Peacock gentleman.

The firft fruits of that part of this parifh which lies upon the river Efke is fet in the faid letters patent at 3 l 11 s 5 d ; and that part which belongs to Nichol foreft at 2 l. And the rectory is now worth upwards of 200 l *per annum* ; though there is no houfe belonging to it, nor the leaft parcel of glebe, the churchyard only excepted.

In

In *Nichol foreſt* is a *chapel* of eaſe, which if it ever had any endowment, hath been loſt (as it is not at all difficult to conceive); but in the year 1744 it received an allotment of 200*l* of queen Anne's bounty, which hath ſince been laid out in lands at Catlowdy, and now yields to the curate about 10*l per annum :* and the preſent rector hath built an houſe for the curate.

The *families* in this pariſh are about 360; of which, preſbyterians (being ſo nigh Scotland) above 100; but no papiſts nor quakers.

THE ancient pariſh of ESTON hath been loſt by the confuſion of times, and is now ſwallowed up by the other two. What we meet with concerning it in the biſhop's archives is as follows :

In the year 1308, king Edward the ſecond, as guardian of the infant heir of Sir John Wake, preſents *Simon de Beverly* to the vacant rectory of Eſton, and inſtitution was given thereupon, with a reſervation of the penſion to the pariſh church of Arthuret, if any ſuch there be.

In 1333, *R. de Berewick* rector of Eſton had a licence of abſence for 3 years granted to him, with permiſſion to let his living to farm for that time.

In 1335, Thomas Wake lord of Lyddale preſents his chaplain *William de Ormeſby* to the vacant rectory of Eſton.

In 1364, *John de Dalton* was collated by lapſe.

The laſt account we have of it is in the year 1384, when immediately upon the death of the ſaid John de Dalton the biſhop collates *John de Morton* to the rectory, as belonging to his collation in full right.

Reginald Graham of Nunnington eſquire, by his laſt will and teſtament proved in the prerogative court of Canterbury in the year 1685, bequeathed to his executors 200*l* to be laid out in lands or other hereditaments for the uſe of the *poor* within the ſeveral pariſhes of Arthuret and Kirkandrews. This money was veſted in the hands of the lords of Eſke, who paid 12*l* yearly for the ſame to the ſchools of the ſaid two pariſhes.

Mrs. Graham bequeathed 20*l* each to the ſaid two pariſhes.

And lady Widdrington by deed in 1754, after reciting the ſaid annual ſum of 12*l* and the ſaid bequeſt of 40*l*, granted to truſtees an annuity or clear yearly rent charge of 40*l*, for the uſe of the ſchools of Arthuret and Kirkandrews upon Eſke.

PARISH OF BEWCASTLE.

BEWCASTLE is the next pariſh; and is divided into four townſhips or conſtablewicks, *viz.* Bewcaſtle quarter, Nixon's quarter, Belbank quarter, and Baily quarter: And contains 240 families all of the eſtabliſhed church, one quaker only excepted.

The pariſh is commenſurate with the manor; and is encompaſſed by Northumberland on the north and north eaſt, by Gillſland on the eaſt and ſouth eaſt, by the foreſt of Lyddall and part of Levington barony on the weſt and ſouth.

weſt, and by Scotland on the north weſt. It contains about 32960 ſtatute acres, and is in length. from ſouth weſt to north eaſt about nine miles, and in breadth from north weſt to ſouth eaſt ſix miles.

It is ſaid to have received its name from one *Bueth* lord or poſſeſſor of the country at and before the Norman conqueſt; who repaired an old Roman caſtle here, and called it after his own name *Bueth Caſtle,* and the country near it *Buethcaſtle Dale.*

Gils-Bueth, or the *ſon* of this *Bueth,* laid claim to ſome part of Gilſland, and Robert de Vallibus lord of Gilſland, ſon of Hubert, ſlew him at a meeting for agreement appointed between them, under truſt and aſſurance of ſafety. Which ſhameful action made the ſaid Robert leave arms, and betake himſelf to the ſtudy of the law, in which he made ſuch proficiency that he became a judge. But this murder ſtill ſtuck upon his mind, until (according to the ſuperſtition of thoſe times) he made ſatisfaction to holy church, by building the abbey of Lanercoſt, and endowing it with that very patrimony which had occaſioned the murder.

Afterwards, Bueth's lands having come to the crown, king Hen. 2. granted the ſame to *Hubert de Vallibus* the laſt of the name at Gilſland, whoſe daughter and ſole heir *Matilda* transferred the inheritance to *Thomas de Multon,* who being alſo lord of Burgh, ſuffered his tenants and vaſſals there to go with their cattle in the ſummer ſeaſon into the large waſtes and mountainous part of Bewcaſtle, the barony of Burgh at that time being well cultivated, and fitting better for corn and meadow. And thereupon it is always found in ancient inquiſitions as parcel of the barony of Burgh, and to be holden of the ſame: but it is not within the ſaid barony; for the two ſeignories of Lyddal and Levington lie between Burgh and it.

Afterwards it came to the *Swinburns,* who held it for ſeveral generations. In the 7 Ed. 1. a market and fair here were granted to *John Swinburn.* In Edward the ſecond's time, *Adam de Swinburn* held it of the lord of Burgh. And in Edward the third's time, Sir *John Strivelin* held it in right of his wife *Jacoba,* Swinburn's daughter.

Afterwards, this caſtle and manor came again to the crown; and king Edward the fourth granted the ſame to his brother *Richard* then duke of Glouceſter.

In the reign of king Henry the eighth and ſome of the ſucceeding reigns, *Jack Muſgrave* captain * of Bewcaſtle (an active man of thoſe times) held the ſame.

Afterwards, king James the firſt in the 12th year of his reign granted the ſame to *Francis* earl of *Cumberland* for the term of 40 years, rendring for the ſame yearly 5*l.*

Finally, king Charles the firſt by letters patent bearing date July 25, in the fifth year of his reign, of his ſpecial grace, and in conſideration of 200*l,* granted to *Richard Graham* knight and baronet all that the caſtle of Bewcaſtle,

* The word *captain* was of a twofold ſignification, denoting either the commander of a company or troop of ſoldiers, or the governor of a town or fort.

to hold to him, his heirs and assigns of the king *in capite* by knights service, that is, by the service of one intire knight's fee, and rendering for the same yearly 7*l* 10*s*.

In the civil war which began in the year 1641, this castle was demolished, and the garrison removed to Carlisle.

In this manor are about 106 tenements, which pay yearly 16*l* 12*s* 4*d* customary rent, 2*l* 17*s* 8*d* quit rents for improvements, and 2*l* 1*s* 4*d* carriage money.—By indenture bearing date May 27 in the sixth year of Charles the first (and confirmed by decree in chancery), between Sir Richard Graham of Eske baronet lord of the manor of Bewcastle and the several tenants, it is agreed that the tenants shall pay a four-penny fine upon change of lord by death and upon change of tenant by death or alienation; and shall pay suit of court, suit at the lord's mill, customary works and carriages, and other boons, duties and services accustomed; and that for a heriot the lord shall have the best beast of which every tenant shall die possessed (the riding horse of such tenant kept by him for the lord's service only excepted); the tenants not to let or mortgage their tenements for above three years, without licence of the lord.

At Bewcastle was a large *Roman* station, of which there are yet some considerable remains. Many Roman coins also have been found here. Mr. Camden tells us he saw a stone in the church made use of for a grave-stone, with this inscription:

·LEG II AUG   Legio secunda Augusta
FECIT   fecit.

Mr. Horsley found another, in the churchyard, at the head of a grave, which was found at first in the bottom of a grave: Which seems to have been an honorary monument erected to Hadrian by the same *Legio Secunda Augusta* and the twentieth legion. It was imperfect, but he takes the reading to be this:

IMP. CAES. TRAIAN.   Imperatori Cæsari Trajano Ha-
HADRIANO. AVG.   driano Augusto legiones secunda
LEG. II. AVG. ET. XX. V. V.   Augusta et vicesima valens vic-
SVB. LICINIO. PRISCO.   trix, sub Licinio Prisco legato
LEG. AVG. PR. PR.   Augustali proprætore.

As the *legio secunda Augusta* was at this place in the reign of Hadrian, so it is most likely that they were quartered here at the time when his *vallum* was built, to cover the workmen, and to bear a share in the work.

The CHURCH is situate on an eminence near the castle. It is dedicated to St. Cuthbert, and is rectorial. The advowson thereof, according to Dr. Todd, was given about the year 1200 by Robert de Buethcastre (perhaps the aforesaid Robert de Vallibus) to the prior and convent of Carlisle; which Robert gave also lands at Buethcastre to the prioress and nuns of Marrig in Yorkshire. The dean and chapter are the present patrons. It is valued in the king's books at 2*l*. It hath little or no glebe except a small garden or two; and the whole

whole prefent revenue (except fome fmall furplice fees) confifts of a prefcrip-
tive payment, as it is called, of 60 *l* a year, in lieu of all tithes, reckonings,
and other dues. Which prefcription, from the largenefs, cannot be very ancient; for at the time that prefcriptions are fuppofed to have commenced, this
fum was not only more than the value of the tithe, but almoft equal to the
value of the other nine parts added to it.

The incumbents of this church, living obfcure in this remote part of the
diocefe, have nothing memorable recorded of any of them. Thofe whofe
names occur in the regiftries follow in this order.—In the year 1306, *Robert de
Southayke* was rector, at the prefentation of the prior and convent of Carlifle;
who, after he had been rector fifty years, exchanged his rectory for that of
Stapleton, whereupon *Henry de Whitebergh* rector of Stapleton was inftituted to
Bothecaftle.—In 1360, *John de Bromfield*; on whofe refignation the next year
fucceeded *Adam Armftrong* —Then one *Robert* is rector.—The next is *John de
Stapilton*, in 1380.—In the year 1580, on the death of *Thomas Aglionby*, alias
Nickfon, the bifhop collates *William Lawfon* by lapfe —In 1623, *Charles Fore-
bench* was prefented by king James the firft, the deanry of Carlifle being then
vacant.—In 1643, *Henry Sibfon*, D. D. was rector, being in that year (amongft
others) a contributor towards the fuftenance of the garrifon of Carlifle.—In
1663, *Robert Lowther*, LL. B. chancellor of the diocefe was inftit.ted.—
Upon his death, *Ambrofe Myers*, M. A. in 1671.—To him fucceeded *George
Ufher*, B. D. in 1673; who was alfo rector of Arthuret. His fucceffor was
James Lamb, M. A. divinity lecturer in the cathedral.—To him, upon his promotion to Appleby, fucceeded *Jeffrey Wybergh*, LL. B. in 1699. Upon whofe
promotion to Caldbeck, fucceeded *Edward Tonge*, A. M. And he refigning
in 1713, *Matthew Soulby* was prefented.—On Matthew Soulby's death in
1738, *Edward Birket*, M. A. fucceeded. And on his ceffion in 1758, *James
Farifh* clerk was inftituted.

In the churchyard of this place, is a *crofs* of one intire ftone, about five feet
and an half high, two feet broad at the bottom, and one foot and an half at
the top, in which top a crofs heretofore was fixed. The lord William Howard
of Naworth (a lover of antiquities) caufed the infcriptions thereon to be carefully copied, and fent them to Sir Henry Spelman to interpret. The tafk
being too hard for Sir Henry, he tranfmitted the copy to Olaus Wormius hiftory profeffor at Copenhagen, who was then about to publifh his *Monumenta
Danica*. This learned antiquary in that book takes notice of the infcription,
and prints it exactly as it was fent to him, but owns at the fame time that he
did not know what to make of it. Bifhop Nicolfon, in the year 1685, in a
letter to Obadiah Walker, mafter of Univerfity college in Oxford, (which
was printed in the Philofophical Tranfactions,) fays of it, that it is wafhed
over, like the font at Bridekirk, with a white oily cement, to preferve it the
better from the injuries of time and weather. On the weft fide of the ftone
are three fair draughts, which evidently enough manifeft the monument to te
chriftian. The loweft of thefe reprefents the portraiture of a layman, with an
hawk or eagle perched on his arm: Over his head are the ruins of the infcrip-

3   tion

tion copied by the lord William Howard; which is again much effaced since his time. Next, is the picture of some apostle, saint, or other holy man, in a sacerdoatl habit, with a glory round his head. On the top stands the image of the blessed virgin, with the babe in her arms; and both their heads incircled with glories. On the north side is a great deal of chequer work, with a decayed Runic inscription. The chequer, the bishop observes, is the coat armour of the family of Vaux or de Vallibus, but this and the other carved work upon the cross (he says) must of necessity be allowed to bear a more ancient date than any of the remains of that name and family, which cannot be run up higher than the conquest. On the east side are nothing but a few flourishes, draughts of birds, grapes, and other fruits; which seem to be no more than the statuary's fancy. On the south, flourishes and conceits as before; and towards the bottom another decayed Runic inscription. When the same learned prelate was again at this church, in the course of his parochial visitation in 1703, he says he tried to recover the Runic inscription on the west side of the cross; but though it looked promising, at a distance, he could not assuredly make out even so much as that single line, which Sir Henry Spelman long since communicated to Olaus Wormius.

PARISH OF STAPLETON.

W E come now to the ancient and extensive barony of GILSLAND, *Stapleton* having been first granted forth as a fee thereof. And as all or most part of the remaining parishes not yet treated of are included within that barony, it is thought fit first of all to set forth the boundary of the said barony of Gilsland, as followeth:

Beginning at the head of Croglin water, and so till it come to Knarhead, as heaven water deals. And from Knarhead unto Blacklawhill, as heaven water deals. And from Blacklawhill unto the Black brook above the Kelds, as heaven water deals. And from Black brook to Biers Pyke, as heaven water deals. And from Biers Pyke descending unto Biers park wall; and so descending the said wall unto the water of Blackburn, where there stands a cross that parts Cumberland and Northumberland. And so descending down the said water unto where Foulpot falleth into Blackburn. And from thence up the Cleugh as Cumberland and Northumberland divide, and so streight forth unto the cross at the head of the said Cleugh. And so from the said cross unto Preaquepot lane. And so from Preaquepot lane unto Edelstone. And from Edelstone through the moss unto Witchcragg, descending Poultross water unto where it falleth into Irding. And so up Irding unto Rodrehaugh, there being two low places having common within the liberty of Tindale. And from the said Rodrehaugh unto the head of Irthing as the water runneth to Fornebeck head. And from Fornebeck head unto Bolclugh. And from Bolclugh, *alias* Kirkbeck, as it falleth into White Levin. And so descending the said White Levin, until it come to Black Levin. And so down Levin unto the Nether end of Sparlin holme, streight overthwart to the great grey stone

ſtone of Croſby moor, within the end of the biſhop's dyke. And from the ſaid grey ſtone unto the Piɛ̃ts wall, ſtreight forth unto the joining of Biſhop's dyke. And ſo following that dyke unto the weſt end of Newby. And from the ſaid end of Newby-down Forſcue ſyke until it fall into Irthing. And ſo down Irthing until it fall into Eden. And ſo up Eden until Norſcue beck fall into Eden. And ſo up Norſcue beck unto Northgill beck head. And ſo to Joane ſyke head. And from Joane ſyke head, as it runneth into the water of Croglin. And ſo up the ſaid water till it come to the head thereof.

Stapleton, Stapilton, or *Stable-town,* (according to Dr. Todd) was the place where the *ſtableſtand* or *buckſtall* was, for the watching of deer, when the country was foreſt. It appears to have been divided into two parts of very ancient time, *viz.* the manor of *Solport,* and the manor of *Stapleton* (which is now called the Gilſland diviſion).

The *Solport* diviſion comprehends the conſtablewicks of *Solport, Trough,* and *Billbank.* In the 34 Hen. 3. *Richard de Levington* (lord of Kirklevington) died ſeiſed of this moiety, from whom it deſcended to *Ranulph de Levington* his bro- ther, who had iſſue *Hawiſe* wife of Sir *Euſtace Baliol. Hawiſe* died without iſſue, whereupon the Levingtons lands fell to her father's ſix ſiſters : So became *Matilda de Carick* her heir of this moiety of Stapleton. *Roland Carick* her ſon ſold it to *Piers Tylliol* in Edward the firſt's time, which deſcended to the *Colvils* and *Moreſbys* heirs of *Tylliol.* Finally, it came to the *Grahams,* in whom it now remains.—The demeſne lands are called the *Shank,* where are the ruins of an old caſtle. The *Trough* is a freehold of about 150*l* a year, which was long in the name of the Forſters, but is now the property of Mr. *Lowes* attorney at law at Hexham. The reſt are cuſtomary eſtates of inheritance, about 39 in number, and pay a yearly rent of 11*l* 14*s* 10*d,* and generally a twenty-penny fine, but ſome have been purchaſed down much lower. They alſo pay heriots, and the lord has the wood. The miln here is alſo held as a cuſtomary eſtate, and the tenants owe ſuit to it, and pay the 16th corn.

The other moiety (being Gilſland conſtablewick) belonged to the *Stapletons. John de Stapleton* was ſeiſed thereof in the 3 Ed. 3. From the *Stapletons* it came to the *Dacres,* and from them to the *Howards* the preſent poſſeſſors.— There are about 24 tenants, who pay 4*l* 18*s* 3*d* yearly cuſtomary rent, 2*s* 11*d* greenhue, and 14*s* ſervice-money. They pay a twenty-penny fine upon change of lord by death, and arbitrary fines upon change of tenant by death or alienation. And the lord has the wood.

The CHURCH of Stapleton is rectorial; valued in the king's books at 8*l* 1*s* 11¼*d*; certified to the governors of queen Anne's bounty at 24*l,* and may now be worth about 40*l per annum.* In the year 1525, John Stapleton granted to Thomas lord Dacre this advowſon; but that, clearly, muſt be underſtood only of his own moiety: for the owners of the other moiety of the manor preſented to the rectory in their turn both before and after.

In the year 1294, Sir *Gilbert de Mancheton* was rector.

In 1296, Sir *Thomas de Leyceſter* was preſented by Sir Robert de Tilliol knight to the church or chapel of Solpard (as the preſentation expreſſeth it)

requeſting

requesting the bishop to institute him as rector of the said church. In the same year Sir *Nicholas de Coventry* was instituted upon a presentation from the lady Sarah de Stavely.

In 1323, *John de Stapleton* was collated by the bishop upon lapse.

In 1338, on the resignation of Sir *Hugh* rector of Stapleton, Sir *John de Kirkby* was presented by John de Stapleton.

In 1356, on an exchange by *Henry de Whitebergh* rector of Stapleton for the rectory of Bewcastle, *Robert de Southayke* was instituted on the presentation of John de Stapleton.

In 1361, *Robert de Bolton* was rector. In 1368, *William de Strickland* was rector; who exchanged with *Nicholas de Stapleton* rector of Ulvesby.

In 1603, *Henry Hudson* was collated by lapse.

In 1686, on the resignation of *William Culcheth*, *Richard Culcheth* was presented by Richard viscount Preston.

In 1714, on the death of Richard Culcheth, *James Jackson*, B. A. was presented by Charles earl of Carlisle.

In 1771, on the death of James Jackson, who had been rector 57 years, *William Graham* was presented by the reverend Mr. Graham of Netherby.

The number of *families* in this parish is about 70; of which 16 are quakers, and 6 presbyterians.

PARISH OF WALTON.

THE parish of WALTON contains only about 60 families in the whole, and is divided into two quarters or constablewicks, *viz.* Walton quarter and the High quarter. The town of Walton was granted by Robert de Vallibus to the priory of Lanercost, at the foundation of the said priory, by the metes and bounds in the grant specified; together with the church also of Walton with the chapel of Treverman; as also pasture for 30 cows in the forest of Walton, and 20 sows with their young of two years, and pasture for their oxen that shall till their lands there *.

After the dissolution of the religious houses, king Edward the sixth, by letters patent bearing date the 28th day of June in the sixth year of his reign, granted to Sir *Thomas Dacre* the elder, knight, (amongst other possessions belonging to the late priory of Lanercost) the rectories and churches of Lanercost, Brampton, and divers others, with the chapel (as it is there called) of Walton, and all tithes belonging to the same, and also the water miln of Wal-

* . . . . . Præterea dedi eis villam de Walton, infra has divisas subscriptas; scilicet, de muro antiquo per longam sicam quæ est contigua Cospatric-leye usque in Irthin, et ita per lithin usque ad locum ubi Camboc cadit in Irthin, sursum per Camboc usque ad sicam quæ descendit de n gra quercu quæ est in via quæ ducit ad Cumynencath, et ex alia parte nigræ quercus usque ad sicam Pelterheved quæ cadit in King, et per King usque ad murum: Et ecclesiam de ipsa Walton, cum capella de Treverman: Et concessi eis habere triginta vaccas ubique in foresta mea de Walton, et viginti sues cum nutrimento duorum annorum, et pasturam boum qui prædictas landas arabunt.— *Regist. Lan.*

ton : To hold to him the faid *Thomas Dacre*, his heirs and affigns, of the king ·
in capite, by the fervice of the 40th part of one knight's fee.

Tryermain (Treverman) aforefaid, was a fee of Gilſland at the .time of the
conqueſt, and one *Gillande* was lord thereof. He ſtood out againſt the conqueror. But his ſon and heir *Gilmore* made his peace with Ranulph de Meſ-
chines lord of Cumberland, and quietly. enjoyed it in king Henry the firſt's
days, and built the firſt chapel there (of wood) by licence of Athelwold firſt
biſhop of Carliſle, and by confent of Enoc then paiſon of Walton Kirk, in
whoſe pariſh it was. He made his coufin Gilmore the firſt chaplain thereof.
After which chaplain fucceeded one Daniel ; and after him Auguſtine, that
lived in the time of Thomas parſon of Walton, which Thomas became a
canon in Lanercoſt, when this rectory became appropriated to that priory.
After the death of Gilmore lord of Tryermaine and Torcroffock, Hubert·
Vaux gave Tryermaine and Torcroffock to his ſecond ſon Ranulph Vaux, which
Ranulph afterwards became heir to his elder brother Robert the founder of
Lanercoſt who died without iſſue. Ranulph being lord of all Gilſland gave
Gilmore's lands to his own younger ſon named Roland, and let the barony
defcend to his eldeſt ſon Robert ſon of Ranulph. Roland had iſſue Alexander,
and he Ranulph, after whom ſucceeded Robert, and they were named Rolands
ſucceſſively that were lords thereof, until the reign of Edward the fourth.——
That.houſe gave for arms ; Vert, a bend dexter, chequy Or and Gules.

The CHURCH of Walton, having been wholly appropriated to the ſaid priory,
is now only a perpetual curacy. In pope Nicholas's valuation, the church of
Walton with the chapel is taxed at *50 l.* In Edward the fecond's valuation it
was not taxed, becauſe it was then totally deſtroyed. In Henry the eighth's ·
valuation, it is not mentioned, as belonging then wholly to the priory ; and
perhaps the country then intirely waſted. In Dr. Todd's time, the revenue
(he ſays) was not more than the wages of a common man ſervant. In 1750,
it was certified at 13 *l* 10 *s per annum.* In 1767, the prefent curate, the reverend John Stamper, purchaſed an augmentation from the governors of queen
Anne's bounty ; whereby an eſtate was bought within the pariſh, of the preſent yearly value of 16 *l.*—Whilſt it was a vicarage (and not totally. appropriated), it was endowed, firſt by Silveſter de Everſden biſhop of Carliſle with
the whole altarage : with which the vicar not being ſatisfied, he appealed to a
ſucceeding biſhop, who ſettled the ſame on the ſame terms, or the ſum of 12
marks at the option of the vicar on his inſtitution.

The laſt vicar was *Robert de Cheſter*, who was inſtituted on the prefentation
of the prior and convent of Lanercoſt in the year ·1380; from which time,
till the diſſolution, the church was ſerved with a regular canon from the
monaſtery. '

. The prefent impropriator and patron is Joſeph Dacre eſquire, heir general of
the aforefaid Sir Thomas Dacre knight grantee of the revenues of the ſaid
priory.

PARISH.

PARISH OF IRTHINGTON.

THE parish of IRTHINGTON is divided into the quarters or conftablewicks of Irthington, Leverfdale, and Newby. It is encompaffed by the parifhes of Brampton, Walton, Wetheral, and Crofby; and confifts of about 146 fa-milies, of which 8 are quakers, and two prefbyterians.

The church of Irthington was given by Robert de Vallibus to the prior and convent of Lanercoft; and after the diffolution of the priory, was granted (amongft other poffeffions of the faid priory) to Sir Thomas Dacre fenior, knight, by king Edward the fixth in the fixth year of his reign.

Within this parifh is the ancient fort of *Petriana*, or *Cambeck* fort, now ufually called *Caftle-fteads*; which Mr. Horfley fays is the only Roman ftation unto which hath been given the name of *Caftle-fteads*, that being the general name which is ufually given to all the milliary *caftella*. At this place many Roman infcriptions have been found, of which Mr. Horfley gives a particular account. One is,

C O H	Cohors
VIIII	nona (pofuit).

Which fhews the ninth cohort of one of the legions to have been there.

Another is,

E CIVITATE CAT	E civitate Cat-
VVELLAVN	uvellaun -
ORVM T OIS	orum Titus Oif-
EDIO	edio (pofuit)

The Caffivelauni were a people of Britain; and this fhews that (amongft the reft) there were Britifh foldiers in the Roman armies.

There is another which Mr. Horfley thinks belongs to this place but was removed to Scaleby. It is on an altar, but partly defaced:

S O L I	Soli
INVICTO	invicto
SEX. SEVE	Sextus Seve-
RIVS. SA	rius Salvator
LVATOR	Præfectus
. . . . AEF	Votum folvit
. . . L M	Libens merito.

The infcription *Soli invicto* is found alfo upon the medals of many of the Ro-man emperors.

The three following alfo were at Scaleby, but generally faid to have come from this fort:

                 DEO

DEO SOLI MITR   Deo Soli Mitræ.

The ancient Perfians held the fun and fire in great veneration, to both of which they gave the name of Mithras. From hence the name was introduced among the Romans. *Deo Soli Mitræ :* that is, To the deity of the fun, whom the Perfians call Mithras.

The next is,

I	Jovi (Optimo maximo)
COH IIII	Cohors quarta
GALLORVM	Gallorum
C P VOLCA . . .	cui præeft Volcati-
VS HOSPEIS	us Hofpes
PR . . . F EQ	Præfeƈtus equitum.

The laft of thofe at Scaleby is,

DEO S BE	Deo fanƈto Be-
LATVCA . .	latucadro
RO AV DO . . .	Aulus Domitius
. . . VLLINVS	Paullinus
VS	Votum folvit.

This Belatucader (as hath been mentioned before) was a local deity; and perhaps may be derived of *Baal* which fignifies a deity, and the Britifh word *eadr* which fignifies valiant; more efpecially, as Belatucader and Mars are underftood to be the fame, as in the infcription found at Netherby, *Deo Marti Belatucadro.*

The late Jofeph Dacre Appleby efquire, owner of the ground in which the fort ftands, employed people for fome time in digging there, whereby he difcovered feveral curiofities, which he removed to his houfe at Kirklinton. Amongft which were two ftones which feem to have ftood contiguous to each other. On one of which is carved in relievo a Viƈtory winged, with the ufual drapery, treading with one foot upon a globe, with a palm branch in her left hand, a mural crown in her right, and underneath, the infcription VICTORIA AVGVSTI. On the other ftone is a fea goat above, and a Pegafus below; the former to denote the maritime fituation of Britain, and the latter to denote the fwiftnefs of the viƈtory.

Another is, a ftone with an infcription,

LEG. VI. V. F. i. e. *Legio fexta viƈtrix fecit.*

Mr. Horfley is of opinion, that thefe legionary infcriptions which have been found in the ftations, were moft of them ereƈted, when Severus's wall was building, at the ftations where the body of the legion quartered; and that the infcriptions of the particular cohorts, that were working upon feveral parts of the wall, were inferted in the face of the wall at thefe feveral places.

Another ftone, with an infcription, removed to Kirklinton, was dug up near the eaft entry of the ftation, where feveral pieces of broken pots or urns, with

other

other reliques of antiquity, were alfo found. · The infcription is fomewhat imperfeſt, but Mr. Horfley reads it, " *Matribus omnium gentium, templum olim* " *vetuſtate conlapſum, Gaius Julius Pitanus provinciæ præſes reſtituit.*"—Mr. Ward thinks the firſt word to be *Victoribus*, and that the rebuilding of, this temple was after the many and great victories gained by Dioclefian and Maximian.

Another infcription belonging to this place is upon an altar which was removed to London, and in Mr. Horfley's time was in the poffeffion of the earl of Hertford:-

DEO SANG M	Deo fancto Marti
ARTI VENVSTIN	Venuftinus Lupus
VS LVPVS VSLM	votum folvit libens merito.

Within this parifh alfo is *Watch-crofs*, which Mr. Horfley takes to be the· *Aballaba* of the Romans, where according to fome was a Roman ftation, others (from its convenient fituation for an extenfive profpect) think it was only an exploratory fort. And to this purpofe it feems to have been made ufe of in more modern times, from its being named *Watch-crofs*. It is about four chains and an half fquare, and is a little detached from the wall to the fouth. At this place have been found two infcriptions; one of them imperfect, which· Mr. Horfley reads " Centuria cohortis Silii Aucinii pofuit." The other is as. follows,

LEG II AVG	Legionis fecundæ Auguftæ
⟩ IVLI. TE	centuria Julii Tertulliani
RTVLLIA	(pofuit) *.

The CHURCH of Irthington (as aforefaid) was granted to the prior and con‑ vent of Laneicoft, who foon got it appropriated to their houfe. And the bifhop Walter Malclerk in the year 1224 taxed the vicarage as follows; viz. the vicar to have the whole altarage, with the corn tithe of the vill of Irthing‑ ton, and all the land belonging to the faid church, with the tithe of hay and mills throughout the whole parifh, with all fmall tithes belonging to the altar‑ age: Saving to the prior and convent yearly three efkeps of oatmeal and two efkeps of malt. Which was afterwards altered by bifhop Chaufe to one efkep and an half of oatmeal.

In pope Nicholas's Valor, the church of Irthington is rated at 13*l* 16*s* 0*d* and the vicarage at 10*l*.—In Edward the fecond's Valor, nothing; becaufe they were totally deftroyed.—In Henry the eighth's taxation, the vicarage of Irthington is rated at 6*l* 1*s* 5¼*d*.—It was certified to the governors of queen‑ Anne's bounty at 30*l*; and may now be worth about 40*l per annum*.

In the year 1224, *William de Meleburn* was inftituted to this vicarage on the prefentation of the prior and convent of Lanercoft.—In 1337, *Laurence de Caldre*; and feveral others afterwards, on the like prefentation of the prior and

* Horfley, 107, 108, 154, 258—265.

convent.

convent.—After the diffolution, on the death of Sir *John Farebarne* vicar of
Irthington, in 1567, inftitution was given to Sir *Robert Hutton* clerk, but the
patron is not named. On whofe death in 1585, Sir *Robert Dobfon* clerk was
collated upon lapfe. And he refigning four years after, *Leonard Scott* was inftituted on the prefentation of Chriftopher Dacre of Lanercoft efquire.

In 1597, on Leonard Scott's death, *Jofeph Lowden*, M. A. was collated
upon lapfe. And on his death in 1612, Sir *Richard Lowden* clerk was prefented by Henry Dacre efquire.

In 1642, on the refignation of *Anthony Salkeld* the late vicar, *Richard Sib-
fon*, B. A. was prefented by Sir Thomas Dacre knight, and inftituted by Ifaac
Singleton and John Hafty, mafters of arts, commiffioners of archbifhop
Ufher.

In 1661, *John Theakfton*, B. A. was prefented by Sir Thomas Dacre. As
likewife *Philip Fielding*, M. A. in 1666.

In 1692, *John Gofling* was prefented by Henry Dacre efquire.

In 1731, on John Gofling's death, *Matthew Wilkinfon* was prefented by
Sufanna Maria Dacre Appleby.

In 1745, Matthew Wilkinfon dying, *James Farifh* clerk was inftituted on a
prefentation by Jofeph Dacre efquire.

In 1763, on the ceffion of the faid James Farifh, *John Stamper* clerk was
prefented by the faid Jofeph Dacre efquire.

PARISH OF BRAMPTON.

BRAMPTON, by Camden and fome others, is fuppofed to be the *Bremetenracum* of the Romans, which being only conjectural from fome fimilitude of
the names, others have rejected this fuppofition, efpecially as there hath appeared no good evidence that ever there was a Roman ftation at Brampton:
And Mr. Horfley places the *Bremetenracum* at *Old Penrith.*—In this parifh (ever
fince the building of Naworth caftle at leaft), was the chief refidence of the
lords of the great barony of Gilfland; whofe hiftory it is proper here in the
firft place to delineate :

I. Ranulph de Mefchiens, in the time of the Conqueror, granted this barony of Gilfland to one HUBERT a Norman, who took his name from the
place. *Gill* in this country dialect fignifies a *dale* or *valley*, which is the fame
as the latin word *vallis*, from whence the French had their word *vaulx*. And
from the time of this grant, the faid *Hubert* was promifcuoufly ftyled HUBERT
VAULX or HUBERT DE VALLIBUS. He had two brothers *Ranulph de Uprightby*
and *Robert de Dalfton*, both of them fo called from the place of their habitation.
From this family at Gilfland did defcend by younger brothers, divers other
families, as *Veulx* of Tryermain, of Ainftapileth, of Catterlen, and of Caldbeck. At the time of the conqueft and before, this barony, or a great part of
it, belonged to one *Bueth*, whofe fon *Gilbert* fon of *Bueth* (commonly called
Gib Bueth) was driven out by the conqueror. And king Henry the firft regranted

8

granted and confirmed Bueth's lands to the faid Hubert and his heirs, to hold
by the fervice of two knights fees, with thol, and theam, and foc, and fac, and
infangthief, and freedom from noutegeld *.

This *Hubert* was a kinfman or follower of the faid Ranulph de Mefchiens,
and ferved under Ranulph's brother William de Mefchiens here in Gilfland.
After he was poffeffed of the barony peaceably, he gave divers parcels thereof
by the name of manors, as Denton to one Wefcop, Farlam to one Wesfalam,
Kirkby to one Odard, and divers other manors and lands there, fome to the
ancient inhabitants, and others to his friends and kinfmen.   Such as he fo preferred, he bound by alliance and marriages to his houfe, and by all other good
means he could devife.   Yet his new reconciled enemies continued but a fhort
time his friends.   For in king Stephen's time, when the Scots under their
king David and earl Henry his fon poffeffed the county of Cumberland, they
ftood with the ancient heir Gils bueth againft Hubert's title.

II. ROBERT DE VALLIBUS, fon of *Hubert,* fucceeded his father.   On king
Henry the fecond's obtaining the crown of England, he took Cumberland
again from the Scots, and *Robert* entred to the barony of Gilfland.   And the
faid king by his charter confirmed the fame to him, as king Henry the firft
had done to Hubert father of the faid Robert.   Witneffes of which grant
were, Bartholomew bifhop of Exeter, Henry elect of Bath, Richard archdeacon of Poictou, earl Geoffrey, and many others :   Dated at Windfor.—And
the fame was likewife confirmed to him by king Richard the firft in the firft
year of his reign.

This *Robert de Vallibus,* at a meeting (then called a *Trift,* that is, in truft
and confidence) for deciding their differences, had bafely murdered the aforefaid Gills-bueth ; of which he forely repented afterwards, and for expiation
thereof founded the priory of Lanercoft in Gilfland.   He was a learned man,
and well fkilled in the laws of this realm ; and in the 24 Hen. 2. was juftice
itinerant in Cumberland with Ranulph de Glanville and Robert Picknell his
affociates.

* Henricus rex Angliæ, dux Normanniæ et Aquitan æ. comes Andegaviæ, archiepifcopis, epif
copis, abbatibus, comitibus, baronibus, juſticiariis, vicecomitibus, m n ſtris, et omnibus fidelibus
fuis totius Angliæ Francigenis et Anglis, falutem. Sciatis me conceffiffe, dediffe, et confirmaſſe
Huberto de Vallibus, in feodo et hæreditate, ſibi et hæred bus ſui , totam terram quam G lbertus
filius Boet tenuit die quo fuit vivus et mortuus, de quocunque illam tenu ffet ; et, de incremento,
Korkeby cum pifcaria et aliis pertinentiis, quam Welcubright filius Wilhelmi Steffan tenuit ; et Kaderleng, cum molendino, quod Uchtredus filius Haldani tenuit : Et totam iftam terram tenebit
ipfe et hæredes fui de me et heredibus meis, per fervicium duorum militum. Quare volo et firmiter
præcipio, quod ipfe et hæredes fui fupradictas terras de me et hæredibus meis habeant et teneant,
bene et in pace, libere, quiete, et integre, et honor fice, cum omnibus pertinentiis fuis, in bofco et
plano, in pratis et pafcuis, in viis et femitis, in aquis et mo'endinis, et pifcariis, et marifcis, et
ftagnis, infra burgum et extra in omnibus rebus et locis, cum thol, et theam, et focha, et facha, et
infangenetheof, et cum omnibus aliis libertatibus et liberis confuetudinibus, quietis ab omni neute-
geldo. Teftibus, R. archiepifcopo Eborum, R. epifcopo Lincolniæ, H. Dunelmenfi epifcopo, F.
comite Norfolciæ, Comite Alberico, Comit Galfrido, Richardo de Lucy, Manafs' Bifet dapifero,
H. de Eflex conftabulario, Hugone Morevil, Roberto de Duftanvil, Willielmo filio Johannis,
Simone filio Petri, Nigello de Broch', Willielmo Malet, Rogero filio Ricardi, Roberto de Stutevill,
Turg' de Ruffedal, apud Novum Caftrum fuper Tinam.

Ia

In the 15 Hen. 2. he paid two marks for two knights fees (whereby he held Gilsland), upon levying the aid for marriage of the king's daughter; and in the 18th of the same king he paid 40s scutage of these knights fees, in regard he was not in that expedition which the king made into Ireland.

In the 21 Hen. 2. he was sheriff of Cumberland, which county that year yielded no benefit to the king by reason of the war. He was also governor of Carlisle at the same time; and after a long siege laid thereto by William king of Scotland, wanting victuals, was necessitated to come to this conclusion, *viz.* that if king Henry did not relieve him before Michaelmas, he would then render it. And he continued sheriff of that county from the 22 to the 30 Hen. 2. inclusive.

To the canons of Carlisle he gave the church of Hayton, with one carucate of land there.

In the 23 Hen. 2. he was one of the witnesses to that memorable award then made by king Henry, for appeasing the differences between Aldephonsus king of Castile, and Sanctius king of Navarre, touching divers castles and territories.

He married Ada daughter and heir of William Engaine, and widow of Simon de Morville; and by her had issue a son, *viz.*

III. ROBERT DE VALLIBUS: who in the 12 Joh. gave the king 750 marks for regaining his favour. Wherein he had offended doth not appear; but in the 16 Joh. he gave another fine of 666*l* 13*s* 4*d* to pacify the king.

IV. To this *Robert* succeeded RANULPH DE VALLIBUS, his brother, in the seigniory of Gilsland; who had a son and heir; *viz.*

V. ROBERT DE VALLIBUS, to whom in the 17 Joh. the custody of the county of Cumberland and castle of Carlisle were committed. Which Robert soon after took part with those barons then in arms against the king, as it seemeth: for before the end of that year, all his lands in Cumberland, Norfolk, Suffolk, Somerset, and Dorsetshire were seized on by the king, and given to Robert de Veteripont. But those storms being over, in the 6 Hen. 3. he took upon him the cross, and went on pilgrimage to Jerusalem; having licence to let his lands for the term of three years after he began his journey, according to a constitution of the Lateran council. In this same year he paid four marks upon levying the first scutage of king Hen. 3. for the two knights fees he held in Gilsland. And in the 13 Hen. 3. he paid other four marks for the scutage in that year. In the 18 Hen. 3. he executed the office of sheriff for the county of Devon, for the first quarter of that year.

VI. To this *Robert* succeeded HUBERT DE VALLIBUS his son; who left issue one sole daughter and heir called MAUD, who was married to THOMAS DE MULTON, whereby the barony of Gilsland came to that family.

The arms of Vaux were; Argent, a bend checquy Or and Gules.

This

This *Thomas de Multon* was fon of *Thomas de Multon* by his fecond wife *Ada* daughter and coheir of Sir *Hugh de Morville*. He had by his faid wife *Maud* a fon called *Thomas de Multon* of Gilfland, who died in the 21 Ed. 1. leaving a fon *Thomas de Multon* of Gilfland, who died two years after his father; leaving iffue another *Thomas de Multon* of Gilfland, who died in the 7 Ed. 2. leaving only a daughter MARGARET DE MULTON lady of Gilfland, married to RANULPH DE DACRE of Dacre caftle in Cumberland, whereby that great inheritance was transferred to the *Dacres*; in whom it continued in the male line, till the death of the laft male heir, GEORGE lord Dacre of Gilfland, Grayftock, and Wemm, who left three fifters coheirs, one of whom died unmarried, and the inheritance was divided between the two furviving fifters, *Anne* married to *Philip* earl of *Arundel* eldeft fon of Thomas Howard duke of Norfolk, and *Elizabeth* married to the lord WILLIAM HOWARD third fon of the faid duke of Norfolk. In the partition of the eftate, Gilfland fell to the fhare of the faid ELIZABETH (the younger fifter); in whofe pofterity, by her faid hufband the lord *William Howard* it ftill continues: whofe family therefore we proceed next to deduce.

I. The faid lord WILLIAM HOWARD, third fon of Thomas duke of Norfolk by his fecond wife Margaret daughter and fole heir of Thomas lord Audley of Walden, became poffeffed of Naward caftle and all Gilfland in right of his faid wife *Elizabeth Dacre*; by whom he had iffue, *Philip* and feveral other fons, and three daughters, *Mary* married to Sir John Winter knight, *Elizabeth* married to Sir Henry Beddingfield baronet, and *Margaret* married to Sir Thomas Cotton baronet.

II. Sir PHILIP HOWARD knight, eldeft fon of the lord *William Howard* and *Elizabeth Dacre* his wife, married Mary daughter of Sir John Carrel of Harting in the county of Suffolk knight; and by her had iffue *William* his fon and heir, *John* and *Philip* who were both flain at Rowton heath in the fervice of king Charles the firft, and two daughters, *Elizabeth* married to Bartholomew Fromond of Cheam in the county of Surrey, and *Alathea* married to Thomas vifcount Fairfax of the kingdom of Ireland. This Sir *Philip* died before his father, who was therefore fucceeded by his grandfon and heir, *viz.*

III. Sir WILLIAM HOWARD knight; who married Mary eldeft daughter of William lord Eure of Witton, by whom he had iffue five fons, *William* who died before his father, *Charles*, *Philip*, *Thomas*, and *John*; and five daughters, *Mary* married to Sir Jonathan Atkins, *Elizabeth* to Sir Thomas Gower, *Catharine* to Sir John Lawfon, *Frances* to Sir George Downing, and *Margaret* to Alexander Leflie earl of Leven in Scotland.

IV. Sir CHARLES HOWARD, eldeft furviving fon of Sir *William*, was in 1660 chofen member of parliament for Morpeth; and having been highly inftrumental in the reftoration of king Charles the fecond, was by letters patent bearing date Apr. 20, 1661, created baron Dacre of Gilland, viscount How-ard of Morpeth, and earl of the city of Carlifle.

In 1663, he was fent ambaffador to the Czar of Mufcovy, and in the year following to the kings of Sweden and Denmark. He was afterwards made governor of Jamaica, where he continued fome years, and there died in the year, 1686, and was interred in the cathedral church at York, where a monument is erected to his memory.

He married Anne daughter of Edward lord Howard of Efkrick, by whom he had two fons, *Edward* his fucceffor, and *Frederic-Chriftian* born at Copenhagen and flain at the fiege of Lutzemburgh; and three daughters, *Mary* married to Sir John Fenwick of Wallington in the county of Northumberland baronet, *Anne* married to Sir Richard Graham of Netherby baronet, and *Catharine* who died unmarried.

V. Edward Howard, earl of Carlifle, married Elizabeth daughter and co-heir of Sir Richard Uvedale of Wickham in the county of Southampton knight, and widow of Sir William Berkeley; and by her had iffue *Charles* who fucceeded him, *William* who died unmarried, and a daughter *Mary* who alfo died unmarried. He died at Wickham aforefaid in 1692, and was buried there.

VI Charles Howard earl of Carlifle, fon of Edward, was lord lieutenant and cuftos rotulorum of the counties of Weftmorland and Cumberland, one of the gentlemen of his majefty's bedchamber, deputy earl marfhal of England, firft commiffioner of the treafury, governor of the town and caftle of Carlifle, vice admiral of the fea coafts adjacent, and one of the privy council. He was afterwards appointed governor of Windfor caftle, and lord warden of the foreft of Windfor.

He married the lady Elizabeth Capel, only furviving daughter of Arthur earl of Effex, and by her had two fons and three daughters. The fons were, *Henry*, who fucceeded him; and *Charles*, afterwards Sir Charles Howard knight of the Bath, lieutenant general of his majefty's forces, governor of the caftle and city of Carlifle, and reprefentative of the faid city in parliament during moft part of the reign of king George the fecond. The daughters were; *Elizabeth*, married firft to Nicholas lord Lechmere, and afterwards to Sir Thomas Robinfon of Rookby park in the county of York baronet: *Anne*, married to Richard Ingram lord vifcount Irwin of Scotland, and afterwards to colonel James Douglafs: And *Mary* (1769) unmarried.

VII. Henry Howard, earl of Carlifle, fucceeded his father in 1738. During the life-time of his father, he ferved in feveral parliaments for Morpeth. He married to his firft wife the lady Frances Spencer only daughter of Charles earl of Sunderland by his wife the lady Arabella Cavendifh daughter and coheir of Henry duke of Newcaftle, and by her had iffue two fons and two daughters, *Charles* lord Morpeth, and *Robert*, who both died unmarried, and the ladies *Arabella* and *Diana*, the former married to Jonathan Cope efquire,

8 and

and the latter to Thomas Duncombe of Duncombe park efquire. To his fecond wife he married Ifabella fifter of the prefent William lord Byron, and by her had iffue one fon *Frederick*, and four daughters, *Anne*, *Frances* married to John Radcliffe of Hitchen in Hertfordfhire efquire, *Elizabeth*, and *Juliana*. The countefs their mother married fecondly to Sir William Mufgrave baronet. —The faid earl *Henry* died at York in 1758, and was interred in the Maufo. leum at Caftle Howard.

VIII. FREDERICK HOWARD, the prefent earl of Carlifle, vifcount Howard of Morpeth, baron Dacre of Gilfland, and knight of the moft ancient order of the thiftle, married in the year 1770 Caroline fecond daughter of Gran. ville-Levefon Gower earl Gower.

The ARMS of the earl of Carlifle are; Gules, on a bend between fix crofs crof-flets fitche Argent, an efcutcheon Or, charged with a demi-lion rampant pierced through the mouth with an arrow within a double treffure counterflory Gules, with a mullet for difference.

The *Creft:* On a chapeau Gules, turned up Ermine, a lion guardant (his tail extended) Or, gorged with a ducal coronet Argent.

Supporters: On the dexter fide a lion Argent, differenced by a mullet. On the finifter a bull Gules, armed, unguled, ducally gorged, and chained Or.

NAWARD CASTLE is the principal feat of the barons of Gilfland in thefe parts. It is built fquare, with towers at each corner, and was enlarged and improved out of the ruins of the caftles of Irthington and Kirkofwald. Dr. Todd fays, there were brought from Kirkofwald, and put up on the roof or wooden ceiling of the great hall here, the heads of all the kings of England from Brute to king Henry the fixth, elegantly painted, in good and lafting colours.

In and about the garden at this place, in Mr. Horfley's time, was a good number of fculptures and Roman infcriptions, which have been fince removed, and where they are now to be found we know not. Mr. Horfley's account of them we have inferted in the feveral places from whence they were brought.

King Henry the third, in the 37th year of his reign, granted to Thomas de Multon lord of Gilfland a weekly market at Brampton on Tuefday, and a fair yearly at the feaft of Pentecoft, and the Quindemes of the Affumption of the Bleffed Virgin Mary *. At which place are held annually courts leet and view of frankpledge for the whole barony; *viz.* for the feveral manors of Bramp-ton, Irthington, Leverfton, Newby, Afkerton, Walton wood, Tredermaine, Hayton, Cumwhitton, Carlatton, Caftle Carrock, Cumrew, Farlam, Denton, Nether Denton, and Talkin. The manors of Lanercoft, Brackenthwaite, and Newbiggin are alfo within the limits of the faid barony, but Lanercoft having been formerly granted to the priory of Lanercoft in frankalmoine, and Bracken-thwaite in Newbiggin difmembered by Joan the female heir of Thomas lord

* Todd.

Dacre

Dacre who married Fynes, they are now deemed feparate, their cuftoms different, and only courts baron held in them.

The general cuftoms of Gilfland are, to pay fines arbitrary upon defcents
and alienations, but upon the death of the lord to pay a twenty-penny fine
only. No furrender nor admittance is ufed, but the lands pafs by deed only
with the lord's allowance thereon. Widows are intitled to a third of all the
lands that their hufbands died poffeffed of, but lofe the faid third upon their
marriage. In none of the manors are heriots paid, except only in Nether Denton; and if there are no live goods, they pay 2l in lieu thereof.

In the 12 Geo. 3. an act of parliament paffed, which probably will make a
great alteration in the tenure of thefe manors : It is intitled " An act to im-
" power certain perfons to infranchife feveral cuftomary lands and heredita-
" ments, parcel of the feveral manors of Brampton, Farlam, Upper Denton,
" Nether Denton, Talkin, Irthington, Laverfdale, Newby, Afkerton, Wal-
" ton wood, Troddermain, Hayton, Cumwhitton, Carlatton, Caftle Carrock,
" Cumrew, Brackenthwaite, and Newbiggin, within the barony or reputed
" barony of Gilfland in the county of Cumberland, late the eftate of Henry
" earl of Carlifle deceafed, and fettled to certain ufes by the will of the faid
" Henry earl of Carlifle ; and for other purpofes therein mentioned."

The CHURCH of Brampton is dedicated to St. Martin, and is vicarial. It
ftands about a mile weft from Brampton, and no houfe near to it but the vicar's
manfe. At the foundation of the priory of Lanercoft, it was given by Robert
de Vallibus to that houfe, and foon after appropriated thereto. And about
the year 1220, Hugh bifhop of Carlifle endowed it with the whole altarage,
and the tithes, oblations, and obventions belonging to the faid altarage, and
the lands belonging to the fame with the tithes thereof *.

In pope Nicholas's taxation in 1291, the church of Brampton is valued at
18l, and the vicarage at 8l. In Edward the fecond's taxation in 1318, the
church is valued at 1l, and the vicarage at nothing becaufe it was totally deftroyed. In Henry the eight's valuation the vicarage is rated at 8l; and is
now worth 100l *per annum* or upwards.

After the diffolution of the religious houfes, this church with the advowfon
thereof was granted (amongft the other poffeffions of the priory of Lanercoft)
to Sir Thomas Dacre fenior knight, and is now the property of the right honourable the earl of Carlifle.

In 1334, *Richard de Caldecotes* was vicar; upon whofe death in 1346, *John*
Engge was inftituted upon the prefentation of the prior and convent of Lanercoft.

* Omnibus Chrifti fidelibus ad quos præfentes literæ pervenerint, Hugo dei gratia Karliolenfis
epifcopus æternam in domino falutem. Noverit univerfitas veftra, Nos ad inftantiam et petitionem
prioris et conven us de Lanercoft admififfe Magiftrum Thomam clericum noftrum ad quoddam be-
neficium et a dictus priore et conventu in ecclefia de Brampton collatum ; fcilicet, ad altaragium
totum cum terra ad hoc pertinente et cum decimis ejufdem terræ, et omnibus decimis, oblationibus,
et obventionibus ad altare ejufdem ecclefiæ fpectantibus, *Regiftr. Lanercoft.*

In 1361, on *John Engge*'s death the prior and convent prefent *John de Hayton*: on whofe refignation in 1372, *William de Kirkby* was inftituted on the like
prefentation.

In 1565, on the death of Sir *Chriftopher Davies* vicar of Brampton, Sir
John Rudd clerk is inftituted, being prefented by Thomas Talentyre, notary
public, being a purchafer from the lord Dacre.

In 1579, John Rudd being dead, the next prefentation was claimed by
William Dacre gentleman, fon of Sir Thomas Dacre knight lately deceafed,
who in the caveat is faid to have bequeathed it to him. But it lapfed to the
bifhop, who collated *Robert Beck* clerk.

In 1600, on Robert Beck's death, inftitution was given to *Henry Hudfon*,
S. T. B. on the prefentation of Henry Dacre of Lanercoft efquire.

In 1644, one Mr. *Warwick* was vicar.. In 1670, *Philip Fielding*.

In 1692, *John Cockburn* was prefented by Charles earl of Carlifle.

In 1702, *Richard Culcheth*, M. A. was prefented by the fame patron. And
Theophilus Garencieres, B. A. in 1714. And *John Thomas*, B. A. in 1721, by
the fame patron.

In 1747, on John Thomas's death, *William Plafket* clerk was prefented by
Henry earl of Carlifle.

In 1750, *Robert Wardale*, B. A. by the fame patron.

In 1773, *Charles Stoddart*, M. A. was prefented by Frederic the prefent earl
of Carlifle.

There was an *hofpital* in the town of Brampton founded by the late earl
Edward (or his countefs, who it is fuppofed was the firft mover) and endowed
fo as to fubfift in Dr. Todd's time, 6 poor men and 6 poor women, called
brethren and fifters. The houfe was built into 12 chambers or apartments for
the 12 eleemofynaries, each of whom was allowed 6*l* a year, a long gown,
and wood for fire. And an allowance of 12*l* a year was provided for the fupport of a perfon to perform divine fervice in their chapel, and to teach fchool.
The nomination of the faid poor perfons and curate to be in the earl of Carlifle. But this inftitution was dropt by the late earl or his father. However,
the chapel remains, and the parochial fervice is performed there for the moft
part, the parifh church being at fo great a diftance, and in a very ruinous condition.

Near the town ftands a large round hill, commonly called the *Moat*, of the
height of about 50 yards, gently and gradually tapering from the bafis to the
fummit. At the top there is a trench or ditch round it. Dr. Todd fuppofes
that this regular ftructure was at firft railed by the Britons and ancient idola-
trous inhabitants; and that it was defigned by them for an open confpicuous
public altar or place of facrifice.

The number of families in this parifh is about 250; of which 52 are prefbyterian, papifts 2, and quaker 1.

PARISH OF CUMWHITTON.

THE parifh of CUMWHITTON is bounded by the river Eden on the weft, by Crofby fields in the parifh of Wetheral to Hood's nook on the north, by the rivulet called Carn and by Carlatton and Cumrew on the eaft, and by Croglin water on the fouth.

The earl of Carlifle, as lord of Gilfland, is lord of the manor; has near 80 tenants, who pay 13*l* 9*s* 4*d* cuftomary rent, a twenty-penny fine at change of lord by death, and an arbitrary fine upon change of tenant by death or alienation. They owe fuit to the lord's court, and pay each one fhilling yearly in lieu of other fervices. They alfo pay 1*l* 8*s* 1¼*d* in confideration of paying only half moulter at the lord's mill. And the lord claims the wood.

There are two eftates within this manor that pay 17*s* yearly cuftomary rent to the lord of Corby, and a twenty-penny fine. Alfo feven others that pay about 3*l* yearly cuftomary rent to Mr. Atkinfon of Carlifle, with a twenty-penny fine.

When pope Nicholas's Valor was taken in the year 1291, this CHURCH was rectorial, and valued at 8*l* 14*s* 0*d*. In Edward the fecond's, 1318, it continued rectorial, but was not taxed by reafon of its poverty. Afterwards it was given (but by whom we have not found) to the prior and convent of Carlifle, and wholly appropriated to them. And their fucceffors the dean and chapter now nominate a curate to officiate, who is licenfed by the bifhop accordingly.

They let out upon leafe from time to time all that the rectory or parfonage of Cumwhitton, and all their glebe land, and meadow called Kirk Crofts, together with all tithes, oblations, obventions, offerings, duties, payments, rights, cuftoms, ufages, profits, and advantages, to the fame belonging, under the yearly rent of 15 efkeps of havermeal and 10*s* in money; the curate's houfe and garden not included in the faid leafe, and the leffee to pay to him moreover 10*l* yearly, and to difcharge all dues and duties ordinary and extraordinary. The parifhioners do not pay tithe corn in kind, but certain quantities of meal in lieu thereof.

The curacy has been augmented with 200*l* by lot, which was laid out in lands at Catlowdy within the manor of Nicol Foreft, which yields now upwards of 9*l* a year; and hath fince been augmented with 400*l* more (200*l* whereof was given by the countefs dowager Gower); wherewith lands were purchafed in the parifh of Addingham, of the prefent yearly value of 15*l*.

Within this parifh lies all or a great part of the large wafte called *King Harry*. Upon which wafte the parifhes of Cumwhitton and Ainftable depafture their cattle. And the earl of Carlifle is lord, and has the foil —The village of Cumrew, with fome tenants at Hornfby (or Ormefby) pay 6*s* 8*d* yearly to the faid lord for thatch, flack, and winter rake. The village of Newbiggin, with fome tenements at Croglin, do the fame.

On

On the fummit of the Fell, is a place called the *Grey Yawd*. It confifts of about 88 pretty large fparry ftones fet nearly in an exact circle of about 52 yards in diameter. One fingle ftone, larger than the reft, ftands out of the circle about 5 yards to the north-weft. We have mentioned feveral of the like kind in other places, which by divers good judges of antiquity are underftood to have been places of Druid worfhip.

Upon the face of a rock, about half way up a fteep hill, that hangs over the river Gelt, in this parifh is a Roman infcription, which Mr. Horfley endeavours to make out as follows:

IX X

Vexillatio Legionis fecundæ, Auguftæ, ob virtutem appellatæ; fub Agricola optione.

Apro et Maximo confulibus; ex officina Mercatii, Mercatus filius Firmii.

Aper and *Maximus* were confuls when Severus's wall was built. And from the nature of the ftone, Mr. Horfley conjectures that a large quantity of ftones for the wall was fetched from this place: And that the ninth and tenth cohorts of the *legio fecunda Augufta* were employed in this quarry, and about the wall in thefe parts.—An *optio* was a fort of deputy to a centurion or other officer, who acted for him in his abfence.

The number of *families* in this parifh is about 80; of which two are papifts, two prefbyterians, and one quaker.

PARISH OF LANERCOST.

THE parifh of Lanercost is of a pretty large extent, and is divided into the conftablewicks of *Banks, Burtholme, Afkerton, Waterhead,* and *King water.*

In the year 1169, which was the 16 Hen. 2. Robert de Vallibus lord of Gilfland built here a monaftery of the order of St. Auftin (which was dedicated to St. Mary Magdalen by bifhop Bernard then bifhop of Carlifle); and by his charter granted to the faid monaftery the land of *Lanercoft,* by thefe boundaries, *viz.* Between the Old Wall and Irthin, and between Burgh and Poltros. And by the faid charter he alfo granted to the faid monaftery, the village of *Walton,* and the church of *Walton,* with the chapel of *Treverman;* and the churches of *Irthington, Brampton, Carlatton,* and *Farlam;* and the land of *Warthecolman,* and *Rofwrageth,* and *Apeltrethwayt,* and *Brenfkibeth;* and pafture for 30 cows and 20 fows with their young for two years, and pannage, in the foreft of *Walton;* and the bark of his timber wood in his barony which had been Gils-Bueth's lands, and the dry and fallen wood in his foreft for their fuel; with liberty to have mills and fifhings in *Irthing, King, Hertingburn,* or elfewhere: And this he did, for the foul of king Henry the fecond who granted and confirmed the fame to his father and him, and for the fouls of his father Hubert, and his mother Græcia, and all his anceftors and fucceffors *.

* Regiftr. Lanercoft.

And

And king Richard the first, by his charter, granted and confirmed to God
and St. Mary Magdalen and the prior of Lanercost and the canons regular
serving God there, all the aforesaid grants; and further grants and confirms to
them, by the gift of the said Robert de Vallibus (after his charter of foundation as aforesaid) the two *Askertons*; and the tithes of all the venison of the
said Robert and his heirs as well of the flesh as of the skins, and of the skins
of foxes; and the tithes of his lakes and fisheries, and all the tithes in his
waste lands, of foals, calves, lambs, pigs, wool, cheese, and butter; and if
any of the said waste lands shall be cultivated, the tithes of those lands:—By
the gift of *Ada* daughter of *William Engain* and *Eustachia* (his wife) 30 acres
of land in *Burgh Marsh*, and two acres whereon to build them houses, and
two salt pans, and pasture in the said marsh for 200 sheep, and a free net in
Eden with the drying thereof, and room to make them booths in *Scaddebothes*; and one carucate of land in *Blenecreye*, and common of pasture there,
for daily mass to be said at the altar of St. Katharine in the church of Lanercost for the soul of *Simon de Morvil* her husband; and also 3 marks of silver in
the church of Burgh; and the church of *Leisingby*, and the church of *Grenesdale*, and Little *Harscou* :—By the gift of *David* son of *Terric* and *Robert* son
of *Asketil*, the *hermitage* which Leising held, and common of pasture in *Denton* :—By the gift of *Alexander de Windesoveres*, the tithe of the multure of his
mill of *Korkeby* :—By the gift of *William* son of *Udard*, a toft with some lands
that had belonged to the *hospital* nigh *Korkeby* mill :—By the gift of *Peter de
Tilliol*, a toft and one acre of land in *Scales*; and eight acres and an half there
given by *Simon de Tilliol*; and two acres by *Henry Noreis* :—And by the gift of
Robert son of *Bueth* and *Robert* son of *Asketil* half a carucate in *Denton*, and
pasture for one milking of sheep, 20 cows, and one bull, with their young for
two years *.

A like confirmation they had by king Henry the third, and king Edward
the first. Which said king Edward the first, having kept his residence a good
while in this priory during his attendance on the war in Scotland, thought fit
(as a farewell) to bestow on the prior and convent the churches of *Mitford*
and *Carlatton*, which he desires to have confirmed to them by the pope in the
following letter : " Venerabili in Christo patri domino P. titulo sanctæ Priscæ
" Presbytero Cardinali, et sanctæ Romanæ ecclesiæ vice-cancellario, amico suo
" charissimo, Edwardus, &c. salutem et sinceræ dilectionis affectum. Cum
" prioratus de Lanercost, Karliolensis diocefeôs, situs juxta confinia terræ nos-
" træ Scotiæ, per combustionem domorum et prædationem ejusdem prio-
" ratus, per quosdam Scotos inimicos et rebelles nostros, fines regni nostri
" dudum hostiliter invadentes, inhumaniter perpetratas depauperatus existat
" plurimum et vastatus ; nosque paupertati dilectorum nobis in Christo prioris
" et canonicorum prioratus predicti piis compatientes affectibus, ob specialem
" devotionem quam ad beatam Mariam Magdalenam in cujus honorem illud
" coenobium est fundatum gerimus et habemus; nec non propter diutinam
" moram nostram quam in eodem fecimus prioratu dum adverfa corporis vale-

* Registr. Lanercost.

                                                        " tudine

" tudine premebamur; dederimus eifdem priori et canonicis advocationes ec-
" clefiarum de Mitford et de Carlaton Dunelm' et Karliol' Dioces' quæ de
" noftro funt patronatu, volentes et concedentes quantum in nobis eft, quod
" ipfi ad relevationem ftatus fui eafdem ecclefias, cedentibus aut decedentibus
" rectoribus earundem, canonice affequi valeant in ufus proprios poffidendas,
" paternitatem veftram affectuofe requirimus et rogamus, quatenus ut domi-
" nus fummus pontifex, cui fuper hoc noftras literas deprecatorias duximus
" dirigendas, præfatis priori et canonicis concedere velit in ufus proprios eccle-
" fias memoratas, cum eas vacare contigerit, fibi et fucceffioribus fuis imper-
" petuum poffidendas, opem et operam velitis noftrorum interventu rogami-
" num apponere efficaces. Vobis enim exinde fpeciatim teneri volumus, ad
" ea quæ vobis grata fuerint et accepta. Datum apud Karliolum 17 die
" Martii (1307)."—This is copied from *Prynne's Chron. Vind.* Tom. iii. p. 1159.
Where alfo (p. 1192) is a copy of the king's grant, of the fame date, of the
premiffes to the faid prior and convent. The king's letter to the pope on this
occafion, mentioned in this epiftle to the cardinal, is alfo extant in *Rymer*,
Tom. ii. p. 1047. And in the year following the bifhop of Carlifle gave his
confent for the appropriation of the great tithes of the church of Carlaton, after
the death of the then incumbent.

Befides the above mentioned poffeffions, they had divers others, as recorded
in their regifter, which feem to have been obtained for the moft part pofterior
to the aforefaid grants and confirmations: Which, reduced into alphabetical
order, are as follows.

Aftineby. William fon of Aftin, with the confent of Eva his wife, gave 13
acres of land here; alfo one acre more called Kirk acre.

Ainftapellyth. Adam fon of Michael gave five acres.

Beaumond. Ralph de la Ferte gave one toft and two acres of land in this
village.

Brampton. Maud de Multon gave common of pafture here.—Thomas de
Multon and Maud his wife gave fix acres called Tenterbank.—Robert fon of
Adam gave lands at Northwode.—They had alfo lands called Crofsflat.

Burdofwald. Walter Benny gave one improvement here by metes and
bounds.

Caftlecayroc. Euftace de Vallibus gave one carucate of land, *viz.* 64 acres.
—Robert de Caftlecayroc gave pafture for 200 fheep, 20 cows, and their
young for one year, 8 oxen, one bull, 2 horfes, and 30 goats; with one fhield-
ing at Brendfcal.—William Laveile gave his body to the priory, with a toft
and croft at Caftlekairoc containing 2 acres and 1 rood; and half an acre at
Suninebrokeil, with common of pafture.

Camboc. Robert de Vallibus, fon of Ranulph, gave common of pafture.

Carlifle. Walter Pykering gave a yearly rent of 1s iffuing out of his houfe
adjoining to the fofs of Carlifle caftle.—John de Buethby gave a meffuage in
Fifher-ftreet.—William Marefchal and his wife gave a meffuage and tenement
in Carlifle.—Robert de Tybay gave all his tenements in Botchergate, and alfo
a yearly rent of 26s 8d.

Clovefgill. Walter de Wyndefover granted lands 'here; which were after-wards releafed by Theffania Weiry and Margaret her fister.

Crechok. Matilda de Vallibus gave a well or fpring towards Crechok.

Croglin. William de Croglin gave 8 acres of land there.

Cumquenach. Robert de Vallibus gave this place, by the boundaries in the grant fpecified.—And Walter Banny gave half a carucate of land there.

Denton. Robert de Vallibus and Robert fon of Anketill gave the church of Over Denton —Robert fon of Bueth gave a carucate of land, with common of pafture.—John fon of John de Denton gave all the bark of his oak trees in Gilfland.

Farlam. Walter de Windefover gave all his demefne at Farlam.—Robert de Carlatton gave all that land which Richard fon of Gilechrift held of him in Little Farlam; alfo all that land at Farlam called Ympegard.—And Chriftian daughter of Adam fon of Hermer gave 5 acres called Biggarth.

Gamelfby and *Glaffonby.* William de Ireby gave common of pafture upon the mountains belonging to thefe townfhips; which was confirmed by Robert de Bius lord of Annandale.

Greenwell. Euftachius de Vallibus gave a carucate of land, containing 64 acres.

Grinfdale. William le Sor gave all the land which Gowline the prieft held; alfo one acre on Haverig with common of pafture; alfo all that land and meadow lying between the Wall and the land belonging to the church, except Orme's acre.

King river. Alexander fon of Roger fon of Baldwin gave 7 acres lying between this river and the Wall.

Kingfgill. Alice daughter of Henry the chaplain gave 6 acres here, which were held of the convent.

Kirkofwald. Adam Salfarius gave a meffuage here.

Knoveran. Matilda de Multon in her viduity gave all her lands and tenements near this river, particularly bounded, late in the poffeffion of Roger de Mora.

Lazonby. Herbert Bunce gave three acres and an half.—And Thomas fon of Thomas fon of Raynburch gave lands here.

Milnholme. Walter de Flamant gave 5 acres on the weft fide of Milne-holme.

Newbiggin. Walter de Sauvage gave half a carucate of land.

Newcaftle. Thomas Brune gave a burgage houfe here, with a rent of 4s.

Preftover. Thomas de Multon gave with his body all his lands at Preftover (in the parifh of Irthington).

Quinquathill. William de Mora and Agnes his wife releafed all their land with the appurtenances in Little Camboc, viz. one third part of Quinquathill.

Scaleby. Simon de Tilliol gave a toft and 8 acres of land; and Jeffrey Tilliol releafed the fuit to his mill.

Scotland. They had divers lands there, given by feveral benefactors.

Talkan. Alan fon of Gilbert de Talkan gave feven roods and an half of his demefne there, with a croft called Mariock croft.—Adam fon of Gilbert de

Talkan

Talkan gave 5 acres with the appurtenances.—Alan fon of the faid Gilbert gave more lands in Talkan, with common of pafture, and to be moulter free and hopper free.—And Richard Haldanefeld and Avyfe his wife gave all their land on the eaft fide of Talkan, and one acre at Ragarth.

Ulvefby. William fon of William de Ulvefby gave 25 acres of land there. Adam de Crakehove gave 8 acres, with wood and meadow adjoining.—Richard de Ulvefby gave 10 acres of his demefne.—And Eudo de Skirwith granted a yearly rent of half a mark of filver out of her lands at Ulvefby.

Walton. Alicia daughter of Henry the chaplain gave lands in the territories of Walton, called Smithelands and Cumhewerin. And Alexander fon of Robert fon of Baldwin gave lands here, and a rent of 4 s.

Warthwyc. William fon of Odard gave a toft and land near the bridge at Warthwyke.

Moreover, Hugh de Morvill gave them one free net in Eden, with liberty to dry the fame. And Ranulph de la Ferte gave another free net there.

Ranulph de Dacre releafed to them all his right of pulture.

Walter fon of William de Ireby granted to them Walter fon of Simon of Gamelfby, with all his iffue and cattle.—Anfelm de Newby gave Henry fon of Ledmere, and all that belonged to him.—Robert de Caftelcayrock gave Gamel de Walton and all his iffue.—And Robert de Vallibus gave Jeffrey Pitch, his wife, and pofterity for evermore.

The *patronage* of the priory was originally in the founder, who in his lifetime granted the fame to the convent †.

In the year 1315, *Henry de Burgh* prior of Lanercoft being dead, the fubprior and his brethren petition the bifhop of Carlifle, then refiding at Horncaftle, to grant a commiffion to fome within his own diocefe to confirm their choice of a new prior, that they might not be put to the trouble and expence of a long journey for fuch confirmation : Whereupon the bifhop immediately fends fuch commiffion to his official. The prior that was chofen upon this occafion was *Robert de Meburn.*—The manufcript Chronicle of Lanercoft in the Britifh Mufeum reports that the abovefaid *Henry de Burgh* was a famous poet : But none of his works have reached to our time.

In 1337, on the death of the prior *William de Southayke*, the convent chufe *John de Bowetbby*, a canon and facrift of their church, and prefent him to the bifhop; who decrees the election to be canonical, confirms it, and fends out his mandate for the inftallation of the new prior.

† Robertus de Vallibus, filius Huberti de Vallibus, univerfis, fanctæ matris ecclefiæ filiis ad quos literæ præfentes pervenerint, falutem. Noverit univerfitas veftra, me conceffiffe et hac præfenti charta confirmaffe canonicis de Lanercoft liberam electionem. Quare volo quod obeunte D. priore, vel quolibet fucceffore ejus, ille fit prior quem jam dicti canonici, vel major pars eorum et fanior, fecundum Deum eligerint. Et ut hæc mea conceffio rata permaneat et illibata, eam præfentis fcripti patrocinio, et figilli mei appofitione corroboravi. Hiis Teftibus ; Roberto archidiacono Karliolenfi, Waltero priore, Roberto Ankitell, Roberto clerico de Leventon, Henrico et Radulpho prefbyteris, Alexandro de Wyndefover, Willelmo filio Odardi, Bernardo de Leverfdale, et multis aliis.—*Regiftr. Lanerc.*

In the very next year, on Saturday before St. Luke's day, the fubprior and convent met capitularly, and chofe *John de Bothcaftre* to be their prior, in the place of the faid *John de Bowethby* deceafed. Whereupon the fubprior imme-diately in the chapter houfe declared and pronounced, in the name of himfelf and all his fellow canons, the faid *John de Bothecaftre* to be duly elected. Af-terwards, application was made (as ufual) to the bifhop, who confirmed the election, and gave a mandate to the vicar of Brampton (one of the cañons) for his inftallation.

  In the year 1354, the faid *John de Bothcaftre* refigned in form in the chapter houfe before the bifhop, who was called thither as their vifitor on that occa-fion. The caufe affigned was old age and infirmities, fuch as rendered him incapable of continuing in the government. Whereupon the vifitor decrees him decent lodgings in the priory, a competent allowance of other neceffaries and conveniences for life, to which the convent oblige themfelves by their unanimous fubfcription. And in his place was chofen *Thomas de Hextildefham*; to whom the bifhop (as ufual) adminiftred the oath of canonical obedience, and moreover obliged him by folemn promife not to frequent public huntings, nor to keep fo large a pack of hounds as he had formerly done.—The oath of canonical obedience was in this form : " In Dei nomine, Amen. Ego " frater Thomas de Hextildefham, prior prioratus de Lanercoft, ordinis " fancti Auguftini, Karliolenfis diocefeôs, ero fidelis et obediens vobis vene-" rabili in Chrifto patri ac domino meo Domino Gilberto Dei gratia Karlioli-" epifcopo et fucceforibus veftris canonice intrantibus, officialibus, et mini-" ftris, in canonicis et licitis mandatis : Sicut Deus me adjuvet et hæc fancta " Dei evangelia. Et hoc propria manu mea fubfcribo."

  In the very next year, the faid prior *Thomas* died. And the canons of La-nercoft had great difputes and heats among themfelves concerning the choice of a fucceffor; infomuch that the bifhop thought it neceffary to fend letters requifitory, under pain of the greater excommunication, commanding them to pay an exact canonical obedience during the vacancy to the fubprior : Who with his party demanded *Richard de Rydal*, a canon regular of St. Mary's Car-lifle to be their prior; whilft another party declared that themfelves had fairly chofen a canon of their own priory one *John de Nonyngton* into the place. The bifhop was appealed to, and the caufe heard at Rofe; where fentence was given for *Richard de Rydal*, and his poftulation confirmed. And he fwore canonical obedience as above.

  In the year following, whether on occafion of the laft year's tumults, or otherwife, the bifhop folemnly vifited the prior and convent of Lanercoft; and his monition, appointing a certain day for their attending him for that purpofe in their chapter houfe, bears date at Rofe the 6th of May 1356. And in the very next fummer the bifhop vifits this houfe again, as well as the priory of St. Mary's Carlifle, and the cell at Wetheral.

  In 1360, prior *Rydal* abfenting himfelf from his priory, the bifhop conftitutes *Martin de Brampton* one of the canons guardian thereof during his abfence; with a charge of faithfully accounting for his adminiftration, when thereunto lawfully.

lawfully required.—And this is the laft account of the priory that is to be found in the regifters of the bifhops of Carlifle at Rofe.

After the diffolution of the religious houfes, king Henry the eighth, by letter patent bearing date Nov. 22. in the 34th year of his reign, granted to Thomas Dacre of Lanercoft efquire, in confideration of his true and faithful fervices, all that the houfe and fite of the late monaftery or priory of Lanercoft, and all meffuages, houfes, yards, ftables, buildings, lands, tenements, dove-coats, gardens, orchards, waters, ponds; alfo all that water mill with the appurtenances in Lanercoft nigh unto the fite of the faid priory; alfo one clofe of pafture and wood called the Park, containing by eftimation 5 acres; one clofe called Windhill banks, containing by eftimation 4 acres; one clofe called Keldholme, containing by eftimation 8 acres; one clofe called Burthe-flatt, containing by eftimation 9 acres; one clofe called Barkhoufe-flat; containing by eftimation 10 acres; all lying and being in Lanercoft aforefaid: One building called Tanhoufe in the parifh of Lanercoft aforefaid; one mef-fuage and tenement called Stonehoufe in Wath Colman in the faid parifh, 50 acres of meadow and 11 acres of arable land in Lanercoft, and all that pafture and common of pafture in the moor called Banksfield in Lanercoft, belonging to the faid meffuage called Stonehoufe; one meffuage and tenement called Seebie Neefe in the faid parifh, and 26 acres of meadow, and common of pafture to the faid Seebie Neefe belonging; alfo all that meffuage and tene-ment called Fullpots with the appurtenances. (Saving and excepting out of the faid grant, the parifh church of Lanercoft and the churchyard thereof, and the manfion houfe called Uttergate, with the ftable, granary, and garden thereto belonging, for the dwelling of the curate or vicar.) To have to the faid Thomas Dacre, and the heirs male of his body lawfully begotten or to be begotten for ever: And to hold of the king *in capite* by the fervice of the 20th part of one knight's fee; rendring for the fame yearly to the king 9s fterling.

Afterwards, king Edward the fixth, by letters patent bearing date June 28, in the 6th year of his reign, granted to the faid *Thomas Dacre*, then Sir Tho-mas Dacre fenior knight [The younger Sir Thomas was fon and heir apparent of William lord Dacre of Gilfland and Grayftock, brother of this Thomas Dacre of Lanercoft]—all thofe the rectories and churches of Lanercoft, Grenefdale, Farleham, Lafingby, Brampton, and Irthington, and the chapel of Walton, and the advowfon, free difpofition, and right of patronage of the vicarages and churches of Lanercoft, Grenefdale, Farleham, Lafingby, Bramp-ton, and Irthington, with all their rights, members and appurtenances in the county of Cumberland, late belonging to the priory of Lanercoft in the faid county; and all the tithes of corn, grain, and fheaves, and other tithes what-foever, with the appurtenances, lying in Lanercoft, Grenefdale, Farleham, Lafingby, Brampton, Irthington, and Walton, in the faid county of Cumber-land, belonging to the faid priory: Alfo all houfes, buildings, barns, ftables, dove-coats, gardens, orchards, glebe lands, meadows, paftures, woods, com-mons, underwoods, tithes of fheaves, corn, grain, hay, wool, lambs, calves, flax, hemp, and other tithes whatfoever, oblations, obventions, fruits, commodities,

modities, emoluments, and hereditaments whatfoever, with the appurtenances,
in Lanercoft, Grenefdale, Farleham, Lafingby, Brampton, Irthington, and
Walton, and elfewhere in the faid county of Cumberland, to the faid rectories
and the faid chapel of Walton belonging, parcel of the poffeffions of the faid
priory : And alfo the water mill with the appurtenances in Walton in the faid
county of Cumberland, late in the tenure of William Pennyfon knight deceafed, to the faid priory belonging, with all houfes, buildings, lands, meadows, paftures, waters, watercourfes, dams, profits, commodities, and hereditaments whatfoever, with the appurtenances, to the faid mill belonging, or
with the fame demifed : And all meffuages, mills, lands, tenements, meadows,
feedings, paftures, woods, underwoods, moors, marfhes, waters, fifhings,
waftes, furze, heath, and other hereditaments whatfoever, with the appurtenances, in Walton, Thorney moor, Withehill, Wall, Dofecote, Burtholme,
Banks, St. Mary-holme, Waltholme, Irthing, King, Brampton, Harefkew,
Denton, and Carlifle, in the faid county of Cumberland, to the faid late priory belonging : And one rent of 9s iffuing out of the houfe and fite of the
late priory of Lanercoft, and out of the demefne lands of the fame priory in
the faid county of Cumberland, by letters patent of our lord Henry the
eighth late king of England dated the 22d day of November in the 34th year
of his reign, given and granted to the faid Thomas Dacre and the heirs male
of his body lawfully begotten : And all fairs, markets, courts leet, views of
frankpledge, waifs, eftrays, goods of felons and fugitives, and of felons of
themfelves, and perfons put in exigent, deodands, and other jurifdictions,
liberties, and privileges whatfoever, in Lanercoft, Grenefdale, Farleham, Lafingby, Brampton, Irthington, Walton, Thorney moor, Withehill, Wall,
Dofecote, Burtholme, Banks, St. Mary holme, Waltholme, Irthing, King,
Harefkew, Denton, and Carlifle, in the faid county of Cumberland, to the
faid late priory of Lanercoft belonging : To have and to hold to the faid
Thomas Dacre knight, his heirs and affigns for ever. To be holden of the
king *in capite* by the fervice of the 40th part of one knight's fee ; rendring for
the fame (together with other particulars) 55l 17s 7d to the king, his heirs
and fucceffors, for all rents, fervices, and demands.

This Sir *Thomas Dacre* went commonly by the name of *Baftard Dacre,* being
an illegitimate fon of Thomas lord Dacre of the North. Hence the Dacres
of Lanercoft bore in their arms the bar of difference, or baftard bar.—In the
year 1559, this Sir Thomas repaired the manfion houfe, and caufed the following verfes to be painted in the glafs of the window in the dining room,
(which are now in the eaft window of the parifh church):

> *Mille et quingentos ad quinquaginta novemque*
> *Adjice, et hoc anno condidit iftud opus*
> *Thomas Dáker eques, fedem qui primus in iftam*
> *Venerat, extincta relligione loci.*
> *Hæc Edoardus ei dederat, devoverat ante*
> *Henricus, longæ præmia militiæ.*

                                                                        Whether

Whether it was a mistake of the author of these quaint lines, or Sir Thomas Dacre intended to have it understood that king Edward the sixth gave unto him the priory, and that king Henry the eighth only intended to have done so; or that king Henry the eighth gave it, and king Edward the sixth confirmed the same to him; it is certain this was not the case. The objects of the two grants were separate and distinct. King Henry gave the priory with the demesne and other lands in the parish of Lanercost. King Edward gave the rectories and advowsons of the churches. The difference was; king Henry's grant was to him and the heirs male of his body, king Edward's grant was absolute to him and his heirs.

The pedigree of the said Sir Thomas Dacre is as follows :

Sir THOMAS DACRE of Lanercost knight married a daughter of Denton, and by her had issue two sons, *Christopher* and *John*; the latter of whom died without issue.

CHRISTOPHER DACRE of Lanercost esquire, son and heir of Sir Thomas, married Alice daughter of Knevet, with whom he had a lease of Scaleby for a term of years. By her he had issue an only child *Henry*.

HENRY DACRE of Lanercost esquire married a daughter of Salkeld of Corby, and by her had issue, 1. *Thomas*. 2. *Humphrey Dacre* of Haltwhistle, who had two sons both of whom died without issue, and a daughter *Mary* married to George Yates rector of Croglin. 3. *Richard*, who was created baneret by king Charles the first in the field; and died without issue. 4. *Mary*, married to Thomas son and heir of Sir Timothy Fetherstonhaugh of Kirkoswald. 5. *Anne*, married to Musgrave of Crookdake.

Sir THOMAS DACRE knight, son and heir of Henry, married Dorothy daughter of Sir Thomas Brathwaite of Warcop knight, and by her had issue, 1. *Patric*, who died before his father, without issue. 2. *Henry*. 3. *Thomas*, who died without issue. 4. *Mary*, married to Basil Fielding gentleman. 5. *Dorothy*, married to John Child rector of Bromfield. 6. *Catharine*, who died unmarried.

HENRY DACRE of Lanercost esquire, second son and heir of Sir Thomas, married first Mary daughter and heir of Henry Sibson, D. D. rector of Bewcastle, and by her had issue, 1. *Thomas*, who died before his father, and unmarried. 2. *Dorothy*, married to Joseph Appleby of Kirklinton esquire.—To his second wife he married Margaret daughter of William Charleton of Haselside in Northumberland esquire, and by her had issue two sons, *William* and *James*, and a daughter *Elizabeth* married to Sir Patric Maxwell of the kingdom of Scotland knight, who died without issue.

WILLIAM DACRE of Lanercost esquire, son and heir of Henry by Margaret his second wife, married a daughter of Sir John Swinburn of Capheaton in

2   the

the county of Northumberland baronet, and by her had only a daughter *Margaret*, who died in her infancy, and unmarried.

JAMES DACRE of Lanercost esquire, second son of Henry by Margaret his second wife, succeeded as heir to his brother *William*; which *James*, dying without issue, left the lordship of Walton and some other estates to *Joseph Appleby* esquire son of his half sister *Dorothy* aforesaid, with request that he would take and use the name of Dacre, which *Joseph* was grandfather of the present *Joseph Dacre* of Kirklinton esquire, heir general of this family of the Dacres of Lanercost.

Dr. Todd says, upon the death of the said *James*, it was disputed, and a controversy was then depending in law, to whom the right of the site and demesne of the dissolved priory did belong. But from the tenor of the aforesaid grants it appears, that this being within the grant of king Henry the eighth, which was only to the heirs male of the body of Sir *Thomas Dacre*; and the male line here failing, it reverted to the crown, and is now in lease to Frederic the present earl of Carlisle.

Courts baron are held here in the name of the said earl. There are about 13 freeholders, and 64 customary tenants. The latter pay a twenty-penny fine certain, and no heriots or other services. The lands pass by deed, surrender, and admittance. Widows are intitled to thirds of what their husbands die possessed, but lose the same if they marry.

The conventual church has been large, and somewhat magnificent. A small part of it is now only used by the parishioners; the rest is in ruins. Having been wholly appropriated to the priory, it remains only a perpetual curacy, and was certified to the governors of queen Anne's bounty at 14*l* 5*s*, and hath since received an allotment of 200*l* from the said bounty. The earl of Carlisle is patron (probably by purchase from the Dacres).

The number of families in this parish is about 300; whereof 15 are presbyterians, 2 quakers, 2 anabaptists, and 2 papists.

BURDOSWALD, the AMBOGLANA of the Romans, is in this parish, and is a very large and remarkable fort, at which place more inscriptions have been found, than at any other Roman station Mr. Horsley exhibits no fewer than twenty-five that had been found here, but several of them removed from hence to Naward, Scaleby, and other places. They are mostly upon altars, and near one half of them inscribed to *Jupiter Optimus Maximus* and other deities, by the *Cohors prima Ælia Dacorum* which was stationed here. Many of them are very imperfect. Those which are most perfect, or otherwise remarkable, are as follows:

I O M	Jovi Optimo Maximo
C O H I A . . .	Cohors prima Ælia (Dacorum)
C P R E M . .	cui præest Maximus
X I M V	Tribunus.
T R I B V	

8

This

This was found at Willoford, about half a mile from Burdofwald, built up in a chimney, near the top of it: The letters that are wanting being covered with part of the wall.

I O M	Jovi Optimo Maximo
...H I AEL DAC	Cohors prima Ælia Dacorum
....C PRAEEST	cui præeft
...RELIVS FA...	Aurelius Fabius
...S TRIB	Tribunus
...PETVO	Perpetuo
COS	Confule.

This, by the name of the conful, appears to have been erected in the year 237.

The next, which follows, is yet compleat and perfect:

I O M	Jovi Optimo Maximo
CoH Ī AEL	Cohors prima Ælia
DAC. C. P	Dacorum, cui præeft
STAT LoN	Statius Lon-
GINVS ℞ B	ginus Tribunus.

Another, in the former part, is very legible, and fhews the contractions or combination of letters in the later empire:

PRO SALVÆ	Pro falute domini
D. N. M X M AC	noftri maximi ac
FORT. M̄P. CAES	fortiffimi imperatoris Cæfaris
M AVRℒ	Marci Aureli ...

The next, Mr. Horfley fays, is a very fine and beautiful infcription, and from the fimplicity of the character he takes it to be as ancient as the time of Hadrian.

LEG V̄Ī	Legio fexta,
VIC P F	victrix, pia, fidelis,
F	Fecit.

At a place called *Shaws* in this parifh, from the foot of a rock breaks out a medicinal fountain, which from the beneficial virtues of its water is called *Holywell*. Dr. Todd fays, it is deeply impregnated with faline and fulphureous particles, and on that account has a cathartic and emetic virtue. Perfons who are affected with cutaneous diforders, refort hither in great numbers in the fummer months, and commonly go away relieved. Dr. Short claffes it amongft the fulphureous waters, and fays it contains a very confiderable proportion of fulphur, a fmall quantity of fea falt, and a very little earth.

PARISH OF KIRK-CAMBOCK.

Kirk-Cambock is (or rather was) a fmall parifh, encompaffed by thofe of Lanercoft, Bewcaftle, and Stapleton. In Henry the fecond's time one *Alfred de Cambock* held it. Afterwards, in Henry the third's time, the *Tirryes* (or *Tyrers)* held it. And in Edward the firft's time one *Richard Tyrer* held it of Thomas de Multon then lord of Gifland, by the 8th part of one knight's fee. After him, *Thomas de Leverfdale,* and *Thomas* his fon. In the 36 Ed 3. *Robert de Leverfdale* and *William Stapelton* held it. And by an inquifition *poft mortem* in the 36 Hen. 6. it is found, that *William Stapleton* died feifed of the manor of Camboke with the advowfon of the church there, holden of Thomas lord Dacre lord of Gilfland, but by what fervices the jurors know not. It is now holden of Frederic earl of Carlifle, as part of Gilfland; and the cuftomary tenants pay an annual rent of 1 l 2 s 6 d, and a twenty-penny fine upon change of lord by death, and a fine arbitrary upon change of tenant by death or alienation.

The *church* of Kirk Cambock is rectorial; and was given to the prior and convent of Carlifle, but when or by whom we have not found. In pope Nicholas's Valor it is rated at 8 l. In king Edward the fecond's, nothing. In king Henry the eighth's it is not mentioned, being then wholly appropriated to the priory, and the parifh almoft deftroyed and ruinated by the Scots.

In the year 1259, *Randolph de Tylliol* was rector of Camboke, in which year a boundary was fettled between this parifh and that of Lanercoft †.

In 1304, on the death of *Simon de Tyrer* rector of Camboke, two prefentations were made to the bifhop. The prior and convent of Carlifle prefented *Alexander de Crokedake,* and Richard de Tyrer prefented another *Simon de Tyrer.* By an inquifition *de jure patronatus* it was found, that Henry de Tyrer father of the faid Richard prefented the laft incumbent, his own fon; but that there was an agreement, under feal, between the prior and convent of Carlifle and him the faid Henry, concluding an alternate right of prefentation. This inftrument being produced and fubmitted to, it was determined that the faid prior and convent have the prefent turn, and the faid Richard and his heirs the next. Whereupon inftitution was given to *Alexander de Crokedake.* And in the year following, the church becoming vacant, *Symon de Tyrer* was inftituted on the prefentation of Richard de Tyrer; faving to the prior and convent of the cathedral church of Carlifle a yearly penfion of 2 s due and of old time accuftomed.

In 1386, bifhop Appleby collated *John de Southwell* by lapfe. And this is the laft account that is given of this church in the bifhops regifters.

The fabrick of the church hath long been in ruins, nothing remaining of it but part of the old walls. No curate is appointed to take care of the parochial duties. For the rites of baptifm and fepulture, the people commonly repair to the church of Lanercoft; and for their inftruction in religion, they go thither, or to Stapleton, or Bewcaftle, or where they think fit.

The rectory is granted by the dean and chapter of Carlifle, by leafe for 21 years, by the defcription of " All that their church or chapel of Kirkcam- " mock, with all houfes, glebe lands, oblations, obventions, profits, and " commodities whatfoever to the faid church or chapel belonging or apper- " taining;" under the fmall yearly rent of five fhillings: And the leffees cove- nant to repair the faid church or chapel and houfes; and alfo to find and pro- vide an able and fufficient curate to ferve the place during the term of the leafe, and yearly to allow the ftipend or wages which the ordinary for the time being fhall appoint and think fit; and alfo to difcharge all other duties ordi- nary and extraordinary to the faid church or chapel belonging or apper- taining.

Why this church hath not been certified to the governors of queen Anne's bounty, and thereby put into a way of augmentation, we have heard no reafon affigned.

PARISH OF FARLAM.

FARLAM is a fmall parifh, in the very extreme parts of Gilfland towards the eaft. It was granted in king Henry the fecond's time by the lord of Gilfland to one *Walter de Windfor*, brother of *Alexander de Windfor*. The faid *Walter de Windfor* had iffue another *Walter*. And his fon, called *Adam de Farleham*, held this land in Edward the fecond's time. And in Edward the third's time, *John de Farleham* held it; who, having no children, devifed the fame to *Ra- nulph de Dacre* and *Margaret Multon* (lady of Gilfland) his wife, and to their heirs. And from thenceforth it hath continued as demefne to the lords of Gilfland.—The Arms of thefe Windfors were; Argent, a faltier Sable.

John de Windfor, brother to the fecond *Walter*, enjoyed Little Farleham. He had iffue *Rayner* and *Solomon*. And *Rayner* had *Bernard*, father of *Ri- chard*, who endowed the houfes of Wetheral and Lanercoft with lands in Little Farleham.

The *church* of Farleham is dedicated to St. Thomas; and was given by Robert de Vallibus to the priory of Lanercoft.

In the year 1251, Silvefter de Everfham bifhop of Carlifle, having fet out a portion for the vicar, viz. all the profits of the church except the tithe corn and except a moiety of the glebe lands, afterwards thinking that too little, he afligns to him the other moiety alfo, except one acre, in the following form: " Omnibus Chrifti fidelibus præfentes literas infpecturis, Silvefter miferatione " divina Karliolenfis epifcopus minifter humilis, falutem in domino. Noverit " univerfitas veftra, quod cum ex officio noftro ad taxationem vicariæ de Far- " lam procederemus, et eidem vicariæ omnes proventus ecclefiæ prædictæ " præter decimas garbarum et præter medietatem terræ ad eandem ecclefiam " pertinentis affignaremus; poftea, nimis exilem ejufdem vicariæ portionem

T t t 2 " perpen-

" perpendentes, aliam medietatem terræ prædictæ, de confensu prioris' et
" conventus de Lanercoft, eidem vicariæ literis præfentibus affignavimus;
" præter unam acram terræ eifdem priori et conventui ad ædificandum quan-
" dam grangiam affignandæ †."

In 1316, on the death of Sir *Simon de Walton* vicar of Farlam, *William de Richardby* was inftituted on a prefentation by the prior and convent.

In 1361, on the death of the vicar Sir *Thomas de Derby*, Sir *Thomas Roke* was inftituted on a like prefentation.

In 1373, Sir Thomas Roke refigns; and Sir *Robert de Hayton* chaplain is in like manner prefented and inftituted.

After the diffolution of the priory this church was granted by king Ed. 6. to Sir Thomas Dacre; and after feveral mefne conveyances, is now the pro-perty of Mr. Henry Smith the impropriator, who nominates the curate, and pays him 4*l* yearly, which with a lot of 200*l* from queen Anne's bounty and the furplice fees, is the whole endowment, and doth not exceed 10*l per annum*. For wherever any of thefe religious houfes became eftablifhed, they fwallowed up the revenues of almoft all the churches about them: Which revenues, at the diffolution, were not reftored to the churches, but given away to the king's favourites, or fold to fupply his neceffities.

The families in this parifh are about 60 in number; four of which are prefbyterian.

PARISH OF DENTON.

DENTON lies in the utmoft north-eaft limits of Gilfland; and is divided into *Nether-Denton* and *Over-Denton*. They are ftrictly two parifhes, but we will firft treat of them jointly. The word *Denton* fignifies a town in a deep valley. The Irifh call *deep* in their language *dæn*, which hath fome affinity with the Saxon word *den*. *Over-Denton* ftands beyond the great bottom or valley, and *Nether-Denton* in the low grounds. *Hubert de Vallibus*, lord of Gilfland, gave Denton to one *Weßkopp*, and he to *Gilßbueth* (or *Bueth* fon of *Gilfrid*), which *Gilßbueth* had iffue *Robert* fon of *Bueth*, who died without iffue, and *Gilßbueth*'s two daughters were his heirs; one married to *Addock* lord of Bothcaftre, the other to *Euftachius de Vallibus* lord of Hayton. The former had *Over-Denton*, and the latter *Nether-Denton*, which became two moieties then by partition.

OVER-DENTON, in the 7 Ed. 1. was in the poffeffion of *Richard Stonland*, who in that year (together with Elena his wife) granted the fame to *John Witherington*, in whofe family it long continued. From them it came to the *Tweedales*, and fo to the earls of Carlifle. The lands are cuftomary, and pay an arbitrary fine on the change of tenant by death or alienation, and a twenty-penny fine on change of lord by death: Alfo an heriot at the death of the

† Regiftr. Lanercoft.

tenant;

tenant; and if there be no live cattle, then 40s in lieu thereof. They like-wife pay one shilling each yearly in lieu of services.

This *Over Denton*, though in the county of Cumberland, is deemed to be in the diocese of Durham, and was given by Robert de Vallibus and Robert son of Anketil to the priory of Lanercost, and appropriated to that house by Hugh bishop of Durham (who presided in that see at the foundation of the said priory and 28 years after); as appears by the following instrument in the Lanercost Register: " H. Dei gratia Dunelmensis episcopus, omnibus clericis
" totius episcopatus sui, salutem. Sciatis nos dedisse, concessisse, et confirmasse
" priori et canonicis de Lanercost, ad præsentationem Roberti de Vallibus et
" Roberti filii Anketilli, ecclesiam de Veteri Denton tenendam. Ita quod
" ipsi canonici præsentabunt nobis et successoribus nostris, quoties ipsa ecclesia
" vacaverit, perpetuum vicarium qui prædictæ ecclesiæ deserviat, et nobis et
" successoribus nostris episcopales consuetudines reddat; qui etiam victum per-
" cipiat a prædictis canonicis, annuam pensionem dimidium tantum marcæ per-
" solvat, nisi eis nos vel successores nostri, ex nostra auctoritate, juxta ipsius
" ecclesiæ augmentum et facultatem in posterum plus percipere concesserimus.
" . . . . Quare volumus, ut prædicti canonici memoratam ecclesiam teneant
" libere et quiete, sicut eam tenendam concessimus. Salvis in omnibus epis-
" copalibus consuetudinibus nostris. Hiis testibus; Willielmo summo came-
" rario, Magistro Ricardo de Coldingham, Willielmo filio archiepiscopi et
" aliis."

This parish hath been so totally ruinated, that there are now only about fifteen families; the curate is named by the earl of Carlisle, who is impropri-ator, and receives all kinds of tithes great and small, and allows the curate 20s yearly.

NETHER-DENTON, as is aforesaid, came by marriage to *Euftachius de Val-libus* lord of Hayton. It was afterwards granted to *John de Denton* son of Ro-bert son of Ankitill; which *John* had a son *John*, who had a son *Richard Den-ton* knight, whose daughter and heir *Margaret* was married in the 17 Ed 2. to *Adam Copele* of Bateley in the county of York. *John*, son of the said *Adam*, had issue *Richard Copeley*; whose daughter and heir *Isabel* was married to *Adam Denton* son of *Thomas del Hall* in Henry the fourth's time; which *Adam Denton* had a son *Thomas*, who had a son *Richard*, whose son *John Denton* exchanged this purparty of Denton in Henry the seventh's time with the lord *Dacre* for *Warnell*, and was ancestor of the present family of the *Dentons* of *Warnell*. And from that time it descended in the posterity of the *Dacres*, and is now the inheritance of Frederick earl of Carlisle.

The *church* of Nether Denton is dedicated to St. Cuthbert, and is rectorial.

The aforesaid *Robert* son of *Bueth* gave it to the monks of Wetheral. He also by the advice and consent of his wife and friends gave to the church some of his lands that lay near to it, and eight acres besides as well without as within the village: Which grant was confirmed by John and Elias sons of David de Denton, and appropriated to the finding a light or candle before the altar of the holy trinity in the church of Wetheral.

After-

After his death, one *David* fon of *Terry* and *Robert* fon of *Ankitill* gave this fame church to the priory of Lanercoft; whereupon did arife great fuit, till the controverfy was ended by mediation of the pope's legate, who divided the profits between them, and gave the prefentation and advowfon of the rectory to the bifhop.

The fhare which each of the faid houfes had out of this rectory was two marks and an half. And in the year 1266 the prior and monks of Wetheral releafed their part to the bifhop and his fucceffors; of which an entry appears to be made in their Regifter.

In 1304, *Robert Oriel* was collated by bifhop Halton to the rectory of Denton, with a faving to the bifhop and his fucceffors of the penfion of 33s 4d, and the like fum to the prior and convent of Lanercoft. And again in 1306, on the collation of Sir *Adam de Kale*, there is a like refervation of five marks, *viz.* two and an half to the bifhop and his fucceffors, and two and an half to the prior and convent of Lanercoft.

In 1309, at an ordination held in the parifh church of Stanwix, *John de Culgaytb* rector of Denton was ordained prieft. After him Sir *John de Abering-ton* was collated in 1317.—Sir *Richard de Brocton* in 1385.

After the reformation, Sir *Edward Bell* the rector died in 1567, and was fucceeded (on the collation of bifhop Beft) by Sir *Chriftopher Lowther* clerk; on whofe refignation in 1576, Sir *Miles Matmaugh* was collated by bifhop Barnes.—Next, Sir *William Thompfon* clerk was collated in 1586.—Sir *Roland Baxter* in 1597.—After him, Sir *Ralph Snowden*; on whofe death in 1633, *Nicholas Dean*, B. A. was collated.

In 1692, *William Culcheth* was rector, and refigned. After him, *Richard Culcheth*; on whofe ceffion in 1703, *Thomas Pearfon*, B. A. was collated by bifhop Nicolfon.

In 1718, on Thomas Pearfon's death, *Nicholas Reay* was collated by bifhop Bradford.

In 1736, Nicholas Reay dying, *William Hefket* was collated by bifhop Fleming.

This church is rated in the king's books at 8l 5s 5d. It was returned to the governors of queen Anne's bounty at 16l 1s 6d. In 1761, it had an augmentation of 400l (200l whereof was given by the countefs dowager Gower). And having 40 acres of glebe land or upwards, it may now be worth between 50l and 60l *per annum*.

In this parifh are about 50 families; two whereof are prefbyterians.

PARISH OF CUMREW.

CUMREW is a fmall parifh, bounded by the parifhes of Croglin, Cumwhitton, Carlatton, and Caftlecarrock.

The *manor* belongs to the earl of Carlifle; who has about 26 tenants, who pay a free rent of 1l 9s 8d, indenture rent 2l 3s 11d, and cuftomary rent

6*l* 10*s* γ¼*d*.　The cuftomary tenants pay a twenty-penny fine upon change of the lord by death, and an arbitrary fine upon change of tenant by death or alienation.　The tenants alfo pay each 1*s* yearly to the lord for fervice money.

The *church* here being wholly appropriated to the dean and chapter of Carlifle, they nominate a curate, who is licenfed by the bifhop.　He has a leafe from the dean and chapter of " All thofe the houfes and glebe lands, tithes, " fruits, oblations, obventions, profits, and commodities, whatfoever, belong- " ing or appertaining to the chapel of Cumrew," under the yearly rent of ten efkeps of haver meal, and one pound in money free of all taxes.　The leffee to repair the chancel, houfes, and buildings.

In lieu of tithe corn, the parifhioners pay 119 bufhels of meal; and inftead of tithe hay, a prefcription of 1*l* 5*s* 2*d*.　It was certified to the governors of queen Anne's bounty at 13*l* 12*s* 10*d*; and hath fince received an allotment of 200*l* from the faid governors, wherewith lands were purchafed in the parifh of Ainftable, of the prefent yearly value of 7*l*.

In this parifh are about 41 families; all of the church of England.

About a quarter of a mile fouth-eaft from the church, are the ruins of a large caftle or building, fituate on a rifing ground, very near the bottom of Cumrew fell.　This feems to be *Dunwallogbt* caftle mentioned in Dugdale's Baronage, vol. 2. p. 22. as fituate on the marches towards Scotland, and belonging to the Dacres.　For there are two little manors here, Brackenthwaite and Newbiggin, which did belong to that family, till the earl of Suffex's heirs fold them to Sir Chriftopher Mufgrave baronet, and he to the earl of Carlifle, grandfather of the prefent earl.

PARISH OF CASTLE CARROCK.

CASTLE CARROCK *(Caftle Crag*, or rock) is a fmall parifh within the barony of Gilfland, at the foot of the great mountain Crofs-fell, and confifts only of one conftablewick.　*Hubert de Vallibus*, lord of Gilfland, gave this manor, and alfo Hayton, to one *Euftace de Vallibus*.　Which *Euftace* gave a carucate of land at Caftle Carrock, and another at Hayton, to the priory of Lanercoft.

In Henry the fecond's time, it was the inheritance of *Robert de Caftle Carrock*, and after him fucceffively it defcended to *Robert* his fon, and to *Richard* his grandfon, whofe fon *Robert de Caftle Carrock* was the laft of that name inheritor thereof. He died in Edward the firft's time, and left three daughters coheirs, which he had by his wife Chriftian de Crokedake aunt and one of the two coheirs of John fon of John fon of Adam de Crokedake.　The faid three daughters were *Johan* wife of Thomas Newbiggin, *Chriftian* wife of Michael Appleby, and *Margery* wife of William Eglesfield.

Newbiggin's part, which was that of *Johan* the eldeft fifter, defcended to three daughters and heirs, *Hellen* married to Richard Hale, *Margaret* married

to

to Thomas Hale, and *Alice* married to John Hale, all of the parish of Kirkby Thore. *Hellen's* part came to *William Kitchen*, who fold the fame to *Ranulph de Dacre*, that married the heirefs of Gilfland. *Margaret's* part came by a daughter named Alice, the wife of Collinfon, to two daughters Johan married to Gilbert Carleton, and Margaret married to John Betham of Thrimby; and in the fourth defcent Elizabeth Betham, then heir, wife of Robert Salkeld, had iffue Roger Salkeld, who fold it to Lough.

The purparty of *Chriftian de Caftle Carrock* wife of Appleby, went by her daughter named Chriftian to William Ritfon, and by their daughter Mariot to Thomas Alanby, and by their daughter to John de Weft Levington, and by his daughter Elizabeth to Alexander Highmore, whofe heir in the 3d or 4th defcent fold it to Dacre.

What became immediately of the third purparty of *Margery de Caftle Carrock*, wife of Eglesfield, we have not found. But in the 12 Cha. 2. Sir John Ballentine knight and Anne his wife conveyed the manor of Caftle Carrock to Charles earl of Carlifle grandfather of Frederic earl of Carlifle the prefent owner.

There are about 12 tenants in this manor, who pay a yearly cuftomary rent of 2*l* 12*s* 6*d* to Armathwaite caftle, and arbitrary fines.

The *church* of Caftle Carrock is rectorial, and in the patronage of the dean and chapter of Carlifle, unto whom it pays an annual penfion of 2*s*. It is valued in the king's books at 5*l* 12*s* 11*d*, was certified to the governors of queen Anne's bounty at 42*l.* and is not yet worth much more than 50*l per annum.*

In the year 1312, *Robert de Helpefton* was inftituted to the rectory on the prefentation of the prior and convent of Carlifle, faving to the faid prior and convent a yearly penfion of 2*s* due and of old time accuftomed.

In 1346, *John de Beghokirk* was prefented by the prior and convent to the vacant rectory.

In 1356, Sir *Adam* rector of Caftlekayroke is cited to fhew caufe why (being feized with a leprofy to fuch a degree that his parifhioners dare not refort to divine fervice) he ought not to have a coadjutor affigned him.

In 1380, *Thomas de Carleton*, rector of Caftelkayroke, makes his laft will, and bequeathes feveral remarkable legacies in twinter fheep (bidentes), lambs, ftones of wool, bows and arrows, and (amongft the reft) to the vicar of Edenhall his book called Placebo Dirige. And foon after, *John Colt* was inftituted by William rector of Bownefs the bifhop's vicar general.

In 1571, *John Richardfon* clerk, on the death of *John Richardfon* fenior, had inftitution on the prefentation of William Vale of the city of Carlifle, who (with others) had procured a grant of this avoidance from Lancelot Salkeld (the firft) dean and chapter of Carlifle.

In 1586, *John Stodart* was prefented by the faid dean and chapter. In 1589, *Leonard Milburn.* In 1635, *Chriftopher Gibfon.* In 1672, *Henry Skarrow.* In 1679, *Chriftopher Rickerby.* In 1722, *Jofeph Pattinfon.*

In

In 1739, upon the death of *Joseph Pattinson*, *John Pearson* clerk was instituted to the rectory, on the presentation of the said dean and chapter.

In this parish are about 42 families, six whereof are presbyterian.

PARISH OF CARLATTON.

THE parish of CARLATTON (or, *Carleton*) is surrounded by those of Castlecarrock, Combwhitton, and Hayton. It contains within it 1550 acres of arable land, but hath few inhabitants, and hath had no parish church for several ages, and it is only known by tradition where the church stood.

In Henry the second's time one *Gospatric* son of *Macbenck* held it of the king, and paid 50 marks. This *Macbenck (Mac-ben-og)* was an Irishman and took part with king Stephen, therefore his son *Gospatric* compounded with king Henry for his father's life. After him, king John gave it to *Robert de Ross* of Werk in Tindale, and also Sowerby and Hubertby, until the said *Robert de Ross* should recover his lands in Normandy, which he lost in the king's service. Henry the third took them from him, and gave them to *Alexander* king of *Scots* and his successors who held the same until king Edward the first seized them for the revolt of John Baliol king of Scots, and granted the same to *Anthony Beck* the military bishop of Durham who had assisted king Edward greatly in his wars in Scotland, but the parliament some years after obliged the king to resume that grant. Since which time Carlatton continued royal demesne, until king Richard the second's time, who granted the same to *Ralph Nevil* earl of Westmorland and Johan his wife. After him it descended to *Richard* his son earl of *Salisbury*, and from him to *Richard* earl of *Warwick* his son, who was slain at the battle of Barnet. After whose death, king Edward the fourth gave it to his brother *Richard* duke of *Gloucester*, afterwards king. Henry the seventh, upon his obtaining the crown, granted it to some of his friends who had been sufferers in the Lancastrian cause. And it still remains as crown land, and is held upon lease, together with Gelfton forest adjoining, by the earl of Carlisle.

The *church* of Carlatton was given by Robert de Vallibus to the priory of Lanercoft, and by bishop Halton (with the consent of king Edward the first) totally appropriated to that house. The reasons given for the appropriation were, that the Scots had destroyed the monastery by fire and sword, and that the king's army for some time had lived upon free quarter amongst the tenants of the priory, to their great damage and impoverishment; and it was upon condition, that the prior and convent should endow the vicarage in an honourable manner, and have a vicar constantly resident upon the place.

Robert de London was rector when this appropriation was made, and it was not to take place till after his death. He was presented by the aforesaid Anthony Beck bishop of Durham; upon which presentation, the bishop awarded (as was usual) a *jus patronatus*, and the inquisition finds that Alexander king of

Scotland prefented laft, that the bifhop of Durham is owner of the village of Carleton, but whether he is owner of the church the jurors know not.

After the refumption of the grant to the bifhop, the advowfon was granted by the faid king Edward the firft to the prior and convent.

In the year 1320, *Henry de Newton* was prefented by the faid prior and convent to the vicarage of Carleton, and thereupon inftituted.

In 1344, Sir *William de Stockdale* was inftituted on the like prefentation.

In 1380, Sir *Richard Hogge* was in like manner prefented by the prior and convent, and inftituted thereupon.—And this is the laft account that we meet with thereof in the bifhops regifters. After the diffolution of the priory, the whole revenues of this church came to the crown, and in confequence thereof all the tithes great and fmall are now in the leffee.

PARISH OF HAYTON.

THE parifh of HAYTON is circumfcribed by the parifhes of Cumwhitton, Wetheral, Warwick, Irthington, Brampton, Farlam, and Caftle Carrok; and includes in it the two manors of *Hayton* and *Talkin*, both within the barony and belonging to the lords of Gilfland.

Hayton confifts of about 93 cuftomary tenements, which pay yearly 18 *l* 12 *s* 3 *d* ancient rent; every ancient tenement pays alfo 1 *s* in lieu of fervices. They pay alfo 23 *l* yearly free rent, for their commons divided in 1704.

The manor of *Talkin* confifts of about 20 tenements; the yearly cuftomary rent 6 *l* 9 *s* 0 *d*. And every tenement pays 2 *d* for greenhue, and 1 *s* yearly in lieu of fervices.

The tenants of both the faid manors pay fines upon death and alienation according to the general cuftom of the barony of Gilfland.

The *church* of Hayton was given by Robert de Vallibus to the prior and convent of Carlifle, and foon after appropriated to that houfe. The dean and chapter are the prefent impropriators and patrons, and leafe out the tithes for 21 years, referving the yearly payment of 17 efkeps of good haver meal, and the leffee covenants to pay the curate and all dues and duties ordinary and extraordinary, and to repair the chancel. They alfo grant to the fame leffee all the tithe of corn, grain, and hay of the new improvements, for the like term, and under the yearly rent of 10 *s*.

The curate is endowed with feveral parcels of land, and a ftipend of 5 *l* from the dean and chapter's leffee; and in the year 1751 this church received an augmentation of 200 *l* by lot from the governors of queen Anne's bounty, and again in 1757; which being laid out in lands, the whole revenue amounts to upwards of 30 *l* a year.

The *families* in this parifh are about 150; whereof 3 are papifts, 2 prefbyterians, and 1 quaker.

APPENDIX.

APPENDIX.

No. I.

Partition of the Debatable Land.

UNIVERSIS et fingulis, ad quos præfentes literæ indentatæ pervenerint, falutem et fidem certam eifdem adhiberi. Quoniam poft hominum
memoriam nulla res, bello præfertim inter populos finitimos exercito, vel in-
dignior vel etiam acerbior extitiffe videatur, quod fi qua forte (quantumvis
juftas ob caufas) intercidat, eo fane melius ceffiffe intelligendum fit, quanto
citius honeftæ pacis conditionibus propofitis reprimatur, ne animi civium
affiduis hinc inde incurfuum ac rapinarum violentiis efferati, pacis artibus minus idonei reddantur; merito fane quin immortales Deo optimo maximo gra-
tias ardentiffimis animis Scotorum et Anglorum nationes nobiliffimæ agere
teneantur, quod poft longum illud fuperiorum annorum bellum, pax fanéta et
optata fœdere demum inter utriufque ipfarum principes iéto fubfequuta fit,
cum illud etiam fingulari laude efferre ac prædicare, quod per quos primum
divino nutu pax illa conftitit, iidem illius nutriendæ, augendæ, ac conftabiliendæ finceriffimos authores ac vere principes fefe præbeant, dum non bella
folum fed bellorum etiam occafiones ac femina (quantum humana id ope queat
perfici) tam folicite modis omnibus extingui atque e medio tolli annitentur, ut
inter alia præfentiffimum belli redintegrandi fomen illud ac pabulum nunc
tandem removendum cenfuerint, quod de agri cujufdam dubii ac incertæ conditionis ad quem ipforum pertineret proprietate nimis diu interceffërat; enim-
vero quum eis ager utriufque regni fines occidentales prope maris fretum vel
eftuarium (quod vulgo *Solway* dicitur) interjacens, mirandos magnofque, fi
quis illius ambitum non adeo magnum refpiciat, motus inter utramque gentem
levibus ab initiis fæpius excitarit, hominum potiffimum perditorum ac flagi-
tioforum fentina poft ipforum ex alterutro regno profcriptionem aut fugam eo
tanquam ad afylum confluente, qui ubi nullis fe legibus neque ullo pœnæ
timore, neutro ibi principum imperium exercente, cohiberi cernerent, eo
audaciæ prorumpebant, ut ex rapto vivere, fubditofque utriufque principis

fpoliare

fpoliare vel ad fpoliandi confortium allicere, ac denique ea omnia pergebant
facere quæ ad pacem turbandam fpectabant; opportunum atque etiam utriufque principis ac populi amicitiæ conftabiliendæ vifum eft neceffarium, fic
de agro illo dividendo, quoniam aliter poft longum annorum curriculum, ob-
fcurior juris (quod quifque in eo prætendebat) explicatio non finebat, miffis
eo infpectoribus ftatuere, ut honore ambarum partium falvo, utilitatem etiam
multo quam antehac uberiorem fubditi ibidem ex non recte fubditis effecti
caperent, ac tales denique pacis diffolvendæ fegetes quales ex illius agri abufu
fuccrefcebant de cætero amputarentur: HINC eft quod NOS *Jacobus Douglas* de
Drumlangrig miles, et *Richardus Maitlande* de *Lethington*, illuftriffimæ et excel-
lentiffimæ principis *Mariæ* Dei gratia Scotorum reginæ commiffarii et deputati
fpeciales, fufficientem poteftatem ad infra fcripta habentes, cum nobilibus et
egregiis viris *Thoma Wharton* equite aurato domino de *Wharton*, et *Thoma*
Challoner itidem equite, fereniffimi, potentiffimi, et excellentiffimi principis
domini *Edwardi* fexti regis *Angliæ*, oratoribus, ambaffatoribus, commiffariis et
deputatis fpecialibus, fufficienti poteftate fulcitis, Convenimus, concordavimus,
et conclufimus, authoritateque commiffionum noftrarum, quarum tenores inferius
inferuntur, convenimus, concordamus, et concludimus articulatim prout fequitur.
AC PRIMUM, Quum dictus ager nunc variabilis, nunc litigiofus, nunc terra
contentiofa vocari folitus, communi vero utriufque gentis vocabulo nuncupatus THE DEBATABLE LAND, quafi quis dicat terram de cujus jure tam *Angli*
quam *Scoti* decertare ac contendere fint foliti, forma oblonga atque inæquali
protendatur ab occidente in orientem, Initium, fcilicet, capiendo ab oftiis
duorum fluviorum in Eftuarium præfatum de *Solway* exonerantium (quibus
nomina *Efk* et *Sark* vernaculo accolarum fermone funt indicta) ac deinde furfum verfum progrediendo, donec ad alteram dicti agri extremitatem qua orientem fpectat deveniatur; Quandoquidem loci ipfius natura et fitus habitan-
tium ibidem animos ad hujus vel iftius regni partes fovendas eo modo difpo-
nere videatur, ut qui occidentalem agri præfati plagam occupant *Angliæ* fe
conjunctiores quam *Scotis* commonftrarint, orientales vero ejufdem incolæ
Scotorum potius in clientelam femet condixerint, idcirco conventum, conclufum, et concordatum eft, inter nos commiffarios et deputatos præfatos, quod
antedicti agri feu terræ contentiofæ pars occidentalior, talibus fub metis, terminis, five finibus, quales hic fubexponentur, *Anglorum* regum ditioni ac im-
perio perpetuo impofterum fubjaceat. Ac ut melius et certius pars hæc occidentalis ab altera difcernatur, conventum et conclufum eft inter nos commiffarios et deputatos præfatos, ut in ipfo utriufque partis difcrimine, trames
linearis rectus tranfverfim ab *Efk* ad *Sark* fluvium ducatur, foffa vel fulco
veftigium ipfius denotante; ac præterea, fingulæ pyramides lapide quadrato
fingulis ipforum *Efk* et *Sark* fluviorum ripis interius imponantur, in ipfis potiffimum (quoad ejus fieri poteft) locorum punctis conftruendæ ac collocandæ,
ubi linea feu trames ille tranfverfus hac illac extendetur. Quos quidem locos,
quo planius dinofcantur, ut fi quo vetuftatis aut doli mali vitio pyramides
corruerint, nihilo fecus locorum veftigia ad ipfarum reparationem innotefcant,
in hunc modum hinc defcribendos putavimus: Locus igitur pyramidi *Efk*
fluvii ripæ imponendæ is efto, ubi fluvii ipfius curfus finuofe incurvatus eft,

ad

ad campi cujufdam (vulgari fermone vocati *Dimmifdaill*) latus occidentale, qua torrens feu rivulus quidam vicinus (vernacule nuncupatus *Dimmifdaill fyke*) in fluvium jam dictum præcipitat. Similiter, pyramidi *Sark* fluvii quæ imponetur ripæ is efto locus, qui clivo rubro fitus eft, e regione loci vocati *Kirkrigg* in *Scotia* paulum fupra le *Eatgyw'*, ubi viciffim *Sark* fluvii alveolus in finus incurvatur. Ab altera igitur ad alteram harum pyramidum, quas a loco movere aut deftruere neutri principum præfatorum aut fubditorum fuorum liceat, foffa vel fulco tranfverfo qualem diximus ambas partes interfecante, deinde fubtus ipfas pyramides alveis præfatorum fluviorum *(Efk* videlicet et *Sark)* utrinque deorfum verfum fretum fequutis, quoad in Æftuarium vel fretum præfatum devolvantur, Quicquid agri, foli, fortalitiorum, molendinorum, ædificiorum, fylvarum, pratorum, arvorum, pafcuum, fluviorum, rivulorum, aquarum ftagnantium, morarum feu camporum paluftrium, pifcariarum, advocationum, donationum, juriumque patronatus ecclefiarum et facellorum, aut denique aliarum rerum quarumcunque intra jam defcriptos hofce limites vel fines partis occidentalis comprehenduntur aut comprehendentur, pure, mere, feparatim, et immediate ad dictum fereniffimum *Angliæ* regem fuofque hæredes ac fucceffores, directo jure, titulo, et dominii proprietate pertinebunt, ac pofthac perpetuis futuris temporibus tanquam portio regni *Angliæ* pertinere cenfebuntur; ita hanc dictam agri præfati feu terræ contentiofæ partem occidentalem una cum ejufdem pertinentiis præmiffis poffidere, eifdemque pro libito uti et frui, dictus fereniffimus rex et fucceffores fui poffit et valeat, poffint et valeant, adeo plene et integre et hoc abfque dictæ illuftriffimæ reginæ, hæredum, fucceiforum, vel denique fubditorum fuorum juris prætenfione, aut alio impedimento quocunque in contrarium movendis, quam fi regni Angliæ territorium id antiquum atque indubium ab initio in hunc ufque diem indefinenter extitiffet. Similiter, conventum, conclufum, et concordatum eft inter nos commiffarios et deputatos præfatos, quod reliqua agri five terræ contentiofæ pars (fcilicet orientalis tractus extra metas præfatas conftitutus) incipiendo a dictis pyramidibus ubi foffa aut fulcus ille tranfverfus exiftit, ac femper orientem verfus procedendo, pure, mere, feparatim, et immediate ad dictam excellentiffimam *Scotiæ* reginam, ipfiufque hæredes et fucceffores, directo jure, titulo, et dominii proprietate pertinebit, ac dehinc perpetuis futuris temporibus, tanquam portio regni *Scotiæ* pertinere cenfebitur; ita ut agri præfati orientalem hanc partem, una cum omnibus et fingulis fortalitiis, ædificiis, molendinis, fylvis, agris, pratis, arvis, pafcuis, fluviis, rivulis, aquis ftagnantibus, moris five campis paluftribus, pifcariis, advocationibus, donationibus, juribufque patronatus ecclefiarum et facellorum, nec non aliis denique rebus quibufcunque extra jam defcriptos limites vel fines partis occidentalis conftitutis et comprehenfis, dicta illuftriffima regina, hæredes et fucceffores fui poffidere, iifdemque pro libito uti et frui poffit ac valeat, poffint et valeant, adeo plene et integre, abfque dicti fereniffimi regis, hæredum, fucceiforum vel fubditorum fuorum juris prætenfione, aut alio impedimento quocunque in contrarium movendis, quam fi regni *Scotiæ* territorium id antiquum atque indubium ab initio in hunc ufque diem indefinenter extitiffet. Item, quia jacto felici hoc fundamento non operæ pretium nobis vifum fuerit

circa

circa fingula quæ hic defignantur, præfertim quod ad metas ponendas attinet, moram terere; conventum et conclufum eft inter nos commiffarios præfatos, quod Guardiani feu Locumtenentes Weftmarchiarum *Angliæ* et *Scotiæ*, communibus opera et expenfis, quamprimum id fieri poffit, foffam vel fulcum illum tranfverfum effodi curabunt, aut ubi loci afperitate terra fodi non poffit, lapides faltem ingentes pro terminis conftitui, ac præcipue pyramides ipfas in locis a nobis fuperius defcriptis fundari atque erigi. Quibus ambabus hoc infuper adjiciendum fancivimus, uti arma feu principum prædictorum infignia infculpantur; ita fcilicet, ut quod latus utriufque pyramidis quod occidentem fpectat, dicti fereniffimi *Angliæ* regis infigniatur armis, quodque orientem refpicit præfatæ illuftriffimæ reginæ *Scotiæ* armis condecoretur; atque in hunc modum honori principum bene de patria meritorum, tum etiam commodo rudioris populi, quo melius ex iftis fignis divifionis hujus difcrimina percipiant, confultum efto.—*Rymer, tom.* 15. *p.* 315.

No. II.

PRIVILEGES of the Order of SEMPRINGHAM.

HENRICUS Dei gratia, rex *Angliæ* et *Franciæ*, et dominus *Hiberniæ*, Omnibus ad quos præfentes literæ pervenerint, falutem. Infpeximus cartam domini *Edwardi* nuper regis *Angliæ* progenitoris noftri factam in hæc verba: EDWARDUS Dei gratia, rex *Angliæ*, dominus *Hiberniæ*, et dux *Aquitaniæ*, Archiepifcopis, epifcopis, abbatibus, prioribus, comitibus, baronibus, jufticiariis, vicecomitibus, præpofitis, miniftris, et omnibus ballivis et fidelibus fuis, falutem. Infpeximus cartam bonæ memoriæ domini *Henrici* quondam regis *Angliæ* proavi noftri in hæc verba: HENRICUS Dei gratia, rex *Angliæ*, dominus *Hiberniæ*, dux *Aquitaniæ*, et comes *Andegaviæ*, Archiepifcopis, epifcopis, abbatibus, prioribus, comitibus, baronibus, jufticiariis, foreftariis, vicecomitibus, præpofitis, miniftris, et omnibus ballivis et fidelibus fuis, falutem. Sciatis, nos recepiffe in noftram propriam manum et cuftodiam et protectionem et defenfionem, domum de SEMPRINGHAM, et omnes domos ejufdem ordinis, videlicet, de *Haverbolm*, de *Chikefand*, et de *Catteleio*, et de *Lincoln*, et de *Ormefby*, et de *Alvingham*, et de *Novoloco*, et de *Watton*, et de *Malton*, et de *Sancto Andrea de Eboraco*, et de *Marefeia*, et de *Huldam*, et de . . . . . . cum omnibus membris ad prædictas domos pertinentibus, et magiftros ipfius ordinis, et omnes priores et canonicos et fanctimoniales et fratres illius ordinis, et homines eorum, et fervientes, terras et poffeffiones, et omnes res fuas, ficut dominicam et fpecialem et liberam eleemofynam noftram. Quare volumus et firmiter præcipimus, ut omnia tenementa fua teneant bene et in pace, libere et quiete, et integre, et plenarie, et honorifice, in bofco et plano, in pratis et pafcuis, in aquis et pifcariis, et vivariis, in ftream et ftrande, in foreftis, in molendinis et ftagnis, in toftis et croftis et virgultis, in viis et femitis: Et fint quieti, tam ipfi quam homines eorum, in civitate et

2   burgo,

burgo, in foris et nundinis, in tranfitu pontium et maris portuum, et in
omnibus locis per totam *Angliam* et *Normanniam*, et per omnes terras noftras
et aquas, de thelonio, et pontagio, et paffagio, et pedagio, et leftagio, et
ftallagio, et hidagio, et carucagio, et wardis, et operibus caftellorum et pontium et parcorum et wallorum et foffarum, et vectigalibus, et tributis, et
exercitu, et equitatione ad . . . . averia foreftæ, et de efcapio . . . .
. . . ubique in . . . . et in *Nottinghamfhire*, et in *Weftmerland*, per
totam terram noftram de *Malreftang* ; et de omnibus geldis, et danegeldis, et
wodegeldis, et fengeld, et horngeld, et fotgeld, et penigeldis, et thendıng-
peny, et hundredefpeny, et de mifkenning, et de thenagio, et de hevedpenny,
et buckftall, et triftris, et de omnibus mifericordiis, et merciamentis, et
forisfacturis, et auxiliis, et wapentaciis, et civitatibus, et tridingis, hundredis,
et fciris, et thenemanetale, et de murdro, et latrocinio, et conceylis, et ut . .
. . . . . hamfoka, grithbritch, blotwit, futwit, et forftall, et hengwite, et
lairwite ; et fint liberi de fcotto, et wardepenny, et bordefhalpenny, et ab
omni carreio, et fumagio, et navigio, et domuum regalium ædificatione, et
omnimoda operatione, et de omnibus auxiliis vicecomitum et miniftrorum
fuorum, et fcutagio, et affifis, et donis, et fummonitionibus, et tallagiis, et
franceplegiis, et de borthevenlig, et omnibus placitis, et querelis, et occafionibus, et confuetudinibus, et de averiis fuis in namium capiendis, et de omni
terreno fervicio et feculari exactione. Sylvæ eorum ad prædicta opera, vel
ad alia aliqua, nullo modo capiantur.   Habeant quoque prædicti canonici et
moniales et fratres curiam fuam et jufticiam, cum faka, et foka, et thol, et
theam, et infangethef, et utfangethef, et flemenefrith, et ordel, et orefte,
infra tempus et extra, et cum omnibus aliis liberis confuetudinibus, et immunitatibus, et libertatibus, et cum omnibus placitis et querelis et quietantiis
fuis.   Præterea concedimus, et regia auctoritate a Deo nobis conceffa confirmamus, ut cum magifter eorum obierit, priores et canonici et fanctimoniales
illius ordinis liberam habeant poteftatem alium ejufdem ordinis fubftituendi,
quem de congregatione fua pars major et fanior canonice elegerit.   Cura vero
et cuftodia prædicti ordinis tam domorum quam grangiarum atque ecclefiarum five fubftantiarum in cuftodia et regimine priorum fit, quoufque fummus
illorum prior eligatur et fubftituatur.   Prohibemus etiam, ut nullus vicecomes
vel minifter feu aliqua perfona magna vel parva infra eleemofynas fuas hominem capere, ligare, verberare, interficere, vel fanguinem fundere, feu rapinam aut aliquam violentiam facere audeat, neque averia eorum de terris
eleemofynæ fuæ aliquis in namium capere præfumat, fuper forisfacturam
noftram, nec nativos et fugitivos fuos vel catalla eorum aliqua detineat nec
homines venientes ad molendina fua ullo modo impediat, nec eos vel homines
eorum pro confuetudine aliqua vel fervicio aut exactione vel pro aliqua caufa
difturbet de rebus fuis, quas hominos eorum affidare poterunt effe fuas proprias ; fed fint quieti de omnibus confuetudinibus et exactionibus et occafionibus quæ funt vel effe poffunt, et generaliter de omnibus rebus in omnibus
modis quæ ad nos vel hæredes noftros et fucceffores noftros pertinent vel
pertinere poffunt : Excepta fola jufticia mortis et membrorum.   Concedimus
etiam eis in perpetuam eleemofynam mifericordias et forisfacturas hominum
fuorum

fuorum de omnibus placitis ubicunque fuerint judicati, five in curia noftra five in alia, quantum ad nos pertinet. Et fi forte damnati fuerint homines eorum ad mortem, vel ad membrorum perditionem, vel in exilium perpetuum, prædicti canonici et moniales omnia catalla eorum habeant fine aliqua contradictione, retenta nobis per ballivos noftros executione jufticiæ de vita et membris, cujus queftum omnimodum eis concedimus. Preterea Sempringhami. enfis ecclefiæ nihil in feudum detur; fed fi opus eft ad cenfum annuum vel ad operationem fecundum utilitatem ecclefiæ folvendum. Hæc autem eis concedimus, cum omnibus libertatibus et liberis confuetudinibus, quas regia poteftas uberiores alicui ecclefiæ conferre poteft. Et prohibemus ne fuper hiis libertatibus aliquis domui de Sempringham vel aliis domibus ejufdem ordinis vel fuis membris moleftiam faciat vel gravamen, vel eorum oves aut animalia capiantur in namium, neque in communi paftura imparcentur, fuper forisfacturam noftram decem librarum, et fuper forisfacturam vicecomitum vigiâti folidorum, ficut confirmatio domini *Johannis* regis patris noftri quam inde habent teftatur. Sufcepimus infuper in cuftodiam et fpecialem protectionem noftram domos fubfcriptas ejufdem ordinis de novo fundatas, videlicet, domos de *Ellerton*, et de *Ferdham*, et de . . . . cum omnibus membris et pertinentiis fuis, ita quod eas teneant bene et in pace, libere et quiete et integre, cum omnibus libertatibus et liberis confuetudinibus fupradictis. Et fi aliquis verfus aliquam domorum prædictarum aliquid de poffeffionibus fuis clamaverit, five eos in aliquo vexare vel in placitum ponere voluerit, prohibemus ne pro aliquo refpondeant, neque in placitum intrent, nec aliquis eos placitare faciat, nifi coram nobis vel hæredibus noftris vel capitali jufticiario noftro vel hæredum noftrorum, vel coram jufticiariis noftris itinerantibus. Hiis teftibus, *Jocelino Bathon'* et *Ricardo Sareft'* epifcopis, *Huberto de Burgo* comite *Kantiæ* jufticiario *Angliæ*, *Hugone de Nevill*, *Martino de Patteftill*, *Radulpho de Trublevill*, *Ricardo de Argent'* fenefcallo noftro, *Henrico de Capella*, et aliis. Datum per manum venerabilis patris *Radulphi Cyceftrienis* epifcopi cancellarii noftri apud *Weftminfter*, fextodecimo die *Martii*, anno regni noftri undecimo.—Nos autem conceffiones et confirmationem prædictas ratas habentes et gratas, eas pro nobis et hæredibus noftris, quantum in nobis eft, dilectis nobis in Chrifto magiftro, prioribus, canonicis, et factimonialibus, ac fratribus illius ordinis et fucceforibus fuis concedimus et confirmamus, ficut carta prædicta rationabiliter teftatur. Præterea volentes eifdem magiftro, prioribus, canonicis, et fanctimonialibus, ac fratribus illius ordinis gratiam facere ampliorem, conceffimus eis et hac carta noftra confirmavimus, pro nobis et hæredibus noftris, quantum in nobis eft, quod licet ipfi vel prædeceffores fui pro fe et hominibus fuis aliqua vel aliquibus libertatum feu quietantiarum in dicta carta contentarum, aliquo cafu emergente hactenus ufi non fuerint, iidem tamen magifter, priores, canonici, et fanctimoniales, ac fratres, et eorum fucceffores, pro fe et omnibus fuis, eifdem libertatibus et quietantiis et earum qualibet de cætero plene gaudeant et utantur, fine occafione vel impedimento noftri vel hæredum noftrorum, jufticiariorum, efcheetorum, vicecomitum, coronatorum, aut aliorum ballivorum feu miniftrorum noftrorum quorumcunque. Conceffimus infuper, et hac carta noftra confirmamus,

pro

pro nobis et hæredibus noftris, eifdem magiftro, prioribus, · canonicis, et fanctimonialibus, ac fratribus prædicti ordinis, quod ipfi et fucceffores fui et eorum homines de omnibus bonis fuis in perpetuum fint quieti de pannagio et muragio per totum regnum noftrum et poteftatem noftram. Sufcepimus, infuper in cuftodiam et fpecialem protectionem noftram, domum Sancti *Edmundi de Cantebrigg* ejufdem ordinis de novo fundatam, ita quod eam teneant bene et in pace, libere et quiete et integré, cum omnibus libertatibus et liberis confuetudinibus fupradictis. Hiis teftibus venerabilibus patribus *H. Lincolnienfi* epifcopo cancellario noftro, et *A: Wigornienfi* epifcopo, *Johanne de Eltham* comite *Cornubiæ* fratre noftro chariffimo, *Johanne de Warnelm*, comite *Gurr'. Rogero de Mortuo mari* comite *Marchiæ*, *Olivero de Ingham*, et *Johanne Mautravers* fenefchallo hofpitii noftri, et aliis. Datum per manum noftram apud *Wodeftock*, tricefimo die Aprilis, anno regni noftri quarto.—Nos autem cartam prædictam de hujufmodi libertatibus, franchefiis, et quietantiis minime revocatis, DE AVISAMENTO ET ASSENSU DOMINORUM SPIRITUALIUM ET TEM-PORALIUM IN PARLIAMENTO NOSTRO apud Weftminfter anno regni noftri primo tento exiftente, acceptamus, approbamus, et dilectis nobis in Chrifto magiftro, prioribus, canonicis, et fanctimonialibus, ac fratribus illius ordinis, et fucceffolibus fuis confirmamus, prout carta prædicta rationabiliter teftatur; prout iidem magifter, priores, canonici, fanctimoniales, ac fratres et præde-ceffores fui libertatibus, franchefiis, et quietanciis prædictis uti et gaudere debent, ipfique et eorum prædeceffores libertatibus, franchefiis, et quietanciis illis a tempore confectionis cartæ prædictæ femper hactenus rationabiliter uti et gaudere confueverunt. In cujus rei teftimonium has literas noftras fieri fecimus patentes. Tefte meipfo apud *Weftminfter* duodecimo die Julii, anno regni noftri fextodecimo.

> Examinatur et concordat cum origine remanente inter evidentias domini regis apud Turrim five Palatium extra muros civitatis Ebor'.
>
> Per me Thomam Sandwick, cuftodem evidentiarum ibidem.

No. III.

Lift of the Provofts of Queen's college in Oxford.

Richard de Retteford, D. D. 1340.
John de Hotham, D. D.
Henry de Whytfield.
Thomas de Carlifle.
Roger Welpdale bifhop of Carlifle.
Walter Bell. 1420.
Rowland del Byrys. 1427.
Thomas Eglesfield. 1439.
William Spencer. 1442.

John Peyrfon. 1449.
Henry Booft. 1473.
Thomas Langton, LL. D. 1489.
Chriftopher Bainbrigge, archbifhop of York and cardinal. 1495:
Edward Rigge. 1508.
John a Pantrey. 1534.
William Devenyfh. 1558.
Hugh Hodgfon, M. A. 1559.
Thomas Francis, M. D. 1559.
Lancelot Shaw, B. D. 1563.
Alan Scott, M. A. 1565.
Bartholomew Bousfield, M. A. 1575.
Henry Robinfon, bifhop of Carlifle. 1581.
Henry Airay, B. D. 1598.
Barnaby Potter, bifhop of Carlifle. 1616.
Chriftopher Potter, D. D. 1626.
Gerard Langbaine, M. A. 1645.
Thomas Barlow, bifhop of Lincoln. 1658.
Timothy Halton, D. D.
William Lancafter, D. D. 1704.
John Gibfon, D. D.
Jofeph Smith, D. D. 1731.
Jofeph Brown, D. D. 1756.
Thomas Fothergill, D. D. 1767.

No. IV.

Perambulation of the foreft of Englewood, 29 Ed. 1.

EDWARDUS, &c. Omnibus ad quos, &c. falutem. Sciatis, quod cum communitas regni noftri nobis conceffit quintam decimam omnium bo_norum fuorum mobilium, quæ habebunt in fefto fancti Michaelis proxime futuro extunc taxandam; quæ quidem quinta decima poft hujufmodi taxationem colligi debet et levari et fideliter nobis folvi: Volumus et concedimus, pro nobis et hæredibus noftris, quod perambulatio facta coram dilectis et fidelibus noftris Johanne de Lythgrenys et fociis fuis ad hoc affignatis per præceptum noftrum de forefta noftra in comitatu Cumbriæ de cætero teneatur et obferve_tur per metas et bundas contentas in eadem perambulatione; cujus tenor de verbo fequitur in hunc modum. Perambulatio foreftæ domini regis de Ingle-wood in comitatu Cumbriæ facta die Sabbati proxime poft feftum apoftolorum Petri et Pauli, anno regis E. filii Henrici xxviij°, coram Johanne de Lyth-grenys, Johanne Byronne, Hafculpho de Clefeby, Michaele de Harclay, Ada de Crukdake, et Ricardo Liffell, in præfentia Hugonis de Louthre loco Ro-berti Clifford jufticiarii foreftarum domini regis ultra Trentham per literas

ipfius

ipfius Roberti patentes pofiti et affignàti, atque per vifum viridariorum foreftæ
de Inglewood et aliorum in eadem forefta ad perambulationem prædictam con-
vocatorum, et per facramentum Thomæ de Derwentwater, Johannis de Lucy,
Roberti de Johnby, Roberti de Wytrigge, Thomæ de Newton, Alexandri de
Baffenthwaite, militum; Roberti de Croglyn, Adæ Hoton, Roberti Tympauron, Johannis Stafold, Adæ Whytebregh, et Willielmi Ofmonderlow: Qui
dicunt fuper facramentum fuum, quod recta perambulatio foreftæ de Inglewood facta eft per metas et divifas fubfcriptas ; viz. Primo, Incipiendo ad pontem de Caldew extra civitatem de Caerlile per magnum iter ferratum ufque
Thorefbie verfus auftrum; et de Thorefbie per idem iter per medium villæ de
Thorefbie ufque Wafpatrickwath fuper ripam de Wathempole; et fic de Wafpatrickwath afcendendo per aquam de Wathempole ufque ad quendam locum
ubi Shauke cadit in Wathempole; et fic de illo loco afcendendo directe ufque
ad caput de Rowland Bek; et fic de illo loco defcendendo ufque ad aquam de
Caldbeck; et fic per illam aquam defcendendo ad locum ubi Caldbeck cadit
in Caldew; et afcendendo ufque ad Gyrgwath; et fic per magnum iter de
Sourbye ufque Stanewath fubter caftellar' de Sourbye; et ita per iter ferratum
afcendendo ad Mabil croffe; et deinde ufque ad collem de Kenwathen; et de
Kenwathen defcendendo per fæpedictum iter per medium villæ de Aleynby;
et ita per idem iter per medium villæ de Blencowe; et item per idem iter
ufque ad Palat; et ita defcendendo per idem iter ufque ad pontem de Amote;
et fic de illo ponte defcendendo per ripam de Amote ufque in Eden; et fic defcendendo per aquam de Eden ufque ad locum ubi Caldew cadit in Eden; et
de illo loco ufque ad pontem de Caldew fupradictum extra portum civitatis
Caerlile. Et quicquid continetur infra divifas præfcriptas dominica foreftæ domini regis E. nunc in forefta remaneat. In cujus rei teftimonium, tam prædictus Johannes de Lythgrenys et focii fui, quam perambulatores predicti,
huic perambulationi figilla fua appofuerunt: Datum apud Penrith, die et anno
fupradictis. Ita quod quicquid per iftam perambulationem ponitur extra foreftam remaneat extra foreftam, et refiduum remaneat in forefta, fecundum
metas et bundas prædictas imperpetuum. In cujus rei teftimonium, has literas
noftras fieri fecimus patentes. Tefte meipfo apud Lincoln xiv die Februarii
anno regni noftri vicefimo nono.

No. V.

Grant of lands in SEATON to the abbey of Holme Cultram.

UNIVERSIS fanctæ matris ecclefiæ filiis, Gunilda filia Henrici filii Arturi,
salutem in domino. Noverit univerfitas veftra me meræ charitatis intuitu,
in libera poteftate et viduitate mea, dediffe, conceffiffe et hac præfenti carta
mea confirmaffe, Deo et beatæ Mariæ de Holmcoltram et monachis ibidem
Deo fervientibus, in liberam et perpetuam eleemofynam, pro falute animæ
meæ et omnium antecefforum et fuccefforum meorum, totam terram meam

quam

quam Henricus pater meus dedit mihi in maritagium et carta fua confirmavit in Lekeley, cum omnibus pertinentiis et aifiamentis ad eandem terram pertinentibus, fine ullo retenemento, in bofco, in plano, in agris, in culturis, in pratis, pafcuis, et pafturis, in aquis et molendinis, et omnibus aliis locis et rebus, libere, quiete, pacifice, integre, et honorifice, ab omni feculari fervitio, confuetudine, exactione (falvo forinfeco fervitio quantum pertinet ad tantam terram de feodo unius militis de tota 'terra quæ eft inter Eſk et Doden). Præterea, dedi et conceffi et hac præfenti charta mea confirmavi eifdem monachis et hominibus ipforum, omnes libertates mihi conceffas per cartam Henrici filii Arturi patris mei, fcilicet ut habeant fcalingas ubi utilius vifum fuerit in Crocherch, et communem pafturam cum hominibus prædicti Henrici filii Arturi et hæredum et fucceſſorum fuorum. Et ut animalia eorum et hominum fuorum tam longe eant ad pafcendum in foreftam prædicti Henrici et hæredum et fucceſſorum fuorum ubi voluerint, ut noctibus poffint redire domum. Et fi forte contigerit animalia fua una nocte in forefta manere abfque confuetudine, fine placito et calumpnia domum redire permittentur. Hanc autem prædictam terram cum omnibus pertinentiis, ego et hæredes et fucceſſores mei warrantizabimus præfatis monachis contra omnes homines in perpetuum. In cujus rei teftimonium, &c.—*Regiſtr. Holme.*

No. VI.

Confirmation of grants to CALDER ABBEY by king Hen. 2.

HENRICUS rex, &c. falutem. Sciatis, nos intuitu Dei et pro falute animæ noftræ et animarum anteceſſorum et hæredum noftrorum, conceffiffe et hac carta noftra confirmaffe abbati et monachis de KALDRA, omnes terras et tenementa fubfcripta; viz. Ex dono *Radulphi Mefchin* terram de *Kaldra*, cum pertinentiis fuis, in qua abbatia de Kaldra fundata eft; et *Bemertone* et *Holegate*, cum omnibus pertinentiis fuis; et unam manfuram in burgo de *Egremount*; et duas falinas de *Withane*; et pifcariam de *Derewent*; et pifcariam de *Egre*; et pafcua ad omnia animalia eorum in forefta ipfius *Radulphi*, quantum eis opus fuerit; et ea quæ neceffaria fuerint falinis et pifcariis fuis, et ædificiis domorum fuarum, et porcis fuis fine pafnagio, per totam terram prædicti *Radulphi*, ficut fuis propriis.—Ex dono *Johannis filii Adæ* et *Matthei* fratris ejus, totam terram de *Stavenerge* cum pertinentiis fuis.—Ex dono *Roberti Bonekill* unam carucatam terræ in *Parvo Gillecruz*, quam Radulphus clericus de Karl' tenuit, cum omnibus pertinentiis fuis; et 12 acras et unam perticatam terræ in *Minori Gillecruz*; et unam acram prati quod eft inter *Minorem Gillecruz* et *Majorem Gillecruz*; et pafturam ad 20 boves et 12 vaccas et 6 equos cum fequela eorum unius anni.—Ex dono *Rogeri filii Willielmi*, totam terram quam habet in *Ikelinton* et *Brachampton*, et totam partem quam habet in molendino de *Brachampton.*—Ex dono *Richardi de Lucy*, medietatem molendini de *Ikelinton*, cum tota fequela ad ipfam medietatem molendini pertinente.—Ex dono *Beatricis*

Beatricis de Molle, quinque bovatas terræ cum pertinentiis fuis in *Minori Gille-cruch,* et quartam partem molendini de *Majori Gillecruch.*—Ex dono *Thomæ filii Gofpatricii* unum toftum fex perticarum & quartæ partis unius perticatæ in longitudine et quatuor in latitudine in *Wirkintone;* et 40 *Salmones* annuatim ad feftum Sancti Johannis Baptiftæ; et unum rete in *Derewent,* inter pontem et mare —Ex dono *Thomæ de Moleton* medietatem villæ de *Dereham* in Alredale, cum advocatione ecclefiæ ejufdem villæ, et cum omnibus aliis pertinentiis fuis. Quare volo, &c. quod prædicti abbas et monachi et eorum fucceffores habeant et teneant omnes terras et tenementa prædicta, bene et in pace, liberæ et integre, cum omnibus libertatibus et liberis confuetudinibus ad prædictas terras et tenementa pertinentibus, ficut cartæ prædictorum donatorum quas inde habent rationabiliter teftantur. Hiis teftibus; H. de Burgo, S. de Sedgrave, Philippo de Albini, Radulpho filio Nicholai, Godefrido de Craucumbe, G. difpenfatore, H. de Capella, et aliis. Datum apud Weftmonafterium 19 die Aprilis.—1 *Dugd. Mon.* 774.

No. VII.

Inquifition post mortem of MAUD DE PERCY.

INQUISITIO capta apud Cockermouth die Lunæ in fefto Sancti Matthei apoftoli, poft mortem Matildis uxoris Henrici de Percy comitis Northumbriæ fuperftitis.—Juratores dicunt, Quod dicta Matildis conjunctim fefita fuit cum prædicto comite fuperftite in dominico fuo ut de feodo talliato per finem, cum licentia regis, de caftro et honore de *Cokermouth* cum fuis pertinentiis; et de manerio de *Papcaftre* cum pertinentiis, quod ad dictum caftrum et honorem pertinet; et de maneriis de *Wigton, Brathewayt, Lowfewater, Dene, Caldbeke,* et *Ulnedale;* et medietate de *Afpatrik;* et de 2 meffuagiis cum fuis pertinentiis in Carlio'o; 4000 acris pafturæ, 4000 acris bofci, cum pertinentiis, in le *Weftwarde* in *Allerdale;* et de reverfione tertiæ partis baroniæ de *Egremond* cum fuis pertinentiis, quam Johanna de Grayftock tenet in dotem ex hæritatione ipforum comitis et Matildis; et de advocatione ecclefiarum de *Dene,* et *Kirkebride,* et *Ulnedale,* et capellæ Sancti *Leonardi de Wigton* in dicto comitatu; et de reverfione alterius medietatis manerii de *Afpatrik* cum fuis pertinentiis; et de reverfione advocationis ecclefiæ de *Ulnedale,* quam Johanna de Grayftock tenet in dotem ad totam vitam fuam, ex hæreditate ipforum comitis et Matildis: Habenda eifdem Henrico et Matildi et hæredibus mafculis de corporibus ipforum exeuntibus, de domino rege et hæredibus fuis per fervitia inde debita et confueta. Ita quod fi iidem Henricus et Matildis fine hærede mafculo de corporibus fuis obierint, tunc omnia prædicta hæredibus de corpore dictæ Matildis exeuntibus integre remaneant. Ita quod, fi prædicta Matildis fine hærede de corpore fuo obierit, tunc omnia prædicta integre remaneant Henrico Percy filio prædicti comitis et hæredibus mafculis de corpore fuo exeuntibus. Ita quod ipfe et dicti hæredes fui mafculi arma prædicti comitis

(quæ

(quæ funt de auro cum uno leone de, azuro rampante) quarteriata cum armis de Lucy (quæ de goulhs cum tribus Lucys argenteis confiftunt) gerat, in om‑ nibus vexillis, penonibus, tunicis armorum, et in omnibus aliis armaturis. quæ de picturarùm, cognitionum, armorum folito competunt adornari, quotiens cognitiones armorum in actibus bellicis vèl alibi oftendere voluerint. Ita quod, fi idem Henricus filius prædicti comitis fine hærede mafculo de corpore fuo exeunte obierit, tunc poft mortem ejufdem Henrici filii prædicti comitis, omnia prædicta integre remaneant Thomæ Percy chr. fratri prædicti comitis et hære‑ dibus mafculis de corpore fuo exeuntibus. Dicta Matildis obiit die Mercurii proxime ante feftum Natalis Domini ultimo præteriti. Et Guillielmus de Mel‑ ton chr. eft ejus proprius hæres, nempe, filius Johannæ de Melton fororis do‑ mini Thomæ de Lucy patris prædictæ Matildis; et dictus Guillielmus eft æta‑ tis 40 annorum et amplius.——*Efcheat.* 22 *Ric.* 2.

No. VIII.

Rules and orders for the Burghers of EGREMONT.

SCIANT tam præfentes quam futuri, quod ego *Richardus de Lucy* dedi, et hac præfenti charta mea confirmavi, burgenfibus meis de Acrimonte et hæ‑ redibus fuis, has fcilicet fubfcriptas leges, libertates, et confuetudines haben‑ das de me et hæredibus meis; fcilicet, Quod iidem burgenfes non debent ire extra portas burgi de Acrimonte per alicujus fummonitionem nifi ad januam caftelli cum domino vel ejus fenefcallo ad namium capiendum vel ftricturam faciendam intra Coupland. Et fciendam eft, quod fi werra advenerit, iidem burgenfes mei invenient mihi et hæredibus meis 12 homines cum armis fuis in caftello meo defendendo de Acrimonte per 40 dies ad eorum proprias expenfas; in cæteris vero, pannos et cibos et aliud mercatorium mihi accredent per dies 40: et fi eis debitum fuum intra terminum non perfolvero, non teneantur mihi alia mercatoria fua accredere, donec debitum fuum reddidero. Item, debent mihi auxilium ad faciendum militem unum de filiis meis: et illud auxilium dabunt ad maritandum unam ex filiabus meis. Item, fi necefle fuerit ad corpus meum vel hæredum meorum redimendum, mihi auxilium dabunt. Item, aliud auxilium mihi facient, quando milites terræ meæ mihi auxiliabuntur, et illud debet fieri per 12 burgenfium. Et dabunt multuram ad molendinum meum, fcilicet tertium decimum vas de proprio blado fuo; de blado fuo vero empto, dabunt fextum decimum. Item, fi quis emerit burgagium, dabit mihi 4 de‑ narios de feifina fua. Item, fi quis burgenfis fummonitus fuerit rationabiliter per leges fuas veniendi ad placita burgi, et defecerit; dabit 6 denarios. Item, burgenfes mei quieti erunt de pannagio fuo, intra divifas fuas de porcis fuis, fcilicet, a Crokerbec ufque ad rivulum de Culderrun (falvo maeremio). Et fciendum eft, quod fi porci fui exeunt prædictas divifas, dabunt mihi panna‑ gium, fc. vicefimum porcum. Et fi forte aliquis burgenfium habeat unum viginti porcos, dabit mihi pro unoquoque porco denarium. Et fi porci fui
venient

venient fine licentia mea in foreftam meam Innerdale, dabunt efchapium. Item, vigiliæ burgi debent incipere a burgenfibus; et fi quis defecerit in eifdem vigiliis dabit mihi 6 denarios. Item, fi burgenfis ceciderit in placito, pro defectu refponfi; dabit 4 denarios domino de forisfacto, et recuperabit placitum fuum. Item, fi convicium apertum dixerit aliquis burgenfis vicino fuo, dabit domino tres folidos pro forisfacto, fi ipfe convictus fuerit inde. Et fi quis percufferit vicinum fuum fine fanguine tracto, dabit domino pro forisfacto tres folidos, fi inde convictus fuerit. Et fi quis traxerit fanguinem de vicino fuo cum armis, dabit domino pro forisfacto 18 folidos, fi convictus fuerit. Item, talis eft confuetudo burgenfium, et viventium omnium fecundum legem villæ, fi latrocinium alicui prædictorum imponitur, purgabit fe per 36 homines, femel, fecundo, tertio, et poftea ejectus erit a communione burgi, et omnia catalla fua et domus ejus et omnia quæ poffidet faifiabuntur in manu domini. Item, fi quis verberaverit præpofitum villæ, dabit domino pro forisfacto dimidiam marcam, fi inde convictus fuerit; et fi traxerit fanguinem de eo, quoquo modo fuerit, dabit domino pro forisfacto 18 folidos, fi inde convictus fuerit. Item, præpofitus debet fieri per electionem burgenfium. Item, fi aliquis burgenfis vendiderit res fuas alicui non burgenfi, et ille noluerit reddere; licet eidem burgenfi capere namium fuum intra burgum, fine alicujus licentia. Item, fi aliquis burgenfis voluerit vendere terram fuam, fc. burgagium fuum, licet ei vendere et ire libere ubi voluerit. Item, fi burgenfis emerit burgagium intra villam et ille tenuerit per annum et diem abfque calumpnia alicujus; terra illi remanebit quieta, nifi aliquis poffit monftrare jus fuum, et extra regnum fuerit in negotiatione vel peregrinatione. Item, fi uxor burgenfis dixerit aliquod convitium vicinæ fuæ, et illa inde convicta fuerit; dabit domino pro forisfacto 4 denarios. Item, omnes burgenfes et liberi eorum quieti erunt a theolonio in tota terra mea de propriis catallis burgenfium. Item, licet burgenfibus ire in forefta mea de Innerdale, ad mercatorium fuum faciendum, fine arcu et fagittis. Item, fi aliquis extraneus venerit in burgum, et fit burgenfis per annum et diem fine calumpnia alicujus; liber deinceps remanebit, nifi fit de dominico regis. Item burgenfes not amputabunt pedes canum fuorum intra divifas fuas: et fi forte aliquis canis fequitur aliquem burgenfem extra divifas fuas in via, excepta forefta mea de Innerdale, non calumpniabitur inde a quoquam. Item, burgenfes non placitabunt pro aliqua re ad me pertinente, extra placitum burgi; nifi de forefta mea, et de corona regis. Item, fi aliquis qui vixerit fecundum legem villæ fornicatus fuerit cum filia alicujus ruftici intra burgum; non dabit merchet, nifi eam defponfaverit. Item, fiquis burgenfis non ædificaverit burgum fuum intra terminum fibi ftatutum, fcilicet intra annum; dabit domino pro forisfacto 12 denarios. Item, affeffus tinctorii, textorii, fullonici debent fieri per vifum 12 burgenfium; et fi quis ftatutum eorum tranfgreffus fuerit, dabit domino pro forisfacto 12 denarios, fi inde convictus fuerit. Item, licet burgenfibus emere quicquid voluerint intra burgum, et vendere, fine calumpnia alicujus. Item, burgenfes qui carucas habent, arabunt mihi uno die, de mane ufque ad nonam, annuatim, ad fummonitionem præpofiti mei; et unumquodque burgagium inveniet unum hominem in autumno ad metendum, et habebunt prandium fuum quando arabunt:

L   bunt:

bunt et metent. Et fciendum eft, quod pro hoc fervitio habebunt communem
pafturam de Corkerbec ufque ad prædictum rivulum de Culdertun, quando
prædicta paftura vacua fit a blado et fœno domini. Item burgenfes capiant neceffaria ad propria ædificia fua intra prædictas divifas, fine vifu foreftariorum
(falvo maeremio). Item, fciendum eft, quod fi forte animalia burgenfium
tranfeant ultra rivulum de Culdertun, dabunt in æftate pro decem animalibus
unum denarium, et pro quinquies viginti ovibus unum denarium. Hiis teftibus ; D. abbate de Chaldra, Roberto priore de Sancta Bega, Henrico filio Arthuri, Alano filio Ketelli, Willielmo fratre ejus, Hugone filio Sywardi, Alano
Benedicto, Gilberto filio Gilberti, Roberto de Haverington, Ada de Land-
plogh, Ricardo Anketill, Roberto de Willona.

No. IX.

Foundation charter of the Priory of SAINT BEES.

WILLIELMUS filius Ranulphi, Turftino Eboraci archiepifcopo, et
omnibus fanctæ matris Eboraci ecclefiæ parochianis, tam clericis quam
laicis, præfentibus et futuris, falutem. Pium eft ut fancta Dei ecclefia, et
filiis et filiabus fuis, dilatetur et amplificetur. Ea propter, dedi et præfenti
chartula confirmavi ecclefiæ fanctæ Mariæ Eboracenfis cænobii, ecclefiam
Sanctæ Begæ, quæ eft fita in Cauplandia, et feptem carucatas terræ quietas et
folutas ab omni feculari fervicio. Reddidi etiam et dedi eidem ecclefiæ parochiam fuam, ficut teftimonio proborum virorum in dedicatione ejufdem ecclefiæ probata eft, viz. quicquid. continetur a *Witchena* ufque ad *Chechel,* et
ficut eadem *Chechel* cadit in mare ; et nominatim, capellam de *Egremund,* quæ
eft fita inter prædictos terminos : Et decimas dominii mei, et omnium hominum meorum qui manent in Egremund : Et decimas pifcariarum mearum de
Cauplandia : Nec non et decimam porcorum, et carnis venationis meæ, per
totam Cauplandiam : Et decimam pannagii mei, et decimam vaccariarum mearum, per totam Cauplandiam. Et fi quis, ex mea permiffione vel donatione,
infra foreftam meam pecuniam * fuam habebit ; ex ea, ficut ex mea, monachi
habebunt decimationem. Et infuper, unoquoque anno 20 folidos de decima
cenfus mei de Cauplandia, five crefcat five decrefcat. Concedo etiam donum
quietum quod *Wallef* dedit eidem ecclefiæ viz. *Stainburn*, et quod *Chetellus*
donavit, viz. *Preftonam* : et quod donavit *Raynerus,* viz. duas bovatas terræ in
Rotingtona; et unum rufticum manentem in eadem villa ; et quod donavit
Godardus, viz. ecclefias de *Witingham* et *Bothele,* cum duabus manfuris et totis
parochiis, et decimas eifdem ecclefiis pertinentes ; et quod donavit *Willielmus*
filius *Gilberti de Lancaftria,* viz. *Swartahef* : omnia quieta in eleemofynam, et
fine omni terreno fervitio. Et fciendum, quod omnes has eleemofynas dedi
prædictæ abbatiæ *Eboraci,* confilio Turftini archiepifcopi, et uxoris meæ Ce-

* fc. cattle.

ciliæ

ciliæ, et hominum meorum, et conceffione Ranulphi filii mei tali conventione et paéto, ut ibi fit cella monachorum ; et abbas Eboraci et capitulum femper mittant et habeant in ecclefia *Sanétæ Begæ* Priorem, et cum eo fex monachos ad minus refidentes, et fervientes ibidem domino. Concedo etiam quicquid homines mei impofterum ibi, confilio meo vel hæredum meorum dabunt. Hanc autem eleemofynam feci, pro falute domini mei Henrici regis Angliæ, et pro anima Matildis reginæ, et Willielmi filii eorum, et pro falute Turftini archiepifcopi, et pro remedio antecefforum meorum et meo et uxoris meæ, et liberorum meorum, et fidelium meorum. Teftibus hiis ; Turftino archiepifcopo, et Willielmo archidiacono, Aufrado et Ricardo capellanis ejus, Rainaldo capellano meo, Siwardo prefbytero, Godardo, Rainero, Wallef, Chetello, Odardo, Ricardo, et multis aliis.— 1 *Dugd. Mon.* 395.

No. X.

Ifland in DERWENTWATER confecrated to ST. HERBERT.

THOMAS permiffione divina Karliolenfis epifcopus, diléto filio vicario de Crofthwaite, &c. Dignum judicamus atque juftum, ut nos, qui ex debito officii noftri teftes veritatis effe tenemur, perhibeamus teftimonium veritati fanæ. Siquidem nobis fuper facras paginas legentibus, inter cætera comperimus, venerabilem Bedam prefbyterum, doétorem famofiffimum, in libro fuo de geftis Anglorum fcripfiffe et teftimonium perhibuiffe, HERBERTUM prefbyterum, difcipulum Sanéti Cuthberti fuiffe, qui in infula fluvii Derwentioris vitam duxit folitariam atque fanétam ; tamen fanétum Cuthbertum femel in anno annis fingulis vifitare, et monita falutaria ab eo recipere. Contigit autem, diétum Sanétum Cuthbertum apud civitatem Luguballiam, quæ nunc Carleolum nominatur, advenire. Quod audiens diétus Herbertus, more folito ad eum acceffit. Cui fanétus Cuthbertus, inter cætera narravit diffolutionem fui corporis infra breve imminere ; et quod hoc fuit fibi divinitus revelatum. Quod audiens diétus Herbertus, ad pedes fanéti antiftitis cum lachrymis fe projecit, deprecans eum et orans, ut a domino impetret, quod ficut ipfi in vita fua uno eodemque fpiritu dominò defervierunt, unò et eodem tempore ac fimul, morte perveniente, ab hoc fæculo tranfmigrarent. Diétus vero antiftes Cuthbertus, fuper cubitum fuum paulifper recubans, cito poft fe erexit, et Herberto prefbytero dixit ; Frater Herberte, gaude gaudio magno, quia quod a domino petivimus impetravimus. Quod non diu poftea fuerat adimpletum. Nam tertio decimo Aprivium, diétus antiftes in infula Pharenfi, et Herbertus in infula fupradiéta, ambo decefferunt. Et quia hoc fanétum faétum plurimis, ac fere omnibus, credimus effe incognitum ; nec bonum effe videtur quod hoc homines lateat, quod dominus ad gloriam fanétorum fuorum dignatus eft patefacere ; Tibi mandamus, firmiter injungentes, quatenus diéto xiii° die Aprivium ad diétam infulam Herberti accedens, et miffam de Sanéto Cuthberto etiam cum nota facias celebrari, et has literas noftras parochianis tuis publicari : adjiciens ad hoc, quod omnibus et singulis dicto die ad locum prædictum causa devotionis, et in honorem Sancti Cuthberti, et in memoriam dicti Herberti accedentibus, quadraginta dies indulgentiæ concedimus per præsentes. Scriptum apud Rosam.—From the *Regiſtr.* of bishop *Appleby.*

No. XI.

Confirmation of APPLETON and BRIDEKIRK to the priory of GISBURNE.

UNIVERSIS Sanctæ Matris Ecclesiæ filiis, ad quos præsens scriptum pervenerit, Domina Aliciâ de Rumeley, filia Willielmi filii Duncani, salutem. Noverit univerſitas veſtra, me in viduitate et libera poteſtate mea, conceſſiſſe et dediſſe, et hac præsenti carta mea confirmaſſe, Deo et ecclesiæ Sanctæ Mariæ de GYSEBURNE, et canonicis ibidem Deo servientibus, pro salute animæ meæ, et patris mei, et matris meæ, et omnium anteceſſorum et succeſſorum meorum, et maritorum meorum Gilberti Pypard et Roberti de Curtenay, villam nomine APELTON in Alnedale et ecclesiam de BRIDEKIRKE cum omnibus peitinentiis suis : Habenda et tenenda in puram et liberam et perpetuam eleemosynam. Unde volo, ut prædicti canonici habeant et teneant predictam villam de Apelton et prædictam ecclesiam, de me et hæredibus meis, ita libere et quiete, sicut aliqua eleemosyna liberius et quietius et honorificentius a viris religiosis in tota terra mea, vel in archiepiscopatu Eborum habetur et tenetur. Ut autem hæc donatio mea rata et illibata permaneat, eam præsentis scripti testimonio, et sigilli mei appositione, corroboravi. Hiis testibus ; Domino R. tunc Karleolenſi episcopo, Domino J. abbate de Fontibus, Domino N. abbate de Furneis, et aliis.—*3 Dugd. Mon. p. 46.*

No. XII.

Grant of FLIMBY to the abbey of HOLM CULTRAM.

UNIVERSIS Sanctæ Matris Ecclesiæ filiis, Cospatricius filius Ormi, salutem. Sciatis, me consilio et conceſſione Thomæ filii et hæredis mei, et Alani filii mei, et aliorum hæredum et amicorum meorum, conceſſiſſe et dediſſe ecclesiæ Sanctæ Mariæ de Holm et fratribus ibidem Deo servientibus, in liberam et puram et perpetuam eleemosynam, quietam ab omni terreno servitio et exactione et consuetudine quæ ad me et hæredes meos pertinent, FLEMINGBY cum omnibus appendiciis suis, per rectas divisas suas ; excepta terra de Waytecrofte, quam prius dederam canonicis de Karliolo : Hiis scilicet divisis, ex illa parte versus Alneburgh sicut spina quædam ducit divisam in tranſverso uſque ad Elisic ; et per Elisic in ascensu uſque ad rectam divisam
inter

inter Flemingby et Ouenrigg; et inde per rectam divifam in tranfverfo inter Waytecroft et Holegill; et inde in afcendendo ufque ad caput de Holegill; et inde ficut via ducit in tranfverfum de Waytecroft ufque ad Scalegill; et poftea in tranfverfum ufque ad Suanefate; et inde in tranfverfum ufque ad Kegill; et fic defcendendo ficut rivulus currit inter duos faltus de Nathwait, per medium bofcum ufque ad Kirnepot. Et communem pafturam de Seton et de Camberton; excepta terra arabili, et pratis, et bofco. Et communem pafturam de Kirnepot ufque ad Fulwic inter bofcum et mare; et ita quod Cofpatricius et hæredes ejus inter bofcum et mare non arabunt, nec pratum facient, nifi ubi prius fiebant, ad gravamen monachorum. Et nos fimiliter communem pafturam habebimus cum monachis in Flemingby; excepta terra arabili, et pratis, et bofco. Si autem forte pecunia monachorum evaferit infra bofcum meum, vel pecunia mea infra bofcum monachorum, ita quod non fit ex confuetudine, utrique parti remittetur abfque gravamine. Hanc autem donationem et conventionem præfcriptam, ego Cofpatricius et hæredes mei warrantizabimus et acquietabimus eifdem monachis contra omnes homines imperpetuum. Ita quod faciemus pro monachis omne forenfe et terrenum fervitium, quodcunque ad dominum regem pertinet, fcilicet, de noutegeld et . . . . et fi quod aliud pertinet ad ejus fervitium, et quodcunque fervitium pertinet ad dominum de Allerdale, fcilicet de feawake et caftleward, et de placitis et auxiliis, et de omni alia terrena exactione et confuetudine. Si vero prædictam donationem et conventionem eis warrantizare non poffumus, eis excambium dabimus ad valentiam infra Cumbreland fi potuerimus; fi vero ibi non potuerimus, nos faciemus excambium de aliis terris ubi magis fuerit ad ayfiamentum monachorum. Sciendum præterea, quod ego Cofpatricius dedi excambium pacabile et ad valentiam ecclefiæ de Camberton in eadem parochia, fcilicet in Seton, conceffione hæredum meorum, pro illa terra de Flemingby quæ adjacebat prædictæ ecclefiæ de Camberton; quam, cum reliqua præfcripta terra de Flemingby, dedi prædictis monachis in puram et liberam et perpetuam eleemofynam. Hæc donatio facta eft in pleno comitio apud Karliolum, coram R. de Vallibus, domini regis Jufticiarii de Cumberland.—*Regiftr. Holme.*

No. XIII.

Grant of free warren in FLIMBY.

EDWARDUS Dei gratia, rex Angliæ, &c. falutem. Sciatis, nos conceffiffe et hac carta mea confirmaffe, dilectis nobis in Chrifto abbati et conventui abbathiæ noftræ de Holm, quod ipfi et eorum fucceffores abbates et monachi ejufdem loci, in perpetuum habeant liberam warrenam in omnibus dominicis terris fuis manerii fui de Fleminby in comitatu Cumbriæ, dum tamen terræ illæ non fint infra metas forefdæ noftræ. Ita quod nullus intret terras illas ad fugandum in eis, vel aliquid capiendum quod ad warrenam

pertineat,

pertineat, fine licentia et voluntate ipforum abbatis et monachorum et fuccefforum fuorum, fuper forisfacturam noftram decem librarum.   Quare volumus
et firmiter præcipimus, pro nobis et hæredibus noftris, quod prædicti abbas et
conventus, et eorum fucceffores abbates et monachi ejufdem abbatiæ, in perpetuum habeant liberam warrenam in omnibus dominicis terris fuis prædictis,
dum tamen terræ illæ non fint infra metas foreftæ noftræ.   Hiis teftibus, &c.
—Regiftr. Holm.

No. XIV.

Grant of the manor of HOLME CULTRAM to the Abbey there, by
Henry fon of David king of Scots.

H ENRICUS comes, filius Davidis regis Scotiæ; Epifcopis, abbatibus,
comitibus, jufticiariis, baronibus, vicecomitibus, miniftris, et omnibus
probis hominibus totius terræ fuæ, clericis et laicis, Francis et Anglis, falutem. Sciatis, me dediffe et conceffiffe, in perpetuam eleemofynam, duas
partes HOLMCOLTRIÆ, abbati et monachis ibidem Deo fervientibus ; quas
ego, et plures homines probi mecum, perambulavimus in primis inter eos et
Alanum filium Waldeff, quando ego tertiam partem prædictæ Holmcoltriæ
prænominato Alano ad venationes fuas conceffi.   Præterea vero, concedo et
hac mea carta confirmo, donationem ejufdem Alani filii Waldeff et Waldeff
filii fui, de illa tertia fua parte Holmcoltriæ, quàm illi ad venationes fuas
conceffeRam ; quam ipfe, in præfentia patris mei et mea et baronum meorum
apud Carliolum, prædicti loci abbati et monachis in perpetuam eleemofynam
dedit et conceffit, et carta fua teftante confirmavit.   Volo itaque, ut abbas
Holmcoltriæ et monachi ibidem Deo fervientes habeant plenarie Holmcoltriam
per fuas rectas divifas, in nemore et plano, pratis et pafcuis, pifcationibus et
aquis : Et Rabi, cum fuis rectis divifis ; ficut ego et barones mei mecum
ipfas perambulavimus, inter prædictos monachos et Afchetillum filium Udardi.
Concedo etiam eis maeremium in forefta de Inglewoda, ad ædificia fua et ad
omnia domi fuæ neceffaria facienda ; et pafturam porcis eorum fine pafnagio.
Cum hiis autem prædictis infra terminos abbatiæ Holmcoltriæ et divifas fuas,
tantam pacem et libertatem conftituo, quantam abbatia de Maylros et abbatia
de Newbotla conceffione patris mei tranquillius et fanctius et quietius poffident
et poffeffionibus fuis infra perfruuntur.   Hiis teftibus ; Adelulpho Carleoli
epifcopo, Waltero priore, Waltero regis cancellario, Engerram comitis cancellario, Hugone de Morvilla, Willielmo de Sommervilla, Willielmo de
Heriz, Willielmo Engaine, Ran' de Soll', Ran' de Lindfeia, Waltero de
Ridale, Cofpatricio filio Ormi, Henrico filio Suani, Waltero filio Alani, Hugone Ridill, Alano de Laceles.——1 *Dugd. Mon.* 886.

No.

No. XV.

Confirmation thereof by David king of Scots.

DAVID rex Scotiæ, Epifcopis, abbatibus, comitibus, baronibus, vice-comitibus, præpofitis, miniftris, et omnibus probis hominibus totius terræ fuæ et filii fui, clericis et laicis, tam prefentibus quam futuris, falutem. Sciatis me conceffiffe, et hac mea carta confirmaffe, donationem filii mei de HOLMCOLTRAM, quam ipfe abbati et monachis ibidem Deo fervientibus donavit et conceffit in eleemofynam. Confirmo etiam eis aliam tertiam partem de Holmcoltram, quam Alanus filius·Waldeff eifdem monachis, pro falute animæ fuæ, dedit et conceffit ; cum·cæteris omnibus quæ carta filii fui continet et teftatur. . Hiis teftibus ; Adelulpho epifcopo Carleolenfi,. Waltero priore, &c.——*3 Dugd. Mon.* 34..

No. XVI.

Grant of lands at KIRKWINNY to the abbey of HOLME CULTRAM.

CHRISTIANUS Dei gratia, epifcopus Candidæ Cafæ, Univerfis fanctæ matris ecclefiæ filiis, tam clericis quam laicis, falutem et benedictionem. Notum fit univerfitati· veftræ,· quod, ,domini opitulante mifericordia, Deo et Ordini Ciftertienfi traditi fumus et domui de Holmcoltram, ubi et corpori noftro fepulturam elegimus : Mandamus igitur univerfitati veftræ, quatenus præfatam domum et ad eam.pertinentia, Grangiam quæ dicitur KIRKEWINNY et omnia quæ ad illam pertinent, manuteneatis et protegatis, ficut Dei et· noftram benedictionem habere defideratis. Quod fi quis contra hæc ire præ-fumpferit, et præfatæ domui de Holmcoltram vel grangiæ de Kirkewinny, vel quibuflibet eorum pertinentiis, dampnum aliquid intulerit, vel inferenti confenferit, tanquam domini Papæ et noftrum excommunicatum, omnipotentis Dei et. noftram [e maledictionem incurfurum,. et æterni incendii pœnas· luiturum fciat, nifi cum fatisfactione congrua emendaverit. Teftibus, &c.—— *3 Dugd. Mon.* 68.

No. XVII.

Grant of the church of KIRKWINNY to the abbey of HOLM CUL--TRAM.

INNOCENTIUS epifcopus fervus fervorum Dei, dilectis filiis abbati et conventui de Holmcoltram Ciftertienfis ordinis, falutem et apoftolicam be-nedictionem.

nedictionem. Sacrofancta ecclefia Romana devotos et humis filios, ex affuetæ pietatis officio, propenfius diligere confuevit; et ne pravorum hominum moleftiis agitentur, eos tanquam pia mater folita eft mifericorditer confovere: Ea propter, dilecti in Domino filii, veftris juftis poftulationibus clementius annuentes, capellam de KIRKEWYNWI in Galwychia, quám per quadraginta annos pacifice poffidetis, liberam et quietam de epifcopalibus et fynodalibus et omnibus aliis exactionibus, ex conceffione Jocelini bonæ memoriæ Glafguenfis epifcopi vobis et ecclefiæ veftræ collatam, ficut in ejus authentico continetur, devotioni veftræ auctoritate apoftolica confirmamus, et prefentis fcripti patrocinio communimus; ftatuentes, ut fi vos in aliquo gravari fenferitis, libere vobis liceat fedem apoftolicam appellare. Nulli ergo hominum liceat hanc paginam noftræ confirmationis infringere, vel ei aufu temerario contraire. Si quis autem hoc attemptare præfumpferit, indignationem omnipotentis Dei et beatorum Petri et Pauli apoftolorum ejus fe noverit incurfurum. Datum Romæ apud Sanctum Petrum, tertio Nonas Februarii, pontificatus noftri anno octavo. *Regiftr. Holm.*

No. XVIII.

Grant of St. SWITHIN's HOLME nigh Penrith to the abbey of HOLME CULTRAM.

OMNIBUS ad quorum notitiam præfens fcriptum pervenerit, Bricius de Penreth ferviens, falutem. Noverit univerfitas veftra me, pro falute animæ meæ et omnium antecefforum et fuccefforum meorum, dediffe, conceffiffe, et hac præfenti charta mea confirmaffe, Deo et Beatæ Mariæ et monachis de Holm, totam illam terram, fine aliquo retenemento, fuper aquam de Amot, quæ vocatur St. SWITHIN's HOLME; fcilicet, a fummitate cofteræ dependentis fuper eundem Holm ufque ad aquam de Amot, in latitudine et in longitudine a fummitate dictæ cofteræ, ficut foffatum extenditur ufque ad Haiam quæ eft fuper dictam aquam de Amot; in liberam, puram, et perpetuam eleemofynam. Tenendam et habendam fibi et domui fuæ de Holm, cum omnibus libertatibus, pertinentiis, et ayfiamentis ad villam de Penreth pertinentibus, cum libero et fufficienti introitu et exitu, per medium terræ meæ de Brawra; et fimiliter cum libero et fufficienti introitu et exitu ab orientali parte ejufdem Holm, ufque ad territorium de Edenhall; libere, quiete, et integre, et folute ab omni feculari fervicio, confuetudine, exactione, et demanda, ficut aliqua eleemofyna liberius, quietius, et melius alicui domui religiofæ poteft conferri. Et ego et hæredes mei dictam terram, cum omnibus pertinentiis fuis, dictis monachis et dictæ domui de Holm, contra omnes homines imperpetuum warrantizabimus et defendemus. Si autem contingat, quod ego et hæredes mei dictam terram dictis monachis et domui de Holm warrantizare non poterimus, dabimus eis tantum pratum in territorio de Penreth, quantum continetur in *Seint Wilfrid Holme*, adeo libere ficut
dictum

dictum Holme eis contuli liberius, vel terram cultam ad valentiam dicti prati; et tantam terram cultam in dicto territorio de Penreth, quanta cultura continetùr in fæpedicto † *Seint Wilfrid holm*, adeo liberam et quietam ficut prædictum *Seint Wilfrid holme* eis liberam et quietam contuli et concessi. In cujus rei, &c.——*Regiftr. Holm.*

No. XIX.

Papal confirmation of grants to the abbey of HÒLME CULTRAM, with further privileges.

CLEMENS epifcopus, fervus fervorum Dei, dilectis filiis Everardo abbati monafterii Sanctæ Mariæ de HOLMCOLTRAM ejufque fratribus, tam præfentibus quam futuris, regularem vitam profeffis in perpetuum. Religiofam vitam eligentibus, apoftolicum convenit adeffe præfidium; ne cujuflibet temeritatis incurfus aut eos a propofito revocet, aut robur (quod abfit) fanæ religionis infringat. Ea propter, dilecti in domino filii, juftis poftulationibus clementer annuimus, et præfatum monafterium fanctæ Dei genetricis et virginis Mariæ de Holmcoltram, in quo divino mancipati eftis obfequio, fub beati Petri et noftra protectione fufcepimus, et præfentis fcripti privilegio communimus : In primis fiquidem ftatuentes, ut ordo monafticus, qui fecundum domini et beati Benedicti regulam, et inftitutionem Ciftertienfium fratrum in eodem monafterio conftitutus effe dignofcitur, perpetuis ibidem temporibus inviolabiliter obfervetur. Præterea, quafcunque poffeffiones jufte et canonice poffidet, aut in futurum conceffione pontificum, largitione regum vel principum, oblatione fidelium, feu aliis juftis modis (præftante Domino) poterit adipifci; firma vobis veftrifque fucceffioribus et illibata permaneant. In quibus hæc propriis duximus exprimenda vocabulis : Ex dono illuftriffimi regis Anglorum Henrici, Dei gratia, totam infulam de *Holm* et *Rabi* cum omnibus pertinentiis fuis, fcilicet per has divifas, Per rivulum qui currit fubtus Kirkebride inter exterius foffatum monachorum et villam de Kirkebride, et cadit in Wathepol; et fic afcendendo per eundem rivulum deforis prædictum foffatum ufque ad Cokkelayk, femper ficut dura terra et muffa fibi invicem obviant; et inde afcendendo in directum ufque ad medietatem muffæ, quæ eft inter Wathie-holme et infulam fancti Lawrentii; et inde per tranfverfum muffæ et nemoris ufque ad Ainterpont; et inde defcendendo per Waver, ad locum ubi Waver et Cromboc fibi obviant; et inde afcendendo per Cromboc, ufque ad locum ubi rivulus de Wytekeld cadit in Cromboc; et inde afcendendo per ipfum rivulum ufque ad ipfum Wytekeld; et inde in directum verfus occidentem ufque ad ficam quæ circuit Middilrigg ex Septentrionali et Occidentali parte et cadit in Polneuton ufque ad locum ubi Polneuton cadit in mare; et inde per circuitum maris ufque ad locum ubi Wathepol cadit in mare; et fic afcendendo per Wathepol ufque ad locum ubi

---

† By this it feemeth that the name *St. Swithin's Holme* has been miftaken in the Chartulary; and the fenfe feems to require that the name throughout fhould be *St. Wilfrid's Holme.*

praedictus

prædictus rivulus qui currit fubtus Kirkebride cadit in Wathepol: Et quicquid
infra prædictas divifas continetur, grangias, et poffeffiones, et liberos introitus
et exitus de abbatia et locis veftris infra et extra prædictas divifas ubique per
mare et per terram, per fabulones et per vaftum, et per vifnetum, et maeremium, et petram, in tota forefta de Englewood, et pafturam, et manfuras
veftras infra muros de Karliolo, et omnia alia ayfiamenta et confuetudines,
cum libertatibus omnibus, a præfatis illuftribus regibus vobis indultis et ipforum cartis confirmatis.—Extra infulam de Holm, ex dono Cofpatricii filii
Ormi et Thomæ filii Cofpatricii, terram et grangiam de *Flemingby*, cum omnibus pertinentiis fuis; et communem pafturam cum vicinis loci illius, ficut in
eorundem donatorum cartis continetur. Capellam quoque in eadem Flemingby, et terram quæ fuit capellæ, pro qua mater ecclefia recepit excambium ad
valentiam a præfato Cófpatricio poffeffore fundi, favente tunc temporis Perfona
Adam; et ceffionem decimarum prædictæ capellæ vobis imperpetuum eodem
Ada favente, et Roberto archidiacono tunc temporis diocefano (vacante epifcopatu) idem teftibus adhibitis carta fua confirmante, coram quampluribus
tam clericis quam laicis.—Ex dono etiam ejufdem Cofpatricii, terram de
Kelton, cum omnibus ayfiamentis et pertinentiis fuis, ficut in ejufdem carta
continetur.—Libertates etiam *ejufdem terræ*, ex dono Willielmi comitis et
Ceciliæ comitiffæ Albemarliæ, ficut in eorundem cartis continetur.—Ex dono
Thomæ filii Cofpatricii, unum *rete* in *Derwent* cum vifneto, et unam *pifcariam*
in *Derwent*, et unam mayfuram in ripa ejufdem fluminis, ficut carta ejufdem
teftatur.—Terram quoque et grangiam in territorio de *Kirkeby Thore* cum
omnibus pertinentiis et libertatibus, ficut cartæ donatorum teftantur; liber-
tátes quoque ejufdem terræ ex dono illuftris Anglorum regis Ricardi vobis
indultas, et ipfius carta confirmatas.—Infuper in *Hibernia*, quicquid comes
Ricardus et Johannes de Curcy et alii nobiles, pietatis intuitu, vobis et domui
veftræ rationabiliter contulerunt, et fuis cartis munierunt, vobis nihilominus
auctoritate apoftolica confirmamus.—Sane laborum veftrorum, quos propriis
manibus aut fumptibus colitis, tam de terris cultis quam de incultis, five de
ortis et virgultis veftris, vel de incrementis animalium veftrorum, nullus a
vobis decimas exigere vel extorquere prefumat.—Liceat quoque vobis, clericos
vel laicos a fæculo fugientes, liberos et abfolutos, ad converfionem recipere,
et eos abfque contradictione aliqua retinere.—Prohibemus infuper, ut nulli
veftrorum, poft factam in eodem loco profeffionem, fas fit abfque abbatis fui
licentia de eodem loco difcedere; difcedentem vero, abfque communium
literarum cautione, nullus audeat retinere: Quod fi quis forte retinere præ-
fumpferit, liceat vobis in ipfos monachos vel converfos fententiam proferre
regularem.——Illud diftrictius prohibentes, ne terras, feu quodlibet benefi-
cium ecclefiæ veftræ collatum, liceat alicui perfonaliter dari, five alio modo
alienari, abfque confenfu totius capituli, vel majoris vel fanioris partis ejufdem:
Si quæ vero donationes five alienationes aliter quam dictum eft factæ fuerint,
eas irritas effe cenfemus.—Adhæc etiam prohibemus, ne aliquis monachus vel
converfus, fub profeffione domus veftræ aftrictus, fine affenfu et licentia
abbatis et majoris partis capituli veftri pro aliquo fide jubeat, vel ab aliquo pecuniam mutuo accipiat, ultra pretium capituli veftri providentia ftatutum, nifi

propter

propter manifeftam domus veftræ utilitatem : Quod fi facere prefumpferit, non teneatur pro hiis aliquatenus refpondere.—Licitum fit yobis præterea, in caufis veftris, five civilem five criminalem contineant quæftionem, fratrum veftrorum teftimoniis uti ; ne per defectum teftium, jus veftrum poffit in aliquo deficere. —Infuper, auctoritate apoftolica prohibemus, ut nullus epifcopus, vel alia perfona, ad fynodos vel conventus forenfes vos ire, vel judicio fæculari de propria fubftantia vel poffeffionibus fubjacere compellat ; nec ad domos veftras, caufa ordines celebrandi, caufas tractandi, vel aliquos publicos conventus convocandi, venire præfumat ; nec regularem abbatis veftri electionem impediat, aut de inftituendo feu removendo eo qui pro tempore fuerit, contra ftatuta Ciftercienfis ordinis et auctoritatem privil giorum veftrorum, fe ullatenus intromittat. Si vero epifcopus, in cujus parochia domus veftra fundata eft, cum humilitate ac devotione qua convenit requifitus, fubftitutum abbatem benedicere, et alia quæ ad officium epifcopale pertinent vobis conferre renuerit ; licitum fit eidem abbati, fi tunc facerdos fuerit, proprios novicios benedicere, et cætera quæ ad officium fuum pertinent exercere, et vobis omnia ab alio epifcopo percipere, quæ a veftro indebite fuerint denegata : Illud adjicientes, ut in recipiendis profeffionibus, quæ a benedictis vel benedicendis abbatibus exhibentur, ea fint epifcopi forma et expreffione contenti, quæ ab origine ordinis noftri funt inftituta et hactenus obfervata, ut fcilicet abbates epifcopis, falvo ordine fuo, præfentari debeant ; er, contra ftatuta ordinis, apoftolicæ fedis privilegio roborata, nullam profeffionem facere compellantur. Pro confecrationibus vero altarium vel ecclefiarum, five pro oleo fancto, vel quolibet ecclefiaftico facramento, nullus a vobis fub obtentu confuetudinis vel alio modo quicquam audeat extorquere ; fed hæc omnia gratis vobis epifcopus diocefanus impendat : alioquin liceat vobis quemcunque malueritis catholicum antiftitem adire, gratiam atque communionem facrofanctæ Romanæ fedis habentem, qui noftra fretus auctoritate quod poftulatis vobis impendat.—Quod fi fedes diocefani epifcopi forte vacaverit, interim omnia ecclefiaftica facramenta a vicinis recipere epifcopis libere et abfque contradictione poffitis ; fic tamen, ut ex hoc in pofterum propriis epifcopis nullum prejudicium generatur.—Quia vero propriorum interdum epifcoporum copiam non poteftis habere ; fi quem epifcopum, Romanæ fedis communionem habentem, de quo plenam notitiam habeatis, per vos tranfire contigerit, ab illo benedictiones vaforum et veftium, confecrationes altarium, ordinationes monachorum, auctoritate fedis apoftolicæ recipere valeatis.—Porro, fi epifcopi vel alii ecclefiarum rectores in monafteria veftra vel perfonas inibi conftitutas, five in mercinarios veftros, pro eo quod decimas non folvitis, vel aliqua occafione eorum quæ ab apoftolica benignitate vobis indulta funt, feu benefactores veftros pro eo quod aliqua vobis beneficia vel obfequia ex caritate præftiterint, fufpenfionis, excommunicationis, vel interdicti fententiam promulgaverint ; eandem fententiam, tanquam contra apoftolicæ fedis indulta prolatam, decernimus irritandam ; nec ullæ literæ firmitatem habeant, quæ tacito ordine Ciftercienfium contra tenorem apoftolicorum privilegiorum conftiterint impetratæ.—Cum vero commune interdictum terræ fuerit ; liceat vobis, claufis januis, exclufis excommunicatis et interdictis, divina officia celebrare.—Paci quoque et tranquilitati veftræ paterna in pofte-

rum folicitudine providere volentes, auctoritate apoftolica prohibemus, ne quis
infra claufuram locorum feu grangiarum veftrarum violentiam vel rapinam feu
furtum facere, hominem capere vel interficere, ignem apponere, vel fanguinem
fundere, aliqua temeritate prefumat.—Præterea, omnes immunitates et libertates, a prædecefforibus noftris piæ recordationis, Innocentio, Eugenio, Alexandro, Lucio, Urbano, et Gregorio, Romanis pontificibus, ordini veftro conceffas, etiam libertates et exemptiones fæcularium exactionum a regibus et
principibus, patrocinio communimus. Decernimus ergo, ut nulli omnino hominum liceat præfatum monafterium temere perturbare, aut ejus poffeffiones
auferre, vel ablatas retinere, feu quibuflibet vexationibus fatigare; fed omnia
integra conferventur eorum, pro quorum gubernatione et fuftentatione conceffa,
fuis ufibus omnimodis profutura : Salva in omnibus Apoftolicæ fedis auctoritate.
—Si qua ergo in futurum ecclefiaftica fæcularifve perfona, hanc noftræ conftitutionis paginam fciens, contra eam temere venire temptaverit; fecundo, ter-
tiove commonita, nifi reatum fuum congrua fatisfactione correxerit, poteftatis
honorifque fui dignitate careat, reamque fe divino judicio exiftere de perpetrata
iniquitate cognofcat, fanctiffimo corpore et fanguine Dei et Domini redemptoris
noftri Jefu Chrifti aliena fiat, atque in extremo examine divinæ ultioni fubjaceat : Cunctis autem eidem loco jura fua fervantibus, fit pax Domini noftri
Jefu Chrifti, quatenus et hic fructum bonæ actionis percipiant, et apud dif-
trictum judicem præmia æternæ pacis inveniant. Datum anno incarnationis
dominicæ MCXC.——*Regiftr. Holm.*

No. XX.

Charter of King HENRY THE THIRD to the city of CARLISLE.

HENRICUS, Dei gratia rex Angliæ, dux Normanniæ et Aquitaniæ, et
comes Andegaviæ, Omnibus ad quos prefentes literæ pervenerint, falutem. Quia accepimus per inquifitionem quam fieri fecimus, quod cives noftri
Carliolenfes quieti fint per cartam Henrici regis avi noftri, quæ combufta eft
per incendium in civitate illa Carlioli per infortunium, de theoloneo, paffagio,
pontagio, et de omnibus confuetudinibus ad nos pertinentibus; et quod habere debent et confueverunt, de mortuo bofco noftro ad ignem fuum faciendum rationabilia eftoveria per diverfa loca in forefta noftra de Carleolo, et fimiliter maeremium ad ædificandum abfque vafta foreftæ noftræ per affignationem
fervientium et foreftariorum noftrorum in diverfis locis annuatim; et quod
fimiliter habent gildam mercatoriam liberam, ita quod nihil inde refpondeant
aliquibus; et quod omnibus fupradictis articulis, libertatibus, et confuetudinibus hucufque libere ufi funt: Nos omnes libertates illas et confuetudines
præfatis civibus noftris concedimus et hac carta noftra confirmamus pro nobis et
hæredibus noftris; volentes, quod omnibus prædictis libertatibus et confuetudinibus de cætero gaudeant et utantur, libere, quiete, bene et in pace, et integre, in perpetuum, cum omnibus aliis libertatibus et liberis confuetudinibus

ad

ad prædictam villam Carlioli pertinentibus. Testibus hiis, Venerabili patre A. Winton' Epifcopo, &c. Datum per manum noftram apud Windfor 26° die Octobris, anno regni noftri 35°.

No. XXI.

King EDWARD THE THIRD's charter to the city of CARLISLE.

EDWARDUS, Dei gratia, rex Angliæ et Franciæ et dominus Hiberniæ omnibus ad quos præfentes literæ pervenerint, falutem. Sciatis, quod cum compertum eft, per inquifitionem per dilectos et fideles noftros Richardum de Denton et Johannem de Harrington de mandato noftro captam et in cancellariam noftram returnatam, quod cives civitatis noftræ Carlioli habuerunt et habere confueverunt, inter libertates et confuetudines ad dictam civitatem fpectantes, plenam returnam omnium brevium, tam fummonitionum in fcaccario, quam aliorum quorumcunque brevium [and other privileges as in the following grant are fpecified] a tempore quo non exiftit memoria, quoufque per Thomam de Lucy, nuper vicecomitem noftrum Cumbriæ anno regni noftri Angliæ 23°, de returna brevium et fummonitionum de fcaccario impediti fûerunt, eo quod libertates in charta regia dictis civitatibus factæ fpecialiter nominatæ et fpecificatæ non fuerunt; ac etiam cives civitatis prædictæ nobis fupplicaverunt, ut fibi dictas libertates, quietantias, confuetudines, et proficua per chartam noftram confirmare velimus : Nos ad præmiffa confiderationem habentes ; et adhoc, quod dicta civitas in frontera Scotiæ ad tuitionem et refugium partium adjacentium contra hoftiles incurfus Scotorum inimicorum noftrorum fituatur ; et jam, tam per peftilentiam mortalem nuper in partibus illis invalefcentem, quam per frequentes acceffus dictorum inimicorum noftrorum in eifdem partibus, et ob alios cafus vaftatur et plus folito fuppreffa eft ; volentes quieti dictorum civium, ne fuper libertatibus, quietantiis, confuetudinibus, et proficuis prædictis, per vicecomitem aut alios miniftros noftros quofcunque impetantur aliqualiter, in futuro prôvidere ; Conceffimus, pro nobis et hæredibus noftris, eifdem civibus, quod ipfi et eorum hæredes et fucceffores, cives civitatis prædictæ, in perpetuum habeant returnam brevium omnium noftrorum et fummonitionum de fcaccario et aliorum brevium quorumcunque ; ac etiam duos mercatus fingulis feptimanis, videlicet, diebus Mercurii et Sabbati ; et unam feriam quolibet anno per fexdecim dies duraturam, videlicet, in die Affumptionis beatæ Mariæ et per 15 dies proxime fequentes : Nec non unam gildam et liberam electionem Majoris et Ballivorum civitatis prædictæ infra eandem civitatem ; et duos coronatores ibidem ; ac emendas affifæ panis, vini, et cervifiæ fractæ ; furcas, infangthef, ac etiam placita coronæ teneant, et omnia quæ ad officium vicecomitis et coronatoris pertinent, in eadem civitate faciant et exerceant ; ac catalla felonum et fugitivôrum dampnatorum, in eadem civitate habeant ; et de omnibus finibus et amerciamentis, comitatibus et fectis comitatûum, et wapentak, fint quieti ; placitaque frifciæ forciæ de libero tenemento infra civitatem illam, fi querela illa infra quadraginta dies poft diffei-

finam

finam factam fuerit attachiata, teneant; etiamque quod ballivi civitatis ejufdem
implacitare poffint coram ipfis breve noftrum de recto patens, ac breve de recto
claufum, fecundum confuetudinem civitatis prædictæ; et habeant cognitiones
omnium placitorum prædictorum: Nec non quod dicti cives et hæredes et fucceffores fui habeant communiam pafturæ, ad omnimoda averia, omni tempore
anni, fuper Moram noftram, et ibidem turbas fodere et abducere licite: Etiam
quod quilibet liber homo plegius alterius effe poteft ad primam curiam in placitis tranfgreffionum, conventionum, vel debitorum: Quodque cives prædicti
quieti fint per totum regnum noftrum Angliæ de thelonio, pontagio, paffagio,
laftagio, kaiagio, cariagio, muragio, et ftallagio, de quibufcunque rebus et
mercionibus fuis: Et etiam quod iidem cives habeant locum vocatum le Battail-holme, pro mercato et feriis fuis; ac tenementa fua in eadem civitate le-
gare poffint: Et quod habeant molendinum dictæ civitatis, et pifcariam noftram in aqua de Eden, ac thelonium intrinficum et forinfecum vocatum Burgh
toll, et firmas, menfuras, gabelgeld, et minutas firmas ejufdem civitatis, ut
parcellam firmæ civitatis illius; prout ipfi cives dictas libertates et quietantias
habere, et molendinum, pifcariam, pafturam, fofforam, et locum cum pertinentiis tenere debent, ipfique cives et anteceffores et prædeceffores fui a tempore cujus contrarium memoria non exiftit femper (quoufque dictis libertatibus
per præfatum Thomam fuere impediti) eifdem libertatibus et quietantiis uti et
gaudere, et prædicta molendinum, pifcariam, pafturam, fofforam, et locum
cum pertinentiis, habere et tenere rationabiliter confueverunt. In cujus rei
teftimonium has literas noftras fieri fecimus patentes. Tefte meipfo apud
Weftmonafterium feptimo die Februarii anno regni noftri Angliæ 26°, regni
vero noftri Franciæ 13°.

No. XXII.

Grant of the churches of NEWCASTLE and NEWBURN to the PRIORY of CARLISLE.

HENRICUS rex Angliæ, archiepifcopo Eborum, et epifcopo Dunelmenfi,
     et vicecomiti de Northumbrelanda, et omnibus baronibus et fidelibus fuis
de Northumbralanda, falutem. Sciatis me dediffe et conceffiffe Deo et Sanctæ
Mariæ de Carliolo et canonicis ejufdem loci, ecclefiam de Novo CASTELLO de-
fuper TYNAM; et ecclefiam de NEWBURNE; et ecclefias quas Richardus de
Aurea Valle de me tenet, poft obitum ejus: et Richardus et clerici qui ipfis
ecclefiis deferviunt, recognofcant de canonicis ipfis, et faciant eis fervicium
quod mihi facere folebant; et poft obitum eorum redigantur ecclefiæ in manus
canonicorum, ita quod clerici qui eis defervient habeant inde neceffaria, et canonici habeant reliquum. Et volo et præcipio firmiter, ut bene et in pace
et quiete et honorifice teneant. T. Willielmo Epifcopo Winton, et Bernardo
epifcopo de Sancto David, et Roberto de Sigillo, apud Roth'.

No. XXIII.

Grant of the churches of WERTHEORD, COLEBRUGE, WITING-
HAM, and RODEBURY to the PRIORY of CARLISLE.

HENRICUS rex Angliæ, Ranulpho Dunelmenfi epifcopo, et Rogero
Picoto, et 'omnibus fidelibus fuis Francis et Anglis, et miniftris de
Northumbreland, falutem. Sciatis me dediffe Ricardo de Aurea Valle,
capellano meo, quatuor ecclefias, de quatuor meis maneriis; fcilicet, Wer-
theorda, et Colebruge, et in Witingeham, et in Rodeberia, tam in terris
quam in decimis et in hominibus qui ad terras harum ecclefiarum pertinent,
cum foca et faca, et tol, et team, et infangethef, cum omnibus fuis confuetudinibus. T. Roberto epifcopo Lincoln, et Willielmo de Werlewaft, et Everardo filio Comitis, et Thoma Capellano, apud Cirenceftriam in Natale S. Joh.
Baptiftæ.

No. XXIV.

Grant of DALSTON to the BISHOP of CARLISLE.

HENRICUS, Dei gratia, rex Angliæ, dominus Hiberniæ, dux Normanniæ et Aquitaniæ, comes Andegaviæ, archiepifcopis, epifcopis, abbatibus,
prioribus, comitibus, baronibus, jufticiariis, vicecomitibus, foreftariis, viridariis, præpofitis, miniftris, et omnibus ballivis et fidelibus fuis, falutem. Sciatis, nos intuitu Dei et pro falute animæ noftræ et animarum antecefforum et
hæredum noftrorum, dediffe, conceffiffe, et hac charta mea confirmaffe, Deo
et ecclefiæ beatæ Mariæ Karlioli, et venerabili patri Waltero Karliolenfi epifcopo, manerium de Dalfton in comitatu Cumbriæ, cum omnibus membris fuis,
tam in dominicis, quam in fervitiis, redditibus, villenagiis, cum advocatione
ecclefiæ, et faca, et foca, et bofcis, et molendinis, pratis, pafcuis, et omnibus
aliis pertinentiis fuis, infra villam et extra, fine aliquo retenemento, Habendum et tenendum, de nobis et hæredibus noftris, eidem epifcopo et fuccefforibus fuis in perpetuum, in liberam, puram, et perpetuam eleemofynam, quietum de omni fervicio feculari, exactione, et demanda. Conceffimus etiam
pro nobis et hæredibus noftris, quod prædictum manerium de Dalfton, cum
bofcis et omnibus pertinentiis fuis, fit omnino deafforeftatum, quantum ad
nos et hæredes hoftros, et quantum ad foreftarios noftros et eorum miniftros,
pertinet vel pertinere poffit, in terris, bofcis, planis, pratis, pafturis, viis et
femitis, in mare, in aquis, et in omnibus rebus et locis. Et quod prædictus
epifcopus et fucceffores fui claudere poffint et parcos facere fi voluerint, et de
bofcis illius manerii vel affartare, capere, dare, et vendere, quantum, quando,
et ubi voluerint, et omnino pro voluntate fua de bofcis illis facere, fine contradictione noftra et hæredum noftrorum, et fine vifu vel contradictione foreftariorum,

orum, viridariorum, regardatorum, et aliorum miniſtrorum noſtrorum, de omnibus quæ ad nos et hæredes noſtros pertinent; et quicquid inde ceperint vel capi fecerint attrahere poſſint et attrahi facere, libere et pacifice, cum libertate chymini, abſque contradictione et reclamatione vel impedimento foreſtariorum quacunque occaſione. Et quod boſci illi cum pertinentiis, et aſſarta inde facta et facienda, quieta ſint in perpetuum de vaſtis, et regardis, et viſu foreſtariorum, viridariorum, et regardatorum. Et quod omnes homines in manerio illo cum pertinentiis manentes ſint quieti, quantum ad nos et hæredes noſtros et foreſtarios pertinet, de ſectis omnium placitorum foreſtæ, et placitis de viridi et venatione, et de omnibus ſummonitionibus, placitis, querelis, occaſionibus, et omnibus aliis quæ ad foreſtam et foreſtarios vel eorum miniſtros pertinent, vel aliquo jure poſſunt pertinere. Et quod idem epiſcopus et ſucceſſores ſui libere poſſint fugare, et venationem ad ſuam voluntatem capere, infra terras et boſcos prædicti manerii. Et quod nullus, ſine prædicti epiſcopi et ſucceſſorum ſuorum licentia, aliquas feras ibi capere poſſit vel fugare, ſuper forisfacturam noſtram decem librarum; ſed prædictus epiſcopus et ſucceſſores ſui habeant ibi foreſtam ſuam, ſicut nos foreſtam noſtram ante illam collationem noſtram ibi habuimus. Invenient autem dictus epiſcopus et ſucceſſores ſui in perpetuum, unum canonicum regularem ad miſſam celebrandam ſingulis diebus in dicta eccleſia Carliolenſi, pro anima patris noſtri et noſtra, et pro animabus anteceſſorum et hæredum noſtrorum.

No. XXV.

Grant of privileges to the BISHOP and PRIOR of CARLISLE by king HꜰNꜰY the THIRD.

HENRICUS, Dei gratia, rex Angliæ, dominus Hiberniæ, dux Nermanniæ et Aquitaniæ, et comes Andegaviæ; Archiepiſcopis, epiſcopis, abbatibus, prioribus, comitibus, baronibus, juſticiariis, vicecomitibus, præpoſitis, miniſtris, et omnibus ballivis et fidelibus ſuis, ſalutem. Sciatis nos conceſſiſſe, et præſenti carta noſtra confirmaſſe, Deo et eccleſiæ Sanctæ Mariæ de Karliolo, et venerabili patri Waltero Karlioli epiſcopo et ſucceſſoribus ſuis, et priori et canonicis Karliolenſibus in eadem eccleſia Deo ſervientibus, omnes terras et redditus, tenementa et poſſeſſiones, jura et dignitates, libertates et liberas conſuetudines, quæ eis a nobis vel anteceſſoribus noſtris, vel aliquibus aliis collata ſunt ſunt vel conferenda; ſicut cartæ donationum rationabiliter teſtantur et teſtabunt. Conceſſimus etiam eidem epiſcopo et ſucceſſoribus ſuis, quod ipſi et prior et canonici Karliolenſes, et eorum ſucceſſores, habeant in perpetuum, per omnes terras ſuas et tenementa ſua, thol et theam, et infangethef, et utfangethef; et quod ipſi et omnes homines eorum, et omnes homines de feodis ſuis, ſint quieti imperpetuum erga nos et hæredes noſtros, vicecomites, conſtabularios, præpoſitos, et omnes ballivos noſtros, de paſſagio, pontagio, leſtagio, ſtallagio, et de conductu theſaurorum, et de operationibus caſtellorum, domorum, murorum, foſſatorum, pontium, calcetorum,

vivariorum,

vivariorum, ſtagnorum, et clauſuriorum parcorum, et de omnibus aliis operationibus, et de ſeĉtis ſchirarum, wapentakiorum, hundredorum, et thretin-
gorum, et de auxiliis vicecomitum, et de murdro, et de francoplegio, et de
viſu franciplegii, et de miſericordiis, et de finibus pro tranſgreſſionibus, et pro
licentia concordandi, et de eſcapiis latronum, et de bobus de ſeiſina, et de placitis, querelis, et omnibus exaĉtionibus, ad nos, vicecomites, conſtabularios,
vel aliquos alios ballivos noſtros pertinentibus. Conceſſimus etiam eidem epiſcopo et ſucceſſoribus ſuis, quod nullus vicecomes, conſtabularius, vel alius
ballivus noſter, ingreſſum vel poſſe habeat in prædiĉtis terris, feodis, vel hominibus, ſed totum ad prædiĉtum epiſcopum et ſucceſſores ſuos et eorum ballivos pertineat; præter attachiamenta de placitis coronæ, ad quæ quidem cum
coronator venerit facienda, ea ita faciant quod in nullo lædatur libertas prædiĉti epiſcopi vel ſucceſſorum ſuorum.   Omnes autem prædiĉtas libertates
conceſſimus ita, quod prædiĉtus prior et canonici Karliolenſes, et omnes ſucceſſores ſui, ſubſint et reſpondeant et ſatisfaciant epiſcopo et omnibus ſucceſſoribus ſuis, ut nulli alii niſi de voluntate ejuſdem epiſcopi et ſuccef-
ſorum ſuorum de omnibus prædiĉtis, ſicut nobis aut hæredibus noſtris aut
vicecomitibus aut conſtabulariis vel aliis ballivis noſtris ſubeſſent et red-
derent et ſatisfacerent de eiſdem, ſi ad nos illa pertinerent. Conceſſimus
etiam, quod idem epiſcopus et ſucceſſores ſui diſtringere poſſint prædiĉtos
priorem et canonicos Karliolenſes, terras et feoda et homines de terris et
feodis illorum, et omnes homines de terris et aliis feodis ipſius epiſcopi et
ſucceſſorum ſuorum, ad omnia prædiĉta, ſicut nos ad eadem eos diſtringere
poſſemus, aut hæredes noſtri, aut vicecomites, aut conſtabularii, vel aliqui alii
ballivi noſtri, ſi prædiĉtæ libertates aut quietantiæ conceſſæ non fuiſſent. Conceſſimus etiam prædiĉto epiſcopo, quod, ſi aliquas libertates aut quietantias ex
hiis quæ continentur in carta iſta conceſſerit priori et canonicis Karlioli, nos eas
confirmabimus. Conceſſimus etiam eidem epiſcopo et ſucceſſoribus ſuis, et
priori et canonicis Karlioli, et eorum ſucceſſoribus, quod omnes homines eorum
ſint liberi et quieti imperpetuum, de omnibus juratis et aſſiſis et recognitionibus faciendis, præterquam in attingendis propriis dominicis noſtris per juratam
ſi opus fuerit infra comitatum ubi manentes fuerint, ſi forte contentio inter nos
ipſos et alios oriatur : ita quod occaſione talis juratæ, ſi forte evenerit, per vicecomites vel alios ballivos noſtros non occaſionentur, nec libertas ejuſdem epiſcopi vel ſucceſſorum ſuorum in aliquo lædatur. Conceſſimus etiam, eidem
epiſcopo et ſucceſſoribus ſuis, quod ſi aliquis homo de terris vel feodis ſuis,
ſive de terris vel feodis prioris et canonicorum Karlioli, pro deliĉto ſuo vitam
aut membrum debeat amittere, vel fugerit et judicio ſtare noluerit vel aliud:
deliĉtum fecerit pro quo debeat catalla ſua perdere, ubicunque juſtitia fieri debeat, ſive in curia noſtra ſive in alia curia; omnia catalla illa ſint prædiĉti:
epiſcopi et ſucceſſorum ſuorum, et liceat eis, ſine diſturbatione vicecomitum
et quorumcunque ballivorum noſtrorum et aliorum, ponere ſe in ſeiſina de
prædiĉtis catallis, in prædiĉtis caſibus et aliis, quando ballivi noſtri, ſi ad nos
pertinerent catalla illa, in manu noſtra ea ſeiſire poſſent et deberent. Conceſſimus etiam eidem epiſcopo et ſucceſſoribus ſuis, quod quotieſcunque aliqui
malefaĉtores capti fuerint in prædiĉtis terris vel feodis, per ballivos ejuſdem
                                                                         epiſcopi

episcopi vel successorum suorum, de quibus non possit vel non debeat fieri judicium in curia prædicti episcopi vel successorum suorum; vicecomites et ballivi nostri recipiant prædictos malefactores sine difficultate et dilatione, super
forisfacturam nostram, quandocunque ballivi prædicti episcopi et successorum
suorum dictos malefactores prædictis ballivis nostris liberare voluerint. Concessimus etiam eidem episcopo et successoribus suis, quod habeant imperpetuum omnia amerciamenta de omnibus hominibus de terris et feodis suis, et de
priore et canonicis Karlioli et eorum successoribus et de omnibus hominibus de
terris et feodis omnibus eorundem, quæ amerciamenta ad nos et hæredes nostros, vel vicecomites aut constabularios vel aliquos alios ballivos nostros possent
pertinere, si ipsa amerciamenta prædictis episcopo et successoribus suis con-
cessa non fuissent: Et quod idem episcopus et succeffores sui habeant potesta-
tem ad distringendum omnes prædictos ad amerciamenta eis reddenda: Prohibemus insuper, super forisfacturam nostram decem librarum, ne quis de prædictis amerciamentis colligendis vel recipiendis, sive districtione inde facienda,
nisi per voluntatem ejusdem episcopi aut successorum suorum, se intromittat.
Concessimus insuper eidem episcopo et successoribus suis, quod licet aliqua libertatum per nos ipsos concessarum, processu temporis quocunque casu con-
tingente usi non fuerint, nihilominus tamen postea utantur libertate eadem,
sine aliqua conditione, non obstante eo quod aliquo casu ea non usi fuerint.
Omnes autem prædictas libertates et quietancias concessimus sæpefato episcopo
et successoribus suis, in liberam, puram et perpetuam eleemosynam. Quare
volumus et firmiter præcipimus, quod prædictus episcopus et successores sui,
et prædicti prior et canonici Karliolenses et successores sui, et omnes homines
eorum, et terræ et feoda et omnes homines de feodis illis, habeant prædictas
libertates et quietancias, bene et in pace, integre et plenarie, in omnibus rebus
et locis imperpetuum, sicut prædictum est. Hiis testibus; Dominis Hugone
Lincolniæ, Jocelino Bathoniæ, Thoma Norwici Episcopis, Huberto de Burgo
comite Kantiæ justiciario Angliæ, Philippo de Albinico, Godefrido de Cran-
cumbe, Hugone Dispensatore, Ranulpho Briton, Waltero de Kirkham rectore
Sancti Martini London, Alexandro Archidiacono Salop, Henrico de Caroll,
Richardo filio Hugonis, et aliis. Datum per manum venerabilis patris Radulphi Cicestriensis episcopi et cancellarii nostri, apud Oxon', 15° die Julii,
anno regni nostri 15°.

No. XXVI.

Another charter of privileges by the same king.

HENRICUS Dei gratia, rex Angliæ, dominus Hiberniæ, dux Normanniæ
et Aquitaniæ, comes Andegaviæ, Archiepiscopis, episcopis, abbatibus, prioribus, comitibus, baronibus, justiciariis, vicecomitibus, forestariis, viridariis,
præpositis, ministris, et omnibus ballivis et fidelibus suis, salutem. Sciatis, nos
intuitu Dei, et pro salute animæ meæ, et animarum antecessorum et hæredum
nostrorum concessisse, et hac præsenti charta nostra confirmasse, Deo et ecclesiæ
Beatæ

Beatæ Mariæ Carliolenſis, et venerabili patri Waltero Karlioli epiſcopo et ſucceſſoribus ſuis, et priori et canonicis Karliolenſibus et eorum ſucceſſoribus,
quod boſci ſui adjacentes maneriis ſuis de Carleton et de Briſcaihe ſint quieti
imperpetuum de vaſtis et regardis et de aſſartis. Conceſſimus etiam eidem
epiſcopo et ſucceſſoribus ſuis, et eidem priori et canonicis Karliolenſibus et
eorum ſucceſſoribus, et omnibus hominibus ſuis, et omnibus hominibus tenentibus de feodis ſuis, quod ſint quieti in perpetuum de eſcapiis averiorum in
foreſta noſtra pertinentibus ad nos vel ad foreſtarios noſtros vel eorum miniſtros. Conceſſimus etiam eidem epiſcopo et ſucceſſoribus ſuis, et eiſdem priori
et canonicis et eorum ſucceſſoribus, et omnibus hominibus ſuis, et omnibus
hominibus tenentibus de feodis ſuis, quod ſint quieti in perpetuum de chimi-
nagio et de chiminio quod vocatur Foreſtage, per totam foreſtam noſtram.
Conceſſimus inſuper eidem epiſcopo et ſucceſſoribus ſuis pro curſu in foreſta
noſtra, videlicet, quod quotieſcunque ipſe vel ſucceſſores ſui vel aliquis de pre-
ſcripta licentia vel voluntate ejuſdem epiſcopi vel ſucceſſorum ſuorum, in foreſta ſua de Dalſton, feras fugavit, et aliqua fera vel aliquæ feræ fugatæ de
foreſta ſua de Dalſton aliquo prædictorum modorum in foreſtam noſtram fu-
gerint, liceat eis cum venatoribus et canibus ſuis feram vel feras ſuas ſequi per
foreſtam noſtram et capere, ſine impedimento et diſturbatione foreſtariorum
vel quorumcunque ballivorum noſtrorum vel eorum miniſtrorum, et cum venatione ſua et venatoribus et canibus, vel ſi forte venationem non ceperint,
cum venatoribus et canibus, licite et ſine impedimento ad propria redire.
Omnes autem prædictas libertates et quietantias conceſſimus pro nobis et hæredibus noſtris, eidem epiſcopo et ſucceſſoribus ſuis, et eiſdem priori et canonicis
Karlioli et eorum ſucceſſoribus, in liberam, puram, et perpetuam eleemoſynam. Quare volumus et firmiter præcipimus, quod prædictus epiſcopus et
ſucceſſores ſui, et prædicti prior et canonici Karlioli et eorum ſucceſſores, et
omnes homines dictorum epiſcopi et ſucceſſorum ſuorum et prioris et canonicorum Karlioli et eorum ſucceſſorum, et omnes homines de feodis ſuis, habeant
prædictas libertates et quietantias, bene et in pace, integre et plenarie, in omnibus rebus et locis imperpetuum, ſicut prædictum eſt. Hiis teſtibus; J. Bathon', Th. Norwicen', et R. London', epiſcopis ; H. de Burgo comite Kantiæ
juſticiario Angliæ, Stephano de Sedyne, Philippo de Albicato, Radulpho filio
Nicholai, et Godfrido de Crancumb, ſeneſchallis noſtris ; Willielmo de Ralegh,
Roberto de Lexington, Willielmo de Ebor', Alexandro archidiacóno Salop,
Hugone de Pateſhull, Johanne de Kirkby, Petro Grimbald, Henrico de Capella, et aliis. Datum per manum R. Ciceſtriæ epiſcopi cancellarii noſtri, apud
Weſtminſter, 18° die Octobris, anno regñi noſtri 15°.

No. XXVII.

Grant of TITHES in the Foreſt of ENGLEWOOD to the PRIORY of
CARLISLE.

EDWARDUS, Dei gratia, rex Angliæ, dominus Hiberniæ, et dux Aquitaniæ, Omnibus ad quos præſentes literæ pervenerint, ſalutem. Sciatis,
quod cum nos, in curia noſtra coram dilectis et fidelibus noſtris Hugone de
Creſſingham et ſociis ſuis juſticiariis noſtris ultimo itinerantibus in comitatu
Cumbriæ, verſus venerabilem patrem Johannem epiſcopum Karliolenſem, et
priorem eccleſiæ Beatæ Mariæ Karlioli, ac Alanum tunc perſonam eccleſiæ de
Thoreſby, advocationem decimarum de quibuſdam aſſartis factis in foreſta
noſtra de Englewood, et aliis minutis parcellis vaſti, tanquam de illis quæ fuerunt extra quarumcunque parochiarum limites, recuperavimus ut jus noſtrum :
Nos, pro ſalute animæ noſtræ et animæ claræ memoriæ Alianoræ quondam
reginæ Angliæ conſortis noſtræ, et animarum anteceſſorum et hæredum noſtrorum, dedimus et conceſſimus pro nobis et hæredibus noſtris, Deo et eccleſiæ
Beatæ Mariæ Karlioli et priori et canonicis ibidem Deo ſervientibus, omni-
modas decimas provenientes tam de aſſartis et parcellis prædictis, quam omnes
decimas proventuras de omnibus aliis landis aut placeis in foreſta prædicta,
extra limites parochiarum exiſtentibus, futuris temporibus aſſartandarum ; re-
cipiendas et habendas eiſdem priori et canonicis et eorum ſucceſſoribus imperpetuum, ſine occaſione vel impedimento noſtri vel hæredum noſtrorum, juſticiariorum, foreſtariorum, viridariorum, aut aliorum miniſtrorum noſtrorum
foreſtæ. In cujus rei teſtimonium, has literas noſtras prædictis priori et canonicis fieri fecimus patentes. T. meipſo apud Weſtminſter 5° die Decembris
anno regni noſtri 22°.

No. XXVIII.

PENRITH boundary on the ſide of CATERLEN.

THE ancient bounds of the cow paſture of PENRITH, proved before the
commiſſioners Henry lord Scroop, John biſhop of Carliſle, John Vaughan
ſenior eſquire, John Swift auditor, Edward Dacre eſquire, Richard Dudley
eſquire, Simon Slingſbye eſquire, and Ambroſe Lancaſter gentleman : It be-
ginneth at one great Grey Stone, otherwiſe called the Picked How, being the
furtheſt part of the franchiſes of Penrith ; and ſo from the ſaid ſtone unto one
other great Grey Stone Weſt lying on the Ring dyke of the corn field ; and
then from that Grey Stone North alongſt the ſaid dyke unto Petterel ; and ſo
over

over Petterel to the Ring Dyke again riding Weſt along the ſaid Dyke unto one old caſten dyke which is caſt overthwart beyond Mellinghow; and then croſſing North alongſt the ſaid old caſten Dyke, being the principal and ancient bounder between the lordſhip of Penrith and Catterlen, which ſaid Old Dyke ſtinteth upon Plumpton Dyke; and then from the ſaid Old Dyke end, alongſt Plumpton Dyke Eaſt over Petterel unto Plumpton park nuke, otherwiſe called Plumpton nuke; and ſo alongſt the ſaid wall as the ſame reacheth North unto Salkeld Yate; and ſo croſſing Eaſt from the ſaid Yate alongſt Yardgill, other-wiſe called Deepgill, as the ſyke runneth to the Weſt end of the long moſs; and then alongſt the ſaid moſs, on the North ſide of the ſame under the Brown-ridge unto the fartheſt end of the ſaid long moſs; and ſo from the ſaid Eaſt ond of the ſaid moſs, until the fartheſt end of the Wandfell; and ſo to the White Raiſe; from thence to Rolley Bank; and ſo overthwart Backey Greene to Stone Gill; and ſo to Amy Dobſon's ſtone; and then overthwart to the Skeugh Dyke; and ſo alongſt the ſame to the Eaſt end of Carleton Louthwait Leeſe.

About ſix witneſſes are examined, who all ſwear to the treſpaſſes by Vaux and tenants only. But Thomas Bacon, Edward Stephenſon, and Thomas Ric-kerby ſwear, that they have been of long time ſtaffe hirds, and driven the cattle of the ſaid town unto their limits and bounds of the ſaid town, which were ridden and renewed as aforeſaid.

Afterwards, the townſhips of Catterlen, New Skelton, and Blencowe came before the ſaid commiſſioners, and alledged, that they ought to have turves, brackens, and common of paſture upon Penreth Fell and the foreſt of Ingle-wood; for which Catterlen pays 52 s, Newton 52 s, Skelton 47 s 10 d, Blen-cow 48 s. And Symon Muſgrave ſhewed two letters patents under the ſeals of England; the one declaring free intercommon for himſelf and his tenants of Edenhall and Dawſonby, with certain ſheep paſture for himſelf within the whole foreſt of Inglewood; and the other giving him free licence to improve and keep ſeveral as his metes and bounds doth reach, within certain places of the bounders of Penreth before ridden.

No. XXIX.

PENRITH boundary on the ſide of EDENHALL.

TO all to whom this preſent award indented ſhall come, William Milbourne of Armathwaite caſtle in the county of Cumberland eſquire, and Joſeph Nicolſon of Hawkeſdale in the ſaid county eſquire, ſend greeting. Whereas ſome diſputes have ariſen between his grace the duke of Portland as lord of the foreſt of Inglewood and manor of Penrith in the county of Cumberland, and Sir Philip Muſgrave baronet as lord of the manor of Edenhall in the ſaid county, touching the bounds and limits of the ſaid manors of Penrith and

Edenhall

Edenhall refpectively, fo far as the fame adjoin and are contiguous to each
other; and alfo touching certain claims made by the faid Sir Philip Mufgrave,
on behalf of himfelf as lord of the faid manor of Edenhall and his tenants
of the faid manor, of a right of common of pafture, and other rights and
privileges within the faid foreft of Inglewood: Which faid difputes and claims
have been fubmitted by the faid duke and the faid Sir Philip Mufgrave to the
award, order, final end and determination of us the faid William Milbourne
and Jofeph Nicholfon: We therefore the faid William Milbourne and Jofeph
Nicolfon, having viewed the ground and heard the evidence produced by both
the faid parties, and likewife confidered of the faid claims and difputes, and
of the boundaries claimed by each of the faid parties, in order that the bounds
and limits of the faid manors of Penrith and Edenhall, as far as the fame adjoin and are contiguous to each other, may for ever hereafter be fixed and afcertained; and for the finally fettling and determining all difputes relating
thereunto between the faid parties for the future; We the faid arbitrators find
and do award, order, and determine, that the bounds and limits of the faid
manors of Penrith and Edenhall, fo far as the fame adjoin and are contiguous
to each other, are as follows; that is to fay, Beginning at a ftone at the end of
the dyke or hedge which divides the fkeugh from Carleton Lowthwaite; and
fo through the fkeugh tarn to a ftone on Skeugh hill marked in the chart or
map hereunto annexed with the letter A, being 322 yards from the faid Skeugh
dyke. And from the faid ftone to a ftone marked in the map with the letter
B, on the north fide of the road leading from Penrith to Edenhall, being 152
yards. And from the faid ftone along the north fide of the faid road, as the
faid road winds to another ftone marked in the faid map with the letter C, alfo
on the north fide of the faid road, being about 390 yards. And from thence
to a ftone marked in the faid map with the letter D, on a hill oppofite to the
faid road being 160 yards. And from thence to a ftone marked in the faid map
with the letter E, below the road leading to Cowrake Quarry, being 200 yards.
And from thence eaftward to another ftone marked in the faid map with the
letter F, below Cowrake Quarry, being 200 yards. And thence to another
ftone marked in the faid map with the letter G, being 57 yards. And from
thence to another ftone marked in the faid map with the letter and figure G 2,
at the eaft end of Cowrake Quarry, being about 39 yards. From thence
northerly to a ftone marked in the faid map with the letter H, being 170 yards.
From thence ftill northerly to a ftone marked in the faid map with the letter I,
in the road leading from Penrith to Langwathby Bridge, being 1100 yards.
And from thence ftill northerly to a ftone marked in the faid map with the
letter K, in Stony Gill, being about 648 yards. And from thence to a ftone
marked in the faid map with the letter L, nearly north, being about 783 yards.
And from thence to Michael Gray's well, marked in the faid map with the
letter M, about 300 yards. And from thence down Liquorice fyke to the
inclofed grounds of the manor of Edenhall. Which faid feveral ftones we the
faid arbitrators have caufed to be fixed and marked with the letter P on the
fide next to the manor of Penrith, and with the letter M on the fide next to
the manor of Edenhall, and have alfo caufed the faid bounds and limits to be laid
                                                                        down.

down and delineated in a chart or map to this our award annexed, and which
we order shall be taken as part thereof. And we do further order and award,
that the said duke of Portland, his heirs and assigns, and all and every his tenants of the said manor of Penrith, their and each of their heirs and assigns,
shall be for ever debarred from any right of common of pasture, or other rights,
royalties, or privileges within the said manor of Edenhall, for or in respect of
their or any of their messuages, lands, tenements, and hereditaments, situate,
lying, or being within the said manor of Penrith or forest of Inglewood: And
also that the said Sir Philip Musgrave, his heirs and assigns, and all and every
his tenants of the said manor of Edenhall, their and each of their heirs and
assigns, shall be for ever hereafter debarred from any right of common of pasture,
or other rights, royalties, or privileges within the said manor of Penrith and
forest of Inglewood, for or in respect of their or any of their messuages, lands,
tenements, or hereditaments, situate, lying, or being within or parcel of the
said manor of Edenhall. In witness whereof, we have hereunto set our hands
and seals the 23d day of November in the year of our lord 1765.

No. XXX.

Agreement between *Hen.* 3. king of England, and *Alexander* king
of Scotland, concerning the lands afterwards called The Queen's-
Haims.

JACOBUS, Dei gratia, Angliæ, Scotiæ, Franciæ, et Hiberniæ rex, fidei
defensor, &c. Omnibus ad quos præsentes literæ pervenerint, salutem. Inspeximus quandam inquisitionem coram domino Thoma de Normanvill nuper
escaetore domini Edwardi nuper regis Angliæ primi citra Trentam, anno regni
sui vicesimo primo captam, in cancellaria nostra infra Turrim nostram London
de recordo remanentem, in hæc verba:

    Inquisitio facta apud Carleolum die Martis in septimana Paschæ, anno regni
regis Edwardi vicesimo primo, coram domino Thoma de Normanvill escaetore
citra Trentam, per Hugonem de Muleton, Hubertum de Muleton, Thomam
de Newton, Robertum de Joneby, Robertum de Croglyn, Adam de Ulvesby,
Adam de Hoton, Adam Turpp, Johannem de Staffholl, Johannem de Salkeld, Robertum de Tympauron, et Thomam de Lowther. Jurati, quantum
terræ *Alexander* rex Scotiæ tenuit de domino rege Angliæ die quo obiit; Dicunt, quod idem Alexander tenuit de domino rege Angliæ die obitus sui in
capite maneria de Penrith, Soureby, Languetheby, Salkild, Carlaton et Scotteby. Quantum de aliis? Dicunt, quod nihil. Per quod servitium? Dicunt,
quod reddendo unum osturcum sorum annuatim ad festum assumptionis beatæ
Mariæ ad castrum Carleoli, et faciendo homagium domino regi Angliæ et hæredibus suis et fidelitatem pro prædictis tenementis. Quantum terræ illæ valeant per annum in omnibus exitibus? Dicunt, quod dicta maneria valent annuatim ducentas libras. Et quis propinquior hæres, et cujus ætatis? Dicunt,
quod

quod *Johannes de Balliolo* eft propinquior hæres ejus, et eft de ætate triginta annorum. In cujus rei teftimonium, prædicti jurati præfenti inquifitioni fi-gilla fua appofuerunt.

INSPEXIMUS etiam tenorem quorundam recordi et proceffus, coram dicto domino Edwardo primo nuper rege Angliæ, et concilio fuo in parliamento fuo dicto anno regni fui vicefimo primo tento, inter ipfum *Edwardum* nuper regem Angliæ et *Johannem* tunc regem Scotiæ habitorum, infra Turrim noftram London de recordo fimiliter remanentem, in hæc verba:

PLACITA coram ipfo domino rege et concilio fuo, ad parliamentum fuum poft feftum Michaelis, anno regni regis Edwardi filii regis Henrici vicefimo primo, incipiente fecundo; fcilicet, *Johannes* rex Scotiæ alias fupplicavit domino regi, quod fibi terras et tenementa cum pertinentiis, de quibus *Alexander* ultimus rex Scotiæ, anteceffor ipfius *Johannis*, fuit feifitus in dominico fuo ut de feodo, die quo obiit, infra regnum Angliæ, videlicet, terras de Tyndall, Penrith, et Soureby redderet, ut vero et propinquiori hæredi præfati *Alexandri*. Propter quod, per breve domini regis mandatum fuit Thomæ de Normanvill efcaetori domini regis ultra Trentam, quod diligentem inde faceret inquifitionem, et domino regi retornaret fub figillo fuo et figillis eorum per quos facta fuer.t prout moris eft, in curia regis. Per quam inquifitionem fic captam, et in parliamento domini regis poft Pafcha anno regni fui vicefimo primo retornatam, compertum fuit; Quod præfatus *Alexander* rex Scotiæ fuit feifitus in dominico fuo ut de feodo, die quo obiit, de prædictis terris et tene-mentis cum pertinentiis, et quod prædictus *Johannes* eft ejus hæres propinquior et plenæ ætatis: Ob quod, nuncii et attornati prædicti *Johannis* regis inftanter petierunt feifinam prædictorum tenementorum domino fuo liberari et reddi, juxta formam inquifitionis retornatæ. Et fuper hoc, venit coram domino rege et ejus concilio *Johannes de Haftings*, dicens, fe effe unum hæredem præfati *Alexandri*, et petiit propartem dictorum tenementorum fibi contingentem de terris et tenementis prædictis fibi liberari, ut uni hæredi præfati *Alexandri*. Ita quod per dominum regem præceptum fuit, tam præfato *Johanni de Haf-tings*, quam nunciis et attornatis præfati *Johannis* regis, quod in craftino venirent coram cancellario et jufticiariis de utroque banco in cancellaria, et. ibidem rationes fuas proponerent, et ibidem fieret eis juftitia, prout de jure et fecundum confuetudinem regni fuit faciendum. Ad quem diem nuncii et attornati præfati *Johannis* regis coram cancellario et jufticiariis venerunt; et præfatus *Johannes de Haftings*, folempniter et pluries vocatus, non venit, nec aliquem pro fe aut nomine fuo mifit. Et iidem nuncii et attornati fupplica-runt, quod ex quo nulla mentio facta fuit de prædicto *Johanne de Haftings* in inquifitione capta, nec idem *Johannes de Haftings* clameum quod appofuit profecutus fuit, quod feifina terrarum et tenementorum prædictorum domino fuo liberentur; dicentes, eundem dominum fuum, præfato *Johanni de Haf-tings* et alii cuicunque in prædictis tenementis aliquid petere volenti, in curia regis prout debuerit libenter velle refpondere: Dixerunt etiam, quod licet præ-fatus *Johannes de Haftings* aliquid in prædictis terris de Tyndall forte petere poffet, ut particeps hæreditatis prædicti *Alexandri*, tamen in prædictis tene-mentis de Penrith et de Soureby cum pertinentiis nihil petere poteft; eo quod

5   terræ

terræ et tenementa illa tantummodo data fuerint cuidam *Alexandro* regi Scotiæ,
anteceffori domini fui, et hæredibus fuis regibus Scotiæ, et non fimpliciter
fibi vel hæredibus fuis: propter quod, nullus hæredum prædicti *Alexandri* in
terris et tenementis illis aliquid petere poteft, nifi tantummodo dominus fuus
ex quo rex eft Scotiæ. Et iidem nuncii et attornati, quæfiti fi quid habent
quod teftatur donum prædictum, dicunt, quod ad præfentes nihil habent; fed
quod carta ipfius doni eft penes dominum fuum in regno fuo Scotiæ, et ad-
citius quod poterunt illam domino regi deferrent et monftrabunt, fi fibi pla-
cuerit et concilio fuo. Et quia prædictus *Johannes de Haftings* clameum quod
appofuit non profecutus fuit, licet pluries et folempniter fuiffet vocatus; et
per inquifitionem de terris de Tyndall captam compertum eft, quod *Alexander*
anteceffor prædicti *Johannis* regis Scotiæ fuit feifitus de terris illis in dominico
fuo ut de feodo die quo obiit, et quod idem *Johannes* rex eft hæres ejus propinquior, nulla facta mentione de alio hærede vel aliis hæredibus ipfius *Alexandri*, qualitercunque præfatus *Johannes de Haftings* fe appofuit; et cum idem
Johannes de Haftings et alii hæredes, fi qui fuerint, recuperare fuum habere
poterunt, fi quid habere debeant, per breve de rationabili parte in cancellaria
domini regis; Mandatum eft præfato efcaetori, quod præfato *Johanni* regi
Scotiæ feifinam terrarum de Tyndall cum pertinentibus plenarie faciat habere:
Salvo jure domini regis et alterius cujufcunque, &c. Ita quod idem rex
Scotiæ inde homagium fuum faciat domino regi in quindecim dies fancti
Michaelis ubicunque, &c. Ad quod homagium tenetur, prout per inquifitionem de terris illis captam compertum eft. Et quoad terras de Penrith et
Soureby cum pertinentiis, &c. eo quod præfati nuncii et attornati afferunt,
terras illas per donum et factum fpeciale in feifinam regum Scotiæ deveniffe,
ideo remaneant terræ illæ in manibus domini regis ufque terminum prædictum,
et tunc deferatur domino regi carta per quam, &c. Ad quem diem venit
prædictus rex Scotiæ, et protulit quodham fcriptum in hæc verba:

" SCIANT PRÆSENTES ET FUTURI, quod ita convenit in præfentia venerabilis patris domini D. T. T. Sancti Nicholai in Carcere Tulliano Diaconi
Cardinalis, et tunc Apoftolicæ fedis legati, apud Eboracum, inter dominum
Henricum regem Angliæ, et dominum *Alexandrum* regem Scotiæ, fuper omnibus querelis quas idem rex Scotiæ moverat vel movere poterat contra
dominum regem Angliæ, ufque ad diem Veneris proximum ante feftum Sancti
Michaelis, anno gratiæ millefimo ducentefimo tricefimo feptimo, fcilicet, fuper
comitatibus Northumbriæ, Cumbriæ, et Weftmorlandiæ, quos idem rex Scotiæ
petiit ficut hæreditatem fuam a dicto rege Angliæ; et præterea de quindecim
millibus marcis argenti, quas illuftris rex *Johannes* pater prædicti *Henrici* regis
Angliæ receperat a domino *Willielmo* quondam rege Scotiæ patre prædicti
Alexandri regis Scotiæ, pro quibufdam conventionibus inter dictos reges initis,
quæ a dicto rege *Johanne* non fuerant obfervatæ, ut idem *Alexander* rex Scotiæ dicebat; et de conventionibus factis inter dictum *Henricum* regem Angliæ
et dictum *Alexandrum* regem Scotiæ, fuper matrimonio contrahendo inter
eundem *Henricum* regem Angliæ et *Margeriam* fororem prædicti *Alexandri*
regis Scotiæ, quod ex parte dicti regis Angliæ non fuit obfervatum, ficut
idem rex Scotiæ dicebat; et de omnibus aliis querelis quas dictus *Alexander*

rex Scotiæ movit vel movere potuit pro se vel antecessoribus suis contra dictum
regem Angliæ usque ad terminum prædictum ;—videlicet, Quod dictus *Alexander* rex Scotiæ remisit et quietum clamavit, pro se et hæredibus suis, dicto
Henrico regi Angliæ et hæredibus suis in perpetuum, dictos comitatus Northumbriæ, Cumbriæ, et Westmerlandiæ, et totam prædictam pecuniam, et
omnes conventiones factas inter prædictum *Johannem* regem Angliæ et prædictum *Willielmum* regem Scotiæ, super conjugiis faciendis inter prædictum
Henricum regem Angliæ vel *Richardum* fratrem suum et *Margaretam* vel *Isabel-
lam* sorores prædicti *Alexandri* regis Scotiæ; et similiter conventiones factas
inter dictum *Henricum* regem Angliæ et dictum *Alexandrum* regem Scotiæ,
super matrimonio contrahendo inter ipsum *Henricum* regem Angliæ et *Margeriam* sororem dicti *Alexandri* regis Scotiæ. Pro hac autem remissione et quieta
clamantia, prædictus *Henricus* rex Angliæ dedit et concessit dicto *Alexandro*
regi Scotiæ ducentas libratas terræ in prædictis comitatibus Northumbriæ
et Cumbriæ, si prædictæ ducentæ libratæ terræ in ipsis comitatibus extra
villas ubi castra sita sunt possunt inveniri ; et si quod inde defuerit, ei perfi-
cietur in locis competentibus et propinquioribus dictis comitatibus Northumbriæ et Cumbriæ: Habendum et tenendum et in dominico retinendum eidem
Alexandro regi Scotiæ et hæredibus suis regibus Scotiæ, de dicto *Henrico* rege
Angliæ et hæredibus suis : Reddendo inde annuatim unum ousturcum sorum
ipsi regi Angliæ et hæredibus suis apud Karliolum per manum constabularii
castri Karlioli quicunque fuerit, in festo Assumptionis beatæ Mariæ, pro
omnibus serviciis, consuetudinibus, et aliis demandis quæ pro eisdem terris
exigi possunt : Ita libere, quod prædictus rex Scotiæ et hæredes sui habeant et
teneant dictas terras et homines dictarum terrarum, cum omnibus libertatibus
et liberis consuetudinibus et quietantiis suis, in bosco et plano, in pratis et
pasturis, in aquis et molendinis, in viis et semitis, in stagnis et vivariis, in
mariscis et piscariis, cum soc et sac, tol et theam, infangethef, outfangethef,
hamesoken, bridebertb, blodewite, flitwite, ferdewite, hengwite, leirwite,
flemensfrith, murdro, et latrocinio, forstall, infra tempus et extra tempus, et
in omnibus locis ; et quod ipse rex Scotiæ et hæredes sui et omnes homines
sui de prædictis terris sint liberi et quieti ab omni scotto, geldo, et omnibus
auxiliis vicecomitum et omnium ministrorum suorum, et de hidagio, carucagio,
danegeld, horngeld, exercitibus, wapentachiis, scutagio, tallagio, lestagio,
stallagio, shiris, hundredis, warda, wardepenny, haverpenny, hundredespenny,
borthalfpenny, thethingpeny ; et de operibus castellorum, parcorum, pontium, claustrorum, et omni careio, fumagio, navigio, et domorum regalium
edificatione, et omnimoda operatione. Et quod prædictus rex Scotiæ et
hæredes sui habeant omnia animalia quæ dicuntur wayf, inventa in prædictis
terris, nisi aliquis ea secutus fuerit qui possit et velit probare quod sua sint.
Concessum est etiam a dicto rege Angliæ, quod omnia placita quæ de
dictis terris de cætero emergent, et quæ coram justiciariis in banco
vel coram ipso rege Angliæ in itinere suo teneri consueverunt, de
cætero placitentur in curia ipsius regis Scotiæ et hæredum suorum
infra prædictas terras, et ibi terminentur per ballivos ipsorum regum
Scotiæ et hæredum suorum, per retornum brevis ipsius regis Angliæ et hæ-

                                                                         redum

redum fuorum, quem vicecomites ipforum iifdem ballivis habere facient, fi
placita. illa ibi per legem Angliæ teneri et terminari poffint; et placita quæ
ibi coram prædictis ballivis per legem terræ terminari nón poterunt, coram·
jufticiariis dicti regis Angliæ et hæredum fuorum itinerantibus ad primas
affifas infra comitatus in quibus terræ illæ fuerint teneantur et terminentur,
in primo adventu ipforum jufticiariorum, priufquam aliqua alia placita
teneantur, fecundum quod juftum fuerit, præfente fenefchallo prædicti regis
Scotiæ et affidente tanquam jufticiario ad illa placita tenenda : ita quod ballivi
vel homines ipfius regis Scotiæ de prædictis terris pro nulla fummonitione
vel aliquo placito exeant comitatus in quibus prædictæ terræ fuerint. Si qua
vero terra affignata fuerit domino regi Scotiæ de prædictis ducentis libratis
terræ infra metas foreftæ, nullus foreftarius regis Angliæ incumbet eandem ·
terram ipfius regis Scotiæ ad manducandum vel hofpitandum vel aliquid
aliud exigendum, nifi tantum pro attachiamentis faciendis de placitis ad foreftam fpectantibus, et hoc per vifum ballivi ipfius regis Scotiæ, fi requifitus
intereffe voluerit.   Placita vero coronæ, cum in prædictis terris emiffa erunt
attachiamenta, per ballivum et coronatores regis Angliæ, præfente ballivo
regis Scotiæ fi requifitus venire voluerit, et placitentur et terminantur eadem
placita coram jufticiariis itinerantibus et prædicto fenefchallo ad primam affifam
ficut prædictum eft de allis placitis.   Ubi fi aliquis hominum fuorum de
prædictis terris convictus fuerit de felonia, poft judicium factum fiat juftitia
per ballivos et homines ipforum regis Scotiæ et hæredum fuorum : Ita tamen,
quod non licebit domino regi Scotiæ vel hæredibus fuis remittere alicui
indicto pœnam ei debitam fecundum legem terræ, nec hæredibus damnatorum
terram per feloniam prædictam forisfactam reddere, nec etiam amerciamenta
remittere hiis qui amerciati fuerint pro quocunque forisfacto.   Omnia etiam
amerciamenta, et efcaeta, et proventus de prædictis terris tam anno et die
dicti regis Angliæ et hæredum fuorum, tam de terris per feloniam forisfactis
quam de omnibus aliis exitibus tam de placitis foreftæ quam de omnibus aliis
placitis homines prædictarum terrarum contingentibus, remaneant ipfi regi
Scotiæ et hæredibus fuis imperpetuum.   Et fi forte contingat aliquo tempore
ipfos reges Scotiæ vel hæredes fuos implacitari de prædictis terris vel de
aliqua parte earundem ; dominus rex Angliæ et hæredes fui eafdem terras,
ficut illas ei dedit, ipfis regi Scotiæ et hæredibus fuis warrantizabit et defendet
in perpetuum : Ita quod propter illud placitum, non oportebit ipfos reges
Scotiæ et hæredes fuos ad curiam regis Angliæ accedere, ut inde alicui refpondeant.   Et dominus rex Scotiæ fecit prædicto *Henrico* regi Angliæ homagium fuum de prædictis terris, et fidelitatem ei juravit.   Scripta vero vel
inftrumenta, fuper prædictis maritagiis et conventionibus a prædicto *Johanne*
quondam rege Angliæ five a prædicto *Henrico* rege Angliæ, et a prædicto
Willielmo quondam rege Scotiæ vel a dicto *Alexandro* rege Scotiæ confecta,
debent hinc inde reftitui ; eo falvo, quod fi in ipfis fcriptis vel inftrumentis
aliqua capitula negotium præfens non tangentia inveniantur, quæ alterutrius
regis utilitatem concernant, debent prædicta capitula per utriufque regis
literas innovari.   Similiter fi quæ chartæ fuper prædictis comitatibus poterunt
inveniri, regi Angliæ reftituentur.   Et fi forte impofterum aliqua inftru-

menta inveniantur de prædictis comitatibus et conventionibus quæ non fuerint restituta, viribus careant et pro nullis habeantur. Hanc autem conventionem fideliter tenendam in perpetuum, prædictus rex Angliæ fecit in
animam fuam jurare W. comitem Warren ; et dictus rex Scotiæ fimiliter in
animam fuam fecit jurare Walterum Comyn comitem de Menetheen. Et
præterea idem rex Scotiæ fecit comitem Maucolmum comitem de Meneteth,
Walterum filium Alani, Walterum Olyfant, Bernardum Fraffer, Henricum
de Bailloull, G. Marifcallum comitem de Penbrok, H. comitem Hereford,
David Comyn, David Marifcallum, Thomam filium Ranulphi, Willielmum
de Torr, Johannem de Bailloull, et Henricum de Haftingg, jurare de pace
ista tenenda, in forma literarum patentium, quas ipfi regi Angliæ inde
fecerunt. Præterea idem rex Scotiæ et barones prædicti jurati pofuerunt fe
jurifdictioni domini Papæ fub hac forma, quod fi dominus rex Scotiæ vel
dicti barones fui aliquo tempore contra prædictum juramentum venerint,
debent fuper hoc a domino Papa canonice coherceri, propter quod etiam
debent ipfe rex Scotiæ et barones prædicti domino Papæ citatorie fignificare,
ut hanc jurifdictionem alicui fuffraganeorum Cantuarienfis Archiepifcopi de
confenfu partium committat. Ad majorem etiam hujus pacis fecuritatem,
facta eft hæc carta inter dictos reges ad modum Cirographi ; ita quod uterque
illorum alterius parti figillum fuum appofuit. Hiis teftibus ; Venerabilibus
patribus, W. Eboraci archiepifcopo, R. Ciceftriæ domini regis cancellario,
W. Carliol, W. Wigorniæ, et W. de Glafgu cancellario præfati regis Scotiæ,
epifcopis : W. Electo Valenc', R. comite Pictau et Cornubiæ, W. comite
Warrenn, J. comite Lincoln conftabulario Ceftriæ, W. comite Albemarl, R.
comite Winton et de Monte Forti, G. Mar. comite Pembr', Comite Patrie,
Comite de Strathern, Comite de Levenath, Comite de Angus, Comite de
Mar, Comite de Atholl, Comite de Roos, Willielmo Longfpee, Radulpho
de Thonny, W. de Roos, R. de Roos, W. de Ferrars, R. Bertheram, H.
Paynil, G. de Umfranvill, Amaur de Sancto Amando, Petro de Malo Lacu,
Magiftro Petro de Burdegal et Magiftro Alt' clericis domini legati, Johanne
filio Galfridi, H. de Vinon, Stephano de Segrave, W. de Lancaftre, W. de
Say, R. de Gray, Thoma de Fournival, Johanne de Lexinton, Johanne de
Pleis, Bartholomeo Pecche, Willielmo Gernon, Richard filio Hugonis,
et aliis."

Et idem rex Scotiæ, in propria perfona fua, in præfentia præfati regis
Angliæ et concilii fui, petiit quod terræ et tenementa illa de Penreth et
Soureby cum pertinentiis fibi juxta tenorem fcripti prædicti liberentur. Et
fuper hoc, idem rex Scotiæ quæfitus fi qua alia fcripta vel munimenta habeat,
per quæ prædicta tenementa petere velit aut poterit, vel fi alio modo ea petat
quam fecundum formam fcripti prædicti, manifefte dicit, quod alia fcripta
feu munimenta inde non habet, nec alio modo ea petit aut habere clamat nifi,
fecundum formam et tenorem fcripti ejufdem. Et quia idem rex Scotiæ
prædictum fcriptum domini *Henrici* regis, patris domini regis nunc, profert
in forma prædicta, figillo ejufdem domini *Henrici* regis fignatum, quod
teftatur, quod terræ et tenementa prædicta data fuerunt prædicto *Alexandro*
regi Scotiæ, anteceffori præfati *Johannis* regis nunc, tenenda fibi et hæredibus

7   fuis

fuis regibus Scotiæ, et idem *Johannes* rex eft hæres ipfius *Alexandri* et rex Scotiæ, nec idem *Johannes* alium ftatum clamat in terris et tenementis illis nifi juxta formam et tenorem fcripti prædicti ; ideo feifina terrarum et tenementorum eorundem fibi liberetur in forma prædicta et juxta tenorem fcripti ejufdem : Salvo femper jure domini regis Angliæ et alterius cujufcunque. Ita quod fi dominus rex Angliæ vel hæredes fui, temporibus futuris, terras et tenementa prædicta cum pertinentiis, verfus prædictum regem Scotiæ aut hæredes fuos petere voluerint ; idem rex Scotiæ et hæredes fui nihil in terris et tenementis illis cum pertinentiis clamare potuerint, nifi fecundum formam et tenorem fcripti prædicti, prout idem rex Scotiæ terras et tenementa illa modo petit.

Et idem rex Scotiæ die Veneris proximo ante feftum omnium Sanctorum, tam pro terris et tenementis illis, quam pro terris et tenementis de Tindale, et etiam pro proparte fua honoris de Huntingdon ipfum regem Scotiæ contingentis, facit homagium domino regi Angliæ ; et Patricius de Graham miles, ipfius regis Scotorum facramentum fidelitatis fecit eidem regi Angliæ in animam præfati regis Scotiæ, de omnibus terris et tenementis prædictis, et de proparte honoris prædicti cum pertinentiis : Et mandatum eft Thomæ de Normanvill efcaetori per breve domini regis in hæc verba : " *Edwardus* Dei gratia, rex Angliæ dominus Hiberniæ, et dux Aquitaniæ, dilecto et fideli fuo ·Thomæ de Normanvill efcaetori fuo ultra Trentam, falutem. Sciatis, quod cepimus homagium dilecti et fidelis noftri *Johannis de Balliolo* regis Scotiæ, de omnibus terris et tenementis quæ idem Johannes tenet de nobis in capite in Anglia, videlicet, de terra de Tyndale, et de manerio de Soureby et Penrith, cum pertinentiis ; quæ per mortem *Alexandri* nuper regis Scotiæ, anteceffuris ipfius *Johannis*, capi fecimus in manum noftram, ac de proparte fua honoris Huntingdon : Et ei terras illas et propartem cum pertinentiis reddidimus ; falvo in omnibus jure noftro et hæredum noftrorum, cum inde loqui voluerimus, et etiam jure alterius cujufcunque. Et ideo vobis mandamus, quod eidem *Johanni* de terris et proparte prædicta cum pertinentiis plenam feifinam perfici faciatis in forma prædicta. Tefte meipfo apud Weftminfter, 29° die Octobris, anno regni noftri vicefimo primo."

INSPEXIMUS etiam irrotulamentum quarundam literarum patentium de confirmatione, gerenda data decimo die Februarii, anno regni domini Richardi nuper regis Angliæ fecundi undecimo, in cancellaria noftra infra Turrim noftram London, de recordo etiam remanente, in hæc verba :

RICHARDUS Dei gratia, rex Angliæ et Franciæ et dominus Hiberniæ, Omnibus ad quos præfentes literæ pervenerint, falutem :

INSPEXIMUS literas patentes domini Edwardi nuper regis Angliæ avi noftri factas, in hæc verba :

" EDWARDUS Dei gratia, rex Angliæ, dominus Hiberniæ et Aquitaniæ, Omnibus ad quos præfentes literæ pervenerint falutem. Supplicaverunt nobis homines et tenentes maneriorum de Peniteth, Salkeld, et Soureby, quæ funt de antiquo dominico coronæ noftræ infra foreftam noftram de Inglewoode habitantes, per petitionem fuam coram nobis et concilio noftro in præfenti parliamento noftro exhibitam, ut cum ipfi pro eo quod terræ et tenementa fua, pro quibus magnam firmam nobis folvere tenentur, per inimicos noftros Scotiæ, ac blada fua in terris fuis ibidem crefcentia per feras noftras foreftæ prædictæ fæpius deftruuntur et devaftantur, ut firmam fuam præd1ctam nobis folvere non poffunt, nifi alias fubveniatur eifdem, velimus eis in auxilium firmæ fuæ prædictæ concedere, quod ipfi communam pafturæ ad omnia animalia in forefta prædicta habere valeant fibi et hæredibus fuis imperpetuum : Nos confideratione præmifforum, et pro eo quod coram nobis in eodem parliamento teftificatum exiftit præmiffa veritatem continere, volentes eifdem hominibus et tenentibus gratiam facere fpecialem, conceffimus eis pro nobis et hæredibus noftris, quod ipfi et hæredes fui habeant et teneant communam pafturæ ad omnia animalia fua in forefta prædicta in perpetuum, prout Prior Carlioli et Willielmus Eng. lifh ac alii tenentes infra foreftam prædictam communam pafturæ ibidem habent ex conceffione noftra et progenitorum noftrorum, fine occafione vel impedimento noftri vel hæredum noftrorum, jufticiariorum, foreftariorum, veredariorum, regardatorum, agiftatorum, ballivorum, et miniftrorum noftrorum foreftæ quorumcunque. In cujus rei teftimonium, has literas noftras fieri fecimus patentes. Tefte meipfo apud Weftmonafterium vicefimo fexto die Octobris, anno regni noftri tricefimo feptimo."

Nos autem literas illas, et omnia contenta in eifdem, rata habentes et grata, ea pro nobis et hæredibus noftris quantum in nobis eft, nunc hominibus et tenentibus maneriorum prædictorum, hæredibus et fuccefforibus fuis, hominibus et tenentibus eorundem maneriorum, acceptamus, approbamus, ratificamus, et tenore præfentium concedimus et confirmamus, prout literæ prædictæ rationabiliter teftantur, et prout ipfi et eorum anteceffores, homines et tenentes dictorum maneriorum communam pafturæ prædictæ ad animalia fua in forefta, prædicta, a tempore confectionis earundem literarum hucufque habuerunt et tenuerunt. In cujus rei teftimonium, has literas noftras fieri fecimus patentes. Tefte meipfo apud Weftminfter decimo die Februarii, anno regni noftri undecimo.

Nos autem tenores præmifforum prædictorum, ad requifitionem Thomæ Carleton armigeri, Willielmi Whelpdale generofi, Thomæ Atkinfon generofi, et aliorum hominum et tenentium manerii de Penreth in comitatu Cumbriæ prædictæ, duximus exemplificandas per præfentes. In cujus rei teftimonium, has literas noftras fieri fecimus patentes. Tefte meipfo apud Weftmonafterium quartodecimo die Maii, anno regno noftri Angliæ, Franciæ, et Hiberniæ decimo nono et Scotiæ quinquagefimo quarto.

No. XXXI.

Foundation charter of the Nunnery in the parifh of *Ainftable*, by king *William Rufus*.

WILLELMUS Dei gratia, rex Anglorum et dux Normannorum, ex mero motu noftro, et intuitu charitatis, fundavimus, conftruximus, et in perpetuum ordinavimus, in puram et perpetuam eleemofynam, unam domum

mum et monasterium nigrarum monialium ordinis Sancti Benedicti, in honorem
Jesu Christi et beatæ virginis Mariæ, pro animabus progenitorum nostrorum et
omnium Christianorum, prout situatur juxta aquam vocatam Croglin in comitatu Cumbriæ. Etiam dedimus, et concessimus monialibus ibidem duas acras
terræ super quas prædicta domus et monasterium situantur. Et etiam dedimus
et concessimus eisdem monialibus três carucatas terræ et decem acras prati,
cum omnimodis communiis, boscis, et vastis eisdem tribus carucatis terræ
quovis modo pertinentibus, jacentibus juxta monasterium prædictum. Etiam
dedimus et concessimus eisdem monialibus et successoribus suis in perpetuum,
ducentas et sexdecim acras terræ existentes infra forestam nostram de Ingle-,
wood, jacentes ex parte boreali cujusdam aquæ vocatæ Tarnwadelyn, cum
omnibus boscis, proficuis, et commoditatibus super easdem existentibus, sive
unquam postmodum crescentibus.

Etiam concessimus eisdem monialibus communiam pasturæ cum omnibus
animalibus suis, pro se et suis ibidem tenentibus, per toram forestam nostram
de Ingilwood, capiendis ibidem sufficientem maeremium pro omnibus suis
ædificiis, quandocunque et quotiescunque necesse fuerit, per deliberationem
forestariorum nostrorum sive eorum unius ibidem existentium. Et etiam
concessimus et confirmavimus eisdem monialibus et successoribus suis quendam annuum reditum xl. solidorum annuatim percipiendorum in perpetuum de tenementis nostris in villa nostra de Karlile, solvendorum eisdem
monialibus et successoribus suis, per manus custodis nostri villæ de Carlile
prædictæ ad festa Pentecostes et Sancti Martini in yeme per æquales portiones. Et etiam concedimus pro nobis et hæredibus nostris, quod prædictæ moniales, tenentes, et sui servientes, liberi sint de tolneto palando per
totum regnum nostrum Angliæ, pro aliquibus bestiis sive rebus quibuscunque,
per eas sive earum aliquem tenentem seu servientem emendis. Et etiam concedimus et confirmamus, quod monasterium et domus prædicta, cum prædictis
tribus carucatis, duabus acris terræ, cum decem acris prati, in omnibus libera
sint et habeant omnes libertates suas, simili modo sicut conceditur nostro monasterio de Westminster, absque vexatione, molestatione, sive aliqua inquieta-
tione seu læsione aliquorum vicecomitum, escaetorum, ballivorum, sive aliquorum ministrorum seu ligeorum nostrorum quorumcunque. Et etiam concedimus eisdem monialibus communam pasturæ cum animalibus suis infra villam et communiam de Aynstaplyth, cum liberis introitu et exitu. Nec non
concedimus, quod prædictæ moniales liberæ sint per totam terram suam, pro
quibuscunque tenentibus, et liberam habeant warrenam, tam pro sectis curi-
arum nostrarum, quam in aquis, boscis, terris, planis, seu metis suis, eidem
monasterio spectantibus, seu quovis modo pertinentibus: Habenda, tenenda,
et occupanda omnia et singula prædicta recitata, præfatis monialibus et successoribus suis in perpetuum, de nobis et hæredibus nostris, in puram et perpetuam eleemosynam, spontanea ita voluntate et concessione AS HERT MAY IT
THINK OR YGH MAY IT SEE. In cujus rei testimonium, has literas nostras
fieri fecimus patentes. Teste meipso apud Westminster, sexto die mensis Januarii, anno regni nostri secundo.—1 Dugd. Mon. 329.

No. XXXII.

No. XXXII.

Confirmation thereof by king EDWARD THE FOURTH.

REX omnibus ad quos, &c. falutem. Sciatis, quod nos ex lamentabili in-
finuatione prioriffæ et monialium domus five prioratus de Armythwhayte
in comitatu Cumbriæ, prope marchias Scotiæ fituati et ædificati, accepimus,
qualiter domus five prioratus prædictus, qui de fundatione inclytorum progenitorum noftrorum quondam regum Angliæ et noftro patronatu exiftit, per
inimicos et adverfarios noftros Scotiæ in domibus, claufuris, et aliis ædificiis
totaliter deftructus et devaftatus, ac de rebus, reliquiis, ornamentis ecclefi-
afticis, libris et aliis jocalibus fpoliatus extitit, et quod deterius eft, omnia
cartæ, fcripta, donationes, literæ patentes, aliaque evidentiæ et munimenta,
dictum prioratum et poffeffiones ejufdem per dictos progenitores eidem priora-
tui antiquitus datas et collatas concernentia, per dictos adverfarios noftros combufta, afportata, et alias elongata fuerunt; ficque magna pars poffeffionum
prædictarum ab eadem domo five prioratu fubftracta, alienata, et detenta exiftit; eoque prætextu, ftatus et proventus ejufdem domus five prioratus adeo
diminuuntur, quod nunc prioriffa et moniales in domo five prioratu prædicto
exiftentes non habent unde vivere ac divina officia et obfequia ac hofpitalitatem
aliaque pietatis opera ab olim ibidem laudabiliter inftituta fundata et ftabilita
fuftinere facereque valeant aut fupportare, quinimo oportebit eafdem prioriffam
et moniales domum five prioratum prædictum, egeftate caufante, infra breve
relinquere, ac divina officia et alia opera prædicta ibidem penitus ceffare, ac
vota dictorum progenitorum noftrorum fundatorum fuorum totaliter effectu
deftrui et defraudari, nifi per nos caritative fubveniatur eifdem; unde eadem
prioriffa et moniales nobis humillime fupplicarunt, ut noftram munificentiam
regiam eis in hac parte gratiofe exhiberi voluerimus: Nos, præmifforum confideratione, earumque inopiam et egeftatem pio compatientes affectu, in aug-
mentationem divini cultus, et ut cædem prioriffa et moniales pro bono ftatu
noftro, et Elizabethæ confortis noftræ, Edwardique percariffimi filii noftri pri-
mogeniti, ac pro animabus noftris cum ab hac luce migraverimus, et pro animabus dictorum progenitorum noftrorum apud altiffimum fpecialius deprecentur
et exorent, ac etiam ut vota et intentiones ipforum progenitorum noftrorum
debitum fortiantur effectum, de gratia noftra fpeciali volentes fecuritati et
quieti dictarum prioriffæ et monialium et fuccefforum fuarum gratiofe providere,
titulum, ftatum, poffeffionem, quos eadem nunc prioriffa et moniales habent
in domo five prioratu prædictis, ac in terris, tenementis, redditibus, et poffeffionibus, et cæteris fuis pertinentiis quibufcunque, quæ habent ex donatione,
conceffione, et fundatione five ratificatione aliquorum progenitorum noftrorum
feu aliorum quorumcunque, et fpecialiter, cujufdam antiqui claufi vocati le
NONNECLOSE, pro nobis et hæredibus noftris quantum in nobis eft acceptamus,
approbamus, ratificamus, et confirmamus; et ulterius, prioratum prædictum
et cætera præmiffa cum pertinentiis, eifdem prioriffæ et monialibus et fuccefforibus

foribus fuis quantum in nobis eft damus et concedimus: Habendum fibi et fucceſſoribus fuis prædiſtis imperpetuum, cum fuis juribus et pertinentiis quibufcunque, juxta primariam fundationem earundem. Nolentes, quod eædem prioriſſa et moniales vel fucceſſores fuæ prædictæ fuper poſſeſſione fuæ domus five prioratus prædicti et cæterorum premiſſorum cum pertinentiis, per nos vel hæredes noſtros, juſticiarios, eſcaetores, vicecomites, feu alios ballivos et miniſtros noſtros quofcunque futuris temporibus occafionentur, impetantur, inquietentur, vexentur, perturbentur, moleſtantur in aliquo feu graventur; aliquo ſtatuto, actu, five ordinatione in contrarium facto, non obſtante: Abfque fine feu feodo nobis, pro literis noſtris prædictis, aut aliqua alia caufa præmiſſa quovis modo concernente, aliqualiter capiendis, faciendis, five folvendis. In cujus, &c. T. R. apud Weſtmonaſterium, ix Aprilis:—1 *Dugd. Mon.* 329.

No. XXXIII.

LIST of KNIGHTS OF THE SHIRE for WEST MORLAND.

26 Ed. 1. Thomas de Derwentwater, Roger de Burton.
28 —— Hugh de Louther, Robert de Waſheton.
30 —— Robert de Aſkeby, Thomas de Bethum.
33 —— Hugh de Louthre, Nicolas de Leaburne.
1 Ed. 2. William de Goldington, Walter de Stirkeland.
2 —— Robert Engliſh, Thomas de Bethum.
4 —— Robert Engliſh, Thomas de Bethum.
5 —— Robert Engliſh, Thomas de Bethum.
6 —— Robert Engliſh, Walter de Stirkeland.
7 —— Robert de Aſkeby, Matthew de Redman.
8 —— Nicholas de Leyburne, Thomas de Hellebeck.
    Robert de Leyburne, Henry de Warthecoppe.
9 —— Nicholas de Morland, John de Kirkby Thore.
10 —— Henry de Warthecop, Robert de Sandford.
12 —— William Engliſh, Robert de Botiler.
15 —— Walter de Stirkeland, Robert de Sandford.
16 —— Walter de Stirkeland, Robert de Sandford.
17 —— Walter de Stirkeland, Robert de Sandford.
18 —— Robert de Sandford, John de Wakethwait.
19 —— Robert de Burton, Robert de Sandford.
1 Ed. 3. John de Lancaſtre, Robert de Sandford.
    John de Stirkland, William Engliſh.
2 —— William Engliſh, Robert de Sandford.
    Roger de Bronoleſheved, Hugh de Moriceby.
    John de Lancaſtre, Robert de Sandford.
3 —— William Engliſh, Robert de Sandford.
    Thomas de Warthecop, Robert de Sandford.
4 —— William Threlkeld, William Engliſh.

5 Ed.

5 Ed. 3. William Englifh, Robert de Sandford.
6 —— Walter de Stirkland, William Englifh.
7 —— William Englifh, Robert de Sandford.
8 —— William Englifh, William de Langwathby.
     William Englifh, Robert de Sandford.
9 —— William Englifh, Robert de Sandford.
10 —— Ralph de Reftwald, William de Langwathby.
     William Englifh, Hugh de Moriceby.
11 —— William de Brampton, William de Langwathby.
     William Englifh, William de Langwathby.
12 —— Richard de Moreland, Roger de Kendal.
     William de Langwathby, Thomas de Sandford.
13 —— William de Brampton, William de Langwathby.
14 —— Hugh de Louthre, Robert de Sandford.
     Roger de Bronolfhewed, Thomas de Mufgrave.
15 —— William Englifh, Thomas de Mufgrave.
17 —— Walter de Stirkland, Robert de Sandford.
     Richard de Prefton, Thomas de Mufgrave.
18 —— William Englifh, Thomas de Mufgrave.
     Robert de Sandford, John de Wakethwayt.
20 —— William de Sandford junior, Thomas de Sandford.
22 —— William Englifh, Thomas de Sandford.
     Robert Boteler, Thomas de Halghton.
27 —— Richard de Prefton junior. (One only fummoned.)
28 —— William de Windefore, Robert de Sandford junior.
29 —— Roland de Thornburgh, Ralph de Bethom.
31 —— Matthew de Redman, Hugh de Louthre.
33 —— Hugh de Louthre, Nicholas de Layburne.
34 —— Rowland de Thornburgh, Thomas de Berwys.
35 —— Henry de Threlkeld, Thomas de Sandford.
36 —— James de Pickering, John de Prefton.
37 —— Thomas de Sandford, Henry de Threlkeld.
39 —— Henry de Threlkeld, John de Prefton.
42 —— Henry de Threlkeld, John de Prefton.
43 —— Gilbert de Culwen, John de Derwentwater.
45 —— Hugh de Louthre, John de Prefton.
46 —— Hugh de Louthre, John de Prefton.
47 —— Rowland de Thornburgh, William de Thornburgh.
50 —— Chriftopher de Lancaftre, Thomas de Warthecop.
51 —— Richard de Roos, John fon of Hugh de Louthre.
1 Ric. 2. James de Pickering, Hugh de Salkeld.
2 —— James de Pickering, John de Louthre.
3 —— William de Threlkeld, John de Louthre.
4 —— Walter de Stirkeland, Thomas de Warthecop.
5 —— William de Threlkeld, Hugh de Salkeld.
     John de Prefton, John de Crakenthorpe.

6 Ric. 2. James de Pickering, John de Kirkeby.
         Richard de Roos, John de Dente.
7 —— Richard de Roos, Robert de Clibbourne.
         Robert de Clibbourne, John de Manfergh.
8 —— Walter de Stirkeland, Robert de Windefore.
9 —— Richard de Roos, John de Crakanthorp.
10 —— John de Derwentwater, Robert de Cliburne.
11 —— Thomas de Blenkanfop, Thomas de Stirkeland.
12 —— Robert de Sandford, Hugh de Salkeld.
13 —— John de Crakanthorpe, Hugh de Salkeld.
14 —— Chriftopher de Morefby, Hugh de Salkeld.
15 —— William de Culwen, William de Thorneburgh.
16 —— John de Crakanthorpe, Hugh de Salkeld.
17 —— William de Culwen, William de Thorneburgh.
18 —— Walter de Stirkland, William de Crakanthorpe.
20 —— John de Lancaftre, Hugh de Salkeld.
21 —— William de Culwen, William de Crakanthorpe.
1 Hen. 4. Thomas de Mufgrave, John de Crakanthorpe.
2 —— William de Thorneburgh, Hugh de Salkeld.
4 —— William de Threlkeld, William de Crakanthorpe.
5 —— Rowland Thornburgh, Richard Ducket.
6 —— Robert de Leyburn, Thomas de Strickland.
8 —— John de Betham, John de Lancaftre.
         Alan de Penington, Thomas de Warthecop.
9 —— Alan de Penyngton, Thomas de Warthecop.
12 —— Robert de Leyburn, Chriftopher de Morefby.
1 Hen. 5. Robert Crakenthorp, John Hoton.
2 —— Thomas de Warcupp, William de Thornburgh.
3 —— Rowland de Thornburgh, Robert de Crakanthorpe.
5 —— Rowland de Thornburgh, Richard de Wherton.
8 —— Alan de Penington, Thomas de Warthecupp.
         William Beauchampe, Thomas Grene.
9 —— John de Lancaftre, William de Blenkanfop.
1 Hen. 6. Robert de Layburne, Thomas fon of William de Blenkanfop.
3 —— Thomas de Bethom, William de Crakanthorp.
5 —— John Dennyfgrave, Robert de Crakanthorp.
7 —— Thomas Stirkeland, Chriftopher Lancaftre.
20 —— Walter de Stirkeland, Richard de Redeman.
25 —— Nicholas Gerlington, George Dacre.
28 —— Thomas Curwen, William Maletts.
29 —— Thomas Paul, John Strete.
6 Ed. 4. William Parr, Chriftopher Morefby.
12 —— William Parr, John Stirkland.
     [N. B. All the indentures, writs, and returns, from this time to the
     firft year of Ed. 6. are loft, except one bundle in the 33 Hen. 8.]
33 Hen 8. Nicholas Leyburn, Nicholas Bacon.

1 Ed. 6. Charles Branden, Thomas Warcop.
7 —— Tho' Warcop, Thomas Fallowfield.
1 Mar. Thomas Warcop, Thomas Fallowfield.
1 & 2 Ph. & Mar. Thomas Warcop.
2 & 3 ——————— Thomas Warcop.
4 & 5 ————————— Anthony Kempe, Thomas Sackville.
1 Eliz. Lancelot Lancaster, Thomas Warcop.
5 —— Walter Strickland, Gerard Lowther.
13 —— Allan Bellingham, Thomas Warcop.
14 —— Thomas Knyvet, John Warcop.
27 —— Francis Clifford, Thomas Warcop.
28 —— Francis Clifford, Thomas Warcop.
31 —— Francis Dacre, Thomas Warcop.
35 —— William Bowes, Edward Denny.
39 —— Walter Harcourt, Henry Cholmley.
43 —— George Wharton, Thomas Strickland.
1 James. Thomas Strickland, Richard Musgrave, knights.
12 —— Thomas Wharton knight, Henry lord Clifford.
18 —— Henry Clifford, Thomas Wharton, knights.
21 —— John Lowther, Robert Strickland, esquires.
1 Cha. John Lowther esquire, Henry Bellingham baronet.
2 —— John Lowther esquire, Henry Bellingham baronet.
3 —— John Lowther knight, John Lowther esquire.
15 —— Philip Musgrave, Henry Bellingham, baronets.
16 —— Philip Musgrave, Henry Bellingham, baronets.
An. 1652. Charles Howard esquire (Only one returned).
     3. Christopher Lister, Henry Baynes, esquires.
   1660. Sir John Lowther bart. Sir Thomas Wharton, knight of the Bath.
     61. Sir Philip Musgrave, Sir Tho' Strickland.
        Sir John Lowther baronet, Alan Bellingham.
     78. Sir John Lowther baronet, Alan Bellingham.
     79. Alan Bellingham, Christopher Philipson.
     81. Sir John Lowther baronet, Alan Bellingham.
     85. Sir John Lowther baronet, Alan Bellingham.
     88. Sir John Lowther baronet, Henry Wharton.
———   Goodwyn Wharton.
   1690. Sir John Lowther, Sir Christopher Musgrave, baronets.
     95. Sir John Lowther (made a lord), Sir Richard Sandford.
        William Fleming, esquire.
     98. Sir Richard Sandford, William Fleming.
   1700. Henry Graham, Sir Christopher Musgrave.
      1. Sir Richard Sandford, Henry Graham.
      2. Sir Christopher Musgrave, Robert Lowther.
       William Fleming.
      5. Henry Graham, Robert Lowther.
       William Fleming.
      7. Sir William Fleming, Robert Lowther.

                                 An.

An. 1708. Daniel Wilſon, James Graham.
    10. Hon. James Graham, Daniel Wilſon.
    13. Hon. James Graham, Daniel Wilſon.
  1714. Hon. James Graham, Daniel Wilſon.
    22. Anthony Lowther, Hon. James Graham.
    27. Hon. Anthony Lowther, Daniel Wilſon.
  1734. Hon. Anthony Lowther, Daniel Wilſon.
    41. Sir Philip Muſgrave baronet, Daniel Wilſon eſquire.
    47. John Dalſton, Edward Wilſon, eſquires.
    54. John Dalſton eſquire, Sir George Dalſton baronet.
  1761. Sir James Lowther baronet, John Upton, eſquire.
    68. John Robinſon, Thomas Fenwick, eſquires.
  1774. Sir James Lowther, and Sir Michael le Fleming, baronets.
James Lowther eſquire.

No. XXXIV.

LIST of BURGESSES for APPLEBY.

26 Ed. 1. Hugh de Graunger, John de Karl.
 28 —— William Grene, William Spavys.
 30 —— William de Goldington, William Berwis.
 33 —— William de Goldington, William Berwis.
1 Ed. 2. Simon de Hoton, Robert de Merket.
2 —— Thomas Franceys, Robert Nevile.
4 —— Richard Simondſon, William de Bray.
5 —— Adam Marchall, John Ware.
6 —— John Scayff, Walter Dobeſmane.
7 —— Alexander Berewiſe, William de la Bray.
8 —— William de Goldington, Robert de Goldington.
12 —— William Goldington, Thomas Franceys.
15 —— William Goldington, William Goldington.
16 —— Walter Dobeſmane, William de Goldington.
19 —— William de Kirkby, William de Bolton.
1 Ed. 3. Adam Dane, Hugh de Bernard Caſtle.
Thomas Naper, John Scayff.
2 —— John Scayff, Walter Roberdeſman.
John Roland, Hugh de Bernard Caſtle.
4 —— William Engliſh, William de Kirkeby.
Simon Kemp, Peter Barbour.
6 —— John Flemyng, Adam Crofton.
Simon Sandford, John de Coupeland.
Robert Sandford, William de Kirkeby.
7 —— William Kirkeby, Thomas Sandford.
9 —— Simon Kemp, Thomas Sandford.
John Hobſon, William Sandford.

6 Ed. 3. Thomas Coufin, John Hobfon.

11 —— Albric Graunger, Thomas de Kitchin.
        John Wynd, Simon Kemp.

12 —— Thomas Sandford, William Sandford.
        Robert de Louthre, Thomas Franceys.

13 —— (Not legible.)

14 —— Thomas de Corbrigg, Thomas Clerk.
        Thomas Sandford, William Sandford.

15 —— Thomas Sandford, William Sandford.

17 —— Thomas Scayff, Eudo Ruffel.

20 —— Simon Sandford, Thomas Dauney.

21 —— Walter de Gouger, Jeremy de Grameftone.

24 —— Robert Sandford, Thomas Dauney.

26 —— Robert Sandford, Thomas Dauney.

29 —— Thomas Fitz-William, Walter Thornburgman.

31 —— William Chamberlain, Patric Croft.

34 —— William Walker, John Prudham.
        John Bennetfon, Roger Miles.

36 —— Thomas Bromfield, Adam Wewat.

37 —— (Not legible.)

38 —— William Stilton, William Brifkowe.

39 —— John Burgh, Thomas del Kitchin.

42 —— Robert Overdees, Thomas Bates.

43 —— Robert Overdees, Thomas Bates.
        Patric Croft, William Walker.

46 —— Robert Overdees, John Penny.

47 —— Robert Goldington, John Whoreworth.

50 —— William Helton, Adam Crofsby.

2 Ric. 2. Thomas Fournes, John . . . . ,

3 —— Robert Overdees, William Coldane.

6 —— John Overdees, Robert Overdees.

7 —— John Overdees, Robert Overdees.

9 —— Adam Crofsby, William de Soulby.

11 —— Adam Crofsby, William de Soulby.

15 —— William Soulby, John de Sourby.

18 —— Robert Yare, William Savage.

20 —— John Helton, John Sourby.

21 —— Chriftopher Culwene, Thomas Chamberlayne.

1 Hen. 4. Thomas Warcop, William Crakanthorp.

3 —— Robert Yare, Robert Ored.

18 —— John Helton, John Soureby.

1 Hen. 5. Robert Sandford, Thomas Stockdale.

2 —— Robert Crakanthorp, John Burkerig.

5 —— Thomas Stockdale, Thomas Burkerig.

8 —— William de Crakenthorp, John Niandfergh.
        William Louther, Nicholas Stanfhawe.

9 Hen.

Hen. 5. Nicholas Stanſhawe, John de Bathe.
Hen. 6. Nicholas Stanſhawe, John Foreſter.
- —— John de Helton, Robert Roche.
7 —— Jeffrey Threlkeld, Robert Leybourne.
20 —— Richard Brady, Robert Ingilton.
25 —— Robert Kelſey, John Harwood.
28 —— William Overtone, John Blackburne..
29 —— Robert Marſton, William Watyr.
7 Ed. 4. John Rayne, Peter Curtays.
12 —— John Scot, Peter Curtays.
. . . .
33 Hen. 8. Clement Horſeley, Thomas John.
1 Ed. 6. Thomas Joly, Robert Wyrley.
7 . . . .
1 Mary. George Giffard, James Banks.
       John Eltofts, William Danbye.
1 & 2 Ph. & M. John Eltofts.
2 & 3 ———— John Eltofts.
4 & 5 ———— John Eltofts, Nicholas Purſlow.
1 Eliz. John Eltofts, Chriſtopher Munkton.
5 —— Chriſtopher Munkton, Robert Atkinſon.
13 —— John Leighton, Richard Wrothe.
14 —— Robert Bowes, George Trewell.
27 —— George Ireland, Henry Macwilliam.
28 —— James Ryther, Robert Conſtable.
31 —— Ralph Bowes, Thomas Poſthumus Hobby.
35 —— Cuthbert Reynolds, Poſthumus Hobby.
39 —— James Colebrand, John Lilly.
43 —— John Morris, Thomas Cæſar.
1 James. John Morris, William Bowyer.
12 —— Arthur Ingram, Thomas Hughes.
18 —— Arthur Ingram, Thomas Hughes.
21 —— Arthur Ingram, Thomas Hughes.
1 Cha. John Hotham, Thomas Hughes.
2 —— William Slingſby, William Aſhton.
3 —— Richard Lowther, William Aſhton.
15 —— Richard viſcount Dungarvon, Richard Lowther..
16 —— Richard earl of Cork, John Brook.
       Richard Salway, Henry Ireton.
An. 1659. Adam Bains, Nathaniel Fielding.
    1660. John Dalſton, Thomas Tufton.
      61. John Dalſton, Thomas Tufton.
      78. Hon. Richard Tufton, Anthony Lowther.
      79. Hon. Richard Tufton, Anthony Lowther.
      81. Hon. Sackville Tufton, Sir John Bland.
    1685. Hon. Sackville Tufton, Philip Muſgrave.

An. 1688. Philip Mufgrave, William Cheyne.
   90. Richard Lowther.
   90. William Cheyne, Charles Boyle.
       Sir John Walter.
   95. Sir William Twyfden, Sir Chriftopher Mufgrave.
       Sir John Walter.
   98. Hon. Gervais Pierpoint, Sir John Walter.
1700. Hon. Gervais Pierpoint, Wharton Dunch.
    1. Hon. Gervais Pierpoint, Wharton Dunch.
    2. Hon. Gervais Pierpoint, James Graham.
    5. James Graham, William Harvey.
    7. James Graham, William Harvey.
    8. Edward Duncomb, Nicholas Lechmere.
1710. Edward Duncomb, Thomas Lutwych.
  13. Thomas Lutwych, Sir Thomas Sandford.
  14. Sir Richard Sandford, Thomas Lutwych.
  22. Hon. Sackville Tufton, Sir Richard Sandford.
                     James Lowther.
  27. Hon. Sackville Tufton, John Ramfden.
       Walter Plummer.
  34. John Ramfden, Walter Plummer.
  41. Sir John Ramfden, George Doddington.
  47. Sir John Ramfden, Randle Wilbraham.
  54. General Honywood, Fletcher Norton.
  61. General Honywood, General Stanwicks.
  68. General Honywood, Charles Jenkinfon.
               Fletcher Norton.
  74. General Honywood, George Johnftone efquire.

No. XXXV.

LIST of SHERIFFS of CUMBERLAND.

  1 Hen. 2. Hildred de Carlifle.
  2 —— Richard de Lucy.
  3 —— Robert Fitz-Troyte, for 16 years.
 19 —— Adam fon of the faid Robert, for 2 years.
 21 —— Robert de Vallibus (Vaux) for 10 years.
 31 —— Hugh de Morewick, for 4 years.
  1 Ric. 1. William fon of Aldeline, for 9 years.
 10 —— William de Taterfhall.
  1 John. William de Stutevill, for 4¼ years.
       Robert lord Courtney, for the remaining half year, and one year
       further.
                                   7 John

7 John. Roger de Lacy, conftable of Chefter, for 5 years.
11 —— Robert de Veteripont, lord of Weftmorland.
12 —— Hugh de Nevill, for 4 years.
16 —— Robert de Rofs of Hamlake.
17 —— Robert de Vallibus.
1 Hen. 3. Robert de Veteripont, for 5 years.
6 —— Walter Mauclerk, bifhop of Carlifle, for 10 years.
17 —— Thomas de Multon of Egremont, for 4 years.
21 —— William de Dacre, for 12 years.
33 —— John de Balyol, baron of Bywell, for 7 years.
40 —— William de Fortibus, earl of Albemarle, for 5 years.
45 —— Robert de Muncafter.
46 —— Euftachius de Balyol, for 4 years.
50 —— Roger de Leyburne, for 2 years.
52 —— William de Dacre.
53 —— Ranulph de Dacre, for 3 years.
1 Ed. 1. Robert de Chauncey, bifhop of Carlifle, for 2 years.
3 —— Robert de Hampton, for 3 years.
6 —— John de Swynburn.
7 —— Gilbert de Culwen, for 4 years.
11 —— Robert de Brus, for 3 years.
14 —— Michael de Harcla, for 12 years.
26 —— William de Mulcaftre, for 5 years.
31 —— John de Lucy, for 2 years.
33 —— William de Mulcaftre, for 2 years.
1 Ed. 2. Andrew de Harcla, for 15 years.
16 —— Anthony lord Lucy.
17 —— Henry de Moulton, for 2 years.
19 —— Robert le Bruyn of Drumbugh caftle.
1 Ed. 3. Peter de Tylliol, for 3 years.
4 —— Ranulph de Dacre, for 6 years.
10 —— Richard de Denton.
11 —— Anthony de Lucy, for 7 years.
17 —— Hugh de Morefby, for 2 years.
19 —— Thomas de Lucy, for 5 years.
24 —— Richard de Denton, for 2 years.
26 —— Hugh de Louthre, for 3 years.
30 —— William de Thirlkeld.
31 —— Robert de Tylliol, for 2 years.
33 —— William de Lancafter, for 2 years.
35 —— Robert de Tylliol, for 2 years.
37 —— Chriftopher de Morefby, for 4 years.
41 —— William de Windefor, for 2 years.
43 —— Adam de Parving, for 3 years.
46 —— John de Denton.
47 —— Robert de Moubray.

48 Ed.

48 Ed. 3. John de Derwentwater.
49 — John de Denton.
50 — John de Derwentwater.
51 — John le Bruyn.
1 Ric. 2. John de Derwentwater.
2 — William de Stapleton of Edenhall.
3 — Gilbert Curwen.
4 — John de Derwentwater.
5 — Amand Monceaux.
6 — Robert Parving.
7 — Amand Monceaux.
8 — John Thirlewall.
9 — Amand Monceaux.
10 — John Thirlewall.
11 — Peter Tylliol.
12 — John Ireby of Ireby.
13 — Richard Redman of Redman.
14 — Chriſtopher Moreſby.
15 — John Ireby.
16 — Thomas Muſgrave.
17. — Richard Redman.
18 — Peter Tylliol.
19 — John Ireby.
20 — Richard Redman.
21 — William Curwen.
22 — Richard Redman.
1 Hen. 4. William Legh of Iſell.
2 — William Lowther.
3 — Richard Redman.
4 — William Oſmunderley of Langrig.
5 — Peter Tylliol, for 2 years.
6 — Richard Skelton of Branthwaite.
7 — William Lowther.
8 — Robert Lowther, for 2 years.
9 — John de la More.
12 — Robert Rotington of Rotington.
1 Hen. 5. Richard Redman.
2 — Iſaac Harrington.
3 — William Stapleton.
4 — Chriſtopher Curwen.
5 — John Lancaſter of Rydall.
6 — William Oſmunderley.
7 — Robert Lowther.
8 — John Lamplugh of Lamplugh.
9 — William Stapleton.
10 — Nicholas Radcliff of Derwentwater.

1 Hen. 6. William Legh.
2 — Chriftopher Culwen.
3 — Chriftopher Morefby.
4 — Nicholas Radcliffe.
5 — John Pennington of Muncafter.
6 — Chriftopher Culwen.
7 — Chriftopher Morefby.
8 — Thomas de la More.
9 — John Pennington.
10 — John Skelton.
11 — John Lamplugh.
12 — Chriftopher Culwen.
13 — John Pennington.
14 — John Broughton of Broughton Tower.
15 — Henry Fenwick of Fenwick Tower.
16 — Chriftopher Curwen.
17 — Chriftopher Morefby.
18 — Hugh Lowther.
19 — John Skelton.
20 — William Stapleton.
21 — Thomas Beauchamp.
22 — Thomas de la More.
23 — Chriftopher Curwen.
24 — John Skelton.
25 — John Broughton.
26 — Thomas de la More.
27 — Thomas Crackenthorp of Cockermouth.
28 — Thomas Curwen.
29 — John Skelton.
30 — Robert Vaux.
31 — Thomas de la More.
32 — . . . .
33 — John Hodelfton of Millum.
34 — Hugh Lowther.
35 — Thomas Curwen.
36 — Richard Salkeld of Corby.
37 — Henry Fenwick.
1 Ed. 4. Richard Salkeld.
2 — Robert Vaux, for 2 years.
4 — John Hodelfton.
5 — Thomas Lamplugh.
6 — Richard Salkeld.
7 — Robert Vaux.
8 — John Hodelfton, for 2 years.
10 — William Legh.
11 — Chriftopher Morefby.

12 Ed 4. William Parr of Kendal Caftle.
13 — John Hodelfton.
14 — William Legh, for 2 years.
16 — Richard duke of Gloucefter, of Penrith Caftle, for 5 years.
 1 Ric. 3. Richard Salkeld.
 2 — John Crackenthorp.
 1 Hen. 7. Chriftopher Morefby.
 2 — . . . .
 3 — Chriftopher Morefby.
 4 — Thomas Beauchamp.
 7 — John Mufgrave of Fairbank.
 9 — Edward Redman.
10 — Richard Salkeld.
11 — Chriftopher Morefby.
12 — Thomas Beauchamp.
13 — Chriftopher Dacre, for 7 years.
20 — Hugh Hutton of Hutton John.
21 — Chriftopher Dacre.
22 — John Hodelfton.
23 — John Radclyffe of Derwentwater.
 1 Hen. 8. Thomas Curwen.
 2 — John Pennington.
 3 — John Skelton.
 4 — John Crackenthorp.
 5 — Edward Mufgrave of Edenhall.
 6 — John Radcliffe.
 7 — John Lowther.
 8 — Thomas Curwen.
 9 — Gawen Eglesfield of Alwardby, efquire.
10 — John Radcliffe, knight.
11 — Edward Mufgrave, knight.
13 — Chriftopher Dacre, knight.
15 — John Radclyffe, knight.
16 — Chriftopher Curwen, knight.
17 — Chriftopher Dacre, knight.
18 — John Radclyffe, knight.
19 — Edward Mufgrave, knight.
20 — William Pennington, knight.
21 — Thomas Wharton of Wharton, knight.
22 — Richard Irton of Irton, efquire.
23 — Chriftopher Dacre, knight.
24 — William Mufgrave, knight.
25 — Chriftopher Curwen, knight.
26 — Cuthbert Hutton, efquire.
27 — Thomas Wharton, knight.

                                          28 Hen.

28 Hen. 8. Thomas Curwen, knight.
29 — John Lamplugh, knight.
30 — John Thwaytes of Thwaytes in Millum, esquire.
31 — Thomas Wharton, knight.
32 — Thomas Dalston of Dalston, esquire.
33 — William Musgrave, knight.
34 — John Lowther, knight.
35 — Thomas Salkeld, esquire.
36 — Edward Aglionby of Aglionby, esquire.
37 — Thomas Sandford of Howgill Castle, esquire.
1 Ed. 6. Thomas Wharton, knight.
2 — John Legh, esquire.
3 — John Lamplugh, esquire.
4 — John Lowther, knight.
5 — Richard Eglesfield, esquire.
6 — William Pennington, esquire.
1 Ph. & M. Thomas Legh, esquire.
2 — Richard Musgrave, knight.
3 — Thomas Sandford, esquire.
4 — Robert Lamplugh, esquire.
5 — John Legh, esquire.
1 Eliz. William Pennington, esquire.
2 — Thomas Dacre senior, of Lanercost, knight.
3 — Thomas Lamplugh, esquire.
4 — Hugh Ayscough, knight; and Henry Curwen, esquire.
5 — William Musgrave, esquire.
6 — Anthony Hodleston, esquire.
7 — Christopher Dacre, esquire.
8 — William Pennington, esquire.
9 — Richard Lowther, esquire.
10 — John Dalston, esquire.
11 — Cuthbert Musgrave, esquire.
12 — Simon Musgrave, knight.
13 — Henry Curwen, knight.
14 — George Lamplugh, esquire.
15 — John Lamplugh, esquire.
16 — William Musgrave, esquire.
17 — Anthony Hodelston, esquire.
18 — Richard Salkeld, esquire.
19 — Henry Tolson of Wood-hall, esquire.
20 — John Dalston, esquire.
21 — George Salkeld, esquire.
22 — Francis Lamplugh, esquire.
23 — John Lamplugh, esquire.
24 — Henry Curwen, knight.
25 — Christopher Dacre, esquire.

26 Eliz. Wilfrid Lawfon of Ifel', efquire.
27 — John Dalfton, efquire.
28 — John Midleton, efquire.
29 — George Salkeld, efquire.
30 — John Dalfton, efquire,
31 — Richard Lowther, knight.
32 — Henry Curwen, knight.
33 — Chriftopher Pickering of Threlkeld, efquire.
34 — John Southaick, efquire.
35 — William Mufgrave, efquire.
36 — Gerard Lowther, efquire.
37 — John Dalfton, efquire.
38 — Lancelot Salkeld, efquire.
39 — Chriftopher Dalfton of Acorn Bank, efquire.
40 — Wilfrid Lawfon, efquire.
41 — Thomas Salkeld, efquire.
42 — Jofeph Pennington, efquire.
43 — Nicholas Curwen, efquire.
44 — William Orfeur of High Clofe, efquire.
1 James. Edmund Dudley of Yanwath, efquire.
2 — William Hutton of Penrith, efquire.
3 — John Dalfton of Dalfton, knight.
4 — Chriftopher Pickering, efquire.
5 — Wilfrid Lawfon, knight.
6 — Chriftopher Pickering, knight.
7 — Henry Blencowe of Blencowe, efquire.
8 — William Hutton, knight.
9 — Jofeph Pennington, efquire.
10 — Chriftopher Pickering, knight.
11 — Wilfrid Lawfon, knight.
12 — Thomas Lamplugh, efquire.
13 — Edward Mufgrave of Hayton Caftle, baronet.
14 — Richard Fletcher of Hutton, efquire.
15 — William Mufgrave of Fairbank, knight.
16 — William Hodlefton, efquire.
17 — George Dalfton, knight.
18 — Henry Curwen, knight.
19 — John Lamplugh, efquire.
20 — Henry Fetherftonhaugh of Kirkofwald, efquire.
21 — . . . . . Dudley, efquire.
22 — Richard Sandford, knight.
1 Cha. Richard Fletcher, knight.
2 — Henry Blencowe, knight.
3 — Peter Senhoufe of Netherhall, efquire.
4 — Chriftopher Dalfton of Acorn Bank, efquire.
5 — William Layton of Dalemain, efquire.

6 Cha.

 6 Cha. William Mufgrave, knight.
 7 —   Chriftopher Richmond of High-head Caftle, efquire.
 8 —   Leonard Dykes of Wardhole, efquire.
 9 —   John Skelton of Armathwaite, efquire.
10 —   William Orfeur, efquire.
11 —   Richard Barwife of Hildkirk, efquire.
12 —   Wilfrid Lawfon, efquire.
13 —   Patricius Curwen, baronet.
14 —   Thomas Dacre of Lanercoft, knight.
15 —   Timothy Fetherftonhaugh, knight.
16 —   . . . .
17 —   Chriftopher Lowther of Whitehaven, baronet.
18 —   Henry Fletcher, baronet.
19 —   . . . .
20 —   . . . .
21 —   Thomas Lamplugh efquire, and Wilfrid Lawfon knight.
22 —   William Brifco of Crofton, efquire.
23 —   William Brifco and Henry Tolfon efquires.
24 —   John Barwys of Waverton, efquire.
Ufurpation.
 1 —   John Barwys, efquire.
 2 —   Charles Howard of Naworth, efquire.
 3 —   William Brifco, efquire.
 4 —   John Barwys, efquire.
 5 —   William Halton of Grayftock efquire, and Wilfrid Lawfon knight.
 6 —   Wilfrid Lawfon knight, for 4 years.
10 —   George Fletcher of Hutton, baronet.
11 —   William Pennington, efquire.
12 Cha. 2. William Pennington, efquire.
13 —   Daniel Fleming of Rydal, knight.
14 —   John Lowther of Lowther, baronet.
15 —   Francis Salkeld of Whitehall, knight.
16 —   John Lamplugh, efquire.
17 —   Thomas Davyfon of Durham, knight.
18 —   William Dalfton of Dalfton, baronet.
19 —   Richard Tolfon, efquire.
20 —   William Layton, efquire.
21 —   Miles Pennington, efquire.
22 —   Thomas Curwen of Camerton, efquire.
23 —   Anthony Bouche of Cockermouth, efquire:
24 —   Richard Patrickfon of Calder Abbey, efquire.
25 —   Bernard Kirkbride of Howe, for 2 years.
27 —   William Orfeur efquire, for 2 years.
29 —   William Blennerhaffet of Flimby efquire, for 2 years.
31 —   Wilfrid Lawfon of Brayton, efquire.
32 —   George Fletcher, baronet.

33 Cha.

33 Cha. 2. Leonard Dyke efquire, for 2 years.
35 — Edward Haffel of Dalemain, knight.
36 — Andrew Hodlefton of Hutton John, efquire.
1 Jam. 2. Richard Mufgrave, baronet.
2 — William Pennington, baronet.
3 — John Dalfton, baronet.
4 — Henry Curwen of Workington, efquire.
1 Will. Edward Stanley of Dalegarth, efquire.
2 — Wilfrid Lawfon of Ifell, baronet.
3 — Richard Lamplugh of Ribton, efquire.
4 — Chriftopher Richmond of Caterlane, efquire.
5 — Jofeph Hodlefton of Millom, efquire.
6 — Henry Brougham of Scales, efquire.
7 — John Ballendyne of Crookdake, efquire.
8 — John Ponfonby of Hale, efquire.
9 — John Latus of Beck in Millom, efquire.
10 — Timothy Fetherftonhaugh, efquire.
11 — Thomas Dawes of Barton, efquire.
12 — Robert Carleton of Carleton hall, efquire.
13 — Thomas Lamplugh, efquire.
1 Anne. Richard Crackemthorp, efquire.
2 — John Dalfton, efquire.
3 — John Senhoufe of Seafcale, efquire.
4 — John Brifco, efquire.
5 — Chriftopher Curwen, efquire.
6 — Robert Pennington, efquire.
7 — Richard Lamplugh, efquire.
8 — Richard Hutton, efquire.
9 — William Ballentine, died 7 July.
Robert Blacklock, efquire.
10 — Robert Blacklock, efquire.
11 — John Fifher of Ulfwater, efquire.
12 — Charles Dalfton, efquire.
13 — Thomas Pattinfon of Melmerby, efquire.
1 Geo. Humphrey Senhoufe of Nether Hall, efquire,
2 — Thos Brougham, efquire.
3 — Henry Blencowe, efquire.
4 — Robert Lamplugh of Dovenby, efquire.
5 — John Ponfonby, efquire.
6 — Thomas Fletcher, efquire.
— John Stanley, efquire.
7 — Jofhua Laithes of Dalehead, efquire.
9 — Peter Brougham of Scales, efquire.
10 — Jofeph Dacre Appleby of Kirklinton, efquire.
11 — John Fletcher of Colehay, efquire.
12 — Thomas Lutwich efquire, merchant in Whitehaven.

13 Geo.

13 Geo. John Ballentine of Crookdake, efquire.
1 Geo. 2. Edward Haffel of Dalemain, efquire.
2 — Richard Mufgrave of Hayton Caftie, baronet.
3 — Edward Stanley of Ponfonby, efquire.
6 — Henry Aglionby of Nunnery, efquire.
7 — John Benn of Henfingham, efquire.
8 — Fletcher Partys of Tallentyre, efquire.
9 — John Dalfton of Acorn Bank, efquire.
10 — William Hicks efquire, merchant in Whitehaven.
11 — John Gafkarth of Hill-top, efquire.
12 — Jofeph Dacre Appleby of Kirklinton, efquire.
13 — Richard Cook of Camerton Hall, efquire.
14 — Montague Farrer of Carlifle, efquire.
15 — Henry Fletcher of Hutton Hall efquire.
16 — Humphrey Senhoufe of Netherhall, efquire.
17 — Jerome Tullie of Carlifle, efquire.
18 — Jofhua Lucock of Cockermouth, efquire.
19 — Chriftopher Pattinfon of Carleton Hall, efquire.
20 — Thomas Whitfield of Claregill, efquire.
21 — Walter Lutwich efquire, merchant in Whitehaven.
22 — Henry Richmond Brougham, efquire.
      John Ponfonby, efquire.
23 — Richard Hylton of Hayton Caftle, baronet.
24 — George Irton of Irton, efquire.
25 — George Dalfton of Dalfton, baronet.
26 — Henry-Curwen of Workington, efquire.
27 — William Fleming of Rydal, baronet.
28 — Timothy Fetherftonhaugh of Kirkofwald, efquire.
29 — Wilfrid Lawfon of Brayton, baronet.
30 — John Stephenfon of Kefwick, efquire.
31 — John Senhoufe of Calder Abbey, efquire.
32 — James Spedding of Ormathwaite, efquire.
      John Gale of Cleator, efquire.
33 — William Dalfton of Millrig, efquire.
1 Geo. 3. John Langton of Cockermouth, efqu're.
2 — John Richardfon of Penrith, efquire.
3 — Henry Aglionby of Nunnery, efquire.
4 — Henry Ellifon of Whitehaven, efquire.
5 — Samuel Irton of Irton, efquire.
6 — John Chriftian of Unerigg, efquire.
7 — Thomas Lutwich of Whitehaven, efquire.
8 — Gilfrid Lawfon of Brayton, baronet.
9 — John Robinfon of Watermillock, efquire.
10 — Michael le Fleming of Rydal baronet.
11 — John Spedding of Ormathwaite, efquire.

:12 Geo. 3. William Hicks of Papcaftle, efquire.
13　—　John Dixon efquire, merchant in Whitehaven.
14　—　George Edward Stanley of Ponfonby, efquire.

No. XXXVI.

LIST of KNIGHTS of the SHIRE for CUMBERLAND.

18 Ed. 1. Walter de Mulcafter, Hubert de Multon.
　　　　　William de Boyvill.
23　—　Robert de Haverington, Hubert de Multon.
25 Ed. 1. Robert de Wittering, William de Boyvill.
28　—　Richard de Slater, Robert de Wittering.
29　—　John de Wiggeton, Robert de Tilliol.
30　—　Robert de Joneby, Nicholas de Aprefby.
34　—　John de Lucy, William de Brampton.
35　—　John de Denton, William de Langrigg.
2 Ed 2. William le Brun, Alexander de Baftenthwait.
3　—　William de Mulcaftre, Alexander de Baftenthwait.
4　—　Robert de Leyburne, Walter de Bampton.
5　—　William de Mulcaftre, Henry de Multon.
　　　　　Robert de Leyburne, Walter de Bampton.
6　—　Andrew de Harcla, Alan de Grinefdale.
8　—　Robert de Tilliol, Henry de Multon.
9　—　Alexander de Baftingthwait, Walter de Kirkbride.
10　—　Robert le Brun, John de Skelton.
12　—　Robert de Leyburn, Alexander de Baftingthwait.
　　　　　John de Boyvill, Adam de Skelton.
17　—　Hugh de Louther, John de Orreton.
18　—　Richard de Denton, John de Skelton.
19　—　Robert de Mulecaftre, Robert Paynwick.
20　—　Robert le Brunn, John de Orreton.
1 Ed. 3. Robert le Brunn, John de Orreton.
　　　　　John de Orreton, Robert Parving.
　　　　　Peter Tilliol, Robert Parving.
2　—　Peter Tilliol, John de Skelton.
　　　　　Robert de Eglesfield, Richard de Salkeld.
　　　　　Peter de Tilliol, Robert Parving.
4　—　Peter Tilliol, John de Orreton.
　　　　　John de Orreton, Thomas de Hardegill.
5　—　Richard de Denton, Robert Parvyng.
6　—　Richard de Denton, John de Haverington.
　　　　　Richard de Denton, Robert Parving.
　　　　　Peter Tilliol, Richard de Denton.

7 Ed. 3. Peter Tilliol, Richard de Denton.
      Richard de Denton, John de Haverington.
8 — Hugh de Moriceby, William Englifh.
      Richard de Denton, John de Haverington.
9 — Peter de Tilliol, Richard de Denton.
11 — Peter de Tilliol, Richard de Denton.
      Richard de Denton, Hugh de Moriceby.
      John de Orreton, Thomas de Skelton.
12 — Thomas de Hardegill, Richard de Bery.
      John de Boyvil, Adam de Skelton.
13 — Peter Tilliol, John de Haverington.
      John de Orreton, John de Haverington.
14 — Alexander de Baftinthwait, Robert le Brunn.
      Peter Tilliol, John de Orreton.
      John de Orreton, John de Haverington.
15 — Peter Tilliol, Hugh de Louthre.
17 — Richard de Denton, John de Orreton.
18 — Hugh de Louthre, Henry de Malton.
22 — John de Orreton, Thomas de Hardegill.
23 — Peter Tilliol, John de Orreton.
24 — Richard de Denton, John de Orreton.
26 — Richard de Denton, Robert de Tilliol.
      Henry de Malton.
27 — Richard de Denton.
28 — Thomas de Rokeby, Thomas de Hardegill.
29 — Richard de Denton, John de Orreton.
31 — John de Orreton, Robert de Tilliol.
      Robert Tilliol, Adam Parving.
34 — John de Orreton, Chriftopher de Moriceby.
      Henry de Malton, Robert de Tilliol.
36 — Robert Tilliol, William Englifh.
37 — William Englifh, Chriftopher Moriceby.
38 — Richard de Tilliol, William Englifh.
39 — Chriftopher Moriceby, William de Stapilton.
42 — John de Pykering, John de Denton.
43 — William Englifh, Richard Moubray.
45 — Robert Curwenne, William de Stapilton.
      Gilbert de Curwenne.
46 — Robert Moubray, John de Denton.
47 — Gilbert de Curwen, Adam Parvyng.
      Gilbert de Curwen, John de Camberton.
50 — Gilbert de Curwen, William Stapilton.
51 — John de Denton, Amand Monceaux.
1 Ric. 2. Robert Moubray, Richard del Sandes.
2 — Peter Tilliol, Clement de Skelton.
      John de Derwentwater, Thomas de Whitrigg.

3 Ric. 2. Richard de Moubray, William de Curwen.
4 —   Peter Tilliol, William de Hutton.
5 —   Gilbert de Curwen, John de Denton.
     Richard de Salkeld, John de la More.
6 —   Clement de Skelton, Thomas Bower.
     Clement de Skelton, Thomas de Dalston.
7 —   Thomas Blenkinsop, Amand Monceaux.
     John de Kirkby, John de Brougham.
8 —   Thomas de Lamplugh, John de Ireby.
9 —   Peter Tilliol, Richard de Beaulieu.
10 —   Amand Monceaux, John de Thirlwall.
11 —   John de Derwentwater, John de Ireby.
12 —   Robert de Mulcaftre, Amand Monceaux.
13 —   William de Threlkeld, Amand Monceaux.
14 —   William Stapilton, Thomas del Sandes.
15 —   Peter Tilliol, John de Louthre.
16 —   Geoffrey Tilliol, John de Louthre.
17 —   Clement de Skelton, Robert de Louthre.
18 —   William de Stapilton, Thomas del Sandes.
20 —   John de Ireby, Clement de Skelton.
21 —   Peter Tilliol, William de Ofmunderlowe.
1 Hen. 4. William de Legh, Rowland Vaux.
2 —   Robert de Louthre, William de Stapilton.
3 —   William de Legh, John de Skelton.
5 —   Robert de Louthre, William de Louthre.
6 —   John de la More, William de Beaulieu.
8 —   Robert de Louthre, John de Skelton.
9 —   William Stapilton, William de la More.
1 Hen. 5. Peter Tilliol, William Beaulieu.
2 —   Robert de Louthre, William de Legh.
     Chriftopher de Curwen, John de Eglesfield.
5 —   Peter Tilliol, Robert de Louthre.
8 —   Peter Tilliol, Thomas de la More.
9 —   Peter Tilliol, Nicholas Randolf.
1 Hen. 6. Peter Tilliol, John Skelton.
2 —   Chriftopher Curwen, William de Legh.
3 —   Peter Tilliol, Chriftopher Curwen.
4 —   Peter Tilliol, Hugh de Lowther.
6 —   Chriftopher Curwen, Nicholas Radcliff.
8 —   Thomas Parr, Thomas de la More.
9 —   Chriftopher Curwen, Hugh de Lowther.
13 —   Thomas Curwen, William Dykes.
15 —   William Stapilton, John Brougham.
20 —   Ralph de Dacre, Thomas Cutwen.
25 —   John Pennington, William Martindale.
27 —   Thomas Curwen, Hugh Lowther.

                                         28 Hen.

28 Hen. 6. John Skelton, Richard Bellingham.
29 — Thomas de la More, Thomas Crackenthorp.
33 — Thomas Colt, Thomas de la More.
38 — Thomas Curwen, William Legh.
7 Ed. 4. John Hodleston, Richard Salkeld.
12 — John Parr, Richard Salkeld.
17 — William Parr, James Morefby:

. . . .
. . . .

1 Ed. 6. Thomas Wharton knight, Richard Mufgrave efquire.
6 — Richard Mufgrave knight, Henry Curwen efquire.
1 Mary. Thomas Wharton knight, Thomas Dacre junior, knight.
        John Leigh efquire, Robert Penruddock efquire.
1 Ph. & M. Thomas Dacre efquire, Robert Penruddock efquire.
2 — Thomas Threlkeld, Henry Methuen, efquires.
3 — Leonard Dacre, John Dalfton, efquires.
1 Eliz. Leonard Dacre, Henry Curwen, efquires.
5 — Leonard Dacre, Henry Curwen, efquires.
13 — Henry Percy, Simon Mufgrave, knights.
14 — Simon Mufgrave knight, Edward Scroop efquire.
27 — Thomas Scroop, Thomas Bowes, efquires.
28 — Robert Bowes, Henry Leigh, efquires.
31 — Thomas Scroop knight, Robert Bowes efquire.
35 — Nicholas Curwen, Wilfrid Lawfon, efquires.
39 — John Pennington, Chriftopher Pickering, knights.
43 — William Hodleston, Gerard Lowther, efquires.
1 James. Wilfrid Lawfon, Edward Mufgrave, efquires.
18 — George Dalfton, Henry Curwen, knights.
21 — George Dalfton knight, Ferdinand Hodlefton efquire.
1 Cha. George Dalfton knight, Patric Curwen efquire.
3 — George Dalfton knight, Patric Curwen, efquire.
15 — George Dalfton knight, Patric Curwen efquire.
16 — George Dalfton knight, Patric Curwen, efquire.
    1655. Charles Howard, William Brifcoe, efquires.
    1657. Charles Howard, William Brifcoe, efquires.
    1659. Sir Wilfrid Lawfon, Colonel William Brifcoe.
12 Cha. 2. Charles lord Howard, Wilfrid Lawfon efquire.
13 — Patric Curwen, George Fletcher, baronets.
        John Lowther efquire.
31 — John Lowther of Whitehaven baronet, Richard Lamplugh efquire.
        Edward lord Morpeth, John Lowther baronet.
32 — George Fletcher, John Lowther, baronets.
1 Jam. 1. Richard vifcount Prefton, John Lowther baronet.
1 Will. 3. George Fletcher, John Lowther, baronets.
2 — George Fletcher, John Lowther, baronets.
7 — George Fletcher, John Lowther, baronets.

10 Will. 3. George Fletcher, John Lowther, baronets.
13 — Edward Haſſel knight, George Fletcher eſquire.
1 Anne. Richard Muſgrave, Gilfrid Lawſon, eſquires.
4 — George Fletcher, Richard Muſgrave, eſquires.
7 — James Lowther, Gilfrid Lawſon, eſquires.
12 — James Lowther, Gilfrid Lawſon, eſquires.
1 Geo. James Lowther, Gilfrid Lawſon, eſquires.
8 — Chriſtopher Muſgrave baronet, Gilfrid Lawſon eſquire.
1 Geo. 2. James Lowther baronet, Gilfrid Lawſon eſquire.
7 — James Lowther baronet, Joſeph Pennington baronet.
14 — James Lowther, Joſeph Pennington, baronets.
21 — James Lowther, John Pennington, baronets.
28 — James Lowther, John Pennington, baronets.
       William Lowther baronet; on Sir James's death.
       William Fleming baronet; on Sir Wm Lowther's death.
1 Geo. 3. James Lowther of Lowther, John Pennington, baronets.
       Wilfrid Lawſon baronet; on Sir James's making his election for
           Weſtmorland.
       Sir James Lowther re-elected, on Sir Wilfrid's death.
8 — Henry Curwen and Henry Fletcher, eſquires.
15 — Sir James Lowther baronet, Henry Fletcher eſquire.

No. XXXVII.

LIST of BURGESSES for the CITY of CARLISLE.

23 Ed. 1. Robert de Greneſdale, Andrew de Seller.
30 — Henry le Spencer, Andrew Serjeant.
33 — Robert de Greneſdale, Alan de Greneſdale.
34 — Alan de Greneſdale.
1 Ed. 2. Andrew Serjeant, Richard de Hubriekby.
2 — William Fitz-Juting, Robert Greneſdale.
4 — John de Croſtone, William Fitz-Henry.
5 — Alan de Greneſdale, Andrew Fitz-Peter.
       Alan de Greneſdale, William de Taillour.
7 — Robert Greneſdale, John Winton.
8 — Robert Greneſdale, Bernard Lecatour.
12 — Robert Greneſdale, Bernard Poulter.
       Robert Greneſdale, Richard Fitz-Ivo.
15 — John de Wilton, Thomas de Callton.
20 — John Fleming, Nicholas le Deſpencer.
1 Ed. 3. John Fleming, Robert de Greneſdale.
       Alan de Greneſdale, John de Capella.
2 — Robert de Greneſdale, Alan de Greneſdale.
       John de Haverington, Simon de Sandford.

2 Ed. 3. Robert Grenesdale, John de Harding.
4 — John Haverington, Robert de Grundon.
6 — John Haverington, Simon Sandford.
7 — John Fleming, Adam Crofton.
8 — John de Pickering, Henry Pepir.
    John Fleming, Adam Crofton.
9 — Thomas Hardull, Thomas Friskinton.
    John de Exlington, Thomas Worthsell.
11 — Thomas de Pardishow, Giles de Orreton.
    John de Denton, Adam Brighton.
12 — Thomas de Pardishow, Giles de Orreton.
    John de Exlington, Thomas de Bardgit.
    Robert Grenesdale, William Fitz-Ivo.
    Thomas Baron, Thomas de Fresington.
14 — John Fleming, Adam Crofton.
    William Fitz Henry, Henry le Spencer.
15 — Thomas Hardgill, John Fleming.
17 — John Chapel, William Chapel.
21 — Adam Crofton, Robert Tebay.
22 — Adam Crofton, Thomas Appleby.
24 — Robert Tebay, John de Haghton.
29 — William Artute, Thomas Stanly.
31 — Thomas Alaynby, William Spencer.
34 — John de Thorneton, Adam de Aglionby.
36 — William Arthureth, William Spencer.
37 — Adam Halden, William Spicer.
38 — William Arthureth, Richard London.
39 — Richard Orfeur, William Clifton.
42 — Adam Aglionby, William de Clifford.
43 — William Arthureth, John de Waverton.
45 — John de Whitlawe.
46 — William Raughton, William Carlisle.
47 — Thomas Tayleur, Richard Denton.
50 — Richard Denton, John de Burgh.
51 — Richard Denton, John de Burgh.
2 Ric. 2. Robert Carlisle, John Levington.
3 — Robert Carlisle, ... Parker.
6 — William Osmunderlaw, John Skelton.
7 — Richard de London, John de Appleby.
    Stephen de Carlisle, Thomas Bolton.
8 — Richard London, John Blenerhasset.
9 — William Aglionby, John Gemot.
10 — Adam de Denton, Robert de Bristow.
11 — Robert de Carlisle, William Aglionby.
12 — John de Corkeby, Nicholas Leveson.
13 — Adam de Kirkbrigg.

15 Ric. 2. John Monceaux, Robert Briſtow.
16 — John Roddeſdale, John de Wek.
18 — John de Brugham, John Monceaux.
20 — John Helton, John Burgham.
21 — Robert Briſtowe, John Briſtowe.
1 Hen. 4. John Helton, Robert Briſtowe.
3 — Thomas Bolton, Robert Briſtowe.
8 — Thomas de Darle, William Mulcaſtre.
1 Hen. 5. Robert de Carliſle, Ralph Blenerhaffet.
2 — Robert de Carliſle, William Cardoyll.
3 — Robert Lancaſtre, William Bell.
5 — Robert Carliſle, William Cardoyll.
9 — William Mancheſtre, John Thompſon.
1 Hen. 6. Robert Cardoyll, Richard Gray.
6 — John Helton, William Càmberton.
8 — Thomas Derwent, Adam Haverington.
9 — Everard Barwick, Robert Clèrk.
11 — Richard Briſkow, Richard Bawleke.
13 — William Northing, Nicholas Thompſon.
14 — Richard Thornburgh, Rowland Wherton.
15 — Robert Maſon, Thomas Mareſcall.
20 — John Blenerhaffet, William Buckler.
25 — Thomas Stanlaw, George Walton.
27 — Robert Carliſle, Richard Alanſon.
28 — Richard Chatterley, Thomas Chatterley.
29 — Richard Alanſon, Alured Maleveter.
31 — John Skelton, Rowland Vaux.
33 — John Bere, Thomas Derwent.
38 — Richard Beverley, Thomas Rukin.
7 Ed. 4. Henry Denton, Richard George.
12 — Robert Skelton, John Cöldale.
33 Hen. 8. William Stapylton, ... : . . .
1 Ed. 6. Edward Aglionby, Thomas Dalſton.
6 — Edward Aglionby, John Dudléy.
1 Mary. John Aglionby, Simon Briſtòw.
Robert Whitley, Richard Mÿnſho.
1 Ph. & M. Richard Whitley, Richard Mynſh'o.
2 — William Middleton, William Wàrde.
4 — Richard Aſheton, Robert Dàlton.
1 Eliz. Richard Aſheton, William Mûlcaſtre.
5 — Richard Aſheton, William Mulcaſtre.
13 — Robert Bowes, Chriſtopher Muſgrave.
14 — Thomas Pattinſon, Thomas Tallentyre.
27 — Edward Aglionby, Thomas Blénerhaffet.
28 — Henry Mac-William, Thomas Blénerhaffet.
31 — Henry Scroope, John Dalſton.

35 Eliz.

35 Eliz. Henry Scroope, Edward Aglionby.
39 — Henry Scroope, Thomas Stamford.
43 — Henry Scroope, John Dudley.
 1 James. Thomas Blenerhaffet, William Barwick.
12 — Henry Fane.
18 — Henry Fane, George Butler.
21 — Henry Fane, Edward Aglionby.
 1 Cha. Henry Fane, Edward Aglionby.
         Henry Fane, Richard Grahme,
 3 — Richard Barwicke, Richard Grahme.
15 — William Dalston, Richard Barwicke.
16 — William Dalston, Richard Barwicke.
    1655. Colonel Thomas Fitch.
    1657. Colonel George Downing.
    1659 Colonel George Downing, Thomas Craifter esquire.
12 Cha. 2. William Briscowe, Jeremy Tolhur.
13 — Philip Howard, Christopher Musgrave.
31 — Philip Howard, Christopher Musgrave.
32 — Edward lord Morpeth, Christopher Musgrave.
 1 Jam. 2. Christopher Musgrave, James Graham.
 1 Will. Christopher Musgrave, Jeremiah Bubb.
 2 — Jeremiah Bubb, Christopher Musgrave.
         William Lowther.
         James Lowther.
 7 — William Howard, James Lowther.
10 — William Howard, James Lowther.
12 — Philip Howard, James Lowther.
13 — Philip Howard, James Lowther.
 1 Anne. Christopher Musgrave, Thomas Stanwix.
 4 — Thomas Stanwix, James Montague.
 7 — Thomas Stanwix, James Montague.
 9 — Thomas Stanwix, James Montague.
12 — Christopher Musgrave, Thomas Stanwix.
 1 Geo. Thomas Stanwix, William Strickland,
         Henry Aglionby.
 8 — James Bateman, Henry Aglionby.
 1 Geo. 2. Charles Howard, John Hylton.
 7 — Charles Howard, John Hylton.
14 — Charles Howard, John Hylton.
         John Stanwix.
21 — Charles Howard, John Stanwix.
28 — Charles Howard, John Stanwix.
 1 Geo. 3. Raby Vane, Henry Curwen,
 8 — Lord Edward Bentink, George Musgrave.
15 — Fletcher Norton, Anthony Storer.
         Walter Stanhope.

                                          No. XXXVIII.

No. XXXVIII.

List of Burgesses for Cockermouth.

24 Ed. 1. William Bully, Peter del Hall.
16 Cha. Sir John Hippefley, Francis Allen.
 1659. John Stapleton, Wilfrid Lawfon.
12 Cha. 2. Richard Tolfon, Wilfrid Lawfon.
13 — Richard Tolfon, Wilfrid Lawfon.
31 — Sir Richard Graham, Orlando Gee.
32 — Sir Richard Graham, Orlando Gee.
33 — Sir Richard Graham, Orlando Gee.
 1 Ja. 2. Sir Daniel Fleming, Orlando Gee.
 1 Will. Sir Henry Capel, William Fletcher.
 2 — Sir Wilfrid Lawfon, Sir Orlando Gee.
 7 — Sir Charles Gerrard, Hon. Goodwin Wharton.
10 — William Seymoor, George Fletcher.
13 — Thomas Lamplugh, William Seymoor.
 1 Anne. James Stanhope, Thomas Lamplugh.
 4 — James Stanhope, Thomas Lamplugh.
 7 — James Stanhope, Hon. Albemarle Bertie.
 9 — Jofeph Mufgrave, Nicholas Lechmere.
 1 Geo. Sir Thomas Pengelly, Nicholas Lechmere.
 8 — Sir Thomas Pengelly, Sir Wilfrid Lawfon.
 1 Geo. 2. Sir Wilfrid Lawfon, William Finch.
 7 — Eldred Curwen, William Finch.
14 — John Mordaunt, William Finch.
21 — John Mordaunt, Sir Charles Windham.
28 — Sir John Mordaunt, Percy Obrien Windham.
 1 Geo. 3. Sir John Mordaunt, Charles Jenkinfon.
 8 — Sir George Maccartney, Charles Jenkinfon.
     Sir James Lowther, George Johnftone.
15 — Fletcher Norton, George Johnftone.
     James Adair, Ralph Gowland.

No. XXXIX.

Proclamation by king James the Second for reftoring to Corporations their ancient charters.

     JAMES R.
     WHEREAS we are informed, that feveral deeds of furrender, which
have been lately made by feveral corporations and bodies corporate, of and in

our cities and towns within our kingdom of *England* and dominion of *Wales*, of their charters, franchifes, and privileges, are not yet recorded or inrolled; and that upon the proceedings and rules for judgment, which have lately been had upon the *Quo Warrantos* or informations in nature of a *Quo Warranto*, judgments are not yet entered upon record; whereupon, notwithftanding new charters have been granted in the reign of our late dear brother and in our reign; which faid deeds (being not inrolled or recorded) do not amount unto, or in law make, any furrender of the charters, franchifes, or liberties therein mentioned; and fuch of the faid corporations or bodies politic, againft which rules for judgments have been made in the life-time of our late dear brother or fince, in our court of king's bench (but no judgments entred upon record) are not difcorporate or diffolved; and that it is in our power to leave fuch corporations in the fame eftate and condition they were in, and to difcharge all further proceedings and effects that may be of fuch rules for judgments, and deeds of furrender: WE do hereby publifh and declare, that upon due fearch and examination made, we have fatisfaction, that the deeds of furrender made by the corporations and bodies politic of the faid cities and towns (except the corporations following, that is to fay, *Thetford, Nottingham, Bridgewater, Ludlow, Bewdley, Beverley, Teukefbury, Exeter, Doncafter, Colchefter, Winchefter, Lanctfton, Lifkerd, Plimpton, Tregoney, Plymouth, Dunwick, St. Ives, Fowy, Eaft-Looe, Camelford, Weft-Looe, Tintegall, Penryn, Truro, Bodmyn, Hadleigh, Leftwytbell, and Saltafh*) are not inrolled or recorded; and that, though rules for judgments have paffed upon informations in nature of a *Quo Warranto* againft the corporations and bodies politic of feveral cities and towns in our faid kingdom and dominion, yet no judgments have been or are entred upon record upon any fuch informations, except againft the city of *London, Chefter, Calne, St. Ives, Pool, York, Thaxted, Llangbour,* and *Malmefbury:* AND we of our mere grace and favour, being refolved to reftore and put all our cities, towns, and boroughs in *England* and *Wales* and alfo our town of *Berwick* upon *Tweed,* into the fame ftate and condition they were in our late dear brother's reign, before any deed of furrender was made of their charters or franchifes, or proceedings againft them or the corporations or bodies politic, in or of the faid cities, towns, or boroughs, upon any *Quo Warranto* or informations in nature of a *Quo Warranto* had: Do hereby therefore publifh, declare, direct, and require, that the faid corporations and bodies politic and corporate, of all the faid cities, towns, and boroughs, whofe deeds of furrender are not inrolled, nor judgments entred againft them as aforefaid, and the mayors, bailiffs, fheriffs, aldermen, common council men, affiftants, recorders, town clerks, magiftrates, minifters, officers, freemen, and all and every others the members of or in every of them refpectively, upon the publication of this our proclamation, take on them and proceed to act as a corporation or body politic, and where places are vacant by death or oth rwife, to make elections, conftitute and fill up the fame (notwithftanding the ufual days and times of elections by the ancient charters and conftitutions fhall happen to be paft), and to do, execute, and perform all and every matter and thing, as they lawfully might and ought to have done, if no fuch deeds of furrender, rules for judgment, or other proceedings, upon any fuch *Quo Warranto* or informations, had been had or made. And for the better effecting our faid intention, we have by order made by us in council, and under our fign manual, and we do alfo by this our proclamation made with the advice of our faid council, difcharge, remove, and difmifs all and every perfon and perfons of and from all offices and places of mayors, bailiffs, fheriffs, aldermen, common council men, affiftants, recorder, town clerk, and all and every office and place, which they or any of them have or claim only by charter, patent, or grant from our dear brother, or from ourfelf, fince the dates of the refpective deeds of furrender or rules for judgment (except fuch corporations whofe deeds of furrender are inrolled, or againft whom judgment is entred); and that all and every fuch perfon and perfons deliver up into the hands and cuftody of the faid perfons hereby appointed and intended to act and execute the faid offices and places, all and every the charters, records, books, evidences, and matters concerning the faid refpective corporations. And we do hereby further publifh and declare, that we have caufed all and every the faid deeds of furrender which can be found, to be delivered and put into the hands of our attorney general, to be by him cancelled and returned to the corporations and bodies politic of the refpective cities and towns whom they concern; and have alfo given to our faid attorney authority, and do hereby warrant and command him, not only not to proceed or enter judgment upon the faid *Quo Warranto's* or informations in nature of a *Quo Warranto*, or any of them, but to enter upon the refpective records *Noli Profequi's* and legal difcharges thereof. And we do hereby publifh and declare our further grace and favour to the faid cities, corporations, and boroughs, at any time hereafter, by any further act, to grant, confirm, or reftore unto them all their charters, liberties, franchifes, and privileges, that at the refpective times of fuch deeds of furrender or rules for judgment made or given, they held or enjoyed.

And in order to the perfecting our faid gracious intentions, we do hereby likewife publifh and declare our royal will and pleafure, as for and concerning the reftoring to fuch of our cities, corporations, and boroughs within our faid kingdom and dominion, which have made deeds of furrender, or have had judgment given againft them, which furrenders and judgments are entred of record, That our chancellor, attorney general, and folicitor general, without fees to any officer or officers whatfoever, upon application to them made, fhall, and they are hereby required to prepare and pafs charters, inftruments, grants, and letters patents, for the incorporating, regranting, confirming, and reftoring to all and every the faid cities, corporations, and boroughs, their refpective charters, liberties, rights, franchifes, and privileges, and for reftoring the refpective mayors, bailiffs, recorders, fheriffs, town clerks, aldermen, common council men, affiftants, officers, magiftrates, minifters, and freemen, as were of fuch cities, corporations, or boroughs, at the time of fuch deeds of furrender, or judgments refpectively given or had, and for the putting them into the fame ftate, condition, and plight, they were in at the times of fuch deeds of furrender, or judgments made or given.

AND

AND whereas divers boroughs, that were not heretofore corporations, have fince the year 1679 had charters of incorporation granted and paffed unto them ; We hereby further exprefs and declare our royal pleafure, to determine and annul the faid laft mentioned charters and corporations : And to that end, we have in purfuance to the power referved in the faid charters, by our order in council, and under our fign manual, removed and difcharged, and we do alfo by this our proclamation, made with the advice of our faid council, remove and difcharge all and every perfon of or in the faid laft mentioned corporations, of and from all offices and places of mayors, bailiffs, recorders, fheriffs, aldermen, common council men, affiftants, and of and from all and every other office and place, from which we have power referved by the faid charters refpectively to remove or difcharge them. And we do hereby promife and declare, that we will do and confent to all fuch acts, matters, and things, as fhall be neceffary to render thefe our gracious intentions and purpofes effectual ; it being our gracious intention to call a parliament, as foon as the general difturbance of our kingdom by the intended invafion will admit thereof.

Given at our court at *Whitehall* the 17th day of October, 1688 ; in the fourth year of our reign.

No. XL.

A CATALOGUE of fcarce or curious PLANTS, growing wild about , *Kendal* and other places within the county of Weftmorland.

ADDER'S TONGUE. Ophiogloffum.
Agrimony. Eupatorium In hedge fides, plenty.
———— Hemp Agrimony. Eupatorium Cannabicum.
Alheal (Clown's). Stachys paluftris. In wet places.
Anemone (Wood). Anemone nemorum.
Angelica (Wild). Angelica Sylveftris.
Archangel (Yellow). Lamium luteum. ·
Arfmart. Perficaria. Of ten forts. In ponds and wet places.
Afarabacca. Afarum.
Afphodel (Lancafhire). Phalangium. In wet grounds.
Avens, or Herb Bennet. Geum urbanum. In thickets.
Baneberries. Chriftophoriana. In woods.
Bafil (Wild). Clinopodium. In hedges and thickets.
—— (Small wild). Acinos. In gravelly places.
Bell flower. Campanula.
Betony. Betonica. In woods and hedges.
———— (Paul's Betony). Veronica ferpyllifolia.
Bindweed. Convolvulus. In moift grounds.
Bird's eye, or wild auricula. In moift grounds.
Biftort. Biftorta. In meadow grounds.

Bird-neft. Nidus avis. Nigh Kendal.
Bloodwort. Lapathum. At Old Hall and other places.
Bramble (Stone). Chamemorus. In Barrowfield wood.
Briony (White). Brionia. At Challon hall.
—— (Black). Tamnus. In hedges, frequent.
Brooklime. In fmall brooks.
Broomrape. Orobanche. At the roots of broom.
Buckbeans. Meny'anthes trifolia.
Burnet. Sanguiforba. In wet lands.
Butchers broom. Rufcus. At Old Hall.
Butter bur (Greater). Petafites major. Nigh Kendal.
Butterwort, or Yorkfhire Sanicle. Pinguicula Gefneri. In wet places.
Carrot (Wild). Daucus. In dry paftures.
Cat mint. Repeta. Nigh Nether Levins.
Celandine (Greater). Chelidonium.
—— (Leffer), or Pilewort. In hedge fides, plenty.
Centory (Leffer). Centaurium. In dry paftures.
Cinquefoil (Common). Pentaphyllum. Creeps on the ground.
—— (Marfh). Growing in wet ditches.
Clary (Wild). Horminum. In ftony places.
Cloudberries. Chamæmorus. In Long Sleddale.
Cockfhead, or St. Foin. Onobrychis. At Sizergh and Old Hall.
Coltsfoot. Tuffilago. In moift ground, frequent.
Columbine. Aquilegia. In woods.
Comfrey. Symphetum. In divers places.
Corn Sallad, or Lamb's Lettuce. Valeriana Locufta.
Cow Wheat. Melampyrum. In woods, near oak trees.
Creffes (Water). Nafturtium aquaticum.
Cranberry. Oxycoccius. On moorifh ground.
Cudweed (Mountain). Gnaphalium. On Kendal Fell.
Crowfoot (Water). Ranunculus Aquaticus. In rivers.
Daffodil (Englifh, wild). Narciffus.
Dames violet (Unfavoury). Hefperis. In Grefmere.
Devil's Bit. In wet places, frequent.
Dock (Water). Lapathum. Nigh Bethom bridge.
Dropwort. Ænanthe. (Hemlock.) Poifonous.
Dyer's weed, or wild Woad. Luteola Refeda. In marfhes.
Elecampane. Helenium.
Eye-bright. Euphrafia. In moift grounds.
Fern (Male Stone) marked with black fpots.
—— (Creeping, water or marfh).
Fleabane (Middle). Conyza media.
—— (Great, or Ploughman's Spikenard).
Fliceweed (Eryfinum). In wet places.
Foxglove (American). Digitalis. At Old Hall.

                                                    Garlick

Garlick (Mountain).   Nigh Long Sleddale.
———— (Broad leaved Mountain).   Nigh Great Strickland.
Gentian (Marſh), or Calathian Violet.   In Foulſhaw.
Gladiole, or flowering raſh Butomus.   At Windermere water ſide.
Globe flower.   Ranunculus globoſus.   In ·moiſt lands.
Goat's beard (Purple).   At Old Hall.
Golden Rod (Marſh).   Virga Aurea.   Near Challon Hall.
Goutweed.   Ægopodium.   Podagraria.
Henbane.   Hyoſcyamus._ Amongſt rubbiſh.
Horehound (White) Marubium.   By highway ſides in rubbiſh.
Hyacinth (White flowered) wild.   At Old Hall.
Jack by the Hedge.   Eriſimum Allieria.   In hedges.
St. John's wort.   Hypericum.
Kidney wort.   In Long Sleddale.
Ladies Bed ſtraw.   Mollugo.   White and yellow.
———— Mantle.   Alchemilla vulgaris.
———— Finger.   Vulneraria.
———— Smock.   Cardamine pratenſis.
——— Slipper.   Calceolus.
Lambs Lettuce.   Valeriana Locuſta.
Lilly of the Valley.   Lillium Convallium.   In woods.
—— (Water).   White.   Nymphæa.
—— (Yellow).   Nymphæa lutea.
Liverwort (Lichen) aſh-coloured.   In wet grounds.
Lungwort, or Mullein.   Verbaſcum.   In paſtures.
Madder (Wild).   Mollugo.
Maiden hair (Black).   Trichomanes.   On walls and rocks.
——————— (White).   Ruta muraria.   The, ſame.
Marjoram (Wild).   Origanum.   In highway ſides.
Marſhmallow.   Althea.   In marſhes near the Sea.
Melilot.   Near Foulſhaw, by Milnthorp Sands.
Mercury (common Engliſh).
——— (Dog's).   Mercurialis.   In hedges.
Milfoil (Water), feathered.   Potamogiton.   In Rowel Beck.
Mint (Water).   Mentha.
—— (Brandy or Pepper mint).
Miſleto.   Viſcum.   On Appletrees in Brigſteer and Lyth.
Moonwort (Leſſer).   Lunaria.   On the moat-at Kendal caſtle.
Moſcatel.   Moſcatellina.   In hedges.
Motherwort.   Cardiaca.   About Kendal.
Muſtard (Wild).
Navelwort.   Cotyledon.   Nigh Windermere.
Nightſhade.   Solanum.   In hedges.
——————— (Deadly).   Near Burton.   Poiſonous.
——————— (Inchanter's).   Circæa.   Common.

Orchis (Sweet smelling) Nigh|Newby.
—— (Scarlet fly.) In Barrowfield wood.
Orpine. Anacampferos. Under hedges.
Osmond, or flowering Fern. In Underbarrow moffes.
Ox-eye. Near End moor.
Pellitory of the wall. Parietaria. At Old Hall.
Penny-royal. Pulegium. In wet places.
St. Peter's wort. Hypericum. In moist ground.
Pilewort, or lesser Celandine.
Pimpernel. Anagallis. Red flowered.
————————————— Yellow flowered.
Plantain (Buckthorn). Plantago.
——— (Water).
Restharro. Ononis. In dry ploughed lands.
Rosewort. Anacampferos. On rocks in Kentmire.
Rue (Meadow). Thalictrum. In woods.
Sage (Wood). Scordium.
Sanicle (Yorkshire). Penguicula vulgaris.
Sawwort. Serratula. In Middleton near Grimeshill.
Saxifrage (Burnet). Pimpinella. At Old Hall.
———— (Meadow). In moist ground.
Selfheal. Prunella. About Kendal.
Shavegrafs. Equifetum nudum. Near Shap.
Sorrel (Round leaved mountain). By Buckbarrow well.
Spignel, or Baldmony. Meum. At Longwell in Selfide.
Sundew. Ros Solis. In moorish ground.
Sunflower, or Dwarf Ciftus. In dry barren grounds.
——— (Hoary dwarf mountain).
Thistle (melancholy). Cirfium. In Long Sleddale.
Thrift, or Sea Gillyflower. Statice Armeria.
Toothwort. Anblatum.
Tormentil. In paftures and mountainous places.
Tutfan, or Park Leaves. Hypericum.
Twayblade. Bifolium. Between Shap and Kendal.
Violet (Water). In Brigfteer mofs.
Wall flower, or wild cheir. On walls.
Willow herb (Yellow). Lyfimachia lutea. In wet ditches.
Woad (Wild), or Dyers weed. Refeda luteola.
Woodroof. Afperula. Near Levens.

No. XLI.

No. XLI.

A CATALOGUE of scarce or curious PLANTS that have been observed growing wild about *Carlisle*, and in some other parts of *Cumberland*.

Achillea: Millefolium. Yarrow or Milfoil.
Aegopodium. Podagraria. Gout weed.
Aethusa. Sinapium. Fool's Parsley.
Agrimonia. Eupatoria. Agrimony.
Ahinanthus. Crista Galli. Yellow rattle or Cock's comb.
Ajuga reptans. Bugle.
Alchimilla. Ladies mantle.
Alisma. Plantago aquatica. Great water Plantain.
Allium vineale. Crow Garlick.
——— ursinum. Ramsons.
Althæa officinalis. Marshmallow.
Anagallis arvensis. Male and female Pimpernel.
Andromeda, polyfolia. Marshlistus, or wild Rosemary.
Anemone, nemorosa. Wood Anemone.
Anthosanthum, odoratum. Vernal Grass.
Anthyllis. Vulneraria. Kidney Vetch, or Ladies finger.
Antirrhinum. Linaria. Yellow Toad Flax.
Artemisia maritima. Sea Wormwood.
Arundo arenaria. Sea Reed grass, or Matweed.
Asplenium. Trichomanes. Common Maiden hair.
——— Marinum. Sea Maiden hair, or Fern.
——— Ruta muraria. White Maiden hair.
——— Adiantum nigrum. Black Maiden hair.
Aster. Tripolium. Sea Starwort.
Athamanta Meum. Spignel or Bald money.
Atropa. Belladonna. Deadly Nightshade.
Balotta nigra. Stinking Horehound.
Beta vulgaris. Sea Beet.
Betonica officinalis. Wood Betony.
Bidens tripartita. Water Hemp Agrimony.
——— Eupatorium. Cannabinum. Hemp Agrimony.
Brassica. Napus. Wild Navew.
——— Erucastrum. Wild Rocket.
Butomus umbellatus. Flowering Rush, or Water Gladiole.
Callibriche verna. Vernal Starwort.
——— autumnalis. Autumnal Starwort.
Caltha palustris. Marsh Marigold.
Campanula rotundifolia. Round leaved Bell flower.

Campanula

Campanula latifolia. Giant Throatwort.
———— Trachelium. Great Throatwort, or Canterbury Bells.
———— glomerata. Leſſer Throatwort.
Carca. Pſeudo-Cyperus. Baſtard Cyperus.
Cardamine. Ladies ſmock, or Cuckow flower.
Carduus Marianus. Milk Thiſtle.
———— Helenioides. Melancholy Thiſtle.
Centaurea, Cyanus. Bluebottles.
———— Scabioſa. Great Knapwood, or Matfellon.
Chærophyllum Sylveſtre. Wild Cicely, or Cow-weed.
Cheiranthus. Wall-flower.
———— Tricuſpidatus. Sea Stock Gillyflower.
Chelidonium majus. Celendine.
———— Glaucium. Yellow horned Poppy.
Chenopodium. Mercury.
Chryſanthemum ſegetum. Corn Marigold.
———— Leucanthemum. The greater Daiſie, or Ox-eye.
Chryſoſplenium oppoſitifolium. Golden Saxifrage.
Circæa Lutetiana, Enchanters Nightſhade.
Clinopodium. Wild Baſil.
Cochleara officinalis. Scurvy graſs.
Conferva rivularis. River Conferva, or Crow ſilk.
———— rupeſtris. Rock Conferva, or Sea beard.
———— rubra. Red Conferva.
Convolvulus. Bindweed.
Cornus ſanguinea. Female Cornel; Dogberry.
Crambe maritima. Sea Colewort.
Cucubalus. Bladder Campion. Spatling Poppy.
Cynogloſſum. Hound's tongue.
Daucus. Wild Carrot, or Bird's neſt.
Draba verna. Whitlow graſs.
Droſer rotundifolia. Sun-dew.
Empetrum nigrum. Crakeberry.
Epitobium anguſtifolium. Roſebay Willow herb.
———— hirſutum. Small flowered hairy Willow herb.
———— montanum. Smooth leaved Willow herb.
———— paluſtre. Marſh Willow herb.
Erica multiflora. Fir-leaved Heath.
Eriophorum polyſtachion. Cotton graſs.
Eryngium maritimum. Sea Holly. Eringo.
Eryſimum officinale. Hedge muſtard.
———— Barbarea. Winter creſſes, or Rocket.
Euphorbia Helioſcopia. Sun ſpurge or Wartwort.
Euphraſia. Eyebright.
Ficaria. Pilewort, or leſſer Celandine.
Fucus veſiculoſus. Sea Oak.

Fucus

Fucus linearis. Sea Thongs.
Galeopfis. Ladanum. Narrow leaved Allheal.
———— Galeobdolen. Yellow Nettle.
Galium. Cheefe reening, or yellow Ladies Bedftraw.
———— Mollugo. Wild Madder.
———— montanum. Mountain Ladies Bedftraw.
Gentiana. Centaurium. Leffer Centory.
Geranium Cicutarium. Hemlock leaved Crane's bill.
———— Mofchatum. Mufked Crane's bill.
———— Robertianum. Herb Robert.
———— Molle. Dove's foot Crane's bill.
Geum urbanum. Avens, or Herb Bennet.
———— rivale. Water Avens.
Glaux maritima. Sea Milkwort.
Glechoma hederacea. Ground Ivy.
Grithmum maritimum. Samphire.
Hordeum Murinum. Wall Barley, or Way Bennet.
Hyofcyamus niger. Henbane.
Hypericum perforatum. St. John's wort.
Ifatis tinctoria. Woad.
Lemna trifulca. Ivy leaved Duck's meat.
Leontodon Autumnale. Yellow Devil's bit.
Leonurus. Cardiaca. Motherwort.
Lithrum. Salicaria. Purple fpiked Loofe ftrip, or Willow herb.
Lobelia Dortmanna. Water Gladiole.
Lychen Geographicus. Map Liverwort.
———— Sanguinarius. Black nobbed Liverwort.
———— Caninus. Afh coloured ground Liverwort.
Lychnis. Flos Cuculi. Mead Pink. Cuckow flower.
Lycopodium clavatum. Club Mofs.
———————— inundatum. Marfh Club Mofs.
———————— Alpinum. Mountain Club Mofs.
———————— Selago. Fir Club Mofs.
Lycopfis arvenfis. Small wild Buglofs.
Lyfimachia nemorum. Yellow Pimpernel.
Malva rotundifolia. Dwarf Mallow.
———— Alcea. Vervain Mallow.
Marrubium. White Horehound.
Matricaria Parthenium. Feverfew.
Melampyrum criftatum. Crefted Cow-wheat.
———————— fylvaticum. Yellow Cow-wheat.
Mentha aquatica. Water mint.
Menyanthes trifolia. Marfh Trefoil, or Buckbean.
Mercurialis perennis. Dog's Mercury.
Myofotis Scorpioides. Moufe ear Scorpion grafs.
Myrrhis odorata. Sweet Cicely.

Narthecium offifragum. Lancashire Asphodel.
Nepeta. Cataria. Nep, or Cat Mint.
Nymphæa lutea. Yellow water lilly.
———— alba. White water lilly.
Oenanthe fistulosa. Water Dropwort.
Ononis. Restharrow, or Cammock.
Origanum vulgare. Wild Marjoram.
Ophioglossum. Adder's tongue.
Ophrys spiralis. Triple Ladies traces.
———— ovata. Tway-blade.
Ornithopus perpasillus. Birds-foot.
Orobanche major. Broom rape.
Osmunda regalis. Flowering Fern.
Ozalis acetosella. Wood Sorrel.
Parietaria. Pellitory of the Wall.
Parnassia palustris. Grass of Parnassus.
Pedicularis sylvatica. Common Lousewort.
———— palustris. Marsh Lousewort.
Phalaris Canariensis. Manured Canary grass.
———— Arenaria. Sea Canary grass.
———— Arundinacea. Reed Canary grass.
Pimpinella Saxifraga. Small Burnet Saxifrage.
Pinguicula. Butterwort.
Plantago major. Great Plantain, or Way-bread.
———— media. Hoary Plantain.
———— Maritima. Sea Plantain.
———— Coronopus. Buckthorn Plantain.
Polygata. Milkwort.
Polygonum. Bistorta. Great Bistort, or Snakeweed.
———— Hydropiper. Water Pepper, or Arsmart.
Polypodium fragrans. Sweet Polypody.
Potamogiton natans. Broad leaved Pondweed.
———— perfoliatum. Perfoliated Pondweed.
———— crispum. Great water Caltrops.
Potentilla Argentina. Silver weed, or wild Tanzy.
———— reptans. Cinquefoil.
Prenanthes muralis. Ivy leaved wild Lettuce.
Primula farinosa. Bird's eye.
Prunella. Self heal.
Pulmonaria maritima. Sea Buglofs.
Ranunculus. Flammula. Lesser Spearwort.
———— sceleratus. Round leaved water Crowfoot.
Rhodiola. Rosea. Rosewort.
Rumex crispus. Curled Dock.
Sagina procumbens. Pearlwort.
Salicornia Europæa. Marsh Samphire.

4

Sambucus

Sambucus Ebulus. Dwarf Elder, or Danewort.
Sanguiforba. Burnet.
Sanicula Europæa. Sanicle.
Saxifraga granulata. White Seagreen Saxifrage.
Scabiofa fuccifa. Devil's bit.
Scandix. Pecten Veneris. Shepherd's needle, or Venus comb.
Scirpus maritimus. Round rooted baftard Cyperus.
Scrophularia nodofa. Knobby rooted Fig-wort.
———— aquatica. Water Fig-wort.
Sedum. Telephium. Orpine, or Live long.
Silene amæna. Sea Campion.
Sifymbrium. Water Creffes.
———— Sophia. Flixweed.
Sium nodiflorum. Creeping water Parfnip.
Solanum Dulcamara. Woody Nightfhade, or Bitter-fweet.
Solidago. Virga aurea. Golden Rod.
Spergula nodofa. Marfh Saxifrage.
Stachys paluftris. Clown's Allheal.
Statice. Armeria. Thrift, or Sea Gilliflower.
Stellaria nemorum. Broad leaved Stitchwort.
Stratiotes Aloides. Water Aloe.
Tamnus. Black Briony.
Thalictrum flavum. Meadow-hue.
Thlapfi campeftre. Baftard Creffes.
———— Burfa Paftoris. Shepherd's purfe.
Thymus. Serpillum. Mother of Thyme.
Tormentilla erecta. Tormentil, or Septfoil.
Tragopogon pratenfe. Yellow Goats-beard.
Trifolium officinale. Melilot.
———— pratenfe. Honeyfuckle Trefoil.
Triglochin paluftre. Arrow headed grafs.
———— maritimum. Sea fpiked grafs.
Triticum junceum. Sea Wheat grafs.
Trollius. Globe flower.
Turritis hirfuta. Hairy Tower Muftard.
Tuffilago. Colt's-foot.
Vaccinium. Myrtillus. Bilberry.
———— Oxycocus. Cranberry.
Valeriana. Valerian.
———— Locufta. Lambs Lettuce, or Corn Sallad.
Verbafcum. Thapfus. Great white Mullein.
Verbena. Vervain.
Veronica officinalis. Male Speedwell.
———— Sepyllifolia. Paul's Betony.
———— Becabunga. Brooklime.

Veronica Chamædrys.   Wild Germander.
———— Hederifolia.   Ivy leaved Speedwell, or small Henbit.
Viola hirta.   Hairy Violet.
———— canina.   Dog's Violet.
———— tricolor.   Heart's ease.

No. XLII.

ACCOUNT of the different VALORS of the diocese of CARLISLE; with a preface by bishop LYTTELTON.

THE following account contains three ecclesiastical Valors of Carlisle diocese, ranged in three columns, for the easier comparing them with each other.
The first, marked N. P. was made by order of pope Nicholas, A. D. 1291
and 92, and taken from a Cotton MS. in the British Musæum (Tiberius C. X.)
intitled, *Regiſtrum Dni Pape de Taxatione Spiritualitat' et Temporalitat' Anglie
et Wallie,* collated with a very fair copy in Litchfield Cathedral library, and
also with the original register of. John de Kirkby bishop of Carlisle, where
(inter folia 452 & 458) the taxation and value of every church, &c. is accurately entered. By this it appears, that the taxation of the *Spiritualia* was
made by Richard de Whitby archdeacon of Carlisle, and Adam de Levyngton
rector of Skelton, *ſecundum verum valorem prout ſolet communiter provenire,* dated
A. D. 1291, 19th of Ed. 1. And that of the *Temporalia* by Peter de Inſula
archdeacon of Exeter, and Adam de Aſton rector of Beckenham, agents for
this buſineſs under John biſhop of Winton, and Oliver biſhop of Lincoln,
appointed by the pope collectors of a ſubſidy *in ſubſidium terre ſanctæ,* dated
A. D. 1292.
   The ſecond, marked Ed. 2. was a re-taxation under a new valuation, the
former being ſo enormouſly high, that the clergy here were unable to pay it.
It was made A. D. 1318, 11 Ed. 2. in conſequence of a royal mandate directed
to the biſhop of Carliſle; which, as it occurs no where but in one of the regiſters of that ſee (from whence alſo this valor was extracted), and is the more
curious, as I do not find the like indulgence was extended to any other dioceſe,
except that part of the preſent dioceſe of Cheſter which lies in the archdeaconry
of Richmond, I ſhall here give it at large : ".Edw^{dus} Dei gratia, Rex Anglie,
&c. Venerab' in Chriſto J. eadem gratia Karl' Epo, ſalutem. Quia plurima
beneficia eccleſiaſtica et temporalia ſpiritualibus annexa, in Dioceſ' veſtra per
hoſtiles aggreſſus Scotorum inimicorum et rebellium noſtrorum vaſtata ſunt, ut
accepimus, et deſtructa; per quod, de decima nobis per Dnm Pontificem
jam conceſſa de dictis beneficiis temporalibus et ſpiritualibus annexis, ibidem ad preſens reſpondere non valent, juxta taxationem decime nunc cur-
rentis prout alias fieri conſueverit: Nos ſuper valorem beneficiorum et tem-
poralium hujuſmodi in dicta dioceſ' veſtra, quantum, videlicet, modo valeant,

certiorari

certiorari volentes, ut decima inde juxta valorem illorum ad opus noſtrum levari poſſit; mandamus, quod ſuper valorem omnium beneficiorum eccleſiaſti-
corum infra dictam dioceſin veſtram, et in temporalibus Prelatorum ibidem
que totaliter ſunt vaſtata, et que ad decimam hactenus taxari conſueverunt,
quantum, videlicet, valeant hiis diebus, inquiratis plenius veritatem; et beneficia et temporalia hujuſmodi prout per inquiſitiones predictas reperiri contigerit, taxari faciatis; et collectores decime in eadem dioces' veſtra de taxati-
onibus hujuſmodi cum facta fuerint conſtare faciatis indilate, ut ipſi decimam
illam juxta taxationes illas ad opus noſtrum levare valeant, ut debebunt; et
nihilominus, taxationes illas cum plenius facte fuerint theſaurario et baronibus
nris de ſcaccario mittatis, et hoc breve. Teſte meipſo apud Ebor' viceſimo
ſexto die Octob' anno regni nri duodecimo.——Per Concilium."

The third, marked H. 8. was made about the year 1546, 27 Hen. 8. and is
here given from the original rotuli (commonly called the king's books) now remaining in the firſt fruits office in London; by which the clergy pay their firſt
fruits and tenths at this day.

On comparing theſe together, it appears, that the livings in general are
rated conſiderably higher in Edward the firſt's time than in Hen. 8th's. Which
is the more remarkable, as within that period trade and manufactures were
improved and had brought an increaſe of ſpecie into the kingdom, and conſequently leſſened the value of money. Agriculture alſo was improved; and
in theſe parts, by the diſafforeſtation of Englewood and other foreſts, many
waſte lands were converted into good paſture and arable, which muſt naturally
increaſe the tithes in many parts of the dioceſe. The temporalia of the biſhoprick, and of the ſeveral religious houſes, particularly of Carliſle priory
and Holm Cultram are rated vaſtly higher in Hen. 8th's valor than that of Edward the firſt, otherwiſe the ſum total of Edward the firſt's valor would have
exceeded that of Hen. 8.

With regard to the valor made in Ed. 2d's time, it falls ſo vaſtly ſhort of
the former, that one cannot but ſuſpect that the biſhop rated the ſeveral preferments conſiderably lower than the true value. The Scots indeed, about
that time, had made ſad devaſtation in this country; and conſequently the
churches, ſituated on the borders, muſt have ſuffered greatly. But it can
hardly be ſuppoſed, that every part of the dioceſe was ſo over-run and deſtroyed, as to reduce the whole in value from 3171 l to 480 l per Ann. The
pope's collectors ſeem to have been of this opinion, and not to have much regarded this latter valuation, till by a ſpecial command of Ed. 3. in the 4th
year of his reign, they were required to make it their rule, as well in that
moiety which was then gathering for his holineſs, as in the other for the king's
uſe. But this command was temporary only, and to continue no longer in
force than till the meeting of the approaching parliament. What was then
done in this affair doth not appear. But it ſeems, that about 30 years afterwards, the old taxation was again the ſtandard, for in biſhop Appleby's regiſter
we have the *taxationes epiſcopatum Anglie*, and there *Karliol'* is rated at 3171 l 5 s
7½ d.

Oct. 1, 1767.   CHA. CARLISLE.

DECANATUS KARLIOL'

N. P.	l.	s.	d.	Ed. 2.	l.	s.	d.	Hen. 8.	l.	s.	d.
Parrio archidiaconi in ecclesia de Dalston -	15	0	0	Ecclesia de Dalston - -							
Portio Prioris Karliol' in ecclesia Beatæ Mariæ -	20	0	0	Portio Prioris Karliol' in ecclesia Beatæ Mariæ - -							
Portio Epi in eadem -	9	9	0	Portio Epi in eadem - -	3	0	0				
Ecclesia Sci Cuthberti Karl' -	17	1	4	Ecclesia Sci Cuthberti Karl' - -	5	0	0				
Portio Epi in Ecclesia de Staynewiggs -	10	8	0	Portio Epi in Ecclesia de Staynwegg's, non taxatur, quia parochia totaliter destruitur.							
Portio Prioris Karl' in eadem -	4	6	8	Portio Prioris Karl' in eadem non taxatur, quia parochia totaliter destruitur.							
Vicaria ejusdem ecclie -	8	10	0	Vicaria ejusdem non taxatur, quia non sufficit pro stipendio unius capellani.		1	0	Stanwykethe vicaria per annum valet - num valet	1 9	1 0	2 0
Ecclesia de Crofhye -	14	0	0	Ecclesia de Crosseby - -							
Vicaria ejusdem -	4	5	0	Vicaria ejusdem non taxatur, quia non sufficit pro stipendio unius capellani.				Crosby vicaria valet perannum clare -	3	11	4
Ecclesia de Denton, nichil, quia non excedit 6 mar', nec rector habet aliud beneficium.				Ecclesia de Denton non taxatur in antiquo,				Denton rectoria valet per annum -	4	5	5
Ecclesia de Walton cum capellis -	50	0	0	Ecclesia de Walton cum capella, non taxatur, quia tota destruitur.							
Ecclesia de Brampton -	18	0	0	Ecclesia de Brampton - -	1	0	0	Brampton vicaria v. per ann.	7	15	4
Vicaria ejusdem -	8	0	0	Vicaria ejusdem -							
Ecclesia de Hirthington -	13	15	0	Ecclesia de Irthington } non taxantur, quia totaliter sunt destructæ.				Irthington vicaria - -	6	1	4
Vicaria ejusdem -	10	0	0	Vicaria ejusdem }							
Ecclesia de Farlam -	7	0	0	Ecclesia de Farlam }							
				Vicaria non taxatur.							
Ecclesia de Grimesal (Kirkby) Grinsdal -	3	4	0	Ecclesia de Grennesdal non taxatur, quia non sufficit pro servitio unius capellani.							
Ecclesia de Hayton -	14	10	0	Ecclesia de Hayton } non taxantur, quia non sufficiunt pro incumbentibus.							
Ecclesia de Coquitington (Kirkby) Cumquitington -	8	14	0	Ecclesia de Cumquitington {							
Ecclesia de Cumrew -	4	10	0	Ecclesia de Cumrew } non taxantur, quia non sufficiunt pro incumbentibus.							
Ecclesia de Rochcliffe -	10	13	4	Ecclesia de Routhcliff {							
Ecclesia de Saburham -	5	0	0	Ecclesia de Seburgham - -	1	0	0				

Ecclesia de Ayketon - - 19 4 0
Ecclesia de Bampton - - 18 10 0

Portio Scolar' Karliol' in ecclesia de Dalston - 16 0 0
Vicaria de Dalston - 12 16 0
Ecclesia de Thoresby - 20 0 0
Ecclesia de Bownes - 30 0 0
Eccl'ia de Burgo sub ... 50 0 0
Vicaria ... 9 0 0
Ecclesia de Beaumont - 10 0 0
Ecclesia de Orreton ... 8 0 0
Ecclesia de ... (non tax') destructa - 80 0 0
Vicaria ejusdem - 9 0 0
Ecclesia de Levington - 42 0 0

Ecclesia de Stapleton - 4 2 0
Ecclesia de Eston (olim destruc') 4 6 8
Ecclesia de Botecastre - 19 0 0

Ecclesia de Cumbak (olim destr') 8 0 0

Ecclesia de Carlaton (olim destr') 6 13 4

Ecclesia de Scaleby - 10 0 0
Ecclesia de Castlekayrok - 6 10 0

Ecclesia de Ayketon

Portio Willmi de Arc in ecclesia de Bampton - 4 0 0
Portio Johan' de Colgaith in eadem - 2 0 0
Portio M. Hosp: S. Nichl in eadem - 1 0 0

Ecclesia de Thoresby
Ecclesia de Bownes
Ecclesia de Burgo
Vicaria ejusdem
Ecclesia de Beaumont   } non taxantur, quia non
Ecclesia de Orreton   } sufficiunt pro stipendio capellani.

Ecclesia de Arthuret
Vicaria ejusdem
Ecclesia de Levington

Ecclesia de Stapleton
Ecclesia de Eston (olim destruc')   } non taxantur, quia non
Ecclesia de Buthcastre   } sufficiunt pro stipendio capellani.

Ecclesia de Cumbok   } non taxantur, quia non sufficit pro stipendio capellani.

Ecclesia de Carlaton, non taxatur, quia non sufficit pro stipendio capellani.

Ecclesia de Scaleby   } non taxatur, quia non sufficiunt pro omnibus incumbentibus.
Ecclesia de Castlekayrok   }

Ayketon rectoria - - 13 13 0
Kirkhampton rectoria - 14 17 10

Dalston vicaria - - 8 18 2½
Thursby vicaria - 11 10 4
Bownes rectoria - 21 13 10½

Burgha cu' super eas - 5 1 9¼
Beaumont al' Beamont & - 8 1 6
Orton ... - 9 0 0

Abbe ... alet per an, pure pacis - 2 0 0
... flore Gare - nihil.
Arth ... vic. t. pacis - 1 2 0
... t. Guerre - nihil.

Kirkleynton or Kirk Levington rectoria, alet per an. t. pacis - 1 1 0
... t. Guerre - nihil.
Stapylton rectoria - 1 9 0

Bewcastell rectoria valet per an' tempore pacis - 2 0 0
tempore guerre - nihil.

Scaylby rectoria - 7 1 0
Castlecayrock rectoria - 5 12 10

DECANATUS KARLIOL'

N. P.	l s d	Ed. 2.	l s d	Hen. 8.	l s d
Rectoria ecclesie de Kirkandres non , edit 4 ms, nec s̄or habet alia beneficia.	3ł 6 0	Ecclesia de Kirkandres, non taxatur in antiquo.		Kirkandrei rectoria	3 11 5
Ecclesia de Wederhall		Ecclesia de Wederhall			
Portio Prioriſſe de Marring in : tdm	3 0 6	Portio Prioriſſe de Marring in eadem non tax-tur, quia totaliter deſtruitur.	1 0 0		
Penſio Dni Epiſcopi in deſia de Denton	1 13 4	Penſio dni Epi in Ecclefia de Denton			
Penſio ejuſdem in eia de Scaleby	1 0 0	Pſio ejuſdem in ecclefia de Scaleby			
Penſio ejuſdem in eia de Staneſwegg	0 6 8	Penſio ejuſdem in celefia de Staneweggys			
Panſio ejuſdem in eia de Croſſebye	0 2 0	Penſio ejuſdem in celefia de Croſſebye			
Penſio ejuſdem in vicaria de Botecaſtre	0 6 8	Penſio ejuſdem in celefia de Bouthcaſtre			
Penſio prioris de Lanercoſt in ecclefia de tam	1 13 4	Penſio prioris de ecclefia de Denton			
		Penſio prioris Karl' in ecclefia de Cambock			
		Penſio idm in celefia de Caſtlecayrok			

{Note bracketed against the Ed. 2. entries for Staneweggys, Croſſebye, Bouthcaſtre, Denton, Cambock, Caſtlecayrok:} Nulle ſunt hiis diebus propterdeſtruſtiones.

Epiſcopatus Karliol' valet in ſpiritual' et temporal' per annum clare - 531 4 11¾

Prioratus beate Marie Karl' valet clare per ann. in ſpirit' et templ' - 418 3 4¾

Cantaria Sci Roche in eccl' parochiali beate Marie Karl' - 2 14 0

Cantaria Sci Crucis in eccl' parochiali perdiſt' - 3 19 0

	l	s	d
Cantaria fce Katherine virginis in eccl' parochiali predict'	3	2	8
Cantaria fci Albani infra civitat' Karliol'			
Prioratus beate Marie Magdal' de Lanercoft valet in fpiritualib' et temporalib'	2	10	4
	77	11	11
Summa totalis Decan' Karl'	1187	13	5¼

Summa totalis Decan' Karl' 740 2 4	Summa totalis Decanatus Karl' 30 10 0

DECANAT' DE ALLERDALE.

N. P.	l	s	d	Ed. 2.	l	s	d	Hen. 8.	l	s	d
Ecclefia de Wyggeton	36	0	0	Ecclefia de Wyggeton	13	6	8	Wigton vicaria	17	19	9¼
								Hofpitale fituat' prope Wigton beate Marie infra ecclefiam de Wigton	2	0	0
Ecclefia de Kyrkebryde	6	0	0	Ecclefia de Kyrkbride	2	0	0	Kyrkbride rectoria	5	6	8
Ecclefia de Brumfeld	7	8	8	Ecclefia de Brumfeld	17	6	8	Bromefielde vicaria	5	0	0
								fca Sci Georgii in ecclefia de Bromefielde	22	0	0
Ecclefia de Afpatrick	30	0	0	Ecclefia de Afpatrick	5	0	0	Afpatryke ona	4	12	0
Vicaria ejufdem	6	12	0	Vicaria ejufdem	1	6	8		10	4	0
Ecclefia de Boulton	18	0	0	Ecclefia de Bolton	8	6	8	Bolton	19	18	2
Ecclefia de Ireby	20	0	0	Ecclefia de Ireby	8	0	0				
Ecclefia de Ulnedale	18	0	0	Ecclefia de Ulnedale	4	0	0	Uldale	17	17	0
Ecclefia de Caldbeck	30	0	0	Ecclefia de Caldbeck	5	0	0	Caldbeck	45	13	6
Ecclefia de Crofthwaite	30	13	4	Ecclefia de Crofthwaite	10	0	0	Crofthwate vicaria	50	8	11¼
Vicaria ejufdem	20	0	0	Vicaria ejufdem	4	0	0	Cantaria bute Marie Magdal' de Kefwyck	4	19	7
Ecclefia de Boekirke hodie Baffenthwaite	9	0	0	Ecclefia de Bekyrke (hodie Baffenthwaite)	1	6	8				
Ecclefia de Thorpenhow	30	0	0	Ecclefia de Torpenhow	5	0	0	Torpenno vicaria	33	4	10

4 H

DECANATOS ALLERDALE.

N. P.	l	s	d	Ed. 2.	l	s	d	Hen. 8.	l	s	d
Vicaria ejusdem	16	0	0	Vi onã ej 6th	3	0	0				
Ecclesia de Isalle	21	14	0	Ecclesia de Isalle	5	0	0	Isal vicaria	8	13	1½
Vicaria ejusdem	6	0	0	Vicaria ejusdem non sufficit pro oneribus ordinariis supportand'							
Ecclesia de Plumbland	18	0	0	Ecclesia de Plumland	4	0	0	Plumbland rectoria	20	14	8
Ecclesia de Gillette (hodie Gilcrux)	2	6	8	Ecclesia de — ece	0	10	0	Gylecrux vicaria	5	14	1¼
Vicaria ejusdem	4	13	4	Vicaria ejusdem non sufficit pro oneribus ordinariis supportand'							
Ecclesia de Brydkyrke	60	0	0	Ecclesia de Brydkyrk	13	6	8	Kyrkbride rectoria	5	0	0
Vicaria ejusdem	13	6	8	Vicaria ejusdem	2	0	0	Brydkirk vicaria	10	8	6
Ecclesia de Crosbye	15	0	0	Ecclesia de Crosby	4	0	0				
Ecclesia de Derham	13	6	8	Ecclesia de — tm	4	0	0	Dereham vicaria	4	10	2
Vicaria ejusdem	4	13	4	Vicaria ejusdem non sufficit pro oneribus ordinariis supportand'							
Ecclesia de Cambirton	200			Ecclesia de Camberton	5	0	0				
								Abbathia sive Mon' de Holme Coltrayne valet per an' in spiritual' et temporal' clare	427	19	3¾
								Newton Arloybe infra dnium de Holme vicar' valet	6	13	4
Summa total Dec' de Allerd' - 503 14 0				Summa total' Decanat' de Allerd' 122 6 1				Summa total' Decanat' de All' 1173 6 4¾			

DECĀNATŪS WESTMER'

N. P.	l	s	d	Ed 2.	l	s	d	Hen. 8.	l	s	d
Ecclesia de Burgo subtus Moram	30	0	0	Ecclesia de Burgo sub Mora	6	13	4	Burgh subtus Moram vicaria	6	8	7
Ecclesia de Kyrkby Stephen	90	0	0	Ecclesia Kirkby Step'	13	6	8	Kirkby Stephan vicar'	48	19	2
Vicaria ejusdem	26	13	4	Vicaria ejusdem	5	0	0				
Ecclesia de Ravenstondal	6	10	6	Ecclesia de Ravenstondal	2	0	0				
Ecclesia de Musgrave	13	6	8	Ecclesia de Musgrave	1	0	0	Musgrave rectoria	16	8	10¼

	£	s	d
Ecclesia de Crosby Gerard	24	0	0
Ecclesia de Warthcoppe	35	0	0
Ecclesia de Askeby	20	0	0
Ecclesia de Overton	40	0	0
Vicaria ejusdem	10	0	0
Ecclesia de Ormeshead	13	6	8
Ecclesia Sci Laurenii de Appleby	15	0	0
Vicaria ejusdem	10	0	0
Ecclesia de Morland	80	0	0
Vicaria ejusdem	26	13	4
Ecclesia Sci Mich de Applebye	30	0	0
Vicaria ejusdem	13	6	8
Ecclesia de Crossby Ravensgarte	40	0	0
Vicaria ejusdem	5	0	0
Ec̄a de Clibburne	13	6	8
Ec̄a de Morton (sic Marton)	20	0	0
Ecl fca de ...	13	6	8
Ec̄a de Newbigging, nihil, quia ... eīt 6 marc' nec rector hēt alib &c'.	40	0	0
Ecl fca de Heppe	20	6	8
Ec̄a de ...	13	0	8
Ecclesia de ...	13	6	8
Ec̄a de ...	35	0	0
Ec̄a de Clifton	10	6	8
Ec̄a de Barton	40	0	0
Brvio prioris de Wartra in eadem	12	0	0
Bo ... de Ebor' in vicar' de Kirkby	1	0	0
Penfio ejm in ecclesia de Mufgrave	0	5	0
Bo ejusdem in vicaria Sci Laur' de Appiebye	1	6	8

	£	s	d
Eccl fca de Crosby Gerard	3	6	8
Ecclesia de Warthcoppe	3	6	8
Ecclesia de Afkeby	3	0	0
Eccl fca de Overton	5	0	0
Vicaria ejusdem ... his ordinariis fu ...			
Ecclesia de Ormefhead	2	0	0
Ecclesia Sci Laur de ... ejusdem ... fus ordinariis fupportand'	4	0	0
Eccl fca de Morland ejusdem	13	6	8
Ecclesia Sci Michaell Appleby	4	0	0
Vicaria ejusdem	5	0	0
Ecclesia de ... by Ravens' ... ejusdem non ... fus ordinariis fupportand'.	5	0	0
Ecclesia de ...	3	6	8
Ecl fca de Merton	4	0	0
Ecl fca de ...	2	0	0
Ecclesia de Kirkby-Thore ... d' Newbiggin, ... in auī ...	5	0	0
Ba de Heppe	2	13	4
Ba de ...	2	0	0
Ecclesia de ...	0	0	0
Ba de ...	5	0	0
Ba de Clifton	1	0	0
Ba de Bruham	2	0	0
Ba de Barton	10	0	0
Portio p' o̅is de Wartra in eadem	5	0	0
Bo abbatis de Ebor' in vicaria de Kirkby	1	0	0
Penfio ejusdem in ecclefia de Mufgrave	0	5	0
Penfio ejusdem in vicaria Sci Laur' de ...	1	6	8

	£	s	d
Crosby Garret rectoria	19	14	4
Warcoppe vicaria	9	5	1½
Ashby rectoria	23	13	4
Orton vicaria	16	17	4
Ormefhedde rectoria	15	9	4
Vicaria ecclefie Sci Laur' de Apulby	9	5	1½
Morland vicaria	11	18	0
Vicaria Sci Mich' de Apulby	20	12	9
Crosby Raynefwraythe vic'	7	13	4
Clyburne rectoria	9	1	4
Marton rectoria	21	15	5¼
Dufton rectoria	19	0	6
Kirkby Thore rectoria	37	17	8¼
Newbigging rectorie	4	10	4
Shappe vicaria	8	15	7
Bampton vicaria	7	1	8
Afton vicaria	4	13	8
Lowthyer rectotia	25	7	3½
Clifton rectoria	8	3	4
Brougham al' Burgham rector	16	10	7¼
Barton vicaria	11	1	0½

4 H

DECANATUS WESTMERL'

N. P.

	l	s	d
Ed. 2.			
Penfio ejufdem in ecclefia de Clib-burn	0	10	0
Penfio ejufdem in vicaria de Mor-land	2	13	4
Penfio pri̅ de Gy Ravenfwath pro decem quart'	2	0	0
Penfio p̅s de Wartra in de Clifton	0	13	4
Bo p̅s Karliol' in	1	6	8
Bo de Kirkby in d fa de Gy	0	6	0
Penfio dni Epi fa de Burgh de Kby Tore in	1	0	0
fa de Newbiggin dñio abbatis de Whitcby in vicar'	0	3	0
de Gy Ravens'	1	0	0
Summa total' Dec' Weftm'	788	10	8

Ed. 2.

	l	s	d
Penfio ejufdem in ecclefia de Cly-burn	0	10	0
Penfio ejufdem in vicaria de Mor-land	2	13	0
Penfio prioris de Wederhal in ecclefia de Crofby Raven'	2	0	0
Penfio prioris de Wartra in ecclefia de Clyfton	0	13	4
Penfio priors Karliol' in ecclefia de fare	1	6	8
Portio vicarii de Kirkby Stephan in eclefie de Crofby	0	5	0
Penfio Epi in defia de Burgo	1	0	0
Penfio eñs de Kirkby Thore in defia de Newbiggin	0	3	0
Penfio abbatis de Whitby in ed de Crofby Ravens'	1	0	0
Summa total' Decan' Weftm'	133	3	0

Hen. 8.

	l	s	d
Schola grammaticalis de Burgh	7	19	0¼
Schola cantator' de Burg	5	0	0
Cantar' five fchola gramaticalis in villa de Appalby	3	11	3
Cant' apud Milborne	4	0	0
Capella de Temple Soureby	1	0	0
Summa total' Dec' Weftmerl'	558	2	3½

DECANATUS CUMBR'

N. P.

	l	s	d
Ecclesia de Edenhal	24	1	4
Ecclesia de Kirkland	40	0	0
Ecclesia de Ulnesbye	11	19	0
Ecclesia de Sourbe	40	11	4
Eccl sie de Ravensfwyke (hodie Remwyk)	6	11	10
Ecclesia de Layfangby	6	13	0
Vicaria ejusdem	7	6	0
Ecclesia de Kyrkofwalde	48	15	5
Ecclesia de Croglin	9	15	4
Ecclesia de Aynftappylith	10	9	5
Vicaria ejusdem	5	4	8
Ecclesia de Melmorbye	13	13	4
Ecclesia de Dalter	50	0	0
Vicaria ejusdem	5	4	8
Ecclesia de Grayftock	120	0	0
Ecclesia de Hoton	4	4	
Ecclesia de Leigham (hodie Adynham)	40	0	0
Ecclesia de Penryth	40	11	8
Vicaria ejusdem	9	6	8
Ecclesia de Skelton	30	0	0

Ed. 2.

	l	s	d
Ecclesia de Ed ehall	6	13	4
Eccl fiaede Kirkland	8	0	0
Ecclesia de Ulvethy	2	0	0
Eccl fiaede Sourby	8	0	0
Ecclesia de Ravenfwyk, non fuffit pro oneribus ordinariis fupportand'			
Ecclesia de Layfenby	1	0	0
Vi ara ejufdem			
Ecclesia de Kırkofwalde	1	0	0
Ecclesia de Croglin, non fuffit pro oneribus ordinariis fupportand'	5	0	0
Ecclesia de Aynftappelith	1	0	0
Vicaria fium non fuffit pro one-ibus fupportand'			
Ecclesia de Melmorby	2	0	0
Ecclesia de Dacre cum vicaria	13	6	8
Ecclesia de Grayftock	20	0	0
Ecclesia de Hoton	2	0	0
Ecclesia de Adynham	10	0	0
Ecclesia de Penryth	6	13	4
Vicaria ejufdem	2	0	0
Ecclesia de Skelton	6	13	4

Hen. 8.

	l	s	d
Edinghall vicaria	17	12	0
Kirkland rectoria	8	10	0
Ulnethy als Oufeby rectoria	13	13	0
Sorebye vicaria	17	10	5
Lafingby vicaria	13	1	2
Vicaria de Kyrkofwald	8	0	0
Croglin rectoria	8	0	0
Aynftabby vicaria	8	8	2
Melmorby rectoria	12	11	4
Rectoria et collegium de Grayftock	40	7	8¼
Ihe vi ina	8	0	0
Ihe in ecclefia	6	13	4
Cantaria fancti predicta	6	13	4
Cantaria Sci Johis Baptifte	6	13	4
Cantaria Sce Katherine i dicti am pred.tam			
Sci Petri in dicta dicta	6	13	4
Cantaria Sci Andree ibidem	6	13	4
Hoton als Hutton rectoria	18	12	7
Adyngham vicaria	9	4	8
Penrith vicaria	12	6	3
Cantaria Sci Andree in eccl' de Penrith	6	0	0
Skelton rectoria	43	2	7

DECANTUS CUMBR'

N. P.		l	s	d
Ecclesia de Salkeld (archid' Karl' appropriata)	-	12	0	0
Pensio prioris Karl' in ecclesia de Kirkland	-	·	0	
Pensio ejusdem in ecclesia de Wolnesby, vel Ulnesby	-	0	6	8
Pensio ejusdem in ecclesia de Hoton	-	0	2	0
Pensio ejusdem in ecclesia de Hedenhall	-			0
Summa totalis Decan Cumbr'		544	2	10
Summa totalis omnium bonorum spiritual' Karliol' dyoc'		2557	9	10

Ed. 2.		l	s	d
Ecclesia de Salkeld Regis	-	2	0	0
Pensio Prioris Carl' in ecclesia de Kirkland	-	1	0	0
Pensio ejusdem in ecclesia de Uldby	-	0	6	8
Pensio ejusdem in ecclesia de Hoton	-	0	2	0
Pensio ejusdem in ecclesia de Edenhal	-	0	4	0
Synodalia et incerti proventus archidiac' Karl'	-	2	0	0
Summa Decan' Cumbr'.		100	19	4

Hen. 8.	l	s	d
Cantaria bie Marie virginis in Skelton Salkeld dicta	4	11	11
Rectona ac colleg' de Kyrkofwald et Dacre	22	10	8
Capellani in dco collegio I ùt fer, et quilt eor' ùt pro pencone annua de magistro dci collegii	27	17	0
	6	13	4
Cantaria bie Marie de Edinghall	4	5	4
Ca bie Marie in ecclesia de Hton	6	14	10
Domus sialis Monalium de Armethuate in spiritual' et tèpl'	18	18	8
Sma Decanat' Alleridal et Karl'	2360	19	10½

Ed. 2.

N. P.

Taxatio bonorum temporalium dñi Karl' ēpi et religios' omnium ejufdem facta anno dñi MCC et nonag' fecundo, per magiftros Petrum de Infula archidiac' Exon' et Adamū de Afton rectorem eccles' de Beckenham, gerentes in hac parte Ebor' Dunelm' et dict' Karl' dioc' vices venerab' patrum dominorum J. Dei gratia Wynton' et O. Lincoln' eporum, executor' negotii terræ fanctæ a fede apoftolica deputator', quoad decimam dño E. illuftri regi Angl' in fubfidium terræ fanctæ conceffam.

							l	s	d
Epūs Karl' habet	-	-	-	-	-	-	126	7	7
Abbas de Heppe habet	-	-	-	-	-	-	46	13	4
Prioriffa de Ermyngtheweit	-	-	-	-	-	-	10	0	0
Prior de Lanercoft habet	-	-	-	-	-	-	74	12	6¼
Prior de Wederhale habet	-	-	-	-	-	-	52	17	6
Abbas de Holm Cultram habet	-	-	-	-	:	-	206	5	10
Prior Karl' habet	·	-	-	-	-	·	96	19	0
Summa totalis bonorum temporalium	·	·				·	613	15	9¼
Summa totalis omnium bonor fpiritual' et temporal'					-	-	3171	5	7¼

						l	s	d
Temporalia Ēpi Carliol'	-	-	-	-	-	20	0	0
Temporalia Abb' de Heppe	-	-	-	-	-	2	0	0
Temporalia Prioriffe de Ermithwaite non taxantur, quia funt deftructa.								
Temporalia prioris de Lanercoft non taxantur, propter eandem caufam.								
Temporalia prioris de Wederhale	-	-	-	-	-	4	0	0
Temporalia abbatis de Holme	-	-	-	-	-	40	0	0
Temporalia prior' Karliol'	-	-	-	-	ſ	20	0	0
Summa bonorum temporalium	-	-	·	∴		86	0	0
Summa bonorum fpiritual' et temporal'	-	-	·	-	-	480	19	0

A

G L O S S A R Y

O F

ANTIQUATED WORDS occurring in the foregoing WORK.

A.

ACOLITE, *acolithus*; an inferior church fervant, who next tunder the fub-deacon *followed* and waited upon the prieft and deacons in feveral parts of the divine offices.

AGISTER, in the king's foreft; an officer to take an account of the cattle *agifted* therein, and to collect the money due for the fame.

ASSART is, cultivating ground in the foreft by grubbing up the wood, where-by the covert for deer is deftroyed: and freedom from affart is an exemption from a fine or penalty for fo doing.

ASSISA, a rent or *affeffment* in general.

AUSTURCUS, a gofs or foar hawk.

AVERIA, beafts, cattle.

AVERPENY, money paid towards the king's carriages by land, inftead of fer-vice by the beafts *(averia)* in kind.

B.

BARNEKIN, the outermoft ward of a caftle, within which were the *barns*, ftables, and cowhoufes.

BASLAERD, a poniard or dagger.

BERCARIA, a fheepfold or other inclofure for keeping fheep.

BLOODWITE, an amercement for bloodfhed.

BORDESHALFPENY, money paid for fetting up *boards* or a ftall in a fair or market.

BORTHEVENLIG, feems to have been an exemption from attendance at the *borow* or leet court.

BOSCAGE, is that food which trees and wood yield to cattle: Alfo it fignifies a duty paid for windfall wood in the foreft.

VOL. II.   4 I   BOSCUS,

Boscus, wood.

Bovate (*oxgang*) of land: as much as one yoke of oxen can reasonably cultivate in a year.

Bredbrich, *brideberth*; jurisdiction of punishing the *breach* of the assize of *bread*.

Bredwite, a fine or penalty for default in the assize of *bread*.

Buckstall, a service in the forest in attending at a certain *station* to watch deer in hunting.

C.

Calcetum, a causeway.

Cariage, *carreius*; a service of the tenant's *carrying* the lord's goods in *carts* or waggons.

Caruca, a plough.

Carucage, a tax paid for every *carucate* of land.

Carucate of land, from *caruca* a plough, signifies as much land as can reasonably be tilled in a year by one plough.

Chiminage, a toll due by custom for having a way through a forest.

Civitas: An immunity *de civitatibus* was a privilege from attendance at the city courts.

Cleugh, *clough*; a gill or valley.

D.

Danegeld, a tax on land for keeping out the *Danes*, and afterwards imposed to prevent other invasions, or on any other extraordinary occasion.

Dapifer, a purveyor for the houshold.

Donum, a benevolence; sometimes called an aid.

E.

Escape, *escapium*, was the punishment or fine of those whose beasts were found trespassing in the forest.

Eskep, a measure of corn; differing in different places.

Exclusagium, a *sluice* for carrying water to the lord's mill.

Expeditating mastiffs in a forest, is cutting off the three claws of the forefoot clean off by the skin.

F.

Fengeld, a tax imposed for the repelling of enemies.

Ferdwite (from *ferd* an army) a penalty for not going out on a military expedition.

Flemensfrith, receiving or relieving a fugitive or outlaw.

Flitwite, *fledwite*, *flightwite*; an amercement where a person, having been a fugitive, returns of his own accord, or without licence.

Footgeld, an amercement for not expeditating dogs within the forest.

Footwite, the same as *footgeld*.

Forestall: An immunity from *forestall*, was an exemption from amercements for forestalling.

Forray,

FORRAY, an inroad or invasion by plundering parties.

FOSTER rent, *foster* corn; the word seems to be a contraction of *forester*, being the same as *forestage*, a duty paid to the foresters.

FRIDSTALL, *freedstall*, (from *frid* peace, and *stall* a station) a seat or place of peace, whereunto a criminal flying should be in safety; a sanctuary.

FRISCA FORCIA, fresh force; a jurisdiction of force newly committed within a city or other franchise.

FURCA, the gallows; a jurisdiction of trying and punishing felons.

G.

GAVEL, *gabel*; a toll or tribute.

GELD, a fine, tax, or tribute.

GREENHUE, any thing that bears a green leaf in the forest.

GRITH, peace.

GRITHBRECHE, *gridbreke*, *gridelbreke*; breach of the peace.

H.

HAIA, an hedge.

HAMSOKEN, was a franchise granted to lords of manors, whereby they held pleas of the violation of a man's house or *home*.

HAVERPENY; the same as *Averpeny*.

HAYBOTE, a liberty to take wood for hedging.

HEADPENY, *hevedpeny*; a small sum of money at so much a head, a poll tax, paid to the lord of the leet.

HENGWITE, *Hangwite*; a penalty for suffering a felon to escape.

HIDAGE, a tax paid for every hide of land.

HIDE of land, seems to be the same as an oxgang, being as much as one yoke of oxen can reasonably plough in a year.

HOBLERS, *hobelarii*; light horsemen.

HORNGELD, a tax paid for *horned* beasts in the forest.

HOUSEBOTE, an allowance of timber for repairing of houses.

HOUSGABEL, *husgavel*, *husgabulum*; house rent, or a tax laid upon houses.

HUNDREDSPENY, a tax or aid paid to the officer of the hundred for the support of his office and dignity.

HUNDREDUM, a tax or payment due to the hundred.

I.

INFANGTHIEF, a privilege of lords of manors to judge any thief taken within their fee.

INSEIGHE (insight), household goods.

J.

JACK; armour worn by horsemen. not made of solid iron, but of many plates fastened together. The boots usually worn with the said armour are still called jack boots.

JAMPNUM,

JAMPNUM, gorfe or furze.

K.

KAIAGE; a toll paid for loading or unloading goods at a *key* or wharf.

L.

LAIRWITE, *legerwite, leirwite*; a fine for adultery or fornication.

LASTAGE, or *leftage*; a cuftom or duty for goods in a market or fair fold by the *laft*, as corn, wool, herrings, pilchards, and the like.

LATRICINUM; an immunity *de latrocinio* was a privilege of non-attendance at the courts which had fole jurifdiction of robbery in a particular place.

LIBRATE of land, is a quantity containing four bovates or oxgangs.

M.

MAEREMIUM, any fort of timber fit for building.

MAIL, a rent.

MARCIUS, a lake or great pond that cannot be drawn dry.

MARCHET, *marchetum*, was a pecuniary payment, in lieu of the right which the lord of the manor in many places claimed and had, of lying with his tenant's wife the firft night after their marriage. It is faid that this fervice, in fome parts of the Highlands of Scotland, is not yet intirely gone into defuetude. And from this perhaps originally might arife the ftrict adherence and connexion of the clan as one great family; for if the firft born child fhould come fo as to correfpond with the time of the marriage, the prefumption would be that the lord was the father of fuch child.

MISKENNING; an unjuft or vexatious citation into the courts.

MULTO, a *mutton* or fheep, a wether.

MURAGE, a toll taken for a cart or horfe laden going through a walled city or town, for repairing the *walls* thereof.

MURDRUM: An exemption *de murdro* was a privilege from attending the courts of thofe that had the fole jurifdiction of murder in a particular place.

N.

NAMIUM, diftrefs.

NATIVUS, a fervant or bondman, fo *born*.

NAVAGE, a duty on the tenants to carry their lord's goods in a *fhip* or veffel.

O.

ORDELE, a trial of offences by fire or water, as paffing barefooted and blindfold amongft red-hot ploughfhares; or being put into water, wherein if they funk they were adjudged innocent, if born up by the water they were taken for guilty.

ORESTE, feems to be a jurifdiction of holding courts in cafes penal.

OSTURCUS, *afturcus*; a gofs hawk or foar hawk.

OUTFANGTHIEF, a privilege of the lord of a manor to call any inhabitant of his manor to judgment in his court for felony, though he were apprehended *out* of his manor.

CxGANG of land, as much as one yoke of oxen can plough in a year.

P.

PANNAGE, *pafnage*, is that food which fwines feed on in the woods, as the maft of beech or acorns. And freedom from pannage is privilege from paying any thing for the fame in the king's forefts.

PASSAGE, a duty paid for *paffing* over a river.

PEDAGE, a duty paid for paffing by foot or horfe through any country, to be employed fot the protection of the paffenger.

PENIGELD, a tax paid in money; a filver *penny* was the current coin of the ancient Saxons, and was equal in weight to our 3 *d*.

PETARIA, peatmofs (for fuel).

PICCAGE, money paid for breaking up ground for a ftall in a fair or market.

PLANUS, level ground or ground cleared of wood.

PLOUGHLAND, as much as can be cultivated in a year by one plough.

PONTAGE, a toll taken for paffing over a bridge, to be employed towards the repair of fuch bridge.

PREEKE; to prick at, to fkirmifh.

PREIFFE; proof, trial.

PULTURE, *puture*, a cuftom claimed by keepers or other officers in forefts, to take man's meat, horfe meat, and dog meat of the inhabitants within the foreft.

PURPRESTURE, in the foreft, is every incroachment made therein by building, inclofing, or ufing any liberty, without lawful warrant.

R.

REGARD, was the view and inquiry of offences within the foreft by an officer called the *regarder:* And to be free from the regard of the foreft, was an exemption from his jurifdiction.

REIF; plunder, robbery, or any other taking by violence.

S.

SAC, *faka*, a privilege of the lord of holding a court.

SALET, a head-piece.

SKEP, *fkep*, a meafure of uncertain quantity: In a furvey of the foreft of Englewood in 1619, it is defined to contain 12 bufhels, and every bufhel (Penrith meafure) 16 gallons and upwards.

SCYRA; an immunity *de fciris*, was an exemption from attending the fhire or county court.

SCOTTUM, a tax or contribution, a *fhot*.

SCUTAGE, a tax on thofe that held lands by knights fervice towards furnifhing the king's army.

SENESCHAL, fteward.

SEQUELA]

SEQUELA, fignified the wife and children, goods and chattels, of a tenant in villenage.

SEWER, in old evidences, the fame as *dapifer*, purveyor or caterer for the houfhold.

SKEUGH, *fcewgh, fhaw;* a wood-ground upon the flope of an hill.

SOKE, *foc;* power to hold courts and adminifter juftice.

SORUS, a for or foar hawk.

SPEIR (Scotch), to inquire.

STAGNES, *ftagna;* pools of ftanding water.

STALLAGE, money paid for erecting a ftall in a fair or market.

SUBBOSCUS, underwood.

SUMAGE, a fervice of the tenants carrying the lord's goods on horfeback.

T.

TALLAGE, a tax in general.

TEAM, *theam;* a privilege of the lord of a manor for ordering of bondmen and villeins, with their children, goods, and chattels.

TENMENTALE, *thenementale:* An exemption from *tenmentale* is a privilege of not attending the court of the *decennary* or *tithing.*

THELONIUM, toll.

THENAGE, fervice to the *thain* or lord of a manor.

THENDINGPENY, *thethingpeny, trithingpeny,* an aid or fubfidy paid to the fheriff or other officer of the *tithing,* for the fupport of his office and dignity.

TOLL, *thol,* in a grant to the lord of a fair or market, fignifies a power to take toll.

TREWES: Days of *trewes* were, when the commiffioners of both kingdoms met for the redrefs of grievances, during which time there was a *truce* or cef-fation of hoftilities. Alfo the articles agreed upon were ftyled the laws of trewes.

TRIDINGA, *trithinga;* an immunity *de tridingis* was a privilege of non-attend-ance at the trithing courts.

TRIST, an intercommoning, alliance, or friendfhip.

TRISTRIS, an obligation to attend the lord of a foreft in hunting, as to hold a dog, to follow the chafe, or ftand at any place appointed.

U.

UTFANGTHIEF, the fame as *Outfangthief.*

V.

VACCARY, an houfe or place to keep cows in, a cow pafture.

VAUMURE, an outwork or bulwark for defence againft an enemy.

VERDERER, an officer to take care of the *vert* in the foreft.

VERT, any thing that bears a green leaf in the foreft.

VILLENAGE, a fervile kind of tenure by bondmen or villeins, of whom there were two forts, one termed a villein *in grofs,* who was immediately bound to

the

the perfon of the lord; the other, a villein *regardant to a manor*, being bound to his lord as a member belonging to and annexed to his manor.

VIRGATE of land; a *yard* land confifting (as fome fay) of 24 acres, whereof four virgates make an hide, and five hides make a knight's fee.

VISNETUM, *vifne, vicinetum*, a neighbouring place; *vaftum et vicinetum*, far and near.

VIVARY; a place where living creatures are kept, as in a park, warren, fifh-pond, or the like.

W.

WAPENTAC, an obligation to attend the wapentake or hundred courts.

WARDA, a duty of attendance in the keeping of a town or caftle.

WARDPENY, money paid for watch and ward.

WHARFAGE, money paid for fhipping or landing goods at a *wharf*.

WOODGELD, a payment in lieu of fervice to be performed in cutting or carrying wood in the king's forefts.

INDEX.

I N D E X.

John's

FINIS.

Lightning Source UK Ltd.
Milton Keynes UK
UKHW020030160219
337399UK00010B/561/P